Third Edition

The Handbook of

Canadian Public Administration

Edited by

Christopher Dunn

OXFORD

UNIVERSITY PRESS

OXFORD
UNIVERSITY PRESS

Oxford University Press is a department of the University of Oxford.
It furthers the University's objective of excellence in research, scholarship,
and education by publishing worldwide. Oxford is a registered trade mark of
Oxford University Press in the UK and in certain other countries.

Published in Canada by
Oxford University Press
8 Sampson Mews, Suite 204,
Don Mills, Ontario M3C 0H5 Canada

www.oupcanada.com

Library and Archives Canada Cataloguing in Publication
The handbook of Canadian public administration / edited by
Christopher Dunn. — Third edition.

Includes index.
Issued in print and electronic formats.
ISBN 978–0–19–902616–6 (softcover). —ISBN 978–0–19–902617–3 (PDF)

1. Public administration—Canada—Textbooks. 2. Textbooks.
I. Dunn, Christopher J. C., 1948-, editor

JL108.H34 2018   351.71   C2017-906732-X
C2017-906733-8

Cover image: shaunl/E+/Getty Images
Cover and interior design: Sherill Chapman

Oxford University Press is committed to our environment.
Wherever possible, our books are printed on paper which comes from
responsible sources.

Printed and bound in Canada

1 2 3 4 — 21 20 19 18

Contents

Preface and Acknowledgements

This book came about at the request of colleagues who had used the first and second editions and made it the touchstone of their graduate and undergraduate public administration programs. Their feedback told of the strengths of the collection: informative pieces, written by expert contributors, that reflect new developments in the field; a consistent style throughout; and a certain edginess, namely a willingness to point out where the field is lacking and where it should be going. I am grateful to such colleagues and to their students.

This book was greatly shaped by the enthusiasm of the contributing authors. In the first book, I assembled a dream team that lent the book a sense of authority—with style. The same dynamic has repeated itself in the second and third editions.

Once again I have thoroughly enjoyed working with Oxford University Press. The professionalism and thoroughness of the staff has lent the same seamlessness and style to this edition as to the first. Kerry O'Neill, assistant editor in Oxford's Higher Education Division, coached the project along and saw to the slimming of the manuscript in a masterful way. Susan Bindernagel provided sensible and sensitive copy-editing. Steven Hall, the production coordinator from the Creative Services Division of Oxford, and expert indexers smoothed out the wrinkles in the text. To these and others I may have missed, I offer thanks.

Memorial University has provided me with a wonderful environment for teaching and research. Its Political Science Department has provided collegiality and inspiration, as well as leadership in the discipline. Its students are among the finest and most talented people I have met.

And lastly, to the people I do this all for. To Hilda, the love of my life; to Christopher, whose passion for life and learning is an inspiration; and to James, the beautiful one born the year of the first book, who gives me a new way of seeing the world.

Contributors

Carl Baar is professor emeritus of political science at Brock University and an adjunct professor of political science at York University.

Luc Bernier is the Jarislowsky Chair in Public Sector Management at the Graduate School of Public and International Affairs, University of Ottawa. He was formerly a professor of public policy at the École nationale d'administration publique (ENAP) of the Université du Québec, as well as director of education and research between 2001 and 2006.

Jacques Bourgault is a former professeur de science politique à l'Université du Québec à Montréal, now adjunct professor at ENAP, consultant in public management and former research fellow at the Canada School for Public Service (CSPS).

Kathy L. Brock is a professor in the School of Policy Studies and Department of Political Studies at Queen's University; she is also past president of the Canadian Association of Programs in Public Administration.

David C.G. Brown is a visiting professor in the School of Political Studies at the University of Ottawa, a former federal public servant, and a president of the International Institute of Administrative Sciences (IIAS).

Michele Campolieti is Professor, Department of Management, University of Toronto at Scarborough and Centre for Industrial Relations and Human Resources, University of Toronto.

Jonathan Craft is a cross-appointed Assistant Professor in the Department of Political Science, and School of Public Policy and Governance at the University of Toronto, specializing in comparative public policy and administration, policy analysis, and Canadian politics.

Bryan Evans is a professor in the Department of Politics and Public Administration at Ryerson University and Director of the Centre for Policy Innovation and Public Engagement.

Tammy Findlay is associate professor and chair at Mount Saint Vincent University's Department of Political and Canadian Studies. She is the author of *Femocratic Administration: Gender, Governance and Democracy in Ontario*.

John Erik Fossum is a Professor, ARENA Centre for European Studies, University of Oslo, Norway. He was previously professor at the Department of Administration and Organization Theory, University of Bergen and has published widely on the EU and Canada.

Ian Greene is a professor emeritus and university professor in the School of Public Policy and Administration, York University, and a former Master of McLaughlin College.

Morley Gunderson is the CIBC professor of youth employment with the Centre for Industrial Relations at the University of Toronto, where he is a member of the Department of Economics and the Centre for Industrial Relations. He is also a fellow of the Royal Society of Canada.

Robert Hebdon is a professor emeritus, Faculty of Management at McGill University.

Michael Howlett is Burnaby Mountain Chair in the Department of Political Science at Simon Fraser University and Professor in the Lee Kuan Yew School of Public Policy at the National University of Singapore. He specializes in public policy analysis, political economy, and resource and environmental policy. He is currently co-editor of several political science and public policy journals and serves on the boards of several international associations in the public policy field.

Kenneth Kernaghan was a professor emeritus in the Political Science Department at Brock University. Dr. Kernaghan was President of the Institute of Public Administration of Canada for 1987–8, and from 1979 to 1987 he served as Editor of *Canadian Public Administration*. He was named to the Order of Canada on 30 December 2008.

Alexandre Laurin joined the C.D. Howe Institute in 2008 and became Director of Research in 2014. From 1999 to 2008, he was with the Parliamentary Information and Research Service.

Evert Lindquist is a professor at the School of Public Administration, University of Victoria. He served as the Director of the School until 2009 and again from January 2012 to 2015. He is the Editor of *Canadian Public Administration*, the journal of the Institute of Public Administration of Canada (beginning January 2012).

Heather MacIvor is a Content Development Associate at LexisNexis Canada. Before starting law school in 2011, Heather spent nearly two decades as a political scientist. She clerked at the Divisional Court in Toronto and articled at the Constitutional Law Branch in Ontario's Ministry of the Attorney General. Heather is also active in the Ontario Bar Association's Administrative Law Section.

Alex Marland is a professor of political science and an associate dean of arts at Memorial University of Newfoundland and is a leading researcher of political communication and marketing in Canada. He is the co-editor of the UBC Press series Communication, Strategy, and Politics (with Thierry Giasson). In 2017 he was awarded both the Donner Prize for best public policy book by a Canadian and the Atlantic Book Award for scholarly writing for his book *Brand Command: Canadian Politics and Democracy in the Age of Message Control*.

John L. Nater is the MP for Perth-Wellington in the House of Commons, Parliament of Canada.

Michael J. Prince is Lansdowne Professor of Social Policy in the Faculty of Human and Social Development, University of Victoria. Before that, he taught in the School of Public Administration, Carleton University. He has advised departments, civil society, and four royal commissions.

Alasdair Roberts is Professor of Public Affairs at the Truman School of Public Affairs, University of Missouri. Previously he was the Jerome L. Rappaport professor of law and public policy at Suffolk University Law School.

William B.P. Robson has been the President and CEO, C.D. Howe Institute, since July 2006. He previously served as the Institute's Senior Vice President since 2003 and Director of Research since 2000. He is a Senior Fellow at Massey College and teaches at the University of Toronto.

Christopher Rootham is a partner with Nelligan O'Brien Payne LLP, Ottawa, and practises in the Labour Law and Employment Law groups. He is the author of *Labour and Employment Law in the Federal Public Service*, covering laws and regulations governing the federal public service in Canada.

Andrew Sancton is a professor emeritus in the Department of Political Science at the University of Western Ontario.

Matti Siemiatycki is an associate professor, Department of Geography and Program in Planning, University of Toronto and holds a Canada Research Chair in Infrastructure Planning and Finance. From 2006–8, he was Research Fellow, Department of Urban Studies, University of Glasgow.

Robert P. Shepherd is an associate professor in the School of Public Policy and Administration at Carleton University and President of the Canadian Association of Programs in Public Administration (CAPPA).

John Shields is a professor in the Department of Politics and School of Public Administration at Ryerson University and a member of the Yeates School of Graduate Studies.

Paul G. Thomas is a professor emeritus in the Department of Political Studies at the University of Manitoba and a former Duff Roblin Professor of Government. He has led or participated in various public inquiries dealing with health care, economic growth, urban governance, electoral reform, and access to information.

Allan Tupper is a professor of political science at the University of British Columbia. He has been President of the Canadian Association of Programs in Public Policy and Public Administration (CAPPA) and Editor of *Canadian Public Administration*.

David Zussman is a former Jarislowsky chair in public sector management at the University of Ottawa, and is Senior Fellow at the Graduate School of Public and International Affairs at the University of Ottawa, and an adjunct professor, School of Public Administration, University of Victoria.

Tribute to Dr Christopher (Chris) Dunn

On 7 November 2017, my esteemed colleague and dear friend Dr Christopher Dunn (simply Chris to me) passed away. News of his passing brought great sorrow and an outpouring of tributes within Memorial University, in the academic community of Canadian Politics, Policy, and Public Administration across the country, within the provincial and national public services, among the generations of students that he taught, and among his numerous friends in Canada and beyond.

Chris Dunn was a remarkable scholar, teacher, public servant, and family man. He never saw those four categories as separate and distinct; for him, they overlapped and intersected. His scholarship served a teaching purpose. Theory could help to inform practice. Academics, he believed, should not stand detached on the sidelines, but instead they should be engaged with public affairs. As a teacher, he believed that how you behaved as a person, including how you treated students, was as important, if not more important, than your academic credentials and your most recent publications. Chris was a wonderful husband, father, brother, uncle, and a generous friend. He was also somewhat of a private person, and so I reached out to his sister Catherine to learn about the more personal aspects of his rich life. I thank her sincerely for sharing her thoughts at this difficult time.

Chris began his academic preparation at the University of Manitoba, where he completed his BA (Hons.). This is where I first met him, and I was so impressed by his talent that I asked him to be my research assistant. We became lifelong friends, even though our contact fluctuated based on our busy lives. After a stint in the planning secretariat serving the NDP government of the day, Chris went on to obtain his MA and PhD from the University of Toronto.

This early government experience led Chris to a lifelong interest in the executive side of government and the processes of executive federalism. His dissertation became a book, *The Institutionalized Cabinet: Governing in the Western Provinces* (MQUP, 1995), which was nominated for a prestigious prize. He also wrote *Canadian Political Debates: Opposing Views on Issues that Divide Canadians* (OUP, 1995), a book that reflected his strong conviction that democratic dialogue required knowledge of contending arguments and evidence. An active researcher until his untimely passing, he was also one of three co-authors of *Canada's Politics: Democracy, Diversity and Good Government* (Pearson, 2017).

Reflecting his belief that scholarship could be a valuable teaching tool, Chris became well known for his inspiration and execution of several edited books dealing with relatively neglected topics in the Canadian politics and public administration/policy fields. This handbook, his edited volume *Provinces: Canadian Provincial Politics*, and his text *Deputy Ministers in Canada: Comparative and Jurisdictional Perspectives* (co-edited with Professor Jacques Bourgault) have all become indispensable sources to faculty, students, and practitioners in government. Both the ideas for such volumes and the efforts to bring them to completion represent major accomplishments.

Chris was a superb editor. He often persuaded academic colleagues from several disciplines to write original chapters for the volumes. Reflecting his collegial and helpful nature, he collaborated with and counseled contributors. He wrote the introductions and produced the other supporting material that made the volumes more valuable as teaching resources. And, of course, he had to master the task of "herding academic cats," who notoriously reside in their own worlds and are unmindful of deadlines. Too often solo publications are heralded as top accomplishments and insufficient recognition is given to the intellectual effort and impact of a volume of edited essays like the present one and the others that Chris produced.

Chris was a dedicated teacher who spent three decades in the classrooms and seminar rooms of Memorial University helping young—and not so young—adults to embark on their careers and more generally realize their potential. He was strongly committed to the intellectual development and personal growth of his students. For him, a student at his office door was not an interruption of his research. On one occasion, a mature student visited his office to withdraw from his course because she could not master the course material while managing the workload of a civil service job. Chris retrieved her most recent essay, immediately read it, and persuaded her that, given some flexibility, she definitely had the capability to undertake university studies. She completed her degree and progressed in her civil service career. Teachers like Chris seldom know in their lifetimes where their positive influence on the lives of others begins and ends.

Chris was also a public servant in the broadest sense of that term. He loved to contribute original policy ideas to journals like *Policy Options*, which are targeted at decision-makers in legislatures and government. With his detailed knowledge of constitutional government issues and their machinery, he was regularly consulted by public officials. According to the judge who headed the inquiry, Chris played a crucial role in the 2007 report of the Review Commission on Constituency Allowances and Related Matters. As someone who was paid from the public purse, Chris felt an obligation to share his knowledge and insights with the media. His was always an informed, balanced voice of reason.

Beyond all these qualities and accomplishments, Chris was a fine, caring person. Throughout his busy life, he exhibited the virtues of thoughtfulness, respect, civility, consideration, and generosity towards others. We regularly shared drafts of work in progress and he offered me advice and encouragement in his late night (not so late where I was) emails from "The Rock." I wondered sometimes whether he was getting enough sleep. As a friend, and as a member of the academic community that held him in such high esteem, I will miss him greatly.

Our sadness is nothing compared to that of his family. His wife Hilda, sons Christopher and James, sister Catherine, and other members of his family are dealing with the loss of a wonderful husband, father, brother, uncle, and friend. Those closest to him must take some comfort in the hundreds of people from all walks of life that filled St Pius X Church in St John's, Newfoundland and Labrador, for his funeral mass on 11 November 2017. This was a sign of the deep respect and genuinely warm affection that so many people felt towards a brilliant, respectful, honest, and compassionate individual.

Paul Thomas
University of Manitoba
December 2017

To the memory of my mother, Patricia Mary Gracia Dunn,
a former federal public servant who saw the potential in
all people and helped it flourish. And to that of my father,
D'Arcy Dunn who spoke the language of music. I love you.

Introduction

Parts I–V

The third edition of *The Handbook of Canadian Public Administration* reviews both the enduring structures of public administration and the challenges posed by new issues.

Part I, Mapping the Canadian Public Service, provides an introduction to the wide vistas of Canadian public administration, with several authors drawing taxonomies of the federal public service itself.

Part II, The Central Institutions, reviews stability and change in the major institutions of government—the central executive, Parliament and the public service, judicial administration, provincial and local public administration, departments, and the deputy minister cadre—and their capacity to learn from each other.

In Part III, The Broad Public Sector, the articles discuss some of the organizational forms outside the walls of the departmental public services, namely Crown corporations; agencies, boards, and commissions (ABCs or arm's-length agencies); and Indigenous public administration.

Part IV, The Processes of Canadian Public Administration, contrasts the twentieth- and twenty-first-century visions of public administration in

Canada and considers the innovations that have come about in service delivery and employee relations.

Part V, Changing Expectations of Government, deals with societal pressures on the public service to deliver values-based government, equality-based public administration, justice for the third sector, balancing of the roles of exempt staff, regular public service, and horizontal management.

All this amounts to a large order. The *Handbook* does not have all the answers. But we believe it asks most of the right questions.

The *Handbook*'s Conceptual Framework*

Public officials work in a multiplicity of organizational forms. The most familiar are government employees who work in departments under the political direction of a cabinet minister and the administrative direction of the deputy minister. However, central agencies and central departments have developed a considerable influence over the direction of government departments. Further, a variety of Crown corporations and semi-independent agencies, boards, and commissions do not operate according to the traditional departmental model of public

*The rest of this introduction is adapted from Dunn, Christopher, "The Public Bureaucracy," in *Canada's Politics: Democracy, Diversity and Good Government*, 3e, eds Eric Mintz, Livianna Tossutti, and Christopher Dunn. 2016. Pages 419–49. Reprinted with permission by Pearson Canada Inc.

administration. When we think of the staff of the various governing institutions, we often ignore those who work for Parliament and the courts. Of particular importance has been the establishment of various Officers of Parliament who, with their staffs, help Parliament in trying to hold the executive accountable for its actions and assist people who have complaints about government. With different forms come different issues.

Public Sector Bureaucracies

There is no Public Administration of Canada. There are multiple public administrations, and together they add up to what can be termed the "public sector of Canada." In other words, there are different components to the public sector, and they have developed according to different historical rhythms and multiple factors. This whole dynamic also exists at the provincial level. The most familiar component has been that of the departmental public service. There also exist public administrations for the legislatures and judiciary, and also for the health and education sectors, the Crowns, and various ABCs. Ironically, those bodies outside the departmental service often attract more public scrutiny than does the departmental service. However, both have been the object of significant attempts to calibrate the correct balance between representativeness, *neutral competence*, and executive leadership.

This introduction is meant to offer a conceptual overview of the public sector at large and some of the issues that preoccupy it.

In this introduction, the term *public sector bureaucracies* is used to refer to the staff of a variety of governing institutions. Governing institutions require sizable staff to be effective.

A New Way to Understand Bureaucracy

Beyond the departmental public service, a wide variety of organizations can be found whose staff also support the workings of the political executive (prime minister and cabinet). In addition, legislative and judicial institutions receive support from their own bureaucratic organizations and officials. In other words, bureaucracies take on many differing forms.

Since understanding the rather labyrinthine federal public service is a challenge, even for public servants themselves, this text takes a different conceptual approach. It arranges the public service according to a "rule of threes." The way to understand the shape of the service is to see it as a series of influences and bodies arranged in sets of three. In other words, there are

- three sectors of Canadian society,
- three national influences on the bureaucracy in Canada,
- three bureaucracies (executive, legislative, and judicial),
- three categories of executive institutions,
- three categories of executive departments,
- three levels of bureaucratic elite in departments,
- three kinds of officials in parliamentary institutions, and
- three kinds of officials in judicial institutions.

This is a unique and simple way to present complex information.

The Three Sectors of Canadian Society

Public bureaucracies exist in a specific context, namely a tripartite division of Canadian society. It is common to talk of the private (or market) sector, the public (or governmental) sector, and the third (or voluntary non-profit) sector. The *private sector* exists in a competitive environment and strives to maximize profit for private owners, be they corporations, family-owned businesses, or self-employed individuals. The *public sector*, which consists of the institutions and agencies of the state, is ideally concerned with acting in the public interest. The *third sector* consists of voluntary non-profit organizations that contribute to the general good of the public. This sector includes, among others, charitable organizations, religious and cultural institutions, and non-profit childcare facilities and nursing homes (see the Evans and Shields chapter in this collection).

There is also a tendency for one sector to influence another sector's administrative practices. In the last quarter century, the public sector has been deeply influenced by something called new public management, a school of public administration that modelled itself on private-sector precepts. The financial practices of the public sector (such as the accounting systems and planning and budgeting tools) more and more resemble approaches in the private sector.

For its part, the third sector depends increasingly on the public sector for funding. One implication of this trend is that non-profit organizations have begun spending more of their time and resources on meeting the reporting and accountability requirements that come with dependence on public financing. Some non-profit organizations even complain that such efforts side-track them from their core missions. As well, the third sector tends to mimic the private sector in its financial management practices: "Many voluntary organizations operate as if they were profit-and-loss entities, with cash flows (from fundraising, endowments, or fees charged for services) that dictate the scope of their activities in a similar way to [private-sector] firms that are fully revenue-dependent. While their objectives are public in a broad sense, they can act like private organizations from a money-management perspective" (Graham, 2007, p. 8).

The Composition of the Public Bureaucracy

The federal bureaucracy is just one among many in this country. Statistics Canada indicated at one point that over 3.6 million Canadians were employed in the many different public organizations. Indeed, the federal general government bureaucracy accounts for only a small proportion of total public sector employment (in 2011, 427,000 of 3,631,837) (Statistics Canada, 2012).

Some Canadians think of government as a collection of minister-directed departments, but this is only part of the picture. Andrew Graham (2007) insists it is necessary to define government expansively,

given the extensive reach of the public sector in modern times. For example, he points out that there is a "shadow government": people working for the private sector under government grants or grants to non-profit organizations. As well, government often achieves its aims by using a variety of governing instruments, some of which are practices that depend on the private sector for their implementation, such as regulations, inducements, and persuasion designed to change private-sector behaviour.

The Three Origins of the Public Bureaucracy in Canada

There have been three national influences on the bureaucracy in Canada. The public bureaucracy, especially the departmental bureaucracy, owes its origins to British and American sources and to the Canadian nation-building ethos, which carried with it some aura of patronage and doing what was necessary.

British Influence

The traditional British style of public administration, modified by Canadian practice and convention, came to be known as the Whitehall Model. It consisted of a number of interrelated principles (see Table I.1).

The British model was a subject of both pride and consternation to Canadians. It offered a familiar and relatively workable set of principles that could be passed from generation to generation, but it also proved to resist easy change.

Table I.1   The Traditional Whitehall Model and Its Canadian Application

Traditional Whitehall Model	Modifications by Canadian Practice and Convention
Parliamentary supremacy	Subordinate (delegated) legislation
Ministerial responsibility	Answerability and accountability
Public service anonymity	Accounting officers Boards of Crown corporations and commissions Media access to public servants
Public service neutrality	Rights to engage in various forms of political activity
The secrecy norm	Access to information or freedom of information
The rule of law	Canadian Charter of Rights and Freedoms
The merit principle	Employment equity Representative bureaucracy

Source: Reprinted with permission by Pearson Canada Inc.

American Influence

American influences have also left a lasting mark in Canada. In the late nineteenth century, the Progressive movement, spearheaded by individuals like Woodrow Wilson, sought to break the "spoils system" (in which the winning political party gave government jobs to its supporters) by making the public sector at all levels more business-like and shielding it from the political realm. The Progressive movement had its strongest effect at the local and state levels, where the patronage-ridden political "machines," the target of the Progressives, had their greatest hold. Among the Progressive movement's effects in Canada were the creation of city managers for urban governance, the foundation of special-purpose bodies to manage some politically sensitive services, and reforms in public budgeting.

Around the turn of the century, the second American influence, the scientific management school, first set in motion by Frederick Taylor (1856–1915), gained in popularity.[1] Frederick Taylor was a member of the New England upper class who was accepted to Harvard but instead chose to become immersed in the burgeoning American manufacturing sector, first as an ordinary worker, then as an engineer, then as what would be called today a "management consultant." Tireless study of the nature of work and management led him to publish his immensely popular work *The Principles of Scientific Management* in 1911.

Taylor's ideas on the organization of work found many expressions throughout his career; practitioners have tended to seize on discrete elements of his thought and use them as they see fit. He reckoned that the job of managers was to acquire the knowledge of work that traditionally belonged to workers and to organize it so as to make it available to current and future managers. He rather optimistically referred to this as "scientific management," by which he simply meant the organization and quantification of such knowledge as well as finding "the one best way" to perform tasks.

Scientific management principles influenced the federal public administration for the better part of the twentieth century. In particular, the Civil Service Commission (established in 1908) ultimately adopted an extensive employee classification system based on a report by American consultants (Dawson, 1929).

New Public Management

A third American influence was to come. In the final decades of the twentieth century, ideas and practices from Britain, the United States, and New Zealand influenced thinking about public administration: new public management (NPM), the adaptation of the practices of private business to the administrative activities of government (see Table I.2). It emerged as the result of two overlapping influences: rational choice theory and principal-agent theory. Rational choice theory (also known as public choice theory) assumes that all individuals, including bureaucrats, are self-interested. Principal-agent theory is based on the idea that the bureaucrat (the nominal agent, or "servant") who is supposed to follow the will of the

Table I.2   Principles of NPM versus Bureaucratic Government

Principles of New Public Management (NPM)	Traditional Bureaucratic Government
Entrepreneurial government	Emphasis on spending
Steering rather than rowing	Concentration on one or a few governing instruments (or means)
Competition	Monopoly
Performance measurement	Rule-driven
Customer-driven government	Ministerial responsibility
Decentralization	Centralization
Market orientation	Command and control
Empowerment	Service

Source: Reprinted with permission by Pearson Canada Inc.

principals (the minister or the legislature) often uses specialized knowledge to thwart this arrangement. The emphasis of NPM was on establishing institutional and behavioural counters to these two alleged tendencies.

Other factors were at play as well. Ideologues such as British Conservative Prime Minister Margaret Thatcher and US Republican President Ronald Reagan convinced many people that behind poorly performing governments were self-serving bureaucrats who in some areas had scaled the heights of power and needed to be checked. The book *Reinventing Government* by David Osborne and Ted Gaebler (1992) was key to popularizing entrepreneurial government in Canada. In particular, Osborne and Gaebler argued that governing should involve "steering"—setting the policy direction— rather than "rowing"; the delivery of services should instead be contracted out to private business as much as possible. NPM was seen as the opposite of the traditional bureaucratic form of government. In fact, it was hailed as an antidote to bureaucratic ills, which, it was claimed, resulted in inefficient governing.

Canadian Development

Although influenced by British and American ideas, the Canadian public bureaucracy has developed, to some extent, in its own way. Until 1917, there was only nominal attention to the merit principle (the right person for a specific job) and more to patronage (a public-service job seen as a political favour to be bestowed on those who supported the governing party). For the next 50 years (1918–67), the merit system-focused Whitehall Model largely dominated. Since 1967, collective bargaining by public service unions and the adoption of the Charter of Rights and Freedoms have modified the Whitehall Model. For example, strict restrictions on the political activities of public servants to maintain their political neutrality were struck down by the Supreme Court as a violation of the freedoms protected by the Charter. New public management also had an effect—although not to the same extent as in some other countries. The long-term effect of these developments is the current blend of rights-based, bargaining-based, and entrepreneurial-based management.

The Three Bureaucracies (Executive, Legislative, and Judicial)

People often think of bureaucracy as involving the standard public service, with the employees in each department answering to a cabinet minister. However, there are many kinds of bureaucracies, and only one kind answers to ministers. The three powers or branches of government—the executive (prime minister and cabinet), Parliament, and the judiciary— each have their own bureaucracies with a variety of specific aspects.

The Three Categories of Executive Institution

Executive institutions are those that are tasked with the implementation of laws passed by the Parliament. They fall into three categories:

1. executive departments headed by cabinet ministers;
2. semi-independent public agencies: Crown corporations and assorted agencies, boards, and commissions; and
3. alternative service delivery (ASD), a variety of different methods for delivering public services.

Executive Departments Headed by Cabinet Ministers

Ministers preside over executive departments. Executive departments are those listed in Schedule I of the Financial Administration Act (FAA), a list that may only be amended by Parliament and not at the discretion of the minister or cabinet. Departments are financed through parliamentary appropriations. As of March 2017, there were 19 departments. Ministers, in the language of most of the acts creating departments, have "direction and management" of the department. According to convention, ministers are individually responsible to Parliament for implementing the mandate that is conferred upon them by the act.

A minister may have personal responsibility to Parliament for personnel management, staffing, and finances of the department, but does not in fact exercise direct responsibility over the employees or finances of the department. The Public Service Commission is given exclusive responsibility for the staffing of departments under the Public Service Employment Act, which came into effect in 2005. This power is often delegated, but it is delegated to the deputy minister, not to the minister of the department. Personnel management other than staffing is the responsibility of the Treasury Board and the department's deputy minister, not the minister. Similarly, control over financial administration is shared between the Treasury Board and the department's deputy minister under the Financial Administration Act, and the minister is excluded. The reason for these exclusions is historical: in the past, ministers enjoyed much greater powers, but they abused them, aggrandizing the power of their departments, their parties, and themselves. Christopher Rootham in Chapter 1 deals with these and other acts that attribute responsibilities in the public sector.

Semi-Independent Public Agencies

The semi-independent public agency, the second type of executive institution, differs from its departmental counterpart in important ways. Although both have a designated minister, Parliament does not usually scrutinize the agency's affairs to the same extent. Ministers will generally submit less readily to questioning in the House of Commons on matters related to boards, commissions, or Crown corporations. These agencies generally have more freedom from central controls in their budgeting and staffing practices. Some are advisory agencies, some perform regulatory functions, and some engage in commercial or business activities—all activities that are rare for departments to perform.

ABCs (or arm's-length agencies). A wide variety of agencies, boards, and commissions (ABCs) serve a number of functions, which may overlap to a large extent. They may have *adjudicative* roles, such as the role played by the Canadian Human Rights Tribunal, which decides cases arising from the Canadian Human Rights Act. Some *regulate* particular industries. For example, the Canadian Radio-television and Telecommunications Commission (CRTC) determines which companies can have broadcasting licences and sets requirements for Canadian content in the broadcast media. Other agencies have *operating* responsibilities, like those undertaken by

the Canadian Food Inspection Agency, whose mandate is to safeguard food, animals, and plants and to provide overall consumer protection. Some federal agencies have *research responsibilities*. For example, the National Research Council (NRC) conducts scientific research and development. Others combine *research and funding responsibilities*. For example, the Canada Council for the Arts, the federal government's arm's-length arts funding agency, provides funding to artists, endowments, and arts organizations and performs research, communications, and arts-promotion activities. Allan Tupper writes about arm's-length agencies in this *Handbook*.

Various rationales have been offered for the use of the agencies, boards, and commissions that generally operate at arm's length from government. One common rationale for the non-departmental form has been the alleged inability of departments to undertake business functions or similar activities, and the need for the organizational flexibility that these independent agencies provide. Some agencies have been set up in part to allow for freedom in personnel and wage policy that supposedly would not have been possible with directions by the Public Service Commission or the Treasury Board. As well, businesspeople and certain researchers may feel uneasy in highly organized departmental structures and prefer to join organizations that are less foreign to their experience and more open to expressions of opinion.

A second reason cited is the need to take away some functions from the controversial political arena. Some functions might be inefficient if too much political interference were allowed. It is argued that pricing policies, monetary policy, capital installation locations, and extension of services should be decided in a non-partisan environment.

A third related justification is to remove quasi-judicial functions from the political realm so that a specialized impartial body with no particular interest in the outcome can make the decisions after holding hearings in a court-like manner.

Other reasons for adopting the non-departmental form include the desire to have an "umbrella organization" to deliver services that involve different government departments or different levels of government. For example, the Canada Revenue Agency was transformed from a department (Revenue Canada) to agency status in 1999. This agency administers federal, provincial, and territorial tax programs and other services. It is managed by a board of management with 15 members appointed by the cabinet, 11 of whom are nominated by the provinces and territories.

Crown corporations. Crown corporations are legal entities set up by the government to pursue commercial or other public policy objectives. The type of Crown corporation most Canadians are familiar with is called a parent Crown corporation. A parent Crown corporation is a legally distinct entity wholly owned by the Crown and managed by a board of directors. As of December 31, 2014, there were 45 parent Crown corporations, excluding subsidiaries (Treasury Board Secretariat, 2014).

Some of these affect Canadians directly every day, like the Canadian Broadcasting Corporation (CBC), Marine Atlantic, or the Bank of Canada, whereas others have a more indirect impact, like the Business Development Bank of Canada, Atomic Energy of Canada, and the International Development Research Centre (IRDC).

Crown corporations report through specific ministers to Parliament, but the relationship between corporation and minister is not as close or direct as is the case with ministers and departments. The reason the Crown corporations came into existence in the first place was to free them from the rules and political control that are evident in the regular bureaucracy. However, the arm's-length relationship raises difficulties for those used to thinking in terms of the orthodox doctrine of ministerial responsibility, where the minister is responsible for all matters administrative and political. This has been the problem Parliament has dealt with in various reform efforts over the past several decades. Accountability frameworks for Crown corporations are dealt with by Luc Bernier in this collection.

Alternative Service Delivery (ASD)

The third kind of executive organization features alternative service delivery (ASD). This category is aimed particularly at improving the delivery of government services, reducing the role of government, increasing flexibility, improving coordination among government departments and programs, and generally making government more business-like and responsive to the needs of the recipients of services.

ASD usually means turning to unusual organizational forms and instruments that do not fit the traditional view of government instruments. They may include establishing new organizational forms within departments or outside traditional departmental structures, termed *special operating agencies* (such as the self-financing Passport Canada). Alternative service delivery may also involve setting up partnerships with business and voluntary non-governmental organizations, commercializing the provision of services, or contracting out services to private business or to former government employees (Inwood, 2009).

The Three Types of Executive Departments

Three types of executive government departments exist:

1. central agencies and central departments;
2. central coordinating departments; and
3. line departments.

Central Agencies and Central Departments

Central agencies, the Privy Council Office (PCO) and the Prime Minister's Office (PMO), are headed by the prime minister and perform service-wide policy, facilitative, and control functions. Their authority comes from the statutory and conventional authority of cabinet itself, and their roles are to assist the prime minister directly and to help with the setting of objectives by cabinet. They have a formal or an informal right to intervene in or otherwise influence the activities of departments. The *central departments* (Department of Finance and the Treasury Board Secretariat) also perform these service-wide functions, but they are headed by ministers rather than by the prime minister, their authority comes from statute, and their objectives are usually collectively set or influenced by cabinet. They also have the right to intervene in or otherwise influence the activities of other departments. The term *central agency* is often used to refer to both types of structures. However, differentiating between the two can be useful, since one type, central agencies, provides a venue for direct prime ministerial power and the other, central departments, does not. In fact, one of the central departments, Finance, occasionally jockeys with the prime minister and the central agencies for relative influence.

In contrast, *line departments* are charged with delivering the basic services of government, such as health and defence. Line departments do not normally have a mandate to intervene in the affairs of other departments. Although the central agencies and central departments exert great influence over government policies and actions, they do not have as large a staff or budget as most government departments do. Despite their importance, the central agencies and central departments are the organs of government that parliamentarians (and most Canadians) know least about and whose workings are the least transparent, compared with the others.

Table I.3   Roles and Functions of Central Agencies and Central Departments

Central Agency/ Central Department	Role	Functions
Prime Minister's Office	The PMO gives partisan political advice to the prime minister and is staffed by supporters of the party in power. Staff are hired under the Public Service Employment Act (PSEA) but classified as "exempt staff" in order to free them from normal public service hiring practices.[2]	Advising on political strategy and prime minister's senior appointments Organizing the prime minister's correspondence and timetable Liaising with ministers, caucus, and national party
Privy Council Office	This central agency provides non-partisan policy advice to the prime minister and cabinet.[3] It serves as the secretariat for the cabinet and its committees The Clerk of the Privy Council serves as the prime minister's deputy minister, the secretary to the cabinet, and (since the early 1990s) the head of the public service, responsible for matters relating to public-service renewal.	Facilitates the cabinet decision-making process and implementation of government's agenda Acts as main designer and adviser for machinery-of-government issues Advises the prime minister (by Clerk) on the appointment of deputy ministers Coordinates strategy for federal–provincial and territorial (FPT) relations.
Treasury Board Secretariat	The Treasury Board Secretariat (TBS) is a central department that serves the central management board for the public service, the Treasury Board. The Treasury Board establishment and mandate is outlined in the Financial Administration Act, which gives the department responsibility for general administrative policy, financial management, human resources management, internal audit, and public service pensions and benefit programs. It also has responsibilities under a number of other acts, such as the Public Service Employment Act, the Official Languages Act, the Access to Information Act, and the Employment Equity Act.	In general, the responsibilities of the TBS include the following: • setting management policies and monitoring performance; • directing expenditure management and performance information systems; and • serving as principal employer of the public service. The Office of the Chief Human Resources Officer (OCHRO) within the TBS, centralizes human resources policy, and acts as the employer in relations with public-service employees.
Department of Finance	The most influential department in the government, Finance sets policy in the most important transfer and economic programs, as well as setting the annual federal budget.	Finance is instrumental in setting policy for • taxes, tax expenditures, and tariffs; • federal borrowing; • transfer payments to provincial and territorial governments; • Canada's role within international financial institutions such as the International Monetary Fund, the World Trade Organization, and the World Bank; and • major economic issues.

Central Coordinating Departments

In addition to the central agencies and central departments that are key actors in virtually all policy decisions and play a major role in coordinating government decisions, there are *central coordinating departments* that also have a coordinating role. For example, the Department of Justice has been responsible for "Charter-proofing" federal legislative proposals across government. Likewise, the minister (in effect, the department) of Public Works and Government Services is allocated exclusive jurisdiction under the Department of Public Works and Government Services Act of 1996 and under the Defence Production Act of 1985 to procure goods for other departments, as well as for the Armed Forces. Other departments are sometimes placed in this category.

Line Departments

Line departments are the third type of organization found in the executive government. They function as the backbone of government, delivering most of what we have come to expect in the way of services from government, from the military to the protection of aviation. As noted, they do not usually intervene in the affairs of other departments.

There are conflicting images of line departments in the literature. Line departments have often been portrayed as the drab, unexciting area of government. They are said to be the most driven by bureaucratic rules, the most dominated by politicians—their own ministers and the prime minister—and the most in need of, but at the same time the most deeply resistant to, basic reform (A.W. Johnson, 1992). At a broad level, there has been an almost constant tension between the need for rigorous accountability on one hand and the desire for creative and flexible management on the other (PCO, 2007).

However, others consider the line bureaucracy as a more independent and a more challenging place to work. Some theorists of the rational choice school, or those who are attracted by the principal-agent theory, see the average bureaucrat as a significant power-seeking agent, one whose nominal superiors do not under normal circumstances have enough information or resources to control their employees. The move to the new public management approach

to public-sector organization and management is a sign of just how much politicians fear the power of the bureaucracy in Canada and Britain (Aucoin, 1995, and Aucoin chapter in the first edition of this *Handbook*, 2002).

The Three Levels of Bureaucratic Elite in Departments

Three levels of bureaucratic elite characterize departments:

1. the deputy minister (DM) level (and in some departments, associate deputy ministers),
2. the assistant deputy minister (ADM) appointments, and
3. director-level appointments.

Deputy Minister

Deputy and *associate deputy ministers* are called Governor-in-Council (GIC) appointments because they are made by the Governor General upon the advice of the cabinet (acting in the name of the Privy Council). In practice, it is the prerogative of the prime minister, not the minister of the department, to appoint these individuals. In doing so, the prime minister takes into account the need to ensure that the appointees can be trusted to carry out his or her will and see to the needs of the government of the day. The Clerk of the Privy Council provides advice to the prime minister on these appointments.

Despite being chosen by the prime minister and closely associated with the policies of the government, most deputy ministers are retained even when a new government is elected. The deputy minister is expected to be politically neutral and impartial—neither for the government nor against it, but rather the guardian of the administrative order. The task at hand is to advise, to speak truth to power, and to supply the government with the best and most cautious information in spite of how unpalatable this may be politically. The deputy minister controls the management of the department. Although traditionally it is the minister, rather than the deputy minister, who is responsible to Parliament for the actions of the department, the Financial Administration Act (2007) has modified this tradition. Specifically, the deputy minister is the accounting officer for the department and, as such, is legally obliged to appear before parliamentary committees to report on conformity to that act (Inwood, 2009). Thinking about the role of the deputy minister has evolved in recent years, as Bourgault's article in this collection shows.

Assistant Deputy Ministers

Assistant deputy ministers are the second level of the administrative elite. Generally, they are charged with managing branches within a department. They are not Order-in-Council (OIC) appointments, but merit-based positions competitively chosen in recent years by the Office of the Chief Human Resources Officer.

Directors General

Directors general and directors are the third level. These are also merit-based appointments and are often considered to be the middle management level of the federal service. Several hundred individuals operate at this level. For example, reporting to the assistant deputy minister for science and technology at Environment Canada in mid-decade were five directors general (water, atmospheric, wildlife and landscape, science and risk assessment, and strategies) as well as a director of the Environmental Science and Technology Centre.

The Three Kinds of Officials in Parliamentary Institutions

In the Canadian Parliament, three sets of institutional players keep the institution running: political officers, officers of Parliament, and procedural officers. Although all play important roles, Officers of Parliament have gained the most public attention in recent years.

Political Officers (House Officers)

Political officers are not bureaucratic officers in the normal sense, but because they do some routine administrative work—administering rules, scheduling, monitoring, rendering accountability, and so forth—they might be considered part of the bureaucracy

of Parliament. The political officers of the House of Commons, including parliamentary party officials such as the Speaker, the Deputy Speaker, the party House Leaders, and the party whips, have come to be known as *House Officers*. These individuals are at once politicians and administrators, in the sense of making the routine machinery of Parliament work. It should also be added that many of them have individuals working for them as well. The Speakers, for example, have legal and financial officers attached to their offices, who assist in deciding on matters of parliamentary law and in administering the precincts of Parliament.

Officers of Parliament

Officers of Parliament, along with the offices they head, have sometimes been called servants of Parliament, parliamentary watchdogs, or the parliamentary control bureaucracy. Paul Thomas (2003) has described them as "independent accountability agencies created first to assist Parliament in holding ministers and the bureaucracy accountable and, second, to protect various kinds of rights of individual Canadians" (Thomas, 2003: 288). As servants of Parliament, as they are sometimes called, these are officers that serve and are responsible to the legislative branch rather than the executive, and to that end they have been freed from the normal constraints that bind the executive government.

One of the most pre-eminent of the Officers of Parliament—and certainly the oldest, established in 1878—is the Auditor General (AG) of Canada. The AG audits departments and agencies, most Crown corporations, and other federal organizations as well as the three territories, and his or her reports are presented directly to Parliament. Since 1977, when the Auditor General Act was broadened to include "triple-E reporting"—commenting on whether government is implementing policies economically, efficiently, and with adequate means for judging their effectiveness (also referred to as "value-for-money [VFM] auditing")—the auditor's reports have become central to Canadian political life.

Over time, the category of officers has tended to expand, as have some of their powers. The present list of officers is Auditor General of Canada (established 1878), Chief Electoral Officer (1920), Commissioner of Official Languages (1970), Information Commissioner (1982), Privacy Commissioner (1982), Conflict of Interest and Ethics Commissioner (2007), Public Sector Integrity Commissioner (2007), and Commissioner of Lobbying (2008).

Although the federal level has no exact equivalent to the post of ombudsman, a post found in many provinces and other jurisdictions, some of the federal officers have quasi-ombudsman roles. (There is, however, an Office of the Ombudsman for the Department of National Defence and the Canadian Forces.) In other words, they take complaints from citizens and public servants regarding the failure of government to perform duties it has taken on itself. Such analogies can be made with regard to the Commissioner of Official Languages, the Information Commissioner, the Privacy Commissioner, and the Public Sector Integrity Commissioner. Paul Thomas covers these officers and other aspects of parliamentary functioning elsewhere in this *Handbook*.

The Harper government also created another official, who was like an Officer of Parliament but not designated as such, called the Parliamentary Budget Officer (PBO). The PBO was an independent officer of the Library of Parliament who reported to the parliamentary librarian who, in turn, reported to Speakers of both chambers. The new Liberal government promised to increase the powers and independence of the PBO. The Office of the Parliamentary Budget Officer provides non-partisan financial and economic analysis to support Parliament's oversight role and to provide budget transparency.

Procedural Officers of Parliament

Procedural officers of Parliament are essentially the public servants of Parliament, providing the equivalent of department-like services to the House of Commons and the Senate. The key figures in the House who furnish these services are the Clerk of the House, the deputy clerk, the clerk assistant, the law clerk and parliamentary counsel, and the sergeant-at-arms. In the Senate there are analogous procedural officers.

The Clerk of the House is the senior permanent official responsible for advice on the procedural aspects of the plenary (whole) House and looks after the ongoing administration of the House of Commons. The Clerk of the Senate performs an analogous role for the Senate. The clerks' roles are comparable to the role of deputy ministers in the executive departments. In the Commons, the clerk is the permanent head responsible for the management of staff and daily operational affairs. The clerk takes direction from the Speaker in relation to policy matters. In turn, the Speaker takes overall direction in management from the Board of Internal Economy (BIE), an all-party committee statutorily charged with administering the House. In parliamentary matters, within the House itself, the Speaker is supreme and takes direction from no one in particular, except the will of the House.

Three Kinds of Officials in Judicial Institutions
Registrar

The Supreme Court of Canada, the Federal Court, the Federal Court of Appeal, the Tax Court, and the Court Martial Appeal Court are administered federally. Reflecting the principle of judicial independence, the administration of these courts operates at arm's length from the executive government.

The staff of the Supreme Court of Canada is headed by the registrar who is responsible to the chief justice of the court. The registrar and deputy registrar are Governor-in-Council appointees who oversee a staff of nearly 200 public servants who manage cases and hearings; provide legal support to the judges; edit, translate, and publish judgments; manage the flow of documents; and perform a variety of other essential tasks.

Courts Administration Service

Support for the four other federally administered courts is provided by the Courts Administration Service. The chief administrator, a Governor-in-Council appointee, is responsible for the overall operations of these four courts and their staff of about 600 public servants. The chief justice of any of the four courts may issue binding directives to the chief administrator.

Judicial Administrator

There is also a kind of third administrative option. In addition to the above, each chief justice has authority over such matters as determining workloads and court sittings and assigning cases to judges, and may appoint a judicial administrator from among the employees of the service for such duties as establishing the time and place of court hearings. Carl Baar and Ian Greene cover matters of judicial administration elsewhere in this *Handbook*.

Conclusion

These are just some of the contemporary questions that have given rise to the spirited debate in Canada about public bureaucracy; there are several others. They concern such matters as whether the federal spending power should be limited (dealt with by Dunn in the *Handbook*); whether the federal–provincial spending and taxing balance is appropriate (a matter Robson and Laurin cover); whether private/public partnerships, third-sector arrangements, Crown corporations, and arm's-length agencies are sufficiently accountable (Siemiatycki/Evans and Shields/Bernier/Tupper); plus others. How does one design a budgeting system (Prince)? Ethical frameworks tailored to the public sector (Brock and Nater)? What is the relationship between political staff and the regular bureaucracy (Craft) or between political staff and deputy heads (Bourgault)? We encourage the reader to pursue such avenues; they are of immense importance, as the coming years will prove.

Public-sector bureaucracies are necessary for the achievement of good government. A large, professional staff is required to administer the multitude of government programs. Designing how they work together is the overriding issue. It is to this we now turn.

Notes

1   The term *scientific management* was coined by lawyer Louis D. Brandeis in hearings before the Interstate Commerce Commission.
2   Each cabinet minister also has a small political staff separate from the public servants in the department.
3   The PCO's name comes from the Queen's Privy Council for Canada.

References

Aucoin, Peter. 1995. *The New Public Management: Canada in Comparative Perspective*. Montreal: Institute for Research on Public Policy.

R. M. Dawson. 1929. *The Civil Service of Canada*. London: John Wiley & Sons, Ltd.

Graham, Andrew. 2007. *Canadian Public-Sector Financial Management*. Kingston: McGill-Queen's University Press.

Inwood, Greg. 2009. *Understanding Canadian Public Administration: An Introduction to Theory and Practice*. 3rd edn. Toronto: Pearson-Prentice Hall.

Johnson, A.W. 1992. *Reflections on Administrative Reform in the Government of Canada 1962–1991*. Ottawa: Office of the Auditor General.

Osborne, David and Gabler, Ted. 1992. *Reinventing Government*. Addison-Wesley Publishing Co.

PCO. 2007. Internal review.

Statistics Canada. 2012. *Public sector employment, wages and salaries*. Retrieved from www.statcan.gc.ca/tables-tableaux/sum-som/l01/cst/govt54a-eng.htm.

Thomas, Paul. 2003. "The Past, Present and Future of Officers of Parliament." *Canadian Public Administration* 46, 3, pp. 287–314.

Treasury Board Secretariat. 2014. "Parent Crown Corporations Grouped by Ministerial Portfolio." Retrieved from https://www.tbs-sct.gc.ca/reports-rapports/ cc-se/crown-etat/ccmp-smpm-eng.asp.

Part I

Mapping the Canadian Public Service

I t is a challenge to outline, or map, the public service of Canada. It is a complex network of legislation, subordinate legislation, conventions, and governmental practices. The following authors attempt to untangle the complexities for students of the field.

Christopher Rootham maps the legislative framework of the core and broader public service. He conceives of the federal public sector as a series of concentric circles, some of which overlap in interesting or challenging ways. The key legislation in this topic is the Financial Administration Act, which defines sections of the public service and then sets out who is responsible for what and in particular the Treasury Board's level of control. There is also the Public Service Rearrangement and Transfer of Duties Act, which is about how to transfer units around the public service. He then examines collective bargaining and terms and conditions of employment with a historical overview of two main topics: collective bargaining laws in the federal public service, and the legal status of Crown service, mainly concentrating on the Federal Public Sector Labour Relations Act (FPSLRA). His third part is a historical overview of staffing matters (such as hiring, transferring) in the federal public service, concentrating almost exclusively on the evolution of the Public Service Employment Act (PSEA) over time, with particular emphasis on the merit principle. His fourth topic deals with legislative protection of fundamental freedoms of public servants, such as political activities in the PSEA; whistle-blowing and public criticism, both common law and, post-Gomery, the Public Servants Disclosure Protection Act (PSDPA); human rights and pay equity, mainly the Canadian Human Rights Act (CHRA); and official languages. The fifth part provides a historical look at federal public service pensions. The sixth and last section covers legislation involving people we would think of as public servants who are not governed by the PSLRA or PSEA. These are military personnel (National Defence Act, and others), RCMP members (RCMP Act), parliamentary employees under the Parliamentary Employment and Staff Relations Act (PESRA), ministerial staff ("statutory orphans," but some PSEA rules apply when trying to get into the public service), and Governor-in-Council appointments (covering such persons as deputy ministers, heads of various tribunals and agencies, and so forth).

William B.P. Robson and Alexandre Laurin offer a comprehensive overview of most fiscal arrangements between Canada's federal and provincial governments. They review the history of various intergovernmental transfers and examine the rationales used in the literature to explain and/or prescribe particular aspects of Canadian fiscal arrangements. Prominent among them include subsidiarity, the Tiebout hypothesis, public choice, externalities, economies of scale, regional redistribution to standardize services, and mitigating harmful internal migration. However, theory sometimes takes second place to fiscal stresses and political responses in particular circumstances. They strongly favour the principle of hard fiscal constraints and more closely aligning the revenue-raising and spending powers of governments in Canada.

Continuing with the intergovernmental theme, Christopher Dunn traces the checkered history of the federal spending power. Sometimes popular, sometimes denounced, the spending power has always been a central concern of federal and provincial politicians. The chapter traces the factors that have determined the rise and fall and then rise again of the use of the instrument. The spending power was an instrument of nation building after WWII, then a focus of the "constitutional reform industry" from the late sixties to the early nineties, followed by a drive for non-constitutional strategies to limit the power that culminated in the Harper Open Federalism policy. Justin Trudeau may be resurrecting the early Liberal tradition of vigorous use of the spending power.

Heather MacIvor contributes an important chapter to the collection, stressing the importance of administrative law to the practice of government. The decision-making power of public officials is derived from statutes enacted by the legislature and regulations issued pursuant to those statutes by the Governor-in-Council or Lieutenant-Governor-in-Council. MacIvor explains the key principles of administrative law for students of public administration. The case studies illustrate the concepts of jurisdiction, statutory powers of decision, the standard of review, and the rule of law. The chapter situates Canadian administrative law in its constitutional and legal framework. It focuses on the power of the Superior and Federal Courts to enforce the rule of law by ensuring that tribunals in the executive branch adhere to their legislative mandates.

"The key lesson for students of public administration," she says, is this: "if you want to know what government can do with a particular file, don't just look at the fiscal data or the latest managerial theories. Read the law. Start with the Constitution, then look at the enabling statute(s) and the applicable regulation(s). Which administrative structures are tasked with implementing the file? What powers do they have? How broad is their discretion? . . . Read the case law. You may find that where government documents are silent on key aspects of public administration, courts have spoken." This is important to remember.

As Kenneth Kernaghan reminds us in Chapter 5, different eras in public sector reform are distinguished by different sets of values. Recently *traditional values* in the public sector (accountability, efficiency, integrity, neutrality, responsiveness, and representativeness) have been challenged by *new values* (service, innovation, quality, teamwork). Yet values are not the only core ideas in Canadian public service: constitutional conventions are intimately linked with public service values. The three conventions integral to the Canadian system (the East Block conventions) are (1) ministerial responsibility, (2) public service anonymity, and (3) political neutrality. Kernaghan traces the action of all three in constructing Canada's values and ethics regime since 2003.

A Legislative Map of the Federal Public Service

Christopher Rootham

Chapter Overview

Canada is a country dedicated to the maintenance of the rule of law. One consequence of this dedication is that actions of the executive branch of government must be authorized by a statute enacted by Parliament or a regulation made in accordance with some legislative grant of authority.[1] The federal public service is therefore set up by an interlocking web of legislation, and administered by individuals acting pursuant to legislative power. This chapter is meant to map out the broad outlines of that legislative web.

Three major statutes establish the federal public service, and then a number of other statutes impact the federal public service sufficiently to warrant mentioning in this chapter. Those three major statutes are as follows:

1. the Financial Administration Act (FAA). The FAA is the statute that builds the fundamental architecture of the federal public service. It creates the Treasury Board of Canada and gives the Treasury Board the responsibility to regulate financial and human resources in the federal public service. The FAA also sets out the basic division of the public sector between the portions managed directly by Treasury Board on the one hand and separate agencies on the other. The FAA also contains financial management rules for Crown corporations.
2. the Federal Public Sector Labour Relations Act (FPSLRA). The FPSLRA sets out the rules for collective bargaining between public sector unions and the federal public service. It also sets out a regime for individual dispute resolution for both unionized and non-unionized federal public servants.
3. the Public Service Employment Act (PSEA). The PSEA establishes the rules for appointments in most of the federal public service, including statutory codification of the principle that appointments should be made on the basis of merit. The PSEA also establishes rules governing political activity by federal public servants.

In addition to those major statutes, other statutes regularly touch on the lives of federal public servants. The most important of those statutes, discussed very briefly below, include:

1.   the Canadian Human Rights Act, which protects federal public servants against discrimination and requires pay equity;
2.   the Public Servants Disclosure Protection Act, which permits whistle-blowing and protects whistle-blowers against reprisals;
3.   the Official Languages Act, which gives public servants in certain regions of Canada the right to communicate in the official language of their choice while at work;
4.   the Privacy Act, which prohibits the collection, use, and disclosure of certain personal information without consent, and gives public servants the right to access their personal information; and
5.   the Public Service Superannuation Act, which sets out the pension benefits for federal public servants.

Finally, there are certain portions of the public service (such as the Canadian Armed Forces, Royal Canadian Mounted Police, and parliamentary employees) that have specific statutes governing their human resources.

Chapter Objectives

By the end of this chapter, students will be able to do the following:
•   Understand and describe the broad outlines of legislation governing the federal public service.
•   Outline the differences between collective bargaining in the private sector and the federal public service.
•   Explain the merit principle and its enforcement.
•   Describe some of the ways in which legislation protects and limits the fundamental rights and freedoms of public servants.

Topic One: What Is the Federal Public Service?

The first step in a legislative overview of the federal public service is to define and delineate the topic of this chapter—what is the federal public service? To do so, it is necessary to define four categories or subsets of the federal public sector:

1.   the core public administration;
2.   separate agencies;
3.   departmental corporations; and
4.   Crown corporations.

The first two categories are referred to collectively as the federal public administration—in this chapter, however, they will simply be referred to as the federal public service. The fourth category is not part of the federal public service.

As described further below, the third category of departmental corporation often overlaps with the previous two categories. It may also be useful to think of these four categories as concentric circles moving away from the core of the federal public sector, or as categories that move further and further away from central government control.

These categories (and the different level of central control exercised over each of these categories) are set out in the Financial Administration Act.[2] This statute, as the name implies, establishes rules for financial and human resources administration in the federal public sector—in particular, who is responsible for various aspects of financial and human resources for each of those four categories.

Nature of Crown Employment (or the Legal Status of a Public Servant)

Before defining those four categories, it is probably useful to discuss—in the briefest of terms—the theoretical underpinnings of employment by the Crown.

The concept of employment with the Crown was, for several centuries, considered a question of status. This meant that the rules governing employment with the Crown were set out either by statute or unilateral decisions by the Crown in the exercise of its prerogative. Until the eighteenth century, public servants were considered to be the personal servants of the reigning monarch. The monarch appointed his or her officials by letters patent. In the eighteenth century, the situation evolved so that public servants were appointed directly by their particular minister. They were also paid out of the revenues generated by that particular ministry.

Eventually, by the middle of the nineteenth century, the early versions of the Civil Service Act[3] created a system whereby public servants were servants of the Crown instead of their particular department or minister. Crown servants were still considered to be servants, however—meaning that their relationship with the Crown was based on status instead of the normal rules of contract that govern the modern employment relationship.

In the past three decades employment with the Crown has evolved away from a status-based relationship into a relationship based on contract. The leading case with respect to the status of Crown servants is *Wells v. Newfoundland*.[4] In that case, a former member of the Newfoundland Public Utilities Board was appointed to hold office during good behaviour until the age of 70. The Board was abolished by the Newfoundland Legislature, and Wells was not reappointed to the new board. He brought a claim for damages equal to lost salary up until age 70 (plus associated loss of pension benefits). The Supreme Court of Canada upheld his claim on the basis of contract. The Supreme Court of Canada reviewed earlier cases holding that junior civil servants were employees governed by either collective agreements or contracts of employment. It decided to apply those earlier cases to senior civil servants as well, stating:

In my opinion, it is time to remove uncertainty and confirm that the law regarding senior civil servants accords with the contemporary understanding of the state's role and obligations in its dealings with employees. Employment in the civil service is not feudal servitude. The respondent's position was not a form of monarchical patronage. He was employed to carry out an important function on behalf of the citizens of Newfoundland. The government offered him the position, terms were negotiated, and an agreement reached. It was a contract.

As Beetz J. clearly observed in Labrecque, supra, the common law views mutually agreed employment relationships through the lens of contract. This undeniably is the way virtually everyone dealing with the Crown sees it. While the terms and conditions of the contract may be dictated, in whole or in part, by statute, the employment relationship remains a contract in substance and the general law of contract will apply unless specifically superseded by explicit terms in the statute or the agreement.

The Supreme Court of Canada then set out the limited scope for exceptions to its rule for judges, ministers of the Crown, and others who fill constitutionally defined state roles.

The fact that employment with the Crown is contractual in nature does not, by itself, serve to identify the employer for a Crown servant. Nor does the contractual nature of Crown employment mean that the relevant statutory provisions prescribing their terms and conditions of employment are less important than they were before this recognition of the contractual nature of their employment. The Supreme Court of Canada has recognized that, at the very least, these statutory provisions form part of the terms and conditions of the contract of employment.[5] Lower courts have concluded that, despite the contractual nature of Crown employment, certain terms and conditions of employment may be amended without consideration or without the acceptance or approval of an employee—contrary to the normal approach to contracts of employment.[6] This is to say that the *nature* of the employment relationship with the Crown is contractual, but the *terms and conditions* of employment are an amalgamation of the rules of contract and various statutory and regulatory conditions.

This raises the question of who constitutes the employer of public servants. This question can be answered by reference to four principles:

1. in the executive branch of the federal government there is only one employer and that is Her Majesty the Queen in right of Canada;
2. as a general rule, Her Majesty does not exercise her functions of employer herself or through the Governor-in-Council; instead she delegates her functions as the employer to either the Treasury Board of Canada or to another agency;
3. Parliament has adopted an objective, simple, and easily verifiable test to determine those persons in respect of whom Her Majesty will be represented as employer by the Treasury Board and those in respect of whom she will be represented as employer by a separate employer; it has drawn up two lists in the Financial Administration Act; and
4. Parliament has chosen to indicate by legislation rather than by regulation the persons for whom the Treasury Board, on behalf of Her Majesty, will be the employer and those for whom it will not; any change of status in this regard therefore can only be made by legislation.[7]

In short, public servants are employed by the Crown (Her Majesty in right of Canada) through the agency of either the Treasury Board of Canada or a separate agency. Further, the Financial Administration Act delineates whether a particular worker is an employee of the Crown as represented by Treasury Board or the Crown as represented by a separate agency.

Category One: Core Public Administration

The core public administration refers to those departments and agencies listed in Schedules I and IV of the Financial Administration Act. More practically, public servants in the core public administration are employed by the Treasury Board instead of their particular department or agency. Most federal public servants are employed in the core public administration. As of March 31, 2016, for example, the core public administration had 197,354 employees (or 76 per cent of the federal

public service) compared to 61,625 (or 24 per cent) in separate agencies.[8]

Treasury Board

The **Treasury Board** is a subcommittee of the Queen's Privy Council for Canada established pursuant to section 5 of the Financial Administration Act consisting of the president of the Treasury Board, the minister of finance, and four other members of the Queen's Privy Council (i.e., cabinet ministers). The Treasury Board, broadly speaking, is responsible for overseeing the administration of the federal public sector. The specific responsibilities of the Treasury Board for human resources are set out in sections 7 and 11.1 of the Financial Administration Act and include determining pay and allowances, determining the human resources requirements of the public service (i.e. headcount), classifying positions, and preparing policies for departments to follow when implementing human resources decisions. The Treasury Board is also the employer for collective bargaining purposes in the core public administration.[9]

The Treasury Board is also responsible for financial management generally in the federal public service, and for exercising powers under various other statutory instruments. The most notable of the Treasury Board's powers outside of the Financial Administration Act is its administration of the Public Service Superannuation Act; one less notable power is that it is responsible for auditing the Office of the Auditor General.[10]

Category Two: Separate Agencies

The second area of the public service comprises the separate agencies listed in Schedule V of the Financial Administration Act. The Crown has delegated to each individual separate agency the power to act as the employer for employees within each separate agency. The Treasury Board is **not** considered to be the employer of employees of a separate agency. The separate agencies all have their own constituting statutes. Those constituting statutes establish—with greater or lesser degrees of particularity—that each separate agency has the power to appoint staff and fix their remuneration.

The Treasury Board still exercises some supervision over separate agencies. For example, a separate agency may only enter into a collective agreement with the approval of the Governor-in-Council.[11] In 1967, the Governor-in-Council[12] decided that separate employers could exercise the same power over their own employees as Treasury Board exercised over employees in the core public administration. However, that authority was subject to two limits: (1) the separate employer had to consult with Treasury Board before making or implementing new policies; and (2) the separate employer had to obtain the terms of reference (or a mandate) from Treasury Board before entering into collective bargaining negotiations.[13] Therefore, the Treasury Board indirectly controls the collective bargaining for separate employers by controlling the mandate for negotiations and the development of policies.

When it comes to determining terms and conditions of employment outside of collective bargaining, some separate agencies are still subject to approval by the Governor-in-Council before they can fix remuneration,[14] while other separate agencies retain that power in their own right;[15] and still others retain that power but must consult with the Treasury Board before setting pay and allowances.[16]

Since separate agencies can be created (or abolished) by a simple amendment to the Financial Administration Act, public servants have often been transferred en masse from the core public administration to a separate agency (or vice versa). When a new separate agency is created, the rules are set out in the statute creating that separate agency. When a group of employees are transferred from one portion of the public service (either a department or a separate agency) to another, the government need only enact a regulation to effect that transfer.[17]

Departmental Crown Corporations

The federal public sector includes a special type of corporation called a "departmental corporation." **Departmental corporations** are created by Acts of Parliament and are listed in Schedule II of the Financial Administration Act. They report to Parliament through a minister and are designed to function with greater autonomy than ministerial departments. Their governing bodies have roles specified in their constituting statutes. Some departmental corporations are also separate agencies; some are part of the core public administration; and some are outside of the federal public administration and considered a separate corporate entity.

A departmental corporation is treated as a department for the purposes of financial accounting and reporting required under the Financial Administration Act.[18] This means that Treasury Board is responsible for the financial management of departmental corporations, including "estimates, expenditures, financial commitments, accounts, fees or charges for the provision of services or the use of facilities, rentals, licences, leases, revenues from the disposition of property, and procedures by which departments manage, record and account for revenues received or receivable from any source whatever" as well as the review of annual or longer term expenditure plans and programs.[19] This control over financial management *does not* extend to control over human resources: in other words, a departmental corporation is not automatically subject to Treasury Board on human resources issues.

The funding of departmental corporations is supposed to be a combination of parliamentary appropriations and revenues earned through services performed by the departmental corporation.

Crown Corporations

Finally, there are **Crown corporations**. A Crown corporation is a "corporation that is wholly owned directly by the Crown, but does not include a departmental corporation."[20] Crown corporations are managed and operated by a Board of Directors,[21] who in turn are appointed by the responsible Minister with the approval of the Governor-in-Council.[22] The Treasury Board must approve the annual operating budget[23] and the capital budget of a Crown corporation.[24] The Treasury Board also sets some procedures for financial accounting (such as the types of forms used for audits of a Crown corporation).[25] Otherwise, Crown corporations are independent from Treasury Board and instead are accountable to Parliament and the Governor-in-Council through their minister.

Some Crown corporations derive most or all of their revenue from commercial activities, while others are largely or almost completely dependent upon parliamentary appropriations.

Finally, employees of a Crown corporation are subject to the same labour and employment laws as employees in the federally regulated private sector—in particular, the Canada Labour Code.[26]

Topic Two: Collective Bargaining and Terms and Conditions of Employment

Early Version of Collective Bargaining: The National Joint Council

Collective bargaining came later to the federal public service than to the private sector. The notion that the Crown could engage in collective bargaining with its servants was seen as antithetical to Crown sovereignty. According to this theory, the government needs to have free control of the public service in order to protect its capacity to govern.

Unionism among public servants dates to the late nineteenth century, with the formation of the Railway Mail Clerks' Association in 1889 and a union of letter carriers, the Canadian Postal Employees Association (a predecessor of the current Canadian Union of Postal Workers), in 1891. The Civil Service Association (an early predecessor of the Public Service Alliance of Canada) was formed in 1907, and the Professional Institute of the Public Service of Canada was formed in 1920 by public service professionals as a reaction against a job classification scheme.

Until 1944, wages and other terms and conditions of employment continued to be set unilaterally without negotiation or consultation with public sector unions. A strike by letter carriers in 1924 did nothing to change this legal regime—the government resolved the strike by announcing "bonuses" outside of the normal pay system, preserving a facade that there was no negotiation of wages.

In 1944, the government created the **National Joint Council** (NJC).[27] The NJC was based in part on the Whitley Council system then in place in the United Kingdom. Under the Whitley Council system, public service associations negotiated terms and conditions of employment and, if negotiations were unsuccessful, the disputes were referred to binding arbitration. The NJC did not go that far. The NJC was a council of two sides: employer and association. The NJC operated on the basis of consensus and

consultation; there was no binding dispute resolution mechanism, so that the government retained control over the final outcome and could ignore or change the recommendations reached by the NJC. The NJC was also prohibited from dealing with compensation.

Despite these defects, the NJC was partially successful as a vehicle through which public servants could advance their interests. Through the NJC, public service associations won a reduction to a 5-day (40-hour) workweek, premiums for overtime pay, and dues deductions for members.

The NJC continues to exist to this day, despite the introduction of collective bargaining in 1967 (discussed below). The NJC is a council of public service unions and the various employers (including Treasury Board), tasked with addressing issues that ought to be dealt with similarly across the public service instead of permitting distinctions between bargaining units. While public service associations can (and have) opted out of various NJC Directives (as the agreements are called),[28] the NJC continues to deal with a number of issues outside of more regular collective bargaining. The NJC Directives, for example, set out rules for travel expenses, health-care plans, and the bilingualism bonus available to public servants.[29]

Collective Bargaining in the Federal Public Service: 1967–Present

Collective bargaining in the federal public service became a political issue in the 1960s. The Conservative government of John Diefenbaker permitted consultation on issues of pay for the first time in 1961, but then refused to implement a pay increase that had been decided upon through this consultation in 1963. In the subsequent election, the Liberal Party promised to introduce collective bargaining in the federal public service. When it was elected in 1965, it struck a committee to report on implementing collective bargaining in the federal public service. This committee prepared the so-called Heeney Report in 1965.[30] The government acted on most of the Heeney Report's recommendations, and introduced the Public Service Staff Relations Act[31] in 1967. Interestingly, one recommendation that was not acted upon was the Heeney Report's recommendation that strikes be prohibited in the federal public service. As a response to that recommendation, inside postal workers went on strike and, after resolving that strike, announced that they would defy any prohibition against strikes in the future. This strike convinced the government that a total prohibition against strikes would be counterproductive: it would simply make strikes illegal for groups that were determined to strike regardless of what the law said. Therefore, the government decided not to ban strikes in the new Act.

The Public Service Staff Relations Act was amended in 1992[32] as part of an initiative called Public Service 2000. The Act was then repealed and replaced with a substantially similar statute called the Public Service Labour Relations Act in 2005 as part of the Public Service Modernization Act, which was in turn re-named the Federal Public Sector Labour Relations Act (FPSLRA) in 2017.[33] The FPSLRA was amended in 2013[34]; as of the date of publication, many of those amendments are in the process of being undone by the current federal government. Rather than explore in detail the historical evolution of these statutes, this chapter will attempt to provide a brief overview of the main features of the FPSLRA.

The FPSLRA is divided into two main parts. The first part deals with labour relations—the legal rules governing the relationship between unions and the employers in the federal public service. The second part deals with grievances—the method by which individual employees challenge certain decisions by the employer concerning their terms and conditions of employment.

The FPSLRA follows the standard Wagner Act model of labour relations that is common throughout Canada. The features of the Wagner Act model are as follows. A union may apply to become the certified bargaining agent on behalf of a group of employees called a bargaining unit. If the majority of employees in the bargaining unit wish to be represented by the union, then that union becomes the certified bargaining agent on behalf of the entire bargaining unit. This means that the union is the exclusive representative of the employees in the bargaining unit. The union and employer negotiate the terms of a collective agreement. If they are unable to reach an agreement, then the union may go on strike or the employer may lock out its employees to force the union to compromise until they reach an agreement. The union is also responsible for policing the collective agreement: any dispute with the employer may be grieved and then referred to a neutral arbitrator for resolution. Certain employees are excluded from this regime—typically managers and employees with duties that are confidential to the employer's labour relations strategies

and decisions. Finally, the whole system is administered or regulated by a labour board—in the federal public service, this board is named the Federal Public Sector Labour Relations and Employment Board.

As stated above, the FPSLRA broadly follows the standard Wagner Act model. There are, however, some areas in which the FPSLRA departs from, or modifies, the normal legal rules that have developed in conjunction with the Wagner Act model. This chapter will set out four of those ways.

1. The Bargaining Unit

In a standard Wagner Act model, the bargaining unit comprises employees who share a community of interest. In some workplaces, this is an entire plant or workplace; in others, different crafts or jobs have their own bargaining unit.

When Parliament first introduced collective bargaining into the federal public service, it considered four possible alternatives. First, it considered simply applying the community of interest test—but rejected that alternative in order to avoid disputes between unions about the composition of each bargaining unit and therefore ensure an orderly transition to collective bargaining. It considered geographically based bargaining units—so that employees in a certain geographic region (province, city, or other location) would comprise a bargaining unit. It also considered a department-based bargaining unit, so that employees in different departments would constitute a bargaining unit. Parliament ended up rejecting these alternatives to ensure that federal public servants would be paid the same regardless of their department or location.[35]

Parliament adopted the fourth alternative and defined bargaining units on the basis of job classification. Each public service position has a corresponding classification depending upon the type of work performed. Bargaining units are determined by those classifications so that all (for example) auditors, veterinarians, or program administrators are in their own bargaining unit. This means that bargaining units in the federal public service are, for the most part, significantly larger than units in the private sector.

2. Scope of Bargaining

In the private sector, unions and employers are free to collectively bargain all issues concerning terms and conditions of employment, save for proposals that are illegal in the sense that they violate a general law of Canada. The FPSLRA changes that approach and limits the topics that may be bargained. Section 113 of the FPSLRA states that a collective agreement may not alter any term or condition of employment if doing so would require an amendment to another statute, or if the term or condition is one established under the PSEA (i.e., dealing with appointments, layoffs, and political activities of public servants), the Public Service Superannuation Act (i.e., pensions), and the Government Employees Compensation Act (i.e., workers' compensation for workplace injuries).

This prohibition means that federal public service unions do not bargain pension-related issues. It also means that there are no seniority provisions in federal public service collective agreements—i.e., there are no provisions about laying off more junior workers before longer-service workers, and no provisions guaranteeing more senior workers first access to promotions. Some issues straddle the line between negotiable and non-negotiable. For example, the choice of which employees are laid off is non-negotiable, but the compensation paid to laid-off employees is negotiable.

3. Resolution of Bargaining Disputes

Bargaining disputes in Canada can be resolved in one of three ways: the union goes on strike, the employer locks out the employees, or the dispute is resolved by interest arbitration. Bargaining disputes in the federal public service are different.

First, nothing in the FPSLRA permits the employer to lock out its employees. Between the expiry of the last collective agreement and the start of the new collective agreement, the employer is prohibited from changing the terms and conditions of employment for its employees. This means no lockouts and no unilateral changes during bargaining.

Second, the right of unions to call a strike is limited in the federal public service by a corresponding obligation on the part of employees to continue to perform essential services. Essential services are those services that are necessary to preserve the safety and security of the public. Strikes in many Canadian jurisdictions—particularly in the public or broader public sectors—are limited by an obligation

to continue to perform essential services. There are, broadly speaking, three different models for dealing with strikes and essential services:

1. *the "no strike" model.* Strikes are illegal and disputes are resolved by compulsory interest arbitration. This model is common for employees who perform extremely essential services, such as police officers and firefighters.
2. *the "unfettered strike" model.* There are no restrictions on strikes.
3. *the "designation model."* Strikes are permitted, but certain essential workers must remain at work during strikes to provide essential services to the public.[36]

The FPSLRA was, until 2013, the prototype of the designation model in Canada. Before commencing a strike, unions and employers had to enter into an essential-services agreement identifying the service that was essential, the level of service (which was determined exclusively by the employer), and the specific employees who had to remain at work to perform the essential service. In 2013, the government amended the FPSLRA so that it could unilaterally decide issues relating to essential services; the government in 2017, however, has indicated that it will be repealing that legislation and returning to the pre-2013 essential-services regime.

Third, until 2013 federal public service unions could choose whether bargaining disputes would be resolved by a strike or by binding interest arbitration.[37] Interest arbitration refers to a system whereby a neutral arbitrator decides the content of a collective agreement. In most systems the choice between strike and arbitration is determined by statute; the federal public service is unique in giving unions a choice between the two dispute resolution regimes. The trade-off, if you will, is that there are some limits on arbitration: an arbitrator may not make an award that affects the assignment of duties, classification of positions, or the organization of the public service.[38] When the FPSLRA was first enacted, the expectation was that most bargaining agents would elect arbitration instead of striking to resolve bargaining disputes. That has not turned out to be the case: partially as a result of the limits of topics that may be referred to arbitration, most bargaining units have elected to strike instead of arbitrate their bargaining disputes.

Fourth and finally, the federal government has imposed legislated wage restraints during a number of periods, effectively suspending collective bargaining on wages for those periods. This includes the periods 1975–8 as part of the anti-inflation program,[39] 1982–3 with the "six and five" program,[40] 1991–7 with legislated wage freezes as a deficit-reduction measure,[41] and finally from 2006–11 as a response to the financial crisis of 2008.[42] This on-again, off-again treatment of collective bargaining has become a regular and unfortunate feature of collective bargaining in the federal public service.

4. Range of Employees Covered Permitted to Collectively Bargain

Fourth, the scope of coverage of collective bargaining is less than in unionized workplaces in the public and private sectors. The FPSLRA sets out a number of categories of workers who are not employees—i.e., are not covered by the Act for collective bargaining purposes.[43] For example, casual workers (those employed for less than 90 working days) are excluded. The FPSLRA also excludes managerial and confidential employees—as do all other collective bargaining statutes in Canada. The difference, however, is that the FPSLRA sets out a comprehensive list of categories of managerial and confidential employees that excludes a larger number of employees than in other workplaces. There is no federal public service equivalent to AMAPCEO, for example, which represents mid-level managers in the Ontario public service.[44]

Individual Disputes—The Grievance System

The dispute resolution mechanism for federal public servants is unique in Canada. Part II of the FPSLRA sets out a grievance procedure for federal public servants. All public servants, even executives and other employees who are not covered by a collective agreement, may grieve anything affecting their terms and conditions of employment—unless there is another avenue of redress set out in another statute except for the Canadian Human Rights Act. For example, if the employee's complaint is about his or her failure in a promotional exercise, the PSEA sets out a complaint procedure for those complaints—which in turn means that the employee may not file a grievance under the FPSLRA. Grievances are decided by the deputy head (i.e., deputy minister or equivalent) of the employee's department or separate agency.

Assuming that the grievance has been denied, there are two alternatives. Some grievances can be referred to adjudication—an arbitration system run by the Federal Public Sector Labour Relations and Employment Board. Other grievances may not be referred to adjudication; instead, a disappointed grievor must apply to the Federal Court for judicial review of the deputy head (or delegate's) decision. The rules about topics that may be referred to adjudication are also different for separate agencies than for the core public administration.

All employees may refer grievances about the following topics to adjudication:

- discipline resulting in termination of employment, a suspension, or a financial penalty (i.e., a fine); and
- grievances alleging a breach of the collective agreement.

Employees in the core public administration may refer the following additional topics to adjudication:

- demotion or termination for unsatisfactory performance;
- termination of employment for other reasons, except for layoffs or other dismissals under the PSEA; and
- deployments without the grievor's consent.

Finally, some separate agencies have been designated for special treatment under the FPSLRA.[45] Employees in those separate agencies may refer grievances about non-disciplinary termination of employment to adjudication.

The final eccentricity of the grievance system in the federal public service is that it is mandatory. Regardless of whether the grievance may be referred to adjudication, an employee must use the grievance system to complain about anything affecting his or her terms and conditions of employment. In other words, public servants cannot sue their employer in civil court, despite the fact that their grievance may be finally decided by the deputy head of the department who did the thing being grieved in the first place.[46]

Topic Three: Staffing

Public services throughout the world have wrestled with the problem of the best way to hire public servants. The problem is typically expressed in terms of a tension between two schools of thought. The first school of thought, sometimes referred to as the Jacksonian school (after US President Andrew Jackson, who once famously said "if you have a job in your department that can't be done by a Democrat, abolish the job"), is that public servants should be hired based on their political affiliation. This way, elected officials can be certain that public servants will support their policies and fully implement their goals. The second school of thought, championed by US President Woodrow Wilson, is that public servants should be hired solely on the basis of merit. Since the early twentieth century, the Canadian federal public service has followed the second, merit-based school.

Appointments, deployments (i.e. permanent transfers to a position with the same classification), and layoffs in the core public administration and some smaller separate agencies[47] are regulated through the PSEA. The PSEA creates an entity known as the Public Service Commission of Canada (PSC). The PSC is responsible for making all appointments to the core public administration and a small number of separate agencies. The PSC also has the power to investigate and determine whether other separate agencies are appointing employees in accordance with merit. The PSC makes appointments on the request of the deputy head of a department, who in turn may delegate this power down to managers to request that the PSC make an appointment.

Unlike in the private sector, an appointment by the PSC is a legal precondition for a person to become an employee in the federal public service. For other employers, the question of whether a person is an employee is a question of fact instead of formality: persons are employees if they are sufficiently dependent and under the control of their employer, regardless of whether the employer has attempted to characterize them as contractors instead of as employees.[48] In the federal public service, by contrast, there is no

such thing as a de facto public servant. Therefore, the thousands of contractors who work exclusively on a full-time basis for the federal government are not considered public servants despite the fact that they are dependent upon, and under the control of, the federal government.[49]

The pole star of the PSEA is the **merit principle**. The idea of merit evolved subtly in the 2005 changes to the PSEA. Prior to 2005, merit was an absolute value: the PSEA required that the Public Service Commission establish a list of all qualified candidates for a position (called an eligibility list) *and* rank those candidates in order of merit. The PSC would then appoint the most qualified candidate to the position; if he or she declined (or left the position shortly thereafter), the PSC would appoint the next most qualified candidate, and so on. The PSEA was amended in 2005 to change merit from an absolute to a relative value. The term *merit* is now defined as follows:

> **31(2)** An appointment is made on the basis of merit when
> **(a)**   the Commission is satisfied that the person to be appointed meets the essential qualifications for the work to be performed, as established by the deputy head, including official language proficiency; and
> **(b)**   the Commission has regard to
> > **(i)**   any additional qualifications that the deputy head may consider to be an asset for the work to be performed, or for the organization, currently or in the future,
> > **(ii)**   any current or future operational requirements of the organization that may be identified by the deputy head, and
> > **(iii)**   any current or future needs of the organization that may be identified by the deputy head.

In other words, an appointment is consistent with the merit principle so long as the candidate is qualified for the position. The deputy head (who, again, delegates this power to managers) sets two types of qualifications: essential qualifications and asset qualifications. The deputy head then assesses the candidates against those qualifications,[50] and decides which of the candidates meet the essential qualifications of the position. After having done so, the deputy head may select among any of the qualified candidates on the basis of the asset qualifications, and the PSC appoints the selected candidate. Similar rules apply for layoffs: when there is a layoff among a group of similar positions, the selection of the employee being laid off must be in accordance with merit.

The PSEA contains a mechanism for unsuccessful candidates to file a complaint about the results of an appointment or layoff process—either to the Federal Public Sector Labour Relations and Employment Board, or to the PSC, depending on the nature of the appointment. The threshold for a successful complaint, however, is that the complainant prove that the appointment was the result of an abuse of authority. This is a difficult threshold to meet. Abuse of authority requires more than simply errors or omissions. The term *abuse of authority* means one of five categories of abuse:

1. when the decision-maker exercises his/her/its discretion with an improper intention in mind (including acting for an unauthorized purpose, in bad faith, or on irrelevant considerations);
2. when a decision-maker acts on inadequate material (including where there is no evidence, or without considering relevant matters);
3. when there is an improper result (including unreasonable, discriminatory, or retroactive administrative actions);
4. when the decision-maker exercises discretion on an erroneous view of the law; and
5. when a delegate refuses to exercise his/her/its discretion by adopting a policy which fetters the ability to consider individual cases with an open mind.[51]

If the Board concludes that there has been an abuse of authority, the Board may not simply appoint the complainant to the position. The PSEA prohibits the Board from ordering the PSC to make an appointment or conduct a new appointment process. Instead, the Board can order the PSC (or deputy head, as the case may be) to revoke the appointment and take other corrective actions other than an appointment. If the Board revokes an appointment, the PSC may simply appoint that person to another position if he or she meets the essential qualifications for that new position.

Finally, the PSEA states that appointments must be made on the basis of merit and must be free from political influence. The PSC hears all complaints about alleged political influence in a staffing process. Since 2005, the PSC has never found political influence in a staffing process.[52]

In addition to protecting merit, the PSEA sets out some other rules respecting staffing in the public service, including:

*   setting out the probationary periods for employees—typically 12 months;
*   requiring that the PSC (in most cases, actually the department) choose between advertised and non-advertised job competitions, and that this decision not be an abuse of authority;
*   requiring that the PSC (or its delegate) assess candidates in the official language of their choice;
*   creating priorities for employment. The PSEA sets out various categories of candidates who must be appointed in priority to other candidates. For example, employees who have been laid off in the past 12 months have a priority over other candidates for the same position—in other words, if they meet the essential qualifications of the position, they are appointed even if other candidates are more qualified. The priority lists are in turn ranked, so that certain categories of priority candidates are appointed ahead of other priority candidates; and
*   giving unsuccessful candidates a right to informal discussion.

The larger separate agencies appoint their own employees, instead of the PSC. Public servants employed in those separate agencies are eligible for positions that are open only to persons employed in the public service. Some of those employees are also eligible to be deployed (i.e., transferred laterally) throughout the public service, depending upon the wording of the legislation creating those separate agencies.[53]

Topic Four: Legislative Protection of Fundamental Freedoms of Public Servants

Public servants are also citizens or residents of Canada. Like all people in Canada, they have certain fundamental rights and freedoms protected by the Charter of Rights and Freedoms. Public servants also have various rights and freedoms protected or limited by legislation. This topic will provide a brief overview of the most important legislative provisions impacting the rights and freedoms of public servants.

Canadian Human Rights Act—Freedom from Discrimination

The Canadian Human Rights Act[54] prohibits discrimination on the basis of eleven separate grounds.[55] This includes a prohibition against refusing the employ or continue to employ any individual, or to differentiate adversely against an employee in the course of employment, on a prohibited ground of discrimination.[56] The Canadian Human Rights Act applies to all federally regulated employees, including all federal public servants.

A complete discussion of human rights law is beyond the scope of this chapter. However, as a brief overview, there are four types or categories of discrimination:

1. *Direct discrimination.* This is a rule or practice that is discriminatory on its face, such as a rule that only men need apply for a particular job.
2. *Indirect discrimination.* This is a rule or practice that is not discriminatory on its face, but has a disproportionate impact upon an identifiable group on the basis of a prohibited ground of discrimination. For example, a rule that a person be over six feet tall to apply for a job is neutral on its face, but has a disproportionate impact upon women.
3. *Systemic discrimination.* This is a pattern of behaviour, policies, or practices that are part of the structure of an organization and that create or perpetuate disadvantage on an enumerated ground.
4. *Harassment.* Harassment is comments or actions based on an enumerated ground that are unwelcome or should be known to be unwelcome. They may include humiliating or annoying conduct. Harassment requires a course of conduct, which means that a pattern of behaviour or more than one incident is usually required for a claim to be made to the Tribunal. However, a single

significant incident may be offensive enough to be considered harassment.

A practice is not discriminatory if it is based upon a bona fide occupational requirement. To demonstrate that a policy or practice is a bona fide occupational requirement, an employer must demonstrate three things:

1. that it adopted the standard for a purpose rationally connected to the performance of the job;
2. that it adopted the standard in good faith; and
3. that the standard is reasonably necessary to accomplish its purpose. To show that the standard is reasonably necessary, the employer must demonstrate that it is impossible to accommodate the individual employees sharing the characteristics of the claimant without suffering undue hardship. This third criteria is often referred to as the "duty to accommodate."[57]

As mentioned above, public servants are protected by the Canadian Human Rights Act. However, the process they must follow to protect their rights is different from most other employees. The grievance process established under the FPSLRA permits an employee to grieve, and then refer to adjudication, an allegation that the employer has breached the Canadian Human Rights Act. The Canadian Human Rights Act has a separate complaints process, whereby a complainant may file a complaint with the Canadian Human Rights Commission, who will investigate the complaint and decide whether to refer the complaint to the Canadian Human Rights Tribunal for a full hearing and determination. The Canadian Human Rights Commission has the discretion, however, to refuse to investigate a complaint when the complaint could be more appropriately dealt with according to another procedure established by an Act of Parliament. Since the grievance procedure is established by an Act of Parliament, the Canadian Human Rights Commission will refuse to investigate most complaints by public servants and require them to pursue those complaints using the grievance process. The Canadian Human Rights Commission will still, on occasion, investigate a complaint by a public servant if it concludes that the grievance procedure is inappropriate for that complaint, but such cases are rare.

Pay Equity

Pay equity is a broad concept that refers to ensuring that rates of pay are not discriminatory, typically on the basis of gender. There are two types of protection of pay equity. First, there is equal pay protection: an employer may not establish two pay rates for the same job (historically, a men's rate and a women's rate). Second, there is the broader concept of pay equity, namely that it is a discriminatory practice to establish or maintain differences in wages between male and female employees who are performing work of equal value.

The Canadian Human Rights Act protects both the narrow and broad forms of pay equity. Section 11 of the Canadian Human Rights Act states that it is a discriminatory practice to "maintain differences in wages between male and female employees employed in the same establishment who are performing work of equal value." The Canadian Human Rights Commission has also published regulations called the *Equal Wages Guidelines*[58] which, as the name suggests, provides guidelines for how to assess pay equity and ensure equal pay for work of equal value.

Pay equity has been the subject of decades of legal battles in the federal public service, these battles being fought in the Canadian Human Rights Commission, the Canadian Human Rights Tribunal, the Federal Court, and the Federal Court of Appeal. The largest pay equity complaint was filed by the Public Service Alliance of Canada on behalf of clerical workers in the core public administration in 1984; it was finally resolved in 1999, requiring Treasury Board to fix pay rates going forward and pay out retroactive pay back to March 8, 1985—the date a joint pay equity study confirmed the existence of pay discrimination.[59] Since this only covered employees of Treasury Board, other pay equity complaints continued well after 1999 on behalf of employees in separate agencies or employees in other occupation groups.

Unlike other discriminatory practices, pay equity complaints cannot be addressed using the grievance process.

Political Activity

Restrictions on political activities by public servants have existed since 1878. At the time of Confederation, there were no restrictions on partisan political activities by public servants. In 1878, Parliament enacted An Act further securing the Independence of Parliament. That 1878 Act prohibited certain categories of people from sitting as a Member of the House of Commons, including government office-holders (i.e. public servants).

In 1968, as discussed above, Parliament enacted the PSEA. The 1968 version of the PSEA permitted public servants below the rank of deputy head to run for political office (federally, provincially, municipally, or otherwise), provided they obtained permission from the Public Service Commission. The PSEA also prohibited public servants from engaging in work for, or on behalf of, a political party. Public servants could donate money and attend political meetings—but could not go further.

After the advent of the Canadian Charter of Rights and Freedoms in 1985, there was considerable concern that the complete prohibition against political activity violated public servants' right to freedom of expression. As a result, several public servants challenged the constitutionality of the ban on political activity. In a 1991 decision, the Supreme Court of Canada struck down the provisions of the PSEA prohibiting political activity by public servants.[60]

Parliament took no action until it repealed and replaced the old PSEA with the new PSEA, effective December 31, 2005. Among other changes, Parliament overhauled the restrictions on public servants' political activities.

The current PSEA[61] distinguishes between political activity and running as a candidate in an election. The PSEA permits public servants below the rank of deputy head to engage in political activity, so long as that activity does not impair or is not perceived as impairing the public servant's ability to perform his or her duties in a politically impartial manner. The Public Service Commission then has the power to investigate any allegations that a public servant has engaged in an impermissible level of political activities.

The PSEA also sets out a regime for public servants who wish to stand as a candidate for a federal, provincial, territorial, or municipal election. A public servant who wishes to be a candidate, or seek nomination to be a candidate on behalf of a political party, must obtain permission from the PSC.

During the federal, provincial, or territorial election period, a public servant must take an unpaid leave of absence; the PSC may also order that the public servant take a leave of absence prior to the election period. There are also regulations[62] setting out how an employee must apply for permission to run as a candidate and, if necessary, a leave of absence. If the public servant is elected in a federal, provincial, or territorial election, he or she immediately ceases to be an employee on the day he or she is declared elected. For municipal elections, the PSC may require a public servant to take an unpaid leave of absence during the election or if elected. In any election, the PSC may grant permission to run as a candidate only if it is satisfied that the public servant's ability to perform his or her duties in a politically impartial manner will not be impaired or perceived to be impaired in light of the nature of the election, the nature of the employee's duties, and the level and visibility of the employee's position.

Public Criticism and Whistle-Blowing

Public servants, like all employees, owe their employer a duty of fidelity and loyalty. This duty of loyalty is owed to the Government of Canada, not the political party in power at any given time. This duty also limits a federal public servant's right to free speech. As a general principle, public servants have the right to criticize the government; however, their criticism is limited by their duty of loyalty. The degree of restraint expected from public servants depends on the position they hold, the visibility of their position, and the nature of the criticism. For example, measured criticism of government policies that jeopardize the life, health, or safety of Canadians is permitted; sustained and highly visible attacks on major government policies are not permitted. Further, the more senior the public servant, the less scope they have for criticism; for example, a data-entry clerk could attend a protest dealing with childcare funding whereas a deputy minister could not.

Disclosure of government wrongdoing—typically referred to as **whistle-blowing**—is protected by legislation in the federal public service. The **Public Servants Disclosure Protection Act**[63] protects public servants who make a protected disclosure of wrongdoing. A protected disclosure is a good faith disclosure made in one of four ways:

1. in accordance with that Act. The Act sets out three stages or types of disclosure:
   a. an internal disclosure made in accordance with procedures established by the employer;
   b. disclosure directly to the Public Sector Integrity Commissioner, who will investigate the alleged wrongdoing and make a report to the chief executive of an organization if it finds that wrongdoing has occurred and then table that report, along with the chief executive's response, in both Houses of Parliament within 60 days; and
   c. disclosure directly to the public. A public servant may only make a public disclosure when there is insufficient time to disclose the matter internally or to the Commissioner, and when the disclosure concerns an act or omission that constitutes a serious offence under a statute or constitutes an imminent risk of a substantial and specific danger to the life, health, and safety of persons or the environment;
2. in the course of a parliamentary proceeding;
3. in the course of another legal proceeding; and
4. when otherwise lawfully required.

The Act also defines *wrongdoing* as seven specific types of actions, including the broad phrase "gross mismanagement in the public sector."

Finally, the Act protects public servants against reprisals for having made a protected disclosure. A reprisal is a disciplinary measure, a demotion, a termination of employment, a measure that adversely affects employment or working conditions, or a threat to do any one of those things. A public servant may complain about a reprisal to the Public Sector Integrity Commissioner, who investigates and decides whether to refer the complaint to the Public Servants Disclosure Protection Tribunal. The Tribunal then holds a hearing, decides whether there has been a reprisal, and if so corrects the reprisal. The Tribunal can also order a payment of up to $10,000 for pain and suffering experienced as a result of the reprisal.

The Public Servants Disclosure Protection Act remains controversial. The Auditor General, who is responsible for investigating allegations of wrongdoing by the Public Sector Integrity Commissioner, found that each of the first two Commissioners were themselves guilty of wrongdoing under the Act for, among other things, a reluctance to investigate wrongdoing and dilatory investigations.[64] There are also some structural weaknesses with the Public Servants Disclosure Protection Act. For example, the Commissioner may not deal with a disclosure of wrongdoing if a person or body acting under another Act of Parliament is dealing with the subject matter of the disclosure[65]—even if they are dealing with it poorly. The fact that wrongdoing is defined, instead of being an open list, has also been criticized.[66] As a result of these factors, there is a sense of frustration among many public servants or government critics that the Public Servants Disclosure Protection Act does not go far enough to promote a culture of accountability within the federal public service.

Official Languages

A federal public servant has various rights in respect of the use of her or his chosen official language (i.e., English or French). Those rights are predominantly set out in the Official Languages Act.[67] That Act prescribes that English and French are the languages of work in all federal institutions, and all employees have the right to use either official language in accordance with that Act.[68] More specifically, the Act prescribes several regions of the country—including the National Capital Region—where employees have the right to receive information and services at work in either official language.[69]

As a result of this statutory right, Treasury Board has enacted a policy whereby all executives who supervise bilingual positions or play a significant role in the management of the institution must be functionally bilingual.[70] Many other positions also require that the employee be functionally bilingual. To reward bilingual employees, there is an annual bilingualism bonus of $800 for employees who occupy bilingual positions.

The Official Languages Act is enforced by the Official Languages Commissioner. Any person may make a complaint to the Official Languages Commissioner if her or his right to receive government services in the official language of her or his choice has been violated. The Commissioner investigates the complaint and makes a report to the President of Treasury Board and the deputy head of the institution concerned. If no action is taken, the Commissioner may transmit the report to the Governor-in-Council, and then to Parliament. Finally, the complainant or the Commissioner has the right to proceed to Federal Court to obtain a formal court order requiring the institution to remedy the breach of the Official Languages Act.

Privacy

Finally, federal public servants have some rights to privacy. The Privacy Act[71] limits the government's right to collect, use, and disclose personal information about an individual—including public servants—without that person's consent. The term *personal information* has a lengthy definition in the Privacy Act, and that definition has in turn been the subject of numerous court cases. A complete discussion of the term *personal information* is beyond the scope of this chapter. It is sufficient to note that personal information does not include information that relates to the positions or functions of a public servant—such as the business address, salary range, or personal views of the individual given in the course of employment. In addition to the protection against disclosure of personal information, public servants (like all Canadian citizens and permanent residents) also have a right to access personal information about themselves held by the government.[72]

The Privacy Act is enforced by the Privacy Commissioner. If a government institution has improperly disclosed personal information, or refused access to personal information, the affected individual may file a complaint with the Privacy Commissioner. The Privacy Commissioner investigates the complaint and makes a finding about whether or not the Privacy Act has been violated. If the complaint concerns a right of access to personal information, the complainant or the Privacy Commissioner may proceed to Federal Court to obtain a court order requiring the government institution to provide a copy of that personal information to the complainant.

Topic Five: Pensions

One of the significant benefits of being a public servant is that public servants receive a pension upon retirement. The pension for federal public servants is a statutory pension plan established by the Public Service Superannuation Act[73]—meaning that the terms of the pension are not negotiated individually or with a union. A full description of the federal public service pension is well beyond the scope of this chapter. In short, however, the pension provided under the Public Service Superannuation Act is 2 per cent for each year of pensionable service (to a maximum of 35 years) multiplied by the retiree's average salary over the best five consecutive years of service.

The Public Service Superannuation Act divides public servants into two categories: Group 1 and Group 2. Group 1 are all those hired before January 1, 2013; Group 2 are all those hired after January 1, 2013. The difference between the two groups is the date on which they are eligible for a full retirement pension. Group 1 employees can retire with an unreduced pension at age 60, or age 55 with 30 years of service; they can take "early retirement" starting at age 50, but with a penalty of 5 per cent for each year they are short from the full retirement age. Group 2 employees have to wait an extra five years for full retirement (i.e., at age 65, or age 60 with 30 years of service, or early retirement starting at age 55).

Public servants also receive a death benefit of twice their salary if they die before the age of 65, and then a steadily-reduced death benefit if they die before the age of 75. Public servants are also eligible for a disability pension if they must retire for medical reasons; essentially, they receive the basic pension with no reduction for retiring early.

Finally, there are a myriad of technical rules about buying back pensionable service with other employers or with the federal public service if there has been a break in service, and rules about other issues for that matter. The Public Service Superannuation Act recognizes that pensions are complicated and even the experts can get it wrong; therefore, there are provisions allowing public servants to correct mistaken decisions or elections when they have been given erroneous advice.

Topic Six: Non-Traditional Public Servants

The five topics discussed above relate mainly to traditional public servants. There are a number of what may be called non-traditional public servants—in other words, people who work within the federal government in jobs that take them outside of the normal rules applicable to public servants. Those non-traditional public servants are subject to distinct laws and statutes unique to their category.

Military Personnel

Military personnel—i.e., members of the Canadian Armed Forces—are governed by the National Defence Act.[74] Their terms and conditions of service, system of internal discipline, and even criminal justice system are set out entirely in that statute or in the orders, regulations, and policies determined by the appropriate level in the military chain of command. Members of the Canadian Armed Forces have the right to grieve issues concerning their terms and conditions of service, using an internal grievance system culminating in a decision by the Chief of Defence Staff. Finally, military personnel have a different pension from the rest of the public service, permitting earlier retirement in recognition of the serious physical toll of military service.[75]

RCMP Members

Police officers are typically treated differently from other public servants throughout Canada. Likewise, the Royal Canadian Mounted Police are treated differently from other federal public servants. Their terms and conditions of service are established by Treasury Board under the auspices of the Royal Canadian Mounted Police Act. RCMP members have a distinct disciplinary system, as well as a grievance system culminating in a decision by the Commissioner of the RCMP (or a delegate of the Commissioner). RCMP members also have a different pension from the rest of the public service that permits earlier retirement, again in recognition of the physical toll of police work.[76]

Until very recently, RCMP members were not permitted to join an employee association or attempt to engage in collective bargaining. In 2015, the Supreme Court of Canada struck down that prohibition against collective bargaining as unconstitutional.[77] As of the date of publication, members of the RCMP have not yet certified a bargaining agent.

Parliamentary Employees

There are a number of employees employed directly by the Senate, House of Commons, Library of Parliament, Senate Ethics Officer, the Conflict of Interest and Ethics Commissioner, and the Parliamentary Protective Service. These employees are governed by the Parliamentary Employment and Staff Relations Act (PESRA).[78] PESRA is very similar to the FPSLRA: it sets out a framework for collective bargaining similar to the FPSLRA, and it also contains a grievance process for all of these parliamentary employees.

There is no equivalent to the PSEA for parliamentary employees. This means that there is no statutory merit principle in place in Parliament: any rules about competitions can be negotiated in collective agreements, or are set out by policies enacted by the five parliamentary employers.

Parliamentary employees are employed directly by those five employers. Individual Members of Parliament or Senators also have a budget with which to hire employees. Those employees who are hired directly by Members of Parliament or Senators are not governed by PESRA—and in fact are not governed by any statute.

Finally, there is a category of employees referred to as "ministerial staff," i.e., those people employed directly by a minister or the Leader of the Opposition. The PSEA permits ministers to appoint their staff; it also states that ministerial staff with at least three consecutive years' service may participate in advertised internal (i.e., only open to public servants) competitions for the period of one-year after they ceased to be a ministerial staff.[79] Otherwise, ministerial staff are statutory orphans[80] without any legislative protection, subject to terms and conditions set unilaterally by Treasury Board.

Governor-in-Council Appointments

A Governor-in-Council appointment is an appointment made by the Governor General on the advice of the Queen's Privy Council of Canada, represented by cabinet. There are approximately 3500 Governor-in-Council appointments made by the federal government. Of those, there are approximately 1000 judges, 100 heads of foreign missions (including ambassadors and high commissioners), and some 500 full-time and 1900 part-time appointments to a wide array of agencies, boards, commissions, Crown corporations, and government departments. Deputy ministers, heads of agencies, and the CEOs and directors of Crown corporations are all Governor-in-Council appointees.

There are, broadly speaking, two types of Governor-in-Council appointments: appointments at pleasure and appointments for a fixed term during good behaviour. An appointment at pleasure can be cancelled at any time, subject only to a requirement that the office-holder be given relatively modest procedural rights to respond to any allegation of wrongdoing if this wrongdoing is the reason for terminating the appointment. An appointment on good behaviour, by contrast, may only be terminated for cause or incapacity on the part of the office holder.

The process for appointing these office holders has always had an element of political patronage—or, to be more kind, has always involved a political judgment. Several governments have promised reform while in opposition, only to abandon those efforts once elected. The Conservative government, for example, created a Public Appointments Commission in 2006 to put in place a more merit-based appointments process; however, its first nominee for commissioner was rejected in 2006 during a minority Parliament, and it never nominated a second commissioner—quietly abolishing the office in 2012. The Liberal government elected in 2015 has implemented what it calls a new approach to Governor-in-Council appointments, making a commitment to a more inclusive and merit-based appointment process. This was simply announced as a policy change, and there are no legal rules requiring a truly neutral appointment process.

Finally, Governor-in-Council appointees are bound by the Conflict of Interest Act[81] to avoid conflicts of interest during their period of office and for one year after their last day in office.

Important Terms and Concepts

Crown corporations

departmental corporations

merit principle

National Joint Council

Public Servants Disclosure
Protection Act (PSDPA)

Treasury Board

whistle-blowing

Study Questions

1. What is the role of the Treasury Board in the federal public service?
2. What are the important differences between collective bargaining in the private and federal public sectors?
3. What is the merit principle and how is it protected?
4. What sorts of political activities are permissible for public servants?
5. What are some of the fundamental rights and freedoms of public servants that are protected by legislation?

Notes

1   The Crown has a very limited number of prerogatives unsupported by legislation, such as issuing passports and conferring honours.

2   Financial Administration Act, RSC 1985, c F-11.

3   An Act for improving the organization and increasing the efficiency of the Civil Service of Canada, (UK), 1857, 20 Vict. c 24. This was the forerunner of the Public Service Employment Act, SC 2003, c 22, ss 12, 13.

4   [1999] 3 S.C.R. 199.

5   *Vaughan v. Canada*, 2005 SCC 11 at para 1: "The terms and conditions of employment of the federal government's quarter of a million current workers are set out in statutes, collective agreements, Treasury Board directives, regulations, ministerial orders, and other documents that consume bookshelves of loose-leaf binders."

6   See *Babcock et al. v. Attorney General of Canada*, 2005 BCSC 513 and *Peck v. Parks Canada*, 2009 FC 686 among other cases.

7   These four principles are paraphrased from the Federal Court of Appeal decision in *Gingras v. Canada*, [1994] 2 F.C. 734.

8   http://www.tbs-sct.gc.ca/psm-fpfm/modernizing-modernisation/stats/ssen-ane-eng.asp. In case you were wondering, this means that 0.7 per cent of Canadian citizens are employed in the federal public service, or 1.4 per cent of Canadians in active employment.

9   Federal Public Sector Labour Relations Act, S.C. 2003, c. 22, s. 2, s. 111.

10   Answering the question "*quis auditoris, ipsos auditoris.*"

11   FPSLRA, s. 112.

12   Record of Cabinet Decision, November 30, 1967. This instrument is the delegation instrument contemplated by s. 11.2 of the Financial Administration Act.

13   This requirement to seek a Treasury Board "mandate" is also sometimes set out in statute: see Canada Revenue Agency Act, S.C. 1999, c. 17, s. 58.

14   See, for example, National Research Council Act, R.S.C. 1985, c. N-15, s. 5(g) and the National Capital Act, R.S.C. 1985, c. N-4, s. 8(3).

15   See, for example, the Canadian Food Inspection Agency Act, S.C. 1997, c. 6, s. 13(2).

16   Canada Revenue Agency Act, SC 1999, c-17, s 51(1)(d).

17   Public Service Rearrangement and Transfer of Duties Act, RSC 1985, c P-34.

18   The Financial Administration Act includes a departmental corporation in the definition of the term *department*: s. 2(1) "department" paragraph (d).

19   Financial Administration Act, s. 7(1)(c) and (d).

20   Financial Administration Act, s. 83.

21   Financial Administration Act, s. 109.

22   Financial Administration Act, s. 105.

23   Financial Administration Act, s. 123(1), (5). A small number of Crown corporations listed in Part II of Schedule III to the Act are exempt from this requirement.

24   Financial Administration Act, s. 124(1), (8).

25   Financial Administration Act, s. 132(3).

26   Canada Labour Code, RSC 1985, c L-2.

27   The NJC was created by Order in Council P.C. 3676, 16 May 1944. It still exists, as amended by various Orders in Council: P.C. 1966–37/2106 of November 10, 1966; P.C. 1980–2413 of September 5, 1980; P.C. 1981–2443 of September 3, 1981; P.C. 1987–884 of April 30, 1987; and P.C. 1994–2/752 of May 5, 1994.

28   The NJC Directive on "work force adjustment" (i.e., layoffs), in particular, has been modified in a number of collective agreements.

29   A complete list of NJC Directives is available on its website; http://www.njc-cnm.gc.ca/directive/index.php?lang=eng. For a more thorough discussion of the National Joint Council, see Richard P. Chaykowski, "Advancing Public-Sector Labour-Management Relations through Consultation: The Role of the National Joint Council of the Public Service of Canada" in Bruce Kaufman & Daphne Gottleib Taras, eds., *Nonunion Employee Representation* (Armonk, NY: M.E. Sharpe, 2000) 328; and Robert Vaison, "Collective Bargaining in the Federal Public Service: The Achievement of a Milestone in Personal Relations" in Barbara W. Carroll et al., eds., *Classic Readings in Canadian*

Public Administration (Toronto: Oxford University Press, 2005) at 197. Vaison's article was originally published in 1969.

30   Canada, *Report of the Preparatory Committee on Collective Bargaining in the Public Service* (Ottawa: Queen's Printer, 1965).

31   SC 1966–67, c 72.

32   Public Service Reform Act, SC 1992, c 54.

33   SC 2003, c 22.

34   SC 2013, c 40.

35   The federal public service does have some extra allowances for isolated locations, and certain Toronto employees are paid more than their colleagues in other locations, but generally pay remains constant across Canada.

36   For a more detailed discussion of these three models, see B. Adell, M. Grant, & A. Ponak, *Strikes in Essential Services* (Kingston: IRC Press, 2001).

37   Again, the government elected in 2015 has indicated that it is going to repeal the 2013 changes and revert to the pre-2013 version of the FPSLRA on this point.

38   FPSLRA, s 150.

39   Anti-Inflation Act, SC 1975, c 75 limited wage increases to 10 per cent, 8 per cent, and 6 per cent in those three years – below the prevailing rate of inflation.

40   Public Sector Compensation Restraint Act, SC 1980–1983, c 122, limiting wage increases to 6 per cent and 5 per cent for those years.

41   The Public Sector Compensation Act, SC 1991, c-30 imposed a 2-year wage freeze, which was then extended to 1995 by the Government Expenditure Restraint Act, SC 1993, c-13 and extended again by the Budget Implementation Act, 1994, SC 1994, c-17 to 1997. Arbitration was suspended until 2001 in a further attempt to keep wages down.

42   Expenditure Restraint Act, SC 2009 c-2, s 393. This Act legislated maximum wage increases of 1.5 per cent for the 2008–9 through 2010–11 fiscal years. It also retroactively legislated maximum wage increases for the 2006–7 and 2007–8 fiscal years for those bargaining agents that were still bargaining for those periods.

43   The full list is in the definition of "employee" in s. 2 of the FPSLRA.

44   See Crown Employees Collective Bargaining Act, 1993, SO 1993, c 38, ss 22–24.

45   At the time of publication, there are only two designated separate agencies: the Canadian Food Inspection Agency and the Canada Revenue Agency.

46   The Supreme Court of Canada concluded that there was nothing unfair about this system in *Vaughan v. Canada*, 2005 SCC 11.

47   As of the time of publication, there are five separate agencies where the PSC has the power to make appointments: the Financial Consumer Agency of Canada; Indian Oil and Gas Canada; the National Energy Board; the Correctional Investigator of Canada; and the Office of the Superintendent of Financial Institutions Canada.

48   See, for example, *McCormick v. Fasken Martineau DuMoulin LLP*, 2014 SCC 39.

49   The Supreme Court of Canada established this principle in *Canada (Attorney General) v. Public Service Alliance of Canada*, [1991] 1 SCR 614.

50   Typically this assessment is done by a group of managers commonly referred to as a "selection board."

51   *Tibbs v. Canada (National Defence)*, 2006 PSST 8.

52   The PSC has only investigated two such complaints; neither complaint was founded.

53   The Canada Revenue Agency Act, SC 1999, c 17, s 55, for example, states explicitly that employees of the Canada Revenue Agency have mobility rights within those parts of the public service governed by the PSEA, and vice versa.

54   Canadian Human Rights Act, RSC 1985, c H-6.

55   Those grounds are: race, national or ethnic origin, colour, religion, age, sex, sexual orientation, marital status, family status, disability, and conviction for an offence for which a pardon has been granted or in respect of which a record suspension has been ordered. Canadian Human Rights Act, RSC 1985, c H-6, s 3(1).

56   Canadian Human Rights Act, RSC 1985, c H-6, s 7.

57   *British Columbia (Public Service Employee Relations Commission) v. BCGSEU*, [1999] 3 SCR 3.

58   *Equal Wages Guidelines, 1986*, SOR/86-1082

59   See *Canada (Attorney General) v. Public Service Alliance of Canada (1999)*, [2000] 1 FC 146 for a Federal Court decision affirming the finding of discriminatory pay.

60   *Osborne v. Canada (Treasury Board)*, [1991] 2 SCR 69.

61   These provisions of the PSEA apply in the core public administration, and also apply to many separate agencies, including the Canada Revenue Agency and Parks Canada.

62   *Political Activities Regulations*, SOR/2005-373.

63   SC 2005, c 46.

64   *Report of the Auditor General of Canada to the House of Commons—Public Sector Integrity Commissioner of Canada*, December 2010, online: http://www.oag-bvg.gc.ca/internet/docs/parl_oag_201012_e_34448.pdf and *Report of the Auditor General of Canada under the Public Servants Disclosure Protection Act—Office of the Public Sector Integrity Commissioner of Canada*, April 2014, online: http://www.oag-bvg.gc.ca/internet/docs/parl_otp_201404_e_39215.pdf.

65   Public Servants Disclosure Protection Act, SC 2005, c 46, s 23(1).

66   Commission of Inquiry into the Sponsorship Program and Advertising Activities *Restoring Accountability: Recommendations* (Ottawa: Commission of Inquiry into the Sponsorship Program and Advertising Activities, 2006) at 186 [the Gomery Report].

67   Official Languages Act, RSC 1985, c 31 (4th Supp).

68   Official Languages Act, RSC 1985, c 31 (4th Supp) s 34.

69   Currently, those regions are the National Capital Region, New Brunswick, parts of Montreal, parts of Quebec, and parts of Eastern and Northern Ontario: see Treasury Board and Public Service Commission Circular No. 1977-46 of September 30, 1977, in Annex B of the part entitled "*Official Languages in the Public Service of Canada: A Statement of Policies.*"

70   Treasury Board, *Directive on Official Languages for People Management*, November 19, 2012, online: https://www.tbs-sct.gc.ca/pol/doc-eng.aspx?id=26168.

71   Privacy Act, RSC 1985, c P-21.

72   Privacy Act, RSC 1985, c P-21, s 12.

73   Public Service Superannuation Act, RSC 1985, c P-36.

74   National Defence Act, RSC 1985, c N-5.

75   Canadian Forces Superannuation Act, RSC 1985, c C-17.

76   Royal Canadian Mounted Police Superannuation Act, RSC 1985, c R-11.

77   *Mounted Police Association of Ontario v. Canada (Attorney General)*, 2015 SCC 1.

78   Parliamentary Employment and Staff Relations Act, RSC 1985, c 33 (2nd Supp).

79   Public Service Employment Act, SC 2003, c 22, ss 12, 13, s 35.2. Parliamentary employees have a similar right.

80   L. Benoit, "Ministerial Staff: the Life and Times of Parliament's Statutory Orphans" in *Restoring Accountability: Research*   *Studies Vol. 1* (Ottawa: Commission of Inquiry into the Sponsorship Program and Advertising Activities, 2005).

81   Conflict of Interest Act, SC 2006, c 9, s 2.

References

Adell, Bernie, Grant, Michel, & Ponak, Allen. 2001. *Strikes in Essential Services.* Kingston: IRC Press.

Bartkiw, Timothy J. & Gene Swimmer. 2008. "Federal Public Sector Labour Relations under the Liberals and Conservative Governments." *How Ottawa Spends 2007-08*, edited by B. Doern, McGill Queens University Press, pp. 200–220.

Lee, Ian & Cross, Philip. 2016. "Reforms to the Federal Public Service during the Harper Years, 2006–2015." *How Ottawa spends 2015–2016*, edited by B. Doern & C. Stoney, School of Public Policy and Administration, Carleton University.

Rootham, Christopher. 2007. *Labour and Employment Law in the Federal Public Service.* Toronto: Irwin Law.

Sossin, Lorne. 2005. Speaking Truth to Power? The Search for Bureaucratic Independence in Canada. *The University of Toronto Law Journal*, 55, 1, pp. 1–59.

Swimmer, Gene. 1995. "Collective Bargaining in the Federal Public Service of Canada: The Last Twenty Years." *Public Sector Collective Bargaining in Canada: Beginning of the End or the End of the Beginning*, edited by Gene Swimmer & Mark Thompson, Kingston: IRC Press.

Swimmer, Gene & Sandra Bach, S. 2001. "Restructuring Federal Public Service Human Resources." *Public Sector Labour Relations in an Era of Restraint and Restructuring*, edited by Gene Swimmer, Oxford University Press, pp. 178–211.

Adaptability, Accountability, and Sustainability

Intergovernmental Fiscal Arrangements in Canada

William B.P. Robson and Alexandre Laurin

Chapter Overview

This chapter is a comprehensive overview of most fiscal arrangements between Canada's federal and provincial governments. It describes the history surrounding the current division of taxing and spending powers and various intergovernmental transfers. It pays particular attention to the justifications that have been advanced in federalist and public economics literature to explain and/or prescribe particular aspects of Canadian fiscal arrangements. Prominent rationales have included subsidiarity, the Tiebout hypothesis, public choice, and public finance (public economics) theories of fiscal federalism. Public finance theories include externalities, **economies of scale,** regional redistribution to standardize services, and mitigating harmful internal migration. The authors stress that these theoretical guidelines are not always realistic guides to what happens in fiscal federalism, which may be affected just as much by fiscal stresses and political responses in particular circumstances. They strongly favour the principle of hard fiscal constraints and more closely aligning the revenue-raising and spending powers of governments in Canada.

Chapter Objectives

By the end of this chapter, students will be able to do the following:
- Explain the importance of the division of powers in intergovernmental finance.
- List the major program landmarks in the evolution of intergovernmental finance in the nineteenth, twentieth, and twenty-first centuries.
- Understand how important theory is to what actually happens in intergovernmental finance.

continued

- Understand how important centralist and decentralist forces are in Canadian fiscal federalism.
- Explain the relative importance of fiscal discipline in intergovernmental finance.
- List the principles that are important in the design of federal/provincial/local finance.

Introduction[1]

Amounts raised and spent by different levels of government in Canada have never coincided: the federal government has always raised more, and provincial, territorial, and local governments less, than required for their own programs. Accordingly, transfers from the federal government to other levels of government have been a feature of Canadian fiscal policy since Confederation.[2]

Initially modest relative to Canada's economy, **intergovernmental transfers** grew as the role of governments in providing services and redistributing income grew through the 20th century. They now occupy a major place in the budgets of Canadian governments: about one-third of the spending of the federal government and almost one-fifth of the revenues of recipient governments. They are correspondingly prominent in public and official discussions. The 2015 federal budget devoted 11 pages to a survey of intergovernmental transfers and federal/provincial spending and taxing powers, and most provincial budgets that year also devoted considerable attention to the topic.

Transfers from central to sub-central governments are common throughout the world. Because they are particularly visible in federations, scholars and other commentators in federations, including Canada, have been prominent in elaborating possible justifications for divisions of taxing and spending powers, and for intergovernmental transfers for various purposes, including closing any fiscal gaps a particular division of powers creates. That literature naturally responded to the circumstances, including the specific mixes of taxes, programs, and transfers, that prevailed at the time. As a result, positive

observations about what was happening have tended to be tightly interwoven with normative statements about what should be.

This chapter begins by describing the history that shaped Canada's current system, then reviews various insights about potential uses of federal–provincial transfers and comments on the degree to which they justify current practices. It next describes potential future evolutions of spending and revenue at the federal and provincial levels. It closes with some comments on how different types of intergovernmental transfers may affect the efficiency, accountability, and sustainability of Canadian fiscal policies and major programs.

An important theme in this survey is the fact just mentioned: particular circumstances, including fiscal stresses at either level of government, and the political responses to those circumstances, have been central in shaping Canada's arrangements. Notwithstanding the insights from public economics about how intergovernmental transfers can address externalities within a federation and provide public goods on a national scale, nothing in economic logic dictates that the gap between revenue and spending at the federal and provincial levels should be as large as it now is in Canada, nor that the gap must grow as it has done, nor that the transfers that bridge it should be structured along current lines.

A second key theme is that the key principle that federal and provincial governments are sovereign in their respective spheres coexists uneasily with federal–provincial transfers, especially when they are large and complex. A focus on the provincial autonomy that is desirable in a federation, as well as on responding effectively to challenges at each level of government, and limiting potentially adverse influences of intergovernmental transfers on budgetary policy, would point towards smaller, simpler intergovernmental transfers. We see a strong case for more closely aligning the revenue-raising and spending powers of governments at each level.

The History and Current State of Intergovernmental Transfers in Canada

Canada's division of revenue and spending powers between the senior governments, and the transfers that reconcile gaps between revenue and spending at each level, have evolved in response to changing concerns and political pressures.

The Nineteenth Century

As is well known, the British North America Act—now formally termed the Constitution Act, 1867—and key political and legal decisions shortly after Confederation gave Canada a system in which the federal and provincial governments are sovereign in their respective spheres.

Looking first at responsibilities, some powers, notably those related to defence, money and banking, navigation, Indians, immigration, and criminal law, became federal matters. Others, notably those related to property and civil rights, natural resources,[3] municipalities, charities, and services now generally referred to as health care and education, became provincial matters.[4]

As for the resources to finance those responsibilities, the 1867 Act granted the federal government power to implement "any mode or system of taxation."[5] It granted the provinces "direct taxation within the province"[6]—a formulation intended partly to preclude tariffs on interprovincial trade, and which has been interpreted so elastically as to allow a variety of indirect taxes. As a result, the tax bases of the federal and provincial governments largely overlap. Both levels have legally unlimited power to borrow to finance any activity.

By today's standards, late nineteenth-century government spending was small relative to the economy. In peacetime, federal infrastructure—such as the national railway and other projects providing benefits on a national scale—was expected to dominate government spending. The indirect taxes—customs, duties, and fees—that then provided the bulk of

revenues were also federal, and accounted for about 80 per cent of all government revenues (Hogg, 1997).

Responding to arguments that the provinces' revenue-raising capacity, largely dependent on property taxes from relatively rural populations, was inadequate to finance their responsibilities, the 1867 Act provided for transfers from the federal government. Originally, these included funding for public administration as well as per-capita transfers to reduce regional disparities. In addition, these transfers contained an incentive to control public debt.[7]

The federal transfers were originally fixed total sums or fixed dollar amounts per head, so growth of the economy and government budgets had reduced their importance in provincial revenues by the end of the century. From nearly 6 in 10 dollars of provincial revenue in 1874, federal transfers had fallen closer to 4 in 10 dollars by 1896 (Perry, 1997).

The Twentieth Century

Federal and provincial spending and revenues changed markedly over the course of the twentieth century.

Two world wars created a need, and demonstrated a capacity, for governments to mobilize resources on a much larger scale. The nineteenth-century model of relatively small governments mainly providing infrastructure and internal and external security transitioned to the post–Second World War welfare state. By the end of the century, health care, education, and social services—areas of provincial responsibility—had become major government programs in Canada, as in other developed democracies.

On the revenue side, Ottawa introduced personal and corporate income taxes in stages during the First World War. Many provinces started taxing corporate and personal incomes for the first time in the 1930s to finance the needs created by the Great Depression. Concerns about the complicated structure of taxes going into the Second World War, and then the fiscal stresses of the war itself, produced important changes in income taxes. Under **tax rental agreements**, the provinces vacated the personal and corporate income tax fields in return for federal transfers. After the war, **tax collection agreements** supplanted the tax rental agreements. Provinces progressively regained tax-policy autonomy, as long as they conformed to shared definitions of the base for taxable income. As provincial spending responsibilities grew, the provincial share of personal income tax revenues increased. One formal change in tax fields occurred in 1980, when the federal government vacated the lottery and gaming field in return for an annual payment from the provinces (Desjardins, Longpré, & Vaillancourt, 2012).

As revenue and spending arrangements changed, intergovernmental transfers changed too. Notably, federal transfers became more incentivizing. An early example was a federal subsidy for technical education during the First World War. In 1927, long before the 1951 constitutional amendment that made old-age income supports a federal responsibility, Ottawa began paying half their cost. The Great Depression tested many provinces' access to credit, with Alberta defaulting in 1936. The federal government's superior access to credit, backed after the creation of the Bank of Canada by the power to monetize debt, increased its attractiveness as a subsidizer of provincial programs. In particular, Ottawa provided extensive supports for the unemployed, before the transfer of responsibility for unemployment insurance to the federal government in 1940.

During the late 1950s and 1960s, the appeal of federal support for national social programs was strong in most parts of the country, and rapid growth in the economy and federal revenues made relatively open-ended support of provincial programs seem affordable. Federal payments geared to half of aggregate provincial spending on publicly funded doctor and hospital care developed during those years. Ottawa replaced direct grants to universities with transfers to provincial governments, likewise geared to half of aggregate provincial spending on post-secondary education. Ottawa also supported provincial welfare programs through the Canada Assistance Plan (CAP), which underwrote half of relevant expenditures in each province individually.[8]

An exception to this general move towards **conditional grants** was the 1957 establishment of a formal **equalization program**. Equalization's essence is to top up the revenues of provinces that have lower-yielding tax bases.[9] The representative tax base used to determine equalization entitlements changed several times in later decades, reflecting a variety of tensions as the fortunes of specific provinces rose and fell, and as the federal government found its obligations under the program easier or harder to meet.

Another notable exception to the general narrative of federal inducements to provinces to expand their programs by subsidizing them was a series of federal offers, in 1964, 1968, and 1973, to withdraw from certain cost-shared programs and transfer tax room to the provinces instead. (At that time, provincial income taxes—with the exception of Quebec—were computed as percentages of federal income taxes, which gave rise to the terminology of "tax points"—each percentage point being one tax point.) Most provinces preferred the shared-cost subsidies; Quebec was the exception. Since 1965, Quebec taxpayers have received a special tax abatement in lieu of cash transfers Ottawa would otherwise have made.[10]

The end of the rapid growth of the 1950s, 1960s, and early 1970s put the federal budget under pressure and prompted changes to federal grants in support of health care and post-secondary education. New **Established Programs Financing** (EPF) arrangements replaced cost-sharing arrangements with a formal transfer of tax base ("tax points") and a cash transfer. These changes reduced federal subsidization and exposure to provincial spending decisions: no longer were the provinces collectively spending "50-cent dollars" on these programs.[11] To make its leverage over provincial health-care policy more explicit, the federal government passed the *Canada Health Act* in 1984, providing a formal basis for reduced transfers to provinces that did not adhere to its principles.

Ottawa's fiscal problems intensified during the 1980s, and the economic downturn of the early 1990s pushed its deficit and debt higher on the national agenda. The mid-1990s effort to balance the federal budget had a major impact on intergovernmental transfers. Ottawa first capped its CAP subsidies to several provinces. It then combined grants for health care and post-secondary education with the Canada Assistance Plan in one block fund, the **Canada Health and Social Transfer** (CHST), eliminating the last of the "50-cent dollars" provinces had been spending on welfare programs. The total CHST was initially smaller than its predecessor programs—part of Ottawa's effort to eliminate chronic deficits. These changes were a rude shock to the provinces. After increasing in line with the economy in the early 1990s (Figure 2.1), federal transfers fell sharply in 1996/97 and 1997/98. Although they grew again as Ottawa's budgetary situation improved, provincial governments and other advocates were complaining of a fiscal imbalance as the twentieth century drew to a close.

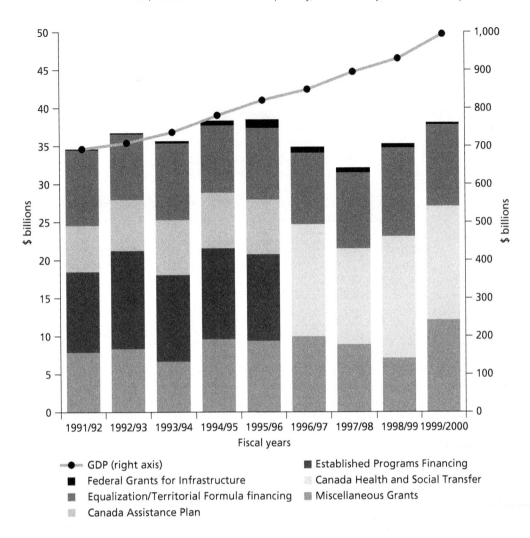

Figure 2.1 Federal Transfers to PTL Governments, by Major Category, 1991/92 to 1999/2000

Note: Data adjusted to take into account the effect of the Quebec tax abatement: federal cash transfers to Quebec are increased by the value of the federal income tax abated under the Alternative Payments for Standing Programs (13.5 tax points).

Sources: Government Finance Statistics (Statistics Canada 2015), Public Accounts of Canada RCG various years), and Canada (2015); authors' calculations.

The Twenty-First Century

In the early twenty-first century, the formal structures of spending and revenue-raising, and the intergovernmental transfers that bridge the gaps between spending and revenue, have changed relatively little, but the dollar amounts have changed markedly. In the 20 years from the early 1990s to the early 2010s, provincial, territorial, and local (PTL) governments increased their share of consolidated government spending—excluding intergovernmental transfers—from 63 to 72 per cent. They also increased their share of revenue, with their own-source revenues—that is, excluding intergovernmental transfers—rising from 56 to 60 per cent of the national total (Figure 2.2).

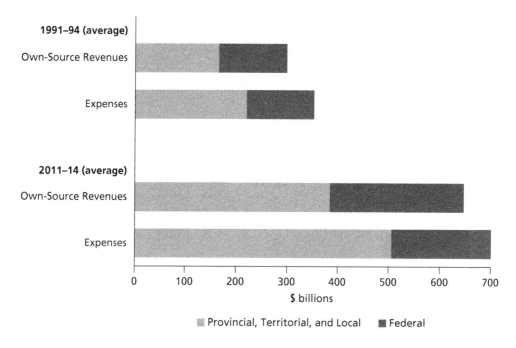

Figure 2.2 Consolidated Revenues and Spending by Levels of Government (Excludes Intergovernmental Transfers), 1991–4 and 2011–14

Note: Data adjusted to take into account the effect of the Quebec tax abatement: Quebec tax revenues are reduced by the value of federal income tax abated under the Alternative Payments for Standing Programs (13.5 tax points) and the discontinued Youth Allowances Program (3.0 tax points); federal revenues are increased by the same amount.

Sources: Government Finance Statistics (Statistics Canada 2015); authors' calculations.

Program Spending by Types

At present, and going a layer deeper, PTL governments currently make about 85 per cent of expenditures on operations—payments to employees, contractors, utilities, and so on—reflecting their role as public service providers. PTL governments also manage about 85 per cent of public infrastructure expenses, and hand out about 80 cents per dollar of business subsidies (Figure 2.3).

Ottawa continues to dominate transfer payments to households through employment insurance, benefits for seniors and families with children, and other purposes. About 70 cents of all government payments to individuals are now federal.

Revenues by Tax Bases

Turning to revenues (Figure 2.4), property taxes—still a field exclusive to the provinces—continue to raise a substantial amount of their revenue. By contrast, Ottawa's

exclusive jurisdiction over customs and other levies on international trade and transactions has become less important as international trade has become freer.

As for shared tax fields, Ottawa is still the largest collector of personal and corporate income taxes, raising about two-thirds of the total. The provinces collect about two-thirds of consumption tax revenues, up markedly over the last 20 years, thanks to rate cuts at the federal level and rate increases at the provincial level.

Miscellaneous non-tax revenues—mainly investment incomes, profits of government business enterprises, royalties, user fees, fines and other penalties, asset sales, and various other sources—are important for PTL governments. The federal government collected only about one-eighth of such revenues in 2014.

Contributions to social insurance schemes and provincial payroll taxes that flow into consolidated revenue[12] now yield roughly equal amounts to each level. Ottawa has recently collected something less than

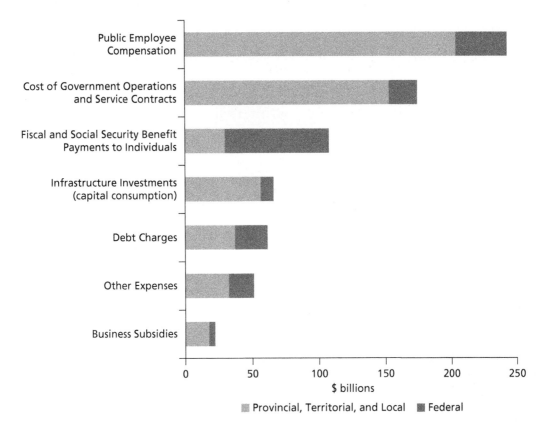

Figure 2.3 Government Spending at Federal and PTL Levels, by Category, 2014

Sources: Government Finance Statistics (Statistics Canada 2015); authors' calculations.

two-thirds of contributions to social insurance schemes related to employment, workplace injuries, and health care, down from more than three-quarters in the early 90s. This change reflects slower growth in federal employment insurance payouts and revenues than in provincial workers' compensation and drug programs.

Intergovernmental Transfers

The fact that provinces have increased their share of spending more than their share of own-source revenues since the 1990s implies that federal transfers have increased and/or that their budget balances have deteriorated relative to the federal balance. Both developments have occurred.

Improved federal fiscal health and pressure for larger transfers spurred faster growth in payments after 2004. Ottawa split the CHST into a Canada Social Transfer (CST) and a Canada Health Transfer (CHT).

The former continued to grow with the economy, but the latter—responding to the higher public profile of health-care spending—grew faster. The net result was that federal transfers outpaced GDP. They also rose relative to PTL spending, from about 15 per cent after the cuts of the late 1990s to around 17 per cent recently. And they rose relative to Ottawa's resources: roughly one in three dollars raised by federal taxes recently has financed intergovernmental transfers (Figure 2.5).

Current Transfers and Commitments

That account brings us to the present, and a review of the current configuration of transfers and their likely growth. The largest single intergovernmental transfer is the CHT—$32 billion in 2014/15, expected to grow to $41 billion in 2019/20. The CST is also sizeable—$13 billion in 2014/15, expected to reach $15 billion in 2019/20

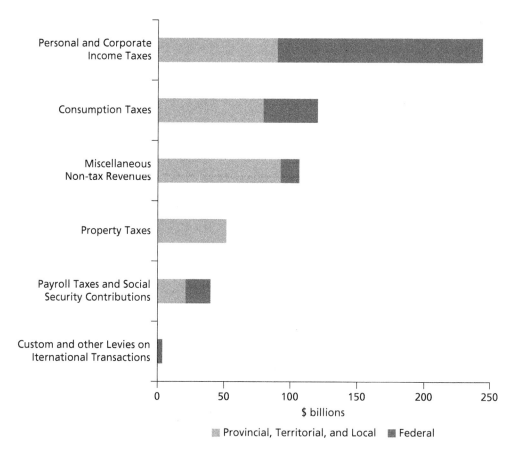

Figure 2.4 Government Revenues at Federal and PTL Levels, by Category, 2014

Note: Data adjusted to take into account the effect of the Quebec tax abatement: Quebec tax revenues are reduced by the value of federal income tax abated under the Alternative Payments for Standing Programs (13.5 tax points) and the discontinued Youth Allowances Program (3.0 tax points); federal tax revenues are increased by the same amount.

Sources: Government Finance Statistics (Statistics Canada 2015); authors' calculations.

(Figure 2.6). The CHT is legislated to continue its 6 per cent annual escalation until the 2016/17 fiscal year, and thereafter to increase at least 3 per cent annually up to the rate of growth of the economy. The CST is legislated to continue its 3 per cent annual growth.

The CHT and the CST, paid on a per-capita basis, are formally earmarked to support provincial spending on health care, post-secondary education, childcare, social assistance, and other social services. In practical terms, however, they resemble unconditional transfers. The money is fungible and can help provinces spend on anything, provide tax relief, or improve their budget balances. There are no recent instances of Ottawa withholding material amounts to penalize a province for deficiencies in its programs.

Rounding out the three largest transfers are the Equalization and the Territorial Formula Financing (TFF) programs—a combined $20 billion in 2014/15, expected to reach $24 billion in 2019/20. The equalization formula reflects differing yields of tax bases among provinces; TFF reflects differing tax yields among all 13 jurisdictions. A desire to create a predictable obligation has led Ottawa to gear total equalization payments to GDP since 2009.

Alongside these programs, Ottawa transfers several billion dollars annually for public infrastructure,

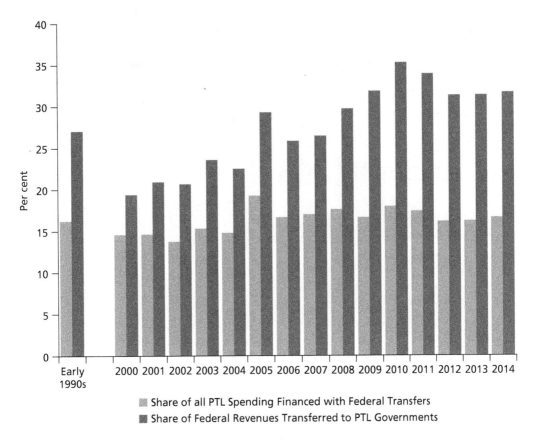

Figure 2.5 Federal Transfers Relative to PTL Spending and Federal Revenue

Note: Data adjusted to take into account the effect of the Quebec tax abatement: federal revenues are increased by the value of federal income tax abated under the Alternative Payments for Standing Programs (13.5 tax points), whereas federal cash transfers to Quebec are increased by the same value. "Early 1990s" represents the average of years 1991 to 1994.

Sources: Government Finance Statistics (Statistics Canada 2015); authors' calculations.

largely through the Gas Tax Fund, the Goods and Services Tax Rebate for Municipalities, and the Building Canada Plan. Infrastructure grants amounted to a few hundred million dollars per year up to the mid-2000s, after which they increased rapidly (Figure 2.6). With the $1 billion annual grant for public transit committed in Budget 2015, federal infrastructure grants are scheduled to reach about $7 billion per year by 2023/24.

The major transfers and infrastructure grants just described make up about 80 per cent Ottawa's transfers to other governments. The remaining grants are for a host of specific purposes, among them the Canada Quebec Accord on Immigration, Wait Time

Reduction Transfers, payments to provinces regarding sales tax harmonization, and payments under Canada Job Fund Agreements.

Theories of Federalism and Intergovernmental Transfers

Canada's historical and current division of revenue and spending powers, and intergovernmental transfers, was not primarily guided by formal theories of federalism. Economists and others have, however, illuminated forces driving the evolution of federal systems, including Canada's. We now turn to those—drawing insights

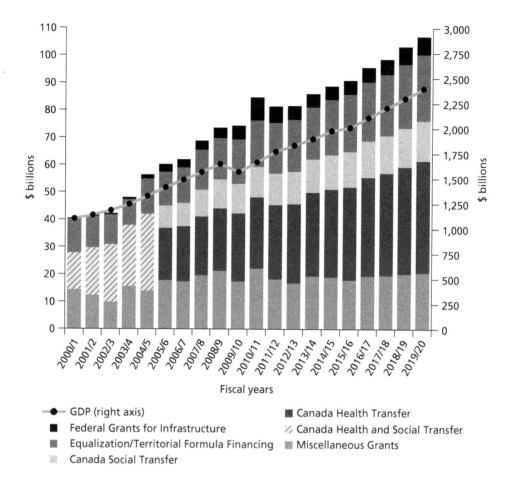

Figure 2.6 Federal Transfers to Other Governments, by Major Category, 2000/1 to 2019/20

Note: Data adjusted to take into account the effect of the Quebec tax abatement: federal cash transfers to Quebec are increased by the value of federal income tax abated under the Alternative Payments for Standing Programs (13.5 tax points).

Sources: Government Finance Statistics (Statistics Canada 2015), Public Accounts of Canada (RCG various years), and Canada (2015); authors' calculations.

from public economics about important goals that fiscal federalism can help achieve, and about the implications of practices that have evolved for other reasons.

Subsidiarity and the Case for Provincial/Local Government

It helps to start by asking why Canada, or any country, has more than one government. The high-level answer is that sub-central governments are better providers

of many things people want. The division of powers at Confederation reflected a desire among many of the new country's citizens for provincial management of numerous things they wanted governments to do.

The case for sub-central provision and regulation is stronger when sub-central tastes and conditions vary. In Canada's case, differences in language, religion, and much else resulted in a federation that was less centralized than some founders wished, with the realities of negotiation among entities that could have remained separate if they chose making the desire for provincial control highly influential.

In a democracy with freedom of movement, organizing public affairs at the most decentralized, competent level—a principle often referred to as **subsidiarity**—has a key further feature. People can move among jurisdictions in response to differences in government programs and taxes. An influential early exploration of these dynamics by Charles Tiebout (1956) described how competition among sub-central governments levying taxes on their residents that are akin to prices for the programs they provide can foster efficient provision of public goods and services. Residents of one jurisdiction who prefer the benefits provided and prices charged by another one can move there, so people of differing tastes can locate in jurisdictions that suit them better.

A complementary dynamic noted by scholars who emphasize incentives and self-interest in the public sector—generally known as the **public choice** school—is that competition among jurisdictions can protect citizens from people in, and interest groups working through, government who seek to benefit themselves (see, for example, Brennan and Buchanan, 1980). This view sees horizontal competition among sub-central jurisdictions, as well as vertical competition between the two levels of government, as a spur to accountability, more efficient services, and a support for democratic government more generally.

National Interests and the Case for Federal Programs and Taxation

What, then, determines what gets done at a central level? Classical public economics—a large part of what Oates (2005) terms "First Generation Theory" of fiscal federalism—tended to stress four broad categories of reasons for assigning functions to the central government in a federation: externalities, different scales for the provision of different public goods, regional redistribution to achieve certain standards of public services and other programs, and mitigating potentially harmful internal migration.

An uncontroversial example is defence against external aggression: a public good primarily organized on a national scale. Others are major elements of international trade and immigration policy. In countries with small pools of talent suitable for public administration, the central government may have an advantage in delivering services (as argued, for example, by

Prud'homme, 1994)—though, happily, we think this argument has limited applicability to Canada.

On the economic front, most major countries give central governments exclusive control of currency and related financial regulation. Because monetary policy and fiscal policy are both tools of macroeconomic management, moreover, a substantial central-government capacity to tax, spend, and borrow is widely seen as helpful in counter-cyclical demand management.[13] A similar argument supports central-government responsibility for insurance against unemployment, more effectively pooling risk across sectors, and over time.

Public-Finance Rationales for Intergovernmental Transfers

If subsidiarity alone dictated assignments of responsibility among different levels of government, locating responsibilities at the lowest level with the competence to discharge them and assuring that each level financed its own activities would make sense. Accountability at the sub-central level would spur sub-central governments to respond more fully to their citizens' preferences, whether expressed by voting with ballots or with feet. Accountability at the central level would let citizens across the country express their preferences with their ballots, knowing the taxes they paid to the central government were financing services delivered by it.

Both levels would budget knowing they would need to cover their own costs, now and later, promoting sustainable fiscal policies.

In practice, however, spending responsibilities and revenue raising do not line up, and examinations of why not have generated an enormous literature.

Economies of Scale as a Public Good
The attraction of assigning some revenue raising to the central government, even when the programs those revenues will fund are sub-central, is evidently considerable. The reduced administrative and compliance costs of uniform national taxes on income and consumption, administered by one agency, have induced many countries, including Canada, to collect centrally at least some taxes that flow directly to sub-central governments.[14]

Realizing the public good of more efficient revenue collection does not, however, require formal, budgeted intergovernmental transfers. The remittances from Ottawa to the provinces in respect of personal, corporate, or sales taxes attributable to activity in the provinces appear neither as a federal spending program nor as provincial transfer income, and we say no more about them. The transfers of interest here are not simple mechanical allocations: they are formal budgeted programs inspired by other goals.

Externalities

One such goal relates to public goods and services that generate benefits beyond the localities where they are provided—national transportation for example. Interjurisdictional spillover benefits mean that people want more investment in such goods and services than sub-central governments, responding to the costs and benefits within their jurisdictions alone, will provide.

As for negative **externalities**, central government–imposed penalties, which would take the form of reductions in transfers otherwise payable, could respond to similar logic. Provinces can adversely affect each other in many ways, such as transboundary pollution, inadequate law enforcement that supports cross-border criminality, or violations of international agreements that trigger retaliation by foreign governments. Penalties levied by the central government could reduce negative externalities within the federation.

Redistribution, Equity, and Rights of Citizenship

Intergovernmental transfers also respond to the related notions that sub-central governments need resources to discharge their responsibilities and that citizens throughout the country have certain rights.[15]

Law enforcement, for example, is often mainly managed locally, but has national dimensions beyond spillovers. If people in one region are receiving inadequate protection, or suffering abuses from the police and the state, many voters will demand central government action, including financial support of the necessary infrastructure. If the alternative is direct central provision of functions in sub-central jurisdictions, subsidies for the sub-central governments are arguably better for a healthy federation.

Notions of citizenship rights can be quite expansive, getting into areas of positive rights. Many Canadians identify certain government programs as coincident with citizenship. They therefore feel that Ottawa should finance them in whole or in part, to ensure that fiscal capacity to deliver those programs exists across the country, and as a lever to punish provinces that fail to meet the standard they feel is appropriate.

Arguments around regional equity carry weight. They found expression in the Constitution Act, 1982, which expresses commitment to ensuring that provinces have "sufficient revenues to provide reasonably comparable levels of public services at reasonably comparable levels of taxation." Their principal formal expression is the equalization program, but per-capita block transfer programs such as the CHT and the CST also support fiscal equity in this sense.

The public finance literature that emphasizes regional and citizen equity tends to argue for centralization of taxation, especially income taxation. Mobile persons and businesses can more readily escape taxes levied by a sub-central jurisdiction; to escape central government taxes, they would need to emigrate. This dimmer view of the **Tiebout model** or the dynamic described by Brennan and Buchanan (1980) sees centralized collection as preventing what would otherwise be a "race to the bottom" in tax rates and redistributive programs.

Mitigating Harmful Migration

Another interpretation of the practice of subsidizing sub-central jurisdictions that have lower-yielding tax bases is that such transfers reduce incentives for internal migration by businesses or workers seeking better packages of taxes and programs. In this view, actual or potential migration is economically inefficient—if, say, fiscal benefits differ from place to place because of unequal natural resource endowments, rather than reflecting the relative productivity of workers in the two regions (Boadway, 2006).

A supporting argument rests on the observation that taxpayers move more readily among sub-central jurisdictions than across international borders. Without equalizing transfers, this internal mobility could make the distortionary costs of taxation higher at the sub-central level than at the central level, so economic efficiency would justify centralizing some taxation, combined with equalizing transfers to sub-central governments (Dahlby, 2008).

Conclusive evidence of significant differences in tax distortions between central and sub-central governments in the absence of intergovernmental transfers has been elusive, however. Even if equalizing grants can reduce these distortions, moreover, they can also lower the perceived cost of taxation in recipient jurisdictions (Dahlby, 2008; Dahlby and Ferede, 2011). And if underestimation of the cost of raising additional revenues leads to higher sub-central taxes and spending, it will also lead to higher central taxes to finance the resulting higher equalization grants.[16]

Recent Experience and Analysis

The experience of the very late twentieth and early twenty-first centuries has prompted further thinking about the economics of federations and potential prescriptions.

One striking observation is the weak evidence for races to the bottom in tax rates and public services. Even internationally, where central fiscal authority is weak or non-existent, tax rates, public services, and redistribution tended to increase in the advanced democracies after the Second World War, and have been quite stable since, while rising in developing countries. Whatever the effects of competition on tax rates, the overall impact of citizens voting at the ballot box and with their feet seems to have been convergence of taxation and spending around the levels established in the second half of the twentieth century.[17] In Canada, accelerations and decelerations of spending at the provincial level seem easier to explain with reference to the fiscal condition of governments than trends up or down in the intensity of tax competition.

Another noteworthy development during the latter twentieth and early twenty-first centuries is **decentralization**—in Canada, in the more advanced democracies,[18] and in many other parts of the world as well. Notwithstanding the economic and citizenship arguments for centralization, other considerations—including the benefits of sub-central accountability and interjurisdictional competition (as described by Brennan and Buchanan, 1980; Chandra, 2012; and Oates, 2005)—seem to have forestalled any centralizing trend.[19]

As for feelings of national identity and their expression in positive rights of citizenship, there is no denying their power, and central governments often strive to bolster them. Yet citizens have multiple allegiances, and decentralization lets them put subnational identity first when enough of them wish it.

In Canada, differences in the regional intensity of citizens' tendency to identify as citizens of the country rather than as citizens of their province or region are persistent. The fact that only Quebec accepted a transfer of tax points rather than a full subsidy in the 1960s has already been mentioned. Many programs most Canadians would identify as national—such as the mandatory work-related retirement and disability schemes (the Canada and Quebec Pension Plans), Employment Insurance, and medicare—do not work uniformly across the country. These differences are sometimes controversial: many see deviations from uniform treatment across the country as evidence that Ottawa is itself a tool for regionally based special interests to benefit themselves at the expense of Canadians elsewhere. Laudable or not, they indicate the limits of arguments based on rights of citizenship.

What about arguments for interregional transfers to mitigate economic shocks and inhibit inefficient migration? Recent literature underlines that regional insurance through open-ended transfers creates moral hazard—among other things, reducing the incentive for sub-central governments to prepare for and adjust to economic shocks (Oates, 2005). Boadway (2006) argues for providing inter-regional insurance through programs running on proper insurance principles.

Situations where fiscally induced migration into a resource-rich jurisdiction, or migration out of a resource-poor one, are economically inefficient are certainly plausible; so are situations where it is efficient. Many circumstances that let governments offer attractive fiscal packages—such as abundant natural resources, other geographic advantages, or efficiency in delivering services—are likely to correlate with good job opportunities, so differences in net fiscal benefits do not necessarily induce inefficient migration.

Some dysfunctions in federations have also spurred new thinking. Inside Canada, the persistence of regional disparities, and evidence that some intergovernmental grants create problematic incentives for recipients, showed that public choice considerations matter (see, for example, Courchene, 1998). Problematic behaviour by sub-central governments, in Argentina and Brazil for example (Tanzi, 1996), has directed fresh attention to the incentives intergovernmental transfers create, and negative externalities from them. We would note that much of the provincial and local infrastructure spending supported by federal transfers in Canada, on public transit for example, does not provide national-scale public goods or mitigate interprovincial externalities. A more straightforward explanation would be regional vote-buying.

In particular, recent literature highlights the importance of **hard versus soft budget constraints** in fostering sustainable fiscal policy (Oates, 2005). Decentralization with open-ended transfers leads recipients to expect the provider of transfers to finance excesses, either because it has formally committed to do so, or because commitments not to do so will prove practically impossible to keep. If intergovernmental grants permit bailouts, the temptation will be to expand public programs beyond levels that reflect public preferences or are sustainable over time (Rodden, 2002).[20]

A key condition of efficiency and sustainability is that potential lenders must have a clear view of the creditworthiness of potential borrowers. One criterion is the ability of sub-central jurisdictions to raise the revenues they need to finance their expenditures. A second is intergovernmental transfers that are stable and consistent with budgetary discipline, rather than prone to ad hoc adjustments when a sub-central jurisdiction gets into trouble. At the time of writing, the problems the European Union is having with Greece demonstrate the dangers of a unit within a larger system acting on the assumption that it can force a bailout.

Implications for Federal Intergovernmental Transfers

For provinces, the soft budget constraint offered by further hikes in intergovernmental transfers will be tempting. Indeed, the growing importance of federal transfers in most provincial budgets (Figure 2.7) has likely increased their focus on Ottawa as a possible solution to their fiscal challenges.

At a given moment, the formulas for these transfers may make them look firm—that is, provinces may appear to face hard budget constraints that oblige them to manage revenues and spending without a federal bailout. But the many changes in the structure and size of these transfers over time likely softens the provinces' perceived budget constraint.

Provincial governments choose the gap between how much they spend and how much they collect. The more federal transfers appear to respond to provincial fiscal pressures, the weaker are the incentives for provincial governments to raise own-source revenues or manage expenditures efficiently[21]—and the stronger are the incentives to deflect blame for shortcomings in their programs, or unhappiness about the taxes they charge, onto Ottawa and to devote time and energy they should devote to improving services to lobbying for bigger federal transfers instead.

It would be perverse if transfers widely seen as helping provinces perform their functions were actually undermining the provincial autonomy essential for a healthy federation. As Figure 2.7 shows, however, major federal cash transfers make up nearly two-fifths of the budget of some provinces, and are nowhere less than one-eighth. These average levels tell us nothing directly about the changes at the margin that affect decisions, but it is reasonable to worry that they induce provincial governments

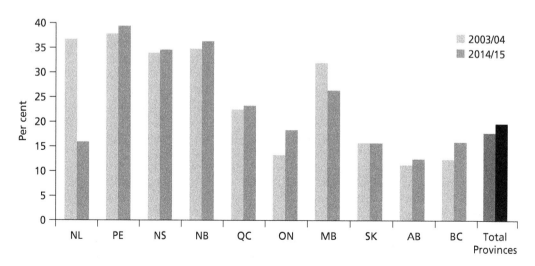

Figure 2.7 Major Federal Cash Transfers as a Share of Total Provincial Revenues 2003/4 and 2014/15

Source: Finance Canada's Fiscal Reference Tables; authors' calculations.

to direct too much attention towards Ottawa at the expense of their own taxpayers and citizens.

The problems created by soft provincial budget constraints may be worse in the future than what Canadians have experienced since the mid-twentieth century. The provinces that will experience above-average stresses from ageing tend to be the provinces that already have larger debt-to-GDP ratios. A heavily indebted province, especially one that is small, might expect Ottawa to step in if it lost access to credit.

If a financing crisis actually occurred, however, the federal government would face a dismal choice. It could allow a default, risking contagion to other fiscally stressed provinces. Alternatively, it could bail the province out, setting a dangerous precedent and potentially undermining even its own credit access, since a bailout of Quebec or Ontario would be much harder to manage than that of a small province. Far better is to ensure that each province sees its budget constraints as hard and manages its taxes, costs, and social-insurance programs to ensure that they are sustainable without additional federal help.

Closing Thoughts

The striking changes in the practice and theory of fiscal federalism over time provide useful context for considering how spending, taxation, and transfers among Canadian governments may evolve in the future. The insights from public economics about different transfers help in understanding their impact, but past changes from unconditional to conditional and back to unconditional grants reveal the importance of circumstances and the limits of normative guidance. In our view, the generally high standard of public services in the Canadian federation, even as federal grants have become less conditional, suggests that Canada would be well served by reforms that give provinces more capacity to raise their own revenues—notably by relying more on consumption taxes.

To the extent that different packages of taxation and spending in different provinces reflect different preferences among their citizens, the case for federal intervention is weakened. Competition among provinces to offer—or not to offer—different packages of taxes and public programs is a strength of a federation, not a problem Ottawa needs to offset. Intervening to reduce the tax-cost of a given program in one province at the expense of others that are charging less relative to the value they are providing their citizens reduces the incentive for each province to provide cost-effective programs.

A focus on improving decision-making at each level of government directs attention away from further increases in transfers from Ottawa to the provinces. Measures to more closely align the revenue-raising and spending powers of governments at each level seem a more promising route to a healthy Canadian federation in the future.

Important Terms and Concepts

Canada Health and Social Transfer (CHST)	Established Programs Financing (EPF)	subsidiarity
conditional grants	externalities	tax collection agreements
decentralization	hard and soft budget constraints	tax rental agreements
economies of scale	intergovernmental transfers	Tiebout model
equalization program	public choice	

Study Questions

1. What is the relative importance of intergovernmental transfers in twenty-first-century Canada?
2. What were the differences in the nature and extent of federal–provincial finance in the nineteenth and twentieth centuries?
3. Outline the kinds of transfers and intergovernmental grants that currently exist and their intended purposes. How did they reach their current configuration—that is, did they previously have a different form and change?

4. "A neat and tidy mind is a crippling disability in understanding Canadian federalism."—Principal J. A. Corry of Queen's University.
    Apply this observation to attempts to provide theoretical foundations for both historical and current divisions of taxing and spending powers and transfers in Canada.

5. What are some past and present examples of public finance rationales in practice in Canadian fiscal federalism? Does Canada's experience suggest that some are more durable than others?

6. What do the authors mean by hard and soft budget constraints in developing fiscal policy? What is their preference? Why? What is your preference? Is there a more nuanced view possible?

7. What tales are told by the figures at the end of the chapter?

Notes

1   This chapter is a revised and condensed version of an eponymous C.D. Howe Institute Commentary (Laurin & Robson, 2015). We thank the editor for comments, and several colleagues and anonymous reviewers for their contributions to and suggestions about previous drafts.

2   Our principal focus is relations and transfers between Canada's senior, sovereign governments: federal and provincial. We treat federal transfers to local governments—which are, in a traditional phrase, "creatures of the provinces"—as part of federal–provincial transfers. We note instances where the data we cite also include transfers to the territories, which are wards of the federal government but in some respects function like provinces.

3   In keeping with the theme of specific circumstances trumping general principles, we note that Alberta and Saskatchewan did not gain control of their sub-soil resources when they became provinces.

4   See sections 91–95 for the complete description of provincial and federal legislative powers. Available at http://laws-lois. justice.gc.ca/eng/const/page-4.html#h-17

5   Constitution Act, 1867, Sec. 91(3).

6   Constitution Act, 1867, Sec. 92(2).

7   Constitution Act, 1867 Sec. 112, 114-116, 118, 119.

8   This activity, not explicitly anticipated in the constitution, was justified by a federal 'spending power' inferred from sections 91(3), 91(1A), and 106. See Hogg (1997).

9   The Constitution Act, 1982 included a commitment in section 36(2) as a transfer to provinces for providing services "at reasonably comparable levels of taxation," that created a constitutional basis for equalization payments to provinces and, arguably, for other major transfers as well.

10 The abatement, originally set at 23 per cent of federal personal tax revenue, has since been reduced to 16.5 per cent on account of changes to federal programs over the years.

11 For clarity, the EPF transfer was calculated with reference to aggregate provincial spending, so no single province enjoyed a 50 per cent subsidy. The CAP transfers continued to be calculated with reference to individual provincial spending, continuing to create 50 per cent subsidies for all.

12 The largest being the Quebec Health Services Fund Contributions and the Ontario Employer Health Tax.

13 The Euro area is an important counterexample, but many people argue that its separation of fiscal from monetary policy is a serious flaw that may doom the arrangement.

14 In Canada, further savings from centralized collection are likely possible. For example, the Canada Revenue Agency has estimated that tax administration costs could be more than $500 million annually lower if Quebec's tax collection services

were consolidated with federal ones, and this figure does not take into account the reduced compliance burden on Quebec taxpayers (Vailles, 2015).

15 A classic pioneering investigation of redistribution within federations is Musgrave (1961). Boadway (2006) identifies three equity-related justifications for equalizing transfers in the absence of interprovincial mobility. Regional fiscal equity aims to provide citizens of different regions but in otherwise similar economic circumstances similar public services for similar tax costs. Interregional insurance aims to insure sub-central governments against temporary shocks to their economies and capacities to generate tax revenues. National standards aim at uniformly high public services.

16 Smart (2007) finds that equalizing grants induce higher average effective tax rates by equalization-receiving governments.

17 In OECD countries, public social spending-to-GDP increased from about 7.5 per cent of GDP in 1960 to 22 per cent in 2014 (see Figure 2 in OECD, 2014).

18 OECD (2013) uses five measures of (de)centralization to compare countries and over time: the ratio of sub-central to general government spending; the ratio of sub-central own revenue to general government revenue; the ratio of sub-central tax revenue to general government tax revenue; sub-central autonomy in setting tax bases and rates; and a measure of decision-making authority over education. The OECD measures indicate that OECD countries have generally decentralized over the past 20 years. Spending decentralization has outpaced revenue decentralization, however, resulting in higher intergovernmental transfers.

19 Contrasts in fiscal arrangements around the world, and changes over time, have supported a great deal of empirical work—but no consensus—on whether centralization or decentralization has any systematic effect on the size of government (Feld, 2014).

20 For a discussion of this problem as it relates to health care–related transfers specifically, see Crivelli, Leive, & Stratmann (2010).

21 Provincial government officials who object to this view should review their own recent experience with recipients of their transfers. Hospitals are a case in point. If hospitals are able, as they often have been, to over-shoot budget targets and get bailed out by provincial transfers, they will not manage their budgets as tightly as they would if deficits directly affected their resources in subsequent years. Soft budget constraints are antithetical to good management wherever they exist.

References

Boadway, Robin. 2006. "Intergovernmental Redistributive Transfers." *Handbook of Fiscal Federalism,* edited by Ehtisham Ahmad and Giorgio Brosio, Cheltenham, UK: Edward Elgar.

Brennan, Geoffrey & James M. Buchanan. 1980. *The Power to Tax: Analytical Foundations of a Fiscal Constitution.* Cambridge: Cambridge University Press.

Canada. 2015, April. *Economic Action Plan.* Ottawa: Department of Finance.

Chandra, Jha Prakash. 2012. *Theory of Fiscal Federalism: An Analysis.* MPRA Paper No. 41769.

Courchene, Thomas J. 1998, September. *Renegotiating Equalization: National Polity, Federal State, International Economy.* Commentary 113. Toronto: C.D. Howe Institute.

Crivelli, Ernesto, Adam Leive, & Thomas Stratmann. 2010, June. *Subnational Health Spending and Soft Budget Constraints in OECD Countries.* IMF Working Paper. International Monetary Fund.

Dahlby, Bev. 2008. *The Marginal Cost of Public Funds: Theory and Applications.* MIT Press.

Dahlby, Bev, & Ergete Ferede. 2011, March. *What Does It Cost Society to Raise a Dollar of Tax Revenue? The Marginal Cost of Public Funds.* Commentary 324. Toronto: C.D. Howe Institute.

Desjardins, Étienne, Mélina Longpré, & François Vaillancourt. 2012, August. *The Topsy-Turvy Sharing of the Gaming Tax Field in Canada, 1970–2010: Provincial Payments, Federal Withdrawal.* Scientific Series. CIRANO.

Drummond, Don. 2011. *Therapy or Surgery? A Prescription for Canada's Health Care System.* Benefactors Lecture. C.D. Howe Institute.

Feld, Lars P. 2014. *James Buchanan's Theory of Federalism: From Fiscal Equity to the Ideal Political Order.* Freiburger Diskussionspapiere zur Ordnungsökonomik, No. 14/06. Freiburg: Leibniz- Informationszentrum Wirtschaft.

Hogg, Peter W. 1997. *Constitutional Law of Canada.* 4th edn, Scarborough, ON: Carswell.

Laurin, Alexandre and William B.P. Robson. 2015, July. *Accountability and Sustainability: Intergovernmental Fiscal Arrangements in Canada.* Commentary 431. Toronto: C.D. Howe Institute.

Milligan, Kevin, & Michael Smart. 2014, September. *Taxation and Top Incomes in Canada.* Working Paper 20489. National Bureau of Economic Research.

Musgrave, Richard A. (1961). "Approaches to a Fiscal Theory of Political Federalism." *Public Finances: Needs, Sources, and Utilization,* edited by Richard A. Musgrave, National Bureau of Economic Research / Princeton University Press. (www.nber.org/chapters/c2274).

Oates, Wallace E. 2005. "Towards a Second Generation Theory of Fiscal Federalism." *International Tax and Public Finance,* 12, 4.

Organisation for Economic Co-operation and Development (OECD). 2013. *Fiscal Federalism 2014: Making Decentralization Work.*

———. (2014, November). *Social Expenditure Update.*

Perry, David B. 1997. *Financing the Canadian Federation, 1867 to 1995: Setting the Stage for Change.* Study 102. Canadian Tax Foundation.

Prud'homme, Rémy. 1994. *On the Dangers of Decentralization.* Policy Research Working Paper 1252. Washington, D.C.: Word Bank.

Receiver General for Canada (RGC). Various years. *Public Accounts of Canada* (Vols I and II).

Rodden, Jonathan. 2002, July. "The Dilemma of Fiscal Federalism: Grants and Fiscal Performance around the World." *American Journal of Political Science,* 46, 3.

Smart, Michael. 2007. "Raising Taxes through Equalization." *Canadian Journal of Economics,* 40, 4, pp. 1188–1212.

Statistics Canada. 2015, April. Table 385-0032: Government Finance Statistics, Statement of Government Operations and Balance Sheet. CANSIM database.

Tanzi, Vito. 1996. *Fiscal Federalism and Decentralization: A Review of Some Efficiency and Macroeconomic Aspects.* World Bank.

Tiebout, Charles M. 1956. "A Pure Theory of Local Expenditures." *The Journal of Political Economy,* 64, 5.

Vailles, Francis. 2015, May 3. De la fusion des deux déclarations de revenus. *La Presse.*

3

The Federal Spending Power

Christopher Dunn

Chapter Overview

The federal spending power allows Parliament to make payments to people or institutions or governments for any purpose, even if it lacks jurisdiction in the area, the one legal restriction being that in doing so it cannot regulate matters outside its jurisdiction. The use, expansion, and control of the federal spending power have occupied generations of practitioners and political observers. The detractors of the spending power, who from the sixties on coalesced into the constitutional reform industry, saw one defeat after another in the latter part of the twentieth century. Early in the twenty-first they secured a measure of victory. The defenders of the spending power, however, may now be reclaiming some influence. Our job in this chapter is to trace the meaning of the spending power; the factors that led to its expanded use, then to its decline, and then to a kind of rebirth; and lastly to the varied attempts to control it. The chapter also offers a template of mechanisms, by era and source, contemplated in efforts to reform the spending power. The key as to whether the detractors or the defenders of the spending power are in the ascendancy lies in its name: spending. When the federal authority is spending expansively, the spending power is not controversial; when its spending contracts significantly, controversy is the order of the day. The complex history of the spending power is easier to follow if one keeps in mind this general rule of thumb, while also considering the supplemental factors that affect it.

Chapter Objectives

By the end of this chapter, students will be able to do the following:
- Define the spending power and outline the various forms it takes.
- Identify the various eras in the rise and decline of the spending power.

- Consider what factors led to those eras and what images of federalism were in play.
- Identify what is meant by the acronyms like SUFA, CHST, CHT, CST.
- Contemplate the relative contributions of various prime ministers to the spending power dossier.
- Assess the relative importance of the open federalism policy.
- Identify and describe the various mechanisms advanced by the constitutional reform industry, 1969–92, and when they were current.

The Spending Power of Parliament

The **spending power of Parliament**, as Prime Minister Pierre Elliott Trudeau noted in 1969, has come to have a special constitutional meaning in Canada. It signifies "the power of Parliament to make payments to people or institutions or governments for purposes on which it (Parliament) does not necessarily have the power to legislate" (Trudeau, 1969: 4). It has justified federal transfer payments in several domains, including conditional or shared-cost programs with the provinces, unconditional equalization payments to provincial governments, payments to institutions (such as universities until 1966) or to industries as incentives for regional development, and, finally, income support payments to individuals. The spending power is also exercised when the federal government enters directly into a field such as resource development or insurance, or establishes commissions for the purpose of exercising direct legislative control over an area (LaForest, 1969: 36).

The spending power served historically as the basis for a wide variety of programs and subsidies to various bodies. Broadly speaking, there have been three kinds of uses of the spending power in the post-war period.

(1) **Payments to individuals and institutions** have been made for purposes that have been or are alleged to have been constitutionally assigned to the provinces. Among these initially were payments to individuals in earlier programs such as federal Family Allowances, Youth Allowances, Canada Council grants, Training Allowances to Adults, and National Research Council grants. Also included were those to institutions and industries, including Area Development Agency grants, research and development incentives for business, plus coal subventions and subsidies. More recently, the spending power has been upheld as the basis for federal loans for student housing, for federal job creation programs involving a federal wage subsidy, and for the tax expenditure provisions of the Income Tax Act (Hogg, 1996: 150–1).

(2) **Shared-cost programs** accounted for the largest percentage of total money paid to the provincial governments and constituted the largest number of programs. These were originally based on the conviction that certain national standards are desirable in areas that relate to the provincial allocation of powers. In other cases decision-makers desired an incentive effect. Federal representatives, by introducing conditions attached to receipt of federal money, hoped either to spur a greater outlay of provincial funds on particular concerns or to encourage the assumption of these or related programs by the provinces. Under this category fell some of Canada's most important and progressive legislation: Hospital Insurance, the Canada Assistance Plan, Medical Care Insurance, the Health Insurance Fund, capital grants to technical schools, and various forms of technical and vocational aid. Shared-cost schemes also gave Canada a comprehensive highway network.

In 1977, federal funding for hospital insurance, medicare, and post-secondary education was grouped into a large block grant called **Established Programs Financing** (EPF). The funding changed from cash grants to a combination of cash and tax points, and federal funding was divorced from the sharing of provincial operating costs. These moves diminished the level of conditionality over provincial programs in health. In 1984, the Canada Health Act reinforced conditions that a province had to meet to obtain the full federal cash contribution: comprehensiveness, universality, portability, public administration, and accessibility. In pursuance of the last condition, it established a prohibition against user fees and extra-billing by imposing financial sanctions against provinces that permitted them. Thus, conditionality was heightened. In 1996, both CAP and EPF were rolled into one federal transfer called the Canada Health and Social Transfer, which provided a block fund to assist provinces in providing health, post-secondary education, social assistance, and social services programs. The new transfer continued the Canada Health Act criteria as well as the former CAP prohibition against making eligibility for social assistance conditional upon a residency requirement.

(3) **Unconditional grants**, apart from statutory subsidies, came to play an important role in the support of provincial revenues. These equalization grants, or fiscal capacity revenue transfers as they are sometimes called, were designed to compensate for the low per-capita tax yield in the less-endowed provinces so that an average Canadian standard of services might be provided that would not otherwise be possible. Canada's commitment to the principle of equalization was finally constitutionalized, and with remarkably little controversy. Section 36(2) of the Constitution Act, 1982 says that "Parliament and the government of Canada are committed to the principle of making equalization payments to ensure that provincial governments have sufficient revenues to provide reasonably comparable levels of public services at reasonably comparable levels of taxation."

Some aspects of the federal spending power are more controversial than others. Equalization payments are generally safe from provincial criticism because of their unconditional nature. Grants to individuals and institutions are generally a modest notch up in controversy, mostly as they relate to Canada–Quebec relations. However, both pale in comparison to federal shared-cost programs in areas of exclusive provincial jurisdiction, which have borne the brunt of most provincial hostility, as we shall see in the rationales for constitutional controls of the federal spending power provided by the "constitutional reform industry."[1]

The criticisms in general, however, fall into two categories: federal theory and public administration. Some hold the spending power as exemplified by the shared-cost program to be a violation of the federal principle. Others claim that the use of the federal spending power blurs accountability, distorts the provinces' ability to set priorities, hinders planning, and creates extravagant administrative and decision-making costs. Either way, some kind of control and/or reciprocity for both Ottawa and the provinces seems to be unavoidable if federal–provincial peace is to exist.

The Era of Federal Dominance, 1945–69

After World War II, the federal government enjoyed a long period of dominance of the intergovernmental scene, largely if not exclusively due to its vastly expanded use of the spending power and of conditional grants in particular. Several factors led to this explosion of federal–provincial shared-cost programs. They involved a combination of economic theory, asymmetries of power, the lack of alternative instruments, and functional consensus.

The first was the **Keynesian consensus** that dominated post-war economic thinking in Canada and many other Western nations. John Maynard Keynes, a noted British economist, had argued that downturns in the business cycle could be counteracted by increasing aggregate demand in the economy. To accomplish this, thought Canadian interpreters of Keynesianism such as Ottawa mandarins O. D. Skelton and W. A. Mackintosh required a commitment to two principles originally floated during the reconstruction planning of World War II: "a strong government that stressed common national interests; and an interventionist role for the state, one that could employ tools such as tax relief, subsidies, and public works to keep employment up when times were hard" (Granatstein, 1982: 166). To a remarkable degree these core beliefs, which also formed the backbone of the Liberal government's influential White Paper on Employment and Income tabled in Parliament in 1945 (Canada, 1945: 808 ff.), persisted throughout much of the next two decades. They also formed an intellectual bedrock for most of the spending programs of this era.

Another factor associated with the rise of the shared-cost instrument was asymmetry in federal and provincial power. Federal actions in this regard were more akin to filling a vacuum than contesting for position or intergovernmental advantage. By 1955, Ottawa collected three-quarters of all tax revenue in Canada, compared to the one-quarter raised by provinces and municipalities (Smiley, 1970: ch. 3). Provincial public services were smaller and preoccupied with basic infrastructure services, whereas Ottawa had a reputation as a bureaucratic powerhouse able to solve problems ranging from the conduct of war and the Cold War to social and economic modernization. Provincial expenditures on matters under their own constitutional jurisdiction had been restricted by a variety of fiscal emergencies, including depression, war, reconstruction, and demographic growth.

Restrictions on the choice of alternative policy instruments were another consideration. Given the opposition of the Premier of Quebec, Maurice Duplessis, to amending the Constitution, not to mention the more recent history of unsuccessful attempts even to agree on an amending formula, federal policy-makers believed that any attempts to amend the Constitution to change the federal and provincial division of powers would be bound to fail. The Judicial Committee of the Privy Council (JCPC) in London, at the time the final arbiter of constitutional matters for Canada, had decided in 1937 that the federal government could not establish a special fund to finance matters that fell under provincial jurisdiction. Critics maintained that it was contrary to the spirit of federalism to use the declaratory power to render provincial works and undertakings matters of general advantage to Canada and therefore matters of federal jurisdiction. Changes in boundaries to capture externalities, or spillovers, were not seriously considered.

A potent factor in the expansion of the spending power was the flexibility inherent in the instrument itself. Richard Simeon and Ian Robinson have argued that most provinces accepted federal incursions into their areas of jurisdiction because the spending power was a malleable and relatively non-threatening mechanism in Canadian federalism. Contrary to the pattern of detailed supervision inherent in American categorical grants, the federal conditions placed only loose conditions on provinces; the conditions themselves were often developed in conjunction with provincial officials who shared professional values with the federal officials; federal shared-cost programs strengthened, rather than weakened, provincial governments by augmenting their revenue base, the size and expertise of their bureaucracies, and their appeal to provincial publics; and, finally, the federal and provincial governments fundamentally agreed on goals, especially in regard to programs the provinces had pioneered themselves, as was the case with hospital and medical insurance (Simeon and Robinson, 1990).

The reciprocal interaction between intergovernmental coordination and departmentalized cabinet organization also facilitated the shared-cost mechanism. Stefan Dupré has commented that cabinet organization at the federal and provincial levels saw three historical modes of operation: the traditional cabinet, the departmentalized cabinet, and the institutionalized cabinet. The **traditional cabinet** predominated in the days before the rise of the modern administrative state; ministers' jobs were to articulate and aggregate matters of local and regional political concern. Between 1920 and 1960 the **departmentalized cabinet** held sway. This, of course, coincided with the rise of the modern administrative state, which saw government departments as the centre of government decision-making, ministers who demonstrated portfolio loyalty, and departmental experts who provided the principal input for government decision-making. Discrete client interests thus focused their attention on the ministers and experts. The **institutionalized cabinet**, which, with some variations, tended to predominate after 1960, featured formal cabinet structures, established central agencies, and new budgeting and management techniques that emphasized shared knowledge, collegial decision-making, and the formation of government-wide priorities (Dupré, 1988: 234–5).

The departmentalized cabinets of the federal and provincial governments promoted shared-cost programs. Ensconced in departmental settings where they were largely masters of their own fate, ministers and officials of the federal and provincial governments could interact with each other in long-term trust relationships according to the functional relations model. Federal and provincial officials who performed analogous functions also shared similar professional values they could transmit to their ministers, and this would result in intergovernmental agreements that were unlikely to be second-guessed by the cabinets or first ministers. Conditional grants formed a financial lubricant that aided the reputations of ministers and the careers of senior officials in both donor and recipient governments; federal–provincial programs tended to be locked in as each level defended against budgetary competition by appealing to the needs of the other level of government or the client group affected by the functional program. To itemize the multiplicity of shared-cost programs is to describe the post-war reconstruction era, as Table 3.1 indicates.

The dominant image of federalism at this time emphasized public administration values. To be sure, clear partisan advantage was gained by expanding the welfare state to serve Canadians who had faced decades of privation, and the indisputable winner in this race was the government party, the federal Liberals. However, for various reasons, most governments—of varied stripes—couched their defence of shared-cost programs in the language of the social sciences. Advocates regularly made reference to functional values, efficiency, containment of externalities, and other related terms. A weaker echo in this debate came from the defensive federalism of Quebec's Maurice Duplessis, who attacked the spending power speaking the language of classical federalism.

Table 3.1   Major Shared-Cost Programs and Years Established

Health Programs		Social Welfare Programs	
1948	Hospital Construction	1937/51	Blind Persons' Allowances
1948	General Public Health	1952	Old Age Security
1948	Tuberculosis Control	1954	Disabled Persons' Allowances
1948	Public Health Research	1956	Unemployment Assistance
1948	Cancer Control	1966	Canada Assistance Plan
1948	Professional Training (Health)		
1948	Mental Health		
1948/53	Medical Rehabilitation and Crippled Children		
1953	Child and Maternal Health		
1957	Hospital Insurance and Diagnostic Services		
1966	Health Resources Fund		
1968	Medical Insurance ("medicare")		

Technical and Vocational Training Programs		Economic Development and Infrastructure Programs	
1937	Student Aid	1900	4H Club Activities
1944	Apprenticeship Training	1909	Railway Grade Crossing Fund
1945	Technical and Vocational Training—Capital Costs Assistance	1913	Premiums on Purebred Sires
		1927	Municipal Airports
1946	Training in Co-Operation with Industry	1944	Urban Redevelopment
1948	Training of Unemployed	1950	Trans-Canada Highway
1950	Training of Disabled	1958	Roads to Resources
1950	Vocational High-School Training	1958	Municipal Winter Works
1953	Rehabilitation of Disabled Persons	1961/5	Agricultural Rehabilitation and Development
1960	Teacher Technical Training	1963	Municipal Development and Loan Fund
1960	Technician Training	1964	Centennial Grants and Projects
1960	Trade and Occupational Training	1966	Fund for Rural Economic Development
1964	Student Loans (interest)	1951/67	Federal Grants to/for Universities

Source: Adapted from Carter (1971: ch. 2); Trudeau (1969); Moore, Perry, and Beach (1966: 114–18). Some programs were folded into others over time. Not all shared-cost programs are listed here.

The Era of the Constitutional Reform Industry: Proposals to Constitutionalize the Spending Power, 1969–92

The spending power proved to be a contentious topic in the next few decades. It was shaped by factors that were the opposites of those that explained its earlier prominence. Keynesian economic prominence faded; provincial power, especially Quebec's power, accelerated; alternative instruments were considered; and the institutionalized cabinet reshaped the policy-making world for federal and provincial governments. These factors came together to promote a new phenomenon: a formidable constitutional industry advocated a grand megaconstitutional reform effort involving a comprehensive renegotiation of the federal bargain struck a century before. It treated the spending power reform as one element of broad reform. During this period, not one but many images of federalism were proffered.

The allure of the Keynesian managed economy began to fade in the 1960s and 1970s as it began to be associated with rising deficits. As Alasdair Roberts demonstrates in this *Handbook*, federal deficits as a percentage of total expenditures increased from 8.5 per cent in 1975 to 15.9 per cent in 1980 and 21.6 per cent in 1985. No longer was it a matter of introducing new shared-cost programs; rather, politicians and bureaucrats sought to limit the growth of programs already in place. This in turn provided provincial treasurers with another in a growing list of complaints about the spending-power instrument, in this case the charge of federal unilateralism. The federal government, keen to control its deficits, introduced the Established Programs Financing (EPF) arrangements in 1977, linking federal contributions to growth in the economy rather than to actual program costs. Later, in both 1986 and 1990, Ottawa changed the formula to reduce the rate of increase in its contributions. In 1990, Ottawa introduced a new "cap on CAP," which put a ceiling on the rate of increase of federal contributions under the **Canada Assistance Plan** (**CAP**) to the so-called "have" provinces (Ontario, Alberta, and British Columbia), which were, coincidentally, the provinces with the highest welfare rates.

Provincial power was on the increase after 1960, and this had important effects on the will and capacity of the federal government to introduce new shared-cost programs. There were in fact three dynamics now at work: country-building, province-building, and Quebec nation-building, each implying "a different sense of community, or collectivity across which benefits are to be maximized and to which primary loyalty or identity will be given" (Evenson and Simeon, 1979: 171). Country-building manifested itself in different forms. The first was the integrative economic provisions of the British North America Act. The second was the Keynesian-inspired federal dominance from the end of World War II to the mid-1960s. Province-building, for its part, was based on a strong sense of regional community and implied major changes: the shift away from shared-cost programs, greater autonomy in economic development and regulation, limitations of the federal spending power and the "peace, order, and good government" clause, and a greater role in the operation of federal institutions and regulatory agencies that affect them (Evenson and Simeon, 1979: 176). Quebec nation-building led to a bureaucratic revolution in the province, featuring massive public sector growth. The Quebec state expanded, requiring new resources and policy levers that were and are under federal control.

Federal, provincial, and Quebec governments therefore began to compete for the allegiance of their respective populations. Evenson and Simeon said this was accompanied by institutional failure: the inability of central institutions to represent and integrate regional interests, and the failure of federal–provincial mechanisms to make collective policy that would reconcile regional and national aspirations. This led to a felt need to re-establish a new equilibrium, and the spending power was a central symbol of jurisdictional power. In this context, the trust relationships of the earlier era dissipated.

Governments began considering alternative instruments—other ways of achieving their aims than the spending power. Equalization had started tentatively in 1957, and provinces began to lobby, often successfully, for increases in the amounts accorded under the program, and to see equalization, with its unconditional nature, as a functional replacement for conditional shared-cost grants. In cases with a de facto concurrent jurisdiction in the so-called "grey areas" of the Constitution, some of the larger provinces argued for the federal government to vacate the area and compensate provinces for running the programs themselves (Strick, 1999: 225). Some, such as Strick (1999: 233), for example, even called for formal changes in the division of powers to give the provinces the constitutional right to govern over certain areas. Others, such as the Beaudoin-Dobbie Report (Canada, 1992b) and the Charlottetown Accord (Canada, 1992a) took the opposite tack and began to consider the notion of federal–provincial partnership in the design and implementation of new national programs that downplayed jurisdictional prerogatives; in some cases the approval of such programs by a reformed national second chamber was seen as a necessary accompaniment (Canadian Bar Association, 1978; Pepin-Roberts Report, 1978).

The institutional cabinet was now in its heyday and it began to shape the way that the federal and provincial governments determined and implemented policy. The involvement of central agencies in the work of federal and provincial functional negotiators laid to rest what had been a series of trust networks dominated by what Dupré described as a workable model of executive federalism. Instead of the fiscal relations model of federal–provincial summitry underpinned by finance ministers and their officials who spoke a common language and focused principally on financial issues, a fundamental reorientation of federal–provincial relations evolved. Summit consultation was circumvented, the role of provincial treasuries was diluted, and different professional norms clashed and prevented fruitful negotiation. Dupré offered a prescription for a once-again workable executive federalism. It was to restrict central agencies' participation in federal–provincial relations to occasional appearances to clarify general policy, taking care to keep them away from ongoing participation in the process of consultation or negotiation and to establish routinized, annual federal-provincial summits (Dupré, 1988).

The notion of a constitutionalized spending power included a number of things. First, of course, it implied the need for a clear description of that power. Other issues also had to be determined: whether the focus was to be on spending-power programs that transferred resources to governments, to institutions, or to individuals; whether new and/or old programs

were to be covered; what threshold of agreement was appropriate for new programs; whether shared-cost or unconditional programs were the focus; whether national objectives were desirable and, if so, what mechanisms should be used to achieve them; and, lastly, what form of compensation, if any, was appropriate for governments that chose not to participate in national programs.

The spending power recommendations of these various reports are summarized in Appendix A of this chapter.

The Partnership Push: 1992–2006 Developments on the Spending Power

Between 1992 and 2006, controls over the federal spending power, which the reform industry had maintained were achievable only through constitutional reform, were now sought by intergovernmental fiat instead. Also, many of the **tests** for the use of the spending power and the **frameworks** for its collective exercise—both of which the reform industry generated—served as guidelines for such intergovernmental efforts. The actors redirected their energies towards new horizons, but the post-1992 agenda was remarkably similar to the pre-1992 agenda.

Federal–provincial discussions and decision-making on the spending power have been shaped by various factors. One was the crisis of purpose experienced by the federal government, as it perceived a public reaction against interventionism and redistribution, and found its policy options increasingly circumscribed by a variety of international agreements. Others involved the continuing, and indeed deepening, fiscal gap between the "have" and "have-not" provinces, combined with the increasing fiscal health of the federal government. Quebec nation-building also remained as a potent force, although it appeared to have waned somewhat by the end of the century. The net result of all these factors was the **Social Union Framework Agreement** (SUFA) of 4 February 1999.

In the latter part of the twentieth century, the federal government experienced a certain crisis of identity and purpose, as Alasdair Roberts notes in Chapter 12. Ottawa, Roberts says, seemed to have found its way to a new role, tentatively, through the notion of enhancing Canada's international competitiveness and its embracing of the knowledge-based economy. However, another version of a new role seems to have come about with the new emphasis on direct transfers to individuals.

The varying condition of the fiscal health of the federal government had a galvanizing effect on the state of the spending power and federal–provincial relations in general. The federal deficit ballooned to $42 billion in 1993–4; its net debt was $508 billion, which represented about 70 per cent of GDP; and its debt charges were close to 33 per cent of revenues. By a combination of financial constraint and improving economic conditions, Ottawa by 1998–9 had managed to achieve a surplus of $2.8 billion; the growth rate of its national debt had declined to the extent that the debt was now close to $577 billion, or 64.4 per cent of GDP; and debt charges were under 27 per cent (Canada, Department of Finance, 1999). The federal government revealed in 1999 that its cumulative fiscal surplus could climb as high as to $95 billion between 2000–1 and 2004–5. The Royal Bank was more conservative in its projections, but still projected a cumulative five-year surplus of over $86 billion (Royal Bank, 1999).

The rise in the economic fortunes of the federal government led to calls for the end to restraint in the transfer field, but the federal government countered with the view that its financial affairs, comparatively speaking, were not healthy enough to allow it to act as the banker for the provinces. Provinces, in the aggregate, were in a similar fiscal circumstance to that of the federal government. Seven provinces posted balanced budgets or surpluses in 1998–9. The Royal Bank of Canada, noted the federal Finance Department, forecast a cumulative fiscal surplus for all provinces of over $46 billion between 2000–1 and 2004–5, and it pointed out that the federal and provincial–territorial revenue growth rates had been virtually identical from 1978 to 1998 and that the federal government's debt burden was over twice as large as the aggregate provincial–territorial debt burden ($246 billion in 1997–8) (Canada, Department of Finance, 1999).

Another factor motivating the federal government was Quebec secessionism. When the Quebec government called for a provincial referendum on sovereignty-association in 1995 and then came within a percentage point of winning a simple majority, the federal Liberal government saw a need

for supplementing its earlier traditional approach of proving the workability of federalism (nicknamed "Plan A" by some observers) with a harder-edged strategy of various warnings about the negative implications of separation (nicknamed "Plan B" by the same). The softer approach would be evident in the devolution of federal program responsibilities and the self-imposed restriction on the spending power undertaken in 1996; the harder version included references to the Supreme Court and a resulting new Clarity Act.

A continuing factor in regard to the spending power was the notion of province-building. Provincial calls continued for autonomy in selected areas of public policy, and a general increase in general-purpose transfers to the provinces allowed them sufficient revenues to fulfill their constitutional responsibilities as they interpreted them. The tendency towards autonomy was strongest in the case of the so-called "have" provinces, who relied comparatively little on federal transfers in the first place, and disputed the moral and political right of the federal authorities to dictate conditions when they contributed so little. Federal specific-purpose cash transfers, for example, amounted to 8 per cent of British Columbia's total revenue, 9 per cent of Alberta's, and just under 11 per cent of Ontario's in 1997–8 (Canadian Tax Foundation, 1997: 8:3). Periodically, these provinces would threaten to opt out of the shared-cost programs and operate the programs themselves. The spending power became the principal object of provincial discontent during this period because it represented everything they disliked about contemporary federalism: federal unilateralism in deciding levels of transfers to the provinces, and the general lack of ability to plan provincial development that this unilateralism implied. In the 1990s the province-building doctrine was expressed in various terms, but with a common element: a vision of equality of the two orders of government, notably in areas where the federal government had previously dominated the agenda.

The road to the Social Union Framework Agreement was strewn with a number of crises and false starts. These included the Canada Health and Social Transfer, the Social Union talks, the 1996 federal spending power commitment, the Calgary Declaration, and events following the 1997 federal general election.

The Canada Health and Social Transfer

In the federal budget of 1995, federal Finance Minister Paul Martin gave notice of the introduction of the **Canada Health and Social Transfer** (CHST). The budget noted that it would "continue the evolution away from cost-sharing in areas of provincial responsibility, which has been a source of entanglement and irritation in federal–provincial relations." It was the financial substance of the CHST, however, that exacerbated historical grievances about the federal spending power.

The CHST amalgamated the two major federal transfer payments, the block funding mechanism for health insurance and post-secondary education known as Established Programs Financing (EPF) and the Canada Assistance Plan (CAP), a social assistance and welfare transfer, into one large transfer, to begin in 1996–7. As was the case with EPF and the CAP, the CHST was to be a combination of cash and tax points. The new transfer was associated with major cuts in the projected entitlement under the former programs. In 1996–7, the funding was set at $26.9 billion, a reduction of $2.5 billion, and in 1997–8 at $25.1 billion, for a total reduction of $4.3 billion in the two-year period. If only cash transfers were considered, the provinces' take would slide dramatically, from $18.3 billion in 1995–6 to $12.5 billion in 1997–8. (During the 1997 election, the Liberals vowed that the cash floor of the CHST would never fall below $12.5 billion, thus ensuring Ottawa a continuing presence in social policy.) The equalization program, which had been renewed for a five-year period beginning in 1994–5, was allowed to rise in line with annual GDP growth. The CHST was still subject to some conditions. Ottawa would continue to enforce the five principles of the Canada Health Act (comprehensiveness, universality, portability, public administration, and accessibility), and the provinces would be required, as they were under CAP, to provide social assistance without any minimum residency requirements. However, the budget invited the provinces to pursue innovation by eliminating restrictions on cost-sharing that the CAP had contained. As to what lay beyond 1997–8, the provinces were invited "to work together, through mutual consent, a set of shared principles and objectives that could underlie the new transfer" (Canada, 1995).

The 1996 Federal Spending Power Commitment

The provinces would indeed begin working together, but it would be within the context of changed federal ground rules. In the Throne Speech of 1996, the federal government made a commitment that it would "not use its spending power to create new shared-cost programs in areas of exclusive provincial jurisdiction without the consent of a majority of the provinces. Any new program will be designed so that non-participating provinces will be compensated, provided they establish equivalent or comparable initiatives." In one stroke the federal government had (1) met the test of no unilateralism in the initiation of new shared-cost programs; (2) established a simple consent formula; (3) opened the door to a consent mechanism and to a more detailed consent formula; and (4) outlined a principle of conditional compensation. (For the meaning of *consent formula*, *consent mechanism*, and other related terms, see Appendix A of this chapter.)

Of course, it did not meet all the tests of the constitutional reform industry. It did not constrain itself against federal unilateralism in established shared-cost programs or fully funded federal programs in areas of provincial jurisdiction. Presumably it was not curtailing its ability to terminate spending power programs or to reduce its funding substantially, as it had in regard to health, education, and welfare programs in the past. It did not constrain federal spending power programs relating to individuals and institutions. Needless to say, it did not meet the continuing demand of the then-Quebec Liberal leader, Daniel Johnson, to add to the Constitution a limitation of the federal spending power. However, progress had been made, and the nine provincial governments other than Quebec saw the measure as a positive step (Provincial/Territorial Council, 1997: 7).

Federal–Provincial Consent Mechanisms after the CHST

One of the more remarkable things about federal–provincial relations in the late 1990s was the extent to which the decision-making structures—both extant and proposed—began to resemble those suggested by the constitutional reform industry. While they did not have elevated names like the Council of the Federation, Federal Council, or reconstituted Upper House, functional counterparts of these entities came into existence.

The premiers, reacting to the new federal ground rules and diminished financial presence, established the Ministerial Council on Social Policy Reform and Renewal at their annual meeting in 1995. (Social policy was defined to include health, post-secondary education, income support, labour market programs, social services, housing, and other specific supports.) In December 1995, the Ministerial Council, on which all provinces except Quebec had participated, reached consensus in a report to the premiers (Ministerial Council, 1995). This report called for a rebalancing of federal, provincial, and territorial roles in social policy and to that end presented 15 principles to guide social policy reform. It also recommended that the report itself serve as a basis for new dialogue with the prime minister, and that the provinces and territories develop a national framework to guide the reform process in areas of provincial/territorial responsibility. The framework would include the 15 principles, the reform agenda being developed by the Council and its sectoral ministerial committees, and a monitoring mechanism that would also aid in settling differences (Ministerial Council, 20).

At their June 1996 first ministers meeting in Jasper, the prime minister and premiers committed themselves to put into practice the Ministerial Council report and established a committee of ministers to study the issues. This would come to be called the Federal/Provincial/Territorial Council on Social Policy Renewal (the F/P/T Council). Human Resources Development Minister Doug Young was the lead federal minister. For their part, the premiers at their August 1996 Annual Premiers' Conference (APC) adopted the *Issues Paper on Social Policy Reform and Renewal* and established a counterpoint body of their own called the Provincial/Territorial (P/T) Council on Social Policy Renewal. The premiers directed their designates to the P/T Council to report in six months with "options for mechanisms and processes to develop and promote adherence to national programs and standards" at both the federal/provincial/territorial and provincial/territorial levels (Provincial–Territorial Working Group, 1996: 16). Significantly, the Council was also to review new

approaches to the use of the federal spending power to ensure that the federal government could not use it to impose conditions unilaterally on social programs. Over time, deadlock would come to characterize the efforts of the joint F/P/T Council, in contrast to the co-operation evident in the P/T Council.

The result of the August 1996 APC mandate was the April 1997 options paper of the Provincial/Territorial Council, *New Approaches to Canada's Social Union*, which presented a broad range of alternatives, including a broad federal/provincial/territorial framework agreement, a framework agreement on a single issue (like the spending power), step-by-step sectoral agreements with no framework, and parallel federal/provincial/territorial and provincial/territorial agreements (Provincial/Territorial Council, 1997). Its most important immediate effect was to popularize the term *social union*.

The premiers seem to have gone for the full-meal deal. At their 1997 conference at St Andrew's-by-the-Sea, New Brunswick, they instructed their Provincial/Territorial Council on Social Policy Renewal to "negotiate with the federal government a broad framework agreement on the social union to address cross-sectoral issues such as common principles, the use of the federal spending power, and new ways to manage and resolve disagreements" (Canadian Intergovernmental Conference Secretariat, 1997a). Parallel fiscal frameworks established by finance ministers and parallel provincial/territorial framework agreements were also mandated for discussion.

Two Faces Have I: Chrétien after the 1997 Federal Election

The provincial approach may have been sophisticated. It may have constituted a phenomenal rebound for a provincial agenda that seemed all but spent with the demise of the Charlottetown Accord. It may have succeeded in luring federal authorities into framework discussions that would have been unthinkable decades before. It may have focused public attention on the spending power in an unparalleled fashion. However, it provided few incentives for the federal government, a government that responded to a far different set of political imperatives. Indeed, there actually were incentives for it to continue interventionism in social policy areas.

What made the renewed federal interventionism initially confusing is that during its first term the Chrétien Liberal government had engaged in a conscious effort to rebalance the federation. As a consequence, it had offered to withdraw from certain areas of provincial jurisdiction, namely labour-market training, social housing, mining, forestry, and recreation. Even though it had decreased cash transfers, the CHST had expanded the freedom of provinces to experiment in social policy, especially in areas previously under the constraints of the Canada Assistance Plan. However, observers were soon able to piece together the motivations for renewed government interest in such intervention. The Liberals cherished their welfare state image, and there was news of an impending social dividend (budget surpluses). Importantly, there was an apparent lack of political payoff for the rebalancing effort. In the 1997 election the Liberals had won fewer seats than in 1993 (155 as opposed to 177); went down in the popular vote to 38.4 per cent from 41.8 per cent; and suffered a decline in regional representation in Atlantic Canada, dropping to 11 seats from 31, and in Western Canada to 15 from 27. In fact, the Liberals in 1997 received the lowest popular vote for a party forming a majority government since 1867, the previous lowest being 40.9 per cent for the Liberals in 1945; won the second lowest seat percentage for a party forming a majority government, the lowest being the 51 per cent for the Liberals in 1945; and attracted the lowest percentage of eligible voters since Confederation— 25.5 per cent—for a party forming a majority government: all of this in an election that featured the lowest voter turnout—66.7 per cent—since 1925 (*The Hill Times*, 1997). To add insult to injury, Quebec took the credit for wresting the rebalanced powers from Ottawa. So what now needed rebalancing, apparently, were Liberal fortunes, not federal and provincial roles.

After the June 1997 federal election, a tendency towards federal intervention would begin to resurrect itself. Jean Chrétien declared himself satisfied with the wording of the Calgary Declaration and the motives of the premiers in calling the late 1997 meeting (Galloway, 1997; Greenspon, 1997). The government did not explicitly renege on the Declaration's partnership theme, but it did not completely honour the spirit of the pledge, either. It unilaterally initiated a spending power program in the form of the Canada Millennium Scholarship Fund, a one-time $2.5-billion program

aimed at increasing accessibility to post-secondary education. The 1998 budget announced the creation of 19,000 internship programs for youth, presumably as a complement to the Millennium Fund. Ottawa continued to discuss with the provinces the idea of initiating the home-care programs touted in the 1997 Liberal Party's Red Book election manifesto, even though the provincial consensus appeared to favour a simpler strategy of reinstating the lost $6 billion CHST cash transfers as opposed to acquiescing to what were informally termed federal "boutique programs." At the same time, however, at their December 1997 meeting the prime minister and premiers agreed to begin negotiations on an F/P/T framework for Canada's social union. The framework would include principles of social policy, collaborative approaches, dispute settlement arrangements, and clarification of roles and responsibilities in social policy.

Parenthetically, some provinces now began to demand that all new major spending power programs, not just the ones involving cost-sharing (as had been the 1996 commitment), should be subject to vetting under a social union framework. Ottawa, for its part, dodged the 1996 commitment bullet by following a strategy of *independence* (initiating transfer programs that did not involve cost-sharing, as with the Millennium Fund) and *integration* (combining resources in a specific policy area, with each government co-operating but retaining separate delivery mechanisms according to areas of expertise, as with the National Child Tax Benefit announced in 1998).

When all provinces—Quebec included, surprising those familiar with Premier Lucien Bouchard's repeated suspicion of the social union concept—finally agreed on the principles of a framework agreement, the federal reaction was predictably muted. At the August 1998 premiers' conference, there was unanimous agreement (nicknamed the "Saskatoon Consensus") on rules the premiers wanted to see in place:

- the federal government should be prohibited from spending money to create or change national social programs without majority provincial consent;
- provinces should be able to opt out of any new or modified national social program with full financial compensation, providing that they provide a program that addresses the priority areas dealt with in the national program;

- there should be a joint role in setting, interpreting, and enforcing national standards for medicare and other national programs; and
- a mechanism should be instituted to give provinces a role in resolving disputes over standards and disagreements when opting-out provinces have met the conditions for receiving compensation (Thompson and Bryden, 1998).

The similarity of some of these suggested rules to those that emerged from the constitutional reform industry phase is striking. However, some of the demands, like that for dispute resolution mechanism involving the provinces, amounted to an advance over what the constitutional reformers had demanded.

Over and above its agreement to sign on to the social union discussions, Quebec made the additional concession of abandoning its traditional insistence that opting-out provinces receive *unconditional* compensation from the federal government. Now Quebec would be obligated to address the same priority areas as did the federal program from which it opted out. Another surprise would lie in store in the course of the fall 1998 Quebec provincial election when Premier Bouchard announced that he wanted a constitutional amendment to the Canadian Constitution entrenching the social union and the right of provinces to opt out of social programs with compensation, even going so far as to call the entrenchment proposal "good for Quebec" (Daly, 1998).[2]

In September 1998 Chrétien refused to accept the premiers' August consensus. In particular, he did not agree to give up the federal government's right to spend on social programs if the provinces did not consent to them, and especially where only federal cash was involved. He would not abandon the federal power to enforce medicare standards. He would not accept the premiers' idea of a joint federal–provincial dispute settlement tribunal, alleging that informal federal–provincial consultation already achieved the same effect as would such a formal mechanism. He would not go further in constraining the federal spending power than what was done in the 1996 Throne Speech commitment. He made reference to some (unspecified) compromises he was willing to make, but warned of a total federal boycott if pushed too far, saying that "if they [the premiers] don't want to take what I'm offering, they take nothing. That's an alternative, too" (Bryden, 1998). The reversal of a

Quebec-sensitive "Plan A" strategy appeared evident in an interview the Prime Minister gave in October 1998 to the Montreal daily, *La Presse*, in which he commented that he had already satisfied Quebec's traditional demands for change, and the Constitution was not a "general store." Bouchard gleefully seized upon this as evidence that the Calgary Declaration was too high a threshold of reform for the Prime Minister.

At long last the battle lines were once again drawn in their traditional form. The provinces wanted a constrained and co-determined spending power. The federal authorities were unwilling to accept this vision, opting instead for a kind of traditional co-operative federalism approach. It seemed that once again Canadians were to be treated to a protracted debate on the pros and cons of the spending power. Yet it would soon appear that these were only bargaining positions. A final agreement, of sorts, was on the way.

A Framework to Improve the Social Union for Canadians

The prime minister and premiers, expressing dissatisfaction with the embarrassingly slow pace of progress achieved on the dossier, took matters into their own hands and emerged from the prime minister's residence on 4 February 1999 with an agreement called *A Framework to Improve the Social Union for Canadians*. Quebec did not sign. The social union agreement was supplemented with a vague Federal–Provincial–Territorial Health Care Agreement that protected medicare and promised an unspecified increase in health funding. The Social Union Framework Agreement included seven sections. Table 3.2 reviews, in summary form, the content of what some have called the "Sussex Accord" or, in more abbreviated form, simply SUFA.

The core importance of SUFA of course lay in its spending power provisions. Regarding the first classification—intergovernmental transfers—the federal government committed to no longer unilaterally introduce new Canada-wide initiatives that were funded through intergovernmental transfers, whether block-funded or shared. This would apply in health care, post-secondary education, social assistance, and social services. Instead, it pledged to collaborate with provinces and territories to identify Canada-wide

Table 3.2   Summary of a Framework to Improve the Social Union for Canadians

Framework Section	Content of the Section
1. Principles	Governments commit to a number of principles within their respective jurisdictions and powers.
2. Mobility within Canada	Governments will ensure that no new barriers to mobility are created in new social policy initiatives.
3. Informing Canadians: Public Accountability and Transparency	Governments' accountability to constituents (*public accountability*) is to be enhanced by a variety of mechanisms: among others, regular reporting to constituents; the development of comparative indicators; explaining the respective roles of governments; and public involvement in developing social priorities.
4. Working in Partnership for Canadians	Building on the demonstrated benefits of the Ministerial Council experience of joint planning and collaboration, governments agree to, where appropriate, joint development of objectives.
	Governments also agree to reciprocal notice, that is, giving each other advance notice when implementing a major change in social policy that affects the other government(s); and to advance consultation before implementing such policy, in order to identify alternative approaches to implementation. As well, for any new Canada-wide social initiative, arrangements made with one province or territory will be made available to all.
5. The Federal Spending Power	In order to promote funding predictability, the federal government will consult at least one year prior to renewal or significant funding changes in existing social transfers, and will build in due notice provisions to new social transfers to provinces and territories.
	For purposes of establishing new constraints, the Agreement makes a distinction between two types of social programs undertaken through the use of the federal spending power: first, new Canada-wide initiatives supported by transfers to the provinces and territories (intergovernmental transfers), and second, new Canada-wide initiatives funded by direct federal spending (federal transfers to individuals and to organizations).
6. Dispute Avoidance and Resolution	Governments commit themselves to working collaboratively to avoid and resolve intergovernmental disputes. Dispute avoidance and resolution, while respecting existing legislative provisions, will apply to existing commitments, and, as appropriate, on any new joint initiative. Sector negotiations to resolve disputes will be based on joint fact-finding, written reports of which will be submitted before completion to the governments involved to provide them opportunity to comment.
7. Review of the Social Union Framework Agreement	Governments will jointly undertake a full review of the Framework Agreement by the end of the third year.

Source: Abstracted and substantially abbreviated by the author from Canadian Intergovernmental Conference Secretariat (1999).

priorities and objectives and to introduce such new initiatives only upon the agreement of a majority of provincial governments. The federal government would no longer impose programs, but allow each province and territory to determine its own program design and mix. The federal government as well would no longer require that the total transfer be devoted to a given objective; a provincial or territorial government that, because of its existing programming, did not need the total transfer to fulfill the agreed objective, might reinvest the balance in the same or a related priority area. The federal, provincial, and territorial governments would agree on an accountability framework for new social initiatives and investments. Provincial and territorial governments would receive their share of available funding if they met or committed to meet the agreed Canada-wide objectives, and agreed to respect the accountability framework.

For the second classification, new Canada-wide initiatives funded by direct federal spending (federal transfers to individuals and to organizations), SUFA had other collaborative mechanisms. For new Canada-wide initiatives funded through direct federal spending for health care, post-secondary education, social assistance, and social services, the federal government would give, prior to implementation, at least three months' notice and offer to consult other governments. The governments participating in the consultations would have the opportunity to identify potential duplication and to propose alternative approaches to achieve flexible and effective implementation.

The provincial gains were not as great as some of those involved in the negotiations had hoped, but the dossier had indeed moved forward. There was a commitment to stable funding for social programs (which materialized as equal per-capita CHST funding in the 1999 federal budget) and a one-year notice provision for changes to existing transfers. In addition, the federal government had made a commitment to joint planning and consultation in social policy. Provinces now had a legitimate right to suggest modifications to federal policy designs. Also, new national shared-cost programs involved greater flexibility in implementation and funding. As long as they honoured the agreed objectives, provinces and territories could arrange the program design and mix of any new national shared-cost program to suit their own needs and circumstances. They could reinvest the extra portion of federal transfers not spent on the program in question in the same or a related priority area. As well, fact-finding and mediation reports could be made public, a useful tool in the perennial struggle of governments for the hearts and minds of Canadians, and a province could demand, and get, within the bounds of practicality, the same arrangement that Ottawa made with another province. And, finally, there was a nod to a kind of equality of status of the provinces with the federal government implicit in the dispute avoidance provisions.

Yet Ottawa had prevailed over the constitutional industry. To a remarkable extent the status quo ante prevailed. The federal authority retained the ability to penalize provinces that did not meet the principles of medicare. The consent formula for the introduction of new Canada-wide, shared-cost programs remained what Chrétien had decreed it to be in 1996; and there was no mention of a consent formula for changing established shared-cost programs. Direct federal spending to individuals and organizations faced no significant new impediments, other than a three-month notice provision accompanied by an offer to consult. There was no mention of federal compensation for early withdrawal from shared-cost programs, and mutual consent was not required for funding changes, only consultation and due notice. The Agreement did not mention the right to opt out with compensation from new national intergovernmental initiatives. There was no binding dispute resolution mechanism, merely a non-binding dispute avoidance and resolution mechanism limited to fact-finding and mediation roles. As well, a host of Quebec demands went largely unanswered.

The advent of a new century did not mute the provincial voices calling for reformed federal decision-making. At their annual premiers' conference (APC) of July 2003, the premiers agreed to the establishment of a Council of the Federation (COF) to provide leadership and to act as an umbrella for provincial/territorial coordinating bodies (CICS, 2003). Premier Jean Charest of Quebec and his intergovernmental affairs Minister Benoît Pelletier forecast that "Ultimately it would be a joint decision-making body, which would oversee areas of overlapping jurisdictions such as health, education, social policy, and interprovincial trade. Mr. Pelletier said it would be funded first by the provinces, which would appoint representatives, with the federal government signing on later" (Aubry, 2003). (Federal membership never came to pass, however.)

During the Chrétien–Martin years, early hits on provincial budgets were somewhat offset by a series of health accords from 1999 on, which rebuilt stable multi-year funding. The culmination of the process was the Health Accord of 2004 which provided $41 billion over ten years and was particularly aimed at reducing patient wait times and enhancing care.

New programming under the spending power also began to take on a more economic hue. The agenda of the Liberal government once had shared with the provinces a concern with place and community prosperity; it now came to be replaced by what might be called "the innovation agenda." This agenda saw the country more in terms of clusters of communities and less in terms of provinces. This was evident in a series of Liberal government policy documents, such as the *Red Book* (Liberal Party, 1993), the 1994 *Jobs and Growth Agenda: Building a More Innovative Economy* (Canada, 1994), the *Innovation Strategy* (Canada, 2002), and a host of throne speeches and budget addresses. This led to a new economic use of the spending power which can be called **urban asymmetry** (Dunn, 2004).

Martin as prime minister emphasized both the innovation agenda and a personal crusade he called "the New Deal for Cities and Communities." His government's Budget 2005 estimated that the goods and services tax (GST) rebate implemented in Budget 2004, the gas tax sharing announced in Budget 2005, and the continuing and enhanced Green Municipal Funds program would provide Canadian communities with over $9 billion between 2005 and 2010. On 1 June 2005, Infrastructure and Communities Minister John Godfrey announced an additional $800 million over two years for public transit at the Canadian Urban Transport Association (CUTA) annual conference.

The Constitutional Reform Industry Cycles into Saigon: Harper's Conservatives and Open Federalism

By the middle of the first decade of the twenty-first century, the spending power had become a political issue skilfully manipulated by the new Conservative Party, a union of the former Canadian Alliance and Progressive Conservative parties. It was emphasized by the leader himself, Stephen Harper, wrapped up in a broader intergovernmental philosophy called **Open Federalism**, made a mainstay of the 2006 federal election, and thereafter a feature of budget announcements and intergovernmental arrangements.

However, the Open Federalism became a vestigial element as the Harper era unfolded, overtaken by other concerns. The second Harper approach was what may be termed "recession federalism," which entailed significant engagement with provinces in the face of the post-2008 economic crisis. The third was "deficit federalism," a mixture of bilateralism and federal unilateralism, including in areas of provincial

jurisdiction. These approaches coincided with the Harper minority governments of 2006–8 and 2008–11 and the majority government of 2011–15, respectively.[3]

Whereas various factors led to the other stages in the history of the spending power, there was just one at the early stage: electoral politics: specifically, coalition-building. Harper and fellow strategists maintained that all winning Conservative coalitions in twentieth-century Canadian history had been built around three main elements: populist reformers, strongest in the West but also present in rural Ontario; traditional Tories, strong in Ontario and Atlantic Canada; and francophone nationalists in Quebec (Flanagan, 2006). The election of 1993 saw Brian Mulroney's grand coalition shatter along these ancient fault lines to form an opposition composed of the Reform Party, the separatist Parti Québécois, and a small (two elected members) Progressive Conservative element. Conservatives, to regain national power, had to reconstruct the coalition.

As it turned out, the members of the coalition were charter members of the constitutional reform industry. Quebec nationalists had had issues with Ottawa's historical use of the spending power for decades; Reform Party western populists cited the legal prohibitions against the use of the spending power, which were included in the party's *Blue Book: 1996–1997 Principles and Policies* statement, as a weapon against Liberal centralizers; and eastern Tories had in fact generated the Meech Lake and Charlottetown accords.

The constitutional reform industry had no end of prescriptions, and Harper found them politically useful, at least initially. The open federalism phase (2006–8) was foreshadowed in a 2004 op-ed piece by Harper, a speech to the 2005 Conservative policy convention, an appeal to Quebecers. and the 2006 Conservative election platform. The most operational detail however came in the 2007 federal budget (Canada, 2007a) which characterized Open Federalism as:

- enhancing the accountability of governments through the clarification of their respective roles and responsibilities;
- using excess federal revenues primarily to reduce taxes rather than to launch new federal

programs in areas that are primarily of provincial and territorial responsibility;

- focusing new spending on areas of federal responsibility and where new initiatives were introduced in areas of primary provincial and territorial responsibility, doing it at the request of provinces and territories;
- limiting the use of the federal spending power by ensuring (1) that new cost-shared programs in areas of provincial responsibility had the consent of the majority of provinces to proceed and that provinces; and (2) territories had the right to opt out of cost-shared federal programs with compensation if they offered similar programs with comparable accountability structures;

- aiding transparency by reporting in all future budgets on new investments (1) in areas of core federal and shared responsibility and (2) in transfers to support provinces and territories.

As it turned out, little actually occurred along these lines. Instead, explicit attention to the fiscal imbalance was the most obvious aspect of early Open Federalism. To this end the Harper Government oversaw a multi-year increase in the Canada Health Transfer (CHT) and the Canada Social Transfer (CST) (see Figure 3.1), and increased equalization payments from $12.9 billion in 2007–8 to $16.7 billion in 2014–15, using escalator clauses in the transfers and broadening the basis for calculating revenues for the

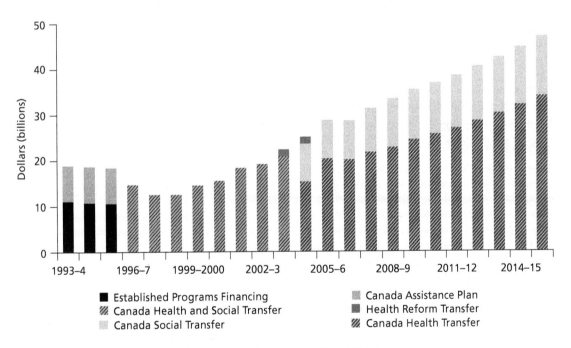

■ Established Programs Financing
▨ Canada Health and Social Transfer
▨ Canada Social Transfer

▨ Canada Assistance Plan
■ Health Reform Transfer
▨ Canada Health Transfer

Figure 3.1 Health and Social Cash Transfers, 1993–4 to 2014–15

Note: CHT includes protection payments (to ensure that a province's total major transfers in one year are no lower than in the prior year) to Newfoundland and Labrador and Nunavut in 2014–15. For Ontario, includes separate payments made in respect of the CHT for 2009–10 ($489 million) and 2010–11 ($246 million) to ensure Ontario received the same CHT cash support as other equalization-receiving provinces. CST does not include a one-time payment for the creation of childcare spaces in 2007–8 (Budget 2007) and the associated Budget 2008 transition protection payments to Saskatchewan and Nunavut. CHT and CST include Budget 2007 protection payments.

Source: Based on figure (Finance Canada) "Total Health and Social Cash Transfers," at https://www.fin.gc.ca/fedprov/his-eng.asp.

purpose of equalization. The intergovernmental peace may have been eased, ironically enough, by significant increases in transfers under *old* shared-cost programs.

Contrary to expectations—many of course generated by the Conservatives themselves—no specific limits on the federal spending power were designed during the 2006–8 Open Federalism period. No significant new federal programs related to areas of provincial jurisdiction were introduced, so at least the intent of the policy had been honoured.

The following period, recession federalism (2009–10), involved extensive multilateralism and specific joint programming, engendered by a serious worldwide recession and political pressure from opposition parties in a pressure-cooker minority government situation. The economic side of the spending power had been evident in the 2007 announcement of $33 billion over seven years to the Building Canada Plan (BCP). Then in 2009 Harper further augmented the BCP by launching Canada's Economic Action Plan and a $4-billion Infrastructure Stimulus Fund (ISF) for provincial–territorial-municipal construction-ready infrastructure projects, bringing total infrastructure funding to $37 billion. There were other collaborative exercises as well.

With the third iteration, deficit federalism (2011–15), Harper focused on his legacy: small government, balanced budgets, and market-enabling federalism. To these ends, Harper unilaterally sought significant alterations in social policy (pensions, medicare, crime), economic policy (securities regulation, training), and institutional policy (Senate reform), most involving provincial jurisdiction. Provincial governments that would not collaborate—and most would not—were either ignored or coerced. The Canada Job Grant (CJG), introduced in the 2012 budget, was a case in point. It was a federally designed training program involving provincial expenses, announced without consultation, and finally altered only after more than a year of widespread, active provincial opposition. Needless to say, it and other programs at this stage were contrary to the spirit of open federalism.

Justin Trudeau: Collaboration or Unilateralism?

Trying to discern Justin Trudeau's approach to the spending power is a challenge. In June 2016, Trudeau pledged to "a wholesale change in relations among levels of government in Canada, after several years when Harper met rarely with the provincial premiers and preferred not to meet directly with municipal governments." The change no doubt meant more collaboration. An IRPP report found that the overall collection of Trudeau's election platform, first ministerial mandate letters, and first budget overwhelmingly used collaborative phrases to describe how his government would relate to provinces, municipalities, and Indigenous communities. There was "working with" (a total of 52 mentions), "partnering with" (19 mentions), "collaborating with" (19 mentions), and "supporting" (30 mentions). "Co-manage" and "[federal] leadership" by contrast only received a total of 2 and 3 mentions each, and were highly qualified (Dunn, 2016.)

All in all, it appeared as if Trudeau was distancing himself from the combination of classical and coercive federalism that Harper had practised, and the spending power approach that applied. The trouble was, unlike Harper, Trudeau never specified the operational details of his collaborative vision, that is, the methods that would put it in to effect. His platform and mandate letters offer little but slogans, so one has to interpret his actions to discern his intergovernmental philosophy, and his approach to the spending power in particular. He is one of the few recent prime ministers not to have enunciated his approach beforehand.

Early actions showed a mix of collaboration and unilateralism. Trudeau accommodated the needs of provinces for flexibility on pipelines, liquefied natural gas, coal-equivalency agreements, and comparative climate indicators. On the other hand, Trudeau announced in 2016 that the provinces have until 2018 to adopt a carbon-pricing scheme or Ottawa will impose one. Moreover, Ottawa recently dictated the terms of a deal on health-care spending. Unilateralism seemed the order of the day, from this perspective.

On balance, there are grounds for seeing a return to federal assertiveness in the spending power dossier. The first sign is the government's approach towards user fees and extra billing, which are illegal under the Canada Health Act, 1984. Provinces not complying with the Act can be penalized with reduced Canada Health Transfer (CHT) payments. However, successive federal governments have been reluctant to invoke their power. As Meili says, "physicians and clinics have quietly been charging extra fees for health services for many years, yet calls for the federal government to enforce the Act have been ignored" (Meili, 2016). Walkom notes that "from the Canada Health Act's inception in 1984 until 2015, Ottawa clawed back a net total of $10 million from five provinces that permitted extra-billing . . . [but] compared to the billions the federal government spent on health transfers over the period, these penalties were pittances" (Walkom, 2016). In this context, the communication by Health Minister Philpott in September 2016 to her Quebec counterpart Gaetan Barrette threatening cutbacks over extra billing, and his pledge to end it by January 2017, is significant since it may presage similar stances to other provinces engaging in analogous practices.

The second sign of federal assertiveness was Ottawa's highlighting of federal priorities for new shared-cost programs. In December 2016 the federal health and finance ministers made an offer for $11.5 billion in new targeted expenditures for provincial and territorial home care and mental health programs over 10 years. (This was over and above the arrangement set in place for a 3 per cent escalator for CHA transfers over a 10-year period.) $6 billion was to be for home care, $1 billion of that for home-care infrastructure, $5 billion for mental health, and $544 million for provincial/territorial drug initiatives and health innovation (Tasker, 2016). Provinces did not accept the package as a collectivity but many signed on ad seriatim in the coming months. Once again federal priorities were shaping provincial programs.

A third sign of assertiveness may be the so-called "medicare model" for new national federal–provincial programs. In a 2015 speech in Calgary Trudeau spoke about a "medicare approach," referring in particular to climate change policy, but mentioning Canada Pension Plan and Medicare antecedents:

> So we will set a national standard in partnership with provinces and territories, one that gives them the flexibility to design their own policies to achieve those targets, including their own carbon pricing policies. And we will provide targeted federal funding to help the provinces and territories achieve their goals, in the same way that federal funding through the Canada Health Transfer is

designed to support provinces and territories in achieving the goals of the Canada Health Act (Trudeau, 2015).

The so-called medicare approach therefore would seem to involve a series of steps: national standards and targets set in some (undefined) partnership fashion, provincial flexibility in setting program goals and design, with targeted federal funding provided under the authority of a federal act and a transfer program designed by federal authorities. However, one national political columnist saw the essence of the medicare model as a national tax for a national program, in this case, carbon pricing. "With provinces slow to join [Medicare], it was Pierre Trudeau's government that finished the deal with the imposition of a national tax for health care that would apply to a province's citizens regardless" (Wherry, 2016). The open question is whether this so-called medicare model will apply to other areas of federal–provincial programs. It is at least likely.

The last point is a conjectural one. In the Liberal program and mandate letters, there were several policy areas where a Liberal government was said to be committed to work with provinces and territories in the future. The areas were labour-market training, post-secondary education infrastructure, health care, early childhood education and daycare, law and order, and housing. It is possible that new shared-cost programs may be coming in at least some of these areas. In those cases, the aforementioned issues of assertiveness and unilateralism may come into play.

Conclusion

The history of the spending power is therefore anything but stationary. There are peaks of both intergovernmental peace and intergovernmental discord. Intergovernmental peace is generally the case when federal funding for spending power programs is generous, particularly in regard to shared-cost programs. Early federal dominance was aided by the fact that provincial expenditures had been battered by depression, war, reconstruction, and demographic growth, whereas Ottawa was the principal revenue generator, committed to welfare state programs, and generous in its cost-sharing ratios. After provincial finances had been decimated by the 1995 federal budget, and

SUFA kept the feds as the senior partner in Confederation, provinces were calmed by a commitment to stable social funding. This materialized in a series of multi-year increases in health-care funding, culminating in the $41-billion, 10-year 2004 Health Accord. Although provinces saw relatively little from Open Federalism promises, they found much to like in the multi-billion-dollar infrastructure programs in the Harper years. Restoring fiscal balance—through various programs—brought intergovernmental peace. Now Justin Trudeau may be able to mollify provinces and territories—upset by his continuation of the Harper-era escalator cap on health funding—with new shared-cost programs in home care and mental health.

Intergovernmental discord tends to increase as federal largesse diminishes. It began a long period of decline with the Established Programs Financing (EPF) arrangements introduced in 1977 as a way to control federal deficits. Federal contributions were linked to economic growth rather than actual program costs. Then Ottawa changed the formula further in 1986 and 1990 to reduce the rate of increase in its contributions. In 1990, the "cap on CAP" put a ceiling on the rate of increase of federal contributions under the **Canada Assistance Plan (CAP)**. This was a fiscal context guaranteed to galvanize the provinces and their sympathizers into action. They created the constitutional reform industry, a set of commentators hostile to an unreformed federal spending power and committed to formal reforms.

Formal constitutional reform, however, failed and was never bruited after Charlottetown in 1992. Fiscal crises continued: a fiscal gap between the "have" and "have-not" provinces, combined with serious federal deficits in the early and mid-1990s. The situation led to the watershed 1995 federal budget with its major transfer cutbacks. This in turn led to provincial pushbacks, manifested in the Calgary Declaration, P/T Council, the Saskatoon Consensus. and the SUFA.

Harper and Trudeau have had relatively similar approaches to CHA escalators, with relatively similar provincial responses. It is probably significant that the 2011 unilateral decision of Finance Minister Flaherty to diminish the future CHA escalator was followed by four years of federal–provincial tension.

It is, however, premature to forecast the effect of Trudeau's continuation of the escalator ceiling, except to say that 2016–17 saw an unusual federal–provincial united front on health funding.

Factors other than financial matters have of course shaped approaches to the spending power in the various eras. They tend to act to shape the opportunities provided by financial largesse. In the 1945–69 era, economic theory, the lack of alternative instruments, and functional consensus complemented and gave meaning to the asymmetries of federal and provincial financial power. From 1969–92, worsening federal finances and the decline of Keynesianism gave openings for the acceleration of provincial power, especially Quebec's; the consideration of alternative instruments; and the role of central agencies in the institutionalized cabinet era. The opening led to megaconstitutionalism and strongly promoted proposals for formal limits on the spending power. The 1992–2006 period and its dependence on non-constitutional reform, especially in the spending power area, was shaped by the continuation of Quebec nation-building alongside a federal crisis of purpose, with the opening provided by early federal deficits and provincial fiscal have- and have-not provinces. The period after 2006 was driven by a combination of electoral politics, resulting in the Open Federalism experiment, international economics, and federal willingness to spend, then to cut back.

The spending power will continue to be an issue, regardless of multiple attempts to relegate it to the back pages of intergovernmental politics. Federal financial fortunes will continue to rise and fall, providing openings for spending power defenders and detractors. Provinces will continue to seek power. And old issues, unresolved earlier, will rise once again, earlier, or later. There is no intergovernmental dispute resolution mechanism, for example. There is no clarity on the status of old shared-cost programs. These may be avenues down which the advocates of provincial power drive. There they may be met once again in battle by the defenders of the use of the spending power and a vigorous federal role. Whether Justin Trudeau's Liberal government will fill this role is an open question. This is not destined to be a quiet area of public policy.

Appendix A The Spending Power and the Constitutional Reform Industry, 1969–92

Report	Scope of Power	Consent Formula	Consent Mechanism	Opt Out with Compensation	Opting Out Conditional	Opting Out Unconditional	National Objectives?	Financial Guidelines
Trudeau (1969)	nsc	yes	no	yes (to taxpayer)		yes	no	no
Molgat-MacGuigan (1972)	nsc	yes	no	yes (to govt)		yes (implicit)	yes (portable; increase of fed $)	no
CBA (1978)	nsc	yes	yes (RUH)	yes (to govt)	yes		yes (portable)	no
Pepin-Robarts (1979)	nsc ffp (esc?)	yes	yes (RUH)	yes (to govt)		yes	no	no
Beige Paper (1980)	nsc	yes	yes (FC)	yes (to govt)		yes	yes	no
Meech Lake (1987)	nsc	no	no	yes (to govt)	yes		yes	no
Shaping . . . (1991)	nsc	yes	yes (COF)	yes (to govt)	yes		yes	no
Beaudoin-Dobbie (1992)	nsc	no	no	yes (to govt)	yes		yes	yes
Charlottetown (1992)	nsc	no	no	yes (or stay)	yes		yes	yes

Scope: Refers to the scope of the spending power involved. Alternatives are new shared-cost (nsc), established shared-cost (esc), fully federal program (ffp), equalization (e), direct transfers to individuals and corporations (i&c). The latter two categories do not appear on this chart, nor does any mention of provincial spending power.

Consent Formula: Refers to what threshold of approval, expressed in numerical terms, should be necessary for the initiation of a spending power program: for example, the consent (1) of a specified number of provinces or (2) of a certain percentage of the delegates in a reconstituted upper house.

Consent Mechanism: Refers to whether or not the provincial consent is to be registered by a new intergovernmental mechanism, whether a reconstituted Upper House (RUH), Federal Council (FC), or Council of the Federation (COF).

Opt Out with Compensation: Refers to whether or not the plan envisages financial or fiscal compensation being offered to governments who do not participate in federal spending power programs and run their own similar program.

Opting-Out Conditionality: Refers to the degree of compulsion associated with the compensation for opting-out provinces: (1) conditional opting out means that compensation depends on the province establishing its own program with objectives compatible with those of the national program; (2) unconditional opting out means that the province receives compensation for opting out, but is not obliged to mount a program with objectives compatible to those of the national program.

National Objectives: Refers to whether or not the opting-out provinces would have to comply with national objectives and whether these would be set federally or co-operatively.

Financial Guidelines: Refers to protections against federal unilateralism, such as notice of withdrawal, compensation for early withdrawal, multi-year funding commitments, and mutual consent for changes.

Important Terms and Concepts

departmentalized
    cabinet
institutionalized cabinet
Keynesian consensus
Open Federalism (Federalism
    of Openness)

payments to individuals and
    institutions
shared-cost programs
Social Union Framework
    Agreement (SUFA)
spending power framework

spending power of Parliament
spending power tests
traditional cabinet
unconditional grants (including
    equalization)
urban asymmetry

Study Questions

1. What are the various kinds of transfers possible under the spending power, and what kinds have various parties promoted while in power?

2. What is meant by the "constitutional reform industry" and what tests and frameworks did it promote as ways to undertake intergovernmental relations in Canada? (See note 1.)

3. To what extent did the Harper government's Open Federalism policies reflect the tests and frameworks of the constitutional reform industry?

4. Why did reform of the spending power prove so difficult to achieve for so many decades?

5. What are the various limits that are possible to place on the spending power, and which have been advocated by what actors over the decades?

Notes

1   The "constitutional reform industry" is a catch-all phrase to describe the main lines of consensus among decentralist forces in Canada from 1968 to 1992. Such reports as Molgat-MacGuigan (Canada, 1972), *Towards a New Canada* (CBA, 1978), Pepin-Robarts (Canada, 1979), the Beige Paper (Quebec Liberal Party, 1980), the Meech Lake and Charlottetown accords, *Shaping Canada's Future Together* (Canada, 1991), and Beaudoin-Dobbie (1992b) would be examples of the reform industry. Over a period of time, this "industry" managed to describe a series of tests for measuring the success of federal–provincial relations. As well, it generated relative consensus on what frameworks were preferable in controlling the federal spending power. Together, these amounted to a thesis that the federal spending power should be constitutionally controlled. Their respective tests and frameworks for Canadian federalism are as follows.

Constitutional Reform Industry Tests

The tests to be applied to federal–provincial relations, if the reform industry had its way, were remarkably consistent from 1969 to 1992. (1) The future use of the federal spending power would have to avoid federal unilateralism in the initiation and termination of fully funded federal programs or shared-cost programs in areas of provincial jurisdiction. (2) Clearly, they would have to be policy areas of overriding national importance, however difficult it was to clarify this concept. (3) A co-operative approach to determining national objectives was preferable to unilateral federal definition; the co-operation could occur along either a federal–provincial or interprovincial axis. (4) The federal principle could be encapsulated in the principle of non-subordination: one level of government should not be subordinated to another in

areas of its own jurisdiction; put another way, this implied the constitutional equality of the two orders of government. (5) Provinces had a right to say "no" to the introduction of new shared-cost programs, and a right (if we can judge from the near-unanimity of most reports on this issue) to reasonable fiscal compensation if they operate a program consistent with the national objectives. (6) The spending power was a two-edged sword; too great an attack on it would harm the potential for attaining overarching national objectives and meeting emergency situations, and too great a reliance on it would result in a drift to duplication, inefficiency, lack of accountability, too much government, and a disregard for the division of powers, which was a protection for provincial ways of life.

Constitutional Reform Industry Frameworks

The frameworks suggested by the various reports of the constitutional reform industry also seemed to suggest some overlapping approaches, if one attempts a comprehensive overview based on Appendix A. This generation of framework recommendations suggests the following. (1) There appeared to be a consensus that the most contentious area is the initiation of new shared-cost programs in areas of exclusive provincial jurisdiction. (2) There was an early preoccupation with mandating a threshold of interprovincial consent for initiation of programs. (3) The threshold-of-consent criterion, however, seems to have ebbed in importance and been replaced by a preference for opting-out rights. (4) There was divided opinion on the notion of tying the use of the spending power to a federal–provincial or (5) interprovincial institution. (6) There was nearly unanimous agreement that non-participating governments should be compensated. (7) There was division on whether this compensation should be conditional on the provinces establishing

programs with compatible objectives, (8) or simply unconditional, but the later initiatives indicated a provincial comfort
level with the former. (9) The new shared-cost programs envis-
aged by the industry tend to feature national objectives, but
the gist of the proposals was towards joint federal–provincial
agreement on the nature of the objectives. Despite the concern with federal unilateralism in program initiation, modification, and termination, until recently there was no concern with
mandating practical solutions such as (10) mandatory notice of
termination, (11) multi-year funding commitments, and (12)
mutual consent for changes. In more recent years, these latter
three seem to have been more generally accepted.

2   Clause 7 of the Calgary Declaration reads: "Canada is a federal
system where federal, provincial and territorial governments

work in partnership while respecting each other's jurisdictions. Canadians want their governments to work together
co-operatively and with flexibility to ensure the efficiency and
effectiveness of the federation. Canadians want their governments to work together particularly in the delivery of their
social programs. Provinces and territories renew their commitment to work in partnership with the Government of Canada
to best serve the needs of Canadians."

3   For more on these stages, see Christopher Dunn, "Harper
without jeers, Trudeau without Cheers: Assessing 10 Years
of Intergovernmental Relations," Research study for the
Insight series of the Institute for Research on Public Policy
(IRPP), September, 2016. http://irpp.org/research-studies/
insight-no8/

References

Aubry, Jack. 2003, April 28. "Quebec Sends Unity Envoy."
     National Post, p. A7.
Bryden, Joan. 1998, September 17. "'Back off,' PM
     Tells Premiers: Chrétien Vows to Keep Social Policy
     Powers." *Ottawa Citizen*.
Canada. 1945, April 12. *House of Commons Debates*.
————. 1972. *Report of the Special Joint Committee of
     the Senate and House of Commons on the Constitu-
     tion of Canada* (Molgat-MacGuigan Report). Ottawa:
     Parliament of Canada.
————. 1978. *Report of the Pepin-Robarts Task Force on
     Canadian unity*. Ottawa: Queen's Printer.
————. 1991. *Shaping Canada's Future Together: Propos-
     als*. Ottawa: Supply and Services.
————. 1992a. *Charlottetown Accord* (draft legal text).
     Ottawa: Privy Council.
————. 1992b. *Report of the Special Joint Committee
     on a Renewed Canada*. (Beaudoin-Dobbie Report).
     Ottawa: Queen's Printer.
————. 1994. *Jobs and Growth Agenda: Building a More
     Innovative Economy*. Ottawa: Government of Canada.
————. 1995. Department of Finance. Archived—The
     Canada Social Transfer http://www.fin.gc.ca/
     budget95/fact/fact_10-eng.asp
————. 1999, December. *The Fiscal Balance in Canada*.
     Ottawa: Department of Finance.
————. 2002. *Canada's Innovation Strategy*. Ottawa: In-
     dustry Canada. Available at: http://dsp-psd.pwgsc
     .gc.ca/Collection/Iu4-5-2002E.pdf.
————. 2007a. *Budget 2007*. Available at: www.budget
     .gc.ca/2007/bp/bpc4e.html.
————. 2007b, October 16. Speech from the Throne.
     Available at: www.parl.gc.ca/39/2/parlbus/chambus/
     senate/deb-e/001db_2007-10-16-E.htm?#7.
Canadian Bar Association (CBA). 1978. *Towards a New
     Canada*. Montreal: Pierre DesMarais.
Canadian Intergovernmental Conference Secretariat
     (CICS). 1997a, August 8. "Social Policy Renewal,"
     news release ref. 850–061/009, St Andrew's-by-the-
     Sea, N.B.

————. 1997b, September 14. "Premiers Agree to Con-
     sult Canadians on Unity," news release ref. 850–
     065/04, Calgary.
————. 1999. *A Framework to Improve the Social Union
     for Canadians*. Available at: www.scics.gc.ca/in-
     fo99/80003701_e.htm.
————. 2000. *New Federal Investments to Accompany
     the Agreements on Health Renewal and Early Child-
     hood Development*. Available at: www.scics.gc.ca/
     cinfo00/80003807_e.html.
————. 2003. "Premiers Announce Plan to Build a New
     Era of Constructive and Cooperative Federalism."
     Communique 850-092/006 of the 44th Annual
     Premiers' Conference, Charlottetown, PEI, July 9–11.
     Available at: www.scics.gc.ca/cinfo03/850092006_e
     .html.
Canadian Tax Foundation. 1997. *Finances of the Nation,
     1997*. Toronto.
Carter, George E. (1971). *Canadian Conditional Grants
     since World War Two*. Toronto: Canadian Tax
     Foundation.
Conservative Party of Canada. 2005. *Policy Declaration*.
     Available at: www.conservative.ca/media/20050319-
     POLICY%20DECLARATION.pdf.
Daly, Brian. 1998, November 5. "Charest Accuses Bou-
     chard of Waffling on Referendum." *Ottawa Citizen*.
Dion, Stéphane. 1998. "A New Social Union: Improving
     the Way Governments Work Together to Serve
     Canadians," notes for an address by the Honourable
     Stéphane Dion, President of the Privy Council and
     Minister of Intergovernmental Affairs, at the Sands
     Hotel, Regina, Sask., 15 Oct.
Dunn, Christopher. 2004, November. "Urban Asymmetry:
     The New Reality in Intergovernmental Relations."
     Policy Options.
————. 2016, September. "Harper without jeers, Trudeau
     without Cheers: Assessing 10 years of Intergovern-
     mental Relations." Research study for the *Insight*
     series of the Institute for Research on Public Policy
     (IRPP). http://irpp.org/research-studies/insight-no8/

————. 2017, January 26. "Is It Time to Pin Trudeau Down?" *Policy Options. http://policyoptions.irpp.org/magazines/january-2017/is-it-time-to-pin-trudeau-down/*

Dupré, J. Stefan. 1988. "Reflections on the Workability of Executive Federalism." *Perspectives on Canadian Federalism.*, edited by R.D. Olling and M.W. Westmacott, Scarborough, ON: Prentice-Hall Canada.

Evenson, Jeff, & Richard Simeon. 1979. "The Roots of Discontent in Canada." *Proceedings of the Workshop on the Political Economy of Confederation,* Institute of Intergovernmental Relations and the Economic Council of Canada, Queen's University, Kingston, 8–10 Nov. Ottawa: Minister of Supply and Services.

Federal/Provincial/Territorial Ministerial Council on Social Policy Renewal. 2003. *Three-Year Review Social Union Framework Agreement* (*SUFA*). June. Available at: www.unionsociale.gc.ca/sufa/Three_Year_Review/e/tyrsufa.html#1_ .

Flanagan, Tom. 2006, May 23. "Harper's Road Map to Power." *Globe and Mail*, p. A15.

Fraser, Graham, & Rhéal Séguin. 1997, December 12. "Nine Provinces to Talk Social Policy." *The Globe and Mail.*

Galloway, Norma. 1997, September 16. "Chrétien Praises Premiers' Plan." *Ottawa Citizen.*

Gouvernement du Québec, Secrétariat aux Affaires Intergouvernmentales canadiennes. 1998. *Québec's Historical Position on the Federal Spending Power, 1994–1998*. Available at: www.cex.gouv.qc.ca/saic/english.htm.

Granatstein, J.L. 1982. *The Ottawa Men: The Civil Service Mandarins, 1935–1957.* Toronto: University of Toronto Press. Reprinted 1998.

Greenspon, Edward. 1997, September 15. "Premiers Use Quebec Unity Proposal to Expand Talks with Ottawa." *Globe and Mail.*

The Hill Times. 1997, June 16. Election Numbers Lowest since Confederation.

Hogg, P.W. 1996. *Constitutional Law of Canada.* 4th student edn, Toronto: Carswell.

LaForest, G.V. 1969. *The Allocation of Taxing Power under the Canadian Constitution.* Toronto: Canadian Tax Foundation.

Liberal Party of Canada. 1993. *Creating Opportunity: The Liberal Plan for Canada* (Red Book). Ottawa: Liberal Party of Canada.

Meili, Ryan. 2016, April 4. "It's Time Ottawa Enforces the Canada Health Act." *Policy Options.* http://policyoptions.irpp.org/2016/04/04/its-time-ottawa-enforces-the-canada-health-act/

Ministerial Council on Social Policy Reform and Renewal. 1995. *Report to Premiers.* Dec. http://www.exec.gov.nl.ca/exec/PREMIER/SOCIAL/ENGLISH.HTM

Moore, A. Milton, J. Harvey Perry, & Donald I. Beach. 1966. *The Financing of Canadian Federation.*

Canadian Tax Papers, no. 43. Toronto: Canadian Tax Foundation.

Provincial/Territorial Council on Social Policy Renewal. 1997, April 29. *New Approaches to Canada's Social Union: An Options Paper.*

Provincial–Territorial Working Group on Social Policy Reform and Renewal. 1996. *Issues Paper on Social Policy Reform and Renewal: Next Steps.* Prepared for the 37th Annual Premiers' Conference, Jasper, Alta, Aug.

Quebec Liberal Party. 1980. *A New Canadian Federation* (Beige Paper). Montreal: Quebec Liberal Party.

Royal Bank of Canada. 1999, September. *Relative Fiscal Power: Ottawa versus the Provinces.*

Simeon, Richard, & Ian Robinson. 1990. *State, Society and the Development of Canadian Federalism.* Toronto: University of Toronto Press.

Smiley, D.V. 1970. *Constitutional Adaptation and Canadian Federalism since World War Two.* Ottawa: Information Canada.

Strick, John C. 1999. *The Public Sector in Canada: Programs, Finance and Policy.* Toronto: Thompson Educational Publishing.

Tasker, John Paul. 2016, December 19. "Ottawa, Provinces Fail to Reach a Deal on Health Spending: Ottawa Offers $11.5B over 10 Years for Targeted Priorities, but Provinces Want Higher Annual Transfers." *CBC News.* http://www.cbc.ca/news/politics/health-accord-meeting-1.3903508

Thompson, Elizabeth, & Joan Bryden. 1998, August 7. "Premiers United on Demands on Ottawa." *Montreal Gazette.*

Trudeau, Justin. 2015, February. "Justin Trudeau Pitches a Medicare Approach to Fight Climate Change in Canada." Speech to the Canadian Club of Calgary. https://www.liberal.ca/justin-trudeau-pitches-medicare-approach-to-fight-climate-change-in-canada/.

Trudeau, Pierre Elliott. 1969. *Federal–Provincial Grants and the Spending Power of Parliament.* Ottawa: Queen's Printer.

Walkom, Thomas. 2016, September 22. "Crackdown on Extra-Billing Is Long Overdue: Walkom." *Toronto Star.* https://www.thestar.com/opinion/commentary/2016/09/22/crackdown-on-extra-billing-is-long-overdue-walkom.html

Wells, Paul. 2016, June 9. "Justin Trudeau vows 'big' infrastructure announcements coming soon," *Toronto Star.* https://www.thestar.com/news/canada/2016/06/09/trudeau-says-collaboration-will-mark-relationships-among-levels-of-government.html.

Wherry, Aaron. 2016. "What Happens When Justin Trudeau Stops Being Polite about Carbon Pricing." *CBC News.* http://www.cbc.ca/beta/news/politics/wherry-trudeau-carbon-pricing-1.3789417

4

An Introduction to Administrative Law

Heather MacIvor

Chapter Overview

This chapter explains the key principles of administrative law for students of public administration. The case studies illustrate the concepts of jurisdiction, statutory powers of decision, the standard of review, and the rule of law. The chapter situates Canadian administrative law in its constitutional and legal framework. It focuses on the power of the Superior and Federal Courts to enforce the rule of law by ensuring that tribunals in the executive branch adhere to their legislative mandates.

Chapter Objectives

By the end of this chapter, students will be able to do the following:
- Identify and explain the key principles of administrative law.
- Explain how the Constitution shapes Canadian administrative law, including the division of powers, the separation of powers, and Charter values.
- Define the substantive and procedural jurisdiction of an administrative decision-maker and explain how the limits of that jurisdiction are determined.
- Define the term *standard of review* and explain the differences between reasonableness and correctness.
- Identify and explain the key principles of procedural fairness and natural justice.
- Explain how a statutory appeal differs from an application for judicial review.

1. What Is Administrative Law, and Why Is It Relevant to Public Administration?

Few non-lawyers are aware of administrative law. The topic receives little attention in public administration courses. Even experienced lawyers (apart from those who specialize in the field) approach it warily, daunted by the complexity of **procedural fairness** and the **standard of review**. At bottom, however, administrative law is pretty straightforward. Every public actor exercises certain powers. Those powers are conferred by statutes or regulations, which limit their purpose and scope. Sometimes a public actor exceeds his or her lawful powers, and thereby causes harm to a specific person or interest. In most cases the injured party can seek a legal remedy via a statutory review or appeal, or a judicial review in court. Ultimately, judges enforce the **rule of law** by ensuring that decision-makers in the executive branch adhere to their statutory mandates from the legislature. Because they directly engage the day-to-day activities of government, these principles of administrative law must be understood by anyone studying governance and public administration. That is why it is covered in this book, and why it should be studied.

The first section of this chapter situates the context of administrative law by examples and common notions. Ideas like delegation, judicial review, jurisdiction, and the rule of law are concepts common to administrative law. Section 2 of this chapter sets out the constitutional framework of administrative law, which consists of three elements. It explains how federalism and the Canadian Charter of Rights and Freedoms affect the scope and exercise of statutory jurisdiction. It then addresses the separation of powers. It contrasts the tidy picture of three branches of government, as portrayed in political science texts, to the more complex reality familiar to administrative lawyers. Section 3 sketches the courts' role in administrative law. It explains how judges analyze an administrative decision subject to a statutory appeal or an application for judicial review. Section 4 concludes the chapter by explaining why a knowledge of administrative law is a vital part of the public administration curriculum.

Let's start with two real-life examples of administrative law in practice.

1. In February 2015 a judge of the Federal Court of Canada heard an application for **judicial review** from Ms. Zunera Ishaq, a permanent resident born in Pakistan. She challenged a federal guideline for conducting citizenship ceremonies. The guideline, issued under the authority of the Minister of Citizenship and Immigration, prohibited anyone from swearing the oath of citizenship with his or her face covered. There would be no exceptions and no accommodations. Whenever she is in public, Ms. Ishaq wears a face veil—in Arabic, a *niqab*—as part of her practice of Islam. She asked the Court to declare the guideline invalid so she could become a Canadian citizen without violating her faith. The case attracted considerable public attention, and *niqabs* became an issue in the 2015 federal election campaign. The political debate focused on Ms. Ishaq's argument that the guideline violated the guarantee of religious freedom in the Canadian Charter of Rights and Freedoms (the Charter). The Federal Court judge declared the guideline invalid.[1] The Federal Court of Appeal unanimously affirmed that declaration in September 2015, in time for Ms. Ishaq to obtain her citizenship and vote in the October federal election.[2] But neither court addressed the Charter issue. So why was the guideline invalid?

2. On April 11, 2014 the governing benchers of the Law Society of British Columbia (LSBC) sparked an uproar among lawyers in that province by deciding to accredit a proposed law school at Trinity Western University (TWU). All of the lawyers practising in a given province are required to take out membership in the provincial law society as a condition of receiving their licences. The benchers are elected by Law Society members to regulate the profession pursuant to the Legal Profession Act (LPA). TWU is a private evangelical Christian university in British Columbia. Many members of the LSBC were concerned about the "Community Covenant" signed by every TWU student, especially its prohibition of intimate relationships between students of the same sex.

On October 30, 2014, in a special membership referendum, a majority of LSBC members endorsed a resolution ordering the benchers to reverse the April decision. There is no provision in the LPA for a binding referendum of LSBC members. Nonetheless, the benchers withdrew TWU's accreditation on October 31. The October decision did not prohibit TWU from opening a law school in the province. But it did mean that a law graduate from TWU—unlike a graduate of any other Canadian law school—would not automatically qualify for the lawyer licensing process in British Columbia. TWU sought judicial review of the October decision in the Superior Court (confusingly called the Supreme Court) of British Columbia. In December 2015 Chief Justice Hinkson ruled that the denial of accreditation was unlawful and set it aside.[3]

Other law societies shared the LSBC's concern about the Community Covenant. On April 24, 2014 the Law Society of Upper Canada (LSUC), which regulates lawyers and paralegals licensed to practise in Ontario, narrowly voted against accrediting TWU law graduates. A majority of benchers refused to recognize a school which, in their view, discriminated against LGBTQ persons seeking access to the legal profession. The Ontario courts[4] rejected TWU's application for judicial review, concluding that LSUC had lawfully denied accreditation to a school with a discriminatory policy.

On April 25, 2014 the governing Council of the Nova Scotia Barristers' Society (NSBS) adopted a resolution barring TWU from recognition in Nova Scotia unless it exempted law students from its Covenant. In July 2014 the NSBS amended its **regulations** in accordance with the resolution. Trinity Western asked the provincial Superior Court to set aside the resolution and the amended regulation. The Nova Scotia courts held that the NSBS could not lawfully refuse to accredit TWU because of concerns about discrimination.[5]

Same case, three provinces, three different outcomes. In Ontario the courts approved the decision to deny automatic access to the lawyer licensing process. The courts in both British Columbia and Nova Scotia held that the denial was unlawful—but for entirely different reasons! Why on earth would three courts reach incompatible conclusions in the same case?

The *Ishaq* and *TWU* cases drew widespread public and media attention. The freedom to wear religious symbols in secular public places is a contentious issue in many Western states. The *niqab* is particularly controversial for many non-Muslims concerned about women's equality. The clash between some religious teachings and the rights of LGBTQ individuals and couples is another hot-button issue. But despite the prominence of rights and freedoms in the public debate, none of the cases just discussed was decided solely on Charter grounds. Instead, all four

were treated as administrative law cases. That distinction is crucial, not just for explaining why each case turned out the way it did, but for understanding the very foundations of Canadian public administration.

- Each case challenged a decision taken by either a government actor (the Minister of Citizenship and Immigration) or a non-government tribunal exercising a statutory power to decide (the three law societies). In this chapter, the word **tribunal** refers to any administrative official or entity that exercises a statutory power of decision.

- Each of the four decision-makers exercised a power delegated to it by the legislative branch. The Minister of Citizenship and Immigration is empowered by the Immigration and Refugee Protection Act (IRPA) enacted by the federal Parliament. The LSUC, LSBC, and NSBS regulate the legal professions in their respective provinces under **statutes** enacted by the provincial legislatures.

- In each case, someone directly affected by the decision sought judicial review. Ms. Ishaq asked the court to set aside the *niqab* ban so she could take the citizenship oath. TWU asked the courts to set aside the denials of accreditation, and order that graduates of its proposed law school be granted automatic access to the licensing process in British Columbia, Ontario and Nova Scotia.

- All four cases revolved around a single question: *did the decision exceed the lawful* **jurisdiction** *of the decision-maker?* The judges of the Federal and Superior Courts did not ask whether banning *niqabs* or refusing to accredit TWU law graduates was a wise or sensible decision. Nor did the judges ask whether they would have made the same decisions. Doing so would have exceeded the courts' own jurisdiction. All the judges could do was determine whether the decision-maker had acted within its statutory authority. When a decision exceeds the lawful jurisdiction of the decision-maker, it is ***ultra vires***—Latin for "beyond the power"—and thereby invalid.

- Finally, each case deals with a fundamental principle in governance and public administration: the rule of law. The courts in *Ishaq* found that a federal minister of the Crown had acted unlawfully. While banning *niqabs* at citizenship ceremonies may have appealed to some Conservative voters, political expediency cannot override the will of Parliament as expressed in statutes and regulations. (See also the discussion of the *Insite* case later in this chapter.) In the TWU cases, the courts ensured that the three law societies operated within the powers delegated by their respective legislatures.

Now that you have some knowledge of administrative law, you may wish to go back and re-read the case summaries at the start of this chapter. Do the court decisions make more sense now? If not, perhaps a summary of the judges' reasons will make things clearer.

- In *Ishaq* the Federal Court set aside the *niqab* ban for lack of jurisdiction. It held that the minister did not have the statutory authority to force someone to bare her face in public as a condition of acquiring Canadian citizenship. Indeed, the *niqab* guideline directly conflicted with the IRPA and the regulations applicable to citizenship ceremonies.[6] The guideline was *ultra vires* and thereby unlawful.
- The NSBS also exceeded its statutory jurisdiction by refusing to accredit potential TWU graduates. In contrast, the LSUC and LSBC acted *within* their respective jurisdictions when they denied accreditation. These contrasting outcomes flow from important differences between the enabling statutes.[7] Under Ontario's Law Society Act, the LSUC has a broad mandate "to protect the public interest."[8] The BC Legal Profession Act requires the LSBC "to uphold and protect the public interest in the administration of justice by . . . preserving and protecting the rights and freedoms of all persons."[9] These broadly worded provisions empower the Law Societies in Ontario and British Columbia to express their disapproval of the Community Covenant by refusing to accredit the proposed TWU law school.[10] In contrast, the corresponding provision in the Nova Scotia statute is restricted to "the public interest in the practice of law." Without proof that the Community Covenant would affect the actual practice of law in Nova Scotia, the NSBS had no jurisdiction to exclude TWU graduates from the licensing process on that basis.[11]

- Even though the LSBC had the substantive jurisdiction to deny accreditation to TWU, its decision-making process violated the rules of procedural fairness (aka "natural justice").[12] The LSBC gave TWU too little opportunity to place its arguments before the membership in advance of the October 30, 2014 referendum vote.[13] There was no evidence that the benchers tried to balance the Charter values of religious freedom and equality when they reversed their decision to accredit TWU on October 31.[14] Consequently, the October decision was *ultra vires*. The court set it aside and restored the benchers' April 2014 decision to accredit TWU's proposed faculty of law.

The next section of this chapter sets out the constitutional framework of administrative law. It explains how federalism and the Canadian Charter of Rights and Freedoms affect the scope and exercise of statutory jurisdiction. Section 2 also addresses the separation of powers. It contrasts the tidy picture of three branches of government, as portrayed in political science texts, to the more complex reality familiar to administrative lawyers.

2. The Constitutional Framework of Administrative Law

This section roadmaps the various constitutional aspects to which administrative law must conform. Any decision taken by or on behalf of government must be consistent with the Constitution of Canada. Otherwise it is *ultra vires* and may be set aside by a court.

> The Constitution binds all governments, both federal and provincial, including the executive branch. They may not transgress its provisions: indeed, their sole claim to exercise lawful authority rests in the powers allocated to them under the Constitution, and can come from no other source.[15]

An administrative decision may conflict with the Constitution in any of three ways:

- by exceeding that government's jurisdiction, as determined by the vertical division of powers;
- by restricting a right or freedom protected by the Canadian Charter of Rights and Freedoms without reasonable justification; and/or

- by intruding into the jurisdiction of a different branch of government, thus violating the horizontal separation of powers.

The next three sections elaborate on all three possible conflicts, and their ramifications, in that order.

At the heart of administrative law lies the concept of jurisdiction. Every government institution, every public official, and every delegated decision-maker is authorized by law to do certain things in certain ways. In legal terms, a grant of statutory authority confers two types of jurisdiction: substantive and procedural. An administrative decision may be set aside—i.e., declared invalid—if the decision-maker (1) did something that the legislature did not authorize it to do (e.g., amending the regulations of the Nova Scotia Barristers' Society to block TWU law graduates), and/ or (2) violated its own rules or the norms of procedural fairness. This distinction between procedure and substance is critically important for understanding administrative law. We will address the principles of procedural justice in Section 3(c), below. This section explains how the Canadian Constitution limits the substantive jurisdiction of executives, legislatures, and courts.

(a) The Division of Powers: Sections 91–96 of the Constitution Act, 1867

The first constitutional aspect to which administrative law must conform is the vertical distribution of powers, or federalism. As every student of public administration knows, Canada is a federal state. It has a national government, usually called the federal government. The country is also divided into ten provinces and three territories, each with its own government. (Because the territories have less legal autonomy, this chapter only refers to the provinces.) The division of powers between the federal and provincial governments is set out in sections 91–96 of the Constitution Act, 1867. Section 92 sets out the substantive jurisdiction of the provincial governments. Section 91 assigns the residual powers to the federal government (the "POGG clause") and lists specific subjects to illustrate the scope of federal jurisdiction. This distinction is neater in theory than in practice; most areas of federal jurisdiction overlap with one or more provincial responsibilities.

The division of powers shapes Canadian administrative law in two ways. *First*, a provincial decision trenching on federal jurisdiction (or vice versa) may be invalidated as *ultra vires*. This is different from finding that a statute is *ultra vires*, which is a question of constitutional law. Administrative law asks whether a particular application of a statute should be set aside on jurisdictional grounds, even though the law itself is *intra vires* (within the jurisdiction of the legislature that adopted it).

The Supreme Court of Canada (SCC) recently addressed the distinction between constitutional and administrative law. In 2008 the federal minister of health announced the impending closure of the Insite safe-injection facility in Vancouver. Since its opening in 2003, Insite had been exempted from prosecution under the federal Controlled Drugs and Substances Act (CDSA). Section 56 of the CDSA provides for such exemptions "if, in the opinion of the Minister, the exemption is necessary for a medical or scientific purpose or is otherwise in the public interest."[16] Insite's exemption allowed addicts to use illegal drugs in a safe place, under medical supervision, without fear of punishment. It also protected Insite's staff from criminal sanctions. The federal Conservative government, first elected in 2006, opposed any measures to soften the CDSA or its enforcement. Consequently, Health Minister Tony Clement announced that he would not extend or renew Insite's exemption after it expired in 2008.

Advocates for injection drug users joined with Insite to challenge the minister's decision in the BC Supreme Court. (The exemption was extended by court order pending the final decision in the case, which was delivered by the SCC in 2011.) Insite's defenders raised two constitutional questions: a division of powers issue (discussed here) and a Charter issue (discussed in Section 2(b)(i), below). Most parties agreed that the CDSA is a valid exercise of the federal government's jurisdiction over criminal law (s. 91[27]). Everyone acknowledged that the provinces can lawfully regulate health-care facilities (ss. 92[7], [13] and [16]). The question was whether the CDSA prevailed over provincial laws allowing the possession and use of illegal drugs at Insite. The SCC said yes: "the federal law constrains operation at Insite and trumps any provincial legislation or policies that conflict with it."[17] Had the court decided the division of powers issue differently, that would have ended the case. After all, if the provincial government could shield Insite from the effects of the CDSA, there would be no need to seek an exemption from the federal minister.

Second, the division of powers indirectly shapes the procedural aspects of administrative law by limiting the jurisdiction of courts to hear certain types of case. There are three types of court in Canada.

- Provincial courts are established and maintained, and their members appointed, by provincial governments (s. 92[14]). They generally deal with purely provincial matters, such as provincial offences and family law (except orders under the federal Divorce Act). They also handle some aspects of criminal procedure and conduct the majority of criminal trials, notwithstanding Parliament's jurisdiction to enact criminal law and procedure. Provincial courts are at the bottom of the judicial hierarchy. Most of their decisions may be appealed to the Superior Court of that province.
- Superior Courts and Courts of Appeal are also established and maintained by the provinces, but their members are appointed by the federal government under s. 96 of the Constitution Act, 1867. They are often called hybrid courts because they straddle the horizontal division of powers. Generally speaking, decisions of Superior Court judges may be appealed to the Court of Appeal in the province. That includes decisions on applications for judicial review.
- Federal Courts are established and maintained solely by the federal government (s. 101). They include the Federal Court and the Tax Court; the Federal Court of Appeal, which hears appeals from those two courts; and the Supreme Court of Canada. The Supreme Court, as its name suggests, is the final court of appeal in all legal proceedings. It reviews decisions of the federal and provincial Courts of Appeal, but only those which it chooses to hear (apart from a few criminal appeals heard as of right).

In administrative law, it can be tricky to figure out which court has jurisdiction to hear a particular case. Recall that the *Ishaq* case was heard as an application for judicial review in the Federal Court. Immigration and citizenship are federal powers under s. 91[25]), but the division of powers alone did not determine which court had jurisdiction. The case belonged in the Federal Court because (1) the decision under

challenge had been made by a federal minister of the Crown; (2) the remedy sought was only available on an application for judicial review; and (3) s. 18(1) of the Federal Courts Act[18] assigns exclusive jurisdiction in such cases to the Federal Court.

While the three *Trinity Western* cases also dealt with applications for judicial review, they were brought in the Superior Courts of their respective provinces. There are two reasons for this. First, regulating the legal profession is a provincial responsibility (ss. 92[13] and [16]), and the three Law Societies acted pursuant to provincial statutes. So the Federal Court had no jurisdiction to grant the relief sought by TWU. Second, the Superior Court in each province is the court of **inherent jurisdiction**. By virtue of its inheritance from the pre-Confederation British courts, the Superior Court has the power to enforce the rule of law.[19] The Nova Scotia and BC applications in TWU were initially heard by single judges. The Ontario application was heard by a three-judge panel of the Divisional Court, a branch of the Ontario Superior Court specializing in administrative law.[20]

The jurisdictional issue in *Insite* is more complicated. Recall that the case challenged the validity of a federal decision in Superior Court, not Federal Court. Had the applicants sought judicial review, the BC Supreme Court would have declined to hear the case for lack of jurisdiction. But instead, Insite's advocates sued for a declaration that the CDSA itself was unconstitutional. The power to determine the constitutional validity of a statute is part of the inherent jurisdiction of the Superior Court. It cannot be taken away, even by express statutory language.[21] In addition, "the provincial superior courts have the authority to consider and rule on the legality of the actions of federal [decision-makers] when doing so is a necessary step in adjudicating claims properly before the superior courts."[22] Finally, s. 17 of the Federal Courts Act permits a case against the federal Crown (other than an application for judicial review) to proceed in either Federal Court or the Superior Court of the province where the matter arises. So the *Insite* case was properly heard in the BC Supreme Court.

(b) The Canadian Charter of Rights and Freedoms

(i) Charter Guarantees

The second constitutional aspect to which administrative law must conform is the Charter and its guarantees.

The Charter's entrenched guarantees of rights and freedoms play a relatively small role in administrative law. Superior Courts have the inherent jurisdiction to grant a full range of remedies for Charter violations. Under s. 52(1) of the Constitution Act, 1982, a court can declare a law invalid if it limits a protected right or freedom and the limitation cannot be justified under s. 1. It can also read in or read down where necessary to make the interpretation of an **impugned** law consistent with the Charter. Section 24(1) of the Charter empowers a "court of competent jurisdiction" to grant "such remedy as the court considers appropriate and just in the circumstances" for a procedural violation.[23]

In contrast, tribunals cannot grant remedies that exceed their statutory powers. For the most part, legislatures have not empowered tribunals to declare laws invalid under s. 52(1).[24] The enactment of the Charter did not automatically expand tribunals' remedial powers.[25] So a litigant who wants to strike down a law should seek a remedy from the Superior Court, not a quasi-judicial tribunal.[26] The most that a tribunal can do, if it finds that a provision in its enabling statute contradicts the Charter, is to refuse to apply it.[27] A tribunal may also have jurisdiction to grant remedies under s. 24(1) "in relation to Charter issues arising in the course of carrying out its statutory mandate,"[28] unless the legislature has expressly prohibited it from doing so.

Despite these limitations on tribunal powers, Charter guarantees occasionally play a role in administrative law. Recall that the Superior and Federal Courts can review decisions to determine whether the decision-maker exceeded his or her jurisdiction. A cabinet minister cannot lawfully exercise **discretion** in a manner that violates a Charter right or freedom.[29] Nor can a legislature authorize a decision-maker to infringe entrenched rights and freedoms.

In the *Insite* case the SCC rejected the argument that the CDSA itself violates s. 7 of the Charter.[30] "If there is a *Charter* problem" with the CDSA, "it lies not in the statute but in the Minister's exercise of the power the statute gives him to grant appropriate exemptions."[31] The Court concluded that the minister's refusal to extend the exemption—in the face of proof that Insite had saved lives—was "arbitrary and grossly disproportionate in its effects, and hence not in accordance with the principles of fundamental justice."[32] The Court chose not to refer the decision back to the health minister for reconsideration. Instead, it imposed the unusual remedy of mandamus: it ordered the minister to grant Insite a new exemption immediately, and to base future decisions on the best available evidence.[33]

(ii) Charter Values

In recent years the SCC has given the Charter a new role in administrative law. It has declared that "administrative decision-makers must act consistently with the values underlying the grant of discretion, including Charter values."[34] This means that "where a discretionary administrative decision engages the protections enumerated in the Charter—both the Charter's guarantees and the foundational values they reflect—the discretionary decision-maker is required to proportionately balance the Charter protections to ensure that they are limited no more than is necessary given the applicable statutory objectives that she or he is obliged to pursue."[35]

How does a decision-maker exercising a statutory power of decision ensure consistency with the Charter values applicable to the particular issue at hand? First, he or she determines whether the dispute engages one or more of the values protected by the Charter. Second, the decision-maker identifies the legislature's purpose in conferring jurisdiction on him or her to make that particular decision. Finally, he or she asks "how the Charter value at issue will best be protected in view of the statutory objectives."[36] If the decision is subjected to judicial review, the Superior Court must determine "whether, in assessing the impact of the relevant Charter protection and given the nature of the decision and the statutory and factual contexts, the decision reflects a proportionate balancing of the Charter protections at play."[37] An administrative decision will be considered reasonable, and affirmed on that basis, where "in exercising its statutory discretion, the decision-maker has properly balanced the relevant Charter value with the statutory objectives."[38]

This approach has attracted criticism. Some lawyers argue that Charter values are vague and largely undefined, whereas the actual Charter guarantees are well understood after more than 30 years of judicial interpretation.[39] As a result, the resort to Charter values introduces unnecessary confusion and unpredictability into Canadian administrative law.

Despite this concern, reviewing courts have had little apparent difficulty in applying Charter values to discretionary administrative decisions. The Divisional Court ruling in the Ontario TWU case illustrates the method to be followed.

- First, the Court identified two conflicting Charter values engaged by the facts of the case. It held that the Community Covenant infringed the equality rights of LGBTQ students (among others),[40] while the LSUC's denial of accreditation infringed the religious freedom of TWU and its potential law students.[41]
- Next, it found that the legislature's objective was clear. It had granted the LSUC a broad "duty to protect the public interest."[42] Over the years, the LSUC has interpreted that duty as a mandate to ensure equality of access to the legal profession in Ontario. It has progressively dismantled arbitrary and discriminatory barriers to aspiring lawyers, as the Charter value of equality required it to do.[43] The LSUC is also bound by section 6 of the Ontario Human Rights Code, which prohibits a self-regulating profession from denying membership on the ground of sexual orientation.[44] The Code is quasi-constitutional legislation, which prevails over any conflicting Ontario statute.[45] The legislature has explicitly directed courts to interpret other provincial laws consistently with the Code's requirements.
- After considering the arguments and evidence, the panel unanimously concluded that "in balancing the interests of the applicants to freedom of religion, and of the respondent's members and future members to equal opportunity, in the course of the exercise of its statutory authority, the respondent arrived at a reasonable conclusion."[46] The Court also rejected TWU's claim that the benchers had ignored the religious freedom of the university and its students and thus failed to balance the contending Charter values at issue.

In contrast, the BC Supreme Court found that the benchers in that province had failed to weigh Charter values when they reversed themselves following the October 2014 membership referendum. That failure, along with the other violations of procedural justice discussed below, rendered the October decision invalid.[47]

(c) The Separation of Powers

The third constitutional aspect to which administrative law must conform is the separation of powers doctrine. The conventional wisdom in political science depicts three distinct but partially overlapping branches of government: legislative, executive, and judicial.

- The legislative branch enacts the laws. The federal legislative branch includes the House of Commons, the Senate, and the Crown (represented by the Governor General). A similar structure operates in each province, except that the legislatures are unicameral and the Lieutenant Governor represents the Crown. The legislative branch debates and passes statutes, and holds the political executive to account. As the only elected branch of government, the legislature is considered to be supreme over the other two branches.
- The executive branch crafts and enforces the laws passed by the legislature. It comprises the Crown, the political executive, and the permanent executive. The prime minister or premier leads the political executive, also called the cabinet. He or she selects cabinet ministers from among the other elected members of the party with the most seats in the legislature. Each minister is responsible for a particular department or ministry (e.g., health, finance, or justice). Ministers sponsor government bills through the legislative process. The permanent executive is made up of public servants working in various ministries, agencies, and Crown corporations. Some public servants advise ministers on policy and develop the bills considered by legislators. Others deliver services to the public. Still others regulate specific fields of activity. Finally, some public servants enforce the law. These include the police and regulatory agencies. In most of these activities, members of the executive branch exercise a measure of discretion.
- Judges interpret and apply the law to resolve specific disputes between two or more parties. They conduct hearings, consider evidence and legal arguments, determine the facts, and draw legal inferences. Then they decide the case, or the specific issue before them, and give written reasons to explain the decision. Judges are appointed by the political executive and hold office until they turn 75. They are expected to be independent of the other branches of government, and to treat all parties before them with fairness and impartiality.

This conventional depiction of the separation of powers is reasonably accurate, as far as it goes. But from the perspective of administrative law, the political science model overlooks three important features of Canadian government. First, it overstates Parliament's role in law-making. Second, and related to the first, it understates the law-making powers of the executive and judicial branches. Third, the conventional picture overlooks the quasi-judicial functions assigned to certain parts of the permanent executive. These generate the lion's share of cases in administrative law.

Let us deal, in turn, with each of these qualifications to the way the separation of powers works in practice to affect administrative law.

(i) Regulations and other Subordinate Legislation

Parliament and the provincial legislatures play a smaller role in law-making than the conventional separation of powers would suggest. First, the executive branch controls the legislative process. Government bills—written by the permanent executive, approved by the political executive, and steered through the legislative process by ministers—are more or less guaranteed to become law. This is particularly true for money bills, whose defeat in the legislature forces the political executive to resign. Very few private members' bills ever make it to a final vote.

Second, the legislature only makes *some* of the laws. True, the statutes passed by Parliament and the provincial legislatures are the most important laws (after the entrenched Constitution). But the subordinate law-making powers of the executive branch are more extensive and significant than is generally realized. The exercise of those powers is a key element in administrative law.

At first glance, statutes may appear dauntingly specific. To take an extreme example, the federal Income Tax Act runs to more than 3000 pages. Even so, a statute cannot provide for all the minute details of policy implementation. Nor can it be quickly amended or repealed in response to unexpected events. The legislative agenda is crowded. An amending bill can sit on the order paper for months awaiting a final vote. As a result, most bills empower a particular minister, or the cabinet as a whole—called the Governor-in-Council or Lieutenant-Governor-in-Council—to make detailed regulations for the purpose of implementing and adapting the law. These regulations are called **delegated legislation** because the legislative branch delegated part of its law-making authority to the executive branch. Regulations are also referred to as **subordinate legislation**, reflecting their inferior status vis-à-vis statutes.

The power to issue binding regulations is not confined to the executive branch of government. Legislatures also delegate rule-making powers to non-governmental agencies with a mandate to regulate a specific group or activity. For example, a college of physicians can make binding rules for its members in the conduct of their practice. A member who fails to obey such a rule can lose his or her licence.

The jurisdiction to enact subordinate legislation is constrained by the regulation-making provisions in the enabling statute. A regulation that exceeds that jurisdiction is *ultra vires* and consequently invalid. In practice, however, courts rarely invalidate subordinate legislation. Judicial reluctance to intrude on the powers of the legislative and executive branches is a cornerstone of constitutional and administrative law. Judges presume that a regulation is *intra vires* unless the party challenging its validity can prove otherwise. If possible, they will interpret the regulation in a way that makes it consistent with the enabling statute. Only if the regulation is "'irrelevant,' 'extraneous,' or 'completely unrelated' to the statutory purpose" will it be declared *ultra vires*.[48] As mentioned at the start of this chapter, the Nova Scotia courts found that the Legal Profession Act did not empower the NSBS to enact a regulation barring TWU graduates from the licensing process in that province. The regulation was *ultra vires* the enabling legislation and set aside on that basis.[49]

(ii) The Judicial Branch: Making Law and Policing Statutory Powers

The assumption that law-making is confined to legislators also obscures the immense body of law generated by judges. When a judge decides a dispute between two parties, his or her written reasons become part of the **common law**. A common-law rule is binding on all persons to whom it applies unless the legislature explicitly overrules it in a statute.

One common-law rule, *stare decisis*, underlies the power of all the others. Under *stare decisis*, a judge hearing a case is expected to follow the principles applied in similar decisions (called "precedents") by the same court. A precedent from a higher court is binding on a lower court until the higher court explicitly modifies or overrules its earlier decision. So when the Supreme

Court of Canada declared that a minister's discretionary decisions must be consistent with the Charter, the impact of that declaration was felt far beyond the walls of Insite. It was binding on all cabinet ministers when they exercise their statutory powers of decision, and on all lower courts asked to judicially review discretionary decisions engaging a Charter right or freedom.

Of particular relevance to this chapter are the common-law rules of natural justice or procedural fairness, discussed in Section 3(c) below. Today the general rules of natural justice are codified in statutes, such as Ontario's Statutory Powers Procedure Act.[50] A tribunal may also adopt detailed rules and procedures appropriate to its powers and clientele, usually in the form of guidelines or practice directions. These tribunal-specific rules are called **soft law**. (Unlike procedural jurisdiction, a tribunal's substantive jurisdiction is entirely defined by the legislative and executive branches via statutes and regulations.) A tribunal's failure to meet the standard of procedural fairness applicable to a particular case is considered an error of law; the resulting tribunal decision may be set aside on that basis.

In addition to making law, courts enforce the rule of law by invalidating *ultra vires* tribunal decisions. They may do so in either of two ways, which are described at greater length in Section 3.

- A Superior Court may hear an appeal from the final decision of a tribunal, if the relevant statute provides for such appeals. The party seeking to have the decision modified or set aside tries to persuade the reviewing court that the tribunal erred in fact and/or in law. The appellant must prove such errors on a balance of probabilities—in other words, it is more likely than not that a particular finding is erroneous. The appellant must also establish that such errors led to an unjust result. If the appellant succeeds, the reviewing court may set the decision aside and either refer the case back to the tribunal for reconsideration or substitute its own decision.
- Where a statutory appeal is unavailable, the party affected by an administrative decision may apply to the Superior Court for judicial review.

(iii) Administrative Tribunals: Quasi-Judicial Decision-Making in the Executive Branch

The conventional separation of powers suggests that judicial functions are confined to judges. That is no longer the case. Today, disputes between certain parties—such as landlords and tenants, doctors and their regulatory colleges, or unions and management—are usually resolved by specialized quasi-judicial tribunals. So are proceedings under particular types of statute. Complaints under human rights codes are generally adjudicated by Human Rights Commissions or Tribunals, whether the respondent is a private person or a government agency.

There are hundreds of administrative tribunals in Canada, regulating every imaginable field of activity. The executive and legislative branches created those tribunals and gave them the power to make administrative decisions potentially affecting every Canadian (or every resident of a province). Tribunals are supposed to apply specialized policy expertise, as distinct from judges' legal expertise, to issues falling within their particular jurisdictions. Tribunals tasked with quasi-judicial functions are also expected to resolve disputes more quickly and cheaply than courts.

While it is risky to generalize about such a diverse set of institutions, all of the tribunals discussed in this chapter share three important features.

1. Each has its own unique statutory mandate. A tribunal cannot make a decision that exceeds its *vires*. For example, it cannot award a benefit or impose a penalty without the explicit power to do so. As we saw in *Ishaq* and the Nova Scotia *TWU* case, such decisions may be invalidated for lack of jurisdiction.

2. Each tribunal exercises some discretion in the performance of its statutory mandate. It makes little sense to speak of an administrative *decision* if the law admits of only one outcome. Broadly speaking, the degree of discretion varies with the decision-maker's status in the executive branch. A minister is afforded the widest sphere of discretion, whereas a front-line public servant delivering services to the public may have little or none. As previously noted in the discussion of *Insite*, s. 56 of the CDSA only requires a minister to form an opinion before he or she grants an exemption for the prescribed purposes. But as *Ishaq* and *Insite* demonstrate, even a minister must exercise his or her powers in conformity with the Constitution and the purposes of the enabling statute.[51]

3. Tribunals, even those with quasi-judicial functions, belong to the permanent executive. This raises concerns about independence and impartiality. Unlike judges, most tribunal members are appointed for fixed periods and some can be dismissed at will.[52] Instead of being autonomous, tribunals are beholden to ministers for their budgets and personnel.

It might be assumed that a quasi-judicial tribunal, which functions like a court and exercises some of the same powers, should be equally independent of the political executive. But the constitutional guarantee of judicial independence does not apply to tribunals in the executive branch. Consequently, a legislature can dispense with such protections for certain types of administrative decision-maker and the courts must defer to that choice.[53] Having said as much, tribunals whose "primary purpose is to adjudicate disputes through some form of hearing" will generally require more stringent safeguards of procedural fairness than policy-making tribunals. Quasi-judicial tribunals, in other words, may require "a high degree of independence from [the rest of] the executive branch."[54] The SCC has declared that "the content of the requirements of procedural fairness applicable to a given tribunal depends not only upon the enabling statute but also upon applicable quasi-constitutional and constitutional principles."[55] Consequently, a statutory or soft law rule that falls short of the required degree of procedural fairness may be subject to modification by a court.

3. From Tribunal to Courtroom: Statutory Appeals and Judicial Review

(a) Introduction

Administrative law both restrains and remedies unlawful and damaging exercises of public power. We have seen that the Superior Courts have the inherent jurisdiction to determine the lawfulness of administrative decisions by hearing applications for judicial review. They also have the statutory jurisdiction to hear appeals from certain tribunals. The Federal Court also has a statutory jurisdiction to hear some appeals and judicial reviews from federal tribunals. Whether on appeal

or judicial review, courts are required to determine whether a part of the executive branch—including a quasi-judicial tribunal—has exceeded the purposes for which the legislative branch empowered it to act.

Judges are reluctant to set aside tribunal decisions. This is a crucial point that should not be obscured by the five cases discussed in this chapter. In four of those five cases (the exception being the Ontario TWU case), the courts overruled the statutory decision-maker and substituted their own decision. This is by no means a representative sample. Such outcomes are relatively rare. Members of the judicial branch generally defer to the other two branches of government in matters requiring policy expertise. Courts also respect the choice by cabinets and legislators to create specialized tribunals and give them jurisdiction over certain legal matters.

> Judicial review seeks to address an underlying tension between the rule of law and the foundational democratic principle, which finds an expression in the initiatives of Parliament and legislatures to create various administrative bodies and endow them with broad powers. Courts, while exercising their constitutional functions of judicial review, must be sensitive not only to the need to uphold the rule of law, but also to the necessity of avoiding undue interference with the discharge of administrative functions in respect of the matters delegated to administrative bodies by Parliament and legislatures.[56]

Despite this deferential attitude, the Superior Courts have a constitutional mandate to ensure that statutory decision-makers stay within their respective jurisdictions. Their enforcement function "cannot be removed from the superior courts by either level of government, without amending the Constitution."[57] This inherent jurisdiction "comprises those powers which are essential to the administration of justice and the maintenance of the rule of law."[58] Under s. 96 of the Constitution Act, 1867, Parliament and the provincial legislatures cannot immunize a tribunal from judicial review. To do so would give the tribunal the final word on the scope of its own jurisdiction, which would be incompatible with the rule of law.[59]

The court's role in a statutory appeal or judicial review is not to re-hear the case. In this sense, its jurisdiction is more limited than that of the tribunal. The court may only determine whether the decision-maker acted lawfully—that is, within its substantive and procedural jurisdiction. We have already seen that a decision may be *ultra vires* where

- the decision-maker exceeded its statutory mandate (*Ishaq*, the Nova Scotia *TWU* case), or
- the decision-maker's exercise of statutory discretion conflicted with the Constitution (*Insite*).

Ishaq, *Insite*, and the Nova Scotia *TWU* case revolved around errors of law. In each case the decision-maker's incorrect assumption about the scope of its jurisdiction led it to make an unlawful decision. As explained in Section 3(b), such true errors of jurisdiction may be set aside on judicial review. Most statutory appeals also focus on alleged errors of law, although a court may consider errors of fact if the enabling statute so provides.

This section examines two additional grounds for a court to declare an administrative decision invalid.

- The court can find that the substance of the decision is unreasonable, where reasonableness is the applicable standard of review. Courts presume that "a legislature does not intend the power it delegates to be exercised unreasonably."[60] Hence a tribunal exceeds its jurisdiction by making a decision that a reasonable and well-informed person would not have made, or one that falls outside the "margin of appreciation" that courts generally accord to specialized tribunals with policy expertise in the subject-matter covered by their statutory jurisdiction.[61]
- The court can find that the tribunal forfeited its jurisdiction by violating the principles of natural justice (as in the BC *TWU* case). "Procedural fairness is a cornerstone of modern Canadian administrative law."[62] Even if the substance of the decision is reasonable, it may be set aside on evidence that the tribunal violated a principle of natural justice or ignored its own rules.

Four concepts are fundamental when courts consider their relationship to administrative tribunals:

- the standard of review,
- natural justice/procedural fairness,
- statutory appeals from tribunal decisions, and

- judicial review of tribunal decisions: the remedial powers of courts.

We will now deal with each of these in turn.

(b) The Standard of Review

The standard of review refers to the degree to which a court is likely to defer to the decision of a tribunal, either on appeal or regarding an application for judicial review. It is a notoriously difficult and unsettled issue in administrative law.[63] Before a court can review the substance of a tribunal decision, it must decide whether the applicable standard is reasonableness or correctness. A court or tribunal that chooses the wrong standard of review makes an error of law and is liable to reversal on appeal or judicial review.[64] In some cases, the outcome is determined by the preliminary finding on the standard of review. Because this determination is so important, the differences between reasonableness and correctness must be clearly understood. The following table summarizes and contrasts the two standards of review.

As the table suggests, the reasonableness standard stacks the deck against statutory appellants and applicants for judicial review. In the vast majority of cases where reasonableness applies, reviewing courts defer to tribunal decisions—even those that the court itself, with its legal expertise, would never have made. While some tribunal members have legal training, many do not. They are experts in the activity regulated by the tribunal, not in statutory interpretation or the rules of evidence. Even with the assistance of legal counsel, a tribunal sometimes misinterprets its own statute or writes unintelligible reasons for decision. The reasonableness standard directs a reviewing court to affirm the resulting decision as if these errors had not been made. This high degree of deference does not always square with the courts' duty to enforce the rule of law. But it is consistent with the SCC's emphasis on specialized subject-matter expertise of administrative tribunals and its reluctance to interfere with the legislative and executive branches of government.[74]

(c) Natural Justice/Procedural Fairness

Table 4.1 identifies one major exception to the reasonableness standard: an alleged breach of procedural justice is generally reviewed on the stricter standard

Table 4.1   Reasonableness and Correctness

Characteristic	Reasonableness	Correctness
Deference to the tribunal	High	Low
Applicable subject-matter	Factual, legal, and policy questions within the tribunal's expertise, including the interpretation of the tribunal's home statute[65] and the application of Charter values[66]	"True questions of jurisdiction"[67] Important legal questions beyond the tribunal's expertise,[68] including constitutional questions[69] Alleged breaches of procedural fairness[70]
Definition	The decision "falls within a range of possible, acceptable outcomes which are defensible in respect of the facts and law"[71] and in light of the purposes for which the decision-making power was conferred by the legislature[72] "reasonableness is concerned mostly with the existence of justification, transparency and intelligibility within the decision-making process"[73]	There is only one correct answer. The tribunal correctly identified the applicable legal principles and applied them to the facts before it.
How often applied	Almost always	Rarely
Available remedies	Setting aside the decision Remitting the case back to the tribunal for a fresh decision	Setting aside the tribunal decision and substituting its own findings

of correctness. When a tribunal fails to follow its own procedures, and thereby causes harm, the affected party may apply for judicial review on that basis. Over and above the soft law specific to each tribunal, "there is, as a general common law principle, a duty of procedural fairness lying on every public authority making an administrative decision which is not of a legislative nature and which affects the rights, privileges or interests of an individual."[75]

There are three core common-law principles of natural justice.

- *Audi alteram partem*: an adjudicator must hear from both sides to a dispute before reaching a final resolution. This rule does not necessarily require a formal in-person hearing for all matters before the tribunal. Depending on the matter in issue, it may be sufficient to invite the parties to make written submissions or to participate in a conference call. The *audi alteram partem* rule also requires that each party be given notice of any hearing, and that it be fully informed of

the case it has to meet.[76] Like the other principles of procedural justice, this rule "is eminently variable and its content is to be decided in the specific context of each case."[77] But if the record shows, on a balance of probabilities, that the decision-maker failed to give either party a fair chance to state its case, a reviewing court may quash the decision. In the BC *TWU* case, Chief Justice Hinkson found that "By refusing to allow TWU to present its case to the members of the LSBC on the same footing as the case against it was presented, the LSBC deprived TWU of the procedural fairness to which it was entitled."[78]

- *Nemo judex in sua debet esse*: no one can make a binding decision in a case which engages their own self-interest. Put differently, a tribunal must be—and must be seen to be—impartial and independent. An otherwise lawful decision may be set aside if the record discloses a reasonable apprehension of bias for or against one of the parties. A mere unfounded suspicion, or a subjective sense of injustice, is not enough to overcome the presumption of impartiality. The perception of bias "must be a reasonable one held by reasonable and right minded persons, applying themselves to the question and obtaining thereon the required information."[79] The test is "what would an informed person, viewing the matter realistically and practically—and having thought the matter through—conclude. Would he think that it is more likely than not that [the decision-maker], whether consciously or unconsciously, would not decide fairly[?]"[80] Only if this stringent standard is met will a court set aside the decision. The requirement of impartiality varies with the type of tribunal. A quasi-judicial tribunal, like a court, must appear (and be) scrupulously even-handed, whereas an elected politician is permitted to express an opinion before deciding on a matter as long as the record shows that he or she kept an open mind[81] and the decision is not otherwise unlawful (recall *Ishaq* and *Insite*).

- *He who hears must decide and he who decides must hear*.[82] A tribunal may not allow a decision to be taken by anyone who lacks the statutory mandate to make it.[83] If the legislature delegated a power of decision to a specific individual or group, that recipient may not sub-delegate it to someone else. In the BC *TWU* case, the benchers of the Law Society—the only group entrusted with decision-making power under the Legal Profession Act—considered themselves bound by the result of the October 2014 membership referendum. By reversing their April 2014 decision, the benchers improperly sub-delegated the decision to the members at large and breached the rules of natural justice.[84] This principle also bars a tribunal from fettering its own discretion. Unlike courts, quasi-judicial tribunals are not bound by *stare decisis*. They are supposed to decide each case by applying their expertise to the facts before them. On the other hand, most tribunals have rules and guidelines to promote consistency and transparency in their decision-making. But if a tribunal treats its soft law as binding, and consequently fails to consider relevant evidence, it may violate procedural fairness.[85]

In some cases, particularly where a quasi-judicial tribunal makes a decision affecting the rights of an individual,[86] a fourth principle applies: *the decision-maker must provide written reasons explaining how the decision was reached*. Otherwise a reviewing court may be unable to determine whether the decision is reasonable or correct. The absence of written reasons may constitute a breach of procedural fairness, and thus an error of law to be reviewed on a standard of correctness.[87] But a lack of reasons does not constitute a "stand-alone basis for quashing a decision," as long as the court can deduce the decision-maker's reasoning from the record of the case.[88] In the Ontario *TWU* case, the LSUC did not issue formal written reasons for its decision to deny accreditation to the proposed law school. But it did transcribe the debates among its benchers at two meetings leading up to the April 2014 vote. The Divisional Court found the transcript sufficient to disclose "the basis upon which the decision was reached, and the analysis that was undertaken in the process of reaching that decision."[89] Where a tribunal does give reasons, it need not provide a detailed explanation and justification for every aspect of the decision. But in extreme cases, where there is no intelligible and transparent justification for the outcome, a reviewing court may set aside the tribunal's decision and substitute its own ruling in the case.[90]

This flexible standard for assessing written reasons reflects a broader tension in the judicial review of procedural fairness. While courts are right to insist that important decisions be made fairly, they also recognize that requiring unduly stringent and complicated procedures would defeat the legislature's purpose for creating tribunals. Quasi-judicial decision-makers are supposed to resolve disputes more quickly, simply, and inexpensively than courts.[91] Increasingly, their rules and procedures are designed to accommodate people who cannot afford legal representation. So a balance must be struck between a user-friendly process, accessible to people without legal training, and the technical requirements of natural justice familiar to lawyers and judges.

> Tribunals should adopt procedures that enable them to consider each case on its merits. They should avoid becoming bogged down with procedural formalities and technicalities as these may cause unnecessary delay and expense and may defeat the statutory purpose. This is especially true of lay tribunals whose members are drawn from the community with an expectation that

they will apply their judgment acquired through knowledge and experience. . . . Common sense should prevail over legal formalism.[92]

On an application for judicial review, the court must be satisfied that the tribunal fulfilled its duty of procedural fairness. "The question, of course, is what the duty of procedural fairness may reasonably require of an authority in the way of specific procedural rights in a particular legislative and administrative context and what should be considered to be a breach of fairness in particular circumstances."[93] The answer to that question varies with the subject matter of the decision, the statutory mandate of the decision-maker, and the relationship of the tribunal to the person most affected by the decision. The following considerations, called the *Baker* factors after the leading SCC case on this issue, are generally relevant to determining what the duty of procedural fairness looks like in practice.

- The first factor is "the nature of the decision being made and the process followed in making it." The more closely the structure and purpose of the tribunal resemble a court, "the more likely it is that procedural protections closer to the trial model will be required by the duty of fairness."[94]
- The second factor is the tribunal's statutory mandate and "the role of the particular decision within the statutory scheme." Courts demand more stringent procedural protections where the decision is final and there is no avenue of appeal.[95]
- The third factor is "the importance of the decision to the individual or individuals affected. The more important the decision is to the lives of those affected and the greater its impact on that person or those persons, the more stringent the procedural protections that will be mandated."[96] A law society discipline panel deciding whether to revoke a lawyer's licence to practice must provide stronger procedural protections than a regulator considering a tiny increase in a user fee.
- Fourth, "the legitimate expectations of the person challenging the decision may also determine what procedures the duty of fairness requires in given circumstances."[97] The doctrine of "legitimate expectations" does not mean that everyone is entitled to the outcome most favourable to him or her. Nor does it "create substantive

rights" or "fetter the discretion of a statutory decision-maker."[98] It is purely procedural, relating solely to "the content of the duty of fairness owed to the individual or individuals affected by the decision."[99]

- The fifth and final *Baker* factor relates to "the choices of procedure made by the agency itself, particularly when the statute leaves to the decision-maker the ability to choose its own procedures, or when the agency has an expertise in determining what procedures are appropriate in the circumstances."[100] In other words, a court should not be too quick to second-guess the procedures adopted by a tribunal to serve its particular statutory mandate.

(d) Statutory Appeals from Tribunal Decisions

There is no such thing as a freestanding right to an appeal in any field of law. An appeal is only available where, and to the extent that, it is provided for in statute.[101] In Ontario, for example, there is no right of appeal from a final decision of the Human Rights Tribunal.[102] Section 45.8 of the Human Rights Code states that, with a few minor exceptions, "a decision of the Tribunal is final and not subject to appeal and shall not be altered or set aside in an application for judicial review or in any other proceeding unless the decision is patently unreasonable." This **privative clause** signals the legislature's intent to give the tribunal the final word in matters within its jurisdiction. It also tells a reviewing court to defer to the tribunal, and not to substitute its own decision unless the adjudicator really made a hash of things.[103] As noted above, however, a privative clause cannot strip the Superior Court of its inherent jurisdiction to enforce the rule of law: "judicial review is constitutionally guaranteed in Canada, particularly with regard to the definition and enforcement of jurisdictional limits."[104]

Other enabling statutes do grant a right of appeal. An Ontario lawyer who has been found guilty of professional misconduct by the Law Society Tribunal may appeal a final decision to the Divisional Court on any question of fact or law.[105] Other statutes provide for a narrower scope of appeal, limited to pure questions of law.[106] In some statutory regimes, an appeal tribunal has the power to review and amend an initial decision. In others, there is a right to appeal an initial decision to a separate tribunal. If the Alcohol and Gaming Commission of Ontario suspends a bar's liquor licence because an inspector found intoxicated underage patrons on the premises, the licence holder can appeal to the Licence Appeal Tribunal—but only on a question of law.[107]

On a statutory appeal to a court, the parties (or their lawyers) file written submissions setting out their evidence and legal arguments. The party seeking to overturn the tribunal's decision is called the appellant; the other party is the respondent. The appellant bears the onus of persuading the court, on a balance of probabilities, that the decision is unreasonable (in rare cases, incorrect). The court will normally schedule a hearing for the parties to make oral arguments. Appeals are generally heard by a panel of three judges, who question the lawyers (or the parties, if self-represented) during the hearing. The final decision may be given orally ("from the bench") at the end of the hearing, or it may be reserved to a later date. The decision is always accompanied by written reasons.

(e) Judicial Review of Tribunal Decisions: The Remedial Powers of Courts

As previously explained, the power to judicially review the decisions of administrative tribunals derives from the inherent jurisdiction of the superior courts to enforce the rule of law. The common-law remedies available on judicial review are derived from the prerogative writs issued by the British Crown to remedy abuses of state power against the monarch's subjects. Three[108] such writs continue to play an important role in Canada.

- *Certiorari*: the decision-maker is ordered to produce the record of the proceeding against the applicant and submit it to the appropriate court for judicial review. The court may "set aside a decision for error of law on the face of the record on an application for an order in the nature of certiorari,"[109] in addition to granting any other type of relief permitted by statute. Most applicants for judicial review request certiorari. Such orders are potentially available "wherever a public body has power to decide any matter affecting the rights, interests, property, privileges, or liberties of any person."[110]
- *Prohibition*: the decision-maker is ordered to refrain from proceeding with a matter before it, on the ground that it lacks jurisdiction. Today, such writs are rarely granted. They conflict with both the courts' deferential attitude towards tribunals and the doctrine of prematurity (discussed below).[111]
- *Mandamus*: the court orders the decision-maker to perform a legal duty owed to the applicant. Mandamus is rarely available, because courts cannot order an administrative decision-maker to exercise a discretionary power. On occasion, however, mandamus "may be used to force the decision-maker to act in a way that is not unreasonable and which takes relevant factors into account."[112] Where, for example, the record shows that the tribunal ignored relevant facts and/or relied on irrelevant facts in making its decision, an order of certiorari (setting aside the decision) may be combined with a mandamus order directing the tribunal to reconsider the decision in accordance with the court's directions.[113] Where the decision is set aside on Charter grounds, as in *Insite*, the Court may decline to refer the matter back to the decision-maker. The SCC's mandamus order in *Insite* directed the minister to renew the exemption, because no other conceivable exercise of his statutory discretion would comply with s. 7 of the Charter.[114]

In addition to their common origin in the English common law, these remedies share another important feature: they are discretionary, meaning that no one can claim a legal right to certiorari or mandamus. Even if the record discloses a significant error of law, the court will not order a remedy unless it would be just, appropriate, timely, and consistent with the public good.[115] A court may refuse to set aside a decision if the record shows that the applicant acted in bad faith[116] or failed to pursue an adequate alternative remedy within the statutory regime. For example, a student at the University of Regina applied for judicial review of a decision requiring him to withdraw for poor academic performance. He was entitled to appeal the decision to the University Senate, but chose not to do so before seeking relief in the Superior Court. The SCC ultimately held that he was not entitled to an order of certiorari because he had not exhausted all of his potential remedies within the laws applicable to the University of Regina.[117]

Courts are also loath to grant judicial review prematurely. They generally wait for the statutory process to run its course before hearing an application. "This prevents fragmentation of the administrative process and piecemeal court proceedings, eliminates the large costs and delays associated with premature forays to court and avoids the waste associated with hearing an interlocutory judicial review when the applicant for judicial review may succeed at the end of the administrative process anyway."[118] A reviewing court may only depart from the prematurity rule under exceptional circumstances, where:

- "the tribunal clearly lacks jurisdiction to proceed";
- a preliminary decision effectively determined the outcome; or
- "proceeding with the hearing would result in an unfair hearing or a breach of natural justice."[119]

Even a clear violation of procedural fairness in the midst of an administrative proceeding will only result in judicial review if there is no other remedy available, such as a statutory right of appeal.[120]

The procedure on judicial review resembles an appeal, in that the evidence and legal argument are presented to the court in written form. The evidence on a judicial review is contained in the record, which shows the reviewing court how the tribunal functioned and what evidence was before it when it made its decision. Counsel for the parties also make oral submissions, beginning with the applicant (who carries the burden of proof). "The focus of judicial review is to quash invalid government decisions—or require government to act or prohibit it from acting—by a speedy process."[121]

However, a judicial review application differs from an appeal in that the reviewing court does not consider the merits of the impugned decision.[122] The question before the court, as illustrated by the cases discussed in this chapter, is whether the administrative decision-maker exceeded its substantive jurisdiction (by making a decision that the legislature did not intend it to make) or its procedural jurisdiction (by violating one or more principles of natural justice).

The applicable standard of review determines the degree of deference owed to the decision-maker. Where reasonableness applies, as it usually does, the court will affirm a decision that falls within a range of acceptable alternatives. If the decision is found to be unreasonable, the court usually sets it aside (by granting an order in the nature of certiorari) and remits

the matter back to the tribunal, sometimes with a stipulation that the re-hearing be conducted by a different member or panel. In the rare cases where correctness is the appropriate standard of review, the court does not defer to the tribunal. Where it finds an error of law, the court may set aside the decision and substitute its own ruling on the case. An excess of jurisdiction is always an error of law, generally resulting in an order in the nature of certiorari. In *Ishaq* the Federal Court concluded that reasonableness was the applicable standard of review. The Nova Scotia Supreme Court made the same finding in *TWU*.[123] But no amount of judicial deference could save a guideline that conflicted with the minister's enabling statute (*Ishaq*) or a regulation that the NSBS had no legal authority to make.

Where the only issue is an alleged breach of procedural fairness, there is no need to conduct a standard of review analysis. Instead, the reviewing court applies the *Baker* factors to determine whether the tribunal fulfilled its duty of fairness towards the applicant.[124] If the duty of procedural fairness was breached, the court generally sets aside the decision. It may also grant an order in the nature of mandamus, requiring the tribunal to respect its duty of natural justice when it re-hears the matter.

4. Conclusion: Public Administration and the Rule of Law

This chapter covered a number of aspects of administrative law. They can be arranged along four axes. (These also reflect the chapter objectives established at the outset.)

The first part of this chapter was concerned with identifying the key principles of administrative law. Administrative law involves challenges to decisions taken by either a government actor or a non-government tribunal. A tribunal is any administrative official or entity that exercises a statutory power of decision. These actors may exercise powers delegated to them by the legislative branch under statute. Those who challenge their decisions may do so by seeking judicial review or an application for appeal from a tribunal decision. The jurisdiction of the decision-maker is important, that is, determining whether the decision-maker had acted within its statutory authority. When a decision exceeds the lawful jurisdiction of the decision-maker, it is *ultra vires*—Latin for "beyond the power"—and thereby invalid. The rule of law is a fundamental principle in governance and public administration: political expediency cannot override the will of Parliament as expressed in statutes and regulations. Courts see to it that tribunals operate within the boundaries of the rule of law.

The second part of this chapter explained how the Constitution shapes Canadian administrative law, concentrating on the division of powers, Charter values, and the separation of powers. The division of powers affects administrative law in two ways. First, administrative law seeks to determine whether a particular application of a statute should be set aside on jurisdictional grounds, even though the law itself is *intra vires* (within the jurisdiction of the legislature that adopted it). Second, the division of powers indirectly shapes the procedural aspects of administrative law by limiting the jurisdiction of courts to hear certain types of cases. In recent years the SCC has given the Charter a new role in administrative law. This means that where a discretionary administrative decision engages Charter protections, the discretionary decision-maker is required to proportionately balance the Charter protections to ensure that they are limited no more than is necessary.

Administrative law is also affected by the separation of powers doctrine. According to this, there are three powers, or branches of government: legislative, executive, and judicial. The separation of power viewpoint overstates Parliament's role in law-making (because of the phenomenon of subordinate legislation). Second, it understates the law-making powers of the judicial branch (which determines an immense body of common law—notably regarding natural justice and procedural fairness), and enforces the rule of law by invalidating *ultra vires* tribunal decisions. Third, the conventional picture overlooks the quasi-judicial functions assigned to certain parts of the permanent executive, which generate the greatest share of cases in administrative law.

The third part of this chapter elaborated the courts' role in administrative law. It explained how judges analyze an administrative decision subject to a statutory appeal or an application for judicial review. It reviewed the four concepts that are fundamental when courts consider their relationship to administrative tribunals: the standard of review; natural justice/procedural fairness; statutory appeals from tribunal decisions; and judicial review of tribunal decisions.

The standard of review refers to the degree to which a court is likely to defer to the decision of a tribunal, either on appeal or regarding an application for judicial review. A court or tribunal must choose correctly between the standards of reasonableness or correctness, the wrong choice being an error of law liable to reversal on appeal or judicial review. Regarding the second topic, it is useful to observe that there are three core common-law principles of natural justice that are common in administrative law: (1) an adjudicator must hear from both sides to a dispute before reaching a final resolution; (2) no one can make a binding decision in a case that engages their own self-interest; and (3) a tribunal may not allow a decision to be taken by anyone who lacks the statutory mandate to make it.

The final two topics are judicial review and appeals. They differ in purpose. Appeals are not a freestanding right; legislatures may or may not give a tribunal the final word in matters within its jurisdiction. The focus of judicial review, on the other hand, is to quash invalid government decisions—or require government to act with dispatch or prohibit it from acting. An application for judicial review differs from an appeal in that the reviewing court does not consider the merits of the impugned decision. Judicial review simply asks whether the administrative decision-maker exceeded its substantive jurisdiction (by making a decision that the legislature did not intend it to make) or its procedural jurisdiction (by violating one or more principles of natural justice).

The importance of administrative law to the practice of government should now be clear. The decision-making power of public officials is derived from statutes enacted by the legislature and regulations issued pursuant to those statutes by the Governor-in-Council or Lieutenant-Governor-in-Council. Even where the law grants a measure of discretion, the decision-maker must act consistently with the Constitution, the enabling laws, and the principles of natural justice. Failure to abide by the limits of one's jurisdiction is an error of law. Where there is no avenue of appeal, the aggrieved party can seek judicial review in the Superior Court under its inherent jurisdiction to enforce the rule of law.

Our fourth and concluding section explains why a knowledge of administrative law is a vital part of the public administration curriculum. The key lesson for students of public administration is this: if you want to know what government can do with a particular file, don't just look at the fiscal data or the latest managerial theories. Read the law. Start with the Constitution, then look at the enabling statute(s) and the applicable regulation(s). Which administrative structures are tasked with implementing the file? What powers do they have? How broad is their discretion? Who are the statutory decision-makers, and what are the precise contours of their substantive and procedural jurisdiction? Are there any quasi-judicial tribunals in this field? Have the courts been asked to define their jurisdiction on appeal or judicial review? Read the case law. You may find that where government documents are silent on key aspects of public administration, courts have spoken.

Tribunals of the sort described in this chapter play a larger role in some policy fields than in others. Immigration, social benefits, and human rights directly affect the well-being of individuals and families. They are replete with quasi-judicial tribunals, which produce their own case law and often generate court decisions. But even a technical field like international trade is governed by law. Disputes between Canadian governments and foreign investors are heard by specialized tribunals with their own soft law (usually modelled on conventions crafted by the United Nations Commission on International Trade Law). Energy, transportation, natural resource development, industrial policy—all are highly regulated, and all are governed by the principles of administrative law discussed in this chapter.

Important Terms and Concepts

common law	privative clause	soft law
discretion	procedural fairness,	standard of review
impugned	aka natural justice	statute
inherent jurisdiction	regulations (aka delegated	tribunal
judicial review	or subordinate legislation)	*ultra vires*
jurisdiction	rule of law	

Study Questions

1.　What are the most important principles of Canadian administrative law? Define each, preferably in your own words.
2.　How does the division of powers shape Canadian administrative law?
3.　Name and briefly explain three ways in which the reality of administrative law differs from the conventional picture of three distinct branches of government.
4.　What role, if any, does the Canadian Charter of Rights and Freedoms play in Canada's administrative law?
5.　What is a tribunal? How would you determine the substantive jurisdiction of a particular tribunal?
6.　Imagine that you were planning to appear before a tribunal. How would you know what procedures to follow?
7.　Imagine that the tribunal ruled against you. How would you know whether or not it had treated you fairly?
8.　What is the standard of review? What are the two possible standards, and how do they differ from each other? If you were trying to persuade a court to overturn the tribunal's decision against you, which standard of review would you want the court to apply, and why?
9.　You discover that the tribunal's decision is protected by a privative clause. What does that mean? Does the privative clause leave you without a remedy? Why or why not?

Notes

1   *Ishaq v. Minister of Citizenship and Immigration*, 2015 FC 156 ["Ishaq FC"].

2   *Minister of Citizenship and Immigration v. Ishaq*, 2015 FCA 194 ["Ishaq FCA"].

3   *Trinity Western University v. The Law Society of British Columbia*, 2015 BCSC 2326 ["TWU BCSC"].

4   TWU first applied to the Ontario Divisional Court for judicial review of the LSUC decision. That application failed: *Trinity Western University v. Law Society of Upper Canada*, 2015 ONSC 4250 ["TWU Div Ct"]. The Divisional Court is discussed later in this chapter. TWU appealed unsuccessfully to the Ontario Court of Appeal: *Trinity Western University v. The Law Society of Upper Canada*, 2016 ONCA 518 ["TWU ONCA"].

5   A single judge of the Nova Scotia Supreme Court (the name for the Superior Court in that province) set aside the refusal to accredit TWU: *Trinity Western University v. Nova Scotia Barristers' Society*, 2015 NSSC 25 ["TWU NSSC"]. The Nova Scotia Court of Appeal affirmed the lower court decision on appeal: *The Nova Scotia Barristers' Society v. Trinity Western University*, 2016 NSCA 59 ["TWU NSCA"].

6   Ishaq FC, *supra* at paras 53-57.

7   TWU Div Ct, *supra* at para 129.

8   Law Society Act, RSO 1990, c L.8, s 4.2.

9   Legal Profession Act, SBC 1998, c. 9, s 3.

10 TWU Div Ct, *supra* at paras 55-58; TWU BCSC, *supra* at para 108.

11 TWU NSSC, *supra* at para 166; TWU NSCA, *supra* at paras 55-68.

12 TWU BCSC, *supra* at paras 112-125 and 148.

13 TWU BCSC, *supra* at paras 40-41 and 148.

14 TWU BCSC, *supra* at para 151.

15 *Reference re Secession of Quebec*, [1998] 2 SCR 217 at para 72 ["Secession Reference"; citation omitted].

16 Controlled Drugs and Substances Act, SC 1996, c 19, s 56(1).

17 *Canada (Attorney General) v PHS Community Services Society*, 2011 SCC 44, [2011] 3 SCR 134 at para 72 ["Insite"]. The Court added (at para 81) that "Insite cannot operate without a federal exemption, not for lack of constitutional powers in the Province, but for the practical reason that neither workers nor clients will come to the facility, making it effectively impossible to offer the proposed health services." The Court relied on the constitutional law doctrine of federal paramountcy.

18 Federal Courts Act, RSC 1985, c F-7, s 18(1).

19 *Canada (Human Rights Commission) v Canadian Liberty Net*, [1998] 1 SCR 626 at paras 26-27.

20 See the Courts of Justice Act, RSO 1990, c C.43, ss 18-21, and the Judicial Review Procedure Act, RSO 1990, c J.1 ["JRPA"].

21 *Attorney General of Canada v Law Society of British Columbia*, [1982] 2 SCR 307 at 326-329; *Canada (Citizenship and Immigration) v Khosa*, 2009 SCC 12, [2009] 1 SCR 339 at para 34.

22 *Strickland v Canada (Attorney General)*, 2015 SCC 37, [2015] 2 SCR 713 at para 22.

23 See *R v Ferguson*, 2008 SCC 6, [2008] 1 SCR 96 at paras 49-50 and 58-66.

24 *Nova Scotia (Workers' Compensation Board) v Martin; Nova Scotia (Workers' Compensation Board) v Laseur*, 2003 SCC 54, [2003] 2 SCR 504 at para 31 [Martin]; *Mouvement laïque québécois v Saguenay (City)*, 2015 SCC 16, [2015] 2 SCR 3 at para 153 [Saguenay]; *Power v Ontario (Community and Social Services)*, 2015 HRTO 26 at para 12.

25 Christopher D. Bredt and Ewa Krajewska, *"R. v. Conway: UnChartered Territory for Administrative Tribunals"*, (2011), 54 *Supreme Court Law Review* (2d) 451 at 464.

26 Sometimes a legislature divides jurisdiction between the Superior Court and a specific tribunal. For example, s. 46.1 of the Ontario Human Rights Code, RSO 1990, c H.19, permits a person to bring a civil suit alleging human rights violations as part of a broader legal claim. This directs a person hoping for remedies under both the Charter and the Code to bypass the Tribunal in favour of an action for damages in the Superior Court. Otherwise he or she could only seek a full range of legal remedies by bringing simultaneous proceedings in two separate fora, thereby incurring significantly higher legal costs.

27 *Martin* at paras 39-48; *R v Conway*, 2010 SCC 22, [2010] 1 SCR 765 at para 77 [Conway].

28 *Conway*, *supra* at para 22.

29 *Suresh v Canada* (Minister of Citizenship and Immigration), 2002 SCC 1, [2002] 1 SCR 3 at para 77.

30 Section 7 reads as follows: "Everyone has the right to life, liberty and security of the person and the right not to be deprived thereof except in accordance with the principles of fundamental justice." The Court held that the applicable sections of the CDSA deprived Insite's clients and staff of their rights under s. 7. But there was no constitutional violation, precisely because the Act empowers the Minister to grant exemptions where necessary to protect the health of drug users or the broader public interest.

31 *Insite* at para 114.

32 *Insite* at para 127.

33 *Insite* at paras 150-153. Mandamus orders are explained in Section 3(e) of this chapter.

34 *Doré v Barreau du Québec*, 2012 SCC 12, [2012] 1 SCR 395 at para 24 [Doré].

35 *Loyola High School v Quebec (Attorney General)*, 2015 SCC 12, [2015] 1 SCR 613 at para 4 [Loyola].

36 *Doré* at paras 55-56.

37 *Doré* at para 57.

38 *Doré* at para 58.

39 Christopher D. Bredt and Ewa Krajewska, "Doré: All That Glitters Is Not Gold", (2014), 67 *Supreme Court Law Review* (2d) 339; Matthew Horner, "Charter Values: The Uncanny Valley of Canadian Constitutionalism", (2014), 67 *Supreme Court Law Review* (2d) 361.

40 TWU Div Ct, *supra* at paras 102-114.

41 TWU Div Ct, *supra* at paras 73-90.

42 TWU Div Ct, *supra* at paras 28-30 and 94-95.

43 TWU Div Ct, *supra* at paras 96-100.

44 TWU Div Ct, *supra* at paras 102 and 110. There are similar provisions in the Nova Scotia and BC human rights statutes, but the courts in those provinces did not cite them in their reasons.

45 Human Rights Code, *supra*, s 47(2).

46 TWU Div Ct, *supra* at para 123.

47 TWU BCSC, *supra* at paras 126-151.

48 *Katz Group Canada Inc v Ontario (Health and Long-Term Care)*, 2013 SCC 64, [2013] 3 SCR 810 at paras 25 and 28 [Katz].

49 *TWU NSCA* at para 68.

50 Statutory Powers Procedure Act, RSO 1990, c S.22; see also BC's Administrative Tribunals Act, SBC 2004, c 45, and the Alberta Administrative Procedures and Jurisdiction Act, RSA 2000, c A-3.

51 See also *Baker v Canada (Minister of Citizenship and Immigration)*, [1999] 2 SCR 817 at para 53 [*Baker*].

52 For a detailed critique of the relationship between administrative tribunals and the rest of the executive branch, see Ron Ellis, *Unjust by Design: Canada's Administrative Justice System* (Vancouver: UBC Press, 2013), particularly Chapter 4.

53 *Ocean Port Hotel Ltd v British Columbia (General Manager, Liquor Control and Licensing Branch)*, 2001 SCC 52, [2001] 2 SCR 781 at paras 20 and 22.

54 *Bell Canada v Canadian Telephone Employees Association*, [2003] 1 SCR 884, 2003 SCC 36 at paras 21-24 [*Bell Canada*].

55 *Bell Canada*, *supra* at para 27.

56 *Dunsmuir v. New Brunswick*, 2008 SCC 9 (*Dunsmuir*) at para 27.

57 *Reference re: Residential Tenancies Act 1979 (Ontario)*, [1981] 1 SCR 714; *MacMillan Bloedel Ltd v Simpson*, [1995] 4 SCR 725 at para 15 [*MacMillan Bloedel*]; *Ontario v Criminal Lawyers' Association of Ontario*, 2013 SCC 43, [2013] 3 SCR 3 at para 18 ["*Criminal Lawyers*"].

58 *MacMillan Bloedel*, *supra* at para 38; *Criminal Lawyers*, *supra* at para 19.

59 *Crevier v Québec (Attorney General)*, [1981] 2 SCR 220; *McEvoy v New Brunswick (Attorney General)*, [1983] 1 SCR 704; *Reference re Young Offenders Act (PEI)*, [1991] 1 SCR 252 at para 14.

60 *Catalyst Paper Corp v North Cowichan (District)*, 2012 SCC 2, [2012] 1 SCR 5 at paras 12 and 15 [*Catalyst*].

61 *Dunsmuir*, *supra* at para 47.

62 *Dunsmuir*, *supra* at para 79.

63 See the recent *cri de coeur* from a Justice of the Federal Court of Appeal: "Our administrative law is a never-ending construction site where one crew builds structures and then a later crew tears them down to build anew, seemingly without an overall plan." David Stratas, "The Canadian Law of Judicial Review: A Plea for Doctrinal Coherence and Consistency" (2016) at 1 (accessed at https://papers.ssrn.com/sol3/papers.cfm?abstract_id=2733751). This discussion can barely scratch the surface; interested readers are advised to check the current state of the law.

64 As of 2015, a single standard of substantive review applies to all administrative law cases in the Superior Courts: "Where . . . a statute provides for an appeal from a decision of a specialized administrative tribunal, the appropriate standards of review are . . . the ones that apply on judicial review, not on an appeal." *Saguenay*, *supra* at para 29. Previously, statutory appeals from tribunals were subject to the same standard of review as appeals from lower courts; see *Housen v Nikolaisen*, 2002 SCC 33, [2002] 2 SCR 235.

65 *Alberta (Information and Privacy Commissioner) v Alberta Teachers' Association*, 2011 SCC 61, [2011] 3 SCR 654 at para 39 ["*Alberta Teachers*"]; *Dunsmuir*, *supra* at para 54.

66 *Doré*, *supra* at paras 45-54.

67 *Dunsmuir*, *supra* at para 59. See the earlier discussion of the Superior Court's inherent jurisdiction to enforce the rule of law by ensuring that statutory decision-makers operate within their respective mandates. Arguably, three of the cases discussed in this chapter—Ishaq, Insite and the Nova Scotia TWU case—engage "true questions of jurisdiction" in this sense.

However, that phrase does not appear in *Ishaq* or *Insite*. Campbell J. of the Nova Scotia Superior Court suggested that the TWU case raised a "true question of jurisdiction," but concluded that the reasonableness standard applied to the question of whether the NSBS had exceeded its mandate by enacting the Regulation (at paras 154 and 159). Justice Campbell's conclusion is consistent with the SCC's insistence that "the category of true questions of jurisdiction is narrow indeed" and its recent suggestion that "the time has come to reconsider whether, for purposes of judicial review, the category of true questions of jurisdiction exists": *Alberta Teachers*, *supra* at paras 33–34. But the Nova Scotia Court of Appeal disagreed: it held that the standard of review for the amended regulation was determined not by *Dunsmuir* but by *Katz* (see footnote 48, above).

68 *Dunsmuir*, *supra* at para 55.

69 *Dunsmuir*, *supra* at para 58.

70 *Newfoundland and Labrador Nurses' Union v Newfoundland and Labrador (Treasury Board)*, 2011 SCC 62, [2011] 3 SCR 708 at para 22 ["Newfoundland Nurses"].

71 *Dunsmuir*, *supra* at para 47.

72 *Catalyst*, *supra* at paras 16-18.

73 *Dunsmuir*, *supra* at para 47.

74 A recent SCC ruling suggests that the Court is moving towards a less rosy view of subject-matter expertise. In *Edmonton (City) v. Edmonton East (Capilano) Shopping Centres Ltd.*, 2016 SCC 47, the five Justices in the majority followed the prevailing trend in administrative law: "expertise is something that inheres in a tribunal itself as an institution" (at para 33). But four dissenting Justices, including Chief Justice McLachlin, adopted a more nuanced approach: "an administrative decision maker is not entitled to blanket deference in all matters simply because it is an expert in some matters. An administrative decision maker is entitled to deference on the basis of expertise only if the question before it falls within the scope of its expertise, whether specific or institutional." (at para 83)

75 *Cardinal v Kent Institution*, [1985] 2 SCR 643 at para 14 [*Cardinal*]; *Moreau-Bérubé v New Brunswick (Judicial Council)*, 2002 SCC 11, [2002] 1 SCR 249 at para 75 [*Moreau-Bérubé*].

76 *IWA v Consolidated Bathurst Packaging Ltd*, [1990] 1 SCR 282 at 322 [*Consolidated Bathurst*].

77 *Moreau-Bérubé*, *supra* at para 75; quoting *Baker*, *supra* at para 21, and *Knight v Indian Head School Division No 19*, [1990] 1 SCR 653 at para 46.

78 TWU BCSC, *supra* at para 148.

79 *Committee for Justice and Liberty v Canada (National Energy Board)*, [1978] 1 SCR 369 at 394 ["*Committee for Justice and Liberty*"].

80 *Committee for Justice and Liberty*, *supra* at 394. This passage appeared in a dissenting (i.e., minority) judgment, to which the doctrine of *stare decisis* does not apply. It has subsequently acquired binding force, having been adopted by majorities in several Supreme Court rulings. See, for example, *Wewaykum Indian Band v Canada*, 2003 SCC 45, 2003 2 SCR 259 at para 60.

81 *Newfoundland Telephone Co v Newfoundland (Board of Commissioners of Public Utilities)*, [1992] 1 SCR 623 at para 27.

82 *Consolidated Bathurst*, *supra* at 322.

83 *Therrien (Re)*, 2001 SCC 35, [2001] 2 SCR 3 at para 93.

84 TWU BCSC, *supra* at paras 119-120.

85 *Thamotharem v Canada (Minister of Citizenship and Immigration)*, 2007 FCA 198 at paras 55-89.

86 *Baker, supra* at paras 39-43.

87 *Newfoundland Nurses, supra* at para 22; *Mission Institution v Khela*, 2014 SCC 24, [2014] 1 SCR 502 at para 79.

88 *Newfoundland Nurses, supra* at para 14.

89 TWU Div Ct, *supra* at para 49.

90 For an example, see *Novick v Ontario College of Teachers*, 2016 ONSC 508 (Div Ct).

91 *Roosma v Ford Motor Co of Canada Ltd*, (1988), 66 OR (2d) 18 (Div Ct) at para 26; quoted in *Ackerman v Ontario (Provincial Police)*, 2010 ONSC 910 (Div Ct) at para 14 [Ackerman].

92 Sara Blake, *Administrative Law in Canada*, 5th ed (Toronto: LexisNexis, 2015), Part I.2.B.

93 *Cardinal, supra* at para 15.

94 *Baker, supra* at para 23.

95 *Baker, supra* at para 24.

96 *Baker, supra* at para 25.

97 *Baker, supra* at para 26.

98 *Moreau-Bérubé, supra* at para 78.

99 *Baker, supra* at para 26.

100 *Baker, supra* at para 27.

101 For example, appeals from convictions for indictable offences are governed by Part XXI of the Criminal Code.

102 Human Rights Code, *supra*, s 45.8.

103 *Dunsmuir, supra* at para 52.

104 *Dunsmuir, supra* at para 31.

105 Law Society Act, RSO 1990, c. L.8, s 49.38. Note that this provision refers to a decision of the Tribunal's Appeal Division. There is a statutory right to appeal a decision of the Tribunal's Hearing Division, but only to the Appeal Division of the same Tribunal. There is no statutory avenue of appeal from a collective decision of LSUC's benchers. That is why TWU applied for judicial review to set aside LSUC's denial of accreditation to its proposed law school.

106 See, e.g., Licence Appeal Tribunal Act, 1999, SO 1999, c 12, Schedule G, s 11; Residential Tenancies Act, 2006, SO 2006, c 17, s 210(1).

107 Licence Appeal Tribunal Act, 1999, SO 1999, c. 12, Sched. G, s. 11.

108 A fourth prerogative writ, *habeas corpus*, is not discussed here. It provides an important check on the exercise of public power, but only in criminal and correctional matters. It requires the authority holding an individual in state custody to bring that individual to court shortly after his or her detention, and to justify his or her continuing incarceration as both lawful and necessary. *Habeas corpus* is also used by prison inmates to challenge the conditions of their detention, e.g., an extended period of solitary confinement.

109 JRPA, *supra*, s 2(2).

110 *Martineau v Matsqui Institution*, [1980] 1 SCR 602 at 622-623.

111 See the discussion of prohibition in *Halifax (Regional Municipality) v Nova Scotia (Human Rights Commission)*, 2012 SCC 10, [2012] 1 SCR 364.

112 Guy Régimbald and Matthew Estabrooks, *Halsbury's Laws of Canada - Administrative Law* (2013 Reissue), section VI.3.(3).

113 *Oakwood Development Ltd v St-François Xavier (Rural Municipality)*, [1985] 2 SCR 164 at 176-177.

114 *Insite, supra* at paras 141–153. See also *Loyola, supra* at paras 163–165.

115 See the discussion of remedial discretion by Stratas J.A. in *Paradis Honey Ltd v Canada (Attorney General)*, 2015 FCA 89 at para 138.

116 *Homex Realty and Development Co v Wyoming (Village)*, [1980] 2 SCR 1011.

117 *Harelkin v University of Regina*, [1979] 2 SCR 561.

118 *CB Powell Ltd v Canada (Border Services Agency)*, 2010 FCA 61 at paras 31-32. "Interlocutory" is a legal term meaning "interim" or "preliminary."

119 *Ackerman, supra* at para 19 (citations omitted).

120 *Haigh v College of Denturists of Ontario*, 2011 ONSC 2152 (Div Ct) at para 25; Christopher D. Bredt and Ewa Krajewska, "The Doctrine of Prematurity: A Trend Towards Deference in the Procedural Decision-Making Process," (2013) 26 *Canadian Journal of Administrative Law & Practice* 275 at 279 and 281.

121 *Canada (Attorney General) v. TeleZone Inc.*, 2010 SCC 62 at para 26.

122 In practice, it is difficult to see how a court could assess the reasonableness of a decision without weighing the merits.

123 Wrongly, according to the Nova Scotia Court of Appeal; see footnote 67, above.

124 *Moreau-Bérubé, supra* at paras 74-75.

References

Blake, Sara. 2015. *Administrative Law in Canada*. 5th edn, Toronto, ON: LexisNexis.

Bredt, Christopher D. & Ewa Krajewska, Ewa. (2011). *R. v. Conway*: UnChartered territory for administrative tribunals. 54 *Supreme Court Law Review* (2d) 451.

———— & ————. 2014. *Doré*: All that glitters is not gold. 67 *Supreme Court Law Review* (2d) 339.

Ellis, Ron. 2013. *Unjust by Design: Canada's Administrative Justice System*. Vancouver, BC: UBC Press.

Horner, Matthew Horner. 2014. Charter Values: The Uncanny Valley of Canadian Constitutionalism. 67 *Supreme Court Law Review* (2d) 361.

Régimbald, Guy & Matthew Estabrooks. 2013. *Halsbury's Laws of Canada—Administrative Law*. Toronto, ON: LexisNexis.

Stratas, David. 2016. The Canadian Law of Judicial Review: A Plea for Doctrinal Coherence and Consistency. Accessed at https://papers.ssrn.com/sol3/papers.cfm?abstract_id=2733751

East Block and Westminster

5

Conventions, Values, and Public Service

Kenneth Kernaghan

Chapter Overview

This chapter outlines the central conventions and values of Canada's public service. *Westminster conventions*, the constitutional conventions or non-legal rules of the British constitution, are central to the operation of Canada's parliamentary democracy. They define "major non-legal rights, powers and obligations of office-holders in the three branches of government, or the relations between governments or organs of government" (Marshall, 1984: 210). They endure but are subject over time to gradual change in their interpretation and application; to distinguish the Canadian version of these three conventions from usage in Britain and in other Westminster-style democracies, the conventions are described here, symbolically, as the *East Block* conventions. Three constitutional conventions—ministerial responsibility, public service anonymity, and political neutrality—have extremely important implications for the public service in Canada's federal and provincial governments.

These conventions are closely related to **public service values,** which are enduring social, cultural, and ideological beliefs that influence the choices public servants make from among available means and ends. For analytical purposes, this essay classifies public service values into four categories: **ethical values, democratic values, professional values**, and **people values**. Some values can be found in more than one category. Each of these categories can in turn be divided into traditional values and new values. Most of the new values fall into the category of professional values. Note: This chapter should be read in conjunction with that by Brock and Nater, which serves to update selected aspects of this chapter by the late Kenneth Kernaghan.

Chapter Objectives

By the end of this chapter, students will be able to do the following:
- Define conventions and values.
- Explain what is meant by East Block conventions.

continued

- Discuss the meaning of public service values.
- Give examples of ethical values, democratic values, professional values, and people values, as well as old and new values.
- Discuss political neutrality as an ideal-type model, and review the evolution of East Block conventions.
- Assess the impact of private sector values on Canada's public services.
- Review some predictions and prescriptions that have been made for public services in Canada.

Introduction

Westminster conventions, that is, non-legal rules of the British constitution, are central to the operation of Canada's parliamentary democracy. Indeed, the preamble to Canada's founding constitutional document—the British North America Act, 1867—states that Canada is to have "a constitution similar in principle to that of the United Kingdom." **Constitutional conventions** are "rules that define major non-legal rights, powers and obligations of office-holders in the three branches of government, or the relations between governments or organs of government" (Marshall, 1984: 210). These conventions are frequently described as principles or, less commonly, as doctrines, traditions, or customs. While they are crucial components of the constitution, they are not set out in written form. They are of enduring importance but they are subject over time to gradual change in their interpretation and application.

Three constitutional conventions—ministerial responsibility, public service anonymity, and political neutrality—have extremely important implications for the public service in Canada's federal and provincial governments. These governments, unlike municipal governments, are modelled on the Westminster system of cabinet–parliamentary government. To distinguish the Canadian version of these three conventions from usage in Britain and in other Westminster-style democracies, the conventions are described here, symbolically, as the *East Block* conventions. The East Block "is the oldest essentially unaltered structure on Parliament Hill. . . . in the course of more than a century most government departments at some time were centred there. . . . In the year of Confederation, it was even possible to have thirteen branches of government housed within it" (Pearson, 1967).

The East Block conventions provide a framework for determining the nature and propriety of relationships among politicians, public servants, and the public. These conventions are closely related to public service values, which are enduring beliefs that influence the choices public servants make from among available means and ends. The conventions are especially tightly linked to such *democratic* values as accountability, loyalty, and impartiality. In fact, the conventions themselves are sometimes treated as values in that they constitute enduring beliefs that influence public servants' attitudes, actions, and choices. Political neutrality, in particular, is often referred to as a public service value as well as a constitutional convention.

In general, three features of the East Block conventions distinguish them from public service values. First, the conventions have constitutional status. Second, they are interdependent parts of a coherent system: a change in one usually results in a change in one or both of the others. While some public service values (e.g., representativeness and responsiveness) can be interdependent, values are often in a state of tension or conflict (e.g., accountability versus efficiency). Like the East Block conventions, public service values have considerable staying power, but changes in their meaning and application occur over time—and new values emerge. Third, public servants do not commonly perceive the East Block conventions as values; none of them appeared among the top 20 values in a 1994 study of public organizations in

Canada (Kernaghan, 1994a: 620). However, accountability, which is closely tied to the convention of ministerial responsibility, ranked near the top of the list.

The interpretation and application of public service conventions and values are influenced by a wide variety of political, economic, and social factors. For example, the decision by political executives to restructure and downsize the public service led to the adoption of new forms of organization and new approaches to management that, as explained later, have significant consequences for conventions and values. This chapter examines these conventions and values, both separately and in relation to one another, with particular reference to recent and anticipated public service reforms. The chapter begins by explaining the meaning and evolution of the conventions of ministerial responsibility, political neutrality, and public service anonymity. The second section outlines the meaning and evolution of the concept of public service values. The third section examines the implications of public sector reforms for conventions and values, and the final section outlines predictions and prescriptions for the future.

The East Block Conventions

The East Block Conventions Defined

The essence of each convention is set out below. It will be evident that in practice both cabinet ministers and public servants have departed, sometimes significantly, from the requirements of these conventions.

Ministerial responsibility has both a collective dimension and an individual dimension. **Collective ministerial responsibility** (often described as cabinet responsibility) requires that ministers, in their capacity as members of the cabinet, are responsible for the policies and management of the government as a whole. If the government loses a vote of confidence in the legislature, it is required to resign. In addition, ministers are obliged to resign if they cannot support government decisions in public (or at least refrain from publicly criticizing them), regardless of their personal views about the decisions. **Individual ministerial responsibility** has two closely related components. First, ministers must resign in the event of a major error that they have personally committed or that has been committed by public servants in their department. Second, ministers must answer to

the legislature, in the form of explanation or defence, for their own actions and for all of the actions of their departmental public servants.

Public service anonymity is a corollary of individual ministerial responsibility. It requires that public servants provide advice to ministers in confidence and refrain from activities that bring them into the public spotlight or involve them in public controversy. _Political neutrality_ requires that public servants not engage in activities that impair or seem to impair their impartiality or the impartiality of the public service as a whole.

East Block Conventions and the Political Neutrality Model

As noted above, the East Block conventions are interdependent. For example, if a minister does not answer publicly for the actions of public servants, the latter may be drawn into the political arena to explain or defend those actions, in part perhaps by criticizing the minister. The result would be a diminution in their political neutrality and their anonymity—and, in all likelihood, their career prospects.

The intertwining of the conventions can be demonstrated by reference to an ideal model of **political neutrality** (Kernaghan, 1976). This model is composed of the East Block conventions. It provides an analytical framework for examining relationships between public servants and politicians, especially cabinet ministers, in a parliamentary democracy of the Westminster variety. The model is not ideal in the sense of most desirable; rather, it is an _ideal-type_ construct depicting the characteristics of a public service that is neutral in an absolute or pristine sense. The components of the model are these:

1. Politics and policy are separated from administration; thus, politicians make policy decisions and public servants execute these decisions.
2. Public servants are appointed and promoted on the basis of **merit** rather than of party affiliation or contributions.
3. Public servants do not engage in partisan political activities.
4. Public servants do not express publicly their personal views on government policies or administration.

5. Public servants provide forthright and objective advice to their political masters in private and in confidence; in return, political executives protect the anonymity of public servants by publicly accepting responsibility for departmental decisions.

6. Public servants execute policy decisions loyally, irrespective of the philosophy and programs of the party in power and regardless of their personal opinions; as a result, public servants enjoy security of tenure during good behaviour and satisfactory performance.

As a public service or a particular public organization departs in practice from each of these characteristics, it becomes more politicized. The term *politicization* refers here to the involvement of public servants not only in partisan political activities but also in politics in the broad sense of the authoritative allocation of social values through policy advice and policy implementation.

Evolution of the East Block Conventions

The evolution of the East Block conventions since Confederation is explained below by reference to each of the six components of the model of political neutrality.

Separation of Politics, Policy, and Administration

One of the most famous statements in the history of public administration is the 1887 assertion by Woodrow Wilson (later President of the United States) that "the field of administration is a field of business. It is removed from the hurry and strife of politics . . . administrative questions are not political questions. . . . 'Policy does nothing without the aid of administration,' but administration is not therefore politics" (Wilson, 1966 [1887]). This statement of what is widely described as the **politics–administration dichotomy** was preceded by a more narrow but similar statement of a House of Commons Select Committee, which emphasized in 1877 the importance of separating politics from administration so as to promote the values of political neutrality and efficiency:

As a general principle appointments, promotions and the whole management of the [public] service should be separated as far as possible from political considerations. The service should be looked upon merely as an organization for conducting the public business and not as a means of rewarding personal political friends. (Canada, House of Commons, 1877: 5)

There was recognition at this time also of the inevitability of public servants exercising power in the policy process and the likelihood of this power being used on occasion to obstruct the will of elected officials. George Casey, the head of the Select Committee, noted that:

We all speak with horror of government by "bureaucracy," but we forget that we can never wholly get rid of its influence. Every official must have some freedom of action in the interpretation and performance of his duties, some power to obstruct, facilitate, or prevent the operation of those laws with whose execution he is charged. (Casey, 1877: 83)

Thus, it was clear more than a century ago that politics and policy cannot in practice be easily separated. It soon became clear also that while elected officials have final authority over policy decisions, public servants have considerable influence on these decisions and exercise substantial power through their dominance of the policy implementation process. The balance of power between politicians and public servants was a constant issue during the twentieth century. As governments grew larger and more complicated, ministers became increasingly dependent for policy advice on the knowledge and experience of public servants. Over the period 1935–57, a small number of federal senior public servants, known as "the mandarins," played an especially influential policy role in Canadian government (Granatstein, 1982; Kernaghan and McLeod, 1982). They were at the same time, however, strong proponents and practitioners of the East Block conventions.

By the early 1960s, the policy role had begun to be shared by a larger group of public servants. By this time also, the power of the public service had been more openly acknowledged. The Glassco Royal Commission on Government Organization concluded in 1962 that "permanent officials are also participants in the exercise of power, rather than mere instruments through which it is wielded by ministers" (Canada,

Royal Commission on Government Organization, 1962, vol. 5: 74). And Professor J.E. Hodgetts noted in 1964 that "the shift from laissez-faire to collectivism has been accompanied by an unprecedented shift in the balance of real power, discretion and initiative— away from courts, legislatures and even cabinets to public servants" (Hodgetts, 1964: 421). The power of public servants in relation to other political actors has ebbed and flowed since the 1960s, depending to a large extent on the determination of the governing party to exercise political control over the public service. This story has been told elsewhere (Aucoin, 1995; Mitchell and Sutherland, 1997; Savoie, 1994). It is a story that demonstrates the difficulty, in practice, of separating politics and policy from administration.

Merit, Not Patronage

The pre-Confederation practice of appointing and promoting public servants on the basis of partisan political considerations rather than of merit continued unabated after Confederation. Vigorous efforts by reformers over a 50-year period led to the formal abolition of **patronage** appointments in the federal sphere by the Civil Service Act of 1918 (Canada, 1918). These efforts served the twin objectives of promoting the political neutrality and the efficiency of the public service.

A substantial number of patronage appointments continued to be made after 1918, but they were gradually reduced to the point where by the early 1960s such appointments had been largely eliminated from the regular departments of the federal government (Canada, Royal Commission on Government Organization, 1962: 371). However, in the provinces, most governments by this time still presented "only the facade of a **merit system**, while combatting charges of patronage and personal favouritism in their public services" (Hodgetts and Dwivedi, 1976: 347). The provincial performance gradually improved after the mid-1960s, but some provinces have continued to make patronage appointments to the lower levels of the public service, and, on occasion, with a change in the governing party a substantial number of senior public servants have been replaced by political appointees.

In both the federal and provincial spheres, patronage appointments are still made to semi-independent agencies, boards, and commissions. While the hope is that governments will not risk embarrassment by appointing incompetent partisans to these bodies, there is less concern about these appointments than about the practice of appointing partisans to senior positions in regular government departments. Among the arguments against this practice is that political appointees block the career path of permanent public servants and they bring into government persons who may not share or understand the conventions and values of the public service.

No Political Partisanship

As a basis for assessing the propriety of public servants' participation in partisan politics, it is helpful to specify what kind of participation is at issue. For public servants, involvement in partisan politics can take the form of such modest activities as casting a vote or being a silent spectator at political meetings; but it can also take the form of such highly visible and potentially controversial activities as door-to-door fundraising and seeking elected office.

To combat patronage, public servants were prohibited from participation in virtually all forms of **partisan political activity** for a very large portion of Canadian history. The 1918 Civil Service Act provided, on pain of dismissal, that no deputy minister or other public servant "shall engage in partisan work in connection with any election or contribute, receive or in any way deal with any money for party funds." Despite the gradual decrease in patronage appointments after that time, these restraints were maintained until they were loosened somewhat by the Public Service Employment Act of 1967 (Canada, 1966–7). Under this Act, all public servants, with the exception of deputy ministers, were allowed to stand for election so long as the Public Service Commission was satisfied that the person's usefulness as a public servant would not be impaired. In addition, public servants were allowed to donate money to a political candidate or party and to attend political meetings. All other forms of political activity were prohibited until 1991, when the Supreme Court of Canada decided that most of the remaining constraints on the political rights of public servants were unduly restrictive (*Osborne v. Canada*, 1991).

The challenge has always been to achieve the greatest possible measure of **political rights for public servants** while maintaining the political neutrality and efficiency of the public service. The traditional arguments for *restricting* the political rights of public servants are these:

Why do we value such neutrality?

1. To preserve public trust in government, public servants must be—and must appear to be—politically impartial in the development and implementation of public policy. Members of the public must be assured that political affiliation is not a consideration in any dealings they may have with public servants.

2. Public servants must be—and must appear to be—politically impartial so as to retain the trust of political superiors who are dependent on them for objective policy advice and for effective policy implementation.

3. Opposition parties must have trust in the political impartiality of public servants so that there will not be a politically motivated turnover of public servants with a change of government.

4. The expansion of political partisanship may result in the re-emergence of the patronage system of hiring and promotion with a consequent decline in merit and in public service efficiency and effectiveness. Both the public and public servants must be assured that appointment and advancement in the service are based on merit rather than on party affiliation.

5. Public servants must be protected against financial or other forms of exploitation by political or administrative superiors who are affiliated with a specific political party or candidate.

The traditional arguments for *expanding* the political rights of public servants are these:

1. Public servants should be permitted to exercise the fundamental rights of freedom of expression and of association guaranteed to all citizens; they should not be treated as second-class citizens.

2. Limits on the political activities of public servants deprive both the general public and political parties of valuable information and insights on public affairs.

3. Limits on the political activities of public servants restrict the involvement in partisan politics of a large percentage of the labour force.

4. The application of the merit principle protects the public service against political or bureaucratic patronage based on the partisan affiliation of public servants.

5. Knowledgeable and skilled persons whose talents are needed in government will be unwilling to accept employment in the public service if their political rights are unduly restricted (Kernaghan, 1991: 220–31).

Over the past decade, in the provinces as well as in the federal sphere, the current has been running strongly in the direction of increased political rights for public servants. As a result, the substantial variation in political rights regimes that used to exist from one government to another has been considerably reduced.

No Public Comment

The term *political rights* refers not only to partisan political activity but to **public comment** as well. Traditionally, public servants have been prohibited from criticizing or praising government policies or personalities in public. Clearly, it is tougher for public servants to follow this admonition if they are actively engaged in partisan politics. Several of the arguments for and against political activity outlined above also apply to public comment. On the one hand, there is concern that public servants be seen as politically neutral by politicians and the public; on the other hand, there is a danger of restricting unduly the political rights of a large body of well-educated and well-informed citizens.

It has proved difficult for governments to develop specific rules regarding the permissible limits of public comment, in part because there are so many types of public comment and in part because there is considerable debate as to what types should be permitted and what types should be prohibited. There is general agreement that public servants should be allowed to comment publicly by providing information and analysis of a technical or scientific nature, describing the machinery of government, and explaining the content of policies. There is general agreement also on the risky or prohibited nature of such activities as providing even constructive criticism of government policies, denouncing these policies, or making overtly partisan statements.

There is, however, a grey and controversial area that includes such activities as discussing, within the framework of settled policy, the solution of problems through new or modified programs, commenting on issues on which policy has not yet been decided, explaining the political and policy process in government, and proposing reforms in the machinery of government (Kernaghan, 1991: 252). Nevertheless, as with partisan political activity, the trend is in the direction of extending the permissible rights of public servants to engage in public comment.

Ministerial Responsibility and Public Service Anonymity

As early as a decade after Confederation, the extent to which ministers could effectively monitor the details of departmental administration was a subject of parliamentary debate (Canada, 1878: 1588, 1610, 1614–15). The growth in the scale and complexity of government during the twentieth century, especially after 1945, meant that ministers could not reasonably be required to resign to atone for public servants' errors about which they had no personal knowledge. Indeed, in Canadian political history, no minister has ever resigned in response to mistakes made by his or her public servants.

However, ministers have, with a few exceptions (Kernaghan, 1979; Sutherland, 1991), adhered to the second component of individual responsibility: they have usually answered to the legislature for all of the acts of their department. They have thereby protected public service anonymity—the anonymity of individual public servants. Nonetheless, public service anonymity has been eroded somewhat by other developments, including expanded media coverage of public servants' activities and their frequent appearances before legislative committees, sometimes to testify about politically controversial issues.

When the issue of individual ministerial responsibility is raised in a partisan context, it quickly becomes evident that where one stands on this issue often depends literally on where one sits. Legislators sitting on the opposition benches interpret the convention in a way that will support their calls for a minister's resignation while government members insist that the opposition has misunderstood or misapplied the requirements of the convention of ministerial responsibility. In addition, some commentators argue that ministerial responsibility is a myth. This argument is based largely on the "corrosive and unhelpful" nature of "the proposition that a minister of a department is responsible for everything that happens in the department" (Segal, 1998: 232). The argument is also based in part on the belief that the convention protects both

ministers and public servants from being held adequately accountable for their decisions. Critics of the convention often suggest that public servants should be held directly accountable to the legislature for their decisions (Segal, 1998: 238), but they fail to draw out the full political and public service implications of this suggestion and to provide a realistically viable option to the convention of ministerial responsibility.

Those who support the preservation of the convention usually present the following arguments regarding its meaning and importance:

- The convention is intended to protect the authority and accountability of ministers for government decisions.
- It is a positive and pervasive force for accountability in the myriad day-to-day operations of government.
- The meaning and application of the convention are often distorted by undue emphasis on ministerial blame and calls for resignation. While ministers are responsible for answering to the legislature for the errors of administrative subordinates, they do not thereby accept personal blame for these errors.
- It is unreasonable to hold a minister personally responsible, to the extent that she or he must resign, for the errors of administrative subordinates.
- Ministers usually resign in the event of serious personal misconduct or in cases where they have directed public servants to take a specific action that turns out to be a serious mistake.
- Public servants answer to legislative committees for administrative matters, but not for policy or politically controversial matters; this answerability takes the form of explanation, not defence, of departmental actions.
- Ministers have a commitment to protect the conventions of political neutrality and public service anonymity (Kernaghan, 1998: 229–30).

Tenure in Office

The issue of security of tenure for public servants demonstrates well the interdependent nature of the East Block conventions. Traditionally, public servants have enjoyed permanence in office "during good behaviour and satisfactory performance." Their security can be tenuous, however, if they become too closely associated with certain policy decisions, if they were appointed on partisan grounds and there is a change in the governing party, or if they engage too actively in partisan political activity or make controversial public comments on government policies.

In general, public servants have served the government of the day with loyalty and impartiality regardless of their personal opinions about the government's policies and decisions. In response, public servants have usually been secure in their positions despite a change of government. In some provincial governments, however, a change in the governing party has led to the removal of a considerable number of senior public servants and their replacement by patronage appointees, as occurred in Ontario in 1990 with a newly elected NDP government. The danger here, for advocates of a professional, non-partisan public service, is that the next government will be tempted to replace these appointees with its own supporters.

Since the mid-1980s in particular it has become clear that public servants can be dismissed for reasons unrelated to acceptable performance and appropriate behaviour. A large number of public servants have lost their jobs as a result of the staff reductions accompanying the downsizing of government. Moreover, the notion of lifelong employment that has historically been associated with the concept of a career in public service is now widely questioned, and the expectation is that employees will move frequently during their careers between the public and private sectors. We shall see below that there is a close connection between these East Block conventions and certain public service values.

David Good (2008) has affirmed that the behaviour of politicians and public servants does depart substantially from the ideal model of the doctrine of political neutrality outlined above. Indeed, since the model was first formulated in the mid-1970s, pressure to depart in practice from its requirements has increased substantially. Good concludes that:

> the widening gap between the ideal model and actual practice is more than stretching the limits of those who are responsible for interpreting the doctrine. It also appears to be giving licence to some for the way in which they practice the

doctrine and subsequently report on their practice. As the interpreters or enforcers of the doctrine struggle to provide meaningful guidance to public servants and politicians in a world that is changing in fundamental ways, their interpretations are finding less resonance. (Good, 2008: 81)

Public Service Values

Values are an enduring and pervasive element of intellectual enterprise and daily experience (see Kernaghan, 2000). Several academic disciplines are centrally concerned with the concept of values. Political science is concerned with the practice of politics as the authoritative *allocation of social values*. Psychology studies how *individuals* develop, understand, and use human values. Sociology adds a *group*-based dimension by examining the impact of social experience on human values. And philosophy brings a *normative* dimension by asking what values people should hold (Gortner, 1994: 375ff.). The study of public administration draws ideas and insights on values from each of these disciplines.

D.B. Dewar, a former federal deputy minister, has explained the practical use of values:

- They help us to visualize ideal outcomes and thus to establish goals.
- They motivate and energize us to work towards these goals.
- They serve as standards to help us measure progress, decide perplexing questions, and choose between alternative courses of action.
- By doing all this, they help us to define who we are and how we should relate to the world.

Dewar has explained also that values tend to be long-lasting and resistant to easy change but should be "open to change for compelling reasons. . . . The toughest questions about values arise when we are confronted by circumstances that force a choice between two values in our framework—between loyalty and integrity, for example" (Dewar, 1994: 2–3). And Ralph Heintzman has observed that "public servants who do not realize they function in a world in which, say, democratic values may be in tension with, say, professional values are stumbling in the dark" (Heintzman, 2007).

Types of values ↴

Types of Public Service Values

For analytical purposes, this essay classifies public service values into four categories: **ethical values** (e.g., integrity), **democratic values** (e.g., rule of law), **professional values** (e.g., innovation), and **people values** (e.g., caring). Some values can be found in more than one category. For example, accountability is usually considered to be both an ethical value and a democratic value—and some commentators include it in the professional category as well. Each of these categories can in turn be divided into traditional values and new values. Among the major **traditional values** are accountability, efficiency, effectiveness, integrity, neutrality, responsiveness, and representativeness (Kernaghan, 1978). Among the most important **new values** are service, innovation, quality, and teamwork. Most of the new values fall into the category of professional values.

Evolution of Public Service Values

Values have long been an important concept in scholarly writings on public administration, especially in the United States (Kaufman, 1956; Gilbert, 1959).

Since the mid-1980s the concept of values has become increasingly central to the study and practice of public administration in many countries around the world, including Canada. This heightened interest in values has resulted from five main developments.

First, the public sector experienced the spillover effect of the private sector's emphasis on the concept of corporate culture, and statements of values. Second, some public organizations have been successfully transformed by focusing on a change in their values rather than in their structures (Denhardt, 1993). Third, the increased emphasis on *results* than on *process* favoured values over the more intrusive alternative instruments of rules, directives, and guidelines. Fourth is the concern about the perceived undermining of traditional public service values by some public-sector reformers.

A fifth and final explanatory factor has been the steadily rising interest since the late 1960s in **public service ethics**—a concept so tightly intertwined with that of public service values that many commentators use the terms *values* and *ethics* interchangeably. However, not all values are ethical values, that is, not all values relate to questions of right and wrong,

good or bad. It is helpful, therefore, to distinguish ethical values from democratic, professional, and people values.

While the relative significance of the traditional values noted above has changed over time, their overall significance has endured. Reference to these traditional values provides a framework for explaining and assessing past, present, and anticipated public service reforms. For example, several reforms between Confederation and 1918 were designed to promote the values of neutrality and efficiency; the 1960 Glassco Royal Commission was concerned with promoting efficiency, economy, and improved service; and the 1978 Lambert Commission focused on accountability (Kernaghan, 1997).

During the past two decades, new values (e.g., innovation, quality) have risen to prominence and certain traditional values (e.g., accountability) have become relatively more important. The Public Service 2000 White Paper published by the federal government in 1990 noted the continuing importance of traditional values such as accountability, integrity, and fairness, but recommended reforms reflecting the growing emphasis on such professional values as innovation and empowerment. Similar mixtures of values are found in other reports and statements.

Reforms, Values, and Conventions

Private Sector Influence on Public Sector Reform

Since the mid-1980s, a strong wind of public sector reform has swept through many countries. The major means by which this reform has been accomplished include partnerships, empowerment, restructuring, re-engineering, information technology, citizen-centred service, and continuous learning (Kernaghan, Marson, & Borins, 2000). Most of the scholarly literature on this reform movement has focused on its organizational, managerial, and political implications. Much less attention has been paid to its implications for public service values and ethics.

Several of the new public service values (e.g., service, innovation) are identical to prominent private sector values. This reflects the fact that many of the recent public sector reforms have been inspired by private sector experience. Concern has arisen about the impact of this private sector influence on the ethical values and constitutional conventions of the public service. The public sector has been affected not only by certain business values (e.g., risk-taking) but also by increased business involvement in the conduct of government activities (e.g., contracting out, partnerships). Several scholars have argued that this business influence will undermine the ethical performance of the public sector (Frederickson, 1993; Doig, 1995). The British parliamentary Committee on Standards in Public Life warned in 1994 that public sector functions are increasingly being performed by those, notably business persons, who have not been socialized to core public service values: "it cannot be assumed that everyone in the public service will assimilate a public service culture unless they are told what is expected of them and the message is systematically reinforced" (United Kingdom, 1994: 16).

There is particular concern about the extent to which it is possible to infuse program delivery agencies (e.g., service agencies in Canada) with core public service values, especially if the organizations are headed by persons brought in from the private sector to manage them on a more "business-like" basis. The creation of agencies at arm's length from ministerial control raises concern as to ministers' responsibility for the agencies' decisions. Moreover, the appointment of business people to head public agencies and the increased mobility of employees between the public and private sectors threaten political neutrality by increasing the likelihood of partisanship and patronage (Canada, Deputy Ministers' Task Force, 1996).

Old and New Values

Value conflict is a pervasive reality for public administrators. There are frequent tensions and clashes among democratic, ethical, professional, and people values, and between old and new values. In assessing the value implications of public service reforms, administrators have to consider both the relative merits and the compatibility of a wide range of pertinent values. As explained below, it is helpful to identify core public service values and to establish priorities among them so as to narrow the range of values that decision-makers are obliged to consider. The 1994 study mentioned above found that the value statements of 93 public organizations contained a total of 164 different values (Kernaghan, 1994a: 630).

There was substantial agreement among the organizations on the top dozen values but most organizations also espoused values related to their particular responsibilities (e.g., safety for a transportation agency).

From among the several means mentioned earlier whereby public organizations can carry out reform, we shall focus here, by way of illustration, on partnerships. Partnerships involving public organizations and various non-governmental entities (especially business organizations) are widely viewed as an effective means of promoting citizen-centred service, collaboration, decentralization, non-departmental forms of organization, and cost recovery. Partnerships are also promoted as an effective means of pursuing such traditional professional values as efficiency and effectiveness and such new professional values as service and innovation. A major impetus for the widespread creation of partnerships since the mid-1980s has been the need to respond to the public's demand for more or better service with fewer resources. Many of these partnerships have been remarkably innovative in meeting this need (Kernaghan, 1993; Rodal and Mulder, 1993).

There is tension between the use of partnerships to pursue these professional values and the need to respect several traditional democratic and ethical values, especially accountability, which may be the dominant value in contemporary public administration. All those individuals and organizations in society who exercise power over us have a duty to account for the proper exercise of that power—and this duty is centrally important for public officials in a democratic system of government. While accountability has long been a central public service value, it has taken on new life and new importance in the context of recent reforms, including the use of partnerships.

Some partnerships—especially truly collaborative ones in which public organizations share power and risk with their partners—have provoked concern about the accountability of the partners to ministers, legislators, and taxpaying citizens. Partnerships in general and innovative ones in particular can be risky, especially for politicians. The political risk is especially problematic in Westminster-style governments like Canada's where, as explained in the earlier discussion of the East Block conventions, cabinet ministers are required to answer to the legislature for the errors of their departmental subordinates. Consider, for example, the political consequences of partnerships in which substantial public money is lost and the business partners cannot, or are not obligated to, bear a reasonable share of the loss.

Partnerships also have significant implications for traditional ethical values like integrity and fairness. The creation of partnerships often involves public servants exercising discretionary authority during protracted negotiations with business firms, thereby increasing the opportunity for conflict-of-interest situations. Fairness is also an issue in partnership arrangements. Thus, if a business firm brings a good partnership idea to government, is it fair to give other firms an opportunity to compete for involvement in the partnership so as to ensure the best possible deal for the taxpayer?

This brief examination of the implications for accountability of using partnerships illustrates the kind of analysis that can be performed for other instruments of reform (e.g., restructuring, technological innovation, empowerment). Reformers need to conduct such analysis so as to take adequate account of both the growing importance of professional values and the enduring importance of democratic and ethical ones.

Predictions and Prescriptions

Predictions

The evolution of the East Block conventions and public service values will depend on a complex mix of political, economic, and social changes that are difficult to foresee. In the absence of a clear statement as to the appropriate meaning and application of the conventions, they may be eroded by certain public service reforms. Paul Thomas (1997: 151–2) has warned against producing the worst of both worlds, that is:

> a serious undermining of the traditional constitutional framework based on misunderstandings and distortions as to how it was meant to operate and how it actually operates, together with a failure to offer an alternative approach to the democratic control of political and bureaucratic power that matched the old framework in terms of its theoretical consistency, practical value and inherent flexibility.

Historical experience in Canada suggests that the relative importance of public service values is likely to shift. The direction and extent of the shift will be determined by the particular features of the environment for governance.

The use of three governance scenarios developed by the federal government (Canada, Deputy Ministers' Task Force on the Future Public Service, 1997: 4) as an analytical tool for strategic thinking and planning provides some insight into possible shifts in the importance of public service values. These scenarios are presented here in a brief and oversimplified fashion. Among the future challenges to government and the public service associated with the *Evolution* scenario are providing basic programs and services with fewer resources, making new management reforms (including new delivery mechanisms and new accountability regimes), and fostering creativity in a risk-averse milieu. The emphasis in this scenario is on the professional values of service and innovation and the democratic/ethical value of accountability. The challenges that arise in the *Market* scenario include fostering private sector innovation and competitiveness, operating in a more business-like fashion, and encouraging mobility between the public and private sectors. This scenario brings to the fore the professional value of efficiency, the democratic value of political neutrality, and the ethical value of integrity (e.g., avoiding the use of public office for private gain). In the final scenario—*Renaissance*—the challenges to government and the public service include promoting collaboration among a wide variety of policy actors; balancing party politics, organizational hierarchy, and ministerial responsibility with partnerships and co-operative working relationships; and recruiting high-calibre employees devoted to the public good. The emphasis in this scenario is on the professional values of collaboration and innovation, the democratic values of accountability and the public interest, and the people values of participation and openness.

Each of the scenarios has different implications for the East Block conventions. For example, the emphasis on risk-taking in the *Evolution* scenario must be balanced by sensitivity to the answerability of ministers for departmental errors; the *Market* scenario's emphasis on mobility between the public and private sectors raises the question of whether short-term employees moving in and out of government will be sufficiently attuned to the requirements of the East Block conventions; and the *Renaissance* scenario's emphasis on collaboration (across departments) must be accompanied by agreement as to which minister(s) will be accountable for results.

Prescriptions

The preceding discussion suggests the need for all policy actors to have as clear an understanding as possible of what the core values and conventions of the public service are and how they should be interpreted. A formal statement of these conventions and values, both for the public service as a whole and for individual public organizations, could provide a foundation for assessing the value consequences of public servants' decisions, including the likely consequences of proposed reforms (Kernaghan, 2003). Montgomery Van Wart (1998: xvii) contends that "being clear about and managing values is an organizational priority of the highest order. . . . Lack of clarity about the values to be endorsed, their priority, their application in different situations, their support, and their enforcement leads to ineffectiveness as employees work at cross-purposes." And Steven Cohen and William Eimicke (1999: 72) argue that public servants are not:

> fully equipped to determine the degree of risk in a particular innovation and accurately assess the ethical questions it may encompass. Nor are they clear about the proper process to follow when seeking to make decisions regarding risk, innovation and ethics. The solution is not to discourage public entrepreneurship but rather to establish practical principles to ensure that it is exercised in an effective and ethical manner.

Several Westminster-style democracies have responded to actual or anticipated problems arising from reforms by drafting or strengthening a **code of conduct**, sometimes called a statement of values or a statement of principles (New Zealand, 2007; United Kingdom, 2006). The experience of these countries suggests that governments need to take careful account of the value implications of reforms before they implement them. There is significant congruence in the core public service values adopted by the Westminster-style democracies of Australia, New Zealand, and the United Kingdom, where ministerial responsibility is a central constitutional convention. The value statements of these three countries contain

a mix of democratic, ethical, professional, and, to a lesser extent, people values. Foremost among the democratic values are accountability and impartiality, while integrity, honesty, and fairness are the most prominent ethical values.

In 2003, Canada adopted a Values and Ethics Code that applies to all federal employees. The Code's purposes are:

- to articulate the values and ethics of public service to guide and support public servants in all their professional activities;
- to maintain and enhance public confidence in the integrity of the public service;
- to strengthen respect for, and appreciation of, the role played by the public service within Canadian democracy.

The Code's four chapters contain a statement of public service values and ethics, conflict of interest measures, post-employment measures, and avenues of resolution. The Code recognizes that public servants' decisions are inevitably influenced by a substantial number of values. The several values in the Code are divided into four categories or "families" of public service values: the democratic, ethical, professional, and people values discussed above. For example, the section "People Values" refers to "demonstrating respect, fairness and courtesy in . . . dealings with both citizens and fellow public servants" (Canada, Treasury Board Secretariat, 2003).

Since 2003, there has been further thinking and action regarding Canada's values and ethics regime. The Public Servants Disclosure Protection Act, which was enacted in late 2005 and came into force in 2007, protects public servants who disclose wrongdoing in government—often described as "blowing the whistle." In addition, the Act's preamble commits the federal government to adopting a Charter of Values of Public Service "to guide public servants in their work and professional conduct" (see Kernaghan, 2006). Moreover, section 4 of the Act requires the Treasury Board to establish a Code of Conduct applicable to the public sector. The heads of departments and agencies are required to establish codes for their organizations that are consistent with the Code.

The emphasis in most current codes is on *traditional* democratic, ethical, and professional values. Few statements reflect the increased importance of new professional values such as innovation and creativity and little effort is made to reconcile traditional and new values. Part of the explanation for these apparent deficiencies is the view of some government officials that the so-called "new" values are a passing fancy or are at best second-order values that are less central to successful governance than the traditional ones. A review of the scenarios discussed above, however, suggests that the importance of certain professional values, especially innovation, is likely to endure. This means that public servants must be mindful of these values when developing codes of conduct and sensitive to the tension between professional values and other categories of values (e.g., innovation versus accountability and integrity). Ontario's 2007 statement, *OPS Organizational Values*, highlights eight values: trust, fairness, diversity, excellence, creativity, collaboration, efficiency, and responsiveness. Elaboration on the value of creativity refers to the importance of public servants being innovative.

A major theme in recent public service reforms is reducing the number of rules so that empowered public servants, who will be held more accountable for results and less accountable for process, can be more creative, and even entrepreneurial. However, some reforms create pressure for more, not fewer, rules (e.g., conflict of interest, non-partisanship). Fostering shared values across the public service and in individual organizations can help to reduce the overall need for rules and to increase the use of guidelines—a less intrusive management instrument. Public servants are then more likely to comply with the rules that remain and to respect the guidelines if they see the connection between the intent of these rules and guidelines and fundamental public service values. For example, one approach to managing conflict of interest is to provide lengthy and detailed rules against it. Another approach is to explain that the need to avoid conflict of

interest is grounded in basic and enduring democratic and ethical values such as impartiality and fairness; to develop broad conflict-of-interest guidelines based on these values; and then to draw from these guidelines a limited number of rules. "The best accountability systems recognize . . . that control is normative . . . rooted in values and beliefs" (Mintzberg, 1996: 81).

Ralph Heintzman, in discussing the relationship between values and rules, notes that "there can never be enough rules to cover every decision a public servant would ever need to make. Which means there will always be lots of discretionary space between the rules, space that can only be filled in by judgment and values." Thus, "even when a due reverence for rules is present, an understanding of their spirit, of the values of public service that underlie the rules, is needed to explain them, and to guide their interpretation and application" (2007: 578).

It is unrealistic to expect that a code of conduct alone will be sufficient to foster shared values and high ethical standards in the public service. A code should be viewed as an essential component of a broad regime for preserving and promoting values-based behaviour (Kernaghan 2003; OECD 1997: 4). This framework could include not only a code of conduct but also such measures as ethics rules and guidelines, ethics training and education, ethics counsellors or ombudspersons, and the evaluation of ethical performance as a basis for appointments and promotions, especially at the senior leadership level. While codes of conduct can serve important purposes, they can be severely undermined by leaders who do not model the organization's values. Public servants are more effectively motivated by concrete examples of values-based leadership than by written declarations of values. Nevertheless, a code of conduct can provide a powerful incentive and complement to exemplary leadership.

Important Terms and Concepts

code of conduct (statement of values)	merit system	politics–administration dichotomy
collective ministerial responsibility	new values	professional values
constitutional conventions	partisan political activity	public comment
democratic values	patronage	public service anonymity
ethical values	people values	public service ethics
individual ministerial responsibility	political neutrality	public service values
merit	political rights for public servants	traditional values

Study Questions

1. Explain the meaning of the three East Block conventions, how they are related to one another, and their connection to public service values.
2. Explain the six components of the model of political neutrality. To what extent does the contemporary behaviour of politicians and public servants depart from this ideal-type model?
3. What are the arguments for and against permitting public servants to exercise full political rights?
4. Assess the importance of the constitutional convention of ministerial responsibility.
5. Explain the meaning and importance of public service values and describe, with examples, the various types of values.
6. Assess the importance of values statements and codes of conduct, with particular reference to Canada's *Values and Ethics Code for the Public Service*.

References

Aucoin, P. 1995. *The New Public Management: Canada in Comparative Perspective*. Ottawa: Institute for Research on Public Policy.

Canada. 1878. *House of Commons Debates*.

———. 1918. *Statutes*. 8–9 George V, c. 12.

———. 1966–7. *Statutes*. c. 71.

———. Civil Service Commission. 1958. *Personnel Administration in the Public Service: A Review of Civil Service Legislation by the Civil Service Commission of Canada*. Ottawa: Queen's Printer.

———. Deputy Ministers' Task Force on the Future Public Service. 1997. *Report*. Ottawa: Privy Council Office. Available at: www.ccmd-ccg.gc.ca/documents/dmtf/intromtf.html.

———. Deputy Ministers' Task Force on Public Service Values and Ethics. 1996. *A Strong Foundation: Discussion Paper on Values and Ethics in the Public Service*. Ottawa: Privy Council Office. Available at: www.ccmd-ccg.gc.ca/publications.html.

———. House of Commons. 1877. *Journals*, Appendix no. 7.

———. Royal Commission on Government Organization. 1962. *Report*. Ottawa: Queen's Printer.

———. Treasury Board Secretariat. 2003. *Values and Ethics Code for the Public Service*. Minister of Public Works and Government Services.

Casey, G.E. 1877. "Civil Service Reform." *Canadian Monthly*, 11, Jan., pp. 83–91.

Charih, M., & A. Daniels, editors. 1997. *New Public Administration and New Public Management in Canada*. Toronto, ON: Institute of Public Administration of Canada.

Cohen, S., and W. Eimicke. 1999. "Is Public Entrepreneurship Ethical? A Second Look at Theory and Practice." *Public Integrity*, 1, Winter, pp. 54–74.

Denhardt, R. 1993. *The Pursuit of Significance: Strategies for Managerial Success in Public Organizations*. Belmont, CA.: Wadsworth.

Dewar, D.B. 1994. "Public Service Values: How to Navigate in Rough Waters." *Values in the Public Service*, Ottawa: Canadian Centre for Management Development, pp. 1–13.

Doig, A. 1995. "Mixed Signals? Public Sector Change and the Proper Conduct of Public Business." *Public Administration*, 73, Summer, pp. 191–212.

Frederickson, H.G. 1993. "Ethics and Public Administration: Some Assertions." *Ethics and Public Administration*, edited by Frederickson, New York: M.E. Sharpe.

Gilbert, C.E. 1959. "The Framework of Administrative Responsibility." *Journal of Politics*, 21, pp. 373–407.

Good, David. 2008. "An Ideal Model in a Practical World: The Continuous Revisiting of Political Neutrality and Ministerial Responsibility." *Professionalism and Public Service: Essays in Honour of Kenneth Kernaghan*, edited by David Siegel and Ken Rasmussen. Toronto, ON: University of Toronto Press, pp. 63–83.

Gortner, H.F. 1994. "Ethics and Values." *Handbook of Administrative Ethics*, edited by T. L. Cooper, New York, NY: Marcel Dekker, pp. 373–90.

Granatstein, J.L. 1982. *The Ottawa Men: The Civil Service Mandarins, 1935–1957*. Toronto, ON: University of Toronto Press.

Heintzman, Ralph. 2007. "Public-Service Values and Ethics: Dead End or Strong Foundation?" *Canadian Public Administration*, 50, 4, Winter, pp. 573–602.

Hodgetts, J.E. 1955. *Pioneer Public Service: An Administrative History of the United Canadas*. Toronto, ON: University of Toronto Press.

———. 1964. "Challenge and Response: A Retrospective View of the Public Service." *Canadian Public Administration*, 7, Dec., pp. 409–21.

———, and O.P. Dwivedi. 1976. "Administration and Personnel." *The Provincial Political Systems: Comparative Essays*, edited by D.J. Bellamy, J.H.

Pammett, and D.C. Rowat, Toronto, ON: Methuen, pp. 341–56.

Hondeghem, A., editor. 1998. *Ethics and Accountability in a Context of Governance and New Public Management*. Amsterdam: IOS Press.

Kaufman, H. 1956. "Emerging Conflicts in the Doctrines of Public Administration." *American Political Science Review,* 50, 1, Dec., pp. 1059–73.

Kernaghan, K. 1976. "Politics, Policy and Public Servants: Political Neutrality Revisited." *Canadian Public Administration,* 19, Fall, pp. 432–56.

———. 1978. "Changing Concepts of Power And Responsibility in the Canadian Public Service." *Canadian Public Administration,* 21, Fall, pp. 389–406.

———. 1979. "Power, Politics and Public Servants: Ministerial Responsibility Revisited." *Canadian Public Policy,* 3, Summer, pp. 383–96.

———. 1991. "The Political Rights of Canada's Federal Public Servants." *Democratic rights and electoral reform*, Royal Commission on Electoral Reform and Party Financing, vol. 10, edited by M. Cassidy, Toronto, ON: Dundurn Press, pp. 213–67.

———. 1993. "Partnership and Public Administration: Conceptual and Practical Considerations." *Canadian Public Administration,* 36, Spring, pp. 57–76.

———. 1994a. "The Emerging Public Service Culture: Values, Ethics and Reforms." *Canadian Public Administration,* 37, Winter, pp. 614–30.

———. 1994b. "Rules Are Not Enough: Ethics, Politics and Public Service in Ontario." *Corruption, Character and Conduct: Essays on Canadian Government Ethics*. edited by J. Langford and A. Tupper, Toronto, ON: Oxford University Press, *pp.* 174–96.

———. 1997. "Shaking the Foundations: Traditional versus New Public Service Values." *New Public Administration and New Public Management in Canada,* edited by Charih and Daniels, Toronto: Institute of Public Administration of Canada, pp. 47–65.

———. 1998. "Is the Doctrine of Ministerial Responsibility Workable?" *Crosscurrents: Contemporary Political Issues,* edited by M. Charlton and P. Barker, Toronto, ON: Nelson, pp. 222–31.

———. 2000. "The Post-Bureaucratic Organization and Public Service Values." *International Review of Administrative Sciences,* 66, 1, Mar., pp. 91–104.

———. 2003. "Integrating Values into Public Service: The Values Statement as Centerpiece." *Public Administration Review.* 63, November–December, pp. 711–19.

———. 2006. "Encouraging "Rightdoing" and Discouraging Wrongdoing: The Case for a Public Service Charter and Disclosure Legislation." Study for Gomery Commission of Inquiry into the Sponsorship Program and Advertising Activities, *Restoring Accountability*. Research Studies, vol. 2, pp. 71–114.

———, & T.H. McLeod. 1982. "Ministers and Mandarins in the Canadian Administrative State." *The Administrative State,* edited by O.P Dwivedi, Toronto, ON: University of Toronto Press, pp. 17–30.

———, Marson, B., & S. Borins. 2000. *The New Public Organization*. Toronto, ON: Institute of Public Administration of Canada.

Marshall, G. 1984. *Constitutional Conventions*. Oxford: Oxford University Press.

———, and G.C. Moodie. 1967. *Some Problems of the Constitution*. 4th edn, London: Hutchinson.

Mintzberg, H. 1996. "Managing Government: Governing Management." *Harvard Business Review,* May–June, pp. 75–83.

Mitchell, J. R., & S. L. Sutherland. 1997. "Relations between Politicians and Public Servants." *New Public Administration and New Public Management in Canada,* edited by Charih and Daniels, Toronto: Institute of Public Administration of Canada, pp. 181–97.

New Zealand, State Services Commission. 2007. *Standards of Integrity and Conduct: A Code of Conduct Issued by the State Services Commissioner*. Wellington: State Services Commission. Available at: www.ssc. govt.nz/upload/downloadable_files/Code-of-conduct-StateServices.pdf.

OECD. 1997. "Ethics Infrastructure." *Public Management Focus,* 4, Mar.

Osborne v. Canada (Treasury Board) (1991), 82 D.L.R. (4th) 321 (S.C.C.).

Pearson, L.B. 1967. "Foreword." *The East Block of the Parliament Buildings of Canada*. edited by R.A.J. Phillips, Ottawa: Department of Public Printing and Stationery.

Rodal, A., & N. Mulder. 1993. "Partnerships, Devolution and Power-Sharing: Issues and Implications for Management." *Optimum*, pp. 27–48.

Savoie, D.J. 1994. *Thatcher, Reagan, Mulroney: In Search of a New Bureaucracy*. Toronto, ON: University of Toronto Press.

Segal, H. 1998. "Ministerial Responsibility: Confronting the myth." *Crosscurrents: Contemporary Political Issues,* edited by M. Charlton and P. Barker, Toronto, ON: Nelson, pp. 232–9.

Sutherland, S.L. 1991. "Responsible Government and Ministerial Responsibility: Every Reform Is Its Own Problem." *Canadian Journal of Political Science,* 24, pp. 91–120.

Thomas, P. 1997. "Ministerial Responsibility and Administrative Accountability." *New Public Administration and New Public Management in Canada,* edited by

Charih and Daniels, Toronto: Institute of Public Administration of Canada, pp. 141–63.

United Kingdom. Committee on Standards in Public Life (Nolan Committee). 1994. *First Report.* London: HMSO. Cmd. 2850–1.

———. 2006. *The Civil Service Code*. London: Cabinet Office. Available at: www.civilservice.gov.uk/documents/pdf/cscode/cs_code.pdf.

Van Wart, M. 1998. *Changing Public Sector Values.* New York, NY: Garland.

Wilson, W. 1966 [1887]. "The Study of Administration." *Classics of Public Administration, edited by* Jay M. Shafritz and Albert C. Hyde, Chicago, IL: Dorsey, pp. 10–25.

Part  II

The Central Institutions

An important part of public administration is describing the organizational dimension. Often it is a matter of describing both the forest *and* the trees. One must be able to offer a significant amount of detail on the machinery of government, but also grasp big picture views of new developments in governance. The *Handbook's* contributors manage to do this nicely.

Christopher Dunn, in Chapter 6, seeks to explain the nature of the central executive in Canada, trace the significant degree of innovation and experimentation that it has experienced in the last half century, and discuss the difficulties involved in drawing lessons from such a record. The central executive refers to the collectivity of political and non-political members of the executive who perform coordinate central policy functions. He poses a question about where change in the federal central executive is headed. His chapter asks whether or not cabinet has evolved to a new stage. It is by now fairly standard to argue that there were two stages of cabinet development in the latter part of the twentieth century: (1) the unaided (or departmental or unstructured) cabinet, and (2) the institutionalized (or structured) cabinet. Many scholars are now saying that a new stage has been entered, some even suggesting the restructuring process redounds to the benefit of the prime minister. This new prime minister–centred cabinet would then be the third stage in cabinet development. Dunn hesitates to accept this conclusion, drawing instead on J.T. Lewis' hybrid model of both a strong first minister and the existence of departmental autonomy and collegial cabinet decision-making processes.

In Chapter 7, Paul G. Thomas provides a comprehensive look at Parliament and the Canadian public service(s) and considers the often problematical relationships between them. Although Thomas examines at length the problems inherent in trying to steer the modern ship of state with an institution that dates back about 800 years, he concludes on an optimistic note.

Public service reform and parliamentary accountability should logically reinforce each other, but in contemporary Canada they have not. Such reform, Thomas notes, historically has been somewhat contrary to longstanding parliamentary traditions, and this has been in evidence in three recent sets of reforms: the "steering not rowing" slogan, the adoption of special operating agencies (SOAs), and the various related elements of the recent orientation towards the private sector, including privatization, contracting out of service delivery, and public–private partnerships. Thomas notes that Parliament has given very little attention to debates or issues regarding public-sector reform. Annual reports of the head of the public service and the chair of the Public Service Commission, even reports of prestigious Royal Commissions, such as the Lambert Report (1979) and Public Service 2000

(1990), engender little interest in parliamentary circles. This is obviously a bad portent for parliamentary supervision of the public bureaucracy. A reversal of this situation, Thomas believes, is paramount for reformers.

Although many texts ignore this area, public administration extends even to the judicial system. As Carl Baar and Ian Greene explain in Chapter 8, the study of judicial administration did not really exist in Canada until the 1970s. Baar and Greene outline the history of judicial administration in the United States and Canada, examine the different parameters that bound it, and review some outstanding issues in judicial administration. Paradoxically, despite being the youngest in the public administration family, in some ways judicial administration has become a model for it.

Some of the interesting work being done in judicial administration involves caseflow management, the relationship between courts and the public, alternative dispute resolution, and integrated justice. *Caseflow management* posits the primary responsibility of the courts and judges for determining how cases proceed, as opposed to the traditional assumption of common-law procedure, that of party (in effect, lawyer) control of the process. Such a management approach thus requires an integrated series of processes and resources necessary to move a case from filing to disposition. Just as it focuses attention on new types of procedural reforms, the concept of judicial administration offers new perspectives on the relationships of *courts and the citizenry*. It highlights the importance of concepts like broadened access to justice, the differential effects of law on different segments of the population, and heightening public trust and confidence. *Alternative dispute resolution* (ADR) is one sign of a new commitment to increasing access to justice. ADR means finding alternatives to the court itself or else moving to alternatives *within* the court. *Integrated justice*, which involves the use of computer technology to facilitate court procedures, is the most innovative and ambitious concept in modern judicial administration. It means, as Baar and Greene say, "seamless automated processes with a single point of entry."

Andrew Sancton's Chapter 9 is composed of two complementary parts. The first part covers the basics of local government in Canada, reviewing the various forms of, and functions of, local government, provincial controls over local government, growth of local governments by incorporations and annexations, notable experiments in two-tier systems of urban government, and patterns of municipal amalgamations and de-amalgamations. The second part reviews the basic outlines of municipal public administration. Notable management developments are covered, such as the role of city managers and chief administrative officers (CAOs), contracting out of government functions, public–private partnerships (P3s), and municipal finance. The chapter shows that urban areas have become so economically dominant that Canadian federal and provincial governments must be just as concerned with the well-being of cities as are urban municipalities.

One of the major change agents in the governance of Canada and the provinces is among the most traditional management figures: the deputy minister. No one knows more about deputy ministers in Canada than Jacques Bourgault. In Chapter 10, he examines the many and varied roles of deputy ministers (DMs), all of them placing the DM at or near the nexus of change in the public sector. Deputies are designated by the prime minister and appointed by the Governor-in-Council to signify the appointment is made by the whole cabinet (that is, of the highest significance). With some exceptions, DMs exercise power through the cabinet minister's authority. They incorporate cabinet priorities into departmental priorities and answer to the minister, but are ultimately accountable to the prime minister. Recently, evolution in the DMs' role obliges them to answer questions posed by parliamentary committees, within the context of ministerial responsibility. However, the role of the DM has become more complex, and has been changed by myriad factors, in recent decades: new approaches to accountability; changes in state–citizenry relations; a greater emphasis on fiscal responsibility; the public management movement; challenges of new technologies; globalization; and the changing nature of the DM's role from managing to empowering others. This complexity can only increase in the future. One major change is the added role of accounting officer to the panoply of the DM's responsibilities.

The Central Executive in Canadian Government

6

Searching for the Holy Grail

Christopher Dunn

Chapter Overview

This chapter seeks to explain the nature of the central executive in Canada, trace the significant degree of innovation and experimentation that it has experienced in the last half century, and discuss the difficulties involved in drawing lessons from such a record. The central executive refers to the collectivity of political and non-political members of the executive who perform coordinate central policy functions. As such it involves cabinet and its committees and the central agencies and central departments of government. The literature describes the evolution of cabinet in a number of stages from traditional, to departmentalized or unaided, then to institutionalized, and then to prime minister–centred. There are grounds to suggest that a new hybrid form has evolved and is exemplified by the Justin Trudeau central executive. Developments at the federal level have been roughly similar to those in the provinces and territories, subject to important qualifications. Because the first minister has the task of organizing government as well as organizing cabinet, judging the utility of different forms of cabinet government is difficult. However, maintaining the integrity of the decision-making process is an important function of cabinets and central agencies.

Chapter Objectives

By the end of this chapter, students will be able to do the following:
- Explain the difference between the dignified and efficient executive.
- List the similarities in federal and provincial cabinets.
- List the differences in federal and provincial cabinets.

continued

- Describe the stages that the executive has experienced in Canadian history.
- Discuss the scholarly debates at work regarding the nature of the central executive.
- Acknowledge the contradictory lessons that can be drawn from the evolution of the executive.

Introduction

The central executive is the fulcrum of governance in the cabinet–parliamentary system. It provides leadership, coordination, and facilitation. As such, it is an appropriate focus for public administration.

First things first, however. Of what earthly good is it to study a relative handful of people so earnestly and in such depth? One answer is simple, if deceptive. First, it is part of the search for the Holy Grail. Much of this chapter is an attempt to render lessons of good governance from the massive experimentation of 11 jurisdictions and a complex world of reform of governance. Second, it also attempts to render lessons from what many, but not all, consider to be bad governance, the over-domination of the executive in Canada. It therefore examines executive dominance and alternatives to it. By necessity some of these two topics overlap in the following text.

The focus here is not on the whole of executive government, but the central executive. The **central executive** refers to the collectivity of political and non-political elements of the executive who are engaged in generating and coordinating central policy. It can be said to include the cabinet, its committees, the Prime Minister's Office (PMO) (the Premier's Office, or similar entity, at the provincial level), the Privy Council Office (PCO) (Executive Council Office at the provincial level), the Department of Finance, Treasury Board Secretariat, and other relevant central agencies and central departments.

This chapter starts with an introduction to the basic machinery of cabinet governance. It will investigate the constitutional position and organizational design of the federal and provincial executives, describe the various paradigmatic frameworks of the central executive, review what generations of

observers have held to be the lesson of design of the machinery of government, and end with a prognosis for the future.

The Constitution and the Executive

It is one of the great paradoxes of the Westminster or parliamentary system that the prime minister (or premier) and cabinet exercise enormous power while they do not exist in a constitutional sense. Their roles have evolved through convention over centuries due to the exigencies of leadership and parliamentary performance in Britain and its former colonies.

The Constitution Act, 1867 does not refer to cabinets by name at either the federal or provincial levels, consistent with constitutional convention. The Act does, however, provide for their legal foundations. "The Queen's Privy Council for Canada" is established by virtue of section 11 "to aid and advise in the Government of Canada." Executive councils in Ontario and Quebec are created by section 63. Since these provinces were being created *de novo*, section 63 specified the composition of the initial cabinets of each: Attorney General, Provincial Secretary, Provincial Treasurer, Commissioner of Crown Lands, Commissioner of Agriculture and Public Works, with the addition of two more for Quebec: the Speaker of the Legislative Council and the Solicitor General. The executive authorities in Nova Scotia and New Brunswick were to continue as they had existed at the Union (section 64), an arrangement duplicated in later instruments admitting British Columbia, Prince Edward Island, and Newfoundland.

Statutes creating Manitoba, Saskatchewan, and Alberta similarly established executive authorities in those provinces. Of course, section 92(1) of the 1867 Constitution dealing with amendment of provincial constitutions implied that the composition of the executive councils and indeed the structure of the executive government (save for the office of Lieutenant-Governor) was a matter of purely provincial jurisdiction. Section 45 of the Constitution Act, 1982 replaces section 92(1).

To understand cabinet government it is useful to think in terms of dichotomies: first, power and authority, and second, the **dignified executive** and the **efficient executive**. It is also helpful to remember that the dichotomies themselves did not always exist. In the era of the autocratic monarch they were unnecessary, since the king exemplified the unity of formal and informal power structures. Over time, as the king's power became constrained by Parliament, it became necessary to distinguish between *authority*, the formal designation of who was enabled to perform public acts, and *power*, the informal political influence that made sure they got performed. A crude differentiation is to say that authority was possessed by the dignified executive and power was possessed by the efficient executive. This dichotomy between dignified and efficient is the simplest way to understand the structure of the federal and provincial executives. As well, each of the two executives has further subdivisions, as Table 6.1 shows.

There is, in the dominion and provincial constitutions, a distinction between cabinet and the Privy Council (or executive council for the provincial executives). The *Privy Council/executive council* is the formal or dignified executive. The Lieutenant-Governor-in-Council "shall be construed as referring to the Lieutenant Governor of the Province by and with the Advice of the Executive Council thereof" (section 66, Constitution Act, 1867). The **cabinet** is the effective executive in that it is the main policy-initiating and -administering body and operates according to constitutional conventions that are more or less similar in all Commonwealth countries.

Table 6.1   The Executive

The Dignified Executive	The Efficient Executive
Queen	Prime Minister (Premier)
Governor General (Lieutenant-Governor)	Cabinet
Privy Council (Executive Council)	Public Service

Source: Dunn, 2006, p. 216.

The executive council can be considered the provincial analogue of the Privy Council. The main difference between federal and provincial executives is that federal ministers do not relinquish membership in the Queen's Privy Council for Canada upon resignation from cabinet, although for reasons of convention ex-ministers do not participate in actual executive power. In provinces, membership in cabinet and membership in the executive council are synonymous.

First Ministers and Cabinets: Federal and Provincial Comparisons

The provincial executives are not miniature versions of their federal counterparts. They have separate and unique traditions and histories. A study of the federal and provincial cabinets is essentially a comparative search for the Holy Grail of the machinery of government. First, let us deal with some similarities between the two levels of government.

Federal and Provincial Similarities

The first similarity is that the federal and provincial governments adopted the **institutionalized cabinet** model (a highly structured cabinet, discussed later) at about the same time in the 1960s and 1970s. The instigators of the institutionalized cabinets were Pierre Trudeau (government of Canada), W. R. (Bill) Bennett (British Columbia), Peter Lougheed (Alberta), T. C. Douglas (Saskatchewan), Duff Roblin (Manitoba), William G. (Bill) Davis (Ontario), the first government of Robert Bourassa (Quebec), Richard Hatfield (New Brunswick), G. I. Smith (Nova Scotia), Alexander (Alex) Campbell (Prince Edward Island), and Frank Moores (Newfoundland). Appendices A shows the inexorable historical march towards institutionalization at both the federal and provincial governments. (To make sense of the term *institutionalization*, the reader may feel compelled to skip ahead in this chapter to "Stages of Cabinet Development.")

A second area of similarity is the virtually identical *conventional and political powers* enjoyed by prime ministers and premiers. The prime minister (or premier) is the sole interlocutor between cabinet and the Governor General (or Lieutenant-Governor). Only he or she can choose cabinet ministers and hence has the power to make or break careers (Mallory, 1984: 89). The first minister is the sole architect of the general machinery of government (cabinet size, cabinet committees, central agency support and procedures, and the number and roles of departments). The first minister can advise the Governor to dissolve or prorogue the legislature. The party depends disproportionately for its electoral fortunes on the popularity of the first minister, giving him or her a privileged bargaining chip—or alternately, a tenuous hold on power. The prime minister is also the prime dispenser of patronage. The first minister enjoys the instant attention of the press and, with it, the possibility of shaping the public policy agenda. Thus, both premier and prime minister have at hand the five Ps of power: prerogative, Parliament, party, patronage, and press.

A third area of federal and provincial similarity relates to the conventions of cabinet government, most notably those involving cabinet formation, individual responsibility, and collective responsibility. Conventions dictate the process of **cabinet formation**. The Governor first appoints a prime minister or premier. Whom to choose is usually obvious: in the case of a majority government, the parliamentary leader of the majority party. In a minority situation, the Governor has the right to consult with parliamentary leaders to ascertain which leader is likely to command a durable majority in the House. The prime minister or premier then, by convention, has the sole right to advise the Governor on who shall be selected as ministers in the new government. The general practice, both federally and provincially, is to choose ministers from among those who have been elected to the House, but there are exceptions. It is possible for senators to enter the cabinet. Generally, there will only be one senator in cabinet, but in governments in which some regions have not elected enough (or any) government-side members, the number may go as high as three or four, as was the case with the Clark (1979–80) and Trudeau (1980–4) governments. As well, there are several precedents for appointing non-elected ministers— but these individuals are expected to seek election soon thereafter.[1] There are several provincial cases of temporarily non-elected officials entering cabinet as well.[2]

The convention of *sectional or regional representation* in the federal cabinet is so basic that it has been called the fundamental characteristic of government in Canada (Mallory, 1984: 89). There is not much formal literature on the matter of regional provincial cabinet balance. However, research has determined that a similar convention indeed holds in each province. (See Dunn, 2006.)

The last two editions of this *Handbook* suggested that "Textbooks on Canadian cabinets may one day refer to a convention of *gender equality* in provincial cabinets." This now seems overly optimistic on one level, but totally appropriate on another. Appropriate because of course Justin Trudeau rationalized gender parity in his first cabinet as long overdue ("because it's 2015"), joining other administrations that had already introduced it—Jean Charest in Quebec (2007 and 2008); Rachel Notley in Alberta, 2015; Kathleen Wynne hypothetically in Ontario—Wynne announced gender parity for cabinet and provincial agencies when conditions permitted (Blackley, 2016). Optimistic because former federal administrations and most current provincial administrations demonstrate a staggering lack of concern with the notion of equal representation of women and men in cabinet. Despite an uptick in representativeness of cabinets overall around the turn of the century and after,[3] by 2016 more than half (six) had the same or even fewer absolute numbers of women in cabinet as in 2000 and roughly the same proportion. (Table 6.2 does not show the pool of elected government caucus members from which to choose, but in most jurisdictions it is substantial.)

Rules regarding gender representation are still in the formative stage, and the party recruitment environments that affect this differ among regions. It is interesting that observers who make comments about the danger of injuring the merit principle when questions of gender parity are mentioned are silent as to merit when the importance of regional representativeness is discussed.

Individual ministerial responsibility holds at the provincial cabinet level as well as the federal. The concept involves the duty of the minister to lead, to defend, and, if deemed necessary, to resign. The minister is responsible or accountable to the House for the proper leadership of a governmental department. The minister must defend his actions and those of his or her departmental officials; the minister bears full political and legal responsibility for officials' actions regardless of any lack of foreknowledge of them. The minister must resign for a serious breach

Table 6.2   Women in Canadian Cabinets, 2000, 2008, and 2016

First Minister in 2016	Number of Women in Cabinet 2000	Total Number in Cabinet 2000	Number of Women in Cabinet 2008	Total Number in Cabinet 2008	Number of Women in Cabinet 2016	Total Number in Cabinet 2016
Justin Trudeau, Canada	8	27	5	27*	15	30***
Christy Clark, British Columbia	8	20	5	23	9	22****
Rachel Notley, Alberta	4	21	7	24	10	19
Brad Wall, Saskatchewan	5	19	4	18	4	17
Brian Pallister, Manitoba	5	15	6	18	4	13
Kathleen Wynne, Ontario	6	26	8	28	12	30
Philippe Couillard, Quebec	8	26	9	19	12	30
Stephen McNeil, Nova Scotia	1	12	3	18	6	17
Brian Gallant, New Brunswick	3	15	2	19, 1 MoS**	3	15
Wade MacLauchlan, Prince Edward Island	1	10	2	11	2	10
Dwight Ball, Newfoundland and Labrador	5	16	5	17	3	13

*Did not include 4 Secretaries of State, two of which were men and two were women
**Minister of State
***As of Aug. 19, 2016
**** The last changes on this table provincially, before going to press, dated from: BC, Dec. 11, 2015; AB, Feb. 2, 2016; SK, Aug. 23, 2016; MB, May 3, 2016; ON, June 16, 2016; QC, 2015; NS, Jan 12, 2016; NB, June 6, 2016; PE, Jan. 7, 2016; NL, Dec. 2015.

of ethics or a serious mistake in policy, with the premier, effectively, being the final judge. A special case of individual responsibility involves the culpability of the finance minister for any release of a budget prior to the official budget day, but this convention is as hard to enforce at the provincial level as it is at the federal.

Similar to the federal case, the doctrine of ministerial responsibility has proven to be hard to define in practice. Some situations are more likely to generate successful calls for the resignation of the minister, as

Andrew Heard has revealed. Wrongdoing by departmental officials and administrative ineptitude appear not to constitute convincing thresholds for ministerial resignation. However, the allegation of conflict of interest and violations of the personal code of ethics of the minister appear to be more formidable reasons (Heard, 1991: ch. 3).

Collective responsibility, as Heard reminds us, has three aspects: first, the responsibility of the cabinet to the monarch; second, to itself (through cabinet solidarity and cabinet secrecy); and third, to the elected House (Heard, 1991: 62). The first is marked when the Governor loses confidence in the cabinet and asks it to resign. This, for example, occurred in reaction to political corruption in Quebec in 1891 with the Mercier government and in British Columbia in 1903 with the Prior government; and the Lieutenant-Governor threatened to do so in Manitoba with the Roblin government in 1915 unless it appointed a Royal Commission to investigate the legislative building scandal. It did.

In the second sense, provincial cabinets have made significant, if inadvertent, contributions to establishing the parameters of the venerable, once thought absolute, convention of cabinet secrecy. In *Smallwood v. Sparling* (1982), the court refused former Premier Joseph Smallwood a general injunction based on cabinet secrecy as a form of Crown immunity (or public-interest immunity). The decision stated that Crown immunity is not absolute but relative, involving the balancing of injury to the public interest and injury to the administration of justice. In *Carey v. The Queen* (1986) a court ordered that Ontario cabinet documents relating to Minaki Lodge be revealed; cabinet documents, as *Sparling* had established, did not enjoy immunity as a class and must be revealed unless disclosure of them would interfere with the public interest. Cabinet secrecy is supposed to aid proper functioning of government, not improper conduct by the government. In 1988, the Nova Scotia Supreme Court, Appeal Division, maintained in favour of the Donald Marshall Inquiry that cabinet ministers could be compelled to testify about the general nature of discussions in cabinet. Provinces have even begun to follow in the example of British Commissions, as well as the McDonald Commission, which was the first Canadian inquiry to get access to federal cabinet papers. In 2002 Ontario's Walkerton Commission Report asserted that its mandate "constituted a waiver of Cabinet privilege by the province" (Ontario, Walkerton, 2002: 486–87). D'Ombrain shows that Walkerton "had the effect of gaining the commission access to whatever documents it wanted subject to procedures for putting them into evidence" (D'Ombrain, 2004: 357, fn. 48). Nevertheless, disclosure of cabinet papers is the exception rather than the rule.

Collective responsibility is as much a provincial convention as a federal one. Federal governments have been forced to resign due to losing votes of

confidence in 1873 (Macdonald, in the Pacific Scandal), 1926 (King, after a customs scandal), again in 1926 (Meighen, in legislative realignments after a short four days in power), 1963 (Diefenbaker, in a vote of confidence), and 1979 (Clark, after losing a budget vote). There have been fewer cases of governments losing the confidence of provincial assemblies, and hence fewer cases about which to theorize and to compare. A notable, somewhat bizarre case was the fall of the Howard Pawley government in Manitoba in 1988 occasioned by NDP MLA Jim Walding voting against his own government in a closely balanced budget vote.

Federal–Provincial Differences

Many of the dissimilarities between federal and provincial cabinets involve political dynamics arising from the pursuit of politics on a smaller scale. One difference is the degree to which the size of the cabinet can be and is used as a control mechanism in the provincial context. Federal cabinets regularly comprise around 10 per cent or less of the size of the Commons, whereas a much larger percentage of the provincial assembly is covered by cabinet membership. The percentage of the governing caucus covered by cabinet membership is even greater, often with more people in cabinet than there are backbenchers. These two sets of factors give a significant degree of power to the cabinet, and the premier who appoints them, as against the backbenchers on both sides.

Second, there are *different types of ministers* at the federal and provincial levels. At the federal level, one found a distinction in the Martin government (2003–6) between the cabinet and the ministry; in the former were the traditional cabinet ministers, and in the latter were secretaries of state, who were members of the Privy Council but not of the cabinet, and like cabinet ministers were bound by the convention of collective responsibility. They earned three-quarters of the salary of a cabinet minister, their job being to assist ministers in specific areas of their portfolios. Harper retained this "in the ministry but not the cabinet" distinction but further provided that each of the secretaries of state attend the cabinet committee meetings pertaining to their area of responsibility. They represent ministers at events, stakeholder meetings, parliamentary committees, and question periods and demonstrate policy leadership in areas specified by the PM or minister but do not preside over any area of the public service. The Trudeau government dropped all references to ministers of state in its *Open and Accountable Government*, the Privy Council Office's directions to ministers and associated officials (Canada, Privy Council Office, 2015).

Provinces have varying arrays of ministers to augment the standard form of departmental minister. Quebec has had a long history of using ministers of state (Lévesque and Bourassa), delegated ministers and associate ministers (Bourassa), two-tiered ministers, that is, line ministers and ministers of state (under Parizeau), and "superministers"—expansive roles given to senior ministers for economy, employment, and natural resources (with Lucien Bouchard). The Charest Liberal government had both traditional and new aspects. There were three types of ministers in Quebec's conseil executif: "minister of" (regular line minister), "minister for" (minister of state), and "minister responsible for" (autonomous policy ministers). New Brunswick under Frank McKenna introduced junior ministers called ministers of state in order to develop ministerial talent. Alberta had associate ministers at various times over the last quarter century. They became relatively less common in the new millennium. Klein had three of them in 2000, eliminated one of them in a 2000 reorganization, and then eliminated the other two in a 2001 reorganization. Ed Stelmach had three associate ministers briefly from June 2007 to February 2008. Rachel Notley appointed an Associate Minister of Health, Brandy Payne, in February of 2016.

In Ontario, there has also been some modest experimentation. Premier Rae expanded upon Peterson's modest use of ministers without portfolio. Since 2000, there has been a new type of minister introduced to the Ontario cabinet system. The Harris and Eves cabinets included associate ministers assigned to support a portfolio minister. These individuals were first appointed by the Lieutenant-Governor as ministers without portfolio and then named by Order-in-Council (O/C) as associate ministers. The responsibilities could be assigned by the premier and portfolio minister or else by an O/C, which assigned specific duties and/or statutory responsibilities. One associate minister was assigned at the end of the last Harris Government in 2001, and four in the Eves Governments. Both Eves and Harris established the chief government whip as a minister without portfolio. Dalton McGuinty did not continue these examples

for five years, but finally on June 20, 2008, appointed Gerry Phillips as minister without portfolio, given responsibility as chair of cabinet. Kathleen Wynne's cabinet had one associate minister, of education.

Visibility is also a difference between federal and provincial cabinets. With a few exceptions, provincial cabinet ministers tend to be higher profile than their federal counterparts. This is not due to any personal failings on the federal side, but rather to reasons of scale, policy, and perception. Provincial ministers are more involved in operational matters, and are seen more often in their communities. Provincial ministers for the most part defend their departmental estimates on the floor of the legislature, whereas the federal estimates are parcelled out to committees.

Territorial Executives

While one is on the subject of interjurisdictional differences, one should also take a look at the territorial executives and in what ways they are similar to and different than their federal and provincial counterparts. The Yukon, Northwest Territories (NWT), and Nunavut all share certain characteristics of southern Canada/Westminster executive forms and norms. All operate according to the principles of collective and individual responsibility. All adhere to the norms of cabinet secrecy, cabinet solidarity, and cabinet confidentiality. Some, like Yukon, also include government caucus members on cabinet committees, as some provinces do. All have premiers (in 2016, Peter Taptuna, Nunavut; Bob McLeod, NWT; Darrell Pasloski, Yukon) who play important policy and coordination roles. As elsewhere in Canada it is possible for governments to fall.

There is even an analogue of the provincial Lieutenant-Governor in each territory, called the commissioner. The commissioner historically served in a more direct administrative role as the representative of the federal government, and later not only chose but chaired the executive council; however, the introduction of responsible government in the late twentieth century ended these practices. In 1985, the practice of chairing the executive council ended, the commissioner being replaced by the government leader (until that year called the leader of the elected executive). The government leader was called the premier starting in 1994. The commissioner is now a symbolic figure who is chosen by the Governor-in-Council and performs many of the roles of provincial governors except that of representative of the monarch.

The territories show signs of institutionalization along southern Canada models. There are cabinet committees, institutionalization, and central agencies. Yet they also demonstrate significant differences in the institutions involved.

There are cabinet committees. The NWT cabinet has eight cabinet committees, including a Priorities and Planning Committee. Unlike southern counterparts, each NWT cabinet minister has the right to attend meetings of committees of cabinet other than the ones to which he or she is formally assigned. In Yukon, there is Fiscal Relations and Management Board, established by statute, and a Legislation Committee. There is a cabinet committee in Nunavut on quality of life, to deal in part with the suicide problem in the territory.

All have institutionalization of their cabinets—there are principal secretaries/chiefs of staff, cabinet secretaries, secretariat analysis of ministerial proposals, records of decisions and so forth. Several central officials attend cabinet, as necessary. The Yukon government has an Executive Council Office. In Nunavut, the deputy minister of executive is the secretary to cabinet and advises cabinet under the direction of the premier.

There are central agencies as well. Central agencies support the premier and executive council in the decision-making process and the shaping of policy. In Yukon, central agencies are the executive council office (ECO) and a management board secretariat. All cabinet submissions are in fact reviewed by a hybrid body named the Policy Review Committee (PRC), which is chaired by the director of policy in the ECO but composed of policy directors from all the departments. It is actually a subcommittee of the Deputy Ministers' Review Committee (DMRC). In the NWT, there is an expansive definition, as several bodies are considered central agencies: Department of Executive, Financial Management Board Secretariat, and the departments of Human Resources, Finance, Justice, and Aboriginal Affairs and Intergovernmental Relations (Northwest Territories. 2014). In Nunavut the central agencies are the Department of Executive and Intergovernmental Affairs, which provides support to cabinet and policy coordination, and the Department of Finance, which provides advice on fiscal and economic management.

Yet there are significant differences, even among the territories themselves. The cabinet and legislature of Yukon operate on the basis of party politics, whereas NWT and Nunavut both operate as consensus governments. In Yukon, each of the Progressive Conservatives (now Yukon Party), New Democrats, and Liberals have formed the government since 1979. In each of NWT and Nunavut, there is no party system and no official opposition, each member running as an independent. The legislative assembly, acting under the authority of the Legislative Assembly and Executive Council Act in each territory chooses the premier and members of the executive council by secret ballot, but ministerial assignments are assigned by the commissioner in executive council, who acts upon the advice of the premier. It is thus possible to be a member of executive council, in effect cabinet, but not a minister. Executive domination does not figure to the same extent as in the south, since the legislature is an active elective chamber, and the cabinet is in a minority, necessitating constant compromise with members of the assembly and its committees. The dynamics are somewhat like those in coalition governments, but with Indigenous consensus traditions added.

Stages of Cabinet Development

Cabinets, like many other social creations, have not remained static. They have evolved from relatively small bodies with modest purposes to large institutions with a multiplicity of roles. This is the case at both the federal and provincial levels. The one characteristic, however, that unites the cabinets of all eras is that they were collective organisms, bodies that tended to make decisions in plenary form. There is now a tendency among some observers to see a pathology in modern cabinet governance: the notion that cabinet, rather than being the driver of government decision-making, is becoming (or has become) irrelevant. The first minister now steers the ship of state, or so the theory goes.

The modes of cabinet operation have been succinctly summed up by J. Stefan Dupré. In 1985 Dupré noted that the federal and provincial cabinets had gone through three historical modes of operation, which he called the traditional cabinet, the departmentalized cabinet, and the institutionalized cabinet. The latter two were associated with greater and lesser workability of executive federalism (that is, relative conduciveness to negotiation, consultation, and exchange of information among intergovernmental actors in Canada) (Dupré, 1985: 1–32). The **traditional cabinet** predominated in Canada before the rise of the administrative state, that is, at a time when the role of government was modest and executive federalism was not yet the practice, the federal cabinet being the primary mechanism of federal–provincial adjustment. The main business of cabinet ministers was to aggregate and articulate regional and local concerns, and to dispense patronage. It lasted from about 1867 to the 1920s.

The next stage was that of the **departmentalized cabinet** (1920s–1960s). In this era, government departments and ministers were the engines of public-sector expansion. Ministers were accorded a significant degree of decision-making autonomy and demonstrated portfolio loyalty—or primary commitment to their departments—because they were judged primarily by departmentally oriented client groups and relied on departmental experts for policy formulation and implementation (Dupré, 1985: 1–5).

Some have termed the departmentalized cabinet the **unaided cabinet** and added some additional characteristics. The unaided cabinet is simple in structure, with few standing committees, and features restricted collegiality (that is, limited collective decision-making and power-sharing as regards departmental policy). The prime minister or premier is the architect of personnel choice and is usually, but not always, the dominant politician. There are central departments: departments that perform a service-wide facilitative and coordinative role but are headed by a minister other than the premier. There are few cabinet-level staff. Budgeting has narrow aims—usually fiscal control predominates—and employs narrow means. Planning is seen as an optional rather than essential function of government. The unaided cabinet promotes a decision-making style featuring few sources of alternative advice to cabinet other than deputy ministers. Restricted collegiality is the order of the day (Dunn, 1995: ch. 1).

Beginning around the sixties (or, in the case of Saskatchewan, the forties) and lasting into the nineties, the **institutionalized cabinet** came to replace the unaided cabinet. This cabinet, Dupré notes, had "various combinations of formal committee structures, established central agencies and budgeting and management techniques [combined] . . . to emphasize shared knowledge, collegial decision making,

and the formulation of government-wide priorities and objectives" (Dupré, 1985). There were now central agency ministers who reflected the collective concerns of cabinet and special interest ministers who continued the older pattern of special interest politics.

The institutionalized cabinet, as has been noted elsewhere, has a complex cabinet structure with many standing committees and expanded collegiality (that is, greater collective decision-making and power-sharing as regards departmental policy). The prime minister or premier's role is expanded to include the responsibilities of organizational architect as well as architect of personnel choice. There are now both central departments and **central agencies**, the latter being those service-wide facilitative and coordinative bodies directly responsible to the prime minister or premier. Cabinet receives both partisan (PMO-type) and policy/technocratic (PCO-type) input. Cabinet-level staff are relatively numerous. Budgeting features wider aims and wider means than the control-oriented budget process of the traditional cabinet. Planning is still considered optional by cabinet, but there is generally more recourse to it. A planning–budgeting nexus, or explicit link between the two functions, is common. There are alternative sources of information to cabinet other than the responsible minister and his or her deputy. Decision-making is more centralized in the structured cabinet. Cabinet makes a wider range of decisions and central bureaucrats monitor departments to a greater extent. Not surprisingly, there is almost constant tension between the centre and the departments (Dunn, 1995).

Several writers have contended, implicitly or explicitly, that the days of the institutionalized cabinet have ended; others qualify this observation, emphasizing jurisdictional patterns. Observers also differ as to the causes for, and processes involved in, a post-institutionalized world. We can classify the approaches as court government, the differentiated centre, the hybrid interpretation, and the political communication approach.

Court Government

Donald Savoie's *Governing from the Centre* (1999) was the most extensive critique of the institutionalized model then mounted. Savoie argued that the cabinet decision-making process (i.e., institutionalized cabinet process), which was designed to be a collective one, and specifically managed as such by central agencies, now belonged to the prime minister and was emphatically not a collective one (Savoie, 1999: 325).

Savoie said that power had shifted away from the ministers and their departments towards the centre, and at the centre, away from cabinet and cabinet committees to the prime minister and his senior advisers. Cabinet committee decisions were rarely challenged in the plenary cabinet, but this did not imply cabinet minister power, the chairs of these committees being hand-picked, process-oriented choices of the prime minister. Central agencies, rather than being neutral facilitators of collective decision-making, became engaged as actors in the process itself as extensions of the prime minister. Comprehensive policy agendas gave way to prime ministers governing by "bolts of electricity"—a handful of key objectives they pursued and pushed through the system. In pursuing these priorities, the first minister, finance minister, and central agencies essentially made the decision-making system a bifurcated one: there was one set of rules for the (nominal) guardians like the prime minister, finance minister, and president of the Treasury Board (whose major job traditionally was to protect the public purse) and another for the spenders (who traditionally tried to evade them). The priority programs of the guardians sailed through with little difficulty, whereas those of regular line ministers were subject to the regular cabinet committee decision-making process, where they were subject to the contending wishes of other ministers and the control of the central agencies (that is, the prime minister) and seldom emerged as their drafters originally intended. What was involved, Savoie says, was widespread institutional failure. The relevance of Parliament was even further cast in doubt; the power and influence of cabinet were threatened; the media became actors, not narrators; and the public service became an instrument for protecting the interests of the prime minister.

Nearly a decade later, Savoie was making a somewhat similar argument about "court government" (meaning a **prime minister–centred government**), the difference being in degree of centralization (Savoie, 2008). The cabinet had become marginalized in a context that could only be characterized as like a kind of [presumably medieval] court government. Cabinet government in both Canada and the United Kingdom has been moved away from by stealth and "all but destroyed" (Savoie, 2008: 229). "Individuals now rule, starting with the prime minister and his most trusted courtiers, carefully selected ministers, and senior civil servants, and they have more power in a court-style government than they do when formal policy and decision making processes tied to cabinet decision making are respected" (Savoie, 2008: 230). Instead of a collective ethos ruling, there is differentiation of status within cabinet. "Ministers now have to learn to work with the prime minister's court more than they have to learn to work with cabinet and cabinet colleagues" (238).

The contrast between the unaided (departmental), institutionalized, and court government prime minister–centred cabinets is presented in Appendix A.

The Differentiated Centre

David Good offers a more nuanced perception, arguing in effect for a differentiated centre in which some agencies have aggrandized power more than others. In this *Handbook* and elsewhere (Good, 2007), he analyzes budget behaviour from the perspective of stylized roles rather than from institutionalized organizations. Good notes that the so-called spender–guardian dichotomy is outmoded, and that public spending in the federal government is actually affected by four sets of actors. Spenders are generally spending ministers (and occasionally the prime minister and finance); guardians are finance and Treasury Board; priority setters are the prime minister, PMO, and PCO; and the principal watchdog is the Office of the Auditor General (OAG), to which has been added a host of new Harper-created watchdogs: the parliamentary budget officer, the chief audit executive in each department, accounting officers in each department, an independent procurement officer, and a public sector integrity commissioner. The watchdogs exercise a kind of cautionary control of public spending. All have different interests, but guardians and priority setters have, despite their differences, arranged to combine to control the effects of spenders and watchdogs (Good, 2007: 294).

The Ottawa that Good describes seems to be a different place than Savoie's. Departments are not as dominated by the centre as Savoie indicates; if they do their homework, develop a clientele, think like guardians, and develop ties to key sectoral and regional ministers, they may convince the prime minister to adopt their concerns as priorities. Savoie, one of the major popularizers of Schick's spender–guardian dichotomy in earlier books, does not mention it in his 2008 *Court Government* book. Good on the other hand does mention it, noting that it applied the "old village" but has been rendered inoperative in the "new town" of complex four-way multilateral relationships. This allows Good to highlight where the "centre" is weak—for example that one of the guardians, Treasury Board, is now virtually a non-actor because of its lack of control over the departmental A-bases and decades of decentralization of management prerogatives to departments. It also allows him to emphasize the challenge function of the PCO, which sees itself as a counterbalance willing to challenge the spending proposals of both finance and the departments, and occasionally even the prime minister, to weed out risky proposals and to make sure that the policy is needed, costed, workable, and likely to be effective (Good, 2007: 109–10). There is not much mention of the challenge function in Savoie.

The Communications Theory Approach

A new approach to discerning and explaining centralism in the central executive comes from the field of communications theory as applied to the public sector. One of the country's experts in this field is Alex Marland of Memorial University. Marland has a nuanced explanation for centralization in the country's central executive. He maintains that two complementary forces are at work: one promotes centralization, and the other supplements institutional forces that engender it.

Political economist H. A. Innis and media theorist Marshall McLuhan held that communications technology was more important that communications content; non-durable media such as electronic communications are prone to expansion and thus to the mass coordination that is a forerunner to centralized power. But it is not just technological determinism at work. Institutional characteristics common to Westminster systems like extreme party discipline, executive dominance, and public management techniques combined with the potency of communications technology allow power to gravitate to the centre. Rather than causing it, communications technology hurries along existing trends. Governments

tend to push issues that strengthen the party's brand while advancing the party's agenda, and alter course away from those that do the opposite.

When pushing issues to the forefront, governments use the tools of modern political communications. Communications theory as applied to the public sector can be said to include such aspects as political marketing (the use of private-sector advertising and marketing techniques by public-sector actors); political communications (the aligning of messages in the public sector among a variety of platforms) and political branding (the establishment of intense discipline in image management, simplicity in policy messaging to maximize effect, and attempts to engage the public at an emotional level). All of these, Marland maintains, reached new levels of sophistication in the Harper era and can be counted on to develop further in the Trudeau years.

The Hybrid Interpretation

Of course, not all observers agree that it is a post-institutionalized world we are talking about when we discuss the Canadian central executive. J. P. Lewis maintains that both federal and provincial executives display important elements of both the institutionalized and prime minister–centred cabinet style.

> The results of this survey suggest that a pan-Canadian cabinet culture exists that functions as a collegial body within the autocratic model, therefore reflecting a number of previous cabinet decision-making models.... Savoie may have been accurate when he said that "court government has taken root in Canada" ... but based on my findings, effective power still rests within the cabinet in a manner that reflects a hybrid autocratic-collegial decision-making model. (Lewis, 2013)

The hybrid model meant that cabinet government drew upon all the previous models. The hybrid model was "reflected in respondents' acknowledgement of both a strong first minister and the existence of departmental autonomy and collegial cabinet decision-making processes" (Lewis, 2013: 815–16).

Lewis' finding of a "common executive culture across jurisdictions and levels of government" should be taken seriously, given the extensiveness of his research. He surveyed 105 former federal and provincial cabinet ministers who served between 2000 and 2010. It in addition has utility in describing the cabinet of Justin Trudeau (2015–).

The Cabinet of Justin Trudeau

The early Trudeau central executive shows signs of channelling this hybrid model. This is evident from the prime minister's commentary and the modifications to the roles of cabinet, cabinet committees, central agencies, and individual ministers. There are also notable structural innovations that exemplify how versatile the organizational architecture at the centre can be.

Role of the Prime Minister

There is a strong prime minister, but it is expressed in a different manner. In a discussion with *Forbes Magazine*, Trudeau was asked how his operating style differed from that the micromanagement of Stephen Harper. He summarized it as helicopter leadership—the notion of hovering above the battlefield and dropping down to the detail level only when there are problems, to motivate officers (ministers) to solve the problem.

> For me, being able to engage with the details when necessary, when there's a challenge, when there's a particularly important pivot, yes, you have to do that. But in general, a leader needs to trust their commanders, needs to trust the team they've assembled, to actually execute in the right way. (*Forbes*, 2015)

It is now part of Ottawa legend to describe the central executive of Stephen Harper as hypercentralist. We described the literature which alleged that government operations were designed to focus on the program of the prime minister and his inner circle. Cabinet met infrequently and was more a sounding board than a decision-making body. The PMO was the pre-eminent central agency and had a large role in designing government communications and formulating messages and programs for individual ministers.

"Cabinet government is back"

The new prime minister, first, made a point of distinguishing the operating style of his government and the previous one. "Government by cabinet is back," Trudeau said upon taking office, apparently taking aim at the prime minister–centred outlook that had been Harper's trademark, but that had roots in the governments going back to Trudeau Sr. (Van Dusen, 2015). Elsewhere he referred to having a cabinet that "actually decides."

The Role of Cabinet

There has been a movement away from the Harper model towards modest cabinet institutionalization and a more fulsome role for individual ministers. First, there is a significant number of cabinet committees. The first Trudeau cabinet had nine cabinet committees, one subcommittee, and one ad hoc committee. By the next cabinet redesign the latter two had been transformed into full committees so there were now 11 committees. (See Tables 6.3 and 6.4). This is getting towards the high end of committee numbers. Harper's last cabinet by contrast had six committees and one subcommittee (Canada, 2016).

One sign of institutionalization and the collegial part of the hybrid interpretation is the existence of a core of cabinet members who share authority at the centre. This appears to be the case with the members of the Agenda, Results and Communications Committee, the functional equivalent of the Harper Priorities and Planning Committee. Of the 11 members of the 2015 Agenda and Results Committee, five were chairs of other cabinet committees and six were vice-chairs. There are five chairs and four vice-chairs outside this circle. Of the ten members of the 2016 Agenda, Results and Communications Committee, six were chairs of other cabinet committees and six were vice-chairs. There were three chairs and four vice-chairs outside this circle.

Prime minister–centred cabinets meet infrequently and tend to be mere sounding boards for centralized authority. By contrast the Trudeau cabinet is a more hybrid one, meeting more often as effective decision-maker. Reports corroborated the decision-making focus shifting from the Priorities and Planning Committee (as under Harper) to cabinet, with full cabinet meeting more often (seven meetings from November 2015 to August 2016) and cabinet returning to its traditional collaborative role (Abma, 2016).

Table 6.3 Trudeau's Nine Cabinet Committees, Two Subcommittees, and Membership, November 4, 2015

	Agenda and Results	Treasury Board	Open and Transparent Government	Inclusive Growth, Opportunities and Innovation	Diversity and Inclusion	Canada in the World and Public Security	Intelligence and Emergency Management	E, CC & E	PA	CITW: SC on US	DP Ad hoc
Trudeau, Justin	X (C)						X (C)				
Bains, Navdeep Singh	X			X				X		X	X
Duclos, Jean-Yves	X	X		X (VC)	X						
Foote, Judy	X		X (C)						X (VC)		X
Goodale, Ralph	X		X			X (C)	X			X (VC)	
Freeland, Chrystia	X			X		X		X (VC)		X (C)	
Joly, Mélanie			X	X	X (VC)				X		
Leblanc, Dominic	X		X	X			X		X (C)		
Morneau, Bill	X	X	E-O	X	E-O	E-O	E-O	E-O	E-O	E-O	X
Sajjan, Harjit Singh	X					X	X	X		X	X
Wilson-Raybauld, Jody	X		X		X	X (VC)	X (VC)			X	
Brison, Scott		X (C)	X	X	E-O	E-O	E-O	E-O	E-O	E-O	X (VC)
McKenna, Catherine		X		X		X		X		X	
McCallum, John		X (VC)			X (C)	X				X	
Philpott, Jane		X					X				
Qualtrough, Carla			X (VC)		X						
Duncan, Kirsty								X			X

continued

Table 6.3   (Continued)

	Agenda and Results	Treasury Board	Open and Transparent Government	Inclusive Growth, Opportunities and Innovation	Diversity and Inclusion	Canada in the World and Public Security	Intelligence and Emergency Management	E, CC & E	PA	CITW: SC on US	DP Ad hoc
Hajdu, Patricia			X		X						
Lebouthillier, Diane			X	X							
Mihychuk, MaryAnn			X	X					X		
Monsef, Maryam			X		X				X		
Bennett, Carolyn				X	X			X			
Carr, James Gordon				X		X		X		X	X (C)
Chagger, Bardish				X	X					X	
MacAuley, Lawrence				X				X	X	X	
Sohi, Amarjeet				X				X			
Bibeau, Marie-Claude					X	X					
Hehr, Kent					X				X		
Dion, Stéphane						X	X	X (C)		X	
Garneau, Marc						X			X	X	X
Tootoo, Hunter								X	X		X
# OF MEMBERS	11	6	11	15	11	10	8	10	9	12	9
# of WOMEN	4	2	8	9	8	4	3	4	4	4	2

Notes: The Ad Hoc Committee on Defence Procurement was in existence from February 22, 2016 to August 21, 2016. Women were clear minorities in six of ten committees, but clear majorities in others.

E-O means Ex-Officio	CITW: SC on US means Canada in the World and Public Security: Sub-Committee on Canada–United States Relations	DP Ad hoc means Defence Procurement (Ad Hoc)
C means Chair	E, CC & E means Cabinet Committee on Environment, Climate Change and Energy	PA means Cabinet Committee on Parliamentary Affairs
VC means Vice-Chair		

Table 6.4   Trudeau's 11 Cabinet Committees and Their Membership, as of January 29, 2018

	Agenda, Results and Communi-cations	Treasury Board	Open and Transparent Government and Parliament	Growing the Middle Class	Diversity and Inclusion	Canada in the World and Public Security	Canada-US Relations	Intelligence and Emergency Management	E, CC & E	DP	Litigation Mgmt
Trudeau, Justin	X (C)							X (C)			
Bains, Navdeep Singh	X	X (VC)		X					X	X	
Duclos, Jean-Yves	X	X		X (C)	X						
Goodale, Ralph	X					X (C)	X (VC)	X			
Freeland, Chrystia	X					X	X				
Joly, Mélanie	X		X		X (VC)				X (C)		
Leblanc, Dominic	X		X					X	X		X (C)
Morneau, Bill	X	X	E-O	X	E-O	E-O	E-O	E-O	E-O	E-O	X
Sajjan, Harjit Singh	X					X	X	X		X	
Brison, Scott	X	X (C)	E-O	X	E-O	E-O	E-O	E-O	E-O	X (VC)	E-O
McKenna, Catherine						X (VC)	X		X		X
Philpott, Jane		X						X			
Qualtrough, Carla			X		X					X	X
Bibeau, Marie-Claude			X		X	X					
Chagger, Bardish			X	X	X		X				
Petitpas Taylor, Ginette		X			X			X			

continued

Table 6.4 (Continued)

	Agenda, Results and Communi-cations	Treasury Board	Open and Transparent Government and Parliament	Growing the Middle Class	Diversity and Inclusion	Canada in the World and Public Security	Canada-US Relations	Intelligence and Emergency Management	E, CC & E	DP	Litigation Mgmt
Garneau, Marc	X		X			X	X (C)	X		X	
Hajdu, Patricia			X (C)	X							X (VC)
Gould, Karina			X (VC)				X	X	X		
MacAuley, Lawrence			X			X	X	X			
O'Regan, Seamus			X				X			X	
Monsef, Maryam			X		X						
Wilson-Raybauld, Jody			X		X			X (VC)			X
Bennett, Carolyn				X	X				X		X (C)
Carr, James Gordon				X			X		X	X (C)	
Lebouthillie, Diane				X	X	X					
Sohi, Amarjeet				X (VC)	X (C)	X	X		X		
Hussen, Ahmed D.					X	X	X				
Duncan, Kirsty									X (VC)	X	
Champagne, François-Philippe						X				X	
# of members	12	6	12	12	13	11	13	11	9	9	7
# of women	4	2	8	5	10	5	5	5	5	3	5

Notes: Women were clear minorities in three of eleven committees, but in clear majorities or parity, at or approaching parity, in the eight others.

E-O means Ex-Officio   E, CC & E means Cabinet Committee   DP means Defence
C means Chair   on Environment, Climate Change and   Procurement
VC means Vice-Chair   Energy

Role of the PMO

Along hybrid lines, there were also changes to central agencies to bolster collegial decision-making. One important change concerned the role of the PMO. During the 2015 campaign he said he liked the symmetry of being the person who would end the pattern of Prime Minister's Office becoming gradually more powerful that had begun when Pierre Trudeau came to office in 1968. Justin Trudeau noted that:

> One of the things that we've seen throughout the past decades in government is the trend towards more control from the Prime Minister's Office. . . . Actually it can be traced as far back as my father, who kicked it off in the first place. And I think we've reached the endpoint on that. . . . "I recognize that, and I think I actually quite like the symmetry of me being the one who'd end that," Justin Trudeau told Mansbridge. (Kennedy, 2015)

Lobbyists seeking to approach the new PMO under the assumption they are primary decision-makers are now apparently told that the responsible minister is the key person for policy dossiers.

Not only has there been an attempt to downplay PMO power in the system, but the PMO has become a more level authority. When Pierre Trudeau took over from Pearson, there were about 40 professional staff in a disorganized PMO. Trudeau gave it more staff, structure, and hierarchy, trends that were continued by most if not all prime ministers up to Harper, who had a very hierarchical Office with 100 staff. Justin Trudeau's PMO is "a less centralized and regimented, more open and collaborative decision-making process than Ottawa has been conditioned to expect," less Pearsonian than "trying to stay in touch with the more fluid management practices of the Google era—something . . . that some insiders compared to launching a start-up," the same pattern that he had used to modernize the Liberal Party structure (Kennedy, 2015).

Role of the PCO

If there is to be increased collegiality in a cabinet setting, a strong PCO is vital. Tellingly, Prime Minister Harper, not a strong believer in broad collegiality,

diminished both role and funding for the PCO. Trudeau has increased both. The first federal budget included $99 million spread over fiscal years 2016–17 and 2017–18 for new staff to provide IT upgrades and to aid the work of the prime minister and cabinet.

The Liberals intend to shift emphasis from the political staff in the PMO to non-partisan civil service agencies like the PCO (Payton, 2016). Public administration theory and practice will now have a higher profile.

One practice the PMO will emphasize in the first term is a "results approach." This is a new name for aligning implementation with objectives. The Liberal platform and ministerial mandate letters were apparently heavily influenced by the results approach, which is based on the work of Michael Barber, the first head (2001–5) of British Prime Minister Tony Blair's Delivery Unit (Barber, 2008, 2015). Matthew Mendelsohn heads a unit in the PCO spearheading the effort (May, 2016). It is politically directed by the Cabinet Committee on Agenda, Results and Communications, chaired by the prime minister himself in order to give it political heft.

Departmental Autonomy Augmented

The hybrid approach makes mention of the existence of departmental autonomy. Trudeau's government does in fact involve more leeway for ministers and departments than was the case under Harper. There are more routine press scrums by ministers. Departmental scientists were told at the beginning of the administration that they would be free to have public discussion of their findings. Notices for cabinet meetings include ministerial availability notices such as this: "Itinerary for the Prime Minister, Justin Trudeau, for Tuesday, October 18, 2016: Ottawa, Ontario 9:30 a.m. The Prime Minister will attend the Cabinet Meeting. Note for media: Ministers will be available to media in the House of Commons Foyer as of 12:00 p.m." This availability would have been unthinkable in the Harper years, when only a handful of ministers were trusted to speak independently.

Structural Innovations

It would be an unusual prime minister that did not innovate in structural terms. This Trudeau has done in his departures from past practice, and new roles for cabinet committees.

Some past practices have faded. There is no more Priorities and Planning Committee; instead there is an Agenda, Results and Communications Committee that appears to serve more purposes: priorizing, monitoring results, and doing political marketing and communications. There are no more ministers of state; the reasons for this were not stated but probably had to do with the optics of a gender-balanced cabinet—assuring the sexes had equal status. Like Harper, Justin Trudeau has appointed no deputy prime minister, a position that had been in place for several decades.

Another discontinued past practice is having separate ministers for regional development agencies. There were six such regional agencies: Atlantic Canada Opportunities Agency (ACOA), Canada Economic Development for Quebec Regions, Canadian Northern Economic Development Agency, Federal Economic Development Agency for Southern Ontario, Federal Economic Development Initiative for Northern Ontario, and Western Economic Diversification Canada. Each in the past has had separate full-time ministers, ministers of state, or a regional minister. The Trudeau ministry, however, attached the responsibility for each to one minister, Navdeep Bains, the Minister of Innovation, Science, and Economic Development. No reason was given.

It is difficult to consider this a permanent state of affairs, however. Either political pressure for separate dedicated regional development ministers will be successful, or the opposite: they could be eliminated in favour of another economic development model (McHardie, 2016). The latter alternative is unlikely in the short run, or unlikely in certain areas like Eastern Canada, given the complete sweep of Atlantic seats, among other factors.

Other departures are less remarkable, but interesting. A developing pattern is to have cabinet chairs who are not associated with the policy area of the committee. Sports Minister Carla Qualtrough, Health Minister Jane Philpott, Heritage's Mélanie Joly, and Natural Resource's Jim Carr headed committees that were not functionally related to their cabinet area.

As governing becomes ever more complex, cabinet committees have had to evolve. One new cabinet committee, Litigation Management (Canada, 2016), is without precedent. It features an unusual mixture of finance, policy, and law, and is occasioned by the 42,000 legal suits involving hundreds of billions in liabilities facing the federal government, including 29,000 in which Canada is defendant or respondent (Mazereeuw, 2016). The committee was the idea of Justice Minister Jody Wilson-Raybould and aimed at devising cohesive political strategies and possibly minimizing confrontation, for example with First Nations.

The Provinces and the Institutionalized Cabinet

Whether or not the provinces have passed beyond institutionalization to a new phase of cabinet evolution is a natural question. One the one hand, there are some indications that the degree of provincial institutionalization has decreased. On the other, there are signs of the hybridization Lewis talked about.

- *Diminished numbers of cabinet committees from the seventies to the nineties.* In British Columbia, Premier Bill Vander Zalm had 12 committees, but the beginning of the Harcourt administration saw only eight; in September 1993, Harcourt reduced it to five committees. In Alberta, Ralph Klein reduced the total number of committees to five, including Treasury Board. In 1990, New Brunswick and Nova Scotia each had five cabinet committees; but by 1995 they and PEI got by with only two committees, Policy Board (Policy and Priorities in New Brunswick) and a Board of Management (Treasury Board in PEI). The later Bourassa government, like the Lévesque government before it, had several standing (or permanent) committees (Lachapelle et al., 1993: 241–4). The Parizeau government, however, reduced the number of committees to four: a (reactivated) Priorities Committee, the Treasury Board (retained), the Legislation Committee (retained), and a special committee for greater Montreal.
- *Static or growing numbers of cabinet committees from the nineties to 2016.* When surveyed between 1995 and 2016, the provincial cabinets revealed a tendency towards equilibrium. There were static or growing numbers of cabinet committees between 1995 and 2008. Three provinces had increased the numbers of committees, four had retained the same number of committees, and only three had reduced the numbers. Most provinces still had significant numbers of cabinet committees. Table 6.5 shows the evidence.

Table 6.5   Numbers of Provincial Cabinet Committees, 1995–2016

Province	Number of Cabinet Committees					
	1995	1998	2004	2008	2013	2016
BC	4 (and 4 "working groups")	5 (and 3 "working groups")	5	8	6 (and 2 "working groups")	6 (and 3 "working groups")
AB	8	10	10	10	5	6 "Government Committees"
SK	6	9	5	3	6	?
MB	12	7	6	6	5 (2014)	?
ON	8 (and 2 subcommittees)	4 (and 4 subcommittees)	8	8	8 (4 and 4 "standing policy" committees (2014)	2
QC	4	7	5	6	6 (2014)	6 Ministerial Standing Committees
NB	2	2	6	6	6	5
NS	5	1	1	5	5	3
PE	2	3	5	3	3 (2014)	2
NF	6	6	5	5	5	5

Sources: Dunn (1998, 2006, 2016); Privy Council Office (1998); Correspondence with Clerks of the Executive Councils, February–June, 2008; Provincial Executive Council Websites, accessed June 2008 and July 2016.

On the other hand, there are some clues that **many** provinces have remained in the institutionalized phase, with meaningful recognition given to the collective nature of executive decision-making:

• *Academic reviews of provincial cabinets.* Some academics see Savoie's picture replicated at the provincial level,[4] but several do not. Graham White, for example, does not believe in the myth of the autocratic first minister in Canada, especially at the provincial level, and quotes several premiers to that effect (White, 2001). The concept of collegiality can exist within the administration of an influential premier, as Lewis discovered. What some outside observers may see as autocratic behaviour by a first minister may be misleading.

Even Ontario, which some authors gave as an example of a premier-centred executive in the nineties, in fact oscillated between institutionalized and premier-centred patterns. The determining factor in the Mike Harris years, between June 1995 and March 2002, contends Ted Glenn, was the premier's assessment of the state of the economy and the deficit (Glenn, 2005). The last Progressive Conservative cabinet, under Eves, had a plethora of cabinet committees. Of Quebec, Bernier says, the power of the premier has been seriously attenuated since the 1960s because of the tendency for the governing parties to turn against premiers who are electoral liabilities and for PQ governments to be riven by intra-party and intra-caucus challenges (Bernier, 2005). Dunn says the strong premier tradition of Newfoundland was mitigated by the tendency of premiers to lose influence the longer they stayed in office (Dunn, 2005).

In Saskatchewan, maintain Rasmussen and Marchildon, the legacy of the institutionalized cabinet in the province continues to be a powerful presence and there endured over a half century an institutionalized legacy: three poles of influence. "These three cabinet committees—the Planning Board, the Government Finance Office and the Treasury Board—and their central agency support structures, formed a planning troika that has remained an enduring feature of the Saskatchewan system" (Rasmussen & Marchildon, 2005: 191).

- *Internal cabinet hierarchy.* One of the historical tendencies of federal and provincial institutionalized cabinets was towards a hierarchy in the committee structure. Whereas this may not in and of itself reveal collegiality, it demonstrates that the premier has to share authority with at least a handful of fellow ministers, and is therefore not the only power in cabinet. All provinces in both 1995 and 1998, except Manitoba, had some version of the planning and priorities type of cabinet committee. These committees characteristically regroup all the most powerful ministers in cabinet and include the chairs of the standing committees of cabinet. The existence of cabinet committees implies power dispersion as well as functional necessity. In 2008, there were priorities committees in Quebec, Alberta, Saskatchewan, and Newfoundland and Labrador. In 2016, there were even more provincial cabinet priorities committees—seven, in British Columbia, Ontario, Quebec, Nova Scotia (Treasury and Policy Board), New Brunswick, Prince Edward Island, and Newfoundland and Labrador—or eight, if one counts the NWT cabinet. This state of affairs is consistent with the hybrid executive and its degree of collegiality.
- *The use of deputy premiers.* While not perhaps a hallmark of institutionalization per se, the practice of having deputy premiers became a fixture of most provincial cabinets in the nineties, after having earlier started in central Canadian provinces. Deputy premiers are not merely administrative conveniences; progressively, they have become more institutionalized actors whose presence denotes another power centre in cabinet. They can therefore further the power-distribution effects of cabinet institutionalization.

What Have We Learned from Experiments with the Central Executive?

Students of Canadian public administration and political scientists have poured an inordinate amount of time into the study of the central executive. Not all have explained why. This chapter suggests that the metaphor of the Holy Grail is useful when trying to explain the fascination with the subject. The notion of attaining a satisfactory decision-making structure is irrepressibly attractive, but always seems beyond discovery by ordinary mortals. Even though they may not enunciate this goal, at its base, most people study the central executive to search for this particular Grail. What we have learned so far is that cabinet evolution is contradictory, subject to personalities and variances, and amounts to a series of quests for balance.

One impression above all strikes the student of this literature: the contradictions. Before the 1960s, cabinet committees were not common in the federal or provincial administrations, but later they were quite acceptable as ways of dealing with the complexities of public policy. When first used, committees were not supposed to be garbed with decision-making powers, ostensibly to safeguard collective responsibility; then they were, even to the extent that collective cabinet came to make few real decisions. Individual ministerial autonomy was once highly prized, then it was an inconvenience to be offset by the collective authority of cabinet committees. The control culture of central agencies, especially that of Treasury Board, was stifling initiative and entrepreneurialism, then when Treasury Board gave too much control to departments, this was bemoaned. Some suggested that there be an uncommitted majority in cabinet, by keeping numbers in cabinet committees small; others called for an involvement by most in cabinet on committees, to the extent that there were sometimes a dozen committees. Some first ministers felt compelled, often by regionalism, to have large cabinets; others were compelled by the dictates of austerity to have smaller ones. For every Savoie who says that dominant first ministers are the problem, there will be a Bakvis or a White saying that the problem is overrated, as are the needs for exaggerated reforms. Even Savoie feels that cabinet government can be salvaged at the beginning of the decade, only to despair of the notion at the end of it, and deciding to fix the prime minister's role instead. What is one to make of all this?

The blanket characterization of cabinet governance as prime minister–centred needs to be tempered. The design of government is remarkably personalistic. First ministers come and go. Chrétien perceived himself hindered by the offshoots of the Pierre Trudeau institutional cabinet—excessive use of ministerial time, excessive paperwork, weakening of strong ministers (Chrétien, 1994: 84)—but a future prime minister, unencumbered by such personal experiences, may revert to the institutional approach. Paul Martin, successor to the centralist Chrétien, had a more inclusive mode of governing. Martin, at nine, had more cabinet committees than Chrétien ever had, and garbed them with important policy and financial management roles; included parliamentary secretaries as privy councillors; created new secretariats and roles in the PCO; and juxtaposed these arrangements with a new democratic action plan for Parliament that was nominally aimed at lessening executive domination. This was institutionalization redux. Even the same first minister might reverse himself/herself. Glenn (2001) says the Harris government in Ontario first decreased, then increased cabinet institutionalization. Of course, Martin was followed by the hypercentralist Harper, but this probably speaks to a notion of a rhythm of centralization giving way periodically to a more collective cabinet.

Ian Loveland reminds us that such a rhythm has been the case in the United Kingdom. There has been support in some quarters for Crossman's thesis (Crossman, 1975–7) that most of cabinet had to go along with decisions taken by the "inner cabinet." Cases include Attlee concealing his atomic weapons policy from cabinet, Callaghan directing economic policy by his "Economic Seminar," Thatcher bypassing her first cabinet and its "wet" ministers, as well as Blair governing in a "command and control" style. Yet there were cases of collective governance: Wilson made significant use of cabinet committees in decision-making, and John Major also shifted to a collective cabinet (Loveland, 2006: 321–6). By 2008, even Gordon Brown, having been one-half of the Blair-Brown duopoly that dominated cabinet government, found himself as a prime minister beset by bad polls, tolerating an end to ministerial submissiveness (Richards, 2008). Could there be lessons for Canada in all this?

In some ways such contradictions are to be expected. The design of the central executive is largely (although not entirely) a prerogative of the first minister. And consistency, as Ralph Waldo Emerson said, is the hobgoblin of little minds: first ministers often bring a great deal of creativity, hence variation, to the design of government and it would be a surprise if they all thought alike.

Most eras of cabinet development have been attempts to regain a balance that had been lost. The departmental cabinet prized ministerial initiative and departmental expertise, and ignored the importance of cabinet-level coordination. The institutionalized cabinet, on the other hand, prized coordination and saw the need for a system of central-departmental counterweights. However, as the system matured, perceptions grew about its increasingly dysfunctional nature: too many ministers, departments, and cabinet committees, too much interest-group influence, but too little policy coherence, regionally sensitive input, and attention to cost control. The apparent concern in the prime minister–centred era is that the pendulum has swung too far towards the power of the first minister and that, if counterweights are to be constructed, they should in fact be put in place against him/her in the form of formal, institutionalized roles for the prime minister, Parliament, parties, and departments. Provincial reviews see this as less of a problem and tend to see maintaining the collective aspect of decision-making as the main challenge.

To the extent that prime ministerial government is deemed problematic, cures are provided. Three major categories of literature speak to the subject. First there are those who perceive the problem as one of Parliament's role being overshadowed by the executive, who propose measures to bolster the former's status. Others suggest that the problem is the prime minister's domination within the executive, and propose balancing reforms within government restructuring of the public-sector bargain. Others also see the problem as being executive-centred, but propose measures that balance power between government and society.

Federal and provincial jurisdictions can learn from the experiences of each other. For the federal government, the lessons from the provincial governments are that the demise of the institutionalized cabinet may be premature; that Ottawa is notoriously inward-looking and it is useful to learn from provincial experience with central decision-making processes; that pragmatism and personalities must be taken into consideration in cabinet decision-making processes; and that there is room for caucus involvement in the work of cabinet. For the provincial governments, the lessons from the federal government have to do with enhancing the policy capacity of the central executive and encouraging policy communities that transcend the boundaries of government.

For all the contradictions and inconsistencies, however, there are enduring principles, as our review of the lessons of federal and provincial government have taught us. They amount to a distillation of the wisdom of the Westminster system.

- The engagement of the first minister is a necessary part of the success of government's policy initiatives.
- Cabinet functions best when it functions collectively, with neither the first minister nor departmental visions dominating, but, rather, a collective vision, collectively generated.
- The job of cabinets and central agencies is to maintain the integrity of the decision-making process, namely, to facilitate the disinterested, open-minded consideration of available public policy options.
- Policy coherence entails both horizontal coordination (not being constricted by departmental boundaries) and vertical coordination (involving provincial and regional officials in the policy-making process).
- The departments are normally the repository of policy and implementation expertise and should be allowed leeway by central agencies, but pragmatically, in proportion to their relative expertise.

The above are not radical propositions, but are reiterations of decades of experience of cabinet–parliamentary systems.

In another sense they are a wakeup call to those promoting prime-ministerial government. To the extent that it is a problem—and the jury is still out on that one—these principles offer a rebuke to the centralization that such government implies. Prime-ministerial government violates the principles of procedural fairness and threatens to undermine the legitimacy of the political system. This is the message of a US domestic policy council chief of staff, as well as research by Tyler: "Individuals who felt that they played a role in the decision-making process were more accepting of the outcome, regardless of its nature . . . Those who felt that the process was biased, or that their views were not being considered by those responsible for policy development, were more apt to exit from the formal decision-making process and evade its decisions." (Pierson, 2000: 9; Tyler, 1990: 163.)

In a sense, we have come full circle in the examination of the central executive. Seeking new lessons in governance from experimenting in the machinery of government, governments and their attentive publics have discovered the canons of cabinet government that were there all along. The job of first ministers is to lead; the job of cabinets is to deliberate; and the job of officials is to help both to do their jobs. It is not the Grail, but it is advice that will have do until we find it.

Acknowledgement

Information for a small portion of this chapter came from Dunn (1996). Permission to use this was received from the former Broadview Press and is gratefully acknowledged.

Appendix A   The Unaided, Institutionalized, and Prime Minister–Centred Cabinets

Unaided or Departmental Cabinet	Institutionalized Cabinet	Court Government (Prime Minister–Centred Cabinet)
PRIME MINISTER AND CABINET		
Personnel choice by first minister	First minister now has two jobs in the institutionalized cabinet (IC): personnel choice plus design of the machinery of government	Same two jobs as in the IC; but PM now has policy-making role in any dossier as well
Dominant first minister		Dominant first minister who holds court
Restricted collegiality		Cabinet is a discussion forum and not a decision forum
Simple cabinet structure	Greater collegiality Complex cabinet structure	Cabinet structure streamlined, less complex
		It is not clear what types of decisions require collective cabinet deliberation; PM and his "courtiers," (carefully selected ministers, senior civil servants) decide, picking and choosing their issues at will.

CENTRAL AGENCIES

Central departments Few cabinet staff Little cabinet-level analysis	Central agencies as well as central departments More cabinet staff Extensive cabinet-level analysis	Same central bodies; large numbers of staff in Prime Minister's Office and central agencies develop ideas and provide extensive central agency analysis for PM's pet projects and purposes; proposals they are not interested in are subject to extensive, slow, porous, and consultative (often intergovernmental) decision-making process. The civil service, beset with conflicting demands, has "lost its way."

BUDGETING AND PLANNING

Budgeting centralized; major role played by first minister Budgeting aim: mostly control Budgeting means: traditional (annual budget cycle) Planning: optional, but either project-oriented or indicative Short-term coordination by first minister or finance minister	Budgeting collegial Budgeting aim: broader than control Budgeting means: both traditional and political/off-budget controls Planning: still optional, but where practised is collective, comprehensive Planning–budgeting nexus (balance, complementarity of the two functions)	Not much mention is made by Savoie of internal governmental budget decision making, but there are hints that practices revealed in the 1999 book still hold: Budgeting centralized under the PM and finance minister; most priorities made by PM and court, with cabinet deciding matters of lesser importance; planning not a noticeable feature. There is little attention to the traditional challenge function of the bureaucracy and presentations of options is no longer standard practice. No mention of the 1999 book's guardian/spender dichotomy and its two sets of rules: one for guardians (no collective constraints) and one for spenders (collective constraints).

DECISION-MAKING MODES

Hierarchical channels of policy advice, from senior officials to the cabinet with no competing sources Decentralized decision-making: departmental autonomy favoured over power of the central executive	Alternative channels of policy advice for cabinet and committees Centralized decision-making: power of the central executive favoured over departmental autonomy	Nothing happens in Canadian (and UK) governments without a strong central push. Centralized decision-making means the PM's power is favoured over that by full cabinet, line ministers, and the federal bureaucracy. Horizontal government makes it difficult for ministers to influence policy. Policy advice and briefing are primarily for the PM and the PM's delegates, media play an inordinately influential role. The centre announces new policies and initiatives, instead of line ministers, because the latter lack profile and the policies would go unnoticed. The majority of cabinet documents are now prepared by consultants rather than by the bureaucracy.

Source: Abstracted and modified from Dunn (1995, 1998) and Savoie (1999, 2008).

Important Terms and Concepts

cabinet committees	departmentalized (unaided)	institutionalized cabinet
cabinet formation	cabinet	prime minister–centred cabinet
central agencies	dignified executive	traditional cabinet
central executive	efficient executive	
collective responsibility	individual ministerial responsibility	

Study Questions

1. What is the difference between the "dignified executive" and the "efficient executive"?
2. Are federal and provincial cabinets more alike than they are different?
3. Considering the various models of cabinet development, which one best describes the current state of the federal central executive? What proof can you offer?
4. Review some guidelines that have been offered for successful cabinet operations, and assess if they are realistic or not.
5. "Cabinet design is an exercise in balance." Discuss.

Notes

1 Between 1867 and 1984, 76 people entered the federal cabinet who were neither MPs nor senators (Heard, 1991: 49) The most recent examples have been Michel Fortier, appointed Minister of Public Works and Government Services in February of 2006; Brian Tobin, Minister of Industry in October 2000; Stéphane Dion, Minister of Intergovernmental Affairs, January 1996; and Pierre Pettigrew, Minister for International Co-operation, January 1996. A few weeks after entering the cabinet, Fortier was made a temporary appointment to the Senate on the condition that he step down and run in the next general election. Tobin was subsequently elected in the general election of 2000 and the latter two in March 1996 by-elections. For a complete list of outsiders entering the federal cabinet, see the parliamentary information site (PARLINFO) found at http://www2.parl.gc.ca/parlinfo/Compilations/FederalGovernment/OutOfParliamentMinisters.aspx?Language=E

2 Newfoundland, British Columbia, and Quebec can be used to demonstrate provincial cases. Joseph R. Smallwood chose the then unelected Clyde Wells, John Crosbie, and Alex T. Hickman for his cabinet in 1966 and all three successfully won seats in the general election of September of that year. In 1971 the mayors of St John's and Corner Brook, William Adams and Noel Murphy, were elevated to cabinet directly from the mayoralty. Ed Roberts entered the Wells cabinet in February 1992 and was subsequently elected in a by-election in June of that year. Since 1882 there have been 15 unelected people appointed to BC cabinets. An "outsider" had not been appointed since 1952 when Bill Vander Zalm was appointed Premier and Finance Minister in August 1986. He went on to win seat in a general election two months later. In October 2000 Premier Ujjal Dosanjh appointed Grand Chief Edward John, a former Carrier-Sekani Tribal Council chief, to his cabinet (Canadian Press newswire, 2000). The list of people made cabinet ministers before being elected in Quebec is long: Premier Jean Lesage chose Eric Kierans for Labour Minister; Jean-Jacques Bertrand picked Jean-Guy Cardinal as Education Minister; Robert Bourassa selected Claude Castonguay

to Health and Jean Cournoyer to Labour; and René Lévesque made Francine Lalonde the Status of Women Minister. Pierre-Marc Johnson chose four civilians (Louise Beaudoin, Jean-Guy Parent, Lise Denis, and Rolande Cloutier) for his cabinet in 1985 (Lachapelle et al., 1993: 240).

3 Given the availability of qualified female government caucus members, the premiers of the 1990s began to make efforts to achieve increased gender balance in the cabinet. The situation was about the same at the federal and provincial levels in the year 2000, as indicated in Table 6.2. By 2008, there had been marginal improvement in the proportional representation of women in five provincial cabinets; two provinces had maintained respectable percentages (Manitoba and Newfoundland and Labrador) and three had actually slipped (British Columbia, Saskatchewan, and New Brunswick).

4 A minority of contributors to the Bernier et al. book *Executive Styles in Canada*, (2005) adopt what might be called the "Savoie perspective." The evidence on the other side is mixed. Norman Ruff says that BC's Liberal government under Gordon Campbell has a different administrative style than its Premier's Office-dominated predecessors. "If there is a newly emergent BC administrative style," he says, "it is that of a 'corporate collegiality' facilitated by the shared political mandate which must be referenced by every cabinet member and that in turn informs the sweeping Core Services Review and the rolling three year Strategic Plans begun in 2002." He also notes that there has been a growth of somewhat fragmented central departments and central agencies. Despite this collegial aspect, Ruff saw a counter tendency: "Beneath its organizational jigsaw, British Columbia had many of the characteristics of what Dunn has described as a post-institutionalized cabinet with an increase in the already considerable concentration of power within the Office of Premier at the expense of Cabinet." In a similar vein, Keith Brownsey maintains that the institutional cabinet once dominated in Alberta, but its reign was restricted to the eras of Peter Lougheed (1971–85) and Don Getty (1985–92).

References

Abma, Derek. 2016. "Trudeau's cabinet style: he gives his ministers 'as much rope,' but pulls it back if they do something wrong." *Hill Times*, 10 August 2016.

Aucoin, Peter. 1986. "Organizational Change in the Machinery of Canadian Government: From Rational Management to Brokerage to Brokerage Politics." *Canadian Journal of Political Science* 19, 1, pp. 3–27.

———. 1994. "Prime Minister and Cabinet." *Canadian Politics*, 2nd edn, edited by James P. Bickerton and Alain-G. Gagnon. Peterborough, Ont.: Broadview Press, pp. 267–87.

———. 1995. "The Prime Minister and Cabinet." *Introductory Readings in Canadian Government and Politics*, edited by Robert M. Krause and R. H. Wagenberg. Toronto: Copp Clark, pp. 169–92.

——— and Herman Bakvis. 1988. *The Centralization-Decentralization Conundrum: Organization and Management in the Canadian Government*. Halifax: Institute for Research on Public Policy.

——— and ———. 1993. "Consolidating Cabinet Portfolios: Australian Lessons for Canada." *Canadian Public Administration* 36, 3, pp. 392–420.

Bagehot, Walter. 1867. *The English Constitution*. 1963 Edition. London: Fontana.

Barber, M. 2008. *Instruction to Deliver: Fighting to Transform Britain's Public Services*. London: Methuen.

Barber, M. 2015. *How to Run a Government So That Citizens Benefit and Taxpayers Don't Go Crazy*. London: Allen Lane.

Bernier, Luc. 2005. "Who Governs in Quebec? Revolving Premiers and Reforms." Bernier, Brownsey, and Howlett. Toronto: University of Toronto Press, pp. 152–3.

Bernier, Luc, Keith Brownsey, and Michael Howlett. 2005. *Executive Styles in Canada: Cabinet Structures and Leadership Practices in Canadian Government*. Toronto: University of Toronto Press.

Blakeney, Allan, and Sandford Borins. 1992. *Political Management in Canada*. Toronto: McGraw-Hill Ryerson.

Blackley, Shelby. 2016. "A balanced cabinet: what has gender parity for the Ontario cabinet looked like in the past?" *Globe and Mail*, 9 June 2016. http://www.theglobeandmail.com/news/national/gender-parity-in-ontario-cabinet/article30353122/

Campbell, Colin, and George J. Szablowski. 1979. *The Superbureaucrats: Structure and Behaviour in Central Agencies*. Toronto: Macmillan.

Canada. 1990. *Public Service 2000: The Renewal of the Public Service of Canada*. Ottawa: Government of Canada.

Canada. 2008. Parliament of Canada Information site. *Ministers named from outside Parliament*. Retrieved at http://www2.parl.gc.ca/parlinfo/Compilations/FederalGovernment/OutOfParliamentMinisters.aspx?Language=E

Canada. Parliament of Canada. Library of Parliament. 2016. Cabinet Committees, 1979 to date. http://www.lop.parl.gc.ca/ParlInfo/Compilations/FederalGovernment/ComiteeCabinet.aspx?Section=&Parliament=1924d334-6bd0-4cb3-8793-cee640025ff6&Current=False&Name=&Gender=&CommitteeRole=&CommitteeName=&Province=&Riding=

Canada. Prime Minister's Office. 2016. "The Prime Minister of Canada announces changes to structure and mandate of Cabinet committees." http://pm.gc.ca/eng/news/2016/08/22/prime-minister-canada-announces-changes-structure-and-mandate-cabinet-committees

Canada. Privy Council Office. 2007. *Accountable Government: A Guide for Ministers and Secretaries of State*. http://pm.gc.ca/grfx/docs/guidemin_e.pdf

Canada, Privy Council Office, 2015. Open and Accountable Government. http://pm.gc.ca/sites/pm/files/docs/OAG_2015_English.pdf

Canadian Press Newswire. 2000. "Chief Edward John brings Aboriginal experience to BC Cabinet." 1 Nov. 2000.

Chrétien, Jean. 1994. *Straight from the Heart*. Toronto: Key Porter Books.

Crossman, Richard Howard Stafford. 1975–7. *The Diaries of a Cabinet Minister*. Three volumes (*v1. Minister of Housing, 1964–66; v2. Lord President of the Council and Leader of the House of Commons, 1966–68; v3. Secretary of State for Social Services, 1968–70*). Cape.

D'Ombrain, Nicholas. 2004. "Cabinet Secrecy." *Canadian Public Administration* 47, 3, pp. 332–59.

Dunn, Christopher. 1995. *The Institutionalized Cabinet: Governing the Western Provinces*. Montreal and Kingston: McGill-Queen's University Press.

———. 1996. "Premiers and Cabinets." *Provinces: Canadian Provincial Politics*, edited by Dunn. Peterborough, ON: Broadview Press, pp. 165–204.

———. 1998. 'The Utility of the Institutionalized Cabinet', in Paul Barker and Mark Charlton, eds, *Crosscurrents: Contemporary Political Problems*. Toronto: ITP Nelson, pp. 244–63.

———. 2005. "The Persistence of the Institutionalized Cabinet: The Central Executive in Newfoundland and Labrador." *Executive Styles in Canada: Cabinet Structures and Leadership Practices in Canadian Government*, edited by Luc Bernier et al., Toronto: University of Toronto Press.

———. 2006. "Premiers and Cabinets." *Provinces: Canadian Provincial Politics*, 2nd ed. Edited by Dunn, Peterborough, ON: Broadview Press, pp. 215–54.

———. 2016. "Premiers and Cabinets." *Provinces: Canadian Provincial Politics*, 3rd ed. Edited by Dunn, Peterborough, ON: Broadview Press, 315–62.

Dupré, J. Stefan. 1985. "Reflections on the Workability of Executive Federalism." *Intergovernmental Relations*, vol. 63 of the Research Studies for the Royal Commission on the Economic Union and Development Prospects for Canada. Edited by Richard Simeon, Toronto: University of Toronto Press, pp. 1–32.

Dyck, Rand. 1996. *Canadian Politics: Critical Approaches*, 2nd ed. Toronto: Nelson Canada.

Glenn, Ted. 2001. "Politics, Leadership, and Experience in Designing Ontario's Cabinet." *Canadian Public Administration* 44, 2: 188–203.

Glenn, Ted. 2005. "Politics, Personality and History in Ontario's Administrative Style." *Executive Styles in Canada: Cabinet Structures and Leadership Practices in Canadian Government* edited by Luc Bernier et al. Toronto: University of Toronto Press, 155–70.

Goldenberg, Eddie. 2006. *The Way it Works: Inside Ottawa.* Toronto: McClelland and Stewart.

Good, David A. 2007. *The Politics of Public Money: Spenders, Guardians, Priority Setters, and Financial Watchdogs in the Canadian Government.* Toronto: University of Toronto Press.

Heard, Andrew. 1991. *Canadian Constitutional Conventions: The Marriage of Law and Politics.* Toronto: Oxford University Press.

Heeney, Arnold. 1972. *The Things That Are Caesar's: Memoirs of a Canadian Public Servant.* Toronto: University of Toronto Press.

Kennedy, Mark. 2015. "Trudeau says he would 'end' tight PMO control begun by his father." *Ottawa Citizen.* 8 September 2015.

Lachapelle, Guy, Gérald Bernier, Daniel Salée, and Luc Bernier. 1993. *The Quebec Democracy: Structures, Processes and Policies.* Toronto: McGraw-Hill Ryerson.

Lewis, J. P. 2013. "Elite Attitudes on the Centralization of Power in Canadian Political Executives: A Survey of Former Federal and Provincial Cabinet Ministers, 2000–2010," *Canadian Journal of Political Science,* 46, 3, pp. 799–816.

Loreto, Richard, and Graham White. 1990. "The Premier and the Cabinet." *The Politics and Government of Ontario* edited by Graham White, Toronto: Nelson Canada.

Loveland, Ian. 2006. *Constitutional Law, Administrative Law, and Human Rights.* Oxford: Oxford University Press.

Mallory, J. R. 1984. *The Structure of Canadian Government,* rev. edn. Toronto: Gage Publishing.

Marland, Alex. 2016. *Brand Command: Canadian Politics and Democracy in the Age of Message Control.* Vancouver: University of British Columbia Press.

Matheson, W. A. 1976. *The Prime Minister and the Cabinet.* Toronto: Methuen.

May, K. 2016. "Delivering the Goods: Why Matthew Mendelsohn Is Trudeau's Go-To Guy,." *Ottawa Citizen.* 2016 January 15. http://ottawacitizen.com/news/politics/delivering-the-goods-why-matthew-mendelsohn-is-trudeaus-go-to-guy.

Mazereeuw, Peter. 2016. "New cabinet committee signals shift in litigation strategy: Cotler." *Hill Times,* 31 August 2016. https://www.hilltimes.com/2016/08/31/new-cabinet-committee-signals-shift-in-litigation-strategy-cotler/78774

McIlroy, Anne. 2000. "Rock's grand plan was news to the PM: Health Minister's home-care program shared with the media before the PMO staff read it." *Globe and Mail,* 4 Mar. 2000, p. A3.

McHardie, Danielle. 2016. "Liberals must offer clear vision without regional development ministers—Prime Minister Justin Trudeau did not name ministers for Canada's 6 regional economic development agencies." *CBC News,* 6 Nov.2016. http://www.cbc.ca/news/canada/new-brunswick/regional-economic-development-agencies-future-1.3306222

Moore, Karl. 2015. "One-on-One Interview with Justin Trudeau: Canada's New Prime Minister." *Forbes.* 2015 November 4.

Northwest Territories. 2014. Executive Council Submissions Handbook. http://www.executive.gov.nt.ca/wp-content/uploads/Executive-Council-Submissions-Handbook-Dec-2015.pdf

Ontario, Walkerton Commission of Inquiry. 2002. *Report: Part One: The Events of May 2000 and Related Issues.* Toronto: Queen's Printer, pp. 486-87.

Organisation for Economic Co-operation and Development (OECD). 1996. *Building Policy Coherence: Tools and Tensions.* Public Management Occasional Papers No. 12. Paris: OECD Publications Service.

Osbaldeston, Gordon. 1989. *Keeping Deputy Ministers Accountable.* Toronto: McGraw-Hill Ryerson.

———. 1992. *Organizing to Govern.* Toronto: McGraw-Hill Ryerson.

Pal, Leslie. 2004. "Political Carpentry: The New Federal Cabinet and an 'Integrative Prime Ministership.'" *Public Management.*

Payton, Laura. 2016. "PCO gets $99 million boost to spending capacity." *IPolitics.* 22 March 2016. http://ipolitics.ca/2016/03/22/pco-gets-99m-boost-to-bottom-line/

Privy Council Office. 1998. *Decision-Making Processes and Central Agencies in Canada: Federal, Provincial and Territorial Practices.* Ottawa: Privy Council Office.

Rasmussen, Ken & Gregory P. Marchildon. 2005. "Saskatchewan's Executive Decision-Making Style: The Centrality of Planning." *Executive Styles in Canada,* edited by Howlett and Brownsey, Toronto: University of Toronto Press.

Richards, Steve. 2008. "Gordon Brown cannot stand alone in the storm - he needs his cabinet." *The Independent,* 29 April 2008.

Roberts, Alasdair. 1997. "Worrying about Misconduct: The Control Lobby and the PS 2000 Reforms." *Canadian Public Administration* 39, 4, pp. 489–523.

Robertson, Gordon. 1971. "The Changing Role of the Privy Council Office." *Canadian Public Administration* 14, pp. 487–508.

Royal Commission of Inquiry into Certain Activities of the RCMP (McDonald Commission). 1981. *Report.* Ottawa.

Royal Commission on Financial Management and Accountability (Lambert Commission). 1979. *Final Report*. Ottawa: Supply and Services Canada.

Royal Commission on Government Organization (Glassco Commission). 1962. *Report*. Ottawa: Queen's Printer.

Savoie, Donald. 1999. *Governing from the Centre: The Concentration of Power in Canadian Politics*. Toronto: University of Toronto Press.

Savoie, Donald. 2008. *Court Government and the Collapse of Accountability in Canada and the United Kingdom*. Toronto: University of Toronto Press.

Schacter, Mark, with Phillip Haid. 1999. *Cabinet Decision-making in Canada: Lessons and Practices*. Ottawa: Institute on Governance.

Stewart, Edward E. 1989. *Cabinet Government in Ontario: A View from Inside*. Halifax: Institute for Research on Public Policy.

Trudeau, P. E. 1968. *Federalism and the French Canadians*. Toronto: Macmillan.

Tyler, Tom. 1990. *Why People Obey the Law*. New Haven, CT: Yale University Press.

Van Dusen, Lisa. 2015. "'Government by cabinet is back': Trudeau, ministers sworn in at Rideau Hall." *IPolitics*, 4 Nov. 2015. http://ipolitics.ca/2015/11/04/crowds-gather-to-watch-justin-trudeau-and-cabinet-sworn-in-at-rideau-hall/

White, Graham. 2001. *Cabinets and First Ministers*. Vancouver: University of British Columbia Press.

Young, Walter D., and J. Terence Morley. 1983. "The Premier and the Cabinet." *The Reins of Power: Governing British Columbia*. edited by Morley et al., Vancouver: Douglas & McIntyre, pp. 45–81.

7

Parliament and the Public Service

Paul G. Thomas

Chapter Overview

This chapter provides a comprehensive look at Parliament and the Canadian public service(s) and considers the often problematical relationships between them. Public service reform and parliamentary accountability have not always reinforced each other. This been in evidence in three recent sets of reforms: the "steering not rowing" slogan, the adoption of special operating agencies (SOAs), and third, the various related elements of the recent orientation towards the private sector, including privatization, contracting out of service delivery, and public–private partnerships. Parliament moreover has given very little attention to debates or issues regarding public-sector reform. Annual reports of the head of the public service and the chair of the Public Service Commission, and even reports of prestigious Royal Commissions, engender little interest in parliamentary circles. This does not bode well for parliamentary supervision of the public bureaucracy. Reversing this situation is paramount for reformers.

Chapter Objectives

By the end of this chapter, students will be able to do the following:

- Distinguish between Parliament and provincial legislatures and their relations to their respective public services.
- Describe the constitutional context for Parliament and the public service.
- Describe the constitutional role of the public service.
- List and explain Parliament's functions in the political system.
- List and discuss the complexities inherent in respect to Parliament's roles in relation to the public service.

Introduction

Parliament's relationship to the public service is not a widely examined aspect of Canada's political system. In general, relations between **Parliament** and the **public service** are informal, indirect, changeable, and often characterized by mutual wariness. The nature of the relationship derives from three main sources: a set of constitutional principles that are largely unwritten; a limited number of statutory provisions; and the dynamic context of the wider political system, particularly the nature of the issues before government and the state of party competition during a particular time period.

With limited recognition for the role of the public service in constitutional and statutory law, its relations with Parliament have been mainly based on the changing interpretation of a series of unwritten constitutional conventions. These conventions were derived from the parliamentary experience of the United Kingdom and were adopted in Canada in the latter part of the nineteenth century when the activities of government were limited and the public service was a small, largely unprofessional entity. As the public sector expanded and became more complicated during the twentieth century, Parliament found it difficult to cope with the rise of a sprawling administrative apparatus wielding growing power. There were from time to time expressions of concern about potential conflicts between **bureaucracy** and democracy, but for many decades Parliament changed little in terms of its structures and procedures to cope with the increased volume and complexity of public policy and public administration.

The contemporary challenge of directing and controlling the bureaucracy is partially conveyed by some basic descriptions of its size and costs. (See Thomas, 2014 for a more extensive analysis). In 2016, the national public bureaucracy comprised 282 departments, agencies, and other organizations, employing over 493,000 people. Total spending by the government of Canada in 2015 was nearly $300 billion. The public service administered 800 Acts passed by Parliament, as well as over 2600 regulations adopted to implement those Acts. Every year another 200–300 regulatory proposals to create new rules to constrain behaviour in the private and the public sector are reviewed inside of government (Wernick, 2016).

This chapter examines the two issues of how public bureaucracies can be held accountable through the parliamentary process, and how this task has been complicated by political change and reforms to how the public service is structured and operates. The discussion proceeds as follows. First, the historical and constitutional context in which Parliament developed its relations with the bureaucracy is discussed. Second, a number of interrelated functions of Parliament are identified. The review of existing policies and the surveillance of administrative performance are tasks that compete with other, more politically rewarding activities. Third, five roles played by Parliament in relation to the public service are identified. Fourth, the aims and impediments to the conduct of a more thorough parliamentary review of the activities of the public service are discussed. Finally, the chapter speculates on Parliament's future relations with the public service in light of recent trends and likely future developments.

The chapter focuses on the Parliament of Canada. In popular usage, Parliament refers to the 338 members of the House of Commons. Under the Fair Representation Act, 30 additional MPs were added to the Commons membership after the October 2015 election. There are two other parts to Parliament: the 105 members of the Senate and the Governor General as the representative of the Crown. In terms of legislative authority, the Senate is almost coequal to the House of Commons in the sense that all bills must be approved by the upper chamber. However, the fact that senators are appointed (rather than elected) by the Governor General on the recommendation of the prime minister and serve until the age of 75 means that the Senate is often seen to lack democratic legitimacy. Also, as appointees, senators from the governing party were seen to be loyal to the prime minister and seldom questioned government policies. Critics insisted that this arrangement seriously compromised the original role of the Senate as a voice for regional concerns and as a source of independent judgment of government actions and inactions. To enhance the independence, effectiveness, and legitimacy of the Senate, the Liberal government of Prime Minister Justin Trudeau fulfilled a 2015 election promise by creating a new appointment procedure in which members of the public could apply and/or be nominated for a Senate appointment and a panel of distinguished citizens would recommend names to the prime minister who in turn would recommend individuals to the Governor General. The first of several rounds of appointments under the new procedure was made early in 2016. There have been few, if any, appointments of party campaign chairs and fundraisers, which occurred under the old procedure. Instead appointees have been highly qualified and accomplished individuals, without Liberal Party backgrounds, although the critics note most of the new appointees bring a small-l liberal mindset to the Senate. In the near future a majority of the Senate members will sit as independents and, as discussed later, this could lead to more scrutiny of government performance.

Any discussion of Parliament as if it were a unified institution is misleading. Several divisions exist within Parliament. The most important dividing lines are between political parties. All important aspects of Parliament's organization and procedures are dominated by the fact of competition among disciplined political parties. Under the fused cabinet–parliamentary model, the cabinet is a part of Parliament. It represents the leadership of the governing party, which usually holds a majority of the seats in the Commons. Most of the initiative in terms of bills, spending proposals, and other business comes from the government and it seeks to exert tight control over the agenda and proceedings of Parliament. Opposition parties are expected to debate government proposals and to expose flaws in the government's performance. Most of the ideas, energy, and intensity of parliamentary life come from the adversarial process of parties competing for public support. Nearly all issues tend to be viewed and acted upon on the basis of partisanship, not upon an objective or neutral search for the truth.

While the clash between the government and the opposition represents the main division within Parliament, there are also disagreements within parties on matters of substance and process. Such disagreements are expressed mainly in the privacy of party caucuses, which meet on a weekly basis when Parliament is in session. Intra-party divisions can be along ideological, policy, and regional lines, as well as between the parliamentary leadership of each party and its backbench followers. In June 2015 Parliament passed the Reform Act that among other things gave MPs in a party caucus the power to trigger a leadership review and allowed for more free votes without party discipline. (See Bryden, 2016.)

In summary, notwithstanding constitutional rhetoric to the contrary, Parliament seldom acts on a collective basis, all members of Parliament are not equal, and not all of them wish to see the institution

strengthened, if this means a loss of cabinet control or a reduction of the prominence of the party leadership in its proceedings. How Parliament approaches its dealings with the bureaucracy and its success in providing oversight of bureaucratic performance are significantly affected by these inter- and intra-party dynamics.

Provincial governments operate on the same principles of cabinet–parliamentary government as the Government of Canada and these principles play a major part in shaping the role of provincial bureaucracies. However, it would be wrong to generalize from the national level to the provincial level about relations between legislatures and public services. Each province represents a distinctive history, set of political traditions and cultures, patterns of party competition, and contemporary political dynamics. Most provincial political systems are much smaller than the national political system, including the size of the bureaucracies involved. Other important differences between the national and the provincial political systems include: some provinces have experienced long periods of one-party rule; cabinets often represent a more domineering presence in **provincial legislatures**; control over nearly all aspects of legislative life is considered a prize for winning power; procedural, organizational, and staff resources to ordinary legislators tend to be limited; legislative sessions are typically shorter; committee systems are less extensive and active in the smaller provincial legislatures; there are no upper houses at the provincial level; and, in terms of the themes of this chapter, there is more political control by the cabinet at the provincial level over the public service (White, 2006). We cannot conclude from these characteristics that provincial legislatures never exert control or influence on governments and public services. Generally, however, provincial legislatures face even greater political and procedural obstacles than does the House of Commons in holding ministers and public servants accountable on an ongoing basis. The remainder of the chapter focuses on the relations between Parliament and the public service at the national level.

The Constitutional Context

The level of bureaucratic accountability achieved within any political system is a function of numerous factors. **Accountability** refers to an obligation to explain and to justify how an individual or an institution discharges its responsibilities, the origins of which may be constitutional, political, hierarchical, or contractual (Thomas, 2008). There is not the space here to analyze the different types and mechanisms of accountability that have emerged within the Canadian political system. Suffice it to say that accountability has become a dynamic, multifaceted process and that public servants, in a given set of circumstances, may face a number of competing accountability requirements.

The starting point for an understanding of accountability is the Constitution. The Canadian Constitution consists of both legal rules and political conventions (Heard, 1991). Both sets of provisions are meant to be binding upon politicians and public servants. Constitutions promote the rule of law by setting forth the parameters of public power, describing the relationships that ought to exist among the various institutions of government, and defining the relationships between individuals and the state. By doing this, constitutions are meant to protect and to promote the rule of law, which means, in simple terms, that no one, no matter how important or powerful, is above the law, and this includes the government and the bureaucracy.

Important parts of the Canadian Constitution consist of unwritten conventions that have emerged from longstanding political practices. These constitutional conventions vary in the extent to which they are seen as morally binding on ministers, parliamentarians, public servants, and others in public life. Although recognized by the courts, conventions must be enforced through political rather than legal processes. Given the unwritten and non-legal nature of conventions and the fact that we live in a cynical age, many Canadians believe that politicians and public servants cannot be trusted to accept responsibility for breaches of the written and unwritten rules of government.

Under Canadian constitutional arrangements public servants are not directly and personally accountable to Parliament. Instead, the preservation of the rule of law and the promotion of bureaucratic accountability are sought through the principles of **collective responsibility** and individual **ministerial responsibility**. These principles represent a statement of the relationships that ought to exist between cabinets and parliaments, between cabinet ministers and the public service, between the public service and parliaments, and between all office-holders and the citizens they serve. Collective and individual ministerial responsibility is based mainly on political conventions rather than on statutory provisions.

Centralization of power and secrecy are inherent in the cabinet–parliamentary system. Collective ministerial responsibility concentrates authority for policy formulation and for the provision of leadership to the public service in the hands of the prime minister and the cabinet. The cabinet–parliamentary system then seeks to hold this small group of partisan politicians accountable to the elected representatives of the public on a continuing basis through a number of mechanisms, most notably through the so-called confidence rule. This rule requires that at all times a government must maintain the support of the majority of MPs in the House of Commons or it can be forced to resign and/or to request dissolution of Parliament leading to a general election. In the case of straight votes of no confidence presented by the opposition parties in response to the Throne Speech (outlining the government's legislative program), the Budget Speech (which presents its taxing and spending decisions), and certain opposition supply motions (in which government policy as reflected in spending is criticized), there is no question that the government must resign. Apart from such explicit votes of no confidence, uncertainty and controversy surround the defeat of particular bills or items of spending. The consensus among authorities is that governments are left to decide the seriousness of such political setbacks and resignations seldom occur. In fact, with a majority government and party discipline, defeats of any kind are rare.

In short, in practice today the prime minister and cabinet largely control Parliament, the opposite of what the pure theory of cabinet–parliamentary government implies. However, governments are still obliged to explain and to defend their actions and inactions before the public's elected representatives through events like the daily Question Period. The constitutional principle of collective ministerial responsibility has been weakened by the rise of disciplined parties and by increased prime ministerial power. While collective ministerial responsibility represents a less-than-perfect accountability system, there is still value in focusing responsibility on a readily identifiable group of political office-holders, in combination with the requirement that they "boast and confess" in public on a regular basis.

Individual cabinet ministers are made legally responsible for the departments they lead under the statutes passed by Parliament that create those departments (see Chapter 2). This legal arrangement provides a basis for holding ministers politically answerable before Parliament for the performance of those departments. Orthodox constitutional theory insists that all actions of public servants within a department are done in the name of the minister and that she or he can be forced to resign from cabinet for serious policy mistakes or major administrative errors. There has been a gradual retreat from this strict theory of individual ministerial responsibility as a result of a number of trends and developments:

- The policies that ministers and their departments carry out often reflect the wishes of the prime minister and the cabinet, and if these policies become controversial the conventions of cabinet solidarity and partisan competition lead the governing party to protect the minister under attack.
- Departments have become large and complicated undertakings in which ministers are involved with only a small percentage of the decisions made daily in their name.
- In addition to their departments most ministers answer to Parliament for the activities of several semi-independent, non-departmental bodies, such as Crown corporations and regulatory agencies, which make up part of the minister's portfolio.

The result of these trends is that individual ministers seldom resign in the face of parliamentary criticism of the policies or administrative actions of their departments. From these facts, critics conclude that individual ministerial responsibility has become a myth and no longer provides a reliable basis for holding ministers (directly) and public servants (indirectly) accountable for their joint efforts in policy formulation and implementation.

Defenders of the existing practices insist that the flexibility of the convention of ministerial responsibility has enabled Parliament to assign it a different meaning under changing circumstances. They insist that individual ministerial responsibility never operated the way that the pure theory implied. Sharon Sutherland (1991a) examined the historical record

and could find only two examples of ministers leaving office for reasons of maladministration in their departments. Most ministers resigned for career changes, policy problems, or personal transgressions. In other words, individual ministerial responsibility has not died—it never lived, at least not in the way that orthodox theory implied. Today, it is seen as no longer realistic to assign absolute responsibility to ministers for all administrative actions and to insist that they resign when mistakes, or simply unforeseen and unwanted developments, take place. Loss of political reputation, not loss of office, has become the real sanction behind ministerial responsibility. In the tough league of the House of Commons, the risk of damaging one's career causes most ministers to keep in touch with the activities of their departments and the other components of their ministerial portfolios.

Defenders of the status quo insist that ministers continue to be answerable before Parliament. They are expected to take corrective actions when problems within their departments are identified, they can still be forced to resign for purely personal transgressions, and it is not unheard of for prime ministers to remove ministers from cabinet who have become a liability to the government. Clearly there is life left in the doctrines of collective and individual ministerial responsibility, but the widespread public perception today is that the Canadian political system lacks real accountability because neither ministers nor public servants appear to pay a serious price when mistakes occur. Shortly after taking office in November 2015 the Liberal Government of Prime Minister Trudeau issued a document titled *Open and Transparent Government* that, among other reforms, promised to strengthen the understandings and practices of both collective and individual ministerial responsibility to make government more accountable to Parliament and the public.

The Constitutional Role of the Public Service

This brings us to the constitutional conventions respecting the role of the public service within the cabinet–parliamentary system. Although developed separately, the conventions respecting the public service reinforce the principles of ministerial responsibility. These conventions stress the value of an anonymous, neutral, professional, and relatively permanent public service appointed and operated on the basis of merit and competence so that it can provide intelligent and objective policy advice to ministers and deliver programs in an efficient and impartial manner. In traditional constitutional terms the public service is said to serve the Crown, which in practical terms is taken to mean the government of the day. Recently, it has been argued that the public service should be recognized in public law as a separate entity with a measure of independence from the government of the day and an obligation to defend the public interest when it is threatened by short-term, opportunistic political decision-making or undue political interference in the administrative process that might impair the rule of law (Heintzman, 2014; Sossin, 2005). This controversial reform notion is discussed near the conclusion of the chapter.

Historically, public servants have shunned publicity and practised a discreet reticence in sharing their knowledge with those outside of government. There is an implicit bargain between public servants and the ministers they serve. In return for the best policy advice the public service can provide and the professional implementation of programs, ministers are expected to avoid blaming in public individual public servants for mistakes. Such matters are to be dealt with privately within the department. Unfortunately, the internal and often confidential nature of such disciplinary action creates the false impression for parliamentarians, the media, and the public that there are no negative consequences for public servants when errors are made or abuses of authority occur.

Just as wider trends within the political system have altered the practices of ministerial responsibility, a number of developments are modifying the conventions of an anonymous, neutral, and permanent public service:

- the difficulty of providing objective policy advice during a period of ideological disagreement over the future role of government;
- changing concepts of political and bureaucratic representation reflected in programs to ensure the public service is more representative of the various publics it serves and is more open and responsive to outside influences through various consultative mechanisms;
- greater fragmentation of the public sector through the creation of new-style organizations (such as special operating agencies) and the

growing reliance on the private sector (through contracting out and public–private partnerships) to deliver public programs;
- increased parliamentary surveillance of the public service through the estimates process, performance reporting, and wider auditing processes;
- greater transparency respecting bureaucratic performance produced by access to information and the whistle-blower protection laws and the rise of a more adversarial media;
- a growing role for the courts under the Charter of Rights and Freedoms and other statutes to review the actions of administrative agencies to ensure that they act on the basis of public law, respect Charter principles, and dispense natural justice; and
- the promotion of a new entrepreneurial public service culture in which such values as leadership from public servants, innovation, risk-taking, rewards for results, revenue generation, and service contracts supplement or displace traditional values such as loyalty to the minister, reticence in sharing their views publicly, prudence, process compliance, and trusteeship of the public interest (Mitchell and Sutherland, 1999; Thomas, 2008).

Under these conditions, what it means to be a professional, responsible, and accountable public servant has become more complicated, problematic, and controversial (Kernaghan and Langford, 2014). Public servants must balance respect for the law, loyalty to the minister, compliance with internal rules and procedures, the enforcement and respect for contracts with outside parties, responsiveness to various groups, and adherence to their own internalized norms and standards of professionalism. Increasingly, how well this balancing act is performed by senior public servants has become the subject of publicity and controversy. From the 1980s onwards the application of the New Public Management (NPM) approach within the public service has added to the strain on both ministerial responsibility and the conventional understandings of the relationship between public servants and Parliament. Canada never embraced NPM as enthusiastically and fully as other countries like Australia and New Zealand and in recent decades new approaches to political and administrative management of the governing processes have been adopted.

Parliament's Functions in the Political System

The constitutional framework described above creates both opportunities and constraints for Parliament in dealing with the public service. Under the doctrine of ministerial responsibility, the organization of government is an executive prerogative. In fact, it has become a recognized right of the prime minister to determine the size of cabinet, the composition of ministerial portfolios, and the makeup of various departments in terms of combinations of organizational components and programs. Primary responsibility for leadership, direction, and control over departments resides with ministers, both collectively and individually. While Parliament cannot be ignored, it normally has limited influence on the organization and management of the public service. Concentration of authority in the hands of the prime minister and cabinet means that in theory the public service is subject to unified political direction and does not face competing demands. In contrast, the system of divided powers and checks and balances contained in the US Constitution means that the public service looks to both the president and Congress for mandates and money and consequently exhibits divided loyalties.

In analyzing Parliament's relations with the public service we must start, therefore, with the fundamental fact that Parliament is limited to scrutiny and influence, not direct control and real power. We must also recognize that scrutiny of the performance of the public service is only one of a number of functions performed by Parliament within the Canadian political system.

Table 7.1 sets forth a list of functions commonly attributed to legislatures. Simply put, **functions of the legislature** represent the contribution to and the effect upon the political system made by Parliament. A list of particular activities that contribute to the performance of these functions is also shown in Table 7.1. Some functions are formally recognized or explicit, whereas others are implicit or latent in the activities of Parliament. The functions overlap in practice—particular activities can contribute to more than one function and inclusion of any function or activity in the table suggests nothing about how successfully or unsuccessfully Parliament performs in this dimension.

The point of this discussion of legislative functions is that scrutiny of the performance of the public service has traditionally not been a high priority for

Table 7.1   Functions of Legislatures
I Policy-Making Functions
• making laws
• exercising control over taxing and spending
• scrutinizing the government and the bureaucracy
II Representational Functions
• recruiting and identifying leaders
• dealing with the bureaucracy on behalf of constituents
• educating the electorate by clarifying policy choices
III Systems/Maintenance Functions
• creating governments
• making the actions of governments legitimate
• mobilizing public support for the outcomes of the policy process
• managing conflict within the political system
• contributing to integration within the political system

Parliament. Overseeing the administration has not developed as a well-defined function. As a consequence Parliament's efforts have been sporadic, unsystematic, issue-oriented, short-term, ad hoc, shallow, and marginal in terms of impacts. There appear to be several reasons why Parliament has not taken its scrutiny function seriously. First, the Constitution may have represented an obstacle since the conventions of public service anonymity and confidentiality represent a protective shield against parliamentary inquiry. Second, governments were not likely to welcome Parliament poking and prying around in administrative matters, not least because most such scrutiny activity would be led by opposition MPs who could be counted on to seek maximum political advantage from any embarrassing discoveries. Not surprisingly, governments have been reluctant to provide Parliament with the procedural opportunities, the relevant information, and the staff resources needed to conduct more extensive and thorough investigations into how programs and departments are performing. There was also the fact that governments often ignored reports from parliamentary committees dealing with deficiencies in departments and programs, and this pattern produced a sense of futility among MPs.

Despite this, it would be naive to assume that, were there no constitutional inhibitions or restrictions imposed by governments, the majority of MPs would jump into the scrutiny function with both feet. As is explained below, the job of reviewing bureaucratic performance is usually difficult, often tedious, frustrating, low-profile, and therefore politically unrewarding work. Not surprisingly, only a minority of MPs exhibit a sustained interest in this function.

Numerous factors, both inside and outside of the political system, can potentially affect the effectiveness of Parliament in performing all of its functions. There is not the space here to discuss these factors in detail. Again at the risk of oversimplification, four broad sets of factors potentially affect the strength of Parliament within the Canadian political system:

- the constitutional arrangements, the incentives they create for parliamentarians to engage in certain kinds of behaviour, and the opportunities available within the political system to change these written and unwritten rules of the political game;
- the types of issues that arise within society and make it onto various institutional agendas of government in any given period and over time;
- the social backgrounds, personal qualities, motivations, and aspirations of parliamentarians;
- the internal organization, procedures, and resources of Parliament, particularly staff and informational resources.

The problem for would-be reformers who want to strengthen Parliament within the policy process is that only the fourth broad set of factors can be "easily" changed in a deliberate and planned fashion. Strengthening Parliament is difficult because it is dominated by competitive political parties who see procedural and organizational arrangements as tactical devices to be used in the *permanent* election campaign, which is the essence of much, though not all, Commons activity. Obviously, most governments do not wish to upset the existing political equilibrium in ways that might work to their disadvantage.

During the three decades from the 1960s to the 1990s, the House of Commons underwent more study and reform than during any previous time in its history, but the payoffs in terms of enhanced parliamentary influence were marginal at best. C.E.S. Franks (1987) and others have described the long list of reforms. Without examining them in detail, it can be argued plausibly that the reforms all amounted to tinkering; they did not change the basic power relationships of the cabinet–parliamentary system, which clearly gives the prime minister and the cabinet the upper hand. Many reformers naively assumed that they could increase Parliament's influence without detracting from the government's control. Dissatisfaction with political process, declining respect for all public officials (especially politicians and to a much lesser extent public servants), and concern about the undue concentration of power within government led, during the 1990s, to a shift in focus away from parliamentary reform in favour of democratic reform involving more public input into policy-making and more direct accountability of public servants to citizens. More recently, during the 2015 national election, the Liberals promised more consultative federal policy-making.

Parliament's Roles in Relation to the Public Service

Based on the functions/activities identified above, five broad **roles of Parliament in relation to the public service** can be identified (Slatter, 1982): legitimization, policy-maker, creator, financier, and scrutineer. Parliament's involvement in the first four of these roles is more formal than real; it consists mainly of ratifying and sometimes refining decisions taken within government. Accordingly, these four roles will be considered only briefly and the following discussion will focus mainly on the purposes, impediments, and techniques of parliamentary surveillance of the bureaucracy.

Parliament plays an important but not easily measured role in *legitimizing* the actions of government. Legitimacy refers to the satisfaction and support of citizens for the processes, decisions, and outcomes of government. There are both procedural and substantive dimensions to legitimacy. Not only must decisions be made according to recognized and well-accepted rules and procedures, they also must reflect and be consistent with widely held values in society. In other words, legitimacy goes much deeper than the latest public opinion polls showing levels of public support for a particular government. It entails the principles and values upon which we agree to be governed. It appears from sophisticated opinion research that governments in Canada began losing legitimacy with their citizens over the three decades from the 1960s to the 1990s. The causes of this erosion are numerous and controversial (Nevitte, 1996). Increased public cynicism and declining trust and confidence are targeted mainly at political institutions, but they also affect the esteem of the public service.

Public bodies wield considerable power over the operations of private organizations and over the lives of individual citizens. They dispense benefits and impose burdens. They set standards of behaviour and coerce compliance through sanctions. They make judgments about the competing claims of various interests within society, often on the basis of private negotiations and complicated factual and ethical calculations about what is in the public interest. Public servants can only do these things, or do them effectively, if they are perceived to be acting in a legitimate manner on the basis of public law that has been approved by Parliament. Parliament is not the only, or even the most important, source of legitimacy, but administrative agencies will not be successful over time if Parliament finds their policies and practices unacceptable.

A second role of Parliament is *policy-making*. To understand this role requires a brief description of the wider context in which it occurs. The conditions under which governments operate today mean that policy-making at the national level in Canada has become complicated, extended, specialized, fragmented, interdependent, and uncertain. In institutional terms, power is concentrated in the hands of the prime minister, central agencies, and, to a lesser extent, cabinet and the bureaucracy. In broader process terms, however, power is increasingly shared and exercised collaboratively with outside pressure groups, provincial governments, and supranational and international institutions. Governments also face the challenge of combining elite-based decision-making with the public's demands for more consultative and participatory approaches. In short, governments are to some extent tied down by multiple linkages to the economy, society, and other parts of the political system.

More and more leadership and power are exercised collaboratively rather than unilaterally. So even though the appearance of prime-ministerial rule remains and the prime minister potentially has firm control over issues once they reach the institutional agenda of government, the image of one-person rule tends to neglect the wider situational constraints that face all governments today. As more issues move upward to international bodies, or downward to provincial, local, and non-governmental bodies, there is a loss of policy-making capacity for both cabinet and Parliament at the national level. Achieving coherence in national policy-making was also complicated by experimentation during the 1980s and 1990s with alternative service delivery mechanisms (discussed below) that made direction and control from the centre of government more difficult.

All of this being said, it is still the case that the cabinet–parliamentary model concentrates decision-making on issues before government in the hands of a relatively small number of political and bureaucratic insiders. The growing power of the prime minister, the fact of party discipline, the cabinet's access to the expertise of the public service, the limited access to information and staff resources by parliamentarians, and the government's use of procedural devices to ensure the completion of its business all reduce Parliament to a marginal, albeit still important, role in the policy process.

During most of the twentieth century, long periods of rule by the Liberal Party, combined with close relationships between the party and the senior ranks of the public service, led some commentators to suggest that power had shifted first from Parliament to cabinet and subsequently from the cabinet to the bureaucracy. Table 7.2 lists some of the other factors usually cited to explain the growing influence of senior public servants within the policy process. The list reflects the fact that policy-making is usually an extended process, involving several different stages and decision-making on a number of different levels. In terms of stages in the policy cycle, the initial formulation of policy tends to be undertaken by public servants in various departmental and interdepartmental bodies. Policy formulation often reflects pressures and advice from individuals and institutions outside of government. The actual selection or adoption of policy to be presented to Parliament in the form of bills, budgetary measures, and other actions is the prerogative of ministers and cabinets, although those choices are clearly influenced by the advice flowing from the public service.

Another level of policy-making in government involves the medium- and lower-level policy-making that takes place daily within departments, Crown corporations, regulatory commissions, and other administrative agencies. In these instances, Parliament has

Table 7.2   Sources of Bureaucratic Influence

- the professional backgrounds and relative permanence of senior public servants compared to ministers and other parliamentarians
- the possession of expert knowledge and specialized information
- the ongoing relationships between the public service and pressure groups, which represent a source of ideas and legitimacy for their policy advice to ministers
- the role of public servants in the important field of intergovernmental and international negotiations, which obliges governments to grant them autonomy to bargain over policy and its implementation
- the weakness of Canadian political parties as vehicles for the development of public policy, which means whether in government or opposition, parliamentarians have a restricted range of alternatives to the policies being presented by the bureaucracy
- the limits of Parliament's own policy-making capabilities due to the partisan theatrics that govern its proceedings and its reliance on vague policy in legislation, with the details to be provided by the bureaucracy through delegated legislative authority

passed laws in very general language and it is left to the bureaucracy to refine and to carry out the statutory purposes. On the basis of such delegated legislative authority enormous discretion is granted to public servants (acting presumably under the supervision of responsible ministers) to formulate and to apply rules of various kinds. In quantitative terms, based upon the hundreds of thousands of small rules that they formulate and apply, public servants have become the real lawmakers. Parliament has a committee to supervise the exercise of this discretionary power but, as is discussed later, there are limits to its effectiveness.

Only under very fortuitous circumstances can Parliament play a role in delaying or modifying the policy proposals of ministers. If this takes place, it happens in the private meetings of the government caucus, which consists of all the MPs and senators on the government side of Parliament or, less frequently, in the standing committee of the House of Commons where bills are sent for review after second reading (Thomas, 2008). Under the Conservative Party of Canada governments led by Prime Minister Stephen Harper from 2006–15, the committee system fell under tight government control and became rather dysfunctional due to the intense partisanship involved with their work.

In summary, it is necessary to be realistic, but not completely dismissive, concerning Parliament's policy-making role. For constitutional and practical reasons Parliament must be content with discussing, approving, and perhaps refining policies that

are formulated initially elsewhere, usually within the bureaucracy, often in collaboration with outside interest groups. There is less excuse, however, for Parliament's weak performance in terms of the review of existing policies, which is a theme of the later discussion of Parliament's role as a scrutineer of the bureaucracy.

A third and related role of Parliament is that of *creator* of administrative bodies. Since departments and non-departmental bodies such as Crown corporations, regulatory agencies, and special operating agencies have a statutory basis, Parliament plays a role in creating these. However, as already mentioned, there is a recognized right for the prime minister to initiate organizational changes and a number of statutes enable the cabinet to set up new administrative agencies. The general practice has been to create such new entities by statute, and therefore there is the opportunity for Parliament to debate the organizational format (departmental or non-departmental), the mandate, and the powers of new undertakings. In practice such debates may occur well after the fact, as was the case with the major 1993 reorganization of the federal bureaucracy. This reorganization saw the number of departments reduced from 32 to 23. Parliament did not approve all the legislation confirming the consolidations for three or four years, long after the new mega-departments were operational. In the interim the cabinet was free to act under the Public Service Rearrangement and Transfer of Duties Act, which allows for the transfer of duties between ministers and departments.

This Act does not apply to independent administrative agencies such as regulatory bodies. Prior to 1984 the cabinet was free to create Crown corporations by Order-in-Council, but amendments to the Financial Administration Act passed in that year require that Parliament approve the creation of all new Crown corporations and the privatization of existing corporations.

In summary, it is an exaggeration to state that Parliament creates the administrative machinery; it is more accurate to say that it reviews ministerial decisions respecting the mandate, organizational format, and powers of the different types of organizations used by government. During the 1980s governments began to experiment with alternative organizational designs such as large consolidated departments, special operating agencies, mixed enterprises, and public–private partnerships. These developments are discussed in the later section of this chapter on future trends. The implications for parliamentary control of the move away from the traditional, integrated department have received little attention, including within Parliament itself.

A fourth role for Parliament in relation to the bureaucracy is that of *financier*. Parliament has three main functions in the field of public expenditure. The first involves authorizing sufficient spending to allow the government to carry on its activities. This is done through the debate and passage of appropriation bills. All new spending must originate with the government (or more formally, the Crown). Motions to reject or to reduce expenditures have been viewed by governments as matters of confidence and party discipline applies. The result is that while constitutional theory places Parliament at the centre of the expenditure process, in practice its direct control and even its indirect influence have been minimal.

Second, it is part of Parliament's financial role to submit expenditure proposals to scrutiny as part of a more general questioning of government policy and management of the public service. Under the rules of the House of Commons, 22 days are allowed in each parliamentary session when the opposition parties can introduce motions criticizing the government, and on six of these—so-called supply or opposition days—the debate ends with a vote of no confidence. Such debates tend to be wide-ranging and rarely focus exclusively on fiscal matters. In October 2001 the rules were changed to allow the leader of the opposition to select two departments or agencies to have their estimates debated before the full House of Commons, an occasion that would bring more publicity to opposition complaints of mismanagement than scrutiny conducted in the committees. In summary, the supply process represents an opportunity for Parliament to convey its views to the government and the various administrative agencies. Detailed examination of the estimates of the various departments is supposed to take place in the 24 standing committees of the Commons. Although they are theoretically free to recommend changes to the government's financial plans, the committees rarely do this, mainly because they are under tight government control. Government control is lost or reduced in minority government situations, such as existed from January 2006 to May 2011, when the Harper Conservatives achieved majority government status.

Several reforms have been introduced since the late 1960s to streamline and revitalize the supply process. In 1968 the detailed examination of the estimates was transferred to the standing committees of the House of Commons with the hope that a more constructive approach involving an actual examination of spending would occur. Instead, the partisan policy debates of the past were simply carried over from the full House of Commons into the committees. In 1982 a new three-part format for the estimates was introduced with the promise of allowing MPs to examine the substance of departmental performance and future plans by reporting on accomplishments against planned results. Under the new system the committees faced a juggernaut of several hundred documents annually; few MPs became comfortable working with the new documents, departments were frustrated that there was little or no informed interest in their work, and the whole exercise resembled a largely futile make-work project since government maintained tight control on both the committees and spending.

A new Expenditure Management System announced by the Liberal government in February 1995 dealt mainly with reforms to the process within the executive, but it also promised Parliament and other interested parties "improved information on program performance to aid in decision-making and to facilitate accountability" (Canada, Treasury Board Secretariat, 1995). For the purposes of enhanced accountability to Parliament and to allow it influence over future spending, departments began to publish "outlook" documents, which are condensed and expurgated versions of internal business plans. These documents, subsequently renamed Reports on Plans and Priorities, are referred to the relevant standing committees of the Commons during the spring when the government's estimates are before Parliament. For the fall sitting of Parliament, departments present the committees with performance reports, which ideally track the progress of departments and programs. Well over 100 performance reports now flow into the Commons committee system each September, and theoretically the review of these documents allows the committees to offer advice to the government about expenditure priorities for a budget to be presented in February or March of the following year.

The most recent attempt to reform the supply process arose from a report tabled in June 2012 by the House of Commons' Standing Committee on Government Operations and Estimates. The committee made 16 recommendations, all of which related to the timing and content of the financial information placed before Parliament. (See House of Commons' Standing Committee on Government Operations and Estimates, Strengthening Parliamentary Scrutiny of Estimates and Supply, June 2012). Little action came from this most recent attempt to reform the supply process, which remains probably the weakest part of the parliamentary process. All governments, regardless of partisan stripe, have sought to protect their dominance over the budgetary process, not just for the obvious political advantage that control brings but also because of the sensible belief that 338 MPs, pursuing the interests of their constituencies and their own re-election prospects, could not be counted on to make the tough, disciplined decisions involved with balancing spending and taxing.

Parliament's Financial Watchdog: The Office of the Auditor General

The third financial duty of Parliament is the retrospective scrutiny of the Annual Public Accounts. It performs this task with the support of the Office of the Auditor General of Canada (OAG), which has existed almost since the country was founded. As a parliamentary watchdog on spending, the OAG has become an important actor in the parliamentary system. Traditionally, the role of the OAG consisted of financial and compliance auditing, which meant that

the office assisted Parliament in ensuring the legality and accuracy of expenditures. As the auditor of the Public Accounts of Canada, the OAG examines annually the financial records of departments and agencies and files reports to Parliament that are automatically referred to the House of Commons Standing Committee on Public Accounts, chaired by an opposition MP. The Public Accounts Committee considers the OAG's report and presents its own conclusions and recommendations to the House of Commons.

Since 1977 the OAG has also been authorized to practise comprehensive or value-for-money auditing (VFM). VFM examines the legality and efficiency of expenditure transactions, but more importantly it evaluates the adequacy of the management and information systems used to ensure economy, efficiency, and effectiveness in government decision-making.

The OAG insists that it does not conduct actual program evaluations because to do so would potentially entangle it in partisan controversy. It claims to limit itself to the issue of whether information is available or could be made available to answer questions about program effectiveness. However, in refining the VFM approach the OAG has moved well beyond strictly financial matters and outside the parameters of its lead discipline of accountancy. Fully one-third of the OAG's staff now have backgrounds in fields other than accountancy. In addition to widening the scope of its audits, the OAG has added a number of other activities to its repertoire: the review of the sustainable development strategies of departments, special examinations of the performances of Crown corporations, and progress reports on the various public service reform initiatives introduced in recent years. By broadening the scope of its activities, the OAG has contributed to the functioning of Parliament beyond supporting its financial duties. Originally the work of the OAG was mainly used in the Standing Committee on Public Accounts because the annual report focused on issues of financial management. Today the OAG's staff work with many parliamentary committees and its various reports are cited in Question Period, debates on legislation, the supply process, committee inquiries, and media reports.

In providing support to Parliament the OAG is required to perform a balancing act. To ensure parliamentary, media, and public attention for its findings, it must present reports that are controversial enough to be noticed. At the same time it must avoid drifting into policy controversies and focusing only on negative developments because such approaches will produce a backlash and lack of co-operation from ministers and departments. There is also a balance to be maintained between identifying waste and error, and emphasizing constructive criticism and organizational learning.

The expanded scope of the legislative audit has taken the OAG into politically sensitive areas and, not surprisingly, made it the target of criticism. A list of the challenges to the Office would include the following points:

- By using the term *audit* loosely the OAG creates a false aura of objectivity and validity for its findings.
- The OAG presumes clear and measurable objectives for departments and programs and on this basis promotes a shallow, managerialist conception of accountability.
- The OAG fails to recognize that policy is made on several levels within government and ends up violating its own rule of not commenting on policy.
- The OAG does not recognize sufficiently the political and bureaucratic constraints faced by public servants and ends up distorting the principle of ministerial responsibility by placing blame where it does not belong, i.e., with public servants rather than ministers.
- By its emphasis on mistakes, the assignment of blame, and the promotion of a mentality of error-free administration, the OAG is a part of a control lobby within government that has stifled the emergence of a less rule-bound, less risk-averse, and more entrepreneurial public service.
- With its $92.4 million budget for 2014–15, large professional staff (approximately 570 employees), and capacity to generate publicity for its findings, the OAG ends up setting the agenda of Parliament, especially of the Public Accounts Committee, rather than taking direction from and responding to the concerns of parliamentarians.
- By promoting the notion that all its reports reflect scientific auditing principles and practices applied in a completely objective manner, the OAG claims to speak "the truth" and by doing so elevates certain kinds of information and knowledge over other modes of inquiry and analysis.

Of course, the OAG denies many of the concerns of its critics. In terms of its relationship to Parliament, the OAG represents a potentially valuable resource to parliamentarians (Aucoin, 1998; Holmes, 1996; Power, 1997; Roberts, 1996; Sutherland, 1980; Thomas, 1999). If Parliament, especially through its committees, fails to provide direction to the OAG and if its reports disappear into a parliamentary black hole, the OAG probably has no choice but to act unilaterally to bring matters to the attention of parliamentarians, only a small minority of whom has exhibited sustained interest in financial and managerial issues.

Parliamentary Scrutiny of the Public Service

The fifth role of Parliament is that of *scrutineer* of the public service. This role is implicit in the previous four. Until the last three decades this role received little definition and separate attention from Parliament. As the consensus grew that ministerial responsibility was inadequate as an accountability mechanism and that ministers were unable to manage the public service, Parliament began to develop the scrutiny function. In general, Parliament saw that it had a duty to probe the operations of the bureaucracy, to make its operations more transparent, to deter the misuse of power, and to galvanize the norms of responsible behaviour on the part of public servants. Table 7.3 presents a list of more specific purposes behind the various mechanisms used by Parliament to provide surveillance of the bureaucracy.

Table 7.3   The Purposes of Parliamentary Surveillance of the Bureaucracy

- to ensure that laws are implemented as intended
- to review whether laws, policies, programs, or activities of government need to be changed
- to promote accountability among permanent public officials
- to discover waste and mismanagement, and to promote economy, efficiency, and effectiveness in public programs
- to discover and to prevent abuses of discretionary authority
- to allow parliamentarians to act as liaison agents with the bureaucracy on behalf of their constituents

Since the mid- to late 1960s Parliament has adopted a variety of procedural and organizational measures to strengthen its surveillance function. An implicit bargain has often been at the heart of these reforms. In return for speedier passage of its business, the government was prepared to allow Parliament, mainly through its committees, to inquire into the performance of the bureaucracy, but only if this was done in a politically non-threatening fashion. To some extent governments also wanted to use Parliament as an ally in the struggle by ministers to force the bureaucracy to be efficient and accountable. On these grounds governments agreed to Commons rules obliging them to furnish Parliament with certain kinds of information on a regular basis and to respond to parliamentary opinion, such as the requirement that governments respond to committee reports within 150 days.

Parliament has also been allowed to create a number of auxiliary agencies (usually called **Officers of Parliament**) to assist it with the task of holding ministers and public servants accountable (Thomas, 2003). Examples of such agencies are the **Office of the Auditor General**, the **Office of the Information Commissioner**, the **Office of the Privacy Commissioner**, and the **Canadian Human Rights Commission**. In response to the so-called sponsorship scandal, in December 2006 Parliament passed the **Federal Accountability Act (FAA)**. The FAA introduced a consistent appointments process for Officers of Parliament with a more meaningful role for parliamentarians in reviewing the qualifications of nominees; added a Public Sector Integrity Commissioner to oversee a whistle-blower protection law; created a **Parliamentary Budget Officer (PBO)** to assist Parliament with its financial duties; announced a Public Appointments Commission (it was never established) to review cabinet appointments to agencies, boards, and commissions; expanded the Access to Information Act to cover all Crown corporations and their subsidiaries; ended the practice of giving priority treatment to political staff of ministers when they apply to join the public service; created a new, independent Commissioner of Lobbying with stronger powers to oversee lobbying rules; and introduced a new conflict of interest code to be enforced by a new Conflict of Interest and Ethics Commissioner. It also strengthened the internal auditing regime within departments and gave the Auditor General serving Parliament more authority to audit public foundations

and to follow money for grants and contributions to third parties outside of government. Finally, the FAA introduced the **accounting officer** model for deputy ministers, a reform that is discussed more fully below. Based on complaints from the first PBO that the location of his office within the administrative framework of the Library of Parliament created limits on his authority/resources, the Liberal Party promised during the 2015 election to make the PBO into an independent officer of Parliament with greater control over its own staffing and budgets.

Table 7.4 presents a summary listing of the main surveillance mechanisms now available to Parliament. Impressive in number, it must be remembered that all the mechanisms operate in a political context of partisan competition where the government is

Table 7.4 Parliamentary Techniques for Surveillance of the Public Service

- Question Period
- members' statements
- debates of bills and periodic reviews of legislation
- review and approval of spending
- creation of standing committees that cover broad policy sectors and are somewhat independent of the executive
- the conduct of general inquiries by parliamentary committees and the requirement that ministers reply to reports
- requirements that ministers present Parliament with information on a regular basis, e.g., the annual report on the public service and the annual report on the Crown corporation sector
- the provision of professional staff to committees and to individual parliamentarians
- the creation of the Joint Committee on the Scrutiny of Regulations to review the exercise of delegated law-making authority
- the adoption of an Access to Information Act to promote openness in government
- the appointment of a number of Officers of Parliament to assist Parliament with its scrutiny function for various purposes, such as the Auditor General, the Office of the Information Commissioner, the Privacy Commissioner, the Commissioner of Official Languages, the Public Sector Integrity Commissioner, and the Commissioner of Lobbying

usually in charge. On the other hand, these surveillance mechanisms do force governments to explain themselves on a regular basis before the elected representatives of the public—which is not an insignificant requirement in a democracy.

Question Period, members' statements, and debates of various kinds can be used as spot checks to bring administrative issues before Parliament, but they do not allow for systematic, in-depth coverage. The best opportunities for such scrutiny come through the work of parliamentary committees. The Commons currently has 24 standing committees, each with 10 members, whose terms of reference cover broad policy sectors. (See Appendix A for a listing.) The committees perform three broad functions: the examination of bills after second reading, the review of the estimates, and the conduct of general inquiries. Reference is made elsewhere in this chapter to how the committees undertake these functions. In all cases there is a tension between the government's insistence on tight control over committee proceedings and the aspiration of parliamentary reformers to create independent and influential committees. Since a more active committee system was created in the late 1960s, successive governments have used their majorities on the committees, the appointment of government MPs as chairpersons, and the insistence on party discipline to restrain committees in the use of their newly acquired powers (Docherty, 2003; Franks, 1987).

On paper the Commons committees have significant powers to review departmental performance. The rules of the House of Commons allow committees to initiate inquiries and to report on all matters related to the mandate, management, and operations of departments. They have the authority to summon witnesses, compel testimony, and order documents to be provided. On several occasions in recent years public service witnesses have been asked to swear an oath before a committee that they will tell the truth. In the past, it was presumed such witnesses would always be truthful within the limits of the rules respecting public service confidentiality. To provide some sense of the volume of work done in committees, from April 2015 to March 2016 (a year during which Parliament took a break for the October 2015 election), there were 475 committee meetings, 1490 witnesses appeared before committees, and 110 reports were presented to the House of Commons and the government (Canada, 2015–16).

Of course, activity does not necessarily represent accomplishment in terms of parliamentary influence on policy and administration. Committees can require a government response to their reports and recommendation within 150 days, but, of course, they cannot force governments to take their views seriously. A 2008 report from the Public Accounts Committee documented the lack of meaningful responses by government to its reports and made a number of recommendations to improve the situation. Committee influence depends on a fortuitous combination of circumstances, such as the willingness of ministers and senior public servants to receive advice, the quality of that advice, the degree of cross-party support for reports, the existence of outside pressures for the recommended changes, and so on.

Over the years since 1968, when the standing committees were made the main working units of the Commons, there have been occasional examples of committees demonstrating independence from the government. This has occurred mainly when committees were conducting inquiries into departments and evaluations of programs deemed to be in trouble. In these instances the responsible ministers may have allowed the inquiries in order to shake up their departments. There have also been cases where government MPs, who had perhaps forsaken the possibility of a cabinet posting, provided aggressive leadership as chairpersons of committees. For example, during the 35th Parliament (1993–7), George Baker, a Newfoundland Liberal MP, led a study by the Commons Committee on Fisheries and Oceans. The Committee compelled departmental representatives to appear and produced a stinging report blaming the Department of Fisheries and Oceans for the collapse of the east coast cod fishery. In a similar fashion, the Commons Committee on the Environment issued several reports critical of the Chrétien government's environmental policies and the Justice and Human Rights Committee conducted a useful study of the operations of the controversial Young Offenders Act. These cases are the exception, however.

A fundamental limitation on Parliament's capacity to enforce bureaucratic accountability is the sheer size of the surveillance task. No matter what procedures it adopts, no matter what organizational arrangements it creates, and no matter how many professional staff it employs, Parliament can never come close to providing continuous scrutiny over the wide range of administrative decision-making taking place on a daily basis. Also, beyond some not easily identified point, parliamentary involvement with administrative matters becomes counterproductive if it robs the public service of the flexibility to apply its professional expertise in the most efficient manner possible. Close relations between departments and parliamentary committees with real power to dispense rewards and punishments would potentially leave senior public servants serving two masters—the minister and the designated parliamentary committee. We need look no further than the Congress in the United States to see the danger of micromanagement of the public service and the divided loyalties this produces when powerful legislative committees exist. There is little danger of such relationships developing in Canada; if anything, the greater risk is too little rather than too much parliamentary scrutiny of the bureaucracy, especially scrutiny that is systematic and constructive.

Obstacles to Parliamentary Surveillance of the Bureaucracy

In addition to the vast scope and technical complexity of the public sector, which complicate the surveillance task, Parliament faces other obstacles, some of which have been alluded to earlier. The constitutional framework concentrates authority over the public service in the hands of ministers, and the governing party exercises tight control over the standing committees of the House of Commons, which represent the main forums where systematic examination of bureaucratic performance might take place. Elected as part of a team, having participated in caucus deliberations, and conscious of the potential damage to their prospects of entering cabinet, government MPs are naturally reluctant to embarrass the minister and the government by exposing mismanagement or the abuse of power. This means that most of the serious challenges on bureaucratic performance come from opposition MPs, who can usually be counted on to interpret any revelation of a problem in the worst possible light. This focus on error identification and blaming causes ministers, government MPs, and public servants to adopt a protective stance. Frustrated by the shallowness and distortion of parliamentary performance reviews conducted mainly on a partisan basis, public servants tend to be less than candid and forthcoming in providing information to committees for fear that

it might embarrass the minister and damage the department's or their own reputation.

It is often suggested that parliamentarians suffer from a lack of information, but this is not really accurate. The real problem is that they are often faced with voluminous and complicated information that does not relate to the issues of public policy and public management making headlines at the time. There is, in fact, more information around today than most MPs and senators have time to consume, and not all of it is relevant, reliable, or easily understood. Packaging information to serve the needs of 338 MPs and 105 senators is a huge challenge because of the diverse and shifting interests of parliamentarians. There is also the complication that parliamentarians do not approach the gathering and use of information on the performance of the bureaucracy in a completely objective manner; they are often more interested in vindicators that reinforce their partisan positions than they are in indicators that accurately report on performance.

Whereas parliamentary committees were once forced to get along with only the services of a clerk who provided advice on procedural matters, they can now seek research support from a number of sources: the Research Branch of the Library of Parliament, the Parliamentary Budget Officer (which was established in March 2008), lawyers from the Legislative Counsel Office, outside consultants (hired from budgets provided to committees), research staffs provided to the party caucuses, and the assistants who work in the offices of individual MPs and senators. As part of its overall budgetary restraint policy, the Liberal government had after 1993 cut the budget of Parliament, and one impact was to curtail committee activity involving paid consultants and travel. Even though Parliament remains better off in terms of information and analytical capability than it was during earlier decades, it still remains no match for the government, which has access to the vast storehouse of accumulated public service knowledge.

To gain greater access to that storehouse of knowledge, Parliament has adopted a number of procedures to oblige the public service to share information. One such approach is to bring public servants before parliamentary committees. This has been done with increasing frequency over the past three decades in conjunction with the examination of bills after second reading, the review of the estimates, and the conduct of general inquiries into matters of public policy. Normally, public servants voluntarily appear before committees, but there have been several instances where they have been summoned. The rules of engagement for such encounters between neutral public servants and partisan politicians are not entirely clear. In constitutional terms, public servants appear on behalf of their minister and not on their own behalf. They are expected to be honest and forthcoming with information (thus respecting the role of Parliament) and at the same time respect their obligations to the minister not to disclose confidential policy advice or sensitive information regarding administrative matters (thus respecting ministerial responsibility). To help public servants balance these considerations a number of guidelines have been published and courses are offered to senior public servants on how to prepare for appearances before committees. While helpful, such devices are inevitably general and are no substitute for the situational judgment that public servants develop through actual experience before parliamentary committees.

Since parliamentary committees are primarily political forums, there are risks for public servants in appearing there. There are few clear rules governing the behaviour of parliamentarians in their encounters with public servants. To avoid entanglement in partisan controversy or embarrassment to the minister, public servants may refuse to answer certain questions. In most cases, parliamentarians accept the reasons given by public servants for refusing to answer. Such reasons include commenting on government policy, providing information about matters outside of a public servant's responsibility, providing a legal opinion, and providing an answer that could affect a commercial transaction (McInnes, 1999). Ministers (when they are present in committees), parliamentary secretaries (who are government MPs serving as assistants to ministers), and chairpersons of committees (who are normally government MPs or senators) will normally protect public servants against political attacks. The usual assumption might be that public servants need protection exclusively from opposition MPs who are determined to embarrass the government, but this is not true. Both Liberal and Conservative MPs when their party was in office have accused public servants of withholding information and misleading committees.

Under rules of the House of Commons adopted in 1985, Commons committees have the authority to summon all nominees for non-judicial Order-in-Council appointments (such as deputy ministers, presidents of Crown corporations, and chairpersons of regulatory commissions) to review their qualifications. Unlike congressional committees in the United States, the Commons committees cannot veto such appointments; they can only report their views on candidates. Back in 1985 the new procedure took Parliament into uncharted constitutional waters and during the first few years of its operation both the government and the opposition sought partisan advantage from the process (Colwell & Thomas, 1987). As a result the procedure was used less and less often.

On a limited but growing number of occasions ministers have failed to uphold their obligation to protect public servants against political attacks and have even blamed individual public servants. The most notorious example was the so-called Al-Mashat affair, involving the fast-tracking of the entry of a former ambassador from Iraq into Canada. In this case Conservative ministers used their majority on a parliamentary committee to shift the blame to a career public servant. According to Sharon Sutherland (1991b) this case was unprecedented and damaging because a parliamentary committee driven by the government majority bypassed ministerial responsibility and criticized the behaviour of a career public servant, sending a chill throughout the public service.

Another such instance was the investigation by the Public Accounts Committee into the so-called billion-dollar boondoggle of the Human Resources and Development Canada's (HRDC) grants and contributions programs that saw a parliamentary committee attack the actions and reputations of public servants for flaws in programs that were highly political in their origins, content, and operations (Good, 2003). The most drastic potential action in relation to public servants is to hold them in contempt for misleading Parliament, which is a rarely used sanction. From 1913 to 2008 it was never used, although in 2003 it was threatened in relation to Canada's Privacy Commissioner who was found by a parliamentary committee to have misused his staffing and budgetary authority. It was actually used on 10 April 2008 when a vote in the House of Commons found the deputy commissioner of the RCMP in contempt for testimony she gave during an inquiry by the Public Accounts Committee into the misuse of the Mounties' pension and insurance funds. After the earlier HRDC, privacy, and sponsorship scandals, MPs were determined to send a strong message that they would not tolerate being misled or being given less than the full story.

The Senate

As an appointed body whose members were, until recently, selected mainly on the basis of political patronage, the Senate lacks democratic legitimacy and credibility with the public. Following a scandal involving misspending by senators with both Liberal and Conservative backgrounds, the Liberal Party in opposition dropped their senators from the parliamentary caucus and in the 2015 election the Liberals promised to create non-partisan and independent Senate by, in part, reforming the process of appointment of senators. As of 2016, appointments to fill vacancies in the Senate would be made by a blue-ribbon panel of distinguished Canadians and individual Canadians could apply to become a senator. The panel would recommend names to the prime minister, who in turn would recommend nominees to the Governor General, whose formal authority to appoint was preserved. The early selections under the new appointment procedure has not brought forth the typical party organizers and fundraisers of the past, but because the prime minister retains the real power of appointment, the perception of the Senate as a partisan body will likely persist for most Canadians.

The Senate is seen to have been a failure in terms of performing the three roles officially ascribed to it: it has failed to provide an effective voice for regional concerns because party loyalty has to take precedence; it has failed to serve as a body of sober second thought and a check on government because the patronage appointees of the prime minister have shown their gratitude, and the government could usually take Senate approval for granted; and finally, it has failed to protect the rights of minorities. Over the past century and a quarter, numerous schemes to reform the Senate have been proposed, but all failed the tests of constitutional and political feasibility. With the recent exclusion of senators from the Liberal caucus and the appointments made under the new procedure, the majority of senators will soon not be part of an organized party caucus system. Of course this will not prevent like-minded senators from working together. The Liberal government has promised to break from the tradition of exercising relatively tight control over the Senate and its committees. With independent senators and less government control,

the Senate committees, which have always been the main working units of the institution, could become far more freewheeling and influential in conducting reviews of the operations of government policies and programs. (See Appendix B for a list of the current Standing Committees of the Senate.)

There are a number of reasons for the success of Senate committee investigations. Many senators have experience and knowledge of public policy issues from their previous careers. Senators approach investigations in a more non-partisan manner than occurs in Commons committees. The Senate has the time and can take a longer-range view of issues than the Commons, which faces re-election pressures. Lastly, Senate investigations do not suffer from excessive media attention, which would promote political grandstanding (Franks, 1987: 188–90; Thomas, 2003: 189–228). It should also be noted that unlike Royal Commissions of inquiry, senators often exhibit a greater sense of political feasibility in their recommendations and remain in office to lobby for their implementation. Measuring the influence of Senate committees on government and bureaucratic thinking is difficult, but they do add to a climate of opinion in the country (Pattee & Thomas, 1985).

Public Service Reform (PSR) and Parliamentary Accountability

As indicated above, the increasing scope and complexity of government during the twentieth century produced strains on the conventions of ministerial responsibility, public service anonymity, and parliamentary accountability. Beginning in the 1980s there was increasing talk about rethinking and reinventing the role of government within the society and the economy. Rising annual deficits and accumulated debts came to be a preoccupation of many governments throughout the world; shrinking the size of the bureaucracy was one response. Another popular response was public service reform. In addition to dealing with a so-called fiscal crisis, other aims of PSR were improving service quality, promoting citizen engagement, and restoring the professional pride and commitment of public servants. Increased accountability by ministers and public servants was not central to PSR in practice, although it was featured at times in the rhetoric selling various types of reform. Indeed a plausible argument can be made that the new managerial approaches tried over the past three decades government were not consistent with parliamentary traditions and with the political culture of Parliament. To illustrate this point, three sets of reforms will be discussed briefly.

During the 1990s the reinventing government movement produced the idea that "steering" should be separated from "rowing," a vague notion that led governments to narrow the scope of ministerial responsibility by identifying a zone of managerial activity where senior public servants would be held directly and personally answerable before Parliament for the performance of the organizations they administer.

The culmination of this line of thinking was the adoption of the accounting officer model in the Federal Accountability Act passed by Parliament in December 2006. Put simply, this concept makes deputy ministers directly and personally accountable before Parliament for the prudent financial management of their departments. However, working out the operational meaning of the concept has proven to be contentious. In opposition during the sponsorship scandal, the Conservative Party of Canada had endorsed a pure version of the concept in which deputy ministers would be personally answerable before parliamentary committees. In office, however, Conservative Prime Minister Harper (based, it appears, on the advice of the Privy Council Office) eventually took the view that when deputy ministers appeared before the Public Accounts Committee to answer questions related to financial management, they were appearing on behalf of their ministers. The opposing view, which is represented by the Public Accounts Committee, is that deputy ministers should answer on their own behalf for the exercise of managerial prerogatives delegated to them under the Financial Administration Act. Controversy persists over how far Parliament can and should go in insisting on a modification to the principle of ministerial responsibility to enforce direct bureaucratic accountability.

Second, the adoption of **Special Operating Agencies** to deliver programs in a more business-like manner, the privatization of Crown corporations, the contracting out of service delivery to third parties, and the development of public–private partnerships were all prominent features of the PSR process during the decades of the 1990s and early 2000s. All of these approaches involved the splitting of policy and operations, faith in competition, efforts to create market-type conditions in the public sector, and

greater reliance on private-sector management techniques. They also involve transferring or sharing of public power with private parties. By definition they involve a reduction in the scope of political accountability operating through Parliament. How ministerial responsibility applies within the shifting contours of the public sector is not at all clear. Unless governments are clear in their aims, invest seriously in the capability to monitor performances of the third parties, and are able to take action to protect the public interest, ministers will not be in a position to render a satisfactory accounting to Parliament. When such reforms took place, Parliament paid little systematic attention to the implications for its role in providing oversight of the political executive and the bureaucracy.

Performance measurement and reporting is a third prominent feature of PSR. Since 1995 the Government of Canada has required departments and agencies to produce business plans, to develop performance measures, and to present performance reports to Parliament. In the spring of each year as part of the supply process, departments make available to the relevant standing committees of the House of Commons an "outlook" document—a condensed and sometimes expurgated version of its business plan, which is used for internal purposes only. The outlooks are meant to explain significant resource shifts and initiatives over a three-year horizon. In contrast to the future orientation of the outlook document, the performance reports made available in the fall, when consultations on the next year's budget are underway, are meant to focus on measures of performance in relation to results of commitments. Today there are hundreds of reports on plans and performance tabled in Parliament annually. The hope was that such documents would shift parliamentary debates and investigations away from the sensational and often trivial aspects of spending and program operations and lead to more focus on substantive outcomes.

To state that Parliament has found it difficult to practise results-based accountability would be a gigantic understatement. The documents produced at considerable cost in terms of both staff time and money are seldom referred to in debates and committee proceedings. There are several explanations for this non-use of performance data. First, there is such a vast amount of information in printed and electronic form and it is so overwhelming, complex, or irrelevant, parliamentarians have found it difficult to work with the material.

Second, most of the data deal with inputs and outputs (such as the levels of services provided) rather than the real-world outcomes or impacts that most interest MPs. Third, performance data are open to conflicting interpretations and parliamentarians do not approach information with completely open minds. As partisan politicians operating in a competitive arena, MPs tend to be more interested vindicating their parties' positions than measuring performance. Finally, as was already mentioned, Parliament is problem-oriented, short-range, and shifting in its approach; the new information system presumes that it can become systematic, priority conscious, and more objective in its approach to the review of government performance.

Technological change and globalization were powerful forces, among others, that drove PSR. The information and communications technology revolution also had great impacts on how politics was conducted and, because of the overlap between politics and administration, there were impacts on the role of the public service. The late Peter Aucoin used the phrase "new political governance" (NPG) to describe these developments. (See Aucoin, 2012 and Aucoin, Bakvis, & Jarvis, 2013.) Put simply, NPG involved hyper-partisanship in the form of a permanent campaign where winning all the time became the goal. The techniques of campaigning became not just part of, but central to, the processes of governing. There was an increase in the number and the influence of exempt political staff (appointed outside of the merit system of the public service) serving the prime minister and other ministers. Another component of NPG during the Conservative government of Stephen Harper was even more pervasive and tighter control by the prime minister and his political staff over nearly all aspects of governing. A final component was the adoption of sophisticated approaches to communications and the control over information that were meant to protect and enhance the reputation of the prime minister and his government (Thomas, 2013). There was the expectation of enthusiastic support for partisan policies by the senior public service, undermining its traditional role of fearless advice and impartial implementation of policy.

The impact of NPG on politics is one thing, but the concern here is the way that it risked undermining the professionalism and impartiality of public service. Aucoin identified the emergence of promiscuous partisanship in the senior ranks of the public service, by which he meant that deputy ministers and other senior officials became reluctant to speak truth to power and were pressured to become part of attempts at "spin" that sought to promote "good news" and minimize the "bad news" regarding the performance of the party in power. Information for Parliament and its committees was harder to obtain and public servants appearing before parliamentary committees were expected to withhold information and opinions that might be damaging to the government of the day.

Critical of the centralizing and controlling practices of the Harper government, the Liberals promised less centralized decision-making in the PMO, more openness in providing Parliament with information, more autonomy for committees, and greater independence for a less partisan Senate. Enthusiasm for parliamentary reform is always greater when a party is in opposition than when it becomes government. Another development with implications for parliamentary accountability is the adoption at the centre of the Trudeau government of so-called deliverology, a model for central decision-making based on clarifying objectives, measuring results, and coordinating implementation across government. Some of the components of the new approach include a cabinet committee on Agenda, Results and Communications (ARC); a mandate letter to all ministers directing them on their contribution to government priorities; and support from a Central Delivery Unit to help departments organize for results and to ensure that evidence on results becomes part of cabinet decision-making. At the time of writing (November 2016) there is limited experience with the new approach. In terms of the focus of this chapter, it is unclear how the deliverology approach will affect the relationships between ministers, the public service, and Parliament.

Conclusion

Historically the relationships between Parliament and the public service have been shaped by unwritten, vague constitutional conventions, most notably the principles of ministerial responsibility and the related concepts of a neutral, anonymous public service, and by the changing parliamentary practices that reflect the shifting issues of the day. Always characterized by a certain amount of mutual wariness, those relationships have become over the past two decades more suspicious, negative, and blame oriented, as evidenced by the examples of parliamentarian attacks on senior public servants noted earlier in this chapter. Both long-term trends and short-term developments, outside and inside of government, have caused this deterioration: a series of scandals; a strong anti-politics public mood; political attacks on the public service; an increased likelihood that ministers will name public servants when something goes wrong rather than assume ministerial responsibility; access-to-information laws and a greater insistence on transparency; more oversight bodies whose sole job is to publicize mistakes and wrongdoing; more aggressive media; and new management doctrines that treat government as a business and seek to put operational matters beyond political influence, leading to a generally blurred accountability picture.

In response to these trends there is an emerging acceptance of the idea that the public service is a separate constitutional entity with its own identity and ethos. Public service is no longer seen as a neutral instrument that owes unconditional loyalty to the government of the day. It is expected to be responsive to the government in office, but it is also expected to show **bureaucratic independence** in providing policy advice and in delivering programs in a professional, impartial manner without undue political interference. This line of thinking implies that the public service is a fourth branch of government—joining the legislature, the political executive, and the courts—and that it is expected to contribute to defining the public interest and upholding the rule of law. Logically this leads to recommendations to codify the constitutional role of the public service and to develop domains and mechanisms of parliamentary accountability for it outside the boundaries of ministerial responsibility. The adoption of the accounting officer role for deputy ministers is the leading practical example of this trend. Reducing the scope of ministerial responsibility to acknowledge separate accountability for public servants entails the risk that ministers will not ask about operational matters and deny knowledge of problems when they arise. Whatever the weakness of ministerial responsibility, it does pinpoint responsibility and thereby contributes to democratic accountability by requiring an identifiable individual to answer before the public's elected representatives in Parliament.

When it comes to the public service, discussion, publicity, and influence are the extent of Parliament's involvement except when it is asked to approve legislative and budgetary initiatives of the government. If we think of Parliament as mainly a discussion forum rather than a decision-making body, we can identify several possible contributions it might make to the future of public service reform. These contributions derive from what is often seen as a weakness of the institution, namely, its non-technical approach to issues of public management. As part of their ongoing efforts to demonstrate political responsiveness, parliamentarians are particularly attuned to the problems, concerns, and opinions of their constituents. On this basis they can bring to the discussion of public organizations and their programs, insights and sensitivities that are beyond the perception and direct knowledge of experts, even those in the public service who manage programs on the basis of pressure group representations and client surveys.

The discussions of government performance that take place in Parliament represent a potentially valuable source of education for ministers, public servants, the media, interest groups, and the public at large. However, the central importance of the concepts of opposition and adversarial politics within the parliamentary systems puts a premium on error avoidance and defensiveness within the cabinet and the senior public service. Generally parliamentarians assign a low priority to the systematic scrutiny of bureaucratic performance. This is mainly an opposition function, because members of the governing party are not encouraged to probe into possible weakness of policies and programs. Even for the opposition parties the incentives to assign time, resources, and energy to scrutiny are weak, unless there is a case that will draw media and public attention and detract from the reputation of the government. So long as Parliament most resembles a permanent election campaign, where the focus is mainly on error identification and blaming, governments will remain reluctant to grant the public service the degree of autonomy implied by the rhetoric of the contemporary public management literature. Reconciling modern public management approaches with the traditions and practices of parliamentary accountability represents a serious challenge. Parliament's ability to engage in a constructive dialogue with the public service will depend less on institutional innovation and more on a shift in attitudes among parliamentarians in the direction of a less partisan and less adversarial approach.

Appendix A

Standing Committees of the House of Commons (23), April 2016

Indigenous and Northern Affairs

Access to Information, Privacy and Ethics

Agriculture and Agri-Food

Canadian Heritage

Citizenship and Immigration

Environment and Sustainable Development

Finance

Fisheries and Oceans

Foreign Affairs and International Development

Government Operations and Estimates

Health

Human Resources, Skills and Social Development and the Status of Persons with Disabilities

Industry, Science and Technology

International Trade

Justice and Human Rights

Liaison

National Defence

Natural Resources

Procedure and House Affairs

Public Accounts

Status of Women

Transport, Infrastructure and Communities

Veteran Affairs

Appendix B

Standing Committees of the Senate (15), April 2008

Aboriginal Peoples

Agriculture and Forestry

Banking, Trade and Commerce

Ethics and Conflict of Interest for Senators

Energy, the Environment and Natural Resources

Fisheries and Oceans

Foreign Affairs and International Trade

Human Rights

Internal Economy, Budgets and Administration

Legal and Constitutional Affairs

National Finance

National Security and Defence

 Rules, Procedures and Rights of Parliament

Social Affairs, Science and Technology

Transport and Communications

Appendix C

Standing Joint Committees (3), April 2008

Library of Parliament

Official Languages

Scrutiny of Regulations

Important Terms and Concepts

accountability

accounting officer

Auditor General

bureaucratic independence

Canadian Human Rights Commission

collective responsibility

Federal Accountability Act

functions of the legislature

ministerial responsibility

Office of the Information Commissioner

Office of the Privacy Commissioner

Officers of Parliament

Parliament

Parliamentary Budget Officer

performance measurement and reporting

provincial legislatures

public service

roles of Parliament in relation to the public service

Special Operating Agencies

Study Questions

1. Provincial legislatures should not be simply amalgamated with Parliament in discussions of public service reform. What distinguishes them?

2. What leads Thomas to conclude that "clearly there is life left in the doctrines of collective and individual ministerial responsibility, but the widespread public perception today is that the Canadian political system lacks real accountability"?

3. What is the nature of the implicit bargain between public servants and the ministers they serve, and what developments have made this bargain hard to maintain as a central organizing concept?

4. Outline the meaning of each of the parliamentary roles in relation to the public service—legitimizer, policy-maker, creator, financier, scrutineer—and the relative *effectiveness* of each role.

5. Considering the evidence presented, as well as additional evidence you may be able to muster, what answer would you give to the question "Does Parliament play a meaningful role in controlling the public service?"

6. Are there arguments for strengthening the first four parliamentary roles that are usually dismissed as formal (legitimizer, policy-maker, creator, financier)? Offer some arguments both for and against this notion.

References

Aucoin, Peter. 1995. *The New Public Management: Canada in a Comparative Perspective*. Montreal: IRPP.

_____. 1998. *Auditing for Accountability: The Role of the Auditor General*. Ottawa: Institute on Governance.

_____. 2012. "New Political Governance in Westminster Systems: Impartial Public Administration and Management at Risk." Governance: An International Journal of Policy, Administration and Institutions. 25, 22, pp. 177–99

Aucoin, P., Bakvis, H. and Jarvis, M. 2013. "Constraining Executive Power in an Era of New Political Governance." *Governing: Essays in Honour of Donald J. Savoie*, edited by J. Bickerton and B.G. Peters, Montreal: McGill-Queen's University Press, pp. 32–50.

Bryden, Joan. 2016,."Michael Chong's Reform Act passed by the Senate." Toronto Star, 22 June 2016.

Canada, House of Commons, Subcommittee on the Business of Supply. 1997. *Completing the Circle of Control*. Ottawa.

Canada, Office of the Information Commissioner. 1999. *Annual Report, 1998–1999*. Ottawa.

Canada, Parliament of Canada. Report on Parliament, 2015–16, p. 10.

Canada, Treasury Board Secretariat. 1995. *The Expenditure Management System of the Government of Canada*. Ottawa: TBS.

Colwell, R., and Paul G. Thomas. 1987. "Parliament and Patronage." Journal of Canadian Studies 22, 2 (Summer), pp. 163–76.

Docherty, David C. 1998. *Mr Smith Goes To Ottawa: Life in the House of Commons*. Vancouver: University of British Columbia Press.

_____. 2003. "Canada: Political Careers between Executive Hopes and Constituency Work." *Politics as a Profession*, rev. English edn., edited by Jens Borchert and Juergen Zeiss, Oxford: Oxford University Press.

Franks, C.E.S. 1987. *The Parliament of Canada*. Toronto: University of Toronto Press.

_____. 1997. "Not Anonymous: Ministerial Responsibility and the British Accounting Officers." *Canadian Public Administration* 40, 4 (Winter), pp. 626–52.

Good, David. 2003. *The Politics of Public Management: The HRDC Audit of Grants and Contributions*. Toronto: University of Toronto Press.

_____. 2007. *The Politics of Public Money: Spenders, Guardians, Priority Setters and Financial Watchdogs inside the Canadian Government*. Toronto: University of Toronto Press.

Heard, Andrew. 1991. *Canadian Constitutional Conventions: The Marriage of Law and Politics*. Toronto: Oxford University Press.

Heintzman, Ralph. 2014. Renewal of the Federal Public Service: Toward a Charter of the Public Service. Ottawa: Canada 2020.

Holmes, J.W. 1996. "The Office of the Auditor General and Public Service Reform: An Insider's Perspective." *Canadian Public Administration* 39, 4 (Winter), pp. 524–34.

Kernaghan, Kenneth., and John Langford. 2014. The Responsible Public Servant. 2nd edn, Toronto: Institute of Public Administration of Canada.

McInnes, David. 1999. *Taking It to the Hill: The Complete Guide to Appearing Before (and Surviving) Parliamentary Committees*. Ottawa: University of Ottawa Press.

Mitchell, J.R. 1997. "Reply to C.E.S. Franks." *Canadian Public Administration* 40, 4 (Winter): 653–7.

_____, and S.L. Sutherland. 1999. "Ministerial Responsibility: The Submission of Politics and Administration to the Electorate." *Public Administration and Policy: Governing in Challenging Times*, edited by Martin W. Westmacott and Hugh P. Mellon, Scarborough, ON: Prentice-Hall Allyn and Bacon Canada, pp. 21–38.

Nevitte, Neil. 1996. *Decline of Deference: Canadian Value Change in a Cross-National Perspective.* Peterborough, ON: Broadview Press.

Pattee, R.P., and Paul G. Thomas. 1985. "The Senate and Defence Policy: Subcommittee Report on Maritime Defence." *Parliament and Canadian Foreign Policy*, edited by David Taras, Toronto: CIIA, pp. 101–20.

Power, Michael. 1997. *The Audit Society: Rituals of Verification.* Oxford: Oxford University Press.

President of the Treasury Board. 1998. *Managing For Results, 1998.* Ottawa.

Roberts, Alisdair. 1996. "Worrying About Misconduct: The Control Lobby and Bureaucratic Reform." *Canadian Public Administration* 39, 4 (Winter), pp. 489–523.

Royal Commission on Financial Management and Accountability. 1979. *Final Report.* Ottawa: Supply and Services.

Savoie, Donald J. 1999. *Governing from the Centre: The Concentration of Power in Canadian Politics.* Toronto: University of Toronto Press.

Slatter, Frans F. 1982. *Parliament and Administrative Agencies.* Ottawa: Law Reform Commission of Canada.

Sossin, Lorne. 2000. "Speaking Truth to Power? The Search for Bureaucratic Independence in Canada." *University of Toronto Law Journal* 55, 1, pp. 1–59.

Sutherland, S. L. 1980. "On the Audit Trail of the Auditor General: Parliament's Servant, 1973–1980." *Canadian Public Administration* 23, 4 (Winter), pp. 616–44.

_____. 1991a. "Responsible Government and Ministerial Responsibility: Every Reform Is Its Own Problem." *Canadian Journal of Political Science* 24, 1 (March), pp. 91–120.

_____. 1991b. "The Al-Mashat Affair: Administrative Responsibility in Parliamentary Institutions." *Canadian Public Administration* 34, 4 (Winter), pp. 573–603.

Thomas, Paul G. 1979. "Theories of Parliament and Parliamentary Reform." *Journal of Canadian Studies* 14, 2 (Summer), pp. 57–67.

_____. 1991. "Profile of the Private Member." *Canadian Parliamentary Review* 14, 2 (Summer), pp. 12–15.

_____. 1993. "Effectiveness of Parliamentary Committees." *Parliamentary Government* 44 (Aug.), pp. 10–12.

_____. 1994. "Parties and Parliament: The Role of Party Caucuses." *Canadian Parties in Transition*, 2nd edn, edited by Alain-G. Gagnon and A. Brian Tanguay, Toronto: Nelson.

_____. 1996. "Evaluation of Information Disclosure Standards for the Improved Reporting to Parliament Project." Paper prepared for the Treasury Board Secretariat, Ottawa.

_____. 1997. "Ministerial Responsibility and Administrative Accountability." *New Public Management and Public Administration in Canada*, edited by Mohamed Charih and Arthur Daniels, Toronto: IPAC.

_____. 1998. "Contracting Out: Policy and Management Issues." *Managing Strategic Change: Learning From Program Review*, edited by Peter Aucoin and Donald J. Savoie, Ottawa: CCMD, pp. 169–222.

_____. 1999. "Change, Parliament and the Future of the Legislative Audit." Paper prepared for the Office of the Auditor General of Canada.

_____. 2003. "The Past, Present and Future of Officers of Parliament." *Canadian Public Administration* 46, 3 (Fall), pp. 287–314.

_____. 2008. "The Swirling Meanings and Practices of Accountability in Canadian Government." *Power, Professionalism and Public Service: Essays in Honour of Kenneth Kernaghan*, edited by David Siegel and Ken Rasmussen, Toronto: University of Toronto Press, pp. 43–75.

_____. 2013. "Communications and Prime Ministerial Power." *Governing: Essays in Honour of Donald J. Savoie*, edited by James Bickerton and B. Guy Peters, Montreal: McGill-Queen's University Press, pp. 53–84.

_____. 2014. "Two Cheers for Bureaucracy." *Canadian Politics*, edited by James Bickerton and Alain-G. Gagnon, Toronto: University of Toronto Press, pp. 177–98

United Kingdom, House of Commons, Public Service Committee. 1996. *Ministerial Accountability and Responsibility.* London: HMSO.

Wernick, Michael. *Clerk of the Privy Council and Secretary to the Cabinet, Twenty-Third Annual Report to the Prime Minister on the Public Service of Canada.* Downloaded from http://www.clerk.gc.ca/eng/feature.asp?pageId=450 on November 22 2016.

White, Graham. 1996. "Comparing Provincial Legislatures." *Provinces: Canadian Provincial Politics*, edited by Christopher Dunn, Peterborough, ON: Broadview Press, pp. 205–28.

_____. 2006. "Evaluating Provincial and Territorial Legislatures." *Provinces: Canadian Provincial Politics*, edited by Christopher Dunn, Peterborough: Broadview Press.

8

Judicial Administration

Carl Baar and Ian Greene

Chapter Overview

This chapter introduces what is to many a new field—judicial administration. It traces the relatively recent roots of the field in the United States and Canada, and explores the concepts and institutions that animate it. Despite being a young subdiscipline, judicial administration honours concepts that are as old as the courts themselves, such as judicial independence and judicial impartiality, and seeks to structure administrative arrangements to protect them. It also brings to the fore some new and innovative concepts, such as integrated justice, alternative dispute resolution (ADR), the multi-door courthouse, mediation, and restorative justice. The paradox of the field is that it has much to teach the older strains of public administration.

Chapter Objectives

By the end of this chapter, students will be able to do the following:

- Understand the historical timeline for the introduction of judicial administration in the United States and Canada.
- Describe the federal and provincial aspects of judicial administration in Canada.
- Describe the judicial hierarchy and how has it evolved since Confederation.
- List some important innovations in court structures in recent decades.
- Discuss the nature of judicial independence and how it impacts the practice of judicial administration.
- Describe some important innovations in judicial administration in recent decades.

Introduction

Judicial administration refers to the organization, management, and operation of courts and court systems. It is a specialized field of study within the broader discipline of public administration. There are two major factors that make judicial administration unique. The first is that the constitutional principle of **judicial independence** means that those administering the courts are constrained by the contours of that principle. The second is that, whereas in most fields of public administration both the public and public administrators want their department to operate as efficiently and effectively as possible, there are some lawyers and litigants who use delay as a tactical weapon. These two factors pose unique problems for those involved in judicial administration.

Judicial administration as a field of study is quite recent in Canada. Perhaps the first comprehensive examination of the area was the three-volume *Report on the Administration of Ontario Courts* published in 1973 by the Ontario Law Reform Commission, and the first scholarly book in the field was *Judicial Administration in Canada* by Judge Perry Millar and Professor Carl Baar, published in 1981 as part of the Canadian Public Administration Series.

Judicial administration was already established as a field of study in the United States, but even there its origins have usually been traced only as far back as 1906, when Roscoe Pound, later to become Dean of Harvard Law School and the most prolific writer in sociological jurisprudence, gave his famous and controversial address to an American Bar Association meeting in St. Paul, Minnesota: "The Causes of Popular Dissatisfaction with the Administration of Justice." By mid-century, a text (W. P. Willoughby's *Judicial Administration*) and a law school casebook (Maynard Pirsig's *Judicial Administration*) had been published, along with major reports by the American Bar Association (e.g., Vanderbilt, 1949) and articles by Pound and other law reformers. The American Judicature Society had been founded in 1913, and its journal, originally the *Journal of the American Judicature Society* and for many years simply *Judicature*, had provided a forum for scholarly and professional writing on the reform of judicial selection, bar governance and discipline, and court organization and procedure. New Jersey Chief Justice (and former ABA president) Arthur Vanderbilt had just completed constitutional reform of his state's court system, and in 1951 would found the Institute of Judicial Administration at New York University Law School.

A new surge of interest in the field would begin in the mid-1960s with the growing American concern about crime, marked by the 1967 publication of the report of the presidential crime commission, *The Challenge of Crime in a Free Society*. By 1973, when the Ontario Law Reform Commission's report was completed, the flagship American text in the field, *Managing the Courts*, by Ernest C. Friesen, Jr, Edward C. Gallas, and Nesta M. Gallas, was in widespread use. New centres of research and education had been established—the National Judicial College, founded in 1960; the Institute for Court Management (ICM), founded in 1969; and the National Center for State Courts, founded in 1971. Three specialized master's degree programs in judicial administration were in operation, at the University of Denver Law School, the School of Public Administration at the University of Southern California, and American University in Washington, DC. And a new refereed journal, the *Justice System Journal*, sponsored by ICM, was about to begin its first volume.

In fact, the practice and problems of judicial administration could be traced back well before the twentieth century. While references to the eternal verity of the law's delay are often sprinkled through the orations of judges and lawyers, efforts to address these and other central concerns of the administration of justice go back thousands of years. Chapter 18 of the Book of Exodus describes how Jethro, concerned that his son-in-law Moses has kept the people of Israel waiting "from the morning unto the evening" to ask him how to resolve their disputes in accordance with God's law, advises Moses to appoint a number of "able men" to decide the large number of routine cases, leaving only the most difficult matters for Moses himself (Exodus 18: 13–27).

Furthermore, while court administration as a profession has only begun to emerge over the past 30 to 40 years, administrative officials have always played key roles in the support of judicial power. When Michel Foucault introduces his classic *Discipline and Punish* with an account of a public execution in 1759 in France, he describes how the clerk of court is called when the executioner is unable to carry out the sentence; the clerk returns to the courthouse and confers with the judges about how to draw and quarter the man before he is hanged (Foucault, 1979: 3–5). When former Ontario Premier E.C. Drury is rewarded at the close of his political career with a patronage post as Local Registrar of the Supreme Court, Sheriff of Simcoe County, and Clerk of the Simcoe County Court in Barrie, he still must arrange in the late 1940s for construction of a gallows to execute a person convicted of a capital offence in the county (Drury, 1970).

While these local court officials played important roles, they were not part of a larger coherent administrative system. Thus when two neophyte senior court administrators in Manitoba decided to assemble their provincial counterparts at a small conference in September 1975, the two did not even know whom to contact in the other provinces. There were clearly identified senior officials (though varying in title, rank, and legal qualifications) in British Columbia, Saskatchewan, Ontario, Quebec, New Brunswick, and Nova Scotia, but Alberta, Newfoundland, and Prince Edward Island still divided responsibility for court support services among diverse officials (as British Columbia, Ontario, and Nova Scotia had done until only a few years earlier). Following some early stops and restarts, these officials have become the core of a national organization (The Association of Canadian Court Administrators) that met annually in locations across Canada until 2012, when for financial reasons it was transitioned to a more centralized body known as the Heads of Court Administration.

As late as 1980, when Brock University initiated Canada's first graduate-level course of study in court administration, there wasn't even general agreement on an appropriate label for the field. The Brock program was referred to as an MA degree specializing in Judicial Administration, while the national organization's members settled on court administration, naming their group the Association of Canadian Court Administrators (ACCA). One ACCA leader felt that the term *judicial administration* was confined to those matters within the responsibility of the judges themselves, and excluded a variety of court support services in the hands of court administrators. Judge Perry Millar, who had attended the inaugural meeting in Winnipeg of what was to become ACCA, felt that the term *court administration* was too close to the earlier term *court services*, and that many officials who held the title "Director of Court Services" needed to bring a broader managerial perspective to their work.

He felt the term *judicial administration* did in fact encompass both the traditional court support functions and the new managerial requirements (Millar & Baar, 1981: 17–18). Today, in fact, both terms—*judicial administration* and *court administration*—are used widely and interchangeably, reflecting the emergence of a coherent field of study and practice. In 2000, when York University created its Graduate Diploma in Justice System Administration, the thinking was that the name of the new program would signal both *judicial administration* and *court administration*, and would also empower the program to examine administrative issues in parts of the justice system beyond courts.

The purpose of this chapter is to introduce some of the major terms, topics, and preoccupations of the field of judicial administration. At the same time, the chapter will also argue that the field, although non-existent less than 40 years ago in Canada, and seen as backward and marginal in the United States, has emerged today as a model for other areas of public administration in an era when the ability to manage professionals, to manage flexibly, to manage contextually, and to deliver specific programs effectively is critical to success in managing a wide range of public-sector initiatives.

Provincial Responsibility

In Canada, authority over judicial administration lies largely with the provinces and is therefore affected by the managerial and fiscal environment of provincial and territorial governments. This differentiates judicial administration from many of the larger, older, and more established areas of public administration, and reinforces its distinctive character.

Provincial authority is easily understood and explained, because the administration of justice has been a provincial responsibility since Confederation in 1867, as specified in section 92(14) of the British North America Act (today known as the Constitution Act, 1867). Prior to that time, courts had been organized within each province from the time of the earliest permanent civilian settlements. Upper Canada (now Ontario) gets its own special footnote in North American history, for in 1795, within a few years of the establishment of its first courts, a group of lawyers met in Niagara-on-the-Lake, the province's first capital, and set up the Law Society of Upper Canada as the governing body of the legal profession; the Law Society is now the oldest group of self-governing lawyers on the continent, and was the model for integrated bar reforms in the United States in the first half of the twentieth century (McKean, 1963: 33).

Four caveats are necessary to modify the general statement that court administration is a provincial responsibility. First, the judges of the superior courts of each province (the judicial hierarchy is discussed below) are appointed, and their salaries and expenses paid, by the federal government. Thus, an important aspect of the responsibility for and administration of the courts is divided between federal and provincial authorities. No similar system would be conceivable in either the American or Australian federations. In fact, the Canadian approach would be unique had not the Indian Constitution of 1949 borrowed and entrenched it in their fundamental law. No principled reason for this division can be gleaned from Canadian Confederation debates of the 1860s, and the general view is that federal appointment power reflected the patronage preferences of key political allies Macdonald and Cartier. In retrospect, federal appointment may reinforce the separation of the judges from a key source of potential dependence on governments responsible for day-to-day administration of the courts, but there is no sign that the Constitution's framers had Locke or Montesquieu in mind when the judicature provisions (sections 96–101 of the Constitution Act, 1867) were drafted.

Second, criminal law and procedure are federal responsibilities under section 91(27), so that provincial efforts to address issues of court delay, for example, must either stay away from changes in the federal Criminal Code or await support and co-operation from Ottawa, speaking through the Department of Justice Canada, before being able to act. For example, grand juries have long been seen as antiquated; once provinces had replaced citizen-initiated prosecution with professional prosecutors, the citizen grand jury no longer provided real protection for persons accused of crime or meaningful participation of the public in the law enforcement process. But provinces that sought to eliminate the grand jury often had to wait many years for federal parliamentary concurrence (Nova Scotia was the last, in 1992). Today, provincial attorneys general often call for an end to preliminary inquiries that take up many hours of Provincial Court time, arguing that the Supreme Court of Canada's post-Charter decision requiring pretrial disclosure of evidence by Crown prosecutors (*R. v. Stinchcombe*, 1991) makes the preliminary hearing redundant. Criminal defence lawyers, however, disagree, and Justice Canada has refused to act on recommendations that go back over 35 years.

Third, the federal government is responsible for the administration of certain specialized courts set up by federal statute under the authority of section 101 "for the better Administration of the Laws of Canada." Earliest among these were the Supreme Court of Canada and the Exchequer Court of Canada. (It is interesting to realize that the Supreme Court itself was not created until 1875, a full eight years after Confederation. Presumably there was no rush, since a final appeal could still go to five members of the House of Lords in England, sitting as the Judicial Committee of the Privy Council.) While the Supreme Court has become the jurisprudential leader in reality as well as formality, the Exchequer Court, with its specialized jurisdiction over federal tax matters, was abolished and replaced in 1971 by the Federal Court of Canada, with broader authority to handle appeals from federal administrative agencies and other matters under federal law (see, generally, Russell, 1987). Later in the 1970s, the existing Tax Review Board was transformed into the Tax Court of Canada. Each of these three courts has had its own administrative apparatus, including professional administrators charged with overall responsibility for managing the records, the staff, and the courthouse space; and **registrars** and trial coordinators who deal with the day-to-day movement of cases and courtroom proceedings. In 2002, federal legislation created the Courts Administration Service (CAS) by merging the administrative staffs of the Federal Court, Tax Court, and Court Martial Appeal Court, and placing the CAS at arm's length from the Ministry of Justice; the innovation has been noticed and praised as far away as Australia (Alford et al., 2004: Ch. 7). The Supreme Court remains a separately administered body. The chief administrator is the Registrar, who is appointed by cabinet on the recommendation of the Chief Justice, and is accountable to the Chief Justice (Supreme Court of Canada Act).

Finally, federal institutions have developed in recent decades to support the common efforts of provincial judiciaries. Thus the Canadian Judicial Council, founded in 1971, includes all federally appointed chief justices and associate chief justices, even though the vast majority of them sit on provincially administered superior courts. The Council has statutory responsibility for discipline of section 96 judges, and has also supervised important research on issues and policies of direct concern to the administration of justice. The Canadian Centre for Justice Statistics was established in 1981 as a satellite of (or section within) Statistics Canada and operates today under the guidance of liaison committees of provincial justice officials. The National Judicial Institute was established in 1988 to provide judicial education programs for all judges, regardless of whether they are appointed by the federal or provincial government.

The Judicial Hierarchy

Courts throughout the world are organized in hierarchies that reflect the process of litigating cases and making authoritative decisions. Cases proceed from trial to appeal; since appellate courts have the last word in a case, they are referred to as "higher courts." Trial courts are typically categorized into superior and inferior courts; the former are often given the statutory name of Superior Court (*cour superieure* in Quebec). The two types of courts, properly identified by more neutral terminology as **courts of general jurisdiction** and courts of limited jurisdiction, are often distinguished by the seriousness of the cases they handle, but there are numerous and growing exceptions.

The hierarchical distinction remains important in legal terms, especially in common-law countries where past decisions establish precedents binding in future cases. Thus, whether a judgment constitutes a binding precedent depends first on the hierarchical relationship of the court that set the precedent and the court that is asked to follow the precedent. A decision of a provincial court of appeal is binding on all the trial courts of that province. A decision of the Supreme Court of Canada is binding on all other Canadian trial and appellate courts. In turn, the decision of a provincial superior court is binding on all other trial courts within that province. (For the names of the various provincial trial courts, see Dunn, 2006: 287.)

The decisions of common-law courts that are not legally superior to one another are not binding, but may be persuasive. Thus, the judgment of a court of appeal in one province is often cited in the courts of appeal of other provinces as a rule that ought to be followed, but it does not govern. Similarly, a superior court judge need not follow the precedent set by another judge on the same superior court.

Constitutionally, **superior courts** also have what is legally termed *inherent jurisdiction*, which is derived from their link to superior courts in England and their constitutional entrenchment in section 96 of the Constitution Act of 1867. Thus superior courts, unlike trial courts whose jurisdiction is limited to powers conferred by statute, have inherent authority to enforce their own orders (e.g., through use of the contempt power).

Historically, appeals in Canadian provinces were not handled by a separate court, but by superior court judges assembled to review the original judgment of one of their fellow judges. As provinces grew in size, courts of appeal became differentiated entities with judges appointed specifically to those tribunals. Newfoundland's superior court had only three judges from its inception in 1825 until 1963; as a result it was not unusual for a trial judge to sit on a three-judge panel reviewing one of his own decisions (Goodridge, 1991). In Alberta, the historic link between its current Court of Appeal and Court of Queen's Bench is such that trial judges often sit by special appointment to hear appeals (but never from their own judgments).

The superior courts were supplemented by a set of county courts and district courts in the nine English-Canadian provinces. These courts, also staffed by federally appointed judges, did the bulk of the civil and criminal trials in county towns throughout the country. Over time, the work of the county and district courts came to overlap the work of the superior trial courts, and beginning in 1973, the two courts were merged to form a single section 96 trial court in each of the provinces.

At the lowest level of the judicial hierarchy stood the **Magistrate's Courts**. In the first half of the twentieth century, it would have been appropriate to apply the term *inferior courts* to them in more than a formal legal fashion. Magistrates themselves were sometimes called police magistrates, reflecting their role in criminal cases—and typically their location in local police stations (where their successors were found until much later in the century). Magistrates were usually non-lawyers (the first women judges in Canada were non-lawyer magistrates, including Emily Murphy of the "Persons Case," whose criminal sentences could be notoriously harsh), serving on a part-time basis, often paid on a piecework basis (the more warrants signed, the higher the pay), and serving at the pleasure of the government. In pioneer Alberta, the local magistrate could be the commander of the local RCMP detachment. Until 1939 in British Columbia, magistrates were paid only when they entered a conviction; the practice continued for some matters until 1960 (Watts, 1986: 79–81).

Beginning in Quebec and Ontario in the 1960s, these courts were transformed over two decades in every province into modern, professional **Provincial Courts**. Their work today is primarily in criminal matters, but some have been given expanded jurisdiction in civil matters (originally small claims but now extending up to claims currently as high as $50,000 in Alberta, $30,000 in Saskatchewan, and $25,000 in British Columbia, Nova Scotia, Newfoundland and Labrador, and Ontario) and in family law. All of these courts have exclusive jurisdiction over young offenders under the federal Young Offenders Act. The criminal jurisdiction of Provincial Courts has expanded to the point where a large majority of serious offences (termed *indictable offences* in Canada, generally parallel to *felonies* in the United States) are tried in these courts. Thus, in practice, superior courts have tended to specialize in civil litigation, Provincial Courts in criminal matters, limiting the salience of the superior-inferior legal relationship between the two levels of trial courts.

These changes, coupled with the desire of Provincial Court judges to erase the difference in status between the two levels, have led to proposals for a **unified criminal court** at the superior court level. The unified criminal court would replace the current division, whereby only superior courts can hold jury trials and Provincial Court judges cannot preside at murder trials. Twenty years ago, the proposal received the unanimous support of provincial attorneys general, but opposition by superior court judges and the Canadian Bar Association stopped the proposals. (For a detailed analysis of the issues, see Baar, 1991.) Renewed interest surfaced again early in this century, and a major national conference was held on the topic in 2002 (see Russell, 1987).

A more successful innovation has been the **unified family court**, designed so that litigation on family issues (divorce, separation, custody and access, division of property) would no longer be divided between superior courts and Provincial Courts.

Specialized family courts with unified jurisdiction now operate in seven provinces.

The existence of a legal hierarchy has had important administrative consequences. In a sense, judicial administration is inherently non-hierarchical in character. The most difficult administrative work is often at the front end of the system. Visualize the paperwork (or computer capacity) necessary to support the activities in a criminal intake court that hears first appearances, deals with applications for pretrial release, takes guilty pleas, metes out sentences, and schedules dates for trials and preliminary hearings. Or consider the support work at the counter in a civil court, where many claims are filed and judgments issued without a case ever going before a judge. The pressure and complexity of this work reflect the fact that **court administrators** must manage processes and smooth the flow of incoming work. Yet the existence of a judicial hierarchy, in which the courts with the greatest legal authority handle fewer cases than courts in a legally subordinate position, could distort administrative priorities.

In the United States, critics have noted that because judicial salaries increase as judges move up the legal hierarchy, so do the salaries of court administrators, meaning that courts with the largest volume of cases, as well as the largest amount of fee and fine collection, are managed by administrators with the lowest salaries and status (Stott, 1982). The chief justices of state supreme courts can often dictate administrative policy in high-volume **courts of limited jurisdiction**. As court administration has evolved as a distinct field and the professional requirements for court managers are increasingly recognized, processes for court governance are likely to evolve that separate the requirements for a hierarchy of legal judgments from the requirements for effectively administering justice.

Judicial Independence

Judicial independence is the central concept in understanding how courts are administered. This independence reflects the fundamental values of the judiciary as a distinct public institution. It is seen as a necessary condition for any court system to perform its functions (in current terminology, achieve its mission). It is also a constraint on the management of courts and a challenge to court administrators everywhere.

The concept refers to the ability of the individual judge to perform his or her adjudicative function, whether sitting in court hearing cases or sitting in chambers writing judgments and hearing motions, free from external interference. Historically, that interference took the form of pressure from government on the judiciary to hand down decisions consistent with governmental preferences, and that pressure is still visible today in many countries throughout the world (including Canada and the United States). Judicial independence can also be undermined by interference from outside pressure groups, or even from inside interference, for example, if the chief judge of a court criticizes the work of one of that court's judges and perhaps threatens to take that work away (see *Chandler v. Judicial Council of the Tenth Circuit*, 1970, in the United States, and *Reilly v. Wachowich*, 2000 in Canada; for related commentary, see Marshall, 1995.)

This is not to say that judges do or should operate free from external influences when they hear and decide cases. Governments are the most frequent litigators (parties) in court. Every criminal case is prosecuted by a Crown attorney (a full-time government official) or a person that Crown attorney designates. Federal and provincial governments are parties or intervenors in every case arising under the Canadian Charter of Rights and Freedoms. Numerous interest groups participate in litigation as well. But these roles are clearly defined and public. Parties argue for their positions, both orally and in writing, through formal processes that are either public, or conducted with all contending parties present (e.g., proceedings under the Young Offenders Act), or subject to review and appeal (e.g., *ex parte* proceedings brought by one party alone on an emergency basis). Thus, if a government lawyer meets privately with a judge to discuss a pending case, as occurred during a war crimes proceeding in the Federal Court of Canada, that meeting is seen as a violation of judicial independence (*Canada [Minister of Citizenship and Immigration] v. Tobiass*, 1997; and see Baar, 1998).

Judicial independence is closely linked to the concept of **judicial impartiality**: that a judge is bound to decide only on the relevant law and facts presented in court. Interference by any individual or official not playing a formal role in the proceeding (that is, someone who is not a witness, advocate, or adjudicator in that case) could prevent the judge from coming to an impartial judgment. Thus judicial independence

is seen as a necessary condition for an impartial tribunal. However, it is not a sufficient condition, since an independent adjudicator might still not act impartially. If that occurs, judicial independence requires that it be remedied through appropriate formal procedures (e.g., an appeal to a higher court, or a motion by a party that the judge recuse him/herself from the case, or a complaint to a judicial disciplinary body), not by a personal attack from a government official or members of the public.

Similarly, judicial independence and impartiality do not prevent politicians, academics, or citizens from criticizing the judgments of a court on the grounds that the court misread the law or misconstrued facts, or made policy best left to others (or declined to make policy when a legitimate opportunity arose to do so). Judges are not accountable in the sense that employees in a government department are; they are not required to follow orders that restrict their exercise of judicial discretion. But judges are accountable in the sense that their discretion is subject to review, whether by a higher court or by those who follow their work and question its quality.

In a liberal democratic theory of society and politics, judicial independence is critical to the ability of courts to do justice by the impartial application of the law to parties in individual cases. It is also a legitimate and important constraint on governments that is often missing in non-democratic regimes, where judges sit and apply the law but may be sanctioned when their judgments are seen to undermine the government in power.

In the Charter era, the constitutional guarantees surrounding judicial independence have been given additional meaning, particularly in the context of disputes over the salaries of provincial court judges in the 1990s. As a result of disputes in four provinces, the Supreme Court of Canada, in the Reference re Remuneration of Judges, 1997, imposed constitutionally required salary commissions in each province to limit negotiation between elected officials and judges. (See McCormick's excellent article [2004] on these developments.) Following criticism of the breadth of the holding in the Remuneration Reference, the Court subsequently modified its judgment [*Provincial Court Judges' Assn. of New Brunswick v. New Brunswick*, 2005].

But how does the fundamental concept of judicial independence fit into the study and practice of judicial administration? First, the preservation and enhancement of judicial independence becomes one of the purposes of court administration (see Friedland, 1995). At an operating level, clerical employees must know what documents need to go in a case file for the judge to review before going into court, and court administrative staff often becomes a buffer between the judiciary and the public. Those who design courthouses have to ensure that jury rooms are private and that judges can move in and out of court without passing through public hallways where parties to a case could make statements not properly in evidence. Those who prepare the court's budget must ensure that officials with fiscal authority do not act to undermine judicial independence.

Second, the management of an organization whose core activities are performed by autonomous professionals becomes a challenge for court administration. Unlike most parts of the public sector, in which civil servants deliver services to the organization's clients in the community, the justice services of the court are not provided by public servants but by independent judges not subject to direct supervision by any manager. In many provinces, court administration defines its clients as the judges themselves rather than the public, only to find that many judges react unkindly to that label.

Third, court administration is made even more challenging in Canada because administrators in every province are part of executive branch ministries responsible to the government of the day. Thus, court administrators must serve two masters—judiciary and government—and two potentially conflicting principles: judicial independence and responsible government. This conflict has been addressed differently in various judicial systems. Courts in the United States are conceived as a third branch of government, so that court administrators are responsible to the judges of their courts—either to a Chief Justice, the court as a whole, or a judicial council. Until 2006, courts in England and Wales were administered by an executive department, the Lord Chancellor's Department (LCD), but the Lord Chancellor was himself both a judge and a cabinet minister. Legislation replacing the LCD by a Department for Constitutional Affairs (now Ministry of Justice) was very controversial and created difficulties for court administration. In Australia, a number of courts have evolved arm's-length relationships to the government of the day, so

that their administration resembles that of independent agencies in Canada. In Ireland, an innovative Irish Courts Service has shifted responsibility for court administration from the government to an independent board of judges, lawyers, court administrators, and public representatives. Elsewhere in Europe, Asia, and Latin America, where government has traditionally played a central role in court administration, a diverse array of countries—including Sweden, Singapore, India, and Cuba—have developed administrative forms separate from the executive.

Canada has traditionally separated adjudication from court administration, so that judges and administrators can define distinct spheres of activity. Judges expect government to provide them with the necessary staff and material resources to conduct legal proceedings, but they have no authority to hire or fire administrative staff or to supervise the purchase of necessary equipment. However, procedural and technological changes urged by judges to reduce delay and increase efficiency are often delayed or denied by government ministries responsible for court administration—usually provincial ministries of the attorney general that are also responsible for prosecuting criminal cases in those courts.

Beginning in 1981, when the late Chief Justice Jules Deschenes of the Quebec Superior Court wrote a 198-recommendation report, *Masters in Their Own House*, many students of the courts have called for some form of judicial **administrative independence** that reflects the unique role of the courts within a traditional cabinet system. But no major change has been accomplished. British Columbia began in 1976 to shift parts of the court administrative staff to a separate judicial administration budget controlled by the judges, but no further shifting of responsibility has taken place in over four decades. In the late 1980s, the Quebec government offered to adopt the principles in the Deschenes Report. The province's three chief justices (from the Court of Appeal, the Superior Court, and the Cour du Québec) were supportive, but the rest of the judiciary resisted, fearing that administrative autonomy would be accompanied by substantial budget cuts that the government would leave the judiciary to implement. More recently, Ontario judges and ministry officials attempted to negotiate a court services agency model similar to that in Ireland, but no consensus was ever reached, and as of 2016 the section 96 chief justices seemed to prefer the existing approach, which is substantially executive-centred. Nevertheless, the position of Executive Legal Officer—a position not in Court Services and directly accountable to the Chief Justice of the Superior Court—has been created to liaise between the Chief Justice and Court Services, and a Memorandum of Understanding between the Office of the Chief Justice and the Attorney General has been negotiated to ensure that the Chief Justice has control over some administrative issues.

While a new set of practical issues has led to increased collaboration between judiciary and government in a number of provinces, the issue of administrative autonomy remains a lightning rod for executive-judicial conflict. A major report of the Canadian Judicial Council, *Alternative Models of Court Administration*, was released in fall 2006. It tried to reopen the issue by showcasing a wider variety of alternative approaches, including a funding model that would utilize a dispute resolution process in the event of a disagreement between the government and the judiciary about the court system's proposed budget. However, any breakthrough is still pending, as noted by the Chief Justice of Newfoundland and Labrador, Derek Green, in 2016 (Green, 2016).

Caseflow Management

Court administration has often been associated with court reform, the periodic efforts of legal and political elites to change the way court cases proceed from initiation to resolution. Roscoe Pound's 1906 address to the American Bar Association, recognized as the beginning of the study of judicial administration, was primarily a comprehensive agenda for procedural and organizational reform of common-law courts.

In the 1990s, court reform moved from a focus on changes in the jurisdiction and organization of courts to the revamping of court processes to reduce cost and delay and to increase access to justice, particularly in civil cases brought by private parties. At the heart of court administrative reforms is the concept of **caseflow management**, which refers to "the continuum of processes and resources necessary to move a case from filing to disposition, whether that disposition is by settlement, guilty plea, dismissal, trial or other method" (Solomon and Somerlot, 1987; see also Church et al., 1978; Mahoney, 1988; and Steelman, 2008). The term was coined in the United

States 40 years ago to convey a new conception of the court's role in the monitoring and supervision of all matters before it.

Caseflow management rests on a set of principles that derive from the notion that courts and judges are responsible for how cases proceed. This may sound trite to those unfamiliar with the internal workings of the judicial system, but it represents a challenge to one of the underlying assumptions of common-law procedure and the **adversary system**: party—and hence lawyer—control of the process (Jacob, 1987). In the traditional common-law proceeding, cases are initiated when one party (the plaintiff in a civil proceeding, the Crown in a criminal proceeding) files an appropriate document with the court. This may be a statement of claim or an application (in civil proceedings), or an information or indictment (in criminal proceedings). Once the defendant has responded (by filing a statement of defence in a civil proceeding or appearing in court to enter a plea in a criminal proceeding), the case then proceeds through preliminary steps taken by the parties (e.g., exchange of documents in civil cases or Crown disclosure in criminal cases). Only when the parties are ready to proceed to a trial, or perhaps earlier to a pretrial conference or a preliminary hearing, do they approach court staff and ask for a trial date (or have the matter placed on a list for trial). Only when a case moves to this stage is the court responsible for expediting its disposition. Thus a case may have been filed in court months or even years earlier, as the parties await medical evaluations in a personal injury case, or additional investigation in a criminal case, or the availability of busy counsel. In this paradigm, lawyer delay is separate from court delay (the number of weeks or months the parties must wait for a trial once they have requested a trial date from the court).

The theory of caseflow management is that the court is responsible for the case from the time it is initiated. Caseflow management rules and procedures typically include a set of time standards for all stages of litigation and a procedure for monitoring those cases that exceed the time standards (Civil Justice Review, 1995). In criminal cases, the Supreme Court of Canada has constitutionalized some of these time standards through use of section 11(b) of the Charter of Rights (*R. v. Askov*, 1990; *R. v. Morin*, 1992, *Barrett Richard Jordan v. Her Majesty the Queen*, 2016). As a result, courts may dismiss cases if the parties do not proceed, or they may force parties on when they believe the litigants are unnecessarily delaying the litigation. By monitoring the flow of cases, courts hope to speed up the pace of litigation, avoid having parties use delay for strategic purposes, and increase the predictability of trial or last-minute settlement in cases that are set down for trial.

Caseflow management may encompass a variety of different techniques and elements. Some courts set general guidelines and standards, for example, by using a fast track for cases that need to proceed more expeditiously. Other courts may establish directions hearings or case conferences at the early stage of a larger or more complex case, so that a customized set of time standards may be established by a judicial officer in consultation with the parties and their lawyers; these procedures are often labelled **case management** or "individual case management." Some courts encourage the use of settlement processes as part of a caseflow management program (e.g., settlement conferences conducted by a judge, or **mediation** conducted by a professional mediator).

While caseflow management projects and procedures have been used in a number of jurisdictions in the United States, and more recently in Canada, parties themselves still typically control the civil litigation process, at least in its preliminary stages. In Canada, criminal case processing is now typically controlled by the courts, although the Crown—and even the police—still play major and perhaps determining roles in setting trial dates.

The concept of caseflow management came later to England, but after a wide-ranging inquiry by Lord Woolf (1995), who later became the Master of the Rolls and then Lord Chief Justice, a comprehensive system of civil caseflow management was initiated in April 1999 throughout England and Wales. The Woolf reforms, as they are known, make up the most important changes in English civil procedure in over a century, and suggest that the changes begun in the United States 50 years ago are likely to continue there and in Canada.

Caseflow management reforms have also shifted the field of judicial administration from its traditional concern with jurisdictional divisions and judicial independence to a focus on operational processes and effective teamwork (both among teams of judges and between judges and lawyers and court staff). In fact, concepts of case management are increasingly used in other fields (e.g., medicine and social services). The field of court administration has thus been in the forefront of widespread public administration efforts to redirect attention away from formal structures and functions over to core processes and purposes.

Courts and the Public

Judicial administration has not only embraced the analysis of operational processes, but has also given increased attention to the relationship of courts and their clientele. A pioneering set of **Trial Court Performance Standards** developed in the 1990s by the National Center for State Courts in the United States focused not only on delay reduction and judicial independence, but also on access to justice and on maintaining public trust and confidence in the courts. Court administration has always been premised on efforts to improve the quality of justice (on court effectiveness rather than more narrowly defined issues of court efficiency). What emerged in the 1990s is a change in the issues courts define as central to achieving and maintaining the quality of justice. Court reform has shifted its orientation from internal professional issues to external public service issues, and from a focus on adjudication in courtrooms and chambers to litigation within and outside the courthouse itself.

One important manifestation has been the recognition that diversity has never been adequately understood or its effects on justice acknowledged. The rule of law is based on principles of universality—rejecting in theory the favouritism and bias that arose when individuals could use their power and influence to exempt themselves from laws that applied to others. But those general laws could have different effects on the population, reflecting historical differences in the treatment of men and women, Indigenous people and settlers, and people of different races and social conditions. The judiciary, made up primarily of men from dominant ethnic groups and economic classes, would be particularly vulnerable to critics of the gap between the theory and practices of legal institutions.

In the United States, a number of state court systems responded to these concerns by creating internal judicial task forces, to consider, first, gender bias and then racial bias (Baar, 1994). The Canadian judiciary lacked the administrative authority to initiate similar inquiries, but provincial law societies initially filled the gap (Law Society of British Columbia, 1992), and the Canadian Bar Association set up a **gender bias task force**, chaired by retired Supreme Court Justice Bertha Wilson, that produced an important and controversial report that spurred the development of judicial education programs on this and related topics (Canadian Bar Association Task Force, 1993: ch. 10). A broader commitment to ensuring access to justice is still new to the field of court administration, but this is increasingly defining the reform agenda (see Hughes, 1988; Zuber, 1987).

Near the beginning of the new century, Ian Greene was invited to join the team of the Canadian Democratic Audit to write a book about the strengths and weaknesses of Canadian courts. His book, *Courts*, reviews the successes and failures of various reforms in the justice system, and concludes that "Canadian courts are doing very well in some areas, such as their contribution to independence and impartiality. But there is a great deal of room for improvement in other areas, such as public participation in court administration and judicial selection, responsiveness to problems of unnecessary delay, support for self-represented litigants, and the respectful treatment of juries, witnesses and litigants" (Greene, 2006: 163). There are signs, however, that the civil justice system in Canada is demonstrating greater concern with the need to respond to public criticism of its inefficiencies. For example, since 2003 the Canadian Forum on Civil Justice, a non-profit independent agency located at York University, and set up to promote improvements to Canada's civil justice system, has an excellent website that provides detailed information on civil justice reform in Canada. And Fabien Gélinas and his colleagues in the Cyberjustice Project in Montreal have suggested new procedural models in civil justice (Gélinas et al., 2015).

Alternative Dispute Resolution (ADR)

The earliest, most visible evidence of this reorientation of court administration was the development of **alternative dispute resolution** (**ADR**) mechanisms. Alternative dispute resolution refers to dispute resolution procedures that occur outside of the regular courtroom procedures, but that normally have the blessing of the judiciary. These were already well-known in other fields: arbitration, which refers to the final settlement of a dispute by an arbitrator who is not a judge, had been a staple of labour relations for decades, and mediation, which refers to a process in which a trained mediator helps disputing parties to find their own resolution, had roots as diverse as religious communities, family counselling processes, and commercial and workplace committees. ADR received added visibility among court reformers in the 1976 Pound Conference in St Paul, Minnesota, convened on the seventieth anniversary of Roscoe Pound's pioneering ABA address. Pilot projects followed under the impetus of the Carter administration's Justice Department, both as freestanding alternatives to the court itself, and as alternatives to adjudication within the court (the beginning of the concept of the **multi-door courthouse**).

Mediation and settlement conferences have become an option—and occasionally a requirement—in Canadian and American trial courts, in civil cases, and in family law matters. What began as a movement proposing a new paradigm for dispute resolution, energized by a culture of peace and a theory of a facilitative interest-based transformative process, has been seen by some as an increasingly professionalized and mainstream option, often rights-based in character and sometimes even staffed by retired judges.

The role of ADR is still evolving. But as the concept of alternative dispute resolution has threatened to go mainstream, it has also been supplemented by a more radical conception of **restorative justice**. Trevor Farrow (2014), in his analysis of ADR in Canada, raises questions about future directions of law practice and court processes. Australian criminologist John Braithwaite, its best-known theoretician, went far enough to identify it as a replacement for a system of criminal justice that he considers one of the worst institutional failures since the Industrial Revolution. For Braithwaite, all disputes require a restoration of the balance of relationships within a community, and thus the participation of members of the larger community in individual cases.

In Canada, the most visible moves towards restorative justice have come in recommendations for separate Indigenous justice systems (Law Reform Commission of Canada, 1991) and the adaptation of traditional sentencing circles for use in Provincial Courts to advise judges on the length and terms of criminal sentences. Other examples are less well-known. Victim–offender rehabilitation programs have been undertaken by Mennonites and Quakers, and courts handling cases under the Youth Criminal Justice Act have used panels of young people to advise the judge on terms of sentences.

Court Technology and Integrated Justice

Judicial administration, like other elements of the public sector, has also responded to the technological changes associated with computerization. Beginning with the advent of automated management information systems in the 1970s (Millar and Baar, 1981: ch. 10), judges and court administrators have worked to adapt a wide range of electronic technology to the justice environment.

Quebec was the early leader in court technology. By the 1970s, the province had replaced traditional court reporters with recording technology—so centralized in the massive Palais de Justice in Montreal that 90 courtrooms were served by a single recording centre. Since then, court reporters in English Canada have upgraded their transcript preparation technology through CAT (computer-assisted transcription) systems, staving off elimination in several provinces and creating the anomalous situation that a province with recording technology may not be able to prepare a transcript necessary for an appeal as effectively as a province with a traditional court reporter.

Today, there are many examples of "paperless" courthouses, with parties and their lawyers filing documents electronically, judges reviewing court records on a computer screen instead of a paper file, and evidence presented on large computer screens in courtrooms -- though many lawyers still tread the halls of justice pulling wheeled suitcases filled with paper. E-filing and similar developments are still at an early stage, and have taken longer to develop than experienced systems engineers expected. But even now, one can walk into an appellate court in British Columbia or Ontario and observe judges listening to oral argument while taking notes on their laptop computers or iPads. And the monitoring and scheduling of cases are automated in every trial centre of any size throughout the country.

The most ambitious concept in the field today is labelled **integrated justice**. It is based on the notion of seamless automated processes with a single point of entry. For criminal cases, integrated justice means that data on criminal charges would move electronically from police to prosecution to courts to corrections, without personnel at each stage having to re-enter the names, charges, and other information about every person accused of an offence. Electronic filing by private parties in civil and family cases is the counterpart of integrated justice in criminal proceedings.

So far, provincial aspirations for integrated justice have run ahead of achievements, as pioneering efforts in British Columbia and New Brunswick were scaled down and large-scale private partnerships were abandoned. Ontario tried to build on these experiences, but its integrated justice project faced added costs necessary to bring courts up to the level needed to begin to move information electronically into and out of the adjudicative process (Baar, 1999), and was finally abandoned. However, by ensuring that all parts of the justice system use the same hardware and software platforms, and by encouraging the police, the courts, and corrections to share information appropriately, British Columbia has achieved a large measure of integrated justice.

New Professionalism

As this account was written, courts faced resource constraints common throughout the public sector. And in some respects, the pressures and constraints on court administration have been even greater. While other government departments can downsize by reducing their complement of senior staff, judges cannot be laid off, and they serve until retirement ages generally well beyond any others (age 75 for superior court judges, Federal Court judges, justices of the Supreme Court of Canada, and some Provincial Court judges). And when judges retire, they are often replaced with appointments by cabinets and governments that have no direct interest in or understanding of the courts' financial needs, or of the reality that justice in individual cases cannot easily be repackaged in bulk, or turned over to the private sector for delivery. As a result, those appointed to the judiciary, like the governments that appointed them, lack a deep understanding of the administrative challenges in the justice system.

Yet court administrators in recent years have approached their work with renewed engagement and a level of professional skill unknown in the past. Previously, experienced clerks familiar with arcane rules of procedure but limited in terms of professional training supervised court services at the local level, while civil servants drawn from other government departments or other fields (with little or no operational experience in the courts or understanding of how management principles must be modified to be effective in a court environment) directed court services provincially. Today, court administrators have developed distinctive skills increasingly important throughout the public sector: how to manage work processes rather than simply directing people (when key people cannot be subject to formal lines of bureaucratic accountability); how to deal with clientele under stress and often in conflict with the system (in the words of a senior management scholar who had studied the US space agency, courts are more complex because on any given day, half the participants don't want them to work); and how to maintain a commitment to broader institutional purposes (to see that justice is done, and is seen to be done).

In the year 2010, the Association of Canadian Court Administrators (ACCA) held its 35th anniversary conference, as it reached a larger membership and expanded its educational and communication activities. Shortly after this, however, funding cuts by the federal and provincial governments, in reaction to the economic downturn at that time, meant that the cost of ACCA membership fees would no longer be covered for government employers, and membership in ACCA declined to the point where the organization could no longer remain viable. Realizing that ACCA had to be dissolved, the ACCA board recommended that the organization be replaced by a more informal group called the Heads of Court Administration (HoCA), and this recommendation was implemented by Canada's provincial, territorial, and federal justice ministers (sometimes known as Attorneys General). HoCA is made up by the head of court administration

services or their designate in each jurisdiction. It meets by conference call every second month, and in person annually. Best practices are shared, and subcommittees to deal with particular issues, such as self-represented litigants, can be established. HoCA reflects both the US model of Conference of State Court Administrators (COSCA), which consists only of state heads of court administration, and the Canadian model of centralized executive direction of court administration. The advantage of HoCA is that its members are in a position to implement recommendations more than the ACCA Board ever was. One downside of the transition from ACCA to HoCA is that there are no conferences for court administrators at lower levels, although these may yet be developed either through HoCA, or the Institute of Public Administration of Canada. Another downside is that now there is no Canadian organization of court administrators to professionalize court administration as a distinct field of management, like the National Association for Court Management in the United States.

York University's Faculty of Liberal Arts and Professional Studies established a Graduate Diploma in Justice System Administration in 2000, building on the original Brock University program in judicial administration. The core course for the diploma is now open to all graduate students interested in judicial administration, including students in York's part-time LLM program, and the Master of Public Policy, Administration and Law program and the core course can be taken in person or by video conference. Seneca College in Toronto runs a well-established Court and Tribunal Administration program primarily designed for university graduates in programs with a law and society background who desire practical training in court services that includes an internship.

The reform agenda for court administration is as challenging as ever, but enhanced skills and a renewed commitment to advance the agenda provide cause for optimism.

Important Terms and Concepts

administrative independence	case management	general jurisdiction trial courts (aka
adversary system	caseflow management	courts of general jurisdiction)
alternative dispute	court administrators	integrated justice
resolution (ADR)	gender bias task force	judicial impartiality

judicial independence

limited jurisdiction trial courts (aka courts of limited jurisdiction)

Magistrate's Court

mediation

multi-door courthouse

Provincial Courts

registrars

restorative justice

superior courts

Trial Court Performance Standards

unified criminal court

unified family court

Study Questions

1. Outline what each of these sections of the Constitution Act, 1867, say, and what the implications are for judicial administration in Canada: s. 96, s. 91(27), and s. 101.
2. Why do the authors think that the superior/inferior characterization sometimes used to characterize higher and lower trial courts in the provinces is misleading? How have reformers sought to erase, or lessen, the difference in status between the two levels? What are the *administrative* consequences of the legal hierarchy?
3. What is the relationship of judicial independence and judicial administration?
4. Spell out in detail the differences in processes under the traditional and caseflow management supervision of court administration.
5. What has been the effect of the Charter on the administration of justice?
6. What seem to be some skills, orientations, approaches and reforms that the larger public administration community could import, to its advantage, from the judicial administration field?

References

Alford, John, Royston Gustavson and Philip Williams. 2004. *The Governance of Australia's Courts: A Managerial Perspective.* Melbourne: Institute of Judicial Administration of Australia.

Baar, Carl. 1991. *One Trial Court: Possibilities and Limitations.* Ottawa: Canadian Judicial Council.

———. 1994. "Independence, Impartiality and Gender Fairness in the Courts." Paper prepared for annual meeting of the Canadian Political Science Association.

———. 1998. "Judicial Independence and Judicial Administration in the *Tobiass* Case." *Constitutional Forum* 9, 2, pp. 48–54.

———. 1999. "Integrated Justice: Privatizing the Fundamentals." *Canadian Public Administration* 42, pp. 42–68.

Barrett Richard Jordan v. Her Majesty the Queen, http://scc-csc.lexum.com/scc-csc/scc-l-csc-a/en/item/14470/index.do

Canada (Minister of Citizenship and Immigration) v. Tobiass, [1997] 3 S.C.R. 391.

Canadian Bar Association Task Force on Gender Equality in the Legal Profession. 1993. *Touchstones for Change: Equality, Diversity and Accountability.* Ottawa: Canadian Bar Association.

Canadian Judicial Council. 2006. *Alternative Models of Court Administration.* Ottawa: Canadian Judicial Council.

Chandler v. Judicial Council of the Tenth Circuit (1970), 398 U.S. 74, 90 S.Ct. 1648, 26 L.Ed. 2d 100.

Church, Thomas, Jr, et al. 1978. *Justice Delayed: The Pace of Litigation in Urban Trial Courts.* Williamsburg, VA: National Center for State Courts.

Civil Justice Review. 1995. *First Report.* Toronto: Ontario Court of Justice and Ministry of the Attorney General.

Deschenes, Jules. 1981. *Masters in Their Own House.* Montreal: Canadian Judicial Council.

Drury, E. C. 1970. *Farmer Premier.* Toronto: McClelland & Stewart.

Dunn, Christopher, editor. 2006. Chapter 9. *Provinces,* 2nd ed. Peterborough, ON: Broadview Press.

Farrow, Trevor. 2014. *Civil justice, privatization, and democracy.* Toronto, ON: University of Toronto Press.

Foucault, Michel. 1979. *Discipline and Punish.* New York: Vintage Books.

Friedland, Martin L. 1995. *A Place Apart: Judicial Independence and Accountability in Canada.* Ottawa: Canadian Judicial Council.

Friesen, Ernest C., Jr., Edward C. Gallas, and Nesta M. Gallas. 1971. *Managing the Courts.* Indianapolis: Bobbs-Merrill.

Gee, Gordon, Robert Hazell, Kate Malleson, and Patrick O'Brien, 2015. *The Politics of Judicial Independence in the United Kingdom's Changing Constitution.* Oxford University Press.

Gélinas, Fabien, Clément Camion, Karine Bates, Siena Anstis, Catherine Piché, Mariko Khan, and Emily Grant. 2015. *Foundations of Civil Justice: Toward a Value-Based Framework for Reform*. New York: Springer.

Goodridge, Chief Justice Noel. 1991. "Remarks to Provincial Judges Association." St John's, Nfld, photocopy.

Green, Derek J. 2016. Remarks by Hon. J. Derek Green, Chief Justice of Newfoundland and Labrador, on the Occasion of a Special Sitting of the NL Court of Appeal to Mark the 40th Anniversary of the First Sitting of the Court and to Pay Tribute to the Judicial Career of the Hon. James Randell Gushue, Court of Appeal, St. John's, NL, March 17, 2016, accessed Aug. 2, 2017, http://www.court.nl.ca/supreme/appeal/pdf/remarks_hon_derek_green_17mar2016.pdf.Greene, Ian. 2006. *Courts*. Canadian Democratic Audit. Vancouver: UBC Press.

Greene, Ian, Carl Baar, Peter McCormick, Geroge Szablowski, and Martin Thomas. 1998. *Final Appeal: Decision-Making in Canadian Courts of Appeal*. Toronto: Lorimer.

Hughes, The Hon. E. N. 1988. *Access to Justice: Report of the Justice Reform Committee*. Presented to the Attorney General of British Columbia.

Jacob, Sir Jack. 1987. "Fundamental Features of English Civil Procedure." *Justice and Comparative Law: Anglo-Soviet Perspectives on Criminal Law, Evidence, Procedure, and Sentencing Policy*, edited by W.E. Butler, Dordrecht: Martinus Nijhoff, pp. 155–69.

Law Reform Commission of Canada. 1991. *Aboriginal Peoples and Criminal Justice*. Ottawa.

Law Society of British Columbia. 1992. *Gender Equality in the Justice System: A Report of the Law Society of British Columbia Gender Bias Committee*. Vancouver.

McCormick, Peter James. 1994. *Canada's Courts*. Toronto: Lorimer.

———. 2004. "New Questions about an Old Concept: The Supreme Court of Canada's Judicial Independence Jurisprudence." *Canadian Journal of Political Science* Vol. 37, pp. 839–62.

McKean, Dayton David. 1963. *The Integrated Bar*. Boston: Houghton Mifflin.

Mahoney, Barry. 1988. *Changing Times in Trial Courts*. Williamsburg, VA: National Center for State Courts.

Marshall, T. David. 1995. *Judicial Conduct and Accountability*. Toronto: Carswell.

Millar, Perry S., and Carl Baar. 1981. *Judicial Administration in Canada*. Montreal and Kingston: McGill-Queen's University Press.

Ontario Law Reform Commission. 1973. *Report on the Administration of Ontario Courts*, 3 vols. Toronto.

Pirsig, Maynard. 1942. *Judicial Administration*. St Paul, Minn.: West Publishing Company.

Pound, Roscoe. 1906. 'The Causes of Popular Dissatisfaction with the Administration of Justice', address to the American Bar Association, St Paul, MN.

President's Commission on Law Enforcement and the Administration of Justice. 1967. *The Challenge of Crime in a Free Society: A Report by the President's Commission on Law Enforcement and Administration of Justice*. Washington: US Government Printing Office.

Provincial Court Judges' Assn. of New Brunswick v. New Brunswick (Minister of Justice); Ontario Judges' Assn. v. Ontario (Management Board); Bodner v. Alberta; Conférence des juges du Québec v. Quebec (Attorney General); Minc v. Quebec (Attorney General), [2005] 2 S.C.R. 286.

Reference re Remuneration of Judges of the Provincial Court (P.E.I.), [1997] 3 S.C.R. 3

Regina v. Askov, [1990] 2 S.C.R. 1199.

Regina v. Morin, [1992] 1 S.C.R. 771.

Regina v. Stinchcombe, [1991] 3 S.C.R. 326.

Reilly, P.C.J. v. Wachowich, C.J.P.C. (2000), 266 A.R. 296–320 (Alberta Court of Appeal).

Russell, Peter. 1987. *The Judiciary in Canada: The Third Branch of Government*. Toronto: McGraw-Hill Ryerson.

Solomon, Maureen, and Douglas K. Somerlot. 1987. *Caseflow Management in the Trial Courts: Now and for the Future*. Chicago: American Bar Association.

David Steelman. 2008. "Improving Caseflow Management: A Brief Guide." Williamsburg VA: National Center for State Courts, Feb 2008. http://contentdm.ncsconline.org/cgi-bin/showfile.exe?CISOROOT=/ctadmin&CISOPTR=1022

Stott, E. Keith, Jr. 1982. "The Judicial Executive: Toward Greater Congruence in an Emerging Profession." *Justice System Journal* 7, pp. 152–79.

Supreme Court Act, S.C. 2002, c. 8, ss. 12–21, accessible at http://laws-lois.justice.gc.ca/eng/acts/C-45.5/FullText.html

Vanderbilt, Arthur T., editor. 1949. *Minimum Standards of Judicial Administration: A Survey of the Extent to Which the Standards of the American Bar Association for Improving the Administration of Justice Have Been Accepted Throughout the Country*. New York: New York University Law Center.

Watts, Alfred, QC. 1986. *Magistrate-Judge: The Story of the Provincial Court of British Columbia*. Victoria: Provincial Court of British Columbia.

Willoughby, W. P. 1927. *Judicial Administration*. Washington: Brookings.

Woolf, The Rt. Hon., Lord. 1995. *Access to Justice*. London: Interim Report to the Lord Chancellor on the civil justice system in England and Wales.

Zuber, The Hon. T.G. 1987. *Report of the Ontario Courts Inquiry*. Toronto.

Local Public Administration

Andrew Sancton

Chapter Overview

This chapter is composed of two complementary parts. The first part covers the basics of local government in Canada, which is more varied than many realize. It reviews the various forms of, and functions of, local government, provincial controls over local government, growth of local governments by incorporations and annexations, notable experiments in two-tier systems of urban government, and patterns of municipal amalgamations and de-amalgamations. The second part reviews the basic outlines of municipal public administration or, as the author calls it, municipal management, which seeks to fulfill the mission of local government. Notable management developments are covered, such as the role of city managers and **chief administrative officers (CAOs)**, contracting out of government functions, public–private partnerships (P3s), and municipal finance. The chapter shows that urban areas have become so economically dominant that Canadian federal and provincial governments must be just as concerned with the well-being of cities as are urban municipalities.

Chapter Objectives

By the end of this chapter, students will be able to do the following:

- Describe the main features of local government structures in Canada's provinces.
- Discuss the ways in which municipal management differs from public management in the parliamentary systems found at federal and provincial levels in Canada.
- List the sources of municipal revenues in Canada.

Introduction

This chapter will investigate the complex world of **local government** in Canada, focusing on the difficult administrative issues that arise at this level. It aims to show that these issues demand increased attention by the public administration community. We begin with a review of the varied forms that local government takes.

The term *local government* does not appear in the Constitution Act, 1867. The closest reference is found in Section 92(8) where the authority to make laws relating to "Municipal Institutions in the Province" is placed under the exclusive jurisdiction of provincial legislatures. Municipalities had existed in one form or another in British North America since 1785, when the City of Saint John, New Brunswick was incorporated by royal charter. All Canadian provinces have enacted laws that provide for the existence of **municipalities**, i.e., corporate entities with defined territories and delegated legal authority to enact bylaws relating to a range of government functions generally considered to be local in nature. Such entities are generally designated as cities, towns, villages, counties, or townships.

Canadian municipalities are at the heart of the country's network of local government. But this network also includes a wide variety of sub-provincial decision-making authorities, some of which are closely associated with municipal governments (police commissions, library boards) and some of which are not (school boards, various forms of regional health authorities). These authorities are usually called **special-purpose bodies**. So local governments in Canada are composed of both municipalities and special-purpose bodies. Like municipalities, special-purpose bodies must have a defined territory, some autonomous decision-making authority, and some guaranteed access to their own source of funds. This means that field offices of the federal and provincial public services are not local governments; nor are local committees that are merely advisory to bodies that do make authoritative decisions. Because of definitional inconsistencies across ten provinces and three territories, it is pointless to attempt to count the number of local governments that are special-purpose bodies.

Counting the municipalities themselves is less problematic, although even here there are difficulties.

For example, New Brunswick contains more than two hundred "local service districts" that provide municipal services to about a third of the province's population, but these districts are not counted as municipalities because they are not subject to the province's Municipalities Act. British Columbia does not have a Municipalities Act. Its Local Government Act (s.5) defines "local government" as comprising the province's 151 municipalities and 27 regional districts. For our purposes, regional districts are considered as municipal governments. They act as municipal governments in (unincorporated) areas of the province that otherwise do not have municipalities and they provide intermunicipal services and regional planning in areas that do. Quebec's 86 "municipal regional counties" act in the same way and are clearly municipalities because they are governed by the Municipal Code of Quebec. Ontario's 30 regional governments and counties are likewise governed by the Ontario Municipal Act, but their territories are made up exclusively of areas that are also covered by lower-tier municipalities. Since 2013, there have been twelve "regional services commissions" in New Brunswick that are very similar to British Columbia's regional districts. In small towns and rural areas near Montreal and Quebec City, there are three separate levels of incorporated municipal government: the local municipality, the municipal regional county, and the metropolitan community, labelled in Table 9.1 as supra-regional governments.

Outside Ontario, Quebec, British Columbia, and New Brunswick, residents either have no municipal government at all (unincorporated areas) or only one level of municipal government. Even in Ontario and Quebec many residents live in areas with only one level of municipal government, the most notable examples being the 2.5 million people in the City of Toronto, a new municipality created in 1998 by a provincial law that amalgamated the upper-tier Municipality of Metropolitan Toronto and its six constituent lower-tier municipalities.

Functions of Local Government

It is impossible to determine municipal functions simply by reviewing provincial legislation for municipalities. Different provinces delegate authority in different ways and many important local functions

Table 9.1   Municipal Governments in Canada's Provinces, 2011

Province	Local Municipalities	Upper-Tier Municipalities	Supra-Regional Municipalities
Alberta	347		
British Columbia	151	27	
Manitoba	196		
New Brunswick	101	12	
Newfoundland and Labrador	280		
Nova Scotia	54		
Ontario	414	30	
Prince Edward Island	76		
Quebec	1,090	86	2
Saskatchewan	787		
Total	3,496	155	2

Source: Sancton, 2015, p. 9. Reprinted with permission of Oxford University Press.

derive from legislation that appears other than explicitly municipal. It might seem safe to assume that garbage collection is always delegated to local government, but in Prince Edward Island it is a provincial responsibility. Generally, however, we can expect local governments everywhere to regulate the built environment and to provide services to real property, including the provision of local roads and sidewalks. Local governments also provide recreational and cultural facilities such as parks, community halls, and public libraries. In more urban areas, local governments provide public transit, regulate taxis, purify and distribute piped water, and provide for sewage collection and treatment.

Except in Newfoundland and Labrador, where urban policing is a responsibility of the Royal Newfoundland Constabulary, urban municipalities generally have a responsibility for policing, although there are varying mechanisms in different provinces to insulate police from the direct control of municipal councils. Some urban municipalities obtain their policing through contracts with the RCMP or with provincial police forces (Ontario and Quebec). The RCMP or provincial police forces generally provide policing in rural areas. Arrangements vary

from province to province concerning the extent to which rural municipalities contribute to the cost. In Ontario, rural municipalities have paid the full cost since 1998.

Provisions for delivery of social services vary widely. Ontario is the only province in which municipalities have the statutory responsibility to provide certain social services (including income-security payments) and to contribute to their funding. In Alberta, the Family and Community Support Services Act allows the provincial government to fund 80 per cent of the costs of approved municipal preventative social-service programs. In British Columbia, larger urban municipalities (especially the City of Vancouver) are engaged in social-planning functions mainly aimed at attracting funding from other levels of government, coordinating the work of non-profit agencies, and providing modest municipal subsidies to various kinds of social-service organizations including community centres and non-profit childcare centres. In other provinces, there is even less municipal involvement in social services, ranging from none at all to minor expenditures for non-recreational social-service programs in community centres and to the staffing of social-planning groups. Quebec and Ontario are the only provinces that delegate any financial responsibility for social housing.

Municipalities in Ontario are responsible for providing land-ambulance services. The City of Winnipeg has a contractual arrangement with the regional health authority to provide ambulance services within its territory, but this is not a municipal responsibility elsewhere in the province.

In some provinces there are aspects of public health that are under local control. The regulation of air quality is a local (regional district) responsibility in British Columbia. Only in Ontario is public health explicitly a local responsibility, often carried out through regional or county public health units. In Manitoba, municipalities have responsibility for the inspection of food-service establishments and for insect control.

Public utilities (other than water supply) are difficult to categorize. For example, electrical distribution in Ontario's urban areas is the responsibility of business corporations, most of which are still owned by municipalities. Some small Ontario municipalities own local telephone companies and the City of Kitchener owns the local natural-gas distribution system. In Quebec, the City of Westmount still operates the local electricity distribution system. Two of Canada's major publicly traded utilities corporations, EPCOR and Telus, can trace their origins to being service providers for the City of Edmonton. Not surprisingly, they are still heavily involved in providing electricity, natural gas, and telecommunications infrastructure within the Edmonton region.

Provincial Controls over Local Government

Provinces do not have written constitutions analogous to the Constitution Act, 1867. This means that it is impossible for Canadian municipalities to have what is known in the United States as **home rule**, a set of provisions in state constitutions that generally prevents the state legislature from interfering with local control over municipal structures and boundaries (Cameron, 1980). Provincial legislatures can do whatever they want with local governments, including abolishing all of them all at once. This possibility applies even to municipalities that predate the provinces in which they are located.

There is in every province at least one general law that establishes the basic rules and structures of municipal government. Such laws are frequently amended as a result of particular issues and problems, many of which were unforeseen when the legislation was originally approved. In principle, municipalities favour broad and general grants of functional authority together with considerable autonomy as to how to structure themselves and regulate their own behaviour. In practice, their actions are more easily defended in courts of law against aggrieved residents and businesses if the legislative authority under which they are acting is clear and explicit.

Some major Canadian cities—Toronto, Montreal, Winnipeg, and Vancouver, for example—are governed by provincial laws specifically tailored for their own purposes. Such laws, often called **charters**, give no more protection to cities against arbitrary provincial legislation than is available under general municipal legislation, but they usually provide for more functional authority than is generally found in smaller places so that these cities can potentially act more effectively in relation to complex urban issues (Sancton, 2016). Not to be confused with special laws for major cities are laws that are routinely passed by provincial legislatures with special provisions for particular municipalities. Sometimes such legislation is so detailed and particular that it is classified as private legislation, meaning among other things that the law is not published alongside the more important public legislation. At the other end of the scale are general provincial laws that apply to municipalities because they apply to all landowners in the province, or to all employers. For example, provincial labour relations law applies to municipalities, meaning that municipalities have no control over the regulation of their own collective bargaining. It is therefore no easy task to list exactly what provincial laws apply to what municipalities.

All provinces except British Columbia have established **quasi-judicial administrative tribunals** to which various types of municipal decisions, usually relating to land use, can be appealed. The scope of such appeals, the procedures under which they are heard, and the extent to which such tribunals can be overruled by ministers vary greatly from province to province. By far the best known and most powerful of these tribunals is the Ontario Municipal Board (OMB) (Moore, 2013). In addition to hearing appeals relating to municipal structures and various financial matters, the OMB has more control over land-use planning than any other such provincial tribunal in the country. Almost every municipal land-use planning decision is subject to an OMB appeal. On controversial decisions in major cities such appeals are routine, meaning that the local politics of land-use planning are quite different in Ontario than in any other jurisdiction in North America. Municipal councillors know that their decision is but a stage in the process leading to final determination by the OMB.

Provincial governments also control municipalities through the power of the purse. The most direct form of financial control is through grants allocated to municipalities for particular purposes but, by legislation and regulation, provincial governments also control the methods by which municipalities raise their own revenues, especially from the tax on real property. To a lesser extent, even the federal government influences municipalities through the conditions it attaches to the relatively limited funds that flow from it to the nation's municipalities. Municipal sources of revenue will be explored in more detail later in this chapter.

Because municipalities are so dependent on policies adopted by other levels of government, they have formed various organizations to protect and advance their interests. At the federal level, there is the Federation of Canadian Municipalities (FCM), which has been especially prominent in recent years because of its successful campaigns to convince the federal government to eliminate the Goods and Services Tax (GST) for municipalities and to share its tax revenues from gasoline with municipalities. But, because the day-to-day intergovernmental issues of most relevance to municipalities remain at the provincial level, it is the provincial associations of municipalities that are generally the most important. In some provinces there are different organizations for different types of municipalities; in others there is just one common association (Shott, 2015). However they are organized, municipalities have difficulty speaking with one voice because the interests of a major city are inevitably going to be different from those of a small rural township.

Incorporations and Annexations: From Rural to Urban

Legislation in most provinces provides for a mechanism whereby property-owners may petition the provincial government to be incorporated as villages, towns, or cities depending on the number of residents involved. Such locally generated incorporations were commonplace in the nineteenth and early twentieth centuries, but the practice has fallen into disuse because ministers of municipal affairs today generally wish to reduce the number of municipalities rather than facilitate their increase. The only exception is British Columbia. On its website, the government of British Columbia provides detailed instructions as to how the locally initiated process of municipal incorporation is expected to happen (http://www.cscd.gov. bc.ca/lgd/boundaries/municipal_incorporation.htm).

The boundaries of newly incorporated urban municipalities usually included a small amount of peripheral urban land to allow for future development. Once land was developed, the urban municipality might have been granted the authority to annex land for development from its rural neighbour. If annexation is to be allowed at all, provincial governments must provide a procedure for it. Such a procedure usually involves some form of local negotiation and agreement.

An alternative to local agreement is for the provincial government to provide that annexation issues be settled by some form of administrative or quasi-judicial tribunal, such as the OMB. The problems here are predictable. Such a process can be very expensive, especially when highly paid lawyers and experts become involved in public hearings. Because municipalities are not constitutionally protected against changes in their boundaries without their consent, provincial governments can always use their legislative authority to sort out boundary disputes.

The best Canadian example of a city that has continually expanded its territory through annexation is Calgary. Annexations from contiguous rural municipalities are almost always on the agenda and are eventually determined by the Alberta Municipal Government Board. Despite the explosive growth of the Calgary metropolitan area in recent years, annexation has enabled the City to include within its borders 90.3 per cent of the 2011 population of what Statistics Canada defines as the Calgary census metropolitan area.

Two-Tier Systems of Urban Government

Continual annexation is often politically difficult, especially when the boundaries of two established urban communities approach each other or when a provincial government wants to maintain the existence of established suburban and rural municipalities that are coveted by central cities. Provincial governments in Manitoba, Ontario, British Columbia, Quebec, and New Brunswick have at various times instead established **two-tier systems** of urban government in which an upper-tier metropolitan or regional authority encompasses the central city and the urbanizing municipalities around it. The main functional purposes of the upper tier have been to regulate and shape the outward expansion while also providing the necessary physical infrastructure, especially roads, sewers, and water-supply systems.

The first Canadian urban two-tier system was the Municipality of Metropolitan Toronto (1954–97), otherwise known as Metro. It became known throughout the world for its success in the 1950s and 1960s in planning and financing the rapid outward expansion of Toronto into the rural townships of Etobicoke, North York, and Scarborough. By the 1970s its problems were mounting, especially when the Ontario government decided that its boundaries would not be extended outwards such that it would continue to encompass most of the Toronto city-region. Instead, the province created the two-tier regional municipalities of Halton, Peel, York, and Durham. During the same period, the province also created new two-tier systems in Ottawa-Carleton, Niagara, Waterloo, Sudbury, and Hamilton.

Between 1960 and 1971 the Corporation of Greater Winnipeg covered the territory of the City of Winnipeg and eleven suburban municipalities and performed similar functions as Metro did in Toronto. Its ten councillors were elected from ten wards deliberately constructed to cross municipal boundaries and to take in both suburban and central-city areas. Innovative as such an arrangement was, it served to intensify conflict between the corporation and its constituent municipalities.

In the mid-1960s, the government of British Columbia established regional districts throughout the province so as to provide municipal services in unincorporated areas and to facilitate regional planning and joint service provision among municipalities within the same region. It is through the regional districts that a light and flexible form of two-tier urban government was established for Vancouver (Greater Vancouver Regional District, now Metro Vancouver) and Victoria (Capital Regional

District). British Columbia's regional districts have existed for fifty years, making them the most durable of all the Canadian regional reforms of the post-war period. Because of the establishment in 2013 of regional services commissions in New Brunswick, there is now a form of two-tier municipal government for New Brunswick cities such as Moncton, Saint John, and Fredericton.

In 1969 the Quebec National Assembly approved laws creating urban communities in Montreal and Quebec City and a regional community for the Outaouais area. Each of these three new institutions (1970–2001) was effectively a form of upper-tier metropolitan government. More recently, in 2001, the province established new supra-regional metropolitan communities for much larger areas around Montreal and Quebec City. What these new institutions gained in territory, they lost in functional authority. Although they are supposed to provide a form of strategic direction to their respective territories, they do not provide any actual services to their inhabitants.

Municipal Amalgamations and De-amalgamations

Many two-tier urban systems established in the post-war period have been replaced by amalgamated municipalities. The first such amalgamation was sponsored in Winnipeg in 1971 by a New Democratic Party government. Known as "Unicity," the Winnipeg amalgamation was designed to promote equity in taxation and service levels and to provide new opportunities for citizen participation. There were fifty small wards whose councillors were grouped into territorially based community committees and assisted by residents' advisory groups elected in open community meetings. Over the years most of the new participatory mechanisms built into the unicity structures have atrophied. For example, the size of the council has been reduced from fifty to fifteen.

The best-known and most extensive program of municipal amalgamations was implemented by the Progressive Conservative government in Ontario in the 1990s. Amalgamations in Ontario were brought about by three separate laws. The first, part of the Savings and Restructuring Act, 1997, provided a mechanism for the minister of municipal affairs, if asked by a single municipality, to appoint a commissioner with the authority to order municipal restructuring if local municipalities could not agree. Although the use of commissioners was limited, their potential appointment prompted hundreds of "voluntary" amalgamations. The second, the City of Toronto Act, 1997, amalgamated the constituent parts of the Municipality of Metropolitan Toronto. The third, the Fewer Municipal Politicians Act, 1999, amalgamated the constituent units of the regional municipalities of Ottawa-Carleton, Hamilton-Wentworth, and Sudbury. The Conservative government justified the municipal amalgamations primarily on the grounds that they would save money, reduce "overlap and duplication," and eliminate the positions of hundreds of municipal politicians.

The Parti Québécois government in Quebec introduced its program for municipal amalgamations in April 2000. Two pieces of legislation followed: one authorizing the minister of municipal affairs to order amalgamations in smaller cities, towns, and villages and another specifying the details of amalgamations in the territories covered by the Montreal and Quebec urban communities and the Outaouais regional community. The Outaouais amalgamation created the new City of Gatineau. These amalgamations came into effect in 2002. Like the Winnipeg Unicity amalgamation thirty years before, the Quebec ones were aimed primarily at eliminating differences in levels of municipal taxation and services within the territories that were amalgamated.

The Liberal opposition leader in Quebec, Jean Charest, committed himself, if elected, to legislate a mechanism for de-amalgamation. The issue became a dominant one in the 2003 provincial election, and the Liberals were elected. They then went on to do roughly what they had promised. De-amalgamation referendums were held in 87 former municipalities on 20 June 2004 within parts of 29 amalgamated municipalities in which ten per cent of eligible voters had petitioned for such a referendum. For a de-amalgamation to be approved, 50 per cent of the votes cast representing 35 per cent of the total eligible voters had to be affirmative. This threshold was met in 31 former municipalities that were part of twelve different amalgamated municipalities. Fifteen of the affirmative decisions for demerger were within the amalgamated city of Montreal. Consequently, difficulties with implementing de-amalgamation were more intense there than anywhere else in Quebec (Trent, 2012).

The result is that Montreal now has an incredibly complex set of relationships between the amalgamated city and the fifteen municipalities that regained their incorporated status in 2005. The system is made even more complex by the fact that, as part of its strategy to prevent de-amalgamation, the City of Montreal went to great lengths to decentralize authority to the "boroughs" that were created at the time of amalgamation. Following de-amalgamation, Montreal has nineteen boroughs, each with its own directly elected mayor who sits on the Montreal city council as well as the borough council. On the island of Montreal (the territory of the former Montreal Island Community), there are now 35 directly elected mayors (Meloche and Vaillancourt, 2013).

From the mid-1990s until the mid-2000s, municipal amalgamations were on the political agendas of almost every provincial government. In some, such as Newfoundland and Labrador, Prince Edward Island, and New Brunswick, plans for amalgamation were modest, and achievements even more so. In Saskatchewan a provincial commission recommended extensive amalgamation in rural areas, but a cautious government decided against implementing a plan that had generated a great deal of local opposition. In 2000 in Alberta, a similar commission explicitly rejected amalgamation for the Edmonton region. Only in British Columbia does the provincial government specifically eschew a policy of forced municipal amalgamation.

Municipal Management

Management is the function that makes all this complex organizational machinery work. Elected councils are charged with making authoritative decisions for municipalities. As with parliaments and legislatures at other levels of government, they receive advice from paid employees, the same people charged with implementing their decisions. Legally speaking, municipal employees are not civil servants because, unlike federal and provincial employees, they are servants of the municipal corporation rather than of the Crown. They are, however, clearly part of the public sector. Statistics Canada reports that 3,632,000 Canadians were employed in 2011 in the public sector, which includes schools, colleges, universities, and hospitals. Of this number, 609,000 worked in local general government (municipal government and associated special-purpose bodies, but not school boards) and another 68,000 worked in local government business enterprises. More people are employed by local general government than by either the federal government or the provincial governments collectively, but school boards and health and social service institutions each employ more people than general local governments (Statistics Canada, 2011).

More so than at the federal and provincial levels, senior municipal managers tend to be functional specialists. Senior civil servants at the federal and provincial levels have usually been educated as generalists and expect that they will move around from one department to another as part of their career progression. Municipal managers often get their first municipal jobs because they were educated as engineers, land-use planners, lawyers, or accountants and then progress through the management hierarchy in the same functional specialization, although not necessarily in the same municipality. By definition, the highest management position in a municipality has no functional specialization, so people initially recruited to such positions often have only limited preparation. Generalists tend to get hired by the very smallest municipalities, which might have only one or two managers in total, or by the very largest, which can afford to hire policy analysts and research assistants in the offices of the very senior managers.

Unlike most federal and provincial civil servants, municipal managers are not responsible to a single political master, a minister of the Crown. In a strong city-manager system, department heads have the luxury of considering themselves to report only to the city manager, but in most municipalities, all department heads also report to the council as a collective entity. Reporting to a group of people rather than a single person makes any manager's job more difficult, especially when various members of the governing body often differ publicly from each other in their basic objectives and priorities. In any event, even in a strong city-manager system, the city manager reports to the council as a whole, which makes the job more politically complex than that of most deputy ministers at other levels.

Municipal councils carry out most of their business in public. Much of this business involves receiving written and oral reports from senior managers. As a result, unlike their federal and provincial counterparts, the work of senior municipal managers is very much a matter of public record, not just in writing but also at locally televised council meetings where they are called on to answer questions from councillors who might not have properly read or understood their agenda material or who wish to use the manager in scoring a political point against an opponent.

The Role of City Managers and Chief Administrative Officers (CAOs)

To understand the positions of city manager and CAO, we must go back to the Progressive reformers at the end of the nineteenth century. The Progressives argued for small municipal councils and non-partisan at-large elections. They wanted as much as possible to remove politics from municipal government. In many ways, their most important municipal innovation was the **council–manager plan**: a system of municipal government in which the mayor's position became largely ceremonial, the council's jobs were to set broad policy and appoint a city manager, and the city manager's job was to do everything else. The establishment of such a position was seen as crucial for removing undue political influence from city administration, breaking the power of the urban political machines, and bringing professional management to urban government.

The first municipal general manager in the United States was appointed for Staunton, Virginia, in 1908. Staunton became the ideal model for the reformers who advocated for the council–manager plan throughout the United States and Canada. Sumpter, South Carolina, appointed a city manager in 1912 and Westmount, Quebec, appointed one in 1913, becoming the third council–manager municipality in North America (Plunkett, 1992: 16). In a pure council-manager system, the manager appoints all the department heads and is directly and solely responsible for all the management documents that flow to council, including the proposed annual municipal budget.

All major Canadian municipalities now have either a city manager or a CAO, or a *directeur-général*, as the position is known in Quebec. Regardless of the title used, the actual authority granted to the holder of the position varies significantly. Municipal acts in the various provinces and the relevant bylaw in each municipality can provide an outline of the legal situation, but even when all this research is done, much depends on the culture of the municipal organization and the management style of the particular individual (Siegel, 2015). In any event, there are no major Canadian municipalities in which the city manager or CAO has as much authority as envisioned by the original designers of the council–manager plan.

Contracting Out

Contracting out is not new. Every time a municipality consults an outside lawyer or expert, it is contracting out, because it is purchasing a service that could in theory be provided by its own employees, current or potential. Often there are extremely good reasons why special expertise is obtained in this way; it would simply be far too expensive to employ highly trained specialists in a particular issue whose special skills might be needed only once every few years. Similarly, if a municipality needs to clean the windows on a high-rise city hall, no one is likely to complain if it hires a specialized company to do the job. No one expects banks to employ window cleaners as permanent employees. Why should anyone expect municipalities to do so?

But what about the idea that municipalities should contract out almost everything they do? This idea has been seriously advanced from time to time, especially in the 1990s when confidence in the ability of governments to do almost anything was at a very low ebb. The issue is politically charged because contracting out is often seen—quite rightly in many cases—as an attack on unionized labour. If municipal workers have high wages because they are unionized, and if a private company can perform the same work at a cheaper price because its workers are not unionized, it is not surprising that unions would fight contracting out.

Garbage collection is a municipal function that causes many battles about contracting out. In 2001, James C. McDavid at the University of Victoria reported on results of a cross-Canada survey about the contracting out of garbage collection. Except in Quebec, he found that contracting out was usually less expensive, especially in smaller municipalities. Lowest costs seemed to be found in municipalities that combined public provision and contracting out, suggesting that direct competition between public and private providers placed downward pressure on costs (McDavid, 2001). But such findings do little to resolve the debate because McDavid did not collect data on

wage levels or ages of workers. Some citizens do not want garbage collectors to be non-unionized young workers who will be let go when they age and become less physically productive. Where municipal workers are doing the job, this is precisely why municipal unions are so resistant to contracting out. In a similar study of residential recycling collection services reported in 2008, McDavid and Mueller found little difference in cost between public and private providers. Notably, private provision predominated: 77 per cent of the providers were private companies (McDavid & Mueller, 2008). As this is a relatively recent municipal service, private providers were often contracted at the beginning, before unions were able to negotiate their own role.

Water services (supply of drinking water and sewage) are considerably more controversial (Furlong, 2015). In Toronto, for example, any hint of moving towards opening the door to private companies has met with immediate resistance from labour unions, environmentalists, and Canadian nationalists concerned with maintaining public control over freshwater resources. But elsewhere there has been considerable movement. Perhaps the best-known case is Hamilton, Ontario, where in 1995 the regional government contracted out the operation of all its water services to a subsidiary of Philip Environmental, a local company. The decision was based as much on a strategy for local economic development as it was on saving money. The idea was that the contract with Hamilton would help Philip develop a national and international presence in what looked like a fast-developing marketplace. The contract guaranteed cost savings to the city, new investment, and the continuation of the unionized jobs in the facilities. But all did not go smoothly. The city underestimated the costs of monitoring the contract. Sewage spills caused lawsuits and embarrassment all around. By the late 1990s Philip was laying off workers, and those who were left were complaining of deteriorating equipment. Most significant of all, Philip Environmental, a company with many other investments, ran into financial difficulty and was acquired cheaply by a subsidiary of Enron Corporation, a company that would soon go bankrupt in circumstances that showed its whole operation to be built on financial fraud. American Water Services Canada, a company ultimately owned by a German utility, took over from the Enron subsidiary and tried to keep the contract. In anticipation of its expiry, Hamilton city council (which had replaced the regional government as a result of amalgamation) voted narrowly to put the contract out for tender, but no company came up with a proposal that was satisfactory to the city. In September 2004 the city council voted to take direct control of the operation of the water services (Loxley, 2010). In retrospect Hamilton's experience with contracting out can only be assessed as disastrous.

But this type of experience has not been universal. A great many Canadian municipalities successfully contract out the management of various parts of their water services. Since 2006, Veolia Water Canada (a French company once known as Vivendi) has managed water services for the municipality of Brockton, Ontario. The initial five-year contract was renewed for another five years in 2011. Brockton is notable because it is an amalgamated municipality that includes Walkerton, the town where, in 2000, contaminated water supplied by a public body run by incompetents killed at least seven people and caused severe illness in hundreds more (Ontario, 2002).

Public–Private Partnerships

Veolia Water Canada has a different kind of arrangement with Moncton, New Brunswick. In the 1990s it designed, built, and paid for a new water treatment facility for Moncton. In return, Veolia obtained the exclusive right to sell water to the city for 20 years (Cameron, 2001: 127–8). This arrangement is just one of many different ways in which partnerships can be worked out. Details will vary with each project, depending in large measure on what municipalities are looking for. In the case of the Moncton project, the city was looking both for specialized expertise in the design and construction of the plant and for a financing mechanism that enabled the city to avoid having to borrow large sums. Although generally recognized as a success, the Moncton–Veolia partnership has been criticized by John Loxley for being more costly to the city than is commonly believed. He claims that the whole project was made financially viable only because Veolia received special treatment from the Canada Revenue Agency concerning how sales-tax expenditures and depreciation would be treated for corporate income-tax purposes. He ultimately argues that Moncton actually would have been better off borrowing the necessary funds and building the plant

itself. Because of the public–private partnership, Moncton technically did not incur any new debt, but the practical impacts on Moncton's financial obligations were the same (Loxley, 2010: 151–9).

In Regina in 2013, municipal voters had an opportunity to decide on whether their municipality would pursue a **public–private partnership** to build a new sewage treatment plant. After receiving a report from consultants in January 2013, the Regina city council voted to begin the process of acquiring a partner for the $224-million facility. Probably the most important reason for making this decision was that a 25 per cent federal subsidy, which was announced in June, required significant private involvement. The Canadian Union of Public Employees (CUPE) countered with its own study which argued that, even after the contribution from the federal government, the partnership option was more expensive. According to CUPE, all of the financial benefits claimed in the city's consultants' report resulted from an overestimation of the cost of the risk to be taken by the private partners. Opponents of the council decision launched a petition calling for a referendum on the subject. City council decided to hold one on 25 September 2013. With a 31 per cent turnout, 57 per cent of the voters approved the project (Regina, 2013). Voters in Regina probably now know more about public–private partnerships than residents of any other city in Canada.

How to quantify risk is a major issue in the assessment of any public–private partnership, including the ones just discussed in Moncton and Regina. A partnership formed in the early 2000s that was mostly about minimizing municipal risk involved the John Labatt Centre (now Budweiser Gardens) in downtown London, Ontario. The arena was a crucial part of the city's plan for downtown revitalization, and the land on which it was built was owned by the municipality. No private company would take on a project like this in downtown London without public backing. The city would not take on the project because it did not want to get into the highly specialized and financially risky business of building and operating an arena. In his study of London's downtown revitalization efforts, Timothy Cobban reports that:

> City council agreed in May 2000 to build the arena with a consortium whose principal partners included Ellis-Don Construction Ltd., a large construction firm with origins in London.

The city's responsibilities under the agreement included providing the land for the arena and $31.72 million of the project's total capital costs. The private sector partners were required to provide $10 million and pay the city $45.5 million over fifty years, with full ownership of the arena transferring to the city at the end of the fifty-year agreement (Cobban, 2003: 240).

The arena is operated by Philadelphia-based Global Spectrum Management (whose parent company also owns the Philadelphia Flyers hockey team and 76ers basketball team), which was also part of the original public–private partnership. Financially, the arena has been a huge success. The city has been criticized for structuring the partnership in such a way that the municipality does not gain directly from this success. But the whole point of the agreement was to protect the city from undue risk if it was not successful. In this sense the partnership met the city's objectives, not to mention the fact that the arena clearly has helped meet the city's revitalization objectives.

A more significant project involving both a $480-million new arena and downtown revitalization was negotiated in 2013 in Edmonton. The partnership is between the city and Daryl Katz, the owner of the Edmonton Oilers hockey team. The new arena was not completed until 2016, so it is too early to make any assessment. The city will own the facility, but it will mainly be paid for by rent from the Oilers, by a special tax (community revitalization levy) that will be paid by neighbouring property owners, and by a surcharge on tickets.

The main lesson to be learned from this discussion of contracting out and public–private partnerships is that today's city managers require a wide variety of skills in order to navigate through all the various tools at their disposal to meet city objectives. They need to understand all the complexities of the kinds of financial arrangements that have just been discussed. They can, of course, receive specialized advice from outside lawyers and accountants, and wise ones will undoubtedly do so for big projects. Ironically, seeking such outside guidance is yet another form of contracting out.

Collective Bargaining

Managers also have to deal with unions. Although unions have no particular interest in the contracting out of specialized professional work, they are highly sensitive to proposals to contract out the work that is normally done by their members. Municipal unions are important for a wide range of reasons, not the least of which is that many citizens think most about municipal services when unions threaten to strike or actually do withdraw the services of their members.

Municipal unions have received very little attention from Canadian political scientists. In 1978, T. J. Plunkett and G. M. Betts wrote a text on Canadian municipal management that briefly treated "Employer–Employee Relations and Collective Bargaining." Their opening paragraph is almost as relevant today as it was then:

> There was a time when local governments as employers established jobs and positions, assigned tasks, set wages, determined hours of work and other working conditions, and promoted, disciplined, and discharged staff at will without reference to their employees. But those days have long since passed in most urban communities. Yet, despite the fact that some groups of public service employees have been organized as trade union locals for more than three decades, elected and appointed officials have been slow to recognize the overall impact that unionization has had, and will continue to have, upon local government administration and practice. As a result, many municipalities still appear to tolerate employee unions as aberrations from the norm and tend to deal with them on an ad hoc basis during contract negotiations rather than develop a cohesive on-going strategy to promote effective and harmonious labour/management relations. (283–4)

Katherine Graham wrote a book chapter entitled "Collective Bargaining in the Municipal Sector" in 1995. She claims that "municipalities' generally narrow approach to the human resource management function was likely a contributing factor to the significant spread of unionization in the municipal public service by the 1960s, with the Canadian Union of Public Employees (CUPE) emerging as by far the most dominant municipal union" (182–3). CUPE is now the largest union in Canada and municipal workers, as well as workers in health and educational institutions, remain its primary base of membership. Graham raises two issues that appear to place municipalities at a disadvantage when bargaining with unions. Both relate to employer disunity. The first variant of the problem is that there are many municipalities and often just one strong union— CUPE. The union provides its local negotiators with considerable data about settlements in other municipalities, and each local attempts to "whipsaw" better settlements than those obtained elsewhere. Naturally, the municipalities respond by sharing information through municipal associations, but they generally do not seem as effective or united as CUPE. In many ways, the most innovative management response to this problem has been in the Vancouver area where Metro Vancouver actually handles labour relations not only for its own employees but also for 27 other employers (municipalities and special-purpose bodies)15 of the 22 constituent municipalities. It manages 49 different collective agreements (http://www.res360.ca/services/collective-bargaining/Pages/default.aspx).

Another source of management disunity derives from what is sometimes called **multilateral bargaining**. In this situation, participants in the bargaining process know that it is ultimately impossible for management to remain united. Unity, or solidarity, is always a potential problem for unions as well, but except in the most unusual of circumstances, local union negotiators are in complete control of the process. Negotiators for municipal management, on the other hand, know that strong elements on the local council, often including the mayor, are not always completely removed from the negotiating process, regardless of what they might say in public. Indeed, some municipal politicians are closely allied to labour interests and are particularly vulnerable to union efforts to crack open an apparently united management position. In contrast, it is rare for a union in the private sector to expect to have allies on a private company's board of directors.

A third problem for municipal management is that some contract settlements are determined by arbitration. Graham does not discuss this scenario directly because she was writing about non-uniformed municipal workers—that is, workers who are not members of police or fire services. Municipal police officers and fire personnel are paid by municipalities mostly from revenues that they must raise themselves. Police and fire personnel have no legal right to go on strike, but they do have very strong local unions, albeit ones that are usually more limited by provincial legislation

in their ability to affiliate with larger organizations like CUPE. In the event that management and union negotiators are unable to reach agreement for police and fire labour contracts, the outstanding issues are usually sent to arbitration. Concerning wage levels, arbitrators frequently award higher settlements than what other unions obtain in the absence of compulsory arbitration. One generous arbitration for one service leads to pressure for others to catch up—which in turn creates higher goals for other unions to strive for. Municipal politicians complain frequently about arbitrated settlements for police and fire, but there appears to be little they can do short of launching a full-scale attack on police officers and firefighters, which is not an attractive option for anyone seeking re-election.

Municipal Finance

In 2015, the Canadian federal government raised approximately $255 billion from taxes and other own-source revenues; the figure for all provincial and territorial governments was $313 billion; and for all local governments, including school boards and Indigenous governments, the amount was $95 billion. Of the $95 billion, $65 billion was from taxes, almost all of which was from a tax on property (Statistics Canada, 2016). The rest was mainly from user fees, from such services as water supply and public transit. Since 2008, Statistics Canada has not collected expenditure data relating for municipalities or for distinct functions of government (e.g. health, education, etc.), so it is difficult to provide meaningful information for the whole country. There is considerable variation by province, especially because of the importance of provincially funded and municipally delivered income-security programs in Ontario. Except for social services in Ontario, municipalities in Canada are remarkably self-sufficient in that they generally finance all of their services from the property tax and user fees.

The details of the property-tax system vary from province to province, but its essentials are that municipal councils annually set property-tax rates within their respective territories and the tax is paid by all property-owners in accordance with the value of their properties as assessed by a provincial or municipal agency. Property taxes are relatively high in Canada compared to most industrialized countries, which means that raising them further causes considerable political difficulties.

This fact reflects constant complaints of Canadian municipal leaders: they are increasingly being forced to pay for local services by relying on their own resources. Provincial support has been declining and federal assistance, although growing, is still relatively insignificant. There are frequent claims from big-city mayors that new types of municipal taxes are needed, but support for such ideas from their own voters and from provincial governments seems limited at best.

Provinces do not allow municipalities to budget for operating deficits. This means that, despite occasional citizen concerns about alleged excessive borrowing, municipal debt levels are relatively low and always relate to real physical infrastructure that has already been built. Municipalities have been pushing for more provincial and federal help with such infrastructure because, if they were forced to finance what is required themselves, they would have difficulty servicing the resulting debt without very painful property-tax increases or new forms of user fees, such as significant tolls on major roads.

Local Governments and the Future of Canadian Cities

Until the end of the First World War, everyone assumed that municipal governments were the governments that exclusively looked after cities. This soon changed when the federal government began providing funding for urban housing to demobilized soldiers. In the 1930s both the federal government and provincial governments stepped in when municipalities proved manifestly incapable of supporting millions of unemployed and indigent citizens. There was another urban housing crisis after the Second World War and once again the federal government, mainly through the Central (now Canada) Mortgage and Housing Corporation, became a key force in Canadian urban development. In the late 1960s, as inner cities in many parts of the United States were being destroyed by rioting and the retreat to the suburbs, the federal government tried to ensure that Canadian cities did not suffer the same fate. The establishment in 1971 of the Ministry of State for Urban Affairs was its most significant initiative, but the ministry was abolished, apparently as a cost-cutting measure, in 1979. There were more federal urban initiatives in the early 2000s. Meanwhile, the involvement of provincial governments in urban affairs became so ubiquitous that it scarcely drew anyone's notice.

Municipal governments are probably less crucial now to the overall well-being of their respective urban areas than they were a hundred years ago. This is not to suggest that municipal governments are not important. It is only to suggest that urban areas have become so economically dominant and so populous that Canadian federal and provincial governments must be just as concerned with the well-being of cities as urban municipalities are. Municipalities continue to shape the fine-grained features of the development and redevelopment of our urban built environment and they continue to finance such crucial services as policing and firefighting. The importance of local government derives from the inherent importance of these traditional functions, not from its alleged potential to displace other levels of government in the eyes of Canada's urban population. Precisely because the traditional functions of local government are so complex and difficult to manage, especially in our largest cities, the challenges for public administrators at the local level in Canada are immense. This chapter has attempted to show that municipal staff work in political and organizational environments that are far more complex than those of civil servants in our federal and provincial governments. This is why local public administration deserves more attention and study.

Thanks to Oxford University Press for permission to use previously published material I have written in Sancton 2010 and 2015.

Important Terms and Concepts

charters	local government	quasi-judicial administrative
chief administrative officer (CAO)	multilateral bargaining	tribunals
council–manager plan	municipalities	special-purpose bodies
home rule	public–private partnership	two-tier systems

Study Questions

1. Why is it not strictly accurate to say that people who work for municipalities are civil servants?
2. What is the constitutional status of Canadian municipalities? Why is it not possible for them to have "home rule" under current constitutional arrangements?
3. For large cities, do you think two-tier systems of municipal government are preferable to the amalgamation of all municipalities in the built-up area?
4. Would you favour the contracting out of the management and operation of the water-supply system in your municipality? Why or why not?

References

Cameron, David. "The Relationship between Different Ownership and Management Regimes and Drinking Water Safety." Discussion Paper for the Walkerton Inquiry, June 2001.

Cameron, David M. 1980. "Provincial Responsibilities for Municipal Government." *Canadian Public Administration*, 23, pp. 222–35.

Cobban, Timothy. 2003. "The Political Economy of Urban Development: Downtown Revitalization in London, Ontario, 1993–2002." *Canadian Journal of Urban Research* 12, 2, pp. 231–48.

Furlong, Kathryn. 2015. *Leaky Governance: Alternative Service Delivery and the Myth of Water Utility Independence.* Vancouver: UBC Press.

Graham, Katherine A. 1995. "Collective Bargaining in the Municipal Sector." *Public Sector Collective Bargaining in Canada: Beginning of the End or End of the Beginning?* edited by Gene Swimmer and Mark Thompson, Kingston, ON: Industrial Relations Centre, Queen's University.

Loxley, John, with Salim Loxley. 2010. *Public Service, Private Profits: The Political Economy of Public-Private Partnerships in Canada.* Halifax and Winnipeg: Fernwood.

McDavid, James C. 2001. "Solid-Waste Contracting-Out, Bidding Practices, and Competition among Canadian Local Governments." *Canadian Public Administration* 44, 1, pp. 1–25.

McDavid, James C., and Annette E. Mueller. 2008. "A Cross-Canada Analysis of the Efficiency of Residential Recycling Services," *Canadian Public Administration* 51, 4, pp. 569–88.

Meloche, Jean-Philippe, and François Vaillancourt. 2013. *Public Finance in Montreal: In Search of Equity and Efficiency.* IMFG Papers on Municipal Finance and Governance, No.15, University of Toronto Munk Centre of Global Affairs.

Moore, Aaron A. 2013. *Planning Politics in Toronto: The Ontario Municipal Board and Urban Development.* Toronto: University of Toronto Press.

Ontario, Attorney-General. 2002. *Report of the Walkerton Inquiry.* Toronto: The Queen's Printer for Ontario.

Plunkett, Thomas J. 1992. *City Management in Canada: The Role of the Chief Administrative Officer.* Toronto: Institute of Public Administration of Canada.

Plunkett, Thomas J., and G.M. Betts. 1978. *The Management of Canadian Urban Government: A Basic Text for a Course in Urban Management.* Kingston, ON: Institute of Local Government, Queen's University.

Regina, City of, 2013, September 25. "Wastewater Treatment Plant Referendum, Official Summary of Results."

Sancton, Andrew. 2010. "Local Government." *The Oxford Handbook of Canadian Politics*, edited by John C. Courtney and David E. Smith, New York: Oxford University Press, pp.131–49.

———. 2015. *Canadian Local Government: An Urban Perspective* 2nd ed. Toronto: Oxford University Press.

———. 2016. "The False Panacea of City Charters? A Political Perspective on the Case of Toronto." SPP Research Papers, Vol. 9, Issue 3, (January 2016), The School of Public Policy at the University of Calgary.

Sancton, Andrew, and Robert Young, editors. 2009. *Foundations of Governance: Municipal Governance in Canada's Provinces.* Toronto: University of Toronto Press.

Shott, Alison Katherine. 2015. *Municipal Associations, Membership Composition, and Interest Representation in Local-Provincial Relations.* London, ON: School of Graduate and Postdoctoral Studies, University of Western Ontario.

Siegel, David. 2015. *Leaders in the Shadows: The Leadership Qualities of Municipal Chief Administrative Officers.* Toronto: University of Toronto Press.

Statistics Canada. 2011. "Public sector employment, wages and salaries (employees)," www.statcan.gc.ca/tables-tableaux/sum-som/l01/cst01/govt54a-eng.htm)

Statistics Canada, 2016, "Government finance statistics, statement of government operations and balance sheet." CANSIM Table 385-0032. http://www5.statcan.gc.ca/cansim/a26?lang=eng&retrLang=eng&id=3850032&&pattern=&stByVal=1&p1=1&p2=-1&tabMode=dataTable&csid=

Trent, Peter. 2012. *The Merger Delusion: How Swallowing its Suburbs Made an even Bigger Mess of Montreal.* Montreal and Kingston: McGill-Queen's University Press.

The Role of Deputy Ministers in Canadian Government

Jacques Bourgault

Chapter Overview

This chapter aims to expose the complexity of the position of federal deputy minister (DM). We begin with a brief description of the profession's context in Canada, then depict its characteristics. The chapter covers many of the Gomery recommendations, since Justice Gomery's report insisted much on the role of the deputy in the federal decision-making system. The chapter also takes into consideration a series of deputy interviews conducted in 2015, just before the federal election.

Chapter Objectives

By the end of this chapter, students will be able to do the following:

- Outline what it means when we say that deputy ministers are appointed "at pleasure," designated by the prime minister, and appointed and dismissed by the Governor-in-Council.
- Describe in detail the changing political context for federal deputy ministers.
- Describe in detail the legal duties and powers of federal deputy ministers.
- Explain the multiple accountabilities of the deputy minister.
- Appreciate the effects of the DM peer group.
- Explain the complications of dealing with accusations of politicization in the DM cadre.

Introduction

What does it mean to be a deputy minister? The deputy minister's position is essential within the Canadian government based on the Westminster tradition, especially in today's ever-changing context. As the linchpin between the public administration and the government, the deputy minister (DM) needs to incarnate knowledge and know-how for his or her minister and to represent the political will to the administration. This prestigious central position carries with it a burden of responsibilities. Now more than ever, the DM's mission is ambitious. Citizens expect more, it affects more resources, and there is more uncertainty surrounding it. In recent years much has been written about the perils of politicization or of professional submission to political masters.

Position in the System

A **deputy minister** (DM) is just below the minister in the departmental hierarchy. The deputy minister's role is to assist the minister in his or her functions within the department and advise the minister. All of the legislation establishing departments stipulates simply that a deputy minister *"may be appointed,"* without specifying the DM's role except for the general designations of *"chief executive officer, deputy head and accounting officer for the organisation."* DMs are the civil servants who are closest to the political level. They are outside the merit appointment system of the Public Service of Canada (PSC) but are subject to most provisions of the Public Service Employment Act.

Designation/Selection/Appointment

At pleasure. Deputy ministers are a category of what are called **discretionary appointments**, along with the CEOs of Crown corporations, board members, and ambassadors; however, deputies and ambassadors hold office for an undetermined period, while the others are generally appointed for a determined period. In theory, any Canadian citizen of sound mind and not under any legal prohibition may be appointed to those functions. Out of respect for democratic principles, the architects of the system wanted the government, which is responsible to the

elected Parliament, to be able to hire and fire the people it wants to advise ministers, run departments, and implement legislation. They were aware that ministers were kept busy by their duties as parliamentarians, MPs, caucus members, and members of cabinet, as well as by their symbolic functions as representatives of the state or the government at local, national, and foreign events. Moreover, it is fair to say that ministers are not always chosen on the basis of their specialized education or experience in the field for which they are to be responsible. As a result, the deputy minister has an important role to play in advising the minister and keeping the department on an even keel.

Designation. Though the prime minister (PM) has full discretion in choosing deputy ministers, today a DM is seldom designated by the prime minister or the minister alone, and never by the governing party per se. Most often, they are civil servants who have been tagged as up-and-comers, groomed over the long term by senior officials and sometimes ministers, and promoted to positions closer and closer to the circle of power. Research by Bourgault indicates that in recent decades only a tiny number of federal deputy minister appointments have been arranged primarily through political channels, which in fact usually means personal networks with a political tinge.

Selection. Up-and-comers are promoted to assistant deputy minister and associate deputy minister before they move up to DM. By convention, the PM makes the selection on the advice of the Clerk of the Privy Council, who in turn is assisted by a senior appointments office that does much of the leg work (assembling a file on the department's needs and on each of the possible candidates). The **Committee of Senior Officials** (COSO) performs two functions in the process, examining departmental succession plans and conducting performance appraisals. The PM may consult others about the Clerk's proposal.

Appointment and dismissal. The statutes establishing departments stipulate that the appointment of DMS is made by the Governor-in-Council (GIC). By convention, the GIC acts on the PM's recommendation. Prime Minister Charles Tupper had a list of prerogatives of the PMO approved by cabinet in 1896; it was subsequently reissued by every prime minister from Laurier to King (for the last time by PC 3374, 25 October 1935) (Canada, Privy Council Office, 1987: 9). It is now considered a convention and need not be written down as long as everyone acts in accordance with the custom. The practice of appointment by the GIC on the PM's recommendation entails a rich and complex balance that affects the exercise of power. This is a cabinet appointment, made after the PM proposes an Order-in-Council, which is not submitted to the full cabinet but does require three other ministerial signatures as well as that of the PM. Such a procedure means that the person appointed retains the confidence of the government, the cabinet, and the PM. It is not a ministerial appointment. Therefore, the PM may try to install a particular DM (for example, a seasoned, bilingual, networked official) to assist a particular minister (a newcomer, or someone who is unaware of the department's workings). Only the PM can make the recommendation, which gives him veto power over all such appointments. The power of appointment provided by the Interpretation Act has been understood to include the power of dismissal of DMS: the PM can ask a DM to resign or recommend that cabinet appoint another person to act as DM in the department. On these matters, the PM is generally advised by the Clerk of the Privy Council. Reasons for dismissal vary. One revealing case was made public by the *Globe and Mail* and related by Plumptre (1987: 379). The PM's note, an unusual document written by the Clerk that may have been requested by the PM's entourage to cover him, stated that the DM in question was "insensitive to the Minister's role" and had "lost control of the Department."

Environment: Prime Minister/ Minister/Chief of Staff

The deputy minister inhabits a politically sensitive sphere. Remote from departmental employees and peers, DMs deal with the prime minister, ministers, and their **chiefs of staff (COSs)**. The chief of staff position, for its part, is highly contested in Canada. The Mulroney Conservatives experienced numerous conflicts between political appointees and career public servants during their first years of power. When the Liberals returned to power in 1993, they downgraded the chief of staff's role and personnel.

The PM recommends the DM's appointment and, accordingly, may at times require the DM's loyalty to counterbalance a minister's tendencies. The PM or his COS may occasionally call the DM for direct information on a matter, to express a position on an issue, to send a signal, to discuss a delicate subject, or to request advice on a related matter. However, direct communications between the PMO and a DM was not the rule: until 2005, a DM would insist on having personal confirmation from the prime minister or the minister and will ask to hear directly from him or her, or to be heard directly. Just as it is not usual procedure for the DM to receive a phone call from the PMO, it would be seen as a fatal error (barring exceptional circumstances) for a DM to call the PM directly, without going through the minister (political channels) or the Clerk of the Privy Council (administrative channels). This is hardly surprising, given the various accountability systems in place. The public service is accountable to the minister or prime minister for advice provided and for the implementation of political decisions. The chief of staff in principle is accountable to the minister as a partisan political actor whose role is to help him or her to gain and maintain power. The chief of staff should not interfere with the minister/DM relationship. To ensure that the accountability chain is not disrupted, the Gomery Report proposed to "adopt a code of conduct for political staff, including a provision that bars them from telling bureaucrats what to do" (Gomery Commission, 2006: Recommendation 11). Harper's government, however, interpreted matters differently. Apart from a handful of influential ministers, ministers were under close observation by the PMO which chose the COS. Not all ministers would play their role to the full. As a result the decision process became a three-way relationship between the DM, chief of staff, and the PMO.

Relations between deputy ministers and their ministers vary according to the minister's personality, its consideration by PM, and their mutual compatibility. In one cynical description, some ministers reached the top of the mountain the day they were appointed and want only to save the seat so they may sit and enjoy the view; others want to roll up their sleeves and get to work on the nitty-gritty details of running a department or hope to leave some monument to the country as their contribution or lasting legacy.

Deputy ministers welcome those differing attitudes with varying degrees of enthusiasm. One frustrated minister once commented, "When you meet the deputy minister for the first time, he is supposed to ask you whether you want to have your main office on Parliament Hill or at the department's HQ. If he insists that you may be better off up on the Hill, near Parliament and colleagues, you may interpret he is afraid of ministerial micro-management" (Bourgault, 1997c: 13).

Times have changed considerably and, by 2000, politicians come to power with a clearer agenda and bold priorities. They expect DMs to deliver this agenda. The DM is to connect the minister with the department and vice versa. For this, ministers have to be capable, interested, and willing to ply their ministerial role. Many DMs interviewed in 2015 for the 2008–15 period had the strong impression their minister was under the PMO's control and in some cases under their chief of staff's control (a PMO's delegation). There was a weekly meeting of chiefs of staff in Langevin block just after the DM's meeting. There was a daily briefing for ministerial communications officers. There was a "four corners dance" (with minister, PMO, DM, PCO), when the PMO was not satisfied the way some issues were dealt with or when some ministerial projects made the PMO worry. Then it was difficult to advise someone "who cannot or was not interested to receive advices, neither to act as a full minister!" as someone put it. Having said this, which did not happen to that extent before, most DMs had to find a way to establish a constructive relation with their minister, and most of them said they did it.

Generally, the minister holds a weekly morning meeting with the COS and DM; depending on the ministers' agenda and preferences, other people, such as the assistant deputy minister (ADM) and senior officials, may also be asked to attend. In addition to this briefing/debriefing, the DM meets with the minister as needed. When there are contentious political issues to be dealt with, when pieces of legislation are before the House, or when budgets or other strategic documents are in preparation (e.g., an appearance before a House committee), meetings with the minister are more frequent and may be held on a daily basis. Relations may also include a daily review of the minister's briefing book for Question Period when the House is sitting. The effect of the modern media cycle and of social media networks have importantly increased the 24/7 communications with ministers: everything can now become an issue for any government.

Legal Duties and Power

Most statutes establishing departments (with the exception of some regulatory departments such as Revenue, Consumer Affairs, Justice, and Immigration) do not stipulate any specific powers to be exercised by the DM. On the contrary, only general powers are dealt with, and they are assigned only to the minister. When the DM's powers are mentioned, it is stated that the DM shall take "general advice" from the minister in these matters (Canada, Privy Council Office, 1987: 17).

DMs may exercise power through the minister's authority, subject to "certain exceptions and constraints" (Canada, Privy Council Office, 1987: 1) as established by the Interpretation Act and convention: "Words directing or empowering a Minister of the Crown to do an act or a thing, or otherwise applying to him by his name of office, include . . . his or her deputy." This provision is followed by an exception for any regulation within the meaning of the Regulations Act (Canada, Privy Council Office, 1987: 24).

As the department's deputy head, the DM is responsible for the management of all of the department's human and financial resources. Those responsibilities were recently expanded as a result of new empowerment approaches adopted by central agencies such as Treasury Board and the Public Service Commission. Briefly put, DMs are now delegated with full responsibility for all decisions as long as they follow the principles and guidelines established by the central agencies. The Canada Revenue Agency may be the most advanced example of this trend. Some powers are delegated to the DM by the central agencies, others by the minister, while in this very case the enabling legislation provides the DM with direct powers. Delegated authority can be subdelegated and the DM delegates signing authority to the ADM and the director general (the individual directly beneath the ADM in rank). The DM's role is then to monitor the system, issuing clear guidelines, fine-tuning them, and following up on their application.

In 2006, the DM's environment was affected by the Federal Accountability Act. The Act created the position of **Parliamentary Budget Officer** and its holder was designated as an officer of the Library of Parliament (section 116). As a consequence, parliamentary committees are gaining slightly more resources to prepare for a DM's appearances before them. The Act also creates a **Public Servants Disclosure Protection Tribunal** to protect victims of reprisal and to order disciplinary actions against the perpetrators of such acts (section 201). Public servants now benefit from a structure promoting disclosure of dubious acts, even those committed by a DM. Interestingly, the spectrum of action of this tribunal is quite vast, since not only criminal acts can be brought to its attention. Finally, the DMs are named **accounting officers** for their departments and they are responsible for internal auditing. An accounting officer is accountable before the committees of the Senate and the House of Commons for organizing the resources of the organization, delivering programs in accord with current policies and procedures, signing accounts for public accounts, and performing duties assigned to the DM by any other Act (Smith,1988).

Each DM must establish and maintain an audit committee for his or her department (section 259). A review is necessary every five years to evaluate the relevance and effectiveness of each program (section 260).

The Deputy Minister's Role in the Political System: Service without Servility

The deputy minister is a public servant subject to the Public Service Employment Act and is therefore a non-partisan official. The DM's functions and duties differ from those of staff in the minister's office. The DM is a public employee with special status in terms of recruitment, appointment, and length of tenure. As a public employee (a function formerly defined as "serving the Crown"), the DM has a duty to the state. The DM performs that duty by loyally and competently serving the government of the day (Kernaghan & Siegel, 1991: 296–7). This means keeping the minister's and cabinet's trust in the DM's professional competency and ethics, and at the same time, as a non-partisan public employee, limiting his or her obedience and acting according to the law. The DM gives advice, protects the minister and the government, acts competently, but will not take any public stance to defend or promote a government policy or decision. Neither will the DM agree to do the minister a favour in violation of the law. Bourgault and Dunn illustrated the evolution of the DM's roles into the federal system, progressively moving from guardian, to administrators of resources, then gurus for policy development, later managers and leaders, and more recently, entrepreneurs and the delivering role (Bourgault & Dunn, 2013).

Incorporating Cabinet Priorities into Departmental Priorities

The deputy minister is expected to know the priorities, sensitivities, and promises of the government of the day and to incorporate these proactively into the department's agenda, where possible (Osbaldeston, 1989: 20). This means developing or modifying policies, programs, and legislation, preparing budget appropriations, and factoring cabinet priorities into discussions with the provinces, with pressure groups, and in international relations. It is the DM's job to make sure that everyone in the department is reading from the same page and that practical steps are taken to achieve the government's objectives.

Serving the Minister

Deputy ministers answer to their minister, not to cabinet. Some DMs do feel that, ultimately, they must heed cabinet, but, as one deputy said, "In the last analysis, it is the PM who holds me accountable. In a more indirect way, it is the Minister" (Osbaldeston, 1989: 18). All DMs recognize direct obligations to the minister as the department head and the department's representative on cabinet (in what Osbaldeston terms a "highly interactive process"; Osbaldeston, 1989: 23). Serving the minister essentially means preparing ministerial decisions, since most decisions concerning the administration of the department and the implementation of vertical (or sectoral) legislation (e.g., agricultural policies, health policies) are formally made by the minister with little time, knowledge, or information. Serving the minister also means providing the minister with knowledge, information, advice, orientations, opinions, corporate memory, and other decision-support materials. Once the minister has established an approach towards a category of decisions, the authority to make decisions of that type can be delegated to save time for the minister.

The DM meets at least weekly, and more often as needed, with the minister and other political aides. Events such as the Throne Speech, the Budget, reports to Parliament, and preparations for the annual executive retreat (strategic planning process) (Osbaldeston, 1989: 34–5) all require detailed preparation by the DM. On a daily basis, the DM is expected to help prepare answers to questions in the House, to gather raw material for speeches, and to reply to technical ministerial correspondence, either under the DM's own name or by preparing drafts for signature by the minister.

The Gomery Report challenges this accepted definition of the relationship between the minister and the DM. It proposes that the DM have the final say in most disagreements with the minister on matters relevant to the DM's accountability. To overrule the position of the DM, the minister would have to invoke an official procedure where he or she would write a letter transmitted to central bodies (Gomery Commission, 2006: Recommendation 5). On the other hand, many "are opposed to increase the power of unelected officials at the expense of Ministers. The result would be confusion as to who was accountable to Parliament for what" (Ardell et al., 2006). Moreover, they maintain that there is no need to create the proposed procedure to prevent ministers from making decisions contrary to the public's interest. When a DM isn't able to convince the minister not to proceed with an improper decision, he will inform the Clerk of the Privy Council of the situation, who will then bring the matter to the attention of the PM. The final decision will then be made by the PM and the minister, and both will be accountable to the Parliament for the outcome (Ardell et al., 2006).

Obligation to Answer

In accordance with a recommendation of the 1985 McGrath report on House of Commons reform, which aimed to revitalize the work of Parliament,

standing committees of Parliament were given authority to call anyone (including DMs) to answer questions. They already had such authority when dealing with areas in which powers are assigned directly to deputy heads, such as financial and human resources matters. That authority was then widened. McGrath's recommendations led to expanded committee powers; the government had to issue guidelines in order to balance the House's right to know and monitor with the House's right to see its Acts implemented effectively. Those guidelines were issued after some difficult official appearances before committees.

The government approved a six-page PCO document, revised in April 2000, that sets out a number of principles regarding the responsibilities of public servants when they appear before parliamentary committees, including the following:

1. The House and Senate, and their committees, have the power to call whomever they see fit, even against the wishes of a minister.
2. Generally, ministers determine which officials will speak on their behalf. It is for ministers to decide which questions they will answer and which questions can be answered by officials.
3. Witnesses testifying before parliamentary committees are expected to answer all questions. However, public servants have a legal responsibility to hold in confidence the information that comes into their possession in the course of their duties. They appear before committees to provide information that ministers could not be expected to provide personally.
4. Public servants have an obligation to behave in a manner that allows ministers to maintain full confidence in their loyalty.
5. When appearing before a committee, public servants must not undermine the principle of ministerial responsibility. They are not directly accountable to Parliament for their actions or for the policies and programs of the government. Matters of policy and political controversy have been reserved for ministers.
6. Public servants have a duty to convey information truthfully to their ministers and, on the minister's behalf, to convey truthfully information that they may properly convey to Parliament.

7. Officials who are asked to be sworn might wish to observe that they are appearing on behalf of their minister to convey factual information and to seek the understanding of the committee for the need to avoid questions that could put them in a position that would conflict with their duty to their minister and their oath of office.

8. Officials have a fundamental duty to advise their ministers frankly on any matters relevant to their departmental and policy responsibilities. Only ministers can properly decide when and to what degree a confidential matter should be disclosed.

9. Testimony under oath could force an official to assume a power of decision in these respects that he or she cannot properly exercise. Committees recognize that the provision of information to committees, beyond that normally accessible to the public, must be a matter of ministerial decision.

10. Officials may give explanations of complex policy matters but they do not defend policy or engage in debate as to policy alternatives.

These principles have generally proven to be workable. There have, however, been some notable exceptions, such as an early case in which the Opposition tried to embarrass the government by attacking a decision by the Deputy Minister of Immigration and overtly politicized the matter. In the famous Al-Mashat affair, senior officials, a minister's assistant, and the Clerk of the Privy Council passed the blame to each other (see Sutherland, 1991). Ministers were generally highly satisfied with the conduct of their deputy ministers before committees (Bourgault, 1997c: 23). Harper's deputies, when interviewed, were all under the impression they did well, although some had to admit flaws: "The best way to deal with this, is to recognize the facts as soon as possible and move on to something else before it becomes a partisan saga," one told. Many others were of the same view and said that ministers and the PMO were generally satisfied with how deputy's appearances went on.

Role within the Department

DMs perform many roles in the department, many of them on behalf of other authorities. For central agencies, they administer resources; for the minister, they implement the organic statutes and vertical laws for which that the minister is responsible and oversee policy-making in those fields; for cabinet, they align the department's priorities with those of the government; on their own authority, they provide the systems, information, and leadership needed to carry out those tasks or, in Mintzberg's terms, they implement the "jobframe," involving information, people, and action (Mintzberg & Bourgault, 2000). Finally, they contribute personally or by means of the department's resources to assisting the minister in his or her duties.

Administering Departmental Resources

On the minister's behalf, the DM administers the departmental resources provided by the budget. On his or her own authority, the DM makes or authorizes decisions on resource allocation. That authority formerly resided more with the central agencies and ministers; the reform of public management has empowered DMs and their subdelegates (directorates and ADMs). A 1993 study showed that the DMs were allocating 19 per cent of their time to immediate subordinates, more than to ministers, pressure groups, and peers; they were allocating 15 per cent of their time to human resources management, more than to policy-making, program implementation, political relations, and public relations (Bourgault, 1997a: 21). Moreover, the number of assistant deputy ministers (and even associate ADMs!) continues to grow. Although supervising them can be time-consuming for the DMs, it is said to be a long-term investment for the public administration, which will benefit from a pool of high-quality administrators to ensure the succession of the actual DMs.

Implementing Vertical Acts

In addition to the Act establishing the department, there can be anywhere from 10 to 100 Acts that apply to any given sphere. Usually, one minister will be responsible for applying each Act; in rare cases, the responsibility may be shared among more than one minister. A DM must see to applying the Acts for which the department is responsible, in accordance with social needs, or to coordinating implementation with governmental and non-governmental agencies.

Implementing vertical Acts entails drafting rules and regulations, monitoring their application, issuing notices, enforcing the rules, fine-tuning policies, developing programs, making rulings and decisions, and taking action. For this purpose, the minister, the DM, and departmental staff consult within and without the government apparatus, provide opinions, sit on committees and working groups, ask for research materials and information for purposes of analysis, etc.

The departments have headquarters and regional offices to implement policies and programs, central capabilities to monitor policy implementation, and central services to communicate and work with headquarters and provincial counterparts. The DM is responsible for ensuring that the entire apparatus functions smoothly. In the late 1980s there were nearly 40 departments. Last reorganizations cut the number of departments by nearly 40%, each responsible for more vertical Acts, more programs and regulations, larger budgets, a larger workforce, and more facilities. These administrative responsibilities consume much of the DM's time.

Policy-Making

Policy-making has always been seen as a key role of the deputy minister; since it is of strategic importance, we expect the department's most prominent manager to be deeply involved in the process. In the past, DMs would spend a larger part of their careers in a given department and became specialists on policy matters. Their position in the organization gives them an overview of developments and makes them the last filter before anything reaches the minister's desk, or in some cases goes to the central agencies. They are at the centre of information processes within the department and between the department and other organizations. This is why Osbaldeston (1989: 17–18) stresses the policy-advisory role and why Swift (1993: 9) considers the advisory role to be so important. Indeed, a DM who is doing his or her job provides official and unofficial advice to many people: the minister, central agency officials, national organizations, etc. A 1993 study found that DMs spend 25 per cent of their time on long-term matters and 5 per cent on evaluation, two functions that fall within the general category of policy-making (Bourgault,

1997a: 21). The 2015 interviews shed light on the fact that the DM's contribution to policy-making has changed: they now have to enter into a deeper conversation with ministers, the PMO, and pressure groups. They have to rely more on science and evidence-based arguments to convince, which will not succeed at all times.

Role within Peer Group

What Is the Peer Group?

Peer groups have been influential since the beginning of the last century. Later, DMs began meeting for a couple of days every year at a retreat 50 kilometres outside Ottawa. In 1940, Clifford Clark, who has been described as "the one who shaped the mandarinate" (Granatstein, 1982: 14–15), officially founded the Five Lakes Fishing Club 30 miles from Ottawa in Gatineau County. The informal get-together helped build relations between the vertical, insular, command-style departments. Until 1939, the measure of cohesion that did exist had been created by the PM more than by the Privy Council Office. After this, the opposite was the case.

The peer group consists of the DMs in all departments and in the PCO. It has varied with the number of departments and the number of special advisers with DM rank in the PCO. More recently, the definition has been broadened to include associate deputy ministers. In all, the group comprises from 35 to 50 people. It is a legacy of the pre-Thatcherian British system, in which Whitehall created a pool of corporate wisdom, the group of permanent secretaries. In Canada, the functional peer group began to emerge in the early 1970s with the need for cohesion and for interdepartmental coordination. The reorganization of the PCO in the late 1960s (Hay, 1982: 15) contributed to the normalization of the peer group, but the main reason for the peer group was the enthusiasm of the Clerk of the Privy Council, Gordon Robertson, for horizontal features. The two main changes in this connection were the creation of ministerial committees, with their mirror committees of deputy ministers, and the initiation of peer-group appraisal of deputy ministers around 1967 (Bourgault & Lemay, 1993).

The functioning of the peer group goes further than horizontal management, however. Its corporate culture implies a holistic and long-term integration effort under the formal authority and coordination of the Privy Council. Under this influence, it is expected that the interests of the government prevail over each ministry's own interests. Its members are to have a shared vision and their actions are coordinated by a corporate plan supported by diverse managerial tools such as the evaluation by peers. The corporate culture is omnipresent, influencing the criteria for selection of the DMs, their formation, and the support available to them, as well as encouraging the DMs to socialize together. It is so pervasive that authors such as Savoie characterize it as "court management" (Savoie, 1999). The leadership of the Clerk of the Privy Council is essential to the functioning of the peer group. As the leader of the DMs' community, he or she creates a common perspective, animates the group, steers their orientation, offers personal support, protects the integrity of the management systems, and ensures their periodic revision (Bourgault, 2007b).

Professional Body

In Canada, unlike France, deputy ministers do not belong to a series of general *grand corps* such as the Inspection générale des Finances, the Ingénieurs des mines, the Préfectoral, or the Conseillers d'État, the Cour des Comptes, to name just a few of the 10 bodies to which the *directeurs de cabinet, directeurs généraux*, and *secrétaires généraux* of the ministries (each of whom has a portion of the role of a DM in Canada) generally belong (Aberbach et al., 1981: 39); in France there is no single bureaucratic head, since the coordination and direction are done through a political aide (*directeur de cabinet*) who is generally on leave from his/her administrative assignment; this person is in charge of all the ministerial cabinet, which includes the political cabinet (headed by a *Chef de cabinet*) and technical and policy assistants; the cabinet coordinates the work of central directors and regional directors, all of whom are subjected to discretionary nominations and, nevertheless, mostly come from within the administration. And unlike their US equivalents, the positions at the senior or deputy minister level in Canada are permanent: they have a reasonable expectation of continuity if they do their jobs properly and behave appropriately. So there is a functional grouping of these strategic officials who are with the government for an extended period. The DM category as such is an administrative classification for officials who occupy the position of administrative department head. On the career path, it comes after the EX category, which consists primarily of assistant deputy ministers and directors. Formally, it is not a professional body one enters at a low level and that then defines the course of one's career. Informally, though, the DM category has taken on some of the characteristics of a professional body over the years: COSO members (DMs) have a say in selection, in the management of the DM group, in individual appraisals, in the development of corporate culture, in operations, and in policies.

Functional Cohesion: Selection, Coordination, Appraisal

The peer group's routine has changed over the past 20 years. At present, the DM breakfast occurs every Wednesday morning from 8:00 to 9:00 a.m. It features the Clerk of the Privy Council and deals with operational issues as well as a debriefing of Tuesday's cabinet meeting. During the 1990s, there was also a weekly DM luncheon. This was a rather social event lasting from noon until two in the afternoon and also involved associate DMs, agency chiefs, and administrative tribunal heads, and was devoted to networking and learning through lectures and discussions. The Coordinating Committee of Deputy Ministers (CCDM) meets for lunch every other Wednesday; it discusses, at alternating meetings, public policy issues and management agenda issues; the meeting is attended by two different sets of DMs. The Treasury Board Secretariat Advisory Committee (TBSAC), made up of some 10–12 DMs, will meet on a monthly basis to make advance comments on the projects contemplated by Treasury Board officers. The Committee of Senior Officials (COSO) meets every three weeks on average, depending on the role the Clerk of the Privy Council wants it to play: it may play a major role, giving advice on matters related to DM staffing policies, identifying up-and-comers who are ready for a DM appointment, overseeing the performance appraisal system for DMs, reviewing the information on each prospective appointee, and advising the Clerk (see Bourgault, 2007b). It has also been used to monitor performance and organizational changes within departments.

The peer group also attends to longer-term issues. In 1974, it began holding annual retreats of approximately four days; some years later, these were replaced by three annual two-day seminars to identify issues and form working groups (in the fall), receive and discuss interim reports (winter), and approve final reports (June). Between those meetings, the seven or eight groups of deputy ministers, assisted by other officials, meet, conduct research, and hold discussions on the matters assigned to them, which include policy issues and organizational and administrative concerns. There may also be ad hoc or technical short-term groups created by a DM to address a specific issue, and other advisory groups created by DMs to provide advice (Bourgault, 1997a). DMs are expected to attend those meetings in person; firm believers in horizontal management, they now devote about a third of their time on government-wide corporate matters.

Of the countries we have studied, Canada has one of the most developed forms of corporate management at the top. It is time-consuming and was perceived by some Conservative governments, like the Mulroney Government, as a techno-bureaucratic threat (Bourgault & Nugent, 1995). Yet, it serves a self-monitoring function and also has the advantage of facilitating interdepartmental coordination and dialogue at the senior level.

Profile of Deputy Ministers

The profile of deputy ministers was studied by Porter (1965) in the late 1950s, Pond and Chartrand (1969) in the late 1960s, and Campbell and Szablowski (1979) in the 1970s. All of these studies looked at various categories of senior executives. Olsen (1980) deals with assistant deputy ministers. Osbaldeston (1989) lists arrivals and departures. Bourgault (2004) traces the professional, political, and socio-economic profile of DMs from 1867 to 2003. Swift (1993) looks at the professional profile of deputy ministers and associate deputy ministers in the 1990s. Zussman and Varette (1996) compare senior executives in the public

and private sectors. We will focus on the studies by Bourgault, Swift, and Zussman and Varette because they are based on homogeneous samples of DMs.

The 2008 federal cohort consisted of 33 DMs. Their average age was 54. Forty-two per cent of them were women. Ten were born in Ontario, ten come from Quebec, and eight are from Western Canada. Two were born in Atlantic Canada and three are immigrants. Sixty per cent speak English as their first language, 31 per cent French, and 9 per cent were raised in another language. Three DMs of the 13 respondents had a parent working in public administration.

As for their education, 12 per cent had completed a PhD, 64 per cent a master's degree, and 21 per cent a bachelor degree. One DM had not specified any degree. Moreover, almost half of them had a multidisciplinary background (14 out of 33). Fifty-two per cent had a background in humanities (political sciences, history, sociology, and geography) and 67 per cent studied management or economics. Specialization was marginal, with 24 per cent of the DMs having studied law and 6 per cent having studied pure sciences.

Most of the DMs attended Ontario universities (67 per cent). Thirty-nine per cent of the DMs studied at Quebec universities—27 per cent at francophone institutions and 18 per cent at anglophone universities—21 per cent studied in Western Canada, and 6 per cent in Atlantic Canada. Twenty-four per cent attended university outside of Canada.

The DMs (as of 30 April 2008) had held their positions for an average of two-and-a-half years. More precisely, 15.2 per cent of the DMs had been in the position for less than one year, 30.3 per cent between one and two years, 24.2 per cent between two and three years, 18.2 per cent between three and five years, 9.1 per cent between five and seven years, and 3 per cent for more than seven years.

Moreover, 39 per cent of the DMs had previously occupied the same position in one or more other ministries, for an average of five years. This means that 21 of the DMs had no previous experience at this level. But all of them had at least some experience as an associate or assistant DM. When they were appointed to their positions, one DM had previously occupied a DM position for less than one year, two between one and two years, two for between two and three years, four between three and seven years, and four for more than seven years. The DM with the longest previous DM experience had previously worked ten-and-a-half years as a DM.

A more recent survey (Bourgault & Gow, 2016: 204) also noted a slight rejuvenation of the DM's community in 2014 with an average age of 52 years arriving into the particular job, multiple MAs replacing most of the PhDs, same proportion of private and public management studies, and having already spent an average of 2.2 years into the job. None of them had come directly from the private sector, although many had had some working experience in that sector more than 10 years before their appointment as deputy minister. A survey conducted in the summer of 2015 tends to confirm those data.

Politicization

Politicization is an ever-controversial issue. Some argue that governments are entitled to appoint whomever they wish and may legitimately choose people whose loyalty and political views they trust; others argue, out of principle or out of envy, that politicization kills morale, creates cliques, and leads to the appointment of people who are unable to think independently and whose competence will always be considered suspect (Bourgault & Dion, 1989c: 109). While Canada has a rocky history in this regard (Simpson, 1988: 378), it has come to consider non-politicization of the public service as a constitutional convention (Canada, Supreme Court, 1991). However, some observers, such as Aucoin (1995: 118), ask whether low levels of politicization are related to political stability and whether bureaucratic patronage is preferable to political patronage. By design and by nature, the position of DM is politicized to some extent. It is just below the minister and part of its function is to make the minister and cabinet perform well and look good: this is the functional and inescapable sense of politicization, which is totally different from ideological and partisan politicizations. It is a discretionary political appointment made by the Governor-in-Council (GIC). On the other hand, DMs must not cross the line into partisan politics. However, the sponsorship scandal raised questions in 2002 about the nature of politicization of some DMs and senior officials. The nature of the scandal, which involved senior bureaucrats administering

contracts designed in the long run to benefit the ruling party, and to promote Canadian unity in violation of election laws, cast doubt on the integrity of those bureaucrats. In his report, Judge Gomery proposed measures to prevent the politicization of the DMs which, despite having triggered controversy, did not lead to concrete measures (Gomery Commission, 2006). Most critics agree that the solutions proposed to address exceptional circumstances were out of proportion (Ardell et al., 2006).

It is difficult to define objective criteria for determining whether politicization exists. Carrying a party membership card, paying membership dues, making financial contributions, or running as a candidate might be considered clear signs, but there are shrewd citizens who contribute to both main parties or switch parties after seven or 10 years. Less formal indicators might include replacing an effective DM without valid reason, appointing someone from outside, especially a relative (even if he or she has no political involvement), or installing someone with compatible views on policy.

In 1988, after the incoming Mulroney government was accused of politicizing the function, Bourgault and Dion conducted a longitudinal study of deputy ministers (1989b: 124–51). A study of all appointments and departures from 1867 to 1988 concluded that the number of departures during the 24-month period after an election in which there was a change in ruling party (which ranged from 2.4 per cent in 1911 to 12.5 per cent in 1984) is not significantly greater than after elections in which there was no change in government or during non-election years (an average of 7.4 per cent per year before 1959 and 9.3 per cent since 1959). The study demonstrated that recruitment was almost entirely internal and that when people leave their functions, they generally do so to retire or to occupy another attractive position in the civil service.

Judge Gomery suggested that the position of Clerk of the Privy Council had become politicized over the past 30 years, as power concentrated around the PM. He recommended the split of the Clerk's functions; the Clerk "should be known as Secretary to the Cabinet and his or her main role should be to represent the public service to the prime minister and the cabinet. The Privy Council Office would be renamed the Cabinet Secretariat. The Secretary of the Treasury Board would assume the title and function of head of the public service" (Gomery Commission, 2006: Recommendation 13). Many disapproved of these recommendations, being of the opinion that the role of this important actor should not be undermined (Ardell et al., 2006). The author concurs neither with the Judge's observation nor the recommendation; at this level the frontier separating politics and bureaucracy does not exist. DMs are employees of the state loyally serving the government of the day within the limits of the law.

Coping with Transitions

Transitions occur when there is a change in the head of government. They are more significant when there is a change in the governing party after a general election, given the time it takes to build trust and the adversarial tone of election campaigns. Transitions bring three types of changes: in politico-administrative structures (such as committees and departments), in agenda (shifting priorities), and in personnel (new ministers, new political aides, and some new senior officials). Transitions are always a key test of politicization: the more highly politicized a civil service is, the more likely it is to be shaken up and for senior officials to be replaced by others of the right stripe who enjoy the confidence of the politicians.

Let us look at what befell deputy ministers in 1984, when the Tories replaced the Liberals in government. The Conservative transition was depicted as having politicized the ranks of DMs. There was a flurry of activity, including some inflammatory statements by the PM and his Conservative entourage, and numerous skirmishes among ministers, DMs, and the ministers' strengthened chiefs of staff (Bourgault & Dion, 1990). But at the end of the day, Mulroney did not fire many more DMs in his first four years in office than Pierre Trudeau had in the previous four years (Bourgault & Dion, 1989a). When Trudeau regained office in 1980 he found all of his former deputy ministers except for four, and when Mulroney first took office in 1984, he found 31 DMs appointed by the previous government. After four years, the Liberals had changed 21 of them and the Conservatives 26; the Liberals had transferred six to other DM positions and the Conservatives four; therefore, only five were still serving the Liberals after four years and one was still serving

the Tories. The bottom line is that the difference is slight. The Tories might well argue that it was easy for the Liberals to look good, since Clark's previous Tory government was in office for only a few months and did not have time to bring in its own people.

To promote stability and to reduce political appointments, Gomery's report recommended commissionning into the same position DMs and senior public servants for a minimum of three years, with the expectation that most appointments would last at least five years (Gomery Commission, 2006: Recommendation 6). Despite the rigidity of this recommendation, the administrative community seemed to support this idea (Ardell et al., 2006). This is already what is generally understood on the Hill. Since exceptions always have to be permitted, it is unclear what this new rule could bring to the process. Some individuals may prefer to retire than go through another transition process with new political officials in place.

Coping with Minority Governments

While a majority government is assured that it will stay in power for a predictable time, a minority government does not have the same control over its lifespan, the procedures of the House of Commons, and the parliamentary committees. The committees may be excessively zealous in questioning bureaucrats and the ministers. A minority government also fears the possibility of a non-confidence vote, which would precipitate an election. Any government would prefer elections to be held when they have a good chance of re-election. All these factors affect the government's expectations of the DMs' performance.

It would be expected that DMs would have a greater influence on their ministers in a minority government because of the ministers' obvious vulnerability. But interviews conducted in 2007 (Bourgault, 2007c) revealed an unexpected relationship. Minority governments avoid controversial policy issues, pay much attention to administrative details, and may exert more control on management and communications. In turn, senior officials may self-censure to avoid controversy and spend more time dealing with crises, and are expected to accommodate short-term solutions that the administration considers less than ideal, but which are necessary political compromises. The minister would expect his DM to offer realistic propositions that can be implemented quickly. DMs are also expected to be very careful in conducting the government's business, as any mistake could bring about the fall of the government.

Ministerial Satisfaction

The discretionary nature of the appointment of DMs and the fact that they serve "at pleasure" have fuelled an ongoing discussion about the merit system in the public service. The Gomery report stimulated debate by proposing that government "adopt an open and competitive process for the selection of DMs . . . where applicants are vetted by a committee of bureaucrats, politicians and outside experts" (Gomery Commission, 2006: Recommendation 12). Judge Gomery agrees that the actual appointment process is an invitation to systemic politicization of the public service, while others claim that Canada is still the country in which politics and administration are the most sharply separated, with an appointment system designed to provide elected officials with compatible senior bureaucrats capable of helping them implement the program they promised the House. Some critics of the Gomery propositions believe that the PM needs to ensure that his or her agenda will be implemented in administrative terms and that appointing DMs is essential to do this (Brown, 2006). Research however revealed that the ministers were not more satisfied with DMs they appointed themselves than with those they kept from preceding governments (Bourgault, 1997c).

Are the politicians really pleased with their DMs? Does it make a difference whether they chose the DMs? With what are they most satisfied and dissatisfied? A 1995 study of former Conservative ministers surveyed half of the 200 or so minister/ DM pairings under the Conservative governments of the 1984–93 period. Twenty-one former ministers were interviewed (Bourgault, 1997c: 19). It was found that 81 per cent of ministers were satisfied or very satisfied with their DMs, comparable to the rate found in 1986 in Quebec among former PQ ministers (Bourgault & Dion, 1989a). Most of the dissatisfaction reported by Conservative ministers was caused by two people closely identified with the Liberals and by two others brought in from outside by the Conservatives themselves. In fact, the overall satisfaction rate was the same for DMs they themselves had chosen as for those inherited from the Liberals.

The Conservative ministers were particularly satisfied with the DMs' loyalty, competence, political judgment, willingness to work, discretion, respect for ministerial authority, and performance before House committees, all but the last of which are traditional values of the Canadian public service. They were less satisfied with the DMs' influence in the bureaucracy (29 per cent), management skills (19 per cent), policy-making capacities (19 per cent), ideological compatibility (19 per cent), decision-making abilities (18 per cent), program evaluation skills (18 per cent), and ability to persuade clients and pressure groups (18 per cent). The ideological gap is not surprising. The dissatisfaction with management, policy-making, and program evaluation skills says a good deal about the disillusionment outsiders may experience after entering government. It may also be consistent with the observations Zussman and Varette (1996) made about the specific career path of DMs; it does not appear that great importance is attached to practical operational experience. What is more surprising is the perceived lack of ability to persuade colleagues, which is the greatest source of dissatisfaction by far. It may be due to normal ministerial impatience with implementing their agenda and removing obstacles, or perhaps to the force of peer power in Ottawa, where an individual DM has to cope with the horizontal system.

Multiple Accountability

The accountability system for deputy ministers has been described as multiple, complex, and at times contradictory. The accountability of the DMs depends on the legal obligations, the powers and the mandates received from the PM, the minister, the Clerk of the Privy Council, central bodies, Parliament, and certain of its agents. A single action can imply different accountabilities on various aspects and contradictions are possible.

Canadian government requires a DM's loyalty to the government's agenda and to the PM as the leader of the government. Moreover, a DM is appointed by cabinet only after being recommended by the PM, so the PM is ultimately the one to whom the DM owes his or her job. The DM is then accountable to the PM for supporting his or her minister and for the application of programs and mandates given by the PM or the cabinet (Bourgault, 2006).

According to legislation, the DM is required to assist and serve the minister by taking charge of the daily management of the ministry. Because of the appointment process, the DM may also owe a debt of loyalty to his or her minister (Bourgault, 2006).

The DM operates under the coordinating umbrella of the Clerk of the Privy Council, who was named "Head of the Public Service" (including DMs) in 1993. Regarded as the "senior Deputy Minister of the Public Service" (Murray, quoted in Bourgault, 2007a), the Clerk assumes the orientation and coordination of the DM's community at the administrative and social level; he or she supervises the coordination of actions, develops long-term vision, ensures adherence to the governmental agenda, watches performance, promotes collaboration between DMs, and organizes social events for DMs (Bourgault, 2007a). The Clerk processes all the preparations for the submission of candidates for DM appointments to the PM and acts as the prime minister's deputy minister, which gives him or her some authority over the other deputy ministers. These considerations, taken together, make the DM accountable to some extent to the Clerk. The DM is accountable to the Clerk for his or her ministry's performance and the DM's own performance, for translating the priorities of the Clerk (and thus the priorities of the PM and government) into the activities of the ministry, and for following any particular instructions given by the Clerk (Bourgault, 2006).

The DM is also accountable to the central bodies, which transmit the directives of the cabinet and the ministerial committees. Since these bodies often delegate powers to the DM, such as those involving human resources, finance, and delivering public goods, he or she is accountable for them (Bourgault, 2006). The Managerial Accountability Framework has been simplified over the years, so as to ease the reporting job, do away with some of the repetitions, and consume less time from the departments and the DM who is to manage the departmental conversation with central agencies.

Some Acts also create specific areas of accountability for DMs; for example, DMs report to Treasury Board on resource management, to the Public Service Commission on staffing processes, and to House

standing committees when called to testify. Moreover, the DM is answerable to Parliament and its committees for the work of his or her ministry (Bourgault, 2006). Finally, in real life, they also report to the DM community as a whole, since their performance appraisal is processed through COSO, and since they must answer questions from their colleagues at the weekly DM community meetings.

The challenge for the DM is therefore to act so as to satisfy the objectives and norms of all these other actors and to be accountable to each of them (Bourgault, 2006)—and still perform coherent and meaningful action.

The multiplicity of DM accountability requirements makes the issue quite complex. "They are marching to several drums," comments Langford (1984), who asks whether they are not creating their own beat. Plumptre, citing the Lambert Commission, observes that "Some deputies maintain that they are, in effect, accountable only to themselves, and claim to measure their performance against their own standards of excellence" (Plumptre, 1987: 374).

To clarify the situation, we should consider the different meanings of the term *accountability*. Accountability means *to account for*. The question then is: account for what, to whom, on what subjects, in how much detail, and with what responsibility for outcomes? British writers have divided the concept into three components: responsibility, reportability, and answerability. DMs are not politically responsible; that responsibility belongs to the minister, who can be asked to resign by a political body. DMs do bear administrative responsibility for their decisions and actions to the minister, the Clerk, and the central agencies administering particular Acts. Center of government has been known to request transfers when things go badly. DMs are responsible for their own personal conduct to the government and the DM community.

DMs are also required to report, which means providing requested information. They report to the minister on all issues the minister may have to deal with, to the House on semi-annual departmental reports and on any matter the House requests, to the Parliamentary Agents' reports such as Auditor General on any matter subject to his jurisdiction; and to the DM community on matters that have been delegated to it.

In addition, DMs are answerable to House committees, which means they have to provide factual information without taking a stand or defending or promoting any political position or governmental policy. They must supply facts and figures and explain why a particular course of action was chosen.

Administrative accountability can be exercised through the MAF reports and through performance appraisals and sanctioned through bonuses, promotions, and constructive reassignments (Bourgault, 1990: 24–5). Canada was the first country to introduce performance appraisals for its most senior personnel (Bourgault & Lemay, 1993). The Canadian process is distinctive in that it is collegial, inclusive, participatory, and, above all, creates incentives and a culture to support collaboration. A DM may write a short report on his or her achievements over the year in terms of his or her mandate, as agreed with the Clerk. A visiting committee formed by COSO will meet with the minister and the DM and report to COSO's evaluation committee, which also receives reports on the person from the central agencies. The committee reports to the Clerk, who makes recommendations to the PM. The PM makes the final decision on the appraisal. The Clerk will then meet with the DM and brief him or her on the results.

Conclusions and Prospects

Deputy ministers are to serve ministers. Ministers' roles and leeway have evolved over the last 20 years. Serving a minister would need a minister to play a genuine ministerial role (making decisions, enjoying leeway to foresee the issues and solutions in a relatively autonomous mode). This is not always the case when the PMO interferes heavily with ministerial decisions. This adds to the puzzling understanding of the DM's main roles in times of real-time issue management due to the multiple media coverages; providing professional advice to the minister, the PM, and the Cabinet; managing the departmental resources; and participating to the corporate management of the Government of Canada. The nature of the DM's job has been affected by recent developments such as new approaches to answerability; state–citizenry relations; fiscal responsibility; public management; the challenges of new media, technologies, and globalization; and the DM's evolving role, which is changing from manager to "empowerer." Ministers need more than ever

to be reassured on a constant basis, which impacts a DM's attention and time.

Under the new systems of answerability, DMs are required to appear before standing committees on behalf of ministers and answer questions without crossing the fine line and engaging in political debate, and they must present reports on goals, outcomes, and resource use.

New conceptions of state–citizenry relations are affecting departmental operations as a whole: policy-making and service-delivery processes are shifting from command-style models to more participative models; more information is being released, making relations with the media, pressure groups, and the provinces trickier for senior officials. The concept of the role of government is evolving from one of emperor to facilitator. DMs must communicate with more people and organizations than ever before, all of whom are claiming the right to be heard: citizens no longer see themselves as subjects of the state; rather, they consider the state to be their servant.

For many years, fiscal constraint has meant budget and program cuts, workforce reductions, and loss of capacity and expertise, making policy decisions more difficult and forcing DMs to deal with external, less predictable resources.

New approaches to public management have ushered in extensive use of contracting as outsourcing and partnering increase. As a result, clearly defined inputs, deliverables, and expected outcomes must be formulated. They have also caused problems with grant management and prompted criticism in cases where resources for the proper control of the use of grants were lacking, even as departments were being asked to deliver more swiftly, more smoothly, and on a more receiver-friendly basis. In this regard, organizational learning is taking place. DMs have to answer complex questions, keep sight of overall objectives, and take corrective action when necessary, upon reports tabled by Agents of Parliament or Central bodies. (One example of the latter is the action plan Minister Jane Stewart brought before the House in response to the Auditor General's report on Human Resources Development Canada in the spring of 2000.)

Globalization is making the DM's job more demanding. DMs no longer control the flow of information; the pressure groups they deal with are able to bypass policy rules through information technology. As a result, DMs must be on their toes and attentive to their own organization's capacities.

Because of all these demands deputy ministers may find themselves overwhelmed and must rely heavily on their staff. They must impart a vision to staff, and that vision must evolve with changing challenges. They must make things happen through people they have enabled and whom they trust and who are now, more than ever, accountable for political and administrative results and conformity to procedures. Building that type of relationship with assistants and subordinates is one of the most critical parts of the deputy minister's new role.

Important Terms and Concepts

accounting officer
chief of staff (COS)
Committee of Senior
  Officials (COSO)

deputy minister (DM)
discretionary appointment
Parliamentary Budget
  Officer

Public Servants Disclosure
  Protection Tribunal

Study Questions

1. How are deputy ministers designated, selected, appointed, and dismissed?
2. What is the nature of the politically sensitive world that DMs inhabit, and how do they manage to survive within it? What are the relative chances of politicization?
3. What duties does the DM owe to the political realm?
4. What is the DM's peer group, and what is their relative importance in his or her professional life?
5. What did Gomery, its critics, and those promoting the Federal Accountability Act have to say about the role of DMs, and what do you think of the chapter's views on this?
6. What is meant by "The accountability system for deputy ministers has been described as multiple, complex, and at times contradictory"?

References

Aberbach, J., R. Putnam, and B. Rockman. 1981. *Bureaucrats and Politicians in Western Democracies*. Cambridge, Mass.: Harvard University Press.

Ardell, Bill, et al. 2006. "Letter to the Prime Minister on the Federal Sponsorship Scandal." IPAC.

Aucoin, P. 1995. "Politicians, Public Servants, and Public Management: Getting Government Right." *Governance in a Changing Environment*, edited by B. Guy Peters and Donald J. Savoie, Montreal and Kingston: CCMD/McGill-Queen's University Press, pp. 113–37.

Bourgault, J. 1990. "Rules and Practices of Dismissal in the Canadian Higher Civil Service." *Getting the Pink Slip*, edited by A. W. Neilson, Toronto: IPAC, pp. 18–44.

———. 1997a. "De Kafka au Net: la lutte de tous les instants pour le contrôle de l'agenda chez les sous-ministres canadiens." *Gestion, revue internationale de gestion* 22, 2, pp. 18–26.

———. 1997b. "La gestion de la performance dans la haute fonction publique: quelques cas issus du modèle de Whitehall." *Performance et secteur public, réalités, enjeux et paradoxes*, edited by M.M. Guay, Montreal: QC, pp. 193–213.

———. 1997c. *The Satisfaction of Ministers with the Performance of their Deputy Ministers during the Mulroney Governments: 1984–1993*. Research Paper No. 22. Ottawa: Canadian Centre for Management Development.

———. 2004. *Le profil des sous-ministres du gouvernement du Canada.* Ottawa: École de la fonction publique du Canada.

———. 2006. "Le rôle du sous-ministre du Gouvernement du Canada: sa responsabilité et sa reddition de comptes." in Canada, *Commission d'enquête sur le programme de commandites et les activités publicitaires. Rétablir l'imputabilité. Études.* Volume 1, Le Parlement, les ministres et les sous-ministres. Ottawa : la Commission, pp. 283–329.

———. 2007a. "Les facteurs contributifs au leadership du greffier dans la fonction publique du Canada." *Administration publique du Canada Canadian Public Administration* 50 (hiver): 541–71.

———. 2007b. "La gestion corporative au sommet des gouvernements: la pratique canadienne." *Revue internationale des sciences administratives* 73 (juin), pp. 283–300.

———. 2007c. "Inaugural Galimberti Memorial Lecture: The Changing Role of the Deputy Minister in Canadian Governments." IPAC Annual Conference, Winnipeg.

———, and S. Dion. 1989a. "Brian Mulroney a-t-il politisé les sous-ministres?" *Canadian Public Administration* 32, 1, pp. 63–84.

———, and ———. 1989b. "Governments Come and Go, But What of Senior Civil Servants? Canadian Deputy Ministers and Transitions in Power (1867–1987)." *Governance* 2, 3, pp. 124–51.

———, and ———. 1989c. "Les gouvernements anti-bureaucratiques face à la haute fonction publique: une comparaison Québec-Ottawa." *Politiques et management public* 7, 2, pp. 97–118.

———, and ———. 1990. "Managing Conflicts in a Context of Government Change: Lessons from the Federal Government of Canada, 1984–1988." *International Journal for Conflict Management* 1, 4, pp. 375–96.

———, and ———. 1991. *The Changing Profile of Federal Deputy Ministers: 1867–1988.* Ottawa: Canadian Centre for Management Development.

———, ———, and M. Lemay. 1993. "Performance Appraisals of Top Civil Servants: Creating a Corporate Culture." *Public Administration Review* 53, 1, pp. 73–80.

———, and P. Nugent. 1995. "Les transitions de gouvernement et la théorie des conflits: le cas de la transition de 1984 au gouvernement du Canada." *Revue Canadienne de Sciences Administratives* 12, 1, pp. 15–26.

Bourgault, J., and C. Dunn. 2013. *Deputy Ministers in Canada.* Toronto: University of Toronto Press.

Bourgault J., and J. I. Gow. 2016. *Les élites administratives sous l'influence de la nouvelle gestion publique,* in L'acteur et la bureaucratie au XXIe siècle, Québec, P.U.L., pp. 193–220.

Brown, Jim. 2006. "Gomery Reform Proposals Spark Backlash among Political, Business Elite." Canadian Press Newswire, 6 Mar 2006.

Burns, R.M. 1961. "The Role of the Deputy Minister." *Canadian Public Administration* 4, pp. 357–62.

Campbell, E.C., and G.J. Szlablowski. 1979. *The Superbureaucrats.* Toronto: Macmillan.

Canada. 1985. *Report of the Special Committee on Reform of the House of Commons* (James A. McGrath, chair). Ottawa: House of Commons.

Canada, Privy Council Office. 1987. *The Office of Deputy Minister,* rev. edn. Ottawa.

Canada, Royal Commission on Financial Management and Accountability (Lambert Commission). 1979. *Final Report.* Ottawa.

Canada, Supreme Court. 1991. *Osborne v. Canada* 2 S.C.R. 69.

Des Roches, J. M. 1962. "The Evolution of the Organization of the Federal Government of Canada," *Canadian Public Administration* 5, pp. 411–23.

Gilmore, Alan. 2010: "The Canadian Accounting Officer: Has it Strengthened Parliament's Ability to Hold the Government to Account?" *The Handbook of Canadian Public Administration,* edited by C. Dunn, Toronto: Oxford University Press.

Gomery Report. Canada, Royal Commission of Inquiry into the Sponsorship Program and Advertising Activities (Gomery Commission). 2005. *Who Is Responsible?* Phase 1 Report. Ottawa.

———. 2006. *Restoring Accountability.* Phase 2 Report. Ottawa.

Granatstein, J. 1982. *The Ottawa Men.* Toronto: Oxford University Press.

Greene, Ian. 1990. "Conflict of Interest and the Canadian Constitution: An Analysis of Conflict of Interest for Canadian Cabinet Ministers." *Canadian Journal of Political Science* 23, 2, pp. 233–56.

Hay, M. A. 1982. "Understanding the PCO: The Ultimate Facilitator." *Optimum* 13, 1, pp. 5–21.

Heintzman, R. 1997. "Introduction." *Public Administration and Public Management: Canadian Experiences.* edited by in J. Bourgault et al., Quebec City: Publications du Québec, pp. 1–13.

Hodgetts, J. E. 1973. *The Canadian Public Service.* Toronto: University of Toronto Press.

Kernaghan, K., and D. Siegel. 1991. *Public Administration in Canada.* Scarborough, ON: Nelson.

Langford, J. 1984. "Responsibility in the Senior Public Service: Marching to Several Drummers." *Canadian Public Administration* 27, 4, pp. 513–21.

Mintzberg, H., and J. Bourgault. 2000. *Managing Publicly.* Toronto: IPAC.

Olsen, D. 1980. *The State Elite in Canadian Society.* Toronto: McClelland & Stewart.

Osbaldeston, G. 1989. *Keeping Deputy Ministers Accountable.* Scarborough, ON: McGraw-Hill Ryerson.

———. 1992. *Organizing to Govern*. Toronto: McGraw-Hill Ryerson.

Plasse, M. 1992. "Les chefs de cabinets ministériels du gouvernement fédéral canadien: rôle et relation avec la haute fonction publique," *Canadian Public Administration* 30, 3, pp. 317–38.

Plumptre, T. 1987. 'New Perspectives on the Role of the Deputy Minister', *Canadian Public Administration* 30, 3: 376–98.

Pond, K.L., and P.J. Chartrand. 1969. "Cheminement des carrières de direction dans la fonction publique au Canada." *Relations industrielles* 4, 2, pp. 318–29.

Porter, J. 1965. *The Vertical Mosaic*. Toronto: University of Toronto Press.

Savoie, D. 1999. *Governing from the Centre*. Toronto: University of Toronto Press.

Simpson, J. 1988. *Spoils of Power*. Toronto: Collins.

———. 2006. "The Gomery Reforms Should First Do No Harm." *The Globe and Mail*, 28 Feb. 2006, A1.

Smith, A.1988. *The Accountability of Accounting Officers Before Parliamentary Committees*. Ottawa, Parliament of Canada, 12p.

Sutherland, S. 1991. "The Al Mashat Affair: Administrative Accountability in Parliamentary Institutions." *Canadian Public Administration* 34, 4, pp. 573–603.

Swift, F. 1993. *Strategic Management in the Public Service: The Changing Role of the Deputy Minister*. Ottawa: Canadian Centre for Management Development.

Zussman, D., and S. Varette. 1996. "Today's Leaders: Career Trends of Canada's Private and Public Sector Executives." Ottawa: Public Management Research Centre and University of Ottawa.

Part **III**

The Broad Public Sector

The broader public sector involves public bodies beyond the walls of the departmental public service. The matters we have chosen to highlight are Crown corporations, agencies, arm's-length agencies, and Indigenous public administration. They are intrinsically interesting because they raise questions of government accountability and control, questions for which moreover there are no easy answers.

Allan Tupper covers an equally complex area, in a somewhat similar fashion. He reviews the multiple definitions of arm's-length bodies, then considers the various rationales for arm's-length agencies. He asks if it is possible for the ABCs (agencies, boards, and commissions) to be simultaneously accountable to multiple principals, independent in their operational activities, yet subject to overall government direction and priorities. The unfortunate conclusion is that major accountability and performance deficits are possible. Yet some improvement is possible, he suggests. Along the way, Tupper considers if semi-independent agencies behave differently than other types of government organizations, the various directions possible to reform public agencies, and what a future research agenda covering them might look like.

Luc Bernier's chapter examines the multivaried nature of Crown corporations. These legal entities set up by the government differ in nature because they pursue a variety of commercial or other public policy objectives. Crown corporations have been used in Canada for a very long time as policy instruments at the unclear border between the public and the private sector. They have both commercial activities and public policies to implement. Their commercial nature distinguishes them from other government organizations. Since the 1980s, many governments have decided to privatize some of them. Nevertheless, many Crown corporations are still used for economic development. Policy objectives other than to generate some economic development are not always clear. This chapter suggests that we should move beyond the discussion of control or governance and look at the idea of public entrepreneurship.

Robert Shepherd covers First Nations' and governments' contrasting expectations of Indigenous governance today. For government officials, community mismanagement stems from the lack of control over financial aid and policy. For First Nations, it occurs as a result of systemic problems associated with financial dependency and outside control over their affairs, which breeds lackadaisical attitudes towards financial and organizational performance. Lack of agreement about the nature of the problem of accountability has led both sides to pose incompatible solutions. For government, it is more stringent bureaucratic controls; for First Nations it is a separation of First Nations and Canadian governance. One important challenge, moreover, derives from the governance models in play. Shepherd examines the complications of promising the inherent right of self-government, only to deliver the weaker delegated self-government model. The latter goes hand in hand with the restrictive New Public Management practised by federal authorities.

Arm's-Length Agencies and Canadian Public Administration

Allan Tupper

11

Chapter Overview

The chapter covers an area that is growing in importance in public administration and in people's lives but is seldom examined systemically. It starts by examining the multiple definitions of arm's-length bodies and highlighting the lack of consensus that pervades them. The various rationales for arm's-length agencies are then explored, some stressing managerial and some political drivers for their creation. The issue of accountability is then approached, considering if it is possible for the ABCs (agencies, boards, and commissions) to be simultaneously accountable to multiple principals, independent in their operational activities, yet subject to overall government direction and priorities. The democratic challenges of semi-independent agencies are then outlined through review of several recent studies. The unfortunate conclusion is that major accountability and performance deficits are possible. Yet improvement is possible.

Chapter Objectives

By the end of this chapter, students will be able to do the following:

- Review the main definitions of arm's-length bodies.
- Examine critically the various rationales for establishing arm's-length bodies.
- Describe the democratic challenges presented by the existence of semi-independent agencies.
- Summarize the existing research on the behaviour of semi-independent agencies.
- Present a research agenda for further research on semi-independent agencies.

Introduction

This chapter examines the role, accountability, and future of arm's-length agencies in Canadian public management. Its theme is that arm's-length agencies are now integral components of the Canadian administrative state at all levels of government. They employ many Canadians, sometimes have large budgets, and make decisions that have major impacts on citizens. As one European author writes of arm's-length bodies: "In modern democracies unelected bodies now take many of the detailed policy decisions that affect people's lives, untangle key conflicts of interest for society, resolve disputes over the allocation of resources and even make ethical judgements in some of the most sensitive areas" (Vibert, 2007: 1).

Arm's-length agencies, also referred to as public agencies and semi-independent bodies in this chapter, are now numerous and diverse in their roles, structures, and behaviour. They range from visible, nationally contentious bodies like the National Energy Board to obscure organizations like the Alberta Irrigation Council and Ontario's Moose and Bear Allocation Committee. Despite criticism and controversy, they continue to proliferate in Canada and abroad. Arm's-length agencies uneasily straddle the worlds of electoral politics, policy implementation, and quasi-judicial administration.

The chapter begins by examining several definitions of arm's-length bodies. It notes that no consensus exists on even this basic question. Different observers employ different criteria and definitions. Governments look at the matter quite differently as well. Analysts and governments also group public agencies into different categories. The heart of the question is really the boundaries between public and private sectors in modern economies.

The rationale for arm's-length agencies is then explored. Again, no consensus emerges. One line of reasoning stresses managerial and organizational forces. The other strand sees political forces as the drivers. In truth, neither explanation is sufficient by itself. In day-to-day public management, many forces explain governments' heavy reliance on semi-independent organizations. For example, students of comparative public management note how government organization and reform are heavily shaped by national histories, administrative cultures, and constitutions. (Pollitt & Bouckaert, 2011: 59–67).

From there we move to the heart of the matter. Can arm's-length agencies simultaneously be accountable to multiple principals, independent in their day-to-day activities and decision-making, yet subject to overall government direction and priorities? What blend of policy processes and oversight institutions are required to reach an ideal or at least satisfactory balance of these conflicting forces?

The democratic challenges of semi-independent agencies are outlined through review of several recent studies. A generous assessment sees their performance as mixed at best. In fact, some recent studies conclude that public agencies fail to deliver the benefits claimed for them. The arm between the government and the agency never seems to be the right length. Sometimes it is too long while often it is too short. Major accountability and performance deficits are possible.

Two major approaches to reform are discussed. A report prepared for the Alberta government, *At a Crossroads: The Report of the Board Governance Review Task Force*, links democratic ideals and modern board governance techniques with the concern that arm's-length agencies are used too frequently (Alberta).[1] Frank Vibert, on the other hand, outlines a different approach (Vibert, 2007). His view is that the problems raised by semi-independent government agencies are too important and complex to be resolved within the executive branch. The semi-independent sector of government must be recognized as a fourth branch of government that is equal to the executive, legislature, and judiciary. His blueprint presents a very different view of the democratic and public management questions posed by agency government. Vibert grapples with the wrenching problems raised by J. A. Corry and J. E. Hodgetts in 1959 when they remarked of **independent regulatory agencies**: "So a board is often at one and the same time, lawmaker, detective, prosecutor, judge and jury" (Corry & Hodgetts, 1959: 537).

The chapter concludes with suggestions for future research and a restatement of its main themes.

What Are Arm's-Length Agencies?

No easy answer emerges to this deceptively simple question. Indeed, problems of definition are highlighted by the diverse vocabulary at play. Our subject is collectively described by such terms as arm's-length agencies; non-department organizations; agencies, boards, and commissions (ABCs as they are sometimes called); and semi-independent government organizations. Different selection criteria yield radically different results. For example, an important study by Carsten Greve et al. reports a United Kingdom government analysis that yielded 309 arm's-length bodies and an academic study that asserts a total of more than five thousand public agencies in the UK (Greve et al., 1999: 134–5)!

An overly loose definition of arm's-length bodies would include such organizations as public–private partnerships (Triple Ps); private firms, like Bombardier, that are national champions in an important sector; and non-government organizations that deliver public services on contract to governments. Also properly excluded are elected bodies whose most visible Canadian manifestation is local school boards in the provinces. A variety of municipal boards, including for example the Vancouver Parks Board, are elected or have a combination of elected and appointed members.

Among the normal criteria used to define arm's-length agencies are that they are established by a government and that they perform an identifiable, often specialized public function. This function might be advisory to the government or civil service, adjudicative, commercial, investigative, or combinations thereof. Another essential characteristic of non-department agencies is that, by definition, they are not part of a government department. However, all arm's-length bodies have a defined and structured relationship to the government proper. Equally, an arm's-length body must have independence from direct ministerial control, although the extent and nature of that independence varies widely. For example, the extent of government financial control can differ greatly. Sometimes public agencies have their own revenue source. In other instances, arm's-length bodies have greater freedom in human resources management than government ministries. In almost all instances, however, board members and/or chief officers of non-department bodies are appointed by the government or with the approval of the government. If properly functioning, arm's-length agencies with decision-making authority are free to judge individual cases without need for advance or post facto political approval.

These criteria yield long lists of public agencies in the Government of Canada and the larger Canadian provinces. Governments have also grouped their agencies into categories for administrative and policy purposes. Alberta's recent report on public agencies presents a useful typology but many alternatives are available (Alberta, 2007; Hodgetts, 1973; UK National Audit Office, 2016; Vibert, 2007; and Wilson, 1981). Alberta has five categories of public agencies. Regulatory/adjudicative public agencies regulate, license, and sometimes make quasi-judicial decisions. Public trusts, a second category, administer provincial government public finances. An important example is the Alberta Investment Management Corporation (AIMCO) that manages Alberta government pensions including the Alberta Heritage Savings Trust Fund. In 2016, AIMCO's total assets were $90.2 B. A third category, corporate enterprises, buy and sell goods and services in market transactions and include ATB Financial, an Alberta bank. Advisory agencies form a fourth large category. The fifth group is service delivery agencies that provide government services to Albertans. The service delivery category is a catch-all that includes, for example, the boards of governors of provincial universities. Alberta's typology, which could easily be applied to other Canadian governments, is an important provincial government effort to see public agencies as a sector of government with distinctive needs and problems.

Rationales for Public Agencies

Why have public agencies proliferated? Why are some government functions administered by arm's-length bodies while others remain under direct ministerial control? In his substantial study of Canadian government organization, J. E. Hodgetts notes that the first two federal public agencies were the Royal Canadian Mounted Police and the Geological Survey of Canada (Hodgetts, 1973: 140). He concludes that they were made semi-independent because their activities were important, specialized, and unrelated to the main duties of government as understood in the late nineteenth century. In short, they were seen as unique organizations that were unlikely to engage major public policy issues or cause political problems.

Public agencies have subsequently proliferated in Canada and throughout the democratic world. A broad explanation relies on organizational and managerial claims. Hodgetts, for example, asserts what might be called an overflow thesis—governments have undertaken many more roles than can be accommodated even in a growing number of ministries (Hodgetts, 1973). A related view, widely articulated in Canadian writings, is that the character of modern government activity demands arm's-length administration. Governments' substantial regulatory role, to be done properly, must be freed from the short-sighted partisanship of democratic politics. Equally, governments now routinely make important decisions about whether citizens, groups, and corporations qualify for particular benefits. Those who are denied benefits can normally appeal decisions. Again, if executive agencies, not courts, are required for these kinds of decisions and appeals, they must be housed in semi-independent structures that are free from direct political control.

Another claim is that government commercial activities, to be done effectively, require freedom from day-to-day ministerial control. If government corporations operate in **competitive markets**, they must not be impeded by cumbersome bureaucratic regulations and reporting obligations. The persons required to run Crown corporations would allegedly not tolerate such restraints. A final managerial claim is that government activities that require specialized expertise and that can be hived off from departments are well-suited to agency administration.

Other authors see more explicitly political forces at work. Writing in 1969, Peter Silcox argued that public agencies were major avenues for patronage and favouritism (Silcox, 1969). Semi-independent agencies can also be politically valuable symbols at critical junctures. Independent regulatory bodies with their apparent independence, and government firms in corporate form, can be used to inspire citizen confidence. Currently, what might be called a "logic of independence" carries weight in modern democratic politics when many citizens hold politics in disdain, when political partisanship is suspect, and when experts and independent agencies seem to be held in higher regard.

Finally, Silcox notes that semi-independent agencies are often partnerships with powerful private interests. The independence and lower profile of the public agencies can make them fertile ground for the incorporation of groups directly into government. As he puts it:

The overall expansion of government activities has brought governments more regularly into contact with each other, with privately operated public service organizations, and with powerful pressure groups. Their partnership in particular areas has often been consummated in semi-independent public bodies. Partnership may be desirable for a number of reasons. It may lead to greater efficiency, allow a government to limit its financial commitment or general political responsibility, or it may be a necessary price for active co-operation and political neutrality. (Silcox, 1969: 159–60)

He argues that the best way to classify public agencies is to determine who wields effective power over them.

Independent agencies are also used simply because another government has successfully used one in a sensitive or complex policy area. Political scientists call this an example of **policy diffusion**. Agnes Batory shows how Hong Kong's independent Anti-Corruption Agency quickly became the worldwide standard for such government agencies (Batory, 2012). Inspired by the United Nations Convention against Corruption and endorsed by the international financial community, Hong Kong was a powerful symbol of a potent, independent public body designed as a fearless opponent of government corruption. Anything less than an agency with Hong Kong's powers and independence would henceforth be deemed as inadequate in the eyes of citizens, especially in democratizing countries.

All that said, little is really known about why Canadian governments use public agencies. Governments have pursued no consistent logic as they have expanded arm's-length governance. Few compelling analyses have been done—the modest corpus of research is primarily suggestive and thinly researched. This gap is puzzling given the importance of arm's-length bodies, their widespread use, and the variety of theoretical frameworks that might be employed to explain their widespread use. Many empirical questions present themselves as do many interesting research methodologies.

A major, unresolved question is whether new public management (NPM) thinking has inspired wider use of semi-independent agencies. At least two intertwined strands of NPM—alternative service delivery and the need for greater government responsiveness to citizens—suggest a preference for, or at least links to, arm's-length bodies. However, many other factors might be at play and NPM may not be a decisive factor.

Arm's-Length Government and Democracy

Semi-independent agencies are haunted by the spectre of arbitrary, uncontrolled government. For critics, they are a form of double jeopardy—expert bureaucrats operating with even less supervision than those in departments. On the face of it, public agencies should be able to balance the conflicting imperatives of government control, legislative accountability, and citizen accountability with the independence required for agency effectiveness. For example, governments almost always have some controls over agency budgets although the extent of such control varies across arm's-length bodies. Similarly, governments control such important matters as the appointment, terms, and renewals of key personnel including board chairs, board members, and agency chief executive officers. Governments sometimes have formal authority to issue binding cabinet directives to semi-independent agencies. Directives, which are almost always publicly issued, oblige an agency to do as directed by the government even if the agency's best judgment is to the contrary. Governments can of course terminate agencies under sunset laws or by their own choice.

Legislatures can examine and debate the annual reports of agencies and question ministers about them as they see fit. Unhappy citizens can also pressure governments to release more information about agencies, to abolish them, or to have decisions reversed. Geoff Mulgan notes that decoupled agency governance may tempt ministers to avoid accountability by hiding behind agency independence: "... when agencies become formally decoupled from their ministers, ministers can legitimately refuse to answer for administrative decisions, instead handing accountability over to the agency and its chief executive" (Mulgan, 2007: 549). He goes on to say, however, that such a strategy is risky because already angry citizens may become more inflamed if they see themselves as pawns in an internal government accountability blame game.

Efforts to balance accountability, government control, and agency independence assume the existence of underlying structures, attitudes, and motivations. Ministers are assumed to have healthy attitudes towards agencies, to be prepared to engage them properly, and to spend time on them. In practice, ministerial attitudes probably range from deliberately indifferent to consciously meddlesome. High-quality board members may not be pursued—less well-qualified party loyalists may be the real targets. Legislatures may lack incentives to undertake careful reviews of agency performance. They may opt to stress spectacular instances of maladministration, to use agency operations as a way to embarrass governments, or more simply to ignore them. Agencies themselves may shirk their obligations and substitute new agency goals for those sought by governments or specified in law. Organization charts, statutory language, and regulations almost certainly require considerable adaptation if the behaviour and accountability of semi-independent agencies are to be improved.

Some evidence suggests that reliance on arm's-length agencies might extract a democratic toll whose costs are greater than its alleged benefits. For example, a recent study by the United Kingdom's National Audit Office on arm's-length bodies (ALBs) in four British departments rings alarms that could well be sounded in Ottawa and the Canadian provinces and territories. No clear idea existed in the departments about the key characteristics of arm's-lengths bodies. Indeed, the four departments defined agencies in different ways. More worrisome was the auditors' finding that confusion reigned about roles and mandates. "*Accountabilities, roles and responsibilities for ALBs are not always clear, risking confusion and tensions* (their emphasis). Given the varying degrees of independence that different ALBs have, it is essential that both departments and ALBs are clear about who is responsible for what" (UK, 2016: 7). In a period of financial restraint, cost-conscious departments frequently resort to agency micromanagement. Such financial micromanagement is at the expense of informed policy discussion and ALBs' need for independence. A more transparent public appointment process for board members, while supported in principle, is in practice cumbersome and so slow that qualified candidates won't apply or persevere through the process. ALBs' on-the-ground expertise is often ignored by departments when they engage in planning and policy discussions.

Government of Nova Scotia guidelines for its provincial public agencies provide a different but also worrisome perspective. It suggests a governance framework where public agencies are not independent in meaningful ways. The Nova Scotia guidelines relentlessly stress that arm's-length bodies are part of the government that must be responsive to government priorities. In fact, the guidelines make no sustained reference to the rationale for agency independence or the means by which independence is attained. Board members and chairs are advised to maintain networks of contacts in the government with whom they should build relationships and share information. Deputy ministers, even when they have no direct line to the agency, should be kept in the loop (Nova Scotia, 2011: 11), as should department staff and central agency officials. Agencies are even provided with a clear statement about their place in the government's overall political communications strategy. "Agencies should always remember the rule of 'no surprises' and ensure that their ministers are advised in advance of all matters in respect to which they may be called upon to answer" (Nova Scotia, 2011: 12). Such a statement is an assertion of the government's view that agencies, like departments, are regular parts of the government apparatus.

The concern that agencies were important but also badly neglected parts of the government inspired Alberta's major 2007 review of provincial public agencies. Telltale signs were the lack of an agreed-on list of provincial agencies or any coherent government sense of the reasons for the creation of arm's-length bodies. The government's major concerns were those typical of the executive branch, notably policy coherence or, put differently, fear of policy fragmentation and agency indifference to provincial priorities. Another worry, in some ways ironic for a government that at the time had held power for 36 years, was that some provincial agencies had become entrenched oligarchies. Board appointments seldom had term limits and reappointment was regular. Ministers seemed unengaged. Another concern, also reflective of central agency concern with consistent policy system coverage, was that important provincial policies on conflicts of interest, financial management, and access to information were unevenly applied in semi-independent provincial agencies.

Many public agencies toil quietly in the background. However, in late 2007, the Canadian Nuclear Safety Commission (CNSC), the federal government's regulatory body for the Canadian nuclear industry, moved to the centre of national attention. In November 2007, CNSC ordered Atomic Energy of Canada Limited's (AECL) Chalk River nuclear reactor closed until its backup safety systems were modernized. The commission feared that the existing backups would not prevent a meltdown during an earthquake. The Chalk River reactor was and remains one of the world's major world suppliers of isotopes that are essential for widely used medical diagnoses and cancer treatments. A long shutdown at Chalk River would have major adverse consequences on human health throughout the world (Galloway, 2007). CNSC was aware of Chalk River's vital role in isotope production but believed that better backup facilities were a higher priority.

The federal government disagreed with the CNSC. It felt that the public interest demanded the immediate reactivation of the AECL reactor. Accordingly, it issued a directive to the CNSC that overruled it and ordered Chalk River reopened at once. CNSC stuck to its guns, however, and refused to issue the required orders. The government therefore went to Parliament and requested immediate passage of an emergency order to reactivate the Chalk River reactor. Shortly thereafter, the government dismissed the commission's president, Linda Keen, although she remained a commission board member. Keen, who was in her second five-year term as president, accused the government of wrongful interference in the business of an expert, arm's-length regulatory agency, a view that was backed by the Liberal opposition of the day (Brennan & Campion-Smith, 2008.)

The CNSC dispute with the Government of Canada evoked surprisingly little public discussion about the broader questions raised about agency governance. For one thing, the case was a classic conflict between the views of an independent, expert body and the public interest as defined by a democratic government. Was the government's action a proper exercise of its powers as defender of the public interest? In this case, the government seemed genuine in its concerns about the grave consequences of a worldwide isotope shortage. No partisan motivation was evident or has been suggested.

The case also highlights the severe consequences when public agency governance fails. In this case, the failure was acute. A legitimate view is that the Canadian Nuclear Safety Commission's board should have itself been able to reconcile the trade-offs between isotope production and the upgrading of the reactor's backups. After all, an effective agency board is supposed to comprise highly qualified persons whose experience gives the agency broad governance capacity, not simply technical and professional expertise. Moreover, the **cabinet's directive power** is to be used when all else fails—that is, exactly in circumstances like these. Yet the commission rejected the directive, leading to Parliament's immediate engagement and the president's dismissal. The government's sole remaining options were the removal of the entire CNSC board and possibly senior staff and/or the wholesale recasting of CNSC's mandate, governing legislation, and relationship to the government and Parliament. Dramatic actions are required when things go badly wrong in arm's-length agencies.

The Behaviour of Arm's-Length Bodies

Do semi-independent agencies behave differently than other types of government organizations? Do they deliver the benefits that are associated with them? A variety of recent studies, taken together, provide some preliminary answers and suggest some interesting theoretical questions. Four quite different studies explore aspects of public agency behaviour. Two studies rely on Canadian experiences while a third is an American case. The fourth case examines 15 European countries.

An insightful Canadian study examines the behaviour of five federal government agencies and six Quebec agencies that were removed from departments and reorganized into special operating agencies, a form of arm's-length body (Bilodeau et al., 2007). The sample included the Canadian Passport Office, Canadian Grain Commission, the Quebec Provincial Police, and Quebec's student finance authority. The study examines the activities of the agencies for their final three years as parts of departments and compares that with their first three years as public agencies. Did their greater independence and narrower mandates as special operating agencies

have a demonstrable impact on employee productivity, organizational outputs, and cost efficiency? In other words, does organizational form have an independent impact on organizational efficiency? The major conclusion is that improvements were noted in these categories but the range of improvement varied widely across the eleven agencies studied. Moreover, the precise causes of the performance improvements were not clear.

A second Canadian study by Kaddour Mehiriz (2015) examines the municipal infrastructure grant program of Infrastructures Transport, a Quebec public agency. Were its grant allocations scrupulously non-partisan or were they responsive to partisan politics and the wishes of the government? Mehiriz's findings suggest that Infrastructures Transport grants were biased towards seats held by government members and to swing ridings that could be electorally decisive. He suggests that such a finding is not surprising given that three board members were members of the civil service.

Carolyn Bordeaux (2007) compares the responses of municipal public agencies to those of municipal government departments in politically charged environmental policy areas. Her focus is the impact on municipalities of major changes in New York state requirements for municipal landfills and garbage incinerators. State-mandated changes imposed major infrastructure costs on municipal governments. They also caused serious local conflicts about the burden of costs, the environmental consequences, and the best location of new garbage facilities. Bordeaux finds that independent public bodies were ineffective in resolving the resultant political struggles in several New York counties; local governments dealing directly with citizens through conventional municipal government organizations were more successful. She argues that in politically contentious areas the strengths of independent bodies—expert knowledge and political neutrality—are their weaknesses. Independent expert bodies, without political resources, are weak. On the other hand, to the degree that autonomous agencies vie for political power, they become conventional political actors and discredit themselves.

A final study by Sjors Overman (2016) compares citizen satisfaction with policing and tax administration in 15 European countries where they are

delivered through different kinds of public organizations. He is particularly interested in whether service
delivery through arm's-length bodies has positive impacts on citizen satisfaction with the quality of policing and tax administration. Despite claims about
greater responsiveness and sensitivity to citizens by
arm's-length bodies, citizens are not more satisfied
with policing or tax administration when delivered
by semi-independent agencies. However, tax administration by semi-independent agencies seems to deflect public dissatisfaction towards the agency and
away from the government. No such impact is noted
in policing. As Overman concludes, in tax management the special agency is a blame-deflecting buffer
for the government.

This section and the preceding one reviewed
recent findings about arm's-length bodies as instruments of governance. The evidence paints an un-
impressive picture although some of the findings are
not Canadian. The UK National Audit Office finds
much to complain about in the British public agencies including ministry micromanagement, confusion
about mandates and responsibilities, and inadequate
agency integration into policy making. The Government of Nova Scotia, on the other hand, sees public
agencies as bodies to be kept on a short leash. Alberta worries that its agencies are proliferating but
essentially adrift without government proper guidance. The case of the Canadian Nuclear Safety Commission shows a crisis between the Government of
Canada and a major regulatory agency. At time of
writing, an equally worrisome, extremely complex,
and very contentious case is unfolding in Alberta
where the government is mounting a legal challenge
about the legality of regulations and administrative
actions of several of its own public agencies. Finally,
a spate of disparate studies show that arm's-lengths
bodies do not seem to behave in particularly distinctive or impressive ways. Arm's-length bodies
can cause major accountability and effectiveness
deficits.

That said, Canadian public administration lacks
a coherent body of rigorous research on public agencies. A balanced perspective is lacking. For example,
in what areas are semi-independent agencies effective? What factors explains their success? How have
accountability deficits been avoided? By what criteria
should arm's-lengths bodies, individually and as a
group, be evaluated?

The Reform of Arm's-Length Organizations

At a Crossroads, the 2007 report of a Government
of Alberta Task Force on provincial public agencies,
is a strong statement of informed opinion about the
reform of semi-independent public organizations
early in the twenty-first century. In contrast, Frank
Vibert, a British scholar, provides an entirely different perspective on the reform of public agencies. His
blueprint rests on the unconventional idea that arm's-
length bodies cannot properly be governed as parts of
the executive branch.

At a Crossroads defines the governance of public
agencies as an important matter for the political
executive. In that sense, it falls squarely within the
tradition of many previous reform initiatives in Westminster democracies. The basic question remains—
how can a balance best be struck between government
control and public agency independence? The report
emphasizes the need for strong government leadership as manifest by a major recommendation for a
single statute that establishes definitions, a working
typology of public agencies, and a set of governance mechanisms that must apply to all provincial
agencies. *At a Crossroads* also applies many insights
from modern corporate governance practices. In this
sense, it blends traditional concerns about responsible government with modern management.

At a Crossroads' premise is that the government
of Alberta has created too many arm's-lengths bodies
without careful thought about their suitability for certain roles. Public agencies have proliferated without
reference to a guiding philosophy, without thought
to their overall impact on government effectiveness,
and with little coherent consideration of their ideal
structure and roles. The report recommends a rigorous review process **prior** to the establishment of any
further public agencies in Alberta. In each case, the
government would be expected to proceed as follows:

> When the establishment of an agency is being
> considered, particular attention should be paid
> to why the agency is being established and
> whether this includes a strong, valid reason for
> it to operate with some level of autonomy from
> the responsible ministry. This might include, for
> example, a need for independent advice or out-
> side expertise, autonomous decision-making that

promotes credibility and public confidence, stewardship of funds and assets, or locating delivery mechanisms within communities. (Alberta, 2007: 13)

The report's recommendation that each future public agency should have its own enabling legislation was an effort to restrain agency proliferation.

At a Crossroads also advocated updated personnel policies in Alberta's arm's-length bodies. It recommended consistent **non-partisan appointment** processes that relied on public advertising of vacancies and made efforts to ensure that boards were representative of Alberta's increasingly diverse population. Term limits were required for board members and chairs. Such positions could not be allowed to become sinecures. No person could serve for more than 10 consecutive years—the norm would be considerably shorter. Semi-independent bodies would be expected to engage in succession planning, to emphasize ethical conduct, and to ensure members were properly qualified in governance practices. In the same vein, other provinces have recently committed to more balanced representation on the boards of their semi-independent agencies. For example, in 2016, the premier of Ontario stated that all provincial agencies will require at least 40 per cent of their board members to be female by 2019 (Taber & Grant, 2016).

At a Crossroads argued that agency governance, to succeed, required clear understanding about roles, responsibilities, and mandates. As it put it: "The Task Force believes that clear statements about roles and responsibilities and precise statements of agency mandates are *prerequisites* to good governance. Precise roles and mandates do not, by themselves, generate perfect results. But without them, effective agency governance is impossible to achieve" (Alberta, 2007: 23). Mandates and roles would be established through legislation and comprehensive mandate statements for each agency that, in dialogue with the government, would be updated annually and reviewed rigorously every third year. All actors—ministers, senior department officials, board chairs, board members, and agency CEOs—would know each other's roles and understand their interdependences. Board performance, as a whole and at the individual level, would be constantly evaluated. A major board role would be to probe the agency's overall effectiveness.

The Alberta report also dealt with two perennial agency problems—whether senior government officials and/or ministers should be board members and whether the roles of CEO and board chair should be fused or separate. Both questions straddled the task force's emphasis on clear mandates and human resource management. Predictably, given its premises, the report argued that government officials, either appointed or elected, should not be board members. Directors who were members of the government faced conflicting obligations. They were obviously appointed to extend government control. At the same time, however, government members have the same statutory and legal obligations as all other directors. That is, they must provide general direction that promotes the public interest and the agency's mandate as outlined in law. Dual role directors might also undercut the board chair's relationship with the minister. Finally, board chairs must not be CEOs because their roles were very different. In fact, boards, not the government, should appoint CEOs who would then be directed and evaluated by boards.

Frank Vibert defines the "agency problem" completely differently. He argues that a new approach to public agency governance will reinvigorate democratic politics. His argument is complex in detail yet straightforward in overview. Vibert sees arm's-length agencies as the cutting edge of modern governance. They are crucial players in a policy revolution that increasingly separates dispassionate policy analysis from ethical and moral judgments about the content of public policy, especially in areas where citizens hold conflicting views. Expert public agencies must be separated from the other branches of government, especially the executive and legislative, whose role it is to judge value-laden policy questions. "What we are seeing being separated out is a new branch within systems of government with a special responsibility for the handling and dissemination of information, the analysis of evidence and the deployment and use of the most up-to-date empirical knowledge" (Vibert, 2007: 12). Vibert also advances a variation of the well-known decline of deference thesis that sees modern citizens as challenging politicians' authority to speak for them. Modern voters are information seekers who insist on evidence-based policy-making and who want to make informed personal choices.

In Vibert's view, the constitutional recognition of an independent information-processing branch of government will improve democracies greatly. His argument is important for students of public administration and for governments themselves who have long defined public agencies as problems in executive branch management. He sees many current public agencies as inappropriate components of the executive branch because they do not undertake administrative or service delivery roles. To the contrary, Vibert sees them in a way reminiscent of some accounts of officers of Parliament, as performing a distinctive mix of executive, quasi-judicial, and investigative roles (Chaplin, 2011). In fact, those positions currently defined as officers of Parliament in Canada would almost certainly be part of the fourth branch. At present, semi-independent agencies straddle the established branches of government and fit uneasily in all of them. Among other things, the constitutional recognition of semi-independent bodies would remove them from the executive branch's strong tendency to suppress and manipulate politically charged information. In this regard, witness the debate in Ontario where the provincial financial accountability officer asserts that the government is deliberately withholding important data from him on such controversial provincial priorities as the Hydro One privatization, health care spending, and infrastructure projects (Morrow, 2015).

Vibert's analysis merits careful consideration. For example, it is easy to envision one or more new Canadian arm's-length agencies whose role will be to judge cases of assisted-dying applicants. Such agencies should be removed from political partisanship and perhaps, for different reasons, from the courts as well. They are possible cases *par excellence* of agencies having unique roles that blend legislative, executive, and judicial roles. Vibert's work also looks at semi-independent agencies as a sector of government that reflects and shapes broader changes in government, society, and public attitudes. That said, his Achilles heel might be that, despite his arguments to the contrary, it rests on a false fact-value dichotomy and that information-generation roles and judgment roles are hard to separate.

Further Research

More and different research is required if Canadian arm's-lengths bodies are to be better understood and improved. Future research needs to be more theoretical. To date, only a few studies have approached public agencies through analytical perspectives that

raise broader questions. For example, arm's-lengths bodies, by their very nature, provide good test cases for many aspects of principal-agent theory.

Greater methodological sophistication is also required. Quantitative research, some of which has been described already, could be used to study certain questions including those concerned with the origins of semi-independent bodies. Qualitative studies, the hallmark of most research on Canadian public management, also have a major role to play. Comparisons between policy areas, between governments, and over time can illuminate many questions as well. Canadian public agencies can certainly be compared with those of other countries. Canadian federalism also offers many interesting research opportunities. Fruitful studies that compare public agencies in several provinces with federal organizations and from province to province can easily be imagined.

Rigorous studies need to be undertaken on the origins and development of public agencies. Agnes Batory's (2012) analysis of anti-corruption agencies in Eastern European countries is a model. She focuses on the interplay between agency structure and resources, political cycles, and the quality of leadership. Batory shows how in Latvia, Poland, and Slovenia these factors interacted in unpredictable ways to shape anti-corruption agencies from their inception. Why do some agencies overcome great obstacles and achieve real autonomy, genuine independence from government, and a capacity to discipline the government, not simply its political opponents? As she puts it: "The agency's de facto operational autonomy will evolve (even if its formal mandate is not redrawn) in a series of attacks, counterattacks, the outcomes of which are shaped by the extent the agency has managed to establish itself as an actor in its own right by this time" (Batory, 2012: 650). Her analysis also highlights the dynamics of arm's-length agencies in controversial policy areas.

Studies that isolate the differences between semi-independent agencies and other administrative forms are also badly needed. What difference does agency governance really make? In this vein, Jack Lucas (2013) suggests that some Ontario municipalities use public agencies to perform public functions that are dealt with directly by municipal councils and civic administrators in other towns. Which mode of delivery is best and by what criteria? The interesting work by Bilodeau, Laurin, and Vining on before-and-after performance of public agencies that have been carved out of departments is instructive. Their focus is on administrative efficiency. Comparable studies might address larger questions about before-and-after service quality. Moreover, Bilodeau et al. see special agencies as organizations that rest uneasily between privatization and government delivery through departments. They advance an important caution when they argue that such undertakings may be the worst of all worlds. Public agencies have less accountability and oversight than departments and, in the absence of exposure to market competition, less efficiency than in privatization. Is this the source of accountability and policy deficits? Overman's European study asks a basic question that could well be replicated in Canada—are citizens more satisfied with public activities undertaken by public agencies? What characteristics of arm's-length governance impress or alienate citizens?

Who runs public bodies? Important research questions concern the socio-economic characteristics and career backgrounds of board members and executive officers. How do agency senior officers differ from board members? Are they primarily drawn from the civil service departments or are their career paths diverse? Are board members generally affiliated with the party in power at the time of their appointment? If they are, how and why does it matter? Has partisanship in appointment changed in governments that now use transparent, merit-based public appointment processes? Do the provincial governments and territories vary? Moreover, how do senior agency officials relate to the broader governmental machinery? Do they have different views about governance than deputy ministers?

In short, given the significance of semi-independent bodies, serious research is required that moves to a broader theory. If public agencies are to be improved, much more needs to be known about why governments use them, where they excel and flounder, and the overall costs and benefits of governance through arm's-length bodies.

Conclusions

Three major points warrant emphasis. First, agencies, boards, and commissions are major aspects of Canadian public administration. Their diverse activities have major impacts on citizens and raise important and difficult governance issues. Second, too little research has been undertaken to permit generalizations about the overall impact and effectiveness of arm's-length bodies. Noteworthy areas for research include careful studies of the rationale for the use of non-department agencies. What combinations of organizational and political forces determine their use in different Canadian governments? Do arm's-length agencies always create accountability and control deficits? Can the proper length of the arm be determined precisely for every case or at least for broad areas of agency governance? Important work also needs to be done on the proper criteria for evaluating agency performance. A particular gap is the determination of circumstances where arm's-length bodies are successful. Finally, armed with a body of rigorous research, students and practitioners of Canadian public administration will be much better equipped to recommend serious reforms.

Important Terms and Concepts

cabinet's directive power	independent regulatory agencies	policy diffusion
competitive markets (Crown corporations and freedom to operate in)	non-partisan appointments	

Study Questions

1. Why is it so difficult to define and catalogue arm's-length (semi-independent) agencies?
2. Why are some government functions administered by arm's-length bodies while others remain under direct ministerial control?

3. Can public agencies balance the conflicting imperatives of government control, legislative account-ability, and citizen accountability with the independence required for agency effectiveness?
4. Do semi-independent agencies behave differently than other types of government organizations?
5. What are the various directions possible to reform public agencies?
6. What do we not know about public agencies; in other words, what more do we have to research about them?

Note

1 The author was a member of the Task Force along with Neil C. McCrank, QC (chair) and Linda Hohol.

References

Alberta, Executive Council. 2007. *At a Crossroads*: Report of the Board Governance Review Task Force. Edmonton.

Batory, A. 2012. "Political Cycles and Organizational Life Cycles: Delegation to Anticorruption Agencies in Central Europe." *Governance*, 25, 4, pp. 639–60.

Bilodeau, N., C. Laurin, and A. Vining. 2007. "'Choice of Organizational Form Makes a Real Difference': The Impact of Corporatization on Government Agencies in Canada." *Journal of Public Administration Research and Theory*, 17, 1, pp. 119–47.

Bordeaux, C. 2007. "Conflict, Accommodation and Bargaining: The Implications of Using Politically Buffered Institutions for Contentious Decision-Making." *Governance*, 20, 2, pp. 279–303.

Brennan, R. and B. Campion-Smith. 2008. "PM blasted for firing nuclear watchdog." *Toronto Star*, 17 January.

Chaplin, A. 2011. *Officers of Parliament, Accountability, Virtue and the Constitution*. Cowansville, PQ: Editions Yvon Blais.

Corry, J. A. and J. E. Hodgetts. 1959. *Democratic Government and Politics*. 3rd edn, Toronto: University of Toronto Press.

Galloway, G. 2007. "Nuclear dispute causing isotope delays." *Globe and Mail*, 11 December.

Greve, C., M. Flinders, and S. Van Thiel. 1999. "Quangos – What's in a Name: Defining Quangos from a Comparative Perspective." *Governance*, 12, 2, pp. 129–46.

Hodgetts, J. E. 1973. *The Canadian Public Service: A Physiology of Government, 1867–1970*. University of Toronto Press.

Lucas, J. 2013. *Hidden in Plain View: Local Agencies, Boards, and Commissions in Canada*. Toronto: Institute on Municipal and Local Finance and Governance and Munk School of Global Affairs.

Mehiriz, K. 2015. "The Influence of Redistributive Politics on the Decision Making of Quasi-Autonomous Organizations. The Case of Infrastructures-Transport (Quebec-Canada)." *Journal of Public Administration Research and Theory*, 25, 4, pp. 1081–98.

Morrow, A. 2015. "Budget Watchdog Warns Hydro One Sale Will Deepen Ontario Debt." *Globe and Mail*, 29 October.

Mulgan, G. 2007. *Good and Bad Power: The Ideals and Betrayals of Governments*. London: Penguin.

Nova Scotia, Executive Council Office. 2011. *Governing in the Public Sector: A Guide for Nova Scotia Government Agencies*. Halifax.

Overman, S. 2016. "Autonomous Agencies, Happy Citizens? Challenging the Satisfaction Claim." *Governance*, 29, 1, pp. 1–17.

Pollitt, C. and G. Bouckaert. 2011. *Public Management Reform: A Comparative Analysis*. 3rd edn, New York: Oxford University Press.

Schrefler, L. 2010. "The Use of Scientific Knowledge by Independent Regulatory Agencies." *Governance*, 23, 2, pp. 309–30.

Silcox, P. in W. D. K. Kernaghan (ed.). 1969. *Bureaucracy in Canadian Government*. Toronto: Methuen, 157–65.

Taber, J. and T. Grant. 2016. "Ontario Wants at Least 40 per cent Women on Provincial Boards by 2019." *Globe and Mail*, 8 June.

United Kingdom, National Audit Office. 2016. *Departments' Oversight of Arm's-Length Bodies: A Comparative Study*. London.

Vibert, F. 2007. *The Rise of the Unelected: Democracy and the New Separation of Powers*. Cambridge: Cambridge U Press.

Wilson, V. S. 1981. *Canadian Policy and Administration: Theory and Environment*. Toronto: McGraw-Hill Ryerson.

Crown Corporations in Canada

"In theory, there is no difference between theory and practice. But in practice, there is."

Luc Bernier

Chapter Overview

Crown corporations have been used in Canada for a very long time as policy instruments at the unclear border between the public and the private sector. They have both commercial activities and public policies to implement. Their commercial nature distinguishes them from other government organizations. Since the 1980s, many governments have decided to privatize some of them. Nevertheless, many Crown corporations are still used for economic development. Policy objectives other than economic development are not always clear. This chapter accordingly suggests that we should move beyond the discussion of control or governance and look at the idea of public entrepreneurship.

Chapter Objectives

By the end of this chapter, students will be able to do the following:

- Understand how and why Crown corporations are used by governments in Canada.
- Use the chapter as a framework to do the analysis/case study of a Crown corporation.
- Think about how Crown corporations as policy instruments are selected.
- Improve understanding of the structures of government in Canada.
- Appreciate how organizations are made not only of structures but also of culture and managerial volition.

Introduction

Yogi Berra, the former baseball personality from whom the aphorism in the title comes, is usually neglected as a scholar of public administration. It is unfortunate; his quote is accurate about **Crown corporations** in Canada. According to economic theory, they should have been privatized but in practice, they continue to be used by successive governments. Crown corporations have existed since the early days of European settlements. The first iron mill and the first brewery under the French regime were Crown enterprises founded by Jean Talon, the *intendant* of the king for Nouvelle-France. Historians of the Canadian state since Innis (Innis, 1930) have written that intervention by the use of Crown corporations and other instruments was a way to create an integrated transportation infrastructure needed to develop a staple economy on the Canadian vast and empty territory, initially with water canal transportation and later with railways (Borins & Boothman, 1986: 80). Both the national and the provincial governments used public enterprises to take advantage of natural resources and create industries that the private sector could not or did not want to develop on its own. Also, the Canadian government lacked a strong regulation capacity and had to rely heavily on Crown corporations (Roberts, 2010). Many of the public institutions that have distinguished since then Canada from the United States have been Crown corporations: railways, an airline, CBC/Radio-Canada, and the hydro companies in the provinces. Governments continue to use Crown corporations today (Bird, 2015).

Three decades of **privatization** later, Canadian governments have kept many of these complex organizations on the grey line between the public and the private sector. A Crown is an organization that works like a private enterprise in that it has commercial activities, but it also has public policy objectives. While the popularity of special operating agencies or private–public partnerships vanished as instruments of public policy, Crown corporations remain. When confronted by the 2008 financial crisis, the Canadian government with the Ontarian and the American federal government nationalized General Motors (and Chrysler). One of the greatest symbols of American capitalism was suddenly a **state-owned enterprise**. The automobile industry received a $9.7 billion investment (Sharaput, 2010: 120).

Crown corporations are obviously not yet an instrument of the past. A Crown corporation is a remarkably adaptable policy instrument as discussed in this chapter. And in a world where the Canadian government hopes that the current free trade agreements will be maintained and new ones will be signed, they could be again policy instruments with their advantages and limits as discussed here. For students of public administration they raise interesting questions that are not easily answered. Why should some organizations be granted more **autonomy** than others in the public domain? Should the state be involved in economic activities that often could be achieved by the private sector? It is interesting to note that although economic theory generally concludes that Crown corporations are a heresy that cannot work, governments continue to use them in practice. The practice is not perfect, but as developed in the last section of this chapter, other theories should be considered to understand the phenomenon. In this chapter, an historical perspective is offered on the role of Crown corporations in Canada since Confederation at both the federal and provincial levels. The chapter suggests why and how they could be used.

Definitions and raisons d'être

In Canada, public enterprises or state-owned enterprises (SOEs) are referred to as Crown corporations or simply Crowns. We are discussing here "the wholly owned corporations, either directly or indirectly, which have been formally designated as agents of the Crown for the attainment of public policy objectives, and for whose liabilities the state itself is both immediately and directly liable" (Borins & Boothman, 1986: 76). Another way of defining them is Florio's:

a. ultimately owned or co-owned by the government,
b. internalizing a public mission among their objectives,
c. enjoying full or partial budgetary autonomy,
d. exhibiting a certain extent of managerial discretion,

e. operating mainly in a market environment, and
f. for which (full) privatization would in principle or de facto be possible, but for some reasons, it is not a policy option (Florio, 2014: 201).

All the elements of this definition are worth looking at and are discussed in this chapter. The French government, for example, does not own wholly most of its large SOEs but still controls them. Borins and Boothman's definition is in this regard more specific. There has to be a public mission; if there is not, why keep the organization in a public sector that is already very complex to coordinate? The commercial operations of Crowns give them more financial autonomy but, at the same time, they are expected today to make profits. Privatization is always possible for them if they don't. There is a list established by Crisan and Mckenzie of federal Crown corporations that could be sold (see Table 12.1), but sales have been slowing down. We will also come back to managerial discretion in the last section. A government can consider that the entrepreneurship of the private sector is too limited and decide to replace it with **public entrepreneurship.** Studies of Crown corporations have been focused for decades on their privatization but there is a renewed interest to look at their use. Some authors have argued that we should instead study the revision of their **governance** (Bernier & Simard, 2007). This chapter suggests that although governance mechanisms are important, another variable to be included in the equation is the entrepreneurship of their managers. Public entrepreneurship influences strategic decisions, interpretation of government policies, and the organizational culture and thus is essential to the use of these organizations as economic policy instruments.

At their height in the 1980s, there were 57 federal Crown corporations in Canada.[1] They represented 35 per cent of government employment and 26 per cent of all Canadian corporations' net fixed assets (Stanbury, 1994; 167–8). In 2010, there were still 46 federal public enterprises according to the Treasury Board of Canada. At the provincial level, public enterprises had also been important instruments of development (Bernier & Fascal, 2011; Vining & Botterell, 1983; Young et al., 1984). Today there are still many provincial Crowns operating although privatization has

occurred there too. In its study "The Size and Composition of the SOE Sector in OECD Countries," the OECD places Canada in the middle range of countries deploying state enterprises. However, as Crisan and McKenzie (2013) noted, that survey did not include provincial public enterprises. When they are included, they roughly double the size of the Crown sector in Canada. Moreover, the numbers do not reflect the fact that state capitalism in Canada has been important to the nation-building experience. This contrasts markedly with the United States, Canada's close neighbour and trading partner. Canada has a tradition that is closer to the European experience of public enterprises (Laux & Molot, 1988: 41, 78).

In Canada, as explained in other chapters of this *Handbook*, the governmental system is divided into three types of public organizations. There are central agencies in charge of coordinating the whole state apparatus (Bernier & Fortier, 2014). Central agencies, such as the Treasury Board, set the administrative rules for other government agencies. The second type is the ministry or line department which, in the Westminster tradition, is the core organization of the administrative system. They are established by legislation and have broad policy mandates under the control of a minister who is accountable to Parliament. And thirdly, there are various bodies and agencies with specialized functions further away from political control. The latter's day-to-day operations do not require close supervision and thus can be more autonomous. They formally report to a minister, but are not typically closely involved with departmental staff, even if they implement policies formulated by the ministry. Among this third group, the most autonomous are the Crown corporations with commercial activities and autonomous revenues as if operating in a normal commercial market (Hafsi & Koenig, 1988). Contrary to private companies, Crown corporations have immunity from taxation and are thus independent from the other levels of government. These can also establish subsidiary corporations which are even further removed from the ministers and politics in general.

The use of the word "Crowns" is not trivial. Though it serves to remind that Canada is a constitutional democracy, the "Crown" also reflects the power of the state to intervene in society and in the

Table 12.1   Crown Corporations That Could Be Privatized

Crown Corporation	Commercial Revenues	Net Income	Parliamentary Appropriation	Expenses	Debt	Total Assets	Liabilities	NSSB
Business Development Bank of Canada		6	0		13,732	17,680	14,037	No
Canada Deposit Insurance Corporation		−102				1,965	1,108	No
Canada Development Investment Corporation		70				3,546	121	No
Canada Mortgage and Housing Corporation		931	2,613		252,047	272,821	263,558	No
Canada Post Corporation		281	23			6,029	4,213	No
Canadian Broadcasting Corporation	566		1,143	1,700				Yes
Cape Breton Development Corp.	5		60	94				Yes
Export Development Canada		285			24,447	32,898	26,310	No
Federal Bridge Corp. Ltd.	15		31	43				Yes
National Arts Centre Corp.	26		41	66				Yes
Old Port of Montreal Corp.	17		15	32				Yes
Parc Downsview Park Inc.	N/A		N/A	N/A				Yes
Public Sector Pension Investment Board		7,513				49,037	2,768	No
VIA Rail Canada Inc.	294	3	338	506			997	222	Yes
Total (all crown corporations)		6,666						

Source: Boardman, Anthony E. and Aidan R. Vining. 2012. "A Review and Assessment of Privatization in Canada." *SPP Research Papers*, volume 5, issue 4, University of Calgary, The School of Public Policy, p. 21.

economy. A government can choose to have activities done by a department or delegate them "at arm's length" when it is considered not necessary to supervise the day-to-day operations. Also, if revenues can be generated from the activities, the corporate form might be advantageous. How should governments in the Westminster tradition organize their operations for economic development? Should it be under the supervision of an elected minister or further away from politics to avoid political interference and sometimes patronage? Ministerial responsibility as a principle of government was developed in the nineteenth century to ensure in the British tradition that public agencies would not escape the control of elected members of Parliament. This improvement in responsible government came with a side effect: a centralization of control. As a consequence, delegating authority to autonomous agencies such as Crown corporations might be a way to simplify the management of the whole system.

Canadian Crown corporations are supposed to be at arm's length in the Morrisonian tradition (Millward & Singleton, 1995). They are kept distant from the grasp of government so as to be allowed to operate on a day-to-day basis as would a private company. At the same time, they remain in tight alliance with their parent ministries as the instruments of public policy. The Crowns are established by either a special Act of Parliament or by articles of incorporation under the Canada Business Corporations Act. Their governance framework was revised in 2005 by the Treasury Board[2] for the federal ones and in the first years of this century for the provinces (Bernier & Pelletier, 2008). The strategic objectives mentioned in their annual reports are a mix of commercial and policy objectives. The top-down accountability framework in the federal government is relatively strong and the Crowns are responsible for several policies and regulations concerning salaries, equity, languages, future managers, and the Access to Information Act. This has been reinforced over the last decade (Canadian Policy Forum, 2015).

Commercial activities imply, in theory, profitability. In a system where often control and accountability have been considered weak, financial performance is important as a measure of success and *legitimacy* (see Vining & Boardman, 1992). In theory the profit or commercial dimension is essential, but governments have often used the corporate form to supply public services. In areas such as Cape Breton, for example, successive governments have maintained Crown corporations less in pursuit of profitability but to minimize potential social disruption, even at the cost of heavy financial losses. On the profitability issue, it would be interesting to study more in depth the changes over time. Before the 1970s, almost nothing was written on the *efficiency* of Crowns (Borins & Boothman, 1985: 78). Many Crowns were created initially to make sure that the operations would be done. In many cases, profitability became more important in the 1980s. When governments started to use the lack of profitability issue as a reason to privatize, directives were also given to improve economic performance for the remaining Crowns, and it could be argued that the state-owned enterprises that still exist today around the world are rather profitable (Bernier, 2015). One could make the argument that their profitability legitimizes their existence. It proves that they are well-functioning organizations.

Profitability can also be used by the managers to gain autonomy vis-à-vis their government.

The second essential reason for existence is supposed to be the implementation of public policies. Crowns are one policy instrument among others. Whether one uses economic policy or industrial policy, Crown corporations are supposed to be instruments to implement policy as do other public organizations. What differentiates Crown corporations from other government agencies is the profit objective, as already mentioned. Except for profit, implementation can also be delegated to organizations outside the state apparatus. Governments can decide to regulate the activities of the private sector to offer the same service to the population. For example, telephone services are offered in Saskatchewan by a Crown corporation while in Quebec and Ontario, a private company offers the same services under a set of regulations. Crowns are at the border between the public and the private sectors, living in both worlds but controlled by government, as Figure 12.1 illustrates.

Figure 12.1 illustrates the localization in the state machinery. Many Canadian scholars have compared Crown corporations to other policy instruments. Canadian scholars such as Doern and Phidd (1983), Trebilcock et al. (1982) and Hewlett and others (see Eliadis et al., 2005) have studied the choice of policy instruments. They distinguish the instruments by degree of coercion from the least intrusive instrument, exhortation, to expenses, to regulation, to Crown corporations. A government can attempt to change the behaviour of the population or of a part of it by using royal commissions or ministerial speeches, and so forth—that is exhortation. The same government can subsidize research or spend money (expenses) to achieve the same purpose. Similarly, regulations like taxes could be imposed, for example on products like tobacco, or fines be issued if people smoke in public buildings or restaurants.

All these instruments are very often used together, making it difficult to understand their unique impacts. In the energy sector, for example, there is exhortation: publicity on driving more slowly to reduce emissions or reduce the dependency on oil; expenses like subsidies for research for green energy; regulations like taxes on gas for cars; and the creation of the Crown corporation Petro-Canada to have a window on the industry. If a government wants to

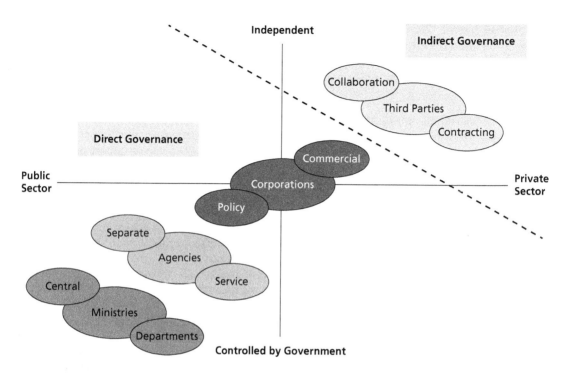

Figure 12.1 Organizations of the Public Sector in Canada

Source: From Wilkins, J. 2011. "Alternative Service Delivery Revisited." Commonwealth Secretariat Discussion Paper No. 10.

make sure something will be done, it can do it itself using a Crown corporation. The new public management era has changed towards the right side of the figure, delegating more delegated activities to the private sector with instruments such as public–private partnerships, for example.

In a capitalist economy such as Canada, state-owned enterprises are supposed to correct market deficiencies. The railway industry is illustrative of the tradition of Crown corporations. From its beginnings, the industry was sustained by various government grants and concessions. Canadian National Railways was created to salvage from bankruptcy three independent railways that linked the country from coast to coast, creating a competitor against the Canadian Pacific Railway, the lone private operator during the First World War. In Canada, continuous state intervention has supported and underwritten the cost of infrastructure. In 1932, the Canadian Broadcasting Corporation/Société Radio-Canada (CBC/SRC)

was created. In 1937, Trans-Canada Airlines followed, eventually becoming Air Canada. During the Second World War, a flurry of public enterprises were created to meet the war demands and to better coordinate the production of military equipment (see Borins in Pritchard, 1983); not least was the Atomic Energy Corporation of Canada (AECL), (today called Atomic Energy Corporation Limited) whose mandate was to mine uranium. After 1945, Canada governments adopted a Keynesian economic policy and used state intervention to assure economic growth and high living standards (Laux & Molot, 1988: 52–9). Propelled by the Liberal government under Louis St-Laurent, a number of agencies were created in the post-war period. In 1950, Canadian Overseas Telecommunications Corporation (COTC, later renamed Teleglobe) was created to develop the infrastructure necessary for expanding communications needs. According to Laux and Molot (1988), there have been three generations: the war industries; reconstruction;

more strategic industries in the 1940s; in the 1960s, managerial or financial enterprises in profitable sectors to compete in the global economy; and in the 1970s, enterprises that were capable of surviving in the global village before privatization became popular.

There might be a very Canadian reason for the use of Crown corporations. Former Prime Minister William Mackenzie King said once that Canada had too much geography and not enough history. Various Crown corporations have been established to diminish regional disparities (Johnson, 2006). One can think for example of the Cape Breton Economic Corporation. Asbestos Corp. Ltd., a Quebec Crown corporation, was created partly in the same spirit, for economic development regionally. The current Société du Plan Nord is built for economic development in the North. The same can be said for Crown corporations in Nunavut and the Northwest Territories. Crown corporations are a very discrete instrument that can be used in a very specific geographic area.

Crown corporations may be created for strategic considerations of local or national interest, or for very pragmatic reasons. There is a long research tradition on the topic (see Gélinas, 1978; Aharoni, 1986). Strategic considerations include the creation of infrastructure for transportation and communication: television or telephone, local or international. Control of monopolies or oligopolies (oil for example), control of inflation, modernization of some sectors, research and development in new technologies, helping bankrupted firms, and availability of risk capital are additional strategic reasons used to justify intervention. Like Petro-Canada, it could be said that the Canadian National Railway was a witness enterprise, allowing the government to learn the workings of the industry. The state obtains in general a lower interest rate when borrowing than the private sector and thus some projects can be launched that would not be profitable for the private sector, supporting research and development and supplying risk capital. Canadians often worry about foreign ownership of private companies, and sometimes public ownership through Crown corporations is the solution.

Pragmatically, it can be easier to supervise some activities than to regulate the private sector. The government can use Crown corporations to develop industrial sectors; subsequent poor performance may be less visible to the public since it is at arm's length.

Another reason could simply be that other policy instruments did not achieve the expected results. There might be reasons more internal to governments such as allocating expenses outside the financial framework. Finally, there is the simple pragmatic opportunity to make money.

Crown corporations such as those related to alcohol have obscure policy objectives. They are money makers for governments, while simultaneously the government creates programs such as "Educalcool" and various programs to control consumption. One could argue that in this sector, regardless of policy objectives, governments should keep the source of revenues.

The reasons to nationalize have varied. In France and the United Kingdom, most state-owned enterprises were previously private enterprises that have been nationalized to foster research and innovation and to implement industrial policy (Millward, 2011). Some industrial sectors were considered strategic or of national interest. Others, like the coal mines in the United Kingdom or steel mills in Sweden, were sectors with too many workers for the state to let them close when they stopped being profitable. In France, some nationalizations came after 1945 to punish private enterprises that had collaborated with the German occupier. France also had a model of economic planning where public enterprises were important. We could also look at the Italian model (see examples in Bernier, 2015). Nationalism also plays a role; but by nationalizing private companies, some governments around the world have had hostile reactions from the private sector—Mexico, for example, with oil companies.

Another reason is to provide bailouts. In addition to profitable areas, governments have also nationalized declining sectors. Coal in the United Kingdom is an example. Asbestos in Canada could also be considered. Asbestos was nationalized in Quebec to fulfill an electoral promise. By the time the party that made this promise got into power, the use of asbestos was already causing health concerns and nationalization should have been forgotten.

Finances are another reason to nationalize. In the United States, as the 2008 financial crisis illustrated, the creation of state-owned enterprises served primarily financial purposes. In Quebec, excluding Hydro-Québec, over time, the use of "sociétés d'État" has been reduced also to financial activities, leaving government competition with the private sector in forest products, mining, or food distribution as relics of the past.

A host of other factors can be in play. Ideology could be important. For many, who often use the case of Saskatchewan as an example, the Douglas government was certainly a case of social-democratic theory in action. Temporal popularity of the instrument is another factor. A recent statistical analysis illustrated that there was a wave of creation of Crown corporations in the Canadian provinces by governments from all parts of the political spectrum (Bernier & Fascal, 2011), followed later by a wave of privatizations. There is also a symbolic use of state-owned enterprises. For example, many countries had for a long period of time invested in airlines that were seldom profitable.

Privatization and After

If Crown corporations don't fulfill policy objectives, why keep them? And worse, what if they lose money? Governments around the world have considered privatization. In Canada, most of the privatization occurred between the mid-1980s and the mid-1990s. The federal government's largest transactions were concentrated in the 1986–8 period. According to Stanbury (1994: 194), 95 privatizations were achieved between 1983 and 1992 but only a handful of large and important federal and provincial Crown corporations were sold. The Canadian National Railway was privatized and has since become a highly successful, publicly traded, international operation. A much smaller Crown corporation, Via Rail, alone provides passenger service to Canadians. Air Canada was sold off. Other privatizations include de Havilland Aircraft, Canadian Arsenals, Canadian National Route, Canadair, Teleglobe Canada, Theratronics International, and Petro-Canada. In the case of Canadair, the federal government ended up paying more than $1 billion to unload the company (Stanbury, 1994: 173–5).

However, sectoral characteristics were important in Canada. The 1985 Conservative budget speech announced that Crowns having a policy purpose would not be sold (Doern & Atherthon, 1987: 133). Public opinion was generally in favour of the Crowns, in particular for energy (Doern & Atherthon, 1987: 138).

The provinces privatized little in comparison with the federal government, and their actions were concentrated over relatively short periods of time. British Columbia started in 1979 but 19 of the 25 privatizations were done in 1988 and 1989. Nine of the 11 transactions in Quebec were done in 1986–8, and 14 of 19 in Saskatchewan in 1987–9. Those provinces were the most active privatizers (Stanbury, 1994: 177). Notable privatization at the provincial level included those of Alberta Energy, the alcohol retail operations of the Alberta government, British Columbia Resources Investment Corporation, Saskatchewan Oil and Gas, Potash Corporation, and provincially owned telephone companies in Alberta and British Columbia.

In many cases, government revenues from privatization were limited because the proceeds went to reduce the long-term debt of the enterprises sold. Many of the privatizations were in commercial businesses such as making buses or refining sugar (Stanbury, 1994: 194). The proceeds to the federal government were $11,968 billion and $9726 billion for the provinces. Petro-Canada alone was sold by the federal government for $5.5 billion (Boardman & Vining, 2012: 4–7).

Privatization was supposed to improve the efficiency of the Crown corporations, assuming that the private sector works better than the public sector. Considering that Crown corporations are already public corporations working similarly to the private sector, it could be that by privatizing them smaller-than-anticipated gains would occur.

There could be other reasons to privatize than financial. State ownership might be a necessity at a specific point in time but not necessarily needed forever. For example, it was considered early on that international telecommunications should be in government hands. In the early 1980s, when technology had evolved, it was one of the first industries where privatization was achieved. Some creations are due to crises that lead governments to intervene in the economy. Later, the necessity of the Crown corporation might not appear as relevant. Petro-Canada was created due to the energy crises of the 1970s (Halpern et al., 1988). Securing the market was one of the reasons why the Canadian government of Liberal Prime Minister Pierre Trudeau decided then to create the Crown corporation. Petro-Canada became the largest Canadian-owned oil company. It was also, in the 1980s, the largest Crown corporation of the Government of Canada. A decade later, the necessity was not considered to exist anymore, and also for political reasons, the Conservative government decided to privatize Petro-Canada.

In the western provinces, the nationalization of oil was not popular and Brian Mulroney had promised to end the involvement of the federal government. Also, the 1980s were the era of privatization in many countries. So Petro-Canada can be used as an example of, first, a flexible instrument (the government can enter and leave a sector); second, of a strategic sector (energy) where a government could decide its presence was essential; third, of movements in general trends such as a global shift in favour of privatization; and fourth, of political factors having an impact. It was also a symbol of Canadian nationalism. Over only a decade, the policy objectives changed from being a window on the industry, securing the availability of oil for Canadians, and economically developing the hinterland to serving as a more, if not exclusively, commercial entity. So Petro-Canada is an interesting example of the flexibility of the instrument. It was sold gradually over the 1990s and the sale was announced in 2004. This example exemplifies also the issue of the role of Crown corporations. If the mission is only commercial, there is no reason to maintain public ownership. It was also a fascinating example of the relations between the federal government and the Western provinces.

Among the survivors is the Canadian Post Office, which was changed from a government department in the 1970s to an agency ("Canada Post/Poste Canada"). It is the largest employer among the federal Crowns with 60,000 employees in 2010, but has been actively reducing its workforce. The second largest employer is the CBC–SRC with 7000 on its payroll. These numbers are also on the decline. The other survivors are much less known to the Canadian public, and mostly act in the shadows of economic activity, but their aggregate activity is surprisingly important. Statistics Canada only counts the economic activity of government agencies that derive at least fifty per cent of their revenues from market activities.[3] In November 2014, the federal government was responsible for 44 Crown corporations, 135 wholly owned subsidiaries, and 27 other subsidiaries and associates. Eleven of the 44

are under the supervision of the Ministry of Transport, three under Industry, and six under Finance. (There are 20 departments, 13 special operating agencies, 51 statutory and other agencies, and 14 departmental agencies in the Government of Canada). The Treasury Board in charge of management and controls was separated from Finance in 1966 and has only one Crown (the Public Sector Pension Investment Board) but 61 subsidiaries.

Control and Governance

Regardless of their economic success, Crown corporations have long been used to establish control (see Gélinas, 1978; Aharoni, 1986; or Stevens, 1993); control has also been used as a reason to privatize the Crowns. The problem of control of large corporations has been described already by Berle and Means (1932). The issue is how to balance the autonomy required to perform the core task and the government's need for control. "The basic raison d'être of the federal Crown corporation has been to separate the management of an activity from continuous partisan intervention and day-to-day government or parliamentary scrutiny and debate" (Gracey, 1978: 28) but still, at some points in time, some control has to exist. In some cases, the Crown corporation is seen as too autonomous, not responding to government demands or forgetting policy objectives or, in other words, being a state within the state. At the other end of the spectrum are government organizations so tightly controlled that there is no room for entrepreneurship:

> First, poor monitoring, excessive intervention and attempts of civil servants to minimize managerial discretion lead to risk aversion, lack of initiative and waste. Second, the persistent tendency of government to use SOEs as conduits for dispensing subsidies or giving political patronage has been a major cause of losses and of inefficiency. Third, at least in some countries, a new managerial class has evolved, attempting to acquire more autonomy and increasing elbow room for independent action. These managers have different values from their private-sector counterparts but also deep-seated different outlooks and goals than civil servants. (Aharoni, 1986: 216)

A middle ground has to be found. This search has usually been considered elusive.

More recent efforts suggest that a broader perspective on governance would be a better way of looking at the issue. The governance perspective takes into account not only the relation between the government and the Crown but also important relations with various stakeholders. At the corporate level, the role of the Auditor General and of the board of directors has been re-emphasized. One of the things that has changed since the days of academic literature on the "control bureaucracy" is the idea that there are other stakeholders and that the government is not always the only owner. The French government, for example, has maintained relative control in many corporations, often with not much more than 25 or 30 per cent of the shares and using a secretariat of its Finance department to coordinate them. Minority owners have to be taken into account. Outside interest groups put pressure on these firms to be involved in sustainable development and have policies in favour of social responsibility.

In 2005, the OECD (2005) proposed guidelines to organize the relation between governments and state-owned enterprises in addition to its guidelines on corporate governance In short, the guidelines specify:

1. The legal and regulatory framework for state-owned enterprises should ensure a level playing field in markets where state-owned enterprises and private-sector companies compete in order to avoid market distortions.
2. The state should act as an informed and active owner and establish a clear and consistent ownership policy, ensuring that the governance of SOEs is carried out in a transparent and accountable manner, with the necessary degree of professionalism and effectiveness.
3. The state and SOEs should recognize the rights of all shareholders and in accordance with the OECD principles of corporate governance ensure their equitable treatment and equal access to corporate information.
4. The state ownership should fully recognize the SOE's responsibilities towards stakeholders and request that they report on their relations with stakeholders.
5. SOEs should observe high standards of transparency in accordance with the OECD principles of corporate governance.
6. The boards of SOEs should have the necessary authority, competencies, and objectivity to carry out their function of strategic guidance and monitoring of management. They should act with integrity and be held accountable for their actions.

In short, the market has to be protected according to the OECD from unfair advantages given to SOEs and best practices do exist. After years of justifying privatization on the basis that SOEs were not efficient, they appear in the OECD documents as a threat to the private sector. After the 2008 financial crisis, although the use of SOEs had been welcomed, very quickly the OECD suggested that re-privatization should follow.

Efforts have been made to improve the corporate governance of the Crown corporations governments decided to maintain. Governments have different ways to organize the governance of their public enterprises. They choose both the members and the president of the board of directors, require strategic plans and annual reports, etc. In theory the board chooses the CEO but it is very unlikely that such a choice would be made without consulting with at least the minister in charge. Moreover, major transactions, borrowing operations, and strategic plans are authorized by the government. Ministers give letters of mission or give instructions.

Some governments in Canada have been active in reforming the governance of the Crowns. Quebec legislated new laws in 2006 covering the accountability practices of 24 public enterprises and other related organizations (Bernier & Pelletier, 2008). The British Columbia government published a good practice checklist in 2011 that covers board composition and responsibilities and a guide about formal relationships and reporting procedures. The government of Ontario, which has been rocked by embarrassing scandals involving Crown corporations (Ontario Lottery and Gaming Corporation, ORNG, E-Health, Hydro One), has, since 2013, made efforts to reduce the number of boards and commissions, but has left remarkably intact the agencies. In Saskatchewan, a province where state ownership has been very important (Rediger, 2004), an alternative arrangement has been the establishment of a holding company, the Crown Investment Corporation, that provides governance and accountability for the remaining Crowns in the province. Generally, most of the reform efforts have been focused on the roles of the board of directors by reinforcing the number of independent members and by creating committees to oversee ethics and governance issues, human resource management, and audit. Governments have also expanded the mandates of their Auditors General to evaluate the performance of the Crowns. It is important to note that these broad policy thrusts emanate from the centre, not from the ministry to which the Crown reports.

Should civil servants be on these boards? There is no simple answer. There has always been asymmetry of information in the relation between the government and the Crown corporation; having a representative on the board of directors is a way to reduce it. Part of the asymmetry has to do with the relative clarity or lack thereof over the mission and objectives of the corporation. As a link to the minister, having the deputy minister as a board member might be a good idea. On the other hand, if this person agrees with a decision of the board, the government has said yes already if eventually there is a disagreement between the government and the Crown. Another perennially unsolved dilemma is the link between policy and implementation in the public sector. Even if the mission of the Crown corporation is essentially commercial, a government representative on the board of directors could be an important link to coordinate policy-making.

Some voices have risen that the relations of the Crowns with the government have not been about policy-making, but rather have been reduced to issues around governance: nominating the members of the board, the role of the chair, the succession of the CEOs, etc. (see Conference Board, 2015 and 2016). Perhaps there is a more political explanation for this state of affairs. Ministers want to avoid risk. They prefer not to answer questions in Parliament about the behaviour of Crown corporations. The tactic has been to seek as much deniability as possible. Involvement in formal processes such as the adoption and approval of the strategic plan could

tie a minister more closely to an agency—perhaps too much so. The consequence is neglect and policy drift. Instead, policy-making is overshadowed by the management of crisis in modern government. There is very little planning but rather fire fighting as officials react to events. In addition, in recent decades, policy has been driven by fiscal reality of declining financial support. Between crisis management and the fiscal imperative, little is left in terms of policy content. Ministers, department staff, and even Parliaments have allowed Crowns to largely operate in a policy vacuum.

From research on Canadian, European, and Algerian public enterprises, Hafsi and Koenig (1988) have suggested that the relationship between the state and a public enterprise follows a pattern. Three possible modes of interaction can be combined into a cycle evolving from mutual dependence and co-operation to autonomy via an adversarial stage. Hafsi and Koenig (1988) have written that "four contextual variables shape the state-owned enterprise (SOE)-government relationship: the SOE's development of a technical core, the SOE's financial self-sufficiency, the structure of government supervision over the SOE, and the agreement on rules of the political game among external groups. The relationship life cycle is then linked to configurations of top management in SOEs, which differ in composition and structure, performance criteria, and critical tasks." In this view, control is only lacking for a period of time. Governments have ways to recreate the co-operation of the beginning. But also, what exactly are the objectives of governments for Crown corporations? The next section considers policy objectives and public entrepreneurship and moves beyond the objectives previously presented and the discussion over control. Is it what is done outside the Crown corporation that matters or what happens inside the black box?

Policy Objectives and Organizational Culture

A Crown corporation is a public organization that has the particular form of a private-sector organization. There is a board of directors, a chief executive officer, and the various services one could expect. What makes a Crown corporation different is its organizational culture. "An organizational culture could be defined as a configuration of shared meanings, symbols and cognitions that characterize the manner in which groups and individuals in a given organization combine to get things done . . ." (Latouche, 1984: 337). The culture defines the texture rather than the structure of the Crown corporation. The culture differentiates the Crown corporation from any private company, or so it should. In a complex organization, the culture helps employees to understand the mission, and in Crown corporations this could be important in finding the equilibrium between commercial and policy objectives. Such a culture has to be transmitted to new employees, as civil servants working for the Department of Global Affairs Canada (originally called the Department of Foreign Affairs and International Trade (DFAIT), among other names) believe they are unique, or that economists at the Department of Finance believe they constitute the best department of economics in the country (Bernier & Facal, 2011).

There will always be the pressure of the core technology. Whether in the public or later in the private sector, Air Canada's core activity is flying airplanes. In the Canadian system, in theory, there is a "ministère de tutelle," a department responsible for the Crown corporation despite the arm's-length relation. In theory, the department has the knowledge needed to control the enterprise. At the same time, the best experts are in theory in the Crown corporation (Parenteau, 1980; Skocpol and Finegold, 1982). Thus the capacity to control what the Crown does—the content of the core activity—is limited. Moreover, international activities in today's economy might diminish the importance of the policy objectives. The core activities of a state-owned enterprise might be far away from the policy objectives of a government.

If Crown corporations are policy instruments, this presupposes clear and understandable policy objectives to implement. These policies have also to be coherent. Or they can be replaced by an appropriate organizational culture. An organizational culture should include a well-developed organizational memory made of some of the following elements: tales, myths, legends, and rituals; a comfortable self-image; a list of heroes; a socialization process; a shared vision of the formal and informal authority structure; a shared vision of all major actors in the environment; an identifiable set of values; and a set of internalized conflicts (real or apprehended) with the government over the autonomy of the SOE (Latouche, 1984: 344–5). Just as it could be difficult to change the culture of a Crown corporation that would be privatized, it could be difficult to change the culture of a nationalized company. In order to solve the financial crisis in 2008, governments nationalized companies. They did do so on a temporary basis for both banks and car manufacturers. They had no intention of keeping these enterprises. But it could have been an opportunity to bring some notion of the public interest to the governance or decision-making of these enterprises.

Province-Building and Crown Corporations

Crown corporations have been an important instrument for province building and at least in these cases the corporate culture was based on relatively clear objectives. Although the OECD places Canada in the middle range of countries deploying such state-owned enterprises, Crisan and McKenzie (2013) noted that when provincial public enterprises are included, they roughly double the size of the public enterprise sector in Canada (for their size, see Table 12.2). The various provinces have created Crown corporations relatively coherently over a short period of time: only a few prior to 1960 and an increasing number from then until 1975. Saskatchewan employed state-owned enterprises as a conscious tool of economic development in the 1940s under a CCF government. After that, their creation decreased until the 1980s when privatization came into vogue. At the end of the 1970s, 233 public enterprises had been created by the provinces (Vining & Botterell, 1983: 363). Seventy-six per cent of them were created after 1960 when province-building hit its stride. After the creation or nationalization of hydro-electric companies in Ontario, Manitoba, British Columbia, and Quebec, public enterprises were created in many provinces for phone companies, for forest products, and for mining such as the Potash Corporation in Saskatchewan. The desire of provinces to maintain some autonomy vis-à-vis Ottawa has made it more difficult for them to privatize. The scope for autonomy is limited. They share instruments such as fiscal policy and subsidies with

Table 12.2 Provincial and Territorial Crown Corporations, All Industries in 2010 (in $ millions)

	Total Assets	Total Liabilities	Equity	Total Revenue	Total Expenses	Gains/Losses, Corporate Taxes and Other Items	Comprehensive Income
Canada	287,385.8	242,025.5	45,360.3	85,448.0	67,192.7	467.0	18,422.1
Newfoundland and Labrador	3,079.0	1,743.1	1,335.8	1,144.1	889.1	(1.0)	259.3
Prince Edward Island	122.2	106.7	15.4	149.4	119.7	(1.2)	28.5
Nova Scotia	1,896.5	1,740.4	156.1	1,105.4	800.6	68.8	373.6
New Brunswick	10,400.5	10,147.5	253.0	2,663.1	2,341.9	(15.1)	178.2
Quebec	101,104.2	80,377.2	20,727.0	20,922.6	16,624.8	225.3	4,158.1
Ontario	73,355.0	68,284.4	5,070.6	27,126.6	21,465.1	150.5	5,767.0
Manitoba	17,495.7	14,164.2	3,331.4	4,561.1	3,531.7	(1.5)	
Saskatchewan	12,288.8	8,480.8	3,808.0	6,705.5	5,656.1	(29)	1,040.0
Alberta	28,009.5	25,798.5	2,211.0	5,963.6	3,614.0	34.3	2,339.7
British Columbia	38,654.4	30,418.2	8,236.2	14,777.3	11,864.8	36.9	3,060.8
Yukon	391.9	324.4	67.6	73.9	59.0	–	14.9
Northwest Territories	397.4	294.9	102.5	154.6	120.5	–	36.2
Nunavut	190.8	145.2	45.6	100.8	105.4	(0.8)	(5.3)

Source: CANSIM Table 3850031—Balance sheet and income statement of provincial and territorial government business enterprises, by North America Industry Classification System (NAICS), end of fiscal year closest to December 31, annually. (http://www5.statcan.gc.ca/cansim/a26)

Ottawa, and have no control over monetary policy. Crown corporations remain flexible instruments that they more fully control.

The first provincial public enterprise was Ontario Hydro, created in 1906. Other provinces followed. Quebec waited until the 1960s Quiet Revolution, a time of catching up with development elsewhere, to establish Hydro-Québec. We will never know how much of the lag in economic development in Quebec vis-à-vis Ontario is due to this difference in timing. In Ontario, Chambers of Commerce asked for hydro nationalization for economic development purposes. In Quebec, a private sector with different views financed political parties that opposed nationalization. After 1960, the trend was reversed, with Quebec becoming the province with the most active industrial policy and a great role for public enterprises (Young et al., 1984).

The post-war period was a time when the investment policy of the state-owned enterprise was becoming more and more active and the pool of available money was growing rapidly. The provinces had established pools of money for economic development and to cover the retirement pensions of their employees following various models, like the Alberta Heritage Fund and the Quebec Caisse de dépôt. These are more classical state-owned enterprises. In Ontario, OMERS and Teachers are huge financial institutions that play a similar role but are not Crown corporations. Saskatchewan has made a great use of Crown corporations to develop natural resources but also in the service sector. In order to coordinate them, the Government Finance Office was created in the 1950s and later became the Crown Investments Corporation, the holding company with oversight of the investments. A more recent venture has been Enterprise Saskatchewan, another effort to foster economic development.

The adaptability of the Crown corporation as an instrument has proved useful for province building. One example is in the electrical field. Canadian public electricity companies that are provincially owned have been able to enter the US deregulated market having both financial resources and power surpluses as their European counterparts cross borders. The low cost of hydro power has avoided competition at home and been a competitive advantage on the US market. Lanthier (2007) studied BC Hydro, Manitoba Hydro, and Hydro-Québec, all of which adopted similar structural changes and confronted similar challenges in their international ventures. The US activities of the three companies are regulated by an autonomous US agency, the Federal Energy Regulatory Commission (FERC). All three have developed expertise in long-distance electricity transportation. The rules of the FERC forced the three companies to dismantle their vertically integrated organizations into three separate entities: production, transmission, and distribution. To succeed in the US market, they created subsidiaries after dismantling their previous offices. They also built partnerships with private companies. In order not to lose their public-interest mission, they emphasized ethical codes of conduct and mission statements as guides for managers' decisions. According to Lanthier (2007: 199), exports helped the three enterprises to maintain low rates on their home market. This is more debatable today with the lower energy prices on the US market due to shale oil. Ontario followed a similar pattern, creating five entities from Ontario Hydro including Ontario One, which distributes the electricity. The Ontario government also created a regulatory agency (Gattinger, 2005).

Public Entrepreneurship as Another Way of Looking at Crown Corporations

Canada has a truncated industrialization, is dependent on trade, and has weak regulatory power; thus, state ownership is a pragmatic response. If creating the Crown is the strategy, once the instrument exists can the economic activity generated be considered the policy? For example, Quebec's successive

governments chose to delegate responsibilities to autonomous public enterprises. They were created to avoid having to establish coherent and comprehensive policies (Parenteau, 1980:195). British Columbia, Saskatchewan, and Alberta have similar histories. More careful research should be done on the link between Crown corporations and economic policies. Policy objectives are not always clear and thus it is difficult to see the relationship between government intentions and what the Crowns do other than having a Crown in charge. Crowns in fact are often part of a broader framework of province-building, of nationalism, and of the volition to catch up with development elsewhere in North America. This was true of Quebec in the 1960s.

Fragmented direction continues to mark the Crowns. Hodgetts (1970: 202), the pioneer of public administration research in Canada, once wrote, "It cannot be said that any unifying philosophy underlies the use of the public corporation in Canada: the whole development has been piecemeal and pragmatic." Is there much else today? Policies do not come anymore from the ministry in charge. The Crowns are caught in a web of rules coming from the Treasury Board, the Privy Council Office, and the Auditor General. The successive Auditors General have repeatedly written in their reports about the Crowns that there has not been enough feedback about strategic plans and annual reports. Other comments are about the lack of measurable indicators of Crown corporation performance, poor benchmarking, and lack of risk management (Bernier and Farinas, 2010). The involvement of Crowns is more financial than it used to be (Lévesque, 2003).

Governments worldwide have chosen to deliver services through organizations with greater autonomy than traditional bureaus. The assumption behind this reliance on agencies is that by giving their managers more autonomy and access to incentive mechanisms, there will be an improvement in efficiency (Vining, Laurin, and Weimer, 2014). But there is more to it. Governments have to decide the policies to be implemented by SOEs but the entrepreneurship (Bernier, 2014) or the strategies are also of importance (Hafsi, 1989; Luke & Verreynne, 2006). In the public sector, entrepreneurial behaviour has long been regarded as either non-existent or aberrant. At the same time, the complexity of the modern state apparatus has made possible the development of entrepreneurs that have taken advantage of the slack available to develop new organizations, new services, and new processes (Bernier & Hafsi, 2007). In theory, this should be particularly true in public enterprises where financial resources are more easily obtained than elsewhere in the public sector.

Linking public entrepreneurship and public enterprises could lead to an improvement in understanding the role that Crown corporations play as instruments of economic policy, in particular in the new context emerging after 2008. Control and governance are only part of the explanation. Enumerating objectives is part of what Crown corporations are supposed to do. Their organizational culture discussed earlier is also important. Is the culture entrepreneurial?

The public sector is viewed as having too many rules or being too risk-averse to offer opportunities to entrepreneurs. But it is possible that within the state apparatus, some organizations are, or should be, a better environment than others for entrepreneurs. State-owned enterprises could be such islands of autonomy and capacity (Skocpol & Finegold, 1982). Enterprise autonomy may be a structural performance driver apart from ownership (Beecher, 2013: 160). The relative autonomy of the state and state capacity are two conditions that offer the potential for public entrepreneurship. It is also possible that entrepreneurship is more important than rules and controls for the success of the state.

Only in a small organization can a single individual perform all entrepreneurial functions. The Schumpeterian entrepreneur as an individual remains in the literature (Schnellenbach, 2007) but later research has been generally more focused on teams of entrepreneurs or lower-level bureaucrats who transformed governments (Borins, 2008; Mintrom & Norman, 2009; Riccucci, 1995).

The British parliamentary tradition has been viewed as a more difficult setting for public entrepreneurship than the American republican system. The British system creates a centralization pressure to avoid mistakes that would embarrass the minister in charge of a department. It could be argued that the closer to the core of government, the more the avoidance of risk and respect for rules will be valued. Entrepreneurship and innovation are thus less likely to occur closer to the centre. Creating

Crown corporations helped insulate managerial teams from the political pressures that existed in ministries. Public enterprises are more likely to be protected from external influences and allow entrepreneurs to innovate under fewer political pressures because of their core activity (Thompson, 1967; Hafsi & Koenig, 1988). Public enterprises might therefore be one of the most promising locations in state apparatuses in which to find and study public entrepreneurship (Luke & Verreynne, 2006). The public enterprises that were not privatized after 1980 are the ones that have been able to build their legitimacy. Public entrepreneurship is both enabled and constrained by a political system and institutional context (Klein et al., 2010).

In Conclusion: Crown Corporations in the Twentieth Century and Future Research[4]

State-owned enterprises now represent approximately ten per cent of global gross domestic product with sales of $ 3.5 trillion around the world (Bruton et al., 2015). In Canada, they have been essential to the development of the country since Confederation and even before. Still today, they are important if we consider both the federal and the provincial governments (Crisan & McKenzie, 2013). Over the years, many governments have decided that the state was too complex and that the Crowns would never work properly, that economic theory had frequently demonstrated that they could not work as well as their private-sector counterparts. Well, they do in practice (Bernier, 2015). Ownership is a dynamic construct; in some contexts Crowns work as well as their private-sector counterparts, while in others privatization can correct the involvement of the state (Bernier & Fascal, 2011; Rentsch & Finger, 2015). Ownership is only one element of a complex system of relations between an enterprise and its institutional environment where the role of the board of directors, the mechanisms of coordination, the role of senior civil servants, etc. come into play.

The Canadian experience with Crown corporations is a fascinating experiment. There is no consensus about the role of these enterprises in a world where privatization, liberalization, and deregulation have changed the institutional environment of SOEs. SOEs can be used as a counter-cyclical tool. Governments used them to face the 2008 economic crisis to rescue ailing firms and to maintain production facilities facing the risk of cessation of activity (Bance & Bernier, 2011; Bance & Obermann, 2015). Their economic role has changed, having become more financial than it was in the twentieth century.

New questions about the public mission have developed over the last decades: questions about social responsibility, sustainable development, and entrepreneurship. Mainstream neoclassical economics and new public management are not comfortable with the idea that state-owned enterprises could perform well. So we have to look for alternative explanations in sociology, public administration, management, etc. SOEs are hybrid organizations that are at the same time market oriented and operate in a business-like manner to offer public services. What institutional theory has to teach us on them has been presented (Bruton et al., 2015).

There are continuing questions about which models, mechanisms, instruments, and processes could be used for the effective and efficient provision of public services (Grossi et al., 2015: 275). Some involve questions like whether or not privatization could be considered passé, why, and how; others concern renationalization or remunicipalization. Others query whether there might be a new trend towards reintegration within the state (Clò et al., 2015). One important issue remains the performance of these firms linked to their organizational structure. Corporate governance of SOEs continues to be a challenge in many countries.

Important Terms and Concepts

autonomy (administrative)
control
corporate governance

Crown corporation
policy implementation
privatization

province-building
public entrepreneurship
state-owned enterprise

Study Questions

1. How are policy instruments selected for implementation?
2. Why would governments choose Crown corporations alone, or use a mix of instruments?
3. What are the pragmatic reasons that could explain privatization?
4. What is public entrepreneurship? Does entrepreneurship make sense in the public sector?
5. What differentiates corporate governance from control?

Notes

1   Part of the historical and statistical analysis presented here has been prepared for an article submitted to the *Annals of Public and Cooperative Economics* in 2017 with Patrice Dutil and Taïeb Hafsi in an article titled "Policy Adrift: Crown Corporations in the 21st Century."

2   *The Review of the Governance Framework for Canada's Crown Corporations,* see http://www2.parl.gc.ca/Content/LOP/ResearchPublications/prb0580-e.htm

3   See http://www.tbs-sct.gc.ca/reports-rapports/cc-se/index-eng.asp

4   Someone interested in further research on the topic could look at CIRIEC's website.

References

Aharoni, Y. 1986. *The Evolution and Management of State-Owned Enterprises*. Cambridge, Ballinger.

Aivazian, V. A., G. Ying, and J. Qiu. 2005. "Can Corporatization Improve the Performance of State-Owned Enterprises Even without Privatization?" *Journal of Corporate Finance*, 11, 5, pp. 791–808.

Bance, P. and L. Bernier, editors. 2011. *Contemporary Crisis and Renewal of Public Action: Towards the*

Emergence of a New Form of Regulation? Brussels: Peter Lang.

Bance, P. and G. Obermann. 2015. "Serving the General Interest with Public Enterprises: New Forms of Governance and Trends in Ownership." *Annals of Public and Cooperative Economics*, 86, pp. 529–34.

Beecher, Janice A. 2013. "What Matters to Performance? Structural and Institutional Dimensions of Water Utility Governance." *International Review of Applied Economics*, 27, pp. 150–73.

Berle, A. A. and G. Means. 1932. *The Modern Corporation and Private Property.* New York: Macmillan.

Bernier, L. 2011, December 4. "The Future of Public Enterprises: Perspectives from the Canadian Experience." *Annals of Public and Cooperative Economics*, 82, 4, pp. 399–419.

Bernier, L., editor. 2015. *Public Enterprises Today: Missions, Performance and Governance, Learning from Fifteen Cases.* Brussels: Peter Lang.

Bernier, L. 2014. "Public Enterprises as policy Instruments: The Importance of Public Entrepreneurship." *Journal of Economic Policy Reform*, 17, 3, pp. 253–66.

Bernier, L. and J. Facal. 2011. "The Ontario Ministry of Finance as an Exception in Canadian Public Administration." *The Guardian: Perspectives on the Ministry of Finance of Ontario*, edited by P. Dutil, University of Toronto Press, pp. 206–25.

Bernier, L. and L. Farinas. 2010. "Les Entreprises Publiques du Gouvernement du Canada." *L'espace canadien: mythes et réalités*, edited by R. Bernier, QC, pp. 403–25.

Bernier, Luc & André Fortier 2014. "Les organismes centraux" *La politique québécoise et canadienne : une approche pluraliste*, edited by Alain-G. Gagnon, Québec, Presses de l'Université du Québec, pp. 239–61. (Politeia).

Bernier, L. and T. Hafsi. 2007. "The Changing Nature of Public Entrepreneurship." *Public Administration Review*, 67, pp. 488–503.

Bernier, L. and M.-L. Pelletier. 2008. "La Gouvernance des Sociétés d'État." *Canadian Journal of Administrative Law and Practice*, 21, 2, pp. 151–92.

Bernier, L. et L. Simard. 2007. "The Governance of Public Enterprises: The Quebec Experience." *Annals of Public and Cooperative Economics*, 78, pp. 455–74.

Bird, M. 2015. "Canadian State-Owned Enterprises: A Framework for Analyzing the Evolving Crowns." *Policy Studies.*

Boardman, A. E. and A. R. Vining. 2012. "A Review and Assessment of Privatization in Canada." University of Calgary: School of Public Policy Paper, vol 5, no 4.

Borins, S. 1998. *Innovating with Integrity: How Local Heroes Are Transforming American Government.* Washington, D.C.: Georgetown University Press.

Borins, S. 2008. *Innovations in Government.* Washington, D.C.: Brookings Institution.

Borins, S. F. and B. E. C. Boothman. 1985 "Crown Corporations and Economic Efficiency." *Canadian Industrial Policy in Action*, edited by D. G. McFetridge, University of Toronto Press, pp. 75–129.

Bruton, G. D., M. W. Peng, D. Ahlstrom, C. Stan, and K. Xu. 2015. "State-Owned Enterprises around the World as Hybrid Organizations." *Academy of Management Perspectives*, 29,1, pp. 92–114.

Canadian Policy Forum. 2015. *Crown Corporation Governance: Seeking the Right Balance between Autonomy and Control.* Ottawa, Spring.

Canadian Policy Forum. 2016. *Crown Corporation Governance: Three Ways to Manage the Tension between Autonomy and Control.* Ottawa, August.

Christiansen, H. 2011. "The Size and Composition of the SOE Sector in OECD Countries." OECD Corporate Governance Working Papers, no. 5.

Clò, S., C. F. Del Bo, M. Ferraris, C. Fiorio, M. Florio, D. Vandone, and C. Fiorio. 2015. "Public Enterprises in the Market for Corporate Control: Recent Worldwide Evidence." *Annals of Public and Cooperative Economics*, 86, pp. 559–83.

Crisan, D. and K. J. McKenzie. 2013. "Government-Owned Enterprises in Canada." University of Calgary: School of Public Policy Paper, vol. 6, no 8.

Del Bo, C. et M. Florio. 2012. "Public Enterprises, Planning and Policy Adoption: Three Welfare Propositions." *Journal of Economic Policy Reform*, 15, 4, pp. 263–79.

Doern, G. B. and J. Atherton. 1987. "The Tories and the Crowns: Restraining and Privatizing in a Political Minefield." *How Ottawa Spends 1987–1988: Restraining the State*, edited by M. J. Prince, Toronto: Methuen, pp. 129–75.

Doern, G. Bruce and Richard W. Phidd. 1983. *Canadian Public Policy: Ideas, Structures, Process.* Toronto: Methuen.

Economic Council of Canada. 1986. *Minding the Public's Business.* Ottawa.

Eliadis, Pearl, Margaret M. Hill, and Michael Howlett, editors. 2005. *Designing Government: From Instruments to Governance.* Montreal: McGill-Queen's University Press.

Florio, M. 2014. "Contemporary Public Enterprises: Innovation, Accountability, Governance." *Journal of Economic Policy Reform*, 17, pp. 201–8.

Florio, M. 2013. "Rethinking on Public Enterprises." *International Review of Applied Economics*, 27, pp. 135–49.

Florio, M. and F. Fecher. 2011. "The Future of Public Enterprises: Contribution to a New Discourse." *Annals of Public and Cooperative Economics*, 82, 4, pp. 361–73.

Gattinger, M. 2005. "Canada-United States Electricity Relations: Policy Coordination and Multi-Level Associative Governance." *How Ottawa Spends:*

Managing the Minority, edited by G. B. Doern, Montreal: McGill-Queen's University Press., pp. 142–62.

Gélinas, A., editor. 1978. *Public Enterprise and the Public Interest : Proceeding of an International Seminar*. Toronto: IPAC.

Gracey, D. 1978. "Public Enterprise in Canada." *Public Enterprise and the Public Interest: Proceeding of an International Seminar*, edited by André, Gélinas, Toronto: IPAC, pp 25–47.

Grossi, G., U. Papenfuß, and M.-S. Tremblay. 2015. "Corporate Governance and Accountability of State-Owned Enterprises: Relevance for Science and Society and Interdisciplinary Research Perspectives." *International Journal of Public Sector Management*, 28, 4/5, pp. 274–85.

Halpern, P., A. Plourde, and L. Waverman. 1988. *Petro-Canada: Its Role, Control and Operations*. Ottawa: Economic Council of Canada.

Hafsi, T., editor. 1989. *Strategic Issues in State-Controlled Enterprises*. Greenwich: JAI Press.

Hafsi T., and C. Koenig. 1988. "The State-SOE Relationship: Some Patterns." *Journal of Management Studies*, 25, pp. 235–50.

Hodgett, J. E. 1970. "The Public Corporation in Canada." *Government Enterprise: A Comparative Study*, edited by W. Friedman and J. F. Garner, London: Stevens and Sons, pp. 201–26.

Huffman, K. J., J. W. Langford, and W. A. W. Neilson. 1985. "Public Enterprise and Federalism in Canada." *Intergovernmental Relations*, edited by Richard Simeon, Toronto: University of Toronto Press, pp. 131–78.

Innis, H. 1930. *The Fur Trade in Canada*. Toronto: University of Toronto Press.

Johnson, David. 2006. *Thinking Government: Public Sector Management in Canada*, 2nd edn, Peterborough: Broadview Press.

Klein, P. G., J. T. Mahoney, A. M. McGahan, and C. N. Pitelis. 2010. "Toward a Theory of Public Entrepreneurship." *European Management Review*, 7, pp. 1–15.

Kowalski, P., M. Büge, M. Sztajerowska, and M. Egeland. 2013. "State-Owned Enterprises, Trade Effects and Policy Implications." *OECD Trade Policy Papers*, No. 147. Paris: OECD.

Latouche, D. 1984. "The Organizational (Counter)–Culture of State-Owned Enterprises: An Explanatory Study of the Quebec Case." *Government Enterprise: Role and Rationale*, Ottawa: Economic Council of Canada, mimeo, pp. 323–78.

Lanthier, P. 2007. "Internationalising Electricity Companies in Canada." *Transforming Public Enterprise in Europe and North-America: Networks, Integration and Transnationalisation*, edited by J. Clifton, F. Comin, and D. Diaz-Fuentes, New York: Palgrave Macmillan, pp. 190–206.

Laux, J. K. and M. A. Molot. 1988. *State Capitalism: Public Enterprise in Canada*. Ithaca: Cornell University Press.

Lévesque, B. 2003. "Fonction de Base et Nouveau Rôle des Pouvoirs Publics : vers un Nouveau Paradigme de l'État." *Annals of Public and Cooperative Economics*, 74, pp. 489–513.

Lewis, E. 1980. *Public Entrepreneurship: Toward a Theory of Bureaucratic Political Power*. Bloomington, IN: Indiana University Press.

Luke, B. and M.-L. Verreynne. 2006. "Exploring strategic entrepreneurship in the public sector." *Qualitative Research in Accounting & Management*, 3, pp. 4–26.

Macdonald, D. A., editor. 2014. Rethinking Corporatization and Public Services in the Global South. London: Zed Books.

Millward, R. 2011. "Public Enterprise in the Modern Western World, An Historical Analysis." *Annals of Public and Cooperative Economics*, 82, 4, pp. 375–98.

Millward, Robert and John Singleton, editors. 1995. *The Political Economy of Nationalisation in Britain, 1920–1950*. Cambridge UP.

Mintrom, M., and P. Norman. 2009. "Policy entrepreneurship and policy change." *Policy Studies Journal*, 37, 4, pp. 649–67.

Molot, M.A. 1988. "The Provinces and Privatization: Are the Provinces Really Getting Out of Business?" *Privatization, Public Policy and Public Corporations in Canada*, edited by A. Tupper and G. B. Doern, Halifax: The Institute for Research on Public Policy, pp. 399–425.

OECD. Organisation of Economic Co-operation and Development. 2005. *OECD Guidelines on Corporate Governance of State-Owned Enterprises*. Paris: OECD.

Parenteau, R. 1980. "Légitimité et Efficacité des Sociétés d'État." *Les Sociétés d'Etat : Autonomie ou Intégration, Document-Témoin de la Rencontre du 8 Mai 1980*, edited by R. Parenteau, Montréal: HEC, mimeo.

Prichard, J. R. S., editor. 1983. *Crown Corporations in Canada: The Calculus of Instrument Choice*. Toronto: Butterworths.

Rediger, P. 2004. *The Crowns: A History of Public Enterprise in Saskatchewan*. Regina: Canadian Plains Research Center, University of Regina.

Rentsch, C. and M. Finger. 2015. "Yes, No, Maybe: The Ambiguous Relationships between State-Owned Enterprises and the State." *Annals of Public and Cooperative Economics*, 86, pp. 617–40.

Riccucci, N. M. 1995. *Unsung Heroes: Federal Execucrats Making a Difference*. Washington, D.C.: Georgetown University Press.

Richards, J. and L. Pratt. 1979. *Prairie Capitalism: Power and Influence in the New West*. Toronto: McClelland and Stewart.

Roberts, A. 2002. "A Fragile State: Federal Public Administration in the Twentieth Century." *The Handbook of Canadian Public Administration*, edited by Christopher Dunn, Don Mills: Oxford University Press, pp. 18–36.

Roberts, A. 2010. "A Fragile State: Federal Public Administration in the Twentieth Century." *The Handbook of Canadian Public Administration*, 2nd edn, edited by Christopher Dunn, Don Mills, ON: Oxford University Press, pp. 219–34.

Schnellenbach, J. "Public Entrepreneurship and the Economics of Reform." *Journal of Institutional Economics*, 3, 2, pp. 183–202.

Sharaput, M. 2010. "Harper Government Industrial Strategy and Industrial Policy in the Economic Crisis." in Doern, G. B. and C. Stoney (2010), *How Ottawa Spends 2010–2011: Recession, Realignment and the New Deficit Era*, edited by G. B. Doern and C. Stoney, Montreal: McGill-Queen's University Press, pp. 109–27.

Skocpol, T. and K. Finegold. 1982. "State Capacity and Economic Intervention in the Early New Deal." *Political Science Quarterly*, 97, pp. 255–78.

Stanbury, W. T. 1994."Privatization by Federal and Provincial Governments in Canada: An Empirical Study." *A Down-Sized State?* edited by R. Bernier and J. I. Gow, Sainte-Foy, QC, pp. 165–219.

Stevens, D. F. 1993. *Corporate Autonomy and Institutional Control: The Crown Corporation as a Problem in Organization Design*. Montreal: McGill-Queens University Press.

Thompson, James D. 1967. *Organizations in Action: Social Science Bases of Administrative Theory.* New Brunswick, New Jersey: *Transaction Publishers.*

Trebilcock, M. J., R. S. Prichard, D. G. Hartle, and D.N. Dewees. 1982. *The Choice of Governing Instruments.* Ottawa: Economic Council of Canada.

Tupper, A. and B. Doern, editors. 1988. *Privatization, Public Policy and Public Corporations in Canada*. Halifax: The Institute for Research on Public Policy.

Vining, A.R. and A.E. Boardman. "Ownership versus Competition: Efficiency in Public Enterprise." *Public Choice* 73, 2, pp. 205–39.

Vining, A. and R. Botterell. 1983. "An Overview of the Origins, Growth, Size and Functions of Provincial Crown Corporations." *Crown Corporations in Canada*, edited by J. Robert S. Pritchard, Toronto: Butterworths, pp. 303–67.

Vining, Aida R., Claude Laurin, and David L. Weimer. 2015. "The Longer-Run Performance Effects of Agencification: Theory and Evidence from Québec Agencies." *Journal of Public Policy* 35, 2, pp. 193–222.

Wilkins, J. 2011. "Alternative Service Delivery Revisited." Commonwealth Secretariat Discussion Paper No. 10.

Young, R. A., A. Blais, and P. Faucher. 1984. "The Concept of Province-Building: A Critique." *Canadian Journal of Political Science*, 17, pp. 783–818.

Indigenous Peoples and the Reconciliation Agenda

13

Funding, Accountability, and Risk[1]

Robert P. Shepherd

Chapter Overview

Reconciliation with Indigenous peoples requires, in part, reconfiguring the models governments use to transfer financial resources. The Final Report of the Truth and Reconciliation Commission provided clearly articulated preferences for reframing this part of the relationship. At a minimum, greater attention should be paid to local flexibility to manage key programs and services such as Indigenous education, training and employment, and living conditions, as opposed to current models that preserve a principal-agent accountability relationship. This chapter surveys changes to the fiscal relationship that have occurred between the 1960s to present day. It concludes that despite changes to funding agreements since 2008 when changes were made to the federal *Policy on Transfer Payments*, there is little evidence to suggest that **accountability** requirements premised on a principal-agent relationship have been altered in any significant way. This means that if reconciliation is to be achieved, more flexible arrangements will have to be found that propel greater local autonomy, capacity-building, and community resilience.

Chapter Objectives

By the end of this chapter, students will be able to do the following:
- Describe the basis of the federal fiscal relationship with Indigenous peoples.
- Describe the implications of the principal-agent accountability relationship on programming.
- Describe the major funding agreements in place with Indigenous communities.
- Explain how the fiscal relationship with Indigenous communities frames local programs and decision-making.

Our history is your history. . .
Until Canada accepts that. . . this
society will never flourish to its
full potential

Chief Ian Campbell (2014)

Introduction

In July 2015, Justin Trudeau, leader of the federal Liberal Party, declared that

> Canadians recognize the urgent need for a renewed nation-to-nation relationship between the federal government and Indigenous Peoples— one built on respect, rights and a commitment to end the status quo. A Liberal government will recognize Aboriginal governments as full partners in the federation, and will work with Indigenous Peoples to create fairness and equality of opportunity in Canada. (Liberal Party of Canada, 2015)

The Liberal Party was elected to a majority government in October 2015, and committed to a sustained program of Indigenous reconciliation in its first budget in March 2016. As a new government, it also committed to adopt and implement the United Nations Declaration on the Rights of Indigenous Peoples (UNDRIP) in May 2016, after the previous government's vote against it in 2007 and endorsement as an "aspirational document" in 2010 (Canada 2010). The announcement to adopt the UNDRIP is attributed, in part, to the June 2015 report of the Truth and Reconciliation Commission (TRC), which examined the effects of residential schools that operated in Canada between 1876 and 1996. Residential schools were government-sponsored religious schools created by the Canadian government (and by New France prior to Confederation) to educate and convert Indigenous youth and integrate them into Canadian society. The Commission provided incontrovertible evidence on the social effects of residential schools on communities and individuals, leading to many calls for governments at all levels to rebuild confidence in the relationship, including the way funding is transferred.

The Commission understood "reconciliation [to be] about establishing and maintaining a mutually respectful relationship between Aboriginal and non-Aboriginal peoples in this country." In order for this positive relationship to occur, "there has to be awareness of the past, acknowledgement of the harm that has been inflicted, atonement for the causes, and action to change behaviour" (Truth and Reconciliation Commission 2015, 6–7). This understanding has framed current federal commitments to a renewed relationship built on action, including new ways to constitute fiscal arrangements. Former Assembly of First Nations (AFN) National Chief Phil Fontaine emphasized that

> The principles of reconciliation, such as mutual respect, coexistence, fairness, meaningful dialogue, and mutual recognition, are not empty words. These principles are about action: . . . they give shape and expression to the material, political and legal elements of reconciliation (Truth and Reconciliation Commission, 2015: 217).

The March 2016 budget committed $8.4 billion over five years to make gains in Indigenous relationship building, programming, and initiatives such as a national inquiry into missing and murdered Indigenous women and girls. The aim of the commitment is to support and expand upon the 2005 Kelowna Accord proposed by then Prime Minister Paul Martin, who sought to improve the relationship by investing in Indigenous education, training and employment, and living conditions. Assumed in the TRC calls to action is a change in mindset regarding the manner in which administrative and funding arrangements are approached by government that respects local judgments on programs and services management. Despite changes to funding agreements since 2008, there is little evidence to suggest that accountability requirements premised on a principal-agent relationship have been altered in any significant way. Despite recent shifts to a risk-based approach to funding that tailors agreements to local capacity, the narrative of the funding relationship remains firmly entrenched in an accountability model that has been in place since Confederation. The Office of the Auditor General (OAG) observed in 2011 that accountability requirements remain rigorous, and that dependence on instruments that reinforce governmental control over funding use may actually be increasing (OAG, 2011: 4.71–4.74).

A key challenge with respect to funding First Nations, Métis, and Inuit governments and organizations has been to balance obligations to the Crown with acknowledging and building the authorities and capacity of communities to manage their own programs, and to being held to account to their members. The current narrative of fiscal control may be out of step with reconciliation premised on mutual respect. In this vein, the chapter describes shifts in funding relationships as extending from the Indian Act along a critical path of governmental accountability, and new public management (NPM) innovations in risk assessment and management. Each of the two discourses of accountability and respectful relationships have generally run in parallel, with principal-agent accountability taking higher priority. Evidence of progress towards reconciliation consists of how well accountability requirements align with approaches akin to a federal–provincial–territorial funding regime, and the extent to which funding authorities that demand high accountability are displaced in favour of those that emphasize local priorities and building management capacity.

The first section provides a description of the role of the Indian Act as it structures the administrative relationship according to sections 91(24) and 35(2) of the Constitution Act. It shows a dichotomy of responsibility between Crown fiduciary obligations under section 91 and limits to them, and obligations to support self-government that could include a shift in focus to a reconciliatory and respectful relationship. The second section provides a brief profile of Indigenous peoples within the Indian Act framework. The next section gives an historical narrative that describes the evolution of the funding relationship between the federal Crown and the three Indigenous constitutional groups, and a dependence on principal-agent accountability. It divides the narrative into pre- and post-2008 Policy on Transfer Payments given that funding agreements changed fundamentally at that time from universal agreements to individualized agreements based on assessment of risk. Finally, the chapter concludes that the current fiscal relationship narrative remains flawed, but reconciliation holds the promise that change is possible given certain conditions.

The Dominant Framework: The Indian Act Relationship

The relationship between the federal Crown and Indigenous peoples is complex, and any narrative will only capture certain critical points in it. With respect to public administration, it conceives of the relationship as administrative extending primarily from a statement of its obligations contained in the Royal Proclamation of 1763. It acknowledged that **Indian** tribes have property rights to their traditional lands, and that these rights were to be respected before lands were opened for settlement. The British North America Act 1867, section 91(24), consolidated these obligations, and provides the federal Parliament with exclusive authority over Indians and lands reserved for them. The Act consolidated numerous pre-Confederation legislation of Upper and Lower Canada, including the Gradual Civilization Act 1857,[2] which governed almost every part of an Indian's life. It set out various rights, privileges, and restrictions; the provisions for local band government; and the creation of reserve lands. Today, the Indian Act continues to play a role in local decision-making because the Minister of Indigenous and Northern Affairs holds the authority to approve local decisions in many areas, including the creation of reserves. Emphasis is placed on this Act in order to set the context of the administrative relationship, although it is by no means the only determinant of that relationship: historical and modern-day treaty obligations also affect the nature of the relationship.

The Indian Act sets the boundaries of federal obligations to support *Indians*, which is a term that has continued to cause much debate about how to identify the Indigenous peoples of Canada, comprising the three constitutional groups: First Nations, Métis, and Inuit. The current 1985 version of the Act defines *Indian* as a person registered as an Indian, or entitled to be registered as an Indian (c. I–5, ss.2–7), and entitled to hold status under that Act. Being registered means that a person is attached, or is a member of a band as recognized by the Department of Indigenous and Northern Affairs Canada (INAC). It also means that a person is on the Indian Register and legally entitled to access federal programming and funding for **status Indian** people. Those who qualify to register under the Act and are recognized under section 91(24) comprise a numerically smaller population than the broader category of constitutional Indians. Defining the scope of federal obligations to Indians has been the subject of many court challenges, as the Crown has attempted to restrict its own obligations to provide a federally protected land base, access to Indian programs and services, or recognition to launch certain types of entitlement or land claims settlements. The federal position is that Métis and **non-status Indians** come under provincial jurisdiction for most constitutional purposes, and do not enjoy the same privileges afforded to status Indians under the Indian Act.[3] The term has also raised conflicting interpretations of whether Indians included in section 35(2) of the Constitution Act 1982 exclude the Inuit and Métis, or whether the category Indians in section 91(24) of the British North America Act includes all of the categories named in section 35(2). The current interpretation appears to be that section 91(24) includes all three of the constitutional groups, but with limitations on the application of the constitution for each, especially given recent court challenges relating to the status of Métis in 2016, and the creation of Nunavut Territory in 1999.

Profile of the Three Constitutional Groups

First Nations

First Nations is used as a generic term to describe Indigenous peoples who are not of Inuit or Métis ancestry, and was first used in 1980 at the newly constituted gathering of the Assembly of First Nations (AFN) in its Declaration of the First Nations (AFN Description). As a legal term, it refers to an organic political and cultural entity or *bands* covered under section 2 of the Indian Act: (a) for whose use and benefit in common, lands, the legal title to which is vested in Her Majesty, have been set apart before, on or after September 4, 1951; (b) for whose use and benefit in common, *moneys* are held by Her Majesty, or (c) declared by the Governor-in-Council to be a band. A band operates through a band council comprising a chief and elected councillors pursuant to section 74 of the Indian Act, or operates through *custom* as afforded under the Act.

The terms *status*, *legal*, and *registered* refer to Indians who come under the jurisdiction of the Indian Act. Aside from those provided status prior to 1985, the Indian Act definition of legal status was extended on a one-time basis to include those individuals, mainly women, who had lost their status through marriage under earlier versions of the Indian Act. It also terminated the status of those who acquired it through marriage, rather than descent. The changes also provided for rules governing entitlement to

Indian registration for children born after April 16, 1985, and the authority for bands to develop and apply their own membership rules (Parliament of Canada, 2003). As a result of such changes, more than 127,000 persons were added to the Indian Register, and 106,000 lost status (RCAP, 1996a: 300–7). The important effect being felt today is that an increasing proportion of marriages on reserves occur with non-status individuals, leading to the concern that, in the near future, reserves will no longer be populated by people who hold status under sections 6(1) or 6(2) of the Indian Act, or who are eligible to access federal programs and services.

The First Nations population comprises the largest proportion of Indigenous peoples at 60 per cent. As of March 2014, there were 617 band governments in Canada, with the majority in British Columbia (198 or 32.1 per cent), Ontario (126 or 20.4 per cent), Saskatchewan (70 or 11.3 per cent), and Quebec (63 or 10.2 per cent). Approximately 59 per cent of First Nations communities have fewer than 500 residents, 8 per cent have populations between 500 and 2000 persons, leaving 33 per cent with populations over 2000 with most under 5000 (INAC 2014a). Membership in a band is maintained in one of two ways: Indian Register maintained by INAC (approximately 59 per cent), or band governments that adopt their own membership code, which is approved by INAC (approximately 41 per cent). Under the second method, it is possible that not all members holding status may be registered. There remain several unrecognized band governments across Canada, explaining why the total number of bands increases annually as recognition is granted by the minister under sections 2 and 6 of the Act.[4] As of December 2015, the median age of the First Nation status and non-status population was 26 years of age, fifteen years younger than the median of 41 years for the overall Canadian population (Statistics Canada, 2015).

Inuit

The broader population of Inuit, which in Inuktitut means "the people," reside mainly in their homeland, Inuit Nunangat, which comprises four regions: Inuvialuit (Northwest Territories and Yukon), Nunavut (independent territory), Nunavik (Northern Quebec), and Nunatsiavut (Northern Labrador). Unlike legal Indians who have enjoyed constitutional recognition under the Constitution Act, the Inuit (Inuk) were defined by way of exclusion, and did not qualify for federal programming under section 91(24). Inuit needs were addressed in the federal territories, and assumed to be a provincial constitutional responsibility. This changed with the 1939 Supreme Court decision in *Reference re Eskimos,* when the federal government was forced to accept that section 91(24) applied.[5] For purposes of identifying Inuit peoples, each Inuk in the northern territories was given a four-digit number in 1941 that entitled them to access federal programs and fishing permits. The system was abolished in 1971, and replaced by a census system and uninsured health benefits lists, which are maintained on the basis of "self-identification and/or community registration" (Furi & Wherrett, 2003). Today, some Inuit possess a negotiated settlement with the federal Crown with the creation of the Nunavut Territory in April 1999. The Inuit, therefore, decided to negotiate the scope of section 91(24) as it applies to them as residing within federal powers.

Métis

The use of the term *Métis* is contestable. When capitalized, it refers to the political body, Métis Nation, which is represented by the Métis National Council (MNC). The MNC defined Métis as "a person who self-identifies as Métis, is distinct from other Aboriginal Peoples, is of historic Métis Nation ancestry, and who is accepted by the Métis Nation" (MNC 2002). Contemporary usage of the term includes people of English- and French-speaking heritage. In *Daniels v. Canada* 2016, the meaning of Métis under section 35(2) of the Constitution Act 1982 was clarified by the Supreme Court, which ruled that the federal government has jurisdiction over Métis people, and that members of the Métis Nation, and non-status Indians (including Métis peoples not belonging to the MNC) are Indians as defined by section 35 (SCC 12). Métis were originally excluded from the Indian Act 1876 because they were not connected to any land grant system under federally constituted Half-breed Scrip Commissions and the Dominion Lands Act. However, there is precedent in 1875 to recognize a Métis community near Fort Frances, which was provided some federal funding. They have also been recognized under such legislation as the Manitoba Act, which afforded Métis access to land as Indians as defined by the Indian Act. Despite these instances of recognition, there has been no national policy on Métis. The *Daniels* decision will likely require the federal government to formulate one. It can only be assumed that the federal government believed this community would integrate into Canadian society, and would not require any formal recognition. With the exception of Alberta, provinces regard the federal government as having responsibility for Métis communities (Morse & Giokas, 1995). Table 13.1 shows the total Indigenous population who self-identified as Indigenous in 2011.

Table 13.1   Indigenous Population by Identity (2011)

Indigenous Identity	Total	Percentage of Group	Percentage of Total
Total Indigenous Population	1,400,685		100.0
First Nations Single Identity	851,560	100.0	60.8
- First Nations (Status)	637,660	74.9	45.5
- First Nations (Non-Status)	213,900	25.1	15.3
Métis (Single Identity)	451,795		32.3
Inuit (Single Identity)	59,445		4.2
Multiple Indigenous Identities	11,415		0.8
Other Indigenous Identities Not Defined or Included Elsewhere	26,475		1.9

Source: Statistics Canada 2011 (https://www12.statcan.gc.ca/nhs-enm/2011/as-sa/99-011-x/2011001/tbl/tbl01-eng.cfm)

Funding Indigenous Communities: Balancing Interests

The narrative of funding Indigenous communities and governments has shifted many times since the Indian Act was proclaimed in 1876. First Nation band governments were created to provide the means by which Canada could recognize individuals qualifying for status under the Indian Act, and therefore, eligible for the benefits contained therein. After amendments to the Indian Act in 1951, the process of transferring program and services management to band councils was initiated as a way of recognizing local self-governing communities. In effect, the federal government created hundreds of local governments to manage federal responsibilities, raising challenges that continue to be experienced today. Some of these challenges include the inconsistent development of local capacity to manage devolved responsibilities, and the obligation of the federal government to transfer funding to local communities. Some First Nation communities have managed well under this system, while others struggle to balance several, and sometimes conflicting, accountability requirements.

Funding is transferred to Indigenous governments and organizations through *funding agreements,* which are written contracts that set out detailed obligations, called terms and conditions, on the part of the federal government and Indigenous *recipients.* Contained in each agreement are a number of *funding authorities* that are voted on by Parliament, and which define a set of specific rules that restrict how money is expended. As such, agreements normally contain more than one *funding authority* that authorizes spending for a defined set of programs over a specified duration. For example, some programs identified in an agreement may be funded for one year or multiple years. In addition, some programs will only be funded under one prescribed authority such as a grant or contribution, or as in the case of current funding agreements, a recipient may qualify for funding under another (usually more flexible) authority based on an assessment of risk. Some authorities demand rigorous accountability, while others are more flexible. Whereas limited options were available to communities before 2008 regarding the authorities assigned to programs, post-2008 authorities are assigned based on the level of assessed risk.

The rules governing the transfer of authorities is outlined through policies, including the federal Policy on Transfer Payments.[6] Such policies determine the vehicles through which funding may be transferred, and the accountability conditions that accompany them. The vehicles through which transfers take place have changed many times in response to shifting demands for accountability, approaches to enforcement of the rules of transfer, and changes in policy direction such as the current reconciliation agenda. The federal Policy on Transfer Payments underwent significant administrative reform in 2008 to reflect a new public management orientation that emphasized delegated approaches to accountability. This resulted in greater use of performance management and risk assessment mechanisms, versus previous orientations that focused on program efficiency instead of outcomes within the context of principal-agent relationships (Harmon, 1995). Due to this shift in direction, the following section examines critical turning points in the funding narrative.

Moving from Line Agreements to Consolidated Agreements

Funding and Assimilation

The period between 1889 to 1968 saw the transition of direct service delivery by the federal government and other agents to one of delegated management. This process of delegation required instruments that would provide the authority to transfer funding, and permit recipients to create and deliver their own programs under the supervision of federal departments. This was a lengthy transition, and many attempts were made to balance the authorities and obligations of the federal Crown with the demand for flexibility and authority at the local level. The narrative begins with the view reflected by Commissioner of Indian Affairs Reed, who reported in 1889 that "The policy of destroying the tribal or communist system is assailed in every possible way and every effort made to implant a spirit of individual responsibility instead" (Canada, 1889: 165). Treaties were regarded as means to a special relationship that were, and some ways are, "assailed" by governments. If the relationship could not be eliminated, then it would have to be managed. Calls for greater accountability were made in the 1940s and 1950s, culminating in the Indian Affairs Branch assuming the responsibility for health and education programs previously held by the churches. Skipping ahead, Indigenous leaders advocated for a new relationship away from control and assimilation to one of integration (Leslie, note 39). A new Indian Act was proclaimed in 1951, which opened the possibility for *self-government*, and the idea that accountability for use of funds would be divided: or **dual accountability**.[7] As a result, local band councils were provided funds for designated programs for the first time in 1968. However, the mechanism used to transfer funding was highly rules-based, emphasizing Crown obligations over local flexibility, which remains the dominant narrative to this day.

The failed 1969 *White Paper*, introduced by Prime Minister Pierre Trudeau and Indian Affairs Minister Jean Chrétien, proposed terminating the legal relationship between Indigenous peoples and the Canadian state, dismantling the Indian Act, converting reserve lands to private property, and transferring federal responsibilities for section 91(24) to the provinces. Its aim was to eliminate *Indian* as a separate legal status, and pass the responsibility for programs to the provinces.[8] Homogenous core funding agreements were created in 1974 to cover costs related to management and administration of some programs no longer delivered by the federal government. Direct transfers were made to band councils for the first time, meaning that the federal department began moving away from direct service delivery to delegated programs to band governments. The system remained rules laden, leading to calls for a new funding regime.

Movement towards "Self-Government"

In 1982, a Special Parliamentary Committee on Indian Self-Government, chaired by Keith Penner, was created "to examine the Government of Canada's total financial and other relationships" with Indian people. The report remains an ideal against which funding agreements are based. Its mandate was twofold: to study the provisions of the Indian Act dealing with band membership and Indian status; and to make recommendations regarding possible provisions for an improved array of administrative arrangements to apply to some or all band governments on reserves (Canada, 1983: 3). It recommended "that Indian self-government must be supported by new funding arrangements that would enable Indian First Nation governments to decide how best to meet their

peoples' needs" (Canada, 1983: 94). It proposed the use of direct grants based on a modified per capita formula, five-year global funding of operational programs, and corrections for infrastructure deficiencies that would place fewer conditions on recipients. Up to this point, individual contractual funding arrangements, called **Contribution Agreements**, were used to provide funding on a program-by-program basis whereby communities were required to manage several individual agreements, often with different rules and reporting requirements. Penner heard from witnesses that this regime was becoming unmanageable as devolution of programs progressed. Although well-suited for one-time funding, they were ill-suited to delivering programs under a self-government orientation as prescribed by Penner, and in later reports, under section 35 of the Constitution Act (INAC, 2008a: 2). Instead, it recommended federal funding be based on a single consolidated agreement that would state the amount of funding and community responsibilities. As a result, INAC created the Alternative Funding Authority (AFA) in 1989, which provided for *block* transfers over five years, but several features of it were abandoned after 2008.

In November 1986, Indian Affairs was granted authority to "devolve, over time, to the greatest extent possible within existing legislation and current administrative arrangements, its programs and services to Indian people" (TBS, 1986). In this period of devolution, new funding arrangements had to be designed to complement the new approach. Its first attempt was the *Community-Based Self-Government Program* introduced that year, which transferred some programs to 135 of 604 communities. The program proposed new funding arrangements, including a block funding mechanism that would allow communities more flexibility to use federal transfers. Ultimately, only bands that met strict eligibility criteria based on management capacity would be able to take advantage of this new agreement. It was ultimately rejected by recipients as a delegated rather than equal self-governing partnership.

Re-defining Federal Obligations to Funding Recipients

With the election of Jean Chrétien in 1993, deep cuts were made to the self-government program, which set the agenda back significantly on improving funding relationships. Two important changes occurred at that time, affecting administrative policies. First, the Department's mandate was amended to focus on "*core* obligations to First Nations . . ." so as to ensure that "basic needs are met."[9] Second, the definition attached to *Indian monies*[10] was dropped and the term *public funds* as defined in the Financial Administration Act was inserted into funding agreements. The distinction meant that all funding was considered public money that could be applied to the conduct of government business, therefore potentially subject to tax, and allocated based on the discretion of ministers. In 1996, a cap of two per cent was placed on all funding agreements for Indigenous recipients as an allowance for inflation and population growth, which was not enough to keep pace with an average annual population increase of four per cent. The cap was removed as of the March 2016 federal budget (INAC 2016).

In 1996, the **Report of the Royal Commission on Aboriginal Peoples** advocated for the regeneration of the approximately 60 to 80 Indigenous nations as the basis for self-determination, and called for the creation of new agreements instead of modifying existing ones. The RCAP Report, INAC evaluation, and other reports made recommendations to improve the financial relationship, including addressing the administrative burden associated with funding agreements. It also cited the proliferation of new programs that were to be funded outside of core agreements by way of proposal-driven arrangements (RCAP, 1996b: 282–8).

Reforming the Funding Relationship: Tailored Risk-Based Agreements

Crown Accountability Placed in Priority

In 2001, the federal government committed to "strengthening its relationship with Aboriginal People" in its Speech from the Throne. As part of the **Indian Act reform**, the First Nations Governance Act 2002, called on First Nations to be more accountable to departments and their members by creating various administrative codes against which departments would measure administrative performance. First Nations regarded the Act as evidence of increased control over local affairs (AFN, 2002). There were also calls at the time by central agencies for a return to Contribution Agreements as the primary authority for transferring funds (Cornell et.al., 11).

A Return to RCAP: Kelowna Accord 2005

Following the tumultuous Indian Act reforms of the early 2000s, Prime Minister Paul Martin committed to a roundtable meeting with Indigenous leadership and first ministers to discuss improving community well-being with a focus on education, employment, and living conditions. The meeting took place in Kelowna in November 2005, and resulted in a proposed accord: First Ministers and National Aboriginal Leaders: Strengthening Relationships and Closing the Gap. The Kelowna Accord, as it became known, was a commitment "to take immediate action to improve the quality of life for the Aboriginal peoples of Canada in . . . health, education, housing and relationships," including a reconstitution of funding arrangements premised on the commitments of the RCAP report (800–844). It pledged $5.1 billion over five years, but was ultimately rejected by the Conservative government in 2006 after they won the election in January that year.

In December 2006, a blue-ribbon panel submitted a report on grant and contribution programs that strongly criticized federal funding agreements and their excessive reporting and accountability regime. Key recommendations in the creation of new instruments were to ensure grants and contributions programs be citizen-focused, simplified, encouraging of innovation, and results oriented (TBS, 2006). The panel recommended reconstituting funding arrangements with Indigenous recipients that emphasized tailoring agreements to local capacity based on enhanced risk assessment. To this point, however, funding arrangements emphasized excessive and Crown-focused accountability that did not serve local Indigenous management, as noted by the Office of the Auditor General in several reports (OAG 2002, 2006). More importantly, it recommended a shift to dual accountability arrangements.

Conservative Government: Recipient Transparency

With the election of the Conservative government in 2006, several priorities were being considered for implementation, including yet another reform effort. First, however, Prime Minister Stephen Harper issued a full apology on behalf of Canadians for the residential school system on 11 June 2008 in which he expressed that the "government now recognizes that the consequences of the Indian Residential Schools policy were profoundly negative, and that

engagement

this policy has had a lasting and damaging impact on Aboriginal culture, heritage and language" (INAC 2008b). The apology set the stage for a series of reforms against the backdrop of the popular Kelowna Accord. The new government believed that reducing paper burden was the way forward to repairing the funding relationship.

In 2012, it launched the Reducing the Administrative Burden on First Nations initiative, which focused on three priorities: (1) consolidate and reduce program reporting requirements on First Nation communities; (2) develop and implement an incentive-based funding system that rewarded communities with strong financial records through more flexible funding arrangements; and (3) re-focus the accountability relationship with an emphasis on local priorities over governmental ones. Each element of the initiative was phased in simultaneously.

The first priority involved consolidating or eliminating redundant information that was already known to INAC through other reporting mechanisms. A simplified annual reporting guide was instituted that combined reporting from several individual reports. Other efforts included the implementation of standardized financial reporting measures for audited financial statements using GAAP standards, more flexible reporting timelines, and the integration of program reporting between different departments that fund Indigenous recipients. Such steps to simplified reporting resulted in a reduced paper burden on recipients as a result of the first phase of the reduction initiative. It also reduced the department's reporting burden on recipients from 4800 internal reports to approximately 800 INAC. 2012).

The second phase constituted the development and implementation of a risk-based funding model, which was enabled under Treasury Board's new Policy on Transfer Payments. The policy came into effect in 2008 but INAC began implementing it in March 2010. The objective of the new policy "is to achieve effective, risk-based approaches to the design and delivery of transfer payment programs and to ensure accountability and value for money for transfer payments" (TBS, 2008a: s. 5.1). With respect to Indigenous recipients, section 6.9.1 of the Directive, "ensur[es] that there is focused and sustained leadership in working towards consistent approaches that are more reflective of the needs of Aboriginal people, with emphasis on the following":

- the recipient engagement strategy;
- the standardization of administrative processes;
- the coordination of recipient audits;
- the reduction of administrative requirements;
- the use of single funding agreements to cover transfer payments from multiple programs;
- the use of multi-year funding agreements;
- the harmonization of transfer-payment programs;
- and, when applicable, consulting with the Treasury Board of Canada Secretariat to facilitate collaboration among departments on these issues (TBS, 2008b).

Departments that engaged with Indigenous recipients were now required to build appropriate risk-assessment tools, construct agreements that consolidated multiple federal funding sources, and transfer funds over multiple reporting periods. INAC, for example, developed the General Assessment (GA) as their risk-assessment tool. The GA evaluates funding recipients on a set of four standardized risk categories: governance, performance history, financial stability, and planning and project complexity.[11] Risk is evaluated according to a set of common benchmarks associated with low, medium, and high levels of risk. For example, a community could be deemed low risk under financial stability if it is able to meet its current financial obligations, it effectively manages long-term debts, and has little to no history of financial mismanagement (INAC, 2014b).

Restructuring funding arrangements was another step under the initiative's second phase. Agreements were restructured to allow for a consistent, systematic, and simplified application of a community's risk profile across each of the various funding agreements. As such, additional and revised funding authorities were constructed in a way that provided incentives for recipients to bear greater risk for the design and delivery of local programs. Under previous universal authorities, there was no incentive to move away from the certainty provided by standard contributions funding towards models that relied on recipients' own management capacity and willingness to bear greater risk for the management of funds (INAC, 2008a). This has been the main challenge in the funding relationship: that federal departments are willing to reduce their accountability requirements, and that Indigenous recipients are willing and able to bear a greater proportion of the risk that goes with designing and managing programs while also showing the confidence necessary to account directly to their constituents.

In the third phase, that of shifting accountability to recipients, the federal government introduced the First Nations Financial Transparency Act (FNFTA) in March 2013. Its aim was to remove INAC from the complaint resolution process between First Nation community members and their community's leadership. Prior to the legislation, community members could only petition the Minister of Indigenous and Northern Affairs to access their community's audited financial statements as they were not required to post them publicly. Under the Act, non–self-governing First Nation recipients, defined under section 2(1) of the Indian Act, are required to make all financial information available directly to their members. The FNFTA was met with significant criticism by some First Nation leaders and Indigenous organizations.

Furthermore, against the backdrop of these reform efforts is an ongoing protest by Indigenous peoples, called Idle No More, initiated in December 2012 by four women, three of whom were of First Nations descent. It was instigated as a reaction in part to the suite of Indian Act legislation contained in budget Bill C-45 tabled in Parliament on 29 March 2012. The bill called for reduced protection of forests and waterways, and a change to sections 39–40 of the Indian Act referring to procedures for "absolute surrender" of Indian lands. The movement was a response to bills such as C-45 that "threaten Treaties and this Indigenous Vision of Sovereignty" to "protect water, air, land and all creation for future generations" (Land, 2013). The movement was also meant to coincide with a hunger strike by Attawapiskat Chief Theresa Spence on Victoria Island in Ottawa regarding the ongoing abuse of the treaty relationship, including the provisions of Bill C-45. Shaun Atleo, then Chief of the Assembly of First Nations, requested a meeting with the prime minister, which was eventually granted in January 2013, and which resulted in a Declaration of Commitment on 23 January 2013. It recognized "the need for fundamental change in the relationship of First Nations and the Crown," including "a revived fiscal relationship . . . that is equitable, sustainable, and includes indexing and the removal of arbitrary funding caps." The federal government indicated that it had already made a commitment to modernizing

the historical treaties, but progress on the fiscal relationship was limited to changes announced in the First Nations Financial Transparency Act. The Idle-No-More movement was a critical turning point in the relationship, as it brought forward individual and collective concerns regarding what it maintained is an equitable relationship that exploits Indigenous lands and resources. Indigenous leaders continue to highlight the effect funding caps have on the ability of local communities to deliver programs and services. They also draw attention to the deleterious effects of operating long-term programs using short-term proposal-driven funding sources, rather than building such funding into "basic programming."

Liberal Government: The Reconciliation Agenda

In June 2015, the Truth and Reconciliation Commission released its Executive Summary, which included major findings from its research and consultations, and 94 Calls to Action intended to provide specific ways the relationship could be repaired. In its final event in December 2015, the federal government committed to implementing the recommendations, including various calls to action to provide stable and reliable funding to address ongoing programmatic failures in the areas of child welfare (1, 2), education (8, 9, 55), language and culture (14, 68, 70), health (21, 23), and justice (31, 34, 72) (TRC, 319–37).

On 13 November 2015, Prime Minister Justin Trudeau made all ministerial mandate letters public, to ensure "Canadians can hold us accountable to deliver on our commitments" (PCO, 2015b). Contained in the mandate letter to the Minister of Indigenous Affairs Dr. Carolyn Bennett is a directive to "work with the Minister of Finance to establish a new fiscal relationship that lifts the 2 per cent cap on annual funding increases, and moves towards sufficient, predictable and sustained funding for First Nations communities," which by extension involves the recrafting of funding instruments for all Indigenous groups (PCO, 2015a). At the time of writing, research was underway to develop new approaches that would provide "predictable and stable funding that respects, at a minimum, the principles of the TRC and the Royal Commission on Aboriginal Peoples" (personal communication, INAC, 2016). In Budget 2016, the 2 per cent funding cap was lifted, and a commitment made to increase total funding for Indigenous programs at 22 per cent above the level of funding that would have been provided under the funding cap. In total, $8.4 billion was committed over five years beginning in 2016–17 "to improve the socio-economic conditions of Indigenous peoples and their communities," with a focus on education, infrastructure, training, and other support programs (INAC, 2016).

The narrative, of course, is ongoing and government continues to commit to reforms of the fiscal relationship as it has done many times in the past. The persistent obstacle to reform has been a demand for rigorous reporting and accountability for *public funds*, on the one hand, with the capacity to respond to such demands through effective and consistent management by recipients on the other. The fact is that donors and recipients have limited confidence that any balance can be struck with respect to treaty obligations, fiduciary duties, recipient capacity, and donor control. The next section provides the iterative technical responses to achieve some of these balances, showing that this narrative has been driven by incremental changes to existing principal-agent accountability-driven funding models, rather than a complete re-orientation that better aligns with funding equivalent to federal–provincial–territorial transfers premised on a partnership approach as recommended by RCAP in the 1990s.

Funding Mechanisms for Indigenous Peoples

The aim of this section is to show the manner in which accountability requirements are structured through the funding agreements and authorities INAC uses. Departmental control over the use of funds is exemplified in the array of funding authorities, which have over time expanded to allow for greater flexibility in the duration of agreements, and to some extent a streamlining of terms and conditions regarding the use of funds. However, to take advantage of such flexibility requires high local management capacity. In addition, some previously dedicated core funding has been reformulated into proposal-based programs, which require recipients to make annual applications that are subject to high accountability requirements. One program subject to such movement of funds to non-core areas is the overall education program, which will be used to describe the lengths to which recipients must attend to access such funding.

The Funding Regime Pre-2008: Universal Menu of Agreements

The period between 1974, when funding was delegated to Indigenous recipients, and 2008–11 culminated in a system of transfers through a menu of standardized funding agreements. The Department of Indian Affairs applied the most innovative of funding arrangements for Indian Act First Nation governments and tribal councils. As such, these are used to exemplify the most optimistic funding relationship with recipients though rooted firmly in the principal-agent approach. The menu comprised four main agreements, which are presented in Table 13.2: Contribution Agreements (CA); Comprehensive Funding Arrangement (CFA); INAC/Canada–First Nations Funding Arrangement (CFNFA); and, the generic Self-Government Transfer Agreement (SGA). The table also shows the funding authorities that comprised each. Most of these agreement types and authorities were available after 1985, and expired in 2011 with the coming into force of the Policy on Transfer Payments, as individual agreements may have been negotiated prior to 2011 when the policy was in transition. Table 13.3 provides a description of the authorities used, and the rules associated with each, including the use of unexpended funding. The Comprehensive Funding Agreement (CFA) relied more heavily on the Contribution Agreements and FTP authorities than the more flexible Canada–First Nations Funding Agreement (CFNFA). The pre-2008 agreements and authorities are described in detail here, in order to demonstrate how closely aligned these are to the current arrangements implemented after 2008.

Based on a general determination of the capacity of recipients conducted by regional offices that began 1986, recipients would sign an agreement that best suited the assessment. If the recipient was regarded as being of average capacity with some management challenges, it was provided the *default* Comprehensive Funding Agreement, and if it was deemed capable and responsible, the more flexible Canada–First Nations Funding Agreement was offered pending a refined assessment. Management-capacity assessments were conducted by regional offices, which often applied inconsistent approaches that resulted in unpredictable funding levels year over year. Equally important, regional budgets varied by annual allocations from

Table 13.2   INAC Funding Arrangements and Funding Authorities (1983–2011)

Funding Arrangement	Funding Authorities	Programs Funded by Authority
Contribution Agreements (CA)	• Contributions—one year	• Band support funding • Special project funding
Comprehensive Funding Arrangement (CFA)—Default Agreement	• Contributions—one year	• Designated core programs, such as social development, capital
	• Flexible Transfer Payment (FTP)—one year (later extended to two years)	• Designated core programs, such as housing, education, post-secondary education, band employee benefits • Self-government negotiations
	• Grant—one year	• Pilot and special projects
INAC/Canada–First Nations Funding Arrangement (CFNFA)	• Flexible Transfer Payment (FTP)—one to three years	• Some core programs such as training, land management
	• Block Funding—Alternative Funding Arrangement (AFA)—one to five years	• Most core programs, including governance and management programs, social development, education, housing, operations and maintenance
	• Targeted Funding (Contribution Agreements)—one year	• Pilot and special projects • Special education, assisted living, youth employment
Self-Government Financial Transfer Agreement (SGA)	• Conditional Grant (negotiated terms in legislation)—five years	• Block funding for all programs, with requirements for audited financial statements

Source: Indian and Northern Affairs Canada. 1996. "Overview of DAEB Evaluation Studies of INAC Funding Agreements." Ottawa: Indigenous and Northern Affairs Canada, October.

Table 13.3   Pre-2008 INAC Funding Authorities

Funding Authority	Key Attributes	Duration
Grant	• A grant can be used in any manner related to the program, project, or initiative being funded. • No performance conditions except for a final report on results. • Unspent funds remain with the recipient.	Any duration
Contribution	• Conditional transfer for non-core projects or programs • Eligible expenses are reimbursed. • Strict performance measurement conditions apply. • Unspent funds (if applicable) must be returned.	Annual
Flexible Transfer Payment (FTP)	• Annual funding is based on a formula or a fixed-cost basis • Funds cannot be used for other projects or programs, unless the department authorizes it. • Surpluses may be retained by the recipient, and carried forward and applied to the same program.	Annual
Alternative Funding Authority (AFA)	• Funds can be redistributed and reallocated to other programs within the block. • Unspent funds may be retained, and reallocated to other projects or programs in the block.	Multi-year—5 years

Source: Indian and Northern Affairs Canada, 1996.

the centre of government, making regional budgets equally unpredictable. Such circumstances are unlikely to change even under the current post-2008 funding instruments.

Funding Agreements

The Contribution Agreement (CA) pre-2008 was a single-year, single-purpose or program contractual funding instrument that involved the greatest degree of accountability and control for government and was used as the main contractual agreement between recipients (all Indigenous groups) and departments between 1950 and 1983.

The Comprehensive Funding Arrangement was the *default* agreement used by INAC to consolidate funding to First Nation governments and tribal councils from the late 1980s to 2011.[12] It used a combination of three funding authorities: Contribution Agreements, Flexible Transfer Payment (FTP), and/or Grants. The FTP funding authority simplified terms and conditions relative to Contribution Agreements, and allocated fixed funding rather than expenses being reimbursed.

The Canada–First Nations Funding agreement was a formal agreement between the Crown and recipients that funded programs for a period of five years. It used two streams of funding programs: block funding using the AFA authority for eligible programs and services, and targeted funding based on a combination of FTP and contributions authorities for other programs. These were referred to as Flexible Transfer Arrangements, and required recipients to undertake a risk-based assessment in order to determine eligibility based on capacity. This type of arrangement for non–self-governing communities came the closest to the Penner recommendations, but was still considered to be highly inflexible for exceptional communities especially (INAC, 2011: 22–3).

Self-Government Financial Transfer Agreements (SGFTA) are still used exclusively with self-governing recipients. They are multi-year grants covering all programs and services. Accountability to the Crown is limited to annual audited financial statements and provisions laid out by the recipient in its constitutional arrangements. Such agreements include provisions to report own-source revenues and revenues acquired through taxation.

In summary, no standardized national risk-assessment process existed during this period, leading to inconsistent regional interpretations of program risk. According to one 2008 INAC assessment report of the funding arrangements, "risk management, accountability and flexibility are not well balanced within funding arrangements, either in terms of the amount of money involved, the nature of the program, or the capacity of the recipients" (INAC, 2011: 2). Moreover, an unintended consequence of program design restricted First Nation recipients from progressing from contributions-type arrangements to the more flexible agreements such as the Canada–First Nations Funding Agreement. As cuts were made to programs between the 1980s and 2000s, discretionary funding was reduced by requiring recipients to apply for what became known as non-core funds. To further control costs, these programs were funded for one year using the Contribution Agreements authority, which were subject to high accountability and reporting requirements. These arrangements imposed burdensome accountability requirements, and reinforced high federal control over the terms and conditions of funding. This had the effect of reducing any probability that recipients would wish to bear the risk for more flexible arrangements that required greater accountability to members.

Post-2008 Funding Regime: Tailored Risk-Based Arrangements

With the introduction of the 2008 Policy on Transfer Payments, federal departments moved towards risk-based agreements that could be tailored to individual recipients using an expanded suite of funding authorities. Agreements after 2010 are constructed on the basis of assigning program funding using risk to determine the appropriate mix of funding authorities for each program, rather than the pre-2010 method which allocated funding to a community through a single agreement with generically assigned funding authorities for each program. The net change from the shift in Transfer Payments Policy is that individual programs are assessed for risk, and a determination is made by the department regarding the level of financial flexibility afforded to communities using a menu of authorities. For programs considered to be "low" risk, the most flexible of authorities is assigned in the overall agreement.

Several new funding agreements were created based on the requirements of the Policy on Transfer Payments, which are listed and described in Table 13.4. As of 2016/17, INAC utilized six funding agreements with Indigenous recipients. These agreements have been tailored to suit both program- and project-based needs. Likewise, new or revised funding authorities were created and combined with previous ones to offer a total of five funding authorities to be consistently applied across all funding agreements. They are: Set, Fixed, Flexible, Block, and Grant and described in Table 13.5, with the corresponding previous version for comparative purposes. The revised authorities were created as a way to reward fiscally responsible recipients, and create incentives for recipients to assume higher risk for program and services design and delivery.

Under fixed contribution and multi-year authorities, the Policy on Transfer Payments was amended to stipulate that any unspent funding may be used for other programs or activities, but a plan outlining how funds will be used must be submitted to the department no later than 120 days after the end of the project, program, or agreement. Under the previous regime, any unspent funds were automatically carried forward on behalf of the recipient. The new provisions add more accountability requirements to already rigorous provisions. They also place greater onus on recipients to manage their agreements closely, which assumes higher management capacity.

First Nation recipients with average or below-average risk scores are placed into the First Nations and Tribal Councils National Funding agreement. With greater capacity and better risk scores, recipients may opt for a more flexible framework agreement such as the Streamlined Funding Agreement, and if of high capability they may use the Canada Common Funding Agreement. Equally important, other Indigenous recipients such as Inuit and Métis communities and organizations are now provided a mechanism to receive ongoing or project-based funding.

Several combinations of funding authorities are possible depending on the funding agreement used, because risk scores determine the combination of funding authorities available to recipients for each program and service, with some standardization for designated

Table 13.4 Current INAC Funding Agreements

Type of Agreement	Description
First Nations and Tribal Councils National Funding Agreement	• Available to First Nation and tribal council recipients. • Considered the "default" and basic agreement, similar to that of the CFA.
Streamlined Funding Agreement Model for First Nations	• Only available to First Nations communities. New agreement type. • An optional agreement that uses plain language, removes complex terminology, and reduces delivery terms and conditions.
Canada Common Funding Agreement Model	• A harmonized funding agreement for First Nation communities and Tribal Councils that receive funding from Health Canada and INAC. Similar to CFNFA. • Requires one set of consolidated audited financial statements instead of two, and combines and reduces the recipient reporting requirements of each department into one set of requirements.
Plain/Simplified Funding Agreement Model for Project Funding	• Similar to the Streamlined Funding Agreement Model for First Nations, but is available for funding recipients that are not a First Nation community or tribal council, and is for proposal-based funding. • Used when a funding recipient does not have any other agreement in place with INAC. Similar to Contribution Agreement (CA).
Funding Agreement Model for Other Recipients	• Used for program, project, or service delivery by a recipient other than First Nation communities and tribal councils (with the exception self-governing First Nations for programs, projects and services not covered by their agreement).

Source: Indigenous and Northern Affairs Canada, 2016.

Table 13.5   Current Funding Authorities

Funding Authority	Key Attributes	Duration
Grant (Same as Grant)	• Can be used in any manner related to the program, project, or initiative being funded. • No performance conditions. • Unspent funds remain with the recipient.	Any duration
Set (Same as Contribution)	• Funding must be spent as stipulated in the funding agreement and cannot be transferred to any other program, project, or service. • Strict performance measurement conditions apply. • Unspent funds (if applicable) must be returned.	Annual
Fixed (Revisions to FTP)	• Funding is based on a formula or a fixed-cost basis. • Funds cannot be transferred to other projects or programs, unless authorized. • Surpluses may be retained by the recipient, and carried forward and applied to the same program.	Annual
Flexible (Variant of FTP)	• Funds can be used within the same cost categories of the program being funded. • An established relationship of two years must exist between the donor and recipient. • Available to communities with a lower range General Assessment score. • Unspent funds remaining upon expiry must be returned.	Multi-year—Up to 10 years
Block (Revisions to AFA)	• Funds can be redistributed and reallocated to other programs within the block as identified in the funding agreement. • Available to communities with a lower range General Assessment score. • Unspent funds may be retained, and reallocated to other projects or programs in the block.	Multi-year—Up to 10 years

Source: Indigenous and Northern Affairs Canada, 2016.

programs. However, a key concern raised by recipients based on comparison of the pre- and post-2008 Policy on Transfer Payments is that there is greater reliance on the Contributions/Set funding authority, and a noticeable shift to proposal-driven program funding as this affords the greatest degree of accountability and control for departmental managers.[13]

An Applied Look at Education Funding

The following illustration explores how education funding is constructed using the funding authorities as applied to each of the funding agreements, regardless of type. Essential, or core funding, is guaranteed to recipients and still covers operations and maintenance, tuitions, and basic support using a mixture of contributions under the Set, Fixed, Flexible, Block, and Grant funding authorities. As with other programs, INAC continues to move towards a proposal-based approach as shown in Table 13.6, and as evidenced with respect to four sub-programs listed as *complementary*

(or optional) under the First Nations Elementary and Secondary Educational Advancement program. Such programs address *targeted*[14] areas for investment, and may be funded mainly using the Set, Fixed, or Flexible funding authorities. These programs are High Cost Special Education Program, New Paths for Education, Education Partnerships Program, and First Nation Student Success Program.

The objective of these *complementary* programs is to support core education funding by providing targeted financial resources to improve literacy, numeracy, and student retention where recipients require this specific funding assistance. The challenge, however, is that although recipient communities welcome the additional resources targeted and complementary programs provide, the programs do not offer long-term sustainability. Access to those funds depends on the quality of the application, and it is provided based on availability of funds and the number of qualified applicants. Increasingly, the demand for

Table 13.6   Targeted Funding for Education Programming

Program Area Description	Funding Authority per Sub-Program		
	Sub-Programs	**Authority**	**Sub-Programs**
Program Purpose: INAC describes the program purpose as "To provide eligible First Nation and Inuit students with support in order to achieve educational outcomes that are comparable to those of other Canadians."	First Nations and Inuit Post-Secondary Educational Advancement	Grant and Contribution	• No application process for contribution funding. • Application process for grant funding. *Proposal Required for the following Complementary Program:* • Post-Secondary Partnership Program (Set)
Provides Funding for: First Nations and Inuit	First Nations Elementary and Secondary Educational Advancement	Grant and Contribution (Set. Fixed, and Block only).	• No application required for core contribution funding. • Application required for grant funding. *Proposal Required for the following Complementary Programs:* • High Cost Special Education (Set) • New Paths for Education (Set) • Education Partnerships Program (Set) • First Nation Student Success Program (Set)
	First Nations and Inuit Youth Participation in Education and Labour Market Opportunities	Grant and Contributions	• Applicant required for: Inuit Cultural Advancement grant. *Proposal Required for the following Complementary Programs:* • Cultural Education Centres Program (Set and Fixed) • First Nations and Inuit Youth Employment strategy (Set and Fixed) • Indspire (Set)

Source: Indigenous and Northern Affairs Canada, 2016.

such funding is growing annually across all regions, and it is conceivable that funding levels can vary significantly from year to year. In the case of education targeted funding, a small proportion of funds is dispersed through grants, normally to cover administrative costs, but the majority of funds is dispersed through more restrictive authorities.

The Standing Committee on Aboriginal People studied the effects of targeted funding in education in 2011, and noted that "statutory funding for First Nations education is necessary to ensure the stable and predictable financing required for planning, teacher retention and recruitment, language instruction, culturally relevant curriculum development, assessment, data collection and management and a range of other critical activities necessary to support

a modern educational program" (Standing Senate Committee on Aboriginal People, 2011: 63). Likewise, the Assembly of First Nations concluded that much-needed language training was outside the core of education programming, which is placing pressure on more vulnerable communities that cannot access targeted funds to the same extent as highly capable communities (AFN, 2012).

Concluding Comments

The chapter First Nations and the Public Sector found in the second edition of this volume concluded that there is a "stubborn single-policy directedness on the part of the federal government with respect to First Nations governance and administrative policy preferences . . . the dominant narrative of federal control continues unabated" (Shepherd, 2010: 344). Despite a shift to risk-based agreements that ideally would tailor agreements to the management capacity of recipients, funding to Indigenous communities and organizations remains driven by high control, rigorous accountability requirements, and significant reporting. Several Auditor General of Canada reports, various special studies conducted by federal departments, a plethora of evaluation studies on the effects of previous agreements and authorities, and parliamentary inquiries and royal commissions have each concluded that a new way to construct fiscal relationships with Indigenous peoples is sorely needed. Except for self-governing communities, accountability continues to be structured using principal-agent approaches, and even this is a contestable conclusion (Shepherd, 2006). Figure 13.1 shows the placement of current funding instruments against principal-agent and dual-accountability constructs, and the degree of discretion afforded to recipients. It sums up the high emphasis on federal accountability requirements, and low flexibility regarding the use of funding as prescribed in the delivery terms and conditions of

funding agreements. RCAP (1996b: 295–311) placed the ideal fiscal relationship as mirroring that of statutory federal–provincial–territorial and local transfer payments, where these jurisdictions are understood constitutionally as separate and equal partners. It also shows that there is much room for development of instruments that can offer intermediate alternatives between current block contributions and self-government agreements.

Overall, federal departments have been reluctant to embrace more flexible funding authorities and agreement frameworks, despite the largely aspirational objectives prescribed in the 2008 Policy on Transfer Payments. It has been consistently observed that departments do not wish to give up control and reduce accountability, which has been routinely criticized in Auditor General and other reports for not delivering on programmatic results. Despite a clear division of responsibility for setting administrative requirements for departments, and recipient responsibilities for program and funding management, the expectation remains that ministers are held to account for local results. As long as such boundary issues go unresolved, it is highly unlikely that ministers will be

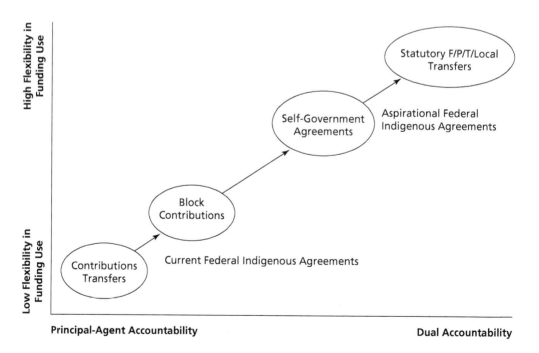

Figure 13.1 Funding Arrangements Relative to Accountability and Flexibility

willing to give up control for recipients' use of funds. Combined with federal fiduciary and treaty obligations to provide support for programs and services to Indigenous peoples, there is a real conundrum that will not be straightforward to resolve. The Royal Commission on Aboriginal Peoples remains a standard against which a new fiscal relationship can be structured, but until local capacity is bolstered, such a vision will be delayed by transition mechanisms such as the ones in place currently. The reality is, however, that such transitions have been occurring for decades with some limited progress towards building capacity, but a coordinated national effort in partnership with Indigenous peoples is needed so that an RCAP or similar vision can firmly take root. At present, the fiscal relationship is focused on satisfying federal policy and programmatic obligations, with very little attention dedicated to recipient policy and program needs and demands, other than creating the conditions necessary for multiple years of funding. That said, funding levels remain inconsistent from year to year, and those levels cannot keep pace with population growth. Nevertheless, there is anticipation that removing the two per cent funding cap will alleviate some of that pressure.

The majority of programmatic funding is still funded under a Contribution Agreements set of authorities with high degrees of accountability and reporting requirements. With such a focus on compliance to delivery terms and conditions, little information is available with respect to outcomes achievement. Although there is greater emphasis in recent reporting guides on results, few recipients are measuring them as there is little incentive to do so. Reporting is intended to provide assurance to funders that they are complying with the rules, especially those related to eligible and ineligible expenditures. As long as this remains the case, most recipients will focus on compliance, and only the most capable of recipients will turn their attention to results achievement as benefits to their communities.

Recipients continue to seek coordination of funding instruments that are harmonized across funding agencies, as funding authorities and rules remain irreconcilable. Recipients view their relationship with Canada, not with individual funding agencies (Goodtrack, 2016). The previous CFNFA, and the most recent Canada-Common Funding Agreement,

attempt to provide a single window for funding, but gaining agreement on harmonized and consistent accountability and reporting requirements from departments and jurisdictions remains elusive. For recipients, this means investing significant time and human resources to satisfy the hundreds of accountability reports required in order to remain eligible for continued funding. Although departmental reporting internally may have decreased, there is no evidence to suggest that recipient reporting has decreased significantly since the Auditor General first reported on this issue in 2002, and updated it in 2011. In fact, the Auditor General actually reported an increase in reporting burden in 2011 for Indigenous recipients due mainly to increased accountability requirements, although the new transfer requirements were still in transition at that time (OAG 2011, at 4.83). INAC reported in 2013/14 that its reporting requirements for recipients had decreased with the implementation of the First Nations Financial Transparency Act, but no reports have been provided to validate the claim.

The narrative provided is not very optimistic, but the reconciliation agenda holds out the hope that change in fiscal relations is possible. There are no simple solutions to move this narrative forward or to change its trajectory. The problem is confounded by urban-rural community differences, high versus low management capacity communities and organizations, differing accountability standards and obligations across governmental and Indigenous organizations, and a general lack of confidence and optimism that change is possible. Transfer payments are not simply vehicles to distribute financial resources, but embody several competing values, including one of mutual respect. Some general conditions are necessary in order for reconciliation to yield tangible benefits.

First, communities and organizations will require dedicated training in management, especially financial management. As more onus is placed on communities and organizations to assume control over programs and services, people will require the requisite skills to manage funding agreements, including preparing budgets, financial reports, and improving accountability arrangements within their communities.

Second, governmental departments in all jurisdictions that work closely with Indigenous peoples should gain some understanding as to the history and conditions surrounding the Indigenous relationship, as the Truth and Reconciliation Commission report suggests. Connections with Indigenous governments and organizations will only increase as greater powers are afforded to those organizations. It will be crucial that those connections, including fiscal relations, are understood and informed.

Third, creating the conditions necessary for self-determination is needed to establish healthy political institutions. At present, governmental focus is on administering reserve-based communities, with limited attention paid to urban Indigenous communities and structures. The fiscal relationship should be premised on satisfying the *needs* of the various communities, rather than on perpetuating a compliance- and rules-driven system that reinforces governmental control under an Indian Act framework. Also important, as explained in RCAP, is the ability to generate own-source revenues, to create tax systems to reinforce local participation in governance, and to renew a resources relationship with Canada and the provinces. Current funding arrangements should rely on fixed funding formulas rather than variable funding formulas, to provide greater predictability in local budgets year over year.

Fourth, accountability arrangements must be negotiated in a way that respects both governmental and Indigenous expectations. It is widely accepted, as the narrative shows, that governmental accountability is excessive, but it is equally the case that reliable and documented accountability measures are needed in Indigenous governments and organizations to provide assurance that resources will be managed effectively. That said, it is accepted that Indigenous peoples themselves demand the highest propriety from their leaders, and are pushing for better accountability processes. Such efforts should be supported, rather than imposing additional rules when improprieties come to light. Such reports should be taken as a sign that community members are engaged, and willing to hold their leadership to account.

The challenge in meeting these conditions is alleviating fear in Indigenous communities that any departure from the status quo will negate or limit application of the treaties, governmental fiduciary obligations, or certainties associated with the *Indian Act* regime. It will take much dialogue to overcome these concerns, but the commitment to Canadian institutions, Charter of Rights and Freedoms, and the

commitment of Canadians and Indigenous peoples to the country will hold as Indigenous aspirations for a new relationship are realized. If anything can be concluded from this narrative, it is that the status quo is not sustainable. The current momentum created as a result of the Truth and Reconciliation Commission, Idle No More, the Inquiry into Murdered and Missing Indigenous Women and Girls, and the federal and provincial reconciliation agendas, should be capitalized upon while public attention is focused on them.

Epilogue

Since this chapter was submitted, three important developments were observed that will influence the funding relationship between the federal Crown and Indigenous communities and organizations. The first significant development was a document released by Justice Canada on 19 July 2017 regarding "Principles respecting the Government of Canada's relationship with Indigenous Peoples" (Justice Canada, 2017). This principles document is intended to provide a guide to implement the United Nations Declaration on the Rights of Indigenous Peoples. The principles themselves are a formal recognition of section 35 of the Constitution Act, 1982, which "holds the promise that Indigenous nations will become partners in Confederation on the basis of a fair and just reconciliation between Indigenous peoples and the Crown." Specifically, principle 8 states that, "The Government of Canada recognizes that reconciliation and self-government require a renewed fiscal relationship, developed in collaboration with Indigenous nations, that promotes a mutually supportive climate for economic partnership and resource development." Such recognition includes fair access to lands, territories, and resources to support traditional economies, and "to share in the wealth generated by those lands and resources." The federal Crown appears open to various revenue-generating mechanisms such as new tax arrangements, fiscal transfers, and the negotiation of revenue-sharing agreements.

The posting of the principles document informed the second development, an announcement made by Indigenous Affairs Minister, Carolyn Bennett, following meetings of the Assembly of First Nations on 25 July 2017 in Regina. The federal minister declared that changes will be made to the funding model for First Nations, stating that "greater fiscal and financial autonomy is necessary for First Nations to provide good governance for their communities and respond appropriately to the priorities and challenges" (CBC, 2017). Specifically, Minister Bennett indicated that funding not used by the end of the fiscal year (31 March) will not have to be returned to the federal government. At present, all funding that uses the contributions authority (Set and Fixed) has to be used in the current year, including most funds for capital projects such as housing. The change would allow First Nations communities and organizations to better plan program and capital fund expenditures based on their own timing, rather than on the federal government's fiscal year. Promises for change to the fiscal relationship were previously made at the 2016 annual meeting of the AFN in Niagara Falls.

The third significant development involved an announcement on 28 August 2017 by Prime Minister Trudeau, that the Indigenous and Northern Affairs Canada (INAC) would be split into two departments. The first department, Crown-Indigenous Relations and Northern Affairs, will be responsible for creating a new relationship with Indigenous peoples. It will lead a consultation process "to determine how best to replace INAC with the two departments [and] will be tasked with better whole-of-government coordination on our nation-to-nation, Inuit-Crown, and government-to-government relationships" (PMO, 2017). The second department, Indigenous Services Canada, will be responsible for improving the quality of services to First Nations, Inuit, and Métis people. This department will carry out much of the work currently performed by INAC, but with greater attention to creating the conditions for Indigenous peoples to support self-determination and self-government. In addition, this new department will consolidate many of the programs for Indigenous peoples currently provided by other federal departments. The approach to a new federal departmental structure was first made by the Royal Commission on Aboriginal Peoples in 1996 to divide federal responsibilities into several parts led by the prime minister, federal Cabinet, Privy Council Office, and two new departments along the lines announced in August 2017 (RCAP, 1996b: 361).

The combination of these major initiatives at the very least demonstrates a concerted willingness and commitment on the part of the federal government to shake up and repair the nature of the relationship with Indigenous peoples. It is equally clear that the current prime minister wishes to leave a legacy of Indigenous reconciliation that will be difficult for future governments to alter. The setting of key principles for implementing the UN Declaration is a positive step that will guide federal relationship building with Indigenous peoples, and the creation of the two departments brings prominence to reconciliation built into federal cabinet structures that is unparalleled by promises made by previous administrations. There will certainly be concerns that splitting INAC will cause bureaucratic turmoil, and that competition for funding could increase. However, such concerns may be offset by the efficiencies of bringing all Indigenous programming under one department, which may have the effect of further focusing federal commitment to Indigenous programming. It is also the case that a shake-up is long overdue in bureaucratic mindsets aimed at fiscal accountability, rather than creating programming that supports reconciliation and a movement towards self-determination.

The challenge will be to follow through on crafting new fiscal arrangements that promote the larger federal agenda for Indigenous self-determination and self-government. The announced changes to the current fiscal authorities is a step in the right direction, but a deeper assessment is necessary that address not only matters of lapsing of funds, but that radically re-thinks the perspective of risk-based management that privileges the reduction of federal risk at the expense of local communities and organizations. More importantly, conditional funding arrangements will have to be re-thought with a view to embracing block funding authorities, considered to be the preferred choice since at least the Penner Report recommendations of the 1980s. In addition, more emphasis will have to be placed on capacity building in financial management and governance with the view to improving local governance. It is not enough to build better financial arrangements: it will be imperative to support capable and sustainable Indigenous governments, which is where the Royal Commission on Aboriginal Peoples ultimately was aiming its recommendations.

Important Terms and Concepts

accountability
Contribution Agreements
delegated authorities
dual accountability

Indian
Indian Act reform
non-status Indian

Report of the Royal Commission on
   Aboriginal Peoples
status Indian

Study Questions

1. What is accountability? What are the variants of accountability that can apply to Indigenous governments and organizations?
2. What are funding authorities? And, why are these important in terms of understanding Indigenous accountability requirements under the funding agreements?
3. Why are there multiple funding agreements in place? Are current arrangements any different from previous versions?
4. What is meant by reconciliation as it applies to Indigenous peoples? What promise does it hold to repair the fiscal relationship?
5. What conditions are necessary to advance the fiscal relationship between government and Indigenous peoples?

Notes

1   The author acknowledges the research and editing effort of Andrew Swift, PhD Candidate, Carleton University. His time and energy on this chapter were much appreciated.

2   The Gradual Civilization Act, 1857 was used to enfranchise male Indians. As an incentive, recipients were offered 50 acres of land (which remained federal land) within the reserve and a share of the principal treaty annuities and other band monies owed. The Act triggered future legislation aimed at defining status Indians and universal approaches to enfranchisement. After Confederation, for example, this Act was replaced by the Gradual Enfranchisement Act, 1869, which was much more invasive.

3   There are exceptions to this statement, because the federal government provides many programs and services to off-reserve Indigenous peoples either directly or by way of provincial transfers. It is contestable as to whether these programs and services constitute recognition of an obligation to Indigenous peoples, or come under the equality provisions of section 15 of the Charter.

4   For more discussion of band recognition, see: Paul A. H. Chartrand and Harry W. Daniels. 2002. *Who Are Canada's Aboriginal Peoples?: Recognition, Definition and Jurisdiction*. Saskatoon: Purich Publishing, pp. 48–51.

5   The Inuit were explicitly excluded from the Indian Act in the 1951 revisions, as they would have been required to organize themselves into bands and conform to the definition of Indian.

6   Note: The name of this policy has changed on several occasions. The previous version was called the Transfer Payments Policy, and came into force in 2000. The current version has been in force since 2008, but provisions related to Indigenous recipients came into force on 31 March 2010.

7   Dual accountability refers to a division of responsibilities between donors and recipients, and an associated framework of accountability for each party's responsibilities. In the Indigenous context, it is seen as a "dual" obligation to account to government for the use of funds, and to the community for the effectiveness of programs and services. It does not mean "shared," but rather obligations assigned to each party.

8   Harold Cardinal referred to the policy as a "a thinly disguised programme of extermination through assimilation" in his 1999 book, *The Unjust Society*.

9   INAC defined basic needs as the provision of water, sewage, basic housing, social assistance, and education in their Outlook on Priorities and Expenditures, 1995–1996 to 1997–1998.

10   Indian Act., s. 2(1) meaning: "all monies collected, received or held by Her Majesty for the use and benefit of Indians or bands."

11   There are variations to these categories depending on the type of funding agreements being considered.

12   The agreement type was developed jointly with Health Canada and Justice Canada.

13   See, for example, concerns regarding education funding: Assembly of First Nations, "Federal Funding for First Nations Schools," Ottawa: AFN, 1 October 2012. http://www.afn.ca/uploads/files/events/fact_sheet-ccoe-8.pdf

14   Targeted funding refers to programs that are not funded automatically in an agreement, and that can be funded using pre-determined funding authorities. For example, under the CFNFA, 17 programs were identified as eligible for targeted funding, of which nine only allowed for Contribution Agreements (i.e., Set) funding.

References

Assembly of First Nations. 2002. "Preliminary Analysis: First Nations Governance Act." Ottawa, 14 June.

Assembly of First Nations. 2012. "Federal Funding for First Nations Schools." http://www.afn.ca/uploads/files/events/fact_sheet-ccoe-8.pdf.

Assembly of First Nations. 2013. "Declaration of Commitment." http://www.afn.ca/en/news-media/latest-news/declaration-of-commitment-january-23-2013.

Assembly of First Nations. n.d. "Description of the AFN." http://www.afn.ca/en/about-afn/description-of-the-afn.

Campbell, Ian Chief. 2014. "Statement to the Truth and Reconciliation Commission of Canada." *Traditional Knowledge Keepers Forum*.

Canada. 1889. "Annual Report of Commissioner Reed to the SGIA." *Sessional Paper No. 12*, 31 October 31.

Canada. 1983. *Indian Self-Government in Canada*. Report of the Special Committee on Indian Self-Government. Ottawa: Queen's Printer.

Cardinal, Harold. 1999. *The Unjust Society*. Vancouver: Douglas & McIntyre.

CBC. 2017. "Changes coming to First Nations funding, feds tell AFN." http://www.cbc.ca/news/indigenous/changes-coming-to-federal-funding-first-nations-1.4220627

Cornell, Steven, Michael Jorgensen, and Joseph Kalt. 2002. "The First Nations Governance Act: Implications of Research Findings from the United States and Canada." *Report Prepared for the Office of the BC Regional Vice-Chief, Assembly of First Nations*. Vancouver: Assembly of First Nations.

Furi, Megan, and Jill Wherrett. 2003. "Indian Status and Band Membership Issues (BP-410E)." Political and Social Affairs Division, Library of Parliament, February 1996. Revised 2003. Ottawa. http://www.lop.parl.gc.ca/content/lop/researchpublications/bp410-e.htm.

Goodtrack, Terry. 2016. "Presentation to IPAC Conference: Accountability," Toronto, ON. 27 June.

Harmon, Michael. 1995. *Responsibility as Paradox: A Critique of Rational Discourse on Government*. Thousand Oaks: Sage Publications.

Indian Act R.S.C., 1985, C. I-5. http://laws-lois.justice.gc.ca/PDF/I-5.pdf.

Indian and Northern Affairs Canada. 1995. "The Outlook on Priorities and Expenditures, 1995–1996 to 1997–1998." Ottawa. http://publications.gc.ca/site/eng/9.657643/publication.html.

Indian and Northern Affairs Canada. 1996. "Overview of DAEB Evaluation Studies of INAC Funding Agreements." Ottawa: Indigenous and Northern Affairs Canada, October 1996.

Indian and Northern Affairs Canada. 2008a. "Special Study on INAC's Funding Arrangements: Final Report." Ottawa. https://www.aadnc-aandc.gc.ca/eng/1100100011584/1100100011589.

Indigenous and Northern Affairs Canada. 2008b. "Statement of Apology to Former Students of Indian Residential Schools." https://www.aadnc-aandc.gc.ca/eng/1100100015644/1100100015649.

Indigenous and Northern Affairs Canada. 2011. "Special Study: Evolving Funding Arrangements with First Nations." https://www.aadnc-aandc.gc.ca/eng/1340036355882/1340036555798.

Indigenous and Northern Affairs Canada. 2012. "Reducing the Administrative Burden on First Nations." http://www.aadnc-aandc.gc.ca/eng/1354134199379/1354134226245.

Indigenous and Northern Affairs Canada. 2014a. "First Nations People in Canada." https://www.aadnc-aandc.gc.ca/eng/1303134042666/1303134337338#fnb1.

Indigenous and Northern Affairs Canada. 2014b. "General Assessment (GA) Workbook." https://www.aadnc-aandc.gc.ca/eng/1390855955971/1390855996632.

Indigenous and Northern Affairs Canada. 2015. "Terms and Conditions for AANDC Transfer Payments." https://www.aadnc-aandc.gc.ca/eng/1385747327206/1385747397222.

Indigenous and Northern Affairs Canada. 2016. "Budget 2016 Highlights – Indigenous and Northern Investments." https://www.aadnc-aandc.gc.ca/eng/1458682313288/1458682419457.

Justice Canada. 2017. "Principles respecting the Government of Canada's relationship with Indigenous peoples." http://www.justice.gc.ca/eng/csj-sjc/principles-principes.html

Kelowna Accord. 2005. "First Ministers and National Aboriginal Leaders: Strengthening Relationships and Closing the Gap, Aboriginal Leaders." Kelowna, 23 November.

Land, Lorraine. 2013. "A Legislative Road Map As Idle No More Revs Up." http://www.oktlaw.com/blog/a-legislative-road-map-as-idle-no-more-revs-up/.

Leslie, John F. 1993. "A Historical Survey of Indian-Government Relations, 1940–1970." Ottawa: Department of Indian Affairs and Northern Development.

Métis National Council. n.d. "Métis Nation Citizenship." http://www.metisnation.ca/index.php/who-are-the-metis/citizenship.

Morse, Bradford, and John Giokas. 1995. "Do the Métis Fall within Section 91(24) of the Constitution Act 1867?" *Report of the Royal Commission on Aboriginal Peoples, Aboriginal Self-Government: Legal and Constitutional Issues*. Ottawa: Supply and Services.

Office of the Auditor General of Canada. 2002. "Chapter 1—Streamlining First Nations Reporting to Federal Organizations." *December Report of the Auditor General*. Ottawa: Supply and Services. http://www.oag-bvg.gc.ca/internet/English/parl_oag_200212_01_e_12395.html.

Office of the Auditor General of Canada. 2006. "Chapter 5—Management of Programs for First Nations." *May Status Report of the Auditor General of Canada*. Ottawa: Supply and Services. http://www.oag-bvg.gc.ca/internet/English/parl_oag_200605_05_e_14962.html.

Office of the Auditor General of Canada. 2011. "Chapter 4—Programs for First Nations on Reserves." *Report of the Auditor General of Canada to the House of Commons*. Ottawa, Supply and Services. http://www.oag-bvg.gc.ca/internet/English/parl_oag_201106_04_e_35372.html

Prime Minister's Office. 2015. "Prime Minister of Canada Makes Ministerial Mandate Letters Public." http://pm.gc.ca/eng/news/2015/11/13/prime-minister-canada-makes-ministerial-mandate-letters-public.

Prime Minister's Office. 2017. "New Ministers to support the renewed relationship with Indigenous Peoples." http://pm.gc.ca/eng/news/2017/08/28/new-ministers-support-renewed-relationship-indigenous-peoples

Privy Council Office. 2001. "Speech from the Throne to Open the First Session of the 37th Parliament of Canada." http://www.pco-pcp.gc.ca/index.asp?lang=eng&page=information&sub=publications&doc=aarchives/sft-ddt/2001-eng.htm.

Privy Council Office, 2015a. Minister of Indigenous and Northern Affairs Mandate Letter, 2015 http://pm.gc.ca/eng/minister-indigenous-and-northern-affairs-mandate-letter

Privy Council Office, 2015b. Prime Minister's Mandate Letters. http://pm.gc.ca/eng/mandate-letters

RCAP, Royal Commission on Aboriginal Peoples.1996a. "Indian Act: Indian Women." *Report of the Royal Commission on Aboriginal Peoples*. Ottawa: Supply and Services.

RCAP, Royal Commission on Aboriginal Peoples. 1996b. "Restructuring the Relationship." *Report of the Royal Commission on Aboriginal Peoples*. Ottawa: Supply and Services.

Shepherd, Robert P. 2006. "Moving Tenuously Toward Lasting Self-Government for First Nations:

Understanding Differences with Respect to Implementing Accountability." University of Toronto. doi:10.3102/00346543067001043.

Shepherd, Robert P. 2010. "First Nations and the Public Sector: Understanding Accountability and Its Impacts on Governance Relationships." *The Handbook of Canadian Public Administration*, 2nd edn, edited by Christopher Dunn, Don Mills: Oxford University Press, pp. 330–49.

Standing Senate Committee on Aboriginal People. 2011. "Reforming First Nations Education: From Crisis to Hope." Ottawa, Parliament of Canada. http://www.parl.gc.ca/content/sen/committee/411/appa/rep/rep03dec11-e.pdf.

Statistics Canada. 2011. "Table 1 Aboriginal Identity Population, Canada, 2011." *National Household Survey*. http://www12.statcan.ca/nhs-enm/2011/as-sa/99-011-x/2011001/tbl/tbl01-eng.cfm.

Statistics Canada. 2015. "Demographics—Aboriginal Statistics at a Glance." http://www.statcan.gc.ca/pub/89-645-x/2015001/demo-eng.htm.

Supreme Court of Canada. 1939. "Reference whether "Indians" includes "Eskimo,"" S.C.R 104.

Supreme Court of Canada. 2016. *Daniels v. Canada (Indian Affairs and Northern Development)*, SCC 12.

Treasury Board of Canada Secretariat. 1986. "Decision of the Treasury Board Meeting of 27 November 1986." Ottawa, 27 November.

Treasury Board of Canada Secretariat. 1989. "Decision of the Treasury Board: Meeting of 26 July 1989." Ottawa, 26 July.

Treasury Board of Canada Secretariat. 2006. "From Red Tape to Clear Results: The Report of the Independent Blue Ribbon Panel on Grant and Contribution Programs." http://publications.gc.ca/collections/Collection/BT22-109-2007E.pdf.

Treasury Board of Canada Secretariat. 2008a. "Directive on Transfer Payments." https://www.tbs-sct.gc.ca/pol/doc-eng.aspx?id=14208

Treasury Board of Canada Secretariat. 2008b. "Policy on Transfer Payments." https://www.tbs-sct.gc.ca/pol/doc-eng.aspx?id=13525.

Truth and Reconciliation Commission of Canada. 2015. "Honouring the Truth, Reconciling the Future." *Final Report of the Truth and Reconciliation Commission of Canada*. Ottawa: Library and Archives.

Part  **IV**

The Processes of Canadian Public Administration

After structures, after organization, there are the processes of government. These are the patterned operations in the public sector that serve the needs of actors at certain stages. The needs can be broad, as in establishing a mission or missions for the public sector, or more narrow, as in budgeting and collective bargaining. Most observers would agree that government processes have changed substantially in the last few decades. Charting the exact nature of the changes, however, is less likely to elicit agreement. In Part 3, the contributors discuss these changes in public administration and the practical reasons for, and visions behind, the changes that have occurred in recent years.

Michael Howlett covers the policy process in the first chapter in this section. He describes it as composing policy cycles and policy styles. A policy-cycle approach says that policy-making occurs over time and as a process rather than as a specific decision or piece of legislation. In his view (and there are many authors' views on this), the cycle involves five elements: *agenda-setting*, *policy formulation*, *decision-making*, *policy implementation*, and *policy evaluation*. Policy styles refer to the methods government uses to create and implement policies. The policy-styles approach is useful in describing the different models put forward earlier in the history of policy studies, such as the rational, incremental, and garbage-can models. Howlett describes the components—the constituent parts—of public policy, provides an historical overview of public policy theory, and considers problems with existing models.

Alasdair Roberts takes a very complex subject—the evolution of the Canadian government—and simplifies it for the reader by considering the history of government in Canada in identifiable periods. Roberts reminds us that a sense of mission marked a number of periods during the evolution of the Canadian public service in the twentieth century. Paradoxically, with a new era of budget surpluses starting as early as the mid-1990s, there was no overarching conception, after so many years of deficits, as to how to spend these surplus government funds. Policy-makers were wary about preaching big government as a panacea for every problem. Promotion of the knowledge-based economy is a likely candidate for the new mission. However, he says, the same problems that bedevilled the last century would likely continue, particularly policy-area disputes between the federal and provincial governments and various international areas of contention, especially between Canada and the United States. Roberts provides both a useful summary of where we have been and a challenge to determine where we should be going.

David Zussman is the country's leading expert on political transitions. Transitions are one of the most fundamental elements that describe a democracy. They involve the peaceful transfer of power from one political leader to another and often involve a change in the political parties that govern a nation. This is either an exhilarating or disappointing experience for the participants—depending on whether you are part of the winning or losing political party. His chapter describes transitions at the federal level from 1984 to the present. It is intended to serve as a primer for those interested in transition planning by looking at best practices in Canada.

Matti Siemiatycki covers in Chapter 17 what has become a growth area. Across Canada, governments of all level have increasingly embraced public–private partnerships (PPPs) as their preferred approach to deliver large-scale public infrastructure. After thirty years of practice, this paper examines the evolving rationales, governance structures, and partnership models that have been used to deliver PPPs in Canada. In particular, the analysis highlights common deal structures, types of risks and responsibilities that are transferred to the private sector, and the significant role that public funding continues to have. Siemiatycki finishes by reviewing outstanding issues facing Canadian PPPs. These include their high upfront costs, limitations placed on meaningful community consultations, and a procurement process that can inhibit design or architectural excellence.

Michael J. Prince surveys major historical phases of budget reform and budget making at the federal level of government from the early twentieth to the early twenty-first centuries. Any budget system in some way addresses a trilogy of aims: the control of spending and taxing, the management of ongoing program activities, and the planning of policy and setting of priorities.

The balance between them, however, may differ as between governments. Prince discusses the contemporary politics of federal budgeting with a focus on the dynamics of recent minority governments, the Stephen Harper era and the Justin Trudeau Government. Every government uses the budget system for establishing public purposes and the public sectors own participation in civil society and the market economy. The Harper and Trudeau Governments evidence shifts in the priority accorded to financial control and strategic planning, while the improvement of management performance remains elusive at the federal level of public administration.

Human resources policy is concerned with public sector labour relations, but as Morley Gunderson, Robert Hebdon and Michele Campolieti emphasize in Chapter 19, collective bargaining is only one aspect of labour relations. Determining the future of public-sector labour relations requires an understanding of where it has been. Labour relations in the Canadian public sector have a mixed history of market determination, collective bargaining, and legislative and regulatory action. Perhaps, as Gunderson, Hebdon, and Campolieti suggest, its development can be considered an evolution from collective begging to collective bargaining, and in the 1990s, as a result of legislated initiatives, a partial return to the begging mode. Initially, small portions of the public sector—for example, in municipal governments—were covered by the same legislation that applied to the private sector. There followed a period of informal bargaining between governments and employee associations, which represented large parts of the public sector workforce, setting the precedent for modern collective bargaining between governments and large employee unions.

Formal collective bargaining in the public sector began in 1944 in Saskatchewan and evolved gradually in other Canadian jurisdictions. Societal impulses combined with increasing power of public-sector employees has resulted in higher unionization rates here (30 per cent) than in the United States (15 per cent). Various legislative options have been used to mediate relations between governments and their employees, including reliance on legislation drafted for private-sector labour relations, modifications of this legislation to accommodate the public sector, and hybrids. Dispute resolution mechanisms have included the right to strike, a limited right to strike, binding arbitration, arbitration requested by either party, and choice of procedure in advance of negotiation. The unfettered right to strike is most common, but no uniform pattern prevails for all of the public service even within one jurisdiction or across all jurisdictions. The differences reflect varying effects of parties, interest groups, special events, and sometimes merely inertia.

Despite the existence of formal strike rights on paper, strikes and collective bargaining can be circumscribed by various means. Designated (or "essential") employees may be prohibited from striking, arbitration chosen by one party may neutralize the strike weapon, and the public-service employer may not have an incentive to settle if it retains its revenue-garnering potential during strikes. In the case of broad collective bargaining, there are also structural impediments: a multiplicity of fragmented bargaining units; legalistic, adversarial government attitudes; and a patchwork of narrow job classifications that inhibit teamwork. Even pay-equity legislation can be considered a legislated method of wage determination, removing the issue from the sphere of conventional collective bargaining. Without these constraining factors, strike activity in the public sector would be much wider than it has been. At issue is whether the public-sector bargaining model, especially the traditional system of collective bargaining present in Canada today, can deal with the new issues emerging in the public sphere.

The Policy Process

Michael Howlett

Chapter Overview

This chapter argues for analyzing policy development in terms of policy cycles and policy styles. A policy cycle approach says that policy-making occurs over time and as a process rather than as a specific decision or piece of legislation. In this chapter, the cycle is defined as comprising five elements: *agenda-setting* refers to the process by which problems come to the attention of governments; *policy formulation* refers to how policy options are formulated within government; *decision-making* is the process by which governments adopt a particular course of action or non-action; *policy implementation* relates to how governments put policies into effect; and *policy evaluation* refers to the processes by which the results of policies are monitored by both state and societal actors, the outcome of which may be reconceptualization of policy problems and solutions.

Policy styles refer to the methods government uses to create and implement policies. These methods can vary widely between governments, over time, and between states. The policy styles approach is useful in describing the different models put forward earlier in the history of policy studies, such as the rational, incremental, and garbage-can models. It also helps to advance studies of these models by specifying the conditions under which such styles occur. The chapter contends that certain common variables reappear at different stages of the policy cycle and influence the styles found in policy-making.

Chapter Objectives

By the end of this chapter, students will be able to do the following:
- Describe the components—the constituent parts—of public policy.
- Describe how policy is made according to the policy cycle model.

- Provide an historical overview of approaches to policy-making processes.
- Consider problems with existing models.
- Provide a literature review relevant to each stage of the policy process.
- Consider the relative advantages of utilizing the policy cycle and policy styles concepts.

Introduction: Policy Development as Decision-Making Process

Policy-making is a techno-political process of articulating and matching actor goals and means. Policies, themselves, are actions that contain both goals, however poorly identified, justified and formulated, and means, again however poorly specified and articulated, to achieve them. Many organizations and actors create policies but public policies are made by governments, and the actions we are concerned with in this case are government decisions to act or not to act to change, or maintain, some aspect of the status quo (Birkland, 2001: ch. 1).

The Components of Public Policies

Public policies are complex entities made up of a number of constituent parts, since they exist as combinations of goals and means put together and implemented by a variety of authoritative policy actors operating within an environment of multiple interacting actors and organizations.

A pathbreaking effort to specify in more detail exactly what these constituent parts entail can be found in Peter Hall's (1989 and 1993) work comparing the development of economic policies in western countries. This work distinguished between three basic elements or components of public polices: more or less abstract or general policy goals, the more concrete policy instruments used to implement them, and the even more specific operational settings or calibrations used when these instruments are deployed. Although Hall himself suggested that only these three different components existed, the distinction he drew among the three different levels of specificity of goals and means—from abstract to

concrete and specific—means it is possible to discern six elements that go into making up a public policy (Liefferink et al., 2006).[1]

Public policies and public policy-making revolve around the process of articulating and matching up policy goals with preferred policy means. These include discussion and development of both goals and means at the abstract (general or conceptual), program (concrete), and on-the-ground (settings) levels. Thus, for example, in an area such as criminal justice policy, policy-making involves consideration of general abstract policy goals (like reducing crime) and conceptual means (better policing), as well as program level objectives (such as reducing violent or gun-related crime) and mechanisms (by increasing the number of local police stations in high-crime areas), and also the settings and calibrations of policy tools (such as reducing violent crime by 50 per cent over five years and doing so by doubling the number and frequency of police patrols in affected areas (Bannink & Hoogenboom, 2007; Kuhner, 2007) (see Table 14.1).

Describing How Policy Is Made: The Policy Cycle Model

This process of policy-making occurs over time and as a set of activities rather than as a specific decision or piece of legislation. This process is a set of interrelated stages through which some item flows in a more-or-less sequential fashion from inputs to outputs. In the case of policy-making, the process is one in which various demands are made upon governments to act or expend its resources in specific ways, leading it to take some kind of action.

The idea that policy development can be thought of as a series of decision-making processes was first broached systematically in the work of Harold

Table 14.1   A Modified Taxonomy of Policy Components Following Hall
(Cells contain examples of each measure)

		Policy Content		
		High-Level Abstraction	*Program-Level Operationalization*	*Specific On-the-Ground Measures*
Policy Focus	*Policy Ends or Aims*	**GOALS** **What General Types of Ideas Govern Policy Development?** (e.g. environmental protection, economic development)	**OBJECTIVES** **What Does Policy Formally Aim to Address?** (e.g. saving wilderness or species habitat, increasing harvesting levels to create processing jobs)	**SETTINGS** **What Are the Specific On-the-Ground Require-ments of Policy?** (e.g. considerations about the optimal size of desig-nated stream-bed riparian zones, or sustainable levels of harvesting)
	Policy Means or Tools	**INSTRUMENT LOGIC** **What General Norms Guide Implementation Preferences?** (e.g. preferences for the use of coercive instruments, or moral suasion)	**MECHANISMS** **What Specific Types of Instruments are Utilized?** (e.g. the use of different tools such as tax incentives or public enterprises)	**CALIBRATIONS** **What are the Specific Ways in Which the Instrument is used?** (e.g. designations of higher levels of subsidies, the use of mandatory vs. voluntary regu-latory guidelines or standards)

Source: Modified from Cashore and Howlett (2007).

Lasswell (Lasswell, 1956, 1971). For Lasswell, the policy development process began with intelligence gathering, that is, the collection, processing, and dis-semination of information for those who participate in the decision process. It then moved on to the pro-motion of particular options by those involved in the actual decision. In the third stage the decision-makers actually prescribed a course of action. In the fourth stage this course of action was invoked, that is, sanc-tions were developed to penalize those who failed to comply with the prescriptions of decision-makers. The policy was then applied by the courts and the bureaucracy and ran its course until it was termin-ated or cancelled. Finally, the results of the policy were appraised or evaluated against the aims and goals of the original decision-makers. This sequence of stages through which the policy-making process operates is often referred to as the **policy cycle** (Jann and Wegrich, 2007).

This model was highly influential in the de-velopment of the policy sciences (deLeon, 1999) and formed the basis for further work on the subject (Anderson, 1984; Brewer, 1974; Jones, 1984; Lyden et

al., 1968; Simmons et al., 1974). Although not entirely accurate, it helped to advance the policy sciences by expanding the idea of the **policy process** beyond its traditional confines in the actions of governments and their agencies. Eventually, through comparative studies of policy-making processes in many sectors and jurisdictions, a simpler version of the policy cycle emerged that more clearly linked the stages of public policy-making with the logic of applied decision-making (Hupe & Hill, 2006).

The five stages in applied problem-solving and the corresponding stages in the policy process are de-picted in Table 14.2.

In this model, **agenda-setting** refers to the process by which problems come to the attention of governments; **policy formulation** refers to how policy options are formulated within government; **decision-making** is the process by which gov-ernments adopt a particular course of action or non-action; **policy implementation** relates to how governments put policies into effect; and **policy evaluation** refers to the processes by which the re-sults of policies are monitored by both state and

Table 14.2   Five Stages of the Policy Cycle and Their Relationship to Applied Problem-Solving

Applied Problem-Solving	Stages in Policy Cycle
1. Problem Recognition	1. Agenda-Setting
2. Proposal of Solution	2. Policy Formulation
3. Choice of Solution	3. Decision-Making
4. Putting Solution into Effect	4. Policy Implementation
5. Monitoring Results	5. Policy Evaluation

societal actors, the outcome of which may be reconceptualization of policy problems and solutions.

Again, study focused on particular stages of the cycle, examining, for example, the nature of agenda-setting dynamics in the United States and Europe, or comparing the roles played by specific actors—like the media—in each. Other studies examined the manner in which different stages interacted—such as policy evaluation and agenda-setting when a negative evaluation of a policy leads to its revision in subsequent rounds of policy-making (Pierson, 1993). These studies shed a great deal of light on the nature of the policy-making process and highlighted the need to better understand the kinds of actors and dynamics at work in different countries and sectors as policy-making processes unfolded if these forces and determinants were to be understood and controlled.

Who Makes Policy: Policy Actors

The cycle or process model is useful not only because of the way it separates out distinct tasks conducted in the process of public policy-making, but also because it helps clarify the different, but interactive, roles played in the process by specific kinds of policy actors, the institutions in which they operate, and the importance of the ideas they hold about both policy content and process in determining what kinds of policy goals and means are considered and implemented in public policy decision-making (Sobeck, 2003).

Agenda-setting is a stage in which virtually any (and all) policy actors might be involved in decrying problems and demanding government action. These

policy actors—whether all, many, or few—can be termed the *policy universe*. At the next stage, formulation, only a subset of the policy universe—the *policy subsystem*—is involved in discussing options to deal with problems recognized as requiring some government action. The subsystem is composed of only those actors with sufficient knowledge of a problem area, or a resource at stake, to allow them to participate in the process of developing alternative possible courses of action to address the issues raised at the agenda-setting stage. When a decision is being taken on one or more, or none, of these options to implement, the number of actors is reduced even further, to only the subset of the policy subsystem composed of *authoritative government decision-makers*, whether elected officials, judges, or bureaucrats. Once implementation begins, however, the number of actors increases once again to the relevant *subsystem* and then, finally, with the evaluation of the results of that implementation, expands once again to encompass the entire *policy universe* (see Figure 14.1).

Understanding how these different actors interact in policy processes in order to produce specific kinds of policy outcomes is a major subject of contemporary comparative policy research. Different patterns of policy outcomes have been linked to the patterns of behaviour of policy actors and these, in turn, have been linked to the kinds of institutional structures found in different countries and sectors that condition how policy initiatives emerge and how policy advice is generated and deployed (Aberbach & Rockman, 1989; Bennett & McPhail 1992; Bevir & Rhodes, 2001; Bevir et al., 2003; Howlett & Lindquist, 2004; Peled, 2002).

Recent comparative studies of policy-making processes in countries such as New Zealand, Israel, Canada, and Australia, for example, have developed the idea that government decision-makers sit at the centre of a complex web of policy advisers who are key players in affecting how demands made at the agenda-setting stage of the policy process are articulated into specific policy options or alternatives for decision-makers to consider (Dobuzinskis, Howlett, & Laycock, 2007; Eichbaum & Shaw, 2007; Maley, 2000; Peled, 2002). These include both traditional political advisers in government as well as non-governmental actors in NGOs, think tanks, and other similar organizations, as well as less formal or professional forms of advice from colleagues, relatives, and members of the public.

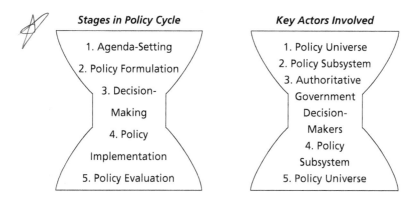

Figure 14.1 The Policy Cycle–Actor Hourglass

Given its reliance on existing institutional configurations, the exact configuration of an advisory system varies not only temporally, but also spatially, by jurisdiction, especially by nation-state and, somewhat less so, by policy sector. That is, the personal and professional components of the policy advice supply system, along with their internal and external sourcing, can be expected to be combined in different ratios in different situations (Halligan, 1995; Hawke, 1983; Prince, 1983; Rochet, 2004; Wollman, 1989). Discerning the underlying patterns of policy analysis, their influence, and their effectiveness in different analytical contexts involves understanding how a policy advice system is structured and operated in different countries, jurisdictions, and sectors of policy activity (Lindquist, 1998; Mayer, Bots, & van Daalen, 2004; Verschuere, 2009) and is a subject of some interest to students of comparative public policy.

Historical Overview of Approaches to Policy-Making Processes: The (Ir)Rationality of Policy Development

Early studies of the policy development process differed considerably in terms of their findings and assumptions about the "rationality" of the process; that is, the extent to which actor deliberations and actions could be understood as ones which tried to optimize the benefits and reduce the costs of specific kinds of potential activity. While a number of studies indicated that policy-makers went about their business in a calm, methodical, and precise fashion aimed at optimizing or maximizing policy outcomes, others found the process to be much more Byzantine, haphazard, and

unpredictable. Several examples of these early works are presented below.

Rational Models

Some early studies of individual policy-making in companies, governments, and organizations, conducted largely by students of public and business administration, found policy-makers attempting to follow a systematic method for arriving at logical, efficient policies. To various extents, they argued that policy-makers established a goal, explored alternative strategies for achieving it, attempted to predict its consequences and the likelihood of each occurring, and then chose the option that maximized potential benefits at least cost or risk (Carley, 1980; Gawthrop, 1971; Ward, 1954; Weiss, 1977).

This model was rational in the sense that it prescribed a standard set of procedures for policy-making that was expected to lead in all circumstances to the choice of the most efficient means of achieving policy goals (Jennings, 1987; Torgerson, 1986). Policy-makers were thought of as neutral technicians or managers who identify a problem and then find the most effective or efficient way of solving it (Elster, 1991).

Limited Rationality Models

Further empirical research into policy-making processes, however, soon led to a rethinking of many elements of the **rational model**. Policy-makers were often found to be neither neutral nor competent and a second wave of models of the policy-making process tended to argue that this was not accidental, or due to avoidable errors made by policy-makers, but an inherent and unavoidable characteristic of the policy-making exercise. The well-known **incremental model** of policy-making developed by Yale University political scientist Charles Lindblom, for example, attempted to capture the elements of a policy process characterized by only limited rationality (Dahl & Lindblom, 1953; Lindblom, 1951, 1958, 1959). Lindblom summarized the elements of his model as consisting of the following "mutually supporting set of simplifying and focusing stratagems":

 a. limitation of analysis to a few somewhat familiar policy alternatives . . . differing only marginally from the status quo;

b. an intertwining of analysis of policy goals and other values with the empirical aspects of the problem (that is, no requirement that values be specified first with means subsequently found to promote them);

c. a greater analytical preoccupation with ills to be remedied than positive goals to be sought;

d. a sequence of trials, errors, and revised trials;

e. analysis that explores only some, not all, of the important possible consequences of a considered alternative;

f. fragmentation of analytical work to many (partisan) participants in policy-making, (each attending to their piece of the overall problem domain). (Lindblom, 1979: 521)

Lindblom argued that policies were invariably developed through a process of successive limited comparisons with earlier policies with which decision-makers were most familiar. As he put it in his oft-cited 1959 article "The Science of 'Muddling Through,'" policy-makers worked through a process of "continually building out from the current situation, step-by-step and by small degrees" (Lindblom, 1959: 83). For Lindblom, this was due to two related aspects of the policy-making situation. First, since policy-making requires distribution of limited resources among various participants, it is easier to continue an existing pattern of distribution than to adopt radically new proposals that alter the established pattern of costs and benefits enjoyed, or borne, by specific actors. Second, the standard operating procedures that are the hallmark of bureaucracy also tend to promote the continuation of existing practices. The methods by which bureaucrats identify options and the methods and criteria for choice are often laid out in advance,

which inhibits innovation and perpetuates existing arrangements (Gortner et al., 1987).

The incremental model hence viewed policy-making as a practical exercise concerned with solving problems through trial-and-error processes rather than through the comprehensive evaluation of all possible means of achieving policy goals (Manzer, 1984). Decision-makers, it was argued, did not maximize policy outcomes in the traditional, rational sense, because they considered only a few familiar alternatives for their appropriateness and stopped their search whenever an alternative acceptable to established policy actors was found.

Irrational Models

Perhaps the most noted critic of the rational model was the American behavioural scientist Herbert Simon. In a series of books and articles beginning in the early 1950s, he argued that several hurdles prevented decision-makers from attaining comprehensive rationality in their decisions (Simon, 1955, 1957). First, Simon noted definite cognitive limits to the decision-makers' ability to consider all possible options, which forces them to selectively consider alternatives. Second, he argued that the model assumed that it is possible for decision-makers to know the consequences of each decision in advance, while, in reality, no one can predict the future with any degree of certainty. Third, he also noted specific policy options usually entail a bundle of favourable and adverse consequences in different areas of social life, which makes comparisons among them difficult. Moreover, since the same option can often be efficient or inefficient depending on the circumstances, it is not possible for decision-makers to arrive at unambiguous conclusions about which alternative is superior.

Simon concluded that public decisions in practice did not maximize benefits over costs, but merely tended to satisfy whatever criteria decision-makers set for themselves. This **satisficing** criterion, as he put it, was realistic given the **bounded rationality** with which human beings are endowed.

A model was put forward by one of Simon's co-authors, James March, and his Norwegian colleague Johan Olsen. March and Olsen (1979) asserted that due to these problems public policy-making was an inherently irrational process. The two authors proposed a so-called **garbage-can model** of decision-making that denied even the limited notion of rationality accepted by incrementalists. They started from the assumption that both the rational and incremental models presumed a level of intentionality, comprehension of problems, and predictability of relations among actors that simply did not obtain in reality. Based on studies they conducted into policy-making exercises carried out in universities and similar large institutions, they argued that policy-making is a highly ambiguous and unpredictable process only distantly related to searching for means to achieve goals. March, Olsen, and Michael Cohen argued that decision opportunities were:

> a garbage can into which various problems and solutions are dumped by participants. The mix of garbage in a single can depends partly on the labels attached to the alternative cans; but it also depends on what garbage is being produced at the moment, on the mix of cans available, and on the speed with which garbage is collected and removed from the scene. (Cohen, March, & Olsen, 1979: 327)

That is, they saw policy solutions as only very loosely related to policy problems and the process of matching solutions to problems as a largely ad hoc one that depended on various unpredictable elements such as the personalities of the actors involved, their presence or absence in specific decision-making instances, and the temporary alliances and arrangements made between them in specific cases. The garbage-can metaphor was used deliberately to strip away the aura of science and rationality attributed to decision-making by earlier theorists. March and Olsen sought to drive home the point that goals are often unknown to policy-makers, as are causal relationships. In their view, actors simply define goals and choose means as they go along in a process that is necessarily contingent and unpredictable.

Problems with Existing Models: False Dichotomies and Corrective Syntheses

As is apparent from the above brief overview, each of these early models was constructed on the basis of certain findings and expectations with respect to the behaviour of policy-makers, especially in regard to how policy-makers characterized acceptable policy outcomes and acted so as to achieve them (Cahill & Overman, 1990). Each model was constructed on the basis of some empirical findings, but inherent in both the incremental and garbage-can models was criticism of the concepts contained in their predecessors. Hence incremental critics of the rational model argued that it would generate maximal results only if all possible alternatives and the costs of each alternative were assessed before a decision was made, while garbage-can critics of incrementalism argued that it assumed a constant set of decision-makers who could learn from past experiences. In both cases, empirical evidence to the contrary was cited to bolster arguments made about the unreality of such assumptions.

Defenders of rational models, however, were unwilling to accept the superiority of alternatives based on limited or restricted notions of rationality. Critics found faults with several aspects of incremental policy-making which, as Forester put it, "would have us cross and recross intersections without knowing where we are going" (Forester, 1984: 23). The model was criticized, for example, for being unable to explain large-scale change and innovation (Berry, 1990; Lustick, 1980; Weiss & Woodhouse, 1992) and for being undemocratic to the extent that it confined policy-making to bargaining within a select group of senior policy-makers (Gawthrop, 1971). By discouraging systematic analysis and planning and by undermining the need to search for promising new alternatives, it was also said to promote short-sighted decisions that can have adverse consequences for society in the long run (Cox, 1992; Hayes, 1992). In addition to criticisms of the desirability of decisions made incrementally, the model was also criticized for its narrow analytic usefulness. Yehezkel Dror, for example, noted that incrementalism could only work when there is a great deal of continuity in the nature of problems that policies are intended to address and in the means available to address them, conditions that do not always exist (Dror, 1964). Incrementalism was also found to be more characteristic of decision-making in a relatively stable environment, rather than in situations that are unusual, such as a crisis (Nice, 1987) and also was seen to be a more likely explanation where large numbers of actors participate in policy development (Bendor, 1995).

The garbage-can model also generated similar criticisms. While it was found by some authors, including John Kingdon (1984) to be a fairly accurate description of how decisions are made at times in some complex organizations, such as legislatures, its application to all instances of policy development was questioned. Guy Mucciaroni, for example, argued that:

> Perhaps the mode of policy-making depicted by the garbage can model is itself embedded in a particular institutional structure. Put another way, the model may be better at depicting decision-making in certain polities than in others. It may be more useful for describing policy-making in the United States, where the institutional structure is fragmented and permeable, participation is pluralistic and fluid, and coalitions are often temporary and ad hoc. By contrast, policy-making in other countries takes place among institutions that are more centralized and integrated, where the number of participants is limited and their participation is highly structured and predictable. . . . [Where this occurs] the result has been a process described as "stable," "predictable," "orderly," "rationalistic," "deliberative" and "planned" quite unlike the garbage can model's image of decision-making that is more open, fluid and ad hoc. (Mucciaroni, 1992: 466–7)

In addition, it was argued that the model did not well explain the existence of fairly long-term patterns in policy-making and exaggerated the gap existing between problems and solutions in most instances (Mucciaroni, 1992).

These limitations led many analysts to continue to look for alternative models of policy-making processes. Some suggested that the shortcomings

of existing models could be overcome by combining elements from each in a new synthetic model. One such effort, for example, suggested that optimal decision-making would consist of both a cursory search ("scanning") for alternatives as suggested by incrementalism, followed by a detailed probe of the most promising alternative, as suggested by the rational model (Etzioni, 1967). However, most efforts took to heart the idea put forward by Lindblom late in his career, that a spectrum of policy-making styles existed (Smith & May, 1980). These ranged from synoptic or rational–comprehensive decision-making to blundering, that is, simply following hunches or guesses without any real effort at systematic analysis of alternative strategies. The spectrum put forward by Lindblom and Cohen in 1979 is illustrated in Figure 14.2.

While Lindblom did not specify under what circumstances a specific option might be used, other authors have since suggested that the manner with which a policy problem or issue would be developed tends to be established on a relatively permanent basis and can usefully be thought of as a policy "style" (Coleman, 1994; Freeman, 1985). Richardson, Gustafsson, and Jordan (1982), for example, defined a **policy style** as a typical process of policy development characterized by "the interaction between (a) the government's approach to problem solving and (b) the relationship between government and other actors in the policy process." Utilizing these two variables, they argued that a limited number of large-scale, typically national, styles could be identified (see Table 14.3).

Several studies applied this concept with great facility to policy-making in various nations and sectors (Tuohy, 1992; Vogel, 1986). However, others found that few governments were consistently active or reactive; nor did any government always work

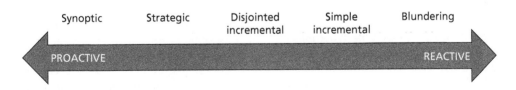

Figure 14.2 A Spectrum of Policy-Making Types

Source: Adapted from Lindblom and Cohen (1979).

Table 14.3   An Early Model of National Policy Styles

Relationship between Government and Society	Dominant Approach to Problem-Solving	
	Anticipatory	Reactive
Consensus	*e.g., German "rationalist consensus"*	*e.g., British "negotiating" style*
Imposition	*e.g., French "concertation" style*	*e.g., Dutch "negotiation and conflict" style*

Source: Adapted from Richardson et al. (1982).

through either consensus or imposition. Rather than think of policy styles as existing at the national level, they argued that a focus on the sectoral level would be more accurate and more productive (Freeman, 1985).

Elements of a Policy Style

Agenda-Setting Styles

In the formal study of agenda-setting, a distinction is often made between the *systemic* or unofficial public agenda and the *institutional* or formal, official agenda. The systemic agenda "consists of all issues that are commonly perceived by members of the political community as meriting public attention and as involving matters within the legitimate jurisdiction of existing governmental authority" (Cobb & Elder, 1972). This is essentially a society's agenda for discussion of public problems, such as crime or health care, water quality or wilderness preservation. The formal or institutional agenda, on the other hand, consists of only a limited number of issues or problems to which attention is devoted by policy elites (Baumgartner & Jones, 1991; Kingdon, 1984).

Each society has literally hundreds of issues that some citizens find to be matters of concern and would have the government do something about. However, only a small proportion of the problems on the public or systemic agenda are actually taken up by policy actors actively involved in policy development. In other words, the public agenda is an agenda for discussion while the institutional agenda is an agenda for action, indicating that the formal policy process dealing with the problem in question has begun.

Over 30 years ago the American political scientists Cobb, Ross, and Ross developed a model of typical agenda-setting styles. They argued that three basic patterns of agenda-setting could be discerned, distinguished by the origins of the issue as well as the resources utilized to facilitate their inclusion on the agenda.

In the **outside initiation** pattern "issues arise in nongovernmental groups and are then expanded sufficiently to reach, first, the public [systemic] agenda and, finally, the formal [institutional] agenda" (Cobb, Ross, & Ross, 1976). In this case issues are first initiated when some part of the public articulates a grievance and demands its resolution by the government. The aggrieved groups attempt to expand support for their demand, a process that may involve submerging the specific complaint within a more general one and forming alliances across groups. Finally, these groups lobby, contest, and join with others in attempting to get the expanded issue onto the formal agenda. If they have the requisite political resources and skills and can outmanoeuvre their opponents or advocates of other issues and actions, they can often succeed in having their issue enter the formal agenda. Thus, as Cobb, Ross, and Ross summarize it:

> The outside initiative model applies to the situation in which a group outside the government structure 1) articulates a grievance, 2) tries to expand interest in the issue to enough other groups in the population to gain a place on the public agenda, in order to 3) create sufficient pressure on decision-makers to force the issue onto the formal agenda for their serious consideration.

The **mobilization** case is quite different and describes "decision-makers trying to expand an issue from a formal to a public agenda." In this model, issues are simply placed on the formal agenda by the government with no necessary preliminary expansion from a publicly recognized grievance. There may be considerable debate within government over the issue, but the public may well be kept in the dark about the policy and its development until its formal announcement. The policy may be specified in some detail or it may just establish general principles whose specification will be worked out later.

In the third, **inside initiation**, pattern, influential groups with special access to decision-makers initiate a policy and do not necessarily want it to be expanded and contested in public. This can be due to technical as well as political reasons. In this model, initiation and specification occur simultaneously as a group or government agency enunciates a grievance and specifies some potential solution to the problem. Expansion is restricted to specialized groups or agencies with some knowledge or interest in the subject. Entrance is virtually automatic due to the privileged place of those desiring a decision. According to Cobb, Ross, and Ross:

> Proposals arise within governmental units or in groups close to the government. The issue is then expanded to identification and attention groups in order to create sufficient pressure on decision-makers to place the item on the formal agenda. At no point is the public greatly involved, and the initiators make no effort to get the issue on the public agenda. On the contrary, they try to keep it off.

From the above discussion, it should be apparent that two of the most critical factors in identifying a typical pattern of agenda-setting in any policy area are the level and extent of public involvement and support for government action (May, 1991), and the response or pre-response of the state in directing, mediating, and accommodating this activity (Majone, 1989). The resulting agenda-setting styles are set out in Table 14.4. As this figure shows, a fourth agenda-setting style—*consolidation*—exists in addition to the three identified by Cobb, Ross, and Ross. In this last style, state actors may initiate debate on an issue with high public support and thus simply

Table 14.4   Basic Agenda-Setting Styles

Initiator of Debate	Nature of Public Support	
	High	Low
Societal Actors	Outside initiation	Inside initiation
State	Consolidation	Mobilization

consolidate this support in moving the issue on for further development.

Policy Formulation Styles

Studies of policy formulation have also emphasized the importance of the kinds of actors interacting to develop and refine policy options for government (Freeman, 1955; Linder & Peters, 1990). But unlike agenda-setting, where the public is often actively involved, in policy formulation the relevant policy actors are restricted to those who not only have an opinion on a subject, but also have some minimal level of knowledge of the subject area, allowing them to comment, at least hypothetically, on the feasibility of options put forward to resolve policy problems.

Scholars over the years have developed a variety of taxonomies to help identify the key actors in these **policy subsystems**, what brings them together, how they interact, and what effect their interaction has on policy development (Jordan, 1981, 1990a, 1990b; Jordan & Schubert, 1992). Most of these distinguish between a larger set of actors with some knowledge of the policy issue in question, and a smaller set in which actors not only have requisite knowledge, but also have established patterns of more or less routine interactions with each other (Knoke, 1993).

Membership in knowledge-based **policy communities** extends to actors such as state policy-makers (administrative, political, and judicial), members of non-governmental organizations (NGOs) concerned with the subject, members of the media who report on the subject, academics who follow or research the area, and members of the general public who, for whatever reason, have taken an interest in the subject (Sabatier 1987, 1988). In many issue areas, the policy community also involves members of other organizations such as businesses, labour unions, or various formalized interest groups or professional associations concerned with government actions in their sector. In some cases, international actors, such as multinational corporations, international governmental or non-governmental organizations, or the governments of foreign states, can also be members of sectoral policy communities (Haas, 1992).

A subset of these actors who interact within more formalized institutions and procedures of government are defined as members of **policy networks** (Coleman & Skogstad, 1990; Marin & Mayntz, 1991; Pross, 1992). These policy networks include representatives from the community, but are inner circles of actors who effectively hold the power to veto many policy options as untenable or infeasible.

In this view, the likely results of policy formulation are contingent upon the nature and configuration of the policy community and network in the specific sector concerned. A key variable, which many observers have argued affects the structure and behaviour of policy networks, is the number of members, which affects aspects of networks such as their level of integration and the types of interactions members undertake (Atkinson & Coleman, 1989, 1990; Coleman & Skogstad, 1990; Van Waarden, 1992). What is important for policy communities, on the other hand, is not the number of participants in the community but the number of relatively distinct idea sets that exist within it. This affects the nature of conflict and consensus in the community and, as a result, affects the behaviour of community actors (Haas, 1992; Hessing & Howlett, 1997; MacRae, 1993; Schulman, 1988; Smith, 1993).

The type and nature of options that come forward to governments from the policy formulation phase are affected by the interaction of networks and communities (Howlett 2002a; Howlett & Ramesh, 1998; Howlett & Rayner, 1995; Smith, 1993, 1994). Table 14.5 presents a model of policy formulation styles based on the manner in which different types of policy networks and communities interact.

In open subsystems where networks have many members and communities sharing many idea sets, it can be expected that a propensity exists for new, radical alternatives to the status quo to be generated in the policy formulation process. In closed subsystems, where networks have few members and communities are dominated by a single idea set, on the other hand, a status quo orientation will emerge in the policy options developed and put before decision-makers. In

Table 14.5   Basic Policy Formulation Styles

Policy Community Idea Sets	Policy Network Membership	
	Few	Many
Few	*Status quo options*	*Marginal/incremental options*
Many	*Contested alternative options*	*Radical alternative options*

subsystems where only a few actors make up the network but communities are open to new ideas, significant alternatives to the status quo may emerge from the formulation process, but usually over the opposition of network members. In subsystems where many actors deal with few ideas, as Lindblom suggested, marginal or incremental options tend to develop.

Decision-Making Styles

In some of their early writings, Lindblom and his co-authors held out the possibility that incremental decision-making could coexist with efforts to achieve more rational decisions. Thus Braybrooke and Lindblom, for example, argued that four different styles of decision-making could be discerned, depending upon the amount of knowledge at the disposal of decision-makers, and the amount of change the decision involved from earlier decisions (Braybrooke & Lindblom, 1963). This generated the two-by-two matrix shown in Table 14.6.

In Braybrooke and Lindblom's view, the overwhelming majority of decisions were likely to be taken in an incremental fashion, involving minimal change in situations of low available knowledge. Three other possibilities existed, however, with the rational model emerging as one possibility and two styles—revolutionary and analytic—also existing as infrequently employed alternatives. Although it was somewhat tautological to use amount of change as a variable to help explain the degree of change each decision-making style entailed, as a description of commonly occurring decision-making styles, this type of model was quite useful. Other authors, like Graham Allison (1969, 1971), also developed similar models of distinct decision-making styles, but also did not specify in

Table 14.6   An Early Model of Decision-Making Styles

| Amount of Change Involved | Level of Available Knowledge | |
	High	Low
High	Revolutionary	Analytic
Low	Rational	Disjointed incremental

Source: Adapted from Braybrooke and Lindblom (1963). Copyright © 1963 by The Free Press; copyright renewed © 1991 by David Braybrooke and Charles E. Lindblom. Reprinted with the permission of The Free Press, a division of Simon & Schuster, Inc. All rights reserved.

any detail the variables that led to the adoption of a particular style (Bendor & Hammond, 1992).

Attempting to improve upon these models, John Forester (1984, 1989) argued that there were at least five distinct decision-making styles associated with a variety of decision-making conditions and contexts. Forester began from the position that "what is rational for administrators to do depends on the situations in which they work." That is, the decision-making style and the type of decisions made by decision-makers varied according to issue and institutional contexts. As he put it:

> Depending upon the conditions at hand, a strategy may be practical or ridiculous. With time, expertise, data, and a well-defined problem, technical calculations may be in order; without time, data, definition, and expertise, attempting those calculations could well be a waste of time. In a complex organizational environment, intelligence networks will be as, or more, important than documents when information is needed. In an environment of inter-organizational conflict, bargaining and compromise may be called for. Administrative strategies are sensible only in a political and organizational context. (Forester, 1984)

Forester suggested that decision-making is affected by the number of agents involved in a decision, their organizational setting, how well a problem is defined, the information available on the problem, its causes and consequences, and the amount of time available to decision-makers to consider possible contingencies and their present and anticipated consequences. The number of agents can expand and multiply almost to infinity; the setting can include many different organizations and can be more or less open to external influences; the problem can be ambiguous or susceptible to multiple competing interpretations; information can be incomplete, misleading, or purposefully withheld or manipulated; and time can be limited or artificially constrained and manipulated.

Recasting Forester's variables allows the development of a simple but effective model of decision-making styles present in the policy development process. Agent and setting, for example, can be thought of as elements of how decision-makers are situated vis-à-vis policy subsystems, while the notions of the definitional, information, and time resources can all be seen as relating to the types of constraints that are placed upon decision-makers. Using these dimensions, the model of styles found in Table 14.7 can be generated.

In this model, decision-makers situated in complex subsystems are expected to undertake adjustment strategies while those dealing with simple configurations of actors and ideas will be more prone to undertake search-type strategies. The nature of the decision criteria, on the other hand, varies with the severity of the informational, time, and other resource constraints under which decision-makers operate. Hence decision-makers faced with high constraints will tend to favour satisficing over optimization, itself an outcome more likely to occur in situations of low constraint.

Policy Implementation Styles

Generally speaking, comparative implementation studies have also shown that governments tend to develop specific implementation styles in areas that they

Table 14.7   Basic Decision-Making Styles

| Severity of Constraints | Complexity of the Policy Subsystem | |
	High	Low
High	Incremental adjustment	Satisficing search
Low	Optimizing adjustment	Rational search

regulate (Hawkins & Thomas, 1989; Howlett, 2002b; Kagan, 1991; Knill, 1998). These styles combine various kinds of instruments into a more or less coherent whole that is consistently applied in particular sectors. More specifically, such styles combine at least one major type of procedural policy instrument with at least one major type of substantive instrument.

Substantive instruments are those directly providing goods and services to members of the public or governments. They include a variety of tools or instruments relying on different types of governing resources for their effectiveness (Peters & Van Nispen, 1998; Salamon, 1989; Tupper & Doern, 1981; Vedung, 1997; Woodside, 1986). A useful way to classify these (see Table 14.8) is according to the type of governing resource upon which they rely: nodality or information; authority, treasure, or financial resources, or administrative or organizational ones (Hood, 1986).

Procedural instruments are different from substantive ones in that their impact on policy outcomes is less direct. Rather than to affect the delivery of goods and services, their principal intent is to modify or alter the nature of policy processes at work in the implementation process (Howlett, 1996; in't Veld, 1998). A list of these instruments is provided in Table 14.9.

Why a particular combination of procedural and substantive instruments is used in particular sectors is a key question. In the case of substantive instruments, Linder and Peters (1989) argued that the features of the policy instruments themselves are important for selection purposes, because some instruments are more suited for a task at hand than are others. They noted that instrument choice was not simply a technical exercise, however, and that variables such as political culture and the depth of its social cleavages could have an impact on instrument selection. They also noted that the choice of an instrument is circumscribed by the organizational culture of the concerned agencies. The context of the problem situation, its timing, and the scope of actors it includes were also cited as having significant potential impacts on choices.

This analysis suggests that the choice of policy instruments is shaped by the characteristics of the instruments, the nature of the problem at hand, past experiences of governments in dealing with the same or similar problems, the subjective preference of the decision-makers, and the likely reaction to the choice by affected social groups. However, in attempting to explain a consistent preference for the use of

Table 14.8   A Taxonomy of Substantive Policy Instruments

Principal Use	Governing Resource			
	Nodality	Authority	Treasure	Organization
Effectors	advice training	licences user charges regulation certification	grants loans tax expenditures	bureaucratic administration public enterprises
Detectors	reporting registration	census-taking consultants	polling policy	record-keeping surveys

Source: Adapted from Hood (1986).

Table 14.9   A Resource-Based Taxonomy of Procedural Policy Instruments

Principal Use	Governing Resource			
	Nodality	Authority	Treasure	Organization
Positive	education exhortation advertising training	agreements treaties advisory-group creation	interest-group funding research and intervenor funding	hearings evaluations institutional-bureaucratic reform
Negative	misleading information propaganda	banning groups and associations	eliminating funding	administrative delay information suppression

particular instruments over a wide range of contexts, the influence of the first three somewhat idiosyncratic variables can be discounted. More significant for such purposes are the preferences of state decision-makers and the nature of the constraints within which they operate (Bressers & O'Toole, 1998). States must have a high level of administrative capacity in order to use authority, treasure, and organization-based instruments in situations in which they wish to affect significant numbers of policy targets. When a state has few of these resources, it will tend to use such instruments as incentives or propaganda, or to rely on existing voluntary, community- or family-based instruments (Howlett & Ramesh, 1995). Similarly, a key feature of procedural instrument choice is a governments' capacity to manipulate policy subsystems. Often used to retain or reacquire the political trust or legitimacy needed for substantive instruments to be effective (Beetham, 1991; Stillman, 1974; Weber, 1958), procedural policy instrument choice is also affected by the size of the policy target and the nature of the constraints under which a state is operating. Whether a government faces sectoral de-legitimation or widespread systemic de-legitimation, especially, is a significant constraint affecting the types of procedural instruments a government will employ (Habermas, 1973, 1975; Mayntz, 1975; Mueller, 1973).

Hence, like substantive instruments, procedural instrument choice is affected by the nature of the constraints under which policy-makers operate and the type of target they are attempting to influence. Putting these two types of instruments and variables together leads to the model of implementation styles found in Table 14.10.

Governments facing a variety of resource or legitimation problems and dealing with large policy targets use low-cost substantive instruments such as exhortation, and procedural instruments such as government reorganization (or "institutionalized voluntarism"), as a preferred implementation style. Faced with lower constraints and similarly large-sized targets, they tend to use direct subsidization involving treasure-based tools, such as offering subsidies to producers of goods and services and extending similar recognition to interest groups to help direct their activities. In a situation where governments face small targets under situations of high constraint, they tend to use forms of authoritative instruments—including such substantive tools as regulation—and procedural instruments such as the extension of financial aid to interest group formation and consolidation, in an implementation style of "representative legalism." Finally, in situations where they face low constraints and the same smaller targets, they use substantive instruments such as public enterprises and procedural instruments such as enhancing public access to information, in a style of "public provision with oversight."

Policy Evaluation Styles

The last stage of the cycle is policy evaluation. For many early observers, policy evaluation was expected to consist of assessing if a public policy was achieving its stated objectives and, if not, what could be done to eliminate impediments to their attainment. Thus David Nachmias (1979) defined policy evaluation as "the objective, systematic, empirical examination of the effects ongoing policies and public programs have on their targets in terms of the goals they are meant to achieve." However, while analysts often resorted to concepts such as "success" or "failure" to conclude their evaluation, as Ingram and Mann (1980) cautioned:

Table 14.10   Basic Implementation Styles

Severity of Constraints	Nature of the Policy Target	
	Large	Small
High	Institutionalized voluntarism (exhortation and information manipulation)	Representative legalism (regulation and financial manipulation)
Low	Directed subsidization (financial and recognition manipulation)	Institutionalized public provision (organization and information manipulation)

the phenomenon of policy failure is neither so simple nor certain as many contemporary critics of policy and politics would have us believe. Success and failure are slippery concepts, often highly subjective and reflective of an individual's goals, perception of need, and perhaps even psychological disposition toward life.

In other words, public policy goals are usually not stated clearly enough to find out if and to what extent they are being achieved, nor are they shared by all key policy actors. Moreover, the possibilities for objective analysis are also limited because of the difficulties involved in the attempt to develop objective standards by which to evaluate government's level of success in dealing with subjective claims and socially constructed problems. Furthermore, the formal, overt goals stated by government typically gloss an array of latent objectives that policy also serves. Thus, for example, while governments may attempt to reduce industrial effluents through raising regulatory standards, they also have an interest in preserving conditions for employment and for economic activity, objectives that can easily conflict with increased regulation (Kerr, 1976).

What is significant in the evaluative process is not so much ultimate success and failure, but, as Lindblom correctly anticipated, that policy actors and the organizations and institutions they represent can *learn* from the formal and informal evaluation of policies in which they are engaged. This can lead them to modify their positions in the direction of greater substantive or procedural policy change, or it can lead them to resist any alteration to the status quo (Majone, 1989). That is, policy evaluations do not necessarily result in policy change. While the concept of evaluation suggests that an implicit feedback loop is an inherent part of the policy cycle, in many cases this loop may not be operationalized (Pierson, 1993). This implies that understanding the conditions under which **policy learning** occurs or does not occur is critical to understanding and modelling evaluative styles.

A significant variable in this regard is the capacity of an organization to absorb new information. As Cohen and Levinthal (1990) argued in the case of the private firm:

the ability to evaluate and utilize outside knowledge is largely a function of the level of prior related knowledge. At the most elemental level, this prior knowledge includes basic skills or even a shared language but may also include knowledge of the most recent scientific or technological developments in a given field. Thus, prior related knowledge confers an ability to recognize the value of new information, assimilate it, and apply it to commercial ends. These abilities collectively constitute what we call a firm's "absorptive capacity."

Of course, this is not the only significant variable, as the organization must also be receptive to new information and capable of its dissemination. Hence, as Cohen and Levinthal also suggested, a second significant variable affecting the potential for administrative learning can be found in the kind of links between administrators and their environments. Table 14.11 presents a model of evaluative styles based on these two variables.

Only when state administrative capacity is high would one expect any kind of learning to occur. However, if a relatively closed network dominates the subsystem, whereby few links join administrators to their environment, then this learning is likely to be restricted to some form of **lesson-drawing** in which policy-makers draw lessons from past uses of policy instruments (Bennett & Howlett, 1992; Rose, 1991). If the links between the network and the community are more open, one would expect other forms of learning, such as **social learning** in which ideas and events in the larger policy community penetrate into policy evaluations. When state capacity is low, one would expect little learning to occur. If the policy

Table 14.11   Basic Policy Evaluation Styles

State Adminis-trative Capacity	Type of Policy Subsystem	
	Open	Closed
High	Social learning	Lesson-drawing
Low	Informal evaluations	Formal evaluations

subsystem in such circumstances is dominated by existing networks, one would expect to find formal types of evaluation with little substantive impact on either policy instruments or goals. If the subsystem is more open to members of the policy community, one would expect a range of informal evaluations to occur, but still find little substantive impact on policy outcomes or processes (Howlett & Ramesh, 1995).

Conclusion: Policy Development as Policy Style

As Lasswell noted in the 1950s, envisioning policy development as a staged, sequential, and iterative process is a useful analytical and methodological device. Methodologically, such an approach reduces the complexity of public policy-making by breaking down that complexity into a small number of stages and substages, each of which can be investigated alone or in terms of its relationship to any or all the other stages of the cycle.

Analytically, as this chapter has argued, adopting such an approach is also useful because it helps to make sense out of the different approaches to understanding patterns of policy development first developed by Lindblom, March and Olsen, and others. More importantly, it also allows the insight of Richardson and his colleagues to be built upon; that is, it is possible to observe and model fairly long-term patterns in policy development processes as *policy styles*, and to construct a general model of sectoral policy development styles on this basis.

The basic components of an overall sectoral policy style are set out in Table 14.12.

Although this implies that there are quite a large number of possible policy styles, the discussion above highlights how these will tend to fall into several common types. That is, certain common variables reappear at different stages of the policy cycle and influence the styles found at these stages. The nature of the policy subsystem, for example, is such a significant, recurring, factor. Since the nature of a subsystem tends to constant over an extended period of time (Baumgartner & Jones, 1991; Blom-Hansen, 1997; Mortensen, 2007), this helps not only to restrict the number of common policy styles, but also to help explain their persistence. This is also true of administrative capacity, a second variable that reappears in various forms as a determining element of the styles found to exist at particular stages of the policy development process.

Analyzing policy development in terms of policy cycles and policy styles is useful for several reasons. Not only does it help to make sense out of the different models put forward earlier in the history of policy studies, such as the rational, incremental, and garbage-can models, it also helps to advance studies of these models by specifying the conditions under which such styles could occur. That is, the type of development process specified by each model is shown not to be a universal one, but rather can be seen as a specific combination or set of styles found at each stage of the process; occurring only in the specific circumstances underlying each stage.

Table 14.12 Components of a Policy Style

Styles Present at Each Stage of the Process	Elements That Combine to Create a Policy Style			
Agenda-setting	Outside initiation	Inside initiation	Consolidation	Mobilization
Policy formulation	Status quo options	Marginal/incremental options	Contested alternative options	Contested alternative options
Decision-making	Incremental adjustment	Satisficing adjustment	Optimizing search	Rational search
Policy implementation	Voluntary improvement	Directed subsidization	Representative legalism	Institutionalized public provision
Policy evaluation	Social learning	Lesson-drawing	Formal evaluations	Informal evaluations

Important Terms and Concepts

agenda-setting
bounded rationality
decision-making
garbage-can model
incremental model
inside initiation
lesson-drawing
mobilization

outside initiation
policy community
policy cycle
policy evaluation
policy formulation
policy implementation
policy learning
policy network

policy process
policy style
policy subsystem
procedural instrument
rational model
satisficing
social learning
substantive instrument

Study Questions

1. What is the policy cycle, according to various observers?
2. How is the policy cycle concept useful in studying public policy?
3. Who are the most notable policy theorists of various stages of the policy cycle?
4. Are there any drawbacks or caveats one must keep in mind when using the policy cycle concept?
5. What are some important models of decision-making?
6. What are some important elements of a policy style?

Note

1   For similar models based on a similar critique of Hall, see Daugbjerg (1997) and Smith (2000). These six categories are inspired from much of the work on applied policy analysis that teach students to break policy down into their "goals," "operationalized" objectives, and specific criteria and to take pains to distinguish policy instruments from "on-the-ground" policy requirements (Weimer & Vining, 1999).

References

Aberbach, Joel D., and Bert A. Rockman. 1989. "On the Rise, Transformation, and Decline of Analysis in the US Government." *Governance* 2, 3, pp. 293–314.

Alford, R.R. 1972. "The Political Economy of Health Care: Dynamics Without Change." *Politics and Society* 2, 2, pp. 127–64.

Allison, Graham. 1969. "Conceptual Models and the Cuban Missile Crisis." *American Political Science Review* 63, pp. 689–718.

Allison, Graham. 1971. *Essence of Decision: Explaining the Cuban Missile Crisis*. Boston: Little Brown.

Anderson, J.E. 1984. *Public Policymaking*. New York: Praeger.

Atkinson, M., and W. Coleman. 1989. *The State, Business, and Industrial Change in Canada*. Toronto: University of Toronto Press.

Atkinson, M., and W. Coleman. 1990. "Strong States and Weak States: Sectoral Policy Networks in Advanced Capitalist Economies." *British Journal of Political Science* 19, 1, pp. 47–67.

Bailey, J. J., and R. J. O'Connor. 1975. "Operationalizing Incrementalism: Measuring the Muddles." *Public Administration Review* 35, pp. 60–6.

Bannink, Duco, and Marcel Hoogenboom. 2007. "Hidden Change: Disaggregation of Welfare Regimes for Greater Insight into Welfare State Change." *Journal of European Social Policy* 17, 1 pp. 19–32.

Baumgartner, F. R., and B. D. Jones. 1991. "Agenda Dynamics and Policy Subsystems." *Journal of Politics* 53, 4, pp. 1044–74.

Baumgartner, F. R., and B. D. Jones. 1993. *Agendas and Instability in American Politics*. Chicago: University of Chicago Press.

Baumgartner, F. R., and B. D. Jones. 2002. *Policy Dynamics*. Chicago: University of Chicago Press.

Beetham, David. 1991. *The Legitimation of Power*. London: Macmillan.

Bendor, Jonathan. 1995. "A Model of Muddling Through." *American Political Science Review* 89, 4, pp. 819–40.

Bendor, Jonathan., and Thomas H. Hammond. 1992. "Re-Thinking Allison's Models." *American Political Science Review* 86, 2, pp. 301–22.

Bennett, Colin J., and Michael Howlett. 1992. "The Lessons of Learning: Reconciling Theories of Policy Learning and Policy Change." *Policy Sciences* 25, 3, pp. 275–94.

Bennett, S., and M. McPhail. 1992. "Policy Process Perceptions of Senior Canadian Federal Civil Servants: A View of the State and Its Environment." *Canadian Public Administration* 35, 3, pp. 299–316.

Berry, William T. 1990. "The Confusing Case of Budgetary Incrementalism: Too Many Meanings for a Single Concept." *Journal of Politics* 52, pp. 167–96.

Bevir, M., and R. A. W. Rhodes. 2001. "Decentering Tradition: Interpreting British Government." *Administration & Society* 33, 2, pp. 107–32.

Bevir, M., R. A. W. Rhodes, and P. Weller. 2003. "Traditions of Governance: Interpreting the Changing Role of the Public Sector." *Public Administration* 81, 1, pp. 1–17.

Birkland, T. A. 2001. *An Introduction to the Policy Process; Theories, Concepts, and Models of Public Policy Making.* Armonk: M.E. Sharpe.

Blom-Hansen, Jens. 1997. "A 'New Institutional' Perspective on Policy Networks." *Public Administration* 75, pp. 669–93.

Botcheva, L., and L. L. Martin. 2002. "Institutional Effects on State Behaviour: Convergence and Divergence." *International Studies Quarterly* 45, pp. 1–26.

Braybrooke, David, and Charles Lindblom. 1963. *A Strategy of Decision: Policy Evaluation as a Social Process.* New York: Free Press of Glencoe.

Bressers, Hans Th. A., and Laurence J. O'Toole. 1998. "The Selection of Policy Instruments: A Network-Based Perspective." *Journal of Public Policy* 18, 3, pp. 213–39.

Brewer, G. D. 1974. "The Policy Sciences Emerge: To Nurture and Structure a Discipline." *Policy Sci.* 5, 3, pp. 239–44.

Brewer, G., and P. deLeon. 1983. *The Foundations of Policy Analysis.* Homewood: Dorsey.

Cahill, Anthony G., and E. Sam Overman. 1990. "The Evolution of Rationality in Policy Analysis." *Policy Theory and Policy Evaluation: Concepts, Knowledge, Causes, and Norms,* edited by S.S. Nagel, New York: Greenwood Press, pp. 11–27.

Capano, G. 2003. "Administrative Traditions and Policy Change: When Policy Paradigms Matter, The Case of Italian Administrative Reform during the 1990s." *Public Administration* 81, 4, pp. 781–801.

Carley, Michael. 1980. *Rational Techniques in Policy Analysis.* London: Heinemann.

Cashore, Benjamin, and Michael Howlett. 2007. "Punctuating Which Equilibrium? Understanding Thermostatic Policy Dynamics in Pacific Northwest Forestry." *American Journal of Political Science* 51, 3, pp. 532–51.

Clemens, E. S., and J. M. Cook. 1999. "Politics and Institutionalism: Explaining Durability and Change." *Annual Review of Sociology* 25, pp. 441–66.

Cobb, Roger W, J.K. Ross, and M.H. Ross. 1976. "Agenda Building as a Comparative Political Process." *American Political Science Review,* 70.

Cobb, Roger W., and Charles D. Elder. 1972. *Participation in American Politics: The Dynamics of Agenda-Building.* Boston: Allyn and Bacon.

Cohen, Michael, James March, and Johan Olsen. 1979. "People, Problems, Solutions, and the Ambiguity of Relevance." *Ambiguity and Choice in Organizations,* edited by James March and Johan Olsen, Bergen: Universitetsforlaget.

Cohen, Wesley M., and Daniel A. Levinthal. 1990. "Absorptive Capacity: A New Perspective on Learning and Innovation." *Administrative Science Quarterly* 35, pp. 128–52.

Coleman, William D. 1994. "Policy Convergence in Banking: A Comparative Study." *Political Studies* 42, pp. 274–92.

Coleman, William D. and Grace Skogstad, editors. 1990. *Policy Communities and Public Policy in Canada: A Structural Approach.* Mississauga, ON: Copp Clark Pitman.

Coleman, W. D., G. D. Skogstad, and M. Atkinson. 1996. "Paradigm Shifts and Policy Networks: Cumulative Change in Agriculture." *Journal of Public Policy* 16, 3, pp. 273–302.

Cox, Robert H. 1992. "Can Welfare States Grow in Leaps and Bounds? Non-Incremental Policymaking in the Netherlands." *Governance* 5, 1, pp. 68–87.

Crenson, M. A. 1971. *The Un-Politics of Air Pollution: A Study of Non-Decisionmaking in the Cities.* Baltimore: John Hopkins Press.

Dahl, Robert A., and Charles E. Lindblom. 1953. *Politics, Economics and Welfare: Planning and Politico-Economic Systems Resolved into Basic Social Processes.* New York: Harper and Row.

Danziger, M. 1995. "Policy Analysis Postmodernized: Some Political and Pedagogical Ramifications." *Policy Studies Journal* 23, 3 pp. 435–50.

Daugbjerg, C. 1997. "Policy Networks and Agricultural Policy Reforms: Explaining Deregulation in Sweden and Re-regulation in the European Community." *Governance* 10, 2, pp. 123–42.

Deeg, R. 2001. *Institutional Change and the Uses and Limits of Path Dependency: The Case of German Finance.* Koln.

Deeg, R., G. Morgan, R. Whitley, and E. Moen. 2005. "Path Dependency, Institutional Complementarity and Change in National Business Systems." *Changing Capitalisms? Internationalization, Institutional Change, and Systems of Economic Organization,* edited by Glenn Morgan, Richard Whitley, and Eli Moen, Oxford: Oxford University Press, pp. 21–52.

deLeon, P. 1999. "The Stages Approach to the Policy Process: What Has It Done? Where Is It Going?" *Theories of the Policy Process,* edited by P. A. Sabatier, Boulder: Westview, pp. 19–34.

Dobuzinskis, Laurent, Michael Howlett, and David Laycock, editors. 2007. *Policy Analysis in Canada: the State of the Art.* Toronto: University of Toronto Press.

Doern, G. B., L. Pal, and B. W. Tomlin, editors. 1996. *Border Crossings: The Internationalization of Canadian Public Policy.* Toronto: Oxford University Press.

Dror, Yehezkel. 1964. "Muddling Through—'Science' or Inertia." *Public Administration Review* 24, pp. 154–7.

Dye, T. R. 1972. *Understanding Public Policy.* Englewood Cliffs, NJ: Prentice-Hall.

Eichbaum, Chris, and Richard Shaw. 2007. "Ministerial Advisers and the Politics of Policy-Making: Bureaucratic Permanence and Popular Control." *The Australian Journal of Public Administration* 66, 4, pp. 453–67.

Eldredge, N., S. J. Gould, and T. J. M. Schopf. 1972. "Punctuated Equilibria: An Alternative to Phyletic Gradualism." *Paleobiology*, San Francisco: Freeman, Cooper, pp. 82–115.

Elster, Jon. 1991. "The Possibility of Rational Politics." *Political Theory Today.* edited by David Held, Oxford: Polity.

Etzioni, Amitai. 1967. "Mixed-Scanning: A 'Third' Approach to Decision-Making." *Public Administration Review* 27, pp. 385–92.

Farr, J., J. S. Hacker, and N. Kazee. 2006. "The Policy Scientist of Democracy." *American Political Science Review* 100, 4, pp. 579–87.

Forester, John. 1984. "Bounded Rationality and the Politics of Muddling Through." *Public Administration Review* 44.

Forester, John. 1989. *Planning in the Face of Power.* Berkeley: University of California Press.

Freeman, Gary P. 1985. "National Styles and Policy Sectors: Explaining Structured Variation." *Journal of Public Policy* 5, pp. 467–96.

Freeman, J. Leiper. 1955. *The Political Process: Executive Bureau–Legislative Committee Relations.* New York: Random House.

Gawthrop, Louis. 1971. *Administrative Politics and Social Change.* New York: St Martin's Press.

Genschel, P. 1997. "The Dynamics of Inertia: Institutional Persistence and Change in Telecommunications and Health care." *Governance* 10, 1, pp. 43–66.

Gortner, Harold, Julianne Mahler, and Jeanne Bell Nicholson. 1987. *Organization Theory: A Public Perspective.* Chicago: Dorsey Press.

Haas, Peter M. 1992. "Introduction: Epistemic Communities and International Policy Co-ordination." *International Organization* 46, 1, pp. 1–36.

Habermas, Jurgen. 1973. "What Does a Legitimation Crisis Mean Today? Legitimation Problems in Late Capitalism." *Social Research* 40, 4, pp. 643–67.

Habermas, Jürgen. 1975. *Legitimation Crisis.* Boston: Beacon Press.

Hacker, J. S. 2004. "Review Article: Dismantling the Health Care State? Political Institutions, Public Policies and the Comparative Politics of Health Reform." *British Journal of Political Science* 34, pp. 693–724.

Hall, P. A. 1989. *The Political Power of Economic Ideas: Keynesianism across Nations.* New Jersey: Princeton University.

Hall, P. A. 1993. "Policy Paradigms, Social Learning and the State: The Case of Economic Policy Making in Britain." *Comparative Politics* 25, 3, pp. 275–96.

Halligan, John. 1995. "Policy Advice and the Public Sector." *Governance in a Changing Environment*, edited by B. Guy Peters and Donald T. Savoie, Montreal: McGill-Queen's University Press, pp. 138–72.

Hawke, G. R. 1993. *Improving Policy Advice.* Wellington: Victoria University Institute of Policy Studies.

Hawkins, Keith, and John M. Thomas. 1989. "Making Policy in Regulatory Bureaucracies." *Making Regulatory Policy,* edited by Hawkins and Thomas, Pittsburgh: University of Pittsburgh Press, pp. 3–30.

Hayes, M. T. *Incrementalism and Public Policy.* New York: Longmans, 1992.

Hessing, Melody, and Michael Howlett. 1997. *Canadian Natural Resource and Environmental Policy: Political Economy and Public Policy.* Vancouver: University of British Columbia Press.

Hood, Christopher. 1986. *The Tools of Government.* Chatham, NJ: Chatham House.

Howlett, M. 1996. "Legitimacy and Governance: Re-Discovering Procedural Policy Instruments." Paper presented to the Annual Meeting of the British Columbia Political Studies Association, Vancouver.

Howlett, M. 2002a. "Do Networks Matter? Linking Policy Network Structure to Policy Outcomes: Evidence from Four Canadian Policy Sectors 1990–2000." *Canadian Journal of Political Science* 35, 2, pp. 235–68.

Howlett, M. 2002b. "Policy Instruments and Implementation Styles: The Evolution of Instrument Choice in Canadian Environmental Policy." *Canadian Environmental Policy: Context and Cases*, edited by D.L. VanNijnatten and R. Boardman, Toronto: Oxford University Press, pp. 25–45.

Howlett, M., and E. Lindquist. 2004. "Policy Analysis and Governance: Analytical and Policy Styles in Canada." *Journal of Comparative Policy Analysis* 6, 3, pp. 225–49.

Howlett, M, and M. Ramesh. 1995. *Studying Public Policy: Policy Cycles and Policy Subsystems.* Toronto: Oxford University Press.

Howlett, M, and M. Ramesh. 1998. "Policy Subsystem Configurations and Policy Change: Operationalizing the Postpositivist Analysis of the Politics of the Policy Process." *Policy Studies Journal* 26, 3, pp. 466–82.

Howlett, M., and M. Ramesh. 2002. "The Policy Effects of Internationalization: A Subsystem Adjustment Analysis of Policy Change." *Journal of Comparative Policy Analysis* 4, 1, pp. 31–50.

Howlett, M, and M. Ramesh. 2003. *Studying Public Policy: Policy Cycles and Policy Subsystems*. Toronto: Oxford University Press.

Howlett, M, and J. Rayner. 1995. "Do Ideas Matter? Policy Subsystem Configurations and the Continuing Conflict Over Canadian Forest Policy." *Canadian Public Administration* 38, 3, pp. 382–410.

Howlett, M., and J. Rayner. 2006. "Understanding the Historical Turn in the Policy Sciences: A Critique of Stochastic, Narrative, Path Dependency and Process-Sequencing Models of Policy-Making over Time." *Policy Sci.* 39, 1, pp. 1–18.

Huitt, R. K. 1968. "Political Feasibility." *Political Science and Public Policy*, edited by A. Rannay, Chicago: Markham Publishing Co., pp. 263–76.

Hupe, Peter L., and Michael J. Hill. 2006. "The Three Actions Levels of Governance: Re-Framing the Policy Process Beyond the Stages Model." *Handbook of Public Policy*, edited by B. Guy Peters and Jon Pierre, London: Sage Publications, pp. 13–30.

in't Veld, Roeland J. 1998. "The Dynamics of Instruments." *Public Policy Instruments: Evaluating the Tools of Public Administration, edited by* B.G. Peters and F.K.M. Van Nispen, New York: Edward Elgar, pp. 153–62.

Ingram, Helen M., and Dean E. Mann. 1980. "Policy Failure: An Issue Deserving Analysis." *Why Policies Succeed or Fail*, edited by Helen M. Ingram and Dean E. Mann, Beverly Hills, CA: Sage.

Jann, Werner, and Kai Wegrich. 2007. "Theories of the Policy Cycle." *Handbook of Public Policy Analysis: Theory, Politics and Methods*, edited by Frank Fischer, Gerald J. Miller, and Mara S. Sidney, Boca Raton: CRC Press, pp. 43–62.

Jenkins, W. I. 1978. *Policy Analysis: A Political and Organizational Perspective*. London: Martin Robertson.

Jennings, Bruce. 1987. "Interpretation and the Practice of Policy Analysis." *Confronting Values in Policy Analysis: The Politics of Criteria*, edited by Frank Fischer and John Forester, Newbury Park, CA: Sage, pp. 128–52.

John, P., and H. Margetts. 2003. "Policy Punctuations in the UK: Fluctuations and Equilibria in Central Government Expenditure Since 1951." *Public Administration* 81, 3, pp. 411–32.

Jones, C. O. 1984. *An Introduction to the Study of Public Policy*. Monterey, CA: Brooks/Cole.

Jordan, Grant 1990b. "Sub-Governments, Policy Communities and Networks: Refilling the Old Bottles?" *Journal of Theoretical Politics* 2, pp. 319–38.

Jordan, Grant. 1981. "Iron Triangles, Woolly Corporatism and Elastic Nets: Images of the Policy Process." *Journal of Public Policy* 1, pp. 95–123.

Jordan, Grant. 1990a. "Policy Community Realism versus 'New' Institutionalist Ambiguity." *Political Studies* 38, pp. 470–84.

Jordan, Grant, and Klaus Schubert. 1992. "A Preliminary Ordering of Policy Network Labels." *European Journal of Political Research* 21, pp. 7–27.

Kagan, Robert A. 1991. "Adversarial Legalism and American Government." *Journal of Policy Analysis and Management* 10, 3, pp. 369–406.

Kay, Adrian. 2006. *The Dynamics of Public Policy: Theory and Evidence*. Cheltenham: Edward Elgar.

Kerr, Donna H. 1976. "The Logic of 'Policy' and Successful Policies." *Policy Sciences* 7, pp. 351–63.

Kingdon, J. W. 1984. *Agendas, Alternatives and Public Policies*. Boston: Little, Brown and Company.

Kingdon, J. W. 1995. *Agendas, Alternatives, and Public Policies*. Boston: Little Brown and Company.

Knill, C. 1998. "European Policies: The Impact of National Administrative Traditions." *Journal of Public Policy* 18, 1, pp. 1–28.

Knill, C. 2001. *The Europeanization of National Administrations: Patterns of Institutional Change and Persistence*. Cambridge: Cambridge University Press.

Knoke, David. 1993. "Networks as Political Glue: Explaining Public Policy-Making." *Sociology and the Public Agenda*, edited by W.J. Wilson, London: Sage, pp. 164–84.

Kuhn, T. S. 1962. *The Structure of Scientific Revolutions*. Chicago: University of Chicago Press.

Kuhner, Stefan. 2007. "Country-Level Comparisons of Welfare State Change Measures: Another Facet of the Dependent Variable Problem within the Comparative Analysis of the Welfare State." *Journal of European Social Policy* 17, 1, pp. 5–18.

Lasswell, H. D. 1956. *Decision Process: Seven Categories of Functional Analysis*. College Park: University of Maryland.

Lasswell, Harold D. 1971. *A Pre-View of Policy Sciences*. New York: Elsevier.

Leach, W. D., N. W. Pelkey, and P. A. Sabatier. 2002. "Stakeholder Partnerships as Collaborative Policymaking: Evaluation Criteria Applied to Watershed Management in California and Washington." *Journal of Policy Analysis and Management* 21, 4, pp. 645–70.

Liefferink, Duncan, Bas Arts, and Pieter Leroy. 2006. "The Dynamics of Policy Arrangements: Turning Round the Tetrahedron." *Institutional Dynamics in Environmental Governance*, edited by Bas Arts and Pieter Leroy, Dordrecht: Springer, pp. 45–68.

Lindblom, Charles. 1951. *Bargaining*. Los Angeles: Rand Corporation.

Lindblom, Charles. 1958. "Policy Analysis." *American Economic Review* 48, 3, pp. 298–312.

Lindblom, Charles. 1959. "The Science of Muddling Through." *Public Administration Review* 19, 2, pp. 79–88.

Lindblom, Charles. 1979. "Still Muddling, Not Yet Through." *Public Administration Review* 39, 6, pp. 517–26.

Lindblom, Charles, and D.K. Cohen. 1979. *Usable Knowledge: Social Science and Social Problem Solving.* New Haven, CT: Yale University Press.

Linder, Stephen H., and B. Guy Peters. 1989. "Instruments of Government: Perceptions and Contexts." *Journal of Public Policy* 9.

Linder, Stephen H., and B. Guy Peters. 1990. "Policy Formulation and the Challenge of Conscious Design." *Evaluation and Program Planning* 13, pp. 303–11.

Lindner, J. 2003. "Institutional Stability and Change: Two Sides of the Same Coin." *Journal of European Public Policy* 10, 6, pp. 912–35.

Lindner, J., and B. Rittberger. 2003. "The Creation, Interpretation and Contestation of Institutions—Revisiting Historical Institutionalism." *Journal of Common Market Studies* 41, 3, pp. 445–73.

Lindquist, E. 1998. "A Quarter Century of Canadian Think Tanks: Evolving Institutions, Conditions and Strategies." *Think Tanks Across Nations: A Comparative Approach*, edited by D. Stone, A. Denham, and M. Garnett, Manchester: Manchester University Press, pp. 127–44.

Lustick, Ian. 1980. "Explaining the Variable Utility of Disjointed Incrementalism: Four Propositions." *American Political Science Review* 74, 2, pp. 342–53.

Lyden, F. J., G. A. Shipman, R. W. Wilkinson, and P. P. Le Breton. 1968. "Decision-Flow Analysis: A Methodology for Studying the Public Policy-Making Process." *Comparative Administrative Theory*, edited by Preston P. LeBreton. Seattle: University of Washington Press, pp. 155–68.

MacRae Jr, Duncan. 1993. "Guidelines for Policy Discourse: Consensual versus Adversarial." *The Argumentative Turn in Policy Analysis and Planning.* edited by Frank Fischer and John Forester, Durham, NC: Duke University Press, pp. 291–318.

Mahoney, J. 2000. "Path Dependence in Historical Sociology." *Theory and Society* 29, 4, pp. 507–48.

Majone, G. 1975. "On the Notion of Political Feasibility." *European Journal of Political Research* 3, pp. 259–74.

Majone, Giandomenico. 1989. *Evidence, Argument, and Persuasion in the Policy Process.* New Haven, CT: Yale University Press.

Maley, Maria. 2000. "Conceptualising Advisers' Policy Work: The Distinctive Policy Roles of Ministerial Advisers in the Keating Government, 1991–96." *Australian Journal of Political Science* 35, 3, pp. 449–49.

Manzer, Ronald. 1984. "Policy Rationality and Policy Analysis: The Problem of the Choice of Criteria for Decision-Making." *Public Policy and Administrative Studies*, edited by in O.P. Dwivedi, Guelph: University of Guelph, pp. 27–40.

March, James, and Johan Olsen. 1979. "Organization Choice Under Ambiguity." *Ambiguity and Choice in Organizations*, 2nd edn, edited by James March and Johan Olsen, Bergen: Universitetsforlaget.

Marin, Bernd, and Renate Mayntz, editors. 1991. *Policy Networks: Empirical Evidence and Theoretical Considerations.* Boulder, CO: Westview Press.

May, P. J. 2005. "Regulation and Compliance Motivations: Examining Different Approaches." *Public Administration Review* 65, 1, pp. 31–44.

May, Peter J. 1991. "Reconsidering Policy Design: Policies and Publics." *Journal of Public Policy* 11, 2, pp. 187–206.

Mayer, I., P. Bots, and E. van Daalen. 2004. "Perspectives on Policy Analysis: A Framework for Understanding and Design." *International Journal of Technology, Policy and Management* 4, 1, pp. 169–91.

Mayntz, Renate. 1975. "Legitimacy and the Directive Capacity of the Political System." *Stress and Contradiction in Modern Capitalism*, edited by Leon N. Lindberg et al., Lexington, MA: Lexington Books, pp. 261–74.

McWilliams, William C. 1971. "On Political Illegitimacy." *Public Policy* 19, 3, pp. 444–54.

Meltsner, A. J. 1972. "Political Feasibility and Policy Analysis." *Public Adm. Rev.* 32, pp. 859–67.

Milner, H. V., and R. O. Keohane. 1996. "Internationalization and Domestic Politics: A Conclusion." *Internationalization and Domestic Politics*, edited by R.O. Keohane and H.V. Milner, Cambridge: Cambridge University Press, pp. 243–58.

Mortensen, P. B. 2005. "Policy Punctuations in Danish Local Budgeting." *Public Administration* 83, 4, pp. 931–50.

Mortensen, Peter B. 2007. "Stability and Change in Public Policy: A Longitudinal Study of Comparative Subsystem Dynamics." *Policy Studies Journal* 35, 3, pp. 373–94.

Mucciaroni, Guy. 1992. "The Garbage Can Model and the Study of Policy Making: A Critique." *Polity* 24, 3, pp. 460–82.

Mueller, Claus. 1973. *The Politics of Communication: A Study in the Political Sociology of Language, Socialization and Legitimation.* New York: Oxford University Press.

Nachmias, David. 1979. *Public Policy Evaluation.* New York: St Martin's Press.

Nice, D.C. 1987. "Incremental and Nonincremental Policy Responses: The States and the Railroads." *Polity* 20, pp. 145–56.

Peled, A. 2002. "Why Style Matters: A Comparison of Two Administrative Reform Initiatives in the Israeli Public Sector, 1989–1998." *Journal of Public Administration Research and Theory* 12, 2, pp. 217–40.

Peters, B.G., and F.K.M. Van Nispen, editors. 1998. *Public Policy Instruments: Evaluating the Tools of Public Administration.* New York: Edward Elgar.

Phillips, S. 1996. "Discourse, Identity, and Voice: Feminist Contributions to Policy Studies." *Policy Studies in Canada: The State of the Art*, edited by

L. Dobuzinskis, M. Howlett, and D. Laycock, Toronto: University of Toronto Press, pp. 242–65.

Pierson, P. 2000. "Not Just What, but When: Timing and Sequence in Political Processes." *Studies in American Political Development* 14, pp. 72–92.

Pierson, Paul. 1993. "When Effect Becomes Cause: Policy Feedback and Political Change." *World Polit.* 45, 595–628.

Prince, Michael. 1983. *Policy Advice and Organizational Survival*. Aldershot: Gower.

Pross, A. Paul. 1992. *Group Politics and Public Policy*. Toronto: Oxford University Press.

Radin, B. A. 2000. *Beyond Machiavelli: Policy Analysis Comes of Age*. Washington DC: Georgetown University Press.

Richardson, Jeremy, Gunnel Gustafsson, and Grant Jordan. 1982. "The Concept of Policy Style." *Policy Styles in Western Europe,* edited by Jeremy J. Richardson, London: George Allen and Unwin.

Rochet, C. 2004. "Rethinking the Management of Information in the Strategic Monitoring of Public Policies by Agencies." *Industrial Management & Data Systems* 104, 3, pp. 201–8.

Rose, Richard. 1991. "What Is Lesson-Drawing?" *Journal of Public Policy* 11, 1, pp. 3–30.

Sabatier, Paul A. 1987. "Knowledge, Policy-Oriented Learning, and Policy Change." *Knowledge: Creation, Diffusion, Utilization* 8, 4, pp. 649–92.

Sabatier, P. A. 1988. "An Advocacy Coalition Framework of Policy Change and the Role of Policy-Oriented Learning Therein." *Policy Sciences* 21, 2/3, pp. 129–68.

Sabatier, Paul A. 1992. "Political Science and Public Policy: An Assessment." *Advances in Policy Studies Since 1950*, edited by W.N. Dunn and R.M. Kelly, New Brunswick, NJ: Transaction Publishers, pp. 27–58.

Sabatier, P. A., and H. C. Jenkins-Smith. 1993. *Policy Change and Learning: An Advocacy Coalition Approach*. Boulder, CO: Westview.

Salamon, Lester M., editor. 1989. *Beyond Privatization: The Tools of Government Action*. Washington: Urban Institute.

Schulman, Paul R. 1988. "The Politics of 'Ideational Policy.'" *Journal of Politics* 50, pp. 263–91.

Simmons, R. H., B. W. Davis, R. J. K. Chapman, and D. D. Sager. 1975. "Policy Flow Analysis: A Conceptual Model for Comparative Public Policy Research." *Western Political Quarterly* 27, 3, pp. 457–68.

Simon, H. A. 1957. *Administrative Behavior: A Study of Decision-Making Processes in Administrative Organization*. New York: MacMillan.

Simon, Herbert A. 1955. "A Behavioral Model of Rational Choice." *Quarterly Journal of Economics* 69, pp. 99–118.

Simon, Herbert A. 1957. *Models of Man, Social and Rational: Mathematical Essays on Rational Human Behavior in a Social Setting*. New York: Wiley.

Smith, A. 2000. "Policy Networks and Advocacy Coalitions: Explaining Policy Change and Stability in UK Industrial Pollution Policy?" *Environment and Planning C: Government and Policy* 18, pp. 95–114.

Smith, Gilbert, and David May. 1980. "The Artificial Debate between Rationalist and Incrementalist Models of Decision-Making." *Policy and Politics* 8, 2, pp. 147–61.

Smith, Martin J. 1993. *Pressure, Power and Policy: State Autonomy and Policy Networks in Britain and the United States*. Aldershot: Harvester Wheatsheaf.

Smith, Martin J. 1994. "Policy Networks and State Autonomy." *The Political Influence of Ideas: Policy Communities and the Social Sciences,* edited by S. Brooks and A.G. Gagnon, New York, NY: Praeger.

Smith, R. A. 1979. "Decision Making and Non-Decision Making in Cities: Some Implications for Community Structural Research." *American Sociological Review* 44, 1, pp. 147–61.

Sobeck, J. 2005. "Comparing Policy Process Frameworks: What Do They Tell Us About Group Membership and Participation for Policy Development?" *Administration & Society* 35, 3, pp. 350–74.

Steinberg, M. W. 1998. "Tilting the Frame: Considerations on Collective Action Framing from a Discursive Turn." *Theory and Society* 27, 6, pp. 845–72.

Stillman, Peter G. 1974. 'The Concept of Legitimacy', *Polity* 7, 1, pp. 32–56.

Thelen, K. 2003. "How Institutions Evolve: Insights from Comparative Historical Analysis." *Comparative Historical Analysis in the Social Sciences*, edited by J. Mahoney and D. Rueschemeyer, Cambridge: Cambridge University Press, pp. 208–40.

Thelen, Kathleen. 2004. *How Institutions Evolve: The Political Economy of Skills in Germany, Britain, the United States and Japan*. Cambridge: Cambridge University Press.

Torgerson, Douglas. 1986. "Between Knowledge and Politics: Three Faces Of Policy Analysis." *Policy Sciences* 19, pp. 33–59.

Tuohy, Carolyn. 1992. *Policy and Politics in Canada: Institutionalized Ambivalence*. Philadelphia: Temple University Press.

Tuohy, C. H. 1999. *Accidental Logics: The Dynamics of Change in the Health Care Arena in the United States, Britain, and Canada*. New York: Oxford University Press.

Tupper, A., and G.B. Doern. 1981. "Public Corporations and Public Policy in Canada." *Public Corporations and Public Policy in Canada*, edited by A. Tupper and G.B. Doern, Montreal: Institute for Research on Public Policy.

Van Waarden, Frans. 1992. "Dimensions and Types of Policy Networks." *European Journal of Political Research* 21, pp. 29–52.

Vedung, Evert. 1997. "Policy Instruments: Typologies and Theories." *Carrots, Sticks and Sermons: Policy*

Instruments and Their Evaluation, edited by Marie Louise Bemelmans-Videc, Ray C. Rist, and Evert Vedung, New Brunswick, NJ: Transaction Publishers.

Verheijen, T. 1999. *Civil Service Systems in Central and Eastern Europe*. Cheltenham: Edward Elgar.

Verschuere, Bram. 2009. "The Role of Public Agencies in the Policy Making Process." *Public Policy and Administration* 24, 1, pp. 23–46.

Vogel, David. 1986. *National Styles of Regulation: Environmental Policy in Great Britain and the United States*. Ithaca: Cornell University Press.

Ward, Edward. 1954. "The Theory of Decision-Making." *Psychological Bulletin*, pp. 380–417.

Weaver, R. K., and B. A. Rockman. 1993. "When and How do Institutions Matter?" *Do Institutions Matter? Government Capabilities in the United States and Abroad*, edited by R.K. Weaver and B.A. Rockman, Washington, D.C.: Brookings Institutions, pp. 445–461.

Weber, Max. 1958. "Politics as a Vocation." *From Max Weber: Essays in Sociology*, edited by Hans Gerth and C. Wright Mills, New York: Oxford University Press.

Weimer, D. L., and A. R. Vining. 1999. *Policy Analysis: Concepts and Practice*. New Jersey: Prentice Hall.

Weiss, Andrew, and Edward Woodhouse. 1992. "Reframing Incrementalism: A Constructive Response to Critics." *Policy Sciences* 25, 3, pp. 255–73.

Weiss, Carol H. 1977. "Research for Policy's Sake: The Enlightenment Function of Social Science Research." *Policy Analysis* 3, pp. 531–45.

Wollmann, Hellmut. 1989. "Policy Analysis in West Germany's Federal Government: A Case of Unfinished Governmental and Administrative Modernization?" *Governance* 2, 3, pp. 233–66.

Woodside, K. 1986. "Policy Instruments and the Study of Public Policy." *Canadian Journal of Political Science* 19, 4, pp. 775–93.

Yanow, D. 1992. "Silences in Public Policy Discourse: Organizational and Policy Myths." *Journal of Public Administration research and Theory* 2, 4, pp. 399–423.

15

A Fragile State

Federal Public Administration in the Twentieth Century

Alasdair Roberts

Chapter Overview

This chapter reviews the development of Canadian public administration in its formative years, the twentieth century. It does this by using periodization as a technique and ascribing a sense of mission (or crisis in mission) to each of the periods. Canada experienced four periods in the last century: the railway state, 1900–28; crisis and drift, 1929–45; building the new social order, 1946–73; and instability and retrenchment, 1974–99. The next transformation is still in formation, he posits.

Roberts says that Canada came to "big government" late. The reasons were four in number: 1) territorial consolidation, 2) the US threat, 3) lagging industrialization in Canada, and (4) the constitutional limits and conflicts inherent in federalism. The results are also four in number: 1) weak regulatory tools, 2) dependence on public enterprise, 3) decentralized social policy delivery, and 4) a tendency for intergovernmental collaboration. As a result we are a country of weak regulatory instruments and decentralized policy delivery.

In the first period, the mission was territorial consolidation. In the second, initial policy drift was the case, then policy divergence. The US fought the depression with public works, Canada with intergovernmental grants; the US increased economic regulation of the private sector and invented new economic planning tools, whereas Canada preferred its belated policies of regulation and planning (undertaken in 1935 by Bennett). King stalled even this. The mission in the third period, 1946–73, was the construction of a new social order, a more activist state. The federal government undertook a wide range of new social and economic responsibilities, largely using financial inducement—most often using the federal spending power.

The last period, 1974–99, was one of crisis in society. What transpired was a crisis for the federal public service as well, brought about by challenges to its concentration of authority, its mounting debt, and the growth of regionalism and secessionism and an overall distrust of government in general. The effects on public administration were a series of checks on the executive government, dismantling of the state apparatus, deregulation, restraint, cutbacks, and public service management reforms.

The next transformation—the finding of a new mission—is on the author's mind. Roberts reminds us that a sense of mission has marked many of the periods of twentieth-century evolution of Canadian public service, but it currently seems to lack one. One thing current policy-makers are wary about is preaching big government as a panacea (general solution) for every problem. Promotion of the "knowledge-based economy" is a likely candidate for the new mission. However, the same problems that bedevilled the last century will likely continue in this one, particularly federal–provincial policy area disputes and competition from the United States and other nations.

Chapter Objectives

By the end of this chapter, students will be able to do the following:

- Outline the four missions of the Canadian public service in the twentieth century.
- Describe in detail the activities undertaken by the state in fulfillment of these missions at various stages of history.
- Appreciate the distinctions between American and Canadian history and levels of development, and their effects on public administration.
- Explain how complications in federalism, and in particular the "Quebec question," have affected Canadian public policy and public administration.
- Assess to what extent the predictions of Roberts have come to pass.

Introduction

Government as we know it today—so-called **big government**, with its extensive array of mechanisms for redistribution of wealth and other modes of social and economic regulation—is a relatively new invention. In fact, it may be the most important invention of the twentieth century, surpassing in significance any of the scientific and technical advances of that period and often serving as a prerequisite for these other advances.

The invention of big government was partly a cultural project and partly an exercise in organizational engineering. The cultural project involved a transformation in popular understandings about the role that the state should play in the regulation of society. The foundation for this transformation was laid in the nineteenth century, when ideas about the sacred nature or **sacrality of the state** became ensconced in popular thought, and the symbols and rituals designed to promote patriotic love of the state—such as flags and anthems—became familiar parts of everyday life.[1] By the latter third of the twentieth century,

the state had become something more than an object of devotion: it had acquired responsibility for regulating broad swaths of social and economic affairs. Furthermore, it had acquired the extensive administrative apparatus needed to fulfill these broad new obligations.

The development of the Canadian federal government followed a path that was similar in many respects to those followed by the central governments of many other capitalist democracies. On the whole, it was characterized by growing confidence among policy-makers about the capacity of government to remedy the defects of an unregulated capitalist economy and the elaboration of programs to manage economic activity and redistribute wealth. However, the story was not a simple one of steady expansion. Instead, it was a story punctuated by crisis and experimentation. Two world wars provided governments with unexpected lessons about the potential of large-scale economic and social planning.

In Canada, the evolution of central government was also shaped by distinctive local conditions. The exercise of consolidating control over territory—the most basic requirement for nationhood—continued in Canada long after it had been completed in other nations. Even after territorial control was established, fears about political and economic sovereignty persisted, driven by the threat of domination by the United States. Urbanization and industrialization, and the pressures that they imposed on government, also occurred later than in other nations. The growth of the national government was moulded as well by the realities of federalism. Except in wartime, the federal government was hobbled by constitutional limits on its powers and by the need to manage conflicts with provincial governments. The result was an administrative apparatus that featured weakly developed tools for economic regulation, a heavy reliance on state-owned enterprises, highly decentralized arrangements for delivery of social benefits, and a distinctive capacity for intergovernmental negotiation and collaboration with economic elites.

A combination of crises struck the Canadian government in the last quarter of the twentieth century, compelling significant changes in its administrative arrangements. Some of these developments—such as increasing popular distrust of political authority, doubts about the competence of government in economic planning, and rapid growth in government indebtedness—were experienced in many nations. In addition, the Canadian government struggled with growing regional alienation and support for secession within the province of Quebec. At the end of the century, the problems of indebtedness and secessionism seemed to have been held in check. However, the federal government's influence in social and economic affairs had declined significantly. There was a sense of uncertainty about its role that had not been experienced since the early years of the Great Depression.

The Railway State, 1900–28

A history of the development of the administrative apparatus of the federal government in the twentieth century can be divided into four parts, each comprising roughly one-quarter of the century and marked by distinctive preoccupations. In the first quarter of the century, the evolution of government was driven by one basic imperative: the drive for **territorial consolidation**. Most of the capitalist democracies with which Canada is now compared had, by 1900, established effective control of the land over which

they claimed sovereignty. Even the United States—the nation whose experience most closely paralleled that of Canada—had divided its western territories into states and linked substantial settlements on both coasts through a system of transcontinental railways.

The Canadian situation was more tenuous. Maps that showed the Dominion consuming a broad swath of North America were highly misleading. Its population of 5.3 million was still largely settled on the southern shores of the Atlantic Ocean, the St. Lawrence River, and the lower Great Lakes. Only 600,000 lived west of the Ontario–Manitoba border.[2] Most of the land over which Canada asserted sovereignty remained under direct federal administration as part of its Northwest Territories. This included all the land that now constitutes the upper halves of Manitoba, Ontario, and Quebec, as well as the land that would later form the provinces of Saskatchewan and Alberta, the Yukon Territory, and Nunavut. Most of the Atlantic coast was claimed by Newfoundland, still a separately administered colony of Great Britain. Canadian ownership of the Pacific coast was contested by the United States.

One way of transforming "Canada" from an assertion to a fact was to settle the vast western territories. Immigration into Canada exploded, from 42,000 persons in 1900 to 401,000 in 1913. The influx was motivated by a growing market for the wheat that could be grown on new western farms. Seventy-three million acres of new farm holdings were established between 1901 and 1921. The steady flow of people into the West—and of grain out of the West—demanded an expansion in transportation facilities. Part of the challenge was an improvement in canals on the St. Lawrence River and Great Lakes to accommodate larger grain carriers. But the larger task was an expansion of national railroads. The railway system was not a legacy of the nineteenth century, as is commonly thought. At its peak in the mid-twentieth century, Canada's rail system comprised about 60,000 miles of track. Only 18,000 miles of track had been built by 1900. Almost all of the remaining track would be laid between 1900 and 1926, as a result of expansion into western and northern lands.

The administrative structure of the federal government in this period was primitive and heavily geared towards the task of territorial consolidation. In 1912, the government employed 15,000 people, excluding the 5100 who worked for the Post Office (Table 15.1). Over 3000 employees worked in customs houses, largely because of the government's support for protectionist trade policies and its dependence on tariffs as its principal source of revenue. Otherwise, most federal employment could be related directly to the expansion of rail and water transportation capacity; the promotion of immigration and processing of immigrants; the sale of federal lands to immigrants; and support to these new farmers.

Employment figures may understate the federal government's preoccupation with the expansion of transportation systems in the years preceding World War I. Between 1901 and 1913, half of the government's total expenditures were dedicated to transportation and communication functions. The bulk of this comprised subsidies to support rail-line expansion by private firms, such as the Canadian Pacific Railway and Grand Trunk Railway. Other inducements—such as federal guarantees for private borrowing and gifts of federal land to private firms—were at least as important but never appeared in the tabulation of federal expenditures. Where inducements failed, the federal government would resort to direct ownership. At the time of Confederation, it had built and operated the Intercolonial Railway; later, it built and leased the National Transcontinental Railway; and, in 1917–19, the federal government took over the bankrupt Canadian Northern and Grand Trunk railways. In 1920, the government

Table 15.1   Largest Departments in the Federal Public Service, 1912–99

1912		1935	
Total employment	20,016	Total employment	40,709
Post Office	5,082	Post Office	10,780
Transport	4,235	National Revenue	5,374
Customs	3,214	Transport	4,678
Public Works	1,400	Public Works	3,620
Interior	1,270	Agriculture	2,280
1945		**1970**	
Total employment	115,908	Total employment	244,197
National Defence	28,137	Post Office	45,482
Post Office	13,770	National Defence	39,027
Finance	12,772	National Revenue	18,967
National Revenue	10,706	Transport	17,556
Veterans Affairs	7,364	RCMP	12,253
1985		**1999**	
Total person-years	260,049	Total employment	186,314
National Defence	37,018	Revenue Canada	43,216
Solicitor General (RCMP)	32,462	Human Resources Development	21,848
National Revenue	29,594	National Defence	18,644
Employment and Immigration	24,823	Correctional Service	12,232
Transport	22,976	Public Works and Government Services	11,418

The Post Office became a Crown corporation in 1981 and was excluded from the public service count after that date. Before 1970 and after 1985, only RCMP administrative staff were included in the public service count.
Sources: Data for 1912 to 1970: (Leacy, 1983). Data for 1985 from Estimates. Data for 1999: (Treasury Board Secretariat, 1999).

consolidated its own operations into the Canadian National Railways, which controlled 40 per cent of all Canadian rail lines.

The evolution of the Canadian government in this period differed significantly from that of the American federal government. Within the United States, the task of territorial consolidation had been completed by the turn of the century; its new challenge was to manage pressures associated with rapid industrialization and urbanization. The American government was pushed by Progressive reformers to expand its regulatory functions to protect the new industrial working class and the growing mass of urban consumers against new concentrations of corporate power. The Progressive era was marked by the assertion of a federal role in assuring safe foods and medicines, regulating labour relations, and breaking up or regulating trusts and monopolies (Eisner, 1994: 161–7).

For a combination of reasons, there was no comparable expansion of federal responsibilities in Canada. One was the slower pace of industrialization and urbanization in Canada. In 1920, most Canadians still lived in unincorporated rural areas or worked in agricultural enterprises. The degree of urbanization already achieved in the United States would not be matched in Canada until 1950. The Canadian government was also hobbled by constitutional restrictions that gave much authority for social regulation to provincial governments. As a senior public servant within the Laurier government, William Lyon Mackenzie King attempted to expand the federal government's role in managing industrial relations and succeeded in persuading Parliament to adopt an Industrial Disputes Investigation Act in 1907 (Robertson, 1991: 112). But the law was struck down as an infringement of provincial jurisdiction.

Nor was the Canadian political climate as favourable to regulatory actions intended to check corporate power. Americans, unworried about the problems of territorial consolidation or foreign economic domination, saw only the abuses that might flow from the emergence of monopolies in key sectors such as oil, steel, or banking. The Canadian government, on the other hand, had concluded from its experience in the development of the railway system that the cultivation of more powerful corporate interests might often be in the national interest. There was no enthusiasm for "trust-busting." Although a Combines Investigation Act had been adopted by Parliament in 1910,

it was poorly drafted and weakly enforced (Brecher, 1960). In one case, western farmers were told that a cartel of grain elevator companies served the public interest by ensuring the "orderly marketing" of grain (Rea, 1999).

Crisis and Drift, 1929–45

Popular opinion about the virtues of King's "prosperity budgets" was badly shaken after the onset of the **Great Depression** in late 1929. The Depression is often regarded as a catalyst that led to a quick and dramatic expansion of governmental responsibilities. In fact, the transformation of government was slow and tentative. The severity of the economic decline—often described, even in its early years, as a "crisis" or "emergency"—was widely understood. There was less agreement on how government should respond. The idea that government might take an active role in economic management did not gain influence for more than a decade, and only after another war provided another public demonstration of the power of central economic planning.

Many factors contributed to the onset of the Great Depression. A glut on the wheat market cut western incomes; this was followed by several years of drought and pestilence. After the crash of the American stock market in October 1929, foreign demand for Canadian natural resources and manufactured goods also plummeted. The economic collapse was unparalleled in its severity. Unemployment increased from 3 per cent in 1929 to 23 per cent in 1933, and almost two million Canadians had no source of earned income at all (McNaught, 1986: 246).

At first, many governments floundered. The King government, like the Hoover administration in the United States, was too firmly committed to the doctrine of budgetary balance to contemplate increased spending for economic relief. Both governments—like many others—had tried to improve conditions by increasing tariffs, but this early experiment at intervention actually exacerbated the economic decline. Each government intended to preserve domestic markets for domestic manufacturers, but the cumulative effect was to close off export markets worldwide.

Only after both leaders were defeated—King in the general election of 1930, Hoover in 1932—did governments become more willing to take steps to ameliorate economic distress.[3] But there was still uncertainty about the best course of action, and significant differences existed in the paths taken in the United States and Canada. The Roosevelt administration dramatically expanded spending on federally run public works projects, such as construction of transportation facilities and improvement of federal lands. The Canadian government, by contrast, put little emphasis on direct spending, choosing instead to emphasize larger grants in support of provincially administered relief projects. Transfer payments to the provinces increased from roughly 5 per cent of federal expenditures in 1929 to a Depression-era peak of 25 per cent in 1937 (Statistics Canada, 1988: Table 44; Strick, 1999: 204; US Bureau of the Census, 1976: 1123–34).

There were other differences as well. As part of its New Deal program, the Roosevelt administration expanded the government's role in regulating economic conditions, introducing new mechanisms to control securities markets, a new law on collective bargaining and conditions of work, and new programs to regulate agricultural production and encourage planning within the manufacturing sector. A system of unemployment insurance and a contributory pension plan were introduced in 1937.

In some of these areas, such as securities market regulation and collective bargaining, there were clear constitutional limitations on the Canadian government's ability to act. In other areas, however, the government's authority was more ambiguous. Shortly before the 1935 election, the Conservative government of R.B. Bennett proposed its own version of the New Deal, including new laws to regulate conditions of work, control the marketing of agricultural products, proscribe unfair trade practices, permit joint planning in the manufacturing sector, and introduce unemployment insurance. King, still reluctant to usurp provincial authority, opposed the proposals, and after his electoral success asked the Supreme Court of Canada for a judgment about their constitutionality. The Court's answer was decisively negative.[4] King then appointed a Royal Commission to consider Bennett's proposals further. The Rowell–Sirois Commission did not issue its report—which included a strong endorsement of constitutional amendments to permit a more active federal role—until after the start of World War II. Provinces fiercely opposed most of the Commission's recommendations. However, a modest constitutional amendment to permit

the introduction of unemployment insurance was adopted in 1940. Parliament adopted its Unemployment Insurance Act a few months later—11 years after the onset of the economic crisis (McConnell, 1968, 1971; McNaught, 1986: 257).

There were other, more modest ways in which the authority of the federal government was expanded in the Depression years. A new central bank—the Bank of Canada—was established in 1935 to improve regulation of private banks and control over the nation's money supply.[5] A federally owned airline—Trans-Canada Airlines (TCA)—was added in 1937, as was a federally owned radio service, the Canadian Broadcasting Corporation (CBC). These were not radical innovations. The Canadian National Railways had set the precedent for government ownership of modes of communication that were thought to be vital to the project of nation-building. TCA and the CBC merely applied the precedent to new technologies.

Building the New Social Order, 1946–73

This second post-war transition was distinctive in other ways as well. The aim at the end of World War I had been a return to pre-war conditions, remembered as a time of expansion and social peace. In 1945, no one wanted a return to the circumstances of the Depression years, which had come to be regarded as proof of the inability of a capitalist economy to regulate itself properly. The success of the wartime effort to manage economic affairs seemed to strengthen the case for an expanded government role in social and economic planning. Furthermore, the federal government now had the administrative capacity to undertake a larger role: over the course of the previous three decades it had built a professional civil service, an ability to collect ample tax revenues, the required statistical services, and improved structures for central decision-making.

The case for a larger federal role could also be rationalized by appeal to a new economic doctrine first proposed by the British economist, John Maynard Keynes. Keynes argued that national governments could have avoided the worst effects of the Depression by taking steps to promote public demand for goods and services. Such steps might have included direct government expenditures like the American public works projects; alternatively, governments could introduce social programs that assured citizens of a minimum income. Keynes's influence was evident in Britain's 1942 Beveridge Report, which advocated a range of new unemployment, welfare, health-care, and pension programs. Canadian bureaucrats and academics, conscious of developments in Britain, argued for similar policies in a succession of wartime reports.[6]

By 1945, Prime Minister King could see that the Beveridge proposals might be good politics as well as sound policy. British voters had already replaced the wartime Conservative government with a Labour government committed to the Beveridge plan. Canada's new social democratic party, the Co-operative Commonwealth Federation (CCF), almost won the 1943 Ontario election and formed a government in Saskatchewan in 1944. Before the general election of June 1945, King's Liberal Party promised a more active role for the federal government in the postwar years. The Liberals, King said, would build a **New Social Order** in Canada (Newman, 1995: 348; Morton, 1997: 231).

However, pre-war realities reasserted themselves at a conference of provincial premiers two months later. In many areas the federal government could not act without the co-operation of the provinces, which balked at the assertion of federal power. Construction of Canada's New Social Order would consequently follow a different path from that in Britain: it would proceed more slowly and unevenly, relying less on direct administration of services by federal departments, and more on financial inducements to encourage action by provincial governments. Nevertheless, the project of building the New Social Order did proceed, encouraged by the high rates of economic growth that typified the next quarter-century. The amount of money the federal government paid directly to citizens increased steadily (see Table 15.2). A Family Allowance program providing federal assistance directly to families with children was begun in 1945. The Unemployment Insurance program begun in 1940 was also expanded, by eliminating rules that restricted eligibility to low-income earners.

Programs to aid elderly Canadians grew as well, although the federal role was checked by constitutional difficulties. A 1951 constitutional amendment permitted the federal government to extend pension programs, but with an important qualification:

Table 15.2 Federal Government Transfers, per Capita, in 1995 Dollars, 1940–95

Year	Payments to Persons	Payments to Governments
1940	$62	$71
1945	$296	$122
1950	$310	$127
1955	$457	$167
1960	$581	$293
1965	$561	$423
1970	$748	$658
1975	$1,267	$912
1980	$1,324	$925
1985	$1,859	$1,163
1990	$2,027	$1,098
1995	$2,388	$1,140

Note: Transfer payments to persons include CPP payments.
Sources: For data on transfer trends, see Statistics Canada (1988) and CANSIM data.

no federal law could override any existing or future provincial pension law. The Old Age Security (OAS) program, established in 1952, provided a basic level of direct financial assistance to any Canadian resident over 70 years of age. A second program—the Guaranteed Income Supplement (GIS)—was added later to provide aid to low-income OAS recipients. In 1966, OAS and GIS were supplemented with a third scheme, the Canada Pension Plan (CPP), providing payments to senior citizens that were tied to contributions made during income-earning years. However, the province of Quebec exercised its prerogative under the 1951 constitutional amendment to establish an independent program, the Quebec Pension Plan. The remaining provinces acquiesced to the federal scheme only when the federal government promised that it would be jointly controlled.[7] In 1970, all three programs were expanded by lowering the threshold for eligibility from 70 to 65 years of age.

The growth of governmental responsibilities entailed an expansion in the federal bureaucracy—and in particular, a burgeoning of the central agencies that formulated policy and coordinated departmental activities. In 1966, the Treasury Board Secretariat—responsible for oversight of departmental spending—was separated from the Department of Finance. In the next decade, its staff increased fourfold. In the same period, the Finance Department's own staff doubled from 3000 to 6000, the Privy Council Office staff grew from 400 to 900, and the Justice Department staff increased from 300 to 1800. Several ministries of state, whose principal responsibility consisted only of coordinating policy among other departments, were established throughout the 1970s (Savoie, 1990: 63). Within departments, the number of staff solely responsible for formulation and evaluation of policy increased as well, partly in response to the new demands emanating from central agencies.

The post-war boom was brought to a jarring halt in 1973, when a cartel of oil-exporting nations raised the price of fuel. An economy that had been built on the availability of cheap energy was hobbled, and began to experience rapid inflation in wages and prices. The 1973 oil shock—and a smaller 1979 oil shock—initially encouraged the federal government to strengthen its capacity for direct management of the economy. The Supreme Court of Canada was persuaded that the government had constitutional authority to impose peacetime wage and price controls, administered by a new Anti-Inflation Board between 1975 and 1978. (A second and less restrictive wage-and-price-control scheme operated from 1982 to 1984.) The government also tightened its hold on the energy sector. A new government-owned corporation, Petro-Canada, was intended to "Canadianize" the industry through acquisition of its foreign-owned competitors (Strick, 1999: 241). The 1980 National Energy Program included a range of subsidies and regulatory reforms aimed at hastening this Canadianization through preferential treatment of domestically owned firms (Foster, 1982: 149–50).

Instability and Retrenchment, 1974–99

In the last quarter of the century, the federal government was challenged in three ways: by popular discontent about the concentration of governmental authority and doubts about its competence in managing the economy; by pressure to restrain the growth of government debt; and by regional disaffection and secessionist pressures. This led, in the last decade of the century, to substantial **retrenchment** within the

federal government and uncertainty about the role it would play in national life in the next century.

During the two world wars, the extension of economic controls and government ownership had been widely accepted as a necessary—and effective—method of responding to emergency conditions. But the experiments of the 1970s were not received so well. On the contrary, they often provoked deep resentment. Some Canadians complained about the emergence of a class of superbureaucrats (Campbell & Szablowski, 1979) whose influence over everyday life seemed contrary to democratic principles. Fears about the expansion of governmental authority were fuelled by the 1976 Lambert Royal Commission, which described "a grave weakening, and in some cases an almost total breakdown, in the chain of accountability" within the federal government.

The Westminster system of government had always been criticized for the degree to which it concentrated political authority in the hands of cabinet ministers and bureaucrats, but now these criticisms seemed to gather new force. This was not simply a result of economic dislocation. Throughout the post-war period, there had been a growing emphasis on the importance of protecting basic human rights against arbitrary government action. Even in Canada, fears about abuse of power were encouraged by the Watergate scandal and the resignation in 1974 of President Richard Nixon.

The result of all these trends was a tightening of legislative and constitutional checks on executive power. In 1977, Parliament amended the Auditor General Act to give the Office of the Auditor General broader authority to determine whether government expenditures were producing value for money. The Canadian Human Rights Act, adopted in the same year, established an independent Commission to provide remedies for discrimination by federal organizations. In 1982, Parliament established two more oversight organizations. The Privacy Act gave the Office of the Privacy Commissioner a mandate to regulate the collection of personal information from citizens by the federal government. The companion Access to Information Act established a limited right of access to federal government records, which is enforced by the Office of the Information Commissioner. Later in the decade, new legislation and administrative codes were adopted to regulate relationships between public officials and lobbyists.

The most important of these new checks on executive power was probably the Charter of Rights and Freedoms, one of several reforms to the Canadian Constitution completed in 1982. The Charter, which proscribes government action that interferes unjustifiably with specified civil liberties, had a profound effect on the formulation of policy within the federal bureaucracy. It also strengthened the role of the federal Justice Department, which provides opinions on the constitutionality of proposed policies and was said to have acquired "a range of power and influence rivalling only that of the Finance Department" (Hiebert, 1999; Monahan & Finkelstein, 1993: 7).

Declining faith in the capacity of the federal government to manage the economy eventually led to a dismantling of much of the administrative apparatus that had been built up in preceding years. The Progressive Conservative government elected in 1984 began to sell off many government-owned enterprises in an attempt to "reduce the size of government in the economy . . . [and] improve market efficiency" (Strick, 1999: 77) (see Table 15.3). The **privatization** program was slowed because of the government's preoccupation with national unity issues and its worry that privatization could lead to job losses and increased regional alienation (Savoie,

Table 15.3   Privatization of Federally Owned Enterprises, 1985–1999

Enterprise	Activity	Year
Northern Transportation	Trucking	1985
de Havilland Aircraft of Canada	aircraft manufacture	1986
Canadair	aircraft manufacture	1986
Canadian Arsenals	munitions	1986
Nanisivik Mines	Mining	1986
Pêcheries Canada	fish processing	1986
Route Canada	Trucking	1986
Teleglobe Canada	telecommunications	1987
Canada Development Corporation	venture capital	1987
Fishery Products International	fish processing	1987
CN Hotels	Hotels	1988
CNCP Telecommunications	telecommunications	1988
Northern Canada Power Commission	electricity generation and distribution	1988
Terra Nova Telecommunications	telecommunications	1988
Air Canada	air transportation	1989
Eldorado Nuclear	uranium mining and processing	1991
Co-Enerco Resources	oil and gas production	1992
Nordion International	nuclear-based industrial and medical products	1992
Telesat Canada	satellite telecommunications	1992
Canadian National Railways	rail transportation	1995
Petro-Canada	petroleum production and retailing	1991–5
Nav Canada	air navigation systems	1996
Canada Communications Group	printing and publishing	1996–7
National Sea Products	fish processing	1997
Theratronics International	radiation therapy equipment	1998

1990: 265). However, the Liberal government elected in 1993 continued the effort. The oldest and most venerable enterprise, Canadian National Railways, was privatized in 1995 (Bruce, 1997).

Other mechanisms for economic regulation also were weakened by the Conservative government. Rules restricting foreign acquisition of Canadian businesses were loosened. The Foreign Investment Review Agency was transformed into a new entity, Investment Canada, with a mandate to encourage foreign investment in Canada. The 1980 National Energy Program was abandoned and the regulatory role of the National Energy Board limited. The federal government surrendered the role traditionally played by the Canadian Transport Commission in regulating competition in the railway and airline industries. However, there was less enthusiasm for deregulation of the broadcasting and telecommunications sectors, given the important role these industries continued to play in maintaining Canada's "identity and sovereignty" (Doern & Wilks, 1998: 124). Cabinet also limited its role in providing direction to the Bank of Canada regarding the development of Canadian monetary policy (Thiessen, 1998).

Since 1945, governments had been negotiating trade agreements aimed at reducing barriers to international trade. In the 1980s, trade liberalization efforts intensified, resulting in a series of agreements—such as the 1989 US–Canada Free Trade Agreement, the 1994 North American Free Trade Agreement, and the 1994 Uruguay Round trade agreements. The immediate effect of these agreements was to limit the capacity of the federal government to protect Canadian industries against foreign competitors through the imposition of high import tariffs. However, the agreements also imposed increasingly tight restrictions on non-tariff barriers, such as government subsidies or regulations that unfairly favoured domestic producers. In 1999, for example, the World Trade Organization directed the Canadian government to dismantle programs run by the Canadian Dairy Commission and the Department of Industry, which it said constituted unfair practices under the Uruguay Round agreements.

These efforts at **economic liberalization** did not solve another growing problem: the imbalance of federal expenditures and revenues following the 1973 oil shock. By the 1980s, the federal government regularly relied on borrowing to finance over 20 per cent of its annual spending. As federal indebtedness grew,

so did the proportion of federal spending that was absorbed on interest charges. The federal government, said Finance Minister Michael Wilson, was on a "treadmill of borrowing money to pay interest on the past debt" (Strick, 1999: 191) (see Table 15.4).

The drive to restrain expenditures was prolonged and painful. By necessity, key targets for restraint included transfer programs, which accounted for the largest proportion of government spending.

Table 15.4   Federal Deficit and Interest Payments as per cent of Total Expenditures, 1974–1998

Year	Deficit (%)	Interest on Debt (%)
1974	26.4	10.3
1975	8.5	10.4
1976	6.7	11.5
1977	14.6	11.6
1978	19.7	13.1
1979	16.3	15.1
1980	15.9	16.0
1981	8.0	18.8
1982	18.3	19.6
1983	22.0	18.8
1984	24.2	20.2
1985	24.7	21.6
1986	18.6	22.5
1987	15.3	22.6
1988	13.3	24.1
1989	13.7	26.5
1990	15.9	27.1
1991	17.2	24.9
1992	16.1	23.5
1993	18.1	22.9
1994	15.3	23.6
1995	13.2	26.1
1996	5.6	26.5
1997	25.2	26.3
1998	25.9	26.1

Source: Statistics Canada, National Economic and Financial Accounts, Catalogue no. 13–001.

Eligibility for the Family Allowance program was restricted in 1989; in 1993, the program was replaced with a new, limited-eligibility Child Tax Benefit. Benefits under the Unemployment Insurance program were reduced throughout the 1990s. (Its name was changed to Employment Insurance in 1996.) Eligibility for the Old Age Security program was also restricted in 1989. In 1996, the federal government attempted to replace this program and the Guaranteed Income Security program with a new, more limited "seniors' benefit," but withdrew the proposal in 1998. Net benefits under the Canada Pension Plan were reduced and a new body, the CPP Investment Board, was established to oversee the investment of CPP funds in the stock market.

Federal payments to provinces were also controlled. In 1977, the federal government adopted a new model for grants, known as Established Programs Financing (EPF), which limited its liability for provincial health and education costs. In 1986 and again in 1990, EPF was amended to control the rate of increase in assistance to provinces. New restrictions on the other major transfer program, the Canada Assistance Plan (CAP), were also imposed in 1990. In 1996, EPF and the CAP were consolidated into a single program, the Canada Health and Social Transfer (CHST). At the same time the federal government announced its intention to reduce CHST payments by 40 per cent over the next three years (Maslove, 1996; Strick, 1999: 213–16).

These efforts at retrenchment caused deep concern, and not only because of the harm that might be done to vulnerable citizens or valued public services. Over 30 years, these social programs had become powerful instruments for promoting a shared identity among the citizens of a weak federal state. The federal government, and other proponents of a stronger federation, used these programs as reifications of a "common Canadian identity" that was said to trump regional and linguistic differences. As a 1991 Ontario government report observed:

A national system of health care, an array of income support programs, free public and secondary education, and affordable post-secondary education are claims that all Canadians make on their governments. Taken together, these programs represent and symbolize Canadians' sense of themselves as members of a community where solidarity and mutual responsibility are fundamental social norms. (Newman, 1995: 343)

The erosion of federal spending on universal social programs led some observers to worry about a concomitant growth in constitutional instability.

Other institutions that had served as instruments for national integration also suffered setbacks. The Canadian Broadcasting Corporation experienced sharp reductions in appropriations, compelling it to reduce services and provoking worries about the threat that might be posed to national culture (Manera, 1996: 21, 187). The Department of National Defence was obliged to abandon an ambitious modernization plan that had been laid out in a 1987 White Paper. It attempted to reduce the impact of budget cuts by deferring acquisitions, contracting out functions, and reducing personnel, but by the end of the 1990s the department still suffered from the twin problems of inadequate equipment and slumping morale.

The last but most serious crisis confronted by the federal government over the last decades of the century arose as a result of the intensification of separatist sentiments in the province of Quebec. The Royal Commission on Bilingualism and Biculturalism (1963–71) described one language-based cause of alienation: the exclusion of francophones from key posts in the federal civil service and the use of English as the language of business within government. (This was one of the unanticipated consequences of the civil service reforms undertaken at the turn of the century [Granatstein, 1998; Roberts, 1999].) The government took steps to improve recruitment and promotion of francophones through the 1969 Official Languages Act, which established French and English as the languages of work in federal institutions and created an Official Languages Commissioner to see that the policy was enforced (Hodgetts et al., 1972: 473 et seq.). Official bilingualism was a contentious policy. In 1976, for example, many pilots went on strike in response to federal attempts to apply the principle to air traffic control within the province of Quebec (Borins, 1983).

The separatist movement shaped the federal bureaucracy in other ways. Following the FLQ crisis of October–December 1970, the federal internal security service—then part of the Royal Canadian Mounted Police—began clandestine operations against political and cultural groups within Quebec that it considered to be potentially dangerous (French & Béliveau, 1979). Public revelations about these operations provoked an independent inquiry and ultimately an overhaul of the RCMP. In 1984, a separate Canadian Security Intelligence Service was set up to be monitored by an independent review agency, the Security Intelligence Review Committee.

The federal government also began to expand its capacity to undertake extensive communications programs. Federal expenditures on advertising increased by 70 per cent in real terms between 1978 and 1992 (Rose, 2000), and the amount spent on polling and market research and other modes of communication probably increased similarly. This period of expansion began with the government's attempt to use mass communications to win over voters in Quebec's May 1980 referendum on sovereignty-association. By 1990, however, it was using similar techniques for other purposes, as in its 1989–90 campaign to quell popular opposition to the new Goods and Services Tax (Rose & Roberts, 1995).

Intergovernmental discussions about constitutional reforms that would respond to the separatist threat intensified in the early 1970s. This contributed to the expansion of staffs specializing in federal-provincial relations. In 1975, the federal government created a new central agency, the Federal–Provincial Relations Office, comprising staff formerly located in the Privy Council Office (Savoie, 1999: 148–53). Traditionally, negotiations on constitutional reform were undertaken by the prime minister and the premiers in closed-door meetings—a mode of decision-making characterized as executive federalism (Smiley, 1987). However, citizens and non-governmental organizations grew increasingly impatient with these processes, calling them undemocratic. The defeat in 1990 of the Meech Lake Accord constitutional reforms was partly attributable to such complaints. In 1992, the federal government used a different approach, emphasizing widespread consultations and employing a referendum for final ratification of yet another set of constitutional proposals. These proposals—the Charlottetown Accord—were also defeated, but it seemed that the federal government had entered a new era in which public consultations on proposed policy changes would become the norm rather than the exception (Boyer, 1992: 223–58; Sterne & Zagon, 1997).

Since 1992, no serious attempts at constitutional reform have been attempted. After Quebec separatists were narrowly defeated in a second referendum in 1995, the federal government sought to devolve powers in other ways. It began to give provinces responsibility for the design and delivery of federally funded labour-market training and social housing programs. New and more independent bodies, such as the Canadian Tourism Commission and the Canadian Food Inspection Agency, were created to encourage closer federal–provincial collaboration in those areas. The government promised that it would only use its spending power to encourage the establishment of new provincial social programs with the consent of a majority of provinces, and with a provision for provinces to opt out by designing distinct, but still federally supported, programs. In contrast to the methods used during the constitutional tumult of the early 1990s, these reforms were made through the traditional method of closed-door negotiations between federal and provincial officials.

The Next Transformation

As the century ended, so, too, did the period of retrenchment within the federal government. The federal budget produced a surplus for the first time in 23 years, with more surpluses expected in following years. The advent of this new era of surpluses produced new calls for a re-expansion of federal programs. The government responded with modest initiatives, including steps to address the "quiet crisis" within the federal public service (Clerk of the Privy Council, 1997). However, policy-makers remained chary of grand gestures that might upset the government's books (Chrétien, 1999). "Never again," Finance Minister Paul Martin told Parliament, "will we allow the spectre of overspending to haunt this land. Never again will we let old habits return—of defining bigger government as better government, of believing that every problem requires another program" (Martin, 1998).

The federal government was not simply bound by fiscal pressures. It also seemed to confront a crisis of mission. In the early years of the century, the central purpose of the federal government—the consolidation of its claim to a vast territory—had been clear enough. By mid-century, the task of territorial consolidation had been largely completed and the federal government had moved on to a second project: the construction of a web of regulatory and redistribution programs designed to remedy the excesses of an unrestrained capitalist economy. But this project now seemed to have exhausted itself—because of disenchantment with the effects of intervention, new proscriptions within international agreements on interventionist policies, and public unwillingness to bear the costs of redistribution. A sense of malaise now seemed to settle on federal policy-makers. Even if surpluses were available, there was no grand conception of government that helped to explain how they might be spent. Observers complained about a policy vacuum within federal institutions (DeMont & Lang, 1999). Even the finance minister seemed to agree that the government was in the midst of another transformation:

> Central governments such as Canada's have become too small to deal with the big, global issues, yet they remain too large and distant to deal with problems of local concern. So the challenge is to redefine the role of central government as an institution that can do a limited number of things well, instead of continuing to pretend it can do everything for everybody. (Newman, 1995: 357)

The unresolved question was how to choose the "limited number of things" that government would do.

The most promising candidate for a new national project was built upon the concept of **competitiveness** within the international trading system (Porter, 1990, 1991). This new paradigm put a premium on lowering trade barriers, promoting overseas trade, and improving the capacity of workers and firms to innovate and adapt to the demands of the global marketplace. The Liberal government explained in its 1999 Throne Speech: "In the global, knowledge-based economy, the advantage goes to countries that are innovative, have high levels of productivity, quickly adopt the latest technology, invest in skills development for their citizens, and seek out new opportunities around the world" (Privy Council Office, 1999).

Many other governments had begun to frame debates about the role of government in similar terms. Many of the traditional functions of government—such as education, health care, and welfare expenditures—were now recast as "investments" designed to create a globally competitive workforce. Social programs that were once defended on humanitarian grounds became "economic assets" instead (DeMont & Lang, 1999: 195). In Canada, however, the project of promoting competitiveness ran afoul of a familiar problem. Jurisdiction over many of the relevant policies remained with provincial governments. For example, the new paradigm emphasized the development of a "highly qualified, well-educated" workforce (DFAIT, 1999), but education was an area of provincial jurisdiction. As a consequence, the federal government proceeded cautiously, going to extraordinary lengths to assuage provincial concerns about incursions on their authority. To run a new national scholarship program, the federal government established a quasi-private institution run by a board appointed in part by provincial governments (Martin, 1998). Even with these precautions, however, the program was attacked as a violation of provincial prerogatives.

Whether competitiveness will prove to be a transient or enduring preoccupation remains an open question. In the twenty-first century, Canada will be confronted with a range of internal and external challenges. The proportion of elderly Canadians will double, and overall population growth will slow significantly. Canada's place in the world, measured either by share of population or by economic activity, will be reduced. Its environment may be dramatically altered as a consequence of global warming. Any of these trends—or events that cannot yet be foreseen—may cause a dramatic transformation in popular opinion about the proper role of the federal government.

Important Terms and Concepts

big government	New Social Order	sacrality of the state
competitiveness	privatization	(or sacralized state)
economic liberalization	retrenchment	territorial consolidation
Great Depression		

Study Questions

1. What was the nature of the territorial challenges Canada faced in its first quarter-century? What were the effects on the federal government's administrative structure, employment figures, and expenditures? Why was the expansion of federal responsibilities in Canada in this period so modest compared with the United States?

2. Over and above the general factors affecting Canada's fortunes in the first part of the twentieth century, there was, of course, World War I (1914–18). What specific effects did it have on federal public administration?

3. How did the Great Depression of the 1930s and then World War II affect federal public administration in Canada?

4. What was the effect of the growth of big government (1946–73) on the federal public administration? Summarize the purposes of the social and economic programs introduced in this era. How many are still with us?

5. In the last quarter of the twentieth century, public administration saw a series of checks on the executive government, dismantling of the state apparatus, deregulation, restraint, cutbacks, and public service management reforms. What programs, policies and administrative moves were examples of initiatives in each of each of these categories?

6. Summarize the missions apparent in each of the last four quarter-centuries in Canada. Is Roberts accurate when he says that the modern public sector tends to lack a mission? Describe what you think what a tenable mission for the next quarter-century could be, based on present trends.

7. Review Tables 15.3 and 15.4. Put into words the significance of these figures and facts. Analyze the trends in the data, and give some probable explanations for them.

Notes

1   The emergence of the sacralized state in the American context is described by Delbanco (1999). A *sacralized state* is one that has become established as a font of important values and as an object of quasi-religious devotion among citizens. Such a state becomes an instrument through which individuals imbue their own lives with meaning. The phrase "true patriots' love" is taken from the 1908 version of "O Canada," written by Alexander Stanley Weir. The last stanza of Weir's lyrics conflated patriotism and religious devotion.

> Ruler Supreme, who hearest humble prayer
> Hold our dominion within thy loving care;
> Help us to find, O God, in thee
> A lasting, rich reward,
> As waiting for the Better Day
> We ever stand on guard.

The original French lyrics by Sir Adolphe-Basile Routhier achieved a similar conflation. In translation:

> Canada! Land of our forefathers
> Thy brow is wreathed with a glorious garland of flowers
> As in thy arm ready to wield the sword,
> So also is it ready to carry the cross.

> Thy history is an epic of the most brilliant exploits.
> Thy valour steeped in faith
> Will protect our homes and our rights
> Will protect our homes and our rights.

2   The statistics in this section are taken from Urquhart (1965). For good surveys of Canadian history in this period, see McNaught (1986) and Morton (1997).

3   The Roosevelt administration, which began in March 1933, was also elected on a commitment to budgetary balance, although it quickly recanted.

4   The Supreme Court's decision was referred to the final judicial authority for Canada at the time, the Judicial Committee of the Privy Council in London. The Judicial Committee affirmed the Supreme Court's decision.

5   The Bank was first established as a privately run entity in 1935, and then nationalized in 1938 (Granatstein, 1998: 49–56).

6   The two most influential were the report of the Advisory Committee on Reconstruction, published in February 1943, widely known as the Marsh Report, and the White Paper on Employment and Income, published in 1945.

7   Changes to the federal plan require the consent of two-thirds of the remaining provinces representing two-thirds of the population.

References

Borins, S.F. 1983. *The Language of the Skies: The Bilingual Air Traffic Control Conflict in Canada*. Montreal and Kingston: McGill-Queen's University Press and Institute of Public Administration of Canada.

Bothwell, R., I. Drummond, and J. English. 1989. *Canada Since 1945*. Toronto: University of Toronto Press.

Boyer, P. 1992. *Direct Democracy in Canada: The History and Future of Referendums*. Toronto: Dundurn Press.

Brecher, I. 1960. "Combines and Competition: A Re-Appraisal of Canadian Public Policy." *Canadian Bar Review* 38, pp. 522–93.

Bruce, H. 1997. *The Pig That Flew: The Battle To Privatize Canadian National*. Toronto: Douglas & Macintyre.

Campbell, C., and G.J. Szablowski. 1979. *The Superbureaucrats: Structure and Behaviour in Central Agencies*. Toronto: Macmillan of Canada.

Canada. 1979. Royal Commission on Financial Management and Accountability. (Lambert.) *Final Report*, Ottawa, 1979.

Chrétien, J. 1998 Notes for an address on the occasion of the 69th Annual General Meeting of the Canadian Chamber of Commerce, Saint John, NB. Office of the Prime Minister, 13 Sept. 1998.

Clerk of the Privy Council. 1997. *Fourth Annual Report on the Public Service of Canada*. Ottawa: Privy Council Office, 3 Feb.

Delbanco, A. 1999. *The Real American Dream*. Cambridge, MA: Harvard University Press.

DeMont, P., and J.E. Lang. 1999. *Turning Point*. Toronto: Stoddart.

Department of Foreign Affairs and International Trade (DFAIT). 1999. *Human Resources in Canada: Our People Make the Difference*. Ottawa: DFAIT, Aug.

Doern, G.B., and S. Wilks. 1998. "No Longer 'Governments in Miniature': Canadian Sectoral Regulatory Institutions." *Changing Regulatory Institutions in Britain and North America*, edited by Doern and Wilks, Toronto: University of Toronto Press, pp. 108–32.

Duxbury, L., L. Dyke, and N. Lam. 1999. *Building a World-Class Workforce*. Ottawa: Treasury Board Secretariat, Jan.

Eisner, M.A. 1994. "Discovering Patterns in Regulatory History: Continuity, Change, and Regulatory Regimes." *Journal of Policy History* 6, 2, pp. 157–87.

Foster, P. 1982. *The Sorcerer's Apprentices*. Toronto: Collins.

French, R., and A. Béliveau. 1979. *The RCMP and the Management of National Security*. Montreal: Institute for Research on Public Policy.

Granatstein, J.L. 1998. *The Ottawa Men: The Civil Service Mandarins, 1935–1957*. Toronto: University of Toronto Press.

Greenspon, E., and A. Wilson-Smith. 1996. *Double Vision: The Inside Story of the Liberals in Power*. Toronto: Doubleday Canada.

Hiebert, J. 1999. "Wrestling with Rights: Judges, Parliament, and the Making of Social Policy." *Choices* 5, 3, pp. 3–31.

Hilliker, J. 1990. *Canada's Department of External Affairs*. Montreal and Kingston: McGill-Queen's University Press.

Hodgetts, J.E., W. McCloskey, R. Whitaker, and V.S. Wilson, editors. 1972. *The Biography of an Institution*. Montreal and Kingston: McGill-Queen's University Press.

Howlett, M., A. Netherton, and M. Ramesh. 1999. *The Political Economy of Canada*. Toronto: Oxford University Press.

Leacy, F.H., editor. 1983. *Historical Statistics of Canada*. 2nd edn, Ottawa: Supply and Services Canada.

Lindquist, E. 1996. "On the Cutting Edge: Program Review, Government Restructuring, and the Treasury Board of Canada." *How Ottawa Spends, 1996–97*, edited by G. Swimmer, Ottawa: Carleton University Press, pp. 205–52.

McConnell, W.H. 1968. "The Judicial Review of Prime Minister Bennett's 'New Deal.'" *Osgoode Hall Law Journal* 6, 1, pp. 39–91.

———. 1971. "Some Comparisons of the Roosevelt and Bennett 'New Deals.'" *Osgoode Hall Law Journal* 9, 2, pp. 221–60.

McNaught, K. 1986. *The Pelican History of Canada*. Harmondsworth, UK: Penguin Books.

Manera, T. 1996. *A Dream Betrayed*. Toronto: Stoddart.

Martin, P. 1998. *Budget Speech 1998*. Ottawa: Department of Finance, 24 Feb.

Maslove, A. 1996. "The Canada Health and Social Transfer: Forcing Issues." *How Ottawa Spends, 1996–97*, edited by G. Swimmer, Ottawa: Carleton University Press, pp. 283–301.

Monahan, P.J., and M. Finkelstein. 1993. "The Charter of Rights and Public Policy." *The Impact of the Charter on the Public Policy Process*, edited by Monahan and Finkelstein, Toronto: York University Centre for Public Law and Public Policy, pp. 1–48.

Morton, D. 1997. *A Short History of Canada*. Toronto: McClelland & Stewart.

Newman, P. 1995. *The Canadian Revolution: From Deference to Defiance*. Toronto: Penguin Books.

Organisation for Economic Co-Operation and Development (OECD). 1997. *Trends in Public Sector Pay in OECD Countries*. Paris: OECD.

Porter, M.E. 1990. *The Competitive Advantage of Nations*. New York: Free Press.

———. 1991. *Canada at the Crossroads: The Reality of a New Competitive Environment*. Ottawa: Business Council on National Issues and Minister of Supply and Services.

Privy Council Office. 1999. *Speech from the Throne*. Ottawa: Privy Council Office, 12 Oct.

Rea, K.J. 1999. Canadian Economic Development: The Prairie Wheat Economy. 30 Aug. Available at: www.chass.utoronto.ca/echist/lecnotes/lec7_p.htm.

Roberts, A. 1996. *So-Called Experts: How American Consultants Remade the Canadian Civil Service, 1918–1921*. Toronto: Institute of Public Administration of Canada.

———. 1997. "Worrying about Misconduct: The Control Lobby and Bureaucratic Reform." *Canadian Public Administration* 39, 4, pp. 489–523.

———. 1999. "The Duelling Commissioners: Linguistic Politics in the Early Public Service." unpublished manuscript.

Roberts, L. 1957. *C.D.: The Life and Times of Clarence Decatur Howe*. Toronto: Clarke, Irwin and Company.

Robertson, B. 1991. *Sir Wilfrid Laurier: The Great Conciliator*. Kingston: Quarry Press.

Rose, J. 2000. *Making "Pictures in Our Heads": Government Advertising in Canada*. Greenwood, Conn.: Praeger Publishing.

———, and A. Roberts. 1995. "Selling the Goods and Services Tax." *Canadian Journal of Political Science* 28, 2, pp. 311–30.

Savoie, D. 1990. *The Politics of Public Spending in Canada*. Toronto: University of Toronto Press.

———. 1992. *Regional Economic Development: Canada's Search for Solutions*. Toronto: University of Toronto Press.

———. 1999. *Governing from the Centre*. Toronto: University of Toronto Press.

Shortt, A., and D.O. Malcolm. 1911. Memorandum on improvements required in the Dominion Public Service, Queen's University Archives, Adam Shortt Papers.

Smiley, D. 1987. *The Federal Condition in Canada*. Toronto: McGraw-Hill Ryerson.

Spence, E.J. 1947. *Wartime Price Control Policy in Canada*. Ottawa: Wartime Prices and Trade Board, Apr.

Statistics Canada. 1988. *National Income and Expenditure Accounts*. Ottawa: Supply and Services Canada.

Sterne, P., and S. Zagon. 1997. *Public Consultation Guide: Changing the Relationship between Government and Canadians*. Ottawa: Canadian Centre for Management Development, May.

Strick, J. 1999. *The Public Sector in Canada*. Toronto: Thompson Educational Publishing.

Taylor, G. 1997. *Canada 2005: Implications for the Public Service Commission*. Ottawa: Public Service Commission, Feb.

Thiessen, G.G. 1998. "The Canadian Experience with Targets for Inflation Control." 1998 Gibson Lecture. Kingston: School of Policy Studies, Queen's University.

Treasury Board Secretariat. 1999. *Employment Statistics for the Government of Canada*. Ottawa: Treasury Board Secretariat.

Urquhart, M.C., editor. 1965. *Historical Statistics of Canada*. Toronto: Macmillan Company of Canada.

US Bureau of the Census. 1976. *The Statistical History of the United States*. New York: Basic Books.

Ward, N. 1962. *The Public Purse: A Study in Canadian Democracy*. Toronto: University of Toronto Press.

Worton, D. 1998. *The Dominion Bureau of Statistics*. Montreal and Kingston: McGill-Queen's University Press.

Transition Planning in Canada

David Zussman

Chapter Overview

Transitions are one of the most fundamental elements that describe a democracy. They encompass the peaceful transfer of power from one political leader to another and often involve a change in the political parties that govern a nation. This is either an exhilarating and disappointing experience for the participants—depending on whether you are part of the winning or losing political party. This chapter describes transitions at the federal level from 1984 to the present. It is intended to serve as a primer for those interested in transition planning by looking at best practices in Canada.

Chapter Objectives

By the end of this chapter, students will be able to do the following:

- Appreciate how transitions are an important element in democratic practices.
- Understand some of the building blocks that constitute a transition plan for any elected government in Canada.
- Develop a transition plan for a prime minister or provincial premier so that they can move from electioneering to governing after a successful election.

There is a tide in the affairs of men,
Which, taken at the flood, leads on to fortune:
Omitted, all the voyage of their lives
Is bound in the shallows and in miseries . . .
And we must take the current when it serves,
Or lose our ventures.

William Shakespeare, *Julius Caesar*

Introduction

A political **transition** is one of the most unique facets of a constitutional democracy and one that can make or break the hopes and dreams of newly elected governments. In its most basic form, a transition occurs when one political leader and often political party, voluntarily and peacefully, gives up power to a successor. When the usual cloak of secrecy that surrounds transitions is peeled back, it reveals insights into a highly complex human drama surrounding the transfer and acquisition of power from an outgoing leader to an incoming one.

But more importantly, a political transition can make or break the effectiveness of a government's first weeks and months in power and sets the government on a trajectory that will likely define the success of the government for years to come. Depending on the degree of preparation, the transition process begins in the months leading up to the dropping of the writ and then moves through the election campaign. The transition continues in the days between the electoral victory and the swearing-in of a new government, followed by a period of consolidation when the new government puts its final stamp on the decisions that were made during the government's early days.

The most intense phase takes place between the tally of the electoral votes and the swearing-in of a new government. It is during this relatively short period of time, which in Canada is around 14 days, that new or returning leaders have the opportunity to put their personal stamp on their government after battling a typical exhausting and bruising election campaign. This is prime ministers'–elect best opportunity to identify the most suitable people to help them manage the government and to institute a decision-making system that reflects their personal needs and approach to governing. It is at this point that leaders take control of the **machinery of government** and take the first steps towards keeping the commitments that were made during the election.

The importance of a smooth transition and the ability to demonstrate a capacity to govern effectively in the first months of power cannot be overestimated. The capacity and commitment for change will never be stronger in a newly elected government, but the implementation challenges are also considerable. In Canada, the dynamics around transition planning are complex because most transition planning is done out of the public eye and in relative secrecy. On the one hand, parties are blamed for being arrogant if they prepare; on the other, they are criticized if they are not ready to govern only days after winning an election. As a result, the transition experience is limited to a small, relatively secret team of people who work in isolation and away from the day-to-day election activities.

As David Cameron and Graham White have pointed out in their insightful description of the Harris government transition in 1995, a successful transition is inherently a function of extensive and thoughtful preparation (Cameron & White, 2000: 21). It is the creation and execution of a strategy and the logical sequencing of events. The transition strategy provides a road map—a step-by-step guide—to identify how the leader intends to reach his or her goals. It should serve as the foundation for the relevant players, so that everyone knows what will happen and what is expected of each of them. When things go in unanticipated directions, as they will from time to time, the transition strategy keeps the team on track as they work towards the swearing-in date and the formal implementation of their plan.

This chapter moves transition planning in Canada out of the shadows and shines a light on the processes, practices, and pitfalls of this crucial period of time for any government. It also details the types and phases of typical government transitions based on the experiences and insights of federal practitioners from the 1984 election of Brian Mulroney to the present day. The chapter concludes with a series of recommendations to ensure that the next generation of transition leaders can learn from the observations of earlier transition teams and maximize the potential that the transition period offers to incoming and returning governments.

Sections of this chapter are adapted from Zussman, David. *Off and Running: The Prospects and Pitfalls of Government Transitions in Canada.* UTP, 2013. Reprinted with permission of University of Toronto Press.

Types of Transitions

Transitions occur within three unique scenarios. The most dramatic transition takes place when an opposition party wins an election and takes over the reins of power from the incumbent government. The Mulroney Conservatives lived through this experience upon winning the election in 1984, as did the Chrétien Liberals in 1993, the Harper Conservatives in 2006, and the Justin Trudeau Liberals in 2015.

The second scenario also occurs as the result of an election, but in this case the governing party remains in power and the leader remains as prime minister. Mulroney's Conservatives won a second mandate in 1988 and Chrétien's Liberals succeeded with second and third mandates in 1997 and 2000. Stephen Harper's Conservative government also transitioned into a second mandate in 2008, governing with a minority during its second consecutive term, followed by a third victory in 2011 in which it won a majority of the seats in the House of Commons.

The third transition scenario is characterized by a change in the leadership of the governing party outside of the electoral context. Kim Campbell was chosen as the leader of the Conservatives in 1993 and immediately became prime minister. Similarly, Paul Martin won the Liberal Party leadership campaign in 2003 and immediately became prime minister before leading his party in a general election the following year.

Not surprisingly, perhaps, the first scenario that shifts leadership of the country to a new political party offers the most opportunity for transformation but has the greatest uncertainty because the new prime minister will likely have only limited experience managing a government. A new prime minister, a freshly minted **cabinet**, and a voter-validated policy agenda represent a unique opportunity to implement major changes in the way a country operates domestically and internationally.

Ironically, in many respects, the transition faced by a re-elected leader can be as challenging as the other two. Prime ministers elected from an opposition party by necessity must build their government from scratch—while a blank slate can be intimidating, it offers endless opportunities. On the other hand, a re-elected government essentially validates its agenda, making it difficult to justify any significant changes in agenda or operations. Under these circumstances it is difficult for re-elected prime ministers to depart in any significant way from their successful path.

Arguably, however, this is the best time to make key changes in personnel and to specific portfolios. After an election, the caucus, the media, and the public expect changes, so it is a missed opportunity if the returning government decides to stand pat with its current lineup of ministers without having prepared for this opportunity.

Kevin Lynch, the former clerk of the Privy Council, maintains that the transition related to returning governments should be as disciplined as one enacted by a new government, if not more so. But more often than not, a re-elected leader engages in a less rigorous transition exercise with the second electoral victory. "That's the wrong way to operate because you don't renew and rethink," Lynch argues. "You actually, in many ways, get more locked into the status quo when leaders should be taking the opportunity to make a fresh start" (Zussman, 2013).

By all accounts, however, transitions within a party have proven to be the most complex and difficult of the three types to lead and implement. This third type of transition scenario occurs without a national election and instead results from a leadership convention within the governing party. By necessity, leadership contests are conflictual and often very bruising experiences for the contestants, leaving many of them dispirited and angry at the end of the process. As result, as soon as newly chosen leaders are sworn into office by the **Governor General**, their immediate task is to beginning the internal healing process by wrapping defeated candidates and their supporters into the workings of the new government. This requires a degree of sensitivity and awareness of human relations that often challenge politicians who are not used to having to cater to the sensitivities of their colleagues.

The Transitional Model—An Introduction
Four Phases of a Transition

All transitions move through four distinct phases of operation. Phase One sees the leader of a party creating a **transition team**, sometimes as much as a year in advance of an election. The focus of this phase is on preparation and the key task is the creation of the transition strategy and plan that will guide the activities of the party, should an electoral victory occur. This preparatory phase also has parallel activities occurring within the public service under the guidance of the **cabinet secretary** in Privy Council Office (PCO).[1] The cabinet secretary has the responsibility to support the government of the day as the prime minister's deputy minister but, as important, as Clerk of the Privy Council Office has the additional responsibility of preparing the public service to welcome a new government in the event the election yields a change in government. The planning phase continues until the writ is dropped.

The second phase spans the entire electoral period, lasting at minimum thirty-six days, and ends on election day. Assuming a transition team has effectively prepared, very little change occurs on the political side of transition planning during an election. The transition team, distinct from the campaign team, remains behind the scenes, closely monitors changing realities, and continues to move through the necessary activities that will ensure a smooth transition of power.

At this juncture, a parallel process begins within the public service as it kicks its transition planning into high gear. In general, cabinet secretaries appoint a senior member of their management team to lead the transition exercise on behalf of the public service writ large, and to coordinate the transition work of the deputy minister community across within the federal government. The transition planning in departments will closely mirror the work being done at the centre as they prepare for all possible election outcomes by monitoring the election platforms and promises made by the campaigning parties and assessing their implications for existing operations.

There is a critical point, however, during the end of the planning phase or the beginning of the election phase, when the cabinet secretary, with the permission of the prime minister, may meet with the transition team of the major opposition parties (i.e., the ones that could form a government in the judgment of the secretary to the Cabinet).[2] The "merging of agendas," a phrase used by the late John Tait, the highly respected deputy minister of justice and deputy solicitor general, captures one of the most critical elements of the transition exercise.[3] Should an opposition party eventually win the election, this single meeting can set the tone for the entire transition exercise and the first months of operations of the government.

At the point where the election results are announced, the post-election phase begins and the transition team takes centre stage in the critical first days following the election. Phase Three lasts an average of ten to fourteen days in Canada and moves the party through to the swearing-in ceremony and the first days in power. It is an exciting time for the transition team and an exhausting one for the politicians as all the planning plays out under the direction of the prime minister–elect.

The process of building a cabinet is a major preoccupation at this stage of the transition. Behind the scenes, methods are developed to identify potential cabinet ministers, judge their suitability for cabinet, negotiate the swearing-in ceremony with the Governor General, set the agenda for the first cabinet meeting, and prepare the **mandate letters** for each minister. This brief period also includes the creation of the Office of the Prime Minister and the critical first Governor-in-Council appointments that have been awaiting the arrival of the newly elected government. Proper planning and preparation by the transition team and the leader in advance of the election will ensure Phase Three runs as smoothly as possible.

First meetings are now underway between the cabinet secretary, the prime minister–elect, and their respective teams. The deputy minister community is also making last-minute adjustments to briefing books based on the outcomes of the election and are eagerly awaiting the announcement of ministerial portfolios.

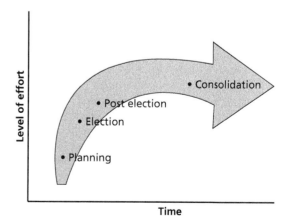

Figure 16.1 Phases of the Transition Process

Source: David Zussman, *Off and Running: The Prospects and Pitfalls of Government Transitions in Canada* (Toronto: UTP, 2013), p. 19.

Phase Four begins the day after the swearing-in ceremony and the first cabinet meeting. It runs through the early days of governing and gives the new government an opportunity to consolidate its hold on the levers of power by monitoring the implementation of the transition plan and adjusting it to the reality of governing. The politicians and public servants are now working closely together to ensure that the promises made during the election campaign are being addressed. Ministers are attending orientation sessions, and their ministers' offices are being staffed and trained. The consolidation of power and the ability to effectively govern during these first weeks and months are a direct outcome of a well-prepared transition strategy and the ability to build new relationships between the politicians and the public service.

Key Players

As the transition moves through its various phases, many people become involved in the vast scope of activities underway. But at its most elemental, the transition revolves around only three players: the prime minister (or leader of an opposition party), their political advisors[4] who may be few or many, depending on the leader's preferences, and the cabinet secretary.

The Prime Minister

The leadership style of the prime minister is the starting point upon which the transition strategy and plan will rest. As a result, one of the most important tasks of a transition team is understanding the leadership style, approach, strengths, and preferences of the prime minister.

Evidence suggests there is no ideal leadership style. Prime ministers need to adapt to the circumstances in which they find themselves—the cabinet they lead, the economic and social circumstances of their era, and, importantly, the problems that arise through the behaviour of their cabinet colleagues. How prime ministers exercise these judgments and how they use their style vis-à-vis their cabinet colleagues affects the fates of their governments as well as their own political futures.

Jean Chrétien created a governing infrastructure that was tailored to his approach and style. He preferred a small cabinet with a minimum of meetings, a very structured and tailored cabinet agenda, and a general orientation that was orderly, professionalized,

and decentralized. The Prime Minister's Office could be heavy-handed on particularly sensitive or crucial issues but Chrétien also gave senior ministers considerable independence to carry out their departmental mandates that regularly updated in light of developments. He trusted his ministers to carry out their responsibilities and contacted them only if they got into trouble (Martin, 2010).

In many ways, Harper and Chrétien shared similar management styles—decisiveness, a reliance on a small number of advisers, an interest in getting at the facts, and a stubbornness to stick with a decision once it was rendered. But not surprisingly, Harper was influenced by the unique characteristics of his early tenure as leader—a newly merged party and the realities of leading a minority government. His approach was to centralize all policy work, especially the communications apparatus, and to limit the influence of his ministers on individual files in their own areas of responsibility.

In the end, prime ministers' decisions are the product of their own life experiences and the benefits that they can derive from both their political and public service advisers following an explicit plan that is well communicated to key players in the decision-making process. Experience has shown that using a generic, off-the-shelf transition plan or operating on an ad hoc basis is a recipe for failure. As Harrison Wellford, one of America's transition experts, has noted: "Good planning, organization, focus, and discipline, taking their cues from the best practices of past transitions, strongly supported by the nominee/president-elect, blessed with a little luck, can greatly increase the chance of success" (Wellford, 2008).

Political Advisers during the Transition Period

The rise of political advisers as permanent actors within the machinery of government is well documented across a broad spectrum of OECD countries. They are here to stay, representing one of the most widespread developments in governance in years. Typically, they are young, relatively inexperienced, and not very knowledgeable about how government works, but they are loyal to their political master and partisan in their approach to their work. They have wide-ranging responsibilities: they prepare correspondence, write speeches, communicate with constituents and citizens, deal with legislation, and advise on policy. When the political leaders whom they serve find themselves in the governing party and the recipient of a coveted ministerial appointment, these political advisers coordinate the minister's work and activities with the Prime Minister's Office (PMO) and connect with the public service at all levels within the minister's portfolio.

Cabinet Secretary

The last set of players that will have a tremendous impact on the success of a prime minister is the senior public service, particularly the secretary to the cabinet. The secretary is traditionally a career public servant chosen by the prime minister to serve as the focal point of his dealings with the vast public service.

It is an understatement to say that the relationship between the prime minister and the cabinet secretary is complex. Traditionally the secretary to the cabinet aspires to become the prime minister's most trusted adviser, especially in policy matters. However, for a number of reasons, the prime minister does not always reciprocate this level of personal intimacy. First, while the cabinet secretary is focused on serving only the prime minister, the prime minister has multiple sources of influence, especially the chief of staff and party apparatus, with which he or she interacts regularly. It is therefore important that the prime minister establish early on in their working relationship how he intends them to interact, so there is no room for misunderstanding.

Pre-Election (Phase I)

As previously discussed, there are four phases to a transition: pre-election, election period, post-election, and consolidation. The purpose of the pre-election phase is to develop a plan that "maximizes the opportunities presented to a newly elected government while seeking ways to reduce the hazards that inevitably lie in wait" (Kumar, 2008). This is the time for creativity, the time to grasp the opportunity to cast the net as widely as possible—to look at new ways of managing government and to enlist a diverse range of knowledgeable people to explore innovative ideas.

Building a Transition Team

Over the past twenty years, each prime minister has reached out to a select group of individuals to take on the responsibility of planning the transition.

The planning period allows a party to thoughtfully discuss and debate issues they will face upon assuming leadership of the nation. A disciplined and strategic approach to the planning period will ensure that the hectic days following an election victory will run smoothly and to maximum benefit for the new prime minister.

There is no hard-and-fast rule for when transition planning should start. Some political parties have begun the transition process more than twelve months before the general election while others, with little apparent chance of winning, don't begin planning until the night before the election when the polls suggest that they will be swept into office. The right timing is dictated by the likelihood of winning the election, the level of interest in planning, and the confidence that the key players around the leader have in the value of the transition exercise as a management tool.

The transition team meetings are discreet and held behind closed doors, leading one to wonder how these people come to be asked to serve in such a capacity. A look back to the Mulroney era and through to our current prime minister reveals that most individuals who are chosen to lead the transition exercise already know the leaders or their senior staff and, as former public servants, academics, or lobbyists, have a good knowledge of how government works. It may come as a surprise to know that, historically, these people are not strong party partisans, but they do bring to the position political instincts that allow them to appreciate the full ramifications of their work.

Jean Chrétien is a case in point. He was never particularly interested in hiring hyper-partisans to work directly for him, although he did recognize the need for people who understood politics. Since his personality and cognitive style was attuned to interpreting every policy issue from a political perspective, as a general rule he preferred to do the political triaging himself, without staff filtering the issues for him. As a result, he hired staff who had had a strong interest in policy in addition to politics.

Once a transition leader is chosen, it is up to him or her to build a cohesive team that can serve the leader through to an eventual victory at the polls or at a leadership convention. The team members are most often engaged because of their specific skills, including the ability to develop and formulate public policy, an understanding of the public service and the machinery of government, skill in political strategy and communications, as well as experience at the centre of government.

Making the choice of the person to head the transition team could logically be seen as the start of the transition process. As is so often the case with personnel issues, the choice is situational, depending to a large degree on the needs and skill set of the leader, the availability of people who have the necessary abilities, and the optics of the choice within the political party. At a minimum, the leader of a transition team needs to have or develop a close relationship with the leader, to understand how government "really" works, to communicate well, to be the public face of the transition after the election, and to be trusted by the campaign team and those who will move into the PMO.

As a starting point, transitions do not include policy development. Policy development is critical to the party and to the leadership of the country, but it is not the role of the transition team to take the lead on developing the policy platform of the party. This is best left to the campaign team and the leader's office. While there is some obvious linkage between the policy agenda and the transition plan, its relationship is sequential. The development of the platform comes first. Then the transition plan lays the groundwork for a smooth transition of power, to ensure that all pieces of government come together to implement the vision and initiatives laid out in the platform.

Tasks of the Transition Team

Serving the Leader

The planning phase is the ideal time to prepare the leader of the party to govern, especially if the leader is a member of an opposition party with no government experience. As I discovered through working with Jean Chrétien on his 1993 transition, even a leader with considerable government experience needs to spend time becoming acquainted with the levers of power and getting up to speed with what has happened in government over the time that the party was in opposition.

As a general rule, it is best to assume that the potential prime minister knows very little about government and governing. Brian Mulroney, Stephen Harper, and Justin Trudeau (except as a child when he accompanied his father) had never been in a cabinet room before they became prime ministers, so their understanding of the importance and functioning of the institutions they were about to lead would have been learned rather informally and theoretically.

This experience, or lack thereof, combined with the leadership style of the individual, requires each transition team to plot its own course during the pre-election phase. Some leaders respond well to evidence-based argumentation grounded in statistics, data, and facts. Some become engaged through anecdotes, stories, and humour, while others prefer tightly scripted logic. The personality and cognitive style of the leader also has an important impact on the choice of cabinet structure and the decision-making system. Some leaders like collaborative decision-making by engaging colleagues in conversation and debate. Other leaders prefer to formulate policy on their own and might prefer to use cabinet as a forum for testing, adjusting, and validating their ideas. Still others use cabinet as a method to communicate their decisions. Understanding these dynamics allows the transition team to outline appropriate options for prime ministers as they decide how best to manage their cabinet.

Elements of a Transition Plan

The transition plan dictates the speed, rhythm, and style of the transition. It is a direct reflection of the leader of the prime minister–elect and should be developed, almost in its entirety, during the planning phase. While decisions specific to some positions may need to wait until election results have been tallied, the transition plan necessarily compels a leader to engage in the difficult process of moving forward with the government's policy priorities and balancing the need for machinery-of-government changes.

Derek Burney remembers the task of preparing the transition plan for Harper: "We met regularly and prepared a detailed transition briefing book," he recalls. "What little reference material on transitions in Canada there might be is not readily shared. So we basically started from scratch, with emphasis on practical need and our own best instincts, drawing heavily on our personal experiences in government. The primary focus was on what a new government needs to know, and above all, what it needs to do initially to get organized as a government" (Burney, 2011).

When Mulroney was presented with his transition plan in 1984, the first page artfully captured the delicate balancing act that encapsulates a transition plan: "This briefing book generally provides two types of information—things you have to do and choices you can make. Where choices exist, we have tried to include reasonable options for your decision, accompanied in most cases by our own advice on which seems preferable. You, of course, are free to choose as you wish" (Neville, 1984: 3).

While there are myriad decisions to be addressed in the planning phase, prime ministers must take into consideration four critical elements that will have direct bearing on their success and that of their government. First is the prime minister's choice of personal staff, but especially the chief of staff, since this person will serve as the "eyes and ears" of the prime minister in countless meetings and interactions with others. The chief of staff plays the position of quarterback for the government, and a great deal of thought needs to go into who might be the best choice for this critical position.

The second set of decisions revolves around the size, structure, and membership of cabinet. While there has been some criticism in recent years about the steady weakening of cabinet and cabinet ministers as a collective decision-making body, the cabinet still can have considerable impact on the direction of a government. Without any formal constitutional anchors, cabinet is still the ultimate decision-making body in the land. For those who go into politics (or government, for that matter) and want to influence policy-making, the cabinet table is the only place to be.

The third key element in the transition plan is the relationship that the government wants to establish with the public service. This decision will be determined by a large number of factors, but it will be crucial in setting the direction of the government, defining its policy agenda, and in implementing its election promises.

The final element in the plan is development of a communications and media strategy for the transition, since anticipation of the swearing-in ceremony and the appointment of cabinet ministers will engender much speculation and comment from the media.

Decision Making in Canada

The prime minister holds enormous power in being able to make recommendations to the Governor General on approximately 600 full-time and 2300 part-time positions in agencies, boards, commissions, departments, and tribunals filled by Governor-in-Council (GIC) appointees. Also, appointed through the GIC system are Lieutenant Governors, judges, and certain ambassadors and high commissioners named usually from the ranks of career public servants. Technically, these appointments are made by the Governor

General, but convention dictates that he or she follow the advice of the prime minister.

Upon gaining office, the prime minister is provided with a list of vacancies in key positions that need to be filled. These appointees can be broken down into four major groups, with approximate numbers for each: (1) 75 deputy ministers and associate deputy ministers; (2) 500 heads and members of agencies, boards, commissions, and tribunals; (3) 50 heads of Crown corporations; and (4) 2300 part-time GICs, such as chairpersons, directors, and members of Crown corporations, federal agencies, boards, commissions, and tribunals.

Finally, judicial appointments are especially significant in Canada, since our justice system plays such an important role in balancing the work of the legislature and of the executive, is historically fiercely independent of the government, and also enjoys high levels of public confidence.

Cabinet

Unless one has worked within the small circle of government that has access to cabinet meetings, few people really understand how the cabinet functions. This is partly because each prime minister has complete authority over building his or her own cabinet. According to Bill Neville, "Of all the prime ministerial prerogatives, none is more powerful—nor more personal—than the leader's right to name those who will serve as ministers in the government" (Neville, 1984: s. 3, p. 1) The prime minister must manage within broad legal requirements, but is essentially unfettered when deciding the number of ministers serving in cabinet, the assignment of portfolios, and the people who will hold them.

The Size of Cabinet

Because cabinet-making brings with it vast personal prerogative, there is no right way to tackle this activity. The road map begins with a decision on the size of the cabinet. Some prime ministers prefer an inclusive approach that allows for as many cabinet positions as is reasonably possible. Others try to minimize the size of cabinet in an effort to make it more manageable. In the end, the transition team must carefully consider the strengths and weaknesses of multiple approaches to the size of cabinet and recommend a configuration that best meets the needs of the leader for the time. As always, the final decision will rest with the prime minister.

Transition teams have the unenviable job of reminding prime ministers of two operational maxims that need to remain top of mind when determining the size of the cabinet. First, in effect, each successive addition to the cabinet is chosen from among a less-suitable and less-competent cadre of potential ministers. And second, with each additional cabinet member, the dynamics around the cabinet table change as the meeting room becomes larger and more people are involved in the decision-making.

Ian Clark, former secretary to the Treasury Board, highlighted this dilemma when, in his analysis of the Kim Campbell government, he pointed out: "The smallest Cabinet in recent history was formed by Kim Campbell bringing only 23 ministers to the table. That is considered small by Cabinet standards, but anyone with leadership experience can attest to the difficulty of discussing anything substantively across a group of over 20 people" (Clark, 1985).

Derek Burney remembers having this conversation with Harper in 2006. "At the time I said, 'Prime Minister, once you cut it down, it's only going to go up! It's not going to go down anymore, so let's get it as slim and trim as we can.' I reminded him that you have all of these egos in the Cabinet room. Instead of having to manage twenty-six, you've got thirty-nine. Well it doesn't make your job easier!" (Zussman, 2013, p. 87).

Cabinet Structure and Organization

Once the size of cabinet has been established, its structure and organization need to be addressed. The transition team will often begin with the structure established by the former regime. The starting point is to determine whether or not it is necessary to change the structure, and if so, to what advantage.

Over the years, prime ministers have structured one-, two-, or three-tier ministries, depending how "equally" they want their ministers to be treated and whether they prefer working with a relatively large or small cabinet. The tradition in Canada is to build a one-tier ministry in which all ministers are members of the cabinet. A two-tier ministry is one in which all ministers are members of the cabinet and others are members of a smaller executive committee, often referred, at the federal level, as Priorities and Planning. The three-tier model has the same features as the two-tier, with the addition of a group of ministers who are not members of the cabinet but are a part of the ministry. The three-tier model has been a fixture

of British government for many years and has been used in Australia as well.

Canadian leaders have chosen to steer clear of a full-scale three-tier model. Although, history does not need to continue to repeat itself. The transition team should present the leader with as many options as logically align with his or her leadership style and approach.

Selecting Cabinet Members

Following considerations of size, structure, and organization comes the difficult task of deciding how best to populate the cabinet positions. When selecting members to a cabinet, a prime minister will take into consideration characteristics such as experience in government, loyalty, professional knowledge, and regional, ethnic, and age representation. There are no hard-and-fast rules that need to be followed—the prime minister has complete authority over who is selected, and, over time, who stays in cabinet.

One of the first decisions to be made is whether to appoint a deputy prime minister.[5] No rules determine whether there is a need for a deputy except that Canadian prime ministers have sometimes used the appointment as a way of recognizing the important contribution of a minister, to shore up political support, or to benefit from the administrative skills of a particularly gifted politician.

While there is some debate about the importance or value of the deputy prime minister position, one indisputable and crucial relationship in the Canadian political system is that between the prime minister and the minister of finance. In essence, the prime minister controls the cabinet decision-making system and the appointment process, while the minister of finance is responsible for government spending, the broad economic management of the country, and fiscal and tax policy. Given the allocation of responsibilities between these two key positions, it is not surprising that the prime minister will spend an inordinate amount of time in choosing a minister of finance.

Following decisions regarding a deputy and minister of finance, leadership of the treasury board and external affairs portfolios are next in line. Other key positions will depend on the priorities of the government and the personal perspective of the leader. When Mulroney was selecting cabinet ministers in 1984, his transition plan provided advice, which continues to hold true today:

You will feel that some of your supporters deserve to be rewarded and that you have an obligation to so reward them. Both feelings undoubtedly have merit in several cases. But the point to be emphasized—and I do so with all my strength—is that cabinet appointments should not be considered rewards for past service. They are simply too critical to your present and future to be assigned on any basis other than choosing the best or most talented people you have available to you. There are a multitude of other "reward" prerogatives at your disposal and I urge you to use them, as you deem appropriate. But, subject only to the broadest requirements of representing regions et al., you truly should choose the best and the brightest for your cabinet (Neville, 1984: ch. 3, pp. 6–7).

Once the decision of "who goes where" is made, prime ministers owe ministers their direct and personal leadership, support, and ear when they need it. Because the making of cabinet is the personal prerogative of prime ministers, they are solely responsible and accountable for its composition and performance.

One of the most effective performance management tools that a prime minister employs is the use of mandate letters for each minister. These letters form the accountability accord for ministers, outlining the overall government priorities, the minister's portfolio responsibilities, and specific personal goals for the minister. The substance of these mandate letters is developed by the transition team during Phase One and then later written by the PCO in Phase Three under the close watchful eye of the transition team.

Chrétien distributed mandate letters that were to the point and strategic, leaving the operational and tactical approach for implementation to the minister and his or her team. Alternatively, the mandate letters developed by Harper and his transition team were more detailed and prescriptive, in keeping with his approach to managing the government. Following the 2006 election, Harper also insisted that the mandate letters be handed out the day of the swearing-in. With so many inexperienced ministers moving into key positions, there was a need to give them a script so they had specific speaking points for the inevitable media scrums (Zussman, 2013).When elected in 2015, Justin Trudeau broke new ground, at the federal level, when he made all mandate letters public so that those interested can follow the progress of each minister in implementing the government's priorities.[6] By explicitly articulating ministerial mandates, the prime minister has demonstrated his commitment to running a more transparent government and making it easier for Parliament and the public to hold ministers and the government to account for their actions (or inactions, as the case may be).

Relations with the Public Service

The bulk of responsibility at the early stages of the transition preparation period within the public service falls to the cabinet secretary, who quarterbacks the coordination of all transition-related activities including the preparation of the crucial briefing materials for incoming ministers. Traditionally, and when the transition will follow a general election, the cabinet secretaries participate in early meetings with the transition teams of the governing party and of the opposition parties so that they can develop an overall sense of their governing priorities, should they win the election.

This is a difficult role for cabinet secretaries, since it places them in the delicate position of preparing for a potential change in government while still serving the government of the day. The fine balancing act is possible only when all players acknowledge the independence and professionalism of the public service in its role to provide the government of the day with "fearless advice and loyal implementation" while simultaneously preparing to welcome a new prime minister.

In practical terms, during the early stages, the cabinet secretary customarily appoints a trustworthy senior official to take the lead on the transition process. At the federal level, this person is often the deputy secretary of plans in the PCO but, regardless of position, this person must bring stature and a sense of service ethic to the exercise. This individual will join the cabinet secretary in meetings with the opposition if they meet before the election, and from that point will become the main contact and will provide a sense of consistency throughout the process.

According to Nicholas D'Ombrain, a former PCO deputy secretary to the cabinet for machinery of government, "PCO must do first-class work, since this is all they have to offer to the new government. If the work is done poorly, they will quickly lose the confidence of the new government." He also cautions about trying to impress a new government by overwhelming it with oral briefings and a high volume of materials. His advice is succinct and clear. "The higher the mountain of material, the less useful it will be. Moreover, the transition team will want to focus on few areas, so don't try to shove your priorities down their throats. It won't work" (Zussman, 2013).

As a general rule, the PCO will cover a wide range of activities in their transition planning—from the most broad and general to narrow and precise ones. As the transition exercise becomes more intense and moves into the electoral period, a larger group of PCO staff becomes involved. These are the people who develop the briefing books that the PCO will hand over to the incoming prime minister and the soon-to-be-appointed PMO staff at their earliest convenience. This team will also coordinate logistical support for the incoming prime minister's transition team and help to coordinate the parallel development of briefing books across government.

Machinery of Government

One of the most important responsibilities of the prime minister is to allocate functions between ministers to ensure that the cabinet and the government are structured in the best way. The general activity of allocating responsibilities and organizational design is referred to as machinery-of-government issues.

Each prime minister has faced the daunting decision of whether or not to reorganize the machinery of government. This is a responsibility that every successful prime minister has taken seriously and is one area in which the transition team must excel. The time to make changes to the structure of government is at the beginning of a mandate, when the reins of power are being taken over and a cabinet is being built. And unless a transition team thoughtfully prepares options in advance of an election, changes to the structure will be almost impossible to accomplish. The complexities and costs involved with these types of initiatives are too important to be done quickly in the wake of an election victory and without the professional advice of machinery experts.

In undertaking an assessment of potential shifts to the structure of government, a transition team should clearly lay out the rationale, benefit, and costs of any restructuring proposals. Restructuring should be considered in order to reduce duplication,

to vacate a policy arena, or to end programs that are no longer necessary or effective. When assessing the costs, leaders need to be cognizant that machinery changes are expensive and can be disruptive to labour management relations, controversial with stakeholders, and distracting for ministers and officials. Changes should be made to reinforce good management principles and not solely for their optics.[7]

Communications and Relations with the Media

The media do not typically have a direct role in transition planning, but any media attention paid to transitions will have some impact on the work of the transition team. Traditionally, transition teams have avoided the media and have done most of their work behind closed doors, both in preparation for their transition work and in the post-election period. But rather than hide behind the wall of silence that normally accompanies federal transitions, leaders should carefully consider and build a media strategy to support and shine a light on transition activities where appropriate. There are many pros and cons to whether a public transition is advisable, but the key elements in deciding to go public would be if the incoming government wants to give a profile to the transition exercise, if it wants to develop a close relationship with the national media, and if there are any policy issues that the prime minister wants to highlight in advance of the swearing-in ceremony.[8]

The ideal time for establishing a solid working relationship with the media occurs during the days immediately following the swearing-in, when the leader and the key players within the political party have the opportunity to provide some insight into the style and characteristics of the newly elected government. Interestingly, while governments in recent years have invested heavily in building a more aggressive communications capacity in order to better target their messaging to the public, there is no indication, at the present time, that either media relations or communications are as core an activity to transition planning as they are to governing.

Election Period (Phase II)

For those involved in planning on both sides of the transition equation—political and public service—the midnight oil is starting to burn bright and the anticipation of the election outcome is top of mind during Phase Two. The political transition team for each party is working to consolidate its overall plan for assuming power. Similarly, the public service under the guidance of the cabinet secretary is directing the work of the central agencies and coordinating the planning being done by the deputy ministers and their teams.

For the vast majority of the public service not directly involved in transition planning, the rhythm of work becomes particularly quiet. As cabinet ministers and their political staff spread out across the country to their respective riding in search of votes, the governance of the country is essentially placed on hold during the election period and a caretaker system kicks in that minimizes the obligations of ministers and limits the scope of their activities.[9]

The way Phase Two plays out very much depends on the expected outcome of the election. As a result, the daily tracking polls affect the rhythm of the work. When the governing party appears to be on the verge of re-election, the PCO and departments prepare for continuity and the resumption of the previous government's agenda. When it looks likely that one of the opposition parties will triumph, attention turns to the fundamentals of governing. The briefing books get larger, and the scope of the work takes a broader perspective to accommodate a new minister from an opposition party.

Political Activities

On the political side, there are actually two approaches to transition planning taking place in the course of the election. The governing party is often reluctant to formalize a transition team and to move ahead with formal planning, since they are the incumbents and may feel there is little need for any formal planning. Unfortunately, we know from experience that too few incumbent governments spend much time planning for their next mandate. Instead, they prefer to spend most of their time and resources finding ways to ensure electoral success. A good case in point is the 2011 election, when virtually no transition planning was done by Stephen Harper or his senior officials in the PMO. Given the rather modest announcements coming out of that election, it appears that little thought was given to reviewing its past practices or to looking forward to governing in a majority government.

However, during the election campaign there is considerable work to be done by the incumbent government's transition team. As a starting point, there is an excellent opportunity to meet with the cabinet secretary to discuss possible changes to the machinery of government, the organization of the Prime Minister's Office, and the viability of platform commitments made during the campaign. This is also a very good time to review the effectiveness of the cabinet system, including the committees and to assess both the personnel in and structure of the prime minister's and ministers' offices.

For the opposition parties, the time between the dropping of the writ and election day is largely, if not entirely, taken up with activities that will result in winning as many seats as possible. Almost all of the leaders' time is taken up with meeting candidates, dealing with the media, and, of course, trying to persuade citizens to vote for the party and its candidates. As anyone who has been involved in the sprint to the finish line will know, it is a gruelling and exhausting experience.

Regardless, leaders recognize that good transition planning will ease the move from electioneering to governing. As a consequence, most opposition parties will continue the work of their transition teams during the election campaign. Since most transition teams are made up of people not normally involved in the day-to-day campaign, this work can continue in parallel with that of the election team.

For the opposition party transition teams, the daily public opinion polls have a significant psychological impact, as well as a real impact on the pace of the work. When the polls show that an opposition party might win the election, the pace of transition planning accelerates. Conversely, when the numbers show little hope in this direction, the level of their activity matches the declining public opinion trend lines.

Public Service Activities

By far the most active planning during the average five-week election campaign takes place within the departments and agencies of the federal government.[10] The transition exercise now takes on the look of a major government initiative, engaging hundreds of policy analysts and planners. Over the course of the campaign, each and every department and agency will have initiated some form of transition planning that will result in hundreds of plans and tens of thousands of hours of professional and administrative time and effort.

Privy Council Office

No formal rules or protocols govern the behaviour of the Privy Council Office and the other central agencies during an election but, overall, every effort is made to minimize any new government work and to limit new spending decisions. While holding a steady hand with the current government, the central agencies also pay particular attention to policy pronouncements during the campaign and begin a careful analysis of all spending promises.

Most important, the election time gives the central agencies an opportunity to coordinate their own activities and to ensure that each department and agency is preparing a transition plan for a possible new minister. In this regard, the agencies work individually with departments and provide templates to deputy ministers who have had limited experience with government transitions.

Departments and Agencies

The deputy ministers of each of the federal departments prepare their own individual transition plans. They are also responsible for all of the agencies, boards, and commissions that report to their ministers. For example, the deputy minister of Innovation, Science and Economic Development Canada has three ministers and eight entities reporting through him or her to the minister. In transition planning the deputy minister is responsible for ensuring that ministers have the appropriate transition materials for their use.

Like their colleagues in PCO, departmental deputy ministers operate under one of three possible scenarios: (1) a new government will be elected that will, by definition, result in a new minister being appointed; (2) the same government will be re-elected, but a new minister will be appointed to head the department; or (3) the same government will be re-elected and the prime minister will choose to reappoint the same minister to his or her former portfolio. In any of these cases, deputy ministers know they will be moving from the planning stage to governing as soon as the swearing-in of the new cabinet is complete. They also know that ministers will rely heavily on departmental advice and human resources until they have completed their own office staffing.

Experience dictates that the average transition period of a new minister after the election takes about six weeks to be fully achieved (including initial meetings with major stakeholder groups). As a result, many deputy ministers develop a timeline for activities, although in certain circumstances the transition planning may be shorter or longer than planned. In any case, deputy ministers must be very flexible in their planning and be prepared to adjust their timing of the different transition elements, depending on changing circumstances.

From the departmental perspective, the time during a general election is precious for the deputy minister. As one veteran federal deputy minister with extensive experience in the Ontario government commented, "You have three weeks to make it work with a new minister. If you don't hit it off with the minister, it can be a very frustrating experience for all" (Zussman, 2013: 115). As a consequence, the preparation time is critical to ensuring that all key elements in a transition plan are prepared in advance so that a trustful working relationship is established early on. Given that there is so little room either for error or for time to remedy things if they go wrong, deputy ministers who have worked on previous transitions have a significant advantage over deputies with no prior experience. This is simply not the time to learn a new craft.[11]

With this in mind, the deputy minister organizes the portfolio to meet the minister's objectives. As a starting point, the departmental transition team may look for issues that have emerged during the election campaign and may have a short-term bearing on the minister's work. Any issues related to the portfolio that were discussed during one of the televised national debates will draw special attention from the transition team since it will attract media attention. Obviously, the election platform will also receive close scrutiny to determine whether policies related to the portfolio are a high priority for the newly elected government.

As a general rule, deputy ministers prepare only one set of briefing materials during the election period. They know that they have only a short time after the election to adjust their briefings to match the ideology or orientation of the incoming government. While it is difficult to describe the complete range of transition briefing materials provided to ministers, they do follow a template. In some ways, a transition book is like a playbook used in professional sports. It contains the equivalent of the first twenty plays in a football game—laying out in precise detail the first few weeks in the life of a new minister, but also including a 100-day (or three-month) horizon.

Each deputy minister is trying to balance the desire to provide as much information as possible to the minister during the early transition period while recognizing that the minister is exhausted from a gruelling election campaign, with only a limited ability to absorb new material, much of which can be complex and overwhelming. Experienced deputy ministers use their best judgment in assembling the briefing books in terms of volume and complexity. Their hope is that the briefing materials will engage the ministers to the extent that they may ask for detailed briefings on the material that particularly interests them. Well-designed briefing materials should be able to parse a minister's particular interests so that the department can then organize and orient itself to the minister's own agenda.

During the election campaign, senior managers of individual departments also prepare special briefing materials in the event that their newly appointed minister has had no experience as a member of cabinet. If that is the case, which is increasingly common, the department usually arranges for briefings on "how government works" and the "craft of being a good minister." They also enlist the help of some former ministers who would be comfortable meeting with and providing insights useful to a newly sworn-in minister in a newly elected government.

Post Election: Getting the Fundamentals Right (Phase III)

This phase is what everyone has been waiting for, and the experience is worth the wait. The post-election phase plays out in a blur of activity and excitement as all the finishing touches are put to the plan. It is also the time when a transition team first learns if all of its work is going to roll out as expected or will come apart when an unexpected event derails the exercise.

The days immediately following the election campaign are filled with activity. At the core, the transition or changeover is a combination of established ritual and the first real—and absolutely critical—exercise of the prime minister's power. As Neville warned Mulroney in 1984, "The decisions

you make in this period, since they centre on the key issue of who will govern with you, are probably the most important you will make. Good decisions will make everything that follows that much easier and productive for the country and the party; less wise decisions will almost inevitably cause you serious problems in the days ahead" (Neville, 1984: s. 2.2: "Media/Communications Requirements," 1).

Shifting from Electioneering to Governing

The transition team begins this phase well rested and ready to start its work. However, the prime minister typically is exhausted physically from a five-week campaign that has included tense, sixteen-hour days and thousands of kilometres of coast-to-coast travel. You can count on adrenaline to keep things moving up to a certain point, but the transition team needs to remember that the prime minister is sleep-deprived and physically drained. Some prime ministers and premiers are energized by their victory, but others are so tired that they are looking for any excuse to find time for some rest and recovery.

Regardless of the exhaustion and need for a good rest at the cottage, the tradition in Canada is to complete Phase Three of the transition in approximately two weeks. In other words, the newly elected government has fourteen days to move from campaigning to governing—from winning an election to being sworn in by the Governor General. This short period of time gives the prime minister–elect little time to work through the hundreds of tasks that have to be completed before taking over the reins of power.

Lawrence Martin captures the mood of the Harper team in 2006 in *Harperland*, his insightful book on Stephen Harper. On the basis of a large number of interviews with key Harper advisers, Martin observed,

> When they finally took power after so long in opposition they were a wary bunch. They knew how to oppose, how to attack, how to pull triggers. But they didn't know how to govern. They had a rookie prime minister, all rookie cabinet ministers except one, and rookie staff. Everything was new and they were in a minority situation. To say the level of anxiety was high was to underestimate the degree of tension. (Martin, 2010: 19)

When an opposition party wins an election, the primary challenge for the transition team in the early hours of the post-election period is to help the prime minister–elect to cross over psychologically from being leader of an opposition party to being the leader of a nation. The prime minister (and all key members of the prime minister's entourage) must make the psychological move from colleague and fellow-combatant with the party faithful to being their leader. This is a relatively easy concept to appreciate, but in practice it has proven to be very complex and difficult for many Canadian prime ministers.

Unfortunately, there is little published material about this phase in the life of a prime minister, but former chief of staff to Stephen Harper, Ian Brodie, provides a fascinating account of the transition of Stephen Harper from opposition leader to prime minister. Brodie vividly recalls the first staff meeting after the election in Calgary and exquisitely captures the drama of the moment when the staff realizes they can no longer address the newly elected prime minister as "Stephen." Brodie remembers how difficult it was to convince some of the staff to change the way they addressed their boss, but he was adamant that the entire staff had to do so, and at once.

> Everyone on the staff called him "Stephen" before and during the election. Then, the day after the election, I insisted everybody call him "Mr. Harper." Once he was sworn in, everyone, including myself, called him Prime Minister. We had to get it through our heads and, more importantly, he had to get it through his head. . . . You could see on his face that he was having great difficulty getting used to this. He never arranged it and I did not talk to him about it. His head would jolt back because it was contrary to our everyday process of calling him Stephen. People didn't seem to appreciate the magnitude of the change that was taking place. For us, the world was changing big time. (Zussman, 2013, p. 133)

Security Steps In

Immediately following an election campaign, the newly elected government swings into action. The first concern of the transition team is the matter of security, the protection of the prime minister. Again, good planning is crucial, and it is helpful if the transition team has already met with the head of security and worked out the logistics. Obviously, returning prime ministers already understand the issue, and more important, will already be comfortable with the security staff. For a newly elected prime minister with little government experience, security is the first tangible sign that things have changed.

The enhanced security also extends to key positions across the government. Before being offered employment in what will become the new PMO, staff must undergo a security check. The PCO will ensure this is done as soon as possible. It normally requires a minimum of forty-eight hours, and some names informally provided will have already been cleared. Initial discussions should also take place with the ethics counsellor, who will advise potential staff on the requirements of the Conflict of Interest Code and other related issues.

First Meetings

From the very first days after the election and throughout the prime minister's tenure as leader of the country, advice and support will come to the prime minister through two distinct channels. First, through the chief of staff, who will be the key political adviser and serve as the prime minister's political anchor to the caucus and the party. The chief of staff will normally provide support in dealing with members of Parliament, prospective ministers, the media, party workers and supporters, and for all the other demands made on the prime minister's time.

The prime minister will also be supported by cabinet secretary, who will serve as the public service anchor for the transition. Early on, the cabinet secretary will offer to meet with the prime minister-elect and the chief political advisers—especially the chief of staff—to signal the need to meet frequently, if not daily, during the days of transition immediately preceding the swearing-in of the new ministry, to ensure proper coordination and communication. This early meeting is crucially important to the cabinet secretary since, as discussed earlier, it will be the first opportunity to build a good working relationship based on mutual respect and co-operation.

In addition to frequent meetings, the ritual of changeover involves a number of essential components that typically follow the sequencing below:

- the first meeting of the prime minister–elect and the transition team following the election victory to put into action the plan that is already in place (and adjust if necessary);
- the meeting between the transition team and the cabinet secretary to meld their respective agendas—the political one, which has been validated by the election results, and that of the public service, which is the custodian of the long-term non-partisan administration of the country;
- the outgoing prime minister calls on the Governor General and indicates his or her intention to resign;
- the prime minister–elect calls on the Governor General and accepts the invitation to form a government;
- soon after, the prime minister–elect calls on the Governor General a second time to outline (as far as possible) the contours of the new ministry;
- a meeting of the prime minister–elect and the outgoing prime minister is arranged (sometimes with some difficulty), so that both parties can agree upon a date for the formal handover; and
- the outgoing prime minister formally resigns, followed almost immediately by the swearing-in of the new prime minister and ministers.

Cabinet Selection and Swearing-In

This phase of the transition is very delicate and requires complete confidentiality on the part of the transition team and the PCO. As well, all potential candidates for the cabinet have to agree that the entire procedure be done "under a cone of silence."

As noted earlier, the first step in the process is to determine the cabinet's size and structure. It is also important during this phase of cabinet-making that the prime minister–elect approves the decision-making mechanisms for the cabinet. This means articulating the role and size of cabinet committees, potentially naming a deputy prime minister, and setting parameters around who will attend what meetings. All this work should have been done in Phase One and Phase Two of the transition process.

As mentioned earlier, when considering whom to appoint to cabinet, several criteria are typically applied. First, prime ministers are mindful of their need to keep the party onside in order to ensure caucus support. In practical terms, this means including key figures in the prime minister's party, even political rivals (such as former candidates for party leadership). The risk of excluding rivals is too high, but to balance the potential impact of including them, efforts are also made to include people who can be counted on to throw their support behind the prime minister. While expertise and experience are important criteria for the job of minister, some consideration must also be given to the ethnic, gender, and regional balance of the cabinet. If there is room for an additional member or two, then the prime minister, looking to the future, may also give some fresh faces the opportunity to demonstrate their potential in the cabinet.

With all of this preparatory work done, the transition team prepares a draft plan of the cabinet, the decision-making process, and the cabinet committee system. This phase may take days if only limited work has been done before the election. Well-prepared teams will have sketched out potential cabinets and cabinet committees well in advance of the election, if only to familiarize themselves with the profile of potential cabinet members and to test the decision-making processes with the clerk of the Privy Council. These draft plans can go back and forth between the prime minister–elect and the transition team many times before the prime minister is satisfied with the overall structure.

Cabinet Interviews and the Vetting Process

The interview process can be organized in three coordinated stages. The first consists of general one-on-one discussions between the prime minister and the candidates. The second phase, known as the vetting process, may involve candidates being interviewed by a committee appointed by the leader that will ask about the candidates' personal, educational, and professional background and will probe for potential problems, especially conflicts of interest. The committee reports its findings back to the prime minister, who assembles them with the other information provided by the security branch of the RCMP, who will have completed their own security checks. In the final stage of this important process, the prime minister advises the potential ministers of the decision shortly before the swearing-in ceremony.

To begin this part of the process, only a few days after the election, telephone calls are made by a member of the transition team or another trusted aide to each of the potential cabinet ministers, asking each to come to Stornoway, to a parliamentary office, or other location at an agreed time. As a general rule, the prime minister meets each potential minister personally to discuss the appointment, unless that person is physically absolutely unavailable.

Here is a selection of the advice provided to Mulroney by Bill Neville in 1984 as preparation for his meetings with potential cabinet ministers:

1. My advice would be not to invite any initiative from the prospective minister on what portfolio he or she might like. Rather, you inform them that you would like them to be a member of your government and minister of X—period. You are exercising your most central prerogative here and, in that sense, bestowing your favour on the minister. These are not bargaining sessions.

2. You are under no obligation to tell any minister who you are proposing to appoint to any other portfolio and I see no reason for you to do so. It just begs comparisons and bargaining—and invites leaks.

3. You do not want at this stage of the process to get into a lengthy discussion about specific plans or policies for the ministry in question. You might simply invite the prospective minister to give some quiet—and private—consideration to the job against the early need and opportunity within the cabinet structure for him to submit his initial analysis and priorities.

4. Ministers should be told that they are not to discuss their appointments with anyone except members of their immediate family and that any breach of that code will be grounds for reconsidering the appointment. You should emphasize that ministers are not to approach potential personal staff and that you have established a process through which ministers must clear their choice of their chief of staff before any approaches are made. This means that ministers will have to endure a short, but essential, delay in approaching potential personal staff.

5. While this is not absolutely necessary, I would strongly recommend that you end the conversation with all but the core ministers with a statement that you will confirm this conversation by brief telephone call on the weekend (i.e., the Saturday/Sunday before swearing-in). It is just possible that one or more of these appointments could come unstuck for some unforeseen reason and this way leaves you at least an opening to make portfolio adjustments if necessary without being open to the charge of "breaking your word."

In 1993, Jean Chrétien introduced a new element in the cabinet selection process. He was very aware that Brian Mulroney had lost eight ministers over the course of his two mandates as a result of ethical lapses. Chrétien was determined that he would ensure, to the extent it was possible, that his ministers act in the best interests of Canada and avoid the ethical potholes that had plagued the Mulroney government. Since all Mulroney appointees had been subjected to a security check by the RCMP, it was apparent that a new system had to be developed that would bring to the light potential problems before they were exposed by the media.

It was decided that each potential cabinet minister would have to agree to be subjected to vigorous questioning from a neutral source about their past behaviour. According to Allan Lutfy, who managed the vetting process with Mitchell Sharp in 1993, five reasons drove the decision to interview each potential cabinet minister before being appointed:

• the process provides a small, first step towards enhancing integrity in government;
• it communicates a clear message to ministers about the importance of integrity in government;
• it may disclose relevant information not otherwise available through the PCO verification process;
• it will assist the government if any personal problems of ministers are disclosed publicly during the mandate; and
• there is a likelihood that many candidates will be first-time parliamentarians and are relatively unknown to the leader.[12]

Once these meetings are completed and the appointments are made, the prime minister faces one optional but very important additional task. It is good manners and probably good politics for the prime minister to take the time to make at least brief telephone calls to those who were not interviewed but were known to be expecting a cabinet post, or who were but did not survive the process, to break the bad news and briefly tell them why they were not chosen, without disclosing the names of those who were. This is not a pleasant task, but I think it pays dividends. And as Bill Neville says in his briefing materials to Mulroney, "Besides, who said being prime minister was all pleasantries?" (Neville, 1984: 11)

Swearing-In

The culmination of the cabinet-making process is the swearing-in ceremony—the most visible manifestation of the change in government. While it is technically the Governor General's event, all details of the swearing-in are negotiated among the PCO, the transition team, and the Governor General's Office. Once the formal procedures and ceremony are concluded, the prime minister and many of the better-known ministers run their first initial media gantlet as they leave. However, as Bill Neville shrewdly comments, "Ministers who at this point say anything substantive about the policy aspects of their new portfolios should have their tongues cut out" (Zussman, 2013, p. 149).

Outgoing Government

The final task immediately after the election is dealing with the outgoing government. While not the direct responsibility of the new prime minister, many loose ends need to be tied up regarding the outgoing group. In some cases, the outgoing prime minister may have a request to make of the new prime minister. In other instances, there may be things a generous prime minister could do to ease the transition of the outgoing government, such as the offer of an ambassadorship that Chrétien made to Kim Campbell after she lost both the election and her seat in 1993.

Staffing of the Prime Minister's and Ministers' Offices

The fundamental challenge faced by a prime minister beginning to staff the PMO is that the people who helped to get you elected are not necessarily best suited to help you govern.

How the prime minister chooses to staff the PMO has wide-ranging implications for government. The

chief of staff is the most visible position, and the incumbent is the most senior official in the office, with the rank of deputy minister. All senior advisers and directors report directly to the chief of staff, who attends all cabinet meetings and receives copies of all PCO and PMO briefing notes to the prime minister. Everything that moves forward to the prime minister must go through the chief of staff.

As mentioned elsewhere, there will be great pressure on the incoming government to hire people who had worked tirelessly during the election to help the party win. Many of them will lobby hard for jobs in the PMO, ministers' offices, or an appointment to the many positions that are available just after the election or soon after. Unfortunately, most of them are not qualified for a government job because they will have little appreciation of the difference between elections and governing. This issue is a universal problem with all newly elected governments, and the degree to which the new government can differentiate between the two skill sets the more likely the transition will succeed.

In the same way that the PMO is closely tied to the prime minister, a minister's staff must bring the necessary skills and experience to the office to support the minister. A minister's office is not nearly as large as that of the prime minister, but it plays a similar function in helping its minister with effective, ongoing management of the political agenda.

This all sounds logical and straightforward. However, put yourself in the shoes of a newly appointed minister for a moment and try to think through the process of staffing your office. You've finished a gruelling election campaign and have just found out you made it into cabinet. You are heading up a department (and a portfolio of related organizations) that spends billions in budget expenditures and may employ up to 40,000 staff. You may be given a portfolio within a policy area you are familiar with— or you may be facing a variety of subject areas that are completely new to you.

The natural tendency will be to staff your office with people you know and trust. You'll tell yourself you're doing this just to get things up and running in the busy and confusing first days as a minister, but the challenge is to push back on that tendency and reach out to find people who can truly make you a better minister and help your office function as effectively as possible. In the same way, a prime minister must realize that the people who helped win an election are not necessarily the right ones to help govern. A minister must also be disciplined enough to look for individuals who have the right mix of skills, experience, and working style to make the task of governing as successful as possible.

Consolidation (Phase IV)

In the end, a successful transition will be judged by the degree to which the prime minister was able to assume the reins of power as seamlessly as possible and if, even if there was an initial period of trial and error, the decision-making system operated to the satisfaction of the prime minister.

A number of crucial milestones fall into Phase Four. These include the early cabinet meetings (which set the tone for future meetings), the first days for a minister as the head of a department, the prime minister's early meetings with the deputy minister community, the distribution of the mandate letters to ministers, dealing with the caucus and defeated candidates, organizing orientation sessions for the cabinet and their staff, and building trust between the public service and the ministers and their staff.

In the case of returning governments it also provides the PMO with an opportunity to evaluate the effectiveness of the office and to determine what changes are needed to successfully implement the government's new agenda. Over time, the consolidation phase fades into a distant memory and the day-to-day challenge of responding to emerging issues and the political pressures of the day will take the work of prime ministers and their staff beyond the reach of the transition team and the advice contained in the briefing materials.

Cabinet Meetings

The cabinet room is the best place for the prime minister to consolidate the transition. It allows for a direct interchange within the ministry and also places the prime minister firmly in charge of the proceedings. Each prime minister brings to the job a unique style of presiding over cabinet. And as discussed in earlier sections, each time a new prime minister is elected, the entire cabinet system shifts to reflect the new leadership style. This is the place for the prime minister to communicate firmly all expectations to cabinet members and, more important, to inform them of the

rules of procedure that will define the way things will be done under the prime minister's leadership.

The prime minister is not simply the chair of the most important committee in the land, but is its spiritual and moral leader who must continually follow the game plan that has been carefully crafted in advance. This role will be most tested in the cabinet room, where the prime minister will be expected to lead. Often, the first meeting will be the most important, so it is especially crucial to be well prepared and in charge of the agenda. If a prime minister abdicates this role, the control of the agenda will move to others in the cabinet room who have the right skill set.

To be successful, a prime minister can and should count on the support of the chief of staff and the cabinet secretary. Their advice is crucial and will help to steer a new leader around unexpected stumbling blocks and bumps in the road. If leadership in the cabinet room is treated by the prime minister as merely another job among many, the government will soon lose its focus and quickly appear rudderless and ineffective.

Early Days as a Minister

The new prime minister is not the only individual who faces a daunting task during the consolidation phase—so do those who have been appointed ministers in the government. Almost overnight, each becomes the equivalent of a chief executive officer of a large, sprawling portfolio of organizations. The first months of their performance can make or break them over the longer term. In politics, there is only ever the smallest margin of error allowed for ministers who are constantly in the public eye.

One approach that a transition team can implement to get ministers started off on the right foot (and to keep them focused on the priorities of the government) is to provide orientation sessions. Despite the fact that new ministers will have a seemingly endless list of tasks to be addressed early in their mandate, it is critical that there be time allocated to training. The life of a politician is immediately changed by the appointment as a minister, and an orientation session can help to make this transition smooth. In 1993, Chrétien put his entire cabinet through a mandatory orientation session, and in 1997 it was mandatory for new ministers and secretaries of state to attend a five-hour orientation program.

For a prime minister to leverage the collective strengths of the appointed team, everything possible must be done to provide them with the tools and information they need to succeed. Minister's school is one tangible and practical way to get them all moving in the same direction.

That being said, orientation sessions can accomplish only so much. Many former ministers will tell you that the orientation session was helpful, but it is always difficult for them to process the massive amounts of information thrown their way in the days after the swearing-in ceremony. As a result, many transition teams have arranged mentoring to support the ongoing development of new ministers. These mentors and advisers are pulled from the ranks of former ministers, who really are the only people who can possibly understand the day-to-day pressures and challenges that are faced in these positions.

First Meeting with the Deputy Minister Community

In the early days, immediately after being sworn in, the prime minister should make an effort to meet with the deputy minister community. This is the prime minister's opportunity to speak frankly about government plans and expectations, to share the government's short-term game plan, and to discuss the long-range view of the challenges the prime minister will be expecting the deputy ministers to manage.

For the deputy ministers, this meeting establishes the importance that the prime minister attaches to the role played by the deputy minister community and the public service, in general. By sharing the government's overall plan, the deputies will be able to organize their departments to reflect the government's needs and better align their activities with government priorities.

Conclusions

It is always important to remember that transitions give life to the most fundamental of our democratic practices—the peaceful transfer of power from one government to another. For this simple reason, we should pay more attention to its well-being and nurture its development in order to ensure that transition planning continues to play a vital role in our pursuit of good government.

In 1984, Bill Neville provided the first step in the professionalization of transition planning in Canada by building on the earlier efforts of the Clark and Trudeau administrations. Since then, transition planning has become a more professional exercise, especially for political parties, but also for the public service. While transition planning continues to take place out of sight and largely invisible to election watchers, there is an increasing appreciation of the importance of the pivotal moment when governments transfer power from an outgoing government to an incoming one—even when it is the same party and leader.

In a nutshell, six elements emerge as cornerstones of a transition exercise:

- developing a leadership style in a world of inexperienced politicians;
- understanding the role of all of the key players;
- establishing respectful and trusting relations among the key players;
- selecting the right transition team;
- making a virtue of planning; and
- consolidating the transition by training and mentoring.

While transition planning has improved in quality and scale over the past thirty years, in the short term, two outstanding issues need to be addressed for Canada to catch up to the practices in other Westminster countries. First, there must be greater clarity about the behaviour of the public service during election campaigns. The independence of the public service from the governing party is a fundamental feature of the Canadian system. While there is a delicate balance to be struck between serving the government of the day and preparing for a new government by meeting with opposition parties before the results of the election are known, there is no evidence that the balance would be disrupted if there were opportunities for the public service to have some contact with the potential governments in waiting. Specifically, rules or protocols have to be established that prescribe appropriate behaviour of the public service with regard to the opposition parties' transition planning.

The second outstanding issue is the immediate need to increase the knowledge base of incoming members of cabinet and their staff. While most members of Parliament are already familiar with election rules and regulations, very few of them have any real experience in governing or managing, either in the private or public sector. As a consequence, most members of Parliament know very little about parliamentary procedure and even less about governing in our Westminster system.

However, these two changes, in the short term, would help Canadian jurisdictions improve the quality of transition work and would reassure Canadians that governments are doing their best in improving the quality of our governance regimes.

Important Terms and Concepts

cabinet
cabinet secretary
Governor General

machinery of government
mandate letters
transition team

transitions
types of transitions

Study Questions

1. What is the purpose of a transition?
2. When should a political party begin to plan for a transition?
3. Is it a good idea to vet potential cabinet ministers?
4. How would you choose a transition team?
5. How and when would you communicate the existence of your transition team?
6. Should a prime minister have management experience?
7. What kind of person would you hire into the Prime Minister's Office?

Notes

1. Cabinet secretaries have a number of different titles depending on their role. They are also the Clerk of the Privy Council, the Head of the Public Service and the Deputy Minister to the Prime Minister. For simplicity, "cabinet secretary" will be used in this chapter to describe the person that performs all of these tasks.
2. The meeting between cabinet secretaries and opposition parties was a convention in Canada until Paul Martin refused to allow the meeting to take place in 2004. Since then, whatever meetings that have taken place have been done surreptitiously and without explicit approval from the prime minister.
3. Alex Himelfarb brought to my attention that John Tait used this terminology in the 1980s when he prepared his departmental staff for a transition.
4. In Canada, political advisers are official designated as 'exempt staff' since they are not part of the public service and are exempted from the rules in the Public Service Employment Act (PSEA) that govern hiring practices, etc.
5. There have been 11 deputy prime ministers serving six prime ministers since Pierre Trudeau.
6. Releasing mandate letters when a government is sworn into office has been a matter of practice in six provinces in Canada and in the UK and Australia for some time.

7. Both Kim Campbell and John Turner made significant machinery changes during the early days of their short-lived governments. This could be a good example of using government reorganization as a way of demonstrating action, despite significant disruption to the overall function of their governments.
8. In 2003, Paul Martin scheduled a press conference so that the media could meet his transition team.
9. The issue of how a government should act during an election campaign is governed by a series of traditions and understandings known as caretaker conventions. The current Trudeau government has made a commitment to have a new set of policies in place before the next federal election.
10. There is no fixed length of an election campaign since the prime minister can request a time frame from the Governor General that is longer than the 36-day minimum time prescribed in the Elections Act. The 2015 federal election campaign was 78 days long.
11. Janice Charette, who was cabinet secretary when Justin Trudeau was swept into office in 2015, spent an enormous amount of time training her deputy minister colleagues since so few of them had any transition experience at all.
12. Allan Lutfy, personal notes, 1993. Personal collection.

References

Aucoin, Peter. 1999. "Prime Minister and Cabinet: Power at the Apex" *Canadian Politics*, 3rd edn, edited by James Bickerton and Alain Gagnon. Peterborough, ON: Broadview, pp. 109–26.

Benoit, Liane. 2006. *Ministerial Staff: The Life and Times of Parliament's Statutory Orphans*. Phase II Report, Commission of Inquiry into the Sponsorship Program and Advertising Activities.

Bernier, L., Brownsey, K., and Howlett, M., editors. 2005. *Executive Styles in Canada: Cabinet Structures and Leadership Practices in Canadian Government*. Toronto: University of Toronto Press, Scholarly Publishing Division.

Bickerton, J. and Gagnon, A.G. 2009. *Canadian Politics*. 5th edn, Toronto: University of Toronto Press, Higher Education Division.

Blakeney, Allan, and Sandford Borins. 1992. *Political Management in Canada*. Toronto: McGraw-Hill Ryerson.

Burney, Derek. 2005. *Getting It Done: A Memoir*. Montreal and Kingston: McGill- Queen's University Press, 2005.

Burney, Derek H. 2011. "Managing Transition in Government," SCDS-CCIS Strategic Analysis Seminar, Ottawa, 2 February.

Cameron, David and Graham White. 2000. *Cycling into Saigon: The Conservative Transition in Ontario*, UBC Press.

Chrétien, Jean. 2002. *Straight from the Heart*. Toronto: Key Porter Books.

Clark, Ian. 1985. "Recent Changes in the Cabinet Decision Making System in Ottawa." *Canadian Public Administration* 28, 2, pp. 185–201.

Dunn, Christopher. 2010. *The Handbook of Canadian Public Administration*. 2nd edn, Don Mills, ON: Oxford University Press.

Dutil, Patrice, editor. 2008. *Searching for Leadership: Secretaries to the Cabinet in Canada*. Toronto: University of Toronto Press.

Goldenberg, Eddie. 2006. *The Way It Works*. Toronto: McClelland and Stewart.

Hennessy, Peter. 1986. *Cabinet*. London: Basil Blackwell.

Hennessy, Peter. 2001. *Cabinet*. 2nd edn, Whitehall. London: Pimlico.

Inwood, Gregory. 2009. *Understanding Canadian Public Administration: An Introduction to Theory and Practice*. 3rd edn, Toronto: Pearson Prentice Hall.

Kernaghan, Ken. 2010. "East Block and Westminster: Conventions, Values and Public Service." *The Handbook of Canadian Public Administration*, 2nd edn, edited by C. Dunn. Toronto: ON: Oxford University Press.

Kumar, Martha. 2008. "Getting Ready for Day One: Taking Advantage of the Opportunities and Minimizing the Hazards of the Presidential Transition." *Public Administration Review* 67, 4 (July/August), p. 603.

Kumar, Martha Joynt, and Terry Sullivan, editors. 2003. *The White House World: Transitions, Organization, and Office Operations*. College Station: Texas A & M University Press.

Martin, Lawrence. 2010. *Harperland: The Politics of Control*. Toronto: Penguin Canada.

Martin, Paul. 2008. *Hell or High Water: My Life in and Out of Politics*. Toronto: Douglas Gibson Books.

Neville, Bill. 1984. *Briefing Book*. Personal collection of Jodi White.

Powell, Jonathan. 2010. *The New Machiavelli: How to Wield Power in the Modern World*. London: Bodley Head.

Privy Council Office. 2003. *Governing Responsibly: A Guide for Ministers and Ministers of State*. Ottawa: Queen's Printer.

Privy Council Office. 2011. *Accountable Government: A Guide for Ministers and Ministers of State*. Ottawa: Queen's Printer.

Privy Council Office. 2015. *Open and Accountable Government*, Ottawa: Queen's Printer.

Public Policy Forum. 1995. *Directions for Reform: The Views of Current and Former Deputy Ministers on Reforming the Ontario Public Service*. Ottawa: Public Policy Forum.

Public Policy Forum. 2012, April. *Towards Guidelines on Government Formation: Facilitating Openness and Efficiency in Canada' Governance*. Final Report. Ottawa: Public Policy Forum.

Rhodes, Rod A.W. 1997. *Understanding Governance: Policy Networks, Governance, Reflexivity, and Accountability*. Bristol, PA: Open University Press.

Rhodes, Rod A.W. 2011. *Everyday Life in British Government*. Oxford: Oxford University Press.

Rhodes, Rod A.W. editor. 2011. *Public Administration: 25 Years of Analysis and Debate, 1986–2011*. Oxford: Wiley-Blackwell.

Richards, David. 2008. *New Labour and the Civil Service: Reconstituting the Westminster System*. London: Palgrave.

Richards, David. 2009. "Sustaining the Westminster Model: A Case Study of the Transition in Power between Political Parties in British Government." *Parliamentary Affairs* 62, 1, pp. 108–28.

Riddell, Peter, and Catherine Haddon. 2009. *Transitions: Preparing for Changes in Government*. London: Institute for Government.

Savoie, Donald. 2010. "First Ministers, Cabinet and the Public Service." *The Oxford Handbook of Canadian Politics*, edited by John C. Courtney and David E. Smith. Don Mills, ON: Oxford University Press.

Savoie, Donald, editor. 1993. *Taking Power: Managing Government Transitions*. Toronto: IPAC.

Sharp, Mitchell. 1994. *Which Reminds Me . . .* Toronto: University of Toronto Press.

Sossin, Lorne. 2010. "Bureaucratic Independence." *The Handbook of Canadian Public Administration*, 2nd edn, edited by C. Dunn. Toronto: ON: Oxford University Press.

Tiernan, Anne. 2007. *Power without Responsibility: Ministerial Staffers in Australian Governments from Whitlam to Howard*. Sydney: University of New South Wales Press.

Wellford, Harrison. 2008. "Preparing to Be President on Day One." *Public Administration Review* (July/August), p. 618.

White, Graham. 2005. *Cabinets and First Ministers: The Canadian Democratic Audit*. Vancouver: UBC Press.

Whittington, Michael, and Richard Van Loon. 1996. *Canadian Government and Politics: Institutions and Processes*. Toronto: McGraw Hill.

Zussman, David. 2008. "The New Governing Balance: Politicians and Public Servants in Canada." The First Tansley Lecture, Johnson-Shoyama Graduate School of Public Policy, University of Regina, Regina, 13 March.

Zussman, David. 2009. *Political Advisors.* Expert Group on Conflict of Interest, Public Governance Committee, Public Governance and Territorial Development Directorate, Paris: OECD, Paris.

Zussman, David. 2013. *Off and Running: The Prospects and Pitfalls of Government Transitions in Canada*. Toronto: The Institute of Public Administration of Canada Series in Public Management and Governance.

Public–Private Partnerships in Canada

Reflections on Twenty Years of Practice

Matti Siemiatycki

Chapter Overview

Across Canada, governments of all levels have increasingly embraced public–private partnerships (PPPs) as their preferred approach to deliver large-scale public infrastructure. After twenty years of practice, this chapter examines the evolving rationales, governance structures, and partnership models that have been used to deliver PPPs in Canada. In particular, the analysis highlights common deal structures, types of risks and responsibilities that are transferred to the private sector, and the significant role that public funding continues to have. Outstanding issues facing Canadian PPPs relate to their high upfront costs, limitations placed on meaningful community consultations, and a procurement process that can inhibit design or architectural excellence.

Chapter Objectives

By the end of this chapter, students will be able to do the following:
- Define what a public–private partnership is and explain how the model works.
- Identify the key rationales for using public–private partnerships in Canada.
- Highlight the strengths and limitations of this model of project delivery.

Introduction

Across Canada, **public–private partnerships** (PPPs) have become increasingly institutionalized as the model of choice for delivering large-scale public infrastructure projects. Between 1990 and 2012, over 195 projects were built, or were in the planning and delivery pipeline. The federal government and most provinces have now set up special-purpose PPP agencies. The Canadian PPP project pipeline bucked the international trend by remaining active throughout the global financial crisis of the late 2000s, making Canada a highly attractive PPP marketplace for the largest global infrastructure firms and investors. Indeed, the Canadian approach to governing, structuring, and delivering PPPs has been identified internationally as a potential model to be emulated, most notably in the United States where PPPs have been slower to take off. Additionally, the British Government pointed to Canada as one of the "examples that the UK should follow" when developing its "new approach to public private partnerships" (HM Treasury, 2012: 9).

With growing interest in Canadian PPPs, it is timely to reflect on the current state of practice in the country, and how this relates to the policy rationales and theoretical understandings of the merits of PPPs. The purpose of this paper is to identify and explain the approach to PPP governance, financing, and project delivery that has emerged in Canada over the past three decades. This assessment provides insights into the merits of PPPs within the country.

The analysis is based on a mixed methodology that includes interviews with over 40 key informants involved in the Canadian PPP industry; a review of dozens of government and corporate documents outlining the policies and rationales for PPPs in the different jurisdictions of Canada; and participation in industry conferences, public forums, and workshops. The evidence presented in the paper shows that the structure of PPPs in Canada challenge theories about the optimal role of the private sector in PPPs, and raises questions about whether the common deals in Canada meet the conventional definition of a PPP.

Defining Infrastructure Public–Private Partnerships

In the most general terms, PPPs are guided by the belief that governments and firms working in meaningful collaboration will deliver projects that have better outcomes than any one party could achieve on their own (Huxham & Vangen, 2000). In practice within the infrastructure sector, PPPs have come to take on a narrower, more specific definition as a form of long-term contracting arrangements between the public and private or voluntary sectors (Tiesman & Klijn, 2002). Garvin and Bosso (2008: 163) provide a working definition of PPPs that will be used in this paper:

> A P3 is a long-term contractual arrangement between the public and private sectors where mutual benefits are sought and where ultimately (a) the private sector provides management and operating services and/or (b) puts private finance at risk.

In contemporary infrastructure project delivery, partnership structures of all kinds are used, and range on a spectrum from greater public-sector responsibility to greater private-sector responsibility. In most PPP models applied in Canada, the facility typically remains publicly owned and regulated. The private-sector partner is offered a long-term bundled concession to undertake some combination of facility design, construction, financing, operations, and maintenance. As the number of project-delivery functions taken on by the private-sector concessionaire expands, so too does the amount of risk it takes on. In return for its participation in the project, the concessionaire is either granted user-fee revenues or paid a pre-determined fee periodically based on the facility being available and in a state of good repair, over a term that can last anywhere from 10 to 99 years (Cohn, 2008).

The Drivers and Rationales for PPPs

The government motivations for delivering infrastructure projects through public–private partnerships have varied by jurisdiction and evolved over time (Hodge & Greve, 2010; Shaoul, 2009). In Canada, identifying a common PPP model or state of practice is

This chapter was originally published in *Canadian Public Administration* and is supported by the Institute of Public Administration of Canada.

complicated by the fact that infrastructure provision is largely the jurisdiction of the provincial and municipal governments rather than the federal government, and each government has been guided by its own objectives and policies. Nevertheless, as presented in Table 17.1, the scholarly literature identifies four primary rationales that have been proposed by policy-makers worldwide to support the use of infrastructure PPPs, each of which have been vigorously contested by scholarly research and in the public discourse. Given the shifts in the justifications for PPPs, Pollock et al. (2002: 142) have questioned whether infrastructures PPPs are in fact "a policy in search of a rationale?"

Significantly, as in Britain and Australia, it is common for researchers examining the Canadian experience with PPPs to distinguish between two distinctive waves of practice (see Conference Board of Canada, 2010; Mussio, 2011; Quiggin, 2004). Differentiating between first- and second-wave PPPs is useful as it highlights how the governance structures, planning processes, and politics have evolved in response to critiques of the first generation of projects, thereby providing a foundation to assess the current PPP practice. It also provides a point of difference to characterize the outcome of the most recent batch of Canadian PPPs.

Table 17.1   Common Rationales for Delivering Infrastructure through PPPs

Rationale	Supporting Arguments	Opposing Arguments
Bring in new money for infrastructure	Concession-style PPPs enable state and local governments to build high-quality infrastructure without taking on additional debt in cases where user fees or other new revenue streams can be pledged to repay initial private-sector investments. This makes them politically attractive (Boardman & Vining, 2010).	Many types of infrastructure do not have new revenue streams to repay private investment. In such instances, PPPs do little to alleviate the financial burden on government. The state sponsor is still responsible for repaying the full cost of the investment unless user fees are levied (Hodge & Greve, 2010; Quiggin, 2004).
Enable off-balance-sheet accounting of infrastructure	Designing PPPs so that they can be treated as off of the balance sheet has been especially prevalent in the European Union, where the Stability and Growth Pact requires member countries to carry minimal public deficits and debt (Brown et al., 2009).	Designing PPP structures simply to achieve off-balance-sheet accounting status can result in projects that have higher costs for government or misallocate risk between the partners (Boardman & Vining, 2012).
Restructure the provision of public services	PPP programs often aim to make infrastructure planning more technocratic by decentralizing decision-making away from elected officials and their line ministries to independent arm's-length agencies and consultants (Cohn, 2008; Engles et al., 2011; Newman, 2013). PPPs have also been promoted as a way to introduce greater marketization and competition into infrastructure provision, leading to improved innovation and risk management (Yescombe, 2007).	Increased reliance on consultants especially financial advisers, during project planning process, has led to the privatization of public policy development and implementation (Shaoul et al., 2007). Limited competition is the result in some sectors of the PPP marketplace, particularly among advisers (Siemiatycki & Farooqi, 2012). Government restructuring supports institutionalization of pro-PPP policy (Rachwalski, 2013; Shaoul et al., 2007).
Drive value for money in public procurement	Bundled PPPs that involve private finance and a long-term operating period deliver public value by stimulating innovation during the project-planning process, encouraging life cycle asset management, and then transferring the risk of cost overruns and operational deficiencies to the private sector (Grimsey & Lewis, 2004).	Government is the ultimate backstop for all risk on public infrastructure in case of poor contractor performance or default (Shaoul, 2009). PPP concessions have been unstable and frequently required renegotiations that favour the contractor (Cruz & Marques, 2013).

The First Wave of PPPs in Canada

The first wave of PPPs in Canada were planned and delivered in the 1990s and the early 2000s, and includes projects such as the Highway 407 long-term lease in the Greater Toronto Area, the development of the Brampton and Royal Ottawa Hospitals in Ontario, the Confederation Bridge linking Prince Edward Island and New Brunswick, a toll road connecting Fredericton and Moncton in New Brunswick, and the development of schools in Nova Scotia and New Brunswick. PPPs were also used to deliver a number of municipal sports complexes and water treatment plants across the country. PPPs planned during this period typically sought to transfer as much responsibility and risk as possible to the private-sector partner, placing them towards the privatization end of the spectrum of partnership models.

During this first wave of projects in Canada, as elsewhere in the world, PPPs were commonly planned directly by government departments, and seen as a strategy to continue building high-quality public infrastructure without adding public debt (Auditor General of New Brunswick, 1998). As such, project planners sought to privately fund (not merely finance) a significant share of the cost of public infrastructure projects by raising new money through user fees or large upfront lease payments (see Quiggin, 2004: 52). In some cases such as the Fredericton-Moncton Highway and the Confederation Bridge, governments also purposely structured the PPP to realize off-balance-sheet accounting so that they could continue to invest in quality public infrastructure without showing provincial deficits (Conference Board of Canada, 2010; Auditor General of New Brunswick, 1998: 170).

Politically, PPPs were aligned with an ideological perspective that private sector firms working in market conditions were more efficient at allocating resources than government, and that PPP arrangements could be used to reduce the role of government in the provision of public infrastructure (Loxley and Loxley 2010). To this end, PPP models were applied that transferred responsibility and risk for supply, availability, operations and demand to the private sector partner. The central rationale surrounding PPPs during this period of bringing in new private money can be seen in the argument that Mike Harris, former Premier of Ontario, put forward in favour of the Highway 407 project: "The sale put $3 billion into

Ontario's coffers and led to our being able to avoid very heavy expenditures on the highway." (Quoted in Paikin, 2012)

Overall, the outcomes from this first wave of PPP projects showed that many did not meet the public interest. Early PPPs in Canada faced scholarly, auditor general, stakeholder and media criticisms about a lack of upfront assessment to support the selection of a PPP, limited government expertise to execute complex concessions, poor transparency and accountability, high private financing costs and profit margins, a loss of public control over crucial infrastructure assets, public opposition to high user fee rates, and contract instability that led to some concessions being renegotiated or terminated (see: Auditor General of New Brunswick, 1998; Auditor General of Ontario, 2008; Auditor General of Quebec, 2009; CUPE 1999). PPPs were also critiqued as being strongly motivated by political objectives such as limiting the power of organized labour (Loxley and Loxley, 2010).

The Second Wave of PPPs in Canada

The experience with the first wave of PPPs in Canada has been central in shaping the configuration of the second wave of PPP projects (Conference Board of Canada 2010). As Cohn (2008, 73) argues, the early 2000s represented a "policy window" for a transformation of PPP practice in Canada due to the alignment of a number of factors. In particular, by the early 2000s, there was ample evidence in the public domain to make policy-makers aware of the limitations of the PPP practice to that point. In the public eye PPPs had become closely associated with privatization, which was a damaged brand. And new Liberal Party governments were elected into office in Canada's three largest provinces (Ontario, Quebec, and British Columbia) around the same time with large parliamentary majorities, and a similar interest in reforming public administration along new public management lines and experimenting with alternative models of service delivery.

As such, the second wave of PPPs was motivated by policy-makers responding to the evidence of administrative processes and project outcomes that were not meeting expectations, and a crop of incoming provincial politicians that had an electoral mandate for change and an interest in revamping PPP mechanisms to make them more politically palatable with the public and key stakeholder groups. Beginning in British Columbia in 2002 with the introduction of the Capital Asset Management Framework and subsequently spreading more widely across the country, governments implemented a constellation of PPP-first policies. These include policies requiring PPPs to be considered for all infrastructure projects over a specified cost threshold, the introduction of new project evaluation tools, and the formation of special purpose PPP agencies with a mandate to promote and deliver PPP projects (Cohn, 2008).

During this second wave of projects, Canada's provincial governments have been the leading users of PPPs to deliver hospitals and health-care facilities, roads and bridges, and justice facilities. A smaller number of provincial and municipal public transit, road, water and waste treatment, education and cultural facilities have also used PPP approaches. Nationally, the most number of PPPs have been delivered in Ontario, British Columbia, Alberta, and Quebec in that order; Canada's other six provinces and three territories have been less consistent in their application of PPPs. Below I outline the key characteristics of the PPP rationales, partnership models, and institutions that comprise this second wave of PPPs in Canada.

Canadian PPPs Are about Delivering Value for Money

In Canada like elsewhere in the world, achieving **value for money** has been identified as the primary rationale for second wave PPPs by their civil service, private sector and political promoters (Garvin and Bosso 2008). This is the principal goal for using PPPs that is identified in contemporary government policy guidance documents and industry reports across the country (sees Infrastructure Canada, 2012; Partnerships BC, 2011; Alberta Treasury Board, 2011; SaskBuilds, 2013; Infrastructure Ontario, 2007; Conference Board of Canada, 2010). In its simplest form, Canadian practitioners of second wave PPPs have defined value for money as a measure of the extent to which cost savings are achieved when delivering a public infrastructure project through a PPP relative to a traditional government-led procurement approach. Proposed drivers of VfM in Canadian PPPs include: enhanced upfront project planning; incentive based bundled contracts that encourage on time

and on budget delivery, as well as innovative facility designs that improve the user experience and save costs; the use of concessions that provide long-term cost certainty and specify the management of the asset over its complete life cycle; and the allocation of project risks to the partner that is best able to manage them, such that governments are protected in case of large cost overruns, revenue shortfalls, or facilities that are unavailable for their users (Infrastructure Canada, 2012).

Importantly, the contemporary emphasis on value for money represents a departure from the first wave of PPPs in Canada, in that it significantly downplays the rationales of using PPPs to bring in new private money to pay for costly public infrastructure or capitalizing on off-balance-sheet accounting. In fact, in the key government policy documents and public statements by PPP proponents, it is now unusual for new money or off-balance-sheet accounting to be identified as a significant motivation for using PPPs (see Alberta Treasury Board, 2011; Partnerships BC, 2011; SaskBuilds, 2013). As one example, the Mayor of Winnipeg provides an explanation for why he supports PPPs, which is similar to the rationales put forward across the country:

> Public–private partnerships promise better value, timeliness and accountability for public infrastructure projects. That's exactly what the City of Winnipeg experienced with our 3.5 kilometre Chief Peguis Trail Extension. The project, including an underpass, multi-use pathway and pedestrian overpass, was completed one year ahead of schedule thanks, in large part, to this innovative approach. (Quoted in Infrastructure Canada, 2012)

The focus on value for money as the driving rationale for PPPs in Canada is the result of both policy and political factors (Cohn, 2008). As shown in Table 17.2, the processes through which second-generation PPPs are carried out are designed to respond to the main criticisms of first-wave PPPs (see Auditor General of Ontario, 2008, 120; Auditor General of British Columbia, 2011: 15). In particular, PPP practitioners in Canada have been especially cognizant to find a balance between transferring project responsibilities and risks to the private sector on the one hand, and on the other maintaining government control and oversight over infrastructure service provision. Nevertheless, the contemporary second-wave PPP models have themselves faced scholarly and stakeholder criticisms as well.

At the same time, the emphasis on using PPPs to deliver value for money has a political imperative, and has been chosen explicitly as part of what Hodge and Greve (2010) refer to as a "language game" to rebrand an unpopular public policy option. For example, an interview with the government minister responsible for rolling out second-wave PPPs in Ontario reveals how political considerations made it necessary to

change the narrative on PPPs to make them about value for money and protecting the public interest.

People's perceptions were clouded and they equated this type of method [first-wave PPPs] to build and finance infrastructure with privatization and so we found that there was really no public appetite for privatization and what we had to do was to change the lexicon—change the language and that is why we came up with and looked for the most boring term that we could possibly find—what we called AFP, alternative

Table 17.2   Characteristics and Critiques of Second Wave PPPs

Critique of First-Wave PPPs	Second-Wave PPP Response to Critique	Contemporary Criticism of Second-Wave PPP
PPP selection is overtly political.	Seven of ten provinces have created special-purpose PPP agencies or departments responsible for making decisions about optimal procurement model independently from government.	PPP agencies may be structured with a bias in favour of PPP if they have a mandate to promote, evaluate, and deliver infrastructure as PPPs (Rachwalski, 2013; CUPE, 2010).
Government lacked the expertise to manage complex infrastructure procurement and operations.	PPP procurement agencies have top-level specialized staff with expertise in project finance, law, business management, accounting, and project management.	PPP agencies have highly paid staff who are incentivized to ensure consistent PPP deal flow in their jurisdiction (Partnerships BC, 2013).
Rigorous assessments were not carried out to evaluate whether the PPP was the optimal procurement model.	The special-purpose PPP agencies have developed standardized procurement processes, assessment methods such as public sector comparators, risk matrices and value-for-money evaluations, and legal contracts that have increased the speed and lowered the transaction cost of using PPPs.	PPP assessment methodologies that have been developed are biased in favour of PPPs over traditional government procurement (CUPE , 2010; Whiteside, 2011).
Procurement process lacked sufficient transparency.	The PPP agencies have developed web sites where they post extensive project documentation such as technical design studies, concession agreements, and summary value-for-money reports, providing a level of data reporting and transparency that has not typically been followed on traditionally procured projects.	Key information not available for stakeholders (and in some cases responsible decision-makers) when needed during the procurement process due to invocation of commercial confidentiality (Siemiatycki, 2007).
Governments lost control over public assets by transferring too many responsibilities and risks to the private sector.	Recent PPPs have retained greater public control than in the past over core service functions such as facility operations and maintenance.	High cost premium is being paid by government in Canadian PPPs to primarily transfer construction risk (Siemiatycki & Farooqi, 2012).

finance and procurement. But we use the same principle basis—although a little bit different. We put up front that first and foremost public interest is paramount—things like that. Value for money must be demonstrated. Process must be fair. All of these kinds of things just as extras, safeguards (Caplan, personal communication, 2012).

In sum, as PPPs have faced similar challenges across the country, most notably union opposition and a healthy dose of public skepticism, the reaction in the second wave of PPPs has been to implement policy procedures and develop political language that emphasizes this procurement model as a driver of value for money.

PPPs as a Procurement Strategy

PPPs in Canada have been conceptualized and applied by governments rather narrowly as a procurement strategy, rather than as part of a broader program to recast the role of the state in the planning and provision of public services. This has two important manifestations, both of which serve to maintain a high level of public control and oversight over infrastructure delivered through PPPs. First, PPPs in Canada typically follow the same formal prioritization and selection processes as traditionally built projects. To this end, in most provinces, prospective provincial infrastructure projects are analyzed and prioritized by civil servants within the line-government ministries and approved by the relevant minister and the Treasury Board. The role of the provincial special-purpose PPP agencies is to provide analysis of whether specific projects are viable as PPPs (which is sometimes required by legislation if the project is above a certain threshold value), and run the PPP procurement and delivery process once the project is approved. As Infrastructure Ontario's Executive Vice President for Major Projects makes clear, "we don't make the decision as to which projects need to be built. We do not make the decision as to where the project is to be built. That is part of the political decision-making process. The politicians decide" (Personal Interview 2012).

Second, the most recent PPP models that have been applied in Canada tend to focus specifically on facility design, construction, financing, and maintenance of the hard physical asset, rather than the private operation of the core public service itself. This is especially the case with regards to social infrastructure (P3 Canada, 2014). Within the PPP hospitals that have been built, all medical and nursing services are publicly programmed and funded in the same way as a traditionally delivered hospital; likewise the guards in most PPP prisons are trained, deployed, and funded through the public correction services; and the teachers and curriculum offered in PPP schools are part of the public education system. Larry Blain, the past CEO and current chairman of British Columbia's PPP agency explains how experiences learned from early PPP projects has directly shaped the current practice:

> The very first hospital we did, we made a very large bundle for facilities maintenance. It included not only looking after the building envelope but also things like janitorial, and even into some quasi-medical areas like diagnostics and imaging and that sort of thing, and food. We've learned over time that we try to minimize now the FM bundle so that it's just essentially the physical asset, because hospitals or regional health authorities, they tend to have their own reasons for wanting to outsource food or janitorial or laundry or some of these things (Blain, 2013).

The application of second-wave PPPs in Canada thus stands in contrast to the experience of other countries where PPPs have been used to more aggressively involve the private sector and reform the role of government in public service delivery (Brown et al., 2009). Nevertheless, the preference in Canada for delivering large infrastructure through PPPs has altered the planning processes, internal government structures, and projects selected. British Columbia, in particular, has undertaken the most significant institutional reforms associated with the launch of their PPP program. The province abolished the central government department responsible for overseeing infrastructure planning while granting key responsibilities for infrastructure PPP promotion and evaluation to the special-purpose PPP agency Partnerships BC (Rachwalski, 2013). Murray (2006) and Rachwalski (2013) contend that this institutional arrangement creates the risk that Partnerships BC has a vested interest in selecting PPPs as this can create more business for the agency.

Similar concerns have been raised in other provinces such as Ontario and Quebec, even though the institutional reorganization to support PPP delivery has been less profound than in British Columbia. In Quebec, the provincial PPP agency faced a critical review by the auditor general that its assessments were biased in favour of PPPs to the detriment of public value in procurement (Auditor General of Quebec, 2009). In response, the agency was ultimately disbanded by the provincial government in 2009 and replaced by a new agency with a broader mandate to provide expertise on all public procurement including PPPs, a retreat from the institutionalization of PPPs that is common across the country.

Not Major Source of New Infrastructure Money

Second-wave Canadian PPPs have not been widely seen or used as a mechanism to raise new sources of funding for critical public infrastructure, or to reduce the need for public investment in such facilities. Most large Canadian PPPs receive substantial upfront government investment in the project totalling millions or even billions of dollars. The private money that is invested in the upfront capital costs of a Canadian PPP deal is most typically repaid directly through government availability payments that come out of general revenues. A common feature of second-wave PPPs is that they do not include new user fees or other revenue streams. Some of the sectors where PPPs have been most commonly applied such as health care and justice do not lend themselves to the application of user fees. Concerns about political acceptability have also limited the application of tolls on transportation projects, where they are more widely used internationally. In the absence of PPPs including new revenue streams, the government ultimately repays all public or private money invested in the project.

The emphasis of Canadian PPP planners on realizing value for money has guided the amount of private capital invested in PPPs, and the structure of the PPP arrangements themselves. Government project sponsors have sought to structure PPP deals so that sufficient private debt and equity is included to ensure that the concessionaire has "skin in the game" and an incentive to manage project risks assigned to them, rather than more broadly as a way of replacing the need for public infrastructure investment. To

this end, given the high cost of private borrowing, with interest-rate spreads ranging from 150 to 400 basis points above those available to Canadian governments, public-sector sponsors of PPPs have combined public and private financing in order to make the projects more affordable. As explained in a report documenting the merits of the financial structure to deliver Winnipeg's Chief Peguis Trail Extension PPP:

> The partial public funding provided by the City is intended to leverage the City's lower borrowing rate, while still requiring the private sector to provide the majority of financing for the Project thereby maintaining the risk transfer benefits associated with private financing. (Deloitte & Touche, 2011: 20)

Beyond conventional long-term PPP concessions, Canadian infrastructure planners have also widely applied shorter-term PPP arrangements designed specifically to incentivize on time and on budget construction. In such deals all private capital invested in the project is repaid by government immediately following the completion of the construction period (see Blain, 2013). Finally, during the financial crisis of the late 2000s, when the global credit markets seized up and the cost of private borrowing rose dramatically, Canadian governments stepped in and converted numerous PPPs in the delivery pipeline to more traditional publicly financed design-build contracts when their private-sector sponsors could not raise sufficient funds at competitive rates. Taken together, the range of PPP models applied reflects more of a pragmatic than ideological perspective on the place of private financing in infrastructure procurement.

Importantly, it is the prospect of attracting federal government funds that is becoming one of the key motivations for municipalities and small provinces and territories to deliver infrastructure through PPPs. In 2008, the federal government created the $1.2 billion P3 Canada Fund, "designed to incent consideration of P3s in public infrastructure procurements, in order to achieve value for taxpayers and other public benefits" (P3 Canada, 2014). In a context where the federal government has no formal statutory role in funding local infrastructure, many municipalities have come to see the use of PPPs as the "only game in town" if they are to attract new federal government funding for their critical infrastructure projects, a view that the federal government has not disavowed. As the federal member of parliament for St. John, New Brunswick explained in 2013, the city's proposal for a critical water treatment project would receive no federal money unless it was delivered through a PPP. "In no uncertain terms we were told two-and-a-half years ago, the only source of funding, the only opportunity to make this happen is through P3 Canada" (CBC, 2012).

On-Balance-Sheet Financing

Following on the experience with the first-wave of PPPs in Canada and abroad, PPP practitioners and politicians have come to the conclusion that off-balance-sheet financing is not an appropriate rationale for delivering infrastructure through a PPP. Canadian provincial governments do not face legislated debt limits like their European counterparts, and are therefore not under the same structural pressure to limit public debt. Moreover, off-balance-sheet financing is not seen by Canadian proponents of PPPs as a strategy to add economic value to the PPP transaction. To this end, the practice of treating PPPs off of the public balance sheet has been largely abandoned during the second wave of PPPs in Canada (Blain, 2013). As the Canadian Council for Public–Private Partnerships, a national industry forum that promotes PPPs, explains in a report, "government officials and business people agree with accountants and auditors that accounting should not drive PPP transactions. Such transactions should be driven by the commercial merits of the deal" (CCPPP, 2008: 2).

Limited Demand Risk Transferred

To date, second-wave Canadian PPPs have been primarily structured to focus on transferring construction and availability risk to the private sector, while only very limited revenue or demand risk has been transferred to the private-sector partner. In most long-term concession style PPPs in Canada, the private concessionaire recoups its initial investment through availability payments paid by the public sector sponsor at scheduled intervals over the life of the concession period, provided performance targets are met. In the case of the Canada Line, for instance, only 10 per cent of the concessionaire's scheduled government

reimbursement depends on ridership targets being met, while factors related to facility availability and service quality determine whether the remainder of the payment is made. Many other Canadian PPP concession agreements have no provision to dock the concessionaire's payments if facility demand is below forecasted levels. This has led Boardman and Vining (2010: 381) to argue "P3s appear to have generally been low-risk for the private sector equity investors." Yet is this altogether negative?

The downside of transferring limited demand risk to the private sector, of course, is that the government partner is exposed to significant financial risk when usage expectations are not met. In the case of the Golden Ears toll bridge in greater Vancouver, for instance, traffic volumes and toll revenues have not met predevelopment forecasts during the initial years of the concession. Because the public-sector sponsor assumed the demand risk, it has been required to subsidize the cost of the availability payments to the concessionaire out of general revenues—reportedly up to $45 million per year (Hager, 2013). This has reduced the public money available for other priorities. Additionally, the potential for private investors to serve as a check on politically motivated but financially unviable projects is eliminated when investors are compensated through guaranteed availability payments rather than user fees.

However, by not attempting to transfer significant levels of demand risk to the private sector partner, Canadian PPP planners have avoided a common source of some of the most acute challenges that PPP projects have faced globally: the loss of government control over fee setting and system-wide planning, and private-sector initiated contract renegotiations when revenues do not meet forecasted levels (Siemiatycki & Friedman, 2012). While it is early in the concession period for most second-wave PPP projects in Canada, none that reached the operational stage have faced a significant threat of financial failure or termination due to poor contractor performance. This stands in contrast to the numerous projects in other large and experienced PPP marketplaces such as Britain, Australia, Spain, and Portugal, where unmet demand expectations on PPP projects have contributed to bankruptcies, uncertainty about the ongoing provision of important public facilities, and in some cases public bailouts (Cruz & Marques, 2013).

Outstanding Issues

Second-wave PPPs in Canada represent a significant evolution in the ideologies, rationales, and partnership models from those used during the first wave of PPPs, and the initial project outcomes show promise. Many Canadian governments, such as those in the provinces of Ontario and British Columbia, boast that the PPP model is revolutionizing infrastructure project delivery, with major second-wave PPPs consistently providing innovative high-quality infrastructure within the expected budget and construction schedule (see Blain, 2009: 1).

Nevertheless, there remain some critical outstanding issues with the way that PPPs are being practised in Canada that challenge the value, public benefit, and in some cases viability of this infrastructure procurement model. First among them is whether Canadian PPPs actually deliver value for money, or whether they pay too high a risk premium to achieve cost and availability certainty. A review of the official ex ante value-for-money studies commissioned by governments across Canada show that PPPs are an expensive way of delivering infrastructure with higher base costs than their traditional public-sector-led alternative (see Siemiatycki & Farooqi, 2012). As shown for a selection of Canadian projects in Table 17.3, it is only after calculations of estimated risk retained by the government associated with each procurement model are considered that PPPs are assessed as providing better value than traditional procurement. Even when the PPP proponent brings forward design innovations that produce cost savings or higher revenues, as was the case in the Canada Line project, they are outweighed by the higher underlying PPP costs (CLRT, 2006).

To be certain, major cost overruns and facilities that do not function as expected are challenges that have commonly plagued infrastructure megaprojects (Flyvberg et al., 2003). Yet the risk premiums assigned to the traditional procurement option when Canadian governments carry out ex ante value for money assessments have varied and sometimes been very high, upwards of 50 per cent of the base construction costs in Ontario and Winnipeg in some cases, with no publicly available data to demonstrate whether such large premiums are empirically warranted (Siemiatycki & Farooqi, 2012). In this context of empirical uncertainty, Boardman and Vining (2012: 125) propose that a key form of value provided by PPPs is in fact "political benefits to governments, from attempting to reduce political risk that can arise from project risk even when this is more costly."

A second concern with contemporary Canadian PPPs relates to the meaningfulness of the stakeholder engagement in the project delivery process. With the goal of second-wave PPPs being highly outcome oriented and focused on design efficiency and risk management, the result has sometimes been PPP planning processes that do not suitably consult with or create enough buy-in from the various stakeholders involved. In some health-care and post-secondary education projects, tensions have arisen between the special-purpose PPP agency running the project procurement process and the local municipality or agency responsible for operating and integrating the new infrastructure into the wider landscape (Personal Interview, Livingston, 2013). Another source of tension has been the invoking of confidentiality of commercially sensitive information during the PPP tendering process. In some cases the lack of information in the public domain has made it difficult for community stakeholders to scrutinize the impacts that projects will have while they are being planned, leading to subsequent public backlashes and legal challenges by groups adversely impacted by the project (Siemiatycki, 2007).

Third, recent PPPs in Canada are not immune to procurement problems, contract management problems, and even outright project failures, regardless of the financing structures followed and incentives and penalties built into the PPP contract. This includes police uncovering evidence of an alleged multi-million dollar corruption scheme on the billion-dollar McGill University Health Centre PPP involving senior executives with the selected PPP concessionaire and the health centre's CEO. It also includes the Herb Gray Parkway project in Ontario where the PPP concessionaire installed steel girders that did not meet Canadian highway building codes, and ultimately was required to replace them at their cost by the procurement agency (CBC, 2013). These experiences highlight that, alongside the incentives and penalties ideally built into the PPP model, project success is dependent on the same factors that impact the outcomes of traditionally procured projects: the skill, experience,

Table 17.3   Calculation of PPP Value for Money (Net Present Value, $millions)

	Durham Courthouse		Chief Peguis Trail		Canada Line	
	Public Sector Comparator	PPP	Public Sector Comparator	PPP	Public Sector Comparator	PPP
Base Costs (CapEx/OpEx)	247	334	105.5	127.9	1822	1959
Transaction/ Admin Costs	8	17	6.2	3.5	98	120
Financing Cost Premium	N/A	N/A	N/A	N/A	0	130
Revenue	N/A	N/A	N/A	N/A	(433)	(581)
Risk-Free Project Cost	**255**	**351**	**110.98**	**131.34**	**1487**	**1628**
Retained Risk By Government	157	25	67.8	16.4	263	30
Risk-Adjusted Project Cost	412	376	178.78	147.8	1750	1658

Sources: CLRT, 2006; Deloitte & Touche, 2011; Infrastructure Ontario, 2007.

integrity, and probity of the public- and private-sector partners involved in the project.

A fourth critique of PPPs is that the procurement process followed is not conducive to achieving architectural or design excellence, which is critical to ensuring the public benefit of large infrastructure projects that will be a part of communities for generations. As the Ontario Association of Architects explains in a public letter outlining their position on PPPs, "the existing process is geared for predictability, minimizing risk, and producing satisfactory (but not exceptional) results" (OAA, 2014: 1). The PPP process, with its value-focused client and large multidisciplinary concession teams, often includes extensive value-engineering exercises that can reduce the creativity and quality of design where it minimizes cost. More importantly, private-sector concessionaires on PPPs are especially risk averse with their facility designs given that they are responsible for construction and availability risk. As such, while PPP projects have been designed by some of Canada's leading architects, to date no second-generation PPP project procured by a Canadian special-purpose PPP agency has been awarded the country's top commendation for architectural quality, the Governor General's Medal.

Finally, despite efforts to rebrand and reform PPPs to address past criticisms, PPPs remain a contentious issue in Canada, with a political consensus about their merit that is far from assured. Canada's

centre-left political party and the country's largest public-sector unions continue to conflate PPPs with privatization and argue that they are more costly than traditional procurement, worsen wages and conditions for service workers, and favour well-capitalized multinational concessionaires over smaller local firms in contract selection (Natyshak, personal communication, 2012; Canadian Labour Congress, 2005; CUPE, 2010). Community-mobilized opposition has also demonstrated the potential to delay PPP project approvals, force politicians to hold referenda on the approval of specific projects, or entirely halt PPPs that are particularly unpopular. In sum, while PPPs have grown in popularity with Canadian governments, they face pockets of resistance that can mobilize broader community opposition if a PPP deal as structured appears to put the public interest in jeopardy.

Conclusions

During Canada's second wave of PPPs, a common set of PPP institutions, models, and practices has emerged across the country. Nearly all private capital invested in PPPs is repaid through availability payments over the life of the concession period and few deals include the transferring of demand or revenue risks. Neither have PPPs been widely used to raise substantial new private funding for infrastructure, nor overhaul the role of government in the provision of public services, nor move the costs of infrastructure funding off of the public balance sheet. Rather, Canadian PPPs are primarily structured as incentive-based contracts designed to transfer construction cost, delivery time, and availability risk to the private-sector partner. To this end, when assessed against the international definition of PPPs provided by Garvin and Bosso (2008), second-wave Canadian PPPs would be at the low end of the spectrum in terms of private-sector responsibility within the partnership.

Indeed, if the second wave of Canadian PPPs can be deemed successful, it is because of the more conservative partnership models and risk-transfer arrangements that have been applied as compared to those common during the first wave of projects. Canadian PPPs have focused on identifying and leveraging the relative strengths of each partner, which in this case has meant maintaining a strong role for the public sector in owning the asset, designing project specifications, and ensuring public control related to key features of their long-term operations. These parameters are a result of both the application of the technical expertise housed in the special-purpose agencies, and the context of public skepticism towards PPPs that has made it politically challenging to implement partnerships that more aggressively transfer responsibility to the private sector.

To be certain, a critical outstanding question remains whether Canadian PPPs are too expensive, and more specifically whether too high a price is being paid to transfer what is effectively construction and availability risk to the private sector. An important area for future study is whether lower-cost alternative approaches to risk management rather than risk transfer exist that do not involve the high cost of including significant private-sector financing. One area for exploration is whether the current special-purpose agencies that are tasked with procuring only PPPs could have their mandates broadened so that their extensive staff expertise could be applied to the delivery of all large infrastructure projects, whether using traditional or PPP models. This is the institutional arrangement that is currently used in Quebec, and may have applicability more widely across the country.

Nevertheless, the overriding strength of the recent Canadian PPP approach is that the partnership models being designed are more like traditional procurements than outright privatizations, and have been applied in most provinces by skilled procurement professionals within the special-purpose PPP agencies. As a result, Canadian PPPs have largely avoided the frequent contract renegotiations and even project bankruptcy or government bailouts that have more frequently plagued projects in other countries that are experienced users of PPPs. The key lesson learned from the Canadian experience with second-wave PPPs is that they do not have to be a radical transformation from traditional procurement approaches in order to be successful.

Important Terms and Concepts

public–private partnership   value for money

Study Questions

1. Define the term *public–private partnership* and explain how this model of project delivery is applied for infrastructure projects.
2. What are the primary rationales that governments in Canada have identified for delivering infrastructure through public–private partnerships?
3. What are the key drivers of value for money in public–private partnerships?
4. Compare and contrast the differences between the first and second wave of public–private partnerships implemented in Canada.
5. Identify the most common critiques that public–private partnerships in Canada continue to face.

References

Alberta Treasury Board. 2011. *Alberta's Public-Private Partnership Framework and Guideline*. Edmonton: Government of Alberta.

Auditor General of British Columbia. 2011. *Audit of the Academic Ambulatory Care Centre Public Private Partnership: Vancouver Coastal Health Authority*. Retrieved March 5, 2014, from www.bcauditor.com

Auditor General of New Brunswick. 1998. *Chapter 13: Fredericton-Moncton Highway*. Report of the Auditor General – 1998. Available from https://www.gnb.ca/OAG-BVG/1998/chap13e.pdf

Auditor General of Nova Scotia. 2010. *Education: Contract Management of Public-Private Partnership Schools*. Retrieved March 5, 2014, from http://oag-ns.ca/index.php/publications?task=document.viewdoc&id=649

Auditor General of Ontario. 2008. "Brampton Civic Hospital Public-Private Partnership Project." *2008 Annual Report*. 102-124. Available from http://www.auditor.on.ca/en/reports_en/en08/303en08.pdf

Auditor General of Quebec. 2009. *Report of the Auditor General of Quebec to the National Assembly 2010–2012. Special report dealing with the watch over the projects to modernize Montreal's University Hospitals*. Available from http://www.vgq.gouv.qc.ca/en/en_publications/en_rapport-annuel/en_fichiers/en_rapport2010-2011-chu.pdf

Blain, L. 2013. "The Partnership Experience in Canada." *Seminar to the Copenhagen Business School*. September 4, 2013. Copenhagen. Retrieved March 2, 2014, from http://cast.cbs.dk/#search_term=blain

Blain, L. 2009. "PPPs Provide Benefits to BC." *Partnerships BC*. Available from http://www.partnershipsbc.ca/files/documents/20090407BCWideOP.pdf

Boardman, A.E. and Vining, A.R. 2012. "The Political Economy of Public-Private Partnerships and Analysis of their Social Value." *Annals of Public and Cooperative Economics* 88, 2, pp. 117–41.

Boardman, A.E. and Vining, A.R. 2010. "P3s in North America: Renting the Money (in Canada), Selling the Roads (in the USA)." *International Handbook on Public-Private Partnerships*, edited by Graeme Hodge, Carsten Greve, and Anthony Boardman. Cheltenham: Edward Elgar.

Brown, J.W., R. Pieplow, R. Driskell, S. Gaj, M.J. Garvin, D. Holcombe, M. Saunders, J. Seiders, Jr., and A. Smith. 2009. *Public-Private Partnerships for Highway Infrastructure: Capitalizing on International Experience*. U.S. Federal Highway Administration. Available from http://international.fhwa.dot.gov/pubs/pl09010/pl09010.pdf

CBC. 2013. "All Herb Gray Parkway Girders by Freyssinet to be Replaced." Available from http://www.cbc.ca/news/canada/windsor/all-herb-gray-parkway-girders-by-freyssinet-to-be-replaced-1.2325566

CBC. 2012. "Saint John Council Votes in Favour of P3 Water Deal." Available from http://www.cbc.ca/news/canada/new-brunswick/story/2013/03/26/nb-p3-water-saint-john.html

CCPPP. Canadian Council for Public-Private Partnerships. 2008. *Public Sector Accounting for Public-Private Partnerships in Canada*. Available from http://www.pppcouncil.ca/pdf/pppfinance_072008.pdf

Canadian Labour Congress. 2005. *Document No. 8 - Public-Private Partnerships (P3s): Against the Public Interest*. Available from http://www.canadianlabor.ca/sites/default/files/pdfs/CLC_Policy_on_P3s.pdf

CLRT. (2006). *Canada Line Final Project Report: Competitive Selection Phase*. Available from http://www.partnershipsbc.ca/files-4/documents/Canada-Line-Final-Project-Report_12April2006.pdf

Cohn, D. 2008. "British Columbia's Capital Asset Management Framework: Moving from Transactional to Transformative Leadership on Public-Private Partnerships or a "Railroad Job"?" *Canadian Public Administration* 51, 1, pp. 71–97.

Conference Board of Canada. 2010. *Dispelling Myths: A Pan-Canadian Assessment of Public-Private Partnerships for Infrastructure Investments*. Available from http://www.fengatecapital.com/DispellingTheMythsRpt_WEB1.pdf

Cruz, C.O. and R.C. Marques. 2013. "Endogenous Determinants for Renegotiating Concessions: Evidence from Local Infrastructure." *Local Government Studies* 39, 3, pp. 352–74.

CUPE. 2010. *Why Privatization Doesn't Work: Useful Research and Analysis about Public-Private*. Available from partnershipshttp://www.cupe.bc.ca/sites/default/files/Critiquing%20privatization%20Updated-Feb2010_0.pdf

CUPE. 1999. *Brief on the Moncton–Fredericton Highway Project*. Available from http://cupe.ca/updir/P3-Highway-NB.pdf

Deloitte & Touche. 2011. *Chief Peguis Trail Extension Project Value for Money Report*. Available from http://www.winnipeg.ca/publicworks/MajorProjects/ChiefPeguisTrail/PDF/2011-11-25-CPTEP-ProjectReportFinal.pdf

Engles, E., R. Fischer, and A. Galetovic. 2011. "Public-Private Partnerships to Revamp U.S. Infrastructure." *Brookings Institution*. Discussion Paper 2011-02.

Flyvbjerg, B., N. Bruzelius, and W. Rothengatter. 2003. *Megaprojects and Risk: An Anatomy of Ambition.* New York, NY: Cambridge University Press.

Garvin, M., and D. Bosso. 2008. "Assessing the Effectiveness of Infrastructure Public–Private Partnership Programs and Projects." *Public Works Management and Policy,* 13, 2, 162–178.

Grimsey, D., and M. Lewis. 2004. *Public Private Partnerships.* Cheltenham, UK: Edward Elgar.

Hager, M. 2013. "Golden Ears Bridge Losing up to $45 Million Each Year." *Vancouver Sun.* Available from http://www.vancouversun.com/business/Golden+Ears+Bridge+losing+million+each+year/8965050/story.html

HM Treasury. 2012. *A New Approach to Public Private Partnerships.* Available from http://cdn.hm-treasury.gov.uk/infrastructure_new_approach_to_public_private_parnerships_051212.pdf

Hodge G., and C. Greve. 2010. "Public–Private Partnerships: Governance Scheme or Language Game? *Australian Journal of Public Administration."* 69 (Suppl. 1), S8–S22.

Huxham, C., and S. Vangen, S. 2000. "What Makes Partnerships Work." *Public–Private Partnerships: Theory and Practice in International Perspective,* edited by Stephen P. Osborne. New York, NY: Routledge.

Infrastructure Canada. 2012. *Infrastructure Spotlight: Improving Canada's Infrastructure through Public-Private Partnerships.* Available from http://www.p3canada.ca/_files/P3_eng.pdf

Infrastructure Ontario. 2007. *Value for Money Assessment Durham Consolidated Courthouse.* Retrieved March 5, 2014, from http://www.infrastructureontario.ca/What-We-Do/Projects/Project-Profiles/Durham-Region-Courthouse/

Infrastructure Ontario. 2007. *Assessing Value for Money: A Guide to Infrastructure Ontario's Methodology.* Toronto: Queen's Printer for Ontario.

Loxley, J. and S. Loxley. 2010. *Public Service, Private Profits.* Winnipeg: Fernwood Publishing.

Murray, S. 2006. "Value for Money? Cautionary Lessons about P3s from British Columbia." *Canadian Centre for Policy Alternatives.* Available from http://www.policyalternatives.ca/sites/default/files/uploads/publications/BC_Office_Pubs/bc_2006/P3_value_for_money.pdf

Mussio, L.B. 2011. *The Present and Future of Public-Private Partnerships in Canada.* Toronto: National Bank Financial Markets Research Paper.

Newman, J. 2013. *The Governance of Public-Private Partnerships: Success and Failure in the Transportation Sector.* Unpublished Doctoral Thesis. Vancouver: Simon Fraser University.

OAA. 2014. *Letter to Glen Murray, Minister of Infrastructure and Transportation.* Available from http://oaa.informz.ca/OAA/data/images/2014-murrayinfrastructurettrjan.pdf

P3 Canada. 2014. *Overview: P3 Canada Fund.* Available from http://www.p3canada.ca/p3-canada-fund-overview.php

Paikin, S. 2012. "Premiers Harris and Peterson Respond." *Inside the Agenda Blog.* Available from http://theagenda.tvo.org/blog/agenda-blogs/premiers-harris-and-peterson-respond

Partnerships BC. 2011. *Understanding Public-Private Partnerships.* Available from http://www.partnershipsbc.ca/pdf/2011-09-02_Understanding-Public-Private-Partnerships.pdf

Partnerships BC. 2013. *Compensation Guidelines.* Available from http://www.fin.gov.bc.ca/psec/disclosuredocs/execcompdisclosure11-12/2011-12%20-%20Partnerships%20BC%20Executive%20Compensation%20Disclosure.pdf

Pollock, A., J. Shaoul, and N. Vickers. 2002. "Private Finance and "Value for Money" in NHS Hospitals: A Policy in Search of a Rationale?" *British Medical Association Journal* 324, 7347, pp. 1205–9.

Quiggin, J. 2004. "Risk, PPPs, and the Public Sector Comparator." *Australian Accounting Review* 14, 2, pp. 51–61.

Rachwalski, M. 2013. "Why We Don't Always Know For Sure if P3s Deliver Benefits over Conventional Government Procurement. Public-Private Partnership (P3)." *Conference Series CBS-Sauder-Monash Second Joint Conference.* Vancouver, June 14, 2013.

SaskBuilds. 2013. *Understanding Public-Private Partnerships.* Available from http://www.saskbuilds.ca/alternative-financing/UnderstandingP3s.html

Shaoul, J. 2009. "Using the Private Sector to Finance Capital Expenditures: The Financial Realities." *Policy, Management and Finance for Public-Private Partnerships,* edited by Akintola Akintoye and Matthias Beck, Oxford: Wiley-Blackwell.

Shaoul, J., A. Stafford, and P. Stapleton. 2007. "Partnerships and the Role of Financial Advisors: Private Control over Public Policy?" *Policy & Politics* 35, 3, pp. 479–95.

Siemiatycki, M. 2007. "What's the Secret? The Application of Confidentiality in the Planning of Infrastructure Using Private-Public Partnerships." *Journal of the American Planning Association* 73, 4, pp. 388–403.

Siemiatycki, M. and N. Farooqi. 2012. "Infrastructure Public-Private Partnerships: Delivering Value for Money?" *Journal of the American Planning Association* 78, 3, pp. 283–99.

Siemiatycki, M. and J. Friedman. 2012. "The Trade-offs of Transferring Traffic Demand Risk on Transit Public-Private Partnerships." *Public Works Management and Policy* 17, 2, pp. 283–302.

Tiesman, G. and E-H. Klijn. 2002. "Partnership Arrangements. Governmental Rhetoric or Governance Scheme?" *Public Administration Review* 62, 2, pp. 197–205.

Whiteside, H. 2011. "Unhealthy Policy: The Political Economy of Canadian Public-Private Partnership Hospitals." *Health Sociology Review* 20, 3, pp. 258–68.

Yescombe, E.R. 2007. *Public-Private Partnerships: Principles of Policy and Finance.* Burlington MA: Butterworth-Heinemann.

Budgeting in Canada

18

Centre Stage of Government and Governance

Michael J. Prince

Chapter Overview

Any budget system in some way addresses the control of spending and taxing, the management of ongoing program activities, and the planning of policy and setting of priorities. This chapter surveys major historical phases of budget reform and budget making at the federal level of government from the early twentieth to the early twenty-first centuries. Contemporary politics of federal budgeting are discussed with a focus on the dynamics of recent minority governments, the Stephen Harper era, and the Justin Trudeau Government. Every government uses the budget system for establishing public purposes and the public sector's own participation in civil society and the market economy. The Harper and Trudeau Governments evidence shifts in the priority accorded to financial control and strategic planning, while the improvement of management performance remains elusive at the federal level of public administration.

Chapter Objectives

By the end of this chapter, students will be able to do the following:

- Describe the three core functions of a budgetary system.
- Outline the political-institutional setting of budgeting in Canada.
- Appreciate the levels of budgetary activities.
- Explain how expenditure and revenue budgeting are at the centre stage of public policy and administration.

Introduction

Budgeting is the most visible and central process of public policy-making, the quantifiable expression of decisions that extract and expend the resources essential for operating government. Budgeting also is a highly institutionalized event in modern Canadian public administration. The quintessential decision that governments make on a regular basis, each budget, on both its expenditure and revenue sides, incorporates values, conflicts, and inconsistencies with which governments must deal. A public budget must respond to or at least appear to recognize the demands of various interests in the population that conflict in numerous ways. At the same time, it must further the government's own agenda and conception of the public interest.

At all levels of government and public-sector governance, budgets are a mixture of politics, economics, and management. Indigenous, federal, provincial, territorial, and municipal governments prepare fiscal plans setting out projected levels and composition of expenditures and revenues, staffing levels, policy priorities, and anticipated deficits, balances, or surpluses. From an analysis of budgets, we are better able to understand many of the processes, politics, and impacts of governing and management. Not all budgetary decisions are big decisions, but in big, moderate, and small choices, budgeting is power—the process of determining who gets what and who pays for what, when, and how. In short, budgets, through exercising authority, shape public and private relationships by conferring benefits and burdens.

This chapter proceeds in four sections. First, it sets out an analytical framework to understand public budgeting in the Canadian political context. Second, major historical phases of budget reform at the federal level of government are surveyed from the early twentieth to the early twenty-first centuries. Third, contemporary politics of federal budgeting are discussed with a focus on the dynamics of recent minority governments, the Stephen Harper era and the Justin Trudeau Government. Fourth, the chapter concludes by suggesting that every government uses the budget system for establishing the direction and character of public purposes and the government's own participation in civil society and the economy. The Harper and Trudeau Governments evidence shifts in the priority accorded to **financial control**

and **strategic planning**. The **management orientation** appears to be the weakest; program evaluation and improvement of administrative performance is the most elusive to achieve at the federal level of public administration.

Analytical Framework for Understanding Budgeting

To better understand public budgeting in Canada the analytical framework set out here consists of three elements: core functions of budgeting; the levels of budgetary activities; and the general institutional setting of cabinet–parliamentary government, federalism, and interest-group politics.

Budget Functions: Control, Management, and Planning

As an instrument of governing, budgeting serves broader public purposes. The threefold function of control, management, and planning and policy choice have formed the basis of a popular typology for studying government budgeting for 50 years (Schick, 1966). According to this approach, any budget system must, and does in some way, address the three functions of the control of spending and taxing, the management of ongoing program activities, and the planning of policy and setting of priorities. Planning and associated budget decisions occur as the first stage of the cycle of management activities and provide, in a sense, the terms of reference for administrative action and accountability. Operationally, these functions may be indivisible as administrative processes, but in practice they are rarely given equal attention because each function requires different skills and different kinds of information and orientations, and these often reside in separate public organizations. Moreover, the accountability terms of reference become more complex as a government moves through these functions. As a consequence, the control, management, and planning functions have tended to be in competition within government budget systems.

Over the sweep of budgetary changes during the past several decades, every major reform has altered, usually deliberately, the balance among these three functions. Every subsequent reform is partly a reaction to and correction of perceived failings of the previous equilibrium among control, management, and planning. No budgetary reform, therefore, is forever. Budgets are simultaneously a reflection of competing values, a record of the past, a form of power, and a set of signals.

Levels of Budgeting: Macro, Micro, and Mezzo

Macro versus **micro budgeting** is a longstanding distinction, particularly in the economics literature, to differentiate big issues and impacts from smaller ones in public finance and policy. In the economics of budgeting, **macro budgeting** is synonymous with stabilization policy and the grand Keynesian-monetarist debate of recent decades, including the debate about deficits and surpluses. Micro budgeting is seemingly everything else. In political science, macro budgeting refers, in part, to such topics as fiscal federalism and the connection between budgets and the electoral cycle. The bargaining between spenders and guardians inside the administrative state is a critical aspect of micro budgeting. In organizational and managerial studies, macro budgeting is equated with the sequence of steps leading to, variously, a statement of priorities, the budget speech, and the tabling and passage of the financial plans. Micro budgeting here embraces the things that go on within departments and other public agencies as well as such activities as auditing and the setting and collection of user fees. While useful, these categories can be misleading, especially when they obscure the significance of middle-level dynamics whose aggregate impact may be growing in importance. These dynamics relate to **mezzo budgeting**.

Much like the macro and micro budgeting, the mezzo level is part of the continuum of budgetary activities that overlap. In part, the mezzo component of the continuum arises from the expansion of the state both internally and externally. Internally, increasing levels of decision-making and interdependence must be accommodated. Policy fields and programs stretch not only across government, but externally to society as well. Budgets are much more than a sum of money calculated annually. They are a set of relationships with interests and individuals and also with different genders and generations of Canadians. If macro budgeting focuses on the aggregates of taxing and spending viewed from the perspective of the government and the economy as a whole, and if micro budgeting is anchored in the world of specific departments and non-departmental organizations and their clientele groups in society, then the remaining middle ground can be extensive indeed.

To understand this middle ground, consider the built-in character of spending within a federal, provincial, territorial, or urban government's own broad categories of budgetary envelopes or sectors. The economic development field typically contains the largest pool of discretionary funds available to politicians to spend on a yearly basis. The higher proportion of grants in this field causes ministers, officials, and interest groups to gravitate to these funds like sharks. Most of the spending in other budgetary policy fields is more rigid, constrained by longer-term legal obligations at the intergovernmental and international levels. Spending on the field of government operations is personnel-intensive, while in the area of defence it is capital-intensive. These and other attributions of mezzo budgeting present different managerial issues and define the amount of room to manoeuvre, which drives some political aspects of the budgetary process.

General Institutional Setting

Budgeting takes place in a general institutional and constitutional context, which has several facets. From cabinet–parliamentary government, budgeting inherits the constitutional principle that only the executive, the cabinet, can introduce money bills—expenditure initiatives and the raising of public funds. It also inherits the notion that elected legislative bodies grant "supply" and hold ministers to account, collectively as a cabinet and as individuals. Cabinets are quasi-representative collections of people, chosen with attention to regional, linguistic, gender, and other criteria in mind, who want to do good things in genuine ways but who also have high expectations of being able to demonstrate, at least on occasion, that they have influence and power. So, too, do their senior public servants and the departments and agencies they head. The budgetary process must in part accommodate these needs, and such accommodation may or may not coincide with desirable program needs or efficiency criteria. Figure 18.1 presents at a macro level, in the parliamentary setting, various steps of the federal budget cycle over the April 1 to March 31 financial year.

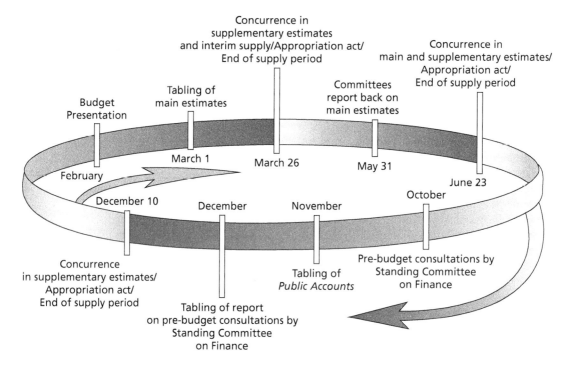

Figure 18.1 Budget Cycle for the Government of Canada

Source: Parliament of Canada, House of Commons Procedure and Practice http://www.parl.gc.ca/procedure-book-livre/document
.aspx?sbdid=f26eb116-b0b6-490c-b410-33d985bc9b6b&sbpid=fda208a7-caa9-40b7-9a42-3f3c5bb83cc7&sbpidx=4

Another institutional aspect is important. In-ternal bureaucratic-executive processes also produce demands for varying definitions of policy analysis so that decisions are carefully considered and consistent with overall priorities and other program areas. This can stretch out the budgeting process. Concerns for timely and decisive budgeting, on the other hand, can lead to demands to shorten the process so that decisiveness can be demonstrated. The cabinet and executive, therefore, produce both an institution-alized and a highly personalized budgetary process as ministers and officials with widely varying bases of power manoeuvre to do public and private good (Doern et al., 2013).

Cabinets are to govern responsibly while oppos-ition parties in legislatures are to counter, criticize, and prevent unofficial and surreptitious governing. Thus, the overall budgetary system within cabinet–parliamentary government is intended to hold elected

ministers accountable and responsible for the deci-sions. Yet the modern process also induces the fre-quent practice of "ministerial irresponsibility." Under this political custom, an entire cabinet or a specific minister selectively accepts credit when good results can be claimed and strenuously deflects blame onto others (previous ministers or governments, other levels of government or other sectors, or even other countries) when bad results are apparent or decisions are unpopular.

A prime minister or premier's explicit budget-ary role varies both among first ministers and under different times and circumstances. A first minister must avoid undermining the minister of finance, but at the same time his or her ultimate agenda is that of the government and the party as a whole rather than that of the budget itself. A first minister's agenda, therefore, is not always precisely the same as that of the finance minister. The premier/prime minister is the chief point of contact for other political leaders, both domestically and internationally, and hence is subject to a range of pressures and personal alliances and obligations of which many of his or her colleagues may not even be aware. Unwritten **constitutional conventions** in our system of parliamentary government enable a prime minister, along with the finance minister, to decide whether any expenditure or revenue plans are contained in a Speech from the Throne; when exactly an annual budget is presented; the form and nature of pre-budget consultations; and whether and when a fiscal update or economic statement is delivered in the House of Commons.

Important differences exist when one relates the above cabinet dynamics to **revenue budgeting** as compared to the expenditure budget process. Essentially, two ministers, the finance minister and the first minister, decide revenue budgets. A far greater concentration of power is practised here than on the expenditure side, where other ministers have some room for input and influence, but some more than others in any given year.

In addition, budgeting is governed by the preferred and perverse dictates of partisanship and the electoral cycle. From time to time, election mandates properly produce democratically desired budgetary decisions. At other times, raw electoral calculus produces behaviour that, while understandable, is not warmly applauded. Political spending increases occur as voters are "bribed" with their own tax dollars; or revenue increases are delayed or underestimated just prior to an election call; or pre-election tactics for restraint speak soothingly of the need to "manage" better, and only after the election do the "draconian details" become apparent. Election mandates, which ought to be the first line of democratic accountability, produce varied budgetary styles and outputs (Maslove et al., 1986).

The ever-evolving system of Canadian federalism is another institutional feature. Budgetary behaviour and norms are influenced by the assignment of powers, major joint spending programs, equalization payments, and constitutional limits on the powers of taxation. The federal government can tax by any mode or means, whereas the provinces can impose direct taxation only (which includes sales tax). The ability of municipalities and school boards to raise revenue is determined by their respective provincial governments. One level of government cannot tax another, a reality that has led, along with other causes, to the use of Crown corporations to capture revenue shares and to disputes between senior levels of government and municipalities for grants in lieu of property taxes on Crown lands. Expenditures are less constrained by purely constitutional features, but the use of the federal spending power in areas of provincial jurisdiction has been controversial. It has, however, helped to produce an elaborate array of federal, provincial, and intergovernmental economic and social programs.

Interest groups and interests are two other key features of the institutional setting of public budgeting in Canada. Whether they are formal associations of business, labour, agriculture, or countless other sectors, interest groups have budgetary expectations to be resolved on the tax side by finance ministries or municipal councils and on the spending side by their department(s), if they have one. Interests include large individual corporations and individual governments that do not have to rely on the lobbying techniques of interest groups. Interests actually possess the power to invest or not invest and to respond or not respond to government incentives delivered through the tax system or through direct expenditures. Interest groups have fewer direct powers, though the power of some can be enhanced by their alliance with key corporate interests or other governments.

Process norms of budgeting call for consultation and participation with affected interests and interest groups. Such groups have widely varying power bases and other resources, and so differ in their capacity to participate and to have an impact. Many interest groups take positions on overall fiscal policy and on particular areas of spending and taxation. They are the beneficiaries of a multitude of different tax and expenditure provisions, but their positions are arguably the least subject to sustained public scrutiny by elected political bodies. Modern budgetary scrutiny requires mechanisms that apply a searchlight on both public and private power (Doern et al., 2013).

Interacting with the above political and governmental institutions are the organizations of international bodies and foreign governments. International organizations, including the Organisation for Economic Co-operation and Development (OECD) and the World Trade Organization (WTO), and foreign government bodies such as the United States Federal Reserve have direct implications for

Canadian public finance and budgeting. The influences exerted include the fiscal policy analysis fostered by the OECD, the moves and countermoves that the WTO prompts in deciding whether, and in what form, subsidies and loans can be allowed under trade law, as well as the interest rate and deficit financing decisions and pressures from the US Federal Reserve. Also part of this international network is the circulation of policy paradigms including Keynesianism and monetarism and their neo varieties as to what constitutes good fiscal management and responsible budgeting

Major Historical Phases of Budget Reform in Canada

An important way to appreciate the links among functions, levels, and institutions in the budgetary process is to see how the roles of key federal government organizations have changed in different periods of budget reform. The major historical phases approximately are as follows: early 1900s to 1940s, the late 1940s to mid-1970s, and the middle years of the 1970s to the early 2000s. These phases of reforms each involved an age of budgeting associated closely to the larger political, economic, and management debates that saw the ascendancy of certain budgetary ideas over others.

Before the 1940s: A Concern for Budgetary Integrity and Control at the Micro Level

The first period can be traced to the early decades of Canadian budgetary systems at all levels of governance, and at least some of its features extend well into the 1960s. The dominant precepts were balanced budgets and honesty and probity in spending. Using the public purse to advance the interests of the party in power—by public works expenditures, by the partisan apportionment of government contracts, or by local improvements at federal expense—were increasingly deemed to be political evils with adverse effects of financial administration. A form of detailed accountability was advocated and adopted, reflected in the precise provisions of the Financial Administration Act, and in competitive tendering and in budgeting by standard objects. The legislation provided for controls that included the approval of the issue of all cheques by a single official of government,

the Comptroller of the Treasury. Standard objects meant that legislative votes for the Estimates were centred on the inputs of spending such as personnel and equipment. Parliament could be reasonably certain that funds would be spent specifically on those objects on which it had voted.

During this period, the Finance Department and Treasury Board were effectively an integrated entity, and key budgetary officials were more likely to be accountants than economists. The Board had a detailed role in controlling spending and its program branch was its nerve centre in the detailed haggling and control function vis-à-vis departments and agencies. The Auditor General complemented the budget system by carrying out a traditional audit function designed to satisfy Parliament that honesty and probity were being practised.

1940s to 1970s: Embracing Macro-Level Planning and Management

This phase encompassed three prominent strands of budgetary reform. The broadest trend was that of Keynesian economics. Beginning in the 1940s, but blossoming in the 1950s and 1960s (before wilting somewhat in the 1970s), the Keynesian paradigm was critical to public finance and policy-making. First, it provided a rationale for government intervention that was otherwise not acceptable in the politics of Western capitalist countries at the time. This enabled in Canada and elsewhere the political promotion of social programs, and the construction of welfare states, as a necessary part of a strategy to stabilize the economy and promote growth. At a more specific level, Keynesianism provided a justification for demand management and counter-cyclical budgeting, and therefore the use of aggregate spending and taxation instruments as fiscal policy tools. Second, Keynesianism provided a more explicit rationale for deficit budgeting. The state was not a private household. It could, within limits, spend more than it took in, as long as some of the eventual balancing took place through surplus budgeting during good times. Third, Keynesianism focused attention on the goals of economic growth, employment, price stability, and short-term stabilization. These ideas and techniques were practised in limited ways both at the federal level and by some provincial governments (Maslove et al., 1986).

The second strand was found in the advocacy of more rational output-oriented management in the public sector. In 1963, the Glassco Royal Commission criticized as excessively detailed the input-oriented control ethos of the federal government's overall budgeting and managerial system. It urged the government to let the managers manage. In short, the Glassco Commission wanted the line departments and agencies of government to be freed from the shackles of dysfunctional controls so that they could then manage more like managers in private firms. In a way, Glassco foreshadowed a very similar message by the reinventing government and New Public Management movement of the 1990s. Later in the 1960s and early 1970s, this ethos was further articulated by an even more pronounced philosophical emphasis on goals and longer-term planning. New acronyms and tools entered the vocabulary and world of bureaucrats, politicians, and students of public administration, acronyms such as PPB to signify planning, programming, and budgeting, and MBO to signify management by objectives. The two strands thus indicated that macro budgeting on the Keynesian scale could be joined by micro budgeting and planning that would no longer be input-oriented but rather goal- and result-oriented.

The main budgetary agencies also changed as a result. The Treasury Board was given its own minister (president) and its secretariat was separated from the Department of Finance. The management of government was to be separated significantly from the management of the economy. That meant a greater attention to control: less spending, less taxation, less bureaucracy. The Treasury Board Secretariat gained responsibilities under the then-new system of collective bargaining as well as more general personnel responsibilities. A new planning branch aggressively pushed the new rationality of output-oriented budgeting. The Finance Department, meanwhile, evolved more into an exclusive macroeconomic department, offering advice and making policy on overall fiscal matters, on the burgeoning system of intergovernmental agreements, and on banking and capital markets.

The third strand of budgetary reform in this period was the rise of the political planning and direction from the centre of federal and provincial governments. In Ottawa, after the coming to power of Prime Minister Pierre Trudeau in 1968, the Privy Council Office (PCO) and the Prime Minister's Office (PMO) were also expanded and asserted their aspects of central coordinating tasks of government. The PCO was the ultimate governmental coordinator in support of the executive as a whole. The PMO was the partisan coordinator, an extension of the prime minister, but with a particular sensitivity to party concerns as well. These developments were not necessarily consistent with Glassco's decentralist creed of "let the managers manage."

The Mid-1970s to Early 2000s: The Rise and Fall and Rise Again of Mezzo Budgeting

Beginning in the mid-1970s, budgetary reform took on still further features of the larger political and economic debate. One feature reflected the growing neo-conservative critique of government. The public sector was demonstrating its inability to carry out certain functions, according to this view, and the only solution was less government. That meant less spending, less taxation, and less bureaucracy. The growing presence of double-digit inflation and unemployment also contributed to the partial rejection of the Keynesian notion of the discretionary anti-cyclical fine-tuning of the economy. Public spending was to be kept at rates of growth that would not exceed the trend-line growth in the gross domestic product (GDP). Beginning with the budget speech in 1975, this goal was officially adopted by the federal government. Another critical goal adopted around the same time was the belief that inflation in Canada was best dealt with, and stable economic growth ensured, through monetary targeting, that is, through watchful (critics would say obsessive and excessive) control of interest rates by the Bank of Canada.

At a more managerial level, but influenced by this larger debate, was the emergence of yet another set of demands to produce rationality in budgets. The Auditor General became a leading advocate of change, and succeeded in obtaining a mandate to conduct value-for-money auditing, allowing federal audit staff to comment on whether government decisions were made with due regard for economy and efficiency in spending. Thus, the prior preoccupation with planning was replaced with a new emphasis on the ongoing and retrospective parts of the budget cycle. Many managers reacted against value-for-money auditing, in part because auditors arrived with criteria for assessment that had never been given to managers at the front end of the cycle. The Auditor General also persuaded the government to establish a new central agency, the Comptroller General, separate from the Treasury Board Secretariat, whose task was to ensure that government departments evaluated their programs in a systematic and continuous way. When the Mulroney Conservatives came to power in 1984, they attempted a wholesale review of federal programs, a process repeated under the impetus of another new government, the Chrétien Liberals in 1993. Both exercises, while different in various respects, resulted in a range of spending cutbacks, program and agency rationalizations, privatizations, commercialization of operations, and much continuity in activities.

Ideas and demands to reform taxation appeared on the budgetary policy agenda a number of times over this period. The practice of demand management, coupled with interest-group pressure, had incrementally produced a flood of tax incentives, each apparently desirable from some standpoint. Indeed, in the 1970s, tax expenditures grew even more rapidly than had regular direct expenditures in federal budgets. Tax reform was visited under the phrase "tax expenditures"—deviations from the general pattern of taxation for a certain class of taxpayers in order to achieve public policy objectives a government considered important. Governments, reformers suggested, should publish tax expenditure accounts to shed light on this relatively hidden side of the fiscal coin. Through the 1980s and 1990s, some federal and provincial governments did publish such accounts. In addition, driven by deficit pressures and calls for greater fairness, several federal tax expenditures were reduced, eliminated, or converted to more equitable non-refundable tax credits. Nonetheless, a large tax expenditure system remains embedded in the corporate and personal income systems and the retail sales tax system. In an effort to reduce the annual deficit and gain better control over the national debt, successive governments raised tax rates and broadened the base of some taxes; for instance, the manufacturer's sales tax was changed to the Goods and Services Tax and extended the application of user fees to more and more federal public services.

These critiques and calls for reform affected the main budgetary agencies in Ottawa. One organizational result was that the Finance Department was restored to greater pre-eminence in order both to control aggregate spending in the interest of the macroeconomy and to enable it to better manage the intricacies of the increasingly interwoven tax and direct expenditure labyrinth. The Clark government of 1979–80 established the Policy Expenditure and Management System (PEMS), dubbed the envelope system of budgeting.

This reform recognized the mezzo level of budgeting by further institutionalizing the middle-level cabinet committees and policy field groupings. Committees were given policy reserves of funds to allocate to proposals generated and discussed within each envelope. New ministries of state for economic development and for social development were established with large secretariats, whose jobs were to better enable the cabinet committees concerned with these areas to link regularly ministerial policy wishes with dollar cost implications. Mirror committees of sector deputy ministers were established to support the ministers and encourage greater horizontal coordination. It was an effort, too, to have **expenditure budgeting** look further ahead over the medium to longer term of a government's mandate. These ministries of state were disbanded by Prime Minister Turner in 1984, out of a concern in part that there were too many central agencies.

Prime Minister Mulroney, in his first government in 1984–8, further simplified the PEMS, consolidating the number of envelopes and streamlining the cabinet papers associated with the priority-setting and budget process. Departmental strategic overviews were no longer requested and the link between operational planning and government-wide strategic planning was weakened. The focus increasingly was on expenditure ceilings and cuts more so than on program goals and results. The five-year fiscal plans previously published in budget papers were reduced to two years.

In his second government of 1988–93, Mulroney quickly abolished the PEMS and the associated economic and social policy sector committees. The PEMS was judged to be too bureaucratic, cumbersome, and ineffective, having largely failed in reducing expenditures and redesigning programs. As well, the prime minister had bypassed the system on a number of occasions to cut spending and to cut deals with ministers or premiers. Such behaviour by the power centre of Canadian government is not rare. The move beyond the envelope system towards a more centralized expenditure budgeting system was reflected in changes made to the cabinet committee system in 1989. An expenditure review committee, nicknamed the search-and-destroy committee in Ottawa circles, was formed, chaired by the prime minister, and given the task of ensuring that the government's expenditures were directed to its highest priorities and that spending control continued to contribute to deficit reduction. Financial officials provided the staff support for the Expenditure Review Committee. With the exception of the Treasury Board Committee, all other cabinet committees were placed under the Planning and Priorities (P & P) Committee. Policy reserves were centralized: only Treasury Board and the P & P Committee were mandated to authorize expenditures. Despite these structural changes to the federal budget process, the deficit and debt both increased over the Mulroney Conservatives' second mandate, with the deficit reaching a historic high of $42 billion in 1993–4.

The Chrétien Liberal government of 1993–7 made several changes to the cabinet and budget systems. The P & P Committee was abolished and the overall cabinet system became less hierarchical and simpler, though still dominated on the fiscal side by Finance, Treasury Board, and the PMO. The Liberals introduced in 1995 a new budget process, the Expenditure Management System (EMS), building on recent developments. The centralization of reserve funds under the purview of Finance and Treasury Board, for example, continued. The policy orientation of the defunct PEMS was now officially absent from the new name of the process, indicating a shift in functions to control and management and away from policy planning. In fact, there was no new money for new policy initiatives. Such policy measures would have to be financed by ministers reallocating resources away from existing programs within their portfolios. There was increased stress on meeting short-run budget goals rather than mapping out longer-term targets. The Finance Department engaged in a very cautious and politically astute style of forecasting deficit targets and then consistently surpassing them with better actual results. This probably helped to moderate public resistance to the initial targets and to revive the reputation of the Finance Department as a forecaster.

Continuing in the pursuit of better control and management, in 1996 the government introduced important changes in the budgetary information provided to Parliament. First, departmental plans and performance reports were tabled with the estimates, making available to parliamentarians and the public better-quality information on the business plans and results of federal programs and policies. Second, the government moved towards full accrual accounting, reporting the cost of government programs in the year in which program activity takes place. These changes represented significant improvements in the budget as an accountability document and have provided the Office of the Auditor General with more opportunity to hold federal agencies and departments to account by reporting and explaining their activities and results.

In addition, the Chrétien Government launched a program review exercise, conducting an in-depth analysis and judgment of the programs, roles, and activities of the federal public service. The macro aims of the review were to meet deficit reduction targets, improve the delivery of services to the public and the management culture that supports that delivery, and clarify the role of the federal government in various policy areas. Influenced by the worldwide new public management movement, the Liberals' rhetorical expression was to "get government right." Results included substantial cuts in program spending, a reduction of over 30,000 federal public servants, and the devolution to provinces and territories of program administration in social housing and labour market policy. Agencies and departments were forced or induced to earn money and fund services through user charges as they differentiated and discovered specific customers. Alternative service delivery agencies, such as the Canadian Food Inspection Agency, were created to achieve savings and to promote a more entrepreneurial approach to public management, including financial administration, but still within the framework of ministerial responsibility and parliamentary accountability. A mezzo-level initiative, the program review had macro and micro consequences that varied greatly across agencies and raised the issue of private funding for public goods.

A single-minded approach to control—aimed at significant deficit reduction and then elimination—was the basis of Liberal fiscal policy and budgeting over this period. This goal was in fact achieved, much sooner than many expected, because of several factors. By the mid-1990s the general public seemed more amenable to accept restraint, particularly from the Liberals, who were viewed with less suspicion than the Conservatives in wanting to attack social programs. Prime Minister Chrétien offered consistently strong support to his finance minister for his budgetary policies and to prevent end runs by line ministers to the PMO. The finance minister was thus able to make deep cuts in expenditures, in fact, absolute declines in program spending, most notably in the 1994 and 1995 budgets. Revenues also increased as a result of some tax increases but even more so from relatively robust and sustained growth in the Canadian economy. Like their Conservative predecessors, the Liberals supported the Bank of Canada's monetary policy of low and stable inflation that meant that low interest rates yielded lower debt-servicing costs for the federal purse.

In a budgetary sense, the Chrétien Liberals in their first mandate had but one policy—deficit reduction. With the 1998–9 budget, the federal government entered the post-deficit (but not post-debt) era. This was the first time since 1969–70 that there was no federal deficit. In their second mandate (1997–2000) and third mandate (2000–4), there was growing financial room and pressure for initiatives on several policy fronts. Ministers and departments marginalized in the previous mandate, and during the longer deficit generation, pushed harder for a more central place on the policy agenda. The idea that Ottawa can and should be an active agent of social and economic change gained greater currency. The Chrétien Liberals committed to allocating every billion dollars of fiscal dividend such that one-half went to a combination of reducing taxes and reducing national debt and one-half to addressing social and economic needs through program expenditures. This principle was applied flexibly from one budget to the next and ultimately applied to the entire mandate. Budgetary surpluses strengthened the credibility of client groups and other interest groups in calling for new spending and/or tax cuts. Fiscal dividend politics, like deficit politics, entails a debate over the appropriate size and

role of the federal government in relation to the provinces, the economy, and civil society.

Recent Politics of Federal Budgeting in Canada

On the contemporary politics of budgeting, consideration will focus on the implications of recent minority governments for budgetary practices and the role of parliamentary as well as on the budgetary styles of the Stephen Harper Conservative governing era and of the Justin Trudeau Liberal Government.

Minority Governments in Ottawa: A Time of Tactical Incrementalism?

Over the 2004 to 2011 period in Canadian federal politics, and for the first time in a quarter century, there was a succession of minority governments in Ottawa: the Liberal **minority government** of Paul Martin (2004–6) and the Conservative minority governments of Stephen Harper (2006–8 and 2008–11).

When a government lacks a majority of the seats in the House of Commons, what it means for federal budgeting is influenced by the tactics and demands of parliamentary parties and their leaders. Typically, in times of majority governments, Parliament's responsibility is to review and debate the budget, as best it can with the time and information available, and then legitimate the expenditure and revenue plans of the governing party as presented by the minister of finance. The dynamics of minority government, David Johnson points put, can include "heated debate, rapidly changing policy developments, shifting political alliances and short-term policy making" (2011: 302). Furthermore, as Gregory Inwood suggests, "In times of minority government, Parliament's role may be enhanced since the executive often must bargain with one or more of the opposition parties to support the budget. In return, those parties may be able to negotiate out of the budget those items they find most objectionable, or have included items close to their own hearts" (2009: 323).

Johnson remarks on two implications of minority government for government budgeting. One is that "the annual budget will have to accommodate a variety of opposition party interests as well as promote the government's policy agenda." A second is that "the government must prioritize items not only in keeping with its own policy objectives but also according to how each item would fare in popular opinion if an election were called" (Johnson 2011: 302). Minority Parliament dynamics thus condition a style of budgeting characterized by centralized decision-making anchored in the Prime Minister's Office and related central agencies, and a short-term time horizon informed by political planning focused on high profile policies and programs. If one can say there is a philosophy of budget making at work in a minority parliament, it might best be described as **tactical incrementalism**. "In reality," as Patrick Malcolmson and Richard Myers observe, "minority government creates a fascinating game of political cat-and-mouse. A government that wishes to stay in power has to try to keep the opposition divided. It typically does so by introducing measures that it hopes at least one of the major opposition parties cannot possibly disagree with" (2009: 48).

Besides the existence or not of a minority government, other factors such as external economic events further condition the politics and management of federal budgeting. For example, in response to the 2008–10 global financial crisis and economic recession in Canada, the second Harper minority government reluctantly adopted a version of Keynesian budgeting: a multi-year economic action plan of spending and deficits to protect jobs and safeguard vulnerable sectors in the economy (Doern et al., 2013).

Budgeting in the Stephen Harper Era: Central Control and Omnibus Acts

For much of the Harper years of both minority (2006–11) and majority governments (2011–15), a control orientation prevailed in matters of federal budgeting and policy making in addition to the leadership style of the prime minister. Initial themes of the Harper Government centred on accountability of administration and adopted a far less ambitious agenda of social policy-making and intergovernmental relations. Each of these themes was in contrast to alleged administrative abuses and to the actual federal state activism of the Martin Government and the final government of Jean Chrétien. In the budgetary process, this meant a subordination of the strategic policy

planning function and a heightened attention to financial and managerial control; a turn from policy analysts and intergovernmental relations officers to auditors and accountants.

Harper Conservatives enacted their control management proclivity through legislative, regulatory, and organizational reforms. The Federal Accountability Act of 2006 among other initiatives designated deputy ministers as the "accounting officers" for their departments in order to ensure compliance with government policies and procedures and be responsible for the systems of internal audits within their organizations. An amendment to the Financial Administration Act now required federal government agencies and departments to evaluate all continuing grants and contributions every five years. The first Harper Government ushered in a wave of new watchdog agencies, including the creation of the Parliamentary Budget Office (PBO). The intent of the PBO is "to bring greater clarity, transparency, and accuracy to federal budget making by giving MPs greater access to current information on the nation's finances (Johnson, 2011: 274)." In 2009, during the second Harper Government, a new Treasury Board policy required all federal departments to assess the relevance and performance of all direct spending programs every five years. Such assessments were to evaluate the utilization of resources in producing outputs and expected outcomes, thus demonstrating the efficiency and effectiveness of federal programs. This cycle of program review operates at the micro level of departmental activities and services, although some programs are quite large in expenditures terms, and, politically, are highly visible in a macro sense. Rules on human and financial resources were also tightened in regards to contracts, travel, purchasing, and hiring with the fundamental aim of ensuring compliance by officials with policies and procedures set by Treasury Board and other central authorities.

Omnibus budget implementation acts, common in the American system of governing, were another notable feature of parliamentary politics practised by the Harper Government. Omnibus budget bills run to hundreds of pages in length comprising scores of statutory amendments to programs and policy measures, many of which have little direct connection to the proposed budget. In minority parliaments, an omnibus budget bill is a stratagem challenging opposition parties to vote against the budget, as a confidence vote in the government, thus potentially triggering a general federal election. It is, as well, a technique to obtain approval for myriad legislative changes under the cover of passing the annual budget. Leading political studies scholars Ned Franks and David Smith call the budget implementation bills in the Harper years as "among the most offensive to the traditions and principles of parliamentary government" (2012: 88). This form of budgetary brinkmanship, unquestionably an expression of new political governance, does little for either respecting or enhancing parliamentary scrutiny of the raising and spending of public money.

With a majority government mandate in 2011, Prime Minister Harper launched a comprehensive program of expenditure cuts to government operations involving 70 federal departments and agencies. Over a three-year period, the program review targeted the elimination of 19,200 public servant positions and more than $5 billion reductions in spending. As a centralized approach to budgeting, Harper "personally signed off on all spending cuts, large and small" identified by departments and reviewed by Treasury Board ministers (Savoie, 2015: 202). In this distinctive process, initiated and overseen by a prime minister, in quite concrete terms the micro, meso, and macro levels of budgetary decision-making came together.

On the Harper reforms on budgetary accountability and control, academic assessments are generally critical. On the accounting officer reform, the verdict is that it is a rather limited positive development and a contested measure for improving Parliament's ability to hold the government or departments to account (Gilmore, 2010; Howard & Phillips, 2012). On the production of performance evaluation reports by federal departments, Savoie maintains most are "relatively bland and harmless" (Savoie, 2015: 200), an indictment that can be made of many reports over many decades, suggesting the underdeveloped state of that management function in government. In our complex world of multiple programs and multiple public and private actors, establishing causal links to a program and then attributing quantifiable impacts are rarely easy in most policy fields. On the effectiveness of the PBO as a new financial watchdog, Johnson's observation aptly describes the experience as a contentious one with its creator: "the PBO has faced

increasing criticism from the Harper government. The PBO challenged the government on the accuracy of its financial estimates. . . . In 2011 the PBO also noted that MPs were not being given sufficient information on the financial implications of law reforms to lengthen prison sentences and limit parole" (Johnson, 2011: 274).

On the web of stricter rules for federal funding and procurement, the impact has been both onerous and worrying for networked governance. For non-profit organizations and small and medium-sized business, the new layers of rules have been "extremely burdensome, producing long delays in the process of approving contracts and contributions as well as high externalities, including additional costs, frustration, and damaged relationships" (Howard & Phillips, 2012: 332). Cosmo Howard and Susan Phillips observe more generally on departmental administration: "the culture that has been firmly embedded over the past decade is an audit culture. Program officers that used to work collaboratively with funding recipients have become more akin to controllers and police" (Howard & Phillips, 2012: 333).

Budgeting in the Justin Trudeau Era: The Return of Aspirational Planning

With the majority Liberal government of Justin Trudeau there appears to be a shift, at the centre of the federal government, in the balance among the control, management, and planning functions of budgeting. In their 2015 election platform, first Speech from the Throne, and early budgets, the Trudeau Liberals are emphasizing a positive and active role for the federal government expressed through strategic planning, deliberate adoption of deficit finances, and stimulus budgeting for their mandate and beyond.

Certain federal budgets are epiphanies marking a sudden and important shift in policy style, policy direction, or both. As a financial and political plan the 2016 budget was such an epiphany. It was a turning point that set out a new (or renewed) conception of the federal role of government and of federal fiscal policy. This confident expression of counter-cyclical budgeting rests on the belief that timely and deliberate investments of public expenditures, especially in a variety of forms of infrastructure (physical, green, and social) throughout the country, can stimulate job creation as well as economic, community, and sustainable development. With this ambition comes a multi-year time horizon in budgeting that extends beyond the life of the government's mandate. In the domain of social policy, the Trudeau Liberals' first budget was an opportunity to introduce major changes to child and family income benefits as well as adjust income tax rates and eliminate several tax expenditures introduced by the Harper Conservatives (Doern & Stoney, 2016). Similarly, the 2017 budget unveiled for people with disabilities a new Accessible Technology Development program of $223 million over five years, a new Early Learning and Childhood Development Framework of $7 billion over 10 years, starting in 2018–19, and a new National Housing Strategy with an investment of $11.2 billion over 11 years (Finance Canada, 2017).

The idea of strengthening and growing the middle class in Canada is not just an expedient political message or an effective campaign slogan in the 2015 election; it is for the Trudeau Government the leitmotif of issue framing, policy-making, and resource allocation in relation to existing programs and new expenditure and revenue proposals. A resurgence of mezzo-level budgeting seems apparent in light of proposals and actions on Indigenous self-government and fiscal relations with the other orders of governance, gender analyses of policies, new investments on innovation and infrastructure, and intergovernmental agreements on labour force development. Such spending—in a thoughtful and democratic way—will require the budget process of governments to give greater priority to strategic planning as well as consultative policy development.

As with previous prime ministers, central agencies in and around Justin Trudeau are playing an important and direct role in priority setting in the budgetary process. Trudeau chairs the cabinet committee on agenda, results and communication (his equivalent of earlier P & P committee), which sets the government's agenda and tracks progress on policy priorities. As with previous administrations, the Treasury Board cabinet committee acts as the management board of the government and employer for the federal public service. Treasury Board also provides oversight of financial management and spending and human resource issues. As a key source for the control function of budgeting, Treasury Board

establishes policies for administrative, personnel, financial, and organizational practices across government. At the same time, in a signal of returning to a more fulsome form of cabinet government and away from a strict governing from the centre, Trudeau has pledged to encourage ministerial initiative, within the context of their mandate letters, to focus on election commitments and shared strategic priorities. The question arises: will this reawaken the traditional competition between spending ministers and fiscal guardians, with increasing demands for more resources coming from departments and their clienteles?

In their Economic Statement and Update, in November 2016, the Trudeau Government announced plans for legislation to ensure more independence for the Parliamentary Budget Officer by establishing that role as an independent officer of Parliament and with an enhanced mandate, and for the Chief Statistician of Canada, to entrench the constitutional convention of independence from the government of the day in the Statistics Act. The March 2017 federal budget allocated $150 million over five years to Statistics Canada to develop a Housing Statistics Framework and for the Canada Mortgage and Housing Corporation to strengthen housing research (Finance Canada, 2017). These reforms, once implemented, go towards bolstering the control and management orientations of the budgeting system by supporting costing and financial analysis work by the PBO and high-quality statistical research and publications by Statistics Canada.

With an espoused interest in adopting new approaches to public issues, the Trudeau Liberals are focusing on the implementation of their political priorities and public policies. And with an interest also in "deliverology"—the art of getting policy goals, program reforms, and service provision effectively and efficiently implemented by government departments and agencies across the federal public sector—the Trudeau Liberals are attempting to link more closely resource allocation decisions and program activities to intended results. In support of this initiative, a delivery unit is housed in the PCO. This represents the latest undertaking by Ottawa in trying to enhance performance management at the micro or operational levels of the public service. There would seem to be new role for program evaluation and evaluators within the public service, implied by deliverology, and heightened accountability for deputy ministers for program results within their portfolios. Time will tell how well they succeed within government in improving the Cinderella status of implementing programs and services, in comparison to the favoured sisters of generating policy ideas and managing the political blame game.

Conclusion

More than money, public budgeting is about relations of authority and influence in governments and governance. Various actors inhabit the stage of the budgetary drama. At the centre stage of governing, the prime minister is the lead public actor. Along with the economic and social conditions of the time, budgeting styles and functions are shaped by the conceptions and practices of governing by a first minister and his or her government. In major program reviews and across-the-board spending-reduction exercises, prime ministers play the critical role. Minority and majority parliaments bestow different opportunities and constraints for governments and for opposition parties in the budgeting process. In both contexts, MPs perform somewhat differing roles; one, as guardians of the public purse, holding the government to account for overall revenue and expenditure choices; the other, as promoters of spending and tax benefits for their own local constituencies.

One constant is the effort by the political executive in exercising top-down direction in determining objectives and in shifting, however slightly, the vast and largely entrenched arrangement of policies, bureaucracies, and programs. Economic challenges and human hardships of the 2008–10 recession and subsequent slow recovery revived political interest in the Keynesian policy-making paradigm. Another constant is the underdeveloped state of the management orientation: program evaluation and improvement of administrative performance remain the most elusive in achieving at the federal level of public administration.

Budgetary processes serve multiple goals and functions and shifts in the priority accorded to control and strategic planning functions of budgeting are evidenced by the Harper and Trudeau Governments. Every government uses the budget system for establishing the direction and character of public purposes and the government's own participation in Canada's disparate economy and diverse civil society. In the Harper era, the range and nature of public policy goals narrowed, in contrast to the previous Chrétien and Martin Liberal Governments, whereas early indications are the Trudeau Government is widening the scope of objectives pursued and shifting taxation and social spending decisions in a more progressive redistributive direction.

Important Terms and Concepts

constitutional conventions	management orientation	revenue budgeting
expenditure budgeting	mezzo budgeting	strategic planning
financial control	micro budgeting	tactical incrementalism
macro budgeting	minority government	

Study Questions

1. Why is public budgeting so central to governments and governance?
2. In Canada's parliamentary system of government, what constitutional conventions relate to budgeting?
3. Besides being a governmental and legislative set of processes, what makes public budgeting a quintessential political activity?
4. How might the status of a minority government influence budget making?
5. Why is the management function arguably the most elusive in achieving?
6. How is the federal budget system changing under the Justin Trudeau Government?

References

Battle, Ken, Sherri Torjman, and Michael Mendelson. 2016. *The Social-Policy-Is-Back Budget.* Ottawa: Caledon Institute of Social Policy.

Doern, G. Bruce, Allan M. Maslove, and Michael J. Prince. 1988. *Public Budgeting in Canada: Politics, Economics and Management.* Ottawa: Carleton University Press.

Doern, G. Bruce, Allan M. Maslove, and Michael J. Prince. 2013. *Canadian Public Budgeting in the Age of Crises: Shifting Budget Domains and Temporal Budgeting.* Montreal and Kingston: McGill-Queen's University Press.

Doern, G. Bruce, and Christopher Stoney, editors. 2016. *How Ottawa Spends 2016–2017: The Trudeau Liberals in Power.* Ottawa: School of Public Policy and Administration, Carleton University.

Finance Canada. 2017. *Building a Strong Middle Class. Budget 2017.* Ottawa: March.

Franks, C.E.S., and David E. Smith. 2012. "The Canadian House of Commons under Stress: Reform and Adaptation." *From New Public Management to New Political Governance: Essays in Honour of Peter C. Aucoin,* edited by Herman Bakvis and Mark D. Jarvis, Eds. Montreal and Kingston: McGill-Queen's University Press, pp. 70–101.

Gilmore, Alan. 2010. "The Canadian Accounting Officer: Has It Strengthened Parliament's Ability to Hold the Government to Account?" *The Handbook of Canadian Public Administration,* 2nd edn, edited by Christopher Dunn, Ed. Toronto: Oxford University Press, pp. 75–84.

Howard, Cosmo and Susan Phillips. 2012. "Moving Away from Hierarchy: Do Horizontality, Partnership, and Distributed Governance Really Signify the End of Accountability?" *From New Public Management to New Political Governance: Essays in Honour of Peter C. Aucoin,* edited by Herman Bakvis and Mark D. Jarvis, Eds. Montreal and Kingston: McGill-Queen's University Press. pp. 314–41.

Inwood, Gregory J. 2009. *Understanding Canadian Public Administration: An Introduction to Theory and Practice.* 3rd edn, Toronto: Pearson/Prentice Hall.

Johnson, David. 2011. *Thinking Government: Public Administration and Politics in Canada.* 3rd edn, Toronto: University of Toronto Press.

Malcolmson, Patrick, and Richard Myers. 2009. *The Canadian Regime: An Introduction to Parliamentary Government in Canada.* 4th edn, Toronto: University of Toronto Press.

Maslove, Allan M., Michael J. Prince, and G. Bruce Doern. 1986. *Federal and Provincial Budgeting: Goalsetting, Coordination, Restraint and Reform.* Toronto: University of Toronto Press.

Savoie, Donald J. 1990. *The Politics of Public Spending in Canada.* Toronto: University of Toronto Press.

Savoie, Donald J. 2015. *What is Government Good At? A Canadian Answer.* Montreal and Kingston: McGill-Queen's University Press.

Schick, Allen. 1966. "The Road to PPB: The Stages of Budget Reform," *Public Administration Review* 26, 4: 243–58.

Collective Bargaining and Dispute Resolution in the Public Sector

19

Michele Campolieti, Morley Gunderson, and Robert Hebdon

Chapter Overview

The evolution of collective bargaining and dispute resolution procedures in the Canadian public sectors is outlined, both across the different jurisdictions as well as over time. Particular attention is paid to the extent of, and pros and cons of, different dispute resolution procedures ranging from the right-to-strike to compulsory arbitration, and the role of government in establishing these procedures. The role of pay equity and employment equity is also discussed since they are important elements in the public sector.

Chapter Objectives

By the end of this chapter, students will be able to do the following:

- Describe the evolution of collective bargaining and dispute resolution in the Canadian public sector.
- Understand the different dispute resolution procedures that are in place across the various jurisdictions and elements of the public sector.
- Understand the difficult role that governments must play in balancing the public interests in designing collective bargaining and dispute resolution procedures in the public sector.

There are three main mechanisms for regulating the employment relationship: (1) the market mechanism (often termed "private ordering" in legal parlance); (2) collective bargaining or other forms of employee representation; and (3) laws and regulations. All three mechanisms are at work to various degrees in the different elements of the Canadian public sector. As discussed subsequently, their relative importance has also changed substantially over time so that the Canadian public sector thereby serves as an interesting laboratory for analyzing the pros and cons of the different mechanisms.

Issues pertaining to collective bargaining and **dispute resolution** in the public sector have taken on increased importance for a variety of reasons, many of which are analyzed in more detail subsequently. The vast majority of the Canadian public sector is covered by collective agreements and the two largest unions in Canada are now in the public sector;[1] hence, it is crucial to understand how collective bargaining operates in that sector. In contrast to collective bargaining in the *private* sector, where Canada has largely followed the US model, Canada's public sector has broken new ground and has a longer and more extensive history of bargaining (Goldenberg, 1988). This longer history and extensive provincial variation (with labour matters falling under provincial jurisdiction) provide a laboratory of natural experiments for analyzing outcomes from collective bargaining and dispute resolution.

With increased emphasis being placed on re-inventing government to be more responsive to the needs of the public and to be complementary to private-sector competitiveness, increased attention is being paid to whether the traditional models of collective bargaining are a hindrance or a help in meeting those objectives. This is especially the case given the increased emphasis on downsizing, **privatization**, and deregulation in various elements of the public sector, as well as the increased use of user charges and private-sector partnerships and delivery systems.[2]

Demands on the public sector will also be changing in the future as a result of the aging population, with longer life expectancy supported by a smaller (and increasingly mobile) taxpaying base of both individuals and firms. This will likely lead to increased emphasis on deinstitutionalization, community-based care, and volunteer activity, all of which will likely place new strains on the collective bargaining system.

Volunteer activity, for example, appears to be taking on increased importance for persons at both ends of the age spectrum—youths and persons who are retiring earlier. The hope is that such activity will help to fill a vacuum both in their own time availability and in the need for public services created by a retrenching role of the state. Yet potential conflicts could develop if, for example, volunteers displace public employees or are the subject of a grievance or are involved in legislative violations.

There is often a perception that the public sector should not be immune to the competitive pressures that have inundated the private sector under globalization, free trade, and increased economic integration. At times, this appears to take on a mean-spirited tone—"if it happened to us, it should happen to them." At other times it is a more reasoned response—that the public sector should be restructured to ensure that it provides the crucial public infrastructure essential for competitiveness of the private sector.

In that vein, governments are under strong pressure to compete with other governments for business investment and the jobs associated with that investment (Gunderson, 1998; Gomez & Gunderson, 2005). With globalization and freer trade, capital is increasingly mobile and able to locate in countries and particular jurisdictions within countries that provide an investment climate conducive to their competitive needs. Governments getting their own house in order with respect to their own public sector can be an important ingredient of that process, especially since governments wear two hats in this area: they set the rules and regulations under which the parties operate; and they are themselves a major employer. This spotlight on the public sector is important not only because of its size (especially in the collective bargaining arena) but also because public-sector activities can have important **spillover effects** on the private sector. The public sector is under strong political pressure to be a **model employer**. At times this can mean progressive practices; at other times it can mean a model of restraint.

Issues of dispute resolution take on heightened importance in the public sector, where there is an emphasis on **alternative dispute resolution** procedures (ADR) to reduce conflict.

In essence, in the 1990s dispute resolution in the public sector took centre stage. This is highlighted by the opening sentence in Swimmer's *Public-Sector Labour Relations in an Era of Restraint and Restructuring*: "The 1990s will probably go down as the most stressful decade for public-sector industrial relations since the inception, 25 years earlier, of collective bargaining for public-sector workers" (Swimmer, 2001: 1). In that setting, it is crucial to understand the process of collective bargaining and dispute resolution in the public sector.

In this restructuring environment another key question is the role of the private sector in the provision of public services and the consequences of privatization for workers, unions, and collective bargaining (Jalette & Hebdon, 2012).

The purpose of this chapter is to provide such an understanding. The evolution of collective bargaining and dispute resolution is first discussed, followed by a description of the current legal framework governing collective bargaining and the alternative dispute resolution procedures. Special attention is paid to arbitration and the increasing role of legislation in circumscribing—indeed, supplanting—collective bargaining. The means for settling disputes in public-sector strikes are then analyzed, followed by a discussion of the growing importance of legislative interventions through pay and **employment equity**. The chapter concludes with a summary and discussion of the key policy issues.

Evolution of Collective Bargaining

The history of bargaining in the Canadian public sector has been described as an evolution from collective *begging* to collective *bargaining*. Prior to the mid-1960s, the terms and conditions of employment in the public sector were generally dictated by the state both as employer and as the entity that establishes laws and regulations. This is epitomized in the statement of one public official that "The Queen does not negotiate with her subjects" (cited in Goldenberg, 1973). Nevertheless, during that earlier period, the foundations were being laid for subsequent collective bargaining. This was done through three main elements.[3]

First, municipal workers in Canada (except for police and firefighters) were generally covered under the private-sector labour relations laws and regulations in each jurisdiction. Hence, they had the same bargaining rights, including the right to strike, as did

workers in the private sector. Since they often provided **essential services** for which there was not a viable private-sector alternative (public transportation, road maintenance, garbage collection, sewage and water), collective bargaining and even strikes in such areas were not unknown. The precedents had already been set for extending such rights to other elements of the public sector.

Second, a precedent for collective bargaining and the right to strike even for the *civil service* had been established in 1944 when a left-wing government in Saskatchewan granted such rights to its own civil service at the same time as its original private-sector labour relations legislation was enacted.

Third, even though formal collective bargaining rights were seldom granted in the public sector, there was the precedent of informal bargaining through consultation between governments and employee associations that represented much of the public-sector workforces. Such associations were generally dominated by white-collar and professional workers who rejected the notion of being members of a conventional union, especially one that would exercise the right to strike. Nevertheless, the employee associations and consultation process did provide the foundations for subsequent bargaining by providing leadership, institutional structure, and bargaining experience that could serve as a springboard for subsequent collective bargaining.

While the foundations and precedents for collective bargaining were present, they required a catalyst to be transformed into genuine collective bargaining. That catalyst was provided by the socio-political-economic environment of the 1960s, characterized by such factors as the civil rights movement, anti-Vietnam War protests, campus militancy, and the Quiet Revolution in Quebec (Ponak & Thompson, 1995: 422). All of these forces questioned the unfettered sanctity of the state and led to a mistrust of government. In such circumstances it was easy to extend that mistrust to the unilateral determination of the wages and working conditions for its employees. If "people power" was expanding to question governance in general, it was a logical extension to expand it to question governance of the workplace. As well, the public sector was expanding rapidly, hiring younger workers with more radical ideas and experiences that were conducive to questioning the idea of being a civil *servant*. The expansion also shifted bargaining power into the hands of public-sector employees who were needed to fill the jobs of the expanding state sector at that time.

The fortuitous combination of the basic foundations for public-sector collective bargaining (established by the precedents of bargaining on the part of municipal workers in all jurisdictions and civil servants in Saskatchewan, as well as the experience of consultation with employee associations) with the catalyst of the socio-political-economic environment, precipitated the legislative initiatives of the 1960s that established broad-based collective bargaining in the public sector throughout Canada. The watershed legislation in this area was the federal Public Service Staff Relations Act (PSSRA) of 1967, which fulfilled a promise made in 1963 by Prime Minister Lester Pearson to grant federal employees broad collective bargaining rights, including the right to strike. This had been preceded by similar legislation in Quebec in 1965. All provincial jurisdictions almost immediately followed suit, although not always granting all employees the right to strike.

By the mid-1970s, the basic structure was in place. Collective bargaining rights had come to the public sector. In fact, collective bargaining dominated the public sector and it was to be the mechanism for determining the terms of employment in the public sector more so than in the private sector.

Interestingly, the divergence of unionization rates in Canada and the United States also began during the mid-1960s (Riddell, 1993; Riddell & Riddell, 2004). Until then, both countries had similar rates of unionization, at around 35 per cent of the non-agricultural paid workforce. Thereafter, unionization rates dropped steadily in the US, so that today less than 15 per cent of the American workforce is unionized. In contrast, in Canada, the unionized workforce has been maintained at about 30 per cent, over twice the US rate. It would be interesting to know if the higher unionization rates in Canada could have been sustained without the legislative boost given to public-sector unionization in the late 1960s and early 1970s.

The Structure of Collective Bargaining

The current structure of collective bargaining in Canada's public sector can best be described by a number of its components: collective agreement coverage, collective bargaining legislation, dispute resolution procedures, arbitration requirements, the restitution of the dominant role of the state, and increased attention to market forces. These components also illustrate the interplay among the three main mechanisms for regulating the employment relationship: the market, collective bargaining, and government legislation and regulation.

Collective Agreement Coverage

As indicated in Table 19.1, about three-quarters of workers in the public sector are covered by a collective agreement, much higher than the 17.5 per cent coverage rate in the private sector. The coverage rate in each of the four main components of the public sector is higher than in any other industry, with the highest rate in the private sector being 41.1 per cent in transportation and warehousing (Uppal, 2011: Table 19.1). When one considers that a large component of the public sector (i.e., managerial personnel) is not eligible for unionization or covered by a collective agreement, the 75 per cent coverage figure suggests that the vast majority of workers in the public sector who could be covered by a collective agreement are covered.

As a result of this high coverage rate, the public sector now also makes up the majority of persons covered by collective agreements in Canada.[4] Clearly, unionization and collective bargaining are important phenomena in the public sector.

Collective Bargaining Legislation[5]

Labour relations in Canada are under provincial jurisdiction, with only about 10 per cent of the workforce under federal jurisdiction (e.g., federal civil service, transportation, communication, banking, and the postal service, with slightly more than half of that total representing private-sector workers). Yukon, the Northwest Territories, and Nunavut also tend to follow the federal jurisdiction. The 11 different jurisdictions (federal plus the 10 provinces) have often followed quite different legislative regimes to govern the conduct of collective bargaining in the various elements of the public sector (e.g., public administration at the federal, provincial, and local levels, education, health, police, and firefighters). The main legislative options include:

Table 19.1   Unionization Rates and Collective Agreement Coverage, Private and Public Sectors, 2011

Sector	Employees (000s)	Union Density (%)	Collective Agreement Coverage (%)
Private	10,907	16.0	17.5
Public*	3,600	71.1	74.7
Education	1,209	67.6	71.6
Utilities	144	63.8	66.2
Public administration	968	66.5	72.0
Health and social assistance	1,831	52.7	54.7

*The public sector refers to employees in government departments or agencies, Crown corporations, or publicly funded schools, hospitals, or other institutions. The subcomponents of the public sector (education, utilities, public administration, health and social services) are ones where the employer usually but not always is a government. Similarly, government employees occasionally are found outside of these industries. For this reason, the sum of employees in those sectors (4,152,000) does not equal the sum in the public sector (3,600,000). Furthermore, the overall collective agreement coverage rate in the public sector, at 74.7 per cent, is higher than the rate in each of those components, since the coverage rate will be much lower for private-sector employers in those components.
Source: Uppal (2011) Table 1, based on data from the Labour Force Survey.

- private-sector labour relations legislation;
- private-sector legislation, but with specific modifications for particular elements of the public sector, usually pertaining to the right to strike and the scope of bargaining;
- separate collective bargaining statutes for different elements of the public sector;
- hybrids of the above.

Although there is almost always an exception, the different elements of the public sector tend to be covered as follows:

- Civil servants tend to be covered by separate civil servant legislation, although in Saskatchewan they are covered by the general private-sector labour relations legislation.
- Teachers tend to be covered by separate statutes, but in some jurisdictions they are covered under the general private-sector labour relations legislation.
- Hospital workers tend to be covered by the general private-sector labour relations legislation, but sometimes by separate legislation and even by the civil service statutes.
- Police and firefighters are sometimes covered by separate statutes, sometimes by separate sections within the private-sector labour relations

legislation, and sometimes by a hybrid of the two, with the private-sector statute covering some aspects of bargaining and special legislation covering other aspects of bargaining.
- Employees of government-owned corporations are usually covered by the relevant private-sector labour relations legislation, but sometimes by separate statutes.

Clearly, there is no uniform pattern across all jurisdictions and with respect to the different elements of the public sector. As such, public-sector collective bargaining legislation in Canada has been described as exhibiting a crazy-quilt pattern. The pattern likely reflects the peculiarities of political pressures, interest groups, special events, and inertia more than it reflects the different needs and circumstances in each jurisdiction. As well, the different legislative regimes can likely deliver similar outcomes even though the process is packaged differently.

Dispute Resolution Procedures, Arbitration, and the Right to Strike

The dispute resolution procedures that prevail across the different elements of the public sector and across the different jurisdictions also exhibit a crazy-quilt pattern. The main dispute resolution procedures are:[6]

- the right to strike, with the same procedures that prevail in the private sector;
- the limited right to strike, where certain designated employees who are regarded as essential are not allowed to strike;
- **binding arbitration** when strikes are not allowed;
- arbitration at the request of either party, and sometimes at the request of the Minister of Labour, for bargaining units with the right to strike;
- choice of procedure where the union is allowed to choose in advance of negotiation either the strike or arbitration route.

As indicated in Table 19.2, the most common dispute resolution procedures in the public sector are the unfettered right to strike, as that right also exists in the private sector, and binding arbitration with no strike (both are 35.9 per cent of cases). As indicated in Campolieti et al. (2016), the right to strike exists for municipal workers in all jurisdictions and it is common for teachers, but is not as available for workers in the civil service or hospitals. Arbitration, with no right to strike, is very prevalent among city police and firefighters, but also is used as a dispute resolution procedure for civil servants, teachers, and hospitals in some jurisdictions. The limited right to strike for non-designated workers (also referred to as the essential-service designation) is also quite prevalent in the public sector and is used primarily in the civil service, hospital sectors, and protective services The **choice of procedure** is not common.

Based on a detailed tabulation of the alternative dispute resolution procedures for the different elements of the public-sector workforce across the different jurisdictions, Gunderson and Hyatt (1996) provide the following generalizations.

1. There is no uniform pattern with any one jurisdiction requiring a single procedure for all elements of the public sector or with any one element of the public sector having the same procedure across all jurisdictions.
2. There is a slight tendency to not allow the right to strike in the most essential services, such as police services and firefighting where compulsory arbitration tends to be used to resolve bargaining impasses, and to allow it in what are considered less essential services, such as municipal services, government enterprises, and teaching, albeit the patterns are certainly not uniform.
3. There is also a slight tendency for some jurisdictions to be more restrictive than others. Alberta, for example, appears to be the most restrictive, allowing the right to strike only for municipal workers and teachers while requiring arbitration in all other sectors. British Columbia, in contrast, allows the right to strike across all elements of the public sector, although general legislation may restrict designated employees from striking.[7]
4. While there are these slight tendencies for some jurisdictions to be more restrictive and for the right to strike to be more limited the more essential the service, there certainly is no strong, uniform pattern.

Table 19.2   Dispute Resolution Procedures in Six Elements of the Public Sector across 11 Canadian Jurisdictions

Dispute Resolution Procedure	Number	%
Right to strike	23	35.9
Limited right to strike, non-designated employees	16	23.4
Binding arbitration with no strike	23	35.9
Choice of procedure	3	4.7
Total (11 jurisdictions, 6 elements* of public sector)	64	100.0

*The six elements of the public sector are civil service, municipal, city police, firefighters, teachers, and hospitals.
Source: Campolieti et al. (2016) Appendix A. Municipal employees and city police are not covered by the federal jurisdiction. Dispute resolution procedures can also vary over time (see Campolieti et al. (2016) page 199, Table 1), so the totals here are as of the end of the period considered by Campolieti et al. (2016).

5. In fact, discrepancies appear to exist even within a jurisdiction in that the right to strike is allowed in what generally would be regarded as an essential service (e.g., police), while it is prohibited and arbitration required in what would be regarded as a less essential service (e.g., civil service).

As with the different legislative regimes that prevail, the pattern of dispute resolution procedures likely reflects the peculiarities of political pressures, interest groups, special events, and inertia more than it reflects the different needs and circumstances in each jurisdiction. It is hard to believe, for example, that police would be more essential than civil servants in one jurisdiction but less essential in another jurisdiction.

The choice of procedure regime, which is an unusual and innovative procedure, is used in the federal jurisdiction and by teachers in Saskatchewan.[8] Under this procedure the union gets to choose, in advance of the negotiation, whether it wants the ultimate dispute resolution procedure to be arbitration or the strike. This is different from where arbitration can be chosen by either party (or sometimes is required by the Minister of Labour), which effectively also allows the employer to choose arbitration and hence to be insulated from the strike. Under the federal regime, the weaker bargaining units initially chose the arbitration route hoping that they would be granted the same wage increases established by the pattern in the more powerful units that chose the strike route. Over time, however, the unions increasingly opted for the strike route, feeling that they could gain more through the ultimate strike threat.

Factors Circumscribing the Strike Weapon in the Public Sector

The data in Table 19.2 could certainly indicate that the right to strike is a very common dispute resolution procedure in the various elements of the public sector in Canada. This is so not only because the right to strike can also be evoked under the limited right to strike procedure, as well as the choice of procedure. In fact, only the arbitration procedure, which exists in 35.9 per cent of the cases, explicitly prohibits strikes.

While the right to strike is an important dispute resolution procedure in many elements of the public sector, its ultimate threat is extremely circumscribed in a variety of ways. As indicated previously, even when the strike is allowed, general legislation often specifies that designated employees may be required to continue to work. When the limited right to strike exists and permanently designated employees are prohibited from striking, the power of the union is emasculated by the fact that the organization can generally carry out its essential tasks with the designated employees.[9] The costs that the union can impose are largely ones of inconvenience. These are not the same as the inconvenience costs imposed in the private sector when customers are forced to shift to a producer not on strike. Here, the producer whose workers are on strike runs the risk of permanently losing customers. In the public sector, there are usually no other producers to shift to, with the non-essential services having to be postponed rather than not provided.

Even under the choice of procedure, where the union can opt for arbitration or the strike, designated employees are not allowed to strike if the strike option is chosen. This is an especially important constraint because the proportion of employees who have been designated as essential has increased substantially over time, amounting to over half of the employees in the bargaining units that have opted for the strike route.[10] If over half of the employees are required to continue working, and these are the workers most essential to the operation, the threat of the strike is clearly circumscribed, especially in the public sector where a permanent loss of customers is not generally involved. This would be analogous in the private sector to bringing in replacement workers (who could immediately do the most important tasks) to fill over half of the jobs, and to restricting customers from going to alternative providers.

Clearly, these subtle institutional features change the picture from one where strikes appear to be the dominant dispute resolution procedure in the public sector to one where the threat from the strike is severely circumscribed. The threat from strikes is further circumscribed by the more general proposition that when strikes occur in the public sector, those on strike lose income but employers generally do not lose revenues even though the services are not provided. This is very different from the private sector where employers lose revenues, perhaps even on a permanent basis if customers shift to other providers. In such circumstances, public-sector employers may not have a financial incentive to settle. In fact, they may have a perverse incentive not to settle so as to reduce their deficits if revenues keep coming in but costs are not incurred during the strike. The threat from strikes may be further reduced by the fact that the public perception, generally, is that the union causes the strike, for the public does not always recognize that it takes two parties to create a dispute. Employers can be just as much the cause of such strikes by refusing to bargain in a meaningful way.

Arbitration

When the right to strike is prohibited or not opted for when the parties can choose to strike, or when the parties are ordered back to work via legislative enactments, binding arbitration is the method of dispute resolution in the public sector. In determining awards the **arbitration criteria** that tend to be used are as follows: (Gunderson, 1983; O'Grady, 1992):

- comparability, especially with private-sector settlements if similar ones exist, but often with other public-sector settlements if private-sector ones do not exist;
- the employers' **ability to pay**;
- cost of living, especially to keep up with inflation;
- productivity increases in the economy as a whole;
- minimum living standards, especially for low-wage groups.

By far the dominant criterion, however, is comparability. This can create a form of de facto **pattern bargaining** since key settlements get emulated across similar groups. Just as in the private sector, however, such pattern bargaining is becoming less prominent, with more attention being paid to local conditions and the employers' ability to pay. In fact, governments have increasingly enacted legislation requiring arbitrators to pay attention to the ability to pay without having to engender tax increases. The subsectors with explicit ability-to-pay criteria in their respective statutes in Canada include police in Newfoundland; police, firefighters, and municipal workers in Quebec; hospital workers, police, and firefighters in Ontario, although the Ontario legislation extends to all public sector disputes that are settled with arbitration not just those settled with compulsory arbitration; teachers in Manitoba; and

all public sector workers in the federal jurisdiction (Campolieti et al. 2016).

Arbitration in Canada tends to be of the conventional type rather than one of the forms of **final-offer arbitration** found in the United States (O'Grady, 1992; Ponak & Falkenberg, 1989). Reasons for this are not obvious, since the pros and cons of final-offer arbitration would appear to apply equally in both countries. Requiring the arbitrator to choose *either* the employer's *or* the union's offer, final-offer encourages the parties themselves to compromise and to settle in advance of the arbitration to avoid the risk of an all-or-nothing settlement. They are under strong pressure to sort out their own internal trade-offs so as to craft a reasonable offer that is likely to be accepted. On the other hand, final-offer imposes a degree of risk, it may lead to unworkable settlements, and it can foster an adversarial win-lose environment.

The win-lose aspect of final-offer arbitration may account for the significantly higher number of job actions of police unions in New Jersey under final-offer versus conventional arbitration (Hebdon, 2005). For unspecified reasons, a number of US states have moved away from final-offer regimes. For example, New Jersey eliminated final-offer arbitration in 1996 for police and firefighters, and Wisconsin for teachers in 2010 (Hebdon, Masters, & Slater 2013).

Hybrid forms of arbitration that combine arbitration and mediation stages have been used in the United States for some time, (Lester, 1984; Stern, 1984). They have also begun to appear in Canada. In particular, mediation-arbitration (med-arb) has been adopted in Ontario and it includes a mediation stage, where a third-party attempts to resolve a bargaining impasse, and if an impasse still remains after mediation it is followed by an arbitration phase, where an arbitrator issues a binding award that resolves the bargaining impasse. Generally, in both the United States and Canada, the mediator and arbitrator in med-arb tend to be same person, although both Fuller (1962) and Devinatz and Budd (1997) argue that med-arb would be most effective when the mediator and arbitrator were not the same individual. The rationale for this hybrid dispute resolution procedure is that it could increase voluntary settlements in the mediation stage since both parties want to appear to be reasonable to the mediator and not take extreme positions since the mediator will then act as an arbitrator if an impasse still remains after mediation. Thus med-arb has been perceived as a way of reducing the reliance on arbitration awards to settle bargaining impasses.

The Pendulum Swings: Legislative Enactments

The previous discussion focused on how the strike threat has been increasingly circumscribed by features such as restricting the strike to non-designated employees and giving employers the option of arbitration. Furthermore, arbitrators are increasingly called on to pay attention to the employer's ability to pay. These, however, are marginal tinkerings with the fundamental mechanism of collective bargaining as it is used to determine employment conditions in the public sector. They are marginal relative to the mechanism of legislation and regulation that has effectively replaced collective bargaining in many elements of the public sector in recent years. While the earlier transformation may be characterized as being from collective begging to collective bargaining, the pendulum may have swung back. Although it may no longer be appropriate to characterize the recent situation as one where "the Queen does not negotiate," it is not a far cry to depict it as one where "the government does not negotiate." This is illustrated in a wide range of legislative enactments with respect to bargaining in the public sector.

Legislative **wage controls** were a common feature of the 1970s and early 1980s.[11] The 1975 wage-control program that applied across the country was applicable to both the private and public sectors, but it had features that made its application more binding in the public sector. As well, public-sector employers are less likely to try to evade legislative initiatives given the scrutiny they are under. The wage-control programs of the early 1980s were restricted to the public sector. They were set off by the federal 6-and-5 program limiting public-sector wage increases to 6 per cent in 1982 and 5 per cent in 1983. Five provinces followed suit with their own programs and the other five provinces limited their spending explicitly to constrain public-sector wages, with Quebec going so far as to institute a 20 per cent rollback.

The public-sector wage control programs of the early 1980s were followed by a series of other legislative and regulatory initiatives in the early 1990s that

effectively controlled public-sector wages. In 1991, the federal government froze wages and suspended collective bargaining for a period that lasted until 1997. The Atlantic provinces as well as Quebec, Ontario, and Manitoba followed with public-sector wage freezes and sometimes even mid-contract wage rollbacks. In some circumstances these were accompanied by so-called **social contracts** where employees were given mandatory unpaid leave days as part of the freezes.

In Saskatchewan, Alberta, and British Columbia public-sector wage restraint was negotiated with the unions, albeit under the obvious shadow of what was happening in the other provinces. The BC negotiations were closest to true negotiations (likely reflecting the NDP government) since they involved extensive consultation and bargaining over a wide range of issues including job security, restructuring, and human resource and workplace practices (Fryer, 1995).

Back-to-work legislation has also increasingly been evoked to settle disputes in the public sector in both Canada (Gunderson & Ponak, 2001; Thompson & Slinn, 2013) and the United States (Lund & Maranto, 1996). Such legislation, which is invariably preceded by a strike, establishes arbitration to set the terms and conditions of the new contract. The importance of legislative enactments (wage controls, the suspension of collective bargaining, social contracts, back-to-work legislation) as a dispute resolution procedure in the public sector is amply illustrated in Table 19.3. During the 1990s, 22.4 per cent of contracts were settled through such legislative enactments. This dwarfed the direct use of arbitration (4.2 per cent) or strikes (3 per cent). In the period 1999–2007, however, legislated settlements dropped to a three-decade low of 2.3 per cent. Legislation intervention increased to 10.1 per cent in the period after 2008. This latter period has been characterized by interventionist wage restraint policies in such jurisdictions as the federal government and Ontario, and a focus by the federal Conservative government on back-to-work laws for disputes at Canada Post and Air Canada. These two laws prompted legal challenges by unions who argued that the federal government was effectively removing their constitutionally protected right to strike. To date the Canada Post case has been heard by the Superior Court in Ontario and the union argument was upheld.

Table 19.3   Proportion of Contracts Settled by Different Means, Public and Private Sectors, 1980–2015

Means of Settlement	Public Sector				Private Sector			
	1980–9 (%)	1990–8 (%)	1999–07 (%)	2008–15 (%)	1980–9 (%)	1990–8 (%)	1999–07 (%)	2008–15 (%)
Bargaining*	74.5	70.4	84.7	74.9	83.8	88.0	85.9	89.4
Arbitration	8.6	4.2	6.3	9.3	0.9	1.6	4.2	6.1
Strike	4.2	3.0	5.2	3.2	15.1	9.5	8.8	4.1
Legislation	12.7	22.4	2.3	10.1	0.2	0.9	0	.4
Conciliation*	N/A	N/A	N/A	N/A	N/A	N/A	N/A	N/A
Other	N/A	N/A	1.5	2.5	N/A	N/A	1	0
Total, all means	100.0	100.0	100.0	100.0	100.0	100.0	100.0	100.0

*Includes settling at the stage of direct bargaining with no third-party assistance, as well as settling at the stages where there was some third-party assistance—conciliation, post-conciliation, mediation, or post-mediation.
Source: Special data request to Employment and Social Development Canada, Labour Program, September, 2016. Data are from Labour Canada's Major Wage Settlements database, for major collective agreements, 500 or more employees.

The state was clearly instrumental in establishing collective bargaining in the public sector in Canada in the mid-1960s, especially through the commitments made in 1963 culminating in the Public Service Staff Relations Act of 1967, as well as legislation in Quebec in 1965. In the 1980s and 1990s, however, the state was equally instrumental in putting the genie back in the bottle through various legislative enactments including wage controls, the suspension of collective bargaining, social contracts, and back-to-work legislation. What the state gives, the state can clearly take away.

As pointed out by Swimmer (2001), some have interpreted this as the end of collective bargaining in the public sector of Canada. For example, Panitch and Swartz (1984, 1993) argue that the government legislative interventions represent the nail in the coffin from a series of government assaults on trade-union freedoms. Others, such as Thompson (1998) and Thompson and Slinn (2013), argue that the basic structure is still in place and can be modified to deal with the new issues.

Nonetheless, *conventional* collective bargaining in the public sector has changed. Warrian (1995, 1996) claims that the end of conventional bargaining in the public sector is a result of the inability of the **Wagner model** of collective bargaining to adapt to the new needs of public-sector bargaining. The Wagner model was designed for the private sector and largely transplanted into the public sector. The

characteristics of the conventional private-sector Wagner model that make it ill-suited for the changing needs of the public sector include:

- a multiplicity of fragmented bargaining units that inhibits unions from bargaining with one voice;
- a legalistic, adversarial orientation that emphasizes the distributive separate nature of employee and employer interests and that therefore inhibits them from joint co-operative win-win initiatives;
- a multiplicity of narrow job classifications and seniority-based work rules that inhibit teamwork and employee involvement in service delivery.

These characteristics may not have had serious negative consequences when the public sector was expanding and not under pressure to restructure. However, they are ill-suited to deal with the new issues of restructuring, downsizing, job security, and flexibility in both wage structures and wage levels.

These are the crucial new issues given the transformation of the public sector and hence of the internal labour markets and workplace practices in that sector. Elements of this transformation include:

- slower employment growth and downsizing;
- a reorientation from government being a service provider to a service coordinator, with a core of

public employees providing policy advice and coordinating service delivery often through the private sector;

- increased emphasis on service delivery and customer orientation in activities where governments are involved;
- increased non-standard employment in such forms as contractually limited appointments and subcontracting;
- privatization of a wide range of conventional public-sector activities and deregulation in others;
- increased performance-based budgeting being applied to public-sector organizations, with that pressure filtering down to performance evaluations of employees;
- pressures to merge units and to restructure for cost-effective delivery.

These and other pressures in turn have important implications for a wide range of industrial relations and human resource practices in the public sector. These include successor rights, transfer rights, merging of seniority lists in newly integrated units, retraining, job classifications, relocation, and work-sharing as an alternative to layoffs. At issue is whether the public-sector bargaining model, with its fragmented bargaining units, narrow job classifications, and adversarial emphasis, can deal with these new issues. What is not at issue, however, is that conventional collective bargaining has been circumscribed by legislative requirements pertaining to such factors as designated employees and impositions on arbitrators to pay attention to ability to pay, as well as more direct interventions in such forms as wage controls, wage freezes, suspension of bargaining, social contracts, and back-to-work legislation.

The Pendulum Swings Back—Perhaps?

The legislative and government actions in the 1980s and 1990s that circumscribed collective bargaining especially in the public sector were bolstered by a series of Supreme Court decisions often referred to as the 1987 Labour Trilogy. Those three decisions (involving *Alberta Reference*, the *Public Service Alliance*, and *Saskatchewan Federation of Labour*) basically concluded that legislative restrictions on collective bargaining and strikes did not violate the freedom

of association guarantees that were protected under the Charter.

These principles began to break down in the 2000s as most evident in the Supreme Court decision in *BC Health Services* in 2007. That decision basically limited the ability of the BC government to invalidate existing collective agreements with health-care workers and to restructure by means of legislation that bypassed the collective bargaining process. It affirmed that the constitutional guarantee of freedom of association in the Charter includes the right to collective bargaining. In that determination, it placed considerable attention to international human rights and labour law whereby freedom of association at work protects the right to organize, the right to collective bargaining, and the right to strike. In effect, its 2007 decision overturned much of the Supreme Court's former Labour Trilogy decisions of 1987.

The BC Health Services decision in 2007 was followed by even further labour protections in what has been labelled the New Labour Trilogy of 2015 (Lynk, 2016). That trilogy involved three major Supreme Court decisions. The *Mounted Police Association of Ontario v. Canada* (2015) guaranteed the right to organize on the part of Mounted Police, opening the door to whether it is constitutional to automatically exclude any occupational group from access to unionization and collective bargaining. The *Saskatchewan Federation of Labour v. Saskatchewan* (2015) decision determined that it was unconstitutional for that provincial government to unilaterally restrict or prohibit strikes in the public sector. The *Meredith v. Canada* (2015) decision further reaffirmed the right to collective bargaining even though it found that the federal government's wage restraint legislation was deemed constitutional in light of the need for austerity measures given the economic crises.

Importantly, these New Trilogy decisions of 2015 interpreted that the freedom of association guarantees under the Charter provided for the right to organize collectively, to bargain collectively, and to strike. Those decisions also relied extensively on international labour law on freedom of association. They also relied heavily on the dissent of Justice Dickinson in the earlier *Alberta Reference* decision of 1987.

These decisions by the Supreme Court were followed by other decisions that favoured the rights of public-sector workers. In 2016, the Ontario Superior Court of Justice negated the 2011 back-to-work legislation imposed by the federal government on postal workers at Canada Post. In 2016, the Ontario Superior Court in *OPSEU v. Ontario* also negated the provincial government's refusal to engage in bargaining by adhering to its austerity program violated the right of workers to bargain collectively and to strike if necessary.

Clearly the pendulum has swung from the earlier 1987 Labour Trilogy with its sanctioning of government legislative restrictions involving wage controls, wage freezes, suspension of bargaining, social contracts, back-to-work legislation, and designating essential workers as not having the right to strike and certain occupation groups as not having the right to organize. The 2007 *BC Health* decision and the 2015 New Labour Trilogy and subsequent decisions have negated, or at least circumscribed, many of these otherwise unfettered actions on the part of governments. This has been fostered by interpretations of the Charter as well as by more attention to international law in areas of human rights and freedom of association.

Whether this pendulum swing is permanent or will foster another pendulum swing in the other direction is an open question. It is also an open question as to whether these court interpretations will breathe new life into the labour movement.

Strikes and Other Settlement Stages in Public and Private Sectors

Table 19.3 also provides additional information on the stages at which collective agreements are settled in the public and private sectors. We have combined direct bargaining with various forms of third-party assistance to create a bargaining category that represents freely negotiated settlements. For only one of the five periods in the table (1999–2007) did the rate of public-sector settlements match that of the private sector. During the rest of the period the public sector freely negotiated settlement rate ranged from 70 to 74.9 per cent while the comparable private sector rates ranged between 83 and 89 per cent. In the most recent period the large difference in public-private settlement rates was due to the higher use of arbitration and more legislative intervention in the public sector. The strike rate in the private sector dropped considerably over the period, from 15.1 per cent in the 1980s to 4.1 per cent in the most recent period 2008–15.

In contrast, in the public sector, strikes have held at relatively low levels with the 2008–15 period showing a rate of only 3.2 per cent. Table 19.4 gives the strike rate for the different elements of the public sector separately for the 1980s, 1990s, and two periods in the 2000s. Over the full period, the public-sector rate was highest in telecommunications and utilities, followed by Crown corporations, and education/health/welfare, all of which

Table 19.4   Strike Rates for Various Elements of the Public Sector, 1980–2015

Element of Public Sector	1980–9	1990–8	1999–2007	2008–15	1980–2015
Parliamentary employees	0.0	0.0	0.0	0.0	0.0
Federal administration	2.7	2.2	8.2	0.0	3.2
Provincial administration	6.2	5.1	4.3	6.7	5.5
Local administration	4.7	4.9	7.1	5.3	5.5
Education/health/welfare	7.1	7.9	8.2	10.8	8.3
Telecommunications and utilities	26.6	12.1	10.6	1.8	15.2
Crown corporations	8.3	6.0	26.1	8.8	10.0
Total public sector	7.2	6.9	8.1	8.7	7.6
Total private sector	25.7	12.5	12.8	7.3	16.7
Ratio public/private	0.28	0.55	0.64	1.20	0.45

Source: Calculations based on special data request from Employment and Social Development Canada, Labour Program, September, 2016. These rates are calculated using data from two sources: Major Wage Settlements of 500 or more employees and the work stoppage dataset. The sub-sector strike rate is estimated as the number of strikes divided by settlements in that sub-sector over the period (×100).

were above the average strike rate of 7.6 per cent of contracts in the public sector. As indicated in the public and private totals for the decades, the strike rate in the public sector rose steadily over the period from being 28 per cent (i.e., 7.2/25.7) of the rate of the private sector in the 1980s, to 55 per cent (i.e., 6.9/12.5) in the 1990s, to 64 per cent in 1999–2007 (i.e., 8.1/12.8) to most recent period where public sector rates were higher than those of the private sector at 1.20 (i.e., 8.7/7.3)

In general all strikes declined steadily from an annual average of 794 in the 1980s to 394 in the 1990s, and time lost from 541 workdays (per 1000 employees) in the 1980s to 233 in the 1990s (Akyeampong, 2006). This trend has continued.[12] For example, between 1995 and 2004 there were a total of 2863 strikes in Canada of which 796 were in the public sector. In contrast, between 2005 and 2014 there were a total of 1533 strikes in Canada with 523 in the public sector.[13]

The growing importance of strikes in the public sector is further illustrated by the distribution of strikes and days lost due to strikes in Table 19.5. Over the 2005–14 period the public-sector components of education, health, and social services and public administration together accounted for 33 per cent of strikes and 34.4 per cent of time lost, which exceeded manufacturing at 22 per cent of strikes and 25 per cent of time lost.

Another important dimension to consider for strikes is the reasons for why they occur. As indicated in Table 19.6 the most common reason for strikes are wages and benefits (21 per cent) of strikes in each of the public and private sectors, and wages and other issues that combine with wages and benefits to account for 30 per cent of strikes in the private sector and 26.1 per cent of strikes in the public sector. The main differences between the public sector and the private sector in Table 19.6 is the higher rate at which strike issues are not reported in the private sector (60.4 per cent) compared to the public sector (38.2 per cent) and that collective bargaining rights are much more important in the public sector (14.3 per cent) than the private sector (0.5 per cent).

Table 19.5   Strikes and Lockouts and Person-Days Not Worked by Major Industry, 2005–14

	Strikes and Lockouts		Work Days Not Worked	
	Number	%	'000s	%
All Industries	1533	100	15,746	100
Primary (Agricultural, Fishing, Mining, Oil)	42	2.7	395	2.5
Utilities	19	1.2	117	0.7
Construction	61	4.0	1,134	7.2
Manufacturing	337	22.0	3,931	25.0
Wholesale and Retail Trade	139	9.1	650	4.1
Transportation and Warehousing	120	7.8	1,216	7.7
Information and Cultural Industries	26	1.7	1,897	12.0
Management and Administrative Support	35	2.3	86	0.5
Finance and Insurance	17	1.1	52	0.3
Real Estate, Rental, and Leasing	21	1.4	31	0.2
Professional, Scientific, and Professional Services	22	0.8	48	0.3
Education, Health, and Social Services	389	25.4	3,528	22.4
Arts and Recreation	40	2.6	252	1.6
Accommodation and Food Services	112	7.3	417	2.6
Other Services (except Public Administration)	46	3.0	96	0.6
Public Administration	117	7.6	1,896	12.0

Source: Authors' computations based on Labour Canada's work stoppage database.

Table 19.6   Strike Issue, Public versus Private Sector, 2005–14

Reason	Public Sector		Private Sector	
	Number	%	Number	%
Job Security	2	0.4	5	0.5
Working Conditions	19	3.6	29	2.9
Wages and Benefits	110	21.0	213	21.1
Wages and Other Issues	47	9.0	50	5.0
Collective Bargaining Rights	75	14.3	5	0.5
Other Issues	70	13.4	98	9.7
Unreported	200	38.2	610	60.4
Total	523	100	1010	100

Notes: Authors calculation based on Labour Canada's Work Stoppage Database. "Wages and Other Issues" can include wages and working conditions, wages and job security. "Other Issues" reflects a combination of issues, e.g., workload and job security.

Pay and Employment Equity Legislation

Legislative interventions have also been important in the areas of pay and employment equity, since these are largely public-sector phenomena. Employment equity legislation requires that employers have the **designated groups** (women, visible minorities, Aboriginal persons, disabled persons) represented throughout the occupational structure of their organization in the same proportion as they are represented in the **external labour pool**. Such legislation exists only in the federal jurisdiction, the federal public service, and for firms that bid on federal contracts.[14]

Pay equity legislation requires that female-dominated jobs be paid the same as male-dominated jobs of the same value, where value is determined by a gender-neutral job evaluation scheme. It exists in all Canadian jurisdictions except Alberta, British Columbia, Newfoundland and Labrador, and Saskatchewan but is confined to the public sector in all jurisdictions except Ontario, Quebec, and the federal jurisdiction (and its territories), where it can also apply to the private sector (McDonald & Thornton, 2015). In those jurisdictions, however, it is still largely a public-sector phenomenon. In the federal jurisdiction (and its territories) and in Quebec until 1998, pay equity required a complaint to be initiated and almost all complaints were from the public sector. In Ontario, where employers were required to have a pay-equity plan whether or not a complaint

had been placed, the wage adjustments were considerably higher in the public sector than in the private sector (Gunderson, 1995).

Pay equity can be an especially important legislative factor influencing wages in the public sector because its applications have been mainly in the public sector and because the wage adjustments have been fairly substantial where they have occurred.[15] Clearly, legislative initiatives have again become an important ingredient of wage determination in the public sector, making them one more step removed from being determined by conventional collective bargaining. It is true that unions are often instrumental in the pay-equity adjustment process and pay equity has become an important instrument in the arsenal of weapons used by unions to garner wage gains. Nevertheless, such gains occur through the legislative route rather than through conventional collective bargaining.

Conclusion

Collective bargaining in the public sector in Canada has been described as evolving from collective begging to collective bargaining. The foundations for the transformation to collective bargaining were established by earlier precedents including the rights of municipal workers in all jurisdictions to bargain and strike and similar rights granted to civil servants in Saskatchewan, as well as by a structure and history of consultation through employee associations. These combined with the socio-economic environment of the 1960s—student protests, the Quiet Revolution in Quebec, and an expanding public service of young persons prepared to question the idea of being civil *servants*. Thus, legislation from the mid-1960s to the mid-1970s essentially established collective bargaining as the dominant mechanism for determining the terms and conditions of employment in the public sector.

The legislation was very diverse across the different jurisdictions and across the different elements of the public sector. The legislative options included the private-sector labour relations legislation; the private-sector legislation with specific modifications usually pertaining to the right to strike and the scope of bargaining; separate statutes for different elements of the public sector; and hybrids of the above. Diverse dispute resolution procedures also prevailed. These included the right to strike; the limited right to strike; binding arbitration; and the choice of procedure.

While legislation and regulations were instrumental in establishing collective bargaining in the public sector, they were also instrumental in severely curtailing that right throughout the 1980s, 1990s, and into the 2000s. This was done through various mechanisms, such as expanding the number of designated workers that were not allowed to strike, requiring arbitrators to pay attention to ability to pay, instituting wage controls and wage freezes, suspending collective bargaining, prohibiting certain groups from bargaining or striking, imposing social contracts, and instituting back-to-work legislation. These were effectively sanctioned by court decisions including a trilogy of Supreme Court decisions in 1987.

The pendulum began to swing the other way beginning with the *BC Health* decision in 2007 and especially with a new trilogy of Supreme Court decisions in 2015 that effectively interpreted the Charter provision on freedom of association as providing for the right to organize collectively, to bargain collectively, and to strike if necessary. Whether this new pendulum swing is temporary or permanent and whether it will breathe new life into the labour movement and public sector bargaining is an interesting and open question.

Over the last several decades, strike activity declined in the public sector but not by as much as it declined in the private sector, so that public-sector strikes now account for a bigger share of overall strike activity than they did in earlier decades.

If contracts settled by back-to-work legislation were added to strike activity on the grounds that the legislation was instituted after a strike, and if social contracts were included as strikes on the grounds that unpaid leave was required (analogous to unpaid strike days), then strikes would be the dominant form of dispute resolution in the public sector when the parties did not settle themselves.

Legislation in the form of employment equity and pay equity has also played a prominent role in the public sector, again highlighting the role of legislation in determining the terms and conditions of employment in that sector.

There is considerable debate over the motivations for the increasing role of governments in using legislation and regulation to circumscribe—indeed supplant—collective bargaining in the public sector. There is also considerable debate over the ability of the traditional system of collective bargaining, which was imported largely from the private sector, to deal with the new challenges facing the public sector. There is little debate, however, over the fact that the twenty-first century will still face challenges in striking a balance over how the public sector will be affected by the three main mechanisms for governing labour relations: the market, collective bargaining, and legislation and regulations.

Important Terms and Concepts

ability to pay	dispute resolution	privatization
alternative dispute resolution	employment equity	social contracts
arbitration criteria	essential services	spillover effects
back-to-work legislation	external labour pool	wage controls
binding arbitration	final-offer arbitration	Wagner model
choice of procedure	model employer	
designated groups	pattern bargaining	

Study Questions

1. Why have strikes not declined in the public sector as much as they have declined in the private sector?
2. What fostered the evolution of collective bargaining in the public sector in Canada from a system of "collective begging" prior to the 1960s to one of viable collective bargaining in the 1970s? How was that altered in the 1980s and 1990s? Is the pendulum swinging back in more recent years so as to foster collective bargaining in the public sector, and if so how?
3. The dispute resolution procedures that prevail across the different elements of the public sector and across the different jurisdictions are described as exhibiting a crazy-quilt pattern. Discuss.
4. While the right to strike is an important dispute resolution procedure in many elements of the public sector, its ultimate threat is extremely circumscribed in a variety of ways. Discuss the various ways in which its threat is circumscribed.
5. What are the pros and cons of final-offer arbitration?

Notes

1   As of 2014, the two largest unions in Canada were the Canadian Union of Public Employees (CUPE) with about 13.3 per cent of total union membership, and the National Union of Public and General Employees (NUPGE) with about 7.2 per cent of total union membership. They are followed by two mainly private-sector unions: the UNIFOR with about 6.3 per cent of total union membership, and the United Food and Commercial Workers (UFCW) with about 5.2 per cent. These figures are based on the authors' calculations using data from Employment and Social Development Canada (2015).

2   For discussions of these issues, see, for example, Auditor General of Canada (1998), Gunderson and Hyatt (1996), Swimmer (1996, 2001), Thompson (1998), Thompson and Ponak (1992), Thompson and Slinn (2013), and Warrian (1995, 1996).

3   Details of the earlier history and evolution of collective bargaining in the public sector, from which this section draws, are given in Finkelman and Goldenberg (1983), Goldenberg (1973, 1988), Gunderson and Hyatt (1996), Ponak and Thompson (1995), Rose (1995), Swimmer (1995, 1996), Thompson and Ponak (1992), and Thompson and Slinn (2013). Those studies also contain references to earlier material on the subject.

4   Applying the 74.7 per cent coverage rate to the 3,600,000 employees in the public sector yields 2,689,200 persons covered, while applying the 17.5 per cent coverage rate of the private sector to the 10,907,000 employees yields 1,908,725 employees covered.

5   Discussions of the statutes governing collective bargaining in the public sector in Canada are given, for example, in Gunderson and Hyatt (1996), Ponak and Thompson (1995), Swan (1985), Swimmer and Thompson (1995), and Thompson and Slinn (2013).

6   Dispute resolution procedures are discussed in the studies indicated in note 5, as well as in Currie and McConnell (1991), Gunderson et al. (1996), and Campolieti et al. (2016).

7   Although British Columbia allows the right to strike for most occupational groups and limited right to strike in the rest, general legislation in that province stipulates that employees requiring essential services may be forbidden from striking.

8   Detailed discussions of the choice-of-procedure regime in the federal jurisdiction are given in Ponak and Thompson (1995), Subbarao (1985), Swimmer (1978, 1989, 1995), and Swimmer and Winer (1993). The choice-of-procedure regime was used more in earlier decades as a dispute resolution procedure for some occupational groups in the public sector, but provinces moved away from its use (Ponak & Thompson, 1995; Campolieti et al., 2016).

9   Court decisions have further enhanced the power of employers with respect to the designation of employees who do not have the right to strike. In *CATCA v. the Queen*, the Supreme Court of Canada held that the employer had the right to determine the level of service regarded as essential—a determination that effectively gives government the power to determine the employees who are designated as providing essential services and hence who will not have the right to strike. Furthermore, that decision indicated that designated employees were to perform *all* of their functions, not just those considered essential.

10 Calculations given in Gunderson and Hyatt (1996: 254) based on data from Swimmer (1995: 379).

11 Discussions of the earlier wage control programs with their relevance to the public sector are given in Fryer (1995), Gunderson and Hyatt (1996), Panitch and Swartz (1984), Ponak and Thompson (1995), Thompson (1988), Thompson and Ponak (1991) and Thompson and Slinn (2013).

12 Low recorded strike rates also do not indicate the absence of conflict. When strikes are suppressed, as is often the case in the public sector, the conflict may simply be redirected to such forms as grievances (Hebdon, 1991; Hebdon & Stern, 1998).

13 Author's calculations based on Labour Canada's work stoppage data base.

14 Employment equity legislation was introduced by the Rae NDP government in Ontario in 1993, but subsequently rescinded by the Harris Conservative government in 1995. In that period it was never actually implemented in a formal sense.

15 Gunderson (1995) indicates that in the early period of the legislation adjustments had been in the neighbourhood of $4000 per recipient or a 20 per cent wage increase, averaging 4 to 8 per cent of payroll. The 1999 Bell Canada settlement of $59 million for 20,000 current and former employees averaged about $3000 per employee. The federal pay-equity settlement with the Public Service Alliance of Canada in October 1999, for a case that started in 1983, was for approximately $3.5 billion and affected 230,000 current and retired federal employees, such as clerks, secretaries, and librarians, in female-dominated positions. That averages to a little over $15,000 per recipient including back pay.

References

Auditor General of Canada. 1998. "Expenditures and Work Force Reductions in the Public Service." *Report of the Auditor General of Canada*. Ottawa: Public Works and Government Services, 1.1 B 1.33.

Akyeampong, Ernst. 1999. "Unionisation: An Update." *Perspectives on Labour and Income* 11, 3, pp. 45–65. Statistics Canada Cat. no. 75–001–XPE.

Campolieti, Michele, Robert Hebdon, and Benjamin Dachis. 2016. "Collective Bargaining in the Canadian Public Sector, 1978–2008: The Consequences of Restraint and Structural Change." *British Journal of Industrial Relations* 54, pp. 192–213.

Currie, Janet, and Sheena McConnell. 1991. "Collective Bargaining in the Public Sector: The Effect of Legal Structure on Dispute Costs and Wages." *American Economic Review* 81, pp. 693–718.

Devinatz, Victor G., and John W. Budd. 1997. "Third Party Dispute Resolution: Interest Disputes." *The Human Resource Management Handbook*, edited by David Lewin and Daniel Mitchell, Greenwich: JAI Press, pp. 95–135.

Employment and Social Development Canada. 2015. *Union Coverage in Canada—2014*. Ottawa: Employment and Social Development Canada.

Finkelman, Jacob, and Shirley Goldenberg. 1983. *Collective Bargaining in the Public Service: The Federal Experience in Canada*. Montreal: Institute for Research on Public Policy.

Fryer, John L. 1995. "Provincial Public Sector Labour Relations." *Public Sector Collective Bargaining in Canada*, edited by Swimmer and Thompson. Kingston: IRC Press, pp. 341–67.

Fuller, Leon L. 1962. "Collective Bargaining and the Arbitrator." *Proceedings of the Fifteenth Annual Meeting, National Academy of Arbitrators* 15, pp. 8–54.

Goldenberg, Shirley B. 1973. "Collective Bargaining in the Provincial Public Services." *Collective Bargaining in the Public Service*, edited by J.F. O'Sullivan, Toronto: Institute of Public Administration of Canada, pp. 11–44.

———. 1988. "Public-Sector Labor Relations in Canada." *Public Sector Bargaining*, 2nd edn, edited by B. Aaron, J. Najita, and J. Stern, Washington: Bureau of National Affairs, pp. 266–313.

Gomez, Rafael, and Morley Gunderson. 2005. "Does Economic Integration Lead to Social Policy Convergence? An Analysis of North American Linkages and Social Policy." *Social and Labour Market Aspects of North American Linkages*, edited by R. Harris and T. Lemieux, Calgary: University of Calgary Press, pp. 309–56.

Gunderson, Morley. 1983. *Economics Aspects of Interest Arbitration*. Toronto: Ontario Economic Council.

———. 1995. "Gender Discrimination and Pay Equity Legislation." *Aspects of Labour Market Behaviour: Essays in Honour of John Vanderkamp*, edited by L.

Christofides, K. Grant, and R. Swidinsky, Toronto: University of Toronto Press, pp. 225–47.

———. 1998. "Harmonization of Labour Policies Under Free Trade." *Relations Industrielles/Industrial Relations* 53, pp. 11–41.

———, and Rafael Gomez. 2005. "Does Economic Integration Lead to Social Policy Convergence? An Analysis of North American Linkages and Social Policy." *Social and Labour Market Aspects of North American Linkages*, edited by R. Harris and T. Lemieux, Calgary: University of Calgary Press, pp. 309–56.

———, Robert Hebdon, and Douglas Hyatt. 1996. "Collective Bargaining in the Public Sector: Comment." *American Economic Review* 86, pp. 315–26.

———, and Douglas Hyatt. 1996. "Canadian Public Sector Employment Relations in Transition." *Public Sector Employment Relations in a Time of Transition*, edited by D. Belman, Gunderson, and Hyatt, Madison, WI: Industrial Relations Research Association, pp. 243–81.

———, ———, and Allen Ponak. 2001. "Strikes and Dispute Resolution." *Union-Management Relations in Canada*, 4th edn, edited by Gunderson, Ponak, and D. Taras, Toronto: Addison-Wesley.

———, and Frank Reid. 1995. "Public Sector Strikes in Canada." *Public Sector Collective Bargaining in Canada*, edited by Swimmer and Thompson. Kingston: IRC Press, pp. 135–63.

Hebdon, Robert. 1991. "Ontario's No Strike Laws: A Test of the Safety-Valve Hypothesis." *Proceedings of the 28th Conference of the Canadian Industrial Relations Association*, edited by D. Carter, pp. 347–57.

———. 2005. "Toward a Theory of Workplace Conflict: The Case of U.S. Municipal Collective Bargaining." *Advances in Industrial and Labor Relations,* Vol. 14, pp. 35–67.

———, and Robert Stern. 1998. "Tradeoffs among Expressions of Industrial Conflict: Public Sector Strike Bans and Grievance Arbitrations." *Industrial and Labour Relations Review* 51, pp. 204–21.

———, Marick Masters, and Joe Slater. 2013. "U.S. Public Sector Collective Bargaining: Tumultuous Times," Chapter 7 in *Collective Bargaining Under Duress: Case Studies of Major US Industries.* Champaign, Il. Labor and Employment Research Association, pp. 255–95.

Human Resources Development Canada. 1998. *Directory of Labour Organizations in Canada*. Ottawa: Canadian Government Publishing.

Jalette, Patrice and Robert Hebdon. 2013. "Unions and Privatization: Opening the Black Box." *Industrial and Labor Relations Review.* 65, 1, pp. 17–33.

Lester, Richard A. 1984. *Labor Arbitration in State and Local Government*. Princeton: Industrial Relations Section Princeton University.

Lund, John, and Cheryl Maranto. 1996. "Public Sector Law: An Update." *Public Sector Employment Relations in a Time of Transition*, edited by D. Belman, M. Gunderson, and D. Hyatt, Madison, WI: Industrial Relations Research Association, pp. 21–58.

Lynk, Michael. 2016. "Rights at Work: Freedom of Association, the 2015 Labour Trilogy and the Future of Canadian Labour Law." H.D. Woods Lecture, Saskatoon, June 1.

McDonald, Judith, and Robert Thornton. 2015. "Coercive Competition: Ontario's Pay Equity Act of 1988 and the Gender Pay Gap." *Contemporary Economic Policy* 36, 4, pp. 608–18.

O'Grady, John. 1992. "Arbitration and Its Ills." Paper prepared for Governments and Competitiveness Research Program, Institute of Policy Studies, Queen's University.

Panitch, Leo, and Don Swartz. 1984. "Free From Collective Bargaining to Permanent Exceptionalism: The Economic Crisis and the Transformation of Industrial Relations in Canada." *Conflict or Compromise: The Future of Public Sector Industrial Relations*, edited by M. Thompson and G. Swimmer, Montreal: Institute for Research on Public Policy, pp. 403–35.

———, and ———. 1993. *The Assault on Trade Union Freedoms: From Wage Controls to Social Contracts*. Toronto: Garamond Press.

Ponak, Allen, and Loren Falkenberg. 1989. "Resolution of Interest Disputes." *Collective Bargaining in Canada*, edited by A. Sethi, Scarborough, ON: Nelson Canada, pp. 260–97.

Ponak, Allen, and Mark Thompson. 1995. "Public Sector Collective Bargaining." *Union-Management Relations in Canada*, edited by M. Gunderson and A. Ponak, Toronto, ON: Addison-Wesley, 415–54.

Riddell, Craig. 1993. "Unionization in Canada and the United States: A Tale of Two Countries." *Small Differences That Matter: Labor Markets and Income Maintenance in Canada and the United States*, edited by D. Card and R. Freeman, Chicago: University of Chicago Press, 109–48.

Riddell, Craig, and Chris Riddell. 2004. "Changing Patterns of Unionization: The North American Experience." *Unions in the 21st Century*, edited by A. Verma and T.A. Kochan, London: Palgrave Macmillan, 146–64.

Rose, Joseph B. 1995. "The Evolution of Public Sector Unionism." *Public Sector Collective Bargaining in Canada*, edited by Swimmer and Thompson. Kingston: IRC Press, pp. 20–51.

Stern, James L. 1984. "The Mediation of Interest Disputes by Arbitrators under the Wisconsin Med-Arb Law for Local Government Employees." *The Arbitration Journal* 39: 41–6.

Subbarao, A. 1985. "Impasse Choice in the Canadian Federal Service: An Innovation and an Intrigue." *Relations Industrielles* 40, pp. 567–90.

Swan, Ken. 1985. "Differences among Provinces in Public Sector Dispute Resolution." *Public Sector Compensation*, edited by D. Conklin, T. Courchene, and W. Jones. Toronto: Ontario Economic Council, pp. 49–75.

Swimmer, Gene. 1978. "The Impact of the Dispute Resolution Process on Canadian Federal Public Service Wage Settlements." *Journal of Collective Negotiations in the Public Sector* 16, 1, pp. 53–61.

———. 1989. "Critical Issues in Public Sector Industrial Relations." *Collective Bargaining in Canada*, edited by A. Sethi, Scarborough, ON: Nelson Canada, pp. 400–21.

———. 1995. "Collective Bargaining in the Federal Public Service of Canada: The Last Twenty Years." *Public Sector Collective Bargaining in Canada*, edited by Swimmer and Thompson. Kingston: IRC Press, pp. 368–406.

———. 1996. "Provincial Policies Governing Collective Bargaining." *Provinces: Canadian Provincial Politics*, edited by C. Dunn, Peterborough, ON: Broadview Press, pp. 351–78.

———, editor. 1996. *How Ottawa Spends 1996–97: Life Under the Knife*. Ottawa: Carleton University Press.

———. 2001. "Public-Sector Labour Relations in an Era of Restraint and Restructuring: An Overview." *Public-Sector Labour Relations in an Era of Restraint and Restructuring* edited by Swimmer, Toronto: Oxford University Press, pp. 1–35.

———, and Mark Thompson. 1995a. *Public Sector Collective Bargaining in Canada*. Kingston: IRC Press.

———, and ———. 1995b. "Collective Bargaining in the Public Sector: An Introduction." *Public Sector Collective Bargaining in Canada*, edited by Swimmer and Thompson. Kingston: IRC Press, pp. 1–19).

Swimmer, Gene, and Stanley Winer. 1993. "Dispute Resolution and Self-Selection: An Empirical Examination of the Federal Public Sector, 1971–1982." *Relations Industrielles/Industrial Relations* 48, 1, pp. 146–62.

Supreme Court of Canada. 2007. Health Services and Support—Facilities Subsector Bargaining Assn. v. British Columbia, 2007 SCC 27.

Thompson, Mark. 1988. "Public Sector Industrial Relations in Canada: The Impact of Restraint." in *Proceedings of the Annual Spring Meeting of the Industrial Relations Research Association*. Madison, WI: IRRA.

———. 1995. "The Industrial Relations Effects of Privatization: Evidence from Canada." *Public Sector Collective Bargaining in Canada*, edited by Swimmer and Thompson. Kingston: IRC Press, pp. 164–79.

———. 1998. "Public Sector Industrial Relations in Canada: Adaptation to Change." Paper presented at the 11th Congress of Industrial Relations, Bologna, Italy, Sept.

———, and Allen Ponak. 1991. "Canadian Public Sector Industrial Relations: Theory and Practice." *Advances in Industrial and Labor Relations*, vol. 5, edited by D. Sockell, D. Lewin, and D.B. Lipsky, Greenwich, CT: JAI Press, pp. 59–93.

————, and ————. 1992. "Restraint, Privatization and Industrial Relations in the 1980s." *Industrial Relations in Canadian Industry*, edited by R. Chaykowski and A. Verma. Toronto: Dryden Press, pp. 284–322.

Thompson, Mark, and S. Slinn. 2013. "Public Sector Industrial Democracy in Canada: Does it Threaten of Sustain Democracy?" *Comparative Labor Law and Policy Journal* 34, 2, pp. 393-414.

Uppal, Sharanjit. 2011. "Unionization 2011." *Perspectives on Labour and Income*. Winter 2011, Statistics Canada Catalogue no. 75-001-X.

Warrian, Peter. 1995. "The End of Public Sector 'Industrial' Relations in Canada?" KPMG Centre for Government Foundation.

————. 1996. *Hard Bargain: Transforming Public Sector Labour-Management Relations*. Toronto: McGilligan Books.

Part **V**

Changing Expectations
of Government

Every edition of this *Handbook* has revealed that Canadians have changing expectations of their government. If anything, they are becoming more exigent. In the second decade, this is particularly noticeable in respect to public sector ethics, gender-sensitive governance, information and technology, political advisers in government, horizontal governance, political marketing, the Third Sector and our future relations with the EU.

Canadians have increasingly rigorous expectations of the ethical behaviour of public officials. Brock and Nater review of the ethics regimes in the federal and provincial jurisdictions in Canada show efforts being made to ensure that Canadians are governed in alignment with fundamental democratic norms. Regimes to control breaches of ethics however are in flux and in a constant state of improvement. The challenges continue, particularly as public sector reforms alter the traditional norms of accountability and Canada becomes more diverse. The chapter chronicles the move away from a compliance-based approach to a values-based approach to ethics—or a combination of the two—and the challenges these engender. Definitions of ethics in the public sector are undertaken first, followed by a review of ethical theories, a compilation of federal and provincial ethics regimes, and an assessment of reasons for mixed results of the ethics regimes put in place over the past 40 years throughout Canada.

Tammy Findlay outlines in Chapter 18 the contributions of feminist analysis to the understanding of public administration. One important way is by gendering it. "Gendering" means making gender differences visible and exposing gender biases. Gendering demonstrates how women's inequality gets reproduced and how both women's and men's lives are restricted by socially constructed gender roles. It allows us to correct faulty assumptions, ask new questions, and assess possibilities for change in governmental processes and policies. The chapter emphasizes that gendering is important for public administration as an academic field, and as a professional practice. Findlay demonstrates how public administration a vital focal point for feminist analysis and action.

This chapter is organized into four, beginning with a general discussion of the relationship between gender, the state, and bureaucracy. It then considers the machinery of government used to represent women. Next, it discusses feminist approaches to public policy analysis. Finally, it explores the gendered character of public sector employment.

David C.G. Brown explores five elements of the story of information and technology in Canadian public administration. He starts by looking at the promise of IT and the discipline that it has spawned, variously described as e- or digital government. The harnessing of information and technology has been a critical underpinning of new public management thinking, and a second part of the discussion is to look at the catalytic effects of a central tenet of NPM, a focus on the citizen. The third section considers – briefly, as it is a topic in itself – politics and policy-making in the electronic environment, in effect what is happening at the front end of public administration. The heart of the chapter is the fourth section, which looks at the spheres and methods of public administration created by IT and IM, and the chapter concludes with a look at their relationship to public sector reform

Jonathan Craft reviews another notable example of changing expectations, this time dealing with the changing expectations of politicians and the public. He examines appointed political staffs in Canada to help understand better what they do and why it matters for contemporary Canadian public administration. An overview is provided of three different types of federal political staffs that serve ministers and MPs, and details the functions they typically perform. The chapter examines why appointed political staff were introduced in the Canadian system, how they have evolved, and reflects on their impact on Canadian public administration.

The chapter by Evert Lindquist reviews and updates the recent initiatives and context for dealing with horizontal initiatives in the Government of Canada. While the motivations behind horizontal initiatives are important and laudable, this chapter depicts the general aspiration of horizontal governance as only of many competing values in Westminster governance systems, and in turn, approaches to fostering or appraising how governments further horizontal governance reflects contending values.

This chapter has four parts. The first reviews how horizontal governance moved to the top of public-sector reform agenda in the late 1990s and early 2000s, and considers different perspectives on enabling horizontal initiatives. The second part considers developments since the mid-2000s, noting that while horizontal strategies continued, dialogue and research on horizontal practice tapered off, despite some academic research and promise. The third part seeks to explain why. It suggesting that increasingly directive governments have nominally embedded horizontal governance as a core value, but have been less interested in furthering open discussions on it. The final section considers whether we want truly horizontal and "zero gravity" governance. It stresses the need to acknowledge competing values, and implications for modernizing governance in the digital era.

Alex Marland introduces students to the importance of communication in public administration. He begins by reviewing key concepts, among them gatekeeping, agenda-setting, news management, information subsidies, and spin. A description of how communications is practised in public administration ranges from examining structural components, such as the strategic communications plan in a memorandum to cabinet, to the ways that Prime Minister Justin Trudeau communicates with the general public. The role of central agencies, notably the Prime Minister's Office and the Privy Council Office, is discussed. Broader theories of access to information, open government and new political governance are touched upon. This review provides a basis for comprehending the emerging theory of public sector branding, which holds that all government communications is becoming centralized.

A shift in government expectations may not yield the changes expected, as B. Mitchell Evans and John Shields explain in Chapter 23, examining the role of the "third sector" in Canadian politics and society. The state has encouraged a new expectation of the third sector—partnership. Partnership implies—in its broadest definition—sharing power, a common forum for dialogue, and multi-actor input into policy development.

This has not happened. The new arrangements—adoption of NPM, a changing conception of governance, and reconceptualization of state, market, and societal boundaries—engendered new expectations of the role of third-sector agencies. Rather than being agents of community, solidarity, and collective responsibility, they are increasingly agents of the state, or "shadow state." As quasi-governmental agents, they often must forgo important research and advocacy to focus on producing the results required by government. Evans and Shields regret that neo-liberal restructuring contributes to deteriorating social cohesion and hampers the development of social capital. Notions of community, solidarity, and collective responsibility are being displaced by an atomized society where the ethic of what C.B. Macpherson critiqued as "possessive individualism" prevails.

John Erik Fossum compares and contrasts Canada and the European Union (EU). The focus is on the broader contexts within which each system's public administration is embedded and not the specific features of each public administration. Globalization and other developments confront political systems with profound challenges pertaining to the fundamentals of political order, community and governing. Europe's attempt at overcoming its traumatic past has given these developments a distinctive shape: the world's first attempt at supranational democratic governance. The issues and challenges facing Europe are about the fundamentals of governing and living together (and apart). The chapter compares and contrasts the EU with Canada on four different themes. The key theme that is tracked through all of these pertains to the pronounced role of executive officials (heads of states and governments and their supportive staffs).

Ethics in the Public Sector

From Compliance to Values or Compliance and Values?

Kathy L. Brock and John L. Nater[1]

Chapter Overview

This chapter reviews and assesses the changing ethics landscape in Canada. It begins with a discussion of the meaning of ethics in the public sector and then charts the rise of the dominant theories in the field. Using this context, the chapter offers a brief scan of ethics laws, codes, and regulations in Canada, followed by a discussion of the challenges posed by three trends in public administration in Canada. The paper concludes with an assessment of the state of public sector ethics in Canada in practice and theory and into the future. It suggests that examples of questionable ethical behaviour can be explained by these trends. However, the solutions to preventing such types of misgovernment are not so easily identifiable.

Chapter Objectives

By the end of this chapter, students will be able to do the following:
- Give examples of contemporary ethics concerns in Canada and abroad.
- Distinguish morality from ethics.
- Discuss the meanings attributed to public-sector ethics.
- Distinguish between compliance-based ethical programs and values-based approach to ethics.
- Give examples of modern compliance-based ethical programs and values-based approaches to ethics in the federal and provincial government regimes.
- Identify and explain the three main ethical theories.

The attainment of the good for one man alone is, to be sure, a source of satisfaction; yet to secure it for a nation and for states is nobler and more divine.

Aristotle (384–322 BCE), *Nichomachean Ethics*

Introduction: Scandals, Scandals Everywhere

Internationally and domestically, 2016 dawned full of promise with the Olympics, American election, and "Sunny Ways" of the newly elected Canadian government. But by the summer, the promises faded as scandals and allegations of corruption swirled. The Olympics opened in Brazil just as the Brazilian Senate reviewed the case for impeachment of the president and the government lay in tatters over accusations of maladministration leading up to the games. The international sports community was dispirited after hearing that high-ranking Russian government officials and its federal security service were implicated in their Olympic athletes' doping scandal. In Britain, the prime minister resigned after the Brexit referendum amidst allegations he mishandled the whole issue.

Canadians were inundated with media coverage of the US election and possible ethics breaches. Democratic presidential candidate Hillary Clinton was dogged first by an ambiguous FBI report on her conduct in deleting and handling government emails when she was secretary of state. The report indicated that there would be no criminal charges against her but that her behaviour had been extremely careless and could have been subject to disciplinary action had she remained a government employee, and that was followed by the FBI decision to reopen the investigation in the final days of the election. This ambiguity around her actions seemed to influence voter intentions and she was unable to break the glass ceiling of US politics. Meanwhile, Republican presidential candidate Donald Trump was mired in controversy with the sitting Democratic President Barack Obama calling him unfit to hold the office, and Mitt Romney, the 2012 Republican presidential nominee, suggesting that there was "plenty of evidence that Mr. Trump is a con man, a fake." By the end of the campaign, Trump's statements on diversity issues and conduct towards women had people openly calling for an investigation into his words and actions. After his electoral win, questions arose about his handling of his extensive private business interests. Maladministration, misjudgment, and corruption seemed rampant around the globe.

In Canada in mid-2016 some glimmers of promise still lingered. The Senate spending controversy resurfaced when Senator Mike Duffy refused to repay the expenses questioned by the Auditor General and the Senate internal economy committee replied that the disputed expenses would be garnished from his salary. The government responded to the reputational damage of the Senate by creating a more open and independent Senate appointment process. Despite the federal government's promise of sunny ways and better days, the Attorney General came under fire for creating an appearance, if not the reality, of bias by attending a $500 Liberal fundraiser with sympathetic lawyers and for her association with a non-profit organization operating in the field of justice. The federal minister of fisheries resigned from cabinet and the Liberal caucus in late May citing addiction issues but in July confessed to resigning because of a "consensual but inappropriate relationship." Also in May it was revealed, in response to the 2015 controversy concerning Prime Minister Justin Trudeau's nannies being paid by public funds, that the prime minister had hired a nanny under the foreign workers program—a program for which he had sharply criticized the Conservative government and that he had promised, during the 2015 federal election, to fix. On a more constructive note, the federal Liberal government used a more transparent appointment process to name Justice Malcolm Rowe to the Supreme Court of Canada. The government announced an inquiry into missing and murdered Indigenous women to address ongoing controversies around the state handling of these cases.

The provinces also had controversies in 2016. The former deputy premier of Quebec was arrested in March under charges of corruption, conspiracy, fraud, and bribery; he was one of a string of politicians, public servants, and Liberal party officials charged in the widespread scandal. On the west coast, a former communications director in the BC Liberal government was charged with breach of trust in a vote-getting scandal and the former BC Liberal party executive director was preparing to defend herself after three criminal charges were filed against her for deleting files in the Ontario gas plant scandal during her previous employment there. Back in Ontario, the Liberal government was still labouring under that scandal and others involving Ontario Hydro, contracting practices under the Green Energy Plan, a $80.5 million payout to the teachers' unions, compensation paid to senior managers in the aborted pension scheme, as well as questionable fundraising events by Ontario cabinet ministers. The tarnished Ontario government was preparing legislation similar to the 2006 Federal Accountability Act passed under the Harper federal Government in an attempt to impose controls and restore legitimacy to government. On the east coast, in March 2016, CUPE requested the New Brunswick Auditor General investigate the awarding of contracts for transportation and construction as part of the privatization initiative. The list goes on.

Is it any wonder that Canadians question the ethical standards of their elected and permanent public officials, despite Canada ranking low on international corruption indices (Atkinson, 2011)? But what Canadians are perhaps too quick to dismiss are the remedies in place and being pursued to address instances of unethical or questionable behaviour by elected and permanent public officials, the very fact that instances of shoddy behaviour and maladministration are brought to public light by an attentive media, and the relative lack of deep embedded corruption in the Canadian political system owing to a vigilant media and public and a generally well-regulated political system. The fact that light shines on such instances of maladministration and misconduct attests to the strength of the ethics regulatory system in Canada.

If the system is well-regulated, then why are these examples of bad behaviour or judgment so often in the media and why do they seem to be becoming more common? This chapter argues that ethical conflicts are erupting into the public view more frequently owing to three trends in Canada. First, the introduction of **new public management** into the Westminster model of Parliamentary government practised in Canada has disrupted traditional methods of **accountability** and notions of responsible government, resulting in new methods being developed and often coexisting uneasily with old norms. Second, the move from **compliance-based ethics** to **values-based ethics**, as part of the first trend, poses new challenges to Canadian governmental institutions. Third, the increasing diversity in Canada

challenges traditional definitions and understandings of ethical behaviour in the public service of Canada.

Defining Ethics in the Public Sector

The definition of **public-sector ethics** is elusive. After reviewing leading sources on ethics in government and public administration, it is tempting to crib from the US Supreme Court definition of pornography and conclude that like pornography, ethics are hard to define but you know ethical and unethical public-sector behaviour when you see it. Ethics is a "proverbial motherhood issue" with everyone for it or at least not against it (Geuras & Garofalo, 2011: Ch. 1: 6; Martinez & Richardson, 2008: 15). Given its elusive nature, numerous authors discuss public-sector ethics without actually defining the concept. But to accept this way out of the difficulty of attempting to define ethics in the public sphere is not satisfying nor is it entirely helpful in understanding proper behaviour in government. A clearer understanding of ethics is necessary to provide a guide to public-sector officials when faced with difficult decisions and dilemmas. In their study of "Democratic Morality," Cynthia and Thomas Lynch remind us of Stephen Bailey's admonition in the 1960s: "Virtue without understanding can be quite as disastrous as understanding without virtue" (2009: 11–12). An informed mental mindset is critical to ethical and moral judgment and behaviour.

It is useful to begin by distinguishing ethics from other closely associated concepts. Ethics and morality are often equated but actually have distinct meanings. **Morality** refers to personal beliefs and standards of conduct whereas **ethics** refers to proper standards of conduct for a category of persons such as public servants or politicians (Martinez, 2009: xii; see also Lynch & Lynch, 2009: 6). This is an important distinction for public office holders to bear in mind because it can help an individual to understand and accept why she or he may be expected to act in a certain way as an office holder that is contrary to the way she or he would normally act in private life. For example, although a government policy analyst might be personally opposed to a policy such as abortion or assisted dying, as a public servant she or he may be expected to advise on how to implement that policy regardless of those personal views.

Similarly, ethics and **integrity** have different connotations. European scholars tend to prefer using integrity because it implies competence, propriety, and a mindset that American scholars equate with professionalism. In contrast, Americans often associate ethics with "doing right or good" or the consequences of policy, which implies an activism that Europeans do not associate with values inherent in the operation of government (Cox, 2009: viii). Consistent with this distinction, in Canada the mandate of the ethics and conflict of interest commissioner doesn't include whistle-blowing, which is a form of "doing right or good." That area lies within the integrity commissioner's mandate.

Ethics also tend to be broadly understood, encompassing other concepts and forms of action but remaining distinct from them. The relationship between corruption and public-sector ethics is complex. The term *corruption* has evolved to mean "the misuse of office for personal gain," and can range from low-level petty corruption (small kickbacks, bribes) to high-level grand corruption that involves creating or moulding the rules or institutions of government to serve private interests. Most forms of corruption, such as bribery, fraud, influence-peddling, and so on, are addressed through criminal law, the police, and courts. While a state with a low score on the international corruption scales might not appear ethical in its practices, a state characterized by ethical practices in government will not be tolerant of corruption. The distinction is that ethics go beyond the misuse of office for personal gain to include taking advantage of privileges that arise because of the office for personal gain or enjoyment (gifts, tickets to hockey games, invitations to cottages) or partisan advantage (benefits to ridings, post-career employment, lobbying). So the Canadian public, using the broader definition of unethical behaviour, tends to believe corruption is widespread in government while elected and permanent public officials do not, because they define corruption more narrowly as misuse of office for personal gain (Atkinson, 2011). In the public mind, public-sector ethics implies more than an absence of high-level corruption.

To be useful, public-sector ethics must provide a guide to policy-makers in their decisions (Barber, 2015: 215–19, 57–9; Gow, 2008; Wolf, 2011). Ethics in public life set standards for good and bad behaviour as well as define good and bad choices in such a way that they assist people in making the right or good choice (Menzel, 2015: 348–9; Snellman, 2015:343–4). Since values are embedded in ethics, context is important in determining what behaviour or choices are favoured in any situation (Kernaghan & Langford, 2014; Lawton et al., 2012: 4–9; Menzel, 2015: 348). In democratic government, ethical principles and behaviour by public officials should result in better decisions that serve the public interest and thus build public trust and confidence (Menzel, 2007: 16–18; Snellman, 2015: 344). Indeed, in his review of leading literature on ethics in public administration, Menzel notes the centrality of the connection between ethical and trustworthy government (2015: 358–9).

The evolving nature of ethics requires them to be defined broadly. For example, Ian Greene and David Shugarman root their understanding of ethical government in the democratic principle of mutual respect (equality + respect) incorporating the five principles of social equality, deference to the majority, minority rights, freedom, and integrity (1997: 3–7), while also in 1997 George Fredrickson based his understanding of ethical public administration on benevolence towards everyone, a noble calling (Lynch & Lynch, 2009: 16). Many authors are not as specific about particular principles but anchor ethics in democratic values more broadly defined, which avoids the appearance of an ideological bias in interpreting ethical actions. In this way, ethics are similar to laws that also set standards for good behaviour and right decisions. In contrast to laws, ethics are contextual, based on particular situations, involve moral conscience and agency, and contravention of ethics may or may not be punishable by the state (Martinez & Richardson, 2008: 16–17). Laws and ethics operate together to sanction acceptable behaviour and decisions.

To summarize: public-sector ethics are distinct from personal morality. They are about doing the right things for the right reasons and may overlap with a sense of professional integrity. In the public sector, ethics mean more than an absence of high-level corruption and are helpful in identifying instances of low-level corruption that are not necessarily captured by legal restrictions. Public-sector ethics set standards and guidelines for public-sector officials that encourage a framework of thinking about decisions that is consistent with serving the public interest. Well-defined public-sector ethics express the fundamental values of government.

In order to develop a more robust understanding of the challenges in building ethical and trustworthy government it is necessary to understand the main theories of public-sector ethics and how they have developed. These theories help explain the current tensions in the model of ethics in the Canadian context. We turn to these theories now.

Ethical Theories and Current Trends

The need for both state-defined rules and individual moral judgment has existed throughout history. Philosophers and practitioners have struggled to create the right balance between prescriptive rules and individual virtuous behaviour to ensure that the public good is served in the business of government. This concern became more acute in western liberal democracies with the growth of the welfare state in the 1960s and 1970s. The huge bureaucratic apparatus challenged the control mechanisms embedded in both congressional and parliamentary forms of democracy. The idea that elected officials could direct the bureaucracy and be held responsible for its behaviour seemed less compelling than in the past. The merit system introduced in the public sector in the early twentieth century had helped curb political patronage and corruption in the public sector up to the 1950s but was less effective as a control as the bureaucracy grew, relations became less personal, career mobility increased, unions developed, and a professional ethos took root.

Three further developments compounded the problem of control and the perception that traditional restraints on public and elected officials were not effective. The shift in government from rowing to steering in the 1990s and 2000s placed more strains on the system as public officials oversaw the granting of large sums of money to outside actors, and partnerships with the private and non-profit sector became a more commonplace means of doing business. The hierarchical form of accountability characteristic of most democratic systems was challenged by horizontal accountability to co-workers, private- and non-profit-sector partners, and the public (Kernaghan and Langford, 2014: 4–5; Roberts, 2009: 262–4; Savoie, 2008: 72–93). The shift in society from a more community-based, publicly engaged society to a more atomistic, individual rights-based society further challenged the sense of corporate loyalty and desire to conform to behavioural norms (Putnam, 2000; Savoie, 2008: 94–123). Finally, an activist media seeking glory by uncovering instances of corruption and bad behaviour only fuelled public suspicion of government. The advent of social media, with its instant and widespread messaging, amplified incidents of wrongdoing or government waste such as the examples cited at the beginning of this chapter. The governments needed to regain control of their image and rebuild public trust.

Compliance and Values

One answer was a renewed emphasis on ethics in government. Initially the response was focused on compliance-based ethical programs. Governments began to adopt ethics codes, codes of conduct, detailed regulations, and other rules often codified in legislation in the 1970s and 1980s. These instruments outlined proper behaviour and penalties for non-compliance. Designated officers, often lawyers or trained specialists, were tasked with interpreting and applying the rules (Roberts, 2009: 262–3). Governments often introduced these rules or legislation in response to scandals or public acknowledgement of wrongdoing as a means of reassuring the public as well as of ensuring the behaviour was corrected (Nastase, 2013: 65). This was certainly the case in Canada when the Conservative federal government enacted the 2006 Federal Accountability Act in response to wrongdoings under the Liberal government and the report of the Gomery commission on the human resources sponsorship scandal. One important advantage of the compliance-based approach to ethics is that it places the onus on individuals and insulates the organizational as whole from liability for bad behaviour or illegal actions of employees (Roberts, 2009:262). Individuals are held accountable by the organization that promotes right action through its rules.

There are four main problems with a compliance-based approach to instilling ethics in the public sector. First, codes, rules, and regulations may become simple window dressing, giving the appearance of propriety rather than being incorporated into institutional decision-making and culture. They may be paid lip service without really changing practices. Systemic problems are not addressed. Second, they may have a perverse effect by creating the impression that if something is not explicitly forbidden or discouraged, then it must be permissible. A very narrow or thin view of ethics can be created by adopting this approach. Third, given that these instruments are normally imposed from the top down or through mandated processes and given that there are authoritative interpretations by designated officers of them, they neither create buy-in by employees nor foster the type of thinking and spirit that breeds ethical action and decisions in the course of daily duties (Nastase, 2013; Roberts 2009: 263–4). Fourth, they can be difficult to enforce. For example, in the Canadian Senate spending scandal that played out between 2011 and 2016, Canadians were shocked by the type of expenses claimed by the senators, the lax administration of expense claims, and by the actions of key officials such as the chief of staff to the Conservative prime minister who gave $90,000 to one of the senators to repay disputed expenses ostensibly to scotch the issue. Everyone knew something was seriously wrong here. However, few punishments were meted out, although the chief of staff did resign. The senator who was most criticized was found not guilty of wrongdoing in a criminal trial. The public was not impressed and the whole affair was a contributing factor to the defeat of the Conservative government.

In part owing to these deficiencies of a compliance-based approach to ethics management, governments have been moving to values-based or integrity-based approaches to ethics. While the compliance-based approaches fit more easily with the traditional command-control structure and hierarchical model of accountability in Weberian bureaucracies, the integrity-based systems are more consistent with the new public management model of employee empowerment and engagement. Garofalo explains that "what many administrators already do in their jobs is exactly what is required for ethical discernment and decision-making, and therefore inculcating the moral point of view into organizations need not be as alien as some might believe" (2008: 352). Integrity-based systems are aspirational and intended to build an ethical culture and environment in which individuals are ethically competent. Borrowing on the Organisation for Economic Co-operation and Development (OECD) definition, Roberts explains that these systems "include (1) the definition of broad aspirational values, (2) "a focus on what is achieved rather than how it was achieved," and (3) "an emphasis on encouraging good behaviour rather than policing and punishing errors or bad behaviours" (Roberts, 2009: 263). They encourage individuals to think about their behaviour or decisions in terms of the organizational values and mission and become moral agents instead of passively accepting norms defined by others (Garofalo, 2008: 347–9).

There are three main weaknesses with the values- or integrity-based approaches to ethics management.

First, the approach requires the organization to cede control of the definition of proper behaviour to individuals and to create the context in which these determinations are made instead. A lack of uniform or "fair" decision-making may result, causing administrators to intervene to ensure that equity applies. Second, these systems may empower ethically challenged individuals at the expense of others or the organization, or they may enable individuals to use the system to their own personal advantage, thus undermining the intent of the ethics system (Roberts, 2009: 263). Third, enforcement is more difficult without clearly delineated rules and regulations. Individuals may not act in the way intended or promoted because they do not have to do so. As a result, these systems have been criticized as too idealistic.

Compliance-based and integrity-based approaches to ethics management have been derived from different ethical theories. However, in practice, a blend of the two approaches is increasingly being adopted. This is not just a pragmatic response but can be justified based on a review of the main ethical theories. The works of both Kernaghan and Langford (2014) and Geuras and Garofalo (2011) promote a more unified approach to ethics management based on their review of these theories. The following discussion of the theories is based upon their works.

Three Leading Ethics Theories

There are three main ethical theories: deontological, teleological, and virtue ethics.

First, deontological theory or duty theory posits that ethical rules and assertions are intrinsic to actions and knowable. Something is ethical because "it is the principle of the thing" or it is unethical because "it is against the rules/it is just not done." The ethics of an action depend on its quality and not on the outcomes or consequences. This type of thinking is associated with Kant, who developed the categorical imperative or absolute moral command as a means of determining moral rightness through a rational thought process. This involves applying three criteria to determine moral rules: a rule is right if it can be made universal; an action or rule is right if it treats people as ends in themselves not means (respect and equality is evoked here); a rule is right if you would have it apply to you ("Do unto others as you would have them do to you" (the golden rule). This school of thought supports the compliance-based approach to ethics management since public servants would look to organization rules for guidance.

"In Canada, the most basic rules for a public servant would be found in the Constitution, the Charter of Rights and Freedoms, the law, regulations, Supreme Court decisions, an oath of office, policy directives and written standards of ethical conduct" (Kernaghan and Langford, 2014: 49–50). Process is important. Actions are right rather than good and individual dignity trumps the greatest good for all in society. A variation of this theory is intuitionism: rules are self-evident to a rational person. The key weakness of duty theory is that the first principles may be disputed or conflictual.

Second, teleological theory or consequentialism posits that ethical rules and assertions must be judged on the observable outcome. An action or decision is justifiable if it results in the greatest good or pleasure for the greatest number of people in a particular situation. Rooted in utilitarian theory developed by Bentham and John Stuart Mill, this theory treats people and their preferences equally. The role of the public servant would calculate the benefits and consequences of each action or policy and then make a decision based on what would maximize happiness in society whether it is in terms of education, health, or other outcomes. The end result justifies the decision in teleological systems, assuming that people are rational and their preferences are informed. In its contemporary form, consequentialism encourages public servants to educate the public so that they can make informed, rational choices and to engage citizen actively in the public policy process. The outcomes of policy should be measurable, thus creating the perception of fairness. Rational choice and public choice theory are variants of this approach to ethics. The core weaknesses of this theory are that cost-benefit or risk-and-feasibility analysis are often complex and vague, and treating all interests as equal may result in perceived inequities. It also subjects the greater good to individual preference.

The third theory of virtue ethics has its roots in Aristotelian thought and has returned as an answer to the weaknesses of both duty and consequential theory. This theory combines public ethics with personal morality and character. An act is deemed good based on the character trait or virtue that the act embodies. For example, helping someone who has fallen is a good act because it demonstrates kindness. These traits are valued because they are part of a greater good such as a happy, peaceful society, or in Canada a political system that promises peace, order, and good government.

In its contemporary manifestation, virtue theory promotes ethics codes that enumerate organizational values and inspire excellence in employees. Treating the public fairly and without discrimination based on race, sex, ethnicity, or sexuality would be good because it demonstrates respect which is essential to a peaceful and happy society. Public servants are expected to reason through a situation and make decisions based on what represents the values of the organization most fully, assigning priority to different values at different times but in accordance with what a reasonable, good person would believe right in that situation. In contrast to duty theory, the public servant actively interprets the values and applies them in situations. The key weakness in this approach to ethics is that values are not well defined or lack a foundation in the purpose of the organization, in this case government. Another weakness is that a cynical or opportunistic public servant may "value shop" to serve his/her own ends.

A possible fourth theory is relativism. It is based on the idea that all values and ethics are relative and there are no absolute or universal morally right actions. While this view allows for a diversity of views on ethics, it is not internally consistent (Geuras and Garofalo, 2011: 46–8).

A Combined Approach

Both Kernaghan and Langford and Geuras and Garofalo recommend a blended approach to ethics in the public sector at the end of their review of the theories. Kernaghan and Langford observe that

> In many cases, applying any of the three approaches would bring you to the same conclusion . . . and efforts have been made to integrate apparently conflicting ethical theories. . . . The key feature of these ethical frameworks is that they force public servants to rise above laziness, bias and the routine of following orders or rules without thought when faced with difficult ethical dilemmas. The most basic duty of a responsible public servant is to pay attention to such dilemmas and be ready to think ethically. (2014: 62)

Geuras and Garofalo go one step further and develop a set of questions incorporating all of these theories that will help a public servant to better understand the issue as a whole rather than from one perspective

(2011: Ch. 3: 25–7). This unified perspective promotes values and ethics education of public servants and their empowerment in making decisions based on organizational values. The end result is "high-performance, high-integrity organizations" (Geuras and Garofalo, 2011: Ch. 16: 1). While compliance mechanisms are still necessary, the emphasis is on a values-based, aspirational system that creates thoughtful, discerning public servants who ask the questions raised by the theories. The weakness in approaches that combine compliance and values or place them on a continuum, as Nastase observes, is that they attempt to unite or render coterminous two approaches based on dichotomous understandings of human nature: what makes people behave well and what ethics are. This can result in inconsistencies and practical difficulties (Nastase,

2013: 69–70), diminishing public trust in institutions rather than building integrity and trust in government.

As the next section demonstrates, the Canadian public sectors have traditionally relied on a compliance-based approach to ethics but seem to be moving towards more emphasis on values-based approaches to ethics. This has caused some tension within the Canadian variant of the Westminster model of parliamentary government. The next section scans the ethics regimes in the various public sectors in Canada.

The Ethics Landscape in Canada

The road to ethics has not been a smooth one in Canada as Table 20.1 shows. As in many liberal democratic jurisdictions, guidelines, legislation, and offices dealing with

Table 20.1   Establishment of Offices of Ethics Commissioners

Federal Government	1974 First Ethics Counsellor (Known as Assistant Deputy Registrar General) 2004 First independent Ethics Commissioner for the House of Commons, Cabinet and Order-in-Council appointments 2005 First Ethics Commissioner for the Senate 2006 Federal Conflict of Interest and Ethics Commissioner
British Columbia	1990 Members' Conflict of Interest Act enacted 1990 First Commissioner Appointed (acting)
Alberta	1991 Bill 40, Conflicts of Interest Act received Royal Assent 1992 First Ethics Commissioner Appointed 1998 Conflict of Interest Act amended to require five-year legislative review of the Act
Saskatchewan	1979 The Members' Conflict of Interest Act comes into force 2014 Conflict of Interest Commissioner serves as Registrar of Lobbyists
Manitoba	2000 Manitoba Law Reform Commission presents report on The Legislative Assembly and Conflict of Interest 2002 Dr. William Norrie appointed as first Conflict of Interest Commissioner 2009 Ron Perozzo appointed as Conflict of Interest Commissioner with additional responsibility as first registrar under The Lobbyists Registration Act
Ontario	1988 Office of Integrity Commissioner created 2016 Amendments to the lobbyist registry come into force
Quebec	2010 Code of Ethics and Conduct adopted by National Assembly 2011 Jacques Saint-Laurent appointed as first Ethics Commissioner
New Brunswick	2000 Office of the Conflict of Interest Commissioner 2000 Stuart G. Stratton appointed as Conflict of Interest Commissioner
Nova Scotia	1997 D. Merlin Nunn appointed as Conflict of Interest Commissioner
Prince Edward Island	1988 Conflict of Interest Act enacted 1999 Office of Conflict of Interest Commissioner created as part-time position 2015 John A. McQuaid appointed as Commissioner
Newfoundland and Labrador	1993 House of Assembly (Amendment) Act proclaimed 1993 Wayne Mitchell appointed as first Commissioner 2016 Bruce Chaulk appointed as Commissioner for Legislative Standards

Source: Modified from Ian Greene, 2009: 2. See also http://www.coibc.ca/links.htm

ethics and conflicts of interest came in fits and starts and tended to be created in response to scandals or public demonstrations of wrongdoing. Born in controversies, they were often controversial themselves, with elected and public officials questioning the need for them and the public suspicious about their effectiveness. Initially Canada tended to embrace a compliance-based approach to ethics but jurisdictions are moving towards values-based approaches while not relinquishing the compliance-based approach. As mentioned above, these two approaches can coexist but often are in tension.

Federal Government

The federal government led the charge to codify ethical issues in the 1970s. The conflict-of-interest guidelines for cabinet ministers introduced in 1973 codified informal policies and introduced new guidelines to address such matters as the use of insider information, outside activities of members, disclosure and divestiture of assets, and so on. Similar guidelines were adopted for different groups of Governor-in-Council appointments and senior public servants at the same time. In 1993, the position of ethics counsellor was created with responsibility for the Lobbying Registration Act and a reporting line to the prime minister (Greene, 2009: 9). However, the idea of one ethics officer for the House of Commons and Senate was rejected soundly by the Senate in 1993, 2004, and again in 2006; the folly of this decision was revealed in the Senate spending scandal that unfolded between 2012 and 2016. The offices remain separate in 2016. In 2006, the newly elected Conservatives made good on their campaign promise to introduce more stringent accountability measures and introduced the Federal Accountability Act, thereby creating the Conflict of Interest and Ethics Commissioner.

The federal government did not stop there. While the Conflict of Interest and Ethics Commissioner (CIEC) is the primary guardian of ethics at the senior levels of government and parliament, Table 20.2 shows that the federal ethics regime now includes the offices of the Conflict of Interest and Ethics Commissioner, the Public Sector Integrity Commissioner, the Lobbying Commissioner, the Privacy Commissioner, and the Information Commissioner, each tasked with separate responsibilities and all as independent agents of Parliament. The Senate ethics commissioner remains a separate body reporting to the Senate. The mandates of these offices are listed in Table 20.2. Although the

CIEC handles conflicts of interest and ethics for the approximately 2200 public office holders which includes cabinet ministers, parliamentary secretaries, ministerial staff, ministerial advisers, deputy ministers and most Governor-in-Council appointments (Dawson, 2016: 1), the public sector integrity commissioner is responsible for public-sector disclosure (whistle-blowing) legislation. Each of these offices has a compliance function as part of its mandate. However, increasingly the mandates reflect public education about values and values- and integrity-based approaches to inculcating the right norms and behaviours in the public sector. This is evidenced by the codes and values being adopted in these offices and the wording of their responsibilities.

Primary responsibility for public-sector ethics and values in the whole of the public service rests with the Treasury Board Secretariat as Table 20.3 demonstrates. Within the Treasury Board Secretariat, the chief human resources officer holds the responsibility for the administration of the federal workforce. This responsibility came through the creation of the office from the former Canada Public Service Agency (CPSA) (Greene, 2009). At the time, the government focused on the creation as a way to "reduce overlap and duplication and give deputy ministers the flexibility they need to better manage, attract, and develop their employees" (Greene, 2009). While the federal public service has transitioned to a consolidated approach to human resources management—together with the values and ethics regimes—the provincial approach varies among jurisdictions.

The Provinces

Each province has established a form of ethics commissioner similar to that of the federal conflict of interest and ethics commissioner. While the titles and responsibilities differ slightly among jurisdictions, the overall mandate and purposes of the office remains the same. In Ontario, for example, while the role of the integrity commissioner does differ from that of British Columbia's conflict of interest commissioner or Newfoundland and Labrador's commissioner for legislative standards, key similarities exist in both function and form.

When the analysis is expanded to the responsibility for ethics for the broader public service, the results are more diverse. While some provinces have adopted a values-based approach combined with vestiges of

Table 20.2   Canadian Officers of Parliament with Duties Related to Ethical Regimes

Office	Statute	Vision/Mandate/Mission	Values
Conflict of Interest and Ethics Commissioner First created 1973 Current version 2006	Conflict of Interest Act Conflict of Interest Code for Members of the House of Commons Parliament of Canada Act	**Application:** current and former public office holders, including ministers, parliamentary secretaries, ministerial staff, ministerial advisers, deputy ministers, and most full- and part-time Governor-in-Council appointees **Mission:** administer the conflict-of-interest rules for members of the House of Commons and public office holders in order to maintain and enhance the trust and confidence of the Canadian public in the conduct of these elected and appointed officials	Respect for people Professionalism Impartiality Integrity
Commissioner of Lobbying Created 2008	Lobbying Act Lobbyists Code of Conduct	**Mandate:** – maintain the Registry of Lobbyists, which contains and makes public the registration information disclosed by lobbyists – develop and implement educational programs to foster public awareness of the requirements of the Act – conduct reviews and investigations to ensure compliance with the Act and the Lobbyists' Code of Conduct	Respect for democracy Respect for people Integrity Stewardship Excellence
Public Sector Integrity Commissioner Created 2007	Public Servants Disclosure Protection Act	**Vision:** enhance public confidence in the integrity of public servants and institutions **Mission:** provide confidential and independent response to – disclosures of wrongdoing in the federal public sector from public servants or members of the public – complaints of reprisal from public servants and former public servants	Respect for democracy Respect for people Integrity Stewardship Excellence Impartiality Confidentiality
Privacy Commissioner First created in 1983	Privacy Act Personal Information Protection and Electronic Documents Act	**Mandate:** oversee compliance with both the *Privacy Act*, which covers the personal information-handling practices of federal government departments and agencies, and the Personal Information Protection and Electronic Documents Act *(PIPEDA)*, Canada's federal private-sector privacy law. **Mission:** protect and promote the privacy rights of individuals.	Strategic Priorities 2015–20 – Economics of personal information – Government surveillance – Reputation and privacy – The body as information
Information Commissioner First created in 1983	Access to Information Act	**Role:** – ensure that Canada's freedom-of-information law is respected – defend the rights of those making information requests by investigating complaints that federal institutions have not respected their rights under the Act	Respect (Values not detailed on website)

continued

Table 20.2 *continued*

Office	Statute	Vision/Mandate/Mission	Values
		– encourage federal institutions to make information more easily available to the public to keep the federal government accountable to Canadians – promote awareness of the importance of open and transparent government	
		OTHERS	
Senate Ethics Officer First created 2005	Ethics and Conflict of Interest Code for Senators	**Mandate:** – *maintain and enhance public confidence and trust in the integrity of senators and Senate* – *provide greater certainty and guidance for senators when dealing with foreseeable real or apparent conflicts of interest* – *establish clear standards and a transparent system so questions relating to proper conduct may be addressed by an independent, non-partisan adviser* **Vision:** through our work, senators will be well-supported in fulfilling their responsibilities under the Ethics and Conflict of Interest Code for Senators in order to maintain and enhance public confidence and trust in the integrity of each senator and in the Senate **Mission:** administer, interpret, and apply the Code and provide sound, timely, independent advice to senators regarding their obligations under the Code in a non-partisan, responsive, and effective manner	Integrity Excellence Respect for people, teamwork, and quality of life

compliance-based approaches, others are mainly compliance based. Regardless of the adoption of a code of ethics or a more formal statement of public ethics and values, all provincial jurisdictions have at the very least adopted some form of value statement outlining the desired values of the public servants and the institutions to which they belong. Table 20.3 outlines the ethics regime in the federal government as well as in each of the 10 provincial jurisdictions.

British Columbia

Under the purview of the British Columbia Public Service Agency, the *Standards of Conduct for Public Service Employees* enumerates six values to which public servants must adhere. Unlike the more aspirational

documents of other provinces, the BC approach includes multiple reporting mechanisms. Within the *Standard*, employees of the public service have a "duty to report" potential situations that could be at odds with the stated values and ethical standards desired in the BC Public Service. While there is no stand-alone reporting mechanism, the use of existing mechanisms through collective bargaining units are maintained with an alternate appeal to the deputy minister where an employee may not fall under one of the two listed bargaining groups. Of the provincial ethics regimes, British Columbia's is among the most regimented, with duties assigned both to management and employees within an organization. There is the option of an external review by designated authorities if the individual is not satisfied with the

Table 20.3   Canadian Public-Sector Ethics

Jurisdiction	Values/Ethics Code? Yes/No Document Name Responsible Agency	Values and Expected Ethical Behaviour	Administration and Resolution Mechanism or Enforcement Process
Federal	Yes *Values and Ethics Code for the Public Sector* Treasury Board Secretariat	Values and Expected Behaviour: Respect for democracy Respect for people Integrity Stewardship Excellence Impartiality Confidentiality	Public servants are provided with the opportunity to report violations of the code to "their immediate supervisor, their senior officer for disclosure, or the Public Sector Integrity Commissioner." Members of the public may also report potential breaches of the code either to a designated representative in an organization or to the Public Sector Integrity Commissioner.
British Columbia	Yes *Standards of Conduct for Public Service Employees* BC Public Service Agency	Loyalty Confidentiality Public comments Political activity Service to the public Workplace behaviour	Administered by individual agencies and departments with responsibilities designated to deputy ministers, line managers, and employees Employees are determined to have a "duty to report" potential situations in accordance with the provisions of the relevant collective bargaining agreement, or in the case where none exists, in writing to the deputy minister. The allegation may be further pursued through an appropriate authority as designated by the Standards of Conduct.
Alberta	Yes *Code of Conduct and Ethics for the Public Service of Alberta* Public Service Commissioner	Impartiality Disclosure Furthering private interests Dealings with others Outside employment Teaching Volunteer activities Investment and management of private assets Acceptance of gifts Political activity Public statements Dealings in Crown land Acquiring permits or licences for Crown minerals or resources	Administered by the Deputy Head of each organization with the option to "issue supplementary departments instructions" provided they are not less restrictive than the Code. Internally, the Code and the appropriate remedies, exemptions, or permissions are obtained through the Deputy Head. A review of a Deputy Head's decision would be undertaken through the Ethics Commissioner. Further clarification is also provided in the Administrative Guidelines to clarify the application of the Code.
Saskatchewan	No *Conflict of Interest Guidelines* and the *Public Interest Disclosure Act (pida)* Public Service Commission	To show respect and integrity To serve citizens To practice excellence and innovation To act as one team	There is no single authority or group of authorities responsible for the administration of ethical behaviour within government. Rather, a number of different documents govern the behaviour of public servants on matters such as conflict of interest and whistle-blower protection.
Manitoba	No. *Value and Ethics Guide* Civil Service Commission	Act in the public interest Act with integrity Act with respect for others Act with skill and dedication	The Value and Ethics Guide is not enforced on a departmental basis. Rather, it is deemed to apply to all civil servants. Individual employees are directed to their manager for additional information. No provision is available within the Guide for complaints or remedies.

continued

Table 20.3   *continued*

Jurisdiction	Values/Ethics Code? Yes/No Document Name Responsible Agency	Values and Expected Ethical Behaviour	Administration and Resolution Mechanism or Enforcement Process
Ontario	No. Numerous directives Treasury Board Secretariat	Trust Fairness Diversity Excellence Creativity Collaboration Efficiency Responsiveness	The Ontario Treasury Board Secretariat houses the various directives related to the ethical actions of Ontario's public servants. Each directive or set of directives offers its own compliance requirements.
Quebec	Yes. *Déclaration de valeurs de l'administration publique Québécoise* and *Regulation respecting ethics and discipline in the public service* Secrétariat du Conseil du Trésor.	Competency Loyalty Impartiality Respect Integrity	The Quebec regulation on ethics in the public service provides for the deputy minister or chief executive officer of a department or agency to ensure compliance with the regulation. Disciplinary measures ranging from reprimands to dismissal are available to the deputy minister. The values declaration provides for no enforcement mechanisms.
New Brunswick	No *New Brunswick Public Service Values and Conduct Guide* Office of Human Resources	Integrity Respect Impartiality Service Competence	This document is presented as a "statement" on public service values. There is no enforcement mechanism and responsibility for its implementation is not formally assigned.
Nova Scotia	Yes *Values, Ethics & Conduct: A Code for Nova Scotia's Public Servants* Public Service Commission	Respect Integrity Diversity Accountability Public good	This document is administered by the deputy head of the individual government department or agency. Within departments, the deputy has the authority to provide additional requirements or guidance depending on the "unique responsibilities or requirements contained in the statutes affecting their specific department." There is no enforcement mechanism within the Code. However, it does emphasize the self-assessment and peer assessment of ethical dilemmas within the workforce.
Prince Edward Island	No. *Human Resource Policy and Procedures Manual* Public Service Commission of PEI.	Respect, diversity and inclusion Collaboration, confidentiality and compassion Dedication and commitment Lifelong learning and development	Without a code of conduct or a guide on ethical behaviour, there is no authority responsible for administration of ethical actions. However, the Public Service Commission does include two documents that tangentially apply to ethical behaviour: the *Human Resource Policy and Procedures Manual* and the 2015–2017 PEI *Public Service Commission Business and Human Resources Plan*.
Newfoundland and Labrador	No. Numerous HR policies Public Service Commission	Fairness Respect Professionalism	Individual policies, including the Conflict of Interest Act, matters relating to political activity and the discipline policy are provided by the Public Service Commission. Each has its own requirements.

original response (Standards of Conduct, 8–9). At nine pages in length, the Standards of Conduct for the BC Public Service focuses on the expansion to a values-based approach while at the same time ensuring a compliance-based approach remains.

Alberta

Similar to the British Columbia's *Standard of Conduct,* the *Code of Conduct and Ethics for the Public Service of Alberta* includes value statements and a reporting mechanism through the Alberta Ethics Commissioner. Of the provincial regimes, the Alberta code is the most comprehensive in terms of value statements as well as more general statements on expected behaviours and guidance in situations where ethical behaviour may be compromised. Four examples of these behaviours are outside employment, teaching, volunteer activities, and political activity. In each of these four situations, employees are advised of the parameters within which they may participate in these activities (Code of Conduct and Ethics, 7–9).

The Code of Conduct and Ethics for the Public Service of Alberta is administered separately in each government department by the individual deputy head. However, an appeal mechanism is available to an employee through application to the Alberta Ethics Commissioner. The Alberta code also contains the option for disciplinary measures, including the option of dismissal in extreme cases (Code of Conduct and Ethics, 13–14). Like Alberta, the values are highlighted, but the compliance remains.

Saskatchewan

Saskatchewan does not have a single document or code containing the ethical actions and duties of its public servants. However, like other provinces, it does offer a series of legislative and regulatory documents related to ethical conduct and action in government by public servants. This includes the *Conflict of Interest Guidelines* as well as the *Public Interest Disclosure Act,* often referred to as whistle-blowing legislation. The whistle-blower legislation stems from the Saskatchewan Party's 2007 platform commitment to strengthen "protection for public servants and whistle-blowers in the workplace by establishing a Public Integrity Commissioner" (Saskatchewan Party, 2007: 42). Despite the lack of a formal code of conduct, the public service itself has statement of core values (Government of Saskatchewan, 2013). While not a codified document, it does reflect the similar values approach of Canadian ethics regimes.

Manitoba

The Civil Service Commission of Manitoba provides public servants with guidance through its *Value and Ethics Guide.* The Guide, implemented in 2007, outlines four broad categories within which public servants are expected to act: act in the public interest, act with integrity, act with respect for others, and act with skill and dedication (Values and Ethics Guide, 2). The Manitoba example is wholly values-based in its approach. There is neither an enforcement nor a disciplinary mechanism directly associated to the *Value and Ethics Guide.* Rather, the guide is provided to "support [civil service members] in all of their work-related and provisional activities" (3). Within each of the four broad categories, civil servants are provided with a definition of the values as well as how those values may be applied in practice. In some cases, other legislation or regulations are cited to provide additional guidance.

Despite the values-based approach, the Guide came under fire from Manitoba's Auditor General in a March 2014 report for its lack of codification. Specifically, the Auditor General recommends the creation of a code of conduct that ensures a role for "senior management in overseeing implementation and compliance with the policy" (Office of the Auditor General – Manitoba, 308). Even within government, this demonstrates the necessity of a codified values-based document with, not only buy-in from senior management, but also clearly defined roles in its implementation.

Ontario

In some cases, the provincial legislation/frameworks reflect the federal approach. This is evidenced not only in the similar value statements, but also in the enforcement and resolution regimes. However, in other cases—most notably Ontario—the provincial regime rests on a compliance-based approach with only tangential statements on values and ethics. While the Ontario Public Service provides eight values that "guide [its] behaviour and relationships" (Ontario Public Service, 2007), it is not contained within a more general discussion of values and ethics in the public service.

As in other jurisdictions, the Office of the Integrity Commissioner applies to only a small fraction of Ontario civil servants: mainly ministerial staff. With no code of conduct or statement of values and ethics, the Ontario Public Service is guided by a series of compliance-based directives issued by the Treasury Board Secretariat (Treasury Board Secretariat, 2016). With a series of directives focused on the nuts and bolts of public service action, the Government of Ontario, once a leader, lags behind its provincial counterparts in its adoption of a blended compliance and values-based ethics regime. However, as mentioned at the beginning of this chapter, Ontario is currently preparing a suite of legislation similar to the 2006 Federal Accountability Act.

Quebec

In 2002, the Government of Quebec moved to consolidate its ethics regime into two documents, thereby solidifying both the compliance-based approach to ethical action in the public service as well as a values-based approach. The first document, the *Regulation Respecting Ethics and Discipline in the Public Service*, addresses both the duties of public servants and the disciplinary measures that accompany a violation of said duties. Through the more aspirational document, the *Declaration of Values in the Quebec Public Service*, public servants are provided five values around which to conduct themselves. This document replaced a previous regulation from 1985. Quebec entwines the two approaches, and in a way mirrors the federal approach. Of note, however is that there are no compliance mechanisms associated with the Declaration of Values.

New Brunswick

The New Brunswick *Public Service Values and Conduct Guide* is more of an aspirational document than a code of ethics. In fact, the document itself states that it is an affirmation of the "fundamental values to which public servants are committed" (New Brunswick Public Service Values and Conduct Guide, 3). However, within each of the five values stated, the Guide does provide a series of specific advice on ways in which public servants ought to conduct themselves (New Brunswick Public Service Values and Conduct Guide, 4–6). As a comparison, the

Manitoba and New Brunswick approaches to values and ethics in the public service are similar. These two examples, if successful, may provide a future basis for a values-based-only approach.

Nova Scotia

Like Alberta's code of conduct, *Values, Ethics & Conduct: A Code for Nova Scotia's Public Servants* is administered by each ministry or agency's deputy head. Each individual deputy head may choose to supplement the code with "procedures and guidance with respect to unique responsibilities and requirements" (Values, Ethics & Conduct, 19). The individual deputy head is accountable through the Treasury and Policy Board. Of the provincial regimes, Nova Scotia's most values the application of the code's values to an ongoing public service setting. The code states that "our five values guide us when making every decision, especially when our decisions are most difficult" (Values, Ethics & Conduct, 16). This code provides the example of the linkages between the values of public service in the abstract and the implementation of ethical values and behaviour in practice.

Prince Edward Island

As a province in the minority without a codified or written ethics document or regime, Prince Edward Island nonetheless has a statement of values for its public service (PEI Public Service Commission Business and Human Resources Plan, 1). However, without an ethics regime to govern its implementation, the task of ensuring ethical behaviour within the PEI Public Service rests with more general documents, including the *Human Resource Policy and Procedures Manual* and the 2015–2017 *PEI Public Service Commission Business and Human Resources Plan*.

Newfoundland and Labrador

Like its Atlantic neighbour, Prince Edward Island, Newfoundland and Labrador does not have a values and ethics code. However, like PEI it does state a series of values to which its public service adheres (Public Service Commission, 2015). Without a values and ethics code, Newfoundland and Labrador is left to manage and encourage ethical behaviour through other means, including education and hiring practices.

The Provinces: A Hodgepodge but Consistent Values

While each province has adopted a provincial approach to an office similar to the federal conflict of interest and ethics commissioner, there has yet to develop a consistent approach to public service values and ethics.

The ethics landscape in Canada continues to evolve. As scandals and controversies ebb and flow, provinces react and implement measures. Whether a consistent approach develops is yet to be seen, however the clear consensus appears to be forming through the use of both compliance and value mechanisms combined with an extensive focus on educational training and learning opportunities. In each province where a values-based code of conduct has been established, the province nonetheless maintains compliance-based enforcement, including conflict-of-interest measures and disciplinary measures for non-compliance.

Whether a province has a values and ethics code, a guide, or simply a statement of its values, the similarities of public service values across jurisdictions demonstrate convergence, which in time will be reflected in the regimes. The themes of confidentiality, respect, professionalism, and integrity appear throughout the different jurisdictions.

Finally, a values and ethics code is only a piece of paper if it is not embraced within an organization and enhanced through training and education. Whether it is through the Canada School of Public Service's educational programming, New Brunswick's i-learn system, or Saskatchewan's online learning portal, the training and education of public servants on ethical conduct provides the link between values in a code or document, and values exhibited by individual public servants. Without a clear values education, the chasm between the expectation of ethical action and the reality of ongoing ethical lapses and scandals will remain wide.

Continuing Problems, Elusive Solutions

When reviewing the ethics regimes put in place over the past 40 years throughout Canada, an observer is struck by the amount of effort, careful thought, and energy expended in creating and operating them. Are they effective, though, if so many scandals come to light that involve elected and permanent public officials? The answer is mixed. According to Ian Greene's study of ethics commissioners in Canada, in the period following the creation of these independent offices (1984–2004), "in every jurisdiction, except Manitoba, there was a drop—quite often dramatic—in the number of substantiated conflict of interest events" (Greene, 2009: 14). He noted that the sample size for Manitoba was too small to be reliable. He attributes the drop in numbers to the ability of public office holders to access the advice of the offices to help them navigate through ambiguous situations and to use that advice to resist party pressures to behave in way that makes them uncomfortable (Greene, 2009: 14).

This trend is consistent with the trend in other countries and regimes. Nastase notes the increase in awareness of ethics in the European Commission, the UK, and the US after hardline approaches to corruption and scandals have been taken (Nastase, 2013: 78–9; Roberts, 2009). However, the general conclusion is that more work needs to be done and these measures have only been partly effective. Some probable reasons for this mixed result in many countries are suggested below.

Mixed Ethics Regimes and Limited Thought

One leading argument for ethics regimes being less effective than expected in many countries including Canada rests in the hybrid nature of ethics regimes. Nastase argues that the blending of compliance-based and integrity-based ethics approaches has meant that there is a diversity of tools available to control misbehaviour and misgovernment. However, it also has meant that there is a continuing tendency to frame ethics management as a cure for corruption rather than as an opportunity to create excellence in people and the public service. The compliance-based approach diminishes the need and desire to move towards a more effective values-based approach that changes the way people think about their work (Nastase, 2013: 76–7, 78–9). The thinking embedded in the ethics regime remains reflexive rather than becoming reflective and proactive with conscious ownership of actions and the consequences.

Atkinson and Fulton would concur with Nastase that more careful reflection is essential to ethical governance. In their study of the sponsorship scandal in Canada, they conclude that the focus of ethics management was on creating rules that would regulate behaviour based on the interests of the actor (compliance, moral agency theory). However, the more effective approach to ethics management lies in effecting a cognitive shift. As they state: "Adherence without reflection imbeds questionable acts inside the organization's operational code; they may require periodic affirmation but they do not require reflective reassessment" (Atkinson & Fulton, 2013: 407). As they proceed to explain, "Where decisions are made that resemble one another, or are part of an established pattern, the result is routinization and normalization that insulate decision makers from confronting alternative interpretations of what their acts mean" (Atkinson & Fulton, 2013: 407). The actors become ethically numb. Even if rules and checks exist, they are brushed aside and bad decisions continue to reinforce one another and the path of behaviour. The "in-group" exempts its members from "publicly proclaimed expectations." They argue that this is the only possible explanation for why the sponsorship scandal was able to continue unchecked for so long (Atkinson & Fulton, 2013: 408).

The only antidote to the creation of these types of perverse subcultures is through active moral engagement, in essence the creation of a learning culture where the values and ethics are "practiced regularly and triggered when necessary" (Atkinson & Fulton, 2013: 407). Webs of rules are not enough. But the antidote is not simply a move to an integrity-based or values-based approach as Nastase (2013), Geuras and Garofalo (2011), and others (Christensen and Laegreid, 2011; Martinez 2009; Martinez and Richardson, 2008) would suggest, because the same pattern of in-group thinking can occur. Instead, the experiences in Canadian, US, and European systems suggest that a combination of rules and values needs to be supplemented by contrarian thinking that prompts deeper critical reflection about decisions in a department or group.

Westminster Model and Ethics for Canadian Public Servants

The introduction of values and ethics in the Canadian public service has had some success. In his study of the effectiveness of recent public management reforms in the federal public service, Phil Charko states

unequivocally that "Values and ethics have changed the culture of public service. The awareness of a conflict of interest and the number of confidential reports has increased. In many departments, there is a healthy dialogue on topics never previously discussed" (Charko, 2013: 108). He offers three examples as evidence: one involving a discussion of the ethical implications of an expected action, another involving a refusal to be pressured to work outside the contracting rules, and last, the fact that bullying is being addressed in the federal public service. This raised awareness leads to better, more conscious decisions. The contrarian thinking desired by Atkinson and Fulton is more present in the public service. Public servants are more likely now to question the alignment of particular policies and decisions with the ethics policy and code and, although the whistle-blowing legislation and integrity offices have not had the transformative effect on government that advocates wished, public servants are empowered to question and identify wrongdoing (Atkinson & Fulton, 2013: 108) In his assessment of values and ethics management, Charko (2013: 108) concludes that progress has been made "but more work needs to be done."

More Work Is Necessary

More work is needed for three key reasons. First, the move towards values and ethics as a means of ensuring public servants perform their work properly and well obfuscates the traditional means of holding public servants accountable. Savoie looks at the ethics and values approach as embedded within the new public management reforms that emphasize performance accountability over procedural accountability, the traditional form of accountability in the Westminster Model. Mark his words:

> By relying on centrally prescribed rules, procedural or administrative accountability had a greater capacity to find the culprit and provide redress in cases of maladministration. Hierarchy enables one to go up and down the organization to see who does what, and centrally prescribed procedures enable one to be able to determine if they have been respected. One can fudge performance and evaluation reports, but it is much more difficult to fudge adherence to rules. (Savoie, 2015: 132)

Introducing a values approach to ethics in this new public management world is particularly dangerous:

> Some outside government have argued that the government should be very careful in replacing a "rules approach" with a "values approach," making the point that, if the role of the public service is limited to supporting and serving the government of the day, then a shift away from a rules-based approach could have significant implications. Values, the argument goes, operate on a higher level of abstraction than do rules and regulations. Accountability requirements are more certain under rules and regulations than under a values-based approach (Savoie, 2015: 135; see also Langford, 2004).

Savoie follows this analysis with a wry commentary on the number of scandals breaking and examples of senior officials seeking their own personal interests at the same time that senior public servants, consultants, and task force members were discussing and promoting values and ethics in government. The move towards a values-based approach to ethics attenuates the lines of accountability in government to the detriment of the public interest. Kernaghan and Langford (2014: 214) counter that classic accountability is not the answer, but the way forward is not clear.

A second problem concerns the definition of values being used. Charko (2013: 108) notes the inconsistency between professional values and democratic values. However, John Langford has offered the most trenchant critique of the values-based approach. He begins with the point made later by Savoie that the abstract nature of values fits a private corporate culture more than a public one (Langford, 2004: 433). When proposed by the ethics task force, the list of values was too long and an incoherent mix of ideas and principles (Langford, 2004). He argues that clustering values results in inconsistencies, value-shopping, and value pluralism. The public servant is left with little firm guidance and no way to prioritize values. Instead of leading to a thoughtful, meaningful exercise, applying the values can be frustrating, subjective, and conflictual if different interpretations result (Langford, 2004: 439–41). In a particularly scathing passage, Langford writes that public servants "cannot see in practical terms what the difference is between an ethical value and values labelled

as 'democratic,' 'professional' and 'people,' and they are confused about the appropriateness of referring to so-called non-ethical values when dealing with ethical choices" (Langford, 2004: 442).

Twelve years later, the clusters and problems remain in the *Values and Ethics Code for the Public Service* (Treasury Board Secretariat, 2016: 7–10). Is it more understandable, then, why progress with ethics in government has been slow and inconsistent? Unlike Nastase and Atkinson, Langford suggests that the better approach to ethics might lie in moving towards the consequentialist or teleological approach to ethics, which is more consistent with the ways that public servants reason. Strict adherence to principles and moral precepts can be too constraining in serving the public interest (Langford, 2004: 443–445). However, as mentioned above, this approach alone has weaknesses as well.

A third important challenge in the ethics regime in Canada concerns the role of the public service in the policy process and its relationship to the democratically elected government. The *Values and Ethics Code for the Public Service* states that:

> The Code should be read in the context of the duties and responsibilities set out in *A Guide for Ministers and Secretaries of State*.
>
> Ministers are responsible for preserving public confidence in the integrity of management and operations within their departments and for maintaining the tradition of political neutrality of the Public Service and its continuing ability to provide professional, candid and frank advice (Treasury Board Secretariat, 2016: 6–7).

This statement is problematic for three reasons. First, it inverts the traditional role of the minister and department. Instead of the minister being responsible and answerable to Parliament and the people for all actions undertaken by the department, the minister is now responsible for preserving public confidence in the operation of the department and protecting public servants—not for preserving integrity of management but preserving public confidence. The minister has in effect become the public relations servant of the public servants.

Second, the minister is to preserve the ability of the public service to provide frank and fearless advice. Does this mean ensuring that the public service is well-funded with what it defines as adequate staffing?

Further, the code does not put offering advice in context or in the traditional administrative-policy dichotomy of the elected government making policy decisions and the public service offering advice on implementation and feasibility. What if the government's chosen policies deviate substantively from the public servant's professional ethics (e.g., advance directives in assisted dying and medical doctors offering advice) or from the public servant's professional opinion of whether they improve the quality of service for the public? Potentially, the ethics code could put public servants in a professional stand-off with the elected government.

This problem is not restricted to the *Ethics Code* but is one of the consequences of new public management as well (Demmke & Moilanen, 2012) . A more empowered, ethically conscious, and activist public service intent on serving the public interest as it defines it rather than as how the elected leaders define the public interest can result in tensions between the public service and government (see also Aucoin, 2008; Kernaghan & Langford, 2014: 219–29; note Jarvis, 2016). The *Ethics Code* encourages the public service to act in accordance with their understanding of professional values. Under democratic values, it reminds them to "loyally implement ministerial decisions" (Jarvis, 2016: 7). The incoherence and contradictions in values noted by Langford are apparent here. How does a public servant reconcile these messages? Interpretations multiply with the *Code* providing limited guidance to resolving dilemmas that arise in the course of doing business. However, if, as Jacob, Imbeau, and Bélanger (2011: 211) conclude in their study of ethics in the Quebec government, public managers have much less discretion, particularly over financial matters, than was promised with the implementation of new public management, then they will have little opportunity to apply the ethics principles or reason to think about them seriously. Savoie's caution that rules and traditional lines of accountability may provide more direction, clarity, and accountability than values-based ethics might be worth considering in either case. Duty ethics become important but also have weaknesses.

Diversity in and of Ethics

A final consideration about the effectiveness of ethics regimes in Canada arises out of the above considerations but is also distinct. As mentioned, ethics codes can encourage subjective interpretations by individuals who must apply them in particular situations. Education and advice by ethics commissioners and integrity officers is limited: recall that the federal commissioner has a mandate to serve 2200 people. As a result, understandings may develop within enclaves as Atkinson and Fulton point out or even on an individual level in the course of work. This tendency towards plural interpretations is reinforced by the increasing diversity of the Canadian public service and Canadian society. Jordan and Gray note that the difficulties of intercultural communication of ethics affect the operation of the public service in an increasingly globalized and cosmopolitan world. Public servants come from deeply different cultural and historical ethical traditions. At the international level but also within states, "public administrators will increasingly encounter norms from other cultures that appear opaque, incomprehensible, and (at extremes) even irrational" (Jordan & Gray, 2011: 12).

Politicians and public servants dealing with people from different racial, cultural, and ethnic backgrounds will increasingly need to learn to apply the values differently if they wish to show respect to all communities. Similarly, colleagues within government may be faced with conflicting values and norms. For example, how are the values of respect and equality to be reconciled if one colleague objects to working with a colleague of another religion or sex on religious grounds? Interestingly, codes tend to be adopted when common understandings of norms are challenged or broken down. This would suggest that the values and ethics being adopted in Canadian governments may be contentious and subject to shifting interpretations and inconsistent implementation for some time.

Conclusion

Scandals, misgovernment, over-government, maladministration, and malfeasance will continue to happen. The media will delight in pursuing these stories both as a part of their democratic duty to inform the public and serve as a check on political ambition and abuse and as a part of their obligation to attract and retain an audience. Canadians will be shocked and dismayed. And more controls will be proposed in government to curb such behaviour. This is the normal cycle of government in Canada as in other countries.

The strength of the Canadian system is that rather than tolerating a relatively low number of significant ethical breaches, its actors attempt to prevent such behaviour from recurring and remain vigilant on the whole. The review of the ethics regimes in the federal and provincial jurisdictions in Canada captures the serious efforts being made to ensure that Canadians are well-governed in accordance with fundamental democratic norms and expectations. However, the means of controlling these breaches of ethics are in flux and in a constant state of improvement. The challenges continue, particularly as public-sector reforms alter the traditional norms of accountability and Canada becomes more diverse. The move away from a compliance-based approach to a values-based approach to ethics is occurring across the country but is fraught with difficulties in itself. Still, the dialogue about ethics and values is promoting awareness and moral engagement as witnessed by the drop in ethical infractions in recent years. More needs to be done but "how?" remains the complex task.

Should Canada continue to embrace the values approach? If so, then the emphasis must be placed on devising a learning culture that will encourage moral engagement and a thoughtful dialogue on integrity and values in the Canadian governing system. Rather than build on one theory of ethics, public office holders might be wise to follow Gueras and Garofalo's advice to apply ethics using questions drawn from the three main ethical theories as well as moral relativism. Virtue theory, consequentialism, and duty theory applied together will provide more insights into issues as they arise and help policy-makers to make the right decision. A system that combines compliance-based ethics with values-based ethics and emphasizes prophylactic procedures such as education, good advice from ethics officers however defined in the system, and contrarian thinking may be the most effective ethics system possible for identifying, preventing, and correcting bad behaviour. A mixed system, as Atkinson and others suggest, will encourage the reflection on right behaviour necessary among public-sector officials, whereas a unidimensional approach may not encourage serious thought and the inculcation of values so critical to making good decisions in the public interest. The mixed system is more likely to capture the grey areas of public behaviour that influence perceptions of ethical governance.

Will scandals still occur? Yes, human nature being what it is, people will go astray. The mixed ethics regime means that some bad behaviour will go on. Will wrongdoing be caught and punished or corrected? Yes, much will but some won't. That is the nature of public life. Will Canadians call for tighter controls and strive for more in governments. Yes, Canadians will continue to muddle through the world of ethics with generally good but occasionally variable results, all the while aspiring to be better. After all, that is what we do best.

Important Terms and Concepts

accountability	integrity	public-sector ethics
compliance-based ethical programs	morality	values-based or integrity-based
ethics	new public management	approaches to ethics

Study Questions

1. Given the plethora of ethics violations in recent years, would you say that past ethics regimes have failed?
2. What have been some advantages of having had ethics regimes in place in Canada in the past several decades?
3. Which of the three leading ethics theories seems the most compelling, if any? Is one closer to your personal sense of ethics?

4. Review the case for compliance-based ethical programs, values-based or integrity-based approaches to ethics, and a combination of the two. Which is the best approach, on balance?
5. Is it an advantage or a disadvantage to have diversity in ethics regimes in Canada?

Note

1   Kathy L. Brock is Professor, School of Policy Studies and Department of Political Studies (Cross-Appointed) at Queen's University, Kingston, Ontario. John L. Nater is an elected member of the Parliament of Canada and a doctoral candidate, Department of Political Science, Western University.

References

Aristotle. 1962. *Nicomachean Ethics*. Translated and annotated by Martin Oswald. Indianapolis: Bobbs-Merrill.

Atkinson, Michael M. 2011. "Discrepancies in Perceptions of Corruption, or Why Is Canada So Corrupt?" *Political Science Quarterly* 126, 3 (Fall), pp. 445–64.

Atkinson, Michael. M. and Murray Fulton. 2013. "Understanding Public Sector Ethics: Beyond Agency Theory in Canada's Sponsorship Scandal." *International Public Management Journal* 16, 3, pp. 386–412.

Aucoin, Peter. 2008. "New Public Management and New Public Governance: Finding the Balance" *Professionalism and Public Service: Essays in Honour of Kenneth Kernaghan*, edited by David Siegel and Ken Rasmussen, Toronto: Institute of Public Administration of Canada and University of Toronto Press, pp. 16–33.

Barber, Michael. 2015. *How to Run a Government so That Citizens Benefit and Taxpayers Don't Go Crazy*. UK: Penguin Books.

Boyce, Gordon and Cindy Davis. 2009. "Conflict of Interest in Policing and the Public Sector." *Public Management Review* 11, 5, pp. 601–40.

Charko, Phil. 2013. "Management Improvement in the Canadian Public Service, 1999–2010." *Canadian Public Administration* 56, 1, pp. 91–120.

Christensen, Tom and Per Laegreid. 2011. "Ethics and Administrative Reforms: A Study of Ethical Guidelines in the Central Civil Service." *Public Management Review* 13, 3, pp. 459–77.

Cox, Raymond W., editor. 2009. *Ethics and Integrity in Public Administration: Concepts and Cases*. Armonk, NY: M.E. Sharpe.

Dawson, Mary (Conflict of Interest and Ethics Commissioner of Canada). 2016. *The 2015–2016 Annual Report in Respect of the Conflict of Interest Act*. Ottawa: Office of the Conflict of Interest and Ethics Commissioner, Parliament of Canada.

Demmke, Christoph and Timo Moilanen. 2012. *Effectiveness of Public-Service Ethics and Good Governance in the Central Administration of the EU-27: Evaluating Reform Outcomes in the Context of the Financial Crisis*. Frankfurt am Main: Peter Lang.

Garofalo, Charles. 2008. "With Deference to Woodrow Wilson: The Ethics-Administration Dichotomy in American Public Service." *Public Integrity* 10, 4 (Fall), pp. 345–54.

Geuras, Dean and Charles Garofalo. 2011. *Practical Ethics in Public Administration*. 3rd edn, Vienna, VA: Management Concepts. E-book version available on Kobo.

Gow, J.I. 2008. "Between Ideals and Obedience: A Practical Basis for Public Service Ethics." *Professionalism and Public Service: Essays in Honour of Kenneth Kernaghan*, edited by David Siegel and Ken Rasmussen, Toronto: Institute of Public Administration of Canada and University of Toronto Press, 99–126.

Greene, Ian and David P. Shugarman. 1997. *Honest Politics: Seeking Integrity in Canadian Public Life*. Toronto: James Lorimer and Company.

Greene, Ian. 2009. "The Evolution of the Office of the Ethics Commissioner in Canada." https://www.cpsa-acsp.ca/papers-2009/Greene.pdf.

Jacob, Steve, Louis M. Imbeau, and Jean-François Bélanger. 2011. La nouvelle gestion publique et l'accroissement des marges de manoeuvre: un terreau propice au développement de l'"ethique?" *Canadian Public Administration* 54, 2 (June), pp. 189–215.

Jarvis, Mark. 2016. *Creating a High-Performing Canadian Civil Service Against a Backdrop of Disruptive Change*. Mowat Research #22. Toronto: Mowat Centre, School of Public Policy & Governance, University of Toronto.

Jordan, Sara R. and Phillip W. Gray. 2011. *The Ethics of Public Administration: The Challenges of Global Governance*. Waco, TX: Baylor University Press.

Kernaghan, Kenneth and John Langford. 2014. *The Responsible Public Servant*, 2nd edn, Toronto: Institute of Public Administration of Canada.

Langford, John W. 2004. "Acting on Values: An Ethical Dead End for Public Servants." *Canadian Public Administration* 47, 4 (Winter), pp. 429–50.

Lawton, Alan, Julie Rayner, and Karin Lasthuizen. 2012. *Ethics and Management in the Public Sector*. New York: Routledge.

Lynch, Thomas Dexter and Cynthia E. Lynch. 2009. "Democratic Morality: Back to the Future." *Ethics and Integrity in Public Administration: Concepts and Cases*, edited by Raymond W. Cox, Armonk, NY: M.E. Sharpe, pp. 5–25.

Macauley, Michael. 2009. "The I That Is We: Recognition and Administrative Ethics." *Ethics and Integrity in Public Administration: Concepts and Cases*. edited by Raymond W. Cox, Armonk, NY: M.E. Sharpe, pp. 26–39.

Martinez, J. Michael. 2009. *Public Administration Ethics for the 21st Century*. Santa Barbara: ABC-CLIO.

Martinez, J. Michael and William D. Richardson. 2008. *Administrative Ethics in the Twenty-First Century*. New York: Peter Lang.

Menzel, Donald C. 2007. *Ethics Management for Public Administrators: Building Organizations of Integrity*. Armonk, NY: M.E. Sharpe.

Menzel, Donald C. 2015. "Research on Ethics and Integrity in Public Administration: Moving Forward, Looking Back." *Public Integrity* 17, pp. 343–70.

Nastase, Andreea. 2013. "Managing Ethics in the European Commission Services: From Rules to Values?" *Public Management Review* 15, 1, pp. 63–81.

Putnam, Robert D. 2000. *Bowling Alone: The Collapse and Revival of American Community*. NY: Simon and Schuster.

Roberts, Robert. 2009. "The Rise of Compliance-Based Ethics Management: Implications for Organizational Ethics." *Public Integrity* 11, 3, pp. 261–77.

Savoie, Donald J. 2008. *Court Government and the Collapse of Accountability*. Toronto: Institute of Public Administration of Canada and University of Toronto Press.

Savoie, Donald J. 2015. *What Is Government Good At? A Canadian Answer*. Montreal and Kingston: McGill-Queen's University Press.

Siegel, David and Ken Rasmussen, editors. 2008. *Professionalism and Public Service: Essays in Honour of Kenneth Kernaghan*. Toronto; Institute of Public Administration of Canada and University of Toronto Press.

Snellman, Carita Lillian. 2015. "Ethics Management: How to Achieve Ethical Organizations and Management?" *Business, Management and Education* 13, 2, pp. 336–57.

Treasury Board of Canada Secretariat. 2016. *Values and Ethics Code for the Public Service*. Ottawa: Minister of Public Works and Government Services. First created in 2003.

Wolf, Jonathan. 2011. *Ethics and Public Policy: A Philosophical Inquiry*. New York: Routledge.

Gendering Canadian Public Administration

Tammy Findlay[1]

Chapter Overview

This chapter outlines some of the ways that a feminist analysis can advance our understanding of public administration by **gendering** it. Gendering means that we consciously aim to make gender differences visible and to expose gender biases. Gendering draws our attention to the ways that women's inequality gets reproduced and how both women's and men's lives are restricted by socially constructed gender roles. It allows us to correct faulty assumptions, ask new questions, and assess possibilities for change in governmental processes and policies.

Gendering is important for public administration as an academic field and as a professional practice. Many scholars and practitioners have drawn attention to the need for a stronger gender lens in public administration (Bacchi, 1999; D'Agostino and Levine, 2011; Findlay, 2015a; Phillips, Little, and Goodine, 1997; Stivers, 1993). And public administration is important for feminism. Women are the majority of workers in the public sector. Women rely more on public services. Women are the primary activists in many areas of policy advocacy (Andrew, 2010; Findlay, 2015a; Rice & Prince, 2013). This makes public administration a vital focal point for feminist analysis and action.

This chapter is organized into four sections. It begins with a general discussion of the relationship between gender, the state, and bureaucracy. It then moves on to review some of the "machinery" that has been created inside governments to represent women. Next, it turns to a discussion of feminist approaches to public policy analysis. Finally, it explores the gendered character of public-sector employment.

Chapter Objectives

By the end of this chapter, students will be able to do the following:
- Understand the differences between the experiences of women and men with the state and with public policy.

- Outline the ways in which the bureaucracy is a gendered institution.
- Explain the impact of new public management (NPM) on women.
- Describe the various types of women's policy machinery and how they have changed over time.
- Compare and contrast gender-based analysis (GBA) and intersectional policy analysis and identify their strengths and weaknesses.
- Define representative bureaucracy, and summarize the debates surrounding it.

Gender, the State, and Bureaucracy

Feminist Analysis of the State

The state is ever-present in our lives. But women's relationship with the state is much different from men's. Rice and Prince (2013) actually refer to "his" and "her" welfare states to draw attention to these vastly divergent realities. Feminist scholars have shown that the state is gendered in its structures, processes, and policies.

Those needs in our lives that are believed appropriate for the state to provide are considered the public sphere. The private sphere generally includes the family and the market. The shifting parameters of this **public/private divide**, and their implications for gender relations, are a principal focus of feminist analysis. Which issues are thought of as public or state responsibilities, and which are left to the private sphere, matters greatly for gender equality. Ideas about how responsibilities are distributed between the public and private spheres depend on ideology. In political science, ideology is defined in terms of a set of beliefs and basic values about "big questions," such as how to structure the economy and society, and what is the proper role of government. What is typically forgotten is that ideas about gender roles and families are equally integral to ideology.

Feminist political economists use the concept of **social reproduction** to name the work that is done for the daily and generational reproduction of the labouring population, such as caregiving and domestic maintenance (Bezanson & Luxton, 2006). In countries like Canada, this work is routinely unpaid or undervalued, done by women, and remains largely invisible to society. However, there is nothing inevitable about this gendered division of labour. It is based on an ideology that views women's responsibility for social reproduction as natural and the state's responsibility as limited. Not all societies hold this ideology to the same degree. Feminist research has identified variations in **gender regimes**, or a particular configuration of gender relations in a given place and time. In some countries, there are much different ideas about women's work and caregiving that result in a different balance of responsibilities requiring the state to play a more active part in the provision of services that support women's caregiving and paid work.

While state intervention can relieve women of some of their unpaid work, Rice and Prince note that it can also be a "mixed blessing" (Rice & Prince, 2013: 247) because women's relationship to the state is marked by a contradictory blend of protection and control. Public policies can increase women's empowerment and autonomy at the same time as they regulate their behaviour and choices.

Feminist research has documented the gendered character of public policy (elaborated later on) and of the state's own structures. A developing area of inquiry, **feminist institutionalism**, is particularly interested in understanding the internal workings of the state and their gendered impact, or "the ways in which political institutions reflect, structure and reinforce gendered patterns of power" (Kenny, 2007: 91). Feminist institutionalism asks:

> How are formal structures and informal "rules of the game" gendered? How do political institutions affect the daily lives of women and men, respectively? By what processes and mechanisms are such institutions produced, both reflecting and reproducing social systems, including

gendered power relations? How do institutions constrain actors, ideas, and interests? Finally, what is the gendered potential for institutional innovation, reform, and change in pursuit of gender justice, and what are its limits? (Krook & Mackay, 2011: 1)

With this work, there is renewed emphasis on detailed analysis of women's experiences with and within specific state institutions such as federalism, electoral politics, or bureaucracy.

Feminist Critiques of Bureaucracy

Max Weber's components of ideal bureaucracy, such as hierarchy, neutrality, impartiality, merit, job tenure, and compartmentalization, influenced the organization of government in most Western countries, including Canada. Feminists have shown that such bureaucratic values are not gender-neutral (Ferguson, 1984; Stivers, 1993). For instance, hierarchical forms of organization may conflict with feminist principles that favour power sharing and diffusion. The expectation of neutrality among bureaucrats can make it difficult to advocate for women's equality from inside government. The compartmentalization of government operations into neat departments (or silos) does not reflect the complex and overlapping nature of women's lives (Findlay, 2015a). Therefore, the role of bureaucracy goes to the heart of longstanding feminist debates about whether to work within or against the state. As we will see below, there are differing perspectives on the place of feminists inside bureaucracies.

New Public Management (NPM)

Changes to the organization of government also have gendered consequences (Brodie & Bakker, 2007; Rice & Prince, 2013). Over the last 40 years, we have seen drastic restructuring of the state and society that some describe as a changing **gender order**. The gender order pertains to the organization of gender relations that prevails in a particular place and time, including the social and cultural constructions of gender, and the institutionalization of power relations. Feminists have traced the transition from a gender order organized around the Keynesian welfare state (KWS) to one based on neo-liberalism. The KWS was contradictory.

It was strongly gendered, based on the male breadwinner model, an ideal of the family in which men earn a wage to provide for a family and women do domestic labour and care for family members in the home. Even though many families (the poor, working classes, single parents, racialized groups, Indigenous peoples, immigrants, and LGBTQ2) did not fit into this family form, public policies, including employment insurance, and pensions, were constructed around this ideal. At the same time, the KWS was built upon a model of entitlement and collective responsibility. The system rested on a foundation of **social rights** that aimed to reduce inequality by redistributing wealth and to guarantee a reasonable standard of living for citizens (Fudge & Cossman, 2002).

The KWS and the ideas associated with it have been eclipsed by neo-liberal **new public management** (NPM), which emphasizes individualism, and the marketization, deregulation, downsizing, and privatization of the public sector. Feminist analysis has demonstrated that the state restructuring brought about through NPM reforms has had serious implications for equality (race, class, gender, sexual orientation, ability, age) by cutting taxes and public services and public-sector jobs for women; off-loading services onto families and the voluntary sector (increasing primarily women's unpaid work); undermining equity-based policies; and reducing support for women's organizations and women's policy machinery (Findlay, 2015a). As NPM is based on the notion that states should be run like businesses, many private-sector management techniques, or "managerialism," were introduced, such as business plans and performance measurement, which have undermined the representation of women in the policy process both inside and outside of the state.

Brodie and Bakker (2007) summarize the consequences of these neo-liberal changes by outlining "the 3Ds of degendering policy capacity: delegitimization, dismantling and disappearance" (2). Through delegitimization, women's voices have been marginalized in the policy process through funding cuts to women's groups and public criticism of feminism by politicians and the media. Through dismantling, many government agencies (federal, provincial, and territorial) for women were downsized, reorganized, downgraded, diluted, defunded, or eliminated. Through disappearance, gender as a frame for policy-making has been erased in favour of a discourse that prioritizes children and families, and individual responsibility over systemic causes. We might add a fourth "D," **decentralization**. With a system of federalism, restructuring has also been achieved by downloading responsibilities for public services from the federal to subnational governments. Because of the historical role that the federal government has played in maintaining social programs (outlined in Chapter 3), decentralization has dovetailed with the neo-liberal agenda of limiting the public provision of goods and services and making room for further privatization (Findlay, 2015a).

Women's Representation in the Policy Process

The Royal Commission on the Status of Women (RCSW)

Although women continue to be under-represented in governance, there are some important historical and contemporary spaces for feminist influence in Canadian public policy with which students of public administration must be familiar. **The Royal Commission on the Status of Women (RCSW)** was appointed in 1967 by the federal government to study the status of women in Canada and to make recommendations on how to advance women's equality. After an extensive public engagement effort, the commission reported on its findings in 1970, offering 167 recommendations related to women's representation in government institutions and a comprehensive set of policy areas including education, employment, divorce, childcare, and reproduction (RCSW, 1970). The year 2020 will be the fiftieth anniversary of the report from the RCSW and it is striking that many of the policy solutions highlighted by the commission continue to be sought by feminists today. As just one example, Canada still has no public childcare system, which puts us far behind most other industrialized countries (Findlay, 2015b ; OECD, 2006).

However, this should not diminish the significance of the RCSW. It played a crucial role in raising public awareness of women's policy issues and in mobilizing women's organizations around a concrete set of policy priorities. Its anniversary also provides an exciting opportunity to take stock of the progress and the gaps in addressing gender inequality in Canada. A group of academic and community-based researchers throughout the country are conducting a project called *Engendering Public Engagement, Democratizing Public Space*, which will foster broad-based public dialogue about the status of women in the twenty-first century. The commission's legacy is long-lasting.

Women's Policy Machinery and Femocrats

One of the central contributions of the RCSW was its attention to government institutions. Flowing from the RCSW's recommendations, federal, provincial, and territorial governments developed structures inside the state to represent women and to provide openings to influence public policy. These structures are commonly called **women's policy machinery**. In 1971, a Minister Responsible for the Status of Women was introduced, followed by the Women's Program in 1972 in the Department of the Secretary of State. In 1973, the Canadian Advisory Council on the Status of Women (CACSW) was appointed. Status of Women Canada was created in 1976 out of the former Office of the Coordinator for the Status of Women in the Privy Council Office (Andrew, 2010; Brodie and Bakker, 2007; Findlay, 2015a). These bodies are staffed by people that are sometimes called femocrats, or feminist bureaucrats.

Throughout the provinces and territories, similar machinery was established, albeit in different combinations of advisory councils, policy and research bureaus, and funding agencies. Some of these include the Nova Scotia Advisory Council on the Status of Women, the Ontario Women's Directorate, and the Conseil du Statut de la femme du Québec. Several municipal governments also have women's structures of representation. In Vancouver, the Women's Advisory Committee (WAC) was struck in 2009 to advise city council on the implementation of the City's gender equality strategy. It was the first municipal women's advisory council in Canada (Vancouver, 2014).

Feminist researchers distinguish between procedural and substantive representation. **Procedural representation**, or formal representation, posits that elected legislatures and the public service should mirror, or be a microcosm of, society (Findlay, 2015a; Tremblay & Trimble, 2003). It seeks to increase the numbers of women in government and administration because studies show a positive connection between the "presence of women in decision-making positions and the likelihood of policy that takes gender into account" (Andrew, 2010: 326). At the same time, there is no guarantee that women will be willing, or able, to advance a feminist policy agenda (Andrew, 2010; Arscott, 1995; Phillips, 1991). Therefore, **substantive representation** seeks representatives who not only resemble their constituents demographically, but who also pursue the concerns and interests of those constituents once in power (Arscott, 1995; Findlay, 2015a). It would ask that we look beyond the much-celebrated gender parity in Prime Minister Justin Trudeau's cabinet to scrutinize whether it is resulting in better public policies for women.

Accordingly, one of the focal points of feminist policy studies involves assessing the extent to which these structures have been able to advance policies that are beneficial to women, or alternatively, whether they have served to co-opt and de-radicalize femocrats into adopting the state's agenda. The reality is likely a bit of both (Findlay, 2015a). The effectiveness of women's policy machinery has also changed over time. The restructuring brought by the NPM has been damaging to women's representation in government. As seen above, many federal and provincial structures that provided a policy voice for women have been cut or eliminated (dismantled) as a result of NPM ideas and practices (Andrew, 2010; Brodie & Bakker, 2007; Findlay, 2015a).

Participatory Policy-Making

The distinction between procedural and substantive representation highlights the need to look at not only *who* makes decisions, but also *what* the results are. However, they say little about *how* decisions are made. Gendering public policy holds the *process* of decision-making in as high regard as the outcomes. For example, Brodie and Bakker discuss the process of budget making and point out that "there is no systematic annual process within government to evaluate budgets from a gender-sensitive perspective" (Brodie & Bakker, 2007: 53). Budgets are clear statements about government priorities and contain decisions about how to allocate valuable public resources. Yet they are closed, secretive, elite-dominated, and shielded from public scrutiny and input. Brodie and Bakker (2007) recommend that gender equality groups receive funding from government to enable them to participate in budget hearings with the Standing Committee on Finance.

Drawing on Dorothy Stetson's framework for gender policy analysis, Newman and White (2006) identify three criteria for evaluating public policy. They ask not only (1) whether women are involved in the process and (2) whether they are able to achieve substantive policy results, but also, (3), *whether women's presence transforms the policy process itself.* Transformation involves reframing policy debates and making the process more inclusive (Findlay, 2015a; Newman and White, 2006). In Lovenduski et al.'s (2005) measurement of the success of women's movements in achieving their goals, and the role of women's policy agencies in that process, "success" includes not only direct policy outcomes, but also the inclusiveness of the policy process, and the ways in which policies are framed. A participatory policy process depends on active and sustained engagement with groups outside of the state.

Scholars of governance have chronicled the shrinking spaces for citizen engagement, consultation, and democratic control in Canada and the corresponding negative impact on public policy (Anderson & Findlay, 2010; Brodie & Bakker, 2007; Jenson & Phillips, 1996; Laforest & Phillips, 2007; Phillips, 1993). Susan Phillips (1993) proposes a series of measures for making a more participatory policy process that would create infrastructure for citizen involvement, level the playing field between the privileged and the disadvantaged, make information more accessible, and build the capacity of community groups. Organized groups are key sources of expertise and accountability and their exclusion impedes policy progress and the rights of citizenship (Brodie and Bakker 2007; Findlay 2015b; Laforest and Phillips 2007).

Feminist Policy Analysis

Gender-Based Policy Analysis (GBA)

The purpose of policy analysis is to improve public policy by identifying problems and proposing solutions. Policy analysis can be conducted using a variety of approaches: value-based, evidence-based, and participatory (Westhues, 2012). **Gender-based policy analysis (GBA)**, a type of policy analysis, ideally combines all three. GBA is a systematic process for assessing the gender impact of all public programs and policies. It considers issues of knowledge, discourse, representation, differential impact, the public/private divide and state, and restructuring, as necessary to analyzing public policy. GBA is intended to address gender insensitivity in government policies, or ignoring "gender as a socially relevant variable in policy-making" (Brodie & Bakker, 2007: 6). It focuses on *all* policies, even (or especially) those that are not obviously gendered, such as climate change and trade policy.

Feminist research demonstrates that women have been excluded from the process of policy-making and that the resulting public policies affect women and men differently. For instance, tax cuts generally benefit men more than women, as men continue to have higher incomes. Cuts to public services hurt women more than men as women have traditionally relied more on the welfare state for social supports and for good employment and are often expected to fill in service gaps with their unpaid work (Brodie & Bakker, 2007; Levac & Cowper-Smith, 2016).

Pal defines public policy as "a course of action or inaction chosen by public authorities to address a given problem or interrelated set of problems" (Pal, 2006: 2). The element of inaction is especially relevant to GBA, as the socially constructed public/private divide has left crucial areas outside of any significant or effective policy intervention. Pressing and persistent policy problems, including the feminization of poverty (women disproportionately live in poverty), the gender gap between women's and men's wages, the double burden of women's paid and unpaid work, and gender-based violence, remain unsolved or inadequately addressed by governments in Canada.

These policy gaps exist even though GBA, or gender mainstreaming as it is also called, has been taken up by governments, including in Canada, as well as in international institutions such as the United Nations (UN) and the World Bank. Canada committed to GBA in its Federal Plan for Gender Equality after signing on to the 1995 Beijing Declaration and Platform for Action from the UN World Conference on Women. It has been adopted by all federal departments, with Status of Women Canada responsible for overseeing it (Brodie & Bakker, 2007).

GBA is an explicit recognition by the state that policies have a differential impact and are not gender neutral. For it to be successful though, there must be resources, institutional capacity, and community input. The restructuring of women's policy machinery outlined earlier has weakened the ability to conduct thorough GBA inside government. There are also concerns that GBA has become an increasingly technical exercise that prioritizes elite expertise over women's movement and community-based input (Rankin & Wilcox, 2004). One of the other critiques of GBA is that its reliance on comparisons between men and women reinforces a binary notion of gender that does not reflect the diversity of gender identities and expressions and that privileging gender excludes other social locations (SWC, 2016). Recently, some analysts have encouraged an expansion beyond only a gender lens and a prioritization of gender to a more complex, intersectional approach.

Intersectional Policy Analysis

There is now a growing field of **intersectional policy analysis**. Hankivsky and Cormier (2011) explain that the

> . . . goal of intersectionality policy analysis is to identify and address "the way specific acts and policies address the inequalities experienced by various social groups," taking into account that social identities such as race, class, gender, ability, geography, and age interact to form unique meanings and complex experiences within and between groups in society. (217)

The Canadian Research Institute for the Advancement of Women (CRIAW) has developed Intersectional Feminist Frameworks (IFFs), which consider "how multiple forces work together and interact to reinforce conditions of inequality and social exclusion" and view women's lives in holistic ways. Status of Women Canada now applies GBA+ "to examine the factors that intersect with sex and gender to shape individual and group experiences and, ultimately, how these experiences influence the achievement of the intended outcomes of initiatives" (SWC, 2016). An intersectional policy analysis takes into account multiple factors including race, ethnicity, class, gender, sexuality, ability, age, geographic location, refugee and immigrant status, and colonialism. It is a multi-level analysis that spans the local, provincial, regional, national, and global scales.

To illustrate, an intersectional analysis can demonstrate flaws in the organization of policy machinery.

Christina Gabriel found that in the Ontario Women's Directorate (OWD) and the Race Relations Department (RRD) "racism and sexism were . . . largely conceptualized as separate and distinct" (Gabriel, 1996: 185). In this compartmentalized arrangement, "women of colour . . . often fall between the mandates of those advocacy offices promoting gender and racial equality" (Gabriel, 1996: 191). Intersectionality also reveals that while the lives of women in general have been regulated by the state through public policy, some groups of women, such as Indigenous women, poor women, or women with disabilities, have experienced very different, and often more intensive and invasive, regulation, surveillance, and coercion.

Some might see intersectional analysis as a threat to GBA, but this is not necessarily so. In many ways, intersectionality builds on the strengths of GBA. One of the central elements of GBA is about knowledge production. Whose knowledge counts as knowledge? Whose knowledge is legitimate? Whose knowledge gets taught in universities? Whose knowledge is taken seriously by policy-makers and the media? GBA uncovers how deeply gendered systems of policy knowledge are, but ideas about expertise, reliable data, and authentic evidence are also heavily shaped by colonialism, racism, heterosexism, and ableism. Is oral history as valued as written records? Is lived experience as valued as formal education? Is qualitative research as valued as quantitative data? Why? These questions animate both GBA and intersectional policy analysis.

They also have in common that the implementation of both GBA and GBA+ by governments is spotty. Let's take a look at a recent example. The 2017 federal budget was touted by the Justin Trudeau government as the first to employ GBA+. The budget included a "Gender Statement" that reads, in part:

> When making decisions that significantly affect peoples' lives, governments must understand to what extent their policy choices will produce different outcomes for all people.
>
> A meaningful and transparent discussion around gender and other intersecting identities allows for a greater understanding of the challenges this country faces, and helps the Government make informed decisions to address those challenges—with better results for all Canadians. (Canada, 2017)

It gave a detailed picture of the persistent gender inequality in Canadian society. However, the budget might more accurately be described as GBA+ minus the "A"—the analysis is lacking. As Anderssen (2017) of *The Globe and Mail*, explains, in other counties, where gender budgets are longstanding practice, the "best examples contain real analysis and rankings to show how spending programs serve men and women of different ages and income levels." Yet in Canada's 2017 budget,

> . . . [t]here's not much analysis,' and no benchmark rankings in this first effort. The Liberals have added a "Gender Statement Chapter," which often reads like budget-splaining a story already known with statistics anyone could find. (Anderssen, 2017)

As a case in point, the finance minister tells us that "Budget 2017 will promote the fair and consistent treatment of women and men under the tax system" (Canada, 2017). How? As stated earlier in this chapter, the tax system produces very different outcomes for men than for women. What will the federal government do to correct this gender insensitivity? Likewise, even though feminist economists show that investments in infrastructure disproportionately advantage men who are concentrated in those sectors of the economy, the "six economic sectors identified as the budget's priorities are all predominantly male employment sectors. There are no parallel investments in predominantly female employment sectors" (McInturff, 2017). Infrastructure will also be built through public–private partnerships, despite the well-known gendered effects of privatization, which raises the costs of services and undermines public-sector employment (Cattapan et al., 2017).

While there are some commitments in the budget to addressing housing, student loans, gender-based violence, judicial education, family justice, job training, female entrepreneurs, parental and caregiving leave, and childcare, much of this includes spending already announced in 2016, or funding where the bulk of it will not be rolled out for 10 years. And a closer look (i.e., the analysis part of GBA+), reveals that the major promises, such as caregiver leave and extended parental leave, delivered through the Employment Insurance (EI) program, will actually exacerbate existing inequalities. Since only 38 per cent of women outside of Quebec are eligible for EI, analysts were quick to point out that the parental leave provisions (which spread out existing benefits over a longer period of time) will benefit only the most privileged women who already qualify for EI and can afford to extend their leave without additional pay (Anderssen, 2017). This is a strange outcome for GBA"+," which is designed to foreground the impact on disadvantaged groups. There is also no added incentive for men to share caregiving responsibilities (Cattapan et al., 2017) and to alleviate the gendered division around social reproduction.

Further, the budget continues Canada's tradition of evidence-less childcare policy. Budgeting $7 billion over 10 years to early learning and childcare initiatives does not follow the research about what is actually required to build a universal childcare system to advance women's equality. It provides little detail about how the money will be spent and how the provinces and territories will be involved.

The budget makes some steps forward on representation, establishing an LGBTQ2 Secretariat within the Privy Council Office to support the prime minister's Special Advisor on LGBTQ2 issues. At the same time, the resources needed in women's policy machinery to do comprehensive GBA+ are still wanting:

> . . . the department that is tasked with supporting gender-based analysis across the entire federal government, Status of Women Canada, continues to be dramatically underfunded. Its budget represents .01 per cent of federal program spending. This year. Last year. Every year for the last decade (McInturff, 2017).

Non-governmental equality-seeking organizations, which are central to accountability for gender-based budgeting, also continue to be underfunded. Overall, federal Budget 2017 indicates that governments have much more work to do if the potential of GBA+ is to be fully realized.

Gender and Public-Sector Employment

Representative Bureaucracy

In the past, the public service was staffed through patronage. Eventually, this approach was rejected in favour of merit-based hiring. Canadian bureaucracy was built around the male-breadwinner form, with women being forced to resign from the public service if they got married up until 1955 (Felice, 1998). In the post-war period, with the rise of the second wave of the feminist movement, women's underrepresentation in the public service became a topic of discussion, building upon earlier debates about increasing the presence of francophones in state administration. Authors considered the merits of "passive" representation (of identity) versus "active" representation (of interests) (Kernaghan, 1978; Wilson & Mullins, 1978), with most public administration scholars at the time accepting the former much more readily than the latter (Findlay, 2015a). Growing demands from equity-seeking groups for both identity and interest-based representation, reinforced through the RCSW, have changed the conversation. Women's policy machinery reflected the notion that structures were needed to provide a voice for marginalized groups inside the state.

At the same time, even the idea of passive representation has met resistance, with some believing that representative bureaucracy conflicts with meritocracy and amounts to reverse discrimination (Kernaghan, 1978: 500, 508–9). In response, researchers and advocates have argued in favour of **representative bureaucracy**, the principle that "the composition of the bureaucracy should reflect in fair proportion certain demographic characteristics of society" (Brooks, 1994: 310) such as gender, race, ethnicity, class, language, ability, and sexuality. They view representative bureaucracy as a reinforcement and extension of merit, by removing barriers that had previously impeded the recruitment of qualified candidates (Kernaghan, 1978; Wilson & Mullins, 1978). Agócs (2012) outlines several justifications for representative bureaucracy. The first is symbolic, underscoring the responsibility of the public sector to act as "model employer." In addition, she maintains that "citizens and taxpayers have a right to expect that they, and their children, can find careers in the public service they support if they so choose and have appropriate qualifications" (Agócs, 2012: 2). Finally, she provides that in the United States, the "literature shows that public organizations with larger proportions of women and/or minorities in decision-making roles are more likely to produce outcomes compatible with the interests of women and/or minorities than similar organizations with fewer women and/or minorities"

(Agócs, 2012: 2). A representative bureaucracy in-volves the active recruitment of women from diverse communities.

Employment and Pay Equity

One of the mechanisms for achieving a representative bureaucracy is **employment equity**. Employment equity grew out of earlier efforts in the 1960s–80s to improve equal employment opportunities in the public service through recruitment, training, pro-motion, and anti-discrimination measures (Findlay, 2015a). The report of Rosalie Abella's Royal Commis-sion on Equality in Employment in 1984 provided a legislative framework for employment equity, not only for the federal government, but also for the provinces. In her report, Abella introduced the con-cept of **systemic discrimination**, demonstrating that discrimination is not always overt and experienced by individuals, but instead is often built into pro-cesses and institutions, acting to disadvantage and marginalize identifiable groups.

This became the basis of the 1986 federal Em-ployment Equity Act, and subsequent provincial legislation and policy. The Employment Equity Act requires that employers take active measures to elim-inate systemic barriers for four designated groups: women, Aboriginal peoples, visible minorities, and people with disabilities and to report on their goals, timelines, and progress. The strongest employment equity legislation in the country was passed in On-tario in 1993. It applied to the provincial government and its agencies, as well as the broader public sector (municipal governments, school boards, universi-ties, hospitals, other health-care facilities) with more than ten employees, the police, and the private sector with more than fifty employees (Bakan & Kobayashi, 2000). This legislation was repealed by the Progres-sive Conservative government in 1995.

Agócs maintains that "employment equity is a transformative process, since in theory it promotes *substantive equality*, not forcing members of desig-nated groups to assimilate to the workplace as it exists, but by changing the culture and structure of the workplace to create fairness for all and remove a bias in favour of white males" (Agócs, 2014a: 5). This does not mean that the policy is working as effect-ively in practice. There are still major limitations in the employment-equity regime. There has been little

progress in the public-sector employment numbers for Indigenous peoples and people with disabilities and a reversal for women (England, 2014; Weiner, 2014). The legislation suffers from weak monitoring and enforcement and inaction by provincial gov-ernments (Agócs, 2014b). The cancellation of the long-form census by the previous Conservative gov-ernment has also damaged the data collection needed to track and measure progress (Agócs, 2014b), though its revival by the current government is a cor-rective step forward.

Employment equity is aimed at the recruitment and promotion of members of designated groups into the public service. But once in the public ser-vice, women also experience a number of challen-ges. The labour market in Canada is characterized by sex segregation, with women and men concen-trated in different job sectors. Women are more likely to be working in jobs that are typically lower paid and insecure, sometimes called pink-collar ghettoes, in both the public and private sectors. In a recent study of public-sector employment, Levac and Cowper-Smith (2016) reported that

> . . . women, and racialized women, are over-represented in term positions and in lower salary categories, and concentrated in cer-tain sectors and positions. Both racialized and non-racialized women are over-represented in public service sectors such as health, education and social services . . . A Parliament of Canada report (2013) finds that women in the federal public service "remain concentrated in adminis-trative support jobs, generally hold lower-paying jobs than men and are over-represented in term appointments" (7).

One of the policy instruments to address such sex segregation in the public sector is **pay equity**, which deals with undervalued wages in female-dominated occupations. Based on the premise that wages are af-fected by systemic discrimination, pay equity seeks to achieve equal pay for work of equal value by re-quiring employers to review and adjust gendered pay disparities (Weiner, 2014). Employers are expected to undertake job evaluations that assess jobs using cri-teria of skill, effort, responsibility, and working con-ditions without gender bias. In some jurisdictions, pay equity has evolved from a thin complaints-based system to a more robust one based on proactive measures that puts the onus on employers to identify and correct inequities (Weiner, 2014).

As with employment equity, there are ongoing issues with pay equity. Gender bias in job evaluations remains stubborn, and many pay-equity settlements have required lengthy court battles. Not all provinces have pay-equity legislation, and it mainly applies only to public-sector employers (Andrew, 2010; LEAF, 2011; Weiner, 2014). Nevertheless, pay equity challenges the idea that assigning value is gender-neutral and best left to the market. A House of Commons Special Committee on Pay Equity recently recommended new proactive federal legislation, and the NDP is urging that it be fast-tracked (Mas, 2016).

Precarity and the Public Service

Despite the gendered job segregation, feminist and labour research frequently shows that the public sector, in comparison with the private sector, provides good jobs for women. "Good" jobs are full-time, well-paid, secure, unionized, and provide benefits (such as a health plan, pensions, and family leaves). Private-sector employment is more often not unionized, lacks employment equity standards and benefits, is lower paid, and is insecure (Bakker, 1996; Levac and Cowper-Smith, 2016). A study based on 2006 census data found that women in the public sector earned an average annual income of $45,821, while women in the private sector earned only $43,841—a 4.5 per cent difference (Sanger, 2011). In addition, "Canada's four employment equity designated groups (Aboriginal peoples, people with disabilities, visible minority (racialized) groups, and women) continue to be present in the federal public service at rates that exceed their workforce availability (according to the 2006 census)" (Levac & Cowper-Smith, 2016: 5).

As discussed earlier, NPM market-based approaches have dominated public administration. Not only has downsizing eliminated many "good jobs" for women, for those left in the public sector, their jobs increasingly resemble private-sector precarity. Public-sector employment (federally and provincially/territorially) is moving to part-time, temporary, casual, contract, insecure work and there is a rise in volunteer and unpaid overtime. Public employers are experiencing growing workloads,

lower pay, physical and mental health issues, and harassment and bullying, and citizens are faced with declining access and service quality, safety, and accountability (Levac & Cowper-Smith, 2016). Women from marginalized groups are disproportionately affected by precarity (Levac & Cowper-Smith, 2016). Agócs (2012) uses 2011 data to demonstrate that in spite of federal employment equity policy, women, Aboriginal peoples, visible minorities, and people with disabilities continue to be over-represented in temporary and lower salary positions in government.

CRIAW, along with four public-sector unions (the Public Service Alliance of Canada, the Canadian Union of Public Employees, the Canadian Union of Postal Workers, and the Canadian Association of University Teachers), the Canadian Labour Congress, and several universities are wrapping up a study that is examining these trends. The project, *Changing Public Services: Women and Intersectional Analysis* is working with communities in four regions of Canada to understand and challenge the negative impacts on women as workers and users of public services (CRIAW, 2016; Findlay et al., 2015).

Conclusion

This chapter reviewed several of the ways that we might gender the study of public administration. Gendering the state reveals the ways in which women's relationship to the state and bureaucracy diverges from men's and how women's relationship with the state has changed over time. Gendering representation allows us to consider the evolution of women's policy machinery since the RCSW, the role of femocrats in the policy process, and the possibilities for more participatory policy-making. Gendering policy analysis through GBA and intersectional policy analysis offers the tools to systematically evaluate the differential impact of government action and inaction. Gendering public-sector employment demonstrates, on the one hand, that efforts have been made, with employment and pay equity, to achieve more representative and fair workplaces in state administration. On the other hand, working in the public sector is marked by growing precarity. The challenges of modern governance demand that students of public administration have a strong grasp of the gendered process and substance of policy-making.

Important Terms and Concepts

decentralization	gender-based policy analysis (GBA)	Royal Commission on the Status of
employment equity	intersectional policy analysis	Women (RCSW)
feminist institutionalism	pay equity	social reproduction
gendering	procedural representation	substantive representation
gender order	public/private divide	systemic discrimination
gender regime	representative bureaucracy	women's policy machinery

Study Questions

1. How does women's relationship to the state and public policy differ from men's?
2. What are some of the ways that the bureaucracy is a gendered institution? Give some examples to illustrate.
3. What is NPM and what is its impact on women?
4. What are the various types of women's policy machinery in Canada and how have they changed over time?
5. What is the difference between gender-based analysis (GBA) and intersectional policy analysis? What are their respective strengths and weaknesses?
6. What is representative bureaucracy? What are the arguments for and against it?

Note

1   The author would like to acknowledge the Social Sciences and Humanities Research Council's Partnership Development Grant and Mount Saint Vincent University's Social Change Through Community-engaged Research Grant. She would also like to thank her students, particularly those in Women, Social Policy, and the Welfare State, whose critical thinking and thoughtful questions helped to cultivate this analytical framework.

References

Agócs. C. 2014a. "The Making of the Abella Report: Reflections on the Thirtieth Anniversary of the Report of the Royal Commission on Equality in Employment." *Employment Equity in Canada: The Legacy of the Abella Report*, edited by C. Agócs, University of Toronto Press, pp. 13–28.

———. 2014b. "Conclusion—Looking Forward: The Unfinished Business of Employment Equity." *Employment Equity in Canada: The Legacy of the Abella Report*, edited by C. Agócs, University of Toronto Press, pp. 306–24.

———. 2012. "Representative Bureaucracy? Employment Equity in the Public Service of Canada." Paper presented at the annual meeting of the Canadian Political Science Association. 13–15 June. http://www.cpsa-acsp.ca/papers-2012/Agocs.pdf

Anderson, L. and T. Findlay. 2010. "Does Public Reporting Measure Up? Federalism, Accountability and Child Care Policy in Canada." *Canadian Public Administration* 53, 3, pp. 417–38.

Anderssen, Erin. 2017. "Liberals Fall Short with First Gender-Based Federal Budget." *The Globe and Mail*. March 22. http://www.theglobeandmail.com/news/politics/federal-budget-2017-women-gender/article34390564/

Andrew, C. 2010. "Women and the Public Sector." *The Handbook of Canadian Public Administration*. 2nd edn, edited by C. Dunn, Toronto: Oxford University Press, pp. 319–29.

Arscott, J. 1995. "A Job Well Begun . . . Representation, Electoral Reform, and Women." *Gender and Politics in Contemporary Canada*, edited by F.P. Gingras, Toronto: Oxford University Press, pp. 56–84.

Bacchi, C. 1999. *Women, Policy and Politics: The Construction of Policy Problems*. London: Sage.

Bakan, A. and A. Kobayashi. 2000. *Employment Equity in Canada: A Provincial Comparison*. Ottawa: Status of Women Canada.

Bakker, I. 1996. "Deconstructing Macro-economics through a Feminist Lens." *Women and Canadian*

Public Policy, edited by J. Brodie, Toronto: Harcourt Brace & Company Canada Ltd., pp. 31–56.

Bezanson, K., and M. Luxton. 2006. "Introduction: Social Reproduction and Feminist Political Economy." *Social Reproduction: Feminist Political Economy Challenges Neoliberalism*, edited by K. Bezanson and M. Luxton, Montreal, Kingston: McGill-Queen's University Press, pp. 3–10.

Brodie, J. and I. Bakker. 2007. "Canada's Social Policy Regime and Women: An Assessment of the Last Decade." Ottawa: Status of Women Canada. March. http://publications.gc.ca/collections/collection_2007/swc-cfc/SW21-156-2007E.pdf

Brooks, S. 1994. "Bureaucracy." *Canadian Politics*, 2nd edn, edited by J. Bickerton and A. G. Gagnon, Peterborough, ON: Broadview Press.

Canada. 2017. "Chapter 5—Equal Opportunity: Budget 2017's Gender Statement." *Budget 2017: Building a Strong Middle Class*. Department of Finance Canada. March 22. http://www.budget.gc.ca/2017/docs/plan/budget-2017-en.pdf

Cattapan, Alana, Cindy Hanson, Jane Stinson, Leah Levac, and Stephanie Paterson. 2017. "The Budget's Baby Steps on Gender Analysis." *Policy Options*, March 27. http://policyoptions.irpp.org/magazines/march-2017/the-budgets-baby-steps-on-gender-analysis/

CRIAW. Canadian Research Institute for the Advancement of Women. 2016. "Changing Public Services: Women and Intersectional Analysis." http://www.criaw-icref.ca/images/userfiles/files/Intersectional%20Feminist%20Frameworks%20Primer.pdf

———. 2006. *Intersectional Feminist Frameworks*. Ottawa. http://criawicref.ca/sites/criaw/files/IFFs%20Primer.pdf

D'Agostino, M. and H. Levine. 2011. *Women in Public Administration: Theory and Practice*. Sudbury, MA: Jones & Bartlett Learning.

England, K. 2014. "Women, Intersectionality and Employment Equity." *Employment Equity in Canada: The Legacy of the Abella Report*, edited by C. Agócs, University of Toronto Press, pp. 71–98.

Felice, M. 1998. "A Timeline of the Public Service Commission of Canada." Public Service Commission of Canada. http://web.archive.org/web/20070703131234/http://www.psc-cfp.gc.ca/research/timeline/psc_timeline_e.htm

Ferguson, K. 1984. *The Feminist Case against Bureaucracy*. Philadelphia: Temple University Press.

Findlay, T. 2015a. *Femocratic Administration: Gender, Governance, and Democracy in Ontario*. Toronto: University of Toronto Press.

———. 2015b. "Child Care and the Harper Agenda: Transforming Canada's Social Policy Regime." *Canadian Review of Social Policy* 71, 1 (Spring), pp. 1–20.

Findlay, T., M. Cohen, and K. vom Scheidt. 2015. "Community-Based Intersectionality: Exploring Participatory Policy Analysis and Advocacy," Paper presented at the Canadian Political Science Association, Canadian Sociological Association, and Canadian Association of Social Work Education, University of Ottawa, June 2–4.

Fudge, J. and B. Cossman. 2002. "Introduction: Privatization, Law, and the Challenge to Feminism." *Privatization, Law, and the Challenge to Feminism*, edited by B. Cossman and J. Fudge, Toronto: University of Toronto Press, pp. 3–37 .

Gabriel, C. 1996. "One or the Other? 'Race,' Gender, and the Limits of Official Multiculturalism." *Women and Canadian Public Policy*, edited by J. Brodie, Toronto: Harcourt Brace & Company, pp. 173–95.

Hankinvsky, O. and R. Cormier. 2011. "Intersectionality and Public Policy: Some Lessons from Existing Models." *Political Research Quarterly* 64, 1, pp. 217–29.

Jenson, J. and S. D. Phillips. 1996. "Regime Shift: New Citizenship Practices in Canada" *International Journal of Canadian Studies* 14, Fall, pp. 111–36.

Kenny, M. 2007. "Gender, Institutions and Power: A Critical Review." *Politics* 27, 2, pp. 91–100.

Kernaghan, K. 1978. "Representative Bureaucracy: The Canadian Perspective." *Canadian Public Administration* 21, 4, pp. 489–512.

Krook, M.L. and F. Mackay. 2011. "Introduction: Gender, Politics, and Institutions." *Gender, Politics and Institutions: Towards a Feminist Institutionalism*, edited by M.L. Krook and F. Mackay, Basingstoke: Palgrave Macmillan, pp. 1–20.

Laforest, R. and S. D. Phillips. 2007. "Citizen Engagement: Rewiring the Policy Process." *Critical Policy Studies*, edited by M. Orsini and M. Smith, Vancouver: University of British Columbia Press, pp. 67–90.

LEAF. Women's Legal Education and Action Fund. 2011. "Pay Equity." http://www.leaf.ca/wp-content/uploads/2011/01/PayEquityFactSheet.pdf

Levac, L. and Y. Cowper-Smith. 2016. *Women and Public Sector Precarity: Causes, Conditions and Consequences*. Canadian Research Institute for the Advancement of Women, Changing Public Services: Women and Intersectional Analysis, April 25. http://www.criaw-icref.ca/images/userfiles/files/Women%20and%20Public%20Sector%20Precarity%20FINAL(1).pdf

Lovenduski, J. et al. 2005. "Conclusions: State Feminism and Political Representation." *State Feminism and Political Representation*, edited by J. Lovenduski et al.,. New York: Cambridge University Press, pp. 260–93.

Mas, S. 2016. "New Democrats Urge 'Feminist' PM to Table Pay Equity Law by End of 2016, *CBC*

News, June, 2016. http://www.cbc.ca/news/pol itics/pay-equity-report-special-committee-1.3624307

McInturff, Kate. 2017. "The Budget is a First Step to Better the Lives of Women in Canada." *The Ottawa Citizen*. March 22. http://ottawacitizen.com/opinion/ columnists/mcinturff-the-budget-will-better-the-lives-of-women-in-canada

Newman, J. and L. White. 2006. *Women, Politics, and Public Policy: The Political Struggles of Canadian Women*. Toronto: Oxford University Press.

OECD. Organisation for Economic Co-operation and De-velopment. 2006. *Starting Strong II: Early Childhood Education and Care*. Paris: Education and Training Policy, Education Division.

Pal, L.A. 2006. *Beyond Policy Analysis: Public Issue Management in Turbulent Times*. 3rd edn, Scarbor-ough, ON: Thomson Nelson.

Phillips, A. 1991. *Engendering Democracy*. University Park: Pennsylvania State University Press.

Phillips, S.D. 1993. "A More Democratic Canada?" *How Ottawa Spends: A More Democratic Canada?* edited by S.D. Phillips, Ottawa: Carleton University Press, pp. 1–41.

Phillips, S. D., B. R. Little, and L. A. Goodine. 1997. "Reconsidering Gender and Public Administration: Five Steps beyond Conventional Research." *Canadian Public Administration* 40, 4, pp. 563–81.

Rankin, P. L. and K. D. Wilcox. 2004. "De-gendering En-gagement?: Gender Mainstreaming, Women's Move-ments and the Canadian Federal State." *Atlantis: Critical Studies in Gender, Culture & Social Justice* 29, 1, pp. 52–60.

RCSW. Royal Commission on the Status of Women. 1970. *Royal Commission on the Status of Women Report*. Ottawa. Queen's Printer.

Rice, J.J. and M. J. Prince. 2013. "Gender and Social Policy: His and Her States of Welfare." *Changing Politics of Canadian Social Policy*. 2nd edn, edited by J.J Rice and M.J. Prince, Toronto: University of Toronto Press, pp. 219–48.

Sanger, T. 2011. *Battle of the Wages: Who Gets Paid More, Public or Private Sector Workers?* Ottawa: Canadian Union of Public Employees (CUPE). December. http:// cupe.ca/updir/Battle_of_the_Wage_ENG_Final-0.pdf

SWC. Status of Women Canada. 2016. "GBA Gender-Based Analysis Plus: The Government of Canada's Approach." http://www.swc-cfc.gc.ca/gba-acs/ approach-approche-en.html

Stivers, C. 1993. *Gender Images in Public Administration: Legitimacy and the Administrative State*. Newbury Park, CA: Sage Publications, Inc.

Tremblay, M. and L. Trimble. 2003. "Women and Elec-toral Politics in Canada: A Survey of the Literature." *Women and Electoral Politics in Canada*. edited by M. Tremblay and L. Trimble, Don Mills: Oxford Uni-versity Press, pp. 1–20.

Vancouver. 2014. City of Vancouver Women's Advisory Committee, *Women's Advisory Committee City of Vancouver 2012–2014 Report*. http://vancouver.ca/ files/cov/women-advisory-committee-2012-2014-report.pdf

Weiner, N. 2014. "Employment Equity in Canada: What Do the Data Show about Its Effectiveness?" *Employ-ment Equity in Canada: The Legacy of the Abella Report*, edited by C. Agócs, University of Toronto Press, pp. 29–50.

Westhues, A. 2012. "Approaches to Policy Analysis." *Can-adian Social Policy: Issues and Perspectives*, edited by A. Westhues and B. Wharf, Waterloo: Wilfrid Laurier University Press, pp. 43–60.

Wilson, S.V. and W.A. Mullins. 1978. "Representative Bureaucracy: Linguistic/Ethnic Aspects in Canadian Public Policy." *Canadian Public Administration* 21, 4, pp. 513–38.

Information, Technology, and Canadian Public Administration

David C.G. Brown

Chapter Overview

This chapter explores five elements of the story of information and technology in Canadian public administration. It starts by looking at the promise of IT and the discipline that it has spawned, variously described as e- or digital government. The harnessing of information and technology has been a critical underpinning of new public management (NPM) thinking, and a second part of the discussion is to look at the catalytic effects of a central tenet of NPM, a focus on the citizen. The third section considers—briefly, as it is a topic in itself—politics and policy-making in the electronic environment, in effect what is happening at the front end of public administration. The heart of the chapter is the fourth section, which looks at the spheres and methods of public administration created by IT and IM, and the chapter concludes with a look at their relationship to public sector reform.

Chapter Objectives

By the end of this chapter, students will be able to do the following:

- Describe the impact that information technology has had on public administration and in particular on government as a knowledge organization.
- Analyze the issues that arise from these developments.
- Discuss the relationship between information technology and new public management.
- Assess how the government is doing in using information and technology to meet the public's and its own needs.
- Comment on public policy issues raised by networked databases and information holdings.

University students today have grown up with smartphones and social media and take them as much for granted as their grandparents took land-line telephones. And yet even they are aware that technology is constantly changing and successive waves of new applications are creating new forms of social interaction, economic activity, and ways of doing things (Tapscott, 2015; Tapscott & Caston, 1993). If technology is having this kind of open-ended impact on daily living, its effects on public administration are at least as profound and unpredictable (Dunleavy et al., 2006).

Information and technology are both new and very old. They have been an integral part of public administration from the earliest forms of empire and social governance to the present day. In ancient times, kings had scribes to record their laws and lesser decisions and to make them known, that they might be obeyed. Information was needed about who the subjects were, where they lived, and what they did. Records were needed to keep track of taxes collected and how they were spent, as well as to memorialize the acts of the kings for posterity. These records helped to define the society to itself and to others and to lay the foundations of the modern state. Over time, the nature of the state has been directly tied to the technology for keeping and transmitting records—an administration based on paper records could be larger and more sophisticated than one where the recording medium was stone tablets (Innis, 1950).

This dynamic relationship between information, its technological medium, and governance continues to be a characteristic of public administration in Canada and every other country in the world (Fountain, 2001a); yet it is in many ways the newcomer in the academic study of public administration, especially when compared with the other foundations of public administration, the management of financial and human resources (for Canadian book-length treatments of this and related topics, see Barney, 2005; Borins et al., 2007; Oliver and Sanders, 2004; and Roy, 2006). This chapter is about that space.

In any discussion, it is important to define the terms used. Two are particularly important for the purposes of this chapter. The first is **information**. The Canadian Oxford Dictionary defines information as "something told" or knowledge. Information theorists refine this to describe a hierarchy—inspired perhaps by atomic theory—of data, information, and knowledge, each level having a "value added" building on the ones below it. Some add a fourth level—wisdom—as a reminder that judgment is increasingly a factor in how information is used as you go up the hierarchy. In any case, these are all terms to describe content or, in the Canadian thinker Marshall McLuhan's characterization, the message (McLuhan, 1964).

The second term is **technology**, which is both the medium and, as political philosophers have observed (Ellul, 1964), the society-shaping dynamic. Our Canadian Oxford Dictionary definition is "the study or use of the mechanical arts or applied sciences." This is a very broad definition that attempts to capture the fact that technology takes many forms and is as old as society. It hints at links to engineering, but at its root is based on the Greek word for art. This multidisciplinary tension between art and science is still very much part of the story.

Our contemporary interest in information and technology comes from the world that has been shaped

Data "is" or "are"?

The word *data*—the foundation of the information hierarchy—is the Latin plural for *datum*: a piece of information or "thing given" according to the Oxford dictionary. The dictionary goes on to say, however, that in English data can be both singular (a body or series of facts, information) and plural (facts or statistics). This creates a subtle but important distinction between focusing on data as a mass of information and as the sum of individual elements, between the information forest and its individual trees. Scientific researchers, who like to build their case from the ground up, tend to emphasize the latter ("data are") while common usage is increasingly on the side of the former ("data is"), with its connotation of big picture and cumulative evidence, which is particularly useful in policy or political debate.

in the past generation by the introduction of the Internet and the convergence between several strands of technology—telecommunications, computing, and broadcasting—that it represents (Rowland, 2006). In North America we tend to refer to these technological forces as **information technology** (IT), even though the term *information and communications technologies* (ICTs) is more accurate and more widely used in the rest of the world. So when the term IT is used in this chapter it should be understood as encompassing the range of technologies that have been the dominant influences since the mid-1990s. By the same token, **information management** (IM) refers to the various methodologies that have emerged for organizing and using information, especially in the environment created by IT. IT and IM are as inextricably linked as yin and yang, but they do represent distinct starting points in the art and science of public administration.

If there is an underlying message in the issues discussed in this chapter it is that we are in a world where everything is new but nothing is new. As Gow and Hodgetts have observed, "The public service is part of the development of society. . . . (I)t reflects the society in which it operates, while acting on that same society, shaping it." (Gow & Hodgetts, 2003: 195). We live in a society that more than ever is shaped by information and technology, and the implications for public administration are enormous.

The Promise of Information Technology

There is a certain inherent optimism in the application of information technology to public administration, sometimes to the point of wishful thinking. Almost by definition, the potential exceeds the reality and certainly the supply of technological "solutions" exceeds the demand for them. It is also an inherently risky field, as invariably the technologies—and thinking about how they can be used—will be different at the beginning of an IT-enabled project or activity than at its end. An important part of this administrative world, therefore, is managing risks and expectations, not to mention costs.

This is not to underestimate the very real and important changes that have been made in public administration in a relatively short period of time or the speed with which change continues to happen. Indeed, government is faced with a dilemma, because it needs to adjust to externally driven technological forces, which influence every corner of Canadian society, while playing a constructive role in helping Canadians adjust to those forces. As discussed later in this chapter, one result is a very different relationship with the private sector than occurs in other areas of public administration. The tapestry is even richer when it is considered that technology is both a focus of public policy (a major industry as well as a shaper of society more generally) and an enabler, an asset to be managed as well as a resource to use in support of other activities, creating a management discipline that maintains an uneasy balance between medium and content.

These competing elements have given rise to a great deal of thought and discussion within government, but it is fair to say that, just as much of the technology has been generated outside government, so too have many (if not most) of the ideas about how it should be used. These can be loosely categorized under the heading of **e-commerce**, which has in turn generated the related discipline of **e-government**. These rapidly evolving disciplines shape much of the day-to-day application of information and technology in Canadian public administration.

e-Commerce and e-Government

The starting point is electronic commerce. (E-commerce is a shorthand that allows speakers at conferences to play with e-variants such as "enabled" or "enhanced.") The term has been in use since the early 1980s and focuses on online sales and other transactions between businesses and their clients as well as their suppliers. The early foundation was electronic data interchange (EDI), which permitted the sharing of digital information over telephone landlines as well as the electronic transfer of funds. The financial industries were leaders in this field and developed applications such as telephone banking and automatic teller machines (ATMs), which combined greater customer control over their finances with cost and efficiency savings for the banks (generated at least in part by the banks transferring basic clerical functions to the customer). These technologies are by now well established, and the ATM and its online offspring in many ways are the gold standard when government provides electronic services to citizens, even though the latter may not always be as straightforward as managing your own bank or credit card account.

The introduction of the Internet in the early 1990s, with its graphic user interface, took e-commerce to another level and created the business models under which governments operate today. In fairly short order, the entire range of transactions involving goods and services was available online, using **electronic service delivery** (ESD) tools and methodologies. These were backed up by bringing into the electronic environment the relationships that companies have with their suppliers (e-procurement and supply chain management) as well as their internal relationships. The process facilitated the growth and integration of global corporations but also allowed for a wide range of employment relationships, including a growth in tele-working and self-employment.

The driving focus, however, was client-relationship management (CRM), supported by computer-enabled consolidation of data about all aspects of the organization's relationship with the customer. At the business end, this led to consolidation of all the ways (channels) in which businesses dealt with their clients—by telephone, mail, fax, self-service kiosk, and in person as well as online—while behind the scenes came the creation of data warehouses to consolidate the information that was collected and of data mining and more recently data analytics to exploit it. This in turn gave rise to a new set of day-to-day headaches and challenges, including meeting requirements for security against hackers and other potential forms of tampering, protection of personal information, and identity management, in order to maintain the integrity and confidentiality of the increasingly valuable data base.

Government was not immune to these developments. From the outset, the private sector has encouraged government to adopt the new methodologies, both in order to modernize public administration—a longstanding private-sector preoccupation—and to establish the public sector as a client for IT goods and services, given that governments are among the largest institutions in the country. While initially not linked to new public management, the use of IT rapidly became an integral part of efforts to reinvent and re-engineer government (Andersen, 1999). Perhaps most importantly, vocal segments of the public began asking government to deal with them in the same way that banks, booksellers, the travel industry, and other successful online service providers do. The clincher was the prospect of major savings,

even "doing more with less," through investments in IT when governments faced a major fiscal crunch in the early 1990s, just at the time that the Internet was coming into the mainstream.

The result has been the emergence of a discipline of *e-government*, the public-sector companion to e-commerce. While definitions of e-government vary, its starting point is the application of technology in the areas of the public sector analogous to where it is used in the private sector. This began with government financial transactions but has included the full adoption of electronic service delivery, client relationship management, and data management methodologies. All governments in Canada are now fully automated environments in their internal communications and information management, closely resembling in that respect large Canadian corporations and universities. This has included moving aggressively towards primarily online environments in the provision of services to government (as discussed later, service to the public is more complicated) and in buying goods and services for government from the private sector (e-procurement).

Consideration of e-government of course has to take account of the differences between government and the private sector and therefore how far the e-commerce model can be applied. A broad view is that IT shapes—and will be increasingly dominant in—all of the state's relationships (Brown, 2005). These are most notably how it interacts with society and the economy, with the citizen and governance institutions, with the international environment, and within the state. The first of these is the focus of public policy, the second raises issues that are addressed under the heading of e-democracy, the third is the stuff of globalization and international relations, while the fourth can be seen as the domain of public administration. The loop is closed, however, as public administration encompasses public-sector institutions and processes that are set up to deal with the three other sets of relationships. It is safe to say that no area is untouched by technology and increasingly technology provides the substance as well as the medium.

This discussion highlights one further terminological point as information technologies rapidly go through successive generations. In barely a quarter century, waves of the Internet have been described as Web 1.0, 2.0, and beyond, with Web 5.0 already a matter of speculation at the time of writing this chapter.

Academic observers have sought terms to capture the essence of these changes, and the vocabulary they use is also evolving. **Digital governance** has come into greater use to evoke the pervasive nature of information technology in all aspects of public administration and the societal governance environment (Dunleavy et al., 2006). This chapter uses e-government and digital government interchangeably, although future versions may, like government itself, go increasingly digital!

An Evolving Public-Sector Environment

The management and use of information technology has long been a feature of Canadian government. The Constitution Act 1867 assigns the federal government responsibility for the postal service as well as for railways and telegraphs that cross provincial lines. This has provided the basis for later court rulings assigning Ottawa jurisdiction over, in turn, telephones, radio, television and, most recently, the Internet. At the same time, provinces developed their own roles in several of these areas that touch on their interests and responsibilities, notably the early establishment of provincially owned telephone companies in western Canada and later provincial educational radio and television initiatives.

This evolution was parallelled by the establishment, in the federal government, of departments and regulatory agencies, notably the establishment of a Department of Communications in 1969 that by 1980 had assumed responsibility for both the hardware and software aspects of telecommunications, broadcasting, and related technologies, anticipating their later convergence. The first Canadian regulatory body, the Board of Railway Commissioners, was given authority over telegraphs and the newly regulated telephone industry when it was established in 1908, a mandate that through several evolutions became a central concern of today's Canadian Radio-television and Telecommunications Commission (CRTC).

These developments were parallelled in the operations of the federal government. It adopted the telephone in the first part of the twentieth century and was also an early user of electronic data processing (computers) after World War II. Based on the advice of the Glassco commission, two common service agencies were established in the 1960s, the Government Telecommunications Agency in the Department of

Communications, which supported the federal government's need to operate across the country, and the Computer Services Agency (CSA) in the Department of Supply and Services. In its earliest form, the CSA provided mainframe computing services to government, although individual departments with large-scale requirements, notably Revenue Canada and National Defence, developed their own computing capacity.

In the 1970s and 1980s, science and technology became an increasingly important part of industrial policy and progressively more integrated with the federal department concerned with that area of public policy. By the early 1990s, the growing role of the telecommunications industry, which includes both cable and telephone companies, and the convergence of computing (a largely unregulated industry) with telecommunications (an area with a long history of government involvement) created a tension between the industry and the communications departments.

The tension was resolved in June 1993 with the reorganization of the machinery of government carried out by Prime Minister Kim Campbell when she formed her cabinet. New prime ministers need to think about how they wish to organize their ministry and the relationships among government departments. Based on briefings from the Privy Council Office, Campbell made an ambitious series of changes, creating several new departments in areas of public policy where government was expected to play a strong role in the future. Three of these were Industry ("a modern industry department that was attuned to the information revolution and the knowledge economy"), including science policy and the hardware side of the old Department of Communications; Human Resources Development (HRDC), concerned with employment policy; and Canadian Heritage, bringing together federal programs relating to Canadian culture and identity (Mitchell, 2002: 3). The latter included the software side of the old Department of Communications, including cultural development in a digital environment.

Apart from some adjustment in nomenclature and in the human resources development portfolio, in particular, these changes have remained in place through subsequent governments of both major political stripes. When the Justin Trudeau government came into office in November 2015, Industry became Innovation, Science and Economic Development and the original HRDC became Employment and Social

Development (ESDC), but their mandates were essentially unchanged, as was that of Canadian Heritage.

These public policy–oriented organizational changes were matched in the Campbell reorganization by changes in central and common service agency responsibilities within government. Drawing on private-sector organizational models, a **Chief Information Officer** (CIO) was appointed within the Treasury Board Secretariat to oversee the use of IT and IM in public administration. In due course this brought together efforts to manage the government's expanding investment in IT, to adopt IT in areas of public administration such as financial and human resources management, and to use technology to improve government services to the public. These were largely policy and horizontal coordination roles in support of Treasury Board ministers.

The development and management of new IT-based services to government was in 1993 assigned to the Government Telecommunications and Informatics Services (GTIS), which combined the previous telecommunications and computer services agencies in a new Department of Public Works and Government Services Canada (PWGSC—renamed Public Services and Procurement in the November 2015 change of government). GTIS was later recast as the Information Technology Services Branch (ITSB), which in turn was replaced in 2011. At that time, a new common service agency, **Shared Services Canada**, was created to consolidate technological infrastructure and internal services in several major areas on behalf of all departments and agencies in the core public service and several other public sector organizations. The services included email, data centres, desktop services, and procurement of IT equipment and applications (PWGSC, 2011). The move was motivated at least in part to save money but proved problematic, attracting critical reviews from the Auditor General (Auditor General, 2015).

The government's recent institutional stability can be explained by policy initiatives that were taken in the aftermath of the 1993 reorganization and that, in retrospect, seem to have captured successfully the sea change that was happening in the larger economy with the introduction of the Internet. Two were of particular importance. The first was the appointment by Prime Minister Jean Chrétien, shortly after coming into office in late 1993, of an Information Highway Advisory Council (IHAC). The IHAC was made up of knowledgeable individuals drawn from the IT industry and a wide range of civil society organizations. It was chaired by David Johnston, who later served as Canada's Governor General. The several hundred recommendations in its two reports, in 1995 and 1997, set a broad policy framework based on four objectives of government policy: a consumer-driven policy environment conducive to innovation; Canadian content online to strengthen Canadian culture; access by all to the information highway; and, better, more affordable government services, with government serving as a model user of the information highway and a catalyst for the move to the information society more generally (IHAC 1995, 1997).

The IHAC reports led to a range of initiatives under the theme of Connecting Canadians to develop electronic infrastructure, digitize cultural holdings, and promote access to the Internet. The latter included programs such as SchoolNet, which succeeded in linking every school in Canada to the Internet, and similar initiatives with respect to Canadian libraries, remote communities, and First Nations bands. Government departments also began to establish a presence on the World Wide Web, and the federal government's Internet portal, the **Canada Site** (https://www.canada.ca/en.html), was established in 1995.

Two other developments played an important part in shaping the federal government's use of technology during this period. The first was the advent of the year 2000, also known as Y2K, and the apprehended "millennium bug." In the early history of computing, memory space for data input was at a premium and the practice developed of using only the last two digits when recording the year in a date. While this was unexceptional in the middle of the twentieth century, there was a growing realization as the end of the century grew nearer that computers using two-digit dates would consider the transition from 1999 to 2000 to be a move back in time rather than forward, with unknown but potentially disastrous consequences. Companies and governments around the world therefore made a major investment, ostensibly to fix the date problem, but in practice to upgrade their computing environments. In the event, there were few problems—whether because the issue had been dealt with or because it was not as serious as originally thought is a matter for debate—but it did provide the occasion for a quantum leap forward in the adoption of information technology by government.

In the wake of the Y2K preparations, the federal government established Government On-Line (GOL), an aggressive effort to place government services to the public on the Internet. Originally launched in 1999, and re-launched with the new millennium on January 1, 2001, GOL continued until March 31, 2006, bridging the Chrétien, Martin, and the beginning of the Harper governments. Led by the Treasury Board Secretariat CIO, GOL's most visible accomplishment was to place the 130 most commonly used government services on line. These included both transactional and information services and involved all the major departments and agencies of government.

A centrepiece of the GOL initiative was the organization of these services into 31 electronic "clusters" that provided a World Wide Web-based electronic single window to the range of government services of interest to groups in society, defined by subject, audience, or life-event (e.g., health, Aboriginal Canadians, or exporting abroad). The clusters were in turn organized into three portals (gateways) for individual Canadians, Canadian business, and the international environment, which became a defining element of the Canada site home page (Brown, 2007). In many areas, provincial and municipal governments provide services to the same groups as the federal sites, and this gave rise to considerable interjurisdictional collaboration in the gateways and clusters aspects of GOL. The success of this strategy played no small part in Canada being awarded top ranking by the consulting firm Accenture for five years, from 2001–5, in its annual international survey of electronic government services to the public (Accenture, 2005).

GOL also provided an opportunity to upgrade the government's electronic infrastructure, and in particular its ability to protect online transactions from interference and compromise through the establishment of a secure channel. A complementary effort was made to establish IT and IM as a focus of public administration and to update the related Treasury Board policies. All of these efforts were coordinated by a committee of deputy ministers, mandated by the cabinet secretary and supported by a tapestry of junior-level committees. For the period that it was in place, GOL was treated as one of the two main initiatives to reform the federal public sector, complementing efforts to modernize public service human resources management.

Later developments have built on the foundation laid by GOL. Within less than a decade it could safely be said that all federal services were available online, backed up by networked databases that were also linked to more traditional service channels (Kernaghan, 2013). Beginning in 2013 the government began a process of redesigning the Canada site to give it an even stronger orientation towards service to the public; this was parallelled by initiatives discussed later in this chapter to enhance public access to government data. Last, but by no means least, in 2013 the Clerk of the Privy Council launched *Blueprint 2020* (PCO, 2014), which sought to enhance the use of social media and other technology tools across the public service; unprecedentedly, this initiative was retained and supported through two changes of Clerk and also the transition from the Harper to the Justin Trudeau governments.

All provincial and territorial governments took their own steps to integrate new technologies into their administrative and public policy environments. Several held their own versions of the IHAC process and all appointed their own Chief Information Officers, who faced the Y2K millennium bug and most of the other management challenges that confronted their federal counterpart (Borins, 2007b). Many consolidated their technology services to government into a single operating environment, some going as far as contracting the work out to the private sector. In addition, all introduced their own Internet home pages and took steps to place services online, usually linked to the establishment of a provincial government service-to-the-public agency. As discussed in the next section, this led to collaboration among jurisdictions at an unprecedented level.

The Citizen as Catalyst

The emphasis in e-commerce on client-centred service has resonated well in the public sector, with its traditional ethos of public service, giving rise to the concept of **citizen-centred service**. It has also built on a history of government initiatives to improve service to the public, which included the language of service provisions of the Official Languages Act passed in 1969, the **Access to Information Act** and the **Privacy Act** in 1983, and the Public Service 2000 task force on service to the public in 1989–90 (Rawson, 1991). All of these emphasized the importance of government meeting members of the public on their rather than the government's terms.

The *Blueprint for the Renewal of Government Services*, issued in 1994 as one of the first initiatives of the new Treasury Board CIO, built on this foundation. Its emphasis on using the citizen as the organizing focus for applying IT and promotion of single-window approaches paved the way for GOL and two companion Treasury Board–sponsored programs, the Service Improvement Initiative (SII) and **Service Canada**. Service Canada in particular was inspired by the creation in several provincial governments of agencies to consolidate the delivery of services to the public on behalf of the entire government, a pathfinder being Service New Brunswick. All provinces and territories have adopted some form of this model, but it was only in 2003 that the federal government followed suit and redefined Service Canada as an operational agency.

An early question for GOL and the SII was whether to aim to shift all government service delivery to the electronic channel. It soon became apparent that this was unrealistic. One important reason was—and remains—that a significant proportion of Canadians do not have access to the Internet or their access is constrained by limitations in local electronic infrastructure or their own computing equipment. This was one of the major concerns of

the IHAC, which devoted considerable attention to the issue of Internet access, giving rise to the Connecting Canadians initiatives described earlier. Twenty years after the IHAC report, the CRTC reported that some 20 per cent of the population still did not have access to broadband Internet, which the CRTC described as a telecommunications basic service for all Canadians (CRTC, 2016). A second reason was that many Canadians in fact prefer to have some kind of personal contact when dealing with government—when offered a choice of service channels, telephone and in-person contact are still ranked high.

Electronic access is most widely seen as an important part of a "suite" of service channels (Flumian et al., 2007; Kernaghan, 2005). Service Canada and its service-to-business counterpart, the **Canada Business Network**, are therefore organized on a multi-channel basis, combining telephone call centres, storefront operations, and mail access. These are complemented by interactive web sites, with all channels backed up by a common information database. A similar pattern has been followed with the consolidation of municipal services to the public, in many areas building on the introduction of a single easily accessible non-emergency telephone number such as 311 (Bontis, 2007a).

Service Nova Scotia—A GST technology back-story

When the federal Goods and Service Tax was introduced in the 1980s, Revenue Canada created a telephone banking facility for businesses to remit the GST they collected. This was expanded to permit businesses to remit Canada Pension Plan and Employment Insurance premiums on behalf of their staff. In Nova Scotia the provincial government decided to contract with Revenue Canada (now the Canada Revenue Agency) to collect their provincial sales tax, which was then combined with the GST to create a streamlined Harmonized Sales Tax (HST). Later, provincial worker's compensation premiums were added to the tax collection single window, further reducing a business's tax remittance costs.

Revenue Canada already collected provincial personal and corporate income tax, and there was very little left for the provincial tax commission to do. It did, however, have a well-established computing environment. So the tax commission moved out of the tax collection business. It amalgamated with the Registry of Motor Vehicles, Vital Statistics, and the Registry of Joint Stock Companies and, later, with parts of the Department of Housing and Municipal Relations, including the Registry of Deeds and Property Assessment. Together, they created the knowledge backbone of Service Nova Scotia, the agency that delivers provincial and municipal services across the province.

These developments have helped nudge government towards a new organizational model integrating government into a single enterprise (Kernaghan, 2007a). This model has three components (Borins, 2007a). The first is the single window to the public, which delivers services on behalf of a number of government departments and agencies. This is sometimes referred to as the front room. In the middle room are departments that continue to have program development and implementation responsibilities, along the lines of the traditional departmental model, but are "joined-up" to work in a networked policy environment. The back room—notably Shared Services Canada, but also the CIO branch of Public Services and Procurement—provides common services to the enterprise, using an integrated technology infrastructure and a common set of technology applications.

While this model is in practice only partially implemented, it does represent a more holistic approach to organizational responsibilities than was the case during the heyday of new public management, with its emphasis on managerial autonomy and empowerment. At the same time, it raises questions about how far the analogy of citizen as client can be taken (Fountain, 2001b). One view is that it works best where the services are optional and desired by the citizen, as opposed to services that are more regulatory in nature, where traditional organizational models may be preferable (Brown, 2007).

Politics and Policy-Making in the Electronic Environment[1]

Public administration takes place in a political environment. Ministers are first and foremost politicians, who have been tested in both the electoral and the parliamentary arenas. Daily they are on duty with the media. They are members of the governing party and they are supported by partisan policy advisers. In the Canadian version of the Westminster system, ministers are the lynchpin in the **accountability** chain between the public service and Parliament and the public. They preside over the policy process, including when their departments consult the public in the context of policy development or implementation.

IT has had a major—although not uniform—impact on all of these aspects of the Canadian political environment (Alexander & Pal, 1998). At first, the political environment was slower than the public service to make full use of IT, and in certain areas the political world is likely to lag permanently behind. In others, any gap has disappeared, although some commentators argue that broader changes are required in our system of governance before the full potential of technology is realized (Barney, 2005). There is also a debate among political scientists about whether Canada's Westminster institutions of governance will be forced to change substantially under the pressure of the networked environment (McNutt, 2014; Roy, 2008). There is little doubt, however, that the experience and attitudes of politicians with respect to technology have an important influence on the environment in which IT and IM issues are addressed in public administration (Malloy, 2003).

To begin with, IT is not inherently a vote-getter. Politicians want to be seen to be addressing the important issues of the day, and these include ensuring that Canada is equipped to meet the challenges of the knowledge society and economy. This is a high-level objective, however, and usually does not translate into political debate. Politicians do want to support the telecommunications and IT industries and to be sure that governments are using technology to improve service delivery. They are wary, however, of the costs of technology and the risks of cost overruns and project failures, which can be dramatic in the case of large technology projects and have attracted close scrutiny from the Auditor General (Auditor General, 2005, 2006, 2010, 2017). They are also sensitive to media stories about cost overruns and security breaches of technology systems and databases and in particular to perceptions of abuse of the personal information of citizens and taxpayers.

As decision-makers, ministers face a major challenge when it comes to technology-linked issues. Very few politicians have a background in computer science or one of the other disciplines involved in technology or information management, but they are often asked to take decisions with a significant technical dimension. As a result, they are more than usually dependent on briefings from their officials,

---

[1] Many of the issues addressed in this section and the following one, on "New Spheres and Methods of Public Administration," are also addressed in a special issue of the journal *Canadian Public Administration*. See: Amanda Clarke, Evert Lindquist and Jeffrey Roy, editors. 2017. "Special Issue on Understanding Governance in the Digital Era: An Agenda for Public Administration Research in Canada" in *Canadian Public Administration*, vol. 60, no. 4 (December 2017): 453–683.

Opening government and its data

The Access to Information Act was introduced in the 1980s to promote government transparency and accountability. In the context of the digital era, the federal government has adopted a three-prong strategy: open government, which promotes greater public involvement in policy-making; open data, which makes government data more accessible to users outside government; and open information, which takes a more systematic approach to making the government's internal records and data available to the public. Canada was also a founding member, in 2011, of the Open Government Partnership, an international collaboration involving governments, multilateral organizations, and civil society organizations that seeks to "secure concrete commitments from governments to promote transparency, empower citizens, fight corruption, and harness new technologies to strengthen governance" (Open Government Partnership, 2017).

and by the same token they are more open to lobbying by the technology industry. The stakes are even higher when it is considered that the IT industry is one of the few in Canada where government purchasing has a major impact on the industry—public administration decisions are also industrial policy decisions.

This being said, all of Canada's political parties are active users of IT, and it has become an integral part of election campaigns, in particular in communications with party members and the media but also with the online public. Candidates routinely have websites and many use blogs and other techniques to good effect (Kernaghan, 2007b). On the other hand, Canada has been very slow to move to electronic voting, perhaps because our first-past-the-post system is comparatively simple and does not involve a major counting effort; experience in the United States, where electronic voting is more common, has also highlighted some of the potential difficulties. It is interesting to speculate, however, whether a generation used to "liking" items on social media will increasingly demand to be able to vote directly on decisions about public policy rather than leaving it to their elected representatives.

Once elected, MPs have personal web sites for dealing with their constituents, although the parliamentary system imposes some inherent limitations on how autonomous they can be in presenting their views (Kernaghan, 2007c). The Parliament Buildings are as thoroughly wired as any government office building, and Parliament itself has an extensive web presence (http://www.parl.gc.ca/). The House of Commons and Senate have been cautious about technology, however,

and IT is not used in conducting parliamentary business, beyond recording for Hansard and broadcast and some experiments in conducting committee hearings.

Public consultations are an important part of the public policy-making process, and both ministers and public servants are involved. The Internet offers considerable potential as a medium for public consultations, and the federal government has established a central Consulting Canadians website to provide information about all such consultations. The site has been particularly important in the regulatory process and other consultations on specialized topics (Borins and Brown, 2007a). This has been complemented by later initiatives under the headings of **open government**, **open data**, and **open information** that seek to provide greater public access to government knowledge holdings and to involve the public more extensively in the public policy process (Clarke and Francoli, 2014). While there are at times concerns about how representative views provided on the Internet are of the larger population there is also evidence that virtual policy communities can in fact be as representative as their in-person counterparts (McNutt, 2006).

A latent political concern about both e-onsultations and electronic service delivery, however, is that their very success in linking public servants with members of the public risks cutting out the middle man or woman—the politician. Known in academic discussions as **disintermediation**, the extent of this phenomenon has not been systematically studied, but its prospect is another reason for politicians to be more cautious in how they approach technology.

New Spheres and Methods of Public Administration

The advent of networked information and communications technologies has given new prominence to some very old disciplines of public administration. IT and IM have taken their place as one of the foundations of modern public administration, alongside financial and human resources management. The related institutions combine traditional and new models. Information and technology have assumed greater importance as assets of government, and the challenges of managing them have created a renewed public administration discipline, one that is characterized by its interdisciplinary nature. Information and technology management also calls for skills and working relationships—within and outside government—that have not had much prominence in the past. In turn, there are implications for traditional accountability models—the link between public administration and the world of Parliament and politics.

The Institutional Response to Information and Technology

Beginning with the 1993 Campbell reorganization—although building on earlier roots—a technology-related institutional environment has emerged in the federal government, with comparable, albeit less elaborate, arrangements in provincial governments. The chief information officer (CIO) is one of the senior officials of the Treasury Board Secretariat and provides central agency leadership to a wide network of IT- and IM-related agencies and government-wide communities of practice that are defined by Treasury Board policies. Every department and agency has its own CIO, usually a member of the senior management team and often involved in internal initiatives to renew services to the public and departmental administration.

The emphasis on service delivery has also produced new institutions. The footprint of the three GOL gateways remains, although each with its distinctive pattern. After some early evolution, Service Canada has settled in as a significant unit within the Department of Employment and Social Development (ESDC), operating the Canada site and providing the single window for delivering government services to individual Canadians. The Canada Business Network,

a unit in the Department of Innovation, Science and Economic Development that operates interjurisdictionally, plays a similar role with respect to Canadian business, especially the medium and small business sectors that have been given new prominence in the information economy. The Department of Global Affairs maintains **Canada's International Gateway**, an Internet portal for Canadians travelling and marketing abroad and foreign residents wishing to know more about Canada. This complements Global Affairs' traditional role of maintaining Canadian diplomatic posts abroad on behalf of the entire government.

In the enterprise model, service to the public is parallelled by service to government. The Department of Public Works and Government Services (PWGSC), and the Government Telecommunications and Informatics Services (GTIS) within it, were set up in 1993 on the **common service agency model** that has prevailed since the 1960s, providing centralized services to government departments where it was considered to be desirable for policy or cost reasons. For a number of reasons—not least the difficulty in predicting where technology is going and therefore the risks involved in putting all its IT resources into one basket—the development of IT services and applications in government initially evolved on a more collaborative basis, with the emphasis on sharing services and best practices among departments rather than one-size-fits-all approaches. As discussed earlier, however, the government later consolidated a number of back-room functions into Shared Services Canada, motivated by the prospect of cost savings. An underlying issue is "make or buy"—whether government should insource, i.e., develop its own IT capacity, or contract out to the private sector (outsource) for its IT capabilities and services.

Other areas of government have also responded to the information age. Three in particular should be noted. The Department of Innovation, Science and Economic Development (formerly Industry), with responsibilities ranging from supporting scientific research to promoting the IT industry, incorporating new businesses, protecting intellectual property, and regulating the radio spectrum (more important than ever in the wireless environment), has since the IHAC report sought to promote the use of technology in support of innovation and competitiveness in the Canadian economy. The Department of Canadian

Heritage is concerned with cultural industries and the use of technology in daily life. One of its agencies, Library and Archives Canada, is leading efforts to digitize cultural and other information holdings, notably those relating to the permanent record—the memory—of government but also of the country as a whole. The Department of Employment and Social Development is concerned with the employment effects of the knowledge economy, including the new literacy—the essential skills—required to live and work in that economy (Wallace et al., 2005).

IT and Information as Assets of Government

Much of public administration theory and practice is about managing people and money as the primary assets of government. In recent years, the government's information holdings and the technology that houses them have joined the list of key public resources (Lenihan et al., 2002). Even so, the situation is still evolving and even somewhat problematic. Although no one would deny the critical importance of the IT infrastructure, traditional accounting carries it on the government's books as a depreciating asset. Program budgeting, with its emphasis on results, treats technology as a means or input, so it is difficult even to track how much is spent on IT in a single year. A published estimate in 2003/4 placed total annual technology-related spending at just under $5B, at the time roughly 10 per cent of total spending on government operations. Almost two-thirds of that amount was on the purchase of IT goods and services from the private sector (Brown, 2007: 63). More recent estimates indicate IT-related spending has remained in the $5B range (TBS, 2016), but the public details are imprecise. The Public Accounts of Canada assign the government's massive inventory of paper files and digital information holdings no value at all! This raises the question of how something that is not valued can be properly managed.

Nevertheless, a considerable effort goes into planning, buying, and running the government's technology and telecommunications infrastructure. Shared Services Canada and Public Service and Procurement's (PS&PC) CIO branch provide the essential backbone, providing both government-wide technology support and mainframe-based computing services for other branches of PS&PC and departments that do not operate their own computing environments. Both PS&PC and other departments have made extensive investments in moving paper-based activities into an electronic environment. These large projects have not always been successful—indeed, by some measures, many if not most of them have problems to at least some degree (Auditor General, 2006, 2010, 2011), with the transition to digitally based long-term archival holdings proving particularly difficult (Auditor General, 2014). One aspect of this track record is that government in Canada generally operates on a larger scale than business, and major government computing projects are generally larger and more complex than those in the private sector.

IM as a Discipline of Public Administration

The management of the government's information holdings represents its own challenge. Traditionally, information was kept on paper records in physical files and filing cabinets. When the Access to Information and Privacy Acts were passed in 1983 they required government institutions to be able to locate and produce any record under their control within 30 days in response to a request from the public. In order to meet this test, Treasury Board administrative policies were introduced that direct departments to manage their records on a life-cycle basis, from creation or acquisition through initial and secondary use to longer-term disposal or retention. Library and Archives Canada is the ultimate resting place of records that are considered to be of enduring value. The Access to Information policy established procedures for the public to request records, working with a central public database of what those records are and where they can be found.

This framework remains in place, but it has become considerably more difficult to administer with the transition to electronic information. Personal computers and networked databases have greatly expanded the volume of information holdings and the range of ways in which they are held, much of it outside of centrally administered registry systems—even increasingly sophisticated electronic ones. Multiple versions of records, both paper and electronic, are common and it is often very difficult to know which one should be used. Email has become ubiquitous in a relatively short space of time, and many records are obscured from view as email attachments.

These challenges are compounded by successive new generations of hardware and software that make it difficult to retrieve electronic files that are more than a few years old. At the same time, court interpretations have made it clear that any retrievable record in any form—including, for example, call logs on government smartphones—is subject to the Access to Information Act. Another dimension has been added with the expansion of the cloud: large-scale, networked information storage that is physically located outside government premises, presenting issues of access and control by government. The issues are compounded when the cloud servers are located outside Canada and not necessarily subject to Canadian law.

These are not the only issues addressed by Treasury Board information management policies. The Access to Information Act makes a distinction between records, which are considered internal to a government institution, and published material, which includes books, press releases and public websites, which are considered to be in the public domain. The policy on Communications and Federal Identity and related directives promote information dissemination and articulate the government's duty to inform citizens so they may exercise their rights and responsibilities; from that starting point it establishes procedures for government publishing and media relations as well as participation in social media. More controversial areas of the policy concern advertising, public opinion research, and sponsorship. The federal identity program sets standards for government signage and visual identity, including with respect to the government's presence on the Internet, in order to facilitate public access and accountability.

Other Treasury Board policies are more oriented towards information protection. The Privacy Act and related policies give Canadians the right to see government files about themselves and establish limits on the extent to which they can be seen by others. It also limits the government's ability to take personal information that was collected for one purpose and use it for another. These restrictions, which are based on international standards, have assumed even greater prominence as networked databases create the potential to link previously unconnected information to build profiles of individuals, groups, and activities in society. Such information is valuable both to government and to commercial interests, and open data and similar efforts to make government data publicly available put pressure on the ground rules governing personal information.

Another set of policies deals with government security: the protection of information and other government assets against perceived threats. Varying levels of assessed threats lead to corresponding levels of security classification and protection, adding to the complexity of information management. Expanding measures in recent years in the name of national security have created an additional pressure to make government information holdings available to security agencies (Geist, 2015).

The People Effect—New Skills

Few areas of public service work have been untouched by the introduction of technology and the move to knowledge-based government. All public-service desktops are connected to internal electronic networks and through them to the Internet. Their users must handle email and manage their own electronic information. Many public servants are able to take advantage of information and communications technologies to establish more flexible work arrangements; many also see them as a kind of virtual prison, blurring the traditional boundaries between work and personal life.

In addition to these environmental effects, a good deal of the substance of public-service work is shaped by information and technology. In addition to the Treasury Board and departmental CIOs, every department has a substantial number of staff whose jobs are defined by Treasury Board information and technology policies or by the management of technology infrastructure and applications. In addition, other administrative disciplines, notably financial management (comptrollership) and human resources management make intensive use of technology in how they do their work. Policy and program work relating to the IT industry or the knowledge economy and society also require technical knowledge, and the government has substantial numbers of computer scientists, engineers, librarians, archivists, and other specialists to carry out this work.

One result of this changing skills profile within government is a requirement for interdisciplinary work teams and for public servants of different academic backgrounds to learn how to work together. Engineers and political scientists may not spend much time with each other as students, but they have to work together in the public service! At the same time, the move towards knowledge work in government places a greater premium on information-finding and -organizing skills as opposed to the application of specialized knowledge (Bontis, 2007b). The open-ended and costly nature of technology, combined with the considerable reliance on private-sector contractors, has brought to the fore skills in areas such as risk management and contract management. All of these demands have also called for new forms of digital leadership (Borins and Brown, 2007b). However, the ability to analyze, synthesize, and advise is as important in public service work as ever.

New Working Relationships

Another skill that is called for in IM- and IT-influenced public administration is relationship management. The networked environment is credited with eliminating time and space and with crossing boundaries. In practice public servants are connected with wide-ranging communities, both within and beyond the traditional departmental structure.

Within government, the growth of service-to-the-public agencies has the effect of separating policy-making from program delivery, often into different ministerial portfolios. This creates practical as well as theoretical issues about accountability and program effectiveness. A similar observation can be made about the consolidation of technology and other administrative services to government in shared or common service agencies, especially when they are in turn contracted out. A related development is the impact of citizen-centred service

on Canadian federalism, which goes well beyond the collaboration noted in the discussion of the GOL Gateways and Clusters (Ambrose et al., 2006).

More than in any other sphere of public administration, the management of information and technology has also created a close working relationship with the private sector (Dutil et al., 2005; Langford & Harrison, 2001). This takes several forms. To begin with, the private sector is the source of most technology hardware and software and many of the applications used in government. Government sales are important to vendors and it is also important for government to keep abreast of the technology that is available or in prospect, and its cost (Brown & Kourakos, 2005). Tendering procedures involve one kind of relationship, contract administration another. The private sector also provides consultants to advise on planning, purchasing, using, and servicing IT goods and services.

With the growing complexity and risks of major IT projects, an issue is whether, in these relationships, government should act as its own technology manager—with government managers or project offices supervising the development of new IT-based systems and running the technology-enabled services. In such situations, the private-sector vendors and consultants are "on tap, not on top." A different dynamic comes into play when project management functions are also assumed, under contract, by the private sector. In such partnerships, public services are being provided to the public or to government, but by the private sector, either jointly with government or on its behalf. This puts a premium on governance arrangements for such projects and on balancing the incentives, risks, accountabilities, and liabilities for both sides of the

The technology-enabled face of federalism

As governments appointed CIOs in the 1990s, they began to meet periodically to discuss common problems and concerns, including dealing with a common vendor community and linking governments on the Internet. The Public Sector CIO Council was formed, made up of the fourteen federal, provincial, and territorial CIOs plus representatives of municipal technology organizations and co-chaired by the federal CIO and a provincial counterpart. In a parallel development, the government service delivery agencies formed the Public Sector Service Delivery Council. The two Councils in turn have sponsored a not-for-profit organization, the Institute for Citizen-Centred Service (ICCS), which conducts research on their behalf.

partnership. The situation is even more challenging to manage in the case of public–private partnerships, where typically the private sector also provides the financing (Siemiatycki, 2015). In all these situations, two important constraints are that even large private-sector firms do not have as deep pockets as government, and government remains ultimately responsible for the decision to involve the private sector and for the results of doing so.

An added dimension to the private-sector relationship is the diversity within the private sector itself. Governments in Canada and around the world deal with a relatively small number of multinational technology and consulting firms, which have broad experience and resources and are skilled at managing large projects, although with a price tag attached. They also tend to offer similar products and services from one jurisdiction to another, with the result that there is considerable similarity in how governments use IT and IM. Their size and importance in developing and providing IT goods and services present governments with a major challenge, in which government itself is not always "on top" (Dunleavy et al., 2006b). Beyond this multinational tier of vendors there is a wide range of firms, with large Canadian-based companies that themselves have international operations at one end, through medium and small firms, many with only a handful of employees, down to a large number of individual consultants at the other end. Governments deal with the full spectrum, sometimes working with firms or individuals on a long-term basis that comes close to traditional public-service employment relationships. Indeed, concern has been expressed about the extent to which contracting for professional services in the IT and other fields has created a "shadow public service" (Macdonald, 2011).

Information Technology and Accountability

The extensive use of technology in government raises many questions about accountability, the spinal cord of public administration. Traditional accountability models are under pressure for many reasons, not just from the effects of IT (Aucoin & Jarvis, 2005). Indeed it can be argued that networked technologies lead to a re-collectivization of accountability, countering the decentralizing tendencies of the new public management (Brown, 2013). One context for such questioning is organizations such as Service Canada, which

provide services to the public on behalf of other government programs. This is a departure from the traditional departmental model, in which a minister is accountable for both policy development and its delivery. It remains to be seen how willing ministers and Parliament will be, in practice, to accept a division of responsibility between these two areas.

A similar issue arises when a minister and department are no longer fully in control of the computing environment supporting the department; this has been a factor in past resistance to the creation of organizations such as Shared Services Canada. A third concern is the increasingly real-time nature of accountability. With current communications technologies, ministers become instantly accountable in Parliament and the media for the actions and statements of their officials, anytime and anywhere these may occur. Such dynamics have created a new centralization of government communications, and in the eyes of some observers a politicization of the communications function and even of the public service (Heintzman, 2014; Thomas, 2013).

Some Conclusions: Information, Technology, and Public-Sector Reform

In justifying new technology projects, terms commonly used by their advocates are *transformation* and *innovation*. These evoke the promise of information technology and of knowledge-based government and in many ways reflect a new reality. Governments in the early 1990s did not plan the introduction of a networked working environment featuring single-window electronic service delivery and backed by powerful databases. They recognized that new technologies and associated management techniques offered considerable potential to improve, even reform, public services as well as to save money. But few would have been able to foretell the extent to which public administration would change, while in other respects retaining many of its traditional features.

It is a nice question whether change invariably represents reform. Many individual changes undoubtedly represent improvements, and Government On-Line can credibly claim to have been a major reform initiative, significantly changing the face of government service delivery. The modern public service builds on a legacy of past reforms, and the challenge is to continue that process.

This challenge can be illustrated in six issues that arise from the nature of information and technology in the public-administration context. The first is the inherent obsolescence of technology. New products and applications are always becoming available along with new ways of using them, generating new social and economic responses (Tapscott & Williams, 2006) and imposing new challenges for public administrators (Kernaghan, 2014a, 2014b). Governments have some limited ability to influence these developments, but they need to become informed and skilled users if they wish to influence, and not just be shaped by, events. Second, they face a particular problem in addressing the fragmented situation of information management in the knowledge-based institution—this is the ultimate testing ground for existing and future technological developments (Brown, 2012).

Closely related to the information management challenge is the institutional immaturity of information and technology management (McDonald, 2002), especially as compared with financial and human resources management. The related statutory framework is limited and there is limited integration among the various administrative disciplines that have been discussed in this chapter—many would not even recognize themselves as being in the same script, never mind on the same page!

A fourth challenge is the one articulated by the Information Highway Advisory Council of maintaining a link between technology strategies and developments for the public sector and those directed at society at large: government is the largest user of the information highway, it also needs to be a model user.

A particular dilemma relates to public communications. Technology has greatly expanded the nature and availability of communications channels and has added immediacy to the relationship between public administration and the public. Communications have become part of the currency of contemporary politics, with the paradoxical effect of isolating the communications function as a discipline within public administration.

This points to the final challenge. Much of the leadership in moving into the world of information- and technology-based public administration has been provided by the public service itself, with only a limited decision-making role taken by ministers. This situation cannot last, however. As politicians become more aware of and experienced with the tools of information and communications technologies, the question will be what conclusions they form about the technology agenda and how they express their political will as a result—whether to encourage technology's further development in public administration or to try to control its use and limit its impact.

Important Terms and Concepts

Access to Information Act	digital governance	open data
accountability	disintermediation	open government
Canada Business Network	e-commerce	open information
Canada's International Gateway	e-government	Privacy Act
Canada Site	electronic service delivery (ESD)	Service Canada
chief information officer (CIO)	information	Shared Services Canada
citizen-centred service	information management (IM)	technology
common service agency model	information technology	

Study Questions

1. What new spheres and methods of public administration have been created by information technology and information management?
2. What issues arise from the nature of information and technology in the public administration context?

3. What is the relationship between information technology and new public management (IT and NPM)?
4. The federal government has adopted information technologies in all areas of its internal and external operations. What is your view of how advanced it is in its use of technology? Where should it go from here? What are the constraints?
5. How important is it for government to protect personal information that it collects in the face of pressures to make use of all it knows (especially using data analytics) in policy-making and in national security situations?

References

Accenture. 2005. *Leadership in Customer Service: New Expectations, New Service.*

Alexander, Cynthia J. and Leslie A. Pal. 1998. *Digital Democracy: Policy and Politics in the Wired World.* Don Mills, ON: Oxford University Press.

Ambrose, Rona, Don Lenihan, and John Milloy. 2006. *Managing the Federation: A Citizen-Centred Approach.* Ottawa: Crossing Boundaries.

Andersen, Kim Viborg. 1999. "Reengineering Public Sector Organizations Using Information Technology." *Reinventing Government in the Information Age: International Practice in IT-Enabled Public Sector Reform,* edited by Richard Heeks, London: Routledge.

Aucoin, Peter and Michael D. Jarvis. 2005. *Modernizing Government Accountability: A Framework for Reform.* Ottawa: Canada School of Public Service.

Auditor General of Canada. 2005. "Chapter 1: Information Technology Security." *February 2005 Status Report of the Auditor General of Canada to the House of Commons.* Ottawa: Public Works and Government Services Canada.

Auditor General of Canada. 2006. "Chapter 3: Large Information Technology Projects." *Report of the Auditor General of Canada to the House of Commons.* Ottawa: Public Works and Government Services Canada.

Auditor General of Canada. 2010. "Chapter 1: Aging Information Technology Systems." *Spring Report of the Auditor General of Canada to the House of Commons.* Ottawa: Minister of Public Works and Government Services.

Auditor General of Canada. 2011. "Chapter 2: Large Information Technology Projects." *Status Report of the Auditor General of Canada to the House of Commons.* Ottawa: Minister of Public Works and Government Services.

Auditor General of Canada. 2014. "Chapter 7: Documentary Heritage of the Government of Canada: Library and Archives Canada." *Fall Report of the Auditor General of Canada to the House of Commons,* Ottawa: Minister of Public Works and Government Services.

Auditor General of Canada. 2015. "Chapter 4: Information Technology Shared Services." *Report of the Auditor General of Canada to the House of Commons, Fall Report,* Ottawa: Office of the Auditor General.

Auditor General of Canada. 2017. "Report 1: Phoenix Pay Problems." *Report of the Auditor General of Canada to the House of Commons, Fall Report,* Ottawa: Office of the Auditor General.

Barney, Darrin. 2005. *Communication Technology.* Vancouver: UBC Press.

Bontis, Nick. 2007a. "Citizen Relationship Management in Canadian Cities: Starting to Dial 311." *Digital State at the Leading Edge,* edited by Borins et al., Toronto: University of Toronto Press, pp. 137–54.

———. 2007b. "Mining the Nation's Intellectual Capital: Knowledge Management in Government." *Digital State at the Leading Edge,* edited by Borins et al., Toronto: University of Toronto Press, pp. 155–82.

Borins, Sandford. 2007a. "Conceptual Framework." *Digital State at the Leading Edge,* edited by Borins et al., Toronto: University of Toronto Press, pp. 14–36.

———. 2007b. "What Keeps a CIO Awake at Night? Evidence from the Ontario Government." *Digital State at the Leading Edge,* edited by Borins et al., Toronto: University of Toronto Press, pp. 69–101.

Borins, Sandford and David Brown. 2007a. "E-Consultation: Technology at the Interface between Civil Society and Government." *Digital State at the Leading Edge,* edited by Borins et al., Toronto: University of Toronto Press, pp. 253–76.

———, and ———. 2007b. "Digital Leadership: The Human Face of IT." *Digital State at the Leading Edge,* edited by Borins et al., Toronto: University of Toronto Press, pp. 277–301.

Borins, Sandford, Kenneth Kernaghan, David Brown, Nick Bontis, Perri 6, and Fred Thompson. 2007. *Digital State at the Leading Edge.* Toronto: University of Toronto Press.

Braibant, Guy, editor. 1977. *Informatics and Administration.* Brussels: International Institute of Administrative Sciences.

Brown, David. 2005. "Electronic Government and Public Administration." *International Review of Administrative Sciences* 71, 2, pp. 24–54.

———. 2007. "Government On-Line," *Digital State at the Leading Edge,* edited by Borins et al., Toronto: University of Toronto Press, pp. 37–68.

Brown, David C.G. 2012. "The Unfulfilled Promise of Information Management in the Government of Canada." *Journal of Parliamentary and Political Law*, 6, 1 (March), pp. 107–127.

———. 2013. "Accountability in a Collectivized Environment: From Glassco to Digital Public Administration." *Canadian Public Administration*, 56, 1 (March), pp. 47–69.

Brown, David and George Kourakos. 2005. *Vendor Engagement Strategy Consultation*, April 2005, Report prepared on behalf of Public Works and Government Services Canada. http://www.ppforum.ca/publications/vendor-engagement-strategy-consultation

CRTC. Canadian Radio-television and Telecommunications Commission. 2016. CRTC *Submission to the Government of Canada's Innovation Agenda, December 21, 2016*. https://www.crtc.gc.ca/eng/publications/reports/rp161221/rp161221.htm

Clarke, Amanda and Mary Francoli. 2014. "What's in a Name? A Comparison of "Open Government" Definitions across Seven Open Government Partnership Members." *eJournal of eDemocracy and Open Government* 6, 3, pp. 248–66.

Dunleavy, Patrick, Helen Margetts, Simon Bastow, and Jane Tinkler. 2006a. "New Public Management Is Dead—Long Live Digital-Era Governance." *Journal of Public Administration Research and Theory*, 16, 3 (July), pp. 467–94.

———, ———, ———, and ———. 2006b. *Digital Era Governance: IT Corporations, the State and E-government*. Oxford: Oxford University Press.

Dutil, Patrice, John Langford and Jeffrey Roy. 2005. *E-Government and Service Transformation Relationships between Government and Industry: Developing Best Practices*. New Directions Series. Toronto: Institute of Public Administration of Canada.

Ellul, Jacques. 1964. *The Technology Society*. New York: Vintage Books.

Flumian, Maryantonnett, Amanda Coe, and Kenneth Kernaghan. 2007. "Transforming Service to Canadians: The Service Canada Model." *International Review of Administrative Sciences*, 73, 4, pp. 557–68.

Fountain, Jane E. (2001a). *Building the Virtual State: Information Technology and Institutional Change*. Washington, D.C.: Brookings Institute Press.

———. 2001b. "Paradoxes of Public Sector Consumer Service." *Governance* 14, 1 (January), pp. 55–73.

Geist, Michael, editor. 2015. *Law, Privacy and Surveillance in Canada in the Post-Snowden Era*. Ottawa: University of Ottawa Press.

Gow, J.I. and I.E. Hodgetts. 2003. "Where Are We Coming From? Are There Any Useful Lessons from Our Administrative History?" *Canadian Public Administration*, 46, 2 (Summer), pp. 178–201.

Heintzman, Ralph. 2014. *Renewal of the Federal Public Service toward a Charter of Public Service*. Ottawa:

Canada 2020. Available at: http://canada2020.ca/wp-content/uploads/2014/10/2014_Canada2020_Paper-Series_Public_Service_EN_Final.pdf

IHAC. Information Highway Advisory Council. 1995. *Connection, Community, Content: The Challenge of the Information Highway*. Ottawa: Minister of Supply and Services.

IHAC. Canada, Information Highway Advisory Council. 1997. *Preparing Canada for a Digital World*. Ottawa: Industry Canada.

Innis, Harold A. 1950. *Empire and Communications*. Toronto: Oxford University Press.

Kernaghan, Kenneth. 2005. "Moving toward the Virtual State: Integrating Services and Service Channels for Citizen-Centred Service Delivery." *International Review of Administrative Sciences* 71, 1, pp. 119–31.

———. 2007a. "Beyond Bubble Gum and Goodwill: Integrating Service Delivery." *Digital State at the Leading Edge*, edited by Borins et al., Toronto: University of Toronto Press, pp. 102–36.

———. 2007b. "Moving Beyond Politics as Usual? Online Campaigning." *Digital State at the Leading Edge*, edited by Borins et al., Toronto: University of Toronto Press, pp. 183–223.

———. 2007c. "Making Political Connections: IT and Political Life." *Digital State at the Leading Edge*, edited by Borins et al., Toronto: University of Toronto Press, pp. 224–52.

———. 2013. "Changing Channels: Managing Channel Integration and Migration in Public Organizations." *Canadian Public Administration* 56, 1 (March), pp. 121–41.

———. 2014a. "Digital Dilemmas: Values, Ethics and Information Technology." *Canadian Public Administration*, 57, 2 (June), pp. 295–317.

———. 2014b. "The Rights and Wrongs of Robotics: Ethics and Robots in Public Organizations." *Canadian Public Administration*, 57, 4 (December), pp. 485–506.

Kernaghan, Kenneth and Justin Gunraj. 2004. "Integrating Information Technology into Public Administration: Conceptual and Practical Considerations." *Canadian Public Administration* 47, 4 pp. (December), 525–46.

Langford, John and Yvonne Harrison. 2001. "Partnering for e-government: Challenges for Public Administrators." *Canadian Public Administration* 44, 4 (Winter), pp. 393–416.

Lenihan, Don, Tony Valeri, and David Hume. 2002. *Information as a Public Resource: Leading Canadians in the Information Age*. Ottawa: Centre for Collaborative Government.

Macdonald, David. 2011. *The Shadow Public Service: The Swelling Ranks of Federal Government Outsourced Workers*. Ottawa: Canadian Centre for Policy Alternatives.

Malloy, Jonathan. 2003. "To Better Serve Canadians: How Technology Is Changing the Relationship between Members of Parliament and Public Servants." *New*

Directions No. 9. Toronto: Institute of Public Administration of Canada.

McDonald, John. 2002. *The Financial Capability Model and the Records Management Function: An Assessment*. Ottawa: Public Policy Forum.

McLuhan, Marshall. 1964. *Understanding Media: The Extensions of Man*. New York: Signet Books.

McNutt, Kathleen. 2006. "Research Note: Do Virtual Policy Networks Matter? Tracing Network Structure Online." *Canadian Journal of Political Science* 39, 2 (June), pp. 391–405.

———. 2014. "Public Rngagement in the Web 2.0 era: Social Collaborative Technologies in a Public Sector Context." *Canadian Public Administration*, 57, 1 (March), pp. 49–70.

Mitchell, James R. 2002. "Changing the Machinery of Government." Ottawa: Sussex Circle.

Oliver, E. Lynn and Larry Sanders, editors. 2004. *E-Government Reconsidered: Renewal of Governance for the Knowledge Age*. Regina: Canadian Plains Research Centre.

Open Government Partnership. 2017. "What Is the Open Government Partnership?" Available at: https://www.opengovpartnership.org/about/about-ogp

PCO. Privy Council Office. 2014. *Blueprint 2020*. Interim report and Website available at: https://www.canada.ca/en/privy-council/topics/blueprint-2020-public-service-renewal.html

PWGSC. Public Works and Government Services Canada. 2011. "Government of Canada to Reduce Information Technology Costs and Save Taxpayers' Dollars." Gatineau QC: Canada News Centre news.gc.ca, 4 August 2011.

Rawson, Bruce. 1991. "Public Service 2000 Service to the Public Task Force: Findings and Implications." *Canadian Public Administration* 34, 3 (Fall), pp. 490–500.

Rowland, Wade. 2006. *Spirit of the Web: The Age of Information from Telegraph to Internet*. Toronto: Thomas Allen Publishers.

Roy, Jeffrey. 2006. *E-Government in Canada: Transformation for the Digital Age*. Ottawa: University of Ottawa Press.

———. 2008. "Beyond Westminster Governance: Bringing Politics and Public Service into the Networked Era." *Canadian Public Administration* 51, 4 (December), pp. 541–68.

Siemiatycki, Matti. 2015. "Public-Private Partnerships in Canada: Reflections on Twenty Years of Practice." *Canadian Public Administration* 58, 3 (September), pp. 343–62.

Tapscott, Don. 2015. *The Digital Economy, Anniversary Edition: Rethinking Promise and Peril in the Age of Networked Intelligence*. McGraw-Hill.

Tapscott, Don and Art Caston. 1993. *Paradigm Shift: The New Promise of Information Technology*. New York, McGraw-Hill

Tapscott, Don and Anthony D. Williams. 2006. *Wikinomics: How Mass Collaboration Changes Everything*. New York and Toronto: Portfolio.

TBS. Treasury Board Secretariat. 2016. Government of Canada Information Technology Strategic Plan 2016–2020: Available at: https://www.canada.ca/en/treasury-board-secretariat/services/information-technology/information-technology-strategy/strategic-plan-2016-2020.html

Thomas, Paul G. 2013. "Communications and Prime Ministerial Power." *Governing : Essays in Honour of Donald J. Savoie*, edited by James Bickerton and B. Guy Peters. Montréal: McGill-Queen's University Press, pp. 53–84.

Wallace, Theresa, Nicole Murphy, Geneviève Lépine, and David Brown, editors. 2005. *Exploring New Directions in Essential Skills*. Ottawa: Public Policy Forum.

Out from the Shadows
Political Staff as Public Administrators

Jonathan Craft

Chapter Overview

This chapter examines appointed political staff in Canada to help better understand what they do and why it matters for contemporary Canadian public administration. An overview is provided of three different types of appointed political staff that serve ministers and MPs at the federal level, and details the functions they typically perform. The chapter examines why political staff were introduced in the Canadian system, how they have evolved, and reflects on their impact on Canadian public administration.

Chapter Objectives

By the end of this chapter, students will be able to do the following:

- Assess how appointed political staffs help us understand inherent tensions between political and non-partisan aspects of public administration.
- Describe what appointed political staff do on a typical day.
- Assess what is similar and different about the work of three different types of federally appointed political staff: those who work in ministers offices (exempt staff), those who work in MPs Ottawa offices (non-ministerial parliamentary staffs), or in MPs local community offices (constituency staff).
- Describe how the role of appointed political staff has evolved over time.
- List the alleged benefits and drawbacks of having appointed political staff as part of the Canadian system of governance.

Introduction

Barbarians at the gate, the people who live in the dark, junkyard dogs, the kids in short pants. These are just some of the harsh epithets used to describe politically appointed staff in Westminster systems. These vivid adjectives are rhetorical flourishes that convey their influence and, at times, their overly zealous political involvement in policy-making and public administration. There has been a growing interest in appointed political staff as they have swelled in numbers and in their perceived ability to influence policy-making and governance (Craft, 2015a; Eichbaum & Shaw, 2010; Esselment et al., 2014). This chapter examines appointed political staff in Canada to help make sense of what they do and why it matters for contemporary Canadian public administration. An overview is provided of different types of political staff that serve ministers and MPs and the functions they typically perform. This is by no means a comprehensive treatment given the confines of a book chapter. For example, Senate staff are omitted, as are political staff working in provincial and municipal political offices. However, the federal waterfront is canvassed through analysis of three types of political staff: (1) appointed political staff who serve ministers of the crown (exempt staff), (2) those who support Members of Parliament who are not ministers (non-ministerial parliamentary staff), and those political staff who work in the local community offices of MPs (constituency staff). This helps further clarify that politically appointed staffs are not a homogenous group, and that they support ministers and members of parliament (MPs) in a variety of ways. More importantly it draws attention to the breadth of these staffs' contributions to Canadian public administration.

The inclusion of a chapter on political staff in the third edition of *The Handbook of Canadian Public Administration* reinforces that key public administration institutions, actors, and practices are dynamic. Further, it helps reinforce that public administration is not the sole ambit of public servants, and allows for some stock-taking of the growing research on political staff functions and impact within Canadian public administration. The chapter begins by setting the stage for when and why political staff became a feature of Canadian public administration, their subsequent expansion and specialization, and then looks at the three categories of political staff outlined above. The key contribution here rests not in the descriptive summary of their genesis and current functions but rather in making the case for seeing these staff as an established component of Canada's contemporary system of public administration. While often overlooked and maligned, political staff add value to the Canadian system by supporting ministers, parliamentarians, and even public servants in their work. They are often key points of contact for Canadians and businesses looking for assistance or to connect with government.

Capacity and Control: Advent and Evolution of Political Appointed Staff in Canada

The earliest catalyst for the addition of personal staff to serve MPs was to provide capacity for MPs to undertake their work. Scheduling, correspondence, constituent meetings, travel, government business, and dealing with the press became too much for individual MPs. The position of MP went from part-time add-ons to their farming, law practice, or businesses to full-time jobs in themselves. Early prime ministers and ministers relied on seconded public servants for support in getting the work of government done (Pickersgill, 1972). Looking at the historical record, one sees clear trends towards the growth in MPs and ministerial staff, and a specialization of their functions that mirror the growing complexity and scope of government itself (Craft, 2016; Savoie, 1983). The record also reveals a qualitative difference in the type of capacity required to accomplish MPs' and ministers' work. Not only do elected officials need help answering the phones, dealing with constituents, and discharging their parliamentary business—and in the case of ministers added burdens of departmental work and cabinet business—they also come from ridings that can present unique needs. For instance, MPs from downtown Montreal or northern Canada have vastly different geographies, local issues, and constituent imperatives to respond to. They will of course still provide information on government services and assist constituents in resolving whatever issues with government they may have, but some MPs may need more than one local constituency office, more staff working on correspondence, passport or employment insurance applications, or bilingual (or multilingual) staff. For their part, as it has famously been noted, ministers are not created equal (Savoie, 1999). Some have particular skill sets and aptitudes that others do not. Further, some ministers sit atop large departments, hold more complex and demanding policy files, are entrusted by the prime minister with political responsibilities for regions, or serve on cabinet or treasury board committees that require particular resources or supports (Bakvis, 1988; Benoit, 2006).

A second qualitative difference in the capacity generated by political staff is that they assist MPs and ministers with the political aspects of their roles: drafting speeches, dealing with local or departmental stakeholders, developing talking points for the media, and dealing with committee and caucus obligations and even MPs in other parties. The expansion and specialization of political staff is in part a product of the need to protect the non-partisan status of the professional public service (Aucoin, 2010). It sounds counterintuitive given the media attention that ministers' office political staff have received in extreme cases where they have been perceived to be pressuring public servants, suppressing the disclosure of reports, or leaving confidential information in bathrooms and other public places (Galloway, 2010; Legault, 2014; Smith, 2009). However, political staffs employed by ministers are termed **exempt staff** because they are exempt from the normal regimes that govern the hiring and comportment of public servants. They are acknowledged political actors who help ministers do the work or politics that is inextricably linked with decisions on resource allocation and value judgments at the heart of cabinet policy-making (Craft, 2016; Wilson, 2016). Successive Privy Council Office (PCO) guides have long acknowledged this reality and clearly articulate the role and function of ministers' offices and distinguish between the status and purpose of minister's office exempt staff and the professional public servants. For example, the guide emphasizes that exempt staff exist in an advisory role for "the political aspects of the Minister's functions but do not play a role in departmental operations" (Privy Council Office, 2015:7). The ideal is for all three sets of actors—public servants, ministers, and exempt staff—to be complementary participants who engage in discreet and overlapping work that produces good governance (Craft, 2016; Zussman, 2009).

The most recent guidance to ministers, updated subsequent to the Liberal majority of 2015, retains longstanding language that states the purpose of establishing a minister's (private) office:

> [T]o provide Ministers with advisors and assistants who are not departmental public servants, who share their political commitment, and who can complement the professional, expert and non-partisan advice and support of the public service. Consequently, they contribute a particular expertise or point of view that the public service cannot provide, and their work is crucial to the effective performance by Ministers of their official duties. (Privy Council Office, 2015, p.89)

The boundaries are of course not as cut and dry as the official guidelines suggest. The terrain at the political-administrative nexus is complex, fluid, and often the product of the personalities and context within which it operates (Savoie, 2003). A **minister's office** can also include seconded public servants, which may seem at odds with the picture painted above of these offices being staffed by politically loyal assistants who tend to the array of ministerial pressures. These seconded public servants join the ministers' office through temporary work assignments often to provide specialized expertise. Additionally, government directories often list a departmental liaison, adviser, or assistant on the minister's office roster. This is in fact a public servant who ensures the smooth communication and flow of business between the department, the minister, and the minister's office. In both cases these are, however, public-service positions and their occupants provide particular support but engage strictly in non-partisan public service work.

The situation with MPs is similar. While their appointed staff do not work on cabinet confidences and departmental policy development they play a supporting role that is distinct from that of the public service. House of Commons policy is also clear that the appointed political staff position "requires [the] utmost trust, particularly because of the politically sensitive and partisan environment in which their duties are carried out" (House of Commons, 2014). This distinction is central as it represents a political liberalization of the abilities of these staffs to assist MPs and ministers with work that public servants cannot perform.

A second key catalyst for the expansion and specialization of political staff in Ottawa has been the search for increased political control in governing. Growing use of political staff has been linked to a broader set of public management reforms aimed at strengthening political control and securing improved responsiveness from the public service and machinery of public administration (Dahlström et al., 2011; Savoie, 1983). This is in part a product of the fact governments have become larger and involved in a wider array of activities. A key function of political staff is to ensure that the government's or individual MP's business does not get lost in the larger churn of government and public administration. Ministers' office staff in particular have become common features in Westminster systems because of their ability to help advance the government's policy agenda and deal with the bumps along the road that threaten to derail all governments (Rhodes et al., 2010). Secondly, a shared concern emerged among politicians in Westminster-style systems that the public service was unresponsive—unwilling to accept and follow the policy preferences of politicians—and instead promoted its own policy and public administration agenda. Canada's leading student of political-administration puts it succinctly, "Indeed, by the 1970s, many politicians and their advisors claimed that permanent public servants were running governments and that their apparent deference to politicians was pure pretense" (Savoie, 2003:7). Shoring up control through a more muscular political arm of government consisting of political staffs was thus a natural response. In fact, it is a phenomenon that stretches past party lines. Successive Liberal, Progressive Conservative, and Conservative governments have used exempt political staff, in different ways, explicitly to try and ensure sufficient political management and public-service responsiveness (Craft, 2016).

The establishment and subsequent institutionalization and specialization of political staff, particularly exempt staff in the **Prime Minister's Office** (PMO) and ministers' offices, has led to criticisms that these actors are part of an unhealthy move away from traditional cabinet government and public administration. For example, in a special report to Parliament, the Public Service Commission asserted, "the traditional relationship between elected officials and the public service has been deeply changed by the emergence of influential ministerial staff" (Public Service Commission of Canada, 2011: 22). Savoie argues that power has drifted to the centre of government and particularly to a small and influential inner court consisting of the prime minister and a select group of ministers, senior officials, and exempt staffs that has displaced Parliament and cabinet (Savoie, 1999). Aucoin's (2012) new political governance (NPG) articulates similar concerns, but goes further suggesting that it is not only political staff in the prime minister's inner circle that are of concern but that political staff are now systemic features of our contemporary system of government. In the wake of the perceived unworkability of traditional public administration in Canada, NPG is argued to involve:

- the concentration of power under the prime minister and her or his court of select ministers, political aides, and public servants;
- the enhanced number, roles, and influence of political staff;
- the increased personal attention by the prime minister to the appointment of senior public servants where the prime minister has the power to appoint;
- the increased pressure on the public service to provide a pro-government spin on government communications; and
- the increased expectation that public servants demonstrate enthusiasm for the government's agenda.

Aucoin's theory was a work in progress and subsequent research has found that it may have been more of an extreme characterization than empirical reality (Craft, 2016; Boston and Halligan, 2012; Wilson, 2016). Nonetheless, the fact that exempt staffs have attracted this type of attention reflects that they are a reality of public administration that needs to be better studied and carefully regulated. Thoughtful analysis has recognized that exempt staffs, and political staff working for MPs, offer much support for the overloaded MPs and ministers they work for. However, it is clear that a more active set of political staff in the system creates opportunities for inappropriate behaviour and role uncertainty that requires clear rules of engagement and oversight (Brodie, 2009; Wilson, 2016). According to one published report, there is widespread agreement that a hierarchy to the political staff class exists, with the order being PMO exempt staff, opposition leader's political staff, ministers' exempt staff, critics' office political staff, a caucus chair's office political staff, a senior MP's office political staff, a senator's office political staff, and finally run-of-the-mill backbench MPs' Ottawa political staff (Carlson, 2011).

Prime Ministerial and Ministerial Exempt Staff

The PMO attracts the most attention as the largest and best resourced ministerial office. It sits at the top of the food chain of exempt staff as the only ministerial office with responsibilities for supporting full cabinet and its committees. It is the only political office that plays an enterprise function in supporting the prime minister as leader of the government and chair of cabinet. Over the years the PMO has been organized in a variety of ways, with new units coming on stream and others falling off that reflect the changing needs of the government and the particular style of the prime minister of the day. As has been written about at length elsewhere (Craft, 2016; Savoie, 1999), the modern PMO owes much to the prime ministership of Pierre Trudeau. His attempts to rationalize policy-making by creating an elaborate system of cabinet committees and a better-resourced PMO aimed to curtail the perceived influence of departmental public service mandarins. The foundation built of a better-resourced and more-involved PMO has stood the test of time, as has its general organization and many of the office's core functions. For example, the PMO has been remarkably consistent in terms of the number of exempt staff it houses at around 100 (see Table 23.1 on page 446). Its core functional units typically include:

- operations;
- policy;
- communications and correspondence units;
- issues management/strategic planning;
- stakeholder relations and outreach;
- appointments and personnel; and
- tour and scheduling.

The PMO is organized hierarchically and led by a chief of staff (formerly principal secretary). Senior PMO exempt political staff (e.g. director of policy,

communications, stakeholder management, etc.) typically report directly to the chief of staff. Chiefs of staff are the most senior advisers to the prime minister, and interlocutors with cabinet, caucus, and the senior levels of the public service. Some PMOs have used deputy chiefs of staff or brought back the principal secretary role, but these have typically managed select files and the strategic agenda of government, with the chief of staff playing a more operational role (Craft, 2016; Zussman, 2013).

The size and influence of each of the PMOs functional lines has waxed and waned but the list provides a good sense of how the PMO is organized and the nature of the support provided by exempt political staff for the prime minister's travel, cabinet business, communications, and government appointments. The precise configuration of the PMO and its exempt staffs' functions are aimed at providing whatever support is needed for the prime minister to do his or her job. Writing in the 1970s, Punette's assessment seems to stand the test of time in describing the three fundamental roles played by the PMO: "Firstly, secretarial and administrative capacity; secondly, a source of political advice to the prime minister of the day; and, thirdly, it provides a supply of factual information about the affairs of government, to enable him to face his ministers from an informed base. If he is to be free from dependence on departmental civil servants, this factual information can only come from a private bureaucracy" (Punnett, 1977:74–5).

The spectrum of files and activities on which PMO exempt staff play points directly to the amount of public administration business that now intersects with PMO and ministers' offices. PMO exempt staff is unique in that they are often more engaged with the major levers of policy-making and the political management of the government's agenda. This can involve advising and supporting work on the big files—cabinet-making, cabinet and cabinet committee agendas, development of memorandums to cabinet on policy matters, and the broader policy and political direction of government as articulated in Speeches from the Throne, budgets, and mandate letters (Craft, 2016; Savoie, 1999). Support is also provided for the day-to-day administration of vetting appointments for approval by cabinet, communications and forward planning, and managing issues that emerge along with the never-ending flow of correspondence to the prime minister from various quarters (Thomas, 2009).

Correspondence and the operations unit of the PMO that arranges for travel, are typically the largest in terms of staffing complements (Brodie, 2012). Others like policy, issues management, and communications are typically smaller but influential. Recent comparative research of Canadian and other Westminster PMO advisers found this subset of staff engage in similar types of work; they "offer counsel on a variety of subjects, propose courses of action, assess political circumstances, manage issues, and at times provide personal and emotional support to the prime minister" (Esselment et al., 2014:13). Indeed, Canadian PMO exempt staff are important actors who help shape the policy agenda of government and move it through the formal public administration institutions and processes. Existing research has however cautioned that, while influential, these actors are limited in terms of the number of files they can engage with and are strategic about their involvement focusing on government priorities (Craft, 2016; Lewis, 2013; Savoie, 1999). A significant source of the PMO's influence is its ability to reach into the various corners of government through its ability to marshal staff in ministers' offices. It also leverages the vast expertise and resources of the public service via the Privy Council Office, which performs a cabinet secretariat function but has evolved to also be the prime minister's department (Craft, 2016; Savoie, 2003).

Table 23.1 confirms that the number of exempt staff in the PMO has been remarkably stable at around one hundred, with most allocated to the management and administration of the office. In recent years there has been a growth in the exempt communications staff. There has also been a growth in the number of PMO exempt staff who help manage the issues of the day and government communications efforts. As depicted in Figure 23.1 below, this compares with about 15 staffers in the Martin PMO and twelve during Chrétien's time in power.

There are clear limits to what we know about how some PMO units work, such as those that manage issues or deal with stakeholders. Research on others is dated, like that on the functions of regional "desks" or assistants (Bakvis, 1991). Other researchers have chipped away at the notion of a centralization of power while still acknowledging an important role for PMO exempt staff (Lewis, 2013). However, we do know that the PMO continues to serves as a clearing house: helping to advance the government's policy and political agenda, coordinate its work with the public service, manage the prime minister's and cabinet's time appropriately, and help manage various events that emerge unexpectedly. Lastly, the PMO also plays a human resources role of sorts in managing the overall exempt staff through assisting (and vetting) ministerial office hires. In some administrations the practice was regimented, requiring sign-off from the PMO chief of staff for filling some positions or vetoing certain appointments in recognition of the

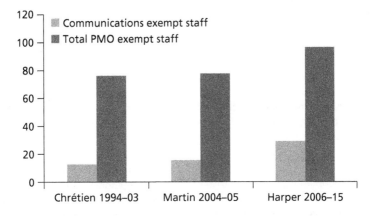

Figure 23.1 Growth of PMO Communications Political Staff, 1994–2015[1]

importance that ministers' exempt staff make for the success of government (Jeffreys, 2010).

Ministers' offices have also evolved significantly from the initial "special assistant" classification created in 1958 to help ministers deal with the press (Mallory, 1967). The contemporary minister's office, like the PMO, is organized hierarchically. It includes a chief of staff, a director of policy, press secretaries, clerical and administrative assistants, and a chauffeur, among others. Table 23.1 highlights that the real growth in the aggregate number of exempt staff working in Ottawa has been in ministers' offices. The particulars of how each minister's office is organized are determined by how ministers spend their discretionary budget for exempt staffing. Official government documents make clear that the purposes of such exempt staff may include "reviewing briefings and other advice prepared by the department; assisting the Minister in developing policy positions, including those that reflect the Minister's political perspective; preparing speeches and politically oriented communications; liaising with other Ministers' offices and caucus . . ." (Privy Council Office, 2015: 46). Indeed, as Robson's (2015) study of ministers' office exempt staff concludes, "Political staff are clearly employed by governments for a reason, or, more likely, several concurrent reasons. Those various reasons seem to be worth about $54 million annually to the federal government" (Robson, 2015: 693).

Recent years have seen a spate of practitioner accounts and scholarly research that has helped to lift the curtain that has long shrouded the exempt staff world. There is also a growing body of official documentation and reports that help flesh out what exactly these offices do, and what particular positions within them undertake. Treasury Board Secretariat (TBS) guides have for some time included an appendix that list various positions and their responsibilities. The following outlines the responsibilities of the minister's chief of staff and the director of parliamentary affairs:

Chief of Staff
- is the most senior political adviser to the minister;
- is responsible for the overall management of the minister's office, including managing the office budget and staff;

Table 23.1   Federal Exempt Staff by Department (31 March 2001 to 31 March 2016)

Year	PMO Exempt Staff Complement	Total Exempt Staff—PMO & Ministers' Offices
1990–1	99	460
1994–5	76	427
1999–2000	80	525
2001	83	461
2002	81	461
2003	77	488
2004	64	428
2005	68	461
2006	65	194
2007	79	414
2008	92	442
2009	94	487
2010	112	532
2011	99	520
2012	95	536
2013	101	570
2014	96	566
2015	95	571
2016	74	391

Source: Adapted from tables provided to the author by Treasury Board Secretariat[2]

- is responsible for developing and implementing strategic plans in order to assist in delivering the department and minister's mandate;
- is responsible, on behalf of the minister, for liaising with senior departmental officials in order to ensure a positive working relationship between the minister and the Public Service; must ensure that the minister is properly briefed and advised on all issues that relate to the government's mandate and the department's objectives; and must liaise, on behalf of the minister, with the Prime Minister's Office and other ministers' chiefs of staff in order to address governmentwide issues.

Director of Parliamentary Affairs

- is responsible for advising and briefing the minister on all legislative issues;
- is responsible, on behalf of the minister, for overseeing all phases of the legislative approval process from the development of legislation within the department to Royal Assent;
- is the point person within the minister's office for implementing the government's parliamentary reform initiative, which includes consulting committee members on proposed legislation;
- is responsible for liaising with caucus and the office of the minister's parliamentary secretary to discuss the department's legislative agenda;
- must liaise with the Prime Minister's Office, other ministers' offices, and caucus members to ensure coordination of government-wide legislative issues; and
- must work closely with the director of policy to ensure consistency between policy and legislative initiatives. (Treasury Board Secretariat, 2011)

Like those detailing the inner workings of the PMO, these are merely guidelines and there is little empirical research to support precisely what these staff do. Detailed examinations do exist for some roles, such as policy advisers. For example, Craft's (2016) book-length treatment documents a high degree of formal advisory work through written and oral partisan-political advice to ministers, and regular engagement with public servants in the development of formal policy-making documents like **memorandums to cabinet**. Ministers' office exempt staffs responsible for policy matters were also found to be key conduits for external stakeholder inputs. Work by Wilson (2015; 2016) has produced a useful profile of exempt staff with policy responsibilities. Contrary to popular accounts, he found this subset of exempt staff to be better educated and older than the moniker of "kids in short pants" suggests. Wilson's (2016) surveys of ministerial policy advisers suggests that they "increase ministers' policy capacity, encourage greater responsiveness from public servants, and generally feel that they enjoy good relations with officials and respect their role" (Wilson, 2016: 337). Unsurprisingly, these staff saw their role as primarily one of giving advice on politics and policy; the survey

supports heavy involvement in formal policy-making instruments with most reporting little to no engagement in constituency case work (Wilson, 2016: 346).

However, like the PMO, exempt staff in ministers' offices engage in more than policy work, supporting ministers in their preparation for events, cabinet, question period, legislative duties, and the various public-facing events that fill up ministers' schedules. The Treasury Board Secretariat has created profiles of the typical positions and functions that exempt ministerial staff undertake. Again, these are guidelines, as ministers will decide for themselves how best to employ their exempt staff. The conclusion of the research on exempt staff completed for the Gomery commission in 2006 was that, in general, exempt staff "by virtue of their political relationship with the party in power and/or the minister they serve, are well placed to influence both the bounce and bobble of bureaucratic political interface and the pace and progress of public policy in Canada" (Benoit, 2006:146). We now have more empirical certainty, particularly related to exempt staff who serve as policy advisers, to support that claim (Craft, 2016; Wilson 2015, 2016). However, a fuller picture of political staff contributions to Canadian public administration can be gained by going beyond the personal offices of the prime minister and ministers to those who serve MPs in Ottawa and work in the local offices of each and every riding across the country.

MP's Ottawa Staff

In 2016, the House of Commons human resources unit reported 2095 active political staff were directly employed by MPs.[3] This includes both those staff that MPs appoint to help them in their Ottawa offices as well as those who staff their local constituency offices, which are examined below. Today's staffing allotments are much more generous than early supports put in place for MPs, which consisted of basic shared clerical supports. As O'Brien and Bosc (2009, footnote 440) detail in the *House of Commons Procedure and Practice* manual, early resources for MPs were basic and often shared:

> In 1913, secretarial assistance was first made available to Members for a few days at a time. Beginning in 1916, Members shared a pool of secretaries who were laid off during periods of

recess and dissolution. In 1958, secretaries became dedicated to individual Members. In 1968, each Member was authorized to hire one full-time secretary. In 1974, a second full-time secretary was authorized for each Member. The same year, constituency offices were established. In 1978, each Member received a staff budget of $58,000, including at least $12,000 for constituency staff, to be used at the Member's discretion for staffing requirements. For the 1999–2000 fiscal year, the base Office Budget was set at $190,000.

Today the House of Commons internal management board, the Board of Internal Economy (BIE), establishes the policies that govern the particulars of MPs' offices, including staff. The 2015–16 member's expenditure report for MPs reveals that, collectively, MPs spent $62,561,319.23 on employees (Parliament of Canada, 2016). This figure masks likely variation in how individual MPs staff their offices in Ottawa and in their constituencies, but indicates the public resources brought to bear to assist MPs in doing their work. An MP's office basic budget amount in 2016 was $349,100. In some cases this basic budget is supplemented by a geographic supplement that can be in the tens of thousands of dollars for larger ridings, or an elector supplement for densely populated ridings.

The BIE has established three types of employees for MPS: regular employees who will be on the payroll for six months or more, short-term employees, and on-call employees. MPs have significant discretion to organize their offices as they see fit, but the BIE has set some restrictions. For example, MPs cannot hire immediate family members or members of a political party executive (House of Commons, 2016). As Dicklin (2016) points out, MPs follow some basic configurations, allocating more staff to the local or Ottawa office depending on whether they are constituency focused or prize their work in the nation's capital. Figure 23.2 below sets out the typical office of an MP that includes both an Ottawa-based staff and the local constituency team in the riding.

What do MPs Ottawa staff do? In some ways they are a pared-down version of ministerial exempt staff. They have responsibilities for the operational matters that touch an MP's life in Ottawa but also broader responsibilities for supporting the profile of their MP. As one recent account put it, staffers "can affect Canadian policy. Policy advisors liaise with industry representatives and lobbyists seeking policy changes, filtering information before it reaches their boss. Some staffers provide briefing notes ahead of meetings and draft questions for key witnesses in committee hearings. By maintaining their bosses'

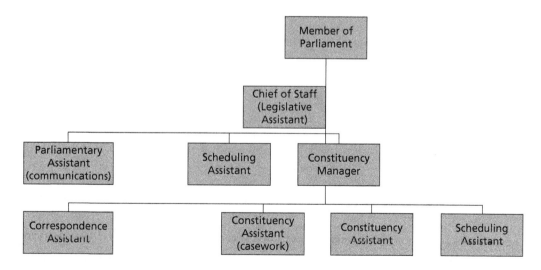

Figure 23.2 Typical Parliamentary Staff Office Organization

Source: Adapted from Dickin 2016, p.14.

Facebook and Twitter accounts, they also have a heavy hand in developing an MP's public persona" (Carleson, 2011). The key distinction is that these MPs do not have cabinet responsibilities or a portfolio to manage. They nonetheless have legislative obligations including member statements and questions along with opportunities to develop private member's bills. They may also sit on House of Commons committees and have various communications and logistical needs. One experienced MP staffer reflected on the gist of the position as follows:

> Staffers work on the MP's social media presence and respond to questions and comments. They prepare the MP for media appearances. They liaise with dozens of stakeholders, public servants, departmental officials, ministerial staff and senior government or opposition staff. Staffers monitor the media. They do research and policy analysis relevant to the MP's interests and portfolio. Staffers write press releases, editorials and website content. They get the MP reimbursed for travel expenses and help make travel arrangements. They "staff" him or her at events, which is to say they act as a personal assistant: carrying wallets, purses, business cards, water and hand sanitizer; taking photos; getting the names and contact information of people the MP wants to follow up with; and doing anything else the MP might need. Whatever you see an MP doing, a staffer helped him or her do it. (Dickin, 2016)

Constituency Office Staff: Government's Unofficial Front Door?

The third set of appointees is those who work for MPs in their constituency offices. Research suggests that MPs take their constituency work seriously and see it as a meaningful part of their overall role as MP. In fact, in the 1970s survey work found that 62 per cent of MPs considered it most important to look after the needs of their constituents. In the 1980s constituency work occupied from 50 per cent to 80 per cent of members' time, and in the 1990s MPs spent about 80 per cent of their time on riding issues (Docherty 1997; Miller 1986; Prince and Mancuso 1995). Some might

be surprised to learn that it was entrepreneurial MPs who recognized the need for help in their ridings, which led to the establishment of informal, and then formal, constituency offices. As one observer notes, Ed Broadbent in Oshawa in the twilight of the 1960s and then Flora MacDonald, who opened and financed out of her own funds a local office in Kingston office staffed by part-time students, inspired the system that now exists to help serve Canadians (MacLeod, 2004). Constituency work can be grouped into three general categories (1) representing general constituency concerns and interests in Parliament and with government; (2) meeting with constituents and community; (3) providing service and help to individual constituents in their dealings with government (Franks, 2007). Staff are vital to an MP's ability to do a lot of that work. Constituency staff are those who answer the phone when you call, upset about a government policy decision, frustrated about the delay in receiving a government benefit or document. Indeed, staff have been expanded as MPs serve ombudsperson-like functions, helping local voters who have issues with government programs or services. This can involve providing general information about where to apply or how to access a service, clarifying federal and provincial responsibilities, or prompting MPs to write to ministers to make them aware of matters or request their assistance. However, MPs and their local staff are more likely to work through less extreme channels. The member's office staff will likely find it more efficient to work at the local level of the relevant department, especially as the files are usually there. When enquiries are made to them, ministers' offices turn to the local office for an update. Working through the bureaucracy frequently provides satisfactory results (House of Commons, 2004).

Research on constituency office staff is limited, which is unfortunate as these staff are for many Canadians the front door to government, a point of access for information about government programs, services, or support in times of need. According to MacLeod's research, the modern constituency office works to balance several core functions, including to "provide service and assistance in dealing with government departments, to engage the public, maintain a presence in the community, provide informal counselling on personal and professional matters, act as brokers and mediators between interests, collate local opinion, and advocate to each level of government and their party on matters concerning specific individuals and their community-at-large" (MacLeod, 2006: 10-11). They will often work their Ottawa counterparts and public servants as needed to help keep their member organized and resolve local files each year. MacLeod summarizes the types of staff who work in these offices and the function they perform:

> The staffers themselves divide easily between lifers and flyers: those who diligently ensure the continuity of operations on the ground and those young and ambitious junior staffers who see the constituency office as a short track to a political life in Ottawa.[4] The best offices tend to be staffed by the former—citizens are rightfully wary of the latter—and over time a dedicated constituency assistant will become a kind of public service sage, a general practitioner capable of parsing application forms and knowing the ins and outs of every department and program, all the while keeping a finger to the wind of public opinion. Predictably, this sustained exposure leads to their developing an acute sensitivity to local need. It's across their desk and over their phones that the most delicate personal details pass: from the plight of a veteran, to the university prospects of a recent high school graduate. (MacLeod, 2006: 10)

Again this provides a sense of the public administration that constituency staff take part in. They are often the front-line face of government when constituency members seek out help. While not political in the sense they are not advising ministers like exempt staff do, they are often key sources for MPs to get the pulse of issues. While this set of staff is appointed at the discretion of the MP, and organized functionally according to the MP's wishes, there are guidelines that spell out the distinction.

> Constituency offices are intended to facilitate the carrying out of Members' parliamentary functions, such as representing their constituents, and may not be used to promote their re-election, to support a candidate or a political party, or to facilitate the internal organization of political parties at any time. Members' offices may not be used at anytime as a rally point for any political or election related activities. (House of Commons, 2016: 7)

Political Staff and Accountability

A final point worth emphasizing regarding political staff is that there have been increasing attempts to better regulate and define the accountability relationships that govern their employment. Convention, policies, and legislation have established accountability relationships for all three categories of political staff. In each case it is very clear that MPs and ministers are accountable for their staff. MPs for instance, are governed by the BIE bylaws that flow from authorities in Section 53 of the Parliament of Canada Act. These are very explicit in noting that that MPs have full responsibility for their staff as the employer:

> Members are the employers of their employees and have full discretion in the direction and control of the work performed on their behalf by employees and contractors. Members are always responsible for actions taken on their behalf. Even where there has been a delegation of authority, Members remain responsible for their employees' actions and decisions. (House of Commons, 2014)

Exempt ministerial staff have also become more regulated; official guidelines and clear language have been strengthened and expanded over time to make clear the limits and requirements that come with that position (Smith, 2008). Like most governments, shortly after assuming office the Justin Trudeau Liberal Government released an updated guide to ministers, ministers of state, and exempt staff called *Open and Accountable Government*. Like previous guides, it makes clear that exempt staff "are subject to a broad range of terms and conditions set by the Treasury Board for the government as a whole and also to the same statutory conflict of interest and post-employment regime and ethical guidelines as Ministers and deputy ministers" (Privy Council Office, 2015: 46). Unlike BIE guidelines, the guide does not explicitly state that ministers are accountable and responsible for their staffs. This is problematic and an area for improvement. This became a public issue when in 2010 the Conservative government made it clear that exempt staff would no longer testify before House of Commons committee probing exempt staff interference with the departmental release of Access to Information Reports. Their stated reason for refusal was that exempt staffs are accountable to ministers who should be the public-office holders to appear (Curry, 2010). The 2015 Open and Accountable Government Guide does, however, include the first ever code of conduct for ministerial exempt staff as an appendix item. This brings Canada in line with other jurisdictions like Britain and Australia, which have had similar codes for some time. Much of the content simply codifies material contained elsewhere, making it clear that exempt staff are paid by public funds and, while political appointees, must engage only in government business, not party business; not inappropriately use government resources; and are not to engage in the operations of departments or direct public servants. The guide adds that political staff are forbidden from deceiving or knowingly misleading Parliament, ministers, public servants, or the public (Privy Council Office, 2015:89–92).

Conclusion: Political Staff and Broader Public Administration

When we think about public administration we may think of Weberian bureaucracy organized in hierarchies with tight spans of control and chains of delegation. Faceless bureaucrats toiling away in cubicles or new-fangled "Office 2.0" set-ups may come to mind. Perhaps we see it as the complex web of policies, staff, and procedures that deliver programs and services, or the big physical institutions like Parliament or the Supreme Court. There are, however, a growing number of public servants who are political appointees who are part of today's public administration reality. These staff are not lifetime professional non-partisan civil servants, but rather temporary appointees hired at the discretion of political actors, be it ministers or MPs. Some sit at the highest levels of government supporting the prime minister and cabinet decision-making. Some draft MP's speeches and keep them organized for committee, and some are on the other end of the phone when Canadians call their local MP's looking for help with their employment insurance applications. It is clear that the political staff world is stratified, with senior political staff in the PMO playing much different roles than the average constituency assistant to a backbench MP. The PMO has gained considerable influence as it has become better resourced and more involved in the diverse array of public administration responsibilities that governments must tackle (Savoie, 1999). Ministers' offices too have become more sophisticated and staffed by a greater number of exempt staff that can be influential for policy, communications, issue management, and stakeholder relations (Craft, 2016). Canada is not alone in dealing with the advent and impact of political staff. Various systems of government are grappling with the implications of an increase in the number and activities of political exempt staff (Eichbaum and Shaw, 2010; Zussman, 2009). However, in better understanding the function and impact of exempt staff it is important not to overlook the political staff who help MPs in Ottawa and their ridings. Together, these three categories of political staff reveal an array of public administration work that is now an increasingly visible feature of Canadian public administration.

Important Terms and Concepts

exempt staff

memorandum to cabinet (MC)

minister's office

Prime Minister's Office (PMO)

Study Questions

1. Why do MPs appoint political staff when MPs can draw upon the support of the public service?
2. Why have the number and type of political staff expanded? Do politicians have sufficient staff? Should the numbers be increased or reduced?
3. What are the benefits and drawbacks of having appointed political staff as part of the Canadian system of governance?

Notes

1   Reproduced with data reported in Esselment and Wilson, 2015
2   Securing figures on federal exempt staff was complicated by the fact that different classification schemes have been used over the years. The data presented for 1990/91 and 1994/95 are drawn from Treasury Board Secretariat (2006). All other years are drawn from a larger table provided to the author by the Office of the Chief Human Resources Officer, Treasury Board of Canada Secretariat in response to request No.

31029, 87685, and 99103. The information provided is for the Core Public Administration (CPA) only. CPA departments and agencies are as detailed in schedules I and IV of the Financial Administration Act. Data includes all employment tenures, active employees, and employees on leave without pay. Data presented as of March 31st of each year.
3   Provided to the author by email.
4   See Peter MacLeod, "The High Cost of Constituency Politics", *Globe and Mail*, November 24, 2004.

References

Aucoin, P. 2010. "Canada." *Partisan Appointees and Public Servants: An International Analysis of the Role of the Political Adviser*, edited by C. Eichbaum and R. Shaw, Boston: Edward Elgar, pp. 64–93. http://dx.doi.org/10.4337/9781849803298.00008.

Aucoin, P. 2012. New political governance in Westminster systems: Impartial public administration and management performance at risk. *Governance, 25*(2), 177-109.

Bakvis, H. 1991. *Regional Ministers: Power and Influence in the Canadian Cabinet*. Toronto: University of Toronto Press.

Benoit, L. 2006. "Ministerial Staff: The Life and Times of Parliament's Statutory Orphans." Commission of Inquiry into the Sponsorship Program and Advertising Activities, Restoring Accountability, Research Studies 1:145–252. Ottawa: Public Works and Government Services Canada.

Boston, J. and John Halligan. 2012.Poltiical Management and New Political Governance: reconciling Political Responsiveness and Neutral Governance, in H. Bakvis and M. Jarvis (eds.), From New Public Management to New Political Governance. Montreal/Kingston: McGill-Queen's University Press. 204–241.

Brodie, I. 2012. "In Defence of Political Staff." *Canadian Parliamentary Review*.

Carlson, Kathryn. 2011. "Kids on the Hill: Young Guns Rule." *National Post*, February 26. http://www.nationalpost.com/news/features/Life-on-the-Hill-Young-guns-rule/4350453/story.html

Craft, Jonathan. (2010). "Do Politicians Control Government?", in *Approaching Public Administration: Core Debates and Emerging Issues*, Roberto Leone and Frank Ohemeng (eds). Emond Montgomery Publications, pp. 54–64.

_____. 2014. "Policy Advice and New Political Governance: Revisiting the Orthodox." *Canadian Public Administration in the 21st Century*, edited by Roberge and Conteh, Boca Raton: CRC, pp. 41–59.

————. 2015a. "Conceptualizing Partisan Advisers as Policy Workers." *Policy Sciences Journal* 48, 2, pp. 135–58.

————. 2015b. "Revisiting the Gospel: Appointed Political Staffs and Core Executive Policy Coordination." *International Journal of Public Administration* 38, 1, pp. 56–65. http://dx.doi.org/10.1080/01900692.2014.928316.

————. 2016. *Backrooms and Beyond: Partisan Advisers and the Politics of Policy Work in Canada*. Toronto: IPAC/University of Toronto Press.

Curry, Bill. 2010. "Ottawa Bars Ministers' Staff from Appearing before Committees." *The Globe and Mail*, May 23. http://www.theglobeandmail.com/news/politics/ottawa-bars-ministers-staff-from-appearing-before-committees/article4189665/

Dahlström, C., B.G. Peters, and J. Pierre. 2011. *Steering from the Centre: Strengthening Political Control in Western Democracies*. Toronto: University of Toronto Press.

Dickin, D. 2016. "Organizing the Halls of Power: Federal Parliamentary Staffers and Members of Parliament's Offices." *Canadian Parliamentary Review* 39, 2, pp. 8–16.

Docherty, David C. 1997. *Mr. Smith Goes to Ottawa: Life in the House of Commons*. Vancouver: University of British Columbia Press.

Eichbaum, Christopher and Richard Shaw. 2010. *Partisan Appointees and Public Servants: An International Analysis of the Role of the Political Adviser*. Northampton: Edward Elgar.

Esselment, A.L., J. Lees-Marshment, and A. Marland. 2014. "The Nature of Political Advising to Prime Ministers in Australia, Canada, New Zealand and the UK." *Commonwealth & Comparative Politics* 52, 3, pp. 358–75.

Esselment, A., and R. P. Wilson. 2015. Political Staff and the Permanent Campaign. Paper presented to the Annual Meeting of the Canadian Political Science Association. Ottawa, Canada, June 4.

Franks, C.E.S. 2007. "Members and Constituency Roles in the Canadian Federal System." *Regional and Federal Studies*, 17, 1, pp. 23–45,

Galloway, G. 2010. "Censoring Report 'Would Save the Requester Money,' Tory Staffer Says." *The Globe and Mail*, May 11. http://www.theglobeandmail.com/news/politics/ottawa-notebook/censoring-report-would-save-the-requester-money/article4389940/

House of Commons. 2004. Organizing your Ottawa and Constituency Offices.

House of Commons. 2014. *Policy on Confidentiality and Conflicts of Interest*, effective February 2014, online: http://www.parl.gc.ca/about/house/boie/pdf/Backgrounder-26-02-2014-E.pdf

House of Commons. 2016. Members Manual. http://www.parl.gc.ca/smartweb/mas/Document.aspx?sbdid=8546E680-EA17-4599-9A7D-F9DB205881F3&sbpid=pdf

Jeffrey, B. 2010. *Divided loyalties: the liberal party of Canada, 1984-2008*. Toronto: University of Toronto Press.

Legault, Suzanne. 2014. Interference with Access to Information: Part 2. Special Report to Parliament from the Information Commissioner of Canada. April.

Lewis, J.P. 2013. "Elite Attitudes on the Centralization of Power in Canadian Political Executives: A Survey of Former Canadian Provincial and Federal Cabinet Ministers, 2000–2010." *Canadian Journal of Political Science* 46, 4, 799–818.

Mallory, J.R. 1967. "The Minister's Office Staff: An Unreformed Part of the Public Service." *Canadian Public Administration* 10, 1, pp. 25–34. http://dx.doi.org/10.1111/j.1754-7121.1967.tb00962.x.

MacLeod, P. 2004. Opinion. *The Globe and Mail*. https://www.theglobeandmail.com/opinion/peter-macleod/article1144423/

MacLeod, P. 2006. How to Organize an Effective Constituency Office. Canadian Parliamentary Review, 29(1): 9-12.

Miller, Bob 1986. "On the Front Lines." *Parliamentary Government*, Vol. 8, pp. 3–5.

O'Brien, Audrey, and Marc Bosc (eds). 2009. *House of Commons Procedure and Practice*, Second edn, 2009. Ottawa: House of Commons.

Parliament of Canada. 2016. Member's Expenditure Summary. http://www.parl.gc.ca/PublicDisclosure/SummaryExpenditures.aspx?Id=MER2016Q4&Language=E

Pickersgill, J.W. 1972. "The W. Clifford Clark Memorial Lectures, 1972 (no 1): Bureaucrats and Politicians." *Canadian Public Administration* 15, 3, pp. 418–27. http://dx.doi.org/10.1111/j.1754-7121.1972.tb01248.x.

Price, Richard and Mancuso, Maureen. 1995. "The Ties That Bind: Parliamentary Members and Their Constituencies." *Introductory Readings in Canadian Government*, 2nd edn, edited by R. Krause and R. Wagenberg, Mississauga: Copp Clarke Pitman, 195-220.

Privy Council Office. 2015. *Open and Accountable Government*. Her Majesty the Queen in Right of Canada.

Public Service Commission of Canada. 2011. "Merit and Non-Partisanship Under the Public Service Employment Act: A Special Report to Parliament." Ottawa.

Punnett, R.M. 1977. *The Prime Minister in Canadian Government and Politics*. Toronto: Macmillan of Canada.

Rhodes, R.A.W., J. Wanna, and P. Weller. 2010. *Comparing Westminster*. Oxford: Oxford University Press.

Robson, J. 2015. "Spending on Political Staffers and the Revealed Preferences of Cabinet: Examining a New Data Source on Federal Political Staff in Canada." *Canadian Journal of Political Science* 48, 3, pp. 675–97.

Savoie, D.J. 1983. "The Minister's Staff: The Need for Reform." *Canadian Public Administration* 26, 4, pp. 509–24. http://dx.doi.org/10.1111/j.1754-7121.1983.tb01042.x.

Savoie, D. J. 1999. *Governing from the centre: the concentration of power in Canadian politics*. University of Toronto Press.

Savoie, D.J. 2003. *Breaking the Bargain: Public Servants, Ministers, and Parliament*. Toronto: IPAC/University of Toronto Press

Smith, J. 2009. "Raitt-gate Rocks Tories." *Toronto Star*, June 4.

Smith, Alex. 2008. *Ministerial Staff: Issues of Accountability and Ethics*. Library of Parliament, International Affairs, Trade and Finance Division, Ottawa: Canada. http://www.lop.parl.gc.ca/content/lop/researchpublications/prb0602-e.htm

Stilborn, J. 2002. *The Roles of the Member of Parliament in Canada: Are They Changing?* Library of Parliament, Political and Social Affairs Division, Ottawa: Canada.

Thomas, Paul G. 2009. *Who Is Getting the Message? Communications at the Centre of Government*. Ottawa: Research Study for the *Oliphant Commission*.

Treasury Board Secretariat. 2006. Expenditure Review of Federal Public Sector. Vol. 2, Compensation Snapshot and Historical Perspective, 1990 to 2003. Ottawa: Treasury Board Secretariat. http://www.tbs-sct.gc.ca/report/orp/2007/er-ed/vol2/vol212-eng.asp#Toc158090277.

_____. 2011, January. *Policies for Minister's Offices*. Ottawa: Treasury Board Secretariat. https://www.tbs-sct.gc.ca/pubs_pol/hrpubs/mg-ldm/2011/pgmo-pldcm12-eng.asp#tocAppA

Wilson, R. Paul. 2015. "A Profile of Ministerial Policy Staff in the Government of Canada." *Canadian Journal of Political Science* 48, 2, pp. 455–71.

Wilson, R. Paul. 2016. "Trust but Verify: Ministerial Policy Advisors and Public Servants in the Government of Canada." *Canadian Public Administration* 59, 3, pp. 337–56.

Zussman, David. 2009. *Political Advisors. Expert Group on Conflict of Interest*. Paris: Organisation for Economic Cooperation and Development.

Zussman, David. 2013. *Off and Running: The Prospects and Pitfalls of Government Transitions in Canada*. Toronto: University of Toronto Press.

The Limits to Defying Gravity

Horizontal Governance and Competing Values in Canada's Westminster System

Evert A. Lindquist

Chapter Overview

This chapter reviews and updates the recent initiatives and context for dealing with horizontal initiatives in the Government of Canada. It depicts the general aspiration of horizontal governance as one of many competing values in Westminster governance systems This chapter not only considers how successive governments, central agencies, and Auditors General have dealt with horizontal initiatives; drawing on the metaphor from Bakvis and Juillet (2004), it invites readers to consider how comfortable we might be with a "zero-gravity" governance environment.

Chapter Objectives

By the end of this chapter, students will be able to do the following:

- Identify past and contemporary examples of horizontal governance.
- Review various rationales advanced for horizontal governance.
- Review the evolution of horizontal governance in recent decades.
- Identify the different and often contradictory drivers of horizontal governance initiatives.
- Explain the competing narratives and values on how to handle diverse horizontal challenges.
- Consider skills and capacity supporting horizontal initiatives.

Introduction[1]

Some ideas—like increasing efficiency, removing duplication and overlap, ensuring merit-based hiring, and improving accountability— are enduring themes of public administration, along with many other themes and values (Dwivedi & Gow, 1999; Lindquist, 1999). During the last twenty years another theme has crept into this basket of values: persistent calls to make government work better across internal and external boundaries, usually under banners such as horizontal management, horizontal policy, joined-up or seamless government, collaborative government, holistic government, and whole-of-government approaches. Although each term has a different focus, in what follows they will collectively be referred to as **horizontal governance**.

Contemporary interest in horizontal governance arose in Canada during the mid-to-late 1990s, as federal and provincial governments sought to restructure and rationalize their programs and finances (Lindquist, 2002). However, over the last hundred or more years elected and public service leaders alike have sought to improve coordination across government, but usually in a top-down manner and aligning the activities of departments with others. Horizontal governance tends to embrace coordination and collaboration for diverse external purposes as well as internal needs, and to cultivate more collaborative cultures and repertoires at all levels of governments (ministers, executives, managers, front-line staff, and other service providers). More recently, the horizontal governance movement has been infused with the possibilities offered by the proliferation of new digital tools (Clarke, Lindquist, & Roy, 2017) and the new public governance (Osborne, 2010), encouraging the use of different kinds of evidence, broader engagement of citizens and stakeholders, and even co-design and co-production of policies and services, leading to more tailored services for citizens and other recipients of government services. Thinking about how government can work from a horizontal perspective, then, can be seen as a new value added to the much larger basket of competing values—many of them enduring values of public administration—which have to be understood and balanced by public-service leaders (Lindquist & Marcy, 2016). Even more interesting is the fact that horizontal governance itself surfaces and reflects many competing values.

One reason why horizontal governance manifests competing values is simply because of the diversity of horizontal initiatives. Table 24.1 provides examples and shows their range. Over time the pool of horizontal initiatives that have been analyzed, held up as exemplars, or debated has evolved, but there has always been an idiosyncratic, diverse mix. Bakvis and Juillet (2004) reviewed the Urban Aboriginal Strategy (1998), the Climate Change Secretariat (1998), the Vancouver Agreement (2000), and the Innovation Strategy (2002). And, for example, the private sector hosted several annual conferences on "Horizontal Policy Management" with its 2006 event showcasing the Canadian Biotechnology Strategy, managing science and technology at the community level, and implementing a cities and communities agenda for Infrastructure Canada (Federated Press, 2006a, 2006b). Its 2012 conference took up topics like Indigenous issues, a northern strategy, policing and public safety, chemicals management, health emergency preparedness across the Canada-US border, and communities of practice to policy research across departments. (Federated Press, 2012). The Harper government's 2009 Economic Action Plan was a cross-government infrastructure and jobs initiative (Canada, Department of Finance, 2009; Good and Lindquist, 2015). In short, the scale, locus, and range of participants in horizontal projects are incredibly diverse and many efforts to develop typologies to make sense of them have not succeeded.[2]

This chapter attempts to make sense of this diversity by reviewing how the discourse on horizontal governance in Canada has evolved not only over time but also from different vantage points, reflecting competing values. As noted above, what we now call horizontal governance was once considered a *coordination* or *structural* challenge, with the prime minister and top officials using more formal, top-down mechanisms such as the mandate and scope of ministerial portfolios and committees; the structure and responsibilities of departments and agencies; monitoring and coordination by central bureaus on government priorities; internal task forces, committees, and working groups

This chapter is adapted from *Crossing Boundaries in Public Management and Policy: The International Experience*, Lindquist, E.A, eds Janine O'Flynn, Deborah Blackman, and John Halligan. Copyright 2013 © Routledge. Reproduced by permission of Taylor & Francis Books UK.

Table 24.1   Horizontal Issues in Canada, Late 1990s

The Canadian Centre for Management Development (CCMD) Roundtable on Horizontal Issues (Hopkins et al., 2001) focused on the following examples:

Team Canada. Prime Minister Chrétien's initiative to launch and coordinate several visits of federal and provincial governments, along with business leaders from across the country, to foreign countries in order to expand markets for Canadian business.

Regional councils. Originally used to encourage information sharing and coordination among federal entities in regions, the councils were increasingly used to implement system-wide reform initiatives, to assist with specific horizontal initiatives, and to serve as sounding boards.

Urban Aboriginal Strategy (Saskatchewan). Sought to better coordinate federal departments, Indigenous communities and organizations, and provincial ministries to deliver and tailor programs and services for urban Indigenous people at risk.

Rural Team New Brunswick. The New Brunswick Federal Regional Council coordinated 13 federal and 7 provincial departments under the Canadian Rural Partnership program to increase leadership, capacity, and access for rural communities and business to government programs.

St. Lawrence Action Plan. A five-year collaborative initiative among 8 federal and 5 Quebec departments and agencies as well as NGOs to improve water quality and coordinate policy in the St. Lawrence River.

Science and Technology (S&T) MOU for Sustainable Development. Initiated in 1995, this initiative involved coordinating five departments to better support science to deal sustainable development issues.

Implementing the Oceans Act (1997). The Department of Fisheries and Oceans worked with 23 federal departments and agencies, provincial governments, and NGOs to develop an Oceans Management Strategy to improve ocean ecosystems, educate children and youth, and promote conservation, economic development, and sustainable communities.

Search and Rescue – Swissair 111 Disaster. The Rescue Coordination Centre (RCC) of the Department of National Defence coordinated seven departments, agencies, and other organizations, and over 1000 people.

Voluntary Sector Task Force. This involved 23 government departments and voluntary sector representatives in discussion tables, leading to the *Working Together* action plan (Voluntary Sector Initiative, 1999).

The Trends Project. The Policy Research Secretariat and the Social Sciences and Humanities Research Council created multidisciplinary networks of policy researchers inside and outside government to identify and probe trends affecting policy-making.

The Leadership Network. This 1998 initiative supported by several central agencies sought to foster leadership and support the Assistant Deputy Minister (ADM) community as part of a broader public service renewal strategy driven by the Clerk.

Additional selected examples come from a study sponsored by CCMD, The Leadership Network, and the federal Quebec Regional Council (Bourgault and Lapierre, 2000): a federal–provincial strategy to improve income security for First Nations in Quebec and Labrador; improving federal presence in Abitibi-Temiscamingue region; a federal strategy in support of Greater Montreal; the Lower St. Lawrence Model Forest with 40 partners, part of a larger national model forests program; the Saguenay–St. Lawrence Marine Park agreement between Canada and Quebec, involving many public partners; and initiatives by federal departments to improve locally shared support services in Shawinigan and Estrie. The Auditor General of Canada (2000) focused on the Family Violence Initiative, the Disability Agenda, and the Canadian Rural Partnership for an audit on horizontal management.

Source: Lindquist 2014, pp 191–2.

with representation from across government to address specific horizontal initiatives; and cross-governmental committees and sector councils to deal with other governments and external stakeholders (Peters, 1998). This rationale and impulse has not disappeared, but other perspectives have since emerged. Sproule-Jones (2000) proposed a bottom-up view of horizontal challenges, focusing on "mutual adjustment" across departments. Lindquist (2002) argued that in the late 1990s and early 2000s central agencies and top executives emphasized fostering a *culture* which would support horizontal initiatives, seeking to inculcate values and repertoires disposed to *collaboration* across the public service. The Auditor General of Canada (1999, 2000) has predictably emphasized a control perspective.

Lindquist (2002, 2012, 2014) suggested that, among these competing perspectives, common ground could be found about the need for sufficient capacity to launch, co-design, and implement horizontal initiatives in the form of budget, human resources, and authorities. But Bakvis and Juillet (2004) usefully and metaphorically reminded us that calls for horizontal governance must always factor in the reality of "pulling against the gravity" of Westminster systems. This chapter, though, goes a step further and encourages readers to reflect on what "zero gravity" for horizontal governance might look like, and whether we really would prefer the nature of such governance. Such tempering of expectations offers a dose of realism about the limits of horizontal and new public governance values in the digital era, and squares with experience over the last twenty years.

This chapter has four parts. The first reviews how horizontal governance moved to the top of public-sector reform agenda in the late 1990s and early 2000s, and considers different perspectives on enabling horizontal initiatives. The second part considers developments since the mid-2000s, noting that while horizontal strategies continued, dialogue and research on horizontal practice tapered off, despite some academic research and the promise of digital tools and approaches (e.g. Conteh, 2016; O'Flynn et al., 2014; Clarke, Lindquist, & Roy, 2017). The third part seeks to explain why, suggesting that increasingly directive governments in over-determined governance environments have embedded horizontal governance as core values for executive teams and public services, but they have been less interested in furthering open discussions on these matters even as they wave the banners of open and digital government. The final section considers whether we want truly horizontal and zero-gravity governance, the need to acknowledge competing values, and implications for modernizing governance in the digital era.

Horizontal Governance in the Late 1990s and Early 2000s

Horizontal governance moved to the top of the public-sector reform agenda during the late 1990s as the government sought to handle cutbacks and avoid further structural change. This section first reviews these developments and efforts to build new skills and culture for this purpose; the second section describes a response emphasizing control and accountability. The third part reviews a need

that transcended these views: building sufficient capacity, enabling horizontal management at all levels for diverse issues in a system of distributed capacities.

Promoting Horizontal Management as Culture and Competency

In 1994, the Liberal Government announced a concerted government-wide **Program Review** process to reduce the federal deficit (Bourgon, 2009). Each department had to meet strict expenditure reduction targets ranging from 20 per cent to as much as 50 per cent over three years. Ministers submitted plans for rethinking or eliminating programs (the phrase "alternative service delivery" vaulted to the top of the lexicon) and decisions were announced in the February 1995 Budget. The Program Review has been hailed as a political and fiscal success (Bourgon, 2009), but in the aftermath public-service leaders worried about the effects on the Canadian public service. First, they wondered what "new" public service would emerge over the longer term. Second, most decisions were "siloed" and not informed by analysis of potential impact on other programs (i.e., two departments cutting back or retaining similar programs for similar clients). Finally, executives wondered if the public service had the capacity to produce high-quality policy analysis and research after a succession of reforms and cost-cutting during the late 1980s and early 1990s.

In late 1995 the Clerk launched several task forces led by deputy ministers on different challenges for the federal public service, including the Task Force on Managing Horizontal Policy Issues. Recognizing that several entities were already dedicated to working across departmental boundaries (e.g. the Council on Administrative Renewal, Personnel Renewal Council, and federal regional councils), the task force focused on better managing horizontal policy issues, not "horizontality" more generally (Canada, Task Force on Managing Horizontal Policy Issues, 1996). It reviewed best practices and recognized that the extent of horizontality for each issue would vary greatly depending on the scope of the problem, the authorities assigned to departments and ministers, their respective capacities, the nature of stakeholders, and whether an issue was a government priority. The review pointed to the importance of properly defining issues, identifying lead institutions, providing proper mandates to lead officials, and securing the right level of support from central agencies (which could be assigned the lead, if necessary). The task force also recognized there had to be realistic time frames and expectations, and sufficient resources to support initiatives. Finally, it called for accountabilities to be delineated in advance, followed by reviews on completion of horizontal policy initiatives.

The task force did not propose structural changes, a reaction to the massive restructuring of the federal public service in June 1993, which dislocated thousands of public servants and was still working through the system. Rather, it sought to strengthen interdepartmental policy-making by streamlining the cabinet and expenditure management systems, better utilizing the Continuing Committee of Deputy Ministers (CCDM) and the Assistant Deputy Minister Forum to manage cross-cutting issues, and striking standing committees or temporary task forces as required. This implied that the Privy Council Office (PCO) should be more collaborative as a strategic coordinator, better engage ministers on horizontal issues, and more systematically use the committees and task forces of the Committee of Senior Officials (COSO).

The Task Force (informed by yet another Task Force on Alternative Service Delivery) concluded there was too much departmental turf protection and too little genuine cross-department collaboration. The proposed remedy was multifaceted. Public servants were to take courses, adopt horizontal perspectives as part of their value system, take up new appointments across departments, and get appraised for how they worked collaboratively. The emerging functional policy community was to foster networking, hold more events to discuss issues, and support professional development. Executives were to model collaborative behaviour, recognize horizontal achievements, and deploy sufficient resources to support horizontal initiatives. Pilots were to be identified by the Continuing Committee of Deputy Ministers' policy committee, and the Treasury Board Secretariat Advisory Committee was to develop more training opportunities. Central agencies had distinctive contributions to make: PCO would anticipate and trouble-shoot on horizontal issues; Treasury Board Secretariat (TBS) would facilitate mobility of executive recruits and incorporate horizontal issues into developing a broader

learning policy; the Public Service Commission would include competencies relating to teamwork and managing horizontal issues for promotion to the executive ranks; and the then Canadian Centre for Management Development would address horizontal issues management in courses and seminars.

The task force recognized that much depended on deputy ministers who would "walk the talk" with staff and other departments. It challenged them to inculcate a new culture in their departments by encouraging executive teams to identify horizontal issues (i.e., designating an assistant deputy minister (ADM) to challenge the department on such issues), initiate reviews of programs and initiatives to determine their horizontal qualities, and adopt a government-wide view on departmental business. Other suggestions included obtaining stakeholder and expert input from inside and outside government; encouraging ADMs to join interdepartmental committees; including performance reviews on horizontal activities, departmental appraisals, and promotion decisions; and cultivating horizontal skills and perspectives through training programs and rotational assignments. Finally, deputy ministers were to assess if their departments had sufficient capacity for short-term policy analysis, longer-term policy research, and longer-term anticipatory thinking.

In short, the task force report focused less on how to better manage specific projects, and more on building an enabling culture across the public service for handling horizontal issues and policy initiatives. As it completed its work, the Clerk created a Policy Research Committee comprising ADMs and other officials to undertake a Canada 2005 scanning exercise—a precursor to the Policy Research Initiative (PRI) and the Policy Research Secretariat (which still later became Policy Horizons Canada, a foresight capability)—that early on reached out across departments, as well as to think tanks and universities, with the Trends Project and other activities (Bakvis, 2000). The themes of horizontal policy development and a "borderless institution" soon appeared in the annual reports on the state of the public service from the Clerk to the prime minister (Bourgon, 1998) and other communications.

Although the task force called for a two-year progress report (Canadian Centre for Management Development, 1994; Canada, 1996), a new president of CCMD (former Clerk, Jocelyne Bourgon) announced in late 1999 a Roundtable on the Management of Horizontal Issues.[3] It concluded that (1) horizontal initiatives were unique, with their character and managerial challenges varying over time; (2) success required leadership, teamwork, and sufficient energy to work across boundaries, particularly given the vertical incentives and accountability of public service systems; and (3) success often depended on building trust among partners, obtaining sufficient financial and human resources, and securing support from executive champions. The roundtable made practical suggestions for initiating and managing horizontal projects in several areas: (1) mobilizing teams and networks predicated on building trust and shared leadership, and crucial support of executive champions in home institutions at critical moments; (2) developing a shared framework and vocabulary on issues, balancing team responsibility with accountabilities to home organizations, and embracing creative ambiguity for unresolved issues; (3) matching support structures to needs, which could change as projects evolved, including possibly setting sunset dates; and (4) maintaining momentum in the face of inevitable setbacks, turnover in members, evolving needs, and unanticipated challenges. Unlike the 1996 task force, the roundtable offered a bottom-up view of how to further horizontal initiatives, producing a guide on how to make horizontal projects work better and ensure other public servants could help further them.

The 1996 task force and 2000 CCMD roundtable each endorsed horizontal, collaborative approaches for dealing with public-service-wide issues, relying on deputy ministerial leadership and ADM-level engagement. They focused more on creating an enabling culture of public service leaders than proposing new structural and coordination solutions. Cultural change would be achieved through better leadership, better training, a broader range of assignments, and appraisal and promotion recognizing horizontal experience. But there was no assessment of how the system might increase the ratio of successes to failures, how to reduce exposure to unnecessary risks without dampening innovation, and how to encourage innovation. Perhaps the most telling observation was that too often "heroic individual effort" must "overcome obstacles that the 'system' could reduce or eliminate" (Hopkins et al. 2001: v).

Horizontal Management and Accountability: Control and Results

The **Auditor General of Canada** has closely observed public-sector reform in Ottawa, often auditing progress using value-for-money precepts. Following the program review, the government entered into alternative service delivery among departments and with other governments and partners. The Auditor General asked tough questions about how well governments managed horizontal arrangements, with an abiding interest in results reporting.[4] They emerged as a strong critic of how horizontal initiatives were managed, fearing that the government had insufficient controls and reporting.

The Auditor General's 1999 report noted the trend towards collaborative government and alternative service delivery arrangements, observing they could be "an innovative, cost-effective and efficient way of delivering programs and services" (Auditor General 1999: 5–7). However, the Auditor worried about increased risk to taxpayers and the public, particularly since the government was typically only one partner in such arrangements, which could potentially dilute accountability to Parliament. The report offered guidance on how to better participate and manage the risks in collaborative arrangements, and questions to inform scrutiny by parliamentarians.

The audits focused on collaborative arrangements jointly managed with other federal entities. The cases included Infrastructure Canada Works, the Model Forests program, the National Action Program on Climate Change, the Labour Market Development Agreements, the Canadian Industry Program for Energy Conservation, and the North American Waterfowl Protection Plan. They did *not* include collaborative arrangements with other governments, conventional contractual arrangements, grants and contributions, or arm's-length entities. This set a low threshold: collaborative arrangements *should* be better managed *among* federal departments and agencies. The Auditor General concluded that collaborative arrangements were more challenging to manage than regular programs because (1) a vision and effective leadership had to be developed among several partners; (2) more complexity existed since each partner has distinct goals, interests, authorities, administrative styles, and accountabilities;

(3) coordination costs were relatively higher with greater potential for conflict, requiring more capacity to manage; and (4) building trust and confidence are essential ingredients for collaboration and take time.

Informed by previous audits of collaborative programs, the Auditor General built a framework around the general themes of serving the public interest, developing effective accountability arrangements, and greater transparency, leading to questions like: Were objectives and the public interest best met by means of collaborative arrangements? Were the objectives, responsibilities, levels of performance, required capacities, and evaluation frameworks specified for each partner? Was sufficient information shared with partners, stakeholders, Parliament, and the public? The Auditor General believed such questions should be answered *before* proceeding with collaborative arrangements, even though horizontal initiatives usually take considerable time and dialogue to build trust, establish a working relationship, and develop repertoires and plans for addressing a complex challenge requiring multiple partners. *But invoking such criteria raised the bar higher than for traditional programs because horizontal initiatives always have higher transaction costs to secure agreements and information.* Not only did the Auditor General argue that departments should maintain reporting obligations to Parliament, they should ensure partners lived up to the reporting standards, even if partners had varying confidentiality needs. The Auditor presumed that parliamentarians, the public, and the media clamour for this information, though evidence suggests otherwise (Lindquist 1998; McDavid & Huse, 2012). In short, the Auditor General strongly emphasized control over the flexibility required for innovation and management.

The Auditor General's next audit was released in early 2001 after a federal election (Auditor General, 2000). One chapter reviewed the government's progress on department results reporting and the challenges for reporting results on horizontal issues. The Auditor General had been closely involved in pilots and roll-out of a new Estimates reporting system under the Improved Reporting to Parliament project (Lindquist, 1998). The audit examined how results were used as a management tool in horizontal initiatives and the barriers to use with case studies of the Family Violence Initiative, the Disability Agenda, and the Canadian Rural Partnership as well as other audit work, again involving only federal departments. They were assessed with respect to (1) coordination and management structures, (2) leadership from senior officials, (3) accountability frameworks, and (4) reporting frameworks.

While the departments had embraced results reporting, the Auditor raised concern about the use of reports for accountability, monitoring, and planning. The Auditor believed that the government and departments failed to clearly set out expected results, and that evaluation was insufficiently used, calling on the government to move beyond a persistent state of planning for results reporting (Auditor General of Canada, 2000: 25). **Treasury Board of Canada** ministers and officials were singled out for not moving results reporting to the next level by sharing information and practices across departments. The report went on to note the recent government commitments that required horizontal policy coordination and implementation, and the recommendations of the 1996 Task Force on Managing Horizontal Policy Issues. The Auditor reminded the government of its commitment to developing an accountability framework, consulting with stakeholders, setting realistic expectations for complex projects, providing sufficient resources, offering incentives and recognition for such activities, and the importance of evaluation and information sharing.

The Auditor recognized that informal coordination might be less burdensome and more productive, but favoured a well-articulated government strategy and structured coordination with shared frameworks, roles, responsibilities, and decision-making protocols. This required a lead department and dedicated staff. The Auditor observed that coordination takes considerable time and energy to achieve, often longer than expected, posing a challenge for results reporting. Like the 1996 task force, the Auditor called for strong executive champions to secure resources and support managers, and suggested formal accountability frameworks would be useful for more complex undertakings, particularly with regard to securing financial or other support for non-centrally funded initiatives. He argued that horizontal managers often do not have access to the incentives and tools to ensure success, and central agencies needed to play a greater role.

The Auditor concluded that little results reporting occurred in the horizontal cases reviewed. Partner institutions had different reporting regimes, it took time to develop credible shared results regimes, and partners resisted developing detailed results frameworks and supplying information. The Auditor called for more systematic reporting on horizontal initiatives by lead departments because there was insufficient knowledge of program delivery costs and staff turnover might lead to insufficient institutional memory to inform subsequent initiatives. Finally, despite acknowledging TBS leadership in identifying and supporting horizontal initiatives, the Auditor worried that not all initiatives received appropriate scrutiny because many did not secure funds or approvals through the submission process—that TBS approached horizontal initiatives in a piecemeal manner. The Auditor called on TBS to exercise strong central and strategic leadership to ensure sufficient resources for coordination and results reporting, and to facilitate sharing lessons and best practices. Like the report on *Collaborative Government*, Chapter 20 on results and horizontal issues set out clear markers for the government, executives, and managers.

Bridging Culture and Control: Building Capacity

That the Auditor General and sitting governments clashed over horizontal governance was not surprising given their institutional histories and interests, despite a common understanding of the challenges managers had to overcome when working across boundaries. However, Lindquist (2002) argued that the government, deputy ministers, the Auditor General, *and* working managers had a common cause in ensuring sufficient capacities and resources were dedicated to horizontal initiatives. A common complaint of managers was that, unless leading a high-profile initiative, they typically managed "off the corner of their desks" (this was before more onerous reporting requirements) and often found it difficult to secure resources and attention from executives and the centre.

Where and how should such capacities be created? The Auditor General felt TBS should be more active, providing greater oversight and support. However, the sheer number and diversity of horizontal initiatives could easily overwhelm central agencies. Indeed, departments are often better positioned to lead many horizontal initiatives. Although the CCMD roundtable was not asked to explore how central agencies could create a more supportive environment

for horizontal initiatives, some follow-up did proceed with reports and courses (Rounce & Beaudry, 2002; Bakvis & Juillet, 2004).

Lindquist (2002) drew together suggestions about how to strengthen system support of horizontal initiatives given the volume and diversity of challenges:

1. *Support a training program on horizontal management* for leaders and staff, informed by case studies and accounts from previous initiatives.
2. *Support a mentoring network on horizontal management* with experienced officials contributing to training courses, providing advice and mentoring on horizontal projects, and increasing awareness of horizontal initiatives.
3. *Develop a central reserve/capacity in tbs to support and recognize horizontal initiatives* with limited-term assistance for staff support and performance pay as well as investment support.
4. *Match machinery to address specific and unique horizontal management challenges* such as regional councils, department headquarters or regional operations, central agencies or deputy minister committees, etc.
5. *Raise awareness of executives and managers about horizontal challenges*, supports, and expectations (also see recognition awards below).
6. *Encourage better reporting and accountability* by identifying ways to assist busy managers and partner organizations to more efficiently meet planning and reporting guidelines, with adaptable templates and other tools.
7. *Enhance existing recognition programs* by establishing a new category to recognize horizontal or collaborative initiatives.

These were presented as an integrated package, to be coordinated by a small Horizontal Management Secretariat in TBS as a focal point for horizontal initiatives and to work with central and other entities to develop training programs, identify priorities for investment support, mentor contacts, and handle communications. However, these elements could be de-coupled and proceed independently; indeed, multiple lines of influence were identified since initiatives emerge and evolve in very different ways, requiring different kinds of engagement and support along the way. This effort to bridge the culture and control views from a capacity perspective provides one framework for evaluating progress from the early 2000s to the present.

From the Mid-2000s and Beyond: Was Horizontal Governance "Business as Usual"?

Since the early 2000s, there has been a significant tapering in the number of reports and commentary on horizontal initiatives, with a modest flurry in the mid-2000s. Interest in horizontal issues seemed well sustained into the 2000s with reports from Canadian Policy Research Networks (CPRN), the Canada School of Public Service (CSPS), and the Auditor General. CPRN published a short study on housing as an example of horizontal social policy challenge (Hay, 2005). CSPS published Smith and Torjman (2004) with two detailed case studies on the National Homelessness Initiative, and Bakvis and Juillet (2004) undertook four detailed case studies for the CSPS on the effectiveness of departments and central agencies in managing horizontal initiatives (the Innovation Strategy, the Urban Aboriginal Strategy, the Climate Change Secretariat, and the Vancouver Agreement). They noted the importance of executive champions, timely support, and appropriate skill sets for enabling horizontal initiatives. However, they found that costs of initiatives were usually underestimated, that staff had insufficient tools and supports, and a lack of clarity about how accountability worked beyond reporting to home departments and agencies. They suggested that central agencies could clarify reporting via mandate letters and streamlined reporting, selectively increase the coordinating and policy capacity of central secretariats, and ensure that performance reviews squarely assessed the horizontal performance of executives. At the departmental level, Bakvis and Juillet (2004) suggested that executive teams could develop internal coordinating units and accountability regimes for horizontal initiatives, more selectively choose initiatives to pursue, and more systematically identify staff with the skills and aptitude for collaborative work.

Lindquist (2004) built on this to suggest central agency horizontal capabilities needed to be better managed for a range of specific upstream and downstream activities, as part of a distributed system. This required assessing departmental capabilities and ensuring central investments were complementary for designing and implementing horizontal initiatives, and for assembling data and analysis. Given the number of initiatives, too many horizontal units might grow at the centre, leading to excessive interference and intermittent culling. Second, while horizontal initiatives could be construed as "soft change" attempts to work with existing authorities and structures (and avoid re-organizations or "hard change"), the transaction costs of work-arounds as well as learning could, in some cases, auger for restructuring.

Revisiting earlier work, the Auditor General released an audit in 2005 on how the federal government handled three high-profile initiatives: the Biotechnology Strategy, the Homeless Initiative, and the Vancouver Agreement, concluding:

> Although there have been some recent improvements, much of the federal government's approach to horizontal initiatives is still on a case-by-case basis. Central agencies have not determined the kinds of circumstances that require a horizontal initiative and the kind of governance needed. They have not developed enough specialized tools for the governance, accountability, and co-ordination of federal efforts in such initiatives and have made little progress in developing means of funding horizontal programs. (Auditor General, 2005: 1–2)

The Auditor General also pointed to insufficient planning for measuring and reporting on results in two cases, and was sharply critical of the PCO and TBS. Since this report there has been no direct follow-up on horizontal initiatives as a cross-cutting theme, except on specific initiatives (see below).

TBS continued and furthered capabilities on horizontal management. It issued a *Companion Guide* on program results and accountability (TBS, 2002), but there were other pertinent corporate initiatives:

- A new results-oriented reporting architecture (Management, Resources and Results Structure or MRRS) was developed to guide Estimates authorization and reporting for departments and agencies, providing a hierarchy of outcomes linked to programs and activities, which could be linked to cross-cutting or horizontal goals (Treasury Board of Canada Secretariat, 2012).

- Renewed effort was made to create an Expenditure Management Information System (EMIS) to provide better data for budgeting, monitoring, and accountability because TBS could not easily pull comparable data from across programs on horizontal issues (i.e., Indigenous, oceans, cities and communities, international, science and technology, etc.) and had to assemble finer-grained data from scratch with departments and agencies (Maloney, 2005).
- The Treasury Board started to conduct horizontal strategic reviews of expenditures in broad policy and administrative areas along with more systematic assessment of department capabilities under the Management Accountability Framework reporting process (Lindquist, 2006b, 2009).
- The Treasury Board continued to publish the government's annual report on *Canada's Performance*, which started in 2001, and introduced a horizontal and whole-of-government framework in the mid-2000s, focusing on a rolling handful of broad policy domains.[5]
- A TBS database of significant formal horizontal initiatives was created, with a small secretariat, since departments and agencies had to formally report on such initiatives in planning and performance documents (Fitzpatrick, 2004).[6]
- TBS continued to house a small secretariat in support of regional councils across Canada to support coordination of regional activities of departments and agencies (Juillet, 2000).

Collectively, these initiatives can be seen as realizing a vision of the Treasury Board as a "management board" arising from the Modern Comptrollership (1996–7) and *Results for Canadians* (Canada, Treasury Board Secretariat, 2000) initiatives. Both sought to improve the ability of the government and the public service to report and work better across boundaries. Whether the initiatives effectively realized the vision remains an open question.

There have been few reports and studies exploring horizontal themes since the mid-2000s. The strategic and operational reviews have not been released as public documents; only selected expenditure reductions and restructuring get announced in subsequent budgets. A task force report on horizontal tools for community investments was produced for Human Resources and Social Development Canada

(Elson et al., 2007), and another examined how official languages programs were managed across the Canadian government (Savoie, 2008), but the Canada School of Public Service's research program atrophied and no additional studies have emerged on horizontal management. The Canada School does not deliver courses focusing on horizontal management, but its offerings for current and aspiring executives rely on the precepts of systems thinking to encourage outward-looking and collaborative strategizing. The Auditor General has not revisited horizontal management as an overarching theme of public-sector reform, although its review of Shared Services Canada progress in developing a common IT infrastructure and services can be seen as a review of an important horizontal initiative (Auditor General, 2015).

Horizontal issues, though, remain salient. Organizations like the Public Policy Forum and the Institute on Governance have hosted events for departments and agencies to discuss horizontal challenges and prospects for collaborative, sustainable, and place-based governance models (e.g., Bourgault, 2010; Canada, Policy Research Initiative, 2010; Crossing Boundaries/Canada 2020 Working Group, 2007; Motsi, 2009; Public Policy Forum, 2008). The Policy Research Initiative was revitalized into Policy Horizons Canada, with a mandate to build a cross-government foresight capability and governed with oversight from a committee of deputy ministers (Policy Horizons, 2011). Reflecting broader trends, scholars have explored how collaboration and social innovation can address policy challenges and associated accountability and performance issues (e.g., Anderson & Findlay, 2010; Caledon Institute of Social Policy, 2009; Fierlbeck, 2010; Rocan, 2009). Howard and Phillips (2012) provide a conceptual analysis of whether horizontal and distributed models of public governance inherently carry accountability deficits. Conteh (2016) considers how accountability is handled across departments for regional economic development. With few exceptions, though, this more recent work has produced new formulations or empirical data on the quality of the contemporary management of horizontal initiatives by Canadian governments, relying heavily on contributions and frameworks from the 1990s and early 2000s (e.g., Ferguson, 2009).

Several changes in the governance environment created a new context for furthering horizontal governance from the mid-2000s to the present. First, the

Human Resources and Development Canada grants and contributions scandal of the early 2000s propelled and ensconced accountability as *the* management issue for government and the public service throughout the decade. It also made it increasingly difficult to use grants and contributions to fund horizontal and collaborative activities with partners because of new approval and reporting strictures (Good, 2003; Phillips et al., 2010). Second, starting in February 2006, the Harper Government instituted a controlling, centralized, and disciplined style of governing, brooking little off-message commentary from government caucus members and public servants alike, a poster-child for Aucoin's new political governance (Aucoin, 2008; Lindquist & Rasmussen, 2012) and, not surprisingly, fewer task forces and roundtables with public reports.[7] Third, the Harper Government balanced its interest in reducing and re-allocating program spending, delegating responsibilities to provinces and territories, and securing marginal votes in elections to secure a majority government. This led to identifying specific initiatives closely aligned to the government's strategic policy and political agenda (e.g., the Economic Action Plan, the 2010 Olympics, etc.). Oversight of major projects and the public service was closely handled by the Prime Minister's Office, which demanded responsiveness and coordination of top priorities. Fourth, the Harper government stopped producing *Canada's Performance* in 2011 which, aside from the TBS horizontal database, was the only cross-government outcome reporting from a horizontal perspective on top government priorities and distinctive in its comparative perspective (Lindquist, 2016). Finally, even when the Auditor General audited government programs like the Economic Action Plan, horizontal management was not identified as a paramount theme to focus on (Canada, Department of Finance, 2009; Good & Lindquist, 2015), even when collaboration across departments and central agencies was considered essential for success.

Stepping back, it seems clear that coordination and control considerations have dominated the landscape leaders of horizontal initiatives must navigate, pushing aside the earlier interest in culture and capacity. And, presumably, in the context of cutbacks and continued high scrutiny and transaction costs associated with grants and contributions so often used for horizontal initiatives (unless they are internal to government), the interest in promoting partnerships with outside groups and other

governments may have waned, unless there is the prospect of genuine innovation in designing and delivering programs. However, if the executive cadre of the public service continues to embrace horizontality and collegiality as an institutional cultural value, and the external governance environment remains difficult in financial and political terms, there may be fertile ground for a quieter and more bottom-up "mutual adjustment" approach for identifying and implementing horizontal initiatives within the federal government, with some potential to work across levels of government.

The success of the Trudeau Liberals in the October 2015 election brought to power a government with not only a different set of priorities, but numerous priorities, a commitment to open government, and a commitment to delivering and measuring results and improved outcomes. Many Liberal election commitments were expansive—just think of climate change, reconciliation, and infrastructure investments, to name a few—each promising to require significant horizontal effort across the federal public service and other levels of government and First Nations. The government's response was to establish a Results and Delivery capability, loosely modelled on the Prime Minister's Delivery Unit from the UK's Blair government (Barber, 2007; Barber et al., 2011). This approach focuses not only on implementation in selected priority areas but also on identifying and managing to short-term outcome indicators. However, this is not the same as taking a government-wide approach to ascertaining the impact of multiple programs on priority outcomes, which was done in a high-level way with *Canada's Performance*. Likewise, at the time of writing (January 2017) the government had yet to indicate which priorities, among scores, it had chosen to focus on. Finally, the Treasury Board of Canada unveiled a new Policy on Results, which took effect on July 1, 2016, aimed to improve tracking and reporting on government commitments and spending. One of the requirements of departments and agencies were to provide "tags" for their programs along with outcome indicators, which presumably would allow the governments and its central agencies to aggregate data and results information for any horizontal initiative, for regions, or for recipient groups. However, the reporting flowing from this new information and reporting regime will likely not be seen until 2018.

Zero Gravity and the Truly Horizontal Organization

There will always be calls for governments to become more horizontal or to adopt whole-of-government perspectives variously, for example, on addressing government priorities, providing tailored services to citizens, or focusing efforts on certain regions or communities. It is common to hear observers who reflect with amazement on the extraordinary way that governments respond to crises or emergencies. They point to the spontaneous collaboration among relevant agencies, elected leaders and officials sharing information and aligning their efforts, leadership from the front line and middle of these public organizations, and willingness to collaborate with volunteers and non-governmental entities. They ask, "Why can't government act and perform like this all of the time?"

The conventional response to such questions often broaches several of the following points. There was concurrence by all actors inside and outside government as to what the priority was; the immediate need and goals were obvious to all, as well as the roles they could play. Various government actors were not asking What are my authorities? and What is my jurisdiction? but rather, What can we do? How can we best help? and Who can I report to? Even the public and normally contending for-profit and non-profit actors and other levels of government ask these questions and act accordingly. The normal authorization and approval processes are suspended because of pressing time constraints and needs. Such exigencies provide fertile ground for spontaneous leadership and sharing of information; decisive action emerges at all levels in the system (executives, middle managers, front-line staff, and volunteers from non-government entities and communities). The focus on clear needs comes with a high tolerance for uncertainty and lack of detailed information at the outset; authorities do not have to have all the answers—they simply have to share what they do know. Focusing attention and aligning effort from so many actors implies inattention to other policy and administrative responsibilities and priorities, pointing to sufficient good will and resilience in the system to permit such diversion of attention and effort.

The short answer to the question Why can't government act like this all of the time? is that the focusing quality of the crisis allows such extraordinary effort. It can't be replicated on every front, all the time, because other crises would emerge and risks would be realized, we would not have the resources to sustain such elevated responses and communication at all levels, and we would expect due process and accountability when things went poorly.

One can take a different tack, and inspired by Wildvasky's (1972) seminal article on the self-evaluating organization, let's briefly consider what a truly horizontal or whole-of-government organization might look like. The public service would have to itemize and address all the priorities of an elected government. All ministers and their departments would have to not only identify their authorities and responsibilities but also those of all other departments, agencies, and other levels of government, and keep them informed on a continuous basis. Using service design lab and techniques, policy and service delivery staff in departments and agencies would have to co-design, co-create, and co-manage services that would be tailored to the specific needs of citizens and communities. All ministers and their departments would have to identify the non-government actors that play in their policy-service domains, and also keep them informed on a continuous basis.

This would mean all departments and policy or program units in public service institutions would essentially function on a matrix basis, responding not only to the priorities of governments and ministers but also to the needs and demands of other departments and agencies, as well as the design needs of citizens and other uses of program services. We know that neither the public nor opposition parties would countenance undocumented initiatives for very long, so, for accountability purposes, a hugely sophisticated and multilevel system of ensuring that all pertinent actors supplied sufficient effort and achieved the desired effect on outcomes (thereby dealing with the "attribution challenge") would have to be put in place. To do this would require knowing what was to be accomplished in each service or policy domain; otherwise the process of discovering what needed to be done or how collaborations might work would lead to ongoing negotiation and adjustment, which would come on top of the anticipated negotiations and adjustments in effort of different parts of the system in response to crises, unanticipated issues, or realized risks. To fully meet all horizontal governance aspirations points to a comprehensive, synoptic public organization, functioning continuously on a 360-degree basis.

Many readers will quickly say that such an imagined state is preposterous but, like Wildavsky's self-evaluating organization, this is the result of unanalyzed implications. Horizontal governance is not inherently a good thing; one can have too much of it or, if attempted, there will be insufficient resources to support the work of all of the implied actors and properly design, deliver, or monitor programs. Digital solutions will neither remove the need for boundaries and choosing among priorities, nor make up for insufficient resources.

This thought experiment quickly flushes out which competing values should be paramount: for example, in democratic systems we believe that the priorities of duly elected governments should matter more than others in the system, which is part of the gravity at play in our systems. Gravity means that societies and governments have to assign priorities and make choices with relatively scarce resources; it means that when governments or crises or public opinion throw up issues that demand attention, non-trivial efforts and alignment can occur because they are not fully deployed to scores of other priorities. We can see that launching horizontal initiatives— whether as a government priority, a "let's try this" pilot from a departmental program lead, or an outside-led approach from a community—always requires non-trivial effort to begin and perhaps to succeed. But the implication is that not all public servants or program areas have sufficient time, imagination, energy, and resources to launch and see through such initiatives; many other services, priorities, and crises need to be tended to across government's waterfront. In this sense, horizontal governance remains a value—often motivated in turn by very different values—competing against many others in our Westminster governance system.

Conclusion: Horizontal Strategies in a Tougher Environment

This chapter reviewed studies and initiatives attempting to improve the quality of horizontal management in the Canadian government. It characterized the impetus towards horizontal governance as only one of many competing values at play in Westminster governance systems, and pointed to competing narratives and values on how to handle diverse horizontal challenges: the coordination, mutual adjustment, culture, control, and capacity perspectives. The studies, initiatives, and narratives of the late 1990s and early 2000s identified myriad enablers for overcoming barriers to collaboration at all levels: leaders of projects, executive champions, departmental executive teams, and central agency leadership focused on building a new public-service culture in support of horizontal management. Since the mid-2000s, horizontal issues have tapered off as a top-of-mind reform challenge, and several explanations were ventured to explain this state of affairs. The drop-off in more public discussion and research does not mean, of course, that ministers and public service executives are less interested in horizontal challenges—indeed, they may have found new, more efficient and effective ways to handle them (and this chapter suggests that "mutual adjustment" might be a possible strategy).

Lindquist (2002) concluded on a speculative note, briefly considering future scenarios in which horizontal governance might proceed, particularly from the vantage point of public servants. The trends remain salient: increasing complexity and interdependence of issues; increasing demands from citizens for better service; the accelerating pace of technological change; and increasing demands for accountability and results reporting. The critical uncertainties for public-sector managers who grapple with horizontal issues also remain salient: the extent to which governments will have more turf-oriented debates or engage in collaboration,[8] and whether citizens and other stakeholders will become more or less engaged in debating and shaping policy development and service delivery as advocated by the new public governance movement.[9] To these trends and uncertainties we can now add the significant pressures on national budgets and economies following the Global Financial Crisis, worry about the stability and finances of the European Union, and the significant policy shifts of the US Trump administration.

This chapter has suggested that horizontal governance is only one of many competing values in our Westminster system, and that the gravity that many horizontal initiatives pull against should be seen not simply as an unwelcome or dysfunctional reality, but rather as a product of striking needed rolling balances of many legitimate governance values in a democratic system—governments needing to be held to account for the allocation of and use of scarce resources. Horizontal initiatives will continue to emerge from various levels of government and from external organizations in response to challenges and uncertainties. As has long been the case, they will be idiosyncratic and often frustrating experiences. In the new governance and fiscal environment in Canada, it will be interesting to see whether decision-making—and particularly longer-term experimentation and solution-finding—becomes on balance more collaborative and horizontal in the directions advocated by the new public governance movement, and whether governments and outsiders fully explore the possibilities of taking advantage of digital tools and the potential willingness of citizens and stakeholders to do things differently and change how government works. Also worth monitoring is whether the public-service executives and managers leading the next waves of horizontal initiatives—whatever their impetus —feel well-supported or have to be heroic, navigating a vertically oriented government system. Providing credible assessments of how these trends and practice are handled by the Canadian government will require a new round of careful, systematic research.

Important Terms and Concepts

Auditor General of Canada   Program Review
horizontal governance   Treasury Board of Canada

Study Questions

1. What are the different motivations guiding horizontal initiatives?
2. Which actors inside and outside government demand or call for better horizontal governance? Whose interests do such initiatives serve?
3. What skills and capacity are required to support horizontal initiatives?
4. How many significant horizontal initiatives can a government successfully support at any time?
5. What other public service values do you think horizontal initiatives are competing with?

Notes

1   This chapter, which draws on and elaborates Lindquist (2002, 2012, 2014), is dedicated to Professor Herman Bakvis in recognition of his wide-ranging scholarship, collegiality, and administrative leadership and service in the field of Canadian public administration from his home institutions of Dalhousie University and then the University of Victoria, and the phrase "pulling against gravity" in the context of horizontal governance. Herman retired from the University of Victoria at the end of 2016.

2   Attempts to produce typologies to categorize horizontal initiatives have proven unsatisfying: if one tries to richly capture their dimensions, the resulting typologies can be as complicated as the challenges; conversely, fewer dimensions cannot capture their distinctiveness and evolution. The first CCMD roundtable explored grouping cases into the categories of service, research, policy, internal support, emergencies, and multifaceted projects. A background report provided typologies based on *function* (information, resources, work,

authority); *goals* (support services, knowledge, policy development, program and service delivery); and *mechanisms* (a menu of formal structures and processes, and informal coordinating devices) (CCMD, 2000). See also the Traverse Group (2006) typology.

3   Three other roundtables proceeded on the Learning Organization, Risk Management, and Social Union Framework. The Management of Horizontal Issues roundtable was led by an associate deputy minister and consisted of ADMs, directors, and two academics supported by a small CCMD secretariat. The group had access to reviews of relevant literature and written summaries and presentations on case studies of horizontal projects, and consulted officials, producing a practical guide. The author was a member of the Roundtable.

4   The Auditor worked with central agencies on improved estimates reporting with a new expenditure management system in 1995 (Lindquist, 1998).

5   *Canada's Performance* reports were published from 2000–11. The archived copies can be found at http://tbs-sct.gc.ca/ems-sgd/esp-pbc/cp-rc-eng.asp.

6   TBS Horizontal Initiatives Database for performance information defines a horizontal initiative as "an initiative in which partners from two or more organizations have established a formal funding agreement (e.g., Memorandum to Cabinet, a Treasury Board submission, federal–provincial agreement) to work towards the achievement of shared outcomes. Partners include other federal departments or agencies, other national governments, non-government and private sector organizations, etc. Major horizontal initiatives include initiatives allocated federal funds that exceed $100 million or are central to achieving government priorities; or have a high public profile." See https://www.tbs-sct.gc.ca/hidb-bdih/home-accueil-eng.aspx.

7   Interestingly, as noted earlier, this was consistent with traditional top-down approaches to coordination backed fully by the authority of the prime minister.

8   Whether public servants can confidently proceed with horizontal initiatives is conditioned by how prime ministers organize and manage their cabinets, and how cabinets work has significant implications for intergovernmental relations (Dupré, 1985) and prospects for collaborative and horizontal government. If supportive and collegial cultures do not emerge at the political level, the leaders of central agencies and operating departments will have more difficulty collaborating, even if a prudent course of action.

9   If buffered from the real work of our governments by technology and intermediaries, citizens will have decreasing knowledge of how public services are delivered; or, they might develop a better understanding due to better access to information and call for greater coordination across institutions.

References

Anderson, L., and Findlay, T. 2010. "Does Public Reporting Measure Up? Federalism, Accountability and Child-Care Policy in Canada." *Canadian Public Administration* 53, 3, pp. 417–38.

Aucoin, P. 2008. "New Public Management and New Public Governance: Finding the Balance." *Professionalism and Public Service: Essays in Honour of Kenneth Kernaghan*, edited by D. Siegel and K. Rasmussen, Toronto: University of Toronto Press, pp. 16–33.

Auditor General of Canada. 1999. "Collaborative Arrangements: Issues for the Federal Government." Chapter 5 in *Report of the Auditor General of Canada to the House of Commons, Volume 1, April 1999*, Ottawa: Minister of Public Works and Government Services Canada.

———. 2000. "Managing Departments for Results and Managing Horizontal Issues for Results." Chapter 20 in *Report of the Auditor General of Canada to the House of Commons, Volume 3, December 2000*, Ottawa: Minister of Public Works and Government Services Canada.

———. 2005. "Managing Horizontal Initiatives." Chapter 4 in *Report of the Auditor General of Canada to the House of Commons, November 2005*, Ottawa: Minister of Public Works and Government Services Canada.

———. 2015. "Information Technology Shared Services." Report 4 in *Report of the Auditor General of Canada to the House of Commons, November 2015*, Ottawa: Minister of Public Works and Government Services Canada.

Bakvis, H. 2000. "Rebuilding Policy Capacity in the Era of the Fiscal Dividend." *Governance* 13, 1, pp. 71–103.

Bakvis, H. and Juillet, L. 2004. *The Horizontal Challenge: Line Departments, Central Agencies and Leadership*, Ottawa: Canada School of Public Service.

Barber, Michael, Andy Moffit, and Paul Kihn. 2011. *Deliverology 101: A Field Guide for Educational Leaders*. Thousand Oaks, California: Sage.

Barber, Michael. 2007. *Instruction to Deliver: Tony Blair, Public Services and the Challenge of Achieving Targets*. London: Politicos.

Bourgault, J. 2010. "Utopia within Reach: Horizontal Collaboration on Place-Based Projects from a Sustainable Development Perspective." *Horizons* 10, 4, pp. 88–94.

Bourgault, J. and Lapierre, R. 2000. *Horizontality and Public Management*. Ottawa: Canadian Centre for Management Development.

Bourgon, J. 1998. *Fifth Annual Report to the Prime Minister on the Public Service of Canada*, Ottawa: Privy Council Office.

———. 2009. *Program Review: The Government of Canada's Experience Eliminating the Deficit, 1994–99: A Canadian Case Study*. London: Institute for Government.

Caledon Institute of Social Policy. 2009. *Collaboration on Policy: A Manual Developed by the Community—Government Collaboration on Policy*. Ottawa: Caledon Institute of Social Policy.

Canada, Department of Finance. 2009. *Canada's Economic Action Plan: First Report to Canadians*. Ottawa: Department of Finance.

Canada, Task Force on Managing Horizontal Policy Issues. 1996. *Managing Horizontal Policy Issues*. Ottawa: Privy Council Office and Canadian Centre for Management Development.

Canada, Policy Research Initiative. 2010. "Sustainable Places." *Horizons* 10, 4.

Canada, Treasury Board Secretariat. 2000. *Results for Canadians: A Management Framework for the Government of Canada*.

Canadian Centre for Management Development (CCMD). 1994. *Continuous Learning: A ccmd Report,* CCMD Report No.1. Ottawa: Canadian Centre for Management Development.

———. (no date, c.2000) *Horizontal Management: Issues, Insights, and Illustrations: A Background Paper,* Ottawa: CCMD.

Clarke, A., Lindquist, E.A., and Roy, J. 2017. Understanding Governance in the Digital Era: An Agenda for Public Administration Research in Canada, Special Issue. *Canadian Public Administration* 60:4, 457–681.

Conteh, C. 2016. "Rethinking Accountability in Complex and Horizontal Network Delivery Systems." *Canadian Public Administration* 59, 2, pp. 224–44.

Crossing Boundaries/Canada 2020 Working Group. 2007. *Progressive Governance for Canadians: What You Need to Know,* Ottawa: Crossing Boundaries/Canada 2020 Working Group.

Dupré, J.S. 1985. "Reflections on the Workability of Executive Federalism." *Intergovernmental Relations* edited by R. Simeon, Toronto: University of Toronto Press, pp. 1–32.

Dwivedi, O.P. and J.I. Gow. 1999. *From Bureaucracy to Public Management: The Administrative Culture of the Government of Canada.* Broadview Press, Peterborough.

Elson, P., M. Struthers, and J. Carlson. 2007. *Horizontal Tools and Relationships: An International Survey of Government Practices Related to Communities: Report of the Task Force on Community Investments.* Ottawa: Human Resources and Social Development Canada.

Federated Press. 2006a. Presentations, Lecture Notes and Visual Aids Delivered at the Federated Press Horizontal Policy Management Course held in Ottawa on January 10 & 11, 2006. Accessed 22 December 2011. http://www.federatedpress.com/FPWeb/Events/ConferenceReports/tabid/308/mid/380/ProjectId/42/wildRC/1/Default.aspx.

———. 2006b. Horizontal Policy Management: Conference held in Ottawa on May 29-31, 2006.

———. 2012. 8th Horizontal Policy Management Conference: Breaking Down the Silos: February 1, 2 & 3, 2012. Ottawa: Brochure, Online. Accessed 22 December 2011. http://www.federatedpress.com/pdf/8HPM1202-E.pdf.

Ferguson, D. 2009. *Research Brief on Understanding Horizontal Governance.* Montreal: The Centre for Literacy of Quebec.

Fierlbeck, K. 2010. "Public health and collaborative governance." *Canadian Public Administration* 53, 1, pp. 1–19.

Fitzpatrick, T. 2004. Reporting on Horizontal Initiatives: Notes for a presentation on April 30, 2004. Ottawa: Treasury Board of Canada Secretariat.

Good, D.A. 2003. *The Politics of Public Management: The HRDC Audit of Grants and Contributions.* Toronto: University of Toronto Press.

Good, D.A. and E.A. Lindquist. 2015. "Canada's Reactive Budget Response to the Global Financial Crisis: From Resilience and Brinksmanship to Agility and Innovation." *The Global Financial Crisis and its Budget Impacts in OECD Nations,* edited by J. Wanna, E. Lindquist, and J de Vries, Cheltenham, UK: Edward Elgar.

Hay, D. 2005. *Housing, Horizontality and Social Policy.* Ottawa: Canadian Policy Research Networks.

Hopkins, M., C. Couture, and E. Moore. 2001. *Moving from the Heroic to the Everyday: Lessons Learned from Leading Horizontal Projects,* Ottawa: Canadian Centre for Management Development Roundtable on the Management of Horizontal Initiatives.

Howard, C. and S. Phillips. 2012. "Moving Away from Hierarchy: Do Horizontality, Partnerships, and Distributed Governance Really Mean the End of Accountability?" *From New Public Management to New Political Governance: Essays in Honour of Peter C. Aucoin,* edited by H. Bakvis and M.D. Jarvis, Montreal and Kingston: McGill-Queen's University Press.

Juillet, L. 2000. *The Federal Regional Councils and Horizontal Governance: A Report Prepared for the Federal Regional Councils and the Treasury Board Secretariat.* Ottawa: Canadian Centre for Management Development.

Lindquist, E. 1998. "Getting Results Right: Reforming Ottawa's Estimates." *How Ottawa Spends 1998–99: Balancing Act: The Post-Deficit Mandate,* edited by L.A. Pal, Toronto: Oxford University Press.

———. 1999. "Efficiency, Reliability, or Innovation: Managing Overlap and Complexity in Canada's Federal System of Governance." *Stretching the Federation: the Art of the State,* edited by R.A. Young, Kingston: Institute of Intergovernmental Relations, Queen's University.

———. 2002. "Culture, Control or Capacity: Meeting Contemporary Horizontal Challenges in Public Sector Management." *New Players, Partners and Processes: A Public Sector without Boundaries?* edited by M. Edwards and J. Langford, Canberra and Victoria: National Institute on Governance and UVic Centre for Public Sector Studies.

———. 2004. "Strategy, Capacity and Horizontal Governance: Perspectives from Australia and Canada." *Optimum Online: The Journal of Public Sector Management,* 34, 4. Online. Accessed 22 December 2011. http://optimumonline.ca.

———. 2006a. *A Critical Moment: Capturing and Conveying the Evolution of the Canadian Public Service.* Ottawa: Canada School of Public Service.

———. 2006b. "How Ottawa Reviews Spending: Moving Beyond Adhocracy?" Ch. 9 in *How Ottawa Spends 2006-07,* edited by B. Doern, Montreal and Kingston: McGill Queen's University Press, pp. 185–207.

———. 2009. "How Ottawa Assesses Department/Agency Performance: Treasury Board's Management

Accountability Framework." *How Ottawa Spends 2009–2010: Economic Upheaval and Political Dysfunction*, edited by A.M. Maslove, Montreal, Kingston: McGill-Queen's University Press.

———. 2012. "Horizontal Management in Canada Ten Years Later." *Optimum Online: The Journal of Public Sector Management* 42, 3. Online. A ccessed16 December 2012. http://optimumonline.ca.

———. 2014. "The Responsiveness Solution: Embedding Horizontal Governance in Canada." *Crossing Boundaries in Public Management and Policy: The International Experience*, edited by J. O'Flynn, D. Blackman, and J. Halligan, London: Routledge, pp. 190–210.

———. 2016. "Performance Monitoring and the Management Accountability Framework: Recent Developments, Perspective, and Insights from the Literature." A report prepared for the Treasury Board of Canada Secretariat.

Lindquist, E.A., and R.T. Marcy. 2016. "The Competing Values Framework: Implications for Strategic Leadership, Change and Learning in Public Organizations." *International Journal of Public Leadership* 12, 2, pp. 167–86.

Lindquist, E. and K. Rasmussen. 2012. "Deputy Ministers and New Political Governance: From Neutral Competence to Promiscuous Partisans to a New Balance?" *From "New Public Management" to "New Political Governance": Essays in Honour of Peter C. Aucoin*, edited by H. Bakvis and M.D. Jarvis, Montreal: Kingston: McGill-Queen's University Press, pp. 179–203.

McDavid, J.C. and I. Huse. 2012. "Legislator Uses of Performance Reports: Findings from a Five-Year Study." *American Journal of Evaluation* 33,1, pp. 7–25.

Maloney, D. 2005. *Expenditure Management Current Challenges, Future Directions*. Notes for FMI Presentation, 22 November 2005.

Motsi, G. 2009. *Two Key Questions for Horizontal Policy Making and Implementation*, Policy Brief 34, Ottawa: Institute on Governance.

O'Flynn, J., D. Blackman, and J. Halligan, editors. 2014. *Crossing Boundaries in Public Management and Policy: The International Experience*. London: Routledge.

Osborne, Stephen, editor. 2010. *The New Public Governance? Emerging Perspectives on Theory and Practice of Public Governance*. Oxford and New York: Routledge.

Paquet, G. and R. Shepherd. 1996. "The Program Review Process: A Deconstruction." *How Ottawa Spends 1996–97: Life Under the Knife*, edited by G. Swimmer, Ottawa: Carleton University Press.

Peters, G. 1998. *Managing Horizontal Government: The Politics of Coordination*, Research Paper No. 21, Ottawa: Canadian Centre for Management Development.

Policy Horizons Canada (2011) *About Us*. Online. Accessed 18 October 2011. http://www.horizons.gc.ca/page.asp?pagenm=pri_index.

Phillips, S.D., R. Laforest, and A. Graham. 2010. "From Shopping to Social Innovation: Getting Public Financing Right in Canada." *Policy and Society* 29, pp. 189–99.

Public Policy Forum. 2008. *Collaborative Governance and Changing Federal Roles: A PPF and PRI Joint Roundtable Outcomes Report*. Ottawa: Public Policy Forum.

Rocan, C. 2009. "Multi-Level Collaborative Governance: The Case of the Canadian Heart Health Initiative." *Optimum Online: The Journal of Public Sector Management* 34, 4.

Rounce, A. and N. Beaudry. 2002. *Using Horizontal Tools to Work across Boundaries: Lessons Learned and Signposts for Success*. Ottawa: Canadian Centre for Management Development.

Savoie, D.J. 2008. *Horizontal Management of Official Languages: Report Submitted to the Office of the Commissioner of Official Languages*. Ottawa: Office of the Commissioner of Official Languages.

Smith, R. and S. Torjman. 2004. *Policy Development and Implementation in Complex Files*. Ottawa: Canada School of Public Service.

Sproule-Jones, M. 2000. "Horizontal Management: Implementing Programs across Interdependent Organizations." *Canadian Public Administration* 43, 1, pp. 93–109.

Traverse Group. 2006. Cross-Organizational Initiatives. Online. Accessed 22 December 2011. http://www.traversegroup.ca/d5/cross-ndash-organizational-initiatives.php.

Treasury Board of Canada Secretariat (TBS). 2002. *Companion Guide: The Development of Results-Based Management and Accountability Frameworks for Horizontal Initiatives*. Ottawa: Treasury Board of Canada Secretariat.

———. 2012. *Policy on Management, Resources and Results Structures*. Ottawa: Treasury Board of Canada Secretariat.

Voluntary Sector Initiative. 1999. *Working Together: A Government of Canada/Voluntary Sector Joint Initiative: Report of the Joint Tables*. Ottawa: Government of Canada.

Wildavsky, A. 1972. "The Self-Evaluating Organization." *Public Administration Review* 32, 5, pp. 509–20.

Communications Concepts and Practices in Canadian Public Administration

25

Alex Marland

Chapter Overview

This chapter introduces students to the importance of communication in public administration. It begins by reviewing key concepts, among them gatekeeping, agenda-setting, news management, information subsidies, and spin. A description of how communications is practised in public administration ranges from examining structural components, such as the strategic communications plan in a memorandum to cabinet, to the ways that Prime Minister Justin Trudeau communicates with the general public. The role of central agencies, notably the Prime Minister's Office and the Privy Council Office, is discussed. Broader theories of access to information, open government, and new political governance are touched upon. This review provides a basis for comprehending the emerging theory of public-sector branding, which holds that all government communications is becoming centralized.

Chapter Objectives

By the end of this chapter, students will be able to do the following:
- Discuss the most important communications terms and concepts.
- Describe the impact on governance of changes in communications technology.
- Explain the new political governance theory.
- Explain public-sector branding.
- Discuss the Savoie thesis and the branding-lens thesis.
- Consider current developments in government communications in the light of the concepts covered in this chapter.

Introduction

Communication is, was, and always will be an essential ingredient in public administration. After all, weak communications can sink well-designed public policy; equally, weak policy results from misinformation and histrionics prattling across the public sphere. Elsewhere, I have argued that related and connected trends running through Canadian public administration—the politicization of government, the centralization of decision-making, and the proliferation of digital media—have coalesced into a **branding** ethos in the public sector (Marland, 2016). It is a theory that all government actors are beholden to messages set by the prime minister's inner circle. Branding and message control characterized Stephen Harper's Conservative administration. Some of the tenets of public-sector branding persist under the Liberal government led by Justin Trudeau, while others appear to be waning. Time will tell whether Liberal interest in de-politicization and de-centralization of communications and government is sincere.

In the meantime, this chapter seeks to acquaint readers with key concepts in public-sector communications, and to introduce them to a strategic game that is immersed in governance. That game, I argue, is characterized by branding strategy. The chapter thus lays the groundwork for understanding the many ways that Canadian public-sector actors are harnessing marketing and communications principles in their approach to governing. Dotted throughout are pertinent examples that generally illustrate that the prime minister is the government's communicator-in-chief. After reading this chapter, a student should be familiar with the importance of communications in governance; the processes and instruments used within public administration to make government information public, including why strategic planning occurs; the theory of public-sector branding; and the reasons why students and citizens should seek information from a variety of sources.

Key Concepts in Public-Sector Marketing and Communications

Most students and scholars of Canadian government are surely unfamiliar with the array of concepts that are common in **political communication** scholarship.[1] Tools such as advertising and social media are reasonably well known because they are highly visible. Other communication tools are obscure because they are not in the public domain, such as direct marketing. This includes mailings, telemarketing, email communication, and texting that reach the recipient without others' knowledge. Some tools are hidden in plain sight. The government is constantly in the news, featuring spokespersons and staged events. Few of us give thought to the work that goes into the planning and execution of these activities. Most of us question neither the motives of public relations (PR) personnel nor the impartiality of journalists' reportage. We also rarely consider the expense of disseminating government information: annual reports are submitted to Parliament about the costs of government advertising and public-opinion research, and ministerial travel expense claims are posted online, but there is no breakdown for media relations. We are exposed to information, formulate a judgment, and (more often than not) move on with our busy lives.

In considering government communications, we must recognize the profound transformation that political and public spheres are undergoing because of digital media. Political journalism is speeding up, as reporters anxiously work to meet mini-deadlines throughout the day in what has quickly become a Web-first and mobile-first environment. E-government adds to this pressure: information that was once obscured is now accessible online from anywhere at any time of day. Citizens are authoring blogs, crowdsourcing can uncover information archived on the Web, Facebook is used to mobilize activists, people chime in to discuss government on Twitter, photos of political gaffes are mocked on Instagram, and political controversy goes viral on YouTube. Equally, the behaviour of politicians and public servants is changing. Squeezing all available communications advantages from public resources is now so commonplace that everyone in Canadian politics and government is thought to be engaged in **permanent campaigning**—a concept that electioneering-style practices that characterize an official election campaign are carried over into governance (Marland et al., 2017). In the frenetic world of 24/7 media and tweets, politicians are drawn into a state of constant communication, as are government communicators. As I shall explain, risk-averse political strategists and public administrators can find refuge in controlled, pre-planned messages.

Before delving into branding we need to appreciate the political structure and social conditions that got us here. In the following pages, I introduce readers to a number of communications theories and strategies that concern the news media industry, public-sector actors, and norms that apply to both journalists and government PR strategists. This offers some baseline awareness of concepts and practices that shape interactions between public servants and institutions, their political masters, journalists, and the Canadian citizenry.

Communications Theories and Strategies

First and foremost, we must dispel notions that the government, politicians, or journalists are impartial purveyors of truth. All political communication is biased. This ranges from what is disclosed to how it is presented, as well as how it is received and interpreted.

Public administrators recognize that information slants are inherent in news production. Complex policy announcements are reduced to an eight-second sound bite, or simplified into a single visual known as an image bite. Journalists and news editors choose what stories to pursue, which ones should lead the news, how much attention to pay to them, who to interview, what editorial angle to apply, and when to dig deeper. Traditionally, elites within the mainstream media have acted as **gatekeepers** who exercise considerable influence over the flow of information between government and citizens (e.g., Bennett, 2004). This power is waning in the digital age, where topics that are trending in social media command attention. Moreover, media economics are such that the business is highly competitive and news operations are chronically under-resourced. News desks are shrinking, media companies are merging, investigative journalism is under strain, and newspapers and magazines are becoming online-only. In Canada, an outlier is the Canadian Broadcasting Corporation (CBC) which, as the country's public broadcaster, enjoys resource stability that is rare in the media industry. Yet the CBC is not immune to budget stresses, market forces, political pressure, or criticisms of bias (Attallah, 2000). Public- and private-sector journalists alike operate in a fast-paced world, and are expected to multitask in ways never seen before. News organizations and their audiences have access to reams of free content, often generated by citizen proto-journalists. Yet, professional journalists have less time to research or think than any of their predecessors. This has implications for governance and how the public service releases information.

Canada's system of democratic government depends on the members of the Canadian Parliamentary Press Gallery (CPPG) to monitor government behaviour. It is such an important role that professional journalists are dubbed the **fourth estate**, implying that the CPPG and its provincial cousins are an honorary branch of government, with the executive, legislative, and judicial branches being the three main ones (e.g., Schultz, 1998). However, reporting on public administration is difficult when Canadians are uninterested in the inner workings of government, or care little about public policy minutia. The amount that advertisers pay is related to the size of the audience; consequently, the news media has a financial incentive to present information in a dramatic manner with story arcs. **Market-oriented journalism** is a problem for good government because the business of governing is dull compared with a multitude of choices for media consumers—think of how a video of cute animals goes viral as compared to the number of view counts of a government official testifying to a legislative committee on a routine issue. Consequently, the media industry is drawn to the business of infotainment, which is to say that news about government and politics is styled to drum up interest among the uninterested (Delli Carpini & Williams, 2001). Minor indiscretions become pseudo-scandals that are quickly forgotten by all but those involved; important public affairs are ignored in favour of a confrontational protest; the clothing and hairstyles of public figures are dissected instead of the implications of policy decisions; and so on. Even the CBC, whose news reporting standards (CBC, 2016) are perhaps the best in Canada, is prone to treat politics and governance as reality TV soap opera.

Wary of negative coverage, the release of information and how it is perceived is managed by politicians, political staff, and public servants—particularly PR personnel. Members of cabinet and parliamentarians on the government side routinely highlight the positives of a throne speech or the tabling of the budget, and they downplay or conceal negatives. Likewise, when faced with questions, a government spokesperson is trained to seek to control the discussion rather than allow a political opponent or a journalist to do so. To offer a single example of communications management, consider the invitation to attend a United Nations climate change conference in Morocco that was sent in October 2016 from the Department of Environment and Climate Change to a number of opposition MPs, First Nations leaders, advocacy groups, business representatives, and other levels of government. The intent was to generate positive optics of the Liberal minister leading a pan-Canadian delegation, supporting the Trudeau government's preferred image of embodying a democratic ethos that rises above partisan politics. This is more inclusive than under the Harper government which, when it did fund the overseas travel of large contingents, tended to restrict participation to Conservative enthusiasts and exemplified permanent campaigning (CTV, 2014). But all is not as it seems. A letter signed by Liberal Environment Minister Catherine McKenna stated that invitees' expenses would be reimbursed only if they signed an acceptance confirmation to "respect the authority" of the minister and "refrain from giving media interviews" (Akin, 2016). Faced with criticism, McKenna's office stated that they would overrule the bureaucrats who had attempted to control the message, and would amend the compliance agreement. This deflected why the minister and the minister's office authorized it in the first place, or why one is necessary.

The unfettered communication of information about government aligns with a principle that citizens in a democratic system have a right to know how they are being governed. But news coverage and social media chatter invites criticism. Among the reasons that this is a problem for public-sector elites is because they are interested in **agenda-setting**, which sits among the most formative stages of the public policy cycle (e.g., Eissler et al., 2014). Multiple times a day, they compete to get their priorities in the news, ideally with prominent and favourable treatment. The thinking is that the greater the quantity and quality of attention that the media pays to an issue or event, the higher the likelihood of citizens agreeing that the topic is important. This in turn will spur policy action that is accepted as a legitimate response to an important public problem. Ergo, issues that are not in the news or that are publicly skewered are unlikely to register positively in public opinion, and are prone to languish in the bowels of public administration.

Thus, obtaining positive coverage and securing a favourable position in the public mindset are integral to running a government and advancing change. Conversely, negativity can derail the best-laid plans. Agenda-setting speaks to why communications control is so important in public administration.

As indicated, the public release of government information involves copious preparation. At the most rudimentary level, this involves what is known as **news management**, which refers to the multifaceted ways that PR practitioners seek to encourage positive media coverage, ranging from setting the ground rules of an interview to staying on message (Street, 2011: 239–42). Generally speaking, planned announcements follow a process that goes something like this: cabinet makes a decision; public servants coordinate launch materials; the minister delivers public remarks, which are supported by media products including prewritten social media posts; messages are circulated to government representatives and publicly via social media; PR personnel monitor the ensuing media coverage; and follow-ups with journalists and critics occur as deemed appropriate. During the planning process, the public service is drawn in to strategize the political optics of each event, a level of detail that reached extremes under Prime Minister Harper and was somewhat devolved to ministers under Prime Minister Trudeau (Marland 2016, 2017). Planners are required to describe the venue and prepare a chronology of what the minister is expected to do. Communications plans and sequence of event plans organize human resources by identifying media spokespersons, event attendees, and photo-op participants. They identify the key messages and establish what the target media market is. Ways that the event will be promoted to media are stated, as are post-event media activities including use of social media. These planning templates work in conjunction with other internal instruments such as briefing notes and cabinet papers.

Unplanned media relations are more sporadic and urgent. Everything from a public emergency to a controversial remark by a public official can rocket to the top of the media's agenda, and thus the governing party's. This includes attempts by opponents to embarrass or discredit the government. **Issues management** involves the firefighting of external events, involving little time to think clearly (Esselment & Wilson, 2017). In these circumstances, planned announcements may be pushed back, and a designated spokesperson is quickly assigned to handle the storm of media enquiries. This buys time for strategists to calculate their next move, until the next calamity arises.

Other forms of news and issues management draw inspiration from the private sector and are honed on the campaign trail. Many of these strategies and tactics are encapsulated in political marketing, an emerging subfield of practice and study (e.g., Marland et al., 2012). Idealistically, the application of marketing to politics and governance is a democratic undertaking, because marketing involves drawing on public-opinion research to inform elites' decision-making. In practice however the more nefarious sides are drawn out. Advertising and direct marketing is attractive to PR strategists because information is not subject to passing through the news media's filter and is delivered unencumbered. The Conservatives were big spenders on television advertising and were criticized for using government resources for partisan persuasion reasons. The Trudeau administration is stealthier. In its first year in office, the Liberal government spent more on Facebook advertising than the Conservatives did in nearly a decade (Fekete, 2016). This is highly targeted and efficient, but it intentionally excludes many citizens and is difficult to scrutinize.

This **microtargeting**, sometimes known as narrowcasting or database marketing, is imported from commerce and the campaign trail. We are in an age of data analytics, which with respect to political communication is the examination of quantitative data to segment audiences and isolate messages that are targeted at narrow groups rather than the population as a whole (Turcotte & Vodrey, 2017). Microtargeting is highly efficient as it introduces a level of precision into the selection of communications vehicles and information, thereby optimizing finite resources. Direct marketing and forms of narrowcasting are used that bypass the mass media, such as cinema advertising, email listservs, podcasts, touchscreen technologies, and hidden forms of social media contact such as Twitter direct messages. Katie Telford, the Liberals' campaign co-chair and Trudeau's chief of staff, has explained the party's digital strategy thusly:

Research, analytics and pathways. We would do the research, hear the analytics, and determine the pathways in [a] meeting, multiple times a week . . . debating every metric. From eyeballs on Facebook versus YouTube videos, to ratios to door knocks to phone calls, from radio ad buys against TV ad buys, and which baseball game more Canadians might be watching. We spent our days and many nights talking about numbers and turning each one of them into a meaningful element of the campaign. (quoted in Boutilier, 2016)

As the capacity to mine and analyze data increases, there is a greater ability to design public policy to cater to narrow subgroups of the population. In turn, this means communicating among select individuals without the public as a whole being aware.

The McKenna compliance agreement outlined earlier shows what happens when government elites move away from controlled advertising to uncontrolled news reports, opinion editorials, blogs, tweets, and other forms of public commentary by non-government actors. Scholars have identified a number of strategic concepts in the daily repertoire of government officials and journalists alike. At the forefront is **media logic**, the idea that organizations and individuals change their behaviour in response to how the media operates; a related concept is the mediatization of communication by journalists (Esser, 2013). Another is a theory that politicians are actors on a stage, who act out different public personas depending on the situation and perform a role for audiences and critics (Goffman, 1959). For instance, the Trudeaus have been acutely aware of media logic and the presentation of self. In private settings during the 1968 Liberal leadership race Pierre Trudeau was something of a policy wonk, but in front of the cameras he "adopted a more playful posture, sliding down banisters, kissing pretty young girls, nibbling at flowers" (Radwanski, 1978: 10). Likewise, even as he promoted an image of delivering a more democratic style of government, Justin Trudeau sanctioned ways to trick the media to ensure perfect visuals on the day of his 2015 swearing-in ceremony (Marland, 2016: xvi).

A longstanding tactic in this area is **image management**, which involves meticulous efforts by PR personnel to influence perceptions of a public figure (e.g., Mayer, 2004). Political strategists are highly aware that a public image that is aligned with voter priorities strengthens a leader's power. A favourable image instills internal cohesion. It influences the ability to advance public policies, and makes a difference on election day. Conversely, an unfavourable image will derail a political agenda and hasten the end of a political actor's time in office. For public servants, image management involves coordinating the corporate identity of the government and its units as an institution. But they must also be cognizant that the prime minister and ministers care about their own image and that of their administration.

Media logic's bearings on public administration and the public sphere creates opportunities for manipulation. The government supplies journalists with information in a manner that meets their practices by offering news releases, Q&As, backgrounders, speeches, and social media posts that include digital photos and video. These are **information subsidies** that package information so that it can be easily reused with maximum economic efficiency (Gandy, 1982). Media logic means that government releases good news on a Monday morning to set the tone for the week; bad news is released late on a Friday when it will be buried and potentially lost in weekend distractions. The most prominent form of subsidies are news conferences and photo-ops. These are referred to as **pseudo-events** because they are bogus events that are staged explicitly for the purposes of optimizing favourable news coverage (Boorstin, 1961). This is why ministers end up standing in front of a podium adorned with a sign, surrounded with a visually compelling backdrop such as a gathering of people and flags, sometimes held indoors at a factory or perhaps outdoors in a wheat field. A government photographer and/or videographer captures images that are uploaded online and disseminated via social media. All of this is coordinated by government PR personnel to maximize the likelihood of reproduction by others, ideally in the mainstream media, which they hope will avoid the critical filter of professional journalism. Whether anyone other than invitees attend the event is immaterial. What matters is the controlled optics.

Given all this, but without invoking conspiracy theories, observers must be careful not to take at face value information that is volunteered by government. Because the creator of an information subsidy controls the mechanism of delivery, that individual or organization also controls what information is released and plans its slant. A minister delivering a speech at an invitation-only event and not taking questions from reporters afterwards is one of many examples of ways

that the fourth estate is flummoxed. The same thing happens in the legislative branch, given that ministers are not compelled to provide direct answers during question period, though they are obligated to reply in writing to questions placed on the order paper. This is a problem if we further consider that the government releases information in a manner contorted to align with the governing party's overarching brand messaging. The practice of spinning information—that is, actively applying a favourable slant to suit one's own political objectives—is universal (Hood, 2010). **Spin** involves framing an issue or object in a certain light, calmly emphasizing the positives and downplaying or hiding negatives. Only a small number of public reporting mechanisms are predominantly factual and can be considered free of spin, such as food safety alerts or weather warnings. Everything else is suspect, and involves mini-battles to control the message.

The Practice of Communications in Public Administration

To begin to appreciate the mind-boggling scope of planned government communications activities on any given day, we can turn to news releases. These are the main instrument of communications officialdom, serving to formally inform Canadians of a course of action, woven with positive spin. On the randomly selected day of July 6, 2016, the Government of Canada issued 40 news releases. Summer is a slower news period than when Parliament is sitting, and is prone to soft news such as funding announcements and ministerial mingling across the country. Even cursory attention paid to these releases offers evidence of news management and agenda-setting behaviour that are conditioned by media logic.

On that particular July day, media advisories informed journalists that a minister, parliamentary secretary, and/or Liberal MP were in a number of different places participating in a pseudo-event. Government officials were present for a review of Employment Insurance programming. The minister of immigration and the minister of natural resources participated in roundtables, while the minister of defence met with industry representatives as part of a policy review process. A progress update about replacing CF-18 aircraft was issued. A fisheries advisory panel's recommendations were received. The minister of veterans' affairs presided over a medals ceremony, and the navy coordinated an event to recognize the opening of training centres. Parks Canada unveiled a plaque recognizing the establishment of ice roads in the Northwest Territories, while also celebrating Parks Day. Federal, provincial, and municipal representatives attended the inauguration of a public fountain. Good news about the Canada Summer Jobs program was trumpeted. A spate of funding announcements were made: for a university, for cancer research, for Francophone organizations and official language programs, for an environmental company, for infrastructure, for drug treatment courts, for health facilities, and for an ecosystem mapping mechanism. The minister of democratic institutions announced the availability of electoral reform online tools. Other media releases were more factual and less prone to spin. Data about Canada's finances were released. A federal court decision was announced. The minister of health signed an order to temporarily allow a form of nasal spray to be imported and sold. The Transportation Safety Board issued an aircraft incident report. The Canadian Nuclear Safety Commission renewed a site's operating licence, while Natural Resources Canada announced that construction began on a bridge to accommodate the storage of radioactive waste. Correctional Service Canada held a change-of-command ceremony. On a sombre note, a minister marked the anniversary of the Lac-Mégantic train derailment disaster, and Correctional Service Canada issued a statement that an inmate at a facility had died. Finally, advance notice was given of ministers' participation in upcoming consultations about official languages policy and about the minister of international trade attending G20 meetings in China. As well, a speech delivered in Colombia by the minister of international development was issued, as was his op-ed that appeared in the *Globe and Mail* the previous day. All of this happened on a single summer's day.

On the surface there is nothing remarkable about all of this; it is routine government business. So how do the broad misconceptions apply? A trained eye can observe bias throughout these news releases, which involve considerable preparation to make ministers, their departments, and their decisions look good. We are not told about problems that are being created, only solutions that the minister and cabinet are championing as part of an agenda. The releases are concise and are often packaged with image bites; providing comprehensive details or unbridled access

to government information would interfere with controlling the message. News editors pick and choose which stories to run with. They find ways to make the stories interesting in order to grab public attention, but in so doing they add another slant and dumb down the reportage. The propensity for simple messages and visuals to fly around social media may generate awareness, particularly among narrow segments of the populace, but it is prone to lack the informed analysis that our system of government requires of the fourth estate. Consequently, citizens do not learn about most government announcements in the first place; as news resources contract there are fewer investigative journalists to pick away at the government's spin; and as digital media evolves there is a bigger canvas for infotainment. The public must be suspect about whatever information they receive. Equally, they should be able to easily locate information that is obscure, such as microtargeted Facebook ads or direct marketing.

Students of government must scan a multitude of information sources if they hope to keep appraised of the latest developments and to peel away bias. Despite the considerable planning and execution, the most noteworthy Canadian public-sector news that July 6 was nothing involving the Government of Canada at all (CTV, 2016).[2] For their part, the Conservatives complained that Trudeau was attending a secretive meeting of business elites in Idaho (Conservative Party, 2016). This helps explain the prime minister's absence from the government's pseudo-events put off that day. It also shines light on the gap in digital photos issued by his office during that period (Prime Minister's Office, 2016a)[3] and why his itinerary stated that his participation in the Idaho conference was "closed to media" (Prime Minister's Office, 2016b). Trudeau's Twitter account issued three public messages that day, with no indication that he was out of the country: remembering the Lac-Mégantic disaster, retweeting a minister's message about her meeting with provincial culture and heritage ministers, and conveying that he had voted for a Canadian snowboarder in an online American sports contest. It is unclear to what extent, if any, Trudeau was involved in the tweets or whether the messages were put out by staff in his name without his knowledge. Would audiences have discerned the difference? Does this happen in ministers' offices? To what extent does it all matter? Regardless, discerning Canadians must evidently play close attention to get past the spin.

Key Structural Components in the Government of Canada

Having established the communications operating environment, in order to understand public-sector branding we must next become acquainted with the internal machinery of government. This brings together strategic planners and PR personnel from central agencies and government departments. Communications is where political staff and the permanent public service mingle, providing an opening for the politicization of government.

At the top of the government communications pyramid is the cabinet, which is headed by the prime minister, the individual who recommends its membership to the Governor General. The cabinet is inevitably involved in communications calculations, though some ministers have more communications sway than others, potentially related to their public profile. For instance, policy priorities are set out in each minister's mandate letter, and all memoranda to cabinet (MCs) are required to feature a two-page strategic communications plan, which is presented as Table 25.1. That annex ensures that consideration is given to the purpose of the communications, what the main issues are, and how the public will likely react. How the cabinet's decision will be announced must be woven into a storyline that considers the government's overarching messages. This works in conjunction with the MC's parliamentary plan annex, which identifies a strategy for issues that might arise in the legislature. The MC complements more detailed department-based planning that identifies target audiences, the likelihood of positive or negative reactions, succinct points that should be repeated in all communications, and intra/intergovernmental and regional sensitivities, among other things. Narrow issues that are of little concern to society as a whole, such as the announcement of a regulatory change that affects a small number of industry stakeholders,

Table 25.1 Strategic Communications Plan in a Memorandum to Cabinet, Government of Canada

STRATEGIC COMMUNICATIONS PLAN
(Two pages maximum)
The strategic communications plan should be provided for all Ministerial Recommendations (MRs). The Annex should be developed jointly by the Minister's Office and the Department.

COMMUNICATIONS OBJECTIVES AND CONSIDERATIONS
Identify 2–3 objectives that will be achieved through the communications plan, outline expected results, and link this initiative to the Government's agenda. Outline significant communications considerations and how these would be managed.

ANALYSIS OF PUBLIC ENVIRONMENT
Assess the public environment and identify risks/opportunities therein, including quantitative and qualitative data available through public opinion research data and analysis of previous stakeholder engagement and consultations, federal–provincial positions, and media coverage. For stakeholders, identify who was consulted, the method of consultation, and their reactions.

ANTICIPATED REACTION
Provide examples of likely positive and negative reactions from various audiences (reference should be made to specific groups rather than to broad audiences such as the general public), including stakeholders.

STORYLINE AND CORE GOVERNMENT MESSAGES
In 5–6 bullets, outline the announcement storyline, relate it to Government priorities, and provide core messages. In plain language, describe the benefits and results for Canadians.

ANNOUNCEMENT STRATEGY
Indicate the profile of the announcement as well as its scope (e.g., national/regional/ international). Include details on planned media and stakeholder outreach, as well as events to support the announcement. Describe measures to sustain the message and a focus on impacts and benefits for Canadians.

Source: Privy Council Office. 2014. Permission granted by the Privy Council Office © Her Majesty the Queen in Right of Canada, 2017.

are generally at the purview of the minister. The rest is submitted to what has become known as the centre of government for review, the components of which are described on the following pages.

In practice, strategic forward-thinking of this nature is delegated to the Agenda, Results and Communications cabinet committee, which is chaired by the PM and attended by key ministers. That committee is also concerned with the tracking of priorities and strategizing how they should be publicized. Preparing to roll out announcements, particularly with respect to bills, falls to the cabinet Committee on Open Transparent Government and Parliament. That body is chaired by the government house leader and is responsible for strategizing about the government's legislative activities. A third important cabinet committee is Treasury Board which, aside from overseeing financial management, sets government communication policies. It is chaired by the president of the Treasury Board. Of note, that minister as well as the minister of finance are automatically members of all cabinet committees.

The **Prime Minister's Office (PMO)** is likewise situated at the apex of government. As a party leader, the prime minister has tremendous appreciation for the importance of news and image management. The PMO is a central support agency that is staffed by partisans, most of whom have a role in communications in some capacity or another. In late 2016, the Trudeau PMO comprised ten units. Among them, the communications unit employed fifteen people in digital content, media relations, photography, speechwriting, and planning; the operations unit housed four writers for the prime ministerial correspondence and five in media advance who scout out offsite pseudo-events; three worked in issues management; two in the research in advertising unit, including a pollster; and a communications adviser for democratic reform (Government of Canada, 2016a). It is a nucleus that includes a chief of staff, a principal secretary, and a director of communications who are in constant contact with the prime minister, seeking direction and offering suggestions—and, in a first, who themselves are public personas due to active use of social media. Invariably, some PMO staff are granted time and space for strategic thinking, while others must contend with the pressure cooker of managing burning issues.

Supporting the PMO, the cabinet, and its committees is the PMO's bureaucratic wing, the **Privy Council Office (PCO)**. The much larger PCO is headed by the Clerk of the Privy Council and employs a number of politically astute public servants. Communications personnel in the PCO inform and act on the strategic wishes of the PMO. For instance, they may be tasked with preparing a speech for the prime minister on a more technical matter than speechwriters in the PMO could, but they would not normally craft a politically charged speech. They act as general managers who coordinate deliverables from across government so that draft materials are submitted for central review on schedule. At a minimum, what is submitted requires finessing, such as double-checking statements and simplifying bureaucratic lingo. Other times a proposed departmental announcement is co-opted by the prime minister or perhaps is denied approval. The PCO employs a number of people involved with access to information, correspondence, digital communications, information technology, media analysis, and web communications (Government of Canada, 2016b).

At the head of each department is a **minister's office (MO)**. A MO comprises a number of political staff, including a director of communications, who support the minister. They participate in strategic planning of departmental announcements and in the issues management of unexpected events. This includes the day to day of fielding media enquiries and media monitoring. MO personnel play an essential role in government because they are where decisions are moved up the line to the PMO. Political personnel in both offices are in constant contact to ensure strategic messaging alignment and logistical coordination. Meanwhile, the PCO is in touch with public-service PR personnel, relaying similar strategic direction. This ensures that everyone is on the same page, in contrast with public pronouncements made at the prime minister's discretion.

One underappreciated way that the PMO, PCO, and MOs coordinate events and synchronize activities is the maintenance of internal communications calendars. Information is constantly fed from departments to the centre so that upcoming announcements and photo-ops can be plotted in a grid. This enables central agencies to see the big picture of government communications. There are the domestic and international schedules of well over two dozen members of cabinet to juggle and prioritize, combined with a litany of travel plans, fiduciary obligations, statutory holidays, and so on—not to mention the prime minister's priorities as well as known external events organized by opponents and non-governmental actors. So-called whole-of-government initiatives that are major priorities and span multiple departments will also be of greater priority than department-specific activities. Generally speaking anything that stems from the throne speech and the budget will be prioritized by the centre.

The other main central agency that provides communications support is the **Treasury Board Secretariat (TBS)**. The agency acts on the direction of the Board president, who is a member of cabinet, as well as the corresponding cabinet committee. It implements central policies that apply throughout the public service. Among these is the Government of Canada's Policy on Communications and Federal Identity, which itemizes the various responsibilities and obligations associated with government communications, a list too long to get into here. Among the philosophies and objectives outlined in the policy are that communications are an essential ingredient in public trust in government; that information must be provided in both official languages; and that new technologies are an important mechanism to reach a diverse public. The apolitical and simplified nature of communications is explained as follows:

> Government communications must be objective, factual, non-partisan, clear, and written in plain language. The communications function entails more than simply providing or receiving information. The way in which the government delivers its communications affects the value of the information, how it is received by the public, and the credibility of its source. Tailoring messages to specific audiences increases the impact of how the information is received. (Treasury Board of Canada Secretariat, 2016)

This is much easier said than done. The government's decision-makers are members of cabinet and they, as with political staff, are partisan. Moreover, all sorts of senior positions throughout government are filled by executive appointment, including the Clerk of the Privy Council and deputy ministers. It is an appropriate ideal to minimize partisanship but a fallacy to suggest that government communication is non-partisan when only some of it is.

The TBS-enforced policy also outlines guidelines related to the management of the government's corporate image. All arms of the government, with a few exceptions such as offices that report to the legislature, are required to use identical visual identity markers. The most prominent is the Canada wordmark, the icon that has the national flag hovering above the final letter in Canada (Figure 25.1). Departments are not permitted to have their own unique logos. There are also strict protocols about the look and feel of government websites. All of this is done with an eye towards eliminating disparity and optimizing efficiency. As a senior adviser of the Federal Identity Program has explained, "visual identity is a complex field, and ongoing attention to key areas can continually improve consistency, application and potential cost-savings" (Treasury Board of Canada Secretariat, 2009). Personnel in the TBS who are responsible for enforcing the corporate identity policy liaise with designated agents within each department. Collectively they ensure that Treasury Board protocols are followed.

Communications flows through public administration in a number of other ways. Public Services and Procurement Canada (previously known as Public Works) is responsible for coordinating the award of advertising contracts and public opinion research contracts. This includes implementing an operating policy that advertising must be monitored and assessed to determine value for money (discussed in the next section). Other government departments that have a hand in communications include finance and heritage. The department of finance is widely considered a central agency in Canadian public administration literature (e.g., Savoie, 1999: 169) but its communications functions are typically limited to the budget, whose announcement is a formidable public event. The release of the budget, roughly each March, follows well-trodden ground. The media clamours for tidbits of information in the days before the event, possibly reporting on information that has

Figure 25.1 Canada Wordmark, Government of Canada

Source: Reproduced with the permission of the Government of Canada.

leaked, which in fact was purposely released by an unnamed high-ranking source in order to draw out attention that will otherwise get lost amid a cluster of major policy announcements. Reporters dutifully record the finance minister's choice of shoes, an odd tradition that is meant to symbolize the type of budget. The budget's contents must be presented to the legislature first, out of respect for the principle of responsible government. To facilitate the timely transmission of information, journalists are given an advance briefing in what is known as a budget lock-in. Their communications devices are turned off as they take notes, with the understanding that information can be broadcast publicly no sooner than when the finance minister delivers a speech. In recent years the department of finance has taken to social media to release information in real time as the minister proceeds. Notwithstanding all this, or the minister's clout, the department of finance is not involved in the cut and thrust of most of the government's communications matters.

By comparison, the department of heritage is immersed in everyday communications of the cultural variety. The arts, sport, commemorative celebrations, public events, national anthem, museums, official languages, Canadian media content, and cultural programs are some of the many tangible and intangible forms of communication that department is concerned with. In essence, matters of national identity and unity flow through Canadian heritage. One example is a pledge made by then-minister Sheila Copps to give away a million flags to Canadians in the aftermath of the 1995 Quebec referendum on sovereignty-association. As we shall see, this ran into trouble with respect to how contracts for the flags were issued.

The Liberal Sponsorship Scandal, Harper's Message Control and Trudeau's Sunny Ways

A further consideration in setting the scene for branding strategy is that the process for awarding government communications contracts has strengthened over time. Up to the late twentieth century, advertising agencies routinely offered their services to political parties during an election campaign, with a quid pro quo expectation that they would be rewarded with lucrative government contracts afterwards. Gradually rules were introduced, including putting out contracts for public tender, and assessing bids against a previously agreed scoring grid. This levelled the playing field for all purveyors of communications services such as advertising, marketing, and public-opinion research although in the early 1990s, the criteria initially favoured companies with ties to the governing party, and procedures were sufficiently slack that people within government were able to work the system in favour of their party (Public Works and Government Services Canada, 2005). This resulted in what is known as the **sponsorship scandal**.

The partisan exploitation of public resources climaxed with the pilfering of communications funds in the late 1990s and early 2000s while Jean Chrétien was prime minister. Journalists initially identified that advertising agencies with ties to the Quebec wing of the governing Liberal party were granted millions of dollars in contracts between 1994 and 2004, but did very little to no work for what they billed. In return, the companies funnelled money and supports back to the party. They did so under the guise of a sponsorship program whereby the federal government was supposed to help finance public events that would increase Quebecers' positive views of Canada. While the large contracts concerned advertising, many smaller instances of phony invoices were uncovered, including for the Canadian flags given away after the Quebec referendum (CBC, 2004).

The affair was so significant that multiple ministers were shuffled and major changes in government operations were initiated as the Liberal cabinet sought to control the scandal. In 2003, the Auditor General released a damning report about government management practices with respect to advertising. A criminal investigation was launched by the police. Separate from that, and without the force of legal consequences, a commission of inquiry was called to identify procedural problems within public administration that contributed to the scandal. New Prime Minister Paul Martin delivered a televised national address to speak directly to Canadians about it, a rare tool that is used only in moments of acute political crisis (e.g., CBC, 2008).

The Commission of Inquiry into the Sponsorship Program and Advertising Activities, led by Justice John Gomery, employed forensic accountants, called witnesses, and hired researchers. Public hearings held between 2004 and 2005 made for dramatic political theatre. Among the over 170 witnesses were Chrétien and Martin, which was extraordinary in itself. The scope of misdeeds and the conclusions of the Gomery Inquiry are instructive even though they were reported over a decade ago. Concerns were raised about the involvement of political personnel in the sponsorship program; insufficient oversight by senior public servants and an unwillingness to confront a manager who was politically connected; the payment of falsified invoices submitted by communications agencies that were connected to party kickbacks and political donations; a culture of secrecy and entitlement; and a lack of general lack of accountability (Canada, 2005: 5–7). All of this pointed to excessive power concentrated in the centre of government and the political influence of top officials.

The scandal was a significant reason why the Liberals were reduced to a minority government in the 2004 federal election, and why they were voted out of office in 2006. A number of advertising officials were criminally convicted and significant changes to public administration practices were instituted. Among them were stricter protocols for government contracting and the aforementioned public tabling of annual reports about government advertising.

Stephen Harper and the Conservative Party promised change and accountability. While in office, procurement practices under the Conservatives were clean, if not always transparent.[4] However, expenditures on government advertising were suspect, with tens of millions spent on ads that were widely derided for being overly partisan. Moreover, communications practices were panned as subversive to good government. Relations between government and the CPPG soured when Harper insisted that his staff be allowed to select which reporters could ask questions (Paré & Delacourt, 2014). The Conservative PMO, via the PCO, required that media products refer to "Canada's new government" and later "the Harper government." Young political staff in the PMO issued orders to all and sundry, including Conservative MPs and senators. Complaints piled up: that ministers were on a short leash; that journalists were kept at bay during pseudo-events where only photography was allowed; that government cheques adorned with a Conservative logo were being handed out at photo-ops; that access-to-information requests were being thwarted; that government scientists were not allowed to speak

publicly; and that parliamentary committees were not always provided with information they had requested (in one case, leading to the Conservatives being found in contempt of Parliament and falling on a motion of non-confidence in 2011). Dubious tactics were employed to advance their political agenda, such as bundling changes into omnibus bills with short deceptive titles; for instance, the 2015 budget bill was dubbed the "Economic Action Plan Act, No. 1" but contained a variety of controversial measures including the power to unilaterally amend aspects of government employee contracts. Communications activities bordered on propaganda, such as the PMO's release of a "photo of the day" or its weekly online video magazine "Stephen Harper: 24/7," all of which featured controlled visuals that presented the prime minister in a positive light irrespective of his critics. Publicity was directed at Conservative-friendly media vehicles, such as small rural news outlets. Public policy was often designed for narrow cohorts of electors so that the party could micro-target segments of the population through direct marketing and narrowcasting. The Tories used targeted tax credits to appeal to electors who were either party supporters or on the margins of switching allegiances. Thus the government created a tradesperson's tools deduction, a volunteer firefighter tax credit, pension income splitting, a public transit tax credit, a first-time home buyers' tax credit, a children's fitness tax credit, and a children's arts tax credit. Marketing played a pivotal role in the creation of these micro-policies, illustrating that communications is so important that it shapes public policy from development to delivery. This is just a snippet of the many ways that political communications calculations were ever-present and directed by senior political operatives.

The command-and-control style meant that the PMO was supreme and MOs were implementers of the centre's directives. The top-down approach was embodied by an internal communications template known as the message event proposal (MEP) that required copious details about a planned public announcement or event. This included what type of photograph was desired and what the ideal news headline would be. The Conservatives required that departments submit a completed MEP many days if not weeks in advance of the event so that it could be considered by the PMO. This weakened departmental and ministerial autonomy because permission had to be sought from the centre. It was the nature of branding supremacy, whereby all ministerial and departmental communications must align with the governing party's overall brand strategy.

The Trudeau Liberals promised to put a stop to this. After his new government was sworn in, Prime Minister Justin Trudeau proclaimed, "Government by cabinet is back." The central control over ministerial affairs was said to be over. Sure enough, Liberal ministers and authorized personnel including select government scientists were available to the media in a manner that had not been seen during the Conservative years. Departments reportedly ceased using the MEP, and were free to craft their own communications plans (Smith, 2016). The government's communications policy was revised to introduce measures to inhibit advertising from taking on a partisan tinge by setting up an arm's-length body to review proposed ads.

This must not be confused with ministerial independence or brand freedom. As indicated, the PMO and PCO remain highly interested and involved with coordinating a common message. They are simply less exacting on minor procedural manners and are content to leave those to the discretion of a minister's office. The grounding of the public service and politics in a default of information secrecy in order to maintain control is slowly eroding, a transformation that the Trudeau Liberals want us to believe they are leading. Time will tell whether the thorny realities of governing get in the way of decentralization.

Access to Information and Open Government

A final point is that the political landscape is evolving in a manner that is critical of government secrecy and centralized authority. Legislation legally compels a timely government response to formal **access-to-information** requests and to release certain internal information that is otherwise not in the public domain. This is balanced against the cabinet's legitimate need to maintain secrecy on sensitive subject matters. What constitutes a "cabinet confidence," and what information should be withheld or redacted, is often a source of debate. There is a significant grey area, because journalists and opponents want to understand topical issues, whereas ministers and public servants want to avoid criticism or

embarrassment. Complaints about delays and withheld information are chronic (e.g., Treasury Board of Canada Secretariat, 2012). Typically, in opposition a political party tends to promote the virtues of transparency and open access, and when in government that same party becomes reluctant.

Another evolution is the increasing expectation that information should automatically be publicly available, negating the need for formalities and delays. Service Canada administers a 1-800 O-Canada call centre and retail locations that act as a one-stop shop and treat citizens with a customer service mentality. Public websites, particularly Canada.ca, have become the default location for posting and accessing government information. Basic matters ranging from the employee directory to details about programs and services are easily located online. The federal **open government** portal (www.open.canada.ca) is an interface for "open data," a repository of datasets that Canadians can analyze themselves; "open information," a clearinghouse for digital records, including the results of completed access-to-information requests and government contracts exceeding $10,000; and for "open dialogue," a pathway to connect citizens with others who share an interest in open government. Recent literature about digital governance suggests that the openness trend is contributing to growing citizen engagement in shaping policy decisions (Clarke & Margetts, 2014: 410). For instance, the release of an obscure dataset and ensuing dialogue among policy wonks can lead to public pressure on government elites to follow a particular pathway, thereby restricting their autonomy to exercise power and a loss of message control. In other ways, government coordination and centralization are in full force. One example is that public servants across Canada use the intranet site Publiservice (http://publiservice.gc.ca), which only they can access. This hiding of information from the public, and the connection of previously disparate units, is related to the central unification of government operations under the umbrella of a cohesive brand.

New Political Governance and Public-Sector Branding

Optimism about the transformative potential of e-government masks a reality that the political apparatus clings to a penchant for spin and quasi-propaganda even as its spokespeople profess otherwise. The standardization of media relations nurtures conditions for political staff to demand the complicity of parliamentarians, public servants, and even ministers. This is a problem for those concerned about the politicization of public administration.

The **new political governance** (NPG) theory put forward by Peter Aucoin during the Harper era holds that institutional conditions in Westminster systems, particularly in Canada, weakens the merit-based, professional public service (Aucoin et al., 2013). The theory encapsulates many of the concepts discussed in this chapter: permanent campaigning, the empowerment of political staff, loyalty of executives appointed to the prime minister's circle, and public servants who are drawn into political activities. It is a model that builds on the work of fellow public administration scholar Donald Savoie, who has argued that power gravitates to the centre of government, and is clustered among a small group with access to the prime minister (Savoie, 1999).

This is where branding strategy comes in. I believe that the **Savoie thesis** and NPG need to be updated to consider the omnipresence of communications in government decision-making. This comes together as branding strategy. Brands are "symbolic constructs that add value or meaning to something in order to distinguish it from its competitors [and] are increasingly used in strategies for managing perceptions in the public sector" (Eshuis & Klijn, 2012: 3). It is a somewhat amorphous concept that unifies all marketing practices with a vision of achieving a strategic competitive image. In politics and governance, it simplifies communications processes, delivering financial and time efficiencies for the public sector and its clients. However, I believe that branding fortifies existing characteristics in the Canadian parliamentary system of message discipline, centralization, politicization, and permanent campaigning—and the downsides of a reduction in parliamentarian independence and ministerial autonomy, increased power concentrated in unelected political staff, and the use of public resources for partisan gain.

Political personnel in the PMO and MOs are responding to the 24/7 digital media environment with a marketing doctrine and minimalism to cope with the onslaught of media enquiries. In this paradigm, the mutual interests of senior political strategists and senior public servants align to ensure that an overarching government message is advanced that supersedes micro-level policy factors. A branding thesis posits that all of the concepts, practices, and structural components discussed in this chapter align within a marketing orthodoxy. Thus, on the one hand we have aspects of digital media (e.g., social media, open government) that suggest political elites are relinquishing communications control, and on the other we have indications that the centre of government is fighting to maintain it amid a communications tsunami. This new model is depicted in Figure 25.2 as an evolution of Savoie's thesis of centralization.

Whether they are aware of it or not, public-sector actors are in the branding business. This carries over to governance. Every action by a governing party, and

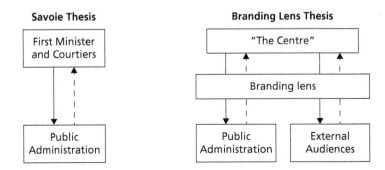

Figure 25.2 The Savoie Thesis and Branding-Lens Thesis

thus actions stemming from public administration, must be both "on message" and consistent with core brand values that are promoted at every opportunity over time. There is an ideological devotion to sticking to the script, reinforcing overarching messages, and protecting the brand. Branding is driven by intra- and intergovernmental desires to align the voices of many different organizations. Within government, civil servants must unofficially consider the context of public policy and issues management within the overall brand image of the political executive and particularly the prime minister. The forces of centralization exist under the auspices that branding is an opportunity to enhance the value-for-money of communications resources. Running everything through a branding lens influences the type of information available to citizens, and the vibrancy of democratic discourse. It stands to reason that over time the number of government and publicly funded organizations that promote messages that are holistic and constant rather episodic and fleeting will increase.

Conclusion

This chapter had two objectives. First, it seeks to acquaint students of Canadian public administration to a variety of concepts in public-sector marketing and communications. This includes permanent campaigning, gatekeeping, infotainment, news and issues management, microtargeting, media logic,

image management, pseudo-events, and spin. It attempts to increase appreciation for the role of communications in agenda-setting and the public policy cycle. It provides examples of Canadian government communications in practice, from the drudgery of daily media relations to the controversy over partisan exploitation of government resources. By reviewing executive offices, and touching on environmental considerations such as access to information, it outlines the internal organizational structure of government communications. Woven throughout is a recognition of the changing dynamics of digital technology that are being brought to bear on government and politics, from social media to data analytics.

The second objective is to build on this foundation by introducing public-sector branding, a growing area of practice and study. In the private sector, branding harnesses all available marketing activities to promote a strategically designed image. This delivers communications efficiencies as each touchpoint reinforces the other. In government, it refers in part to a corporate identity, with the Canada wordmark being a common symbol for all federal departments. This visual unification is possible due to the government's internal structures, and complements parallel branding practices in party politics. Taken together, branding provides another way of explaining the centralization of power in Canadian public administration and political elites' obsession with communications.

Important Terms and Concepts

access to information	market-oriented journalism	political communication
agenda-setting	media logic	Prime Minister's Office (PMO)
branding	microtargeting	Privy Council Office (PCO)
fourth estate	minister's office (MO)	pseudo-events
gatekeepers	new political governance (NPG)	Savoie thesis
image management	news management	sponsorship scandal
information subsidies	open government	Treasury Board Secretariat (TBS)
issues management	permanent campaigning	

Study Questions

1. Why is communication so pivotal in public policy and public administration?
2. What do changes in communications technology imply for governance?

3. Identify and explain the main communications terms and concepts used in this chapter.
4. What do the acronyms PMO, PCO, TBS and MO stand for? More importantly, how do they interact in public administration?
5. In what ways are theories of new political governance and public-sector branding relevant to recent events? In formulating your answer, think about matters that you have noticed in the news, controversies trending online, and/or your own personal interactions with politicians or the government at any level.
6. What are the Savoie thesis and the branding-lens thesis? Discuss.

Notes

1   For an overview, see Lilleker (2010) or the glossary on pages 405 to 414 of Marland (2016).
2   Rather, it was that former Conservative minister Jason Kenney was planning to seek the leadership of the Alberta Progressive Conservative Party.
3   On July 3, Prime Minister Trudeau was shown participating in the Toronto Pride Parade and on July 7 he was depicted

travelling to Poland to attend a NATO Summit. No photographs were issued July 4 to July 6, which were weekdays.
4   For instance, communications secrecy and the use of the Deputy Minister of Public Works as spokesperson were central to the government's successful handling of its announcement that the Halifax Shipyard was awarded a $25-billion government contract after an intense regional competition (Chase, 2011b).

References

Akin, David. 2016. "Bureaucrats Wanted to Muzzle Mps, First Nations Leaders and Others Bound for Climate Change Conference." *National Post*, October 28. http://news.nationalpost.com/news/canada/canadian-politics/bureaucrats-wanted-to-muzzle-mps-first-nations-leaders-and-others-bound-for-climate-change-conference

Attallah, Paul. 2000. "Public Broadcasting in Canada: Legitimation Crisis and the Loss of Audience." *International Communication Gazette* 62, 3–4, pp. 177–203.

Aucoin, Peter, Herman Bakvis, and Mark Jarvis. 2013. "Constraining Executive Power in the Era of New Political Governance." *Governing: Essays in Honour of Donald J. Savoie*, edited by James Bickerton and B. Guy Peters, Montreal and Kingston: McGill-Queen's University Press, pp. 32–52.

Bennett, Lance W. 2004. "Gatekeeping and Press-Government Relations: A Multigated Model of News Construction." *Handbook of Political Communication Research*, edited by L.L. Kaid, Mahwah, NJ: Lawrence Erlbaum, pp. 283–313.

Boorstin, Daniel Joseph. 1961. *The Image: A Guide to Pseudo-Events in America*. New York: Vintage.

Boutilier, Alex. 2016. "Liberals Outline New-Found Digital Muscle." *Toronto Star*, May 28. http://www.thestar.com/news/canada/2016/05/28/liberals-outline-new-found-digital-muscle.html

Canada. 2005. "Who Is Responsible? Summary." Commission of Inquiry into the Sponsorship Program and Advertising Activities. Public Works and Government Services Canada.

CBC. 2004. "Free Flag Giveaway Spawned Phony Transactions." March 19. http://www.cbc.ca/news/canada/free-flag-giveaway-spawned-phony-transactions-1.477155

CBC. 2008. "Addressing the nation: Prime ministers of Canada." http://www.CBC.ca/archives/topic/addressing-the-nation-prime-ministers-of-canada

CBC. 2016. "Journalistic Standards and Practices." http://www.cbc.radio-canada.ca/en/reporting-to-canadians/acts-and-policies/programming/journalism/.

Chase, Steven. 2011b. "How Ottawa Will Reveal Shipbuilding Winners to Yards, Tories and Public." *Globe and Mail*. October 19. http://www.theglobeandmail.com/news/politics/ottawa-notebook/how-ottawa-will-reveal-shipbuilding-winners-to-yards-tories-and-public/article2206613/

Clarke, Amanda and Helen Margetts. 2014. "Governments and Citizens Getting to Know Each Other? Open, Closed, and Big Data in Public Management Reform." *Policy & Internet* 6, 4, pp. 393–417.

Conservative Party. 2016. "Trudeau's Summer Camp Trip." July 6. http://www.conservative.ca/trudeaus-summer-camp-trip/

CTV. 2014. "Conservative MP Begs for 'Million-Dollar Shot' with PM at Jewish Holy Site." January 21. http://www.ctvnews.ca/politics/conservative-mp-begs-for-million-dollar-shot-with-pm-at-jewish-holy-site-1.1649947

CTV. 2016. "5 Things to Know on Wednesday, July 6, 2016." http://www.ctvnews.ca/5things/5-things-to-know-on-wednesday-july-6-2016-1.2974921.

Delli Carpini, M.X. and B.A. Williams. 2001. "Let Us Infotain You: Politics in the New Media Environment." *Mediated Politics: Communication in the Future of*

Democracy, edited by W.L. Bennett and R.M. Entman. Cambridge: Cambridge University Press, pp. 160–81.

Eissler, Rebecca, Annelise Russell, and Bryan D. Jones. 2014. "New Avenues for the Study of Agenda Setting." *Policy Studies Journal* 42, pp. S71–S86.

Eshuis, Jasper and Erik-Hans Klijn. 2012. *Branding in Governance and Public Management*. New York: Routledge.

Esselment, Anna and Paul Wilson. 2017. "Campaigning from the Centre." *Permanent Campaigning in Canada*, edited by A. Marland, T. Giasson, and A. Esselment. Vancouver: UBC Press, pp. 222–40.

Esser, Frank. 2013. "Mediatization as a Challenge: Media Logic versus Political Logic." *Democracy in the Age of Globalization and Mediatization*, edited by. H. Kriesi, S. Lavenex, F. Esser, J. Matthes, M. Bühlmann, and D. Bochsler. Basingstoke, Hampshire: Palgrave Macmillan, pp. 155–76.

Fekete, Jason. 2016. "Liberals Have Spent More on Facebook Ads Than Total Amount Spent between 2006 and 2014." *National Post*, October 10. http://news.nationalpost.com/news/canada/liberals-government-has-spent-more-on-facebook-ads-than-amount-spent-between-2006-and-2014

Gandy, Oscar H. 1982. *Beyond Agenda Setting: Information Subsidies and Public Policy*. Norwood, New Jersey: Ablex Publishers.

Goffman, Erving. 1959. *The Presentation of Self in Everyday Life*. New York: Anchor Books.

Government of Canada. 2016a. Prime Minister's Office. Employee directory. http://www.goc411.ca/en/Employees/IndexByDepartment/112.

Government of Canada. 2016b. Privy Council Office. Employee directory. http://www.goc411.ca/en/Employees/IndexByDepartment/113.

Hood, Christopher. 2010. *The Blame Game: Spin, Bureaucracy, and Self-Preservation in Government*. Princeton, NJ: Princeton University Press.

Lilleker, Darren G. 2010. *Key Concepts in Political Communication*. London: Sage.

Marland, Alex, Thierry Giasson, and Jennifer Lees-Marshment, editors. 2012. *Political Marketing in Canada*. Vancouver: UBC Press.

Marland, Alex. 2016. *Brand Command: Canadian Politics and Democracy in the Age of Message Control*. Vancouver: UBC Press.

Marland, Alex. 2017. "Strategic Management of Media Relations: Communications Centralization and Spin in the Government of Canada." *Canadian Public Policy*, 43, 1, pp. 36–49.

Marland, Alex, Thierry Giasson, and Anna Esselment, editors. 2017. *Permanent Campaigning in Canada*. Vancouver: UBC Press.

Mayer, J. D. 2004. "The Presidency and Image Management: Discipline in Pursuit of Illusion." *Presidential Studies Quarterly* 34, 3, pp. 620–31.

Paré, Daniel J. and Susan Delacourt. 2014. "The Canadian Parliamentary Press Gallery: Still Relevant or Relic of Another Time?" *Political Communication in Canada: Meet the Press and Tweet the Rest*, edited by A. Marland, T. Giasson and T.A. Small, Vancouver: UBC Press, pp. 111–26.

Prime Minister's Office. 2016a. "Photos and video." http://pm.gc.ca/eng/photovideo

Prime Minister's Office. 2016b. "Itinerary." PMO listserve email, July 6.

Privy Council Office. 2014. Memorandum to Cabinet template (July 2014). http://www.pco-bcp.gc.ca/docs/information/publications/mc/docs/mc-eng.doc

Public Works and Government Services Canada. 2005. "Who is responsible? Summary." Commission of Inquiry into the Sponsorship Program and Advertising Activities.

Radwanski, George. 1978. *Trudeau*. Toronto: Macmillan of Canada.

Savoie, Donald. 1999. *Governing from the Centre: The Concentration of Power in Canadian Politics*. Toronto: University of Toronto Press.

Schultz, Julianne. 1998. *Reviving the Fourth Estate: Democracy, Accountability and the Media*. New York: Cambridge University Press.

Smith, Marie-Danielle. 2016. "Federal 'Unmuzzling' Has Gone beyond Government Scientists with scrapping Of Harper-Era System." *National Post*, May 29. http://news.nationalpost.com/news/canada/canadian-politics/federal-unmuzzling-has-gone-beyond-government-scientists-with-scrapping-of-harper-era-system

Street, John. 2011. *Mass Media, Politics and Democracy*. 2nd edn, Basingstoke, Hampshire: Palgrave MacMillan.

Treasury Board of Canada Secretariat. 2009. "FW: Federal Identity Program questions." April 17. Internal email obtained via access to information.

Treasury Board of Canada Secretariat. 2012. "Reducing delays in the processing of access to information." Report of the Access to Information Study Group. March. http://www.tbs-sct.gc.ca/hgw-cgf/oversight-surveillance/atip-aiprp/ai/reduction/reductiontb-eng.asp

Treasury Board of Canada Secretariat. 2016. Policy on Communications and Federal Identity. May 11. https://www.tbs-sct.gc.ca/pol/doc-eng.aspx?id=30683

Turcotte, André and Simon Vodrey. 2017. "Permanent Polling and Governance." *Permanent Campaigning in Canada*, edited by A. Marland, Alex, T. Giasson and A. Esselment, Vancouver: UBC Press, pp. 127–44.

The Third Sector, the Neo-Liberal State, and Beyond

Reshaping Contracting and Policy Advocacy

Bryan Evans and John Shields

Chapter Overview

The third sector, resting between the state and the market, has become an important and recognized presence in contemporary society, fulfilling many important purposes. The ascent of neo-liberalism to hegemonic status over the past forty years has, however, entailed significant implications for the role and function of the third sector in Canada and beyond. The adoption of the methods and perspectives of new public management, the public administrative expression and crystallization of various theoretical components of neo-liberalism, has reshaped the relationship between the state and the third sector from one based upon trust and shared values to one centred around markets and contracts. Consequently, the non-profit organizations that compose the third sector have found their role defined primarily in terms of service delivery. The other consequence is that the policy advocacy role of non-profit organizations has become much more constrained due to limited capacity to engage in the policy process. More significantly this has contributed to a "chill" effect as nonprofits in a competitive contracting context fear that any perceived criticism of government policy or advocacy for policy alternatives may lead to the loss of contracts necessary to the survival of the organization. While new public governance theory contends that the policy process has become more open and inclusive to non-state actors, the reality in the Canadian context is much more equivocal.

Chapter Objectives

By the end of this chapter, students will be able to do the following:

- Define the third sector and identify its size and scope.
- Describe the various functions of the third sector and explain how it contributes to the health of civic society.

continued

- Acquire a strong conceptual understanding of the relationship between non-profit organizations and the state.
- Understand how the macro-level shift in policy paradigm from one based on Keynesian-era–inspired ideas to one of neo-liberalism has reconstructed the role of many third-sector organizations to that of a delivery arm of the neo-liberal state with constrained policy advocacy functions.
- Describe important theoretical perspectives such as new public management, new public governance, and neo-liberalism and how these inform our understanding of the third sector and its policy and service delivery roles.

Introduction

The **third sector**—occupying the space between the state and market where not-for-profit organizations operate—has emerged from the shadows in recent decades to assume a prime space in state-society relations. Non-profit organizations have assumed increased roles to make up for the gaps left by a shrinking state (Amin et al., 2002: vii). There has also been growing awareness of the previously largely invisible role played by the third sector in terms of enhancing civic society and democracy. In a neo-liberal era, however, the third sector has been transformed. As a "partner" with the neo-liberal state, many non-profit organizations are being stripped of their autonomy and reduced to cheap service-delivery agents, potentially negating the third sector's progressive role in society. Neo-liberal forms of governance, however, are currently being challenged by new public governance (NPG), which seeks to restore an independent place for non-profit organizations in governance. This chapter will explore the contemporary role of the third sector and its changing place within Canadian public administration. It will conclude with a consideration of the place of third-sector organizations in the policy process, including advocacy, to assess the influence of NPG over neo-liberalism in contemporary public administration.

What Is the Third Sector?

The idea of a distinctive sector composed of non-profit organizations fulfilling important functions in society has come to be recognized. Identified under various labels—**non-profit sector**, social economy, and charitable sector—the term *third sector* is commonly used in public policy and public administration circles (Milbourne, 2013: 10). While non-profit organizations have long existed, what is new is that the large and growing array of not-for-profit organizations recognize themselves for the first time as distinct bodies with voice within society (Laforest, 2011). The state and other societal actors are also acknowledging the existence of these organizations as a sector.

A useful description of the sector embodied by such labels is provided by the Organisation for Economic Co-Operation and Development (OECD):

> A sector between the state and market, filling both economic and social missions, which pursues a general interest, and whose final objective is not the redistribution of profit. Each of these terms underlines only one aspect of the sector. So, while the term "non-profit sector," born in the USA, refers mainly to the absence of the redistribution of profits, the term "social economy" . . . underlines the socio-economic dimension of the sector, and the term "third sector" highlights its position between the state and the market. (OECD, 2003: 10)

The core defining feature of non-profits are that they are mission-driven organizations motivated by passion for their cause (Emmett & Emmett, 2015: 6).

The values that distinguish the third sector from the business and state sectors are altruism, charity, mutuality, philanthropy (Shields & Evans, 1998: 89), and the ethic of giving and caring. The third sector is very broad-ranging but can be separated into four core categories. *Funding agencies or fundraising intermediaries* (e.g., the United Way) generally do not provide services themselves but "channel resources to those who do." *Member-serving organizations* (e.g., business and professional associations and trade unions) serve their immediate members rather than the public at large. *Public benefit organizations* (e.g., nursing homes, daycares and other social service organizations, cultural institutions) "exist primarily to service others, to provide goods or services (including information or advocacy) to those in need or otherwise to contribute to the general welfare." *Religious organizations* (e.g., churches and religious societies) are involved in the pursuit of "essentially sacramental and religious functions" (Salamon, 1995: 54; Salamon, 2012: 7). The sector embraces a diversity of organizations with varying aims and perspectives. In this paper the focus is primarily on public benefit/service-providing organizations as these are the non-profit organizations that have primarily been "partnered" with the state.

The third sector is large and growing. At a global scale it would employ the equivalent of 4.5 per cent of the world's population (Evans, 2008). In the Canadian context the sector is even larger, although its exact dimension is difficult to account for as the statistical measurement of the sector is imprecise given the voluntary character of much of the sector's activity, the small size of many of the organizations, and the infrequent surveys taken of the sector. In the last survey in 2004 there were some 170,000 formally constituted non-profit bodies in Canada, of which 85,000 were registered charities (Imagine Canada, nd c), with an additional 360 charities added per year (Emmett & Emmett, 2015: 15). If we count informal and unincorporated groups it is estimated that in 2000 there were some 870,000 non-profit bodies in operation (Laforest, 2011: 4). In 2008 non-profits contributed 8.1 per cent of Canadian GDP (Emmett & Emmett, 2015: 10). Measured in terms of its share of the economically active population, Canada's third sector, at 11.1 per cent of the workforce, stands as second largest in the world with only the Netherlands outpacing it (Hall et al., 2005: 9–10).

The vast majority of non-profit organizations are small, with more than half of them having no paid staff. In fact, one per cent of the largest organizations command 60 per cent of all sector revenues (Imagine Canada, nd a). In terms of sources of funding, non-profit organizations receive some 49 per cent of their revenues from government, 35 per cent from earned income, 13 per cent from gifts and donations and 3 per cent from other sources (Imagine Canada, nd b). Service-providing non-profits, however, are far more dependent on government sources of revenue with 85 per cent or more of their funding coming from state sources (Lowe et al., 2017; Baines et al., 2014).

It is also important to note that third-sector organizations are a central part of **civil society**—they are in fact the organized face of civil society. Civil society reinforces:

> . . . the idea that society is more than government, markets, or the economy, and individual citizens and their families. There has to be society—a civil society—where citizens under the rule of law but otherwise self-organizing and self-directed, could come together to pursue their interests and values. (Anheier, 2014: 81–2)

Civil societies act "as a reservoir of caring, cultural life and intellectual innovation," schooling people in the "skills of citizenship" (Edwards, 2004: 14). Strong civil societies help to protect society from excessive power of the state and private market interests (Anheier, 2014: 83). Independent third-sector organizations are critical for healthy civil societies.

The Evolving Role of Non-Profit Organizations in Canada

In the latter 1800s and early 1900s non-profit organizations were actively involved in charitable work addressing the health, socio-economic, and moral issues arising out of rapid urbanization and industrialization in a period of a minimalist state. Much of the voluntary effort at this time was, however, infused with Victorian religious motivation and was, consequently, paternalistic and directed as much, or more, at the social and moral regulation of society as materially aiding the poor and vulnerable (Valverde, 1995). Interestingly the state in Canada did provide funding for non-profit bodies to assist in their charitable efforts. In this period the state resisted directly providing health and social provision in an effort to forestall public pressure for active involvement in human welfare provision (Maurutto, 2005).

The upheavals brought by the Great Depression of the 1930s and the Second World War transformed the state's role in society. Guided by a Keynesian policy paradigm, active state involvement in economy and society was sanctioned. The state took the lead in providing for the health and welfare of Canadians, explicitly displacing the capricious and paternalistic approach to charitable welfare (Murphy, 2011: 253). Non-profit involvement in social service provision, however, did not disappear but rather was reconfigured, as service-based non-profit organizations transformed into community-based partners with the state for welfare provision. The Canadian welfare state was based on a **mixed social economy model** where services were delivered through a combination of state and private/non-profit–run and –administered programs (Valverde, 1995). Non-profit service providers were partnered with the state through public financing of many of the programs they offered.

Under the **Keynesian welfare state**, the third sector continued to play an important role in social provision but as a junior partner to government. Significantly, as the welfare state expanded, the third sector grew in tandem with the state. A symbiotic and dynamic relationship between the state and non-profits emerged, with each building up and enhancing the other (Salamon, 1995). Non-profit service delivery was seen as less bureaucratic, more innovative and flexible (Deakin, 2003: 196), and geographically and culturally close to the communities being served. The third sector was, however, seen as structurally limited in its capacity to deliver comprehensive collective goods to all (Salamon, 1995: 16). Consequently, non-profits were limited to supporting the state and filling service gaps while government provided comprehensive and uniform welfare state supports.

In the Keynesian era the relationship between the state and non-profit service providers was distinguished from the neo-liberal period in a number of important ways: (1) state financing of non-profit service providers was centred on base funding, allowing organizations a good deal of latitude in spending; (2) funding was stable and long-term, allowing non-profits to build capacity and to become deeply rooted in the communities they served; (3) relationships between the state and the third sector were primarily based on trust and mutual respect rather than regulated by the narrow bonds of business contracts and strict accountability measures; (4) non-profit service providers were not meant to replace the state but were to enhance and complement the state's welfare-building role; and (5) relationships between the state and non-profits were not based on a coherent forward-planning vision but were generally ad hoc and uneven (Evans et al., 2005: 76). The relationship that evolved between third-sector organizations and the state, while far from ideal, did represent meaningful **partnerships** where non-profit organizations were respected by the state and allowed scope for autonomous operation.

In the welfare-state era, a number of distinctive roles for the third sector developed. First, the mandate of non-profits is to do good works, to provide **services** to the community (Cappe, 1999: 2). The third sector delivered a wide variety of services that were both tangible (clothing, food, health, shelter, and training) and more intangible (counselling, emotional support, and collective worship). Some of these service activities were in partnership with the state, while others were independent actions. As Casey notes, non-profit service delivery has "the capacity to be more sensitive to the needs of users and to respond in a more effective and innovative manner by providing the population a stake in the governance of public goods and services" (Casey, 2016: 27).

Advocacy is a second area of non-profit activity. In its broadest sense advocacy can take a number of forms, including public education about an issue or societal problem and more direct advocacy/lobbying directed at improving the conditions of a particular client group or aimed at what are considered to be laws or policies that are unjust or against the public good. Third-sector organizations contribute to an ongoing public policy dialogue (Cappe, 1999: 2). The advocacy role of third-sector organizations has been critical for broadening the democratic experience in the post-war period (Edwards, 2004: 78–81), especially for more marginalized groups (advocacy is discussed in greater detail below).

Third-sector organizations can also play a **mediation** role within society; that is, they can bring together people across a spectrum, such as a geographic area involving various neighbourhoods, where they are able to work out issues and help develop a common understanding, a consensus, or compromise (Scott, 1997: 46–7). This mediation role is very much an aspect of third-sector organizations' part in building **social capital**, maintaining **social cohesion** and fostering community building within society. Social capital "refers to features of social organization such as networks, norms, and social trust that facilitate coordination and co-operation for mutual benefit" (Putnam, 1995: 67). Non-profit organizations foster the kinds of relationships that enable groups of people to work together efficiently in the pursuit of their shared goals (Halpern, 2005). Social cohesion is about building shared values and communities of mutual interest (Ratcliffe & Newman, 2011). A cohesive society is one where public, private, and non-profit institutions are able to manage conflict; where institutional supports exist to foster inclusiveness; and where disparities within society are prevented from growing too wide. This is the basis from which strong communities are built.

A fourth role for third-sector organizations is helping to build citizenship and democracy (Phillips & Smith, 2011: 1). **Citizenship** is ultimately about participation and membership in a community (Barbalet, 1988: 2). Moreover, citizenship was seen to encompass a more active dimension involving deep participation within the community/society. As Cappe (1999: 2) notes, third-sector organizations offer "a unique way of social organizing" constructed on the values of "independence (freedom of association), altruism (concern for others), [and] community (collective action)." In addition, what makes community-based organizations different "is that they are as much about participation as provision; as much about citizenship as service" (Nowland-Foreman, 1996: 4). Democracy, of course, is about active participation and the ability to be part of decision-making in the public arena.

The Neo-Liberal Turn

Neo-liberalism emerged out of the economic crisis of the 1970s that undermined the Keynesian policy order. By the late 1980s the neo-liberal paradigm had become hegemonic. At its core, neo-liberalism constitutes a fundamental assault on the Keynesian welfare state. Neo-liberalism seeks to shrink the size and influence of government, giving the market and individual initiative much freer rein. Rather than a concern with greater equality, neo-liberalism promotes more income and wealth inequality fostered by the pursuit of individual gain in a free-market society (Peck, 2010). In order to address the problem of "government failure," neo-liberalism employs a policy agenda focused on **marketization**, deregulation, privatization, and tax cuts centred on the top of the income brackets. David Harvey explains its logic this way: "neoliberalism values market exchanges as . . . it emphasizes the significance of contractual relations in the marketplace. It holds that the social good will be maximized by maximizing the reach and frequency of market transactions, and it seeks to bring all human action into the domain of the market" (Harvey, 2005: 3).

Public Administration and Neo-Liberal "Reforms"

Neo-liberalism demanded a new model of public administration based on a reworked state and administrative structure that mimicked market economics, thus releasing the public sector's productivity capacity (Stewart & Walsh, 1992). The values guiding neo-liberal public administration were fundamentally different from those of the Keynesian period. Neo-liberalism identified a fundamental problem with public administration to be its overly bureaucratic character and the absence of a pricing mechanism for public services, resulting in inefficiencies. Such "structural difficulties are accentuated by the emphasis on formal rules and authority as the guides for action within traditional public organizations, rather than depending upon either market signals or the entrepreneurial spirit of individuals to guide decisions" (Peters, 1993: 10). The OECD criticized this model, contending that organizational effectiveness was impeded by "highly centralised, rule-bound, and inflexible organisations that emphasize process rather than results" (OECD, 1995: 7). Consequently, the restructuring of these characteristics became one of the central objectives of neo-liberalism; although, ironically, new contracting arrangements would impose a government-based web of rules onto non-state actors.

In public administration neo-liberalism was imposed through **new public management** (NPM), which consists of two basic streams: managerialism and modes of control. Managerialism is defined as involving (1) continuous increases in efficiency; (2) the use of ever more sophisticated technologies;

(3) a labour force disciplined to productivity; (4) clear implementation of the professional management role; and (5) managers being given the right to manage (Pollitt, 1990: 2–3). Modes of control deals with the emergence of indirect control or "centralized decentralization" (Shields & Evans, 1998) as a means of managing from a distance and which operates through such means as (1) continuous quality improvement; (2) an emphasis upon devolution; (3) information systems; (4) an emphasis upon contracts and markets; (5) performance measurement; and (6) an increased emphasis on audit and inspection (Walsh, 1995: xiv).

The prominent place that NPM has come to play within the third sector has led to a cultural take-over by stealth of non-profit service provision by business values and practices (Taylor, 2002: 98–9). New funding and accountability measures were designed to solidify funder control of program costs and structure (Handy, 1990: 94). In the process non-profit organizations have been compelled to bend to controlling neo-liberal accountability schemes and human resource strategies (Baines, 2011; Cunningham, 2008).

Neo-Liberalism's Impact on Third-Sector Service Providers

Neo-liberalism has transformed the third sector in numerous ways. Alternative service delivery was employed to help shrink the state and reduce labour costs, and non-profit providers took on a larger role in government-supported service provision. The third sector was also called upon to fill in for social provision abandoned by the state altogether. Neo-liberalism has sought to reduce its social responsibilities by off-loading onto lower-tier governments and calling upon the third sector to take on a greater role through increased voluntary activity and enhanced philanthropic effort (Joy & Shields, 2013). In the UK this approach became known as the big society initiative (Ishkanian & Szreter, 2012) and was guided by the false logic that the existence of the big state crowds out non-profit activity and as the state shrinks extra capacity would open up for the third sector, allowing it to increase its role in society without the need of additional state support (Hardill & Baines, 2011: 158). The neo-liberal rhetoric about a revival of voluntarism and a more participatory civic culture is, in fact, about the process of transferring

many social support functions to the third sector. This speaks to the neo-liberal desire to *disinvest* government responsibilities for various citizenship rights in the social and economic spheres and, in the process, to transform the state's caring role in society. The result is that the third sector has been under constant pressure to do more with less and is being stretched beyond its capacities (Salamon, 2003).

Neo-liberalism labelled its relationship with non-profit organizations as partnerships, but the reality is that they are hierarchical contract-based associations where control rests with the government funder. The new contracting regime introduced under neo-liberalism is about developing a more contractually based relationship with non-profit organizations (to set the government–non-profit relationship on a more commercial footing); the non-profit sector is being significantly and negatively altered (Evans et al., 2005). In short, neo-liberalism is about downsizing the state, slashing state support for programs (including those shifted to non-profit organizations), and placing most other human activities on a more market-based footing.

The market-oriented logic of the system has been the main way in which the neo-liberal state has pushed the restructuring of the third sector. These contracts are (1) competitive (non-profit providers bidding against one another); (2) short-term (usually one-year contracts to maximize funder control and oversight); (3) rigid in terms of how contracted dollars must be spent; and (4) generally inadequately funded (financing fails to fully cover the real costs of program delivery). The model assumes that non-profit volunteers and charitable donations will make up any funding shortfalls (Eakin, 2001: 2). This approach to non-profit financing has been called "hollow core funding" whereby the third sector subsidizes government programming (Eakin, 2005).

This **contract funding** regime has had a number of negative effects on nonprofits, including (1) increasing levels of income instability and vulnerability among non-profit service providers; (2) reducing organizational effectiveness and flexibility as organizations struggle to compete for contracts and meet the narrow rules governing program funding; (3) creating wage depression and precarious employment in the sector because of underfunding and short-term financing; (4) greatly increasing the administrative burden on organizations due to onerous reporting requirements—accountability is only to the funder and notions of non-profit accountability to the community services is downplayed; (5) taking away the ability of many non-profits to engage in rational long-term planning because of the short-term nature of funding; (6) cultivating a climate of "advocacy chill" where non-profits become afraid to voice criticism of government that they depend on financially—neo-liberalism has also identified non-profit organizations as "special interest," generally shutting them out of the policy-making process; (7) commercializing operations by pushing non-profits to impose fee structures and sell other products to make up for funding shortfalls; and (8) creating mission drift as organizations juggle missions and mandates to fit government funding priorities (Baines et al., 2014; Lowe et al., 2017).

The market-based relationships that neo-liberalism created with third-sector organizations fostered a business culture dominated by narrow notions of efficiency (Stein, 2001), funder control, and persistent austerity. The relationship between service-providing nonprofits and their clients was also negatively impacted as providers were compelled to tighten policy contracts and eligibility rules. Dependency on the state for funding has meant that these third-sector organizations have not been autonomous to negotiate on behalf of their client groups. In this process nonprofits are being transformed into one-dimensional alternative service delivery agents and stripped of their multi-purposed origins.

The rigidities and negative externalities created under neo-liberalism has recently opened up a new approach to governance—new public governance (NPG). NPG moves away from market-centred to pluralist relationships between the state and the third sector where advocacy and inclusive processes of public administration and policy-making are promoted (Baskoy et al., 2011). We examine this development in the next section, using the case of non-profit organizations' involvement in the policy process.

New Public Governance and the Case of Third-Sector Organizations in the Policy Process

The roles of non-profit organizations in the policy process have been identified as "(1) identifying issues on the policy agenda; (2) developing policy solutions through research and analysis, i.e. policy-ready research; and (3) promoting particular policy solutions" directly to government (Carter et al., 2005: 6). These roles, and the extent to which non-profits are effective policy actors, have become particularly important because of the presumed displacement of neo-liberal forms of governance with NPG. NPG is "concerned with how policy elites and networks interact to create and govern the public policy process" (Osborne, 2010: 6). NPG scholars contend "we are witnessing a fundamental shift in governing models" marked by a "pluralization of policy making." Through networks, government decision-makers no longer dominate the policy process in a command-and-control manner, but rather occupy a seat at the centre of a "complex 'horizontal' web of policy advisors that includes both 'traditional' . . . advisors in government as well as active and well-resourced non-governmental actors in NGOs, think tanks and other similar organisations" (Craft and Howlett, 2012: 85). These relationships have been characterized as a "reciprocal bestowing of legitimacy" in that non-profit organizations, among other actors, are relied upon by the state to deliver services and to provide a vehicle to carry citizen's voices to the state and by doing so legitimate consequent public policy (Lang, 2013: 17). For many nonprofits, the achievement of their mission involves policy advocacy and engagement with the public policy process. Critics, however, question whether the policy process is "as open and as participatory as this model of 'governance' suggests" (Phillips, 2007: 497) and whether neo-liberal approaches remain dominant.

Policy advocacy is a general term referring to activities intended to influence government policy. This includes research, coalition building, and presenting policy alternatives to policymakers through direct engagement, or indirect engagement through mobilizing public opinion (Pekkanen & Smith, 2014; Jansson, 2016). Tactics employed will vary depending on the status of the organization as an insider or outsider. Most basically, insider tactics involve working directly with government policy staff and decision-makers. Outsider tactics are concerned with working outside the formal advisory system and can involve public education/awareness campaigns, efforts to influence media coverage, and protest events (Onyx et al., 2010).

A variety of factors contribute to constraining or facilitating policy engagement. Mobilization for advocacy is often in response to government actions (Baumgartner et al., 2011). What governments decide to do (or not do) is a significant external factor informing non-profit advocacy. However, the spectrum of relations between government and non-profit actors, and the nature of these relationships, are important in informing decisions affecting policy advocacy. A significant role for non-profit organizations is concerned with the delivery of programs funded by government. The work of nonprofits combines "advocacy with the provision of services" where service delivery is generally the core function (Almog-Bar and Schmid, 2014: 12). A question of concern is to what extent this funding relationship constrains non-profits' role in policy advocacy. A Belgian study of more than 250 nonprofits found that being the recipient of government funds had no effect on policy advocacy (Verschuere and De Corte, 2013). Other researchers observe a "skittishness many nonprofits have about engaging in, much less admitting to, advocacy" (Pekkanen & Smith, 2014: 7). A study of Canadian nonprofits found that advocacy chill was prevalent. Failing to win a government service delivery contract would have dire consequences for the nonprofits' viability. In the Canadian case, a serious degree of politicization, or the perception of such, has come to overshadow the awarding of government contracts at the federal level (Evans & Shields, 2014).

The capacity of a non-profit organization to engage in policy advocacy derives from the internal characteristics of the organization itself. However, "few voluntary sector organizations . . . have the policy capacity to participate effectively" (Phillips, 2007: 498). In a 2005 Canadian survey of several thousand non-profit organizations, fewer than 25 per cent of those responding to the survey indicated they participated in the policy process. Non-participation was linked to inadequate capacity (Carter, 2011: 430–1). The limited policy capacity of non-profit organizations, given years of neo-liberal constraints, runs contrary to the notion that the policy process is as open as NPG suggests. If governments increasingly demand evidence-based policy from external sources, non-profit organizations require enhanced policy capacity to effectively participate. A lack of capacity disadvantages nonprofits in fully engaging with government.

Various Canadian studies find that non-profit organizations are not capable of being fully engaged policy actors. Two national surveys concluded that only a quarter of non-profit organizations participate in public policy processes. This degree of non-participation is not a function of disinterest but rather a lack of capacity to do so (Carter, 2011: 430–1). However, non-profit organizations are often involved in the implementation of public policy regardless of whether they have been active participants in the agenda-setting or design phases of the process (Carter, 2011: 432). Mulholland (2010) reports that the majority of policy related activities by nonprofits occurs around procedural matters and there has been limited input into actual policy development. The survey responses of Canadian government and non-government policy workers suggest that provincial governments tend to invite specific external policy actors and do so frequently, while leaving half or more of the non-government actors either completely out of the policy process or subject to very infrequent invitations to meet and consult (Evans & Sapeha, 2015: 265–66). More troubling was the finding that a sizable portion of non-profit organization participation in the policy process occurred either after key decisions had been made or not at all (Evans & Wellstead, 2013, 2014).

To date the evidence suggests that in the Canadian context NPG has had only limited penetration within public administration and public policy. Neo-liberal approaches to governance still appear to be well entrenched and the impact of years of neo-liberalism has greatly weakened the capacity of the third sector to fully engage in the policymaking process.

Conclusion

The third sector has become a recognized and an increasingly important presence in society. The size, scope and place of the sector has, however, evolved over time. The changed relationship between the state and non-profit organizations has very much influenced the sector's transformation. In an earlier period of the minimalist state, the sector was much smaller with charities providing paternalistic-based interventions in society. The Keynesian welfare state brought about a rapid expansion of non-profit organizations and the movement towards the secularization and professionalization of the sector. The third sector was a junior partner in social provision, and state support encouraged non-profit advocacy and the active engagement of the sector in society fostering the democratic impulses of civil society.

Under neo-liberalism the state's relationship with the sector changed significantly and the autonomy of government-funded non-profit service providers came increasingly to be controlled by the funder through NPM approaches such as competitive contracting. The advocacy role of nonprofits was diminished and the third sector came to be expected to pick up more of the cost of social provision as the state retreated from social responsibilities and the state shrunk in size. Located between the state and the market, the third sector was strategically positioned to facilitate the neo-liberal strategy of the marketization of public goods and services. But the capacity of the sector to fill the vacuum left by a hollowed-out welfare state was too small and under-resourced to do

the job. An over-stretched and stressed third sector resulting from neo-liberal reforms has negatively impacted the development of social capital, social cohesion, and the general health of civil society.

The emergence of new public governance within government policy and administrative circles imagines a renewed role for third-sector organizations promising to restore their autonomy, build meaningful partnerships with the state. and facilitate non-profit advocacy. NPG would mark a significant departure from neo-liberal governance practices that could energize the third sector. In the Canadian context, as suggested by our case study regarding policy-making processes, there is to date limited evidence that NPG has taken root within public administration. In this regard NPG remains a promise but the lived reality is that neo-liberalism remains the dominant governance paradigm.

Important Terms and Concepts

advocacy	mediation	services
citizenship	mixed social economy model	social capital
civil society	neo-liberalism	social cohesion
contract funding	new public governance (NPG)	third sector (non-profit sector)
Keynesian welfare state	new public management (NPM)	
marketization	partnerships	

Study Questions

1. What key roles does the third sector play in contemporary society?
2. Why is it challenging to measure the size and scope of the third sector in Canada?
3. The nature of the relationship of non-profit organizations to the state and public administration has shifted over time. Describe the character of these changes during different time periods.
4. In what ways does neo-liberalism challenge the autonomy of non-profit service providers?
5. Advocacy is an important function for the third sector. In what ways does new public governance promote this advocacy role?

References

Almog-Bar, M., and H. Schmid. 2014. "Advocacy Activities of Nonprofit Human Service Organizations: A Critical Review." *Nonprofit and Voluntary Sector Quarterly*, 43, 1, pp. 11–35.

Amin, Ash, Angus Cameron, and Ray Hudson. 2002. *Placing the Social Economy*. London: Routledge.

Anheier, Helmut K. 2014. *Nonprofit Organizations: Theory, Management, Policy*, 2nd edn, New York: Routledge.

Baines, Donna. 2011. "Restructuring and the Labour Process Under Maretisation: A Canadian Perspective." *Voluntary Organisations and Public Service Delivery*. edited by Ian Cunningham and Philip James, New York: Routledge, pp. 168–84.

Baines, Donna, John Campey, Ian Cunningham, and John Shields. 2014. "Not Profiting from Precarity: The Work of Nonprofit Service Delivery and the Creation of Precariousness." *Just Labour: A Canadian Journal of Work and Society*, 22, Autumn, pp. 74–93.

Barbalet, J.M. 1988. *Citizenship: Rights, Struggle and Class Inequality*. Minneapolis: University of Minnesota Press.

Baskoy, Tuna, Bryan Evans, and John Shields. 2011. "Assessing Policy Capacity in Canada's Public Services: Perspectives of Deputy and Assistant Deputy Ministers." *Canadian Public Administration*, 54, 2, 217–34.

Baumgartner, Frank R., Heather A. Larsen-Price, Beth L. Leech, and Paul Rutledge. 2011. "Congressional and Presidential Effects on the Demand for Lobbying." *Political Research Quarterly* 64, 1, pp. 3–16.

Cappe, Mel. 1999. "Building a New Relationship with the Voluntary Sector." Speech to the Third Canadian Leaders' Forum on the Voluntary Sector, Association of Professional Executives, Ottawa, 31 May. Available at: www.pco-bcp.gc.ca/ClerkSP-MC/voluntary_e.htm.

Carter, S. 2011. "Public Policy and the Nonprofit Sector." *The Philanthropist*, 23. 4, pp. 427–35.

Carter, S., B. Plewes, and H. Echenberg. 2005. *Civil Society and Public Choice: A Directory of Non-Profit Organizations Engaged in Public Policy*. Toronto: Maytree Foundation.

Craft, Jonathan and Michael Howlett. 2012. "Policy Formulation, Governance Shifts and Policy Influence: Location and Content in Policy Advisory Systems." *Journal of Public Policy*, 32, pp. 79–98.

Casey, John. 2016. *The Nonprofit World: Civil Society and the Rise of the Nonprofit Sector*. London: Kumarian Press.

Cunningham, Ian. 2008. *Employment Relations in the Voluntary Sector*. London: Routledge.

Deakin, Nicholas. 2003. "The Voluntary Sector." *The Student's Companion to Social Policy*, edited by Pete Alcock, Angus Erskine, and Margaret May, Oxford: Blackwell, 191–9.

Eakin, Lynn. 2001. *An Overview of the Funding of Canada's Voluntary Sector*. Ottawa: Voluntary Sector Initiative Working Group on Financing, September.

———. 2005. *The Policy and Practice Gap: Federal Government Practices Regarding Administrative Costs When Funding Voluntary Sector Organizations*. Ottawa: Voluntary Sector Forum, March.

Edwards, Michael. 2004. *Civil Society*. Cambridge, UK: Polity.

Emmett, Brian and Geoffrey Emmett. 2015. *Charities in Canada as an Economic Sector: Discussion Paper*. Toronto: Imagine Canada.

Evans, Bryan, Ted Richmond, and John Shields. 2005. "Structuring Neoliberal Governance: The Non-Profit Sector, Emerging New Modes of Control and the Marketisation of Service Delivery." *Policy and Society* 24, 1, pp. 73–97.

Evans, Bryan and Halina Sapeha. 2015. "Are Non-Government Policy Actors Being Heard? Assessing New Public Governance." *Canadian Public Administration* 58, 2, pp. 249–70.

Evans, Bryan and John Shields. 2014. "Nonprofit Engagement with Provincial Policy Officials: The Case of NGO Policy Voice in Canadian Immigrant Settlement Services." *Policy and Society* 33, pp. 117–127.

Evans, Bryan and Adam Wellstead. 2013. "Policy Dialogue and Engagement between Non-Governmental Organizations and Government: A Survey of Processes and Instruments of Canadian Policy Workers." *Central European Journal of Public Policy*, 7, 1, pp. 60–87.

Evans, Bryan and Adam Wellstead. 2014. "Tales of Policy Estrangement: Non-Governmental Policy Work and Capacity in Three Canadian Provinces." *Canadian Journal of Nonprofit and Social Economy Research*, 5, 2, pp. 7–28.

Evans, Chris. 2008, June 24. *Canada's Non-Profit Sector: Get the Facts*. Toronto: MaRS: https://www.marsdd.com/news-and-insights/canadas-nonprofit-sector-get-the-facts/

Hall, Michael, Cathy W. Barr, M. Easwaramoorthy, S. Wojciech Sokolowski, and Lester M. Salamon. 2005. *The Canadian Non-Profit and Voluntary Sector in Comparative Perspective*. Toronto: Imagine Canada.

Halpern, David. 2005. *Social Capital*. Cambridge, UK: Polity.

Handy, Charles. 1990. *The Age of Unreason*. Boston: Harvard Business School Press.

Hardill, Irene and Susan Baines. 2011. *Enterprising Care? Upaid Voluntary Action in the 21st Century*. Bristol: Polity Press.

Harvey, David. 2005. *A Brief History of Neoliberalism*. Oxford: Oxford University Press.

Imagine Canada. nd a. *Key Facts about Canada's Charities*: http://www.imaginecanada.ca/resources-and-tools/research-and-facts/key-facts-about-canada%E2%80%99s-charities

Imagine Canada. nd b. *The Nonprofit and Voluntary Sector in Canada*: http://www.imaginecanada.ca/sites/default/files/www/en/nsnvo/sector_in_canada_factsheet.pdf

Imagine Canada. nd c. *Sector*: http://sectorsource.ca/research-and-impact/sector-impact

Ishkanian, Armine and Simon Szreter, editors. 2012. *The Big Society Debate: A New Agenda for Social Welfare?* Cheltenham: Edward Elgar Publishing Limited.

Jansson, Bruce S. 2016. *Social Welfare Policy and Advocacy: Advancing Social Justice through 8 Policy Sectors*. Thousand Oaks, CA: Sage.

Joy, Meghan and John Shields. 2013. "Social Impact Bonds: The Next Phase of Third Sector

Marketization?" *Canadian Journal of Nonprofit and Social Economy Research/Revue canadienne de recherche sur les OBSL et l'économie sociale* 4, 2, pp. 39–55.

Laforest, Rachel. 2011. *Voluntary Sector Organizations and the State: Building New Relations*. Vancouver: UBC Press.

Lang, Sabine. 2013. *NGOs, Civil Society, and the Public Sphere*. New York: Cambridge University Press.

Lowe, Sophia, Ted Richmond, and John Shields. 2017. "Settling on Austerity: ISAs, Immigrant Communities and Neoliberal Restructuring." *Alternate Routes: A Journal of Critical Social Research* 28, pp. 14–46.

Maurutto, Paula. 2005. "Charity and Public Welfare in History: A Look at Ontario, 1830–1950." *The Philanthropist* 19, 3, pp. 159–67.

Milbourne, Linda. 2013. *Voluntary Sector in Transition: Hard Times or New Opportunities?* Bristol: Policy Press.

Mulholland, Elizabeth. 2010. "New Ways to Keep Up Our End of the Policy Conversation." *The Philanthropist* 23, 2, pp. 140–5.

Murphy, Jonathan. 2011. "The Dark Side." *Third Sector Research*, edited by Rupert Taylor, New York: Springer, pp. 253–68.

Nowland-Foreman, Garth. 1996. "Governments, Community Organisations and Civil Society—A Beginner's Guide to Dissection of a Golden Goose." *The Jobs Letter*, New Zealand. Available at: www.jobsletter.org.nz/art/artn0001.htm.

OECD (Organisation for Economic Co-Operation and Development). 1995. *Governance in Transition*. Paris, France : Organisation for Economic Co-operation and Development; Washington, D.C. : OECD Publications and Information Center [distributor].

———. 2003. *The Non-Profit Sector in a Changing Economy*. Paris: OECD.

———. 2005. *Modernizing Government: The Way Forward*. Paris: OECD.

Onyx, Jenny, Lisa Armitage, Bronwen Dalton, Rose Melville, John Casey, and Robin Banks. 2010. "Advocacy with Gloves On: The "Manners" of Strategy Used by Some Third Sector Organizations Undertaking Advocacy in NSW and Queensland," *Voluntas: International Journal of Voluntary and Nonprofit Organizations* 21, 1, pp. 41–61.

Osborne, Stephen, 2010. "Introduction: The (New) Public Governance: A Suitable Case for Treatment?" *The New Public Governance: Emerging Perspectives on the Theory and Practice of Public Governance*, edited by Stephen Osborne, London: Routledge.

Peck, Jamie. 2010. *Constructions of Neoliberal Reason*. Oxford: Oxford University Press.

Pekkanen, Robert and Steven Rathgeb Smith. 2014. "Introduction: Nonprofit Advocacy: Definitions and Concepts." *Nonprofits and Advocacy: Engaging Community and Government in an Era of Retrenchment*, edited by Tsujinaka et al., Baltimore, Maryland: Johns Hopkins University Press.

Peters, B. Guy. 1993. *The Public Service, The Changing State and Governance*. Ottawa: Canadian Centre for Management Development.

Phillips, Susan D. and Steven Rathgeb Smith. 2011. "Between Governance and Regulation: Evolving Government–Third Sector Relationships." *Governance and Regulation in the Third Sector: International Perspectives*, edited by Susan D. Phillips and Steven Rathgeb Smith, New York: Routledge, pp. 1–36.

Phillips, Susan D. 2007. "Policy Analysis and the Voluntary Sector: Evolving Policy Styles." *Policy Analysis in Canada: The State of the Art*, edited by L. Dobuzinskis, M. Howlett, and D. Laycock. Toronto: University of Toronto Press.

Pollitt, Christopher. 1990. *Managerialism and the Public Services*. Oxford: Blackwell.

Putnam, Robert. 1995. "Bowling Alone: America's Declining Social Capital." *Journal of Democracy* 6, 1, pp. 65–78.

Ratcliffe, Peter and Ines Newman. 2011. "Introduction: Promoting Social Cohesion." *Promoting Social Cohesion: Implications for Policy and Evaluation*, edited by Peter Ratcliffe and Ines Newman, Bristol: The Polity Press, pp. 1–11.

Salamon, Lester M. 1995. *Partners in Public Service: Government–Non-Profit Relations in the Modern Welfare State*. Baltimore: Johns Hopkins University Press.

Salamon, Lester M. 2003. *The Resilient Sector: The State of Nonprofit America*. Washington, D.C.: Brookings Institution Press.

Salamon, Lester M. 2012. "The Resilient Sector: The Future of Nonprofit America." *The State of Nonprofit America*, 2nd edn, edited by Lester M. Salamon, Washington, D.C.: Brookings, pp. 2–86.

Scott, Jacquelyn Thayer. 1997. "Defining the Non-Profit Sector." *The Emerging Sector: In Search of a Framework*, edited by Ronald Hirshhorn, Ottawa: Canadian Policy Research Networks, pp. 43–51.

Shields, John, and B. Mitchell Evans. 1998. *Shrinking the State: Globalization and Public Administration "Reform."* Halifax: Fernwood.

Stein, Janice. 2001. *The Cult of Efficiency*. Toronto: Anansi Press.

Stewart, J., and K. Walsh. 1992. "Change in the Management of Public Services." *Public Administration* 70, pp. 499–518.

Taylor, Marilyn. 2002. "Government, the Third Sector and the Contract Culture: The UK Experience So Far." *Dilemmas of the Welfare Mix: The New Structure of Welfare in an Era of Privatization*, edited by Ugo Ascoli and Constanzo Ranci, New York: Kluwer Academic/Plenum Publishers, pp. 77–108.

Valverde, Mariana. 1995. "The Mixed Social Economy as a Canadian Tradition." *Studies in Political Economy* 47 (Summer), pp. 33–60.

Verschuere, Bram and De Corte, Joris. 2013. "Non-profit Advocacy Under a Third-Party Government Regime: Cooperation or Conflict?" *Voluntas* 24, 4, pp. 222–41.

Walsh, Kieron. 1995. *Public Service and Market Mechanisms: Competition, Contracting and the New Public Management*. New York: St Martin's Press.

Looking Across the Atlantic

The European Union and Canada Compared

John Erik Fossum

Chapter Overview

This chapter compares and contrasts Canada and the European Union (EU). Canada is a full-fledged federation, whereas the EU is a fledgling federation. They share similar values, and have strong links. There are interesting similarities in some of the challenges that they face, even if the two political systems are quite different. The chapter focuses on the broader contexts within which each system's public administration is embedded and not the specific features of each public administration. In today's world, globalization and other developments confront political systems with profound challenges pertaining to the fundamentals of political order, community, and governing. Europe's attempt at overcoming its traumatic past has taken an unprecedented shape: the world's first attempt at supranational democratic governance. Canada has over the last four decades grappled with a range of fundamental questions pertaining to its constitutional fundamentals. These include questions of historical injustice (especially in relation to First Nations), how to deal with cultural and national diversity, the thorny issue of Quebec secession, and how to organize its external and internal economic relations. Many of the issues and challenges facing Europe and Canada are constitutive. With that is meant that they refer to the fundamental rules, principles, and arrangements for governing and living together (and apart). The chapter compares and contrasts the EU with Canada on five different issues. One aspect that runs through all of these pertains to the pronounced role of executive officials (heads of states and governments and their supportive staffs).

Chapter Objectives

By the end of this chapter, students will be able to do the following:

- Explain reasons for undertaking a comparative study of the EU and Canada.
- Outline the five constitutive (central or essential) challenges facing the EU and Canada.

continued

- Explain what disagreement exists over what the EU is, as well as over what it ought to be.
- Show that challenges associated with the nature of the political system spill over to and affect the realm of public administration in the EU, and Canada.
- Describe similarities in constitutional politics of the EU and Canada.
- Describe differences between the EU and Canada as to how executive power is organized.
- Outline similarities and differences in exit/secession arrangements for the EU and Canada.
- Describe the nature of the financial crisis in the preceding decade.
- Describe the core features of CETA and some of the arguments in favour of and against it.

Introduction

This chapter compares the EU with Canada. The two share similar values, and there are important historical and contemporary links between them. The chapter identifies five important challenges facing the two systems, examines these, and shows how executive officials who play a central role in these two political systems grapple with these challenges. The five themes are constitutional contestations; executive-legislative relations; exit/**secession**; the **financial crisis**; and the **Comprehensive Economic and Trade Agreement between the EU and Canada** (CETA). Several of these themes have not been dealt with before through Canada–EU comparison. The first section provides some of the reasons for why it is interesting to compare the EU and Canada, which are further elaborated on in the subsequent sections.

Why Compare the EU and Canada?

Well before the EU's inception in the 1950s, Europeans looked for models to emulate in their quest for a political settlement that would ensure lasting peace on the war-torn continent. Although Canada and the EU share important values and there are strong links between the two, most Europeans have looked past Canada to its southern neighbour, the United States for inspiration and guidance.[1] Europeans eager to unite the European continent could find inspiration

in manifest destiny and American continental expansion. Europeans anxiously seeking to restore Europe's historically central global role would look with envy at the role of the United States as a global hegemon. Europeans have not only been allured by US power; they have pointed to the close affinity and the many values that they share with those on the other side of the Atlantic. It is easy to see how the strong European imprint on America has made many Europeans consider Americans not as "they," but as "us." These and other factors have spawned a debate on what is more likely and preferable: the Americanization of Europe or the Europeanisation of America (Offe, 2005).

The American political-constitutional experience weighs in heavily. The American Revolution heralded in a new revolutionary constitutional tradition, including a new and innovative *democratic* federalism (Ackerman, 1991). The American Revolution marked how Europeans-turned-Americans were able to rid themselves of their oppressive European past. Europeans in the post-war period have been anxiously trying to rid themselves of *their own* European oppressive pasts. One of the main instruments has been European integration.

From this perspective Canada at first glance would appear to have comparatively less to offer to Europeans, even if Canada's European roots are even more entrenched (Resnick, 2005). Whereas Americans broke with the UK, Canada continued its association (formally until 1982 when the Canadian constitution was patriated). It was therefore only quite recently that Canada sought to sever its ties to its European past (and during Stephen Harper's premiership (2006–15) strong efforts were made to symbolically recreate these, especially to the UK). What Seymour Martin Lipset highlights in *Continental Divide* (1990) is a liberal freedom-seeking United States versus a UK loyalist conservative Canada. The implication is that when we set the sights on the Canada–EU comparison, we should not have high normative expectations.

My point of departure is that this is somewhat misleading. With the benefit of hindsight we see that Lipset did not place sufficient emphasis on Canada's own constitutional transformation, notably through the "Charter Revolution" (for different assessments see for instance Morton and Knopff, 2000; Cairns, 2003). That is one of the reasons why the Canada–EU comparison *is* very interesting, in practical-political *as well as* in normative terms.

Perhaps the most important single factor that warrants comparing the EU and Canada pertains to the following paradox. Both are deeply contested entities; both have each in its own way been held up as an example to emulate. How is it that something that is deeply contested, and therefore presumably quite fragile, could be something to emulate? A traditional nationalist perspective would consider the fact that neither the EU nor Canada has been able to develop an unambiguous, substantively robust shared sense of national community as something of a failure and as a major source of instability. Canada has been marked by multiple nationalisms. Authors of books with titles such as *Must Canada Fail* have feared that the nationalisms are irreconcilable. The challenges associated with multiple competing nationalisms are far more pronounced and pressing in today's Europe, since the EU is composed of well-entrenched national democracies anxiously preserving their national identities. Euro-sceptics, and especially Euro-phobes (those that want to dismantle the EU), draw support from the so-called No Demos thesis (Grimm, 1995), which holds that since the EU is not, and cannot, become a nation, it cannot become democratic.

At the same time, Canada and the EU have shown that it is possible to live together and prosper despite deep disagreements on the nature and identity of the polity and the community. The EU and Canada are profoundly different in structure and composition, but they are both multinational and share a fundamental commitment to respect difference and diversity. That is an important reason for why analysts today are less prone to consider multinational and poly-ethnic entities as inherently unstable (Kymlicka, 1995; Gagnon & Tully, 2001). The important point is that Canada and the EU have been held up as examples to emulate not because they have eradicated national and other forms of difference and diversity, but because they have developed ways of living together despite these differences, and have done so through peaceful and democratic means. That is the key to unlocking the paradox.

Five Sets of Issues/Constitutive Challenges

All of the five issues that will be addressed in more depth help to shed light on the constitutive challenges facing the EU and Canada. Of particular importance to this chapter is to show the central role that executive officials play in dealing with these challenges. The most obvious constitutive challenge refers to the difficulties in reaching constitutional agreement among the main stakeholders—the governments of the two systems. Despite comprehensive efforts, neither the EU nor Canada has thus far been able to do so. In the European case, there is not even agreement that the EU is fit for a constitution (Fossum and Menéndez, 2011). The second issue is legislative–executive relations. A key designator is **executive dominance**, which relates to the central role that executive officials play in relation to parliaments and in terms of shaping the fundamental rules and norms of the systems, that is, in constitution making. The third issue of exit or secession of a constituent unit (in Canada: province, in the EU: member state) brings up issues of break-up or even unravelling. In both the EU and Canada these issues are to a large extent assigned to and controlled by executive officials. The fourth issue is the financial crisis. It is interesting to consider the contrast between Canada and the EU here. Whereas Canada never really experienced any crisis, for the EU the financial crisis did not only precipitate a major existential crisis that continues to haunt Europe but has further reinforced the political role of executive officials. The final issue is the recently signed Comprehensive Economic Trade Agreement between the EU and Canada (CETA). It brings up a number of issues, not least the relationship between executive officials (insiders) and parliaments (mainly outsiders) in these comprehensive negotiation processes.

a) Contestations over Constitutional Fundamentals

Both the EU and Canada are marked by constitutional contestation and inability to reach constitutional closure. That has not been for lack of effort. There have been numerous executive-driven attempts at reaching closure, none of which has laid the constitutional issues to rest.[2]

In today's EU, disagreements over the EU range across facts and norms. There is disagreement over what the EU *is*, as well as over what it *ought to be*. Analysts have not been much aided by leaders who have consistently refused to clarify these issues. Jacques Delors, most famously, has designated the EU an *objet politique nonidentifié* (see Schmitter, 2000: 2). Some insist that the EU is a special-function type of international organization that is made up of member states and whose main purpose it is to serve the member states. The underlying vision is that Europe should continue to be based on nation-state–based democracy. Others insist that the EU is a fledgling federation. The underlying vision is that the EU should become a full-fledged federal democracy (whether state-based or not). The third position is made up of those that insist that the EU is a major experiment in transnational governance, (Bohman, 2007; for an overview of the different positions in this debate, see Eriksen & Fossum. 2012).

Disagreements range across four different dimensions: level of governing (state, EU-based, global); structure of governing (hierarchy versus network); mode of community (unified versus composite); and *scope* of polity, i.e., the realm or reach of activities that the EU is (and should be) involved in (Fossum & Pollak, 2015).

It is hardly surprising that this comprehensive debate over the nature of the polity spills over to the realm of public administration. The EU itself has a very limited administration, and the member states effectuate EU decisions. The question is whether member states' public administrations are Europeanized in the sense of being reprogrammed to serve the EU. There are disagreements as to whose interests/concerns the public administrations serve: the EU's interests, the member states' interests, or both. As was indicated above there is a debate over whether the EU is developing as a multilevel system of (hierarchical) government, or whether it is instead developing as

a system of (networked) transnational governance.[3] Trondal argues that "the European Executive Order transforms an inherent Westphalian order to the extent that an intergovernmental dynamic is supplemented by different mixes of supranational, departmental, and/or epistemic dynamics." (Trondal, 2010: 2) An important research challenge is to establish good indicators for determining the magnitude of this transformation.

Disagreements over what the EU is and what it should be straddle the line between state and non-state, between state and international organization, and nature and scope of public administration, which exhibits a complex mixture. Even if the EU has obvious federal features, there is no agreement on a viable EU federalism.[4]

In Canada a key historical problem has been to reconcile nationalism and federalism. But in some contrast to the EU, in Canada these disagreements start from the recognition that Canada is a federation—the issue has been whether the federation should be reformed or whether some portions of it should leave. The nature and scope of the federation and its underlying community and identity have preoccupied Canadians for decades. Canada was also, for close to two decades (late 1970s until late 1990s), involved in mega constitutional politics, which

goes beyond disputing the merits of specific constitutional proposals and addresses the very nature of the political community on which the constitution is based. Precisely because of the fundamental nature of the issues in dispute—their tendency to touch citizens' sense of identity and self-worth—mega constitutional politics is exceptionally emotional and intense. When a country's constitutional politics reaches this level, the constitutional question tends to dwarf all other public concerns. (Russell, 1993: 75)

In this period "Canada surely had a lock on the entry in the Guinness Book of Records for the sheer volume of constitutional talk." (Russell, 1993:177) An important aspect of mega constitutional politics is that it opened up the system of intergovernmental constitutional bargaining to broader segments of the population; hence it contributed to democratization. Patriation and the Charter revolution greatly strengthened the rights-basis of the constitution and reconfigured federal–provincial dynamics. It modified the dominant role of executive officials by empowering citizens. An important vehicle was the Canadian Charter of Rights and Freedoms, which contributed to mobilize citizens to demand access to the constitutional negotiations (Fossum, 2007). The Charter spoke to every citizen as a rights holder and a stakeholder in the constitution, including in the process of constitutional change. This process of Charter-inspired politicization altered the debate on how comprehensive constitutional changes should be organized by reducing the historically dominant control that executive officials had had of these processes (Cairns, 1991, 1992, 1995). The ensuing Charter mobilization greatly increased the number of self-conceived constitutional stakeholders, in particular women's groups, gays and lesbians, Aboriginals, immigrants, and disabled people.

Two striking similarities between the EU and Canada should be highlighted here. One is that the EU and Canada have dealt with their many internal disagreements in the peculiar combination of commitment to core principles (rule of law, rights, democracy, respect for difference, and diversity) combined with lasting disagreement on how these should be consolidated in a constitutional document and a set of institutions. In that sense we could say that Canada and the EU share what Jeremy Webber has referred to as an **agonistic constitutionalism**. It "acknowledges that parties often do disagree over fundamentals—indeed, may push very hard to have their view of the world accepted—and yet find a way to collaborate nevertheless. The principles remain important. The parties are deeply committed to them [. . .] But the parties place the maintenance of the relationship ahead of agreement on the fundamental structure of sovereignty." (Webber, 2015: 263.) The two political cultures are imbued with an accommodation mentality. This mentality is to a large extent sustained by the particular pattern of executive-legislative relations that we find in both entities.

The other important similarity refers precisely to the central role that executives in both the EU and Canada play in constitution-making/change. This is an intrinsic element of the notion of executive dominance that will be spelled out in more detail in the next section.

In Canada the central role of executive officials pertains to the First Ministers' Conferences; the EU parallel is the Intergovernmental Conference (IGC). In the EU, treaty change is being undertaken through the IGC, by executive heads of government and their respective staffs, in a formal system of summitry, with the European Council at its apex. Every member state has veto, whereas the European Parliament has a very limited role in the process. The system of treaty change that emerged in the EU finds an obvious parallel in the Canadian—also intergovernmental— approach to constitutional change. The Canadian near-equivalent to the European Council is the First Ministers' Conference, which consists of the prime minister and the 10 premiers. This body has played the most important role in the numerous efforts at fashioning constitutional change in Canada. In reality, in Canada as in the EU, the heads of governments could operate with very limited parliamentary input into the process of intergovernmental negotiations.

In both cases these systems are multi-purpose in the sense that they deal with constitutional issues *as well as* more mundane policy and political issues, and the boundaries between constitution-making proper and policy-making are often not very clear. That may on the one hand yield an element of flexibility but may on the other hand also increase constitutional uncertainty (and ambiguity) and render the processes more vulnerable to external influences. An important question that was widely debated in Canada and that Europeans are now grappling with is whether these arrangements may contribute to instability.

b) Executive-Legislative Relations

In the EU and Canada alike executives play a central role in shaping/conditioning the nature of constitutional politics and the way in which conflicts are dealt with. In addition, executive-legislative relations are profoundly affected by constitutional politics. The term that denotes the central role of executives in constitutional and routine decision-making alike is executive dominance.

The EU and Canada differ considerably in how executive power is organized. Executive power at the EU-level is fragmented across several institutions: the Commission, the Council configurations, and the European Council.[5] In Canada, executive power is concentrated in the hands of the prime minister and each premier and his or her staff within each government, and then dispersed across the governments of the federal system. Each system—the EU and Canada—thus exhibits its own unique blend of concentration and diffusion of executive power. This manifests itself in three dimensions of executive dominance (Fossum & Laycock, 2013). The first dimension has already been discussed and refers to the central role of executives in constitution-making/change. The second dimension is horizontal and pertains to a very high degree of executive control of decision-making. The third dimension is vertical and pertains to the manner in which executives enjoy direct and privileged access to both main levels of governance, and are therefore able to sideline parliaments. These three dimensions are particularly prominent in the EU given that EU integration from its very inception has been driven by executives and experts. Popularly elected bodies at all three main levels (regional, national, and European) have been trying to catch up; rein in and render the system subject to parliamentary oversight and control; obtain a decision-making presence, formally and substantively, in line with democratic precepts; render the system transparent; and find a way to explain and justify the system to citizens. Even before the financial crisis struck this process was far from completed, especially at the EU level.

The pronounced executive presence in handling constitutional issues is equally present in the procedures that the two systems—EU and Canada—have developed for exit of a member-state (EU) or a province (Canada).

c) Exit/Secession

Both the EU and Canada have procedures for territorial exit or secession. The main difference between them is that in the case of Quebec in Canada the secessionists lost, whereas in the UK in Europe they won.[6] Although the process was never officially launched, Canada's experience, coupled with the efforts made afterwards to establish proper procedures for the secession of a province, make for some interesting parallels between the cases.

The sources of secession relate to the fact that the EU and Canada are deeply contested. In Canada secession provisions were put in place after the failed Quebec 1995 referendum. They were thus a result of Quebec's actions. The trigger was a reference to the Supreme Court that was asked to consider the legality of

secession. The Supreme Court in its advisory opinion in 1998 was careful to underline the political nature of this issue. It stated that Quebec has no legal right—under Canadian or international law—to unilaterally secede from Canada. But it went on to note that:

> Our democratic institutions accommodate a continuous process of discussion and evolution, which is reflected in the constitutional right of each participant in the federation to initiate constitutional change. This implies a reciprocal duty on the other participants to engage in discussions to address any legitimate initiative to change the constitutional order. A clear majority vote in Quebec on a clear question in favour of secession would confer democratic legitimacy on the secession initiative which all of the other participants in Confederation would have to recognize.[7]

The federal government in 1999, through the so-called Clarity Act (An Act to Give Effect to the Requirement for Clarity as Set out in the opinion of the Supreme Court of Canada in the Quebec Secession Reference[8]) established a set of procedural guidelines for how secession might proceed.

In the EU exit provisions (Article 50 TEU) were inserted in the Lisbon Treaty, which entered into force on December 1, 2009. These provisions will be tested in the presently running Brexit negotiations. The UK voted in favour of Brexit on June 23, 2016. Article 50 TEU stipulates that the process only starts when the exiting state formally notifies the European Council of its intention to withdraw, which the UK Prime Minister Theresa May did on March 29, 2017.[9] The European Council at its meeting on April 29, 2017 set out the EU's negotiating guidelines. One important difference between the EU and the situation in Canada in the mid-1990s, then, is that the Brexit process will be conducted in accordance with provisions already laid down in the EU treaties. As noted above, it was only after the Quebec referendum that such procedures were put in place in Canada.

Why do political systems introduce exit provisions? One reason is that such provisions emerge as a result of a long-drawn political struggle, as we saw in Canada. A second reason is that a political system inserts exit provisions as a form of safety-valve to contain conflicts. The EU has long handled conflicts and diversity through differentiated integration (Leuffen et al., 2012), which means that states have not integrated at the same speed. When provisions for special status would no longer be considered adequate, the next step would be for a member state to exit the Union. The UK has had the by far most exemptions in the EU, but this was not enough to placate the EU opponents. A third reason for exit provisions could be to foster consolidation; exit provisions ensure that the least committed members do not tear down the whole building by constantly instigating centrifugal dynamics. Thus, it is possible to interpret the availability of exit as a means of regulating disintegration, but it is also possible to interpret exit provisions as an integrative and/or consolidating measure. The Brexit case—once it has found a settlement, which may take quite a few years—will show us which interpretation wins out in Europe.

An important similarity between the EU and Canada is that the basic procedures for negotiating secession are multilateral. In the EU the non-elected Commission undertakes the negotiations with the UK and does that on behalf of the governments in the European Council. Article 50 TEU provides two years to conclude the negotiations (the deadline can be extended if all member states agree to a request for extension). The negotiation "shall be concluded on behalf of the Union by the [European] Council, acting by a qualified majority, after obtaining the consent of the European Parliament."[10] Note that the "member of the European Council or of the Council representing the withdrawing Member State shall not participate in the discussions of the European Council or Council or in decisions concerning it." In Canada, negotiations with a province would not be bilateral—between the federal government and the relevant province—but would be conducted among all the governments of the provinces and the federal government.[11] Thus, it is important to underline that in both cases the executive officials play a central role in this process.

There is quite a lot of ambiguity surrounding such momentous processes. One pertains to the wording of the referendum question. The 1995 Quebec referendum question was quite ambiguous (Young, 1998), and left a lot of scope for political manoeuvring. It read: "Do you agree that Québec should become sovereign, after having made a formal offer to Canada for a new economic and political partnership, within

the scope of the Bill respecting the future of Québec and of the agreement signed on 12 June 1995?" In fact, the question reflects the fact that secession was the result of a long process of working out whether Quebec should seek a different status either within or without the federation. Quebec sovereignists had long advocated sovereignty-association. It referred to political sovereignty and economic association. It is interesting to note that Quebec sovereignists had earlier advocated an EU-type association for Quebec with the rest of Canada. The increasingly integrated EU post-Maastricht was hardly what sovereignists were dreaming about. The issue Quebecers confront and the UK is also seeing as the Brexit process unfolds is that in a world of tightly interlinked states and communities, the *scope* for autonomous political decision-making is strongly curtailed.

In the UK Brexit case the referendum question was clear but the underlying alternatives had *not* been clarified, as has become readily apparent in the aftermath of the referendum. The main options that were not clarified when the referendum was held included a hard Brexit, which would entail that the UK exits the EU's internal market and customs union; soft Brexit, which would entail that it remains within the EU's internal market and customs union and becomes an EU rule-taker (akin to the EEA states); or a soft-hard Brexit, which would entail a transition arrangement whereby the UK gradually dismantles its EU affiliations. These are very different forms of association and what they would look like is dependent on what the EU accepts. None of this was clarified when the referendum was held.

The Brexiteers who claimed that Brexit entailed "taking back control" immediately reneged on a number of their promises after the referendum. The UK government close to a year after the referendum wants as close a relationship to the EU as possible without being inside the EU internal market and EU customs union, but precisely what that entails is still very unclear. The pro-remain UK Prime Minister Theresa May has repeatedly stated that "Brexit means Brexit," but nobody really knows what that entails. Ironically, when starting the Brexit process the UK first had to pass a law to incorporate all EU legislation in British law, the European Union (Withdrawal) Bill, which involves at least 12,000 EU regulations and directives.[12] Formally speaking that makes the UK extremely EU-integrated because the UK legal system, not the Court of Justice of the European Union, will handle all of these provisions. Concerns are raised that the government, when retooling these provisions to suit the UK, will do so through executive decrees rather than through parliamentary procedures, hence that this will add to executive dominance.

There are several interesting parallels between Quebec and the UK, and Canada–EU with regard to the nature and dynamics of their relationships. With regard to Quebec versus the UK, both cases exhibit a, historically speaking, highly ambiguous relationship to their respective unions. The UK has since the EU's inception had an ambiguous relationship to the EU: when the UK was out it sought to get in, and once it was in it sought to get out (Lord, 2015). A long-drawn-out process of opposition to EU federalization is coupled with support for the EU as a continent-wide internal market. UK visions have varied from the EU as a political to a mere economic community. In both the UK and Quebec their ambiguous historical relationships to their respective unions testify to the difficulties of forging clean breaks.

Another parallel is that in both the Quebec-rest-of-Canada and the UK-EU cases concerns have arisen about fragmentation—of the union that remains but also of the unit that exits. Partitionists claimed that if Canada was divisible then so should Quebec be.[13] In Canada, the lack of a Plan B made analysts worry that Quebec secession could lead to the unravelling of Canada (Cairns, 1997). As was being said in Europe in 2016, if the EU is divisible, so is the UK. That applies in particular to the role of Scotland where a clear majority of the population voted against Brexit and where Scotland's Premier Nicola Sturgeon promised to hold a second independence referendum,[14] and wants to do so as soon as the result of the Brexit negotiations are clear.

For the UK a hard Brexit would be easier to handle the weaker or more divided the EU is. The weaker the EU the better the UK's bargaining position because the EU–UK relationship is quite asymmetrical. Several of the Brexit architects—especially the UKIPers—are anti-EU and would prefer to see the EU dismantled.[15] Former UKIP leader Nigel Farage actively propounded the need to dismantle the EU and has encouraged other states to hold similar exit referenda to spur such a process. The result of the French presidential elections in April-May 2017 was critically important. If Marine Le Pen were to have won the elections, we would have expected at least France to seek to renegotiate its relationship to the EU. That would have been a momentous development because it would have significantly weakened the informal motor of integration, namely the close Franco-German co-operation that has marked the EU since its inception. Macron's election closed off talk of renegotiation.

d) Why Did Canada Escape the 2008 Crisis, whereas in the EU It Helped Trigger a Major Existential Crisis?

Why has Canada put the financial crisis that struck in 2008 behind it, whereas it continues to haunt the EU? The crisis started in the US housing market but spread worldwide. After the collapse of Lehman Brothers in September 2008, governments undertook massive capital interventions to prevent financial markets from completely collapsing, in many instances accumulating massive public debts. It was at this stage, when the crisis turned from a financial crisis to a public debt crisis, that it became crystal clear that the repercussions would be far more profound for the European Union than in the United States, where the crisis originated.

When we compare and contrast the EU with Canada, we see that in Canada it proved possible to contain the US-generated crisis to a financial problem that was dealt with within the banking sector. The Canadian system of banking regulation and organization proved able to deal with this problem in a relatively straightforward manner. Analysts have attributed that to historically entrenched aspects of state structure and banking regulation in Canada. Bordo et al. (2011) note that: "(t)he relative stability of the Canadian banks in the recent crisis compared to the United States in our view reflected the original institutional foundations laid in place in the early 19th century in the two countries. The Canadian concentrated banking system that had evolved by the end of the twentieth century had absorbed the key sources of systemic risk—the mortgage market and investment banking—and was tightly regulated by one overarching regulator."

In the EU, however, what started as a financial and fiscal crisis has developed into a major political and institutional—even constitutional—amalgam of crises (Menéndez, 2013; Fossum & Menéndez, 2014).

Much of that must be attributed to structural faults built into the EU construct: a monetary union without a fiscal union is an inherently unstable construct (Scharpf, 2010).[16]

EU Commission President Jean-Claude Juncker in his 2016 state of the union address acknowledged that the EU is currently facing the worst existential crisis in its existence. Even if the EU is facing a number of challenges there is no question that the financial crisis, or what has come to be termed the Eurozone crisis, has led to a profound structural mutation that threatens to undermine many of the EU's past achievements.

It is readily apparent that the Eurozone crisis and its handling have clearly weakened democratic systems of monitoring and control at all three key levels: EU, member state, and regional. National parliaments have seen their fiscal sovereignty severely constrained, and the European Parliament (EP) has not been given powers to fill the gap (Fasone, 2014). The EP, at least partly sidelined in the crisis response, has been one of the main losers. The crisis response has reinforced technocracy, in the sense that experts have obtained a freer role and are less encumbered by legal and democratic controls. A case in point is the European Central Bank (ECB).

How these challenges are to be addressed requires paying attention to how power relations and patterns of democratic authorization and accountability have been reconfigured by the crisis. Most assessments stress that the crisis has strengthened the EU's intergovernmental elements (Fabbrini, 2015), in particular the role of the executive officials in the European Council. There are, however, also analysts who show how the crisis has strengthened the EU's supranational component, notably in the areas of macroeconomic policy and banking regulation, in which the role of the Commission and the European Central Bank (ECB) has been considerably enhanced (Dehousse 2015).

But in overall terms the crisis and the EU's handling of it have ushered in a shift in the locus of decision-making, with the European Council playing a central role (the so-called Union method). The intergovernmental dimension has been pronounced as reflected in intergovernmental treaties (see Treaty on Stability, Coordination and Governance in the Economic and Monetary Union) and informal intergovernmental bargains (notably between Germany and France). These developments are seen as giving rise to an executive-dominated federalism that is quite impervious to parliamentary oversight and control (Habermas, 2012). These developments spur de-constitutionalization (Menéndez, 2013), amid profound concerns about a general weakening of the legal basis for integration (Joerges, 2014). Analysts have also argued that what initially appeared as a distinctive form of emergency politics may alter what we understand as normality in Europe, with profound democratic legitimacy implications (White, 2015a, 2015b).

e) The Comprehensive Economic and Trade Agreement between the EU and Canada (CETA)

The fifth challenge or constitutive issue is the Comprehensive Economic and Trade Agreement between the EU and Canada. An important question is whether this is an economic question, a matter of how two political systems organized their economic relations, or whether it is a constitutive issue with bearing on more fundamental aspects of the nature and operation of the two political systems. In the following I will first provide a brief overview of CETA and thereafter comment on its broader implications. The aim of CETA "is to increase flows of goods, services and investment to the benefit of both partners. For the EU, CETA represents the first comprehensive economic agreement with a highly industrialised Western economy."[17] The assumption is that the liberalization of trade in goods and services will produce significant economic gains for both the EU and Canada. Improved market access for EU companies would remove the disadvantages they currently experience in relation to US companies. For Canada, a comprehensive trade agreement with the EU would reduce its dependence on the United States. A study in 2008 suggested that CETA would generate an annual real income gain of € 11.6 billion for the EU and € 8.2 billion for Canada, as well as greatly increase the levels of European exports to Canada and Canadian exports to the EU. Other studies are far more negative and suggest that CETA may have obverse social and economic effects in terms of increasing unemployment, raising inequality, and engendering welfare losses (Kohler & Storm, 2016). Other concerns that are raised are the possible implications on sustainable development, the fight against climate change, and food safety.[18]

Labelling this as a comprehensive trade agreement is entirely correct. The agreement is a full 1598 pages, consisting of 30 chapters, and in addition has a number of annexes. It is so comprehensive because it covers both tariff and non-tariff barriers, and mechanisms for dispute settlement.

It is a comprehensive agreement that has taken a long period to negotiate. CETA negotiations started in May 2009. They initially concluded at the EU-Canada Summit on 26 September 2014, but CETA was only signed by the EU and Canada on 30 October 2016. Since the European Parliament approved CETA, provisional application can commence. But adoption of the entire agreement is dependent on parliamentary ratification in EU member states (including in those states, such as Belgium, where regional assemblies also need to give their assent) and in Canadian provinces and territories, and as of early 2017 had still not taken place.

Assessments of the possible implications of CETA vary. That is also because there are different views as to what CETA signifies. One position views binding international co-operation as beneficial not only because it produces economic gains but also because it constrains the scope for public regulation of markets. These are the "globalization optimists." The other position holds that comprehensive agreements, especially those that deeply affect trade in services and all types of non-tariff barriers, constrain the ability of public authorities to regulate markets, and to make up for inequalities and social ills that socially dis-embedded markets inevitably generate.

These are ultimately ideological questions. What is clear about CETA and what both positions would acknowledge is that CETA raises what Dani Rodrik (2012) has referred to as the globalization trilemma: you cannot have strong globalization, national sovereignty, and democracy at the same time—there has to be a trade-off.

In the CETA case, this trilemma does not only pertain to the substance of the agreement; it also pertains to the process whereby it was negotiated.

Here executive officials played a central role. It is an important democratic challenge to ensure that parliaments are adequately involved in such comprehensive negotiation processes.

Conclusion

In this chapter, the aim was to alert students of Canadian politics and administration to the similarities and differences that exist between the EU and Canada. Most people would expect such an assessment to highlight the many differences. They clearly exist but as has been shown here there are a number of parallels that would not appear obvious if one started from the presumption that Canada is a state whereas the EU is an association of states. Nevertheless, the decentralized and government-centred nature of Canadian federalism holds a number of features in common with the EU that were pointed out as early as in 1972 in Richard Simeon's pathbreaking book *Federal-Provincial Diplomacy*. Since then. as the EU has consolidated and engaged in comprehensive processes of executive-driven constitution-making/treaty change, the parallels have become more pronounced and the scope for comparison has increased.

This chapter has provided a brief overview of five quite different themes. Each theme sees a pronounced role of executive officials: how their organization and interaction shape each system. It is only in the theme on the financial crisis that there is no equivalence between the cases in terms of executive presence. That is because Canada is far more robust in socio-economic terms than the EU. Canada is a well-entrenched state with a strong fiscal capacity. Thus, whereas both Canada and the EU have developed comprehensive approaches to accommodating cultural difference and diversity, Canada in contrast to the EU has a socio-economic constitution that enables it to deal with internal and external shocks in a far more coherent and decisive manner than is the case with the EU.

Important Terms and Concepts

agonistic constitutionalism	Comprehensive Economic and Trade Agreement between the EU and Canada (CETA)	executive dominance
		financial crisis
		secession

Study Questions

1. What utility is there in comparing the European Union and Canada, when there has been historically more focus on US-EU relations?
2. What are the similarities and differences in the role of government leaders in constitutional politics in the EU and Canada?
3. Explain what is meant by executive dominance. How does it manifest itself in in the EU and in Canada, in structural terms, and across very different issues?
4. Why were the effects of the financial crisis so different in the EU and Canada?
5. Discuss the implications of CETA for Canada and the EU.

Notes

1   See for instance Cappelleti et al (1986); Fabbrini (2010).
2   In the EU, since the 1980s these are: the Single European Act (1986), the Maastricht Treaty (1992), the Amsterdam Treaty (1997), the Nice Treaty (2001), the Laeken Constitutional Treaty (2004), the Lisbon Treaty (2007) and the Treaty on Stability, Coordination and Governance in the Economic and Monetary Union (TSCG)(2012). In Canada what Russell (2004) terms the period of mega constitutional politics includes the Constitution Act 1982, and the failed Meech Lake Accord (1987), and the Charlottetown Accord (1992).
3   In terms of the latter, some analysts are developing new approaches to the relationship between politics and administration reflected for instance in such notions as experimentalist governance (Sabel and Zeitlin 2010; for assessments see for instance contributions by Fossum 2012; Verdun 2012).
4   Some analysts have sought a way out by discussing the EU as a system of multilevel governance. Hooghe and Marks (2003) discuss two versions of this.
5   Executive officials have long enjoyed privileged process-access through the prominent role of the Council configurations in EU decision-making (especially in the Maastricht pillars II and III), and have seen their role strengthened with the increased salience of the European Council and the build-up of competence in the Council Secretariat. Executives and experts enjoy a privileged role through the Commission's "expert role," the Comitology system, agencification, and the recent institutionalization of the Eurozone, to mention a number of the key components of this system that are particularly designed to cater to executives and experts.
6   Quebec has held two secession referenda, one in 1980 and the other in 1995. In the latter it was pulled back from the brink by a very slight No majority (49.4 per cent voted Yes, whereas 50.58 per cent voted No, the No side won by a mere 54,288 votes). The EU is currently faced with the challenge of Brexit, after 51.9 per cent or 17,410,742 voted Leave whereas 48.1 per cent or 16,141,241 voted Remain in a popular referendum on June 23, 2016 (turnout was 72.2 per cent). http://www.bbc.com/news/politics/eu_referendum/results
7   *Reference Re Secession of Quebec,* [1998] 2 SCR 217.
8   Available at http://laws.justice.gc.ca/eng/acts/c-31.8/fulltext.html
9   UK Prime Minister May's letter to the European Council is available here: https://www.gov.uk/government/uploads/system/

uploads/attachment_data/file/604079/Prime_Ministers_letter_to_European_Council_President_Donald_Tusk.pdf
10 http://eur-lex.europa.eu/resource.html?uri=cellar:2b f140bf-a3f8-4ab2-b506-fd71826e6da6.0023.02/DOC_1&format=PDF
11 *An Act to Give Effect to the Requirement for Clarity as Set out in the Opinion of the Supreme Court of Canada in the Quebec Secession Reference, SC 2000,* c 26, http://canlii.ca/t/j0tj retrieved on 2017-04-17
12 For an explanation see the Government White Paper, available at: https://www.gov.uk/government/uploads/system/uploads/attachment_data/file/604516/Great_repeal_bill_white_paper_accessible.pdf
13 The leader of the Reform Party, Preston Manning, noted that "if Canada is divisible, as long as the process employed respects the rule of law and the principle of democratic consent, then Quebec is divisible by the application of the same processes and the same principles." Remarks by Preston Manning, MP Leader of the Official Opposition, House of Commons - February 10, 1998, printed in Hansard.
14 https://www.theguardian.com/politics/2017/mar/29/scottish-independence-sturgeon-to-press-on-with-referendum
15 http://www.independent.co.uk/news/uk/politics/eu-referendum-nigel-farage-4am-victory-speech-the-text-in-full-a7099156.html
16 Many of the measures are set out in the intergovernmental Treaty on Stability, Coordination and Governance T/SCG/en 1 of 2 March 2012 and the so-called Six-Pack, a bundle of five regulations and one directive that cover fiscal surveillance and macroeconomic surveillance under the new Macroeconomic Imbalance Procedure.
17 European Parliament Research Service: Briefing – International Agreements in Progress, January 2017. PE 595.895 (author Wilhelm Schöllmann). Available at: http://www.europarl.europa.eu/RegData/etudes/BRIE/2017/595895/EPRS_BRI(2017)595895_EN.pdf
18 A comprehensive and critical assessment of CETA that includes European and Canadian voices is "Making Sense of CETA, 2. Edition," published by PowerShift, CCPA et.al. Berlin/Ottawa, 2016. The report is available at: https://www.tni.org/files/publication-downloads/making-sense-of-ceta_22092016.pdf

References

Ackerman, Bruce. 1991. *We the People*. Vol. 1. Foundations. Cambridge, Mass.: Belknap Press.

Bohman, J. 2007. *Democracy Across Borders: From* Dêmos *to* Dêmoi, Cambridge. MA: MIT Press.

Bordo, Michael D., Angela Redish, and Hugh Rockoff. 2011. "Why Didn't Canada Have a Banking Crisis in 2008 (or in 1930, or 1907, or . . .)?" Working Paper 17312 National Bureau of Economic Research, Cambridge, MA.

Crum, Ben. 2013. "Saving the Euro at the Cost of Democracy?" *Journal of Common Market Studies* 53, 5, pp. 614–30.

Cairns, Alan C. 1991. *Disruptions: Constitutional Struggles from the Charter to Meech Lake*. Toronto: McClelland & Stewart.

Cairns, Alan C. 1992. *Charter versus Federalism: The Dilemmas of Constitutional Reform*. Montreal & Kingston: McGill-Queen's University Press.

Cairns, Alan C. 1995. *Reconfigurations: Canadian Citizenship and Constitutional Change*. Toronto: McClelland and Stewart Inc.

Cairns, Alan C. 1997. "Looking into the Abyss: The Need for a Plan C." C.D. Howe Institute Commentary, C.D. Howe Institute, No. 96, September 1997.

Cairns, Alan C. 2003. "The Canadian Experience of a Charter of Rights." *The Chartering of Europe*, edited by Erik O. Eriksen, John E. Fossum, and Agustín J. Menéndez, Baden-Baden: Nomos Verlagsgesellschaft, 93–111.

Cappelletti, Mauro, Monica Seccombe, and Joseph H.H. Weiler, editors. 1986. *Integration Through Law. Methods, Tools and Institutions: Vol 1. Book 1: A Political, Legal and Economic Overview*. Berlin: De Gruyter.

Dehousse, Renaud. 2015. "The New Supranationalism." Paper prepared for presentation at the ECPR General Conference, Montreal, August 26–August 29, 2015.

Eriksen, Erik O. and John E. Fossum, editors. 2012. *Rethinking Democracy and the European Union*. London: Routledge.

EU Commission President Jean-Claude Juncker. 2016. "State of the Union Address 2016— Towards A Better Europe—A Europe That Protects, Empowers and Defends." ec.europa.eu/soteu

Fabbrini, Sergio. 2010. *Compound Democracies: Why the United States and Europe Are Becoming Similar*. Revised ed. Oxford: Oxford University Press.

Fabbrini, Sergio. 2015. *Which European Union? Europe After the Euro Crisis*. Cambridge: Cambridge University Press.

Fasone, Cristina. 2014. "European Economic Governance and Parliamentary Representation. What Place for the European Parliament?" *European Law Journal* 20, 2, pp. 164–85.

Fossum, John E. 2007. "On Democratizing European Constitution Making: Possible Lessons from Canada's Experience." *Supreme Court Law Review*, 37, pp. 343–81.

Fossum, John E. 2012. "Reflections on Experimentalist Governance." *Regulation and Governance* 6, 3, pp. 394–400.

Fossum, John E. and David Laycock. 2013. "Democratic Governance and the Challenge of Executive Dominance in International and National Settings." *Developing Democracies—Democracy, Democratization and Development*. edited by Michael Böss, Jørgen Møller, and Svend-Erik Skaaning. Aarhus: Aarhus University Press, pp. 176–90.

Fossum, John E. and A Agustín J. Menéndez. 2014. "The European Union in Crises or the European Union as Crises?" *ARENA Report* No. 2/14.

Fossum, John E. and Johannes Pollak. 2015. "Which Democratic Principles for the European Union? What Deficit?" *The European Union—Democratic Principles and Institutional Architectures in Times of Crisis*, edited by Simona Piattoni, Oxford: Oxford University Press, pp. 29–45.

Gagnon, Alain-G. and James Tully, editors. 2001. *Multinational Democracies*. Cambridge: Cambridge University Press.

Grimm, Dieter. 1995. "Does Europe Need a Constitution?" *European Law Journal* 1, 3, pp. 282–302.

Habermas, Jürgen. 2012. *The Crisis of the European Union: A Response*. Cambridge: Polity Press.

Hooghe, Lisbeth and Gary Marks. 2003. "Unravelling the Central State, but How? Types of Multi-Level Governance." *American Political Science Review* 97, 2, pp. 233–43.

Joerges, Christian. 2014. "Law and Politics in Europe's Crisis: On the History of the Impact of an Unfortunate Configuration." *Constellations* 22, 2, pp. 249–61.

Kohler, Pierre and Servaas Storm. 2016. "CETA without Blinders: How Cutting 'Trade Costs and More' Will Cause Unemployment, Inequality, and Welfare Losses." *International Journal of Political Economy*, 45, 4, pp. 257–93.

Kymlicka, Will. 1995. *Multicultural Citizenship: A Liberal Theory of Minority Rights*. Oxford: Clarendon Press.

Leuffen, Dirk, Berthold Rittberger, and Frank Schimmelfennig. 2012. *Differentiated Integration. Explaining Variance in the European Union*. Palgrave Macmillan.

Lipset, Seymour M. 1990. *Continental Divide—The Values and Institutions of the United States and Canada*. New York: Routledge.

Lord, Christopher. 2015. 'The United Kingdom, a Once and Future(?) Non-Member State." *The European Union's Non-Members: Independence Under*

Hegemony? edited by Erik O. Eriksen and John E. Fossum, London: Routledge, pp. 211–29.

Menéndez, Agustín J. 2013. "The Existential Crisis of the European Union." *German Law Journal* 14, 5, pp. 453–525.

Morton, F.L. and Rainer Knopff. 2000. *The Charter Revolution and the Court Party.* Peterborough, ON: Broadview Press.

Offe, Claus. 2005. *Reflections on America: Tocqueville, Weber and Adorno in the United States.* Cambridge: Polity Press.

Resnick, Philip. 2005. *The European Roots of Canadian Identity.* Toronto: Broadview Press.

Rodrik, Dani. 2012. *The Globalization Paradox. Democracy and the Future of the World Economy.* New York: W.W. Norton & Company.

Russell, Peter H. 1993. *Constitutional Odyssey: Can Canadians Become a Sovereign People?* Toronto: University of Toronto Press, 2nd edn.

Sabel, Charles F. and Jonathan Zeitlin editors. 2010. *Experimentalist Governance in the European Union: Towards a New Architecture.* Oxford: Oxford University Press.

Scharpf, Fritz. 2010. "The Asymmetry of European Integration, or why the EU cannot be a 'Social Market Economy.'" *Socio-Economic Review* 8, pp. 211–50.

Schmitter, Phillippe. 2000. *How to Democratize the European Union . . . And Why Bother?* Lanham: Rowman and Littlefield.

Simeon, Richard. 1972. *Federal-Provincial Diplomacy: The Making of Recent Policy in Canada.* Toronto: University of Toronto Press.

Trondal, Jarle. 2010. *An Emergent European Executive Order.* Oxford: Oxford University Press.

Verdun, Amy. 2012. "Experimentalist Governance in the European Union: A Commentary." *Regulation and Governance* 6, 3, pp. 385–93.

Webber, Jeremy. 2015. *The Constitution of Canada. A Contextual Analysis.* Oxford: Hart Publishing.

White, Jonathan. 2015a. "Emergency Europe." *Political Studies,* 63, 2, pp. 300–18.

White, Jonathan. 2015b. "Authority after Emergency Rule." *The Modern Law Review,* 78, 4, pp. 585–610.

Young, Robert. 1998. *The Secession of Quebec and the Future of Canada.* Revised and expanded edn, Montreal & Kingston: McGill-Queen's University Press.

Glossary

ability to pay A criterion increasingly used in arbitration settlements wherein the ramifications of settlements on the financial health of the employer are considered. It is sometimes distinguished from "pattern settlements," in which an agreement in one occupational group gets applied across the board. (Chapter 19)

Access to Information Act An Act passed in 1983 that gives the public the right to access government records and states that government agencies must provide the requested records within a reasonable amount of time (30 days). The Act does not apply to records that contain personal information about individual citizens, and sensitive information relating to certain matters of national security may also be exempt. (Chapters 22, 25)

accountability Generally, the assignment of responsibilities, with clear expectations or standards, by a person or body in authority to a specific person or body, who is obligated to answer for performance or non-performance. (Chapters 7, 13, 20, 22)

accounting officers Established by the Federal Accountability Act, this position is given to the deputy minister or head of an agency. The officer is accountable for aspects of the organization and use of departmental resources, but holds less responsibility than similar officers in the UK. (Chapters 7, 10)

administrative independence (judicial administrative independence) Freedom of functioning of courts' administration that reflects the unique role of the courts within a traditional cabinet system. One manifestation would be to shift parts of the court administrative staff to a separate judicial administration budget controlled by the judges. (Chapter 8)

adversary system The dominant legal paradigm in the English legal system, now spread worldwide. It assumes that the parties—and hence lawyers—control the process and that the judge (and jury, if necessary) assesses arguments presented rather than being directly involved in the argumentation of the case. (Chapter 8)

advocacy Public support for laws or policies; non-profit organizations often advocate (lobby) for policies for the good of particular groups and/or society as a whole. (Chapter 26)

agencies Generally, any non-departmental form in government that is freed from the normal day-to-day operational controls by central government, but for which government may set broad policy directions.

agenda-setting The first stage in the policy process; in this stage, a problem is identified by policy actors and a variety of solutions are put forward. Public-sector elites compete to get their priorities in the news, ideally with prominent and favourable treatment, reasoning that the greater the quantity and quality of positive attention that the media pays to an issue or event, the higher the likelihood of citizens agreeing that the topic is important. This in turn will spur policy action that is accepted as a legitimate response to an important public problem. Agenda-setting speaks to why communications control is so important in public administration. (Chapters 14, 25)

agonistic constitutionalism A term coined by Jeremy Webber that can be used to describe a similar tendency of the EU and Canada to deal with their many internal disagreements in the peculiar combination of commitment to core principles (rule of law, rights, democracy, respect for difference and diversity) combined with lasting disagreement on how these should be consolidated in a constitutional document and a set of institutions. Parties often do disagree over fundamentals and yet find a way to collaborate nevertheless. The two political cultures are imbued with an "accommodation mentality" sustained by the particular pattern of executive-legislative relations that we find in both entities. (Chapter 27)

alternative dispute resolution (ADR) Patterns of dispute resolution other than the right to strike, namely, the limited right to strike, binding arbitration, arbitration at the request of either party, and the choice of procedure. The choice of ADR mechanism depends on the effects of political pressures, interest groups, special events, and inertia. (Chapters 8, 19)

arbitration criteria When the right to strike is prohibited or not opted for when the parties can choose to strike, or when the parties are ordered back to work via legislative enactments, binding arbitration is the method of dispute resolution in the public sector. In determining awards the arbitration criteria that tend to be used are as follows: comparability; the employers' ability to pay; cost of living; productivity increases; and minimum living standards. (Chapter 19)

Auditor General of Canada An officer of Parliament often described as the principal financial watchdog in the legislative branch. The Office of the Auditor General is responsible for ensuring the legality and accuracy of expenditures by practising comprehensive/value-for-money auditing; the Auditor General's reports are read by parliamentarians and pundits alike and often set the agenda for public-sector reform. (Chapters 7, 24)

autonomy (administrative) One of the rationales for establishing Crown corporations, the reasoning being that it may encourage efficiency; usually conceived to act in balance with the need for control by central government. Autonomy is to be applied to operational or day-to-day matters, control to matters of general policy. (Chapter 12)

back-to-work legislation Increasingly evoked to settle disputes in the public sector in both Canada and the United States, such legislation, which is invariably preceded by a strike, establishes arbitration to set the terms and conditions of the new contract. It is one of a number of legislative enactments (wage controls, the suspension of collective bargaining, social contracts, back-to-work legislation) designed as dispute resolution procedures in the public sector. (Chapter 19)

big government An era in the evolution of the federal government in Canada, from 1946 until about 1973, characterized by growing confidence among policy-makers about the capacity of government to remedy the defects of an unregulated capitalist economy and the elaboration of programs to manage social and economic activity and redistribute wealth. Some consider it the most important invention of the twentieth century. (Chapter 15)

binding arbitration A method of dispute resolution in the public sector used when the right to strike is not a viable option. An impartial third-party professional determines awards based on such criteria as comparability (the dominant criterion), the employers' ability to pay, and the cost of living. (Chapter 19)

bounded rationality A limited rationality, arising from information costs and uncertainty. (Chapter 14)

branding (political branding) A theory that all government actors are beholden to messages set by the prime minister's inner circle, a phenomenon aided by related and connected trends running through Canadian public administration—among others, the politicization of government, the centralization of decision-making, and the proliferation of digital media. (Chapter 25)

budget In government finance, a key document of an organization's planning process that allocates financial resources in order to achieve policy agendas. Budgets establish internal financial controls and effective cash management.

bureaucratic independence The idea that the public service is an organ of government. This is a reinterpretation of the traditional approach, which holds that the public service is simply the operational arm of the government and, as such, no public servant can make a decision or take any action not authorized by a statute or government directive. Bureaucratic independence recognizes that, while public servants owe a duty of loyalty to the government of the day, certain circumstances may arise that permit them to exercise independence from that government in order to protect the neutrality of the public service and the rule of law. (Chapter 7)

cabinet The leading committee of the executive. (Chapter 16)

cabinet committees Clusters of cabinet ministers, usually grouped on the basis of shared functional responsibilities or, as is the case with committees such as the Treasury Board, brought together to provide coordination of government activities. (Chapter 6)

cabinet formation The process of establishing a responsible government in office, guided by conventions of the Constitution. (Chapter 6)

cabinet's directive power The formal authority to issue binding cabinet directives to semi-independent agencies. Directives, which are almost always publicly issued,

oblige an agency to do as directed by the government even if the agency's best judgment is to the contrary. (Chapter 11)

cabinet secretary The official designated with the responsibility to support the government of the day as the prime minister's deputy minister but, as important, as Clerk of the Privy Council Office, with the additional responsibility of preparing the public service to welcome a new government in the event the election yields a new government. (Chapter 16)

Canada Assistance Plan (CAP) A cost-sharing arrangement for social assistance programs that existed from 1966 to 1996 with conditions attached to federal funding, including the forbidding of a residency period as a condition of eligibility for social assistance or for the receipt of social assistance in the province or territory. The 1995 federal budget announced that the Canada Assistance Plan and Established Programs Financing would be combined into one block fund: the Canada Health and Social Transfer, or CHST. (Chapter 3)

Canada Business Network A unit in the Department of Innovation, Science and Economic Development that operates interjurisdictionally and serves as an Internet portal role for Canadian business, especially the medium and small business sectors which have been given new prominence in the information economy. (Chapter 22)

Canada's International Gateway An Internet portal maintained by the Department of Global Affairs for Canadians travelling and marketing abroad and foreign residents wishing to know more about Canada. This complements Global Affairs' traditional role of maintaining Canadian diplomatic posts abroad on behalf of the entire government. (Chapter 22)

Canada Site The federal government's Internet portal, established in 1995. It provides a vast array of information on government-related programs and services, with links to many government departments. (Chapter 22)

Canadian Charter of Rights and Freedoms Set out in the Constitution Act, 1982, the Charter is designed to regulate the policies and actions of governmental organizations (rather than of individuals, to avoid infringing on individual rights); the Charter covers a wide range of issues that include rights of assembly and association, democratic rights, mobility rights, and minority-language rights. (Chapters 4 and 8)

Canada Health and Social Transfer (CHST) Combined grants for health care and post-secondary education with the Canada Assistance Plan (CAP) in one block fund, beginning in 1996, eliminating the last of the "50-cent dollars" provinces had been spending on welfare programs. (Chapter 2)

Canadian Human Rights Commission Administering under the Canadian Human Rights Act, the Commission ensures compliance with the Employment Equity Act, acts dedicated to achieving non-discrimination in employment and provision of federal services, and assists with equal employment opportunities for designated groups by federally regulated employers. (Chapter 7)

case management   Pre-planning for complex cases, in the form of directions hearings and/or case conferences. (Chapter 8)

caseflow management   An organizational principle under which the court is responsible for the continuation of a case from the time it is initiated. Guidelines generally include a schedule for all stages of the case, a way of monitoring the schedule, and procedures to prevent unnecessary delays (for example, fast tracking, case management, and mediation). (Chapter 8)

central agency   A public-service-wide facilitative and coordination body, directly responsible to the prime minister or premier, established to promote shared knowledge, collegial decision-making, or the setting of government-wide priorities. (Chapter 6)

central executive   The collective political and non-political elements of the executive who are engaged in generating and coordinating central policy. (Chapter 6)

charters   Laws that provide for more functional authority than is generally found in smaller places so that cities can potentially act more effectively in relation to complex urban issues. (Chapter 9)

chief administrative officer (CAO)   The typical form (and title) of appointed administrative managers in Canadian cities. Their main duty is to facilitate relations and communicate information between staff and council. As with all municipal staff in Canada, they report to all councillors collectively. (Chapter 9)

chief information officer (CIO)   One of the senior officials of the Treasury Board Secretariat that provides central agency leadership to a wide network of IT- and IM-related agencies and government-wide "communities of practice" that are defined by Treasury Board policies. The post was started in the Campbell Government in 1993. Every department and agency has its own CIO, usually a member of the senior management team and often involved in internal initiatives to renew services to the public and departmental administration. (Chapter 22)

chief of staff   A senior official in a minister's office who is accountable to the minister as a partisan political actor and whose role is to help the minister gain and maintain power. (Chapter 10)

choice of procedure   A form of dispute resolution, mostly used at the federal level, where the union is allowed to choose in advance of negotiation either the strike or arbitration route. (Chapter 19)

citizenship   Membership in a political community and participation in its affairs. In the first half of the twentieth century, such participation referred to equal political and civil rights; in the second half, it also implied equal entitlement to basic social and economic rights. (Chapter 26)

civil society   The network of voluntary organizations that stands between the state and families/individuals. (Chapter 26)

citizen-centred service (client-centred service)   An approach to service provision that focuses on the individual needs of clients. In government, it means that the government meets members of the public on their own terms (rather than the government's terms). (Chapter 22)

code of conduct (statement of values)   A set of principles meant to guide and support public servants in all professional activities, and to instill public confidence in government and government organizations. In general, codes of conduct help to preserve and promote values-based behaviour. (Chapter 5)

collective ministerial responsibility   See **collective responsibility.** (Chapter 5)

collective responsibility   Responsibilities held by the cabinet as a whole—to the monarch, to itself, and to the House. Responsibility to the House requires that ministers, in their capacity as members of the cabinet, are collectively responsible for the policies and management of the government as a whole. If the government (the cabinet) loses a vote of confidence in the legislature, it is required to resign. (Chapters 6, 7)

Commission of Inquiry into the Sponsorship Program and Advertising Activities (Gomery Commission)   Appointed by the Liberal government in February 2004, in response to the sponsorship scandal. The Commission found evidence of mismanagement, and urged clarification of government accountability. Its recommendations included founding an accounting officer regime, creating a Public Service Charter, providing an open and competitive procedure for the selection of deputy ministers and limiting their terms to no less than three years, increasing the resources of the Public Accounts Committee and encouraging members to stay within the Committee for the duration of the Parliament, and CEOs of Crown corporations be appointed on merit and, if necessary, dismissed by the board of directors of that corporation. The Commission's reports led to the formation of the Federal Accountability Act. (Chapter 25)

Committee of Senior Officials (COSO)   An advisory to the Clerk of the Privy Council charged with giving advice on matters related to deputy ministers' staffing policies, identifying candidates for DM appointment, overseeing the performance appraisal system for DMS, and reviewing the information on each prospective appointee. (Chapter 10)

common law   The body of rules and principles distilled from centuries of judge-made law in Britain and its former colonies. A common-law rule may be enshrined in, or overridden by, a statute passed by the legislature. (Chapter 4)

common service agency model   A model of centralized service provision in which one agency oversees a number of services that are of benefit to many other agencies. In government, this centralization of services is often based on policy or economic factors. (Chapter 22)

competitive markets   A rationale for the creation of arm's-length agencies (ABCs) that stresses the advantages of not having them impeded by cumbersome bureaucratic regulations and reporting obligations, and able to able to access specialized expertise. (Chapter 11)

competitiveness In the late twentieth century, with the emergence of the information economy, the national project emphasized competition in terms of lowering trade barriers, promoting overseas trade, and improving the capacity of workers and firms to be innovative and adapt to the global marketplace. (Chapter 15)

Comprehensive Economic and Trade Agreement (CETA) A 1598-page, 30-chapter agreement between the EU and Canada, deemed comprehensive because it covers virtually all sectors and aspects of Canada- EU trade in order to eliminate or reduce barriers. It covers both tariff and non-tariff barriers, includes innovative mechanisms for dispute settlement, and sets new standards in investment, government procurement, labour and environment, product standards, investment, professional certification, and many other areas of activity. (Chapter 27)

compliance-based ethical programs Governmental ethics regimes that involved adoption of codes of conduct, ethics codes, detailed regulations, and other rules often codified in legislation, largely in the 1970s and 1980s. These instruments outlined proper behaviour and often detailed the penalties for non-compliance. Designated officers, often lawyers or trained specialists, were tasked with interpreting and applying the rules. Governments often introduced these rules or legislation in response to scandals or public acknowledgement of wrongdoing as a means of reassuring the public as well as of ensuring the behaviour was corrected. (Chapter 20)

conditional grants Grants from the federal government to the provinces for various purposes throughout the twentieth century, which saw their greatest rate of expansion during the late 1950s and 1960s, when the appeal of federal support for national social programs was strong in most parts of the country, and rapid growth in the economy and federal revenues made relatively open-ended support of provincial programs seem affordable. (Chapter 2)

constitutional conventions Binding rules of the Constitution that are not set down in writing and that cannot be enforced by the courts. These conventions fill in the gaps in the formal Constitution in order to make it workable. Generally, they define the powers and obligations of government. (Chapters 5, 18)

contract funding (program-based funding) The primary method of financing of non-governmental entities and third-sector organizations through short-term, highly defined contracts with the state. (Chapter 26)

contract or agreement Generally, a means of forming a governmental organization; members of the organization must adhere to the duties set out in the contract or agreement.

Contribution Agreements Contractual financial agreements, many still in effect today, established to connect the federal government with individual First Nations

bureaucracies after the Department of Citizenship and Immigration devolved its program responsibilities to First Nations governments beginning in the 1950s. (Chapter 13)

control The central direction provided by central agencies and responsible ministers. In the case of Crown corporations, autonomy is to be applied to operational or day-to-day matters, control to matters of general policy. (Chapter 12)

corporate governance The term given to different ways governments have chosen to organize the governing of their public enterprises; there is no one standard model, but general trends are apparent. Governments may choose both the members and the president of the board of directors, and require strategic plans and annual reports. In theory the board chooses the CEO but it is very unlikely that such a choice would be made without consulting with at least the minister in charge. Moreover, major transactions are also authorized by the government as are important operations of borrowing. Strategic plans are also approved. Ministers do give letters of mission or give instructions. Measures to improve corporate governance may also include mandating accountability practices, "good practice" checklists, establishing Crown holding companies, reinforcing the number of independent members, creating committees to oversee ethic and governance issues as well as human resource management and audit, and expanding the mandates of their auditors general to evaluate the performance of the Crowns. (Chapter 12)

council–manager plan A system of municipal government in which the mayor's position became largely ceremonial, the council's jobs were to set broad policy and appoint a city manager, and the city manager's job was to do everything else. (Chapter 9)

court administrators Court administrative staff who manage court processes and smooth the flow of incoming work. (Chapter 8)

Crown corporation Crown agencies that have corporate status, generally established in order to provide for independence from external control over financial matters, personnel, and day-to-day activities. Crown corporations include parent Crown corporations, as defined in the Financial Administration Act, along with their wholly owned subsidiaries. (Chapters 1, 12)

decentralization Provision of public services by lower levels of government based on consideration of the benefits of sub-central accountability and interjurisdictional competition. (Chapters 2, 21)

decision-making The third stage in the policy process; in this stage, governments select a particular course of action or non-action. (Chapter 14)

delegated authority Governance authority delegated from the Crown. In relation to Aboriginal governance, it is an alternative to the broad, inherited, inherent right of self-government. (Chapter 13)

democratic values These values include rule of law, accountability, loyalty, and impartiality. (Chapter 5)

departmental corporation A type of organization defined in section 2 of the Financial Administration Act as a corporation. By virtue of section 3(1)(a.1) of the Act, such a corporation is required to be "established by an Act of Parliament" and to perform "administrative, research, supervisory, advisory, or regulatory functions of a governmental nature." (Chapter 1)

departmentalized (unaided) cabinet The form of cabinet that was common at both the federal and provincial levels between 1920 and 1960, coinciding with the rise of the modern administrative state. It featured government departments at the centre of government decision-making and relied on the input of departmental experts. The prime minister (or premier) was dominant, but ministers were relatively autonomous in producing policy, and there was very little government-wide planning. (Chapters 3, 6)

deputy ministers (DMs) Civil servants closest to the political level, DMs are just below ministers in the organizational hierarchy. Their role is to assist and advise the minister. The DM belongs to a category of discretionary appointments. (Chapter 10)

designated groups The four groups (Aboriginal people, persons with a disability, visible minorities, and women) for which employers must identify and remove barriers to employment under the requirements of the federal Employment Equity Act of 1995. (Chapter 19)

digital governance A term that evokes the pervasive nature of information technology in all aspects of public administration and the societal governance environment of which it is a part. The terms e-government and digital government are often used interchangeably. (Chapter 22)

dignified executive The formal executive, the holders of constitutional authority. (Chapter 6)

discretion The power, conferred by law, to choose among two or more outcomes in reaching a decision. Decision-makers in the executive branch are often vested with discretion in the exercise of their statutory powers, but they must exercise that discretion in conformity with the purpose of the statute. A grant of discretionary power is usually signalled by the word "may" in a statute, whereas the word "shall" reflects an absence of discretion. Example: s. 25(1) of Ontario's Law Society Act provides that "The benchers shall annually, at such time as the benchers may fix, elect an elected bencher as Treasurer." The word "shall" signifies that the benchers are required by law to elect a Treasurer every year, while "may" affords them the latitude to choose the time of year when the election will happen. (Chapter 4)

discretionary appointments Appointments at will by the Governor-in-Council who, by convention, acts on the recommendation of the prime minister. This category also includes ambassadors, CEOs of Crown corporations, and members of federal agencies, boards, and commissions. However, DMs (and ambassadors) are appointed for an undetermined period, whereas the others are appointed for a set period of time. (Chapter 10)

disintermediation Cutting out the middle man or woman (e.g., in government–public relations, the politician); a criticism sometimes made of e-consultations and electronic service delivery. (Chapter 22)

dispute resolution Various methods used to end disagreements between employers and employees (and their representatives) when collective bargaining is not successful. (Chapter 19)

dual accountability Dual accountability refers to a division of responsibilities between donors and recipients, and an associated framework of accountability for each party's responsibilities. In the Indigenous context, it is seen as a "dual" obligation to account to government for the use of funds, and to the community for the effectiveness of programs and services. It does not mean "shared," but rather obligations assigned to each party. (Chapter 13)

e-commerce Trade in which products and services are bought and sold via electronic networks. (Chapter 22)

economic liberalization Government's efforts to reduce barriers to international trade and market relations, often in the form of limiting or eliminating import tariffs. In North America, such efforts have led to the North American Free Trade Agreement. (Chapter 15)

economies of scale An argument for allocating some responsibilities to the national government, based on the reduced administrative and compliance costs of uniform services administered by one agency. (Chapter 2)

efficient executive The informal executive, those who hold political power. (Chapter 6)

e-government The use of new technologies, particularly information technology, to facilitate government operations. E-government operations include electronic service delivery, financial transactions, government–client relationship management, and data management. (Chapter 22)

electronic service delivery (ESD) The use of computer networks to provide public services to households and industry. (Chapter 22)

employment equity Legislation that requires an employer to ensure that its workforce is inclusive and representative of the four designated groups in Canada. (Chapters 19, 21)

equalization program. Equalization's essence is to top up the revenues of provinces with lower-yielding tax bases. Section 36(2) of the Constitution Act, 1982 commits Parliament and the Government of Canada to "the principle of making equalization payments to ensure that provincial governments have sufficient revenues to provide reasonably comparable levels of public services at reasonably comparable levels of taxation." (Chapter 2)

essential services Services that are most necessary to the functioning of society and for which there are not viable private-sector alternatives (e.g., police services, firefighting); they are usually distinguished from less essential services (e.g., municipal services, teaching). There is a slight tendency across Canadian jurisdictions to restrict the right to strike in the most essential services and to allow it in the less essential services. (Chapter 19)

Established Programs Financing (EPF)   Arrangements introduced in 1977 that replaced cost-sharing arrangements with a formal transfer of tax base ("tax points") and a cash transfer. These changes reduced federal subsidization and exposure to provincial spending decisions: no longer were the provinces collectively spending "50-cent dollars" on these programs. (Chapter 2)

ethical values   These values include integrity, honesty, and fairness. (Chapter 5)

ethics   Proper standards of conduct for a category of persons such as public servants or politicians, whereas morality normally refers to personal beliefs and standards of conduct. (Chapter 20)

executive dominance   A tendency common to both the EU and Canada, which has three manifestations. One is the central role of executives in constitution making/change. The second dimension is horizontal and pertains to a very high degree of executive control of decision-making. The third dimension is vertical and pertains to the manner in which executives enjoy direct and privileged access to both main levels of governance, and are therefore able to sideline parliaments. (Chapter 27)

exempt staff   Staff who are not part of the public service and are exempted from the rules in the Public Service Employment Act (PSEA) that govern hiring practices; political staff are officially designated as such. (Chapter 23)

expenditure budgeting   Budgeting that concerns the appropriations side of the budget. (Chapter 18)

external labour pool   The labour pool outside that of the designated groups in federal Employment equity legislation. This legislation requires that employers have the designated groups (women, visible minorities, Aboriginal persons, disabled persons) represented throughout the occupational structure of their organization in the same proportion as they are represented in the external labour pool. Such legislation exists only in the federal jurisdiction, the federal public service, and for firms that bid on federal contracts. (Chapter 19)

externalities   Public goods and services that generate benefits (or costs) beyond the localities where they are provided. (Chapter 2)

Federal Accountability Act   Passed in December 2006 in response to the sponsorship scandal and citizens' concerns over the government's ability to manage public services. The Act seeks to improve accountability across the federal government, at the levels of Parliament, departments, and agencies. So far, the Act has introduced a new Public Sector Integrity Commissioner, a Parliamentary Budget Officer, a Public Appointments Commission, an independent Commissioner of Lobbying, and a Conflict of Interest Code. It has also expanded the reach of the Access to Information Act, strengthened internal auditing regimes, and introduced the accounting officer model to federal public administration. (Chapter 7)

Federalism of Openness   see Open Federalism.

feminist institutionalism   An understanding of the internal workings of the state and their gendered impact, that is, how political institutions reflect, structure, and reinforce gendered patterns of power. (Chapter 21)

final-offer arbitration   A situation in dispute resolution in which the arbitrator must choose either the employer's offer or the union's offer; the arbitrator cannot choose a compromise between the two. (Chapter 19)

financial control   Part of a threefold function of control, management, and planning and policy choice that has formed the basis of a popular typology for studying government budgeting for 50 years. According to this approach, any budget system must, and does in some way, address the three functions of the control of spending and taxing, the management of ongoing program activities, and the planning of policy and setting of priorities. (Chapter 18)

financial crisis   In modern times usually refers to the financial crisis that struck in 2008. The crisis started in the US housing market but spread worldwide. After the collapse of Lehman Brothers in September 2008, governments undertook massive capital interventions to prevent financial markets from completely collapsing, in many instances accumulating massive public debts. It was at this stage, when the crisis turned from a financial crisis to a public debt crisis, that it became clear that the repercussions would be far more profound for the European Union than for instance in the United States, where the crisis originated. (Chapter 27)

fourth estate   The name sometimes given to professional political journalists, implying that the Parliamentary Press Gallery and its provincial cousins are an honorary branch of government, with the executive, legislative and judicial branches being the three main ones. (Chapter 25)

frameworks   See spending power frameworks.

functions of the legislature   The contributions to and the effect upon the political system made by Parliament. Some functions are formally recognized or explicit, whereas others are implicit. The functions include policy-making functions, representational functions, and maintenance functions. (Chapter 7)

garbage-can model   A model in which public policy-making is viewed as an inherently irrational process in which decision-makers randomly associate problems with solutions. Actors choose problems from the "garbage," then search for a solution. Solutions are then formed independent from problem analysis, often by individuals who were not involved in identifying the problem, and solutions are often influenced by personal interests and biases. (Chapter 14)

gatekeepers   The traditional role played by journalists and news editors, who choose what stories to pursue, which ones should lead the news, how much attention to pay to them, who to interview, what editorial angle to apply, and when to dig deeper. Traditionally, elites within the mainstream media exercised considerable influence over the flow of information between government and citizens, a power that is waning in the digital age, where topics that are trending in social media command attention, and news operations are chronically under-resourced. (Chapter 25)

general jurisdiction trial courts   (aka courts of general jurisdiction): See superior and inferior courts. (Chapter 8)

gender-based policy analysis (GBA)   A systematic process for assessing the gender impact of all public programs and policies, intended to address gender as a socially relevant variable in policy-making. It focuses on all policies, even (or especially) those that are not obviously gendered, such as climate change and trade policy. (Chapter 21)

gender bias task force   Chaired by retired Supreme Court Justice Bertha Wilson, a task force that produced an important and controversial report that spurred the development of judicial education programs on this and related topics. (Chapter 8)

gender order   The organization of gender relations that prevails in a particular place and time, including the social and cultural constructions of gender, and the institutionalization of power relations. (Chapter 21)

gender regime   A particular configuration of gender relations in a given place and time. (Chapter 21)

gendering   Making gender differences visible and exposing gender biases; in particular, it draws our attention to the ways that women's inequality gets reproduced and how both women's and men's lives are restricted by socially constructed gender roles. It is particularly oriented towards change in governmental processes and policies. (Chapter 21)

Great Depression   The period of economic crisis from 1929 to 1939, caused by a confluence of many factors. The economic collapse was unparalleled in its severity, and unemployment in Canada increased from 3 per cent in 1929 to 23 per cent in 1933. Governments differed in their policy responses, with Canada taking a less interventionist approach than the United States. (Chapter 15)

Governor General   The representative of the Queen. (Chapter 16)

hard budget constraints   In the context of globalized markets, constraints on government taxation and expenditure decisions rooted in international capital markets and bond ratings. (Chapter 2)

home rule   A set of provisions in US state constitutions that generally prevents the state legislature from interfering with local control over municipal structures and boundaries. (Chapter 9)

horizontal governance   The aim of making government work better across internal and external boundaries, usually under banners such as horizontal management, horizontal policy, joined-up or seamless government, collaborative government, holistic government, and whole-of-government approaches. (Chapter 24)

human rights   The right of individuals and groups to not be adversely affected by discrimination based on characteristics such as age, gender, race, or religion.

image management   Involves meticulous efforts by PR personnel to influence perceptions of a public figure. Political strategists are highly aware that a public image that is aligned with voter priorities strengthens a leader's power. A favourable image influences the ability to advance public policies, and makes a difference on election day; conversely, an unfavourable image will derail a political agenda and hasten the end of a political actor's time in office. For public servants, image management involves coordinating the corporate identity of the government and its units as an institution. (Chapter 25)

impugned   A legal synonym for "challenged," e.g., "the law was impugned as a violation of the Charter." (Chapter 4)

incremental model   A model in which policy-making is viewed as a practical exercise concerned with solving problems through trial-and-error processes (often based only on familiar alternatives) rather than through the comprehensive evaluation of all solutions. (Chapter 14)

independent regulatory agency   A public agency enjoying a certain amount of autonomy from government to allow it to make and enforce regulations to protect public safety or well-being. (Chapter 11)

Indian   A person registered, or entitled to be registered, in accordance with the Indian Act. One of three Aboriginal groups recognized as in the Constitution Act, 1982, Indians are often differentiated according to three categories: status Indians, non-status Indians, and treaty Indians. (Chapter 13)

Indian Act reform   Four interrelated pieces of legislation first introduced in the 2001 Speech from the Throne when the federal government committed to "strengthening its relationship with Aboriginal People." In addition to the First Nations Governance Act (Bill C-61, later reintroduced as Bill C-7), this group of reforms included the Specific Claims Legislation Act (Bill C-6), the Land Management Act (Bill C-49), and the First Nations Fiscal and Statistical Management Act (Bill C-19). These bills were designed to replace parts of the Indian Act, as an alternative to reforming the entire Act.

individual ministerial responsibility   See **ministerial responsibility**. (Chapters 5, 6)

information   A hierarchy of data (knowledge) in which each level builds on the one(s) below it. (Chapter 22)

information management (IM)   Refers to the various methodologies that have emerged for organizing and using information, especially in the environment created by IT. IT and IM are inextricably linked, but they do represent distinct starting points in the art and science of public administration. (Chapter 22)

information subsidies   The packaging of information so that it can be easily reused with maximum economic efficiency; typical information subsidies involve things like news releases, Q&As, backgrounders, speeches, and social media posts including digital photos and video. (Chapter 25)

information technology (IT)   Computer-mediated technologies that facilitate the gathering, storage, processing, analysis, and transmission of information. (Chapter 22)

information and communications technologies (ICTs)   See information technology.

inherent jurisdiction: The Superior Court in each province retains the residual jurisdiction of the British Crown courts prior to Confederation (see sections 96 and 129 of the Constitution Act, 1867). The Superior Court may hear and decide any case that has not been expressly assigned to a different court by an act of Parliament (e.g., s. 18(1) of the Federal Courts Act) or that province's legislature. (Chapter 4)

inherent right of self-government   A broad, inherited right not subject to diminution by the Crown, analogous to natural law in the Western liberal tradition; usually distinguished from the weaker alternative: governance through delegated powers.

inside initiation   An agenda-setting style whereby influential groups with special access to decision-makers initiate a policy, presenting both a problem and a solution. Often, these groups want to avoid public discussion and criticism, and the public is not involved in the process. (Chapter 14)

institutionalized cabinet   The form of cabinet that tended to predominate after 1960; it featured formal cabinet structures, established central agencies, and implemented new budgeting and management techniques that emphasized shared knowledge, collegial decision-making, and the formation of government-wide priorities. (Chapters 3, 5, 6,)

integrated justice   A concept based on the notion of seamless automated (electronic) processes with a single point of entry for data in criminal and civil cases. (Chapter 8)

integrity   Ethics and integrity have different connotations. European scholars tend to prefer using integrity because it implies competence, propriety, and a certain mindset which American scholars equate with professionalism. In contrast, Americans often associate ethics with "doing right or good" or the consequences of policy, which implies a certain activism that Europeans do not tend to associate with values inherent in the operation of government. Consistent with this distinction, in Canada the mandate of the ethics and conflict of interest commissioner doesn't include whistle-blowing, a form of "doing right or good." That area lies within the Integrity Commissioner's mandate. (Chapter 20)

intergovernmental transfers   Financial and other transfers arising from the fact that amounts raised and spent by different levels of government in Canada have never coincided since Confederation: the federal government has always raised more, and provincial, territorial, and local governments less, than required for their own programs. (Chapter 2)

intersectional policy analysis   Analysis whose goal is to identify and address the way multiple forces work together and interact to reinforce conditions of inequality and social exclusion and to view women's lives in holistic ways. (Chapter 21)

issues management   The result of unplanned media relations, it involves the firefighting of external events, little time to think clearly, the pushing back of planned announcements, and the assignment of designated spokespersons to handle the storm of media enquiries, buying time for strategists to calculate their next move. (Chapter 25)

judicial administrative independence (administrative independence)   Freedom of functioning of courts' administration that reflects the unique role of the courts within a traditional cabinet system. One manifestation would be to shift parts of the court administrative staff to a separate judicial administration budget controlled by the judges. (Chapter 8)

judicial impartiality   The stipulation that a judge is bound to decide only on the relevant law and facts presented in court. (Chapter 8)

judicial independence   The ability of the individual judge to perform his or her adjudicative function, whether in court or in chambers, free from external interference.

judicial review   The power of courts to review tribunal decisions and to grant remedies in the nature of certiorari, prohibition, and mandamus. Judicial review "is directed at the legality, reasonableness, and fairness of the procedures employed and actions taken by government decision makers. It is designed to enforce the rule of law and adherence to the Constitution. Its overall objective is good governance" (*Canada (Attorney General) v TeleZone Inc*, 2010 SCC 62, [2010] 3 SCR 585 at para 24 [*Telezone*]). This supervisory role is part of the inherent jurisdiction of the Superior Courts. (Chapter 4)

jurisdiction   The core concept in administrative law. Jurisdiction refers to the powers that may lawfully be exercised by a particular institution or government official in a specific set of circumstances. A decision-maker derives his or her jurisdiction from the Constitution and/or the particular statutes and regulations applicable to his or her position within the executive branch of government. (Chapter 4)

Keynesian consensus   The post-war agreement within many Western nations, including Canada, to support the system of economics proposed by John Maynard Keynes. Keynes had argued that governments should be involved in promoting the economy by creating public policies aimed at increasing aggregate consumer demand in times of economic downturn, in an effort to stimulate the economy. (Chapter 3)

Keynesian welfare state   A public-policy organization, developed out of Keynesian economics, that embraces the goal of full employment and a comprehensive social safety net for those unable to achieve self-sufficiency in the market economy. (Chapter 26)

lesson-drawing   Policy-makers drawing lessons from past uses of policy instruments. (Chapter 14)

limited jurisdiction trial courts (courts of limited jurisdiction)   See superior and inferior courts. (Chapter 8)

local government   A broad term that encompasses both municipalities and special-purpose bodies. (Chapter 9)

machinery of government The general activity of organizational design and allocating responsibilities and functions between ministers to ensure that the cabinet and the government are structured in the best way. (Chapter 16)

macro budgeting Budgeting dealing with big issues and impacts. In the economics of budgeting, macro budgeting is synonymous with stabilization policy and the grand Keynesian-monetarist debate of recent decades, including the debate about deficits and surpluses. In political science, macro budgeting refers, in part, to such topics as fiscal federalism and the connection between budgets and the electoral cycle. In organizational and managerial studies, macro budgeting is equated with the sequence of steps leading to, variously, a statement of priorities, the budget speech, and the tabling and passage of the financial plans. (Chapter 18)

Magistrate's Court The court at the lowest level of the judicial hierarchy for much of Canadian history until the middle of the twentieth century; also referred to as inferior courts. Magistrates were usually non-lawyers, serving on a part-time basis at the pleasure of the government. (Chapter 8)

management orientation Part of a threefold function of control, management, and planning and policy choice that has formed the basis of a popular typology for studying government budgeting for 50 years (Schick 1966). According to this approach, any budget system must, and does in some way, address the three functions of the control of spending and taxing, the management of ongoing program activities, and the planning of policy and setting of priorities. (Chapter 18)

mandate letters A performance management tool that a prime minister employs in regard to ministers. These letters form the accountability accord for ministers, outlining the overall government priorities, the minister's portfolio responsibilities, and specific personal goals for the minister. (Chapter 16)

market-oriented journalism Refers to the financial incentive to present information in a dramatic manner with story arcs due to the fact that the amount that advertisers pay is related to the size of the audience; consequently, the news media has a disincentive to report on the inner workings of government, or public policy minutia. Instead, it delivers infotainment, so that news about government and politics is styled to drum up interest among the uninterested. (Chapter 25)

marketization The application of market criteria to allocate public resources and also to measure the efficiency of public service producers and suppliers. The goal is reduced cost and increased quality of service resulting from competition between potential producers. (Chapter 26)

media logic The idea that organizations and individuals change their behaviour in response to how the media operates. (Chapter 25)

mediation The use of professional mediators (or negotiators) not immediately associated with disputing parties to assist in coming to a resolution. In civil society, it is exemplified in such measures as family counselling and workplace committees. (Chapters 8, 26)

memorandum to cabinet (MC) A formal public service document used to seek cabinet approval of a new policy initiative. (Chapter 23)

merit Worth, or deserving of reward. In employment, it refers to hiring the individual who best meets job requirements. This principle has driven hiring processes in the federal government since 1918, and it has been supplemented in the late twentieth century by considerations of representativeness as a subset of merit. (Chapter 5)

merit principle Prior to 2005, merit was an absolute value: the PSEA required that the Public Service Commission establish a list of all qualified candidates for a position (called an eligibility list) *and* rank those candidates in order of merit. The PSC would then appoint the most qualified candidate to the position; if he or she declined (or left the position shortly thereafter), the PSC would appoint the next most qualified candidate, and so on. The PSEA was amended in 2005 to change merit from an absolute to a relative value. Now, an appointment is consistent with the merit principle so long as the candidate is qualified for the position. (Chapter 1)

merit system The systems set up by federal and provincial governments to promote merit and combat patronage in government institutions. (Chapter 5)

mezzo budgeting Budgeting that deals with middle-level matters, that is, those between macro and micro budgeting. It is a level growing in importance. (Chapter 18)

micro budgeting Budgeting that deals with smaller issues and impacts. In the economics of budgeting, micro budgeting is seemingly everything else other than issues of stabilization policy and Keynesian-monetarist debates. In political science, the bargaining between spenders and guardians inside the administrative state is a critical aspect of micro budgeting. In organizational studies, micro budgeting embraces the things that go on within departments and other public agencies as well as such activities as auditing and the setting and collection of user fees. (Chapter 18)

microtargeting Sometimes known as narrowcasting or database marketing, microtargeting is imported from commerce and the campaign trail and involves data analytics, which with respect to political communication is the examination of quantitative data to segment audiences and isolate messages that are targeted at narrow groups rather than the population as a whole. (Chapter 25)

ministerial responsibility The expression of accountability in the political realm. Until the latter part of the twentieth century, a minister was responsible (culpable) for *every* action that took place in his or her department. The modern realist version of the doctrine recognizes a distinction between official acts of which the minister can reasonably be expected to be aware, and those that the minister could not have known about. The minister may be held culpable for failing to take appropriate corrective action in the event he or she learns of an illegal or inappropriate act. A minister may be asked to resign in certain cases: misleading Parliament, authorizing unreasonable use of executive power, or engaging in immoral conduct unbecoming to a minister of the Crown. (Chapter 7)

ministers Members of cabinet, usually given the direction of a governmental department; neither ministers nor the cabinet are not mentioned in the Constitution, but exist by virtue of convention and, in the case of ministers, statute.

Minister's Office (MO) The political office of ministers of the Crown. These are typically staffed by appointed political staffs but may feature public servants seconded or on assignment from the department. (Chapters 23, 25)

minority government A government that lacks a majority of the seats in the House of Commons. There was, for example, over the 2004 to 2011 period in Canadian federal politics, and for the first time in a quarter century, a succession of minority governments in Ottawa: The Liberal minority government of Paul Martin (2004–6) and the Conservative minority governments of Stephen Harper (2006–8 and 2008–11). In minority government situations, federal budgeting is influenced by the tactics and demands of parliamentary parties and their leaders. (Chapter 18)

mixed social economy model A model, prevalent in the Keynesian welfare state, for social service provision in which services are delivered through a combination of state and privately run and privately administered programs. (Chapter 26)

mobilization An agenda-setting style whereby decision-makers try to move an issue from a formal, or governmental, agenda to a public agenda. Government then tries to enlist support for the issue among the general public. (Chapter 14)

model employer An ideal employer; a quality that is expected from governments because, while they are a major employer, they also have the power to set collective bargaining rules. (Chapter 19)

morality Morality normally refers to personal beliefs and standards of conduct whereas ethics more appropriately refers to proper standards of conduct for a category of persons such as public servants or politicians. This is an important distinction for public office holders to bear in mind because it can help an individual to understand and accept why she or he may be expected to act in a certain way as an office holder that is contrary to the way she or he would normally act in private life. (Chapter 20)

multi-door courthouse Alternatives to court adjudication, such as arbitration and mediation. (Chapter 8)

multilateral bargaining A situation, participants in the bargaining process know that it is ultimately impossible for management to remain united. (Chapter 9)

municipality A body, governed by elected officials, that is responsible for various government functions and activities at the local level. (Chapter 9)

National Joint Council (NJC) Created in 1944, the NJC is a council of public service unions and the various employers (including Treasury Board), tasked with addressing issues that ought to be dealt with similarly across the public service instead of permitting distinctions between bargaining units. (Chapter 1)

neo-liberalism An ideological approach to governing and public administration that supports freedom of the market and of the individual. Developed in response to a perceived government failure, neo-liberalism encourages a reduced role of the state in economic and social domains, deregulation of labour and financial markets, and the elimination of trade barriers. (Chapter 26)

new political governance (NPG) A theory put forward by Peter Aucoin during the Harper era which holds that institutional conditions in modern systems, particularly in Canada, weaken the merit-based, professional public service. The theory encapsulates concepts like permanent campaigning, the empowerment of political staff, loyalty of executives appointed to the prime minister's circle, and public servants who are drawn into political activities. (Chapters 25 and 26)

new public management (NPM) A diverse group of ideas and initiatives, originating in the late 1980s and early 1990s, that were inspired by private-sector values; these ideas were increasingly popular in governments who sought to lower costs, provide better service, contain deficits, and incorporate new technologies. These precepts were embedded in earlier post-war reports and reforms but were not as influential or integrated as in the newer NPM literature. (Chapters 20, 26)

new social order The name given in 1945 to the increased federal role in society and economy. The concept was heavily influenced by British intellectuals such as Keynes, who argued that governments could have avoided the worst effects of the Depression by taking steps (in the form of direct government expenditures, social programs) to promote public demand for goods and services. The shift to the new order was not immediate, but over the next quarter century it was reflected in programs such as the family allowance program, employment insurance, and government-based pension plans, all of which dramatically increased the amount of money the federal government paid directly to citizens. (Chapter 15)

new values These values include service, innovation, quality, and teamwork. Most of the new values fall into the category of professional values. (Chapter 5)

news management The multifaceted ways that PR practitioners seek to encourage positive media coverage, ranging from setting the ground rules of an interview to staying on message. (Chapter 25)

non-partisan appointment Processes that rely on some form of arm's-length merit criteria rather than political or party considerations. One example is that of Alberta, whose public agencies are staffed after a process of public advertising and seeking of diversity and whose appointments have term limits and include succession plans. (Chapter 11)

non-status Indian An Indian not registered as an Indian under the Indian Act and therefore not entitled to the same rights and benefits available to status Indians. Non-status Indians consider themselves Indians or members of a First Nation, but are not legally recognized as Indians because they are unable to prove their status, they have lost their status rights, or they have experienced discriminatory practices. (Chapter 13)

Office of the Auditor General See Auditor General of Canada.

Office of the Information Commissioner An office of Parliament that deals with complaints from those alleging denial of rights under the Access to Information Act; officers use statutory investigative and mediation powers, in the fashion of an ombudsman. (Chapter 7)

Office of the Privacy Commissioner An office of Parliament that investigates complaints, conducting audits and pursuing court action, under the Privacy Act and the Personal Information Protection and Electronic Documents Act (PIPEDA). (Chapter 7)

Officers of Parliament Neutral officials independent from the executive government who perform tasks essential to the operation of Parliament, or in the public interest. They report directly to Parliament and not to the executive, and both Houses are involved in some fashion in their appointment. In recent years, their numbers and independence has increased. Currently, the Officers of Parliament are the Auditor General (established in 1868), the Chief Electoral Officer (1920), the Official Languages Commissioner (1970), the Privacy Commissioner (1983), the Access to Information Commissioner (1983), the Conflict of Interest and Ethics Commissioner (2007), the Public Sector Integrity Commissioner (2007), and the Commissioner of Lobbying (2008). Officers of the Legislature are the provincial counterparts. (Chapter 7)

open data See **open government**. (Chapter 22)

Open Federalism (Federalism of Openness) In Canada, the Harper Conservative Party's approach to federalism and in particular the federal spending power, which emphasized accountability and an increased voice for provinces/territories in federal decision-making that affects their jurisdictions. This structure was first discussed at the Conservative Party's founding conference in 2005, and it was most clearly enunciated in the 2007 federal budget. (Chapter 3)

open government A concept that government information should be automatically available to citizens—the conceptual background for the federal government's "open government portal" (www.open.canada.ca) providing an interface for "open data," a repository of datasets that Canadians can analyze themselves; "open information," a clearinghouse for digital records, including the results of completed access to information requests and

government contracts exceeding $10 000; and for "open dialogue," a pathway to connect citizens with others who share an interest in open government. (Chapters 22, 25)

open information See **open government**. (Chapter 22)

outside initiation An agenda-setting style whereby a group outside the government articulates a grievance and tries to gain support from other groups in the population in order to create pressure on decision-makers to force the issue onto the formal agenda. The public is often involved in the process. (Chapter 14)

Parliament The federal legislative power "consisting of the Queen, an Upper House styled the Senate, and the House of Commons" (section 17 of the Constitution Act, 1867). (Chapter 7)

Parliamentary Budget Officer An officer who provides independent analysis of parliamentary financial and economy-related matters; often provides financial estimates for proposed actions. (Chapters 7, 10)

partisan political activity Activities held by, or on behalf of, registered political parties. (Chapter 5)

partnerships A formal arrangement in which government agrees to provide services in partnership with other parties where each contributes resources and shares risks and rewards. (Chapter 26)

patronage The practice of appointing and promoting public servants on the basis of partisan political considerations rather than of merit. By the early 1960s such appointments had been largely eliminated from the federal government, but a few, some say functionally useful, patronage appointments remain (e.g., ministerial staff and Governor-in-Council appointments, although these are outside the merit-based public service). (Chapter 5)

pattern bargaining The tendency to have key settlements emulated across similar groups in the public sector, usually driven by considerations of comparability. Today, considerations of local conditions and the employers' ability to pay have become more prominent than pattern bargaining in dispute settlement. (Chapter 19)

pay equity The comparable-worth guideline, embedded in legislation, that requires equal pay for predominately female jobs of equal value to predominately male jobs; equivalent to the US term "comparable worth." (Chapter 21)

payments to individuals and institutions Payments made by the deferral government to individuals and institutions (usually in the form of grants) in areas related to matters of provincial jurisdiction. (Chapter 3)

people values Primarily, values that involve caring and compassion for others on an individual level. (Chapter 5)

performance measurement and reporting An aspect of public-sector reform that is meant to assist Parliament in its scrutiny function and lead to a sustained focus on substantive policy outcomes. Annually, hundreds of reports on plans and performance are tabled in Parliament, placing a strain on members' ability to absorb and make practical use of all the information. (Chapter 7)

permanent campaigning The concept that electioneering-style practices that characterize an official election campaign are carried over into governance, with politicians and government communicators drawn into a state of constant communication. (Chapter 25)

policy community A type of policy subsystem, generally composed of a relatively large set of actors (including government policy-makers, representatives of non-governmental organizations, members of the media, academics, and members of the general public) with some knowledge of the policy issue in question. (Chapter 14)

policy cycle The stages in policy development, also called policy stages, or the stagist approach. A policy cycle generally involves agenda-setting, policy formulation, decision-making, policy implementation, and policy evaluation. (Chapter 14)

policy evaluation The fifth stage in the policy process; in this stage, both state and societal actors monitoring the results of policies, often leading to the reconceptualization of policy problems and solutions. (Chapter 14)

policy diffusion The spreading of a policy innovation or practice or institutional form from one jurisdiction to another. (Chapter 11)

policy formulation The second stage in the policy process; in this stage, policy options are developed within government, and infeasible options are excluded. (Chapter 14)

policy implementation The fourth stage in the policy process; in this stage, government puts decisions into effect. (Chapters 12, 14)

policy learning The notion that policy actors can learn from the formal and informal evaluation of policies in which they are engaged; this learning often leads actors to modify their positions on issues of policy. (Chapter 14)

policy network A type of policy subsystem, generally composed of fewer actors than in a policy community. Actors are involved with formal government institutions, and they must be knowledgeable about policy areas. Generally, members of the network have established familiar patterns for interaction within the group. (Chapter 14)

policy process Variously interpreted, but usually described as the notion of the policy process as an ongoing cycle in which policies are adapted into new forms. (Chapter 14)

policy style The methods government uses to create and implement policies. These methods can vary widely between governments, over time, and between states. (Chapter 14)

policy subsystem A group of policy actors involved in policy formulation; the relevant policy actors are restricted to those who not only have an opinion on a subject but also have some level of knowledge of the subject area. (Chapter 14)

political communication The use of communication tools by government for political purposes, such as advertising and social media as well as other communication tools not in the public domain, such as direct marketing (mailings, telemarketing, email communication, and texting that reach the recipient without others' knowledge). Some tools are hidden in plain sight. The government is constantly in the news, featuring spokespersons and often staged events. (Chapter 25)

political neutrality The convention that prohibits public servants from engaging in activities that impair or seem to impair their impartiality or the impartiality of the public service as a whole (e.g., partisan political activities). In Canada, the courts have noted that restricting political activities of all public servants is contrary to the *Canadian* **Charter of Rights and Freedoms.** Consequently, the Public Service Employment Act permits political activities by public servants, as long as their involvement does not affect their impartiality. (Chapter 5)

political rights for public servants In Canada, the rights to vote in elections, to contribute to political parties, to canvass on behalf of a political party or political cause, to express political opinions, and to be nominated for and run for public office. (Chapter 5)

politics–administration dichotomy Originally developed to oppose the spoils system and to promote a more professional business-like public service, this idea holds that administrative areas of government have more in common with business practices (technical implementation) than with political activities (the development of laws, policies, and public values). (Chapter 5)

Prime Minister's Office A partisan-oriented central agency whose authority derives from the prerogatives of the prime minister. Staffed by officials sympathetic to the party in power, the Office engages in political intelligence-gathering; organizes the prime minister's media relations, correspondence, and timetable; and acts as the liaison between party, government, and Parliament. It is the prime minister's equivalent of a ministerial office. Staff support the PM as leader of the political party and head of government. (Chapters 23, 25)

prime minister–centred cabinet A theory of cabinet government that holds that the Canadian cabinet has become marginalized in a context that could only be characterized as a kind of [presumably medieval] court government. The prime minister and his most trusted courtiers, carefully selected ministers, and senior civil servants rule, and they have more power in a court-style government than they do when formal policy- and decision-making processes tied to cabinet decision-making are respected. [See also departmentalized cabinet, institutionalized cabinet] (Chapter 6)

Privacy Act An Act passed in 1983 that gives citizens the right to see government documents that contain information about themselves and restricts access to documents that contain other people's personal information. The Act also restricts government agencies from collecting personal information that is not essential to their operations, limits the ability of agencies to share personal information about citizens, and forces agencies to disclose to citizens the reason for collecting personal information. (Chapter 22)

privative clause   A statutory provision denying a right to appeal a tribunal decision to the Superior Court. For example, s. 31(3) of Ontario's Workplace Safety and Insurance Act, 1997 states that "A decision of the Appeals Tribunal under this section is final and is not open to question or review in a court." The inclusion of a privative clause in an enabling statute is interpreted as a signal of the legislature's intent to give the final word to that tribunal. However, the legislature cannot abolish the inherent jurisdiction of the Superior Courts to grant a remedy on judicial review (e.g. an order of certiorari setting aside an unreasonable or incorrect decision). (Chapter 4)

privatization   The selling of government-owned enterprises, assets, or controlling interests to the private sector. There have been waves of privatization at various periods in Canadian history, for example the post-World War II divesting of Crown corporations. (Chapters 12, 15, 19)

Privy Council Office   A non-partisan central agency that serves as the secretariat for cabinet and its committees, and for coordinating policy development for the Government of Canada. It is also responsible for monitoring government priorities and for liaising between cabinet and department and agencies. It is led by the Clerk of the Privy Council, who is also designated as Secretary of Cabinet and Head of the Public Service. (Chapter 25)

procedural fairness   (aka natural justice):   A set of common-law principles governing the exercise of decision-making power in administrative law. (Chapter 4)

procedural instruments   Policy instruments associated with the information and decision-making processes rather than the substance of policy. They support government aims and initiatives by managing state–societal interactions. They indirectly influence the number or nature of actors in the policy subsystems that policy-makers face. Such procedural instruments as government–NGO partnerships, public advisory commissions, roundtables, and information dissemination provide government with means to steer policy processes in its preferred directions by manipulating policy actors and their interrelationships. (Chapter 14)

procedural representation   (formal representation) Posits that elected legislatures and the public service should mirror, or be a microcosm of, society. Procedural representation increases the likelihood, but does not guarantee, that those represented, for example women, will be able to advance a feminist policy agenda. (Chapter 21)

professional values   These values include efficiency, effectiveness, quality, service, innovation, teamwork, and accountability. (Chapter 5)

Program Review   A process begun in 1994 under the Liberal government to reduce the federal deficit. Each department had to meet strict expenditure reduction targets ranging from 20 per cent to as much as 50 per cent over three years. Ministers submitted plans for rethinking or eliminating programs (including alternative service delivery) and decisions were announced in the February 1995 Budget. The Program Review has been hailed as a

political and fiscal success by some, and an unfortunate exercise in downloading of federal responsibilities by others. (Chapter 24)

province-building   The willingness of the provinces to maintain some autonomy and or control vis-à-vis Ottawa. Crown corporations remain flexible instruments over which provinces can exercise more substantial control than, say, fiscal policy and subsidies, which they share with Ottawa, or monetary policy, over which they have no control whatsoever. The province-building motive provides a disincentive for provinces to privatize Crowns. (Chapter 12)

Provincial Courts   Magistrate's Courts were transformed into Provincial Courts, beginning in Quebec and Ontario in the 1960s, and over the next two decades in every province. Their work today is primarily in criminal matters, particularly over young offenders, but some have been given expanded jurisdiction in civil matters and in family law. (Chapter 8)

provincial legislatures   The provincial analogue of the federal Parliament, consisting of the legislative assembly and the Queen. Provincial legislatures usually demonstrate more limited staff resources, shorter legislative sessions, less active committee systems, and more executive (cabinet) domination. (Chapter 7)

pseudo-events   Media events that are staged explicitly for the purposes of optimizing favourable news coverage, coordinated by government PR personnel to maximize the likelihood of reproduction by others, ideally in the mainstream media, which they hope will avoid the critical filter of professional journalism. (Chapter 25)

public choice   a body of theory that holds that competition among jurisdictions can protect citizens from people in, and interest groups working through, government who seek to benefit themselves. (Chapter 2)

public comment   In general, evaluations (particularly of a political nature), positive or negative, made in public. In Canada, public servants have been traditionally prohibited from engaging in public comment on government policies, parties, or personalities, aside from discussions of a technical or scientific nature or to explain already-established governmental procedures and policies. Nevertheless, as with political activity, the trend is in the direction of extending the permissible rights of public servants to engage in public comment. (Chapter 5)

public entrepreneurship   The development of conditions to allow private-sector–type entrepreneurship to flourish in the public sector. The relative autonomy of the state and state capacity are two conditions that offer the potential for public entrepreneurship. The complexity of the modern state apparatus has made possible the development of entrepreneurs who have taken advantage of the slack available to develop new organizations, new services, new processes. The British parliamentary tradition has been viewed as a more difficult setting for public entrepreneurship than the American republican system. (Chapter 12)

public/private divide   Refers to the two spheres of experience and the shifting parameters society holds about the appropriate locus of need fulfilment. Those needs in our lives that are believed appropriate for the state to provide are considered the public sphere. The private sphere generally includes the family and the market. (Chapter 21)

public–private partnerships (P3s)   Governments and firms working in collaboration motivated to deliver projects. In the words of Garvin and Bosso (2008), "A P3 is a long-term contractual arrangement between the public and private sectors where mutual benefits are sought and where ultimately (a) the private sector provides management and operating services and/or (b) puts private finance at risk." (Chapters 9, 17)

public-sector ethics   Some approaches to this concept might endorse certain values, but the evolving nature of ethics requires them to be defined broadly. For example, in their work, Ian Greene and David Shugarman root their understanding of ethical government in the democratic principle of mutual respect (equality + respect) incorporating the five principles of social equality, deference to the majority, minority rights, freedom, and integrity. Many authors are not as specific about particular principles but anchor ethics in democratic values more broadly defined, which avoids the appearance of an ideological bias in interpreting ethical actions. In this way, ethics are similar to laws, which also set standards for good behaviour and right decisions. Laws and ethics operate together to sanction acceptable behaviour and decisions. (Chapter 20)

Public Servants Disclosure Protection Act   Also known as the "whistle-blower act," this accountability act provides protection for public servants who disclose wrongdoing within government. The Act requires public servants to follow established procedures in order to secure the handling of sensitive information. In order to obtain protection, whistle-blowers must make their disclosure to the Commissioner, must disclose no more information than reasonably necessary, and must not violate confidences of cabinet.

Public Servants Disclosure Protection Tribunal   A board, established by the Federal Accountability Act, that is charged with protecting public servants who disclose government wrongdoings by ordering disciplinary actions against the party or parties responsible for any unfair suffering the public servant has faced as a result of his or her disclosure. (Chapter 10)

public service   A multifaceted universe of organizations that can be formed to accomplish almost any purpose or objective the government wishes to achieve, subject always to the constitutional limitations imposed by the Constitution Act, 1867 and to the Charter of Rights and Freedoms. (Chapter 7)

public-service anonymity   The requirement of public servants to provide confidential advice to ministers and to avoid the public spotlight and public attention. (Chapter 5)

public-service ethics   Commonly held value standards under which public servants are expected to operate. In general, ethics refers to questions of right and wrong (e.g., questions of integrity). (Chapter 5)

public-service values   These values involve enduring social, cultural, and ideological beliefs that influence the choices of public servants. (Chapter 5)

quasi-judicial administrative tribunals   Committees to which various types of municipal decisions, usually relating to land use, can be appealed. (Chapter 9)

rational model   A model in which policy-making is viewed as a systematic method in which policy-makers establish a goal, explore alternative strategies for achieving the goal, predict the consequences and likelihood of each alternative, and then choose the option with the most benefits and the least risks. (Chapter 14)

registrars   administrative court staff who deal with the day-to-day movement of cases and courtroom proceedings (Chapter 8)

regulations   (aka delegated or subordinate legislation) A set of detailed provisions designed to implement a specific statute, and issued pursuant to a regulation-making power set out in that statute. For example, s. 48(1) of the Ontario Human Rights Code empowers the Lieutenant Governor-in-Council to make regulations on certain specified subjects. The legislature may also delegate the power to make regulations to an individual minister, or to a governmental or non-governmental agency tasked with regulating a particular field of activity. Section 95(1) of Ontario's Health Professions Procedural Code (appended to the Regulated Health Professions Act) provides that "Subject to the approval of the Lieutenant Governor in Council and with prior review of the Minister," the Council of a medical College (e.g., the College of Physicians and Surgeons or the College of Dentistry) may make regulations on matters requiring medical expertise, such as prescribing standards and qualifications for the issue of certificates of registration. (Chapter 4)

Report of the Royal Commission on Aboriginal Peoples (RCAP Report)   The 1996 Report of the Royal Commission on Aboriginal Peoples (the Dussault–Erasmus Commission), which supported First Nations self-government within the context of the Canadian Constitution. It called for new relationships with government (including an Aboriginal Parliament and the abolition of DIAND), self-determination through self-government, economic self-sufficiency, and personal and collective healing. Sensitive to the differing needs of the various Aboriginal, it advocated three different models for self-government: the national model (for groups with defined memberships), public government (in regions where Aboriginals form the majority of the population), and community-of-interest government (an administrative arrangement to serve urban Indians from diverse backgrounds). In this arrangement, First Nations governments would negotiate with provincial governments on a government-to-government basis and with the federal government on a nation-to-nation basis. (Chapter 13)

representative bureaucracy   The principle that the composition of the bureaucracy should approximately reflect certain demographic characteristics such as gender, race, ethnicity, class, language, ability, and sexuality. Many view representative bureaucracy as a reinforcement and extension of merit, in that it aims to remove barriers that impede the recruitment of qualified candidates. (Chapter 21)

responsibility   A convention of the Constitution by which ministers are answerable before Parliament for the administration of their particular department and/or portfolio.

restorative justice   A replacement popularized by Australian criminologist John Braithwaite for the system of criminal justice, in which all disputes would require a restoration of the balance of relationships within a community, and thus the participation of members of the community in individual cases. (Chapter 8)

retrenchment   The drive to restrain expenditures. It has taken different forms in Canada, but the most effective way of achieving this aim has been the reduction of transfers to people and to provinces. (Chapter 15)

revenue budgeting   Budgeting involving how government will access revenues; in recent years in Canada the revenue budget has become the occasion for major policy announcements. Essentially, two ministers, the finance minister and the first minister, decide revenue budgets, demonstrating that a far greater concentration of power is practised here than on the expenditure side. (Chapter 18)

roles of Parliament in relation to the public service   In relation to the public service, Parliament plays the following roles: legitimizer, policy-maker, creator, financier, and scutinizer. (Chapter 7)

Royal Commission on the Status of Women (RCSW)   A commission, appointed by the federal government, which reported in 1970, offering 167 recommendations related to equality of women, such as representation in government institutions and a comprehensive set of policy areas including education, employment, divorce, childcare, and reproduction. (Chapter 21)

rule of law   The principle that power is exercised according to law, not the self-interest or whims of the powerful. "At its most basic level, the rule of law vouchsafes to the citizens and residents of the country a stable, predictable and ordered society in which to conduct their affairs. It provides a shield for individuals from arbitrary state action" (*Reference re Secession of Quebec*, [1998] 2 S.C.R. 217 at para 70). The rule of law comprises three elements. First, "the law is supreme over the acts of both government and private persons. There is, in short, one law for all." Second, "the rule of law requires the creation and maintenance of an actual order of positive laws." Third, "the relationship between the state and the individual must be regulated by law" (*Reference re Secession of Quebec*, [1998] 2 S.C.R. 217 at para 71). Judicial review enforces the rule of law by ensuring that statutory

decision-makers exercise their powers within the boundaries established by the legislature. (Chapter 4)

sacrality of the state (or sacralized state)   A dominant image in popular thought, promoted by the Canadian state in the nineteenth century, and reflected in the symbols and rituals (flags, anthems) designed to promote patriotic love. (Chapter 15)

satisfycing   A less-than-optimal criterion for choice that decision-makers use in conditions of bounded rationality (when they do not have full information about all alternatives and all consequences). Decision-makers do not opt for the best solution, but for the most satisfactory one, based on the information they have. (Chapter 14)

Savoie thesis   The contention that power gravitates to the centre of government, and is clustered among a small group with access to the prime minister. (Chapter 25)

secession   The detachment of part of a country from whole. Provisions for secessions are rare across the world, but both Canada and the EU have secession arrangements. The Canadian federal government in 1999, through the so-called Clarity Act (An Act to give effect to the requirement for clarity as set out in the opinion of the Supreme Court of Canada in the Quebec Secession Reference, S.C. 2000, c. 26) established a set of procedural guidelines for how secession might proceed. In the EU exit provisions were inserted in the Lisbon Treaty (Article 50 TEU) which took effect in 2009. (Chapter 27)

Service Canada   An alternative service delivery arrangement in which a wide range of government programs and services from across federal departments and other levels of government are integrated to provide citizens with easy-to-access, personalized service. Individual departments concentrate on developing outcomes-focused policies and programs, while Service Canada concentrates on improving the delivery of programs and services. (Chapter 22)

services   Tangible and intangible assistance provided to citizens; some service activities involve partnership between non-profit organizations and the state, while others are independent actions. (Chapter 26)

shared-cost programs   In general, a mutually beneficial program in which the cost is shared between two or more affected parties. In Canada, such programs between provinces/territories and the federal government have often led to controversy over the federal spending power, as they often involve great sums of money being paid to the provincial/territorial governments, but they have also resulted in many beneficial social programs. Initially, provinces/territories were required to adhere to strict conditions attached to the funding, but many of these conditions were eliminated when the federal government began to favour block grants and tax transfers to fund social programs. (Chapter 3)

Shared Services Canada   A new common service agency created in 2011 to consolidate technological infrastructure and internal services in several major areas on behalf of all federal departments and agencies in the core public service and several other public sector organizations as well. The services included email, data centres, desktop services, and procurement of IT equipment and applications. The move was motivated at least in part to save money but proved problematic, attracting critical reviews from the Auditor General. (Chapter 22)

social capital The recognized value of social networks in coordinating for the benefit of individuals, organizations, and society as a whole. (Chapter 26)

social cohesion A sense of inclusiveness in a given society; the shared impression that all are involved in a common enterprise, share common values, face common challenges, and care enough about each other to accept reduction in the disparities of wealth and income. (Chapter 26)

social contracts In Canada, one measure (among many) employed in the 1980s and early 1990s that effectively controlled public sector wages. In the so-called social contracts, employees were given mandatory unpaid leave days as part of the freezes. (Chapter 19)

social learning In relation to public policy, a form of learning in which ideas and events in the larger policy community penetrate into policy evaluations. (Chapter 14)

social reproduction Work that is done for the daily and generational reproduction of the labouring population. (Chapter 21)

social rights Name given to policies that reduce inequality by redistributing wealth and to guarantee a reasonable standard of living for citizens. (Chapter 21)

Social Union Framework Agreement (SUFA) An agreement in the collaborative federalism mode, signed in 1999, between the federal government and the provinces and territories. It addressed social policy concerns, providing guidelines to guarantee an adequate level of social support for all citizens, and to ensure citizens' mobility rights across Canada. (Chapter 3)

soft budget constraints In the context of globalized markets, constraints on government taxation and expenditure decisions rooted in political processes. They include, for example, constraints that are negotiable; subject to bargaining, lobbying, or political pressures; or where the decision-maker has a high expectation of external financial assistance to offset obligations. (Chapter 2)

soft law The catch-all term for the rules and guidelines adopted by tribunals to govern their own work. The soft law applicable to a given tribunal must be consistent with the applicable statutes and regulations, and with the common-law principles of procedural fairness and natural justice. (Chapter 4)

Special Operating Agencies (SOAs) Autonomous service units, at both the federal and the provincial levels, that operate under the Financial Administration Act. A type of alternate service delivery mechanism roughly modelled after the Thatcher–Major-era executive agencies, they are meant to operate in a more independent, business-like manner, involving negotiated agreements between the sponsoring departments and the Treasury Board. In 2010, the federal government had 16 SOAs, most established in the 1990s. (Chapter 7)

special-purpose body (SPB) A body, functioning at the local level, that is usually only responsible for one function (or a set of closely related functions). These bodies are usually very efficient, but can raise issues of accountability, as their managers are sometimes appointed rather than elected. (Chapter 9)

spending power framework A series of issues and considerations that could feature in any broad attempt to reform the federal spending power. For example, what would the threshold of provincial consent be for introduction of new spending power programs? And how strictly would provinces have to follow set guidelines in order to qualify for federal compensation? (Chapter 3)

spending power of Parliament The power of Parliament to make payments to people, institutions, or governments in relation to areas in which it (Parliament) does not necessarily have the power to legislate. (Chapter 3)

spending power tests A series of broad conditions that critics of the federal spending power advanced as matters to be met in any reform of the spending power. For example, national objectives should be determined by a co-operative approach rather than a unilateral federal definition, and the federal principle (the principle of non-subordination of one level of government to another in areas of its own jurisdiction) should be followed. (Chapter 3)

spillover effects The influence of public-sector labour practices on the private sector. The public sector is under strong political pressure to be a model employer. At times this can mean progressive practices; at other times it can mean a model of restraint. (Chapter 19)

spin Involves framing an issue or object in a positive light, and downplaying or hiding negatives. According to some observers, only a small number of public reporting mechanisms are predominantly factual and can be considered free of spin, such as food safety alerts or weather warnings. (Chapter 25)

sponsorship scandal A scandal involving purveyors of communications services such as advertising, marketing, and public-opinion research in 1990s and early 2000s. The criteria for government communications contracts initially favoured companies with ties to the governing party, and procedures were sufficiently slack that people within government were able to work the system in favour of their party. (Chapter 25)

standard of review The degree of strictness that a court will apply to a tribunal decision on appeal or judicial review. (Chapter 4)

state-owned enterprises (SOEs) A term synonymous in Canada with "public enterprises" or commercial Crown corporations. One way of defining them is to use Florio's definition: ultimately owned or co-owned by the government; internalizing a public mission among their objectives; enjoying full or partial budgetary autonomy;

exhibiting a certain extent of managerial discretion; operating mainly in a market environment; and for which (full) privatization would in principle or de facto be possible, but for some reasons, it is not a policy option. (Chapter 12)

status Indian   In legal terms, an individual who is legally recognized as Indian under the Indian Act. (Chapter 13)

statute   A law enacted by the legislative branch, given Royal Assent by the Crown, and proclaimed in effect. (Chapter 4)

strategic planning   Part of a threefold function of control, management, and planning and policy choice that has formed the basis of a popular typology for studying government budgeting for 50 years. According to this approach, any budget system must, and does in some way, address the three functions of the control of spending and taxing, the management of ongoing program activities, and the planning of policy and setting of priorities. (Chapter 18)

subordinate legislation (or delegated legislation)   A subordinate, or secondary, law-making power delegated to the executive by an act of Parliament (in the form of Orders-in-Council or regulations made by a minister or agency); authority for creating the legislation comes from a primary, enabling piece of legislation passed by Parliament. Examples of bodies established by subordinate legislation include commissions of inquiry, advisory committees, and review panels. (Chapter 4)

subsidiarity   In a democracy with freedom of movement, organizing public affairs at the most decentralized, competent level. (Chapter 2)

substantive instruments   Policy instruments that directly provide goods and services to members of the public or governments. (Chapter 14)

substantive representation   Seeks representatives who not only resemble their constituents demographically, but who also pursue the concerns and interests of those constituents once in power. (Chapter 21)

superior and inferior courts   Constitutionally, superior courts have what is legally termed "inherent jurisdiction" (general jurisdiction) in the provinces derived from their link to superior courts in England and their constitutional entrenchment in section 96 of the Constitution Act, 1867. Thus, superior courts have inherent authority to enforce their own orders (e.g., through use of the contempt power). Provincial (inferior) Courts are courts of limited jurisdiction; their jurisdiction is limited to powers conferred by statute. (Chapter 8)

systemic discrimination   A concept introduced by the report of Rosalie Abella's Royal Commission on Equality in Employment in 1984, asserting that discrimination is not always overt and experienced by individuals, but instead is often built into processes and institutions, acting to disadvantage and marginalize identifiable groups. (Chapter 21)

tactical incrementalism   A strategy said to be followed by the governing party in a typical minority government in Canada. The opposition is kept divided by introducing measures at least one of the major opposition parties will disagree with. It is performed in the context of a short-term time horizon informed by political planning focused on high-profile policies and programs. (Chapter 18)

tax collection agreements   Post-war arrangements that supplanted the tax rental agreements, whereby provinces progressively regained tax-policy autonomy, as long as they conformed to shared definitions of the base for taxable income. (Chapter 2)

tax rental agreements   Under tax rental agreements, the provinces vacated the personal and corporate income tax fields in return for federal transfers. Starting in 1941, these federal transfers grew out of concerns about the complicated structure of taxes going into the Second World War, and then the fiscal stresses of the war itself. (Chapter 2)

technology   Both a medium and, as political philosophers have observed, the society-shaping dynamic. The Canadian Oxford Dictionary definition is "the study or use of the mechanical arts or applied sciences." This is a very broad definition that attempts to capture the fact that technology takes many forms and is as old as society. (Chapter 22)

territorial consolidation   An imperative that dominated the first quarter of twentieth-century Canada and put an imprint on federal public administration. By 1900, Canada had not yet established control of the land over which it claimed sovereignty, and the government deemed it necessary to prioritize the expansion of rail and water transportation, along with immigration services, in order to unify the country. (Chapter 15)

tests   See spending power tests.

third sector (non-profit sector)   The sector between the state and market realms where not-for-profit organizations operate. The primary objective of third-sector organizations is not the redistribution of profit, but the pursuance of the public good. (Chapter 26)

Tiebout model   Theorizes about how people move among jurisdictions in response to differences in government programs and taxes. An influential early exploration by Charles Tiebout (1956) described how competition among sub-central governments levying taxes on their residents that are akin to prices for the programs they provide can foster efficient provision of public goods and services. Residents of one jurisdiction who prefer the benefits provided and prices charged by another one can move there, so people of differing tastes can locate in jurisdictions that suit them better. (Chapter 2)

traditional cabinet   The form of cabinet that predominated in the days before the rise of the modern administrative state; ministers' jobs were to articulate and aggregate matters of local and regional political concern. (Chapters 3, 6)

traditional values   These values include accountability, efficiency, effectiveness, integrity, neutrality, responsiveness, and representativeness. (Chapter 5)

transition team   A select group of individuals who take on the responsibility of planning the transition from electioneering to governing, usually involving a substantial planning period to allow a party to thoughtfully discuss and debate issues the prime minister and cabinet will face upon assuming leadership of the nation. (Chapter 16)

transitions   One of the most fundamental elements that describe a democracy, involving the peaceful transfer of power from one political leader to another and, often, a change in the political parties that govern a nation. (Chapter 16)

transitions, types of   Transitions occur within three unique scenarios. One is when an opposition party wins an election and takes over the reins of power from the incumbent government; a second is when the governing party remains in power and the leader remains as prime minister; and the third involves a change in the leadership of the governing party outside of the electoral context, as in a leader becoming in effect prime minister by winning a leadership contest for the governing party. (Chapter 16)

Treasury Board of Canada   A cabinet committee of the Queen's Privy Council for Canada presided over by the president of the Privy Council and composed of at least four other ministers; it may act for the Privy Council on all matters relating to general administrative policy, the organization of the federal public administration, financial management, the review of expenditure plans; human resources management, and internal audits. It is served by its own central department, the Treasury Board Secretariat. (Chapters 1, 24)

Treasury Board Secretariat   A central department charged with improving cross-governmental management performance, examining departmental spending plans, and acting as the principal employer for the core public administration. It is led by the president of the Treasury Board, whose authority derives from statute. (Chapter 25)

Trial Court Performance Standards   A pioneering set of standards developed over a decade ago by the National Center for State Courts in the United States focused not only on delay reduction and judicial independence, but also on access to justice and on maintaining public trust and confidence in the courts. (Chapter 8)

tribunal   An agency, located within the executive branch of government, that exercises a statutory power of decision. Tribunals include individual decision-makers (a minister of the Crown, an arbitrator hearing a labour grievance); regulatory boards and commissions that make and enforce policy (the Canadian Radio-television and Telecommunications Commission (CRTC), the Ontario Energy Board); and quasi-judicial agencies that hear individual applications or complaints and assess individual benefits, remedies or punishments, e.g., the Canadian Human Rights Commission or the Discipline Committee of a Law Society. (Chapter 4)

two-tier systems   Systems of local governance in which both an upper tier (with broader regional interests, such as a county or a municipality) and a lower tier (e.g., a city or a town) are involved in local public administration. (Chapter 9)

ultra vires   Latin for "beyond the power" of a particular official or institution. A statute is *ultra vires* if it exceeds the constitutional jurisdiction of the legislature that adopted it. A regulation is *ultra vires* if it conflicts with the statute under which it was made. (Chapter 4)

unconditional grants (including equalization)   Grants made by the federal government that (apart from statutory subsidies and grants-in-lieu, which are also unconditional but insignificant as a percentage of transfers of this kind) play an important role in the support of provincial/territorial revenues. The most important are equalization grants, which are designed to compensate for the low per-capita tax yield in the less-endowed provinces/territories so that all Canadians have access to an average standard of services. (Chapter 3)

unified criminal court   A reform, proposed in the 1980s, to the current criminal court division in which only superior courts could hold jury trials and Provincial Court judges could not preside at murder trials; it was designed as a way to erase the difference in status between the two levels. (Chapter 8)

unified family court   Specialized family courts with unified jurisdiction now operating in seven provinces of Canada; this organization was designed to overcome the historical division between superior courts and Provincial Courts regarding litigation on family issues. (Chapter 8)

urban asymmetry   The condition wherein the federal government makes decisions and builds relationships based on the unique needs of large urban areas and agglomerations, resulting in unequal (unparallel) treatment of different urban areas across the country. (Chapter 3)

value for money   In its simplest form, Canadian practitioners of second-wave PPPs have defined value for money as a measure of the extent to which cost savings are achieved when delivering a public infrastructure project through a PPP relative to a traditional government-led procurement approach. (Chapter 17)

values-based or integrity-based approaches to ethics   While the compliance-based approaches fit more easily with the traditional command-control structure and hierarchical model of accountability in Weberian bureaucracies, the integrity-based systems are more consistent with the new public management model of employee empowerment and engagement. Integrity-based systems are aspirational and intended to build and ethical culture and environment in which individuals are ethically competent. They encourage individuals to think about their behaviour or decisions in terms of the organizational values and mission and become moral agents instead of passively accepting norms defined by others. (Chapter 20)

wage controls   In Canada, legislated controls over federal and provincial public sector wages, common in the 1970s and early 1980s. (Chapter 19)

Wagner model A framework for labour relations and collective bargaining originating in the United States and imported into Canada, where it gained prominence in the 1940s. First designed for the private sector, and then largely transplanted into the public sector, the model addressed union certification, bargaining over collective agreements, strikes and lockouts, grievance procedures, renegotiation of agreements upon their expiration, and lists of prohibited unfair labour practices. (Chapter 19)

whistle-blowing A good-faith disclosure of wrongdoing that is protected by the Public Servants Disclosure Protection Act. (Chapter 1)

women's policy machinery Structures developed inside the state to represent women and to provide openings to influence public policy. (Chapter 21)

Index

Please note: Page numbers in italics indicate figures.